C# Programming:

From Problem Analysis to Program Design

Fifth Edition

C# PROGRAMMING:

FROM PROBLEM ANALYSIS TO PROGRAM DESIGN

FIFTH EDITION

BARBARA DOYLE

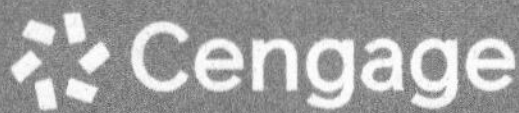

Australia • Brazil • Canada • Mexico • Singapore • United Kingdom • United States

C# Programming: From Problem Analysis to Program Design, Fifth Edition

Barbara Doyle

Product Director: Kathleen McMahon

Product Team Manager: Kristin McNary

Senior Product Manager: Jim Gish

Senior Content Developer: Alyssa Pratt

Product Assistant: Abigail Pufpaff

Marketing Manager: Eric LaScola

Senior Production Director: Wendy Troeger

Production Director: Patty Stephan

Senior Content Project Manager: Jennifer K. Feltri-George

Managing Art Director: Jack Pendleton

Cover image: © zeljkodan/Shutterstock.com

Production Service: SPi Global

Compositor: SPi Global

© 2016, 2014 Cengage Learning, Inc. ALL RIGHTS RESERVED.

WCN: 01-100-101

No part of this work covered by the copyright herein may be reproduced or distributed in any form or by any means, except as permitted by U.S. copyright law, without the prior written permission of the copyright owner.

Microsoft ® is a registered trademark of the Microsoft Corporation.

Unless otherwise noted all screenshots are courtesy of Microsoft Corporation

For product information and technology assistance, contact us at **Cengage Customer & Sales Support, 1-800-354-9706 or support.cengage.com.**

For permission to use material from this text or product, submit all requests online at **www.copyright.com.**

Library of Congress Control Number: 2015937761

ISBN: 978-1-285-85687-2

Cengage
200 Pier 4 Boulevard
Boston, MA 02210
USA

Cengage is a leading provider of customized learning solutions with employees residing in nearly 40 different countries and sales in more than 125 countries around the world. Find your local representative at: **www.cengage.com.**

To learn more about Cengage platforms and services, register or access your online learning solution, or purchase materials for your course, visit **www.cengage.com.**

Notice to the Reader

Publisher does not warrant or guarantee any of the products described herein or perform any independent analysis in connection with any of the product information contained herein. Publisher does not assume, and expressly disclaims, any obligation to obtain and include information other than that provided to it by the manufacturer. The reader is expressly warned to consider and adopt all safety precautions that might be indicated by the activities described herein and to avoid all potential hazards. By following the instructions contained herein, the reader willingly assumes all risks in connection with such instructions. The publisher makes no representations or warranties of any kind, including but not limited to, the warranties of fitness for particular purpose or merchantability, nor are any such representations implied with respect to the material set forth herein, and the publisher takes no responsibility with respect to such material. The publisher shall not be liable for any special, consequential, or exemplary damages resulting, in whole or part, from the readers' use of, or reliance upon, this material.

Printed in the United States of America
Print Number: 14 Print Year: 2022

© zeljkodan/Shutterstock.com

Brief Contents

© zeljkodan/Shutterstock.com

Table of Contents

© zeljkodan/Shutterstock.com

Preface

C# Programming: From Problem Analysis to Program Design requires no previous introduction to programming but only a mathematical background of high-school algebra. The book uses C# as the programming language for software development; however, the basic programming concepts presented can be applied to a number of other languages. Instead of focusing on the syntax of the C# language, this book uses the C# language to present general programming concepts. It is the belief of the author that once you develop a thorough understanding of one programming language, you can effectively apply those concepts to other programming languages.

Why C#?

C# has gained tremendous popularity in the industry. C# is a true object-oriented language that includes a rich set of instruction statements. C# was the language used for development of much of .NET, the Microsoft programming paradigm that includes a collection of more than 2,000 predefined classes that make up the Framework Class Library (FCL). Thus, C# has access to a large collection of predefined classes similar to those available to Java. C# provides tools that make it easy to create graphical user interfaces—similar to the tools Visual Basic programmers have employed for years. C# also provides the pure data crunching horsepower to which C/C++ programmers have become accustomed. However, unlike other languages, C# was designed from scratch to accommodate Internet and Windows applications. C# is an elegant and simple object-oriented language that allows programmers to build a breadth of applications. C# is also a great language for mobile application development. It can run on not only Windows platforms but is very portable and can run on Android and iOS devices. For these reasons, C# was chosen as the language for this book.

Going Beyond the Traditional CS1 Course

This book was written for the Computer Science 1 (CS1) student and includes all of the basic programming constructs normally covered in the traditional CS1 foundation course for the Computer Science curriculum. Readers begin developing applications immediately in the first chapter. It includes lots of examples and figures illustrating basic concepts. A heavy emphasis on illustrating the visual tools that can be used to create applications is included in this edition. However, this book goes beyond what is traditionally found in most CS1 textbooks and, because of the inclusion of a number of advanced applications, this textbook could also be used in an intermediate course for students who have already been exposed to some programming concepts.

Advanced Topics

After building a solid programming foundation, this book presents rapid application development techniques that can be used to build a number of advanced types of applications including Windows, data-driven applications using a database, and Web and mobile applications for smart devices. Generics, delegates, ArrayLists, dynamic data types, abstract classes, interfaces, and many advanced object-oriented concepts are introduced. Readers retrieve data from files and store data both to sequential and binary files. Solutions involving multidimensional arrays and other advanced collection classes are demonstrated. Illustrating the drag-and-drop construction approach used with Visual Studio, Windows, and Web applications are created. Readers are introduced to the event-driven programming model, which is based on interactively capturing and responding to user input on Windows and Web forms. Class libraries, Windows Forms applications, and Windows Presentation Foundation client applications are created. Two full chapters are devoted to programming based on events and then those topics are integrated throughout the remainder of the book. Readers are introduced to ASP.NET for Web applications and ADO.NET for working with databases.

For first-time programmers, this book is unusual in introducing applications that retrieve and update data in databases such as those created using Microsoft Access. A number of visual development tools are illustrated to connect to data sources. Other interesting topics include retrieving data using Language-Integrated Query (LINQ), developing stand-alone .dll components (class libraries), and an introduction to Xamarin for programming applications for mobile devices. All of these advanced features are discussed after the reader has gained a thorough understanding of the basic components found in programming languages.

Changes in the Fifth Edition

C# Programming: From Problem Analysis to Program Design, Fifth Edition, has been revised and updated to reflect the latest release of Visual Studio 2015 and C# 6.0. All examples are streamlined and unnecessary using statements are removed from each chapter. The new improvements to the code editor are highlighted from early chapters and summarized in an appendix. Additional advanced object-oriented concepts are included. Each chapter includes new programming exercises not seen in previous editions. All example programs, exercises, and the solution set have been updated using Visual Studio 2015. All screenshots are updated to the Visual Studio 2015 IDE. The following summarizes some of the changes in the fifth edition.

1. New C# 6.0 language features such as auto-properties, exception filters, and string interpolation are introduced.
2. Beginning with the first example, code is streamlined, reducing the amount of boilerplate code needed. References to static class members are added to all examples throughout this edition to bring static class members directly into scope.
3. Early introduction of Visual Studio 2015 user interface improvements.
4. New debugging tools, new Windows layout features, enhanced colorized tooltips, simplified context menu options, and the new Quick Action Light Bulb editing tools are illustrated.
5. All screenshots updated to reflect change made in Visual Studio 2015.
6. New **Programming Exercises** not found in previous editions added to every chapter. Solutions to all exercises developed by the author.
7. Increased and updated list of Internet sites added at the end of each chapter in the **Resources** section for readers to explore.
8. Additional **Notes** added throughout the book highlighting tips and "catch you" types of topics.
9. Expanded **Glossary** provides a reference for keywords tagged throughout the book.
10. Revised **Appendices** include special sections, Customizing the Visual Studio Development Environment and Code Editor Tools, with updated illustrations and figures.

Approach

A problem-solving methodology based on object-oriented software development is introduced early and used throughout the book. Programming Examples are presented at the end of each chapter, and each example follows a consistent approach: analyzing the problem specifications, designing a solution, implementing the design, and verifying or validating the solution structures.

The author believes that the best way to learn to program is to experience programming. This assumption drives the material presented in this textbook. As new concepts are introduced, they are described using figures and illustrations. Examples are shown and discussed as they relate to the concept being presented. With a hands-on approach to learning, readers practice and solidify the concepts presented by completing the end of the chapter exercises. Readers are also encouraged throughout the book to explore and make use of the more than 2,000 classes that make up the FCL.

Every chapter begins with a list of objectives and a short overview of the previous chapter. Text in each chapter is supplemented with figures and tables to help visual learners grasp the concepts being presented. Each chapter is sprinkled with useful tips and hints as NOTES on the concepts being presented. Code snippets and numbered examples are embedded as new concepts are introduced in each chapter. In addition, each chapter contains complete working programs illustrating an application using C#. Every chapter ends with a Coding Standards section, which provides a summary of acceptable conventions or guidelines pertaining to the chapter's topics that focus on style issues. A list of websites for readers to explore is included in a special Resources section at the end of each chapter. A summary of the major points covered in that chapter and review exercises in both objective and subjective formats are included. Every chapter ends with programming exercises that give readers an opportunity to experience programming.

Using This Book for Two Different Courses

Although this book is primarily intended for a beginning programming course, it will also work well in an intermediate course. For courses introducing students to programming, Chapters 1 through 8 should be covered in detail. Depending on how quickly students are able to grasp the material, the course could end in any of the chapters following Chapter 8. For example, ending with Chapter 9, Introduction to Windows Programming, would give students an opportunity to get excited about continuing their work in programming in upcoming semesters.

For an intermediate course, where the first course was taught using a different language, the last part of Chapter 1 along with Appendices A and B could be read to orient the readers to running an application using Visual Studio. Students could be encouraged to scan Chapters 2 through 7 and review Chapter 8 more extensively. Scanning these chapters, students could compare and contrast the details of the C# language with the programming languages they already know.

For the intermediate course where the first course was taught using C#, Chapters 4, 7, and 8 should be reviewed, because topics covered in these chapters—Creating your Own Classes and Arrays—are often more difficult for the student to grasp. The remainder of the book beginning in Chapter 9 would be included for the intermediate course.

Overview of the Chapters

Chapter 1 briefly reviews the history of computers and programming languages including the evolution of C# and .NET. This chapter explains the difference between structured and object-oriented programming and includes the software development methodology used throughout the remainder of the book. This chapter describes the different types of applications that can be developed using C#. It discusses the basic elements found in a C# program and illustrates how to compile, run, and debug an application.

The focus in Chapter 2 is data types and expressions. Readers gain an understanding of how types, classes, and objects are related. They also learn how to perform arithmetic procedures on the data, how to display formatted data, and how expressions are evaluated using operator precedence. Chapter 3 extends the manipulation of the data through introducing methods and behaviors of the data. Readers learn to write statements that call methods and to write their own class methods. They learn how to pass arguments to methods that return values and to those that do not.

Readers learn to create their own classes in Chapter 4. This chapter introduces the components of a class including the data, property, and method members. Special methods, including constructors, are written.

Chapter 5 introduces control structures that alter the sequential flow of execution. Selection control constructs are introduced in Chapter 5. One-way, multiway, switch, and ternary operators used to make decisions are illustrated. Looping is introduced in Chapter 6. The rich set of iteration operators including while, for, do while, and foreach are explored. Recursive solutions are also explored.

Chapter 7 discusses arrays. This chapter describes how to declare and perform compile-time initialization of array elements. The Array class and its many members are introduced. Methods of the string and ArrayList classes are included in Chapter 8. Multidimensional arrays and other collection classes, including stacks, queues, and hash tables, are also introduced in Chapter 8.

Chapter 9 presents a different way of programming, which is based on interactively responding to events. A number of classes in the FCL that are used to create Windows applications are introduced. Elements of good design are discussed in Chapter 9. Delegates are also explored in Chapter 9. Visual Studio's drag-and-drop approach to rapid application development is introduced and used in these chapters. The Windows Presentation Foundation (WPF) is also introduced in Chapter 10 as an alternative approach to Windows Forms for creating Windows applications.

Advanced object-oriented programming features are the focus of Chapter 11. Readers are introduced to component-based development and learn how to create their own class library files. Inheritance, interfaces, abstract classes, sealed classes, generic types, partial classes, and polymorphic programming are discussed in detail. Advanced features such as overriding, overloading, and the use of virtual methods are also included in Chapter 11. Static versus dynamic typing is also investigated in Chapter 11.

Chapter 12 discusses debugging and exception handling techniques. The chapter introduces one of the tools available in Visual Studio, the Debugger, which can be used to observe the run-time environment, take an up-close look at the code, and locate logic errors. The try. . .catch. . .finally block is discussed for handling exceptions. In addition to discussing .NET exception classes, custom exceptions are designed.

Chapter 13 presents the basics of creating, opening, closing, reading, and writing files. The major classes used to work with file and directory systems are introduced. Chapter 14 introduces a number of new namespaces collectively called ADO. NET, which consists of a managed set of library classes that enable interaction with databases. The chapter illustrates how ADO.NET classes are used to retrieve and update data in databases. The visual programming tools and wizards available with Visual Studio, which simplify accessing data, are covered in this chapter. The LINQ is also introduced in Chapter 14.

The focus of Chapter 15 is on Web applications. Readers explore how the design of Web-based applications differs from Windows applications. They discover the differences between static and dynamic web pages and how HTML and Web server controls differ. Master pages and Cascading Style Sheets are introduced. Also included in Chapter 15 is an introduction to Xamarin used for mobile application development. Chapter 15 illustrates how validation controls can be used to check users' input values and shows how the ADO.NET classes, introduced in Chapter 14, can also be used with Web applications to access database records.

Appendix A presents suggestions for customizing the appearance and behavior of the Integrated Development Environment (IDE). Appendix B discusses the Code Editor features of Visual Studio. Code snippets and refactoring are described. These new features improve programmer productivity by reducing the number of keystrokes required to enter program statements. This appendix also illustrates developing applications visually using class diagrams. Appendix C lists the Unicode and ASCII (American Standard Code for Information Interchange) character sets. Appendix D shows the precedence of the C# operators, and Appendix E lists the C# keywords.

Features

Every chapter in this book includes the following features. These features are both conducive to learning in the classroom and enable you to learn the material at your own pace.

- Multi-color interior design shows accurate C# code and related comments.
- Learning objectives offer an outline of the concepts discussed in detail in the chapter.
- Hundreds of visual diagrams throughout the text illustrate difficult concepts.
- Syntax boxes show the general form for different types of statements.
- Numbered examples illustrate the key concepts with their relevant code, and the code is often followed by a sample run. An explanation follows that describes the functions of the most difficult lines of code.
- Notes highlight important facts about the concepts introduced in the chapter.

- Numerous tables are included that describe and summarize information compactly for easy viewing.
- A Coding Standards section provides a summary of acceptable conventions or guidelines pertaining to the chapter's topic. These coding/programming guidelines help ensure consistency and reduce the number of bugs and errors entered into programming projects.
- Internet sites listed including tutorials that can be used to enhance concepts are presented in the Resources section.
- Programming Examples are complete programs featured at the end of the chapter. The examples contain the distinct stages of preparing a problem specification, analyzing the problem, designing the solution, and coding the solution.
- Quick Reviews offer a summary of the concepts covered in the chapter.
- Exercises further reinforce learning and ensure that students have, in fact, absorbed the material. Both objective and subjective types of questions are included at the end of each chapter.
- Programming Exercises challenge students to write C# programs with a specified outcome.
- The glossary at the end of the book lists nearly 400 key terms in alphabetical order along with definitions for easy reference. Throughout this text, the terms set in bold indicate that they are defined in the glossary.

From beginning to end, the concepts are introduced at a pace that is conducive to learning. The writing style of this book is simple and straightforward, and it parallels the teaching style of a classroom. The concepts introduced are described using examples and small programs.

The chapters have two types of programs. The first type includes small programs that are part of the numbered examples and are used to explain key concepts. This book also features numerous case studies called Programming Examples. These Programming Examples are placed at the end of the chapters to pull together many of the concepts presented throughout the chapter. The programs are designed to be methodical and workable. Each Programming Example starts with a Problem Analysis and is then followed by the Algorithm Design. Every step of the algorithm is then coded in C#. In addition to teaching problem-solving techniques, these detailed programs show the user how to implement concepts in an actual C# program. Students are encouraged to study the Programming Examples very carefully in order to learn C# effectively.

All source code and solutions have been written, compiled, and tested by quality assurance with Visual Studio Professional 2015.

Features of the Book

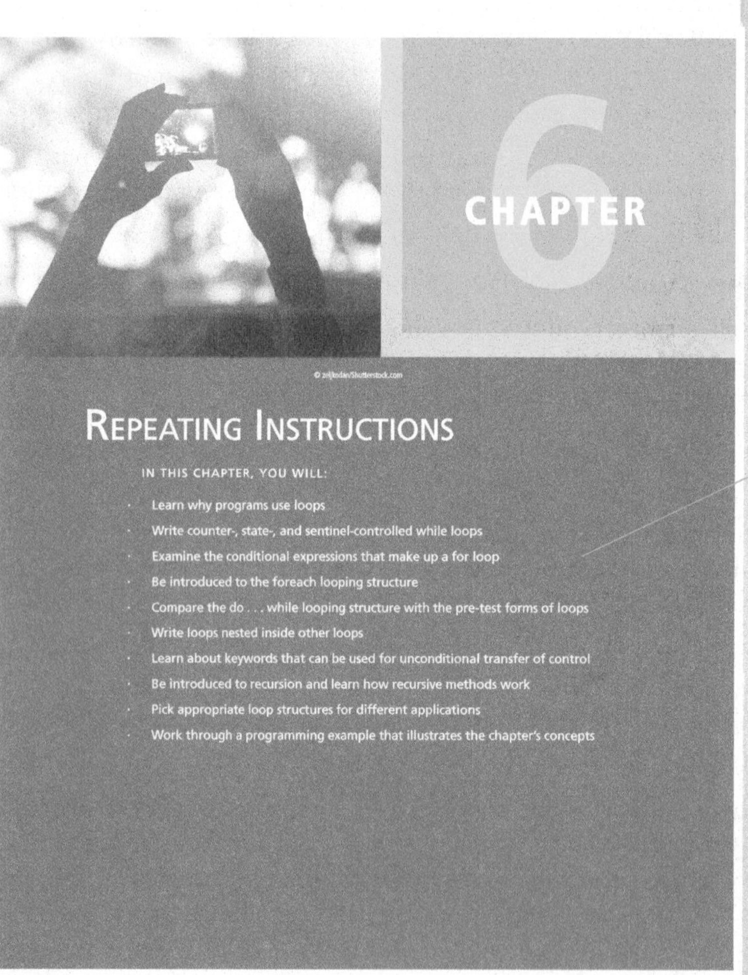

ond class
me of the
of days in
inputs an
ould con-
nd cylin-
d provide
ample, in
ds to cal-
providing
For cylin-
d surface
e user to
priate val-
f the type
anization
arger the
the orga-
splay the
r symbol.
tions are
solution.
rectness?
ned near
ld by the
pplication
nd make a
rice. Test
Once the
CHAPTER
6
Repeating Instructions
IN THIS CHAPTER, YOU WILL:
Learn why programs use loops
Write counter-, state-, and sentinel-controlled while loops
Examine the conditional expressions that make up a for loop
Be introduced to the foreach looping structure
Compare the do . . . while looping structure with the pre-test forms of loops
Write loops nested inside other loops
Learn about keywords that can be used for unconditional transfer of control
Be introduced to recursion and learn how recursive methods work
Pick appropriate loop structures for different applications
Work through a programming example that illustrates the chapter's concepts

Learning objectives appear at the beginning of each chapter.

er)

s");

' " +

ng(
);

pplications
u make

epresent-
5666667).

As you examine Example 7-15, you should observe that the result is stored in a `double`. To avoid doing integer division in the `ComputeAverage( )` method, `total` was defined as a `double` and then divided by an `int` (`pointsScored.Length`). The result is a `double` and it is then assigned to a `double`. The `ToString( )` method was called in the `DisplayStats( )` method of the `PlayerApp` application sending in "F0" as a format specifier. Another option to produce a floating-point result, both variables could have been defined as integers and then one of them could have been cast to a `double`, that is ((`double`) `total` / `pointsScored.Length`).

Figure 7-10 shows how the data from `PlayerApp` is represented in memory.

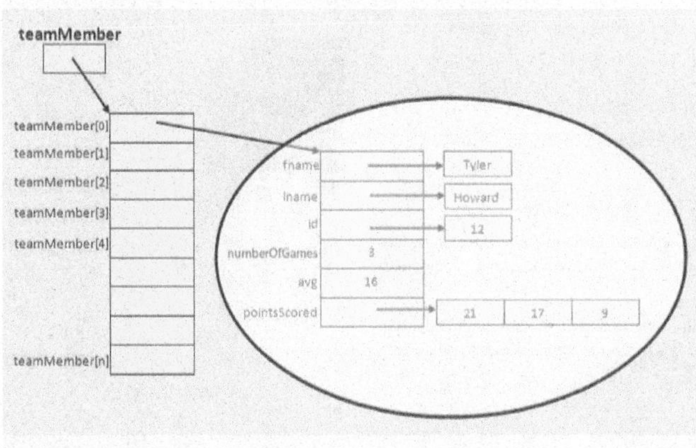

© Cengage Learning

7

FIGURE 7-10 PlayerApp memory representation

As you review the figure, note the difference between value types such as `avg` and `numberOfGames`. Array objects and `string` types contain a reference to the location of the stored values. Many advanced concepts relating to arrays were illustrated in the `PlayerApp` application. Array elements were defined as private data members and local variables. You saw how you could instantiate arrays of user-defined class array objects. Arrays were returned from methods and sent in as arguments to methods. Many of these same features will be revisited with the Programming Example that follows.

Numerous visual diagrams throughout the text illustrate difficult concepts.

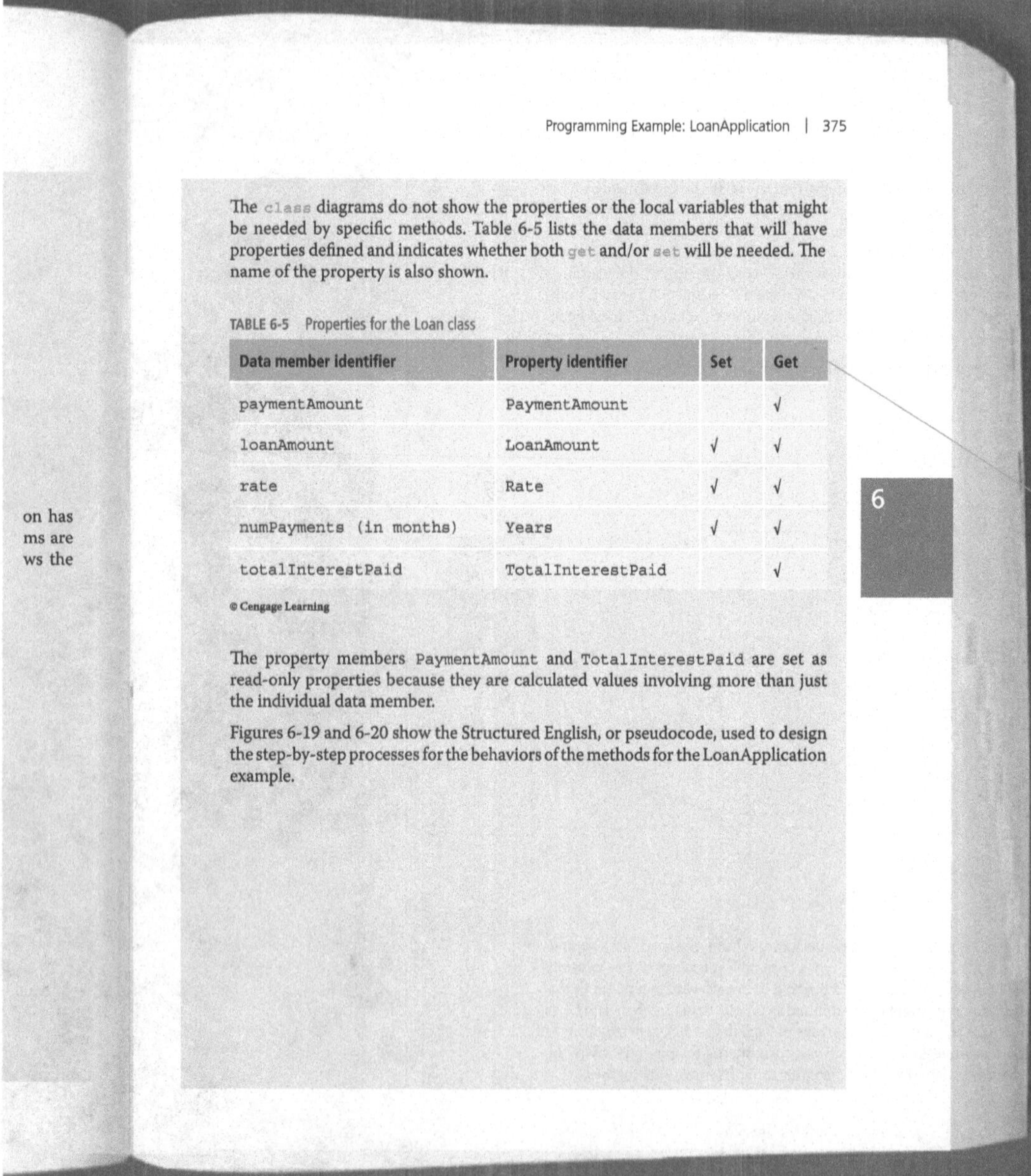

The class diagrams do not show the properties or the local variables that might be needed by specific methods. Table 6-5 lists the data members that will have properties defined and indicates whether both get and/or set will be needed. The name of the property is also shown.

TABLE 6-5 Properties for the Loan class

Data member identifier	Property identifier	Set	Get
paymentAmount	PaymentAmount		√
loanAmount	LoanAmount	√	√
rate	Rate	√	√
numPayments (in months)	Years	√	√
totalInterestPaid	TotalInterestPaid		√

© Cengage Learning

The property members PaymentAmount and TotalInterestPaid are set as read-only properties because they are calculated values involving more than just the individual data member.

Figures 6-19 and 6-20 show the Structured English, or pseudocode, used to design the step-by-step processes for the behaviors of the methods for the LoanApplication example.

6

on has
ms are
ws the

Numerous tables are included that describe and summarize information compactly for easy viewing.

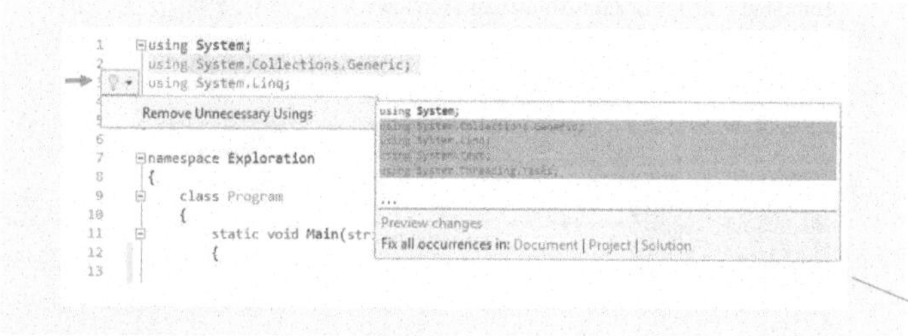

FIGURE B-5 Quick Action Light Bulb recommendation

Four of the five using statements are highlighted in pink in Figure B-5, indicating they could be removed. Under that suggestion, a **Preview changes** link is available. The Quick Action Light Bulb also helps with syntax errors. Figure B-6 provides another illustration. This time `itemCnt` was defined, but `cntOfValues` wasn't. As shown in Figure B-6 three possible options are suggested to correct the problem. The preview window shown on the right in Figure B-6 illustrates how the code will be modified if the third option is selected.

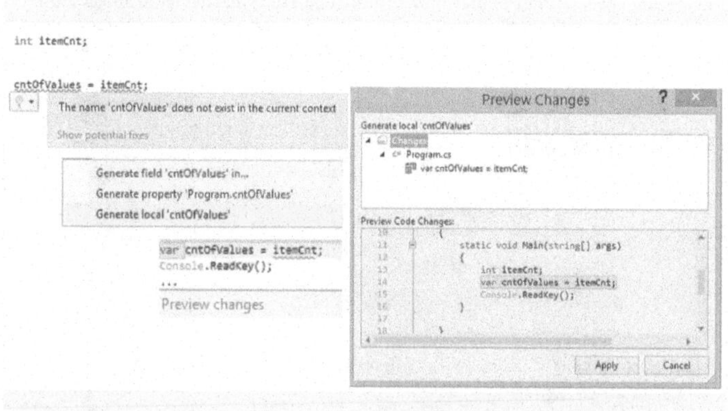

FIGURE B-6 Quick Action Light Bulb changes previewed

Updated screen shots of what readers see in Visual Studio are also included throughout the book.

Non-keyword code appears in a different font throughout the text so readers can quickly distinguish program statements from normal text.

Multi-color interior design shows accurate C# code and related comments. Throughout the book, keywords are shown in blue and comments appear in green.

Numbered examples illustrate the key concepts with their relevant code, and the code is often followed by a sample run. An explanation follows that describes the functions of the most difficult lines of code.

The heading for the class definition can specify not only a base class following the colon but also one or more interfaces as follows:

```
[modifier] class ClassIdentifier : identifier [, identifier]
```

To indicate that the Student class derives from the base class Person and implements the ITraveler interface, Example 11-20 shows that you add ITraveler to the class definition line.

EXAMPLE 11-20

```
public class Student : Person, ITraveler // Base class comes first.
```

If a class implements more than one interface, they all appear on the class definition line separated by commas. The base class is listed first if the class is inheriting from a base class.

NOTE If the interface is part of a project, the namespace for the interface should be the same name as other classes' namespaces in the project. Otherwise, a using statement is needed in classes that implements the interface to reference the interface.

Reviewing Figure 11-15, you see that ITraveler has three abstract methods as part of its definition. Because the Student class is implementing the ITraveler interface, it must define the implementation details for all three methods. Example 11-21 shows the revised Student class. It includes bodies for those methods and the GetExerciseHabits( ) method, which was defined as an abstract method in the Person class. This satisfies the implementation requirements for the methods.

EXAMPLE 11-21

```
public class Student : Person, ITraveler
{
    private string major;
    private string studentId;

    public Student( )
        : base( )
    {
    }

    // Constructor which sends 3 arguments to base class
    public Student(string id, string fname, string lname,
                   string maj, string sId)
        : base(id, lname, fname)
```

Syntax boxes show the general form for different types of statements.

Making Data Constant

When you add the keyword `const` to a declaration, it becomes a constant. Constants are convenient for assigning a value to an identifier; `const` forces the functionality of not allowing the value to be changed. Similar to a variable, the value stored in the memory location can be used throughout the program. However, the value cannot be altered. The general form of constant syntax is

```
const type identifier = expression;
```

Some examples of constant declarations are shown in Example 2-9.

EXAMPLE 2-9

```
const double TAX_RATE = 0.0675;
const int SPEED = 70;
const char HIGHEST_GRADE = 'A';
```

NOTE: An advantage of defining a constant is that the value needs only be assigned once, during declaration. A constant can be used in many statements. If the value must be changed, only one change is required in the program and that is at the constant declaration location. After that change is made, the program must be recompiled.

To call attention to the fact that the identifier `TAX_RATE` is a constant instead of a variable, all capital letters are used. To provide a separator between words, the underscore character is used. This is the standard convention used by programmers for naming constants.

Assignment Statements

Variables can be initialized during declaration, or a value can be assigned to them later in the program. However, in C#, you must assign a value to a variable before it can be used. No default values are assigned when you declare the variable. To change the value of the variable, an assignment statement is used. An assignment statement takes the form of

```
variable = expression;
```

Now any and every class that derives from the Person class must provide the implementation details for the GetExerciseHabits( ) method. That is what adding the abstract keyword does. It is like signing a contract. If you derive from an abstract base class, you sign a contract that details how to implement its abstract methods.

NOTE You will receive a syntax error if you use the keyword static or virtual when defining an abstract method. There is an implicit assumption that the method will be overridden; thus, the keyword virtual is unnecessary in the base class.

Notes provide short quick tips highlighting important concepts and features that might be overlooked.

If the abstract class includes more than one abstract method, derived classes must provide implementation details for every abstract method included in the base class. Abstract classes can include regular data field members, regular methods, and virtual methods in addition to abstract methods. Remember that a virtual method tags the method as being capable of being overridden in a derived class. This does not mean that all derived classes have to provide new implementation details for those tagged as virtual, just that they *can*.

In the derived class, all abstract methods' headings include the special keyword override. Thus, the only change needed for the Student class is a new method, GetExerciseHabits( ), which has an override keyword added to the method heading. The method body must return a string argument. You can see that new method if you look ahead to Example 11-21, which illustrates the completed Student class.

All .NET languages only support **single inheritance**, which means that a class can extend or derive from at most one class. One way languages such as C# and Java work around this is by implementing multiple interfaces, which are the topic for the following section.

NOTE C++ permits multiple inheritances. A class can extend from more than one base class in C++. This is not possible in C#, Java, or any of the managed .NET languages.

11

Sealed Classes

You learned that the abstract keyword enables you to create a class solely for the purpose of inheritance. Abstract classes cannot be instantiated. Objects can only be created using classes derived from the abstract class. The purpose of an abstract class is to provide a common definition of a base class so that multiple derived classes can share that definition. Sealed classes provide a completely opposite type of restriction. They restrict the inheritance feature of object-oriented programming. When you add the modifier **sealed** to a class, the class cannot be a base class. In order to define a sealed class, add the keyword sealed following the access modifier as shown in Example 11-18.

Programming Examples are complete programs featured at the end of the chapter. The examples contain the distinct stages of preparing a problem specification, analyzing the problem, designing the solution, and coding the implementation.

PROGRAMMING EXAMPLE: JoggingDistance

This example demonstrates the use of methods in a program. The problem specification is shown in Figure 3-11.

How far do you jog each morning? You prefer to jog in different locations each day and do not have a pedometer to measure your distance. Create an application to determine the distance jogged given the average number of strides ran during the first minute, average number ran during the last minute, and the total minutes jogging.

Design a modularized solution (with methods) to display the distance traveled.

Pedometers measure the distance you run. However, you can also do a good estimate of the distance if you know your foot stride, how many strides you complete per minute, and the number of minutes you jog. Foot stride is the distance covered by one average step length. Since everyone has a different foot size, strides differ. Many people average 3 feet per step when jogging. For this application, assume the foot stride is 2.5 feet. There are 5,280 feet in a mile.

To establish how many strides per minute, allow the user to input the number of strides made during the first minute jogging and the number of strides made during the last minute of jogging. Use the average of those values to represent the strides per minute. Allow the user to input the total time spent jogging in hours and minutes. Write code that will display the distance traveled in miles.

© Cengage Learning

FIGURE 3-11 Problem specification for JoggingDistance example

ANALYZE THE PROBLEM

You should review the problem specification in Figure 3-11 and make sure you understand the problem definition. Several values must be entered into the program. These values must be entered as `string` variables and then parsed into numeric fields, so that arithmetic can be performed.

Coding/programming style guidelines and suggestions are featured at the end of each chapter.

Coding Standards

It is important to establish and follow good coding standards. The intent of creating a set of coding standards is to have an acceptable list of guidelines that can be followed by all members of a team. The following list of standards is recommended as they relate to methods.

Naming Conventions

- Use Pascal Casing (first character of all words are uppercase; all other characters are lowercase) for method identifiers.
- Use Camel Casing (first character of all words, except the first word, are uppercase; all other characters are lowercase) for local variable identifiers and parameters.
- Use a verb or action clause to name a method. Do not use misleading names. Method names should tell what the method does. If you select a good method name, there is no need for additional documentation explaining what the method does.

Spacing Conventions

- Align curly braces ({ }) up with the method heading.
- Declare each local variable independently on separate lines. It is permissible to reuse the data type, but each variable should be on a separate line.
- There should be one and only one single blank line between each method inside the class.
- Avoid writing long methods. Consider refactoring when the method exceeds 25 lines of code.
- Avoid extremely large source code files. Consider refactoring when the file size exceeds 300–400 lines in a single class.

Declaration Conventions

- Do not have more than one class in a single file.
- Declare and initialize local variables in the method where they are used.
- Try to initialize variables when they are declared.
- Avoid passing too many parameters to a method. If you have more than four to five parameters, it is a good idea to define a class or structure.
- A method should do only one thing: have a single theme.

A special Resources section at the end of each chapter offers a number of web sites for the reader to explore.

Quick Review offers a summary of the concepts covered in the chapter.

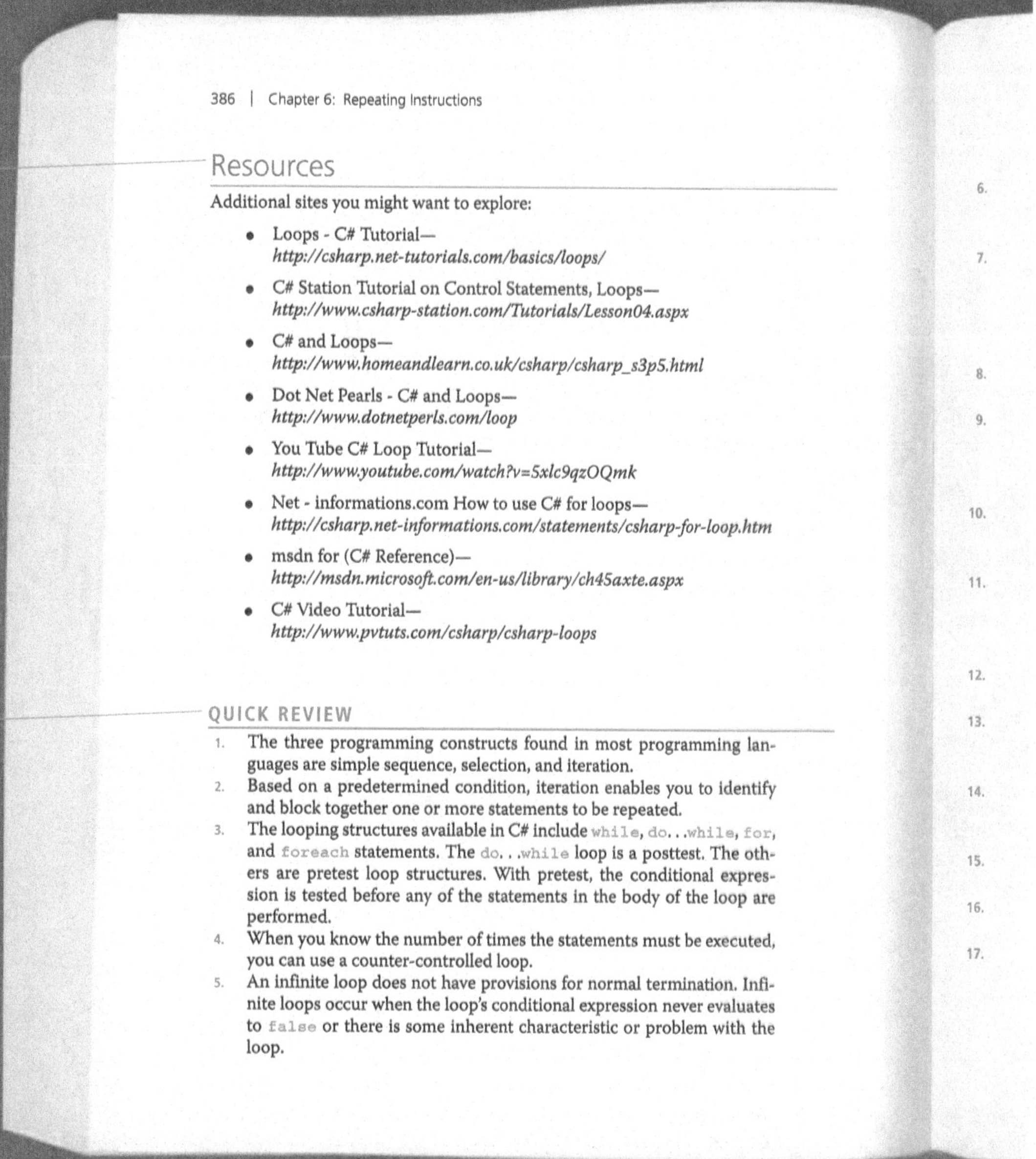

Resources

Additional sites you might want to explore:

- Loops - C# Tutorial—
  http://csharp.net-tutorials.com/basics/loops/
- C# Station Tutorial on Control Statements, Loops—
  http://www.csharp-station.com/Tutorials/Lesson04.aspx
- C# and Loops—
  http://www.homeandlearn.co.uk/csharp/csharp_s3p5.html
- Dot Net Pearls - C# and Loops—
  http://www.dotnetperls.com/loop
- You Tube C# Loop Tutorial—
  http://www.youtube.com/watch?v=5xlc9qzOQmk
- Net - informations.com How to use C# for loops—
  http://csharp.net-informations.com/statements/csharp-for-loop.htm
- msdn for (C# Reference)—
  http://msdn.microsoft.com/en-us/library/ch45axte.aspx
- C# Video Tutorial—
  http://www.pvtuts.com/csharp/csharp-loops

QUICK REVIEW

1. The three programming constructs found in most programming languages are simple sequence, selection, and iteration.
2. Based on a predetermined condition, iteration enables you to identify and block together one or more statements to be repeated.
3. The looping structures available in C# include `while`, `do...while`, `for`, and `foreach` statements. The `do...while` loop is a posttest. The others are pretest loop structures. With pretest, the conditional expression is tested before any of the statements in the body of the loop are performed.
4. When you know the number of times the statements must be executed, you can use a counter-controlled loop.
5. An infinite loop does not have provisions for normal termination. Infinite loops occur when the loop's conditional expression never evaluates to `false` or there is some inherent characteristic or problem with the loop.

6.
7.
8.
9.
10.
11.
12.
13.
14.
15.
16.
17.

19. Which statement could be used in C# to set a `ListBox` object's selection mode to MultiExtended if you did not have Visual Studio's Properties window available? The name for the `ListBox` `object` is `lstBox1`.
    a. `lstBox1.SelectionMode = SelectionMode.MultiExtended;`
    b. `lstBox1 = MultiExtended;`
    c. `SelectionMode = MultiExtended;`
    d. `SelectionMode.MultiExtended;`
    e. all of the above

20. Which property can be set for a form to enable the Enter key to function like a mouse click for a selected `Button` `object`?
    a. `Enter`
    b. `Button_Click`
    c. `EnterKey`
    d. `AcceptButton`
    e. `AcceptKey`

---

21. Describe what is required to make a menu option clickable or a check box functional.

22. When is a `RadioButton` control preferred over a `CheckBox` control? When is a `ComboBox` control preferred over a `ListBox` control?

23. Identify two control options you might add to a Windows form to enable more controls to be available without consuming a lot of additional space.

ed?

e loop

Exercises further reinforce learning and ensure that students have, in fact, absorbed the material. Both objective and subjective types of activities are included at the end of each chapter.

Programming Exercises challenge students to write C# programs with a specified outcome.

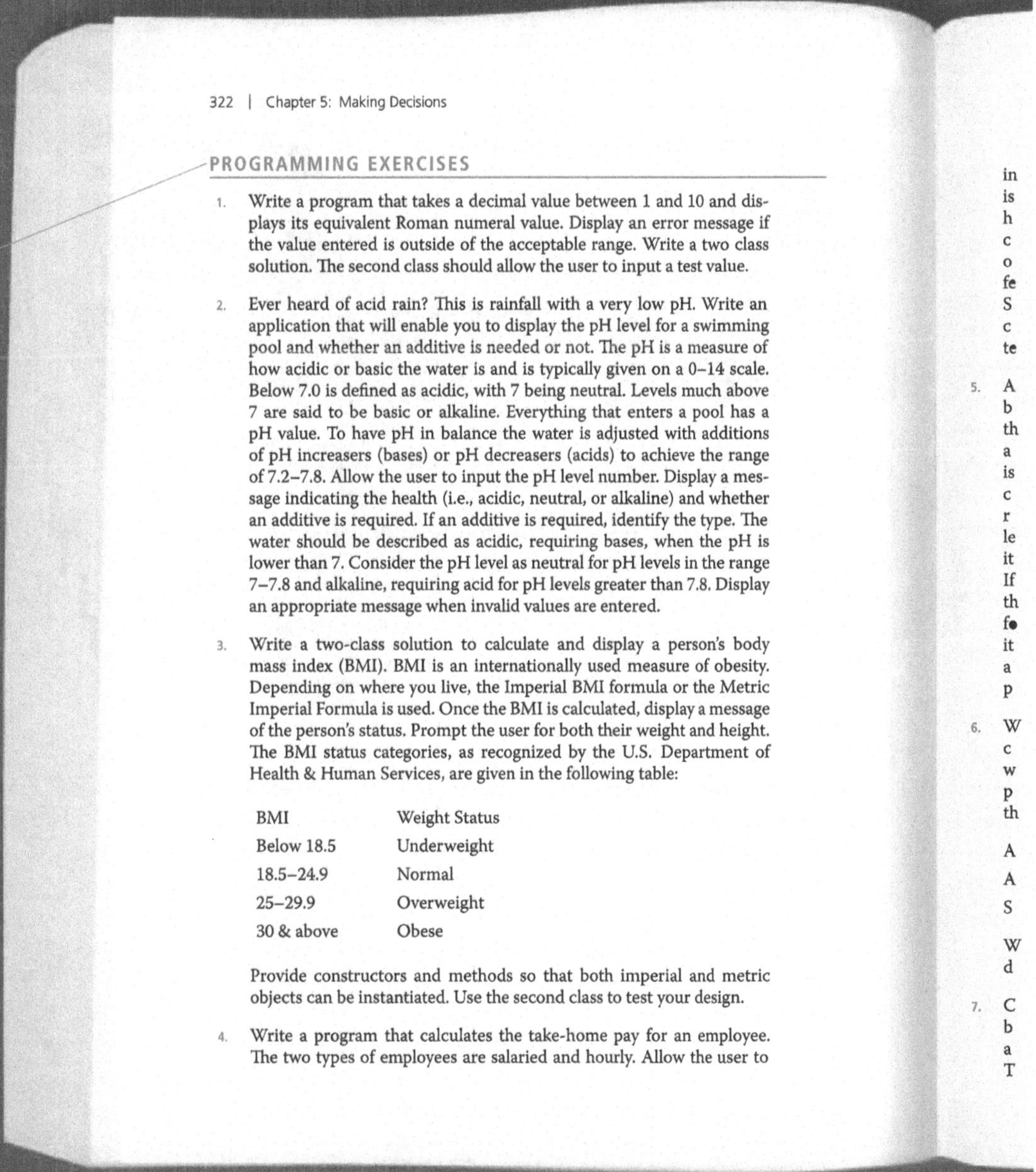

PROGRAMMING EXERCISES

1. Write a program that takes a decimal value between 1 and 10 and displays its equivalent Roman numeral value. Display an error message if the value entered is outside of the acceptable range. Write a two class solution. The second class should allow the user to input a test value.

2. Ever heard of acid rain? This is rainfall with a very low pH. Write an application that will enable you to display the pH level for a swimming pool and whether an additive is needed or not. The pH is a measure of how acidic or basic the water is and is typically given on a 0–14 scale. Below 7.0 is defined as acidic, with 7 being neutral. Levels much above 7 are said to be basic or alkaline. Everything that enters a pool has a pH value. To have pH in balance the water is adjusted with additions of pH increasers (bases) or pH decreasers (acids) to achieve the range of 7.2–7.8. Allow the user to input the pH level number. Display a message indicating the health (i.e., acidic, neutral, or alkaline) and whether an additive is required. If an additive is required, identify the type. The water should be described as acidic, requiring bases, when the pH is lower than 7. Consider the pH level as neutral for pH levels in the range 7–7.8 and alkaline, requiring acid for pH levels greater than 7.8. Display an appropriate message when invalid values are entered.

3. Write a two-class solution to calculate and display a person's body mass index (BMI). BMI is an internationally used measure of obesity. Depending on where you live, the Imperial BMI formula or the Metric Imperial Formula is used. Once the BMI is calculated, display a message of the person's status. Prompt the user for both their weight and height. The BMI status categories, as recognized by the U.S. Department of Health & Human Services, are given in the following table:

BMI	Weight Status
Below 18.5	Underweight
18.5–24.9	Normal
25–29.9	Overweight
30 & above	Obese

   Provide constructors and methods so that both imperial and metric objects can be instantiated. Use the second class to test your design.

4. Write a program that calculates the take-home pay for an employee. The two types of employees are salaried and hourly. Allow the user to

ıse 4 using
erver con-
ect) when
nal details

dd features
and so on.

name, last
m in a text
be stored.
page both
s stored in

epartment
s database
stores the
ent phone
abase table
he name of
by chang-
rid storing

© zeljkodan/Shutterstock.com

APPENDIX A
VISUAL STUDIO CONFIGURATION

To increase productivity, you might want to configure the appearance and behavior of the integrated development environment (IDE) for Visual Studio. This appendix presents suggestions for possible settings.

Customizing the Development Environment

When Visual Studio is launched, it opens the current default **Start Page**. As shown in Figure A-1, you have options of **New Project . . .**, **Open Project . . .**, and **Open from Source Control . . .** from the **Start Page**. Shown below that main level of menu options, you see a heading labeled **Recent**. It shows the last 10 projects opened and enables you to quickly reopen the project from that link without having to browse to the location where the project is stored. Also included on this default **Start Page** are sections enabling you to **Connect to Azure, Discover what's new**, view **Product Videos**, and see **Announcements.**

You can choose to have this page opened each time you run Visual Studio or deselect the checkbox in the extreme left corner and not **Show page on startup**. You can begin customizing your environment even at that point. You can also check the **Keep page open after project loads** if you do want to see the **Start Page** listed as one of the available tabs while you are working on your project.

Special appendices highlight code editor tools and provide suggestion for configuring Visual Studio to maximum productivity.

Instructor Resources

The following teaching tools are available for download at our Instructor Companion Site. Simply search for this text at *sso.cengage.com*. An instructor login is required.

Instructor's Manual. The Instructor's Manual that accompanies this textbook includes additional material to assist in class preparation, including suggestions for lecture topics.

Test Bank: Cengage Learning Testing Powered by Cognero is a flexible, online system that allows you to:

- author, edit, and manage test bank content from multiple Cengage Learning solutions
- create multiple test versions in an instant
- deliver tests from your LMS, your classroom, or wherever you want

PowerPoint Presentations. Microsoft PowerPoint slides are available for each chapter. These are offered as a teaching aid for classroom presentations, either to make available to students on the network for chapter review or to be printed for classroom distribution. Instructors can add their own slides for additional topics that they introduce to the class.

Source Code for Examples. The complete Visual Studio project files for the examples included within each chapter are available for instructors and are also posted for students on Cengage.com. Individual source code files are stored with a .cs extension inside the project subdirectory.

Programming Exercises Solution Files. The complete Visual Studio project files for the solutions to all programming exercises included at the end of the chapters are provided. The individual source code files are stored with a .cs extension inside the project subdirectory.

Acknowledgments

I would like to express my gratitude for the opportunity to complete the fifth edition of this book. Like the other editions, it was a huge undertaking for me. Special thanks go out to Alyssa Pratt, Senior Content Developer, at Cengage Learning, for her positive comments, guidance, and support. She was a pleasure to work with again on this new edition. I am grateful to the Quality Assurance team members who verified that each of the examples and exercise solutions worked properly. Also thanks to the Content Manager and Copyeditor, Jennifer Feltri-George and Andrea Schein, who provided great suggestions as we progressed with the project.

I am very grateful to the following reviewers for their uplifting comments and suggestions for improvements:

Wai Mok: The University of Alabama in Huntsville

Iftikhar Sikder: Cleveland State University

Leslie Spivey: Edison Community College

I hope that the reviewers will see that many of their suggestions were implemented. The textbook is much improved because of their contributions.

CHAPTER 1

© zeljkodan/Shutterstock.com

Introduction to Computing and Application Development

IN THIS CHAPTER, YOU WILL:

- Learn about the history of computers
- Differentiate between system and application software
- Investigate the steps of software development
- Explore different programming methodologies
- Discover why C# is being used today for software development
- Distinguish between the different types of applications that can be created with C#
- Explore an application written in C#
- Examine the basic elements of a C# program
- Compile, run, build, and debug an application
- Create an application that displays output
- Work through a programming example that illustrates the chapter's concepts

Computers have become such an integral part of our lives today that many of their functions are taken for granted. Yet, only a few years ago, mobile apps, text messaging, and cloud computing were unknown. Social media is one of the most powerful sources for news updates through platforms such as Twitter and Facebook. With today's smartphones, many people have the computing power of mini super computers in their pockets. Video-sharing websites such as YouTube can now be accessed with most smartphones. Advances in computing are occurring every day. Expectations are that tablet sales will grow by 200 percent through 2016. Over 100 million units were sold in last year. For most consumers, tablets are not replacements for their conventional computers but are added devices they will purchase.

Much personal computing can now occur on smaller devices. Mobile applications, or apps, for smartphones, tablets, and other wireless devices are increasingly in demand. Today because of smartphone apps, you don't have to worry about being lost, being bored, or alone. To reach this level of complexity, software development has gone through a number of eras, and today technical advances accumulate faster and faster. What new types of computer software will be integral to our daily lives in the future? What types of apps will be on the wearable technology such as wristwatches or glasses for you in the future. The focus of this book is to introduce you to application development. Before beginning the journey into software development, a historical perspective on computing is included to help you see the potential for advancements that awaits you.

History of Computers

Computing dates back some 5000 years. Many consider the abacus to be the first computer. Used by merchants of the past and present for trading transactions, the abacus is a simple calculating device that uses a system of sliding beads on a rack for addition and subtraction.

In 1642, another calculating device, called the Pascaline, was created. The Pascaline had eight movable dials on wheels that could calculate sums up to eight figures long. Both the abacus and Pascaline could perform only addition and subtraction. It was not until the 1830s that the first general-purpose computer, the Analytical Engine, was available.

Charles Babbage and his assistant, Lady Augusta Ada Byron, Countess of Lovelace, designed the Analytical Engine. Although it was very primitive by today's standards, it was the prototype for what is known today as a general-purpose computer. The Analytical Engine included input devices, memory storage, a control unit that allowed processing instructions in any sequence, and output devices.

NOTE In the 1980s, the U.S. Defense Department named the Ada programming language in honor of Lady Lovelace. She has been called the world's first programmer. Controversy surrounds her title. Lady Byron was probably the fourth or fifth person to write programs. She did programming as a student of Charles Babbage and reworked some of his calculations. Babbage is considered the father of the computer since he conceptualized and invented the first mechanical computer in the nineteenth century.

Many computer historians believe the present day to be in the fifth generation of modern computing. Each era is characterized by an important advancement in computer technology. In the mid-1940s, World War II, with its need for strategic types of calculations, spurred on the first generation of general-purpose machines. These large, first-generation computers were distinguished by the use of vacuum tubes. They were difficult to program and limited in functionality. The operating instructions were made to order for each specific task.

The invention of the transistor in 1956 led to second-generation computers, which were smaller, faster, more reliable, and more energy efficient than their predecessors.

The third generation, 1964–1971, saw computers become smaller, as transistors were squeezed onto small silicon discs (single chips), which were called semiconductors. Operating systems, as they are known today, which allowed machines to run many different programs at once, were also first seen in third-generation systems.

As time passed, chips kept getting smaller and capable of storing more transistors, making computers more powerful and less expensive. The Intel 4004 chip, developed in 1971, placed the most important components of a computer (central processing unit, memory, and input and output controls) on a minuscule chip about half the size of a dime. Many household items such as microwave ovens, television sets, and automobiles benefited from the fourth generation of computing.

During the fourth generation, computer manufacturers tried to bring computing to general consumers. In 1981, IBM introduced its personal computer (PC). The 1980s saw an expansion in computer use as clones of the IBM PC made the PC even more affordable. We also saw the development of graphical user interfaces (GUIs) and the mouse as a handheld input device. The number of PCs in use more than doubled from two million in 1981 to 5.5 million in 1982. Ten years later, 65 million PCs were in use.

NOTE According to the 2013 *U.S. Census Bureau's Current Population Survey*, over 83.8% of households in the United States had computers at home. Over 73% reported having a high-speed Internet connection at home.

Widespread use of computer networks and parallel processing, where computers use more than one CPU for faster processing speeds, characterize the current fifth-generation systems. Fifth-generation devices are still in development. Smaller devices with touchscreen capabilities using mobile apps are growing.

The real power of the computer does not lie in the hardware, which comprises the physical components that make up the system. The functionality lies in the software available to make use of the hardware. Computers can now accept spoken word instructions, imitate human reasoning through artificial intelligence, and communicate with devices instantaneously around the globe by transmitting digital media. By applying problem-solving steps, expert systems assist physicians in making diagnoses. Healthcare professionals are now using handheld devices in patients' rooms to retrieve and update patient records. Using handheld devices, drivers of delivery trucks are accessing global positioning systems (GPSs) to verify locations of customers for pickups and deliveries. Sitting at a traffic light or in a restaurant, you can check your text messages, make airline reservations, remotely monitor and manage household appliances, and access your checking and savings accounts. Using wireless networks, students can access a professor's notes when they enter the classroom. These things are all possible because of the software, the applications controlling the hardware devices. Because of the programmability of the computer, the imagination of software developers is set free to conjure the computing functions of the future. Software developers are able to help make ideas come to reality faster. The next section begins the discussion on software, which is the focus of this book.

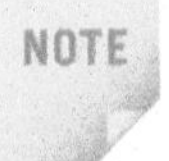

According to the Bureau of Labor Statistics, employment of software developers is projected to grow 22 percent from 2012 to 2022, much faster than the average of all occupations. The Occupational Outlook Handbook also reported the median pay in 2012 for software developers with a bachelor's degree and no work experience was $93,350 per year.

System and Application Software

Software consists of **programs**, which are sets of instructions telling the computer exactly what to do. The instructions might tell the computer to add up a set of numbers, make a decision based on the result of a calculation, or translate a sentence from one language into another. Just as a cook follows a set of instructions (a recipe) to prepare a dish, the computer follows instructions without adding extra salt to perform a useful task. Instructions for computers have also gone through a number of stages or generations.

Machine code instructions, or programs, that were executed directly by the CPU were used with general-purpose machines in the 1940s. Back then instructions were entered through a panel of switches. The instructions were symbolized by 1s and 0s representing whether the switch was turned on or off. This was a tedious error prone endeavor. Assembly language instructions, which were tied to a particular computer's architecture, were next used. Instructions still had to be converted into machine-readable form, but these instructions or programs could be read and written by humans.

In the mid to late 1950s, the software industry that we know today was born with the introduction of languages such as **FORTRAN** (Formula Translator) and **COBOL** (Common Business-Oriented Language). These languages were not hardware dependent and marked the beginning of third-generation languages. They are easier to read, closer to human languages, and further from the machine instructions. Programs written using third-generation instructions can run on different machines. Most popular general-purpose languages of today are considered third-generation high-level programming languages.

Some computer historians identify fourth- and fifth-generation languages with fourth generation being characterized by black box processing and fifth-generation languages designed to have the computer solve problems without a programmer.

The next sections describe the two major categories of software that can be developed using a programming language: system software and application software.

System Software

System software is loaded when you power on the computer. When thinking of system software, most people think of operating systems. **Operating systems** such as Windows, Android, iOS, and Linux are types of programs that oversee and coordinate the resources on the machine. Included are file system utilities, small programs that take care of locating files and keeping up with the details of a file's name, size, and date of creation. System software programs perform a variety of other functions: setting up directories; moving, copying, and deleting files; transferring data from secondary storage to primary memory; formatting media; and displaying data on screens. Operating systems include communication programs for connecting to the Internet or connecting to output devices such as printers. They include user interface (UI) subsystems for managing the look and feel of the system.

NOTE

Operating systems are one type of system software. They are utility programs that make it easier for you to use the hardware.

Other types of system software include compilers, interpreters, and assemblers. As you begin learning software development, you will write instructions for the computer using a **programming language**. Modern programming languages are designed to be easy to read and write. They are called **high-level languages** because they are written in English-like statements. The programming language you will be using is **C#** (pronounced *see sharp*). Other high-level computer programming languages include Java, Visual Basic, C, and C++.

Before the computer can execute the instructions written in a programming language such as C#, the instructions must be translated into machine-readable format. A **compiler** makes this conversion. Compilers are considered types of system software. Figure 1-1 shows what a machine language instruction looks like.

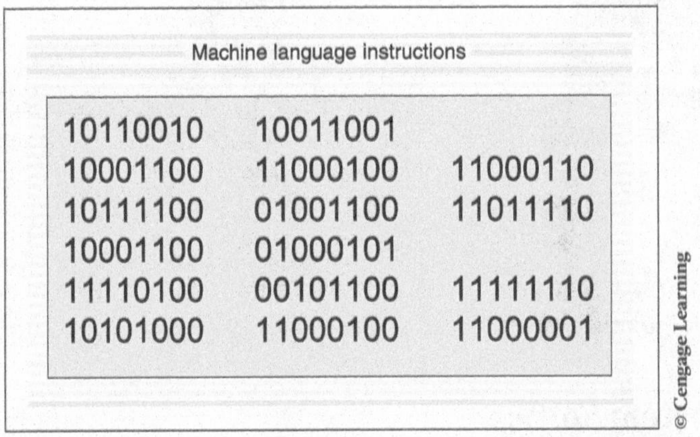

Machine language instructions

```
10110010   10011001
10001100   11000100   11000110
10111100   01001100   11011110
10001100   01000101
11110100   00101100   11111110
10101000   11000100   11000001
```

© Cengage Learning

FIGURE 1-1 A machine language instruction

Just as the English language has rules for sentence construction, programming languages such as C# have a set of rules, called **syntax** that must be followed. Before translating code into machine-readable form, a compiler checks for rule violations. Compilers do not convert any statements into machine language until all syntax errors are removed. Code can be interpreted as well as compiled. Interpreters translate one statement of code into an intermediate form and then execute that line. They then translate the next instruction, execute it, and so on. Unlike compilers, which look at entire pieces of code, **interpreters** check for rule violations line by line. If the line does not contain an error, it is converted and immediately executed. Interpreters are normally slower than compilers. Many languages offer both compilers and interpreters, including C, BASIC, Python, and Lisp. **Assemblers** convert the assembly programming language, which is a low-level programming language, into machine code. Low-level programming languages are closer to hardware. They are not as easy to read or write as high-level programming languages.

Application Software

Application software consists of programs developed to perform a specific task. The games you might play or the search engines you use on the Internet are types of application software. Word processors, such as Microsoft Word, are examples of application software. Word was written to help users create professional looking documents by including a number of editing and formatting options. Spreadsheets, such as Microsoft Excel, are types of application software designed to make numerical calculations and generate charts. Database management systems, such as SQL Server, Oracle, or Microsoft Access, were designed to organize large amounts of data, so that reports could easily be generated. Software that generates payroll checks is considered application software, as is software that helps you register for a class. E-commerce websites with database-driven shopping carts, such as eBay, are forms of application software. Application software is used by the banking industry to manage your checking and saving accounts. Application developers, or programmers, use development languages such as C# to write software to carry out specific tasks or to solve specific problems. The programs that you write from this book will be application software.

Software Development Process

You will soon be writing programs using C#. How do you start? Many beginning programmers just begin typing without planning or without using any organized sequence of steps. This often leads to increased development time and solutions that might not consistently produce accurate results.

Programming is a process of problem solving. Typing the program statements in a language such as C# is not the hardest part of programming. The most difficult part is coming up with a plan to solve the problem. A number of different approaches, or **methodologies**, are used to solve computer-related problems. Successful problem solvers follow a methodical approach with each programming project. Figure 1-2 illustrates the organized plan, or methodology, that is used to solve the problems presented in this book. The following section describes each step.

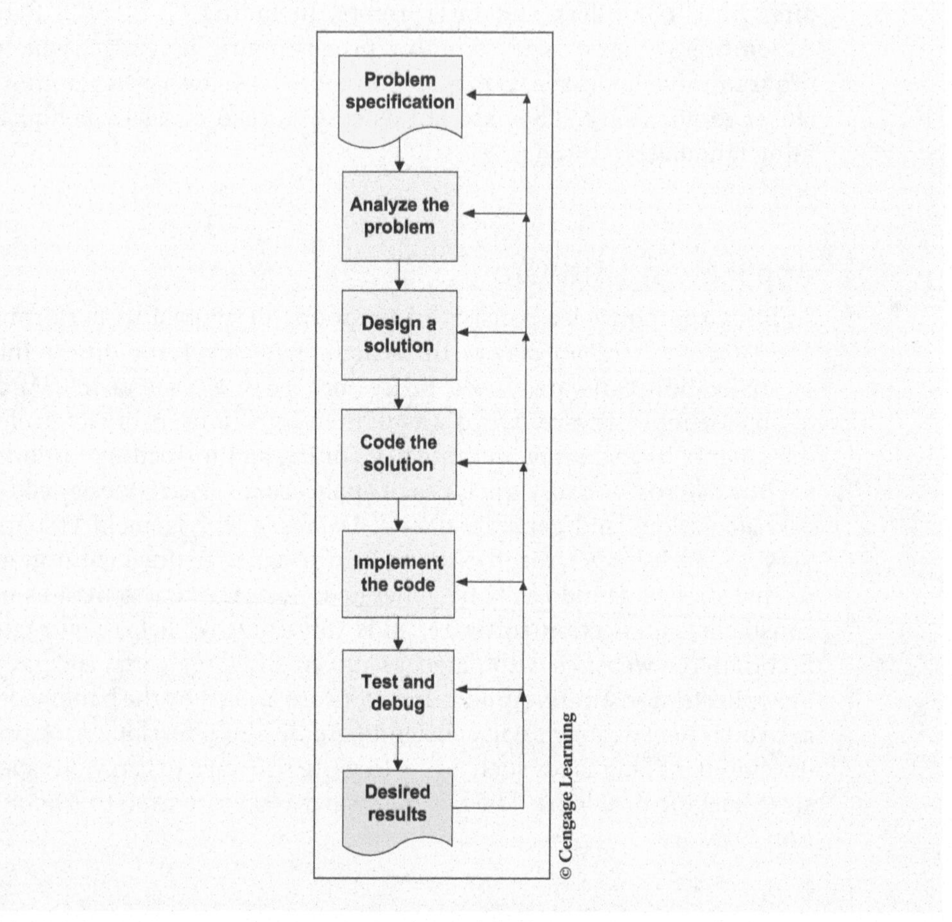

FIGURE 1-2 Steps in the software development process

Steps in the Program Development Process

1. **Analyze the problem.** The first step should be directed toward grasping the problem thoroughly. Analyze precisely what the software is supposed to accomplish. During this phase, you review the problem **specifications**, which describe what the program should accomplish. Specifications often include the desired output of the program in terms of what is to be displayed, saved, or printed. If specifications are ambiguous or need clarification, you might need to ask probing questions. *If you do not know where you are going, how will you know when you have arrived at the correct location?*

NOTE Sometimes one of the most difficult parts of the process is getting clear specifications from the user. Unless you know what the problem is, there is no way you can solve it. Make sure that you understand the problem definition.

A program specification might look like Figure 1-3.

Rapid Ready Car Rental Agency rents four types of vehicles:

Economy
Intermediate
Full size
Specialty-sports

The economy rents for $31.95 per day; the intermediate rents for $41.95 per day; the full size rents for $49.95 per day; and the specialty-sports rents for $59.95 per day.
They offer a 10% discount for rental periods in excess of 7 days. Rapid Ready has a policy that prohibits rental for periods beyond 30 days.
Allow the user to select the type of vehicle and number of total days before displaying the final price.

© Cengage Learning

FIGURE 1-3 Program specification sheet for a car rental agency problem

During this first phase, in addition to making sure that you understand the problem definition, you must also review the program inputs. You should ask the following types of questions:

- What kind of data will be available for input?
- What types of values (e.g., whole numbers, alphabetic characters, and numbers with a decimal point) will be in each of the identified data items?
- What is the **domain** (range of the values) for each input item?
- Will the user of the program be inputting values?
- If the problem solution is to be used with multiple data sets, are there any data items that stay the same, or remain **constant**, with each set?

Before you move to designing a solution, you should have a thorough understanding of the problem. It might be helpful to verbalize the problem definition. It might help to see sample input for each of the data items. Figure 1-4 illustrates how the input data items would be determined during analysis for the car rental agency problem shown in Figure 1-3. Figure 1-4 shows the identifier, or name of the data item, the type, and the domain of values for each item.

Instead of having the user enter the full words of Economy, Intermediate, Full size, or Specialty Sports, the characters E, I, F, and S could be mapped to those categories.

Data identifier	Data type	Domain of values
kindOfVehicle	char (single coded character)	E, I, F, or S
noOfDays	Integer (whole number)	1...30

© Cengage Learning

FIGURE 1-4 Data for car rental agency

2. **Design a solution.** Programmers use several approaches, or **methods**, during design. Procedural and object-oriented methodologies are the two most commonly used design methods. Some projects are more easily solved using one approach than the other. Both of these approaches are discussed in the next section. The selection of programming language sometimes weighs in when determining the approach. The C# language was designed to be very object oriented.

   No matter what size the project is, careful design always leads to better solutions. In addition, careful design normally leads to solutions that can be produced in shorter amounts of time. A **divide-and-conquer** approach can be used with both methodologies. As the name implies, when you divide and conquer a programming problem, you break the problem into subtasks. Then, you conquer each of the subtasks by further decomposing them. This process is also called **top-down design**. Detailed models should be developed as input to subsequent phases.

Using the **object-oriented approach**, the focus is on determining the data characteristics and the methods or behaviors that operate on the data. These logical groupings of members (data and behavior) are referred to as a **class**. These characteristics are placed in a class diagram. Figure 1-5 contains a class diagram for the problem specification given in Figure 1-3.

Rental Car
-kindOfVehicle : char -noOfDays : int
+ComputeCharges() : double

© Cengage Learning

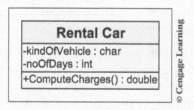

FIGURE 1-5 Class diagram of car rental agency

Figure 1-5 is a class diagram divided into three sections with the top portion identifying the name of the class. The middle portion of a class diagram always lists the data characteristics. Data representing the type of vehicle to rent and the number of days for the rental are important to a rental car agency. The bottom portion of the class diagram shown in Figure 1-5 shows what actions are to be performed with the data items. `ComputeCharges( )` is used to determine the cost of the rental using the type of vehicle and the number of rental days. You will learn more about class diagrams later in this chapter. Procedural designs, which are appropriate for simpler problem definitions, use structure charts to show the hierarchy of modules, and flowcharts or pseudocode listings to detail the steps for each of the modules.

Algorithms for the behaviors (object oriented) or processes (procedural) should be developed for both of these methodologies. An **algorithm** is a clear, unambiguous, step-by-step process for solving a problem. These steps must be expressed so completely and so precisely that all details are included. The instructions in the algorithm should be both simple to perform and capable of being carried out in a finite amount of time. Following the steps blindly should result in the same results every time.

An algorithm for `ComputeCharges( )` multiplies the number of rental days by the rate associated with the type of vehicle rented to produce the rental charge. After the algorithm is developed, the design should be checked for correctness. One way to do this is to use sample data and **desk check** your algorithms by mimicking the computer; in other words, walking through the computer's steps. Follow each step precisely, one step at a time. If the problem involves calculations, use a calculator, and follow your design statements exactly. It is important when you desk check not to add any additional steps, unless you go back and revise the algorithm.

During this phase, it might also be helpful to plan and design the look of the desired output by developing a prototype. A **prototype** is a mock-up of screens depicting the look of the final output.

3. **Code the solution.** After you have completed the design and verified that the algorithm is correct, you translate the design into source code. **Source code** consists of program statements written using a programming language, such as C#.

Source code statements can be typed into the computer using an editor such as Notepad or an **integrated development environment (IDE)**, such as Visual Studio. IDEs include a number of useful development tools: IntelliSense (pop-up windows with completion options), debugging, color coding of different program sections, online help and documentation, and features for running the program.

You must follow the syntax of the language when you code the solution. Whether you speak English, Spanish, or another language, you are accustomed to following language **syntax**, or rules. For example, the syntax of the English language dictates that statements end with periods and include subjects and verbs. When you write in English, you are expected to follow those rules. When you write in the C# programming language, you are expected to follow the rule that every statement should end with a semicolon. It is at this third phase of the program development process (code the solution) that you must concern yourself with language syntax.

Many programmers use an **iterative approach** in the software development process. This means that you might find it necessary to go back to the design stage to make modifications. There might even be times when additional analysis is necessary. If you analyze and design thoroughly before attempting to code the solution, you usually develop a much better program that is easier to read and modify.

4. **Implement the code.** During this phase, the typed program statements (source code) are compiled to check for rule violations. IDEs such as Visual Studio supply compilers within the development environment. The output of the compiler is a listing of the errors along with a brief description of the violation. Before the implementation can go forward, all the syntax errors must be corrected. When rule violations are eliminated, the source code is converted into the **Microsoft Intermediate Language (MSIL)**. All languages targeting the .NET (pronounced dot net) platform compile into MSIL. The language that you will be using in this book, C#, is a language introduced as part of the .NET platform. Like C#, other languages, such as Java, compile code into an intermediate language. Java's intermediate language is called **bytecode**. Intermediate languages facilitate the use of code that is more platform independent than other languages that compile straight into the machine language of the specific platform.

NOTE

If you are using the Visual Studio IDE, you might not be aware of the MSIL's presence. You simply select options to compile, build, and execute the program to see the output results.

The MSIL code is between the high-level source code and the **native code**, which is the machine language code of a particular computer. MSIL code is not directly executable on any computer. It is not in the language of the computer, which means that it is not tied to any specific CPU platform. A second step is required before you see the results of the application.

This second step is managed by .NET's **common language runtime (CLR)**. CLR loads predefined .NET classes used by the program into memory and then performs a second compile, called a **just-in-time (JIT) compilation**. This converts the MSIL code into the platform's native code. The CLR tool used for this is a JIT compiler called **JITer**. JITer reads the MSIL and produces the machine code that runs on the particular platform. Any computer that executes the code must have the CLR installed. The CLR is included with the .NET Framework. Any computer executing .NET code must have the .NET Framework installed. Figure 1-6 illustrates the steps that must be performed for source code written in C# to be executed.

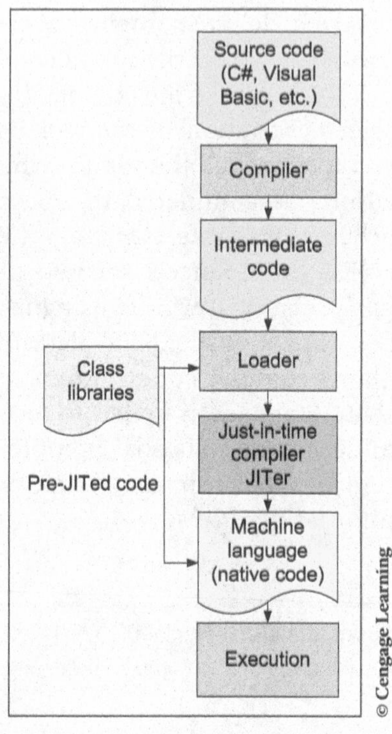

FIGURE 1-6 Execution steps for .NET

5. **Test and debug.** Even though you have no compiler syntax errors and you receive output, your results might be incorrect. You must test the program to ensure that you get consistent results. The **testing** phases are often shortchanged. Only after thoroughly testing can you be sure that your program is running correctly.

   Plan your testing. Good programmers often build **test plans** at the same time they are analyzing and designing their solutions. This test plan should include testing extreme values, identifying possible problem cases, and ensuring that these cases are tested. After syntax errors are eliminated and results are being produced, you should implement the test plan verifying that the results are accurate. If the application is interacting with a user for input of data, run the program multiple times with the planned test values. For calculations, perform the same operations using a calculator, much as you did during the design phase when you desk checked your algorithm. There are software development methodologies built around test development. For example,

Test Driven Development (TDD) is a programming methodology that emphasizes fast, incremental development and writing tests before writing code. With TDD, additional functionality is added only after the first tests are passed. The first cycle normally deals with very simple cases. After you have these very simple tests working, you add more functionality, a bit at a time.

During testing, **logic errors** are often uncovered. Logic errors might cause an abnormal termination of the program or just produce incorrect results. These types of errors are often more difficult to locate and correct than syntax errors. A **run-time error** is one form of logic error. Run-time errors normally cause program crashes (stopping execution) and the reporting of error messages. For example, if you attempt to divide by zero, your program might crash. To further complicate matters, a program might sometimes work properly with most test data, but crash when a certain value is entered. This is why it is so important to make sure that you thoroughly test all applications. When a logic error is detected, it might be necessary to go back to Step 1, reanalyze the problem specifications, and redesign a solution. As you look back at Figure 1-2, notice the figure shows that the software development process is iterative. As errors are discovered, it is often necessary to cycle back to a previous phase or step.

Programming Methodologies

How do you ride a bicycle? How do you drive a car? How do you do your laundry? How do you prepare for an exam? As you think about those questions, you probably have an answer, and your answer will differ from those of other readers. However, you have some strategy, a set of steps, which you follow to get the job done. You can think of a methodology as a strategy, a set of steps, or a set of directions. Programmers use a number of different programming methodologies. The two most popular programming paradigms are structured procedural programming and **object-oriented programming (OOP)**. These approaches are discussed in this section.

Structured Procedural Programming

This approach emerged in the 1970s and is still in use today. **Procedural programming** is process-oriented focusing on the processes that data undergoes from input until meaningful output is produced. This approach is very effective for small stand-alone applications. The five steps for software development—analyze, design, code, implement, and test and debug—which were identified in the preceding section, work well for the structured procedural approach.

During design, processing steps are defined in terms of an algorithm. Any formulas or special processing steps are included in the algorithm. To think algorithmically, programmers use a number of tools. One such tool used is a flowchart. Figure 1-7 shows some of the symbols used in a flowchart for the construction of an algorithm.

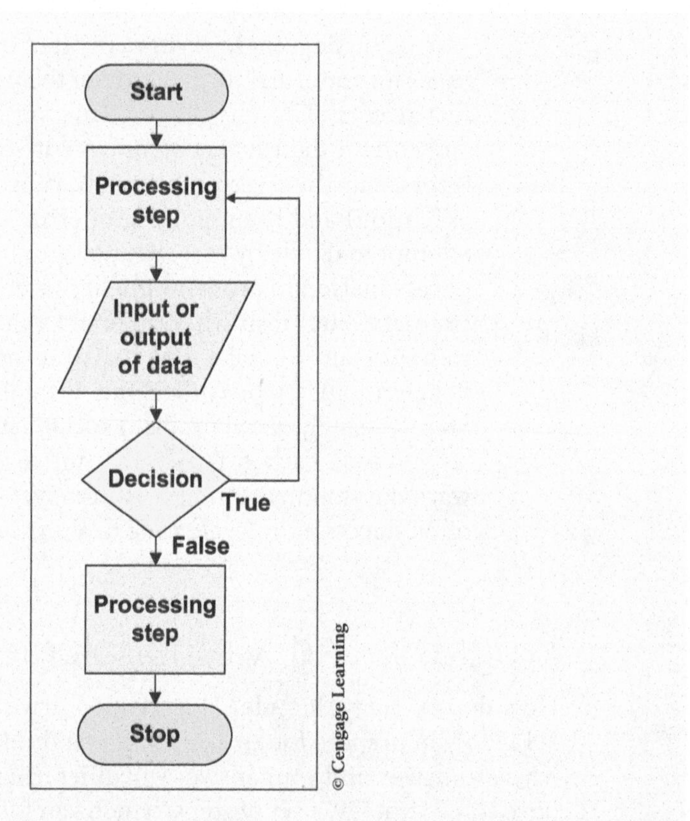

FIGURE 1-7 Flowchart symbols and their interpretation

Another tool used to develop an algorithm during design is **pseudocode**. As the name implies, with pseudocode, steps are written in pseudo or approximate code format, which looks like English statements. The focus is on determining and writing the processes or steps involved to produce the desired output. With pseudocode, the algorithm is written using a combination of English statements and the chosen programming language, such as C#. Verbs such as compute, calculate, sum, print, input, and display are used to imply what type of activity is needed to reach the desired result. While, do while, for, and for each are used to imply looping or that steps should be performed more than one time. When decisions or tests are required, if and if else are used. Indentation is used to show which program statements are grouped together. Figure 1-8 shows example pseudocode for the Rapid Ready car rental problem specification.

```
if (desired number of days > 30)
  display message "Sorry can not rent more than 30 days"
else
{
   if (desired number of days > 7)
      discount percent = 0.10
   else
      discount percent = 0

   if (car type = 'E')
      rate = 31.95
   else
      if (car type = 'I')
         rate = 41.95
      else
         if (car type = 'F')
            rate = 49.95
         else
            if (car type = 'S')
               rate = 59.95
  calculate cost before discount = rate * desired number of days
  calculate discount amount = cost before discount * discount percent
  calculate final charge = cost before discount - discount amount
}
```

FIGURE 1-8 Pseudocode or Structured English for the Rental Car application

Structured programming is associated with a technique called **top-down design** or **stepwise refinement**. The underlying theme or concept is that given a problem definition, you can refine the logic by dividing and conquering. The problem can be divided into subproblems, or procedures. Then, each of the subproblems is furthered decomposed. This continues until you reach subproblems that are straightforward enough to be solved easily at the subproblem level. After you arrive at a solution at the lower levels, these solutions are combined to solve the overall problem.

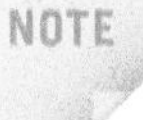

Consider the analogy of building a house. Using top-down design, this problem might be decomposed into Prepare the Land, Construct the Foundation, Frame the Structure, Install the Roof, Finish the Interior, and Complete the Exterior. Then, each of these subproblems could be further subdivided. An overall contractor could be hired for the project and then subcontractors assigned to each of the subproblem areas. Within each subproblem, additional problems would be defined and separate workers assigned to that area. For example, Finish the Interior might be further divided into Walls, Floors, and so on. Walls would be further decomposed into Hang Sheet Rock, Mud the Walls, Prepare for Paint, Paint the Walls, Paint the Trim, and so on. Again, each of these areas could be subcontracted out.

As you think about breaking the Rental Car problem into smaller subprograms, you might consider that the data must be entered or inputted, number of days tested to determine whether you can rent the car or not, type of desired vehicle tested to determine the rate, final calculations made, and then the results displayed. Each of those small subprograms could be further divided into multiple program statements.

Programmers using the structured procedural approach normally write each of the subprograms as separate functions or methods that are called by a main controlling function or module. This facilitates the divide-and-conquer approach. With larger problems, the subprograms can be written by different individuals. One of the drawbacks of the procedural approach involves **software maintenance**. When an application is upgraded or changed, programs written using the procedural approach are more difficult to maintain. Even minor modifications can affect multiple functions and require additional modifications to be made. There is also less opportunity to reuse code than with the object-oriented methodology.

Object-Oriented Programming

OOP developed as the dominant programming methodology in the early and mid-1990s. Today it is viewed as a excellent approach to software development. The concept behind OOP is that applications can be organized around objects rather than processes. This methodology includes a number of powerful design strategies that facilitate construction of more complex systems that model real-world entities. The C# language was designed to take advantage of the benefits of the object-oriented methodology.

With **object-oriented analysis, design**, and **programming**, the focus is on determining the objects you want to manipulate rather than the processes or logic required to manipulate the data. Remember that the procedural approach focuses on processes. One of the underlying assumptions of the object-oriented methodology is that the world contains a number of entities that can be identified and described. An **entity** is often defined as a person, place, or thing. It is normally a noun. By **abstracting out the attributes** (data) and the **behaviors** (processes on the data), you can divide complex phenomena into understandable entities. An **abstraction** is simply a description of the essential, relevant properties of an entity. For example, you should easily be able to picture in your mind, or conceptualize, the entities of people, school personnel, faculty, student, undergraduate student, graduate student, vehicle, car, book, school, animal, dog, and poodle by describing **characteristics** or attributes, and **behaviors** or actions, about each of these.

Consider the case of a student. A student has these characteristics or attributes: student ID, name, age, GPA, major, and hometown. The characteristics can be further described by identifying what type or kind of data might exist in each of them. For example, alphabetic characters would be found in the name attribute. Whole numbers without a decimal would be found in the age attribute, and numbers with a decimal would be in the GPA attribute.

In addition to abstracting the data properties, you should also be able to think about some of the actions or behaviors of each of the entities identified in the previous paragraph. Behaviors associated with a student include actions such as Apply for Admission, Enroll as Student, Get Final Grade, Change Name, and Determine GPA. Using the object-oriented methodology, these attributes and actions (or characteristics and behaviors) are **encapsulated**, which means that they are combined together to form a class.

A **class diagram** is one of the primary modeling tools used by object-oriented programmers. You saw the Rental Car class diagram in Figure 1-5. Figure 1-9 illustrates another diagram using the Unified Modeling Language (UML) notation. The top portion of the diagram identifies the name of the class, which is Student. The section in the center contains the data members and the type of data that would be found in each data member. **Information hiding** is an important component of OOP. The minus symbol (–) to the left of the data member's name refers to the access modifier and indicates that the member is private and accessible to that class only. The bottom portion of the diagram in Figure 1-9 shows actions, or methods, of the Student class. The plus symbol (+) access modifier indicates that the behaviors are public and available outside of the class. You will read more about class diagrams in upcoming chapters. This UML notation is used throughout the book for creating class diagrams.

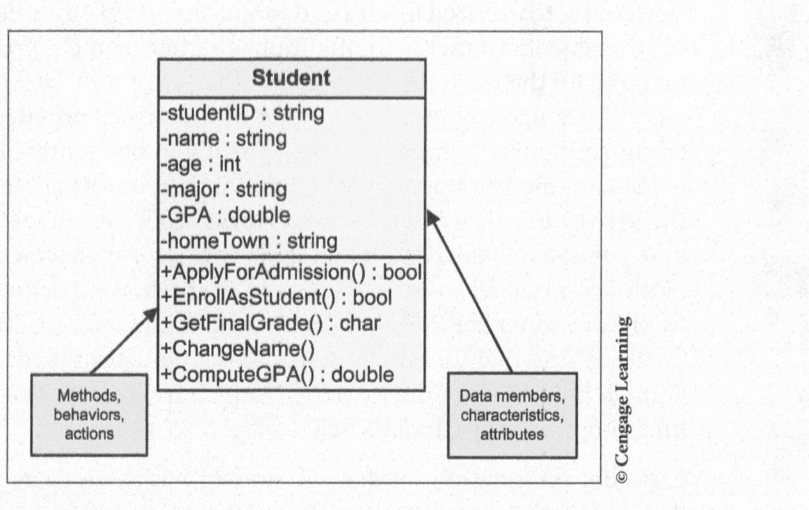

FIGURE 1-9 Student class diagram

A class is like a template. It is similar to a blueprint for a house. Even though you define all the characteristics of a house in the blueprint, the house does not exist until one is built using that template. Many houses can be created using the same template. In object-oriented terminology, the constructed house is one instance (object) of the blueprint or template. You **instantiate** the blueprint by building a house using that template. Many objects of a particular class can be instantiated. Thus, an **object** is an **instance** of the class.

Examine the expanded example of a student with the following data members:

- Student number: 122223
- Student name: Justin Howard
- Age: 18
- GPA: 3.80
- Major: CS
- Hometown: Winchester, Kentucky

When these data members are associated with the class, an object is created or **constructed**. A second object could be instantiated from that class by giving values to its members (e.g., 228221, Elizabeth Czerwinski, 21, 4.0, ENG, Reno, Nevada).

The object-oriented methodology facilitates designing components, which contain code that can be reused by packaging together the attributes of a data type along with the actions of that type. In Chapter 4, you will create your own classes that you instantiate. Through **inheritance**, it is possible to define subclasses of data objects that share some or all of the parent's class characteristics. This is what enables reuse of code. For example, you should be able to visualize that Student is a subset of Person, just as Teacher is a subset of Person. Using object-oriented design, you could abstract out the common characteristics of all people and place them in a superclass. Through inheritance, Student and Teacher can use the characteristics of Person and add their own unique members.

Another important object-oriented concept is polymorphism. Behaviors or methods of parent and subclasses can have the same name but offer different functionality. Through **polymorphism**, you are able to invoke methods of the same name on objects of different classes and have the correct method executed. For example, you might have subclasses of `UndergraduateStudent` and `GraduateStudent`. They could both inherit characteristics from the `Student class`. Both of the subclasses might have their own method that contains details about how to determine their cost of tuition. Both subclasses might name their method `DetermineTuitionCosts( )`. Through polymorphism, the correct method is executed based on which object invoked it. When an object of the `UndergraduateStudent class` is used, the `DetermineTuitionCosts( )` method of the `UndergraduateStudent class` is used. When an object of the `GraduateStudent class` is used, the `DetermineTuitionCosts( )` method of the `GraduateStudent class` is used. You will read much more about object-oriented features in upcoming chapters. In Chapter 11, you will read about advanced OOP features including inheritance and polymorphism. In that chapter, you will write multiclass solutions.

The object-oriented principles are of particular importance when developing applications using C#. No program can be written that does not include at least one class. All program statements written using the C# language are placed in a class.

Whether you are using a procedural or object-oriented approach, you should follow the five steps to program development. As with the procedural approach, the object-oriented development process is iterative. During design and subsequent phases, do not hesitate to reconsider analysis and design decisions.

Evolution of C# and .NET

Programming Languages

In the 1940s, programmers toggled switches on the front of computers to enter programs and data into memory. That is how some of the early programming began. Even when they moved to punching holes in cards to represent the 0s and 1s and reading the cards into memory, it could not have been much fun to be a programmer. It was easy to make an error. In the 1950s, assembly languages replaced the binary notation by using mnemonic symbols to represent the instructions for the computer. Symbols such as MV were used to represent moving the contents of one value in memory to another memory location. Assembly languages were designed to make the programmer's job easier by using these mnemonic symbols instead of binary numbers. However, the instructions depended on the particular CPU architecture. Statements to perform the same task differed from computer to computer. Assembly languages are still considered **low-level programming languages**. As you can see from Figure 1-10, these types of instructions are not easy to read or understand. They are not considered close to the English language, as high-level programming languages such as C# and Java are.

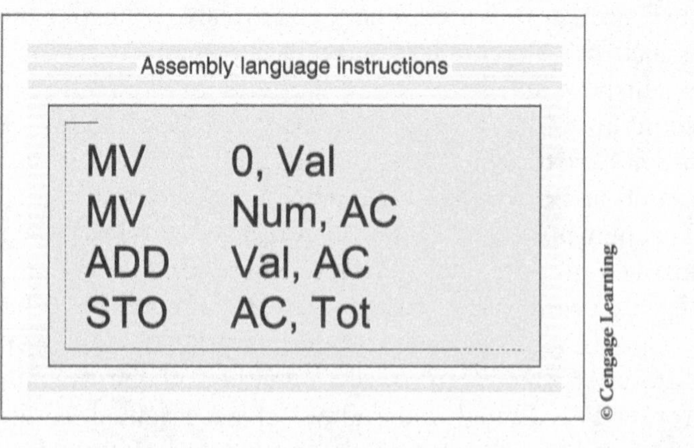

FIGURE 1-10 Assembly language instruction to add two values

As noted previously, high-level languages came into existence in the late 1950s with FORTRAN and later COBOL. These languages were considered **high-level languages** because they were designed to be accessible to humans, easy to read and write, and close to the English language. Since then, more than 2000 high-level languages have come into existence. Some have gone by the wayside, while others have evolved and are still widely used today.

Some of the more noteworthy high-level programming languages are C, C++, Visual Basic, Java, and now C#. C++ is an extension of C, which actually evolved from BCPL and B in 1973. Dennis Ritchie is credited with developing the C programming language; Bjarne Stroustrup at Bell Labs is considered the father of C++ for his design work in the early 1980s. C++ includes features that enabled programmers to perform OOP. C++ is used heavily in the computer industry today.

Smalltalk, considered a pure object-oriented language, was developed at the Xerox Palo Alto Research Center (PARC). Visual Basic, introduced in 1991, derived from the BASIC (Beginners All Purpose Symbolic Code) programming language, a language developed in the 1960s. The earlier versions of Visual Basic did not facilitate development using an object-oriented approach. Earlier versions of Visual Basic did, however, facilitate easy creation of Windows-based GUIs. Visual Basic has been used for a great deal of application development because of this.

Java was introduced in 1995 and was originally called Oak. It was originally designed to be a language for intelligent consumer-electronic devices such as appliances and microwave ovens. Instead of being used for that purpose, the business community used Java most heavily for Web applications because of the nature of the bytecode, which enabled machine-independent language compiling. Because the bytecode does not target any particular computer platform and must be converted into the language of the system running the application, this facilitates development of code that runs on many types of computers.

C# is one of the newer programming languages. It conforms closely to C and C++, but many developers consider it akin to Java. There are a number of similarities between the languages. In 1999, a team lead by Andres Hejsberg built a new language called Cool, which stood for C-like object-oriented language. When it was introduced by Microsoft, it was renamed C#. It has the rapid GUI features of previous versions of Visual Basic, the added power of C++, and object-oriented class libraries similar to Java. C# was designed from scratch to work with the new programming paradigm, .NET, and was the language used most heavily for the development of the .NET Framework class libraries.

Today C# can be used to develop many types of software components, including mobile apps. One of the exciting new uses of C# is in the area of cross-platform mobile development. C# can be used to create not only Windows Phone but also iOS and Android smart device apps. With the Visual Studio 2015 release, Microsoft partnered with a company called Xamarin and included their software with the 2015 edition. Xamarin provides add-ins to Visual Studio that enable you to build iOS and Android apps within Visual Studio. As part of the Xamarin partnership with Microsoft, Xamarin extensions can be downloaded and added to earlier versions of Visual Studio, back to Visual Studio 2010.

C# enables dynamic webpages, database access components, Windows desktop applications, Web services, mobile apps, and console-based applications to be created. You will be using C# for the software development in this book; however, the concepts presented can be applied to other languages. The intent of the book is to use the C# language as a tool for learning how to develop software rather than to focus on the syntax of C#.

.NET

When you think about C#, you should also understand its relationship to .NET. **.NET** is an environment in which programs run and was designed to be a new programming paradigm. It is not an operating system, but rather a layer between the operating system and other applications. As such, it provides a platform for developing and running code that is easy to use. .NET is an integral part of many applications running on Windows and provides common functionality for those applications to run. Microsoft stated that the vision for .NET was to provide a new programming platform and a set of development tools. The intent was for developers to be able to build distributed component-based applications. Before its official announcement in 2000, .NET was in development for over three years. Microsoft distributed a number of beta versions before the official release. A **beta version** is a working version that has not been fully tested and may still contain **bugs** or errors. It was not until February 2002 that Microsoft finally released the first version of Visual Studio, the IDE for developing C# applications. Visual Basic, Visual C++, and Visual C# all use this same development environment. Figure 1-11 shows Visual Studio with a C# program running. The output of the program "Welcome to Programming!" is shown in the small message box on the right of the figure.

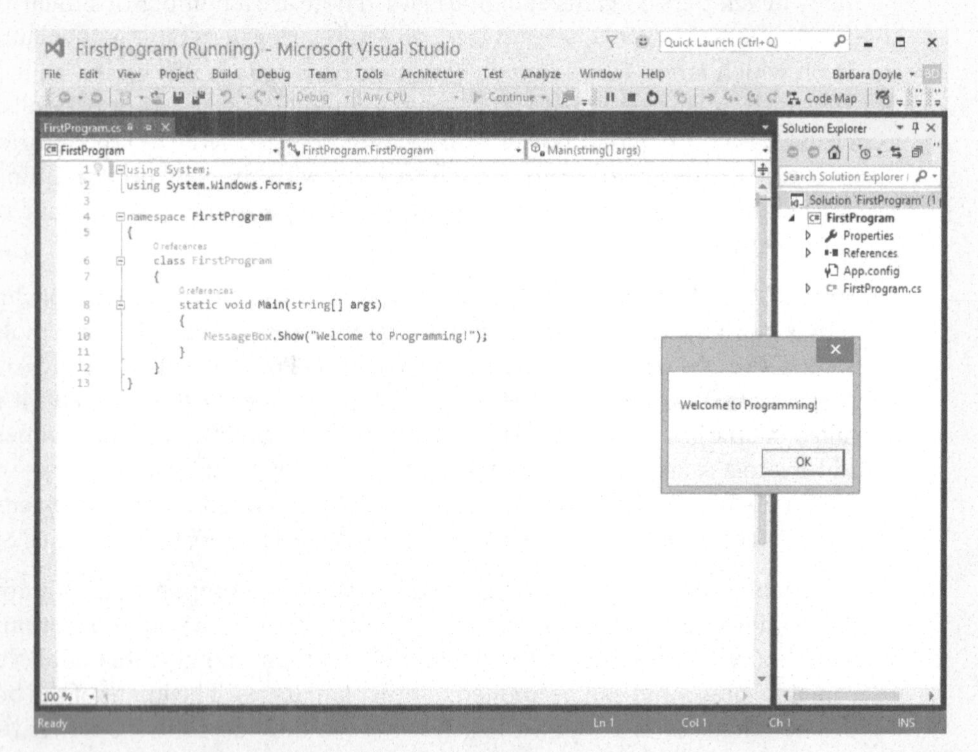

FIGURE 1-11 Visual Studio integrated development environment

Microsoft dropped .NET from the name of Visual Studio for the 2005 version. New releases of the IDE with additional features come out every couple years. Visual Studio 2015 is the most current version at the time this work was published. Visual Studio 2015 supports .NET Frameworks up to 4.6.

Included in Visual Studio are tools for typing program statements, and compiling, executing, and debugging applications. The new concepts introduced as part of .NET are outlined in the following paragraphs.

Multilanguage independence: .NET supports development using a number of programming languages: Visual Basic, C#, C++, Visual F#, Python, and a number of third-party languages. All the code from each of the languages can compile to the common MSIL.

Part of the application might be developed using Visual Basic and another portion developed using C#. When they are compiled, they translate to a common IL. The following list describes some of the common features of the .NET-supported languages:

Framework base classes: The .NET Framework has a class library, which provides a very large collection of reusable types (classes) each of which provide a great amount of predefined functionality available to any .NET language.

Dynamic Webpages and Web services: .NET was written with the Internet in mind; thus, deploying applications over intranets or the Internet becomes an ordinary, day-to-day operation. Using a new technology, ASP.NET, a set of components called ADO.NET, and having XML support makes it easier to access relational databases and other data sources as well as to import and export data through the Web.

Scalable component development: .NET not only facilitates object-oriented development but also takes design one step further. With .NET, true component-based development can be performed better and easier than in the past. Segments of code, created as separate entities, can be stored independently, combined, and reused in many applications. That is the beauty behind .NET—it provides a relatively seamless way for client programs to use components built using different languages. With .NET, component-based development can become a reality.

Why C#?

Compilers targeting the .NET platform are available for the programming languages of Visual Basic, C++, and C#. In addition to Microsoft, a number of third-party vendors are also marketing .NET-compliant languages. Microsoft also introduced a new programming language called Visual F# with Visual Studio 2010. Java is used today by a lot of software developers. Therefore, why use C#? C# was *the* language created for .NET and was designed from scratch to work with .NET. A large number of classes were included as part of .NET. These classes or templates were designed for reuse by any of the .NET-supported languages. They reduce the amount of programming that needs to be done. These classes are called the .NET Framework classes. Most of the .NET Framework classes were written using the C# programming language.

C#, in conjunction with the .NET Framework classes, offers an exciting vehicle to incorporate and use emerging Web standards, such as Hypertext Markup Language (HTML) and Extensible Markup Language (XML). As stated earlier, C# was designed with the Internet in mind. Most of the programming tools that were developed before .NET were designed when the Web was in its infancy and, thus, are not the greatest fit for developing Windows and Web applications.

C# is a simple, object-oriented language. Through using the Visual Studio IDE and the .NET Framework, C# provides an easy way to create GUIs similar to those Visual Basic programmers have been using for years. C# also provides the pure data-crunching horsepower to which C and C++ programmers are accustomed. C# is now an open source language. In April 2014, the C# compiler platform, named Roslyn, was released to the public as open source. Today there are over 1,000,000 developers using C#. Expectations are that opening up the compiler will enable companies like Xamarin, which provide cross-platform mobile development using C# to use the shared C# codebase and that the number of developers targeting C# will continue to grow.

Xamarin's founders started an open-source project called Mono in the early 2000s, which offered an open source implementation of C# on different platforms during the early years. The Xamarin company, founded by Miguel de Icaza and Nat Friedman, was founded in 2011, but has an interesting history. The original company was called Ximian. Ximian was later sold to Novell and when Novell was acquired by Attachmate in 2011, the open-source Mono project came back under the support of its original engineers in the new company named Xamarin.

In November 2014, Microsoft announced that it was partnering with Xamarin and embracing open source as a core principal to enable .NET applications to run on multiple operating systems. The .NET Foundation was created and much of the open-source is now available on GitHub. **GitHub** is a web-based repository hosting service. C# is going to be around for some time. It represents the next generation of languages.

Some characterize C# by saying that Microsoft took the best of Visual Basic and added C++, trimming off some of the more arcane C traditions. The syntax is very close to Java.

Types of Applications Developed with C#

C# can be used to create several different types of software applications. Some of the most common applications are as follows:

- Web applications
- Windows GUI applications
- Console-based applications

In addition to these applications, class libraries and stand-alone components (.dlls), smart device applications or apps, and services can also be created using C#.

1

Web Applications

C# was built from the ground up with the Internet in mind. For this reason, programmers can use C# to quickly build applications that run on the Web for end users to view through browser-neutral user interfaces. As they program in C#, developers can ignore the unique requirements of the platforms—Macs, Windows, and Linux—that will be executing these applications and end users will still see consistent results. Using **Web forms**, which are part of the ASP.NET technology, programmable webpages can be built that serve as a UI for Web applications. **ASP.NET** is a programming framework that lets you create applications that run on a Web server and delivers functionality through a browser, such as Microsoft Internet Explorer. Although you can use other languages to create ASP.NET applications, C# takes advantage of the .NET Framework and is generally acknowledged to be the language of choice for ASP.NET development. Much of the .NET Framework class library (FCL) is written in the C# programming language. After you learn some problem-solving techniques and the basic features of the C# language, Chapter 15 introduces you to ASP.NET. Figure 1-12 illustrates an ASP.NET webpage you will create with C# in Chapter 15.

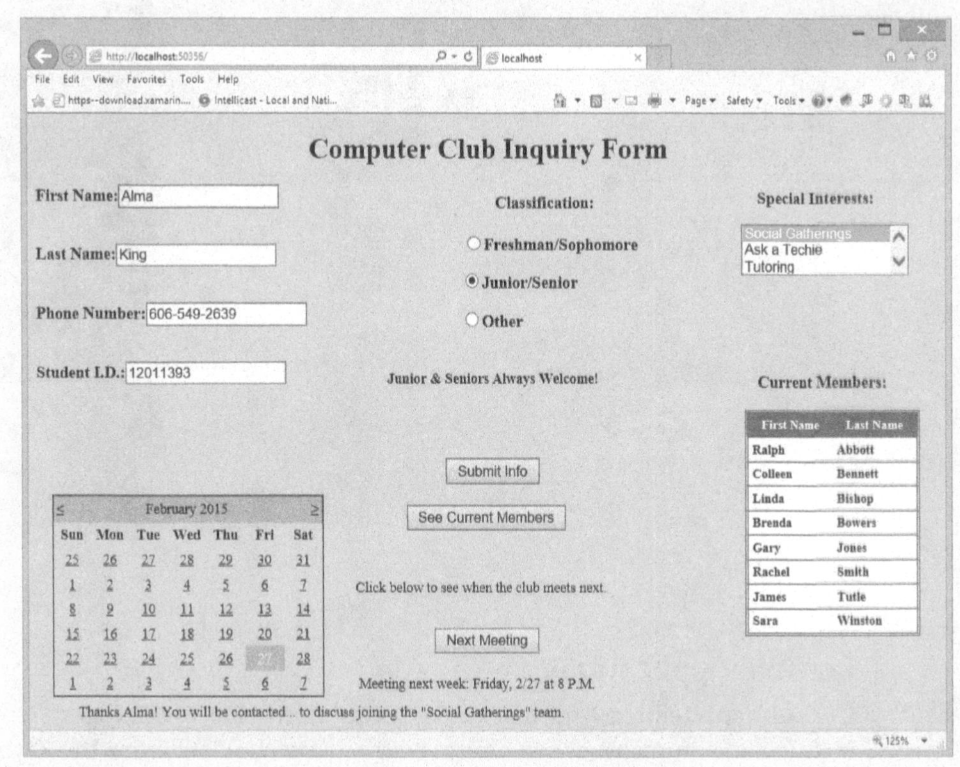

FIGURE 1-12 Web application written using C#

Windows Applications

Windows applications are designed for desktop use and for a single platform. They run on PC desktops much like your favorite word-processing program. Writing code using C# and classes from the `System.Windows.Forms` `namespace` applications can be developed to include menus, pictures, drop-down controls, and other widgets you have come to expect in a modern desktop application. .NET uses the concept of `namespace` to group types of similar functionality. The `System.Windows.Forms` `namespace` is used as an umbrella to organize classes needed to create Windows applications. Using the IDE of Visual Studio, GUIs can be developed by dragging and dropping controls such as buttons, text boxes, and labels on the screen. This same drag-and-drop approach is used to create Web applications with Visual Studio. You will begin creating Windows GUI applications in Chapter 9. Figure 1-13 illustrates a Windows application you will create using the C# language in Chapter 10.

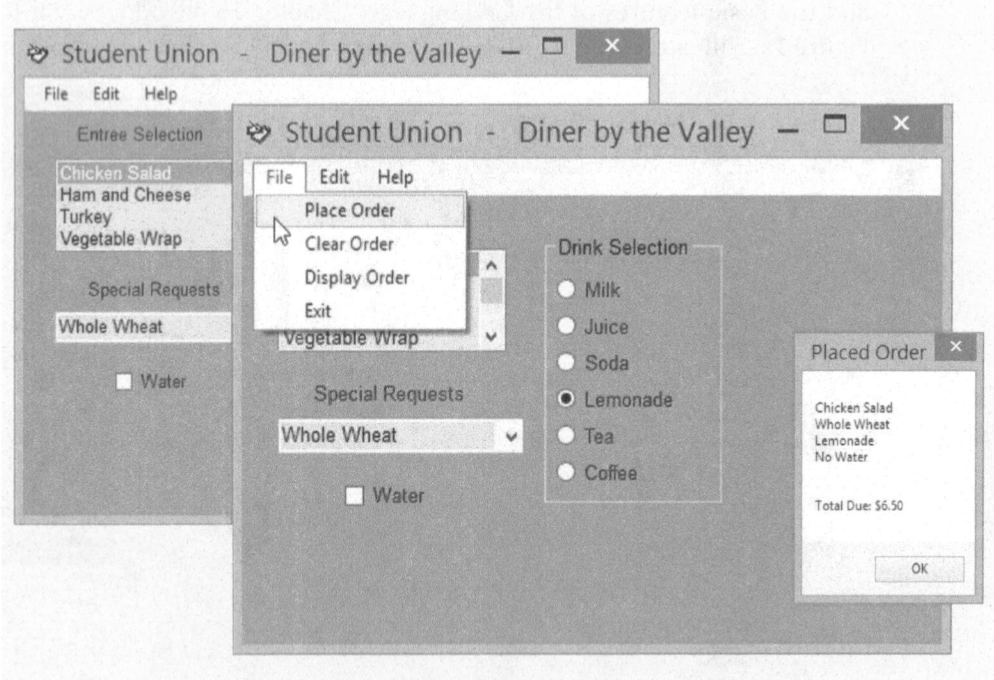

FIGURE 1-13 Windows application written using C#

Console Applications

Console applications normally send requests to the operating system to display text on the command console display or to retrieve data from the keyboard. From a beginners' standpoint, console applications are the easiest to create and represent the simplest approach to learn software development, because you do not have to be concerned with the side issues associated with building GUIs. Values can be entered as input with minimal overhead, and output is displayed in a console window, as illustrated in Figure 1-14. You will begin by developing console applications, so that you can focus on the details of programming and problem solving in general.

The default colors were changed for all Console Applications. As shown in Figure 1-14, the **Screen Background** was set to White. The **Screen Text** was set to Black. This change was made by selecting **Defaults** from the icon on the title bar of the output window when the application was launched. The colors were changed from the **Colors** tab.

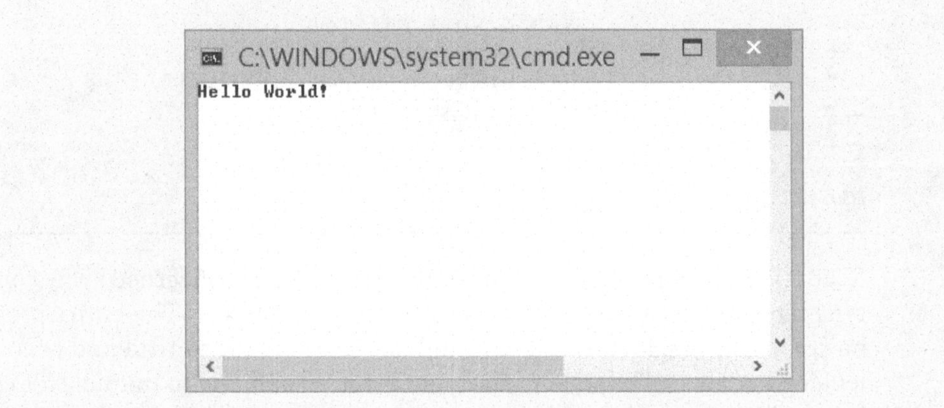

FIGURE 1-14 Output from Example 1-1 console application

As you read in previous sections, programs are the instructions written to direct a computer to perform a particular task. Each instruction must be written in a specific way. The **syntax** rules for writing these instructions are defined by the language in which the program is written. Before results are obtained, these human-readable instructions, called **source code**, must be translated into the machine language, which is the **native code** of the computer. The translation is a two-step process, which begins with the compiler. In this chapter, you will write your first C# program, learn how it is compiled, and explore how the final output is produced.

Each instruction statement has a **semantic meaning**, a specific way in which it should be used. This chapter highlights the purpose of the program statements as they appear in an application, because many of these program elements will be used in all applications that you develop using C#.

Exploring the First C# Program

Since the 1970s when the C language was developed, it has been traditional when learning a new language to display "Hello World!" on the console screen as the result of your first program. The program in Example 1-1 demonstrates a C# program that does exactly that. The sections that follow explain line-by-line the elements that make up this first program.

EXAMPLE 1-1

```
Line 1    // This is traditionally the first program written.
Line 2    using System;
Line 3    using static System.Console;
Line 4
Line 5    namespace HelloWorldProgram
Line 6    {
Line 7         class HelloWorld
Line 8         {
Line 9              static void Main( )
Line 10             {
Line 11                  WriteLine("Hello World!");
Line 12                  ReadKey( );
Line 13             }
Line 14        }
Line 15   }
```

Readability is important. As far as the compiler is concerned, you could actually type the entire program without touching the Enter key. The entire program could be typed as a single line, but it would be very difficult to read and even more challenging to debug. The style in Example 1-1 is a good one to mimic. Notice that curly braces { } are matched and appear on separate lines, by themselves. Statements are grouped together and indented. Indenting is not required but is a good practice to follow because it makes the code easier to read. When you type your program, you should follow a consistent, similar style. The output produced from compiling and executing the program appears in Figure 1-14.

Elements of a C# Program

Although the program statements in Example 1-1 make up one of the smallest functional programs that can be developed using C#, they include all the major components found in most programs. An understanding of the features that make up this program will help prepare you to begin developing your own applications. Examine each segment line-by-line to analyze the program, beginning with Line 1.

Comments

The first line of Example 1-1 is a comment:

```
Line 1    // This is traditionally the first program written.
```

> **NOTE** Comments are displayed in `green` throughout the book.

Writing a comment is like making notes for yourself or for readers of your program. Comments are not considered instructions to the computer and, therefore, have no effect on the running of the program. When the program is compiled, comments are not checked for rule violations; on the contrary, the compiler ignores and bypasses them. Comments do not have to follow any particular rules, with the exception of how they begin and end.

Comments serve two functions: they make the code more readable and they internally document what the program statements are doing. At the beginning of a program, comments are often written to identify who developed the code, when it was developed, and for what purpose the instructions were written. Comments are also used to document the purpose of different sections of code. You can place comments anywhere in the program. Where a portion of the code might be difficult to follow, it is appropriate to place one or more comments explaining the details. In Example 1-1, the only comment is found on Line 1.

```
Line 1    // This is traditionally the first program written.
```

Appendix A suggests ways to customize your development environment. One of the items discussed is how line numbers are displayed. Line numbers are added here to explain the features. This setting is found in Visual Studio at the **Tools**, **Options**, **Text Editor**, **C#** dialog box.

With C#, three types of commenting syntax can be added to a program: inline, multiline, and XML document comments.

Inline Comments

The comment that appears on Line 1 of Example 1-1 is an inline, or single-line, comment. An **inline comment** is indicated by two forward slashes // and is usually considered a one-line comment. The slashes indicate that everything to the right of the slashes, on the same line, is a comment and should be ignored by the compiler. No special symbols are needed to end the comment. The carriage return (Enter) ends the comment.

Multiline Comments

For longer comments, multiline comments are available. A forward slash followed by an asterisk /* marks the beginning of a **multiline comment**, and the opposite pattern */ marks the end. Everything that appears between the comment symbols is treated as a comment. Multiline comments are also called **block comments**. Although they are called multiline comments, they do not have to span more than one line.

Unlike the single-line comment that terminates at the end of the current line when the Enter key is pressed, the multiline comment requires special characters /* and */ to begin and terminate the comment, even if the comment just appears on a single line. Example 1-2 shows an example of a multiline comment.

EXAMPLE 1-2

```
/* This is the beginning of a multiline (block) comment. It can
go on for several lines or just be on a single line. No additional
symbols are needed after the beginning two characters. Notice there
is no space placed between the two characters. To end the comment,
use the following symbols. */
```

C# does not allow you to nest multiline comments. In other words, you cannot place a block comment inside another block comment. The outermost comment is ended at the same time as the inner comment as soon as the first */ is typed.

XML Documentation Comments

A third type of comment uses three forward slashes ///. This is an advanced documentation technique used for XML-style comments. **XML (Extensible Markup Language)** is a markup language that provides a format for describing data using tags similar to HTML tags. When XML-style comments are included, the C# compiler reads them and generates XML documentation from them.

You will be using the inline // and multiline /*   */ comments for the applications you will develop in this book.

Using Directive

You specify which group of classes you want to have access to in your program with `using` directives. The statements that appear in Example 1-1 on Lines 2 and 3 permit the use of members found in the `System` `namespace` and specifically members in the `System.Console` `class`. Line 2 indicates any member of the `System` `namespace` can be referenced in the program. With just Line 2, in order to reference members in the `System` `namespace`, you would need to fully quality your reference. Fully qualifying means that you would specify the name of the `class` first followed by a period and then the member's name.

Adding Line 3 takes this one step further. By typing `using static System.Console;`, any members of the `Console class` can be referenced without having to fully qualify the reference with the `namespace` or the `class` names, that is, `System` and `Console`.

```
Line 2    using System;
Line 3    using static System.Console;
```

Being able to include not only a `namespace` but also a `static class` name is a new language feature introduced with Visual Studio 2015 and the C# 6.0 release. This new language feature reduces the amount of typing needed when you use members of the `class` later in your program. Prior to Visual Studio 2015 and C# 6.0, you could not specify a `class` name, such as `Console` with the `using` statement. Only `namespace` names could be identified with the `using` statement. All calls to methods such as `WriteLine( )` had to include the fully qualified `class` name, as in `Console.WriteLine( )`. Now with this new language feature included, the `class` name can be omitted as you will note is done on Lines 11 and 12 in Example 1-1. This is possible as long as a reference to the `static Console class` name is included with other `using` statement references. The lines are repeated here for your review.

```
Line 11   WriteLine("Hello World!");
Line 12   ReadKey( );
```

Using .NET provides the significant benefit of making available more than 2000 classes that make up what is called the FCL. A `class` contains code that can be reused, which makes programming easier and faster because you don't have to reinvent the wheel for common types of operations. The Framework classes are all available for use by any of the .NET-supported languages, including C#.

Keywords after they are introduced, such as `class`, are displayed in blue throughout this book. *Keywords* are words reserved by the system and have special, predefined meanings. The keyword `class`, for instance, defines or references a C# `class`.

With several thousand .NET Framework classes, it is very unlikely that program developers will memorize the names of all of the classes, let alone the additional names of members of the classes. As you could well imagine, it would be easy for you to use a name in your own application that has already been used in one or more of the Framework classes. Another likely occurrence is that one or more of these Framework classes could use the same name. How would you know which `class` was being referenced? .NET eliminates this potential problem by using namespaces.

EXAMPLE 1-3

Assume you have a class called Captain. You could abstract out characteristics and behavior attributes of a Captain. If you had an application that was being developed for a football team, the characteristics and behaviors of that kind of Captain would differ greatly from those of the Captain in an application designed for a fire department. Moreover, both sets of characteristics differ from those of a boating Captain. The Captain associated with a military unit, such as the Navy, would also be different. With each possible application, you could use the same name for the Captain class. If you gave instructions to a program to display information about a Captain, the program would not know which set of characteristics to display. To clarify whether you are talking about the boat Captain, football team Captain, fire station Captain, or the Navy Captain, you could qualify the keyword by preceding the name with its category. To do so, you could write Boat.Captain, Football.Captain, Fireman.Captain, or Navy.Captain. You would need to precede Captain with its category type every time reference was made to Captain.

By specifying which namespace you are building an application around, you can eliminate the requirement of preceding Captain with a dot (.) and the name of the namespace. If you specify *use the boating* namespace, you do not have to qualify each statement with the prefix name. That is what the using directive accomplishes. It keeps you from having to qualify each class by identifying within which namespace something appears. A using directive enables unqualified use of the types that are members of the namespace. By typing the using-namespace-directive, all the types contained in the given namespace are imported, or available for use within the particular application.

The most important and frequently used namespace is System. The System namespace contains classes that define commonly used types or classes. The Console class is defined within the System namespace. The Console class enables programmers to write and read from the console window or keyboard. The fully qualified name for Console is System.Console. If you removed the using System; and using static System.Console; directives in Lines 2 and 3, it would be necessary for you to replace

```
Line 11   WriteLine("Hello World!");
Line 12   ReadKey( );
```

with

```
Line 11   System.Console.WriteLine("Hello World!");
Line 12   System.Console.ReadKey( );
```

> **NOTE** In addition to the `using static System.Console;` directive, the `using System;` directive also appears. When a console application is created, Visual Studio automatically references and imports the System `namespace`.

Namespaces provide scope, or an enclosing context, for the names defined within the group. By including the `using` directive to indicate the name of the `namespace` to be used, you can avoid having to precede the `class` names with the category grouping. After you add the `using System;` line, you can use the `Console` `class` name without explicitly identifying that it is in the `System` `namespace`. Adding the additional `using static System.Console;` available as a new feature with Visual Studio 2015, facilitates invoking the `WriteLine( )` and `ReadKey( )` methods without not only explicitly identifying the `System` `namespace` but also specifying the `Console` `class` name.

Namespace

Lines 5 through 15 define a `namespace` called `HelloWorldProgram`.

```
Line 5    namespace HelloWorldProgram
Line 6    {
Line 15   }
```

The `namespace` does little more than group semantically related types under a single umbrella. Example 1-1 illustrates how a `namespace` called `HelloWorldProgram` is created. `HelloWorldProgram` is an **identifier**, simply a user-supplied or user-created name. As noted in the previous section, you will create many names (identifiers) when programming in C#. Rules for creating identifiers are discussed in Chapter 2. You can define your own `namespace` and indicate that these are names associated with your particular application.

Each `namespace` must be enclosed in curly braces { }. The opening curly brace ({) on Line 6 marks the beginning of the `HelloWorldProgram` `namespace`. The opening curly brace is matched by a closing curly brace (}) at the end of the program on Line 15. Within the curly braces, you write the programming constructs.

In Example 1-1, Lines 5, 6, and 15 could have been omitted. This program did not define any new programming constructs or names. It is merely using the `Console` `class`, which is part of the `System` `namespace`. No errors are introduced by adding the additional umbrella, but it was not necessary. Visual Studio automatically adds a `namespace` umbrella around applications that are created using the IDE.

Class Definition

Lines 7 through 14 make up the `class` definition for this application.

```
Line 7          class HelloWorld
Line 8          {
Line 14         }
```

As C# is an object-oriented language, everything in C# is designed around a `class`, which is the building block of an object-oriented program. C# doesn't allow anything to be defined outside of a `class`. Every program must have at least one `class`. Classes define a category, or type, of object. Many classes are included with the .NET Framework. Programs written using C# can use these predefined .NET classes or create their own classes.

In Example 1-1, the user-defined `class` is titled `HelloWorld`. The example also uses the Console `class`, one of the .NET predefined classes. Every `class` is named. It is traditional to name the file containing the `class` the same name as the `class` name, except that the filename will have a .cs extension affixed to the end of the name. C# allows a single file to have more than one `class`; however, it is common practice to place one user-defined `class` per file for object-oriented development.

> **NOTE** Most object-oriented languages, including Java, restrict a file to one `class`. C#, however, allows multiple classes to be stored in a single file.

Classes are used to define controls such as buttons and labels, as well as types of things such as Student, Captain, and Employee. The word `class` is a keyword. Like namespaces, each `class` definition must be enclosed in curly braces { }. The { on Line 8 is an opening curly brace, which marks the beginning of the `class` definition. The opening curly brace is matched by a closing curly brace at the end of the `class` definition on Line 14. Within the curly braces, you define the `class` members. A `class` member is generally either a member method, which performs some behavior of the `class`, or a data member, which contains a value associated with the state of the `class`.

Main( ) Method

The definition for the `Main( )` method begins on Line 9 and ends with the closing curly brace on Line 13.

```
Line 9          static void Main( )
Line 10         {
Line 13         }
```

The `Main( )` method plays a very important role in C#. This is the entry point for all applications. This is where the program begins execution. The `Main( )` method can be placed anywhere inside the `class` definition. It begins on Line 9 for this example. When a C# program is launched, the execution starts with the first executable statement found in the `Main( )` method and continues to the end of that method. If the application is 3000 lines long with the `Main( )` method beginning on Line 2550, the first statement executed for the application is on Line 2550.

> **NOTE** All executable applications must contain a `Main( )` method.

The entire contents of Line 9 are the heading for the method. A **method** is a collection of one or more statements combined to perform an action. Methods are similar to C++ functions. The heading for the method contains its **signature**, which includes the name of the method and its argument list. Return types and modifiers, such as `public` and `static`, are part of the heading, but not considered part of the signature. The heading line for the `Main( )` method begins with the keyword `static`, which implies that a single copy of the method is created and that you can access this method without having an object of the `class` available. More details regarding `static` are discussed in subsequent sections. For now, remember that `Main( )` should include the `static` keyword as part of its heading.

The second keyword in the heading, `void`, is placed in the return type location. Typically, a method calls another method and can return a value to the calling method. Remember that a method is a small block of code that performs an action. As a result of this action, a value might be returned. If a method does not return a value, the keyword `void` is included to signal that no value is returned. When the method does return a value, the type of value is included as part of the heading. Chapter 3 introduces you to the different data types in C#.

`Main( )` is the name of the method. Methods communicate with each other by sending arguments inside parentheses or as return values. Sometimes no argument is sent, as is the case when nothing appears inside the parentheses.

> **NOTE** Unlike the lowercase `main( )` method that appears in the C++ language, in C#, `Main( )` must begin with an uppercase 'M'.

In Example 1-1, only two executable statements are included in the body of the method `Main( )`. The body includes all items enclosed inside opening and closing curly braces. When a program is executed, the statements that appear in the `Main( )` method are executed in sequential order. When the closing curly brace is encountered, the entire program ends.

Method Body Statements

The body of this `Main( )` method consists the statements found on Lines 10 through 13.

```
Line 10    {
Line 11        WriteLine("Hello World!");
Line 12        ReadKey( );
Line 13    }
```

Remember that the purpose of the program in Example 1-1 is to display `"Hello World!"` on the output screen. The lines of code in Example 1-1, which have been explained on previous pages of this chapter, are common to most applications you will be developing. Line 11, however, is unique to this application. The body for this method begins with the opening curly brace on Line 10 and ends with the closing curly brace on Line 13.

The statements in the `Main( )` method are calls to a method named `WriteLine( )` and another method named `ReadKey( )`. A method call is the same as a **method invocation**. Like `Main( )`, `WriteLine( )` has a signature. The heading along with the complete body of the method is the **definition of the method**. When called, `WriteLine( )` writes the string argument that appears inside the parentheses to the standard output device, a monitor. After displaying the string, `WriteLine( )` advances to the next line, as if the Enter key had been pressed.

NOTE A quick way to identify a method is by looking for parentheses; methods always appear with parentheses ( ). A call to methods, such as `WriteLine( )` and `ReadKey( )`, always includes a set of parentheses following the method name identifier, as do signatures for methods.

The string of text, `"Hello World!"`, placed inside the parentheses is the method's argument. `WriteLine( )` is defined in the `Console class` and can be called with no arguments. To have a blank line displayed on the standard output device, type:

```
WriteLine( ); // No string argument is placed inside ( )
```

The `Console class` contains the standard input and output methods for console applications. Method members in this `class` include `Read( )`, `ReadKey( )`, `ReadLine( )`, `Write( )`, and `WriteLine( )`. The method `Write( )` differs from `WriteLine( )` in that it does not automatically advance the carriage return to the next line when it finishes. The following lines would produce the same result as the single line `WriteLine ("Hello World!");`

```
Write("Hello");
Write(" ");
WriteLine("World!");
```

An invisible pointer moves across the output screen as the characters are displayed. As new characters are displayed, it moves to the next position and is ready to print at that location if another output statement is sent. Notice the second statement in the preceding code, `Write(" ");` this places a blank character between the two words. After displaying the space, the pointer is positioned and ready to display the *W* in World. The output for both of the preceding segments of code is

```
Hello World!
```

Usually, the characters inside the double quotes are displayed exactly as they appear when used as an argument to `Write( )` or `WriteLine( )`. An exception occurs when an escape character is included. The backslash `('\')` is called the **escape character**. The escape character is combined with one or more characters to create a special **escape sequence**, such as `'\n'` to represent advance to next line, and `'\t'` for a tab indention. A number of escape sequences can be used in C#. This is the same set of escape characters found in other languages such as Java and C++. Table 1-1 lists some of the more commonly used escape characters that can be included as part of a string in C#.

TABLE 1-1 Escape sequence

Escape sequence character	Description
`\n`	Cursor advances to the next line; similar to pressing the Enter key
`\t`	Cursor advances to the next horizontal tab stop
`\"`	Double quote is printed
`\'`	Single quote is printed
`\\`	Backslash is printed
`\r`	Cursor advances to the beginning of the current line
`\b`	Cursor advances back one position (Backspace)
`\a`	Alert signal (short beep) is sounded

© Cengage Learning

When an escape sequence is encountered inside the double quotes, it signals that a special character is to be produced as output. The output of the statement:

```
Write("What goes\nup\nmust come\tdown.");
```

is

```
What goes
up
must come       down.
```

Notice in the `Write( )` method that the argument inside the parentheses has three escape sequences. The backslash is not printed. When the `'\n'` is encountered, the output is advanced to the new line. The space between the words *come* and *down* was placed there as a result of the tab escape sequence `('\t')`.

Three other methods in the `Console` `class`, `Read( )`, `ReadKey( )`, and `ReadLine( )`, deserve explanation. Visually they differ from the `WriteLine( )` method in that they have no arguments, nothing is placed inside the parentheses. `Read( )`, `ReadKey( )`, and `ReadLine( )` methods can all return values and are used for accepting input from a standard input device, such as a keyboard.

NOTE Notice in Example 1-1 that the statements in the body of methods end in semicolons. However, no semicolon is placed at the end of method headings, `class` definition headings, or `namespace` definition headings. Note that semicolons appear on Lines 2, 3, 11, and 12 in Example 1-1.

`ReadKey( )` is often used in a C# program to keep the output screen displayed until the user presses a key on the keyboard. The `ReadKey( )` method is invoked on Line 12 for Example 1-1. Until the user presses a key, the `"Hello World"` message remains on the output screen. The `Read( )` method can also be used and like the `ReadKey( )` method accepts any character from the input device, and as soon as a key is pressed, control passes to the next line in the program. Instead of accepting a single character as the `Read( )` and `ReadKey( )` methods do, `ReadLine( )` allows multiple characters to be entered. It accepts characters until the Enter key is pressed. You will use the `ReadLine( )` method in Chapter 3 to input data values.

Now that you know what elements make up a C# program, you are almost ready to begin developing your own programs. Figure 1-15 shows how `namespace`, `class`, method, and statements are related.

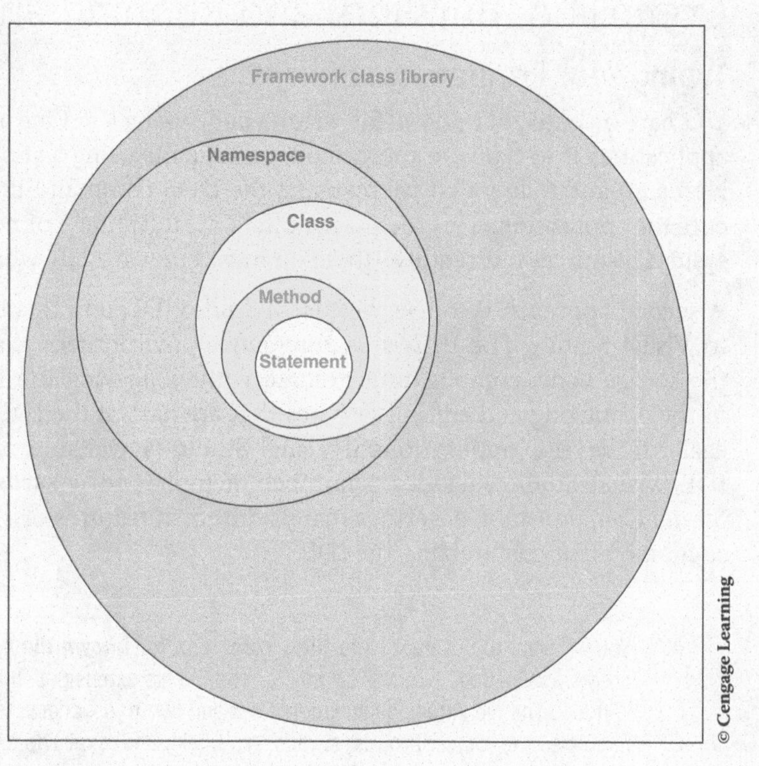

FIGURE 1-15 Relationship among C# elements

The FCL includes a number of different namespaces, such as `System`. Defined within a `namespace` are a number of classes, such as `Console`. Defined within a `class` are a number of methods, such as `WriteLine( )` and `Read( )`. You did not see the statements that made up the `WriteLine( )` method, you saw the `WriteLine( )` method being called. A method can have one or more statements. One of those statements can be a call to another method, such as the case of calling on the `WriteLine( )` method from within the `Main( )` method.

To develop software using C#, the .NET Framework is needed. The Framework includes all the predefined .NET classes. Having so many classes available decreases the amount of new code needed. You can use much of the functionality included in the `class` library. The next section describes how you begin typing your program statements.

Compiling, Building, and Running an Application

Typing Your Program Statements

You have a couple of options for writing code using C#. One approach to developing applications is to type the source code statements using a simple text editor (such as Notepad) and follow that up by using the DOS command line to compile and execute the application. This technique offers the advantage of not requiring significant system resources but requires that you must know exactly what to type.

A second approach is to use the Visual Studio IDE, and this chapter introduces you to Visual Studio. The IDE is an interactive environment that enables you to type the source code, compile, and execute without leaving the IDE program. Because of the debugging and editing features that are part of the IDE, you will find it much easier to develop applications if Visual Studio is available. In addition to the rich, IDE, Visual Studio includes a number of tools and wizards. Appendix A, *Visual Studio Configuration*, describes many additional features of Visual Studio, including suggestions for customizing the IDE.

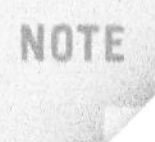

You will want to deselect **Hide file extensions for known file types** so that as you create applications, you will be able to see the file extensions in the **Solution Explorer** Window. The file extension includes a dot and two to six characters following the name. Examples are .cs, .csproj, .sys, .doc, .suo, .sln, and .exe. The extension identifies the type of information stored in the file. For example, a file ending in .cs is a C# source file. It is helpful to be able to identify files by type. You can make this change in the **Control Panel, Folder Options, View** tab.

The preceding sections described the program statements required as a minimum in most console-based applications. To see the results of a program, you must type the statements, or source code, into a file, compile that code, and then execute the application. The next sections examine what happens during the compilation and execution process with and without using the Visual Studio IDE.

Compilation and Execution Process

The **compiler** is used to check the grammar. The grammar is the symbols or words used to write the computer instructions. The compiler makes sure that there are no rule violations in the program statements or source code. After the code is successfully compiled, the compiler usually generates a file that ends with an .exe extension. The code in this .exe file has not yet been turned into machine code that is targeted to any specific CPU platform. Instead, the code generated by the compiler is *MSIL*, often referred to simply as **IL**. In the second required step, the **just-in-time** compiler (**JITer**) reads the MSIL code and translates or produces the machine code that runs on the particular platform. After the code is translated in this second step, results can be seen.

Operations going on behind the scene are not readily apparent. For example, after the compiler creates the IL, the code can be executed on any machine that has the .NET Framework installed. Microsoft offers as a free distribution the .NET Framework Redistributable version for deploying applications only. The **redistributable version** is a smaller download than the SDK and includes the CLR and `class` libraries. Again, this is available at the Microsoft website.

The runtime version of the .NET Framework is similar in concept to the Java Virtual Machine (JVM). Like C#, Java's compiler first translates source code into intermediate code called bytecode. The bytecode must be converted into native machine code before results can be seen from an application. With C#, the CLR actually translates only the parts of the program that are being used. This saves time. In addition, after a portion of your MSIL file has been compiled on a computer, it never needs to be compiled again because the final compiled portion of the program is saved and used the next time that portion of the program is executed.

Compiling the Source Code Using Visual Studio IDE

You can use the built-in editor available with the Visual Studio IDE to type your program statement. You then compile the source code from one of the pull-down menu options in the IDE and execute the application using another menu option in the IDE. Many shortcuts are available. The next section explores how this is done using the Visual Studio IDE.

Begin by opening Visual Studio. Create a new project by either selecting the **New Project** button on the Start page or using the **File, New, Project** link.

As shown in Figure 1-16, a list of project types appears in the middle window. There are a number of templates that can be used within the IDE. To develop a C# console application, select **Visual C#** and **Console Application** for the Template. Using the **Browse** button beside the Location text box, navigate to the location where you want to store your projects. The name of the project is `HelloWorldProgram`. If the check box beside the **Create directory for solution** option is selected in the bottom right corner, an extra folder will be created that bundles the files created for your solution.

> **NOTE** Whatever name you give the project becomes the namespace's name for this project unless this default setting is changed.

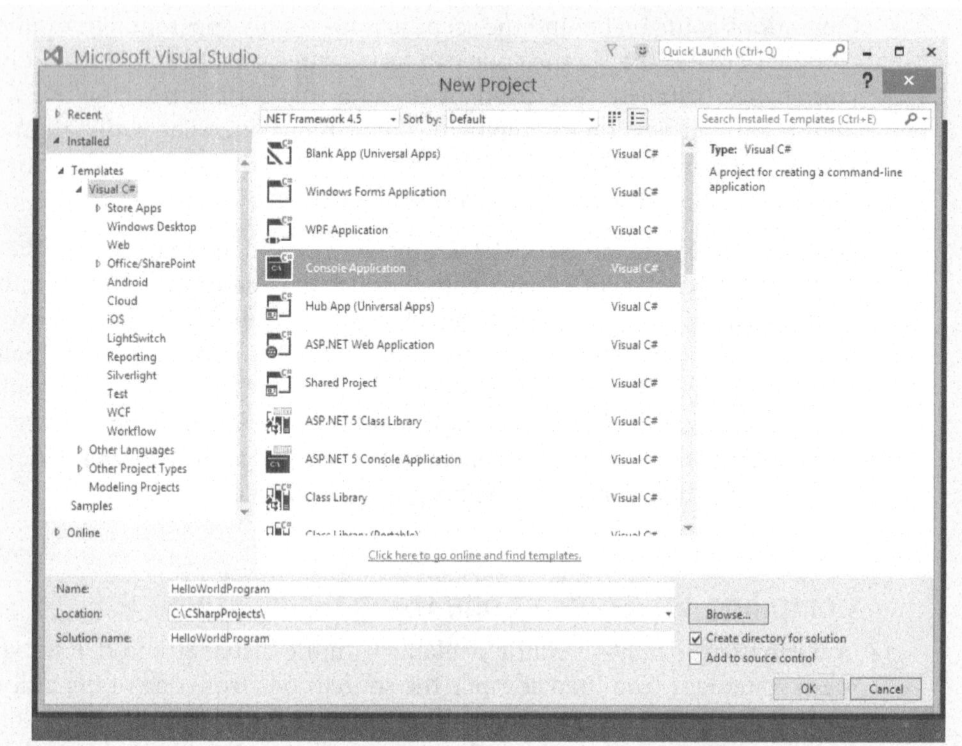

FIGURE 1-16 Creating a console application

Selecting the template determines what type of code is generated by the IDE. Figure 1-17 shows the code that is created automatically when you create a console application.

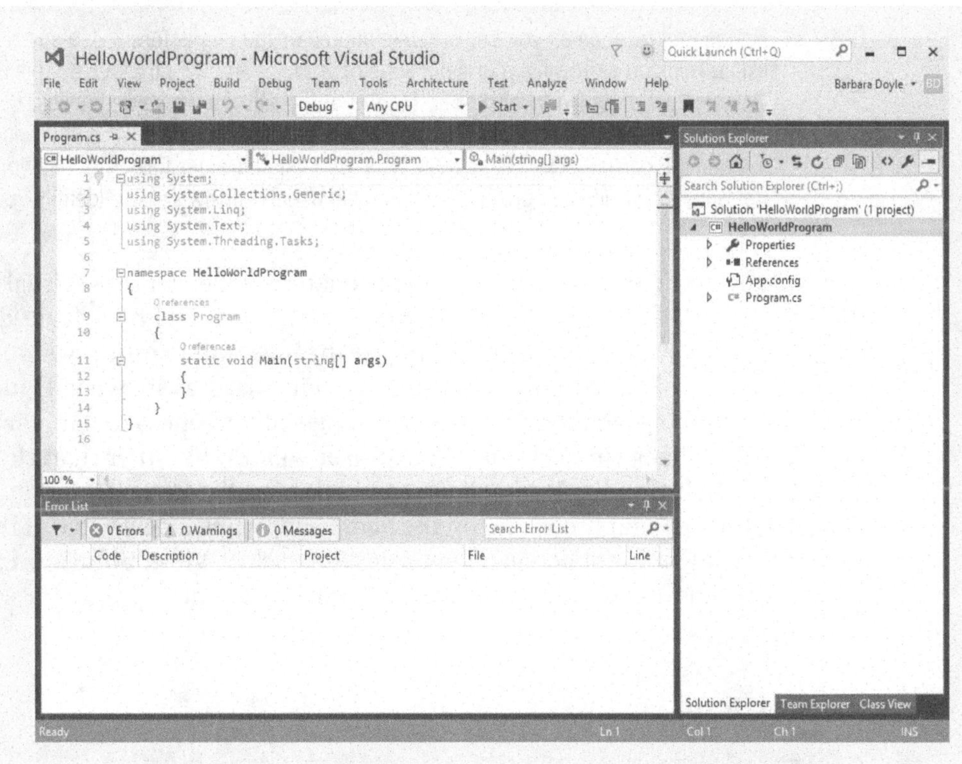

FIGURE 1-17 Code automatically generated by Visual Studio

As you can see from Figure 1-17, having the IDE generate this much code reduces your typing. The only lines that must be added are those specific to the application being developed.

Notice the light bulb to the left on the first line in Figure 1-17 suggesting you remove unnecessary `using` statements. The light bulb is called the **Quick Action Light Bulb** and is new to Visual Studio 2015. It can help identify unnecessary statements, help with errors, and streamline code.

To produce the traditional Hello World program, begin by adding onto the `using static System.Console;` as a new directive under the line that reads `using System;`.

```
using static System.Console;
```

The remaining `using` statements can be deleted.

Move the cursor to the end of Line 9 and press the Enter key to open up a new blank line. Type the following lines between the braces in the `Main( )` method:

```
WriteLine("Hello World!");
ReadKey( );
```

Notice that as soon as you begin typing and enter the characters `Wr`, a smart window listing pops up narrowing your selections of `Write` and `WriteLine`. This is the **Word Correct** option of the **IntelliSense** feature of the IDE. As the name implies, the feature attempts to sense what you are going to type before you type it. When the window pops up, if it has the correct selection, simply type the next character following that word and you will get another IntelliSense pop-up. You can also use the arrow keys to identify your selection.

Next, change the name of the `class` and the source code filename. Visual Studio uses the default name `Program` for each new `class` created and by default identifies the source code file by that same name. If you use the **Solution Explorer** window to change the source code filename to `HelloWorld.cs`, a message, as shown in Figure 1-18, will be displayed asking whether you want to change all references to that new name. You can make this change in the **Solution Explorer** window by either right clicking on the name in the **Solution Explorer** window and selecting the **Rename** option, as is shown in Figure 1-18, or simply clicking on the name and typing a new value. If the **Solution Explorer** window is not active on your desktop, select **View**, **Solution Explorer**. Be sure to leave the .cs file extension when you rename the file.

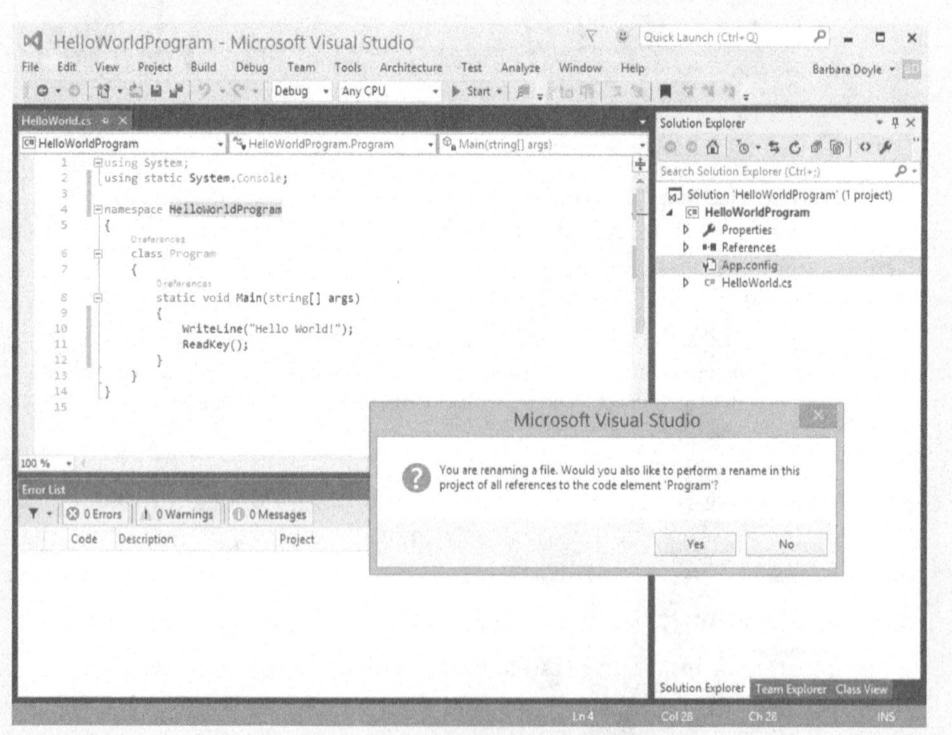

FIGURE 1-18 Changing the source code name from Program

As you review the **Solution Explorer** window shown in Figure 1-18, notice the top level reads **Solution "HelloWorldProgram" (1 project)**. The second line also contains the word "**HelloWorldProgram**." Visual Studio first creates a solution file. `HelloWorldProgram`, which appears on the top line, is the name of the solution file. The solution file may consist of one or more projects. For this application, the solution consists of one project. When you explore the directory where your applications are stored, you will find a folder named using that solution name. Inside the folder, there will be a file ending with a `.sln` extension. This is the solution file and it stores information about the solution. In that same folder, you will also see a file ending with a .csproj extension. This file stores information about the project. Normally when you reopen your application in Visual Studio, you will open the file ending with the `.sln` extension.

If you answer **Yes** to the question shown in Figure 1-18, the name of the `class` in the source code is replaced with the new name.

It is not absolutely necessary to change the names of the source code file and `class`. The application can run without making that change; however, to develop good habits, you should change the name. It can save your time and grief when applications involve multiple classes.

The statements in Example 1-4 appeared in Example 1-1 and are repeated here without the line numbers so that you can see the final source listing.

Visual Studio generates a couple of other unnecessary lines that can be removed. For example, the extraneous `using` statements were removed in the example. They are not needed for most of the applications you will develop. With Visual Studio 2015, you may see a yellow light bulb appear to the left of these extraneous `using` statements, suggesting that they be removed and showing you a preview of the changes. The `using System;` directive could have also been removed since only members of the `Console` `class` were referenced for this simple example. The arguments inside the parentheses for the `Main( )` method were also removed. You will read about these lines later in this book.

As you review Figure 1-18, notice the green bars that appear along the margins. These indicate lines that have been changed. Once you close the file and reopen it, they disappear. Initially a vertical yellow line appears in the margin to mark code that has changed since the file was most recently saved. When you save the changes, the vertical lines become green.

EXAMPLE 1-4

```
// This is traditionally the first program written.
using System;   // This line could have also been removed.
using static System.Console;

namespace HelloWorldProgram
{
      class HelloWorld
      {
            static void Main( )
            {
                  WriteLine("Hello World!");
                  ReadKey( );
            }
      }
}
```

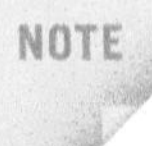

Do remember that C# is case sensitive, meaning that the name HelloWorld is a totally different name from helloWorld, even though only one character is different. Therefore, be very careful to type the statements exactly as they are shown.

To compile the `HelloWorldProgram` project, select the **Build** `HelloWorldProgram` option on the **Build** menu. The name `HelloWorldProgram` follows the **Build** option because `HelloWorldProgram` is the name of the project. Projects that contain more than one `class` are compiled using the **Build Solution** option.

To run the application, you can click **Start Debugging** or **Start Without Debugging** on the **Debug** menu bar, as illustrated in Figure 1-19. If you attempt to execute code that has not been compiled (using **Build**), the smart IDE compiles the code first. Therefore, many developers use the shortcut of bypassing the **Build** step.

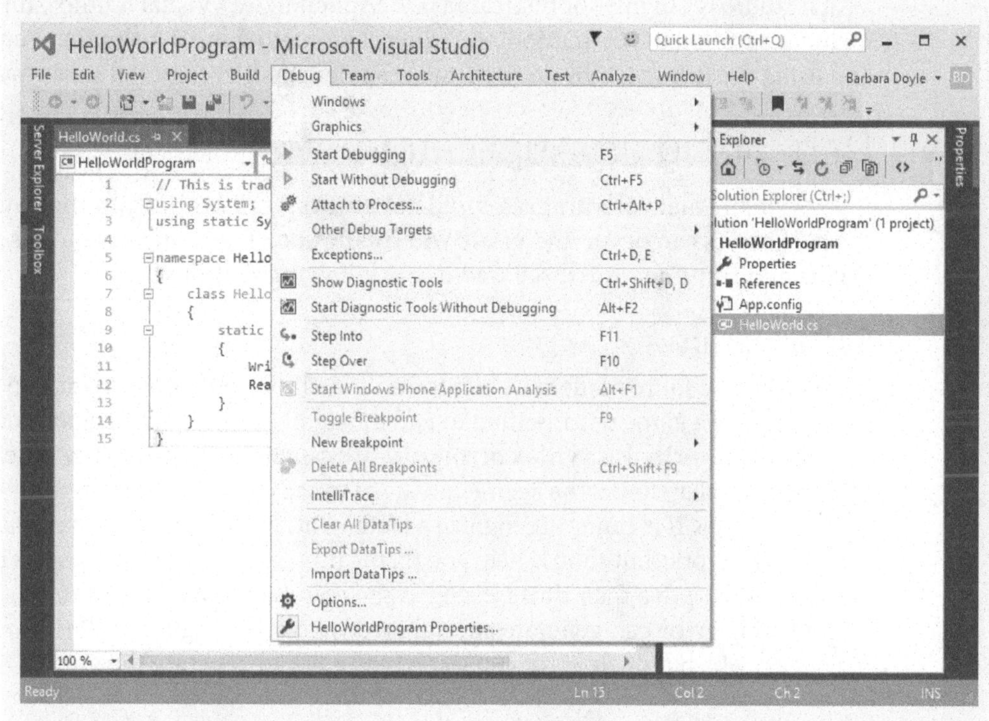

FIGURE 1-19 Execution of an application using Visual Studio

If you ran the application using the **Start Debugging** option without invoking the `ReadKey( )` method, the output flashes on the screen and then disappears. You hold the output screen if you include a call to the `Read( )` or `ReadKey( )` methods. When this line is executed, the program waits for you to press a key before it terminates. Notice the `ReadKey( )` method is invoked as the last statement in the `Main( )` method.

Another option to hold the command windows in Visual Studio is to select **Debug, Start Without Debugging** instead of **Debug, Start Debugging** to execute your program. Notice in Figure 1-19 that **Start Without Debugging** is the option immediately below the **Start Debugging** option. If you select **Debug, Start Without Debugging,** it is not necessary to add the additional `ReadKey( );` statement. When you use the **Start Without Debugging** option for execution, the user is prompted to "Press any key to continue."

Several other shortcuts are available to run your program. Notice as you look at the menu option under **Debug** that Ctrl+F5 is listed as a shortcut for **Start Without Debugging**; F5 is the shortcut for **Start Debugging**. In addition, if you have the **Debug** toolbar icons on your screen, an open right arrow represents **Start Without Debugging**. A closed green right arrow represents **Start Debugging**.

Visual Studio is a highly sophisticated IDE. Appendix A, "Visual Studio Configuration," includes additional information regarding customizing the development environment and using the debugger for development. Reviewing that material now would be wise.

Debugging an Application

It is inevitable that your programs will not always work properly immediately. Several types of errors can occur and cause you frustration. The major categories of errors—syntax and runtime—are discussed in the following sections.

Syntax Errors

When you type source code statements into the editor, you are apt to make typing errors by misspelling a name or forgetting to end a statement with a semicolon. These types of errors are categorized as **syntax errors** and are caught by the compiler. When you compile, the compiler checks the segment of code to see if you have violated any of the rules of the language. If it cannot recognize a statement, it issues an error message, which is sometimes cryptic, but should help you fix the problem. Error messages in Visual Studio are more descriptive than those issued at the command line. However, be aware that a single typing error can generate several error messages. Figure 1-20 shows a segment of code, in which a single error causes the compiler to generate three error messages.

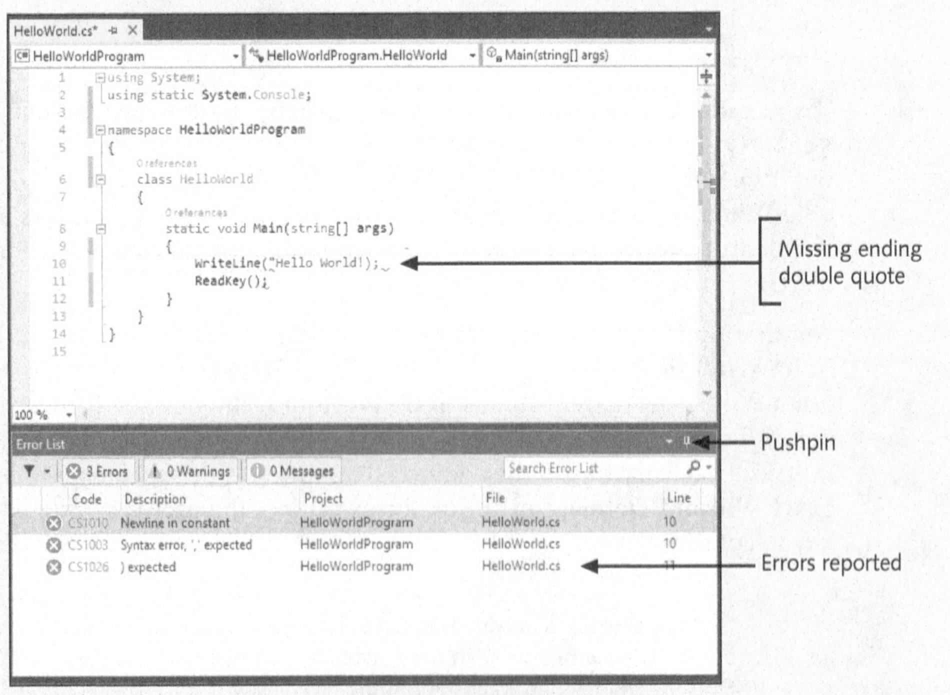

FIGURE 1-20 Syntax error message listing

The error messages are displayed in the **Error List** window found at the bottom of the IDE. The IDE also underlines the supposed location of the problem. You can also double click on any of the error messages to go directly to the line flagged by the compiler. If the **Error List** tab is not visible on your screen, you can select **Error List** from the **View** menu.

A pushpin icon appears in the upper-right corner of all tool windows such as that shown in the **Error List** window. When the pushpin stands up like a thumbtack, the window is docked in place; thus, the **Error List** window is docked in place in Figure 1-20.

NOTE Tool windows support a feature called Auto Hide. If you click the pushpin so that it appears to be lying on its side, the window minimizes along the edges of the IDE. A small tab with the window name appears along the edge. This frees up space so you can see more of your source code.

The syntax error shown in Figure 1-20 is a common mistake. The double quote was omitted from the end of the argument to the `WriteLine( )` method at Line 10. The error message does not say that, however. When you are reviewing error messages, keep in mind that the message might not be issued until the compiler reaches the next line or next block of code. Look for the problem in the general area that is flagged. Some of the most common errors are failing to end with an opening curly brace (`{`) or having an extra closing curly brace (`}`), failing to type a semicolon at the end of a statement (`;`), and misspelling names. As a good exercise, consider purposefully omitting curly braces, semicolons, and misspelling words. See what kind of error messages each mistake generates. You will then be more equipped to find those errors quickly when you develop more sophisticated applications in the future.

NOTE Because one error can generate several messages, it is probably best to fix the first error and then recompile rather than trying to fix all the errors in one pass.

Run-time Errors

Run-time errors are much more difficult to detect than syntax errors. A program containing run-time errors might compile without any problems, run, and produce results. Run-time errors can also cause a program to crash. A program might be written to retrieve data from a file. If that file is not available, when the program runs, a run-time error occurs. Another type of run-time error is division by zero.

Many times, a program compiles and executes without errors but does not perform as expected. If the results are incorrect, the associated error is called a **logic error**. Logic errors are not identified until you look closely at the results and verify their correctness. For example, a value might not be calculated correctly. The wrong formula might be used. Failing to understand the problem specification fully is the most common culprit in logic errors. It is not enough to produce output; the output must be a correct solution to the problem.

Another potential run-time error type will be introduced when you start working with data in Chapter 2. If you are using data for calculations or performing different steps based on the value of data, it is easy to encounter a run-time error. Run-time errors can be minimized during software development by performing a thorough analysis and design before beginning the coding phase. The common strategy of desk checking also leads to more accurate results.

Creating an Application

Now that you understand what is required in most C# programs and how to compile and see your results, work through the following example using the suggested methodology for program development introduced earlier in this chapter. In this section, you will design a solution for the following problem definition.

PROGRAMMING EXAMPLE: ProgrammingMessage

The problem specification is shown in Figure 1-21.

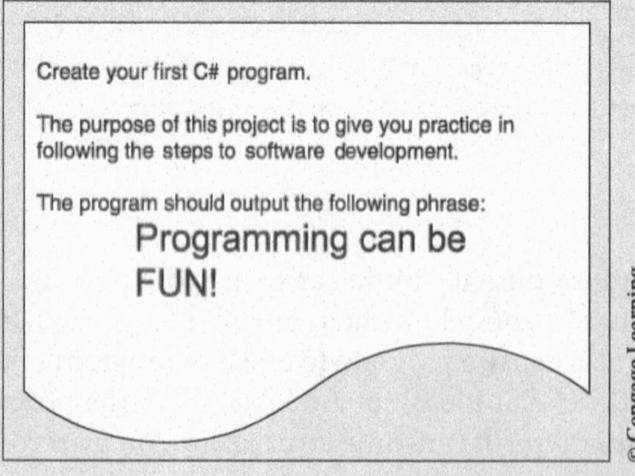

Create your first C# program.

The purpose of this project is to give you practice in following the steps to software development.

The program should output the following phrase:

Programming can be FUN!

© Cengage Learning

FIGURE 1-21 Problem specification sheet for the ProgrammingMessage example

ANALYZE THE PROBLEM

Do you understand the problem definition? This step is often slighted or glossed over. It is easy to scan the problem definition and think that you have a handle on the problem but miss an important feature. If you do not devote adequate time and energy analyzing the problem definition, much time and expense might be wasted in later steps. This is one, if not the most important, step in the development process. Ask questions to clarify the problem definition if necessary. You want to make sure that you fully grasp what is expected.

As you read the problem definition given in Figure 1-21, note that no program inputs are required. The only data needed for this application is a string of characters. This greatly simplifies the analysis phase.

DESIGN A SOLUTION

The desired output, as noted in the problem specification sheet in Figure 1-21, is to display "Programming can be FUN!" on two lines. For this example, as well as any other application you develop, it is helpful to determine what your final output should look like. One way to document your desired output is to construct a **prototype**, or mock-up, of the output. Prototypes range from being elaborate designs created with graphics, word-processing, or paint programs, to being quite cryptic sketches created with paper and pencil. It is crucial to realize the importance of constructing a prototype, no matter which method you use. Developing a prototype helps you construct your algorithm. Prototypes also provide additional documentation detailing the purpose of the application. Figure 1-22 shows a prototype of the final output for the ProgrammingMessage example.

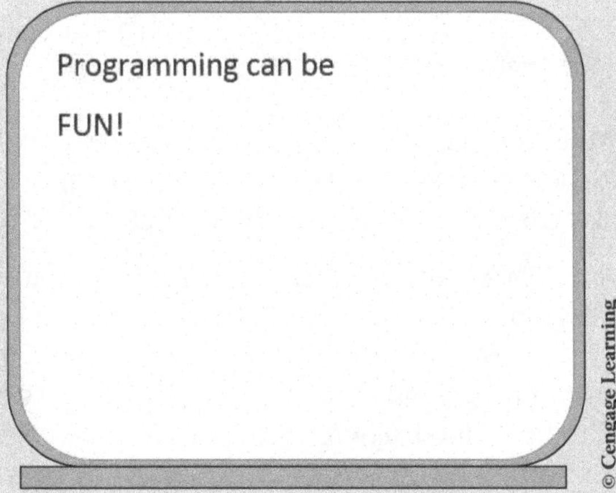

FIGURE 1-22 Prototype for the ProgrammingMessage example

During design, it is important to develop an algorithm. The algorithm for this problem could be developed using a flowchart. The algorithm should include a step-by-step solution for solving the problem, which, in this case, is straightforward and involves merely the output of a string of characters. Figure 1-23 shows a flowchart defining the steps needed for the ProgrammingMessage example.

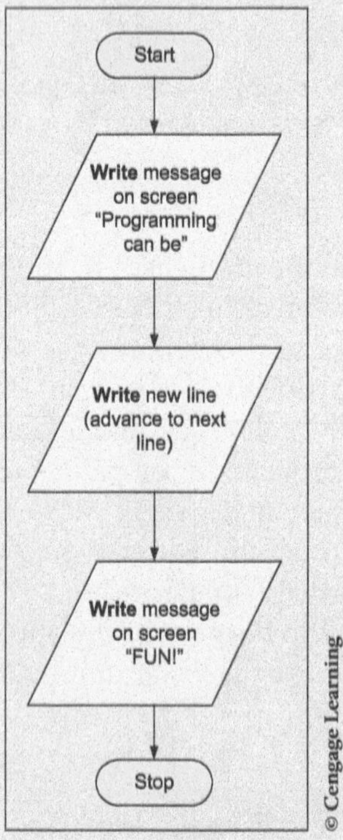

FIGURE 1-23 Algorithm for the ProgrammingMessage example

Another option is to use structured English or pseudocode to define the algorithm. The pseudocode for this problem would be very short. It would include a single line to display the message Programming can be FUN! on the output screen.

Using an object-oriented approach to design, the solutions normally entail creating `class` diagrams. No data members would need to be defined for this problem. The `Console` `class` in the `System` `namespace` already has methods you can use to display output on a standard output device. Thus, no new methods or behaviors would need to be defined. Therefore, if you were to construct a `class` diagram, it would include only a heading for the `class`. Nothing would appear in the middle or bottom portion of the diagram. Because the diagram does not provide additional documentation or help with the design of this simple problem, it is not drawn.

After the algorithm is developed, the design should be checked for correctness. One way to do this is to desk check your algorithms by mimicking the computer and working through the code step-by-step as if you were the computer. When you step through the flowchart, it should produce the output that appears on the prototype. It is extremely important that you carefully design and check your algorithm for correctness before beginning to write your code. You will spend much less time and experience much less frustration if you do this.

CODE THE SOLUTION

After you have completed the design and verified the algorithm's correctness, it is time to translate the design into source code. You can type source code statements into the computer using a simple editor such as Notepad, or you can create the file using Visual Studio. In this step of the process, you must pay attention to the language syntax rules.

If you create the application using Visual Studio, the IDE automatically generates much of the code for you. Some of that code can be removed or disregarded. For example, did you notice that the four `using` statements (`using System.Collections.Generic; using System.Linq; using System.Text;` and `using System.Threading.Tasks;`) were removed in the previous example? The *Quick Action Light Bulb* will help you remove unnecessary `using` statements. You can again remove or disregard these clauses. The `using System;` is the only `using` clause that needs to remain with your program statements for most of the applications that you will be developing. Adding an additional `using` clause (`using static System.Console;`) to reference the `Console` class shortens the amount of typing needed.

Visual Studio also modifies the `Main( )` method's heading from what you saw previously in this chapter. The signature for `Main( )` can have an empty argument list or include `string[ ] args` inside the parentheses. For the types of applications you are developing, you do not need to send the additional argument. Therefore, you can also disregard or completely remove the argument inside the parentheses to `Main( )` at this time.

You might want to change the name of the source code file, and allow Visual Studio to change all references to that name. When you typed `ProgrammingMessage` as the project name, the IDE automatically named the `namespace ProgrammingMessage`. The `class` could also be called `ProgrammingMessage`, and this would cause no name clashing problems such as the `namespace` being given the same name as the `class` name. Figure 1-24 illustrates the changes you might want to make to the code generated by Visual Studio.

```
using System;
using System.Collections.Generic;
using System.Linq;
using System.Text;
using System.Threading.Tasks;

namespace ProgrammingMessage
{
    class Program
    {
        static void Main(string[] args)
        {
        }
    }
}
```

Can delete these using statements

Change the name

Can replace with static void Main()

FIGURE 1-24 Recommended deletions

With the exception of the `using static System.Console;` clause, the only lines that you had to type were found in the `Main( )` body.

```
WriteLine("Programming can be");
WriteLine("FUN!");
ReadKey( );
```

The final program listing looks like this:

```
/*Programmer: [supply your name]
  Date:       [supply the current date]
  Purpose:     This class can be used to send messages to
               the output screen.
*/
using System;
using static System.Console;

namespace ProgrammingMessage
{
     class ProgrammingMessage
     {
          static void Main ( )
          {
               WriteLine("Programming can be");
               WriteLine("FUN!");
               ReadKey( );
          }
     }
}
```

At the beginning of your program, identify the author of the code, and as a minimum specify the purpose of the project. Note that the statements inside the `Main( )` method are executed in sequential order. The `ReadKey( )` method is executed after

1

the two `WriteLine( )` methods. `ReadKey( )` is used in a program to keep the output screen displayed until the user presses a key. After a character is pressed on the keyboard, control passes to the next line that marks the end of the application.

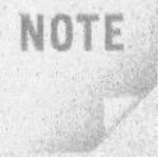

NOTE If you are developing your application with an earlier version of Visual Studio and C#, you would not be able to add the reference to the `static class` (`using static System.Console;`). You would need to fully qualify calls to members of the `Console class`. `WriteLine( )` would be called by typing `Console.WriteLine( )`.

IMPLEMENT THE CODE

During implementation, the source code is compiled to check for rule violations. To compile from within the Visual Studio IDE, use the **Build** menu option. If you have errors, they must be corrected before you can go forward. From within the Visual Studio IDE, select **Start Without Debugging** on the **Debug** menu bar to see the results.

TEST AND DEBUG

Just because you have no compiler syntax errors and receive output does not mean that the results are correct. During this final step, test the program and ensure that you have the correct result. The output should match your prototype. Is your spacing correct?

By following the steps outlined in this chapter, you have officially become a C# programmer. The program you created was a simple one. However, the concepts you learned in this chapter are essential to your progress. In Chapter 2, you will begin working with data.

Coding Standards

It is important to follow coding standards when you design classes. Doing so will lead to better solutions and reduce the amount of time needed when you make changes to your program statements. You should also follow standards while initially designing your algorithms using flowcharts and pseudocode. Following are some suggested coding standards or guidelines as they relate to pseudocode.

Pseudocode

- For arithmetic operations, use verbs such as compute or calculate to imply some form of arithmetic is needed.
- Use words such as set, reset, or increment to imply what type of actions should be performed.
- Use print or display to indicate what should be shown on the screen.

- Group items and add indentation to imply they belong together.
- For statements that should be performed more than one time, use keywords such as while or do while to imply looping.
- Use if or if/else for testing the contents of memory locations.

Developing standards that you consistently adhere to will increase your coding efficiency and make your code more maintainable.

Resources

There are enormous numbers of sites devoted to just C# on the Web. You might start your exploring at one or more of the following sites:

- C# 5.0 Language Specifications—
  http://www.microsoft.com/en-us/download/details.aspx?id=7029
- C# Programmers Guide—
  https://msdn.microsoft.com/en-us/library/67ef8sbd.aspx
- History of Computing Project—
  http://www.thocp.net/
- Pascaline—
  http://www.thocp.net/hardware/pascaline.htm
- The Microsoft .NET Website—
  http://www.microsoft.com/net
- The Visual Studio Home Page—
  http://www.visualstudio.com/
- U.S. Census Data on Computer and Internet Use—
  http://www.census.gov/cps/
- Bureau of Labor Statistics Occupational Outlook Handbook—
  http://www.bls.gov/ooh/Computer-and-Information-Technology/Software-developers.htm
- .NET Foundation for Open Source Development—
  http://www.dotnetfoundation.org/
- GitHub Open Source Repository—
  https://github.com/microsoft/dotnet
- Mono Cross Platform Open Source .NET Framework—
  http://www.mono-project.com
- Xamarin Cross-Platform Mobile Development—
  https://xamarin.com/
- Microsoft Developer Network—
  http://msdn.microsoft.com/en-us/

QUICK REVIEW

1. The power of the computer rests with software, which is the set of instructions or programs that give the hardware functionality.
2. Many consider today's computer technology to be in the fifth generation of modern computing. Each era is characterized by an important advancement.
3. Software can be divided into two categories: system software and application software. Application software is defined as the programs developed to perform a specific task.
4. The type of software most often associated with system software is the operating system. The operating system software is loaded when you turn on the computer. Other types of system software are compilers, interpreters, and assemblers.
5. Programming is a process of problem solving. The hardest part is coming up with a plan to solve the problem.
6. The five problem-solving steps for software development introduced in this chapter include analyzing, designing, coding, implementing, and testing and debugging the solution.
7. Procedural programming is process oriented and focuses on the processes that data undergoes from input until meaningful output is produced.
8. The underlying theme of top-down design or stepwise refinement is that given any problem definition, the logic can be refined by using the divide-and-conquer approach.
9. Software maintenance refers to upgrading or changing applications.
10. Using an object-oriented analysis approach, the focus is on determining the objects you want to manipulate rather than the logic required to manipulate them.
11. Encapsulation refers to combining attributes and actions or characteristics and behaviors to form a class.
12. An object is an instance of a class.
13. Through inheritance, it is possible to define subclasses of data objects that share some or all of the main class characteristics of their parents or super classes. Inheritance enables reuse of code.
14. C# was designed from scratch to work with the new programming paradigm, .NET, and was the language used for development of much of .NET.
15. .NET is a software environment in which programs run. It is not the operating system. It is a layer between the operating system and other applications, providing an easier framework for developing and running code.
16. Through using Visual Studio (which is an IDE) and the .NET Framework classes, C# provides an easy way to create GUIs.

17. C# is being used to develop mobile apps for multiple platforms including iOS and Android.
18. C# can be used to create Web, Windows, and console applications.
19. Webpages can be created using Web forms, which are part of the ASP.NET technology.
20. Windows applications are considered desktop bound and designed for a single platform.
21. Console applications are the easiest to create. Values can be entered and produced with minimal overhead.
22. C# programs usually begin with a comment or `using` directives, followed by an optional `namespace` grouping and then the required `class` definition.
23. All C# programs must define a `class`.
24. Comments are written as notes to yourself or readers of your program. The compiler ignores comments.
25. It is not necessary to end single inline comments (`//`); they end when the Enter key is pressed. Comments that span more than one line should be enclosed between `/* */`. These are considered block or multiline comments.
26. Many classes make up the Framework class library. A `class` contains data members and methods or behaviors that can be reused.
27. The using-namespace-directive imports all the types contained in the given `namespace`.
28. By adding a using directive to a `static class`, you can eliminate the need of preceding a method invocation with the name of the `class`, a dot (.), and the method name. (i.e. `using static System.Console`)
29. Everything in C# is designed around a `class`. Every program must have at least one `class`.
30. A method is a collection of one or more statements taken together that perform an action. In other words, a method is a small block of code that performs an action.
31. The `Main( )` method is the entry point for every C# console application. It is the point at which execution begins.
32. The keyword `static` indicates that a single copy of the method is created.
33. The keyword `void` is included to signal that no value is returned. The complete signature of a method starts with the return type, followed by the name of the method, and finally a parenthesized list of arguments. One signature for `Main( )` is `void static Main( )`.
34. `WriteLine( )` writes a string message to the monitor or a standard output device.
35. Methods communicate with each other through arguments placed inside parentheses.

36. Readability is important. Indenting is not required, but it is a good practice because it makes the code easier to read.
37. To see the results of a program, you must type the statements (source code) into a file, compile that code, and then execute the application.
38. Visual Studio IDE is an interactive development environment that enables you to type the source code, compile, and execute without leaving the IDE program.
39. One way to document your desired output is to construct a prototype, or mock-up, of your output.
40. The `ReadKey( )` method is often used to hold the display screen for viewing. It accepts any character from a standard input device, such as a keyboard. It does nothing with the character.

EXERCISES

1. All of the following are examples of high-level programming languages, except:
   a. C#
   b. C
   c. Java
   d. C++
   e. Assembly
2. The program that translates high-level programming language into machine-readable form is a(n):
   a. application
   b. operating system
   c. C# program
   d. compiler
   e. machine language utility
3. The following strategy reduces the amount of time in development and produces more efficient solutions:
   a. Code the solution as soon as possible.
   b. Design the solution before coding.
   c. Analyze the solution before testing and debugging.
   d. Build a prototype during testing.
   e. Use a simple, low-level language for development.

4. In which phase of the software development process would probing questions be used to verify the problem definition?
   a. analysis
   b. design
   c. coding
   d. implementation
   e. testing
5. Cycling back to previous phases as potential problems are uncovered is an example of:
   a. object-oriented programming
   b. stepwise refinement
   c. intermediate language
   d. iterative development
   e. structured programming
6. After designing your solution, you should _____ before typing any code.
   a. analyze the problem definition
   b. check for run-time errors
   c. do maintenance on the solution
   d. desk check the solution
   e. determine what .NET class to use
7. With the object-oriented methodology, the data members are referred to as:
   a. attributes or characteristics
   b. characteristics or behaviors
   c. methods or attributes
   d. behaviors or methods
   e. attributes or behaviors
8. Which of the following is the name of a namespace needed for Console applications?
   a. using
   b. Console
   c. System.Console
   d. Write
   e. System

9. ASP.NET creates which type of application?
    a. Windows
    b. console
    c. command
    d. Web
    e. services
10. Which beginning symbol(s) indicates the lines that follow will be comments?
    a. `/*`
    b. `**`
    c. `///`
    d. `*/`
    e. `//`
11. System is an example of a(n):
    a. object
    b. `class`
    c. method
    d. `namespace`
    e. directive
12. A(n) _____ groups semantically related types under a single name.
    a. object
    b. `class`
    c. method
    d. `namespace`
    e. directive
13. To mark the beginning and end of a block of code, C# programmers use:
    a. [ ]
    b. { }
    c. ( )
    d. begin end
    e. start stop

14. Which of the following is a keyword?
    a. `Main( )`
    b. `System`
    c. `using`
    d. `WriteLine`
    e. all of the above

15. The fully qualified call to the method that allows the user to input a single character is:
    a. `Console.System.Read( )`
    b. `System.Console.Read( )`
    c. `Console.System.Write( )`
    d. `System.Console.Write( )`
    e. `System.Console.ReadLine( )`

16. A(n)_____ is a mock-up of desired output.
    a. prototype
    b. algorithm
    c. diagram
    d. specification
    e. none of the above

17. What is the name of the feature in Visual Studio that displays in a scrollable list all available methods and properties when the dot is typed after an object name?
    a. Help
    b. Rotor
    c. Mono
    d. IntelliSense
    e. ToolTip

18. To see the results of an application, you _____ the code.
    a. compile
    b. JIT
    c. execute
    d. edit
    e. desk check

19. Which escape sequence can be used to indicate that the cursor should advance to the next line?
    a. newline
    b. escape next
    c. \n
    d. \newline
    e. \r

20. Which of the following is a call to a method?
    a. `Console.Write;`
    b. `Console.Write["ok"];`
    c. `Write.Console("ok");`
    d. `Console.Write("ok");`
    e. none of the above

---

21. Identify one syntax error that might occur when you type Example 1-1 into an editor. Identify one logic error that might occur.

22. What is produced when you run the following application?

```
using System;
using System.Console;
namespace ExerciseI
{
  class Problem2
  {
    static void Main( )
    {
       Write("Go ");
       Write("Forth ");
       WriteLine("and DO");
       Write("Awesome ");
       Write("Stuff!");
    }
  }
}
```

23. What must be changed in the segment of code in Exercise #22 to cause all of the output to be displayed on one line?

24. Using the program segment in Exercise #22, identify line number(s) in which each of the following can be found:

    a. method invocation

    b. `namespace`

    c. `class` name

    d. argument to a method

    e. identifier

25. Identify the syntax error(s) (if any) in the following:

```
Line 1  using System
Line 2  namesspace ExerciseI
Line 3  {
Line 4    Problem2
Line 5    {
Line 6      static Main( )
Line 7      {
Line 8         console.write("ok")
Line 9      }
Line 10   }
Line 11 }
```

PROGRAMMING EXERCISES

1. Write a program that displays the traditional Hello World message on the screen but adds your introduction. The output should be displayed with white background and black text. One possible design is shown here.

```
Hello World! My name is Tyler Howard!
```

   For an added challenge, also display your message using a different language.

   For example, using Spanish, the message might read:

```
In Spanish:
Hello World! Mi nombre es Tyler Howard!
```

2. Develop an application that produces a banner containing information about your project. Items you might include are your programming assignment number, name, date submitted, and the purpose of the

application. Label each item. These are items you might want to include as internal documentation on future programming assignments. The output should be displayed with white background and black text. Your output for your banner might look similar to the following:

```
**********************************************************
**      Programming Assignment #2                       **
**      Developer: Alma King                            **
**      Date Submitted: September 17                    **
**      Purpose: Provide internal documentation.        **
**********************************************************
```

In addition to printing the output screen banner shown in the preceding code segment, be sure to include appropriate comments as internal documentation to your program.

3. Create an application that displays an X as output. Use any characters of your choosing when you design your prototype. The output should be displayed with white background and black text. One possible design is given here.

```
##                                                  ##
        ##                                  ##
                ##                  ##
                        ##      ##
                           ## # ##
                        ##      ##
                ##                  ##
        ##                                  ##
##                                                  ##
```

For an added challenge, use mostly tabs and newline characters as part of your design as opposed to just using the space character.

4. First develop a prototype and then write a program that displays the name of the programming language discussed in this text. The output should be displayed with white background and black text. You should be more creative, but one possible design is given here.

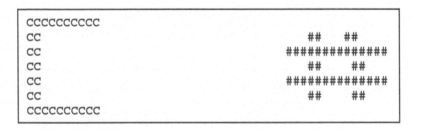

```
CCCCCCCCCC
CC                                              ##    ##
CC                                          #############
CC                                              ##     ##
CC                                          #############
CC                                              ##     ##
CCCCCCCCCC
```

5. Flags are a symbol of unity and invoke special meaning to their followers. Create a design for a flag and write a program that displays your design. The output should be displayed with white background and black text. One possible design follows.

```
*******________________________________________
*******________________________________________
*******________________________________________
*******________________________________________
_______________________________________________
_______________________________________________
```

6. Create an application that produces three different outputs using the same phrase. Select your own favorite popular saying for the phrase. The phrase should first be displayed on a single line. The output should be displayed with white background and black text. Use at least three Write( ) methods—but display the output on a single line.

   Next, print the phrase on three separate lines, again using only Write( ) methods. For your third and final output, print your favorite saying one word per line. Decide which combination of Write( ) and/or WriteLine( ) would be the most streamlined approach. Label each output. Following is an example of what the final output would look like using a favorite saying of the author:

```
Output #1
        Laugh often, Dream big, Reach for the stars!
Output #2
        Laugh often,
        Dream big,
        Reach for the stars!
Output #3
        Laugh
        often,
        Dream
        big,
        Reach
        for
        the
        stars!
```

7. Produce a listing containing information about you. Include items such as your name, hometown, major, hobby, and/or favorite activity. Label each piece of information, place each of the items on separate lines, and place a single backslash (\) after each entry. Begin and end the entire listing with the | character. Include the full listing in a box of asterisks.

Design the solution so that all items are displayed from Write( ) methods. Ensure that your source code is readable and doesn't wrap if printed. The output should be displayed with white background and black text. Your output might look similar to the following:

```
**********************************************
*!      Name: Barbara Doyle\                 *
*       Hometown: Jacksonville\              *
*       Major: CS\                           *
*       Hobby: Biking\                       *
*       Favorite Activity: Swimming\        !*
**********************************************
```

8. Hangman is a favorite childhood game. Design the stick figure for this game and produce a printed listing with your stickman. One possible design follows. You may implement this design or develop an improved version; however, you must include legs and arms that use the backslash symbol as part of your prototyped design. The output should be displayed with white background and black text.

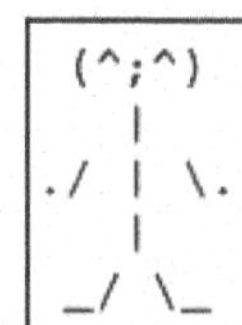

9. Create an application that displays several patterns. You may use any character of your choice to construct the patterns. Design your solution to include at least three different patterns and display the three patterns on the same row. The output should be displayed with white background and black text. One possible solution follows.

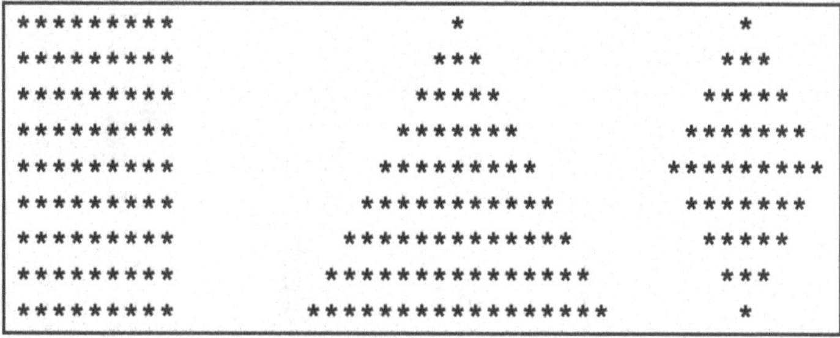

10. Write a program that displays your initials in block characters so that each letter is made up of the character that it represents. Output should consist of at least 10 rows or lines and all initials must appear together in those rows. The output should be displayed with white background and black text. For example, the initials for Benjamin Andrew Jones in block characters are shown below.

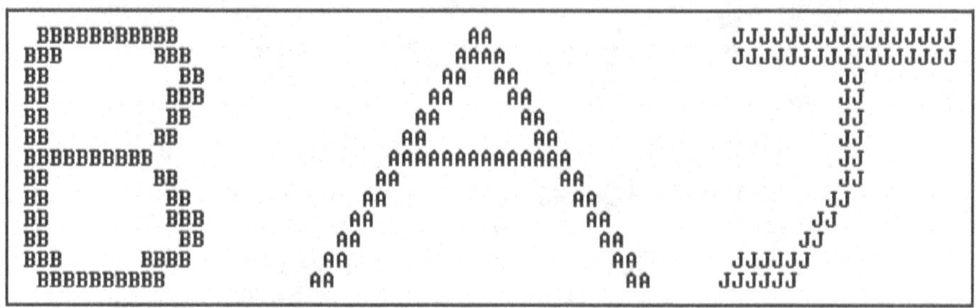

© zeljkodan/Shutterstock.com

Data Types and Expressions

IN THIS CHAPTER, YOU WILL:

- Examine how computers represent data
- Declare memory locations for data
- Explore the relationship among classes, objects, and types
- Use predefined data types
- Use integral data types
- Use floating-point types
- Learn about the decimal data type
- Declare Boolean variables
- Declare and manipulate strings
- Work with constants
- Write assignment statements using arithmetic operators
- Learn about the order of operations
- Learn special formatting rules for currency
- Work through a programming example that illustrates the chapter's concepts

Chapter 1 introduced you to the basic elements of a C# program. You discovered the requirements for developing, compiling, and executing applications. This chapter focuses on data. **Data** is the raw facts, the basic numbers and characters that are manipulated to produce useful information. In this chapter, you will begin to see the power of programming when you write applications to perform calculations. You will learn how to declare variables that hold different types of data in memory and see how arithmetic operators react given different kinds of data.

Data Representation

You might hear someone say that his computer has a 64-bit processor with 8 GB of RAM and 1 TB of hard disk space. Another person tells you her flash memory key holds 64 GB. Exactly what does this mean?

Bits

To begin, the word **bit** is a shortening of the words *Binary digIT*. Binary means two; thus, a binary digit can hold one of two values: 0 or 1. For data representation, the 1 and 0 correspond to on and off, respectively. When thinking about bits, it might help you to picture a circuit (switch) turned on or turned off. The number 1 represents the circuit as being turned on.

Bytes

Computer memories are commonly divided into 8-bit groupings. This 8-bit combination is called a **byte**. In the simplest terms, with each of the switches being known as a bit, it takes a combination of eight switches to represent one character, such as the letter A. With 8 bits representing 1 byte and 1 byte representing one keystroke, it would take 11 bytes to represent the word *programming*. You might wonder why it takes 8 bits to make a byte. The 8-bit byte is a format that people settled on through trial and error over the past 50 years. This use of 8 bits got its start with the IBM System/360 in the 1960s. It gained popularity in the 1980s with the explosion of the home computer, which was also based on 8 bits. Today, we would not think of associating a byte with a variable number of bits; it is commonly accepted that a byte consists of 8 bits.

Binary Numbering System

The computer stores data by setting the switches in a cell of memory to a pattern that represents a character. To represent data, computers use the base-2 numbering system, also known as the **binary numbering system**. Our base-10 numbering system, called the **decimal system**, uses 10 symbols ranging from 0 to 9 to represent a value. Base 2 has only two symbols, the values 0 and 1. Therefore, a binary value might look something like 01101001 because it is composed of only 0s and 1s. How do you determine the decimal equivalent value of the binary number 01101001? If you understand the decimal (base-10) positional numbering system, it is easy to translate those concepts to any other base numbering system. Figure 2-1 illustrates how 1326 is derived in base 10.

10^3	10^2	10^1	10^0
(1000)	(100)	(10)	(1)
1	3	2	6

$$
\begin{array}{lcr}
1 \text{ times } 10^3 \ (1000) & = & 1000 \\
+ \ 3 \text{ times } 10^2 \ (100) & = & 300 \\
+ \ 2 \text{ times } 10^1 \ (10) & = & 20 \\
+ \ 6 \text{ times } 10^0 \ (1) & = & 6 \\
\hline
 & & 1326
\end{array}
$$

© Cengage Learning

FIGURE 2-1 Base-10 positional notation of 1326

Figure 2-2 uses those same concepts with base 2 to illustrate the decimal equivalent of 01101001. In Figure 2-2, you see that the number 01101001 in binary is equivalent to the number 105 in decimal.

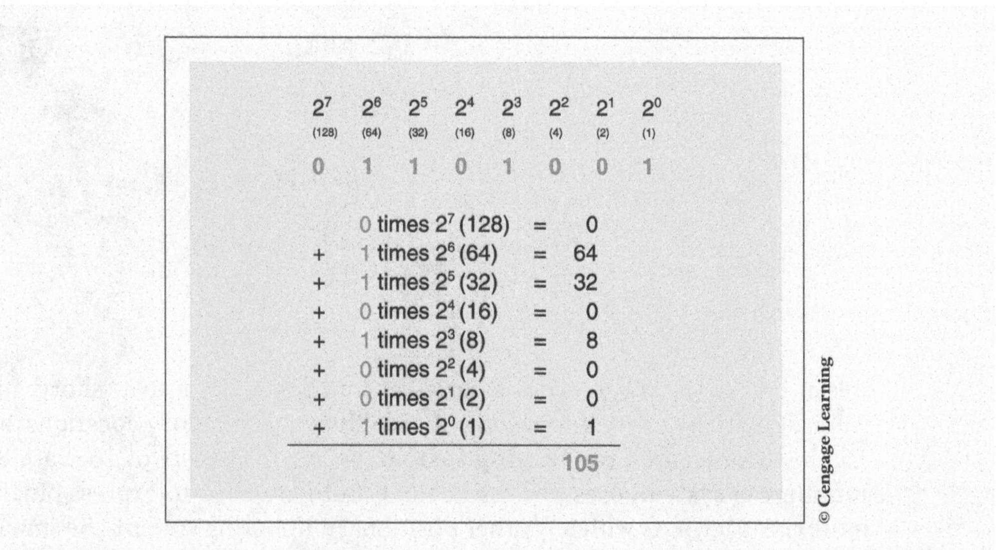

FIGURE 2-2 Decimal equivalent of 01101001

You can see from Figure 2-2 that in the binary numbering system, each bit holds a value of increasing powers of 2. Table 2-1 presents the decimal value when the bits contain various values. As given in the table, when all the bits are turned on with a 1 representation, the equivalent decimal value is 255.

TABLE 2-1 Binary equivalent of selected decimal values

Decimal value	Binary equivalent
0	00000000
1	00000001
2	00000010
3	00000011
4	00000100
5	00000101
6	00000110
7	00000111
8	00001000
...	...
254	11111110
255	11111111

Because it is difficult to read a series of binary numbers, two shorthand versions were developed to make viewing the contents of memory locations easier. Base 16, the **hexadecimal numbering system**, works on powers of 16. Base 8, the **octal numbering system**, uses powers of eight. Both are used to express binary numbers more compactly. As with any other positional numbering system, the smallest symbol is 0, the total number of symbols is equal to the base, and our positional notation is used. Hexadecimal has 16 symbols (0–9, A–F). The decimal value 15 is represented by F in hexadecimal. 2C in hex is 44 in our base 10 numbering system, as shown in the following example:

	2	→	2 times 16^1	→	2 times 16 = 32
+	C	→	12 times 16^0	→	12 times 1 = 12
					44

2

Using the base-10 positional numbering system, the value of each digit depends on its position within the number. The octal numbering system uses eight digits.

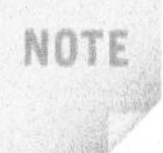

Can you determine the octal representation for the decimal value 9? The answer is 11. 1 times 8^1 + 1 times 8^0 = (8 + 1) = 9

Character Sets

With only 8 bits, you can represent 2^8 or 256 different decimal values ranging from 0 to 255. This is 256 different characters or different combinations of 0 and 1. The binary numbering system is used to represent the language of the computer. The binary number 01000001 is equivalent to the decimal value 65, which represents the uppercase character A. Fortunately, you do not have to retrain yourself to speak that language. The character set used by programmers of C# is called Unicode. **Unicode** is the universal character-encoding schema. It covers all the characters for all the writing systems, both ancient and modern, in the world. Because computers just deal with numbers, they store letters and characters by assigning a number to them. Unicode provides a unique number for every character. Before Unicode was invented, there were hundreds of different coding schemas in use. No single encoding could contain enough characters. When the developers created the Unicode character set, instead of using 8 bits, they used 16 bits. Now, 2^{16} or 65,536 unique characters can be represented. Unicode includes representation of characters for writing in many different languages in addition to English.

A subset of Unicode, the first 128 characters, corresponds to the **American Standard Code for Information Interchange (ASCII)** character set. ASCII consists of the alphabet for the English language, plus numbers and symbols. For both the ASCII character set and Unicode, the first 32 values (0 through 31) are codes for things such as carriage return and line feed. The space character is the 33rd value, followed by punctuation, digits, uppercase characters, and lowercase characters. Appendix C contains a table showing the decimal representation for the ASCII portion of the Unicode character set. Both the C# and Java languages use the Unicode character set.

Kilobyte, Megabyte, Gigabyte, Terabyte, Petabyte. . .

Now back to our 64-bit processor with 2 GB of RAM and 1 TB of hard disk space. When you start talking about lots of bytes, you get into prefixes such as kilo, mega, and giga, as in kilobyte, megabyte, and gigabyte (also shortened to K, M, and G, as in Kbytes, Mbytes, and Gbytes or KB, MB, and GB). Table 2-2 presents the multipliers.

TABLE 2-2 Common abbreviations for data representations

Storage capacity	Size in bytes	Abbreviation
Kilobyte	2^{10} (1,024)	KB
Megabyte	2^{20} (1,048,576)	MB
Gigabyte	2^{30} (1,073,741,824)	GB
Terabyte	2^{40} (1,099,511,627,776)	TB
Petabyte	2^{50} (1,125,899,906,842,624)	PB
Exabyte	2^{60} (1,152,921,504,606,846,976)	EB
Zettabyte	2^{70} (1,180,591,620,717,411,303,424)	ZB
Yottabyte	2^{80} (1,208,925,819,614,629,174,706,176)	YB

Notice that **kilo** is about a thousand, **mega** is about a million, **giga** is about a billion, and so on. So, when you think about a machine that has a 64-bit processor with 4 GB of RAM and 1 TB of hard disk space, you know that the machine can process 64 bits at one time, store approximately 4 billion characters in memory, and has storage capacity for approximately 1 trillion characters on the hard disk.

The first 4 TB hard drive was released in 2011. In August 2014, the first 8 TB hard drive was released.

Memory Locations for Data

Programs manipulate data, and data can take the form of a number, single character, or combination of characters. The following are all examples of data:

18, "Brenda", 'A', 3.25, –7, 36724, and 47.23

By themselves, these data items have no value. The number 18 could be an age, temperature, number of students in a class, number of hours you are enrolled in this term, or could represent something totally different. Without identifying and labeling 18, it is a meaningless number. When working with data, the first task is to use an identifier to name the data item.

Identifiers

Identifiers are names of elements that appear in a program, such as data items. Some identifiers are predefined; others are user defined. You have already seen some .NET identifiers when you wrote your first program in Chapter 1. These were not reserved keywords, but simply names selected and used by the developers of the .NET platform and the C# language. The program in Example 1-1 contained the following predefined identifiers: `System`, `Main`, `Console`, and `WriteLine`.

The `namespace` identifier of `HelloWorldProgram` and the `class` identifier of `HelloWorld` are user-defined identifiers selected by the author of the textbook during the creation of the first project.

Here are the rules for creating an identifier in C#:

1. A combination of alphabetic characters (a–z and A–Z), numeric digits (0–9), and the underscores (_) can be used. Identifiers can be long; however, many systems consider the first 31 characters unique.
2. The first character in the name may not be a numeric digit.
3. No embedded spaces can be placed between the characters. This means you cannot separate words in a name by a space. Normally, you concatenate (append) second and subsequent words onto the identifier by capitalizing the beginning letter of each word after the first.

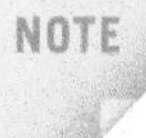

The underscore character is used between words as a separator by languages such as C++. Even though it is a valid character that can be used in C#, the underscore character is used primarily for defining constant identifiers. You will learn about constant literals in this chapter.

4. Tables 2-3 and 2-4 give the **keywords** in C#. Keywords are predefined reserved identifiers that have special meanings to the compiler. They cannot be used as identifiers in your program. Notice that the keywords in Table 2-4 are identified as *contextual keywords*. Contextual keywords are not as powerful as regular keywords. Contextual keywords have special meaning only when used in a specific situation. Other times they can be used as identifiers.

TABLE 2-3 C# keywords/reserved words

Keywords					
abstract	as	base	bool	break	byte
case	catch	char	checked	class	const
continue	decimal	default	delegate	do	double
else	enum	event	explicit	extern	false
finally	fixed	float	for	foreach	goto
if	implicit	in	int	interface	internal
is	lock	long	namespace	new	null
object	operator	out	override	params	private
protected	public	readonly	ref	return	sbyte
sealed	short	sizeof	stackalloc	static	string
struct	switch	this	throw	true	try
typeof	uint	ulong	unchecked	unsafe	ushort
using	virtual	volatile	void	while	

NOTE Contextual keywords only have special meaning when used in a specific context. They were added in an attempt to avoid breaking code that might have been written using earlier standards where one of these words might have been used as a user-defined identifier. For example, `yield` only has a special meaning when it is used immediately before a `return` or `break` statement. Other times, it could be used as an identifier.

TABLE 2-4 C# contextual keywords

Contextual keywords					
add	alias	ascending	asyn	await	descending
dynamic	from	get	global	group	into
join	let	orderby	partial	remove	select
set	value	var	where	yield	

5. It is permissible to use the "@" symbol as the first character of an identifier, but it has special meaning and should be avoided unless you are writing code that will interface with another programming language. When used, the "@" symbol enables keywords to be used as identifiers.
6. It is smart to use the case of the character to your advantage. C# is case sensitive. The identifier `Rate` is different from the identifier `rate` and also different from `RATE` or `rATE`.

   With .NET, there are three conventions for capitalizing identifiers: Pascal case, camel case, and uppercase. Using **Pascal case**, the first letter in the identifier and the first letter of each subsequent concatenated word is capitalized. Classes, methods, namespaces, and properties follow the Pascal case naming convention in C#. Variables and objects follow the camel case convention. With **camel case**, the first letter of an identifier is lowercase, and the first letter of each subsequent concatenated word is capitalized. The convention in C# is to use camel case for variable and object identifiers. Uppercase is used by constant literals and for identifiers that consist of two or fewer letters.
7. Being descriptive is helpful. Use meaningful names that represent the item being described. If the identifier is used to reference a person's age, call it age, not x. The more descriptive your identifiers, the easier it is for you and others to read your code.

Table 2-5 gives examples of valid identifiers.

TABLE 2-5 Valid identifiers

Valid identifiers		
`studentName`	`age`	`numberOfCourses`
`soc_sec_number`	`departureTime`	`course1`
`AmountOwed`	`count_of_Values`	`taxAmount`
`n`	`streetAddress`	`zipCode`
`roomSize`	`courseName`	`x3`
`moreData`	`bookTitle`	`homeRuns`
`pointsScored`	`CLUB_NAME`	`exam4`

The compiler will not catch a violation in rule #7 of the previous list. However, this rule is extremely important, and you should follow it. By using meaningful names that describe their contents, programs you develop are more readable and easier to debug and modify. Table 2-6 gives a list of illegal identifiers and a notation indicating why they are invalid.

TABLE 2-6 Invalid identifiers

Invalid identifiers	Description of violation
`soc sec number`	Embedded space
`int`	Reserved keyword
`3rdDay`	Begins with a digit
`room #`	Special symbol other than underscore and an embedded space
`first-name`	Special symbol other than underscore
`A number`	Embedded space
`class`	Reserved keyword

Variables

For a computer program to process or manipulate data, the characters and numbers must be stored in random access memory (RAM). Variables are the programming elements that facilitate this storage. A **variable** represents an area in the computer memory where a value of a particular data type can be stored. When you **declare a variable**, you allocate memory for that data item in your program.

Declaring a variable requires that you select an identifier and determine what type of data will appear in the memory cell. The syntax for declaring a variable follows:

```
type identifier;
```

At the same time the variable is declared or created, it can be initialized to a value. This is referred to as a **compile-time initialization**. Notice the word initialization. The variable starts off with the initialized value, but it can be changed. The value being assigned to the variable should be compatible with the data type. When the variable is going to be used in arithmetic, it is a good idea to initialize it to 0. The syntax for initializing a variable when it is declared follows:

```
type identifier = expression;
```

The expression can simply be a value such as 0 or 27, or it can include other identifiers in an arithmetic equation.

With both types of declaration, in addition to naming the data item, you must also determine what type of data will be associated with it. This step notifies the computer of how much storage space to set aside for the data item and how the data will be retrieved after it is placed in memory.

Literal Values

A variable's value can change. Literals cannot be changed. **Literals** are the numbers, characters, and combinations of characters used in your program. They can be assigned to a variable or used in an expression. Their values stay constant. The number 17 is always 17. The character A is always A. It is possible to copy the value of a literal into a variable and then change the variable; this does not change the value of the original literal. It is also possible to use literals without assigning them to a specific variable.

Every time you declare a variable in the C# language, you are actually **instantiating** a `class` (creating an `object`). If you declare three variables of `int` type, you are instantiating the `class` three times; three `int` objects are created. The following statement creates three `int` objects:

```
int homeWorkScore1;
int examNumber1;
int numberOfPointsScored;
```

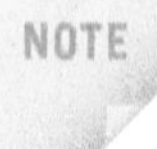

Notice how the camel case naming convention was used to declare the variables of `homeWorkScore1`, `examNumber1`, and `numberOfPointsScored`. The first letter is lowercase. The first character of subsequent words is uppercase. You were instantiating the `int` class when these objects were created. A summary of some of the C# coding standards can be found at the end of this chapter.

Literals are often used to give a value to an object's data portion. This can be done when the `object` is created or later in the program statements. A value such as 100 could be assigned to `homeWorkScore1` using the following statement:

```
homeWorkScore1 = 100;
```

Here 100 is a numeric literal. The contents of the memory location where the variable `homeWorkScore1` stored the value 100 can be changed; however, the literal value of 100 cannot be changed. 100 is always 100.

C# differs from languages that include a default value for variables when they are declared. In C#, every variable must be assigned a value before it is used. Otherwise, a syntax error is issued.

The following sections explain how the concepts of types, classes, and objects are related to data.

Types, Classes, and Objects

C# is an object-oriented language that makes extensive use of classes and objects. The following section explains where types fit into this picture.

Types

C# has a large number of predefined types for use in your programs. When you think about what a type is in the English language, you probably associate type with a label that signifies the sharing of some common characteristics by a group that belongs to that category. Dictionary definitions of the word **type** run something like this: a kind of group that can be differentiated from other kinds of groups by a particular set of characteristics. Example 2-1 should help you build on your understanding of what a type is and the importance of using the correct type.

EXAMPLE 2-1

You might have or plan to own a certain type of vehicle, such as a Hummer or a Corvette. Hummer vehicle types have different characteristics from those of the Corvette. A Corvette can travel at a faster pace than a Hummer. However, the Hummer can travel over much rougher terrain. You would not take the Corvette into a mountainous hiking region with the expectation that it could travel over large rocks, whereas a Hummer might do the trick. You would not want to transport four people in a Corvette, but four people could easily fit into a Hummer. Each is considered a vehicle. If you owned both, you could decide which one to use depending on the situation or destination.

For C# there is more than one type of number. One number type is called an **integer**, or `int`. The `int` type is a whole number, between a certain range of values, and contains no decimal point. It can be positive or negative. Another type of number is a **floating-point value**, which can contain a fractional portion. C# supports two types of floating-point types: `float` and `double`. If you wanted to store your grade point average, it would not be appropriate to put that value in an `int` because an `int` only lets you store the whole number portion. It would be like trying to put more than two people in the Corvette. They just do not fit. If your grade point average is 3.87 and you place the value in an `int` type, it chops off, or **truncates**, the 0.87 and your grade point average becomes 3. You would not be very happy with that, would you?

Classes

Types are actually implemented through classes in C#. The Framework class library (FCL), which is part of .NET, includes over 2000 classes that you can use in your programs. For simplicity, you can think of there being a one-to-one correspondence between a `class` and a type in C#. C# was designed from the ground up to be a true object-oriented language. As you learned in Chapter 1, every program must include a `class`. C# is a strongly typed language. There are number of types built into the language and C# also enables you to write or create your own user-defined data types or classes. In Chapter 11, Advanced Object-Oriented Programming Features, you will also read about another data type called an anonymous data type. In C#, a simple built-in numeric data type such as a whole number is also sometimes referred to as a **primitive type**.

Objects

As previously mentioned, an `object` is an instance of a `class`. It is an occurrence of the `class`. For simplicity purposes, you can think of an instance of the base type `int` as 21 or 3421. However, a `class` includes more than just the data associated with the type. **Class** is the term used to denote the encapsulation of data and behaviors into a single package or unit. The characteristics of the class's behavior and data can be described. The data portion of the `int`, as indicated previously, is always a whole number value. An `int` data type can store values that do not have a decimal portion. The behavior of the int data type can be described by identifying basic arithmetic operations such as addition and subtraction that can be performed on the type. Logical comparisons can determine which is larger than the other, and values can be displayed. These are all behaviors of the int data type. Encapsulating (packaging) these data and behavior characteristics into a single unit allows you to describe the type.

EXAMPLE 2-2

Your current grade point average might be named using an identifier such as `gradePointAverage`. Grade point average normally takes the form of a real number with a fractional component, such as 3.42. In C#, real numbers with decimals are represented using the `double` data type. Your name is another data item composed of a `string` of characters. In C#, the data type `string` is used to represent a grouping of characters. To represent a single character, such as the first initial of your last name, a `char` data type is used. Your age, for example 21, is a whole number without a fractional part. The data type most often used to represent a number without a fractional part is an `int`.

Table 2-7 gives some examples of different data types, with examples of what might be stored in each of these data items.

TABLE 2-7 Sample data types

Description grade	Identifier	Data type	Data
Grade point average	`gradePointAverage`	`double`	3.99
Current age	`age`	`int`	19
Full name	`studentName`	`string`	Elizabeth Hill
Final grade in a course	`courseGrade`	`char`	A

You learned in Chapter 1 that every program must define a `class`. There are thousands of classes that make up the .NET FCL. The following section describes some of the predefined data types that are considered primitive data types in most languages. These value and reference types will be explored: `int`, `double`, `decimal`, `bool`, `char`, and `string`.

Predefined Data Types

The .NET Framework includes a common type system (CTS) that is supported by all .NET languages, including C#. This enables cross-language integration of code meaning a single application can be written using multiple languages, such as C#, Visual C++, and Visual Basic. The types in the CTS are referred to as common types and are divided into two major categories, as seen in Figure 2-3: value types and reference types.

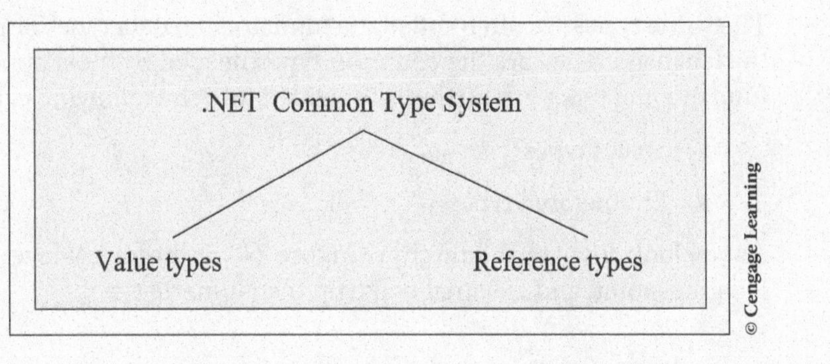

FIGURE 2-3 .NET common types

When placed in memory, value types contain their own copy of data, in binary notation. The data is stored in the actual memory cell that is addressed by the value type's identifier. In contrast, the contents of reference type memory cells are much different. Reference types contain the address or location in which the sequence of bits is stored. Figure 2-4 shows the difference between how value types are stored and how reference types are stored. An integer value type, such as 2012, representing the year a car was manufactured, is stored directly in the memory cell. To store a string of characters, such as the kind of vehicle, the memory location would contain the address in which *Corvette* is located. The `string` data type is a reference type. The memory location associated with the identifier does not contain the characters *Corvette*, but instead the address in which *Corvette* is stored.

C# also supports pointer types in a limited extent. A pointer is a variable that holds the memory address of another type. In C#, pointers can only be declared to hold value types and arrays. You will read more about arrays in Chapter 8.

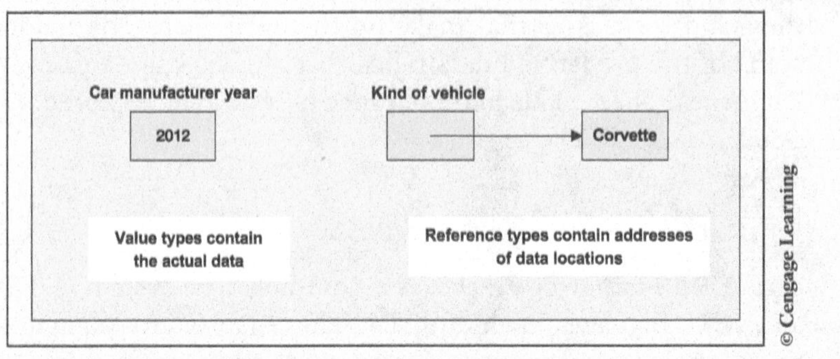

FIGURE 2-4 Memory representation for value and reference types

Value Types

The **value types** are often called the fundamental data types or primitive data types of the language. They are the common types needed by most applications. In C#, these fundamental types are further subdivided into the following categories:

- Struct types
- Enumerated types

As you look down the hierarchy of Figure 2-5, at the lowest level you find that Integral, Floating-point, and Decimal make up the Numeric types.

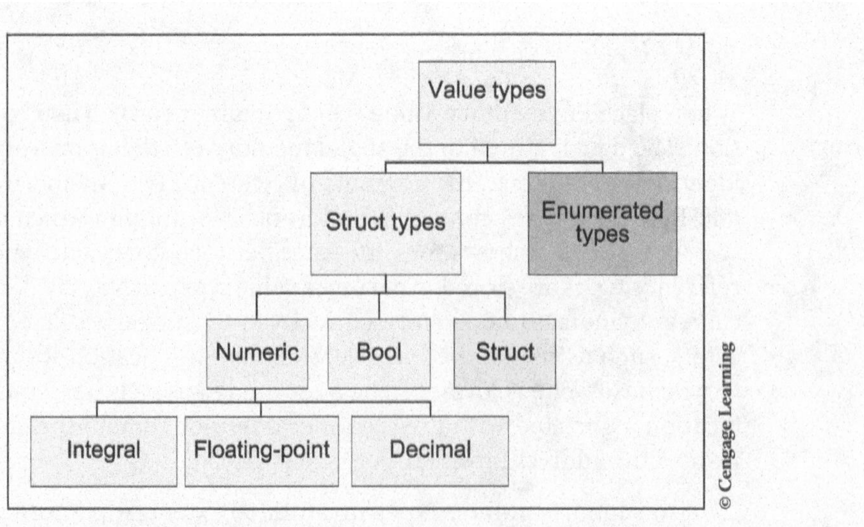

FIGURE 2-5 Value type hierarchy

Twelve types belong to the numeric value type. Nine of them are Integral (whole number types), two are floating-point (numbers that can have a fractional value), and one is a `decimal` type. The `decimal` type is a fairly new data type; it is not found with C++, C, or Java. It was added to C# to eliminate the problems of loss of precision in mathematical operations that occurred in previous languages. The basic C# types all have aliases in the System `namespace`. Table 2-8 gives the keywords for the built-in C# types, including the numeric type each belongs to in the hierarchy, and the aliases in the System `namespace`.

TABLE 2-8 C# value data types with .NET alias

C# type	Numeric type	.NET alias type
`byte`	Integral	`System.Byte`
`sbyte`	Integral	`System.SByte`
`char`	Integral	`System.Char`
`decimal`	Decimal	`System.Decimal`
`double`	Floating-point	`System.Double`
`float`	Floating-point	`System.Single`
`int`	Integral	`System.Int32`
`uint`	Integral	`System.UInt32`
`long`	Integral	`System.Int64`
`ulong`	Integral	`System.UInt64`
`short`	Integral	`System.Int16`
`ushort`	Integral	`System.UInt16`

Integral Data Types

All integral values represent whole numbers—values without decimal notation. The value type `int` is used most often to represent a whole number value and will be the primary type used in this textbook. As Table 2-9 illustrates, a value as small as the negative number –2,147,483,648 and as large as 2,147,483,647 can be stored in the `System.int` data type. The primary difference in the integral types is how much storage is needed and whether a negative value can be placed in the data item.

Type names that begin with *u*, which stands for unsigned, allow only positive values to be placed in the memory cell.

TABLE 2-9 Values and sizes for integral types

C# type	Numeric range	Width in bits
`byte`	0 to 255	8-bit
`sbyte`	128 to 127	8-bit
`char`	U+0000 to U+ffff	16-bit
`int`	2,147,483,648 to 2,147,483,647	32-bit
`uint`	0 to 4,294,967,295	32-bit
`long`	9,223,372,036,854,775,808 to 9,223,372,036,854,775,807	64-bit
`ulong`	0 to 18,446,744,073,709,551,615	64-bit
`short`	32,768 to 32,767	16-bit
`ushort`	0 to 65,535	16-bit

NOTE Commas are included in Table 2-9 to add to the readability. However, only the digits 0–9, +, and – are permitted in numeric data types. No formatting symbols, such as commas, are allowed.

Notice in Table 2-9 that the data type `char` is listed as an integral type; however, the range is listed as U+0000 to U+ffff. The `char` keyword is used to declare storage to hold a single Unicode character. A `char` can hold a single value, such as the letter A. If you want to store the three initials representing your first, middle, and last name, you need three `char` variables. You might want to look at Appendix C, which contains a partial listing of the Unicode characters. Most of the known written languages can be represented with the 16-bit Unicode character set.

Example 2-3 shows examples of integral variable declarations.

EXAMPLE 2-3

2

```
int studentCount;           // number of students in the class
int ageOfStudent = 20;      // age - originally initialized to 20
int numberOfExams;          // number of exams
int coursesEnrolled;        // number of courses enrolled
```

Notice that each declaration ends with a semicolon (;). This is because variable declarations are considered statements in the C# language. All statements end in a semicolon.

In Example 2-3, identifiers are chosen that adhere to the rules listed for naming program items. Every line also contains an inline comment. These comments are unnecessary because the identifiers are self-documenting. If nondescriptive identifiers, such as `x`, `y`, or `s`, are used, comments would be helpful.

Do not place a comment on every line or with every variable declaration because it creates unreadable code. It is best to include comments when a segment of code needs further explanation.

Each identifier in Example 2-3 consists of two or more words. The second and subsequent words begin with an uppercase character. This naming convention is used throughout the textbook for variable and `object` names. The first character of the identifier begins with a lowercase character.

Class and method names, both user-defined and FCL `class` identifiers, begin with an uppercase character. Constants, which are covered later in this chapter, are named with all uppercase characters, using the underline character to separate words. This is the standard style used by C# programmers.

Styles, or conventions, are the set of personal choices adopted by programmers. If you are new to application development, you might want to follow the textbook's style for selecting identifiers. One of the most important things to remember is that after selecting a style, you should use it consistently. Less bugs will enter your solutions. If you're working with a team, having everyone follow the same styles makes work more harmonious. It lets everyone move along the same path.

Floating-Point Types

If you need to keep the decimal portion, the value cannot be stored in an integral data type, such as an `int`. Floating-point values can be specified in scientific notation with an exponent or in standard decimal notation. Very large or small numbers can be specified. The general form of exponential syntax is

```
n.ne±P
```

With the scientific notation syntax in the preceding example, n is the decimal number; P is the number of decimal positions to move left or right; and the + or – indicates the direction in which the decimal should be moved. A plus sign indicates that the decimal is moved P positions to the right to form the standard decimal equivalent value. The syntax rules in C# allow the e to be uppercase or lowercase. The ± in the notation indicates that a +, –, or neither can be added. If there is no + or –, + is assumed. Example 2-4 shows examples of converting from scientific to standard decimal notation.

EXAMPLE 2-4

3.2e+5 is equivalent to 320000

1.76e–3 is equivalent to 0.00176

6.892e8 is equivalent to 689200000

Because the first value includes an "e+5," the decimal is moved to the right five positions. The second statement in the preceding examples moves the decimal position three positions to the left. The last statement moves the decimal to the right eight positions, which places five significant zeros onto the end of the value.

As Table 2-10 indicates, a value with up to 15–16 decimal places can be placed in a `double`. The floating-point types conform to IEEE 754 specifications. For more information, you can read about the IEEE standard at the IEEE site *http://standards.ieee.org/*. The following are examples of floating-point variable declarations.

TABLE 2-10 Values and sizes for floating-point types

Type	Numeric range	Precision	Size
`float`	$\pm 1.5 \times 10^{-45}$ to $\pm 3.4 \times 10^{38}$	7 digits	32-bit
`double`	$\pm 5.0 \times 10^{-324}$ to $\pm 1.7 \times 10^{308}$	15–16 digits	64-bit

EXAMPLE 2-5

```
double extraPerson = 3.50;     // extraPerson initialized to 3.50
double averageScore = 70.0;    // averageScore initialized to 70.0
double priceOfTicket;          // cost of a movie ticket
double gradePointAverage;      // grade point average
float totalAmount = 23.57F;    // note the F placed after 23.57
```

Notice that all but one of the declarations in Example 2-5 uses `double`. In C#, `double` is the default type for floating-point numbers. When a compile-time initialization is included, no suffix is required if you initialize a `double` variable. In the case of the `float`, it is necessary to suffix the number with an `f` or `F`; otherwise, the number is assumed to be a `double`.

If you fail to suffix the number with an `f` or `F` and assign it to a `float` variable as is `float totalAmount = 23.57;`, you get a syntax error similar to that shown in Figure 2-6.

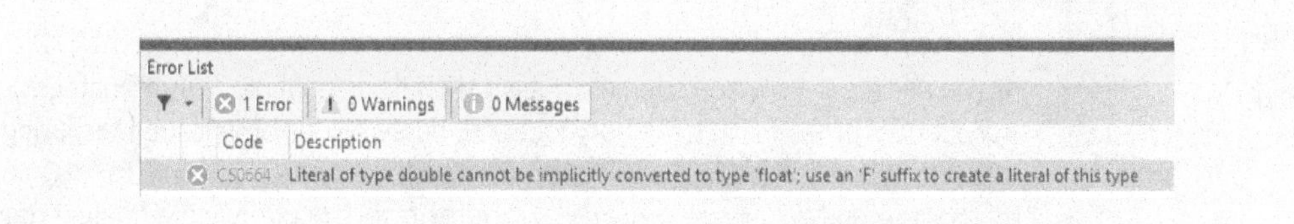

FIGURE 2-6 Syntax error for failing to use F suffix

The `double` type is used throughout the textbook for all numbers that require a fractional value.

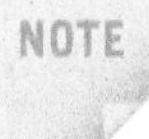

Never place commas, dollar signs, or any other special formatting symbols with numbers when they are assigned to value types.

Decimal Types

The `decimal` value type is new to modern programming languages. It is appropriate for storing monetary data items because it allows both integral (whole) numbers and a fractional portion. It provides for greater precision than what is found with floating-point types because 128 bits are used to represent the value.

Numbers ranging from negative –79,228,162,514,264,337,593,543,950,335 to positive 79,228,162,514,264,337,593,543,950,335 can be stored in a `decimal` value type. As you can see in Table 2-11, 28–29 digits are possible with the `decimal`.

TABLE 2-11 Value and size for decimal data type

Type	Numeric range	Precision	Size
decimal	1.0×10^{-28} to 7.9×10^{28}	28–29 significant digits	128 bits

As is the case with the float type, it is necessary to attach the suffix m or M onto the end of a number to indicate decimal, as shown in Example 2-6. Without the suffix, the number is treated as a double. Again, a syntax error message is issued if you try to do compile-time initialization or assign a number to a decimal variable without the suffix. No automatic conversion occurs.

EXAMPLE 2-6

```
decimal endowmentAmount = 33897698.26M;    // note the M
decimal deficit;
```

NOTE

If you assign or do a compile time initialization using a whole number (integer) as the value for float or decimal memory location, no syntax error is issued for failing to suffix the number with an F or M. An implicit conversion occurs from int to float, int to decimal and also int to double. Syntax errors occur when a floating point number (number with a decimal) is assigned to either a float or decimal without the M or F being suffixed onto the end of the value.

Boolean Variables

Boolean is based on true/false, on/off logic. If you look back at the value type hierarchy in Figure 2-5, you see that Boolean inherits from the Value and Struct classes but not from the Numeric type. The only Boolean type in C# is bool. A bool variable can have a value of either true or false. One example of the bool type being very useful is in determining when all data has been processed. The variable can be declared as shown in Example 2-7.

EXAMPLE 2-7

```
bool undergraduateStudent;
bool moreData = true;         // used to indicate when all data is
                              // processed. Originally set to true
```

The `bool` type will not accept integer values such as 0, 1, or −1. The keywords `true` and `false` are built in to the C# language and are the only allowable values.

NOTE Some languages such as C++ allow Boolean types to hold integers. C# does not.

In addition to numeric and Boolean, there are two other value types: enumeration and structures. These allow you to define your own custom classes. They will be used as you advance in your software development.

Declaring Strings

All the types previously discussed were value types. As shown in Figure 2-3, the .NET CTS also includes reference types. The memory location of value types actually contains the data. With reference types, data is not stored directly in the memory location; instead, the memory location contains a reference to the location in which the data is stored.

C# has two built-in reference types: `string` and `object`. The `string` type represents a string of Unicode characters. Example 2-8 shows how `string` variables are declared. The second and third declarations also include compile-time initializations.

EXAMPLE 2-8

```
string studentName;
string courseName = "Application Development I";
string twoLines = "Line1\nLine2";     // newline escape sequence
                                      // character included
```

The other built-in reference type is `object`. This is probably the most important type of all because every type inherits characteristics from it. In Chapter 3, you will investigate the `object class` when you begin writing your own methods.

NOTE All types inherit the methods `ToString( )`, `Equals( )`, `Finalize( )`, and `GetHashCode( )` from the `object class`.

Making Data Constant

When you add the keyword `const` to a declaration, it becomes a constant. Constants are convenient for assigning a value to an identifier; `const` forces the functionality of not allowing the value to be changed. Similar to a variable, the value stored in the memory location can be used throughout the program. However, the value cannot be altered. The general form of constant syntax is

```
const type identifier = expression;
```

Some examples of constant declarations are shown in Example 2-9.

EXAMPLE 2-9

```
const double TAX_RATE = 0.0675;
const int SPEED = 70;
const char HIGHEST_GRADE = 'A';
```

An advantage of defining a constant is that the value needs only be assigned once, during declaration. A constant can be used in many statements. If the value must be changed, only one change is required in the program and that is at the constant declaration location. After that change is made, the program must be recompiled.

To call attention to the fact that the identifier `TAX_RATE` is a constant instead of a variable, all capital letters are used. To provide a separator between words, the underscore character is used. This is the standard convention used by programmers for naming constants.

Assignment Statements

Variables can be initialized during declaration, or a value can be assigned to them later in the program. However, in C#, you must assign a value to a variable before it can be used. No default values are assigned when you declare the variable. To change the value of the variable, an assignment statement is used. An assignment statement takes the form of

```
variable = expression;
```

The expression can be one of the following:

- Another variable
- Compatible literal value
- Mathematical equation
- Call to a method that returns a compatible value
- Combination of one or more items in this list

The syntax requires that the variable that will hold the result of the expression be placed first—on the left of the equal (=) symbol. The = symbol, when used with an assignment statement or a compile-time initialization, is called an *assignment operator*. The value of the expression on the right side of the assignment operator (=) is determined and then that value is assigned to the variable on the left side of the = operator.

Notice that the syntax for an assignment statement requires a variable on the left side of the assignment operator.

If the value on the left side is not compatible with the right side, the C# compiler issues a type mismatch error.

C# is a strongly typed language. It does a good job of verifying type consistency in an assignment statement. The variable receiving the result of an expression must be either of the same type or a type that can hold the result.

Example 2-10 begins by declaring variables that can be used in assignment statements.

EXAMPLE 2-10

```
int numberOfMinutes,
    count,
    minIntValue;
```

If more than one variable is declared of the same type, the identifiers are separated by commas. The semicolon is placed at the end of the list to indicate the end of the declaration statement.

```
char firstInitial,
     yearInSchool,
     punctuation,
     enterKey,
     lastChar;
double accountBalance,
       weight;
decimal amountOwed,
        deficitValue;
bool isFinished;
string aSaying,
       fileLocation;
```

After being declared, these variables can be assigned literal values as illustrated in the following code segment:

```
numberOfMinutes = 45;
count = 0;
minIntValue = -2147483648;
firstInitial = 'B';
yearInSchool = '1';
punctuation = ';';
```

Notice that no commas are included with the literal –2147483648. Although this seems unreadable, you will receive a syntax error message if you add the commas. The variables `firstInitial`, `yearInSchool`, and `punctuation` are of `char` type. Special attention should be paid when using `char` literals. All `char` literals must be enclosed in single quotation marks when used in an assignment statement. Remember, the `char` type can hold any character from the standard keyboard plus many other characters. However, it can only hold one character at a time.

```
enterKey = '\n';                    // newline escape character
lastChar = '\u005A';                // Unicode character 'Z'
```

Both of the previous assignments have more than one entry between the single quotes. However, the combination of symbols represents a single character. The `enterKey` variable is assigned the carriage return using the special escape sequence character. The variable `lastChar` is assigned the character `Z` using its Unicode representation.

Chapter 1 introduced you to some special escape sequences representing characters. You might want to review Table 1-1, which contains many of the valid C# escape sequence characters. The last example in the preceding declarations illustrates how a Unicode character literal can be used to initialize the variable. The numerical value is a hexadecimal number.

```
accountBalance = 4783.68;
weight = 1.7E-3;                    //scientific notation may be used
amountOwed = 3000.50m;              //m or M must be suffixed to decimal
deficitValue = -322888672.50M;
```

NOTE If you attempt to initialize a `decimal` variable and forget to use the `M` or `m` suffix, a compiler error is generated.

```
aSaying = "Today is the first day of the rest of your life!\n ";
fileLocation = @"C:\CSharpProjects\Chapter2";
```

NOTE The at symbol (@) can be placed before a `string` literal to signal that the characters inside the double quotation marks should be interpreted verbatim. This eliminates the need to escape the backslash character using the escape character. Without the @ symbol, the `string` literal for the filename would have to be written as *C:\\CSharpProjects\\Chapter2* with two backslashes for what was previously a single backslash.

```
isFinished = false;        // declared previously as a bool
```

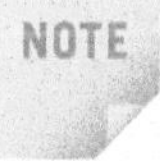

NOTE The only values that can be placed in a memory location declared as a `bool` are `true` and `false`.

It is also possible to assign one variable's value to another variable. This does not impact the variable on the right side of the assignment operator, as illustrated in Figure 2-7. The `25` from `newValue` replaces the `0` in `count`. A variable can hold only one value at a time.

```
int count = 0,
    newValue = 25;
count = newValue;
```

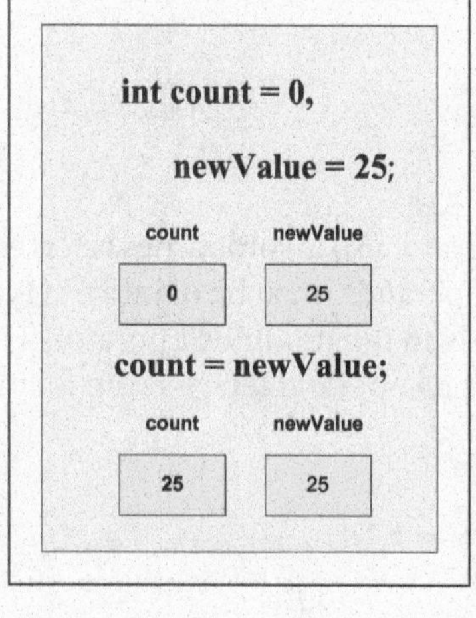

© Cengage Learning

FIGURE 2-7 Impact of assignment statement

Basic Arithmetic Operations

Assignment statements can include mathematical equations. The basic operations of addition, subtraction, multiplication, and division can be performed on real data (floating-point). These operations plus modulation can be performed on integral types. The simplest form of an assignment statement is

```
resultVariable = operand1 operator operand2;
```

The operands may be variables, constants, or literals. The operators are represented by special symbols given in Table 2-12.

Readability is very important when you write code. Always place a space before and after every arithmetic operator, including the equal symbol (=). The compiler ignores the white space, but readers of your code appreciate it.

TABLE 2-12 Basic arithmetic operators

Operator	Operation
+	Addition
–	Subtraction
*	Multiplication
/	Division
%	Modulus

The modulus operator (%) is sometimes referred to as the remainder operator. In most languages, both operands must be of integral type. C# allows you to use floating-point values as operands to the modulus operator. The result produced is the remainder of operand1 divided by operand2. Given the following statements, Figure 2-8 illustrates the results.

```
int firstValue = 67;
int secondValue = 3;
int result;
result = firstValue % secondValue;
```

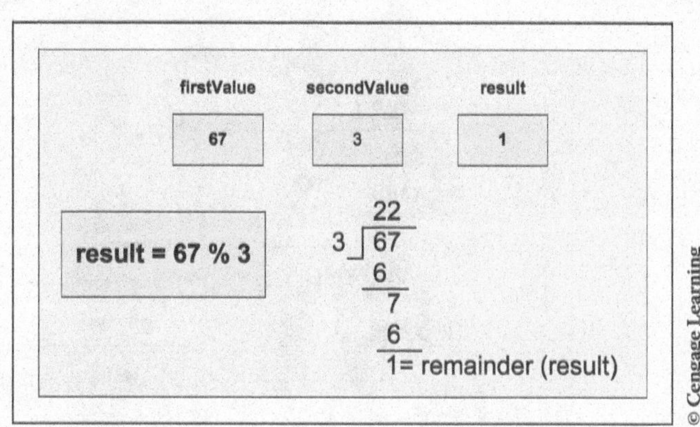

FIGURE 2-8 Result of 67 % 3

The modulus operator can be used with negative values; however, you might consider the results strange. For example: –3 % 5 = –3; 5 % –3 = 2; –5 % –3 = –2; The sign of the dividend determines the result.

The results are as you would expect when you use the plus symbol (+) with numeric data. When the + symbol is used with `string` variables, the + symbol concatenates operand2 onto the end of operand1.

```
string result;
string fullName;
string firstName = "Rochelle";
string lastName = "Howard";
fullName = firstName + " " + lastName;
```

As shown in Figure 2-9, the value referenced by `fullName` after the preceding statements are executed is `"Rochelle Howard"`. Notice that a `string` literal containing a single space is placed between the two variables; otherwise, you would have created a full name of `"RochelleHoward"`.

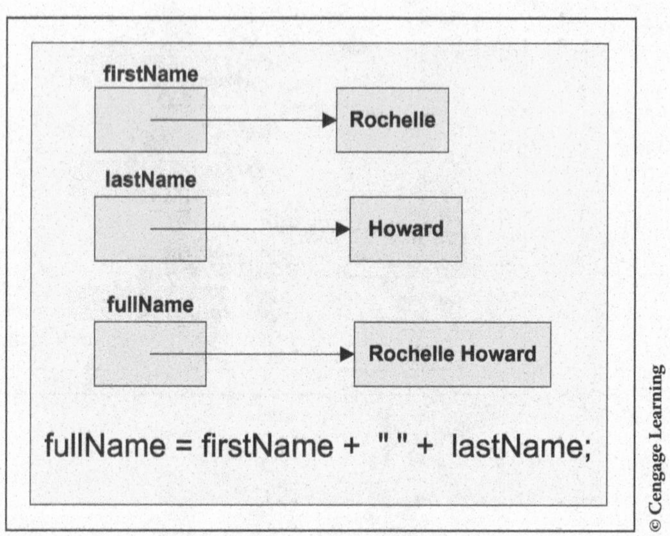

FIGURE 2-9 String concatenation

The + symbol is considered an **overloaded operator**. It behaves differently based on the type of operands it receives. If the operands are numeric, it performs addition. If the operands are strings, it performs concatenation. You will read more about the `string` data type in Chapter 8. The plus operator is the only operator from Table 2-12 that can be applied to `string` data types.

Increment and Decrement Operations

A common arithmetic operation is to add or subtract the number one (1) to or from a memory location. **Increment/decrement operators** are used for this. C#, such as C++ and Java, has a special unary operator that increments and decrements by one. It is considered a unary operator because it requires a single operand. The basic operators explored in the preceding explanations are all **binary** operators that require two operands.

The symbols used for increment and decrement are ++ and --. No space is permitted between the two symbols (++ or --).

```
num++;        // could be written as num = num + 1;
--value1;     // could be written as value1 = value1 - 1;
```

The first statement adds `1` to `num`. The second subtracts `1` from `value1`. The increment and decrement operators are often used in situations in which a counter is needed. They are not used to accumulate values because they always add one or subtract one from the variable.

NOTE
In C#, when you use the increment and decrement operators with floating-point types, no syntax error is generated. C# adds or subtracts the number 1 to the variable. You can also use the ++ or -- with a variable of `char` type.

2

If you use these operators in an arithmetic expression involving additional operands, the placement of the ++ or -- is important. If they appear as prefixes, or to the left of the variable, the increment or decrement is performed before using them in the expression. When placed before the operand, they are called preincrement or predecrement operators; when placed after the operand, they are called postincrement or postdecrement operators. For example, if the following declaration were made and then each of the `WriteLine( )` methods were called, the output for Example 2-11 would be

100

101

102

EXAMPLE 2-11

```
int num = 100;
WriteLine(num++);          // First WriteLine( )displays 100
WriteLine(num);            // num now has a value of 101
WriteLine(++num);          // Pretest increment changes num to 102
                           // before it is used. Displays 102
```

With Example 2-11, the last value printed is 102. If `num` were used following the lines of code in the example, `num` has a value of 102. Notice that the incremented value is displayed here because the ++ operator is placed before the identifier with the last call to the `WriteLine( )` method. The first call to the `WriteLine( )` method did not display the incremented value. The original value is used as the argument and then the value is incremented.

If `x` is declared to be of type `int` and initialized with a value of `100`, the following statement displays 100 102. The new value stored in `x` is `102` when control goes to the statement following the call to the `WriteLine( )` method.

```
WriteLine(x++ + " " + ++x); // Displays 100 102
```

Look carefully at Example 2-12 to make sure that you understand how the placement of the increment and decrement operators impact the result obtained when they are included in an expression involving multiple operations.

EXAMPLE 2-12

```
int count = 0,
    result = 0,
    firstNum = 10;
count++;
result = count++ * --firstNum + 100;
```

Figure 2-10 shows what is stored in the memory locations when the variables are declared. Compile-time initialization is performed on all three variables.

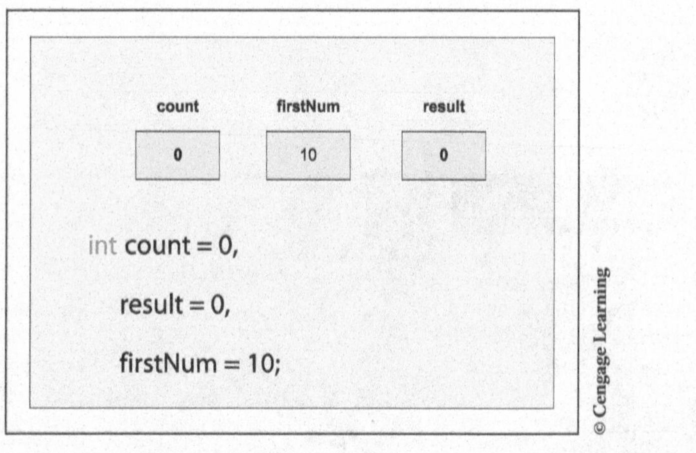

FIGURE 2-10 Declaration of value type variables

The next statement shown in Example 2-12, `count++;`, is not part of another expression. It really does not matter in this situation whether the increment operator (++) is placed before or after `count`. The only memory location affected is `count`'s memory cell. It is incremented by one. Figure 2-11 shows the memory cell after `count++;` is executed.

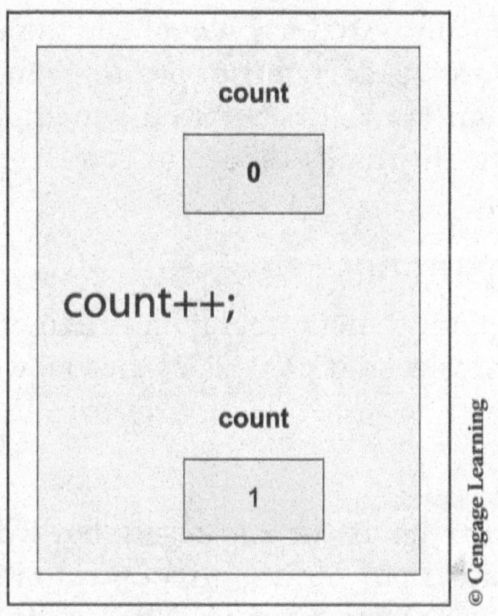

FIGURE 2-11 Change in memory after count++; statement executed

The last statement in Example 2-12, illustrated in Figure 2-12, is of interest:

```
result = count++ * --firstNum + 100;
```

Notice the ++ is placed after `count`. The -- comes before `firstNum`.

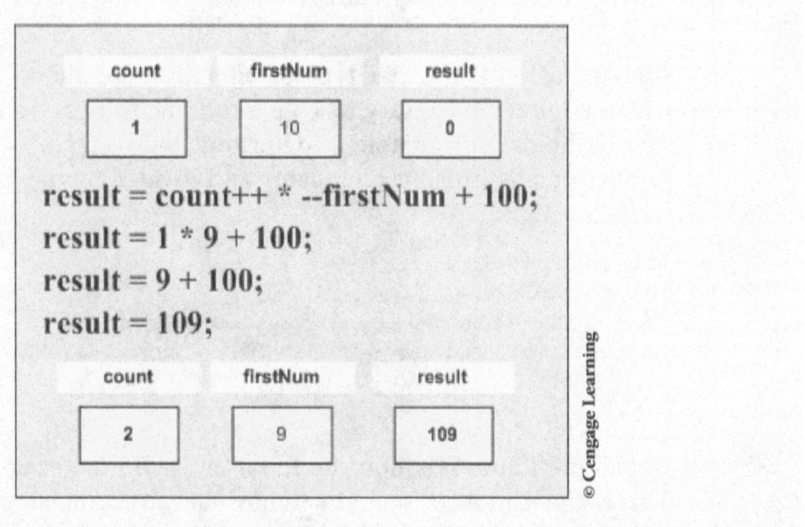

FIGURE 2-12 Results after statement is executed

The current value of count, 1, is used in the multiplication because the ++ comes after the identifier name. After using count in the arithmetic, it is incremented by 1, becoming 2. Because the decrement operator comes before the variable firstNum, 1 is subtracted from firstNum before the multiplication is performed. Thus, 1 is multiplied by 9, and the result is added to 100.

Compound Operations

You commonly write arithmetic operations that modify a variable by using its original value as part of the calculation. Consider the following:

```
answer = 100;
answer = answer + 5;
```

The variable answer holds the end result, but it is also used in the computation. **Compound operators** provide a shortcut way to write assignment statements using the result as part of the computation. The last line in the preceding code segment (answer = answer + 5;) could be replaced with the following:

```
answer += 5;
```

Both statements take the original value of answer, add 5 to it, and store the result back in answer.

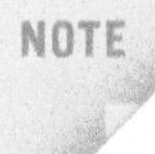

In expressions involving multiple operations, the compound operation is always performed last. For example: answer += 45 * 28 + 37 / 16; is equivalent to answer = answer + (45 * 28 + 37 / 16);. The original value of answer is not added until the expression on the right of the equal sign is complete.

Accumulation is another type of operation commonly found in applications. You will often find it necessary to keep a running total or accumulate values that a single variable holds. For example, to determine the average of a set of values, the values are normally added to an accumulator and divided by the number of entries. Consider the following:

```
int total = 0;
int newValue;
// : Note statements to enable the user
// to enter values for newValue are inserted here

total = total + newValue;
```

If multiple values are input by the user, each newValue could be added to total. This is an example of accumulating values. Accumulators are often used with monetary amounts. For example, to accumulate the total amount of money received or the total for an order that includes a number of items, a variable such as `total` could be defined. These types of variables, functioning as accumulators, normally should be initialized to zero. Then they grow or increase in value with each new addition. The compound operator may be used for these types of situations. Using a compound operator, `newValue` could be added to `total` as shown here:


```
total += newValue;          // same as total = total + newValue;
```

Table 2-13 gives the compound operators available in C#.

TABLE 2-13 Compound arithmetic operators

Operator	Operation
+=	Addition
-=	Subtraction
*=	Multiplication
/=	Division
%=	Modulus

Another example of using a compound operator is illustrated with the remainder or modulus operator:

```
answer = 100;
answer %= 3;            // same as answer = answer % 3;
```

The result of the preceding expression would be `1` because that is the remainder of dividing `100` by `3`. As stated previously, when a compound operator is used in a statement that contains multiple operations, the variable on the left of the assignment operator is not used until the entire expression on the right side of the assignment symbol is completely evaluated. Consider Example 2-13.

EXAMPLE 2-13

```
answer = 100;
answer += 50 * 3 / 25 - 4;
```

The value of `100` is not added until the expression is completely evaluated on the right side of the assignment operator. C# then takes the calculated value and adds `100` to it. The result replaces the original `100`, storing `102` in `answer`. The order in which the calculations are performed is as follows:

50 * 3 = 150

150 / 25 = 6

6 – 4 = 2

100 + 2 = 102

As with the increment and decrement operators, no space is allowed between the compound operator symbols.

The order in which the calculations are performed is called the **order of operations**. The operations are performed from left to right in Example 2-13. The following section explains why this is not always the case.

Order of Operations

When multiple arithmetic operators are included in an expression, execution begins with the operator that has the highest level of precedence. The level of precedence is determined by the rules of the language. The C# precedence level for the operators used thus far is given in Table 2-14.

TABLE 2-14 Operator precedence

C# category	Operators						Associativity
Unary	+	-	++	--			Right
Multiplicative	*	/	%				Left
Additive	+	-					Left
Assignment	=	*=	/=	%=	+=	-=	Right

As Table 2-14 presents, several operators appear at the same level. For example, `*`, `/`, and `%` are considered equals in terms of order of operations. When an expression contains two or more operators with the same precedence, the associativity of the operators controls the order in which the operations are performed. **Left-associative** means the operations are performed from left to right, so as you move from left to right in an expression, the operation that is encountered first is executed first.

The + and – appear as unary operators in row one and binary operators in row three of Table 2-14.

NOTE As stated previously, unary means one, indicating that only one operand is used with the operator. For example, placing a minus symbol in front of a variable is a unary operation.

As unary operators, the – and + operations are executed from right to left negating or indicating that an operand is positive. The binary + and – are left associative. The assignment category operators, in row four, are **right-associative**.

Parentheses can be used to change the order of operations. If you identify an operation that needs to be processed first, enclose that portion of the expression in a pair of parentheses. Parentheses are also added to increase readability of an expression. Figure 2-13 illustrates the order of operations in which multiple operations of the calculations are performed.

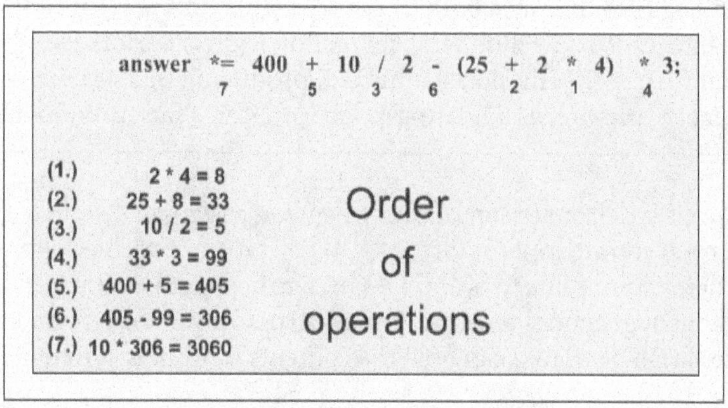

answer *= 400 + 10 / 2 - (25 + 2 * 4) * 3;
7 5 3 6 2 1 4

(1.) 2 * 4 = 8
(2.) 25 + 8 = 33
(3.) 10 / 2 = 5
(4.) 33 * 3 = 99
(5.) 400 + 5 = 405
(6.) 405 - 99 = 306
(7.) 10 * 306 = 3060

Order of operations

© Cengage Learning

FIGURE 2-13 Order of execution of the operators

Before the arithmetic expression is executed, `answer` is initialized to `10`.

```
int answer = 10;
answer *= 400 + 10 / 2 - (25 + 2 * 4) * 3;
```

Mixed Expressions

C# allows you to mix numeric integral types and floating-point types in an expression. When an expression has operands of different types, the statement is considered a mixed mode expression. Examples include the following:

89 + 76 / 3.25

2 * 7.9 – 5 + 67.99

In the first expression, the division operator has operands of `76`, an integral, and `3.25`, a floating-point type. When the operands are of the same type, the result of the operation will be of that type. However, if the binary operation involves a `double` and an `int`, **implicit type coercion**, or conversion is performed. Integral types convert into floating-point types. Automatic coercion, by changing the `int` data type into a `double`, occurs for each of the preceding expressions.

It is important to note what is illustrated in Example 2-14, if all the expressions are of integral type on the right side of the equal operator, you cannot just declare the result type to be of floating-point and get the correct floating-point result.

EXAMPLE 2-14

```
double answer;
answer = 10 / 3;
```

You do not get the results you might expect stored in the answer. The result is 3.0, not 3.333333. Because both of the operands on the right of the assignment operator are integers (whole numbers), integer division is performed. This produces an integer result. After the division is finished, producing 3, it is then assigned to the `double` variable, `answer`, as a floating-point `double`. Thus, `answer` becomes 3.0.

Implicit type conversion occurs when you assign an `int` to a `double`. No conversion occurs if you attempt to store a `double` in an `int` variable. Figure 2-14 shows the syntax error for attempting to assign a `double` to an `int` in Example 2-15. The first assignment statement generates an error. Implicit type conversion occurs in the second statement. The variable `value2` can hold the contents of what is stored in `anotherNumber`.

EXAMPLE 2-15

```
int value1 = 440,
    anotherNumber = 70;
double value2 = 100.60;
value1 = value2;           // syntax error as shown in Figure 2-14
value2 = anotherNumber;    // 100.60 cannot be stored in value1
```

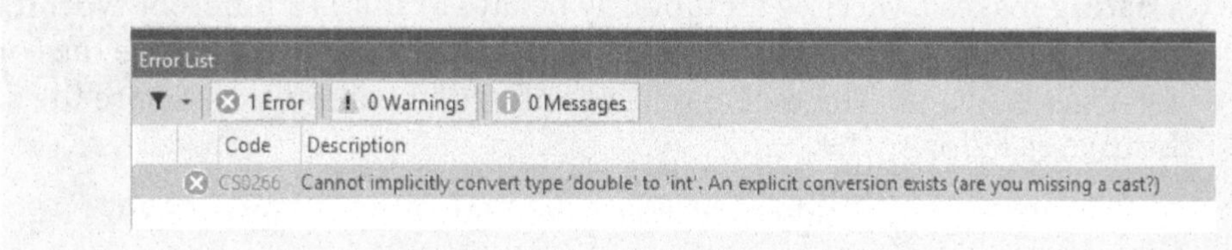

FIGURE 2-14 Syntax error generated for assigning a double to an int

When one of the operands is a number literal, you can make the literal act like a floating-point type by simply affixing a decimal followed by a zero onto the value, as shown in Example 2-16.

EXAMPLE 2-16

```
int exam1 = 86,
    exam2 = 92,
    exam3 = 91;
double examAverage;
examAverage = (exam1 + exam2 + exam3) / 3.0;
```

The result of the preceding assignment statement is 89.666666. Leave off the .0, so that the assignment statement reads as follows:

```
examAverage = (exam1 + exam2 + exam3) / 3;
```

The result is 89. That could mean the difference between your getting an A in the course versus a B. By simply replacing the `3` with a `3.0`, you get the results you would expect. When the division operator gets an integer representing the sum of the scores and a `double` (3.0), the integer value of 269 is converted into 269.0 for the calculation.

This implicit type conversion is made possible by changing the value of the literal. However, this is not always possible. For one reason, you might not have a literal. What if the count of exam scores is stored in a variable? You cannot put a 0.00 onto the end of an identifier because this generates a syntax error.

If you need to make a mixed-mode assignment with variables, one way to avoid the syntax error produced in Figure 2-14 is to cast the variable in the expression, as explained in the following section.

Casts

C# provides an **explicit type coercion**, or conversion through type casting or type conversion that can be used with variables. It takes the following form:

```
(type) expression
```

Casting makes a variable temporarily behave as if it is a different type. If the value 3 is stored in an `int` memory location, a cast is necessary to produce the correct result for `examAverage`. The type `double` is placed in parentheses before the data item to be cast, as follows:

```
examAverage = (exam1 + exam2 + exam3) / (double) count;
```

By performing a cast on the variables in Example 2-15, the syntax errors would be avoided. Example 2-17 illustrates another example.

EXAMPLE 2-17

```
int value1 = 0,
    anotherNumber = 0;
double value2 = 100,
    anotherDouble = 100;
value1 = (int) value2;
value2 = (double) anotherNumber;
```

The cast in the last assignment statement in Example 2-17 could have been omitted because implicit conversion occurs when an `int` is stored in a `double` memory location.

The new keyword `dynamic` was added to C# 4.0 to tell the compiler that a variable's type can change or that it is not known until runtime. You will read more about `dynamic` in Chapter 11.

Formatting Output

You can format data by adding dollar signs or percent symbols. You can separate digits with commas or show the fractional portion of a value. You can suppress leading zeros or you can pad a value with zeros. C# includes a number of special format specifiers that can be used with numbers. One way to use these formatting specifiers is to place them in the `string` argument of the `Write( )` or `WriteLine( )` methods. When you include these special format specifiers as part of the argument to these methods, the `String.Format( )` method is automatically called. You will learn more about calling methods in Chapter 3. Example 2-18 illustrates using the currency format specifier to display a number with commas, decimal, and a dollar symbol.

2

EXAMPLE 2-18

```
double price = 1089.30;
WriteLine("The price is {0:C}.", price);
      // Displays The price is $1,089.30.
```

To indicate that you want to have the value displayed as money with the dollar symbol, comma separators, and two positions to the right of the decimal, the currency format is specified using `C` or `c`. The format specifier is placed inside the curly braces ({ }), thus becoming part of the `string` literal argument for the `WriteLine( )` method.

Notice two values are placed inside the braces. The first value in the curly brace is a placeholder. It indicates which of the arguments that are placed outside of the double quotes you want displayed. The argument formatted in Example 2-18 is `price`, which is the first argument. You will find that most modern computer programming languages use `0` to reference the first entry. After indicating the argument, you can add an optional format specification. In this case, the currency, `C`, specifier was added.

NOTE A `string` is expected for the first argument to the `WriteLine( )` method. To increase readability, the statement can be placed on two lines, with the `string` joined together by the concatenation operator, + sign.

Table 2-15 gives examples using the two most common format specifiers, `c` and `f`.

TABLE 2-15 Examples using format specifiers

Character	Description	Examples	Output
C or c	Currency	`Write("{0:c}", 26666.7888);`	$26,666.79
C or c	Currency	`Write("{0:c}", -2);`	($2.00)
C or c	Currency	`Write("{0:c}", 38.8);`	$38.80
F or f	Fixed point	`Write("{0:F4}", 50);`	50.0000
F or f	Fixed point	`Write("{0:F0} {1}", 50, 22);`	50 22

For illustration purposes, literal values were used as string arguments to the `Write( )` method in Table 2-15; however, variables, constants, and/or expressions can be used in the `Write( )` method as the argument being formatted.

The `F`, fixed point, specifier includes one additional argument. You can indicate how many digits to print to the right of the decimal. The `{0:F4}` indicates that the first argument, argument `0`, should be formatted with a fixed or decimal point and that four digits should be printed to the right of the decimal. As presented in the last row of Table 2-15, when no special formatting is required with an argument, the placeholder is the only entry enclosed inside the curly brace as in `{1}`.

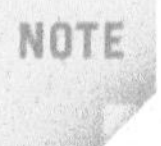

As given in Table 2-15, negative values are displayed in parentheses when the currency format specifier is used.

Format specifiers are positioned in the string at the location where the value is to be printed. Consider the following example:

```
WriteLine("Carpet{0:F0} is {1:C}", 9, 14);
```

The result is as follows:

```
Carpet9 is $14.00
```

No space was printed after the character t in Carpet. The first argument, referenced with a `0` in the argument `{0:F0)`, is `9`. That value, (`9`) is printed followed by a space. It was formatted with a fixed point and zero digits to the right of the decimal. The value `14` is inserted at the location in which the `{1:C}` is inserted. It is formatted with currency. Table 2-16 presents some of the standard numeric format specifiers used to format numbers within a string.

TABLE 2-16 Standard numeric format specifiers

Character	Name	Description	Example
C or c	Currency	Number converted into a string that represents a currency amount with dollar symbols, decimal, and commas. If present, the precision modifier indicates the number of decimal places.	("{0:C3}", 4238.8) – produces $4,238.800
D or d	Decimal	Number converted into a string of integer digits (0–9), prefixed by a minus sign if the number is negative. If required, the number is padded with zeros to its left to produce the number of digits requested in the specifier.	("{0:D5}", 42) – produces 00042

(continues)

TABLE 2-16 Standard numeric format specifiers (*continued*)

Character	Name	Description	Example
E or e	Scientific (exponent)	Number is converted into a string of the form "-d.ddd...E+ddd" or "-d.ddd...e+ddd", where each 'd' indicates a digit (0–9). The string starts with a minus sign if the number is negative.	("{0:E2}", 4238.8) – produces 4.24E+003
F or f	Fixed point	Number is converted into a string of the form "-ddd.ddd..." where each d indicates a digit (0–9).	("{0:F2}", 4238.8) – produces 4238.80
G or g	General	Number is converted into the most compact of either fixed-point or scientific notation, depending on the type of the number and whether a precision specifier is present.	("{0:G}", 4238.8) – produces 4238.8 ("{0:G2}", 4238.8) produces 4.2E+03
N or n	Number	Number is converted into a string of the form "-d,ddd,ddd.ddd...". Thousand separators and minus symbol (if the value is negative) are inserted. The precision specifier indicates the desired number of decimal places.	("{0:N2}", 4238.8) – produces 4,238.80
P or p	Percent	Number is converted into a string that represents a percent. The converted number is multiplied by 100 to be presented as a percentage. The precision specifier indicates the desired number of decimal places.	("{0:P}", 0.123) – produces 12.30 % ("{0:P1}", 0.12783) – produces 12.8 %

If the standard format specifier does not provide the type of formatting you require, you can also create your own custom format string. A standard format string consists of a single alphabetic character, optionally followed by a sequence of digits that form a value between 0 and 99. Table 2-17 lists some of the characters you can use to create custom numeric format strings and their definitions.

TABLE 2-17 Custom numeric format specifiers

Format character	Name	Description	Example
0	Zero placeholder	If the value being formatted has a digit in the position where the '0' appears in the format string, then that digit is copied to the result string. The position of the leftmost '0' before the decimal point and the rightmost '0' after the decimal point determines the range of digits that are always present in the result string.	("{0:00000}", 4238.8) – produces 04239
#	Digit placeholder	If the value being formatted has a digit in the position where the '#' appears in the format string, then that digit is copied to the result string. Otherwise, nothing is stored in that position.	("{0:#####}", 4238.8) – produces 4239
.	Decimal placeholder	The first '.' character in the format string determines the location of the decimal separator in the formatted value.	("{0:#####.##}", 4238.8) – produces 4238.8 ("{0:#####.00}", 4238.8) – produces 4238.80
,	Thousand separator	If the format string contains a ',' character between two digit placeholders (0 or #), the output will have thousand separators inserted between each group of three digits.	("{0:##,###.##}", 4238.8) – produces 4,238.8 ("{0:##,###.##}", 238.8) – produces 238.8 ("{0:00,00.00}", 238.8) – produces 00,238.80
;	Section separator	The ';' character is used to separate sections for positive, negative, and zero numbers in the string. If the value is positive, the first format specifier is used. If the value is negative, the second specifier is used. When the value is zero, the third specifier is used.	("{0:00,000.00; –##,###.00; Zero}", 15) – produces 00,015.00 ("{0:00,000.00; –##,###.00; Zero}", –15) – produces –15.00 ("{0:00,000.00; –##,###.00; Zero}", 0) – produces Zero
'ABC' or "ABC"	String literal	Characters enclosed in single or double quotes are copied to the result string literally and do not affect formatting.	("{0:##,##.00£}", 100) – produces 100.00£

The examples in Tables 2-16 and 2-17 show how the format specifiers can be used as arguments to the `Write( )` or `WriteLine( )` methods. They can also be stored in a string variable and then used as arguments to methods such as the `ToString( )` method. In Chapter 3, you will read about creating your own methods and using many of the predefined ones that are part of the C# language.

Width Specifier

You may specify a width as part of the format specifier. This is especially useful when you want to control the alignment of items on multiple lines. Add the Alignment component following the index ordinal before the colon. A comma is used as a separator. If the number value of alignment is less than the actual length of the formatted string, alignment is ignored and the length of the actual formatted string is used as the field width. Consider the following example:

```
WriteLine("{0,10:F0}{1,8:C}", 47, 14);
```

The result is as follows:

```
        47  $14.00
```

The formatted data in the field is right aligned if alignment number value is positive and left aligned if alignment number value is negative. If padding is necessary, white space is used. The comma is required if alignment is specified.

Consider the following example:

```
WriteLine("{0,-10:F0}{1,8:C}", 47, 14);
```

The result is as follows:

```
47          $14.00
```

Here, the first argument (47) is left justified because the alignment component (–10) is negative. Following the 47, eight blank spaces are displayed and then an additional two spaces are padded to the left of $14.00 since that format specifier was positive 8 and only six character positions are needed to display $14.00.

PROGRAMMING EXAMPLE: CarpetCalculator

This example demonstrates the use of data items in a program. The problem specification is shown in Figure 2-15.

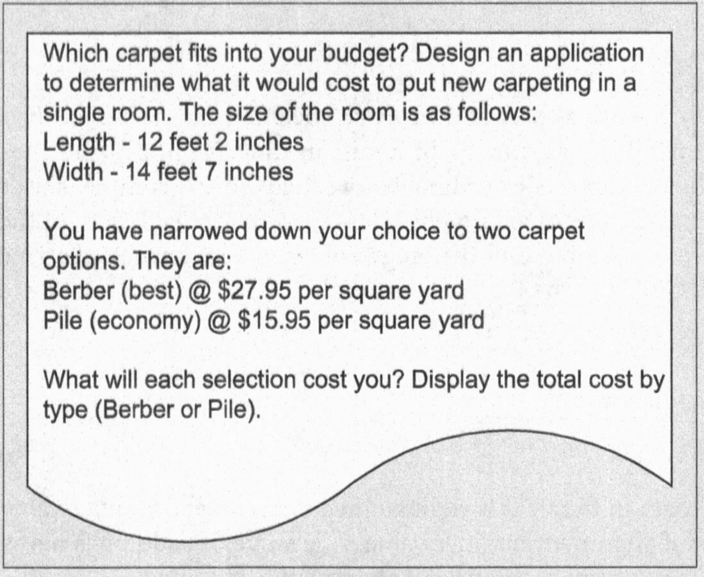
Which carpet fits into your budget? Design an application to determine what it would cost to put new carpeting in a single room. The size of the room is as follows:
Length - 12 feet 2 inches
Width - 14 feet 7 inches

You have narrowed down your choice to two carpet options. They are:
Berber (best) @ $27.95 per square yard
Pile (economy) @ $15.95 per square yard

What will each selection cost you? Display the total cost by type (Berber or Pile).

© Cengage Learning

FIGURE 2-15 Problem specification sheet for the CarpetCalculator example

ANALYZE THE PROBLEM

You should review the problem specification in Figure 2-15 and make sure you understand the problem definition. No program inputs are included in this solution. After you learn how data can be entered into your program, you will probably want to revise your solution so that you can run your application any number of times with different types and prices of carpeting. For now, the problem does not require you to input values.

However, data is needed in the program. Begin by determining what kinds of data. What types of values (i.e., whole numbers, numbers with a decimal point, Boolean, alphabetic characters, or strings) will be in each of the identified data items? Are there any constant data items? What would be appropriate identifiers for the variables and constants? What is the range of values or domain of the data item? These are all questions that should be asked. The items listed here describe the data needs for this problem:

- The dimensions of the room are given in feet and inches—whole numbers and integers—representing both values (i.e., 12 feet 2 inches).
- The carpet prices are given as a price per square yard. This value is a number with a decimal portion (i.e., 27.95).

- To determine the number of square yards, you must calculate the number of square feet.
- Because the width and length are given in feet and inches, you first convert these measurements (feet and inches) into single units for both the width and length.
- A memory location is needed to store the total square yards. However, to get that value, a memory location is needed to hold total square feet.
- A memory location is needed to hold the total cost of the carpet.

2

VARIABLES

Table 2-18 lists the data items needed to solve the CarpetCalculator problem.

TABLE 2-18 Variables

Data item description	Type	Identifier	Domain (range of values)
Length of room in feet	`int`	`roomLengthFeet`	positive value < 50
Length of room in inches	`int`	`roomLengthInches`	positive value < 12
Width of room in feet	`int`	`roomWidthFeet`	positive value < 50
Width of room in inches	`int`	`roomWidthInches`	positive value < 12
Length of room	`double`	`roomLength`	positive value < 100
Width of room	`double`	`roomWidth`	positive value < 100
Number of square feet	`double`	`numOfSquareFeet`	positive value < 10,000
Number of square yards	`double`	`numOfSquareYards`	positive value < 100
Carpet price per square yard	`double`	`carpetPrice`	positive value < 50.00
Total cost of carpet	`double`	`totalCost`	positive value < 1000

CONSTANTS

Because this application is not interactive, which means it does not allow the user to input values, decisions have to be made about what data will not change. The number of inches in a foot never changes; the number of square feet in a square yard never changes. Both of these items are defined as constants. The names of the different types of carpet by category are also defined as constants. Notice in Table 2-19 that all uppercase characters are used as identifiers for constants to delineate the constants clearly from the variables. For readability, the underscore character is used as a separator between words.

The actual prices of the different carpets could be defined as constants. Constant definitions are normally placed at the top of the program to make it easy to locate and modify their values when changes are necessary. Instead of declaring the prices as constants, numeric literals are used to initialize the variable's values. After you learn how to enter values interactively as your program is running, you might want to revise your solution so that the price can be inputted by the user. For now, the `27.95` and `15.95` are used as numeric literals for the price.

TABLE 2-19 Constants

Data item description	Type	Identifier	Value
Number of square feet in one square yard	`int`	`SQ_FT_PER_SQ_YARD`	`9`
Number of inches in one foot	`int`	`INCHES_PER_FOOT`	`12`
String of characters representing the best carpet name	`string`	`BEST_CARPET`	`"Berber"`
String of characters representing economy carpet name	`string`	`ECONOMY_CARPET`	`"Pile"`

DESIGN A SOLUTION

The desired output is to display the costs associated with each kind of carpet, given a specific room size. Figure 2-16 shows a prototype for the final output for the `CarpetCalculator` example. The xxx.xx is placed in the prototype to represent the location in which the calculated values should appear.

© Cengage Learning

FIGURE 2-16 Prototype for the CarpetCalculator example

During design, it is important to develop the algorithm showing the step-by-step process to solve the problem. The algorithm for the `CarpetCalculator` example is first developed using a flowchart. Figure 2-17 shows the steps needed to get the desired output. Notice that ovals are used to indicate the start and stop of the application. Rectangles are used to represent processing that will occur, and parallelograms are used for input or output of data. When a flowchart spans multiple pages, a circle connector is used, as is illustrated in Figure 2-17, to connect the diagrams.

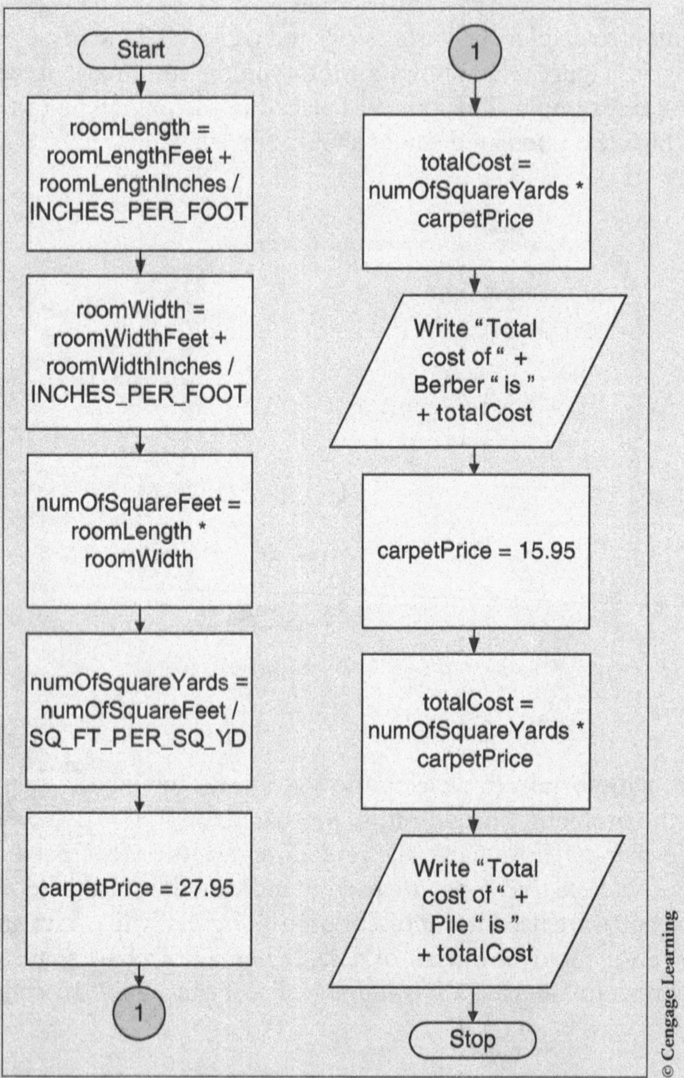

FIGURE 2-17 CarpetCalculator flowchart

There are a number of techniques and tools used to describe process logic. A flowchart is just one of them. Structured English is another technique. This technique also goes by the name of English Narrative and pseudocode. Flowcharts are primarily used when the solution lends itself to being designed using the traditional, structured approach. Structured English is a tool that is used for that approach but is also well suited for the object-oriented methodology.

Structured English is an abbreviated, action-oriented version of the English language. There are no syntax rules with Structured English. The emphasis is to write the steps in English as clearly and concisely as possible without consideration for language details. The focus is on writing *what needs to be done.* Figure 2-18 shows the Structured English design for the `CarpetCalculator` example.

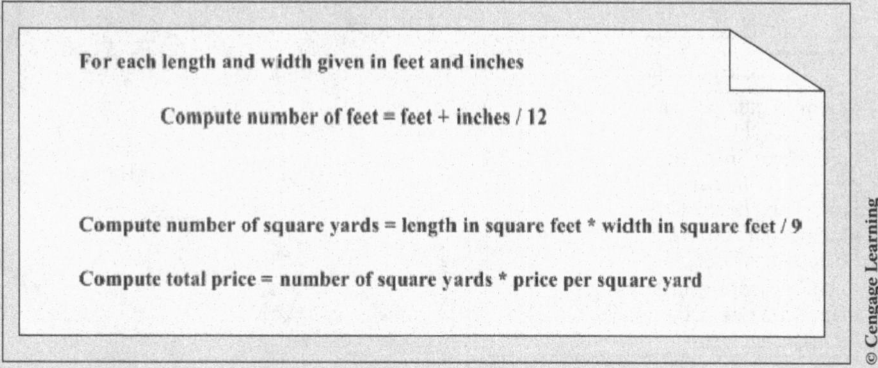

For each length and width given in feet and inches
Compute number of feet = feet + inches / 12
Compute number of square yards = length in square feet * width in square feet / 9
Compute total price = number of square yards * price per square yard
© Cengage Learning

FIGURE 2-18 Structured English for the CarpetCalculator example

Structured English is one of the more common tools used with the object-oriented approach to document the process logic. Decision trees and tables are sometimes used in conjunction with Structured English, especially when the solution requires that a number of alternate paths be developed as part of the solution. Chapter 5 introduces you to these tools.

The object-oriented approach focuses on the objects (persons, places, and things) that exist in our world. Class diagrams help design and document the data items and behaviors of the objects. Figure 2-19 shows the `class` diagram for the `CarpetCalculator` example.

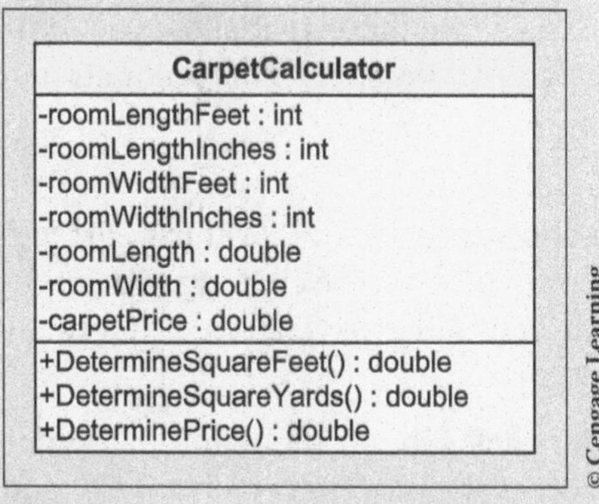

CarpetCalculator
-roomLengthFeet : int
-roomLengthInches : int
-roomWidthFeet : int
-roomWidthInches : int
-roomLength : double
-roomWidth : double
-carpetPrice : double
+DetermineSquareFeet() : double
+DetermineSquareYards() : double
+DeterminePrice() : double
© Cengage Learning

FIGURE 2-19 Class diagram for the CarpetCalculator example

Figure 2-19 includes methods. In this chapter, you learned about the data items. The middle section in the `class` diagram includes the identifiers and their data types. Methods are included in the bottom portion of the `class` diagram. *Methods* are procedures for implementing the behaviors in C#. In Chapter 3, you will learn how to write methods. Figure 2-20 shows a class diagram solution without methods.

For now, this will be how the application is designed. Notice Figure 2-20 includes three additional data members and no method methods.

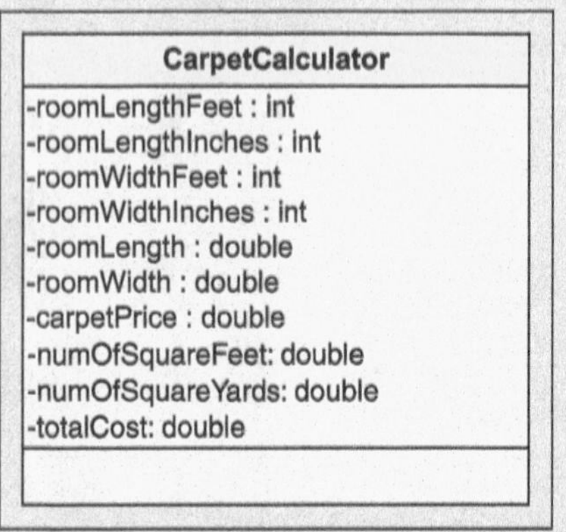

FIGURE 2-20 Revised class diagram without methods

After the algorithm is developed, the design should be checked for correctness. When you desk check your algorithm, use a calculator and write down the results you obtain. After you implement your design, you can compare the results obtained from the program with the calculator results.

At this point, it might seem that it would be easier simply to perform the calculations using a calculator. Remember that the power of the computer comes into play when you write a set of instructions that can be used with many different data sets. In Chapter 3, you will learn to call methods that allow you to input data interactively, such as the carpet price and room sizes. This will add much more functionality to your program.

CODE THE SOLUTION

After you have completed the design and verified the algorithm's correctness, it is time to translate the design into source code. If you are creating your application in Visual Studio, you might want to glance back at Figure 1-26 to review the suggested changes. They included the following:

- After launching Visual Studio, click **File** on the menu bar, point to **New Project**. In the **New Project** window, select **Visual C#**; and in the middle window, select **Console Application**. Type an appropriate name, such as `CarpetCalculator`.
- You may remove the extraneous using statements like `using System.Collections.Generic; using System.Threading.Tasks; using System.Linq;` and using `System.Text;` These namespaces are not needed for this application.

- Add a new `using static` statement directive, `using static System.Console;`. Recall the capability of adding `static` classes to the `using` directive was added with the release of Visual Studio 2015 to enable use of `static class` members without fully qualifying reference to them.
- Change the name of the `.cs` filename from `Program.cs` to a name more representative of the application's operation, such as `CarpetCalculator.cs`. Answer Yes when asked if you would "like to perform a rename in this project of all references to the code element Program."

The final program listing appears as follows:

```
/* CarpetCalculator.cs Author: Doyle
 *  Calculates the total cost of carpet, given
 *  room dimension in feet and inches and carpet
 *  price in price per square yard.
 */
using System;
using static System.Console;

namespace CarpetCalculator
{
    class CarpetCalculator
    {
        static void Main(string[] args)
        {
            const int SQ_FT_PER_SQ_YARD = 9;
            const int INCHES_PER_FOOT = 12;
            const string BEST_CARPET = "Berber";
            const string ECONOMY_CARPET = "Pile";

            int roomLengthFeet = 12,
                roomLengthInches = 2,
                roomWidthFeet = 14,
                roomWidthInches = 7;

            double roomLength,
                   roomWidth,
                   carpetPrice,
                   numOfSquareFeet,
                   numOfSquareYards,
                   totalCost;

            roomLength = roomLengthFeet +
                (double)roomLengthInches /
```

```
                           INCHES_PER_FOOT;
            roomWidth = roomWidthFeet +
                 (double)roomWidthInches /
                      INCHES_PER_FOOT;
            numOfSquareFeet = roomLength * roomWidth;
            numOfSquareYards = numOfSquareFeet /
                           SQ_FT_PER_SQ_YARD;
            carpetPrice = 27.95;
            totalCost = numOfSquareYards * carpetPrice;

            WriteLine("{0,12}", "Carpet App");
            WriteLine( );
            WriteLine("{0,-7}{1,8:C}",
                 BEST_CARPET + ":", totalCost);

            // Second test
            carpetPrice = 15.95;
            totalCost = numOfSquareYards * carpetPrice;
            WriteLine("{0,-7}{1,8:C}", ECONOMY_CARPET +
                 ":", totalCost);
            ReadKey( );
        }
    }
}
```

NOTE Readability is important. Notice how the second lines of statements are indented to indicate that the statement has not been completed.

IMPLEMENT THE CODE

During implementation, the source code is compiled to check to see if any rule violations have been made. To compile the project, click **Build Solution** from the **Build** menu if you are using Visual Studio. To run the application, use the **Start Without Debugging** option available on the **Debug** menu.

TEST AND DEBUG

During this final step, test the program and ensure you have the correct result. The output should match your prototype. Is your spacing correct? Figure 2-21 shows the output generated from displaying the results of the calculations.

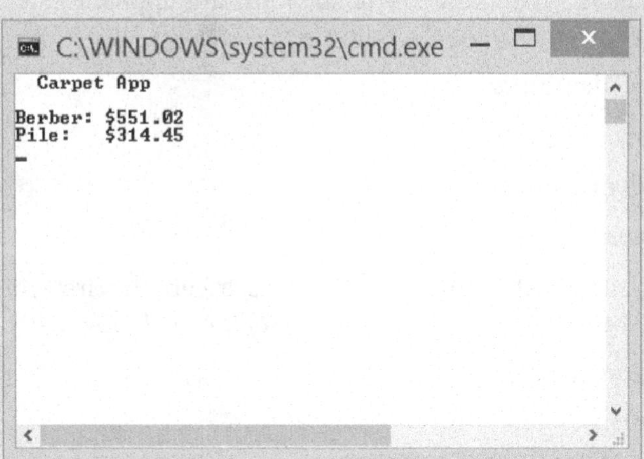

FIGURE 2-21 Class diagram for the CarpetCalculator program

In conclusion, this chapter concentrated on using data. You will use the concepts you learned in this chapter for the remainder of your software development. In Chapter 3, you will learn how to write methods that describe the behavior of the data.

Coding Standards

As you read in Chapter 1, coding or programming style is a term used to describe acceptable conventions for writing source code. It goes beyond the rules of the language and provides guidelines or suggestions that should be followed to ensure consistency among programmers working toward a common goal. Following the guidelines reduces the number of errors or bugs introduced into programming projects. It saves time, increases program maintainability, and helps ensure reliability of code. Naming Conventions, which were discussed earlier in this chapter, are highlighted next.

Naming Conventions

- Use meaningful, descriptive words as identifiers.
- Do not use abbreviations for identifiers unless it is a well-known abbreviation.
- With the exception of variables used as iterators for loops, do not use single character identifiers.

- Use Pascal Casing (first character of all words are uppercase; all other characters are lowercase) for the following:

  Class and type identifiers

  Method names

  Namespace identifiers

  Property names
- Use Camel Casing (first character of all words, except the first word, are uppercase; all other characters are lowercase) for the following:

  Local variable identifiers

  Object identifiers

  Private data members

  Parameters
- Filename should match class name.
- Use all uppercase characters to name constants.
- Do not use an underscore in identifiers.
- Use a noun or a noun phrase to name a class.

Spacing Conventions

- Use tabs instead of spaces for indentation.
- Use white space (one blank line) to separate and organize logical groups of code.
- Place curly braces ({ }) at the same level as the code outside the braces.
- Place curly braces on a new line.
- Declare each variable independently on separate lines. It is permissible to reuse the data type, but each variable should be on a separate line.
- Avoid long lines of code. Lines should not exceed 80 characters.
- If a program statement must be split over multiple lines, use indentation to improve readability.

Declaration Conventions

- Use the built-in C# data type aliases, not the .NET CTS data type.
- Use the simplest data type.
- Declare and initialize local variables close to where they are used.
- Try to initialize variables when they are declared.
- Floating-point values should include at least one digit before the decimal place and one after.
- Use the `const` keyword to define constant values.

Resources

Additional sites you might want to explore:

- Naming Guidelines for .NET—
http://msdn.microsoft.com/en-us/library/xzf533w0(VS.71).aspx
- Guide to Megabytes, Gigabytes, Terabytes. . .—
http://fixitwizkid.com/threads/your-guide-to-megabytes-gigabytes-terabytes-yottabyte-exabyte-petabyte-zettabyte.8062/
- Writing Readable Code—
http://software.ac.uk/resources/guides/writing-readable-source-code
- C# Video tutorials—
http://www.programmingvideotutorials.com/csharp/csharp-introduction

QUICK REVIEW

1. Identifiers are names of elements that appear in a program, such as data items. They can include upper- and lowercase characters a–z, digits 0–9, underscores, and the at symbol (@). The first character cannot be a digit. No spaces can be included between words. Keywords cannot be used as identifiers.
2. Use meaningful names for identifiers by describing what will appear in memory locations when declaring variables.
3. A variable represents an area in computer memory where the value of a particular data type can be stored. Declaring a variable requires that you select an identifier and determine what type of data will appear in the memory cell.
4. Literals cannot be changed. They are the numbers, characters, and combinations of characters used in your program.

5. Types are actually implemented through classes. This means that classes are used to define types.
6. An `object` is an instance of a `class`. It is an example of the `class`.
7. The value types are often called the fundamental or primitive data types. They are the predefined data types of the language.
8. Value types include nine integral (whole number) types, two floating-point types, and the `decimal` type.
9. All integral values represent whole numbers, which are values without a decimal notation. The value type `int` is used most often.
10. Floating-point values allow you to keep the fractional portion of a data item. They can be specified in scientific notation with an exponent or in standard decimal notation.
11. The `decimal` data type is suitable for financial and monetary calculations.
12. A `bool` variable can have a value of either `true` or `false`.
13. `string` type represents a combination of Unicode characters.
14. `const` forces the functionality of not allowing the value to be changed.
15. An assignment statement takes the form of variable = expression.
16. Unary operators require a single operand.
17. Preincrement and postincrement operators of ++ and -- add or subtract the number one (1) to and from a memory location.
18. Compound operators include the assignment operator and are used to modify a variable by using its original value as part of the calculation.
19. The order in which calculations are performed is called the order of operations. Parentheses can be added to an expression to alter the order.
20. Left associative means that the operations are performed from left to right. This means that as you move from left to right in an expression, the operation that is encountered first is executed first.
21. If the binary operation involves both a `double` and an `int`, implicit type coercion is performed.
22. Explicit type coercion through type casting or type conversion takes the form of (type) expression.

EXERCISES

1. Which of the following is a valid identifier?

   a. `int`

   b. jersey girl

   c. 6Values

   d. sampleValue

   e. value-1

2. The number 768.6 is an example of a type.
   a. `bool`
   b. integral
   c. floating-point
   d. struct
   e. `int`

3. Which of the following is a reference type?
   a. `int`
   b. `bool`
   c. `string`
   d. `decimal`
   e. integral
4. The character that cannot be used with an identifier is:
   a. –
   b. $
   c. *
   d. #
   e. all of the above
5. Which of the following is a reserved keyword?
   a. Console
   b. Main
   c. using
   d. System
   e. all of the above
6. One of primary differences between `float`, `double`, and `decimal` is:
   a. `float` is used to represent more significant digits.
   b. `double` is normally used with large monetary values.
   c. `decimal` is not used to display negative values.
   d. `double` does not require suffixing a numeric literal with a value such as `m` or `f`.
   e. `decimal` is primarily used to represent small monetary values that require a $ for formatting.

7. Which of the following is a valid declaration for a variable to store the name of this textbook?
   a. `char` name of book;
   b. `string` nameOfBook;
   c. boolean nameOfBook;
   d. `char` bookName;
   e. `char` book Name;

8. Types are implemented in C# using:
   a. classes
   b. types
   c. objects
   d. namespaces
   e. programs

9. An `object` of the `int` `class` is:
   a. 147.98
   b. 417
   c. `int class`
   d. type `object`
   e. type integral

10. What would be an appropriate declaration for a memory location to be used as a flag to indicate whether a value has reached its upper limit?
    a. `int` upperLimit;
    b. upperLimit reached;
    c. `bool` upperLimit;
    d. Boolean upperLimit;
    e. `string` upperLimit;

11. Adding the keyword `const` to a declaration:
    a. places a value in memory that cannot be changed.
    b. declares variables of the constant type.
    c. must be done by placing it after the identifier in the declaration.
    d. can only be done with the integral types.
    e. is prohibited in C#.

12. Which statement increases the result by 15?
    a. 15 += result;
    b. 15 =+ result;
    c. result =+ 15;
    d. result += 15;
    e. result = 15 +;

13. What is stored in ans as a result of the arithmetic expression, given the following declarations?

    ```
    int ans = 0, v1 = 10, v2 = 19;
    ans = v2 % v1++;
    ```

    a. 1.8
    b. 9
    c. 8
    d. 2
    e. none of the above

14. What is stored in ans as a result of the arithmetic expression, given the following declarations?

    ```
    int ans = 10, v1 = 5, v2 = 7, v3 = 18;
    ans += v1 + 10 (v2 / 5) + v3 / v2;
    ```

    a. 18
    b. 32
    c. 28
    d. 30
    e. none of the above

15. Which of the following formats 86 to display with two digits to the right of the decimal?
    a. {0:C}
    b. {0:c}
    c. {0:f2}
    d. all of the above
    e. none of the above

16. Indicate the order of operations for the following assignment statements by placing a number under the assignment operator, as illustrated in Figure 2-13.

    a. ans = value1 + value2 * value3 – (value4 + 20 / 5 % 2) * 7;

    b. ans += value1-- * 10;

    c. ans = (((value1 + 7) – 6 * value2) / 2);

    d. ans = value1 + value2 / value3 * value4--;

17. Which of the following are valid identifiers? If they are invalid, indicate why.

    a. intValue

    b. value#1

    c. the first value

    d. _value1

    e. AVALUE

18. For each of the following, declare a variable using the best choice for data type.

    a. a counter for the number of correct responses

    b. the amount of money you owe on a credit card

    c. the name of your hometown

    d. the grade you hope to obtain on the next exam

    e. the grade you hope is recorded at the end of the term for this course

19. For each of the following declarations, write an appropriate compile-time initialization.

    a. counter for the number of correct responses begins with zero

    b. amount of money you owe on a credit card is zero

    c. name of the hometown or the city where your school is located

    d. grade on the next exam is 100

    e. grade to be recorded at the end of the term for this course is an A

20. Suppose x, y, and z are `int` variables and x = 2, y = 6, and z = 10. What will be in the memory locations of each of the variables after each of the following statements is executed? (For each exercise, use the original declaration.)

	x	y	z
a. z += ++y % 2;	________	________	________
b. x = y * z / 2 – x * z;	________	________	________
c. x %= --z – y * 2;	________	________	________
d. y = (z – y) * 2 + --y;	________	________	________

21. Suppose x, y, and z are `double` variables and x = 2.5, y = 6.9, and z = 10.0. What will be in the memory locations of each of the variables after each of the following statements is executed? (For each exercise, use the original declaration.)

	x	y	z
a. z * = y++ % 7;	________	________	________
b. x = z / 3 * --y;	________	________	________
c. z /= (`int`)y /x;	________	________	________
d. z = x + y / 4;	________	________	________

22. What will be the output from each of the following statements?
    a. Write("Result is {0:c}", 67);
    b. Write("Number {0:f0} is {1:c}", 1, 3);
    c. Write("{0,-10:f0}–{1,10:c}", 1, 3 * 2);
    d. Write("{0:f0} result " + "xyz {1:f2}", 1, 25);

23. Explain how a variable differs from a constant.

24. Explain the width specifier. Be sure to include both positive and negative numbers with your explanation.

25. The following program has several syntax errors as well as style inconsistencies. Correct the syntax errors and identify the style violations.

```
namespace Chapter2
{
  class converter
  {
  static void main(
{
            CONST int inches = 12;
            int x = 100; y = 10;
            float z = 22.45;
            double ans;
            ans=inches+z*x%y;
            System.write("The result is {f2:0} " + "ans");
}
}
```

PROGRAMMING EXERCISES

For each of the exercises, be sure to include appropriate comments, choose meaningful identifiers, and use proper indentations in your source code.

1. Write a program that converts a temperature given in Celsius into Fahrenheit. Test the program by performing a compile-time initialization of 32 for the original Celsius value. Display the values number aligned. The original temperature should show no digits after the decimal. One position following the decimal should be printed for the converted value. Be sure to provide labels for both values. Go into your source code and change the initialization value to 0. Rerun the application. Select additional test values and rerun the application.

2. Design an application that converts miles into feet and its equivalent metric kilometer measurement. Declare and initialize miles to 4.5. Show your miles and kilometers formatted with two positions to the right of the decimal. Feet should both be shown with no positions to the right of the decimal with comma separators. Be sure to provide labels for values and number align them. Once you get that portion running, go into your source code and change the initialization value for miles. Rerun the application and make sure that your values are still number aligned.

3. Write a program that computes the average of five exam scores. Declare and perform a compile-time initialization with the five exam values. Declare integer memory locations for the exam values. Use an integer

constant to define the number of scores. Print all scores. The average value should be formatted with two digits to the right of the decimal. Rerun the application with different values. Be sure to desk check your results.

4. Write a program that prints the number of quarters, dimes, nickels, and pennies that a customer should get back as change. Declare and initialize all memory locations as integers. On output, show the original change amount as a monetary amount, with two positions to the right of the decimal. Run your program once by performing a compile-time initialization using 92 cents for the value to be converted. Go into your source code and change the 92 to 27. Rerun the application. Be sure to desk check your solutions.

5. Write a program that shows the formatted retail price of shirts when there is a 15% markdown. Test the program by performing a compile-time initialization with an item labeled "Open Collar Running Shirt," which has a wholesale price of $41.00. How much savings is expected with the markdown? Display appropriately labeled retail and markdown values for the shirt. Once you get that running, go back into your source code, add lines of code that will reassign the memory location's values for a Razorback T-Shirt, which has a retail price of $36.00. Add additional lines of code, which will display the new item's information along with the previous item. What happens if the markdown goes to 20% or 10%?

6. Write a program that calculates and prints the take-home pay for a commissioned sales employee. Perform a compile-time initialization and store the name of Joshua Montain in a variable called employeeName. For practice working with the decimal data type, declare all monetary values as decimal. Employees earn 7% of their total sales as a commission. Employees pay federal tax rate of 18%. All employees contribute 10% of their earnings to a retirement program and pay an additional 6% of their earnings to Social Security. If Joshua's sales this month were $161,432, how much money will he take home? Produce a formatted report with your values labeled and number aligned showing the amount for each of the computed items and the sales commission percentage rate. Also show the total deductions. The final take home pay and total sales figure used for the calculations should be formatted with currency. All other values should have comma separators, no dollar sign, and display two positions to the right of the decimal. Select appropriate constants. After you finish displaying Joshua's data, change his sales to 1.3 million and rerun the application.

7. Write a tip calculating applications that can be used to determine what the tip and final charges would be given a total bill charge. Display the tip for 15% and 20% along with totals for each of the percentages. On output, show the original bill charge and each of the tip calculations with a final amount. Be sure to provide labels and number align the values.

8. Write a program that computes a weighted average giving the following weights.

   Homework: 10%
   Projects: 35%
   Quizzes: 10%
   Exams: 30%
   Final Exam: 15%

   Do a compile-time initialization with the following values: Homework: 97; Projects: 82; Quizzes: 60; Exams: 75; Final Exam 80. Display all values, including the weights, appropriately labeled and formatted. Rerun the application with different values.

9. Write a program that computes the amount of money the computer club will receive from the proceeds of their granola sales. They sell the granola bars for $1.50 per bar. Purchases for the granola are in cases, with each case having 100 bars. Each case costs $100.00. They are required to give the student government association 10% of their earnings. Display their proceeds, showing the amount given to the student government association. Show all the values formatted with currency. How much money would they make if they sold 29 cases?

10. In countries using the metric system, many products are sold by grams and kilograms as opposed to pounds and ounces. Write an application that converts grams to pounds and will display the price of the product by pound. Test your application by doing a compile-time initialization of Poutine, a common Canadian dish, made with French fries, which sells for $1.29 per 100 grams. Display both the metric and customary U.S. units. Be sure to provide labels for all values. Once you get that portion running, go into your source code and rerun the application using additional items, such as haricot verts, which are a type of green beans sold at 0.75 per 100 grams.

© zeljkodan/Shutterstock.com

Methods and Behaviors

IN THIS CHAPTER, YOU WILL:

- Become familiar with the components of a method
- Call class methods with and without parameters
- Use predefined methods in the Console and Math classes
- Write your own value- and nonvalue-returning class methods (with and without parameters)
- Distinguish between value, ref, and out parameter types
- Explore the use of named and optional parameters with default values
- Work through a programming example that illustrates the chapter concepts

In Chapter 2, you learned how to declare variables and data members. You discovered that data is stored in memory in variables. You learned how to perform arithmetic procedures on the data and how expressions are evaluated using the rules of precedence. You also learned how to display formatted data. This chapter focuses on methods. Methods provide the operations, or behavior, for the data members of a `class`. Methods facilitate dividing a problem into manageable units for ease of development and reuse of code. You will learn about different types of methods in this chapter, how to call predefined methods, and how to create your own methods and call them. You will write methods that perform processing and return the results of their work and you will write methods that perform procedures without returning a value. You will learn how to pass arguments to methods and learn about the different types of parameters that can be used with methods. You will begin by examining what components make up a method.

Anatomy of a Method

A method is really nothing more than a group of statements placed together under a single name. Methods are defined inside a `class`. As you learned in Chapter 1, a `class` includes a collection of data and methods. Methods are the members of a `class` that perform an action, and through writing methods you describe the behavior of data. Methods are similar to functions, procedures, and modules found in other programming languages. They allow program statements to be grouped together based on the functionality of the statements and to be called on one or more times when needed.

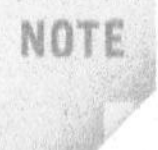

Unlike some languages such as C and C++ that allow methods to be defined globally outside a `class`, C# requires all methods to be members of a `class`.

All programs consist of at least one method. For both console and Windows applications, the required method is `Main( )` in C#. `Main( )` is a method you have already written as the entry point into your program. It does not matter where you physically place the `Main( )` method in your program. When your program runs, the first statement in the `Main( )` method is the first statement executed. Control continues in `Main( )` until the closing curly brace is encountered.

When you wrote programs earlier as part of the body of `Main( )`, you wrote statements that invoked, or called, other methods. Example 3-1 contains calls to two methods: `WriteLine( )` and `ReadKey( )`. `Main( )` is the only user-defined method included in Example 3-1.

EXAMPLE 3-1

```
/* ******************************************
 * SquareExample.cs        Author:        Doyle
 * Computes the square of a variable initialized
 * at compile time.
 * ******************************************/
using System;
using static System.Console;
namespace SquareExample
{
    class SquareExample
    {
        static void Main( )
        {
            int aValue = 789;
            int result;

            result = aValue * aValue;
            WriteLine("{0} squared is {1}", aValue,
                         result);
            ReadKey( );
        }
    }
}
```

The output of Example 3-1 is:

```
768 squared is 589824
```

> **NOTE** The value in the result variable can be formatted using the number format `string` (n or N). By adding the N format argument to the `string` (`{1:N0}`), a comma is inserted so that the value is more readable.
>
> ```
> WriteLine("{0} squared is {1:N0}", aValue, result);
> ```
>
> produces
>
> 768 squared is 589,824
>
> The zero in `{1:N0}` indicates that no digits should be printed to the right of the `decimal` point. When zero (0) is included with the format specifier, the decimal point is not printed either.

The last statement, `ReadKey( )`, in Example 3-1, is a method invocation. The `ReadKey( )` method is added to hold the screen when the program runs. This is necessary if the program is executed in Visual Studio using the **Debug, Start Debugging (F5)** option.

The first line of a method is called the **heading** of the method. Figure 3-1 labels the components that make up the heading.

NOTE

You will notice that no semicolon is placed at the end of method headings, such as `Main( )`. Nor do you place semicolons at the end of the `class` headings (e.g., `class SquareExample`) or `namespace` headings. Semicolons are placed at the end of variable declarations, calls to methods, and assignment statements.

Some programmers refer to the heading for the method as the prototype for the method. The **definition** of the method includes the heading and the body of the method, which is enclosed in curly braces.

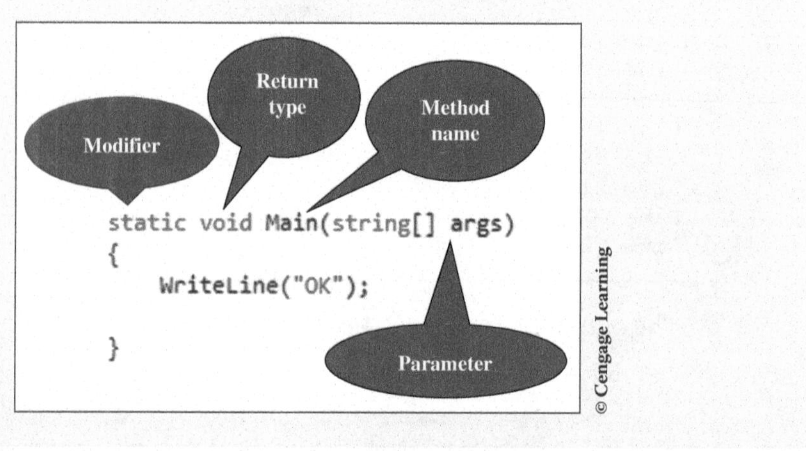

FIGURE 3-1 Method components

The programs you create include definitions for dozens of methods, calls to those methods, and calls to methods that are part of the .NET FCL (Framework class library). The components identified in Figure 3-1 are described in the following section.

Modifiers

Modifiers appear in the headings of methods. They also appear in the declaration heading for classes and `class` members, as shown in Figure 3-1. A modifier is added to a type or a type member's declaration to change or alter it or to indicate how it can be accessed. In Chapter 2, you learned about and used the `const` modifier.

`const` is added to a declaration to indicate that a value is constant and cannot be changed. You have previously seen two other types of modifiers: `static` and access modifiers.

Static Modifier

3

You have already encountered `static` used with the `Main( )` method. All `Main( )` method headings must include the `static` modifier. C# issues an error message if you forget to include `static` when you write a `Main( )` method. `Write( )`, `WriteLine( )`, and `ReadLine( )` are all `static` methods of the `Console` `class`. In order to invoke or call these methods, you have to place the `class` name (`Console`) before the method name as is illustrated in Figure 3-1 or as you saw previously, you can also include an additional using directive that reads `using static System.Console;`. Once this is added to your program, you no longer have to fully quality calls to `Write( )`, `WriteLine( )`, or other `static` members of the `Console` `class`. You can simply type the method's name.

You will soon explore the members of the `Math` `class`. The `Math` `class` is also in the `System` `namespace`. The heading for each of the `Math` `class` members includes the `static` keyword. The method in Example 3-2 raises a value to a specified power. Examine its heading.

EXAMPLE 3-2

```
static double Math.Pow(double, double)
```

Static is used in this context to indicate that a method belongs to the type itself rather than to a specific `object` of a `class`. This means that it is not necessary to instantiate an `object` of the `class` to use the method member. If you want to call a `static` method, which is defined in the same `class` where it is being called from, the method can be called by simply typing its identifier (without an `object` or `class` name). However, if you are calling a `static` method from another `class`, the `class` name normally must be used. For example, to call the `Sqrt( )` method of the `Math` `class`, you would write:

```
double answer = Math.Sqrt(25);
```

You will define nonstatic methods in Chapter 4.

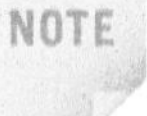

Recall that if you are using Visual Studio 2015 or later, you have the option of adding a reference to `static` classes with the `using` directive. This enables use of its `static class` members of that class without having to fully qualify them.

If you are planning to use a number of methods in the `Math class`, and if you are using Visual Studio 2015 or later, you could add the following directive,

```
using static System.Math;
```

and now execute the method by omitting the qualifier, `Math`, as is shown in the following.

```
double answer = Sqrt(25);
```

Calls to `Write( )` are made throughout the book without qualifying with the `Console class` because `using static System.Console;` is included at the top of program examples.

Methods that use the `static` modifier are called `class` methods. A single copy of the method is made instead of copies for each `object`. Instance methods require that an `object` be instantiated before the method is accessed. You will read more about instance methods in Chapter 4 when you create your own classes. When you write your own methods, the `static` modifier can be added; however, for most classes designed for object-oriented applications, the `static` keyword is rarely used. Much of the power of object-oriented development comes from encapsulating (packaging) methods and data members together so that objects can be defined with their own members and be totally independent of each other. A single copy of a method is created for use with all objects when the method is defined as `static`.

Another type of modifier is an access modifier. It specifies the level of accessibility for types and their members. You will work with access modifiers in Chapter 4. In Chapter 4, you will read about one other type of modifier: `override`. This keyword is added to the heading of a method to declare a new definition for a previously defined method.

Return Type

The `return` type identifies what type of value is returned when the method is completed. Any of the predefined or valid user-defined types can be returned. Methods can return a value when all the statements of the method are complete, or they can simply return control to the method that called them, without bringing a value back.

The `return` type is always listed immediately preceding the name of the method, as shown in Figure 3-1. Methods do not have to return anything; however, they can return at most one data type through the method's name.

If a method does not return a value, the `void` keyword is placed at the `return` type location in the method heading, as shown in the following line of code:

```
void DisplayInstructions( )
```

If a return type other than void is specified in the method heading, there must be a return statement included in the body of the method. The value returned must be a compatible value—one that either matches the type in the heading or can be stored in that type.

The return statement takes the form:

```
return [value];
```

3

Note that value is enclosed in square brackets to indicate that it is optional. If the method heading uses void as the return type, the return statement can be omitted or included as follows:

```
return;
```

Whenever the return type is not void, you must have a return value following the return keyword. This value can be a literal, arithmetic expression, or variable that holds a value. Example 3-3 illustrates returning a calculated value.

EXAMPLE 3-3

```
static double CalculateMilesPerGallon
                (int milesTraveled, double gallonsUsed)
{
    return milesTraveled / gallonsUsed;
}
```

The method heading in Example 3-3 indicates that a double value is returned. This is the double that precedes CalculateMilesPerGallon, the name of the method. Inside the body of the method, the result of the division produces a compatible double value.

The value being returned is sent back to the location in the program that called the method. For example, the value returned from the CalculateMilesPerGallon( ) method is sent back to the WriteLine( ) method for display in the call that follows:

```
WriteLine("Miles per gallon = {0:N2 }",
          CalculateMilesPerGallon(289, 12.2));
```

The output produced from the WriteLine( ) method would be

```
Miles per gallon = 23.69
```

Your programs are easier to modify and debug if your methods have one entry and one exit. This is a problem-solving technique you should try to include in your design. The implication is that you should try to have only one return statement in a method.

Method Name

When naming a method, you follow the rules for creating an identifier, which were described in Chapter 2. Identifiers should be meaningful names that label the overall purpose of the segment of code. Many programmers use the standard convention of naming the method with an action verb phrase. This verb phrase should describe what the method is intending to accomplish. **Pascal case style** is used for `class` and method identifiers. This C# convention specifies that the first character is uppercase when the identifier has at least three characters. Subsequent words that are part of the identifier also begin with an uppercase character. Examples of method identifiers following these style conventions include `CalculateSalesTax( )`, `AssignSectionNumber( )`, `DisplayResults( )`, `InputAge( )`, and `ConvertInputValue( )`.

Parameters

The items inside the parentheses of the method heading are called the parameters, or arguments. Sometimes, a method requires the supply of unique data. For example, if a method is written to calculate the average of three values, the method requires that these three values be sent to it. The `CalculateMilesPerGallon(int milesTraveled, double gallonsUsed)` method in Example 3-3 required two arguments: an `int` value for `milesTraveled` and a `double` value for `gallonsUsed`. It is through parameters and arguments that the data can be sent into a method.

When writing a method, you decide what type of unique data is needed for the method. You then place the data type and an identifier for the data type inside the parentheses. You must include matched pairs of types and identifiers inside the parentheses. The two matched pairs of parameters for the `CalculateMilesPerGallon( )` method are as follows:

```
(int milesTraveled, double gallonsUsed)
```

In the body of the method, the identifiers are used to reference where and when the unique data item should be used. For the `CalculateMilesPerGallon(int milesTraveled, double gallonsUsed)` method, `milesTraveled` and `gallonsUsed` were used in an arithmetic expression. The result of the expression is returned to the calling method.

Some programmers make a distinction between parameters and arguments, using the term **parameter** to refer to items appearing in the heading of the method and **argument** for the items appearing in the call to the method. Others make a distinction between arguments and parameters by adding actual and formal onto the terms. **Formal parameters**, or arguments, appear in the heading of a method. **Actual arguments**, or parameters, appear in the call. Think of the actual argument as being the actual data that is sent to the method. The formal parameters are like placeholders; they formally indicate what type of data is expected to be sent for the method to use. This book uses the term "parameters" to refer to the items in the method heading and the term "arguments" for items sent into the method via a method call. For Example 3-3, the arguments for the `CalculateMilesPerGallon(int milesTraveled, double gallonsUsed)` method are 289 and 12.2. This is actual data or numbers; however, the actual argument used to call the method could be an identifier for a variable. It could be an expression involving an arithmetic statement or a call to another method, just as long as it produces a compatible type.

Similar to `return` types, parameters are optional. If no parameters are included, an open and closed parenthesis is used. If more than one parameter is included, they are separated by a comma.

Some languages place the `void` keyword inside the parentheses in place of the parameter list to indicate that no parameters are needed. C# does not allow this and generates a syntax error.

There are several different types of parameters, which are explored later in this chapter.

Method Body

As you saw in Example 3-1, statements making up the method body are enclosed in curly braces. The body for the following `DisplayMessage( )` method consists of two calls to the `Write( )` method in the `Console class`, one call to the `WriteLine( )` method in the `Console class` and a `return` statement that does not return a value.

```
void DisplayMessage( )
{
    Write("This is ");
    Write("an example of a method ");
    WriteLine("body. ");
    return;   // no value is returned
}
```

Normally, the statements inside the body of a method are executed in sequential order. The body of a method can include statements that declare variables, do arithmetic, and call other methods. These same rules and concepts apply whether you are using your own methods or predefined methods that make up the FCL. When the last statement in the method finishes, control is returned to the method that made the call.

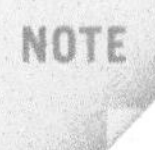

Notice that the `return` type for the `DisplayMessage( )` method is `void`. A `return` statement is included. Return is optional here because no value is returned when the method is finished. Normally you will not include the optional `return` statement when the return type is `void`.

Example 3-2 showed you the heading of the `Pow( )` method. It is repeated here:

```
static double Math.Pow(double, double)
```

This method returns the result of raising a number to a specified power. Inside the parentheses, two parameters of type `double` are required. These values refer to the base number and an exponent in that order. These identifiers are inserted in the body of the method at locations where the calculations on the values should occur. When the method is called, the specific values that are sent as arguments replace the placeholders in the body of the method. For example, if you make the following call:

```
double result = Math.Pow(5, 2); // Requires using System;
```

the value returned when `Pow( )` is finished is stored in `result`. It would be 25 because $5^2 = 25$.

NOTE You did not see the actual statements that made up its body for the `Pow( )` method. This is one of the beauties of object-oriented development. It is not necessary for you to know how the method produces a result. To use the `Pow( )` method, all you need to know is what type of values to send it and what type of value you can expect to receive back. The black box concept of object-oriented programming hides method implementation details from you.

When an application is run, `Main( )` serves as the controlling method. Execution always starts in the body of the `Main( )` method. Execution begins with the first line in `Main( )` and stops when the closing curly brace in `Main( )` is reached. Lots of other methods can, of course, be executed in your application; however, they must be called from either `Main( )` or from a method that has been called from `Main( )`. In Example 3-1, you saw how control was passed to the `WriteLine( )` and `ReadKey( )` methods by calling, or invoking, these methods.

Calling Class Methods

Invoking a method means calling the method. When a method call is encountered, the .NET execution engine, the common language runtime (CLR), halts execution in the current method and transfers control to the body of the method called. After completing the called method's body, control is returned back to the location in the calling method that made the call. A call to the method that does not return a value uses the following syntax:

```
[qualifier].MethodName(argumentList);
```

NOTE

Whenever square brackets are inserted into a syntax reference, the entry is optional. With static methods, the qualifier is the class name. Visual Studio 2015 enables you to avoid qualifying calls to static class members if you add a using directive for the static class. Both Console and Math are static classes found in the System namespace.

```
using static System.Console;
using static System.Math;
```

3

As stated previously, not all methods require an argument list. Both of the following statements are legal calls to the WriteLine( ) method. The first takes no arguments; the second call sends one data item to the method.

```
WriteLine( );      // No arguments. Writes a blank line
WriteLine("Ok"); // Single argument
```

When the argument list contains more than one data item, the values are separated by commas, as follows:

```
WriteLine("Value1({0}) + Value2({1})" +
          " = Value3({2})", 25, 75, (25 + 75));
```

Output from the last call to the WriteLine( ) method would be

```
Value1(25) + Value2(75) = Value3(100)
```

The call included four arguments:

```
1.     "Value1({0}) + Value2({1})" + " = Value3({2})"
2.     25
3.     75
4.     (25 + 75)
```

A call to a method never includes the data type as part of the argument list, but rather the actual data. The actual argument can, of course, take the form of a literal, as shown previously, or it can be a variable or an expression. The expression can be quite sophisticated and even include a call to another method.

If you are developing your applications using Visual Studio, when you call methods you should take advantage of the IntelliSense feature of the IDE. After you enter a class or object name and then type a dot (.), the list of members is displayed. As you move down the member list, a pop-up window displays information about each member. The Console class was typed in Figure 3-2 followed by a dot. Then the WriteLine( ) method member is selected. Notice in Figure 3-2 that two different icons appear to the left of member names. Methods appear with a three-dimensional box. The icon featuring the wrench beside Title and WindowWidth is used to reference a property. You will learn more about properties later in Chapter 4.

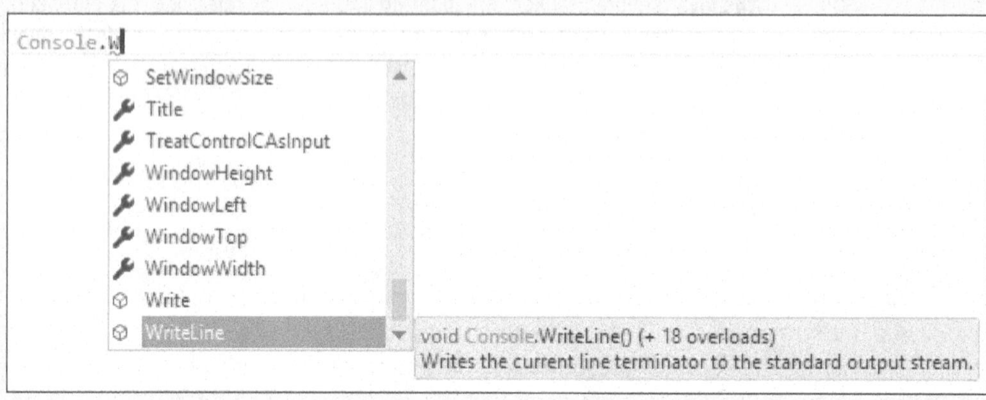

FIGURE 3-2 Console class members

In the sections that follow, you will explore some of the predefined methods you have already seen and used. This should help you gain a better understanding of how to use those and the other predefined methods that make up the FCL.

NOTE IntelliSense lists user-created identifiers as well as .NET identifiers. To open IntelliSense in Visual Studio quickly, type the first character of any identifier. You get a list of members from which to choose. This also works if you type two or three characters. By typing more characters, you reduce the number listed.

Predefined Methods

A key feature of the .NET Framework is the extensive `class` library. Within the library of classes, each `class` has a number of predefined methods. The `WriteLine( )` method shown in Figure 3-2 is a predefined member method of the `Console class`. These .NET methods have been thoroughly tested by the .NET developers and provide a great deal of functionality. Avoid making work for yourself by using predefined methods whenever possible.

In the programs you have already seen and developed, the `using` directive made the `System namespace` available and the `using static System.Console;` reference enabled you to call `static` members of the `Console class` without having to first type the class name as was done in Figure 3-2. The `Console class` provides methods for reading characters from, and writing characters to the console. There are methods for working with individual characters or entire lines of characters. The methods you have used most often are `Write( )` and `WriteLine( )`. They are both **overloaded methods**, which means that there are multiple methods with the same name, but each has a different number or type of parameter. First examine the `Write( )` method.

Write( ) Method

As you saw in Figure 3-2, the IntelliSense feature of Visual Studio shows information about the method in a pop-up window on the right. Use this information to determine how to call the method. The pop-up window includes the signature for the method along with the `return` type and a short description of the member's functionality. The name of the method, the modifiers, and the types of its formal parameters make up the **signature**. Even though the `return` type is displayed first in the IntelliSense pop-up window, the `return` type is not considered part of its signature.

3

With IntelliSense, as soon as the desired member is identified and selected, type the next character following the member's name. For example, when you type *W*, if *Write* is selected, you could next type the left parenthesis following the *W*. This would populate the text editor with *Write(.*, without your having to type the characters *rite*. By learning to use this feature, you won't mind declaring longer descriptive identifiers and you will have fewer typing errors.

To add as much functionality as possible to the methods, they are sometimes overloaded. .NET includes 18 different `Write( )` methods. The `Write( )` method signature shown in Figure 3-3 has one formal parameter, a `string` value. All 18 methods have the same name, but each one has a different signature. Notice how the first line of the pop-up display for Figure 3-3 starts with "10 of 18." This is only one of the eighteen (18) `Write( )` method signatures. Example 3-4 lists four of the other `Write( )` signatures. In addition to these four, there are 14 other `Console.Write( )` methods. The implication is that you can send to the method, as an argument, any of the predefined basic types and get the results you would expect displayed on the console.

EXAMPLE 3-4

```
Write(int)
Write(double)
Write(object)
Write(bool)
```

So how does the CLR know which of these 18 methods to use? The answer is simple, but important for you to understand. When the method is called, the argument used to make the call is matched with the signature to determine which of the methods to execute. Remember, the signature of the method includes the formal parameters, which include the data type that can be used for the method.

In Visual Studio, after you select the `Write( )` member and type the opening parenthesis, IntelliSense displays a drop-down list with a scroll bar that allows the viewing of all 18 signatures. This gives you an opportunity to know what type of argument is needed with a call. Figure 3-3 shows the 10th one of the 18 signatures.

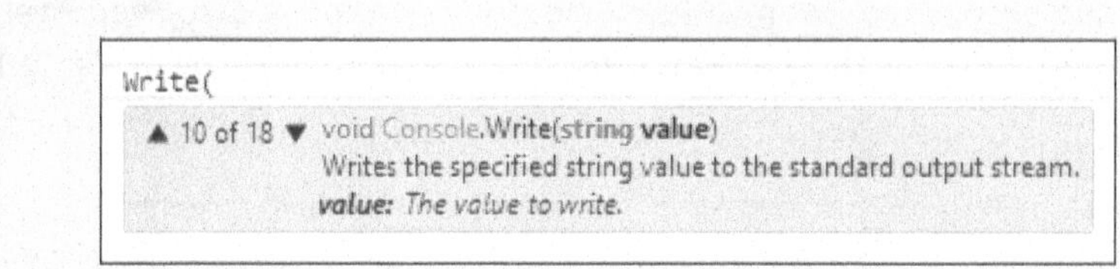

FIGURE 3-3 IntelliSense display

The `Write( )` method in Figure 3-3 is called by entering the name of the method, an open parenthesis, a `string` value, and a closing parenthesis. In the call, the `string` value can be a `string` literal, a `string` variable, or a value of another data type converted into a `string`. From Chapter 2, you learned that a `string` literal is one or more characters enclosed in double quotation marks. A valid call to the `Write( )` method using the displayed overloaded method from Figure 3-3 would be

```
Write("Any string value will work!" );
```

The 18 overloaded `Write( )` methods include parameters for common types, such as `int`, `double`, `decimal`, `bool`, and `object`. You should explore the other options.

WriteLine( ) Method

As shown previously, the `WriteLine( )` method behaves like the `Write( )` method with the exception that it writes the current end-of-line terminator after it displays the arguments. There are 19 overloaded `WriteLine( )` methods. Example 3-5 includes valid calls to the `WriteLine( )` method.

EXAMPLE 3-5

```
WriteLine (45);
WriteLine ("An apple a day" + " keeps the doctor away.")
WriteLine (67.28 + 10000);
WriteLine (true);
WriteLine ("Score on the next exam: {0}", 100);
```

The output generated from each of the preceding statements is

```
45
An apple a day keeps the doctor away.
10067.28
True
Score on the next exam: 100
```

Notice in the output generated for Example 3-5 that True is printed when the `bool` variable is displayed. The first character is capitalized. Yet the valid values for a `bool` variable are `true` and `false`, all lowercase characters. Do not be confused by this inconsistency.

The `Write( )` and `WriteLine( )` methods did not `return` anything when they were called. They performed their tasks and then relinquished control to the next sequential statement in the `Main( )` method. Their task was to write the specified information to the console. No value was returned to the calling method, `Main( )`, when they completed their jobs. Notice that the heading for the `Write( )` method in the pop-up window displayed by IntelliSense shown in Figures 3-1 and 3-2 begins with "`void` ...".

The `Console` `class` also includes methods that allow you to enter values from the keyboard. When entered, these values are returned to the program. Three methods used for console input are `Read( )` and `ReadLine( )`, and `ReadKey( )`. The first two methods are not overloaded.

Read( ) Method

`Read( )` was used previously to hold the output window open until a character from the keyboard was pressed. This enabled the user of your program to leave the output on the screen as long as necessary.

The pop-up window in Figure 3-4 shows the method heading for `Read( )`.

```
int aNumber;

aNumber = Read(
              int Console.Read()
              Reads the next character from the standard input stream.
```

FIGURE 3-4 Console.Read ( ) signature

As Figure 3-4 shows, the `Read( )` method returns an `int` representing the next character input from the keyboard. The heading for the method in the box on the right displayed using IntelliSense begins with the `int` keyword. The `int` is the Unicode representation of the single `char` value entered. Example 3-6 illustrates what is stored in memory when the `Read( )` method is used.

EXAMPLE 3-6

```
// Assumes using static System.Console; directive added
int aNumber;
Write("Enter a single character: ");
aNumber = Read( );
WriteLine("The value of the character entered: " + aNumber);
```

If the user types the alphabetic character a when prompted, the output is as follows:

```
The value of the character entered: 97
```

This might be a good time for you to review Appendix C. Notice that the Unicode decimal representation for the character a is 97.

To display the actual character entered, you could cast the value, as shown in Example 3-7.

EXAMPLE 3-7

```
WriteLine("The value of the character entered: " + (char)aNumber);
```

If the user types the character `'a'` using the cast, the output becomes

```
The value of the character entered: a
```

Notice that because the `Read( )` method returned a value, provisions had to be made for a location to store the value on return from the method. For this, an assignment statement is used. Another option is to include the call to `Read( )` as part of the argument to the `WriteLine( )` method at the location where `aNumber` should be displayed. The single statement in Example 3-8 could replace all four lines from Examples 3-6 and 3-7.

EXAMPLE 3-8

```
// Notice the (char) cast
WriteLine("The value of the character entered: " + (char) Read( ));
```

This single line is possible because the `Read( )` method in the `Console class` allows the user to enter one character. The `Read( )` method returns an `int`. The `int` value is cast to a `char` for display purposes. This value is then concatenated onto the end of the `string`, with the "+" operator. Although the preceding is syntactically correct and works for entering a single character, it is not as readable. It does not prompt users by telling them to enter a character. Another disadvantage of replacing the four lines with the single line is the fact that the entered value is not stored in a variable; thus, it is only available for use with that specific output statement.

`ReadKey( )` method in the `Console class` is another option for holding the screen. `ReadKey( )` obtains the next character or function key from the user. This is the method that has been invoked with previous examples.

ReadLine( ) Method

The `ReadLine( )` method is much more versatile than the `Read( )` method. Any number of characters can be entered using the `ReadLine( )` method, and it returns all characters up to the current end-of-line terminator, the Enter key.

As Figure 3-5 shows, no arguments are included inside the parentheses to the `ReadLine( )` method. `ReadLine( )` is not an overloaded method. It always returns a `string`. Even if numbers are entered, a `string` representing the concatenation of these numbers is returned. When the user types the number 786 at the keyboard, the result returned is '7' + '8' + '6' or the `string` `"786"`. An extra step is needed before any mathematical operations can be performed on the value. The `string` value must be parsed into an appropriate number type.

This feature was probably borrowed from Java. All values are entered as strings in Java. This enables values to be entered as strings and checked for typing errors before parsing or translating them into numbers.

```
string someStringValue;

someStringValue = ReadLine(
                  string Console.ReadLine()
                  Reads the next line of characters from the standard input stream.
```

FIGURE 3-5 Console.ReadLine ( ) signature

Example 3-9 shows calls to the predefined `Write( )`, `ReadLine( )`, `Parse( )`, and `WriteLine( )` methods. An integer is requested. `ReadLine( )` returns a `string` value. An extra step is needed before any arithmetic can be performed on the value that was entered. The string value must be changed or converted into an appropriate number type. The `Parse( )` method does that conversion. It is discussed in the following section.

EXAMPLE 3-9

```
/* ********************************************
 * AgeIncrementer.cs              Author: Doyle
 * Displays age one year from now.
********************************************/
using System;
using static System.Console;
namespace AgeIncrementer
{
    class AgeIncrementer
    {
        static void Main( )
        {
            int age;
            string aValue;
            Write("Enter your age: ");
            aValue = ReadLine( );
            age = int.Parse(aValue);
            WriteLine("Your age next year will be {0}",
                      ++age);
            ReadKey( );
        }
    }
}
```

ReadKey( ) Method

The `ReadKey( )` method obtains the next character or function key pressed by the user. This method can be called if you want the user to press some key to continue processing. It could also be placed as the last line of executable code in the `Main( )` method.

Parse( ) Method

Another predefined `static` method you will use often is the `Parse( )` method. As stated previously, `Parse( )` returns the number representation of its `string` argument. All numeric types have a `Parse( )` method. In Example 3-9, an `int` value is returned when the `Parse( )` method finishes. `Parse( )` can also be called with a `double object`, as illustrated in Example 3-10.

EXAMPLE 3-10

```
/**********************************************
 * SquareInputValue.cs          Author: Doyle
 * Allows an integer value to be input.
 * Computes and displays the square of the
 * value that is input.
 *********************************************/
using System;
using static System.Console;
namespace SquareInputValue
{
   class SquareInputValue
   {
      static void Main( )
      {
         string inputStringValue;
         double aValue;
         double result;

         Write("Enter a value to be squared: ");
         inputStringValue = ReadLine( );
         aValue = double.Parse(inputStringValue);
         result = Math.Pow(aValue, 2);
         WriteLine("{0} squared is {1}", aValue,
                      result);
         ReadKey( );
      }
   }
}
```

Calls to methods `char.Parse( )` and `bool.Parse( )` produce similar results with their respective data types, as shown in Example 3-11.

EXAMPLE 3-11

```
string sValue = "true";
WriteLine(bool.Parse(sValue));    // displays True
string strValue = "q";
WriteLine(char.Parse(strValue)); // displays q
```

If you attempt to parse an incompatible value, a `System.FormatException` error, similar to that shown in Figure 3-6, is generated. The error in Figure 3-6 was generated from `WriteLine(char.Parse(sValue))` when `sValue` referenced `"true"` as shown in Example 3-11.

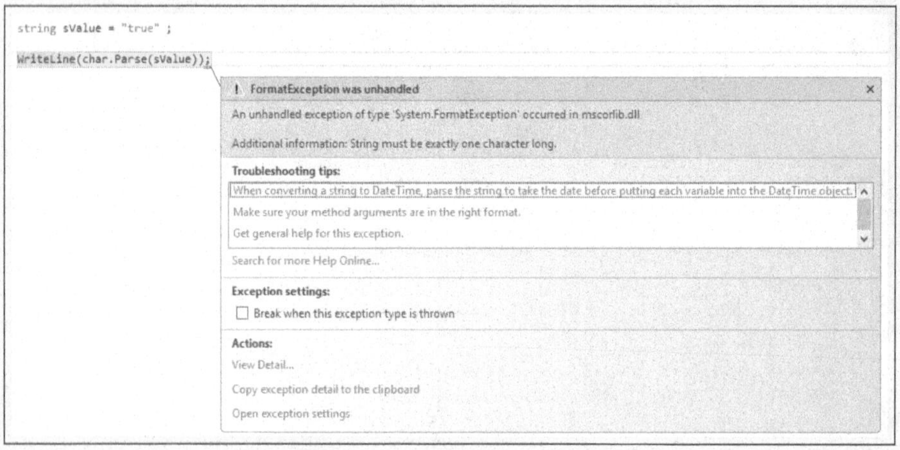

FIGURE 3-6 System.FormatException run-time error

`sValue` is a `string` variable that contains more than one character. The argument to `char`.Parse( ) must be a single-character `string`.

There is more than one way to convert from one base type into another. As part of the .NET FCL, in the `System` `namespace`, a number of `static` methods are found in the `Convert` `class`. These include `Convert.ToDouble( )`, `Convert.ToDecimal( )`, `Convert.ToInt32( )`, `Convert.ToBoolean( )`, and `Convert.ToChar( )`. Used like the `Parse( )` method, they convert data from one base type into another base type. The following converts an entered `string` value into an `int` base type:

```
int newValue = Convert.ToInt32(stringValue);
```

These methods are all overloaded so that the argument to the method can be of varying type. If, for example, you send a `char` argument to the `Convert.ToInt32( )` method and store the result in an `int` variable, you get the Unicode numeric representation for that character.

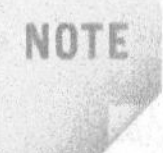

NOTE int.Parse( ) could be replaced by Int32.Parse( ). Int32 is the class in .NET. The int type is an alias for Int32. All .NET-supported languages recognize Int32.

3

You might be wondering whether you should use the Parse( ) methods or methods from the Convert class to convert your string values into their appropriate data types. It is really a matter of choice whichever you use. Both work well if the string is storing the correct data that you are attempting to convert. When you call the Convert.ToInt32( ), it actually calls the Int32.Parse( ) method. Therefore, there is a little more overhead involved in the call to methods in the Convert class. The difference is that if you pass an empty string to the Convert class, it returns 0. If you pass an empty string (null string) to the Int32.Parse( ) method, it creates an error, similar to that illustrated in Figure 3-6, by throwing an ArgumentNullException. You will learn about how to handle exceptions in Chapter 11.

NOTE You might also want to explore the TryParse( ) method. Int32.TryParse( ) attempts to convert a string to an int without throwing an exception.

One advantage the Convert class offers is that it makes it easier to convert between all the base types—not just from a string into another data type. The Parse( ) method only works well for string conversions. For example, Int32.Parse( ) only converts strings into integers. Convert.ToInt32( ) converts any base type into an integer.

Methods in the Math Class

The Math class has a number of predefined static methods you will find helpful. The Math class, such as the Console class, is located in the System namespace. This class provides constants and methods for trigonometric, logarithmic, and other common mathematical functions. The Pow( ) method that you saw previously is a member of the Math class. You learned that the first argument to the Pow( ) method is the base, the number to be raised. The second argument is the exponent, or the specified power value. Table 3-1 identifies, describes, and gives examples of the more commonly used methods from the Math class. The signature and the return type are included in the third column.

TABLE 3-1 Math class methods

Method	Description	Method heading
`Abs`	Returns the absolute value of a specified number. Overloaded—can be used with `int`, `double`, `decimal`, `short`, `float`, `sbyte`, and `long`. Example: `Math.Abs(-88.62)` returns the value `88.62`	`static int Abs(int)`
`Ceiling`	Returns the smallest whole number greater than or equal to the specified number. Example: `Math.Ceiling(88.12)` returns the value `89`	`static double Ceiling(double)`
`Cos`	Returns the cosine of the specified angle measured in radians.	`static double Cos(double)`
`Exp`	Returns e raised to the specified power. e is defined as a constant in the Math `class`. It has a value of 2.7182818284590452354. Example: `Math.Exp(2)` returns the value `7.38905609893065`	`static double Exp(double)`
`Floor`	Returns the largest whole number less than or equal to the specified number. Example: `Math.Floor(88.62)` returns the value `88`	`static double Floor(double)`

(continues)

TABLE 3-1 Math class methods (*continued*)

Method	Description	Method heading
`Log`	Returns the logarithm of a specified number. Two overloaded methods. The first one returns the natural (base e) logarithm of a specified number. It takes a single argument of type `double`. The second one (signature to the right) returns the logarithm of a specified number. Example: `Math.Log(4)` returns the value `1.38629436111989`	`static double Log(double, double)`
`Max`	Returns the larger of two specified numbers. Overloaded with 11 different methods (`byte`, `decimal`, `double`, `short`, `int`, `long`, `sbyte`, `float`, `ushort`, `uint`, and `ulong`). All require the same type for both arguments. Example: `Math.Max(87, 13)` returns `87`	`static double Max(double, double)`
`Min`	Returns the smaller of two numbers. Overloaded—exactly like Max in the previous row. Example: `Math.Min(87, 13)` returns `13`	`static int Min(int, int)`
`Pow`	Returns a specified number raised to the specified power. Not overloaded. Arguments can be entered as `int`. They are implicitly converted. Return value must be stored in `double`; otherwise, you receive a syntax error. Example: `Math.Pow(5, 3)` returns `125`	`static double Pow(double, double)`

(*continues*)

3

TABLE 3-1 Math class methods (*continued*)

Method	Description	Method heading
`Round`	Returns the number nearest the specified value. Overloaded. Can return a number with the specified precision indicated by the second argument, as illustrated with the signature to the right. Example: `Math.Round(87.982276, 4)` returns `87.9823`	`static double Round(double, int)`
`Sign`	Returns a value indicating the sign of a number (–1 for negative values; 1 for positive; and 0 for zero values). Overloaded—each returns an `int`. Argument can be used with `double`, `decimal`, `long`, `short`, `sbyte`, `int`, or `float`. Example: `Math.Sign(46.3)` returns `1`	`static int Sign(double)`
`Sin`	Returns the sine of the specified angle measured in radians	`static double Sin(double)`
`Sqrt`	Returns the square root of a specified number. Return value must be stored in `double`; otherwise, you receive a syntax error. Example: `Math.Sqrt(25)` returns `5`	`static double Sqrt(double)`
`Tan`	Returns the tangent of the specified angle measured in radians.	`static double Tan(double)`

Because each of the methods in Table 3-1 is `static`, calls to them must include the `Math class` name as a qualifier. Or, as noted previously, with Visual Studio 2015, an additional `using static System.Math;` directive must be added at the top of the application.

NOTE You learned about implicit conversion in Chapter 2. C# provides for conversion from smaller data types into larger when you send arguments to methods. For example, implicit conversion occurs from `int` to `long`, `float`, `double`, or `decimal` types. Thus, if the formal parameter enclosed inside the parentheses for the method's heading is a `double`, you can usually send an `int` argument when you call the method. The `int` is converted into a `double` by the CLR.

The following are examples of valid calls to methods of the `Math class`:

```
double aValue = 78.926;
double result1,
       result2;
result1 = Math.Floor(aValue);//result1 = 78
result2 = Math.Sqrt(aValue); //result2 = 8.88403061678651
Write("aValue rounded to two decimal places" + " is {0}",
        Math.Round(aValue, 2));
```

The output for the last statement is

```
aValue rounded to two decimal places is 78.93
```

As you look at the examples using the predefined methods from the `Math class`, you can see that they all have something in common. Each of the methods returns a value. Calls to methods returning values usually are placed in an expression or in an output statement. When the value is returned, there has to be a place for the value to be used.

A `class` can define a `static` method, or a `class` can use a `static` method defined in another `class`. If you are calling a method that is a member of the same `class` from where it is being called, the call statement does not have to include the `class` name. If you are calling a `static` method defined in another `class`, the name of the `class` must be included. When you use the methods in the Math `class`, you are using methods that are defined outside the boundaries of your `class`. `Exp( )` is a `static` member of the `Math class`. In the following example, it returns `e`, the natural logarithmic base, raised to the fifth power. It is necessary to use the `class` name `Math` as a qualifier.

```
double result;
result = Math.Exp(5);
```

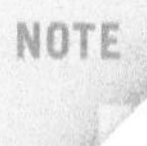

The `Math` `class` also has two `static` data field members defined as constants. A call to `static` field members also requires prefixing the member name with the `class` name. Their declarations follow:

```
const double E = 2.7182818284590452354;
const double PI = 3.14159265358979323846;
```

An example of their use is as follows:

```
circumference = 2 * Math.PI * radius;
```

Calls to value-returning methods must be placed at a location in your code where the value could be accepted when the method is finished. The call can appear anywhere a compatible value of that type can be placed. The statements in Example 3-12 on Lines 4, 5, and 9 illustrate three different places to which the `static` method `Max( )` returns a value.

EXAMPLE 3-12

```
Line 1  int aValue = 200;
Line 2  int bValue = 896;
Line 3  int result;
Line 4  result = Math.Max(aValue, bValue); // result = 896
Line 5  result += bValue * Math.Max(aValue, bValue) - aValue;
Line 6  // result = 896 + (896 * 896 - 200)
Line 7  // result = 803512
Line 8  WriteLine("Largest value between {0} and {1} is {2}", +
Line 9                aValue, bValue, Math.Max(aValue, bValue));
```

The output generated is

```
Largest value between 200 and 896 is 896
```

As given in Table 3-2, the heading for `Max( )` is

```
static int Max(int, int)
```

As shown with the preceding three statements in Lines 4 through 8, values returned from a value-returning method can be returned to any location in your program where a variable of that `return` type can be used. The `int` returned in Line 4 is assigned to `result`. The `int` returned in Line 5 is used as part of an arithmetic expression. The `int` returned in Line 9 is an argument to the `WriteLine( )` method.

Writing Your Own Class Methods

There are many classes containing member methods that make up the .NET FCL. You should explore and make use of them whenever possible. However, for specific tasks relating to building your unique applications, it is often necessary for you to write methods of your own.

The syntax for defining a method follows. The square brackets used with the modifier indicate an optional entry.

3

```
[modifier(s)] returnType MethodName(parameterList)
{
    // body of method - consisting of executable statements
}
```

As noted previously, the `returnType` specifies what kind of information is returned when the body of the method is finished executing. This can be the name of any predefined or user-defined type, such as `int` or `double`. The `returnType` can also be replaced with the keyword `void`. `void` is used to indicate that no value is being returned. Notice that there is only room for one `returnType` per method. Thus, a method can return at most only one value type under its name.

User-defined methods in C# can be classified into two categories:

- Methods that do not return a value, called `void` methods
- Methods that do return a value, called value-returning methods

You will write both types in the sections that follow.

Void Methods

`void` methods are the simplest to write. No `return` statement is needed in the body of the method.

It is permissible to include the `return` keyword as the last statement in a nonvalue-returning method. Some programmers feel this adds to the readability. If you do add a `return` statement, a semicolon is placed after the keyword. No value is sent back with nonvalue-returning methods.

The keyword `void` is used for the `return` type in the heading. Example 3-13 illustrates a nonvalue-returning method. This one does not expect any data to be sent into it. No parameters are included inside the parentheses. The keyword `static` is included so that the methods can be called without instantiating an `object` of the method's `class`.

EXAMPLE 3-13

```
static void DisplayInstructions( )
{
     WriteLine("This program will determine how " +
               "much carpet to purchase.");
     WriteLine( );
     WriteLine("You will be asked to enter the" +
               " size of the room and ");
     WriteLine("the price of the carpet, " +
               "in price per square yards.");
     WriteLine( );
}
```

Nonvalue-returning methods can include parameters. Example 3-14 illustrates a `void` method that requires that data be sent to it when it is called.

EXAMPLE 3-14

```
static void DisplayResults(double squareYards,
                           double pricePerSquareYard)
{
    Write("Total Square Yards needed: ");
    WriteLine("{0:N2}", squareYards);
    Write("Total Cost at {0:C} ", pricePerSquareYard);
    WriteLine(" per Square Yard: {0:C}",
              (squareYards * pricePerSquareYard));
}
```

To call these nonvalue-returning methods, simply enter the method's identifier followed by a set of parentheses. If the method has parameters, the call will include actual arguments inside the parentheses. These methods are `class` methods; they include the `static` keyword in the heading. Calls to methods in Examples 3-13 and 3-14 follow:

```
DisplayInstructions( );
DisplayResults(16.5, 18.95);
```

NOTE The 16.5 and 18.95 could be replaced by `double` variables containing values.

Notice how each of these methods is called without qualifying it with a `class` or `object` name. This is possible when a `static` method is called from within the `class` where it resides as a member. This is different from the calls to methods in other classes, such as `Console` and `Math` classes. Recall you needed to either quality the call to the method with the `class` name and a dot, or add a `using` directive referencing the `class`.

3

Value-Returning Method

Every method that has a `return` type other than `void` must have a `return` statement in the body. A compatible value of the type found in the heading follows the `return` keyword. As stated previously, this `return` does not actually have to appear as the last statement; however, it is good practice to design your methods so they have one entry and one exit. Placing the `return` as the last statement helps you follow this guideline. Example 3-15 illustrates a value-returning method that does not require any arguments. To call this method, no data need to be passed to it.

EXAMPLE 3-15

```
static double GetLength( )
{
     string inputValue;
     int feet,
         inches;
     Write("Enter the Length in feet: ");
     inputValue = ReadLine( );
     feet = int.Parse(inputValue);
     Write("Enter the Length in inches: ");
     inputValue = ReadLine( );
     inches = int.Parse(inputValue);
     return (feet + (double) inches / 12);
}
```

Three variables are declared in the `GetLength( )` method in Example 3-15. They are considered local variables. A local variable exists only inside the method where it is declared. This method is the only place these three variables can be referenced. The term **visible** is often used to indicate where an identifier has meaning and can be used. A variable's life begins with its declaration in a method and ends when it exits the method. **Scope** is very similar to visibility in that it is used to describe where in the program's text the identifier can be used. Thus, the variable's scope covers the location where it is declared to the closing curly brace of the method. The scope of an identifier is simply the region of the program in which that identifier is usable. Scope applies to methods and variables. An attempt to use any of the local variables declared in the `GetLength( )` method in another method results in a syntax error stating that the identifier is unknown.

IntelliSense in Visual Studio will often help you determine when an identifier is visible. If, after typing a dot, you do not see the identifier, it is normally not in scope. Of course, this assumes you have no errors in your program text.

It is possible to use exactly the same name as an identifier for a local variable that has already been used for an instance variable or a parameter identifier. When this happens, the innermost declaration takes scope when you are inside that method. Thus, the local variable would be visible and the other(s) hidden. If, for example, the identifier `feet` is used as a variable in the `Main( )` method and that same identifier, `feet`, is declared as a variable inside the `GetLength( )` method, no syntax error is generated. Instead, the `feet` variable declared in the `GetLength( )` method is visible as long as execution is inside that method. When the method is completed, the `GetLength( ) feet` identifier becomes out of scope. You can think of it as "dying" or no longer existing as soon as the closing curly brace is encountered. As soon as that happens, if control returns back to `Main( )` where the other `feet` is declared, the `Main( )` method's `feet` goes back into scope and becomes visible again.

Be cautious about declaring local variables using a name that is already associated with another variable. This often leads to unreadable code that is more difficult to debug and maintain.

Similar to nonvalue-returning methods, one or more data items can be passed as arguments to these types of methods, as illustrated in Example 3-16.

EXAMPLE 3-16

```
static double DeterminePrice(double squareYards,
                             double pricePerSquareYard)
{
    return (pricePerSquareYard * squareYards); }
}
```

Calls to value-returning methods require a location for the value to be returned. As you saw previously, calls can be placed in assignment statements, output statements, or anywhere a value can be used. If the method has parameters, the call includes the actual data inside the parentheses. Because the `static` keyword appears in the heading, these are still considered `class` methods. Calls to methods in Examples 3-15 and 3-16 follow:

```
double roomLength;
roomLength = GetLength( );
WriteLine("Total cost of the carpet: {0:C}",
          DeterminePrice(squareYards, pricePerSquareYard));
```


An error would be generated if you place a call to a nonvalue-returning method as an argument to the `Write( )` or `WriteLine( )` methods. Both of these methods are expecting to receive a value back from a method so that the value can be displayed. Placing a call to the `DeterminePrice( )` method is an appropriate argument to the `WriteLine( )` method because `DeterminePrice( )` returns a `double`.

Signatures of methods that appeared in Examples 3-13 through 3-16 follow. The signature consists of the name of the method, modifiers, and the formal parameter types.

```
static DisplayInstructions( );
static DisplayResults(double, double);
static GetLength( );
static DeterminePrice(double, double);
```

The complete program listing using the `class` methods introduced as part of the `CarpetExampleWithClassMethods` `class` is shown in Example 3-17. Notice that there is no `GetLength( )` method in the program listing. Instead a method named `GetDimension( )` is used to get both the length and the width. The heading for the method includes a `string` parameter representing which side, length, or width is being entered. This method is called twice. It is called first with the `string` argument of "Length" and second with "Width" as the argument. The value that is returned from the `GetDimension( )` method each time is stored in different variables.

Whenever possible, you should write code that can be reused. Often, if you spend a little extra effort thinking through your design, you can write a generalized solution and reap the benefits later. A simple example of this is writing one method, `GetDimension( )`, to retrieve both the width and the length. It is called two times with different messages or arguments.

EXAMPLE 3-17

```
/* CarpetExampleWithClassMethods.cs
 * Author: Doyle
 * Calculates the total cost of carpet. User
 * inputs room dimensions and carpet price.
 */
using System;
```

```
using static System.Console;
namespace CarpetExampleWithClassMethods
{
     class CarpetExampleWithClassMethods
     {
        static void Main( )
        {
             double roomWidth;
             double roomLength;
             double pricePerSquareYard;
             double noOfSquareYards;
             DisplayInstructions( );
                // Call GetDimension( ) to get the length
             roomLength = GetDimension("Length");
                // Call GetDimension( ) again to get the
                // width
             roomWidth = GetDimension("Width");
             pricePerSquareYard = GetPrice( );
             noOfSquareYards =
                 DetermineSquareYards(roomWidth,
                                      roomLength);
             DisplayResults(noOfSquareYards,
                            pricePerSquareYard);
             ReadKey( );
        }
        static void DisplayInstructions( )
        {
             WriteLine("This program will " +
                       "determine how much " +
                       "carpet to purchase.");
             WriteLine( );
             WriteLine("You will be asked to " +
                       "enter the size of " +
                       "the room ");
             WriteLine("and the price of the " +
                       "carpet, in price per" +
                       " square yds.");
             WriteLine( );
        }
        static double GetDimension(string side )
        {
             string inputValue;// local variables
             int feet,    // needed only by this
                 inches; // method
             Write("Enter the {0} in feet: ",
                   side);
             inputValue = ReadLine( );
             feet = int.Parse(inputValue);
             Write("Enter the {0} in inches: ",
                      side);
```

```
            inputValue = ReadLine( );
            // Note: cast to avoid integer division
            return(feet + (double) inches / 12);
        }
        static double GetPrice( )
        {
            string inputValue; // local variables
            double price;
            Write("Enter the price per " +
                  "Square Yard: ");
            inputValue = ReadLine( );
            price = double.Parse(inputValue);
            return price;
        }
        static double DetermineSquareYards
                    (double width,
                         double length)
        {
            const int SQ_FT_PER_SQ_YARD = 9;
            double noOfSquareYards;
            noOfSquareYards = length * width
                     / SQ_FT_PER_SQ_YARD;
            return noOfSquareYards;
        }
        static double DeterminePrice
                    (double squareYards,
                    double pricePerSquareYard)
        {
            return (pricePerSquareYard *
                       squareYards);
        }
        static void DisplayResults
                    (double squareYards,
                    double pricePerSquareYard)
        {
            WriteLine( );
            Write("Square Yards needed: ");
            WriteLine("{0:N2}", squareYards);
            Write("Total Cost at {0:C} ",
                    pricePerSquareYard);
            WriteLine(" per Square Yard: " +
                      "{0:C}",
                      DeterminePrice(squareYards,
                      pricePerSquareYard));
        }
    }
}
```

Figure 3-7 shows the output produced when the user types 16 feet, 3 inches for `length`; 14 feet, 7 inches for `width`; and 14.95 for `price`.

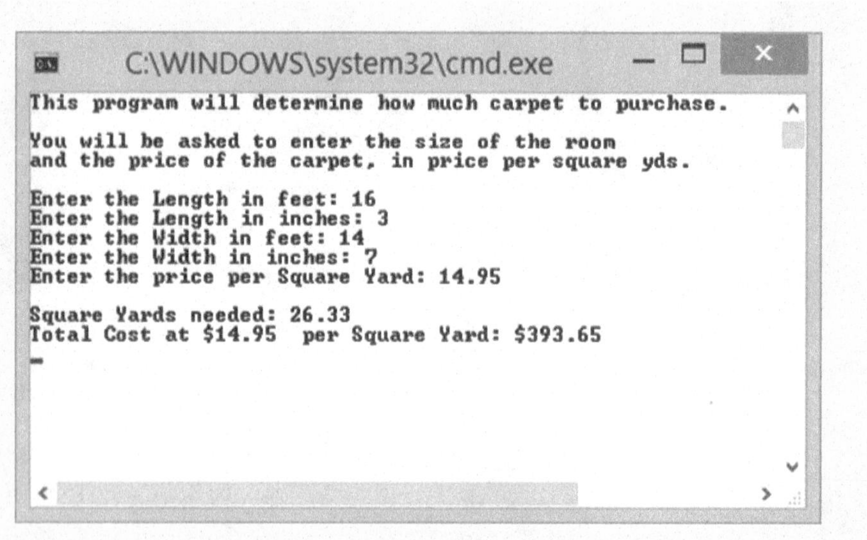

FIGURE 3-7 Output from CarpetExampleWithClassMethods

The **Debug, Start Without Debugging** option (**Ctrl+F5**) holds the output screen without adding the extra call to the `ReadKey( )` method.

The console window screen background and text colors were changed by selecting **Defaults** or **Properties** option from the command window. These selections are revealed by clicking on the icon at the top left corner in the command window. Clear the prompts for input by calling the `Clear( )` method of the `Console class`. This clears the screen and positions the cursor in the top-left corner of the command window.

Types of Parameters

The examples using parameters presented thus far used value parameters. C# offers both call by value and call by reference parameters. Call by value is the default type. With **call by value**, a copy of the original value is made and stored in a separate, different memory location. If the method changes the contents of the variable sent to it, this does not affect the original value stored in the variable from the calling method. The original value is retained when control passes back to the calling method. There are three other types of parameters available in C#:

- `ref`
- `out`
- `params`

The `params` parameter will be discussed when arrays are presented in Chapter 7. The `params` type facilitates sending a varying number of arguments into a method. The other two, `ref` and `out`, are useful now. Earlier, you learned that when a method was called, you could receive only one data type back as a `return` type. This holds true for receiving the value back through the name of the method. Only one `return` type can be specified. However, think about a situation in which you might write a method that allows the user to enter several values. If only one of those values could be returned to the calling segment, how would you decide which one to return? What happens to the other values? If you need a method to return more than one value, the values can be returned through parameters, in particular call by reference parameters. The `ref` and `out` keywords facilitate this process.

Both `ref` and `out` cause a method to refer to the same variable that was passed into the method. Instead of making a copy of the original value and storing the copied value in a different memory location, as happens when you send in a value parameter, when you use `ref` or `out` the method gains access to the original memory location. Both identifiers, the one in the calling method and the identifier in the method, refer to the same area of memory. Any changes made to the data in the method are reflected in that variable when control passes back to the calling method.

When you use the keywords `ref` and `out`, call by reference is assumed. With call by reference, you send the address of the argument to the method. You must include either `ref` or `out` in both the call and in the method's heading parameter list. They must match. In other words, you cannot use `ref` in the heading and `out` in the call. This is different from languages such as C++, in which you just indicate a reference parameter in the method heading. The actual call in C# must also include the keyword.

The keywords differ in that the `ref` keyword cannot be used unless the original argument is initialized before it is sent to the method. This restriction does not exist for `out`. The `out` keyword is useful for methods that allow users to enter the variable's value in a method and have those values available back in the calling method when control returns.

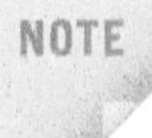

NOTE Java does not have reference parameters. Java's objects simulate call by reference, but the language does not offer call by reference for its primitive types.

All three types, value, `ref`, and `out`, are demonstrated in Example 3-18.

EXAMPLE 3-18

```
/* Parameters.cs
 * Author Doyle
 * This class demonstrates the difference between the
 * default, ref, and out parameter types */

using System;
using static System.Console;

namespace Parameters
{
     class Parameters
     {
            static void Main( )
            {
               int testValue = 1;
               WriteLine("Original Value: {0} ", testValue);

               TestDefault(testValue);
               WriteLine("Upon return from TestDefault " +
                          "Value: {0}", testValue);

               WriteLine( );
               WriteLine("Original Value: {0}", testValue);

               TestRef(ref testValue);
               WriteLine("Upon return from TestRef Value:" +
                          " {0}", testValue);

               WriteLine( );
               // variable not initialized
               // for out parameter type

               int testValue2;
               // however, you cannot display its
               // value yet!
```

```
                // WriteLine("Original Value: {0}", +
                //              testValue2);
                TestOut(out testValue2);
                WriteLine("Upon return from TestOut Value:" +
                        " {0}", testValue2);
                ReadKey( );
            }

            static void TestDefault(int aValue)
            {
                aValue = 111
                WriteLine("Inside TestDefault - Value: {0} ",
                           aValue);
            }

            static void TestRef(ref int aValue)
            {
                aValue = 333;
                WriteLine("In TestRef - Value: {0}",
                           aValue);
            }

            static void TestOut(out int aValue)
            {
                 aValue = 222;
                 WriteLine("In TestOut - Value: {0} ",
                            aValue);

            }
        }
}
```

The output shown in Figure 3-8 illustrates how value parameters remain unchanged. They retain their original value in the calling method. This is because a copy is actually made of the original value. On return to the calling method, the original retained values are visible.

Arguments sent using `ref` and `out` are changed when control is returned to the calling method. The `out` parameter does not have to be initialized before the call; however, the `out` parameter must be assigned a value before the method returns. C# does not allow the use of uninitialized variables.

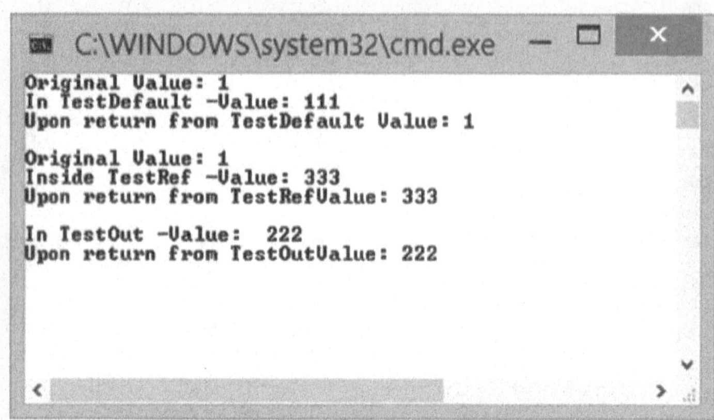

FIGURE 3-8 Output from ParameterClass example

Figure 3-9 illustrates graphically the difference between call by value and call by reference. It also calls attention to the fact that the `out` parameter type does not have to be initialized before the call. Notice that the program statements from Example 3-18 are used for this figure.

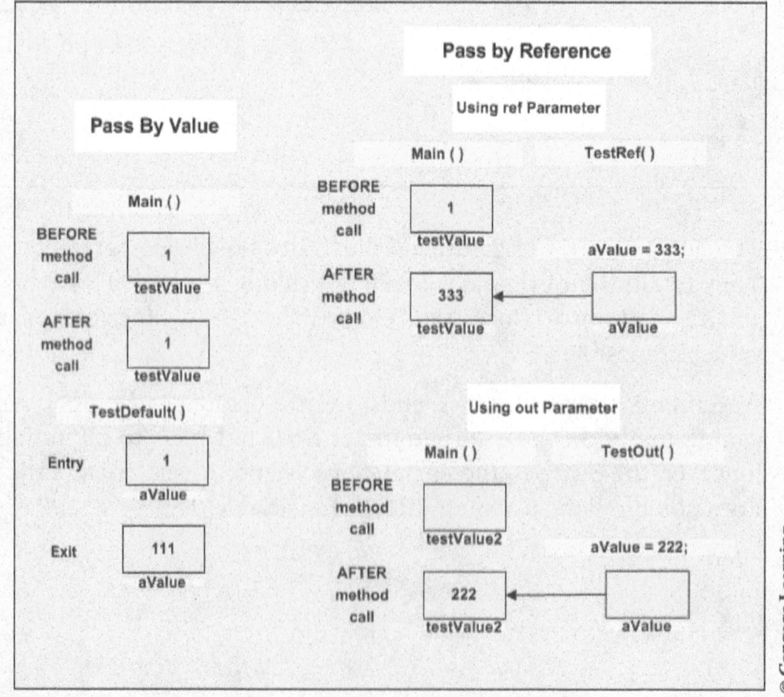

FIGURE 3-9 Call by reference versus value

As you review Example 3-18, notice that the names of the parameters in the method headings differ from the names used as arguments to the call back in the `Main( )` method. This does not present a problem. For the default parameter type, call by value, naming them using a different identifier might help you note that they are referring to two different memory locations. However, you should note, as illustrated in Figure 3-9, `aValue` in the `TestRef ( )` method refers to the same memory location that `testValue` in `Main( )` references. The parameter `aValue` in `TestOut( )` references the same location as `testValue2` in `Main( )`. Calls using the `ref` and `out` keywords, call by reference, can use different identifiers for the parameters in the method heading and the argument in the call. However, they are referencing the same memory location. It would have been appropriate to have used the same name for the parameter identifier as was used for the argument in these calls. Using the same identifiers, when you use the `ref` or `out` keywords, might help you note that they are referring to the same memory locations. When you are designing your solutions, you might want to use the same identifiers for call by reference and different names for call by value parameters.

In the preceding program example, Example 3-18, notice how one of the calls to the `WriteLine( )` method appears as a comment. In Visual Studio, two tools are available that allow you to select a segment of code with only one click, commenting or uncommenting the section. This can be useful during debugging. The icon circled in Figure 3-10 is used for commenting as the ToolTip shows. Uncomment appears to the right.

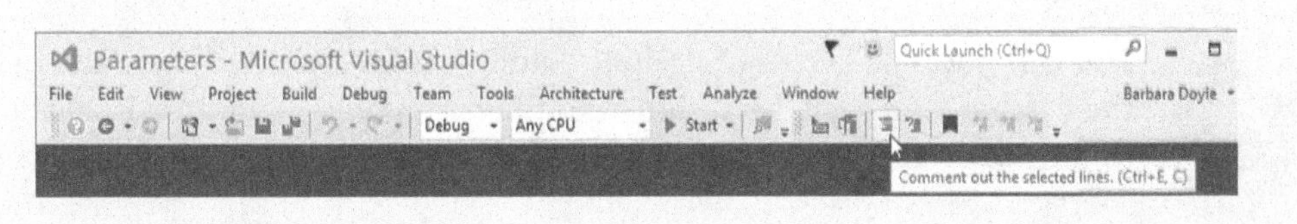

FIGURE 3-10 Visual Studio comment out icon

The lines in the preceding code were commented out to eliminate a syntax error. The contents of `testValue2` could not be displayed until it had a value.

Named and Optional Parameters

With each new version release of C#, new features are introduced. C# 6.0 was introduced with Visual Studio 2015. C# 4.0 included several new features associated with methods. With these new features, you now have the option of naming an argument in a method invocation. This can add to the readability of method calls and also enable you to send in values through using the names of the parameters instead of having to worry about getting the exact order of which argument goes where when you call the method. You may also assign default values to parameters so that a call to the method does not need to send in a value unless it is different from the associated default value. While these features should probably be used sparingly, they are good additions to the language and are discussed in the following sections.

Default Values with Optional Parameters

When you assign a default value to a parameter, it then becomes an optional parameter. You do not have to send in a value every time you call the method. Instead the default value is used if no value is sent in as a parameter. You may have more than one optional parameter associated with a method. However, if you have more than one, the optional parameters must be placed last in the list of parameters, after any required parameters. Example 3-19 illustrates optional parameters with default values.

EXAMPLE 3-19

```
static void DoSomething(string name, int age = 21,
                        bool currentStudent = true,
                        string major = "CS")
{
    // additional program statements go here
}
```

You can now call `DoSomething( )` and send in arguments for the default value or the default values will be assigned to the parameters. Example 3-20 shows valid calls to the `DoSomething( )` method.

EXAMPLE 3-20

```
DoSomething ("Elizabeth Abbott", 20);
DoSomething ("James Gabriel");
DoSomething ("Jonathan Byrle", 25, false, "MS");
```

Default values must be constants. If no arguments are sent for a particular parameter, the default value is used. One of the limitations on using optional parameters is if you need to send in arguments for any of the optional parameters, you must provide arguments for all preceding optional parameters. Thus, the call `DoSomething`

("Gabriella Henson", "MS"); is not a valid call, but DoSomething ("Joe Smith", 20, false); is a valid call. Notice it was not necessary to send a value for the major, but if you need to send a boolean value for currentStudent, you must also send in values for all preceding parameters. In this case, you had to send a value for the optional parameter age.

3

Named Parameters

Named arguments free you from the need to remember or to look up the order of parameters for the method call. The parameter for each argument can be specified using the parameter's name followed by a colon (:) and then the assigned argument's value. Naming parameters also has the added feature that you can send the arguments into the method in any order. Example 3-21 illustrates calls to DoSomething( ) using named parameters.

EXAMPLE 3-21

```
DoSomething (name: "Robert Wiser", age: 20);
DoSomething (name: "Paul Nelson", major: "BIO");
DoSomething (name: "Fredrick Terrell", age: 25, major: "MS");
```

You will notice that optional and named parameters are very useful together. As long as a parameter has a default value, it can be omitted when you use named parameters. You can just supply values for arguments you want to assign new values for.

Optional parameters have been part of Visual Basic for quite a while. With the introduction of C#, 4.0, developers can make use of this feature in C# and also be able to use named parameters.

Optional parameters give you the ability to omit arguments to method invocations, whereas named parameters allow you to specify the arguments by name instead of by position. A lot of material is presented in this chapter. The programming example that follows makes use of most of these new concepts.

PROGRAMMING EXAMPLE: JoggingDistance

This example demonstrates the use of methods in a program. The problem specification is shown in Figure 3-11.

How far do you jog each morning? You prefer to jog in different locations each day and do not have a pedometer to measure your distance. Create an application to determine the distance jogged given the average number of strides ran during the first minute, average number ran during the last minute, and the total minutes jogging.

Design a modularized solution (with methods) to display the distance traveled.

Pedometers measure the distance you run. However, you can also do a good estimate of the distance if you know your foot stride, how many strides you complete per minute, and the number of minutes you jog. Foot stride is the distance covered by one average step length. Since everyone has a different foot size, strides differ. Many people average 3 feet per step when jogging. For this application, assume the foot stride is 2.5 feet. There are 5,280 feet in a mile.

To establish how many strides per minute, allow the user to input the number of strides made during the first minute jogging and the number of strides made during the last minute of jogging. Use the average of those values to represent the strides per minute. Allow the user to input the total time spent jogging in hours and minutes. Write code that will display the distance traveled in miles.

© Cengage Learning

FIGURE 3-11 Problem specification for JoggingDistance example

ANALYZE THE PROBLEM

You should review the problem specification in Figure 3-11 and make sure you understand the problem definition. Several values must be entered into the program. These values must be entered as `string` variables and then parsed into numeric fields, so that arithmetic can be performed.

VARIABLES

Table 3-2 lists the data items needed for the JoggingDistance problem.

TABLE 3-2 Variables for the JoggingDistance class

Data item description	Type	Identifier
Number of strides during first minute	`int`	initialStrideCount
Number of strides during last minute	`int`	finalStrideCount
Jogging time	`int`	hrs, mins, totalMinutes
Average number of strides per minute	`double`	numberOfStepsPerMin
Total distance traveled	`double`	distanceTraveled

CONSTANTS

The stride (feet per step) is set as a constant value. The identifier and preset constant value will be

STRIDE = 2.5.

The number of feet per mile is also set as a constant.

FEET_PER_MILE = 5280;

DESIGN A SOLUTION

The desired output is to display the distance traveled, in miles, for a given jogging session. Figure 3-12 shows a prototype of the desired final output. The xxx.xx is placed in the prototype to represent the location in which the calculated values should appear.

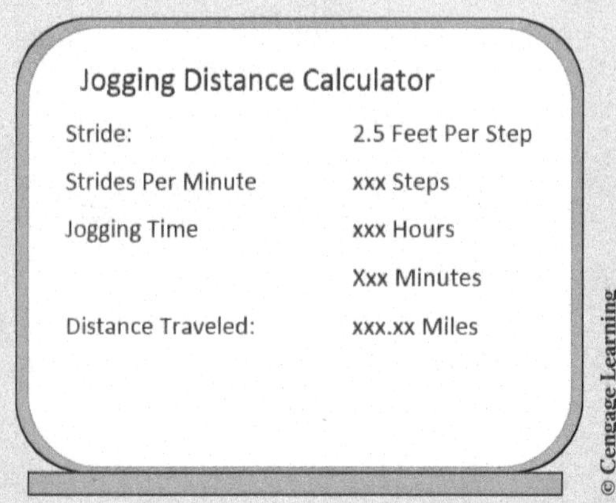

FIGURE 3-12 Prototype

The object-oriented approach focuses more on the `object`. Class diagrams are used to help design and document these characteristics. Figure 3-13 shows the `class` diagrams for the JoggingDistance example.

JoggingDistance
-initialStrideCount : int -finalStrideCount : int -hrs : int -mins : int -totalMinutes : int -numberOfStepsPerMin : double -distanceTraveled : double
+DisplayInstructions() : void +GetNumberStrides(in when : string) : int +InputJoggingTime(out hrs : int, out mins : int) : void +CalculateAvgSteps(in initialStrideCount : int, in finalStrideCount : int) : double +CalculateTime(in hrs : int, in mins : int) : int +CalculateDistance(in numberOfStepsPerMin : double, in totalMinutes : int) : double +DisplayResults(in numberOfStepsPerMin : double, in mins : int, in hrs : int, in distanceTraveled : double) : void

© Cengage Learning

FIGURE 3-13 Class diagram

During design, it is important to develop the algorithm showing the step-by-step process to solve the problem. Structured English, also called pseudocode, is suited for the object-oriented methodology. Seven additional methods, in addition to the `Main( )` method, need to be designed. Figure 3-14 shows the Structured English design for the JoggingDistance example.

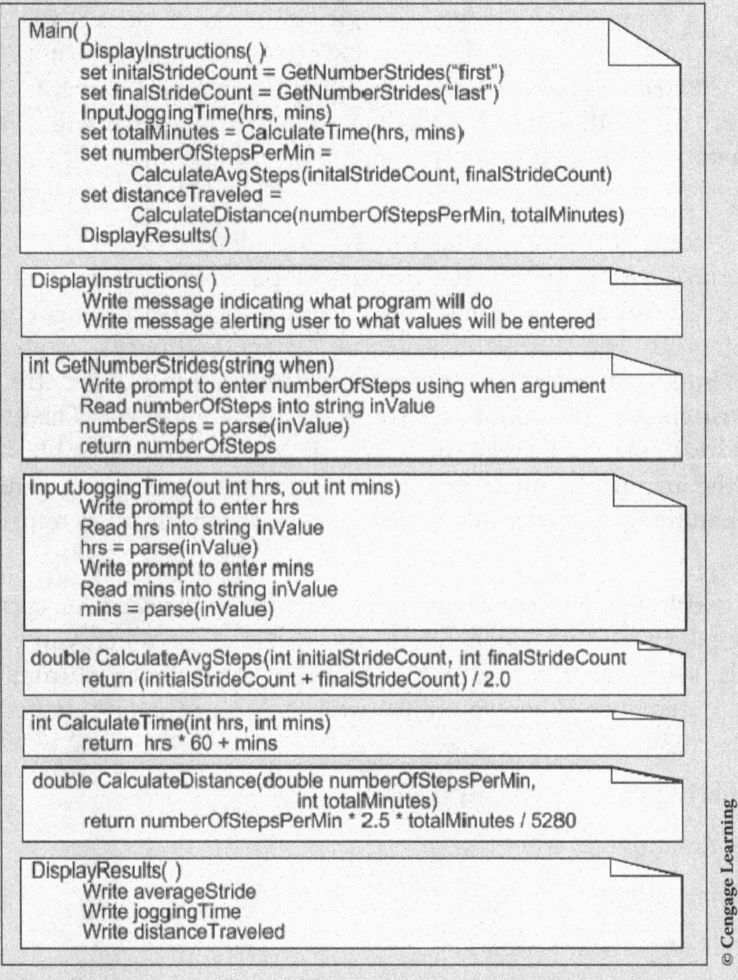

FIGURE 3-14 Structured English for the JoggingDistance example

The methods illustrate both `void` and value-returning operations. Notice that `DisplayInstructions( )`, `InputJoggingTime( )`, and `DisplayResults( )` are all nonvalue-returning methods. When you implement the solution, the keyword `void` appears in their headings. No `return` statement appears in the body of these methods. When the methods' statements are completed, control returns back to `Main( )` from where the methods were invoked.

The other methods (`GetNumberStrides( )`, `CalculateTime( )`, `CalculateAvgSteps( )`, and `CalculateDistance( )`) all return values back to `Main( )`. Instead of having `void` preceding the method name, a data type appears before the method name. This data type describes what will be returned when the method is finished. You also find a `return` statement as the last line in each of these four methods.

Also notice some of the methods have parameters, some do not. The `InputJoggingTime( )` method has two special parameters. A method can only return one value through its name. There can also only be one value following a return statement. The `InputJoggingTime( )` method needs to return hours and minutes both back to `Main( )`. Two separate value-returning methods could have been written. Another option is to use the `out` reference type. This essentially gives the address of the `hrs` and `mins` to the method. Any changes, like inputting values into the memory location, will be available back in `Main( )`. Without the `out` or `ref` parameter type, the values would be lost when control is returned back to `Main( )`.

After the algorithm is developed, the design should be checked for correctness. When you desk check your algorithm, begin in `Main( )`. When you encounter method calls, keep your location in that method, go to the called method, and perform the statements. When you finish with the called method, return back to your saved location.

Test your algorithm with the following data:

Steps during first minute: 185

Steps during last minute: 120

Time spent jogging—Hrs: 1 Min: 12

Use a calculator and write down the results you obtain. After you implement your design, you can compare these results with those obtained from your program output.

CODE THE SOLUTION

After you complete the design and verify the algorithm's correctness, it is time to translate the design into source code.

The final application listing for the file appears here:

```
/* JoggingDistance.cs
 * Author: Doyle
 * This application calculates the jogging distance.
 * Users are asked to enter the number of
 * strides ran during the first and last minute
```

```
 * and the total jogging time. A 2.5 stride is used
 * for calculation.
 */
using System;
using static System.Console;
namespace JoggingDistance
{
    class JoggingDistance
    {
        static void Main(string[] args)
        {
            int initialStrideCount,
                finalStrideCount,
                hrs,
                mins,
                totalMinutes;
            double numberOfStepsPerMin,
                   distanceTraveled;
            DisplayInstructions( );
            initialStrideCount = GetNumberStrides("first");
            finalStrideCount = GetNumberStrides("last");
            InputJoggingTime(out hrs, out mins);
            totalMinutes = CalculateTime(hrs, mins);
            numberOfStepsPerMin = CalculateAvgSteps(
                        initialStrideCount, finalStrideCount);
            distanceTraveled = CalculateDistance(
                        numberOfStepsPerMin, totalMinutes);
            DisplayResults(numberOfStepsPerMin, hrs, mins,
                        distanceTraveled);
            ReadKey( );
        }
        static void DisplayInstructions( )
        {
            WriteLine("How many miles did you jog?");
            WriteLine("Distance (in miles) will be calculated");
            WriteLine("based on stride and number of steps");
            WriteLine("taken per minute. \n");
            WriteLine("You will be asked to enter ");
            WriteLine("your initial and ending strides...");
            WriteLine("OR how many steps you took the ");
            WriteLine("first minute and how many ");
            WriteLine("steps during the last minute.");
            WriteLine("Average stride is calculated " +
            WriteLine("from those entries. \n");
            WriteLine("Calculations are based on a ");
            WriteLine("2.5 feet stride-each step is 2.5 " +
                      "feet long.");
            WriteLine( );
```

```
        WriteLine("\nYou will also be asked " +
        WriteLine("to enter the length ");
        WriteLine("of time (hours and minutes)");
        WriteLine("you jogged.");
        WriteLine( );
        WriteLine("Press any key when you are ready " +
                  "to begin!");
        ReadKey( );
        Clear( );
    }
    static int GetNumberStrides(string when)
    {
        string inputValue;
        int numberOfSteps;
        Write("Enter number of steps taken " +
              "during {0} minute: ", when);
        inputValue = ReadLine( );
        numberOfSteps = int.Parse(inputValue);
        return numberOfSteps;
    }
    static int CalculateTime(int hrs, int mins)
    {
        return hrs * 60 + mins;
    }
    static double CalculateAvgSteps(int initialStrideCount,
                                    int finalStrideCount)
    {
        return (initialStrideCount + finalStrideCount) / 2.0;
    }
    static void InputJoggingTime(out int hrs, out int mins)
    {
        string inputValue;
        WriteLine("\nHow much time did you spend jogging?");
        Write("Hours: ");
        inputValue = ReadLine( );
        hrs = int.Parse(inputValue);
        Write("Minutes: ");
        inputValue = ReadLine( );
        mins = int.Parse(inputValue);
    }
    static double CalculateDistance(double numberOfStepsPerMin,
                                    int totalMinutes)
    {
        const double STRIDE = 2.5;
        const int FEET_PER_MILE = 5280;
        return numberOfStepsPerMin * STRIDE * totalMinutes /
            FEET_PER_MILE;
    }
```

```
        static void DisplayResults(double numberOfStepsPerMin,
                   int hrs, int mins, double distanceTraveled)
        {
            Clear( );
            WriteLine("{0,35}", "Jogging Distance Calculator");
            WriteLine( );
            WriteLine("{0,-25} {1} Feet Per Step ", "Stride:",
                   2.5);
            WriteLine("{0,-25} {1} Steps", "Strides Per " +
                   "Minute: ", numberOfStepsPerMin);
            WriteLine("{0,-25} {1} Hour(s) and {2} Minute(s)", +
                   "Jogging Time:", hrs, mins);
            WriteLine("{0,-25} {1:f2} Miles", "Distance Traveled:",
                   distanceTraveled);
        }
    }
}
```

3

IMPLEMENT THE CODE

Compile the source code. If you have any rule violations, make corrections until no errors are present. Run the application entering the values indicated previously (185, 120, 1, 12).

TEST AND DEBUG

During this final step, test the program and ensure you have the correct result. The output for the test values should match your prototype. Figure 3-15 shows the output generated from the preceding source code.

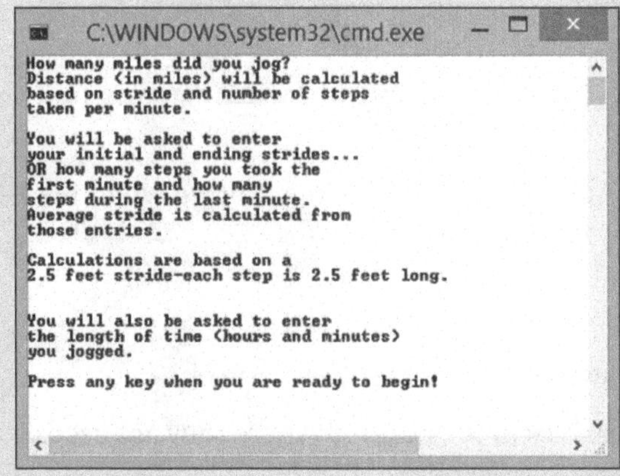

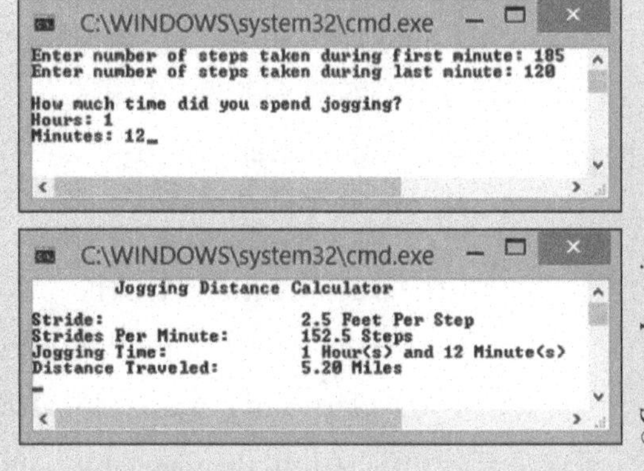

© Cengage Learning

FIGURE 3-15 Output from JoggingDistance example

Coding Standards

It is important to establish and follow good coding standards. The intent of creating a set of coding standards is to have an acceptable list of guidelines that can be followed by all members of a team. The following list of standards is recommended as they relate to methods.

Naming Conventions

- Use Pascal Casing (first character of all words are uppercase; all other characters are lowercase) for method identifiers.
- Use Camel Casing (first character of all words, except the first word, are uppercase; all other characters are lowercase) for local variable identifiers and parameters.
- Use a verb or action clause to name a method. Do not use misleading names. Method names should tell what the method does. If you select a good method name, there is no need for additional documentation explaining what the method does.

Spacing Conventions

- Align curly braces ({ }) up with the method heading.
- Declare each local variable independently on separate lines. It is permissible to reuse the data type, but each variable should be on a separate line.
- There should be one and only one single blank line between each method inside the class.
- Avoid writing long methods. Consider refactoring when the method exceeds 25 lines of code.
- Avoid extremely large source code files. Consider refactoring when the file size exceeds 300–400 lines in a single class.

Declaration Conventions

- Do not have more than one class in a single file.
- Declare and initialize local variables in the method where they are used.
- Try to initialize variables when they are declared.
- Avoid passing too many parameters to a method. If you have more than four to five parameters, it is a good idea to define a class or structure.
- A method should do only one thing: have a single theme.

- Methods that have a return type other than `void` should be invoked from a program statement that can accept a returned value (i.e., assignment statement or output statements).
- Methods should have one entry and one exit.

Commenting Conventions

- Good, readable code will require very few comments. If you use meaningful variables and method names, you will not need many comments.
- Include comments to explain complex or confusing logic in a method that might not be completely understandable.

Resources

Additional sites you might want to explore:

- C# Dev Center—
http://www.csharp.net
- Code Gallery site—
http://code.msdn.microsoft.com
- Methods (C# Programming Guide)—
http://msdn.microsoft.com/en-us/library/ms173114.aspx
- downloadfreetutorial.com—
http://www.downloadfreetutorial.com/how-to-call-a-method-in-c-5-0-with-example-declaration-syntax-with-parameter-tutorial-download

QUICK REVIEW

1. Methods are the members of a `class` that describe the behavior of the data.
2. The `Main( )` method is required for both console and Windows applications.
3. `Main( )` should include the `static` keyword.
4. The heading to a method can consist of modifiers, a `return` type, a method identifier, and parameters. The body of the method is enclosed in curly braces.
5. When the `static` modifier is included with a method, it becomes a `class` method.
6. The `return` type identifies what type of value is returned when the method is completed. Any of the predefined or valid user-defined types can be returned.
7. The `void` keyword specifies that the method does not `return` a value.
8. Many programmers employ the standard convention of using an action verb phrase to name methods.
9. Formal parameters appear in the heading of a method. Actual arguments appear in the call. The actual arguments are the actual data that is sent to the method.

10. The signature of a method consists of the name of the method, modifiers, and the types of its formal parameters. It does not include the `return` type.
11. The `ReadLine( )` method returns all characters up to the current end-of-line terminator, the Enter key. It returns a `string` that must be parsed into a number before the value can be used in arithmetic.
12. Variables declared in the `Main( )` method and other methods are considered local variables and are visible only inside the body of the method in which they are declared.
13. If a value is being returned from a method, such as with an expression or output statement, there must be a location in which the value can be accepted when the method is finished. The call may actually appear at any location where a compatible value of that type can be placed.
14. To call nonvalue-returning methods, simply type the method's name. If the method has parameters, the call includes actual arguments inside the parentheses, without the types.
15. C# offers both call by value and call by reference. Call by value is the default if no keyword is added in the heading. Call by reference is possible through using the `ref` and `out` keywords. They must appear both in the heading and in the call. `ref` requires that the argument be initialized before it is sent.
16. Named arguments enable you to send in values through using the names of the parameters instead of the order of the parameters.
17. When you assign a default value to a parameter, it then becomes an optional parameter.

EXERCISES

1. Which of the following is placed in a method heading to indicate that no value will be returned?
   a. noReturn
   b. `void`
   c. arguments
   d. `static`
   e. `public`
2. Functions or modules found in other languages are similar to __________ in C#.
   a. modifiers
   b. parameters
   c. arguments
   d. methods
   e. classes

3. Which of the following modifiers is the least restrictive?
   a. `private`
   b. `static`
   c. `public`
   d. `internal`
   e. `protected`

4. Which of the following identifiers follows the standard naming convention for a method?
   a. `Calculate Final Grade`
   b. `MilesPerGallon`
   c. `InputValue`
   d. `Report`
   e. `Method1`

5. Which of the following would be the most appropriate way to invoke the predefined `Floor( )` method found in the `Math` `class`?

   ```
   static double Floor (double)
   ```

   a. `answer = Floor(87.2);`
   b. `answer = Math.Floor(87.2);`
   c. `Floor(87.2);`
   d. `Math.Floor(double);`
   e. `Math.Floor(87.2);`

6. Given the following statement, what would be the best heading for the `DetermineAnswer( )` method?

   ```
   int aValue,
       result;
   result = DetermineAnswer(27.83, aValue);
   ```

   a. `void DetermineAnswer(27.83, aValue)`
   b. `int DetermineAnswer( )`
   c. `int DetermineAnswer(double v1, int v2)`
   d. `double int DetermineAnswer( )`
   e. `void DetermineAnswer(double v1, int v2)`

7. After completing the called method's body, control is returned:
   a. back to the location in the calling method that made the call.
   b. to the last statement in the method that made the call.
   c. to the first statement in the method that made the call.
   d. to the `Main( )` method.
   e. to the method that is listed next in the printed source code.

8. Which of the following is a valid method call for `DetermineHighestScore`?

   ```
   void DetermineHighestScore(int val1, int val2)
   ```

   a. `void DetermineHighestScore(int val1, int val2)`
   b. `DetermineScore(int val1, int val2)`
   c. `DetermineHighestScore(val1, val2)`
   d. `DetermineHighestScore(2, 3.5)`
   e. `GetHighestScore( )`

9. What is the signature of the following method?

   ```
   void SetNoOfSquareYards(double squareYards)
   {
       noOfSquareYards = squareYards;
   }
   ```

   a. `void SetNoOfSquareYards(double squareYards)`
   b. `SetNoOfSquareYards(double squareYards)`
   c. `SetNoOfSquareYards`
   d. `void SetNoOfSquareYards(double)`
   e. `SetNoOfSquareYards(double)`

10. Variables needed only inside a method should be defined as:
    a. `private` member data
    b. local variables
    c. properties
    d. arguments
    e. parameters

11. Given the call to the method `ComputeCost( )` shown below, which of the following would be the most appropriate heading for the method? The variable `someValue` is declared as an `int`.

```
someValue = ComputeCost(27.3);
```

a. `static void ComputeCost(double aValue)`

b. `static int ComputeCost( )`

c. `static double ComputeCost(int someValue)`

d. `static int ComputeCost(double aValue)`

e. `static int ComputeCost(int aValue)`

3

12. The following is probably an example of a ________.

```
DisplayInstructions( );
```

a. call to a value-returning method

b. call to a void method

c. method heading

d. method definition

e. call to a method with multiple arguments

13. If you follow the standard C# naming conventions, the local variable names:

a. follow the Camel case convention.

b. should use an action verb phrase.

c. begin with an uppercase character.

d. are named like namespace identifiers.

e. are defined inside parenthesis of the method header.

14. Which of the following would be a valid call to a method defined as shown below?

```
static void InitializeValues( )
```

a. `void InitializeValues( );`

b. `WriteLine(InitializeValues( ));`

c. `int returnValue = InitializeValues( );`

d. `InitializeValues( );`

e. `InitializeValues(aVariable );`

15. Given the following `method` definition, what would be a valid call? The variable `someIntValue` is defined as an `int`.

    `static int GetData(out int aValue, ref int bValue)`

    a. `someIntValue = GetData(aValue, bValue);`

    b. `someIntValue = GetData(out aValue, ref bValue);`

    c. `someIntValue = GetData(out, ref);`

    d. `someIntValue = GetData(int out aValue, int ref bValue);`

    e. `GetData(out aValue, ref bValue);`

16. If a method is to be used to enter two values that will be used later in the program, which of the following would be the most appropriate heading and call?

    a. heading: `void InputValues(out int val1, out int val2)` call: `InputValues(out val1, out val2);`

    b. heading: `void InputValues(int val1, int val2)` call: InputValues(val1, val2);

    c. heading: `void InputValues(ref int val1, ref int val2)` `call: InputValues(ref val1, ref val2);`

    d. heading: `int int InputValues( )` call: `val1 = InputValues( );` `val2 = InputValues( );`

    e. none of the above

17. Which of the following is *not* a modifier in C#?

    a. `int`

    b. `private`

    c. `public`

    d. `static`

    e. `protected`

18. Given the following task, which would be the most appropriate method heading? A method displays three integer values formatted with currency.

    a. `static int int int DisplayValues( )`

    b. `static int DisplayValues(int v1, int v2, int v3)`

    c. `static void DisplayValues( )`

    d. `static void DisplayValues(int v1:C, int v2:C, int v3:C)`

    e. `static void DisplayValues(int v1, int v2, int v3)`

19. Given the following task, which would be the most appropriate method heading? A method receives three whole numbers as input. The values represent grades. They should be unchangeable in the method. The method should return the average with a fractional component.

a.
```
static double DetermineGrade(int grade1, int grade2, int
                             grade3)
```

b.
```
static int DetermineGrade(int grade1, int grade2,
                          int grade3)
```

c.
```
static int DetermineGrade(double finalAverage)
```

d.
```
static double DetermineGrade(ref int grade1,
                             ref int grade2,
                             ref int grade3)
```

e.
```
static void DetermineGrade( )
```


20. Given the following task, which would be the most appropriate method heading? Results have been calculated for `taxAmount` and `totalSales`. Write a method heading that accepts these values as input for display purposes.

a.
```
static DisplayResults( )
```

b.
```
DisplayResults(double)
```

c.
```
static void DisplayResults( )
```

d.
```
static void DisplayResults(double taxAmount,
                           double totalSales)
```

e.
```
static void DisplayResults(taxAmount, totalSales)
```

---

21. Use the following method headings to answer the questions below:

```
static int DetermineResult(int value1, ref double value2)
static void DisplayResult(int value1, double value2)
static int GetValue( )
```

a. How many parameters does each method have?

b. What is the `return` type for each of the methods?

c. Which of the preceding methods will have a `return` statement as part of its body?

22. Write methods to do the following:
    a. Display three full lines of asterisks on the screen.
    b. Accept as an argument your name, and display that value along with an appropriate label.
    c. Accept two floating-point values as arguments. Display the values formatted with three digits to the right of the decimal.
    d. Accept three `int` arguments and return their sum.

23. Write statements to invoke each of the methods defined above in Exercise 22.

24. What will be produced from the following predefined `Math` `class` method calls?
    a. `WriteLine(Math.Pow(4,3));`
    b. `WriteLine(Math.Sqrt(81));`
    c. `WriteLine(Math.Min(-56, 56));`

25. The following program has several syntax errors as well as style inconsistencies. Identify a minimum of five syntax errors and three style violations. For an added challenge, correct all errors.

```
/*************************************
using System;
namespace ErrorExample
{
class ErrorExample
{
static void Main( )
      {
      int VAL1;
      string aValue;
      val1 = GETVal1(aValue);
      WriteLine("value entered, plus one is  {0}",
               ++val1);
      Readkey( );
     }
     static GETVal1( )
     {
           Write("Enter a value: ");
           aValue = readline( );
           val1 = int.Parse(aValue);
           return int VAL1;
     }
}
}
```

PROGRAMMING EXERCISES

1. Design a message display application which will allow users to enter their name and favorite saying. Begin by providing instructions to the user about what the application will be requesting. Include one method for input. Invoke the input method two times. First call the method asking for the person's name. Send a `string` argument indicating what value should be entered. Invoke the method a second time to retrieve the favorite saying. Return the string values back to the `Main( )` method. Call another method, sending the name and saying. From that method, display the message showing the person's name and their saying surrounded by rows of greater than/less than symbols(<><><>).

2. Write an application that includes two additional methods in addition to the `Main( )` method. One method should return a string consisting of four or five lines of information about your school. The other method should return a string consisting of asterisks. First call the method that returns the string of asterisks. Call the method that returns the asterisk a second time after you invoke the method that displays the information about your school. Items you might include are the name of your school, number of students enrolled, and school colors. Include appropriate labels. The display should be aesthetically pleasing so include enough asterisks to surround your listing.

3. Write an application that allows a user to input the height and width of a rectangle. It should output the area and perimeter of the rectangle. Use methods for entering the values, performing the computations, and displaying the results. Results should be formatted with one position to the right of the decimal and printed number aligned in a tabular display.

4. Design an application using methods that convert an integer number of seconds into an equivalent number of hours, minutes, and seconds. Use methods for entering the initial seconds, performing the computations, and displaying the results. You should have separate methods for each computation. Results should be formatted and printed in a tabular display with the values number aligned.

5. Write a program that converts a temperature given in Fahrenheit into Celsius. Allow the user to enter values for the original Fahrenheit value. Display the original temperature and the formatted converted value. Number align values. Use appropriate methods for entering, calculating, and outputting results.

6. Write a program that can be used to convert meters into feet and inches. Allow the user to enter a metric meter value in a method. Provide input,

calculation, and display methods. Be sure to provide labels for values and number align them.

7. Write a program that can be used to determine the tip amount that should be added to a restaurant charge. Allow the user to input the restaurant charge, before taxes. Produce output showing the calculated values including the total amount due for both 15% and the 20% tips. Tax of 9% should be added to the bill before the tip is determined. Write appropriate methods for your solution. Display subtotal showing the amount owed prior to applying a tip. Show each tip amount and the totals with each tip amount. Be sure to provide labels for values and number align them.

8. Write a program that computes the amount of money the computer club will receive from proceeds of their granola bar sales project. Allow the user to enter the number of cases sold and the sale price per bar. Each case contains 12 bars; each case is purchased at $5.00 per case from a local vendor. The club is required to give the student government association 10% of their earnings. Display instructions to the user about the application. Display all inputs and calculated values. Proceeds should be formatted with currency. Modularize your solution by writing appropriate methods.

9. Write a program that calculates and prints the take-home pay for a commissioned sales employee. Allow the user to enter values for the name of the employee and the sales amount for the week. Employees receive 7% of the total sales as their commission. Use 18% as the federal tax rate. Retirement contribution is 15%. Use 9% as the social security tax rate. Define appropriate constants. Write input, display, and calculation methods for each of the deductions. Your final output should display all calculated values, including the total deductions and all defined constants.

10. Write an application that helps landowners determine what their property tax will be for the current year. Taxes are based on the property's assessed value and the annual millage rate. The established millage rate for the current year is $10.03 per $1000 value. Homeowners are given a $25,000 exemption, which means they may subtract $25,000 from the assessed value prior to calculating the taxes. Enable users to enter the property address and the prior year's assessed value. The township has decided to increase all properties' assessed value 2.7% for the current year to add additional monies to the school budget line. Provide methods to compute and return the new assessed value and the proposed taxes for the current year. Provide another method that displays the formatted values.

CHAPTER 4

© zeljkodan/Shutterstock.com

Creating Your Own Classes

IN THIS CHAPTER, YOU WILL:

- Become familiar with the components of a class
- Write instance methods and properties used for object-oriented development
- Create and use constructors to instantiate objects
- Call instance methods including mutators and accessors
- Become familiar with auto property initializers
- Work through a programming example that illustrates the chapter's concepts

In Chapter 3, you examined the anatomy of methods. You learned how to invoke predefined methods and how to write methods that performed some type of specific processing. You wrote methods that returned results and methods that performed procedures without returning a value. You learned how to pass arguments to methods and about the different types of parameters that can be used with methods. In this chapter, you learn how to design classes that include data, method, and property members. You begin by examining concepts as they relate to object-oriented development.

The Object Concept

C# is an object-oriented language. All the code that you wrote for your applications has been placed in a `class`. Thus far, you have not really taken advantage of the object-oriented approach to systems development.

To use an object-oriented approach, the solution is defined in terms of a collection of cooperating objects. Each of the objects is capable of sending messages to other objects and receiving messages from objects. Each object is also capable of processing data. In the simplest terms, you can think of the object as a separate little machine with distinct capabilities. The machine receives a message, it performs its intended role, and then it sends back a message indicating it is finished. This message coming back might also include results from some type of processing.

Recall that an **object** is one instance or example of a class. You cannot create an object until its structure is defined. This is done through defining a class. So, a **class** is like a template. It defines the structure for all objects that are going to be of that class type. When you define the class, you describe its **attributes**, or characteristics or fields, in terms of data and its behaviors, or methods, in terms of what kinds of things it can do. Once a class is created, it can be viewed as a new customized data type, similar to an `int` or a `double`. To define, for example, a `Car` `class`, you might include attributes shared by all cars, such as color, manufacturer, and model year. All cars also have the ability to start, stop, and show fuel consumption. These behaviors become the methods of the `Car` `class`. One example of a car is a Corvette. The `Corvette` might be a red 2016 model with, of course, the abilities to start, stop, and show its fuel consumption. The `object` 2016 `Corvette` then is an instance of the `Car` `class` and the set of values for its attributes is called its state. The red `Corvette` `object` has the abilities or behaviors of starting, stopping, and showing fuel consumption. These behaviors `Start( )`, `Stop( )`, and `ShowFuelConsumption( )` are its methods.

Remember that one of the underlying assumptions of the object-oriented methodology is that a number of entities exist in our world, in our environment that can be identified and described. An **entity**, usually associated with a person, place, or thing, is normally a noun. The entity can be defined in terms of its current state and behaviors. By abstracting out the attributes (data) and the behaviors (processes on the data), you can create a `class` to serve as a template from which many objects of that type can be instantiated. Then, just as you declare objects of the `int` type and use all its predefined methods, after you define your own classes, you can declare objects of your user-defined types and use the methods that you define.

To program an object-oriented solution, a few new concepts are needed. You read about one type of modifier, static, in Chapter 3. Another type of modifier, access modifiers, specifies the level of accessibility for types and their members. C# includes the following accessibility modifiers:

- `public`
- `protected`
- `internal`
- `protected internal`
- `private`

4

Public access offers the fewest access limitations; there are basically no restrictions on accessing `public` members or classes. Notice in Example 4-1 that the `class` definition includes the `public` access modifier. By specifying a `public` access, other classes can reuse your classes in different applications.

Private is the most restrictive access modifier. Private members are accessible only within the body of the `class` in which they are declared. Often in object-oriented design, data is defined with a `private` modifier and methods that access the data are declared to have `public` access. By defining the data members as `private`, you restrict access to the data through the members' methods or properties that you will learn about in this chapter.

Table 4-1 presents the different accessibility levels of access modifiers.

TABLE 4-1 C# access modifiers

Modifiers	Explanation of accessibility
`public`	No restrictions
`protected`	Limited to the containing `class` or classes derived from the containing `class`
`internal`	Limited to current project
`protected internal`	Limited to current project or classes derived from `class`
`private`	Limited to containing `class`

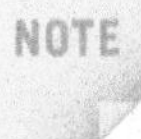

When a `class` or a `class` member does not specify a modifier, the default accessibility level of `private` is assumed.

With object-oriented development, instead of thinking about what processes need to be programmed, begin by determining what objects are needed in the solution. From that, determine what data characteristics will belong to the objects and what kind of behaviors the data will need to perform. When you are defining a `class`, you find that there are common features that are included with your object-oriented solutions, as described in the following sections.

Private Member Data

You learned in Chapter 2 to declare variables. Those variables were defined inside the `Main( )` method. In Chapter 3, you saw how methods other than `Main( )` could define local variables. The variables declared in these methods and in `Main( )` were only visible inside the body of the method in which they were declared. When you define a `class` and determine what data members it should have, you declare **instance variables** or **fields** that represent the state of an `object`. These fields are declared inside the `class`, but not inside any specific method. They become visible to all members of the `class`, including all of the method members. Consider Example 4-1.

EXAMPLE 4-1

```
public class Student
{
      private string studentNumber;
      private string studentLastName;
      private string studentFirstName;
      private int score1;
      private int score2;
      private int score3;
      private string major;
```

Example 4-1 defines a blueprint for `Student` in terms of what kinds of data will be associated with each Student. No actual data is stored with the data members. There might be thousands of students associated with this class definition. Each of the students has different values for their `studentNumber`, `studentFirstName`, `studentLastName`, `score1`, `score2`, `score3`, and `major`. No compile-time initialization, or assignment of initial values, is added to the data member declaration like you did with variables defined in the `Main( )` method. Instead you simply identify what characteristics all students will include. You define the template or the blueprint for the class.

Normally, the data members are defined to have a `private` access. This enables the `class` to protect the data and allow access to the data only through the `class` member methods or properties. Look ahead to Figure 4-3. Figure 4-3 illustrates where the fields or data members (instance variables) are declared. As shown, data fields are declared first inside the body of the class definition. There are a number of tools available in Visual Studio to aid in the development of applications. To add a second class to your solution, use the **File, New, File, Visual C# class** menu or the **Solution Explorer Window**. In the **Solution Explorer Window**, if you select your project file and right-mouse click, the option **Add Class** will be available. **Add Class** is also an option from the **Project** menu. New classes added will not include another `Main( )` method. Only one `Main( )` method can be associated with each solution/project.

When you first create your project, append `App` onto the end of the project or solution name. This will enable you to know where the `Main( )` method is located. For example, when you initially set up a project that will include a `Student class`, the solution will be called `StudentApp`. The `StudentApp.cs` file will now hold the `Main( )` method. You then add another `class` to the `StudentApp` project, called `Student`. The `Student.cs` file will hold your template for student objects.

4

After a project has been created and a new class added to your application, the **Solution Explorer Window** enables you to create a class diagram. When you right-click on the source code file, one option is to **View Class Diagram**. Once the diagram is opened you can define the template for the class without writing any code. Figure 4-1 shows a class diagram for the `Student class` created with Visual Studio.

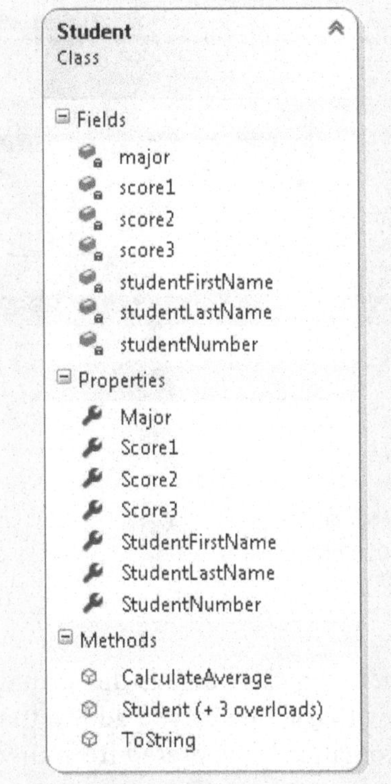

FIGURE 4-1 Student class diagram created in Visual Studio

After the class diagram is created, add the names of data members or fields and methods using the **Class Details** section. Data types can be selected from a drop-down menu. By default, data members or fields are assigned a `private` access modifier. Figure 4-2 shows a snapshot of the Class Diagram tool.

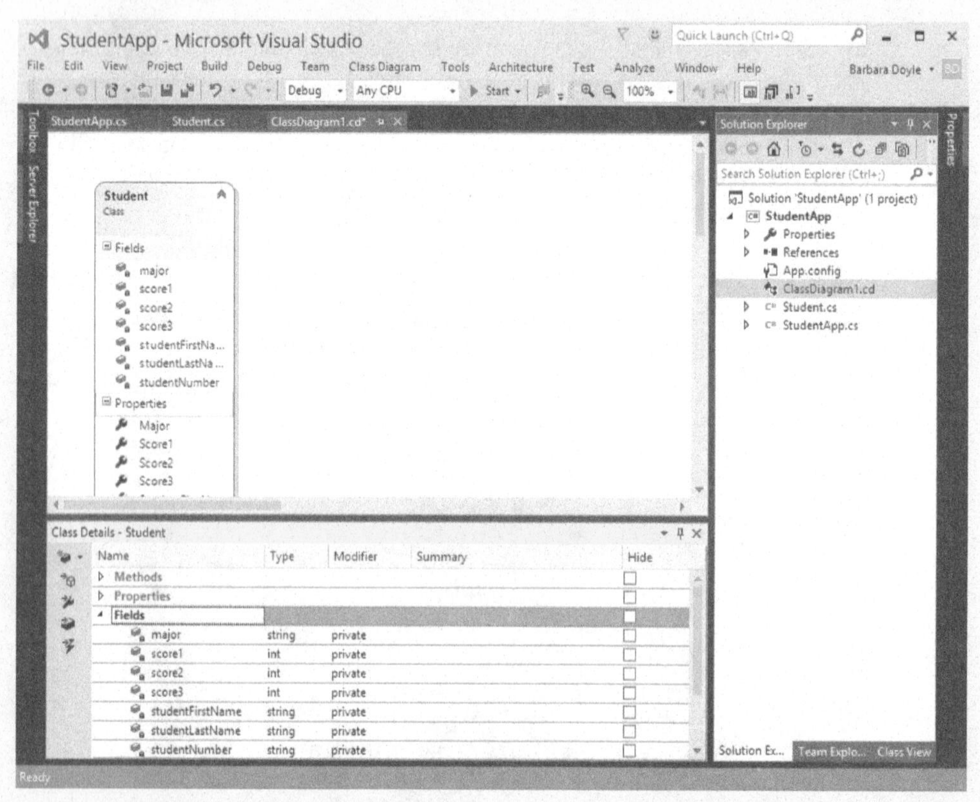

FIGURE 4-2 Student class diagram details

If the **Class Details** pane is not visible, right clicking on the class diagram reveals an option to open the pane.

When you complete the class details illustrated in Figure 4-2, code is automatically placed in the file with each entry you add to the class diagram. Figure 4-3 shows the code that was automatically generated from the Student class diagram.

```
public class Student
{
    //Data members, data fields, or characteristics
    private string studentNumber;
    private string studentLastName;
    private string studentFirstName;
    private int score1;
    private int score2;
    private int score3;
    private string major;

    //Default constructor
    public Student()...

    //Constructor with one argument
    public Student(string sID)...

    //Constructor with three arguments
    public Student(string sID, string lastName, string firstName)...

    //Constructor with six arguments
    public Student(string sID, string lastName, string firstName,
                   int s1, int s2, int s3, string maj)...

    //Properties
    public string StudentLastName...

    public string StudentFirstName...

    public string StudentNumber...

    public string Major...

    public int Score1...
```

FIGURE 4-3 Auto-generated code from Student class diagram

Using the Class Diagram tool in Visual Studio gives you the added benefit of graphically viewing the class. You can define the template for the class just using the code editor as was done with previous applications. However, if you use the Class Diagram tool, you can also switch back and forth between the class diagram and the code window. Each has a separate tab. You will notice in Figure 4-2 that **Solution Explorer** window reveals that file that holds the class diagram has a .cd extension.

Figure 4-3 illustrated where the fields or data members (instance variables) are declared. As illustrated in Examples 4-1 and 4-2, data fields are normally declared first inside the body of the `class` definition. In the examples that follow, the `CarpetCalculator`, from Chapter 3, is revisited using an object-oriented approach.

EXAMPLE 4-2

```
public class CarpetCalculator
{
      private double pricePerSqYard;
      private double noOfSqYards;
:     // The : indicates other lines follow.
```

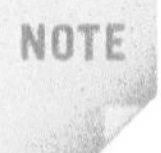

Notice that the `public` access modifier was added to the `class` heading. This will enable the `class` to be referenced outside this file.

Constructor

Constructors are special types of methods used to create objects. Object-oriented design of applications facilitates reuse of code. After the `class` is defined, you create instances, or examples, of the `class`. This is called **instantiating** the `class`. An instance of a `class` is called an `object`. When you instantiate the `class`, you actually create an instance of the `class`, an `object` that takes up space and exists. It is through this special type of method, called a **constructor**, that you create instances of a `class`. Constructors differ from other methods in two ways:

- Constructors do not return a value, but the keyword `void` is *not* included.
- You receive an error message if you type `void` as part of the constructor method heading.
- Constructors use the same identifier (name) as the `class` name.
- Constructors are methods. Similar to other methods, they can be overloaded.

A `public` access modifier is always associated with constructors so that other classes can instantiate objects of their type. When you write a `class`, a constructor is automatically created for you if you do not explicitly define one. This one is called the default constructor. It has no functionality, other than the fact that it can be used to create an instance of the `class`. Default values are assigned to each member data field if the default constructor is used to create an `object` of the `class` type. No parameters are included with the default constructor. It has no body, simply opening and closing curly braces. For a `class` called `Student`, a default constructor is shown here:

```
public Student ( )
{
}
```

Constructors are used to provide initial values for the object's data members. These initial values can be sent as arguments to the constructor method, or the initial values can be hard coded in the body for the constructor. To add full functionality to your classes, you normally write multiple constructors for all classes in which objects will be instantiated. When you explicitly write even one constructor for a class, you lose the default one that is created automatically. When you write your constructors, think about how objects will be created of that `class` type. If you had a `Student class`, you might want a constructor that lets you create a `Student object` when a `studentNumber` is given. You might want another constructor that lets you create a `Student object` when a `studentNumber` and `studentFirstName` and `studentLastName` are given. Another constructor might be useful if you had all of the data (`studentNumber`, `studentFirstName`, `studentLastName`, `score1`, `score2`, `score3`, and `major`). Thus, for a `Student class`, at least four constructors might be designed, as shown in Example 4-3.

4

EXAMPLE 4-3

```
//Default constructor
public Student ( )
{
}

//Constructor with one parameter
public Student (string sID )
{
     studentNumber = sID;
}

//Constructor with three parameters
public Student (string sID, string firstName,
                string lastName)
{
     studentNumber = sID;
     studentFirstName = firstName;
     studentLastName = lastName;
}

//Constructor with all data members
public Student (string sID, string firstName, string lastName,
                int s1, int s2, int s3, string maj)
{
     studentNumber = sID;
     studentFirstName = firstName;
     studentLastName = lastName;
     score1 = s1;
     score2 = s2;
     score3 = s3;
     major = maj;
}
```

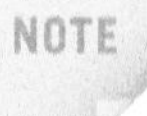

You should design your classes to be as flexible and full-featured as possible. One way to do this is to include multiple constructors. However, it is not appropriate to simply attempt to define a constructor for every possible combination of data members. Identify and design the proper number of constructors based on how other classes might want to instantiate objects of that class.

Notice that the first constructor shown in Example 4-3 is one that takes no arguments. This is the default constructor. As previously noted, you lose the default constructor that is automatically generated when you start writing your own constructors. However, you will normally want to offer the flexibility of allowing an object of your class to be instantiated without any arguments. This is where the default constructor is needed. So, you need to create one.

The body of the constructor methods consists primarily of assignment statements. Notice that the private data member identifier appears on the left side of the equal symbol. A different name, from the data member, is used as a parameter identifier. This is done to avoid using the `this` keyword to reference the data member. You will read more about `this` in upcoming chapters.

Examine the second constructor in Example 4-3. The data member `studentNumber` is assigned the value stored in `sID`. When an object of the class is instantiated using that constructor, data will be passed into the constructor through `sID`.

A fifth constructor could not be designed with the first argument being `firstName`, the second argument being `lastName` followed by the `string` for the `sID`. Its signature would not be different from the constructor that has the `sID` parameter listed first. As with overloaded methods, signatures must differ for constructors. You also could not have one constructor that has the two `string` parameters of `firstName` and `lastName` and then define another constructor that took `string` parameters of `lastName` and `firstName`. Their signatures would be the same. Both would have two strings for their parameter list.

When you write your own default constructor, it does not have parameters. But, it does not have to have an empty body. There could be assignment statements added to a default constructor. These parameterless constructors are useful for assigning default values to data members.

Example 4-4 shows three constructors for the `CarpetCalculator` `class`.

EXAMPLE 4-4

```
// Constructor with no parameters – Default constructor
public CarpetCalculator( )
{
     //empty body
}

// Constructor with one parameter
public CarpetCalculator(double price)
{
     pricePerSqYard = price;
}

// Constructor with two parameters
public CarpetCalculator(double amountNeeded, double price)
{
   noOfSqYards = amountNeeded;
   pricePerSqYard = price;
}
```


All three constructors used the same identifier, that is, the name of the `class`. They each have different signatures. One requires no arguments, one requires one argument, and the third requires two arguments. By writing three separate constructors, more flexibility is offered an application that chooses to use this `class`. An `object` of the `class` can be created by giving a price and the number of square yards needed; an `object` can be created sending it just the price; or, an `object` can be created without any arguments.

It might seem like overkill to write a method that does not have a body, but this is a common practice. If you define at least one constructor, you should write another constructor that takes no arguments, the default constructor. Otherwise, you are limiting the functionality of your `class`. By having a constructor with no arguments, you can create instances of the `class` without setting the current state of its data members. For instance, you can create an object with default values and later give the object other values. When this happens, the default values for the specific types are used. You might want to look ahead at Example 4-11. It illustrates calling or invoking these `CarpetCalculator` constructors.

Writing Your Own Instance Methods

When you define the methods of the class, you are writing instance methods. Instance methods do not use the `static` keyword in their heading. To call an instance method, however, an `object` must be instantiated and associated with the method. There are several special types of methods. They are described in the sections that follow.

Accessor

Another type of special method is an **accessor**. To read the current state or value of an `object` member's data, accessors can be used. Accessors are also referred to as **getters**. They send back the value of a data member, without changing it. Accessors are used because instance variables, data members of a `class`, are normally defined using a `private` modifier. As you read earlier in this chapter, `private` limits access to members of the `class`. However, the idea behind object-oriented development is that objects communicate with each other by exchanging information. Objects that are instances of one `class` might need to access members of another `class`. They do this through calling methods. Because methods are usually defined as `public`, this communication is possible.

An accessor normally returns just the current value of a data member so that the current value can be used by other classes. Many bodies of accessor methods consist of a single `return` statement, as illustrated in Example 4-5.

EXAMPLE 4-5

```
public double GetNoOfSqYards( )
{
    return noOfSqYards;
}
```

NOTE

Java programmers often include an accessor method for each `private` data member that is to be accessible from outside the `class`. This is unnecessary in C#. Property members can be defined. This reduces the number of accessors needed. You will learn about properties later in this chapter.

A standard naming convention is to add "Get" onto the front of the instance variable identifier and use that name for the accessor method name that retrieves the data item. Example 4-5 shows an accessor method for `noOfSqYards`. The identifier for the accessor is `GetNoOfSqYards( )`.

Mutators

To change the current state or value of an `object` member's data, special methods called mutators can be used. **Mutators** are sometimes called **setters**. A mutator is normally written to include one parameter that represents the new value a data member should have. Similar to accessors, mutators are needed because of the `private` accessibility of instance variables. Example 4-6 shows two overloaded mutators.

The first example is the more common way to write a mutator. The body of the method consists of a single assignment statement.

EXAMPLE 4-6

```
public void SetNoOfSqYards(double squareYards)
{
     noOfSqYards = squareYards;
}
public void SetNoOfSqYards(double length, double width)
{
     const int SQ_FT_PER_SQ_YARD = 9;
     noOfSqYards = length * width / SQ_FT_PER_SQ_YARD;
}
```


NOTE Property members also reduce the number of mutators needed.

A standard naming convention is to add "Set" to the front of the instance variable identifier; that name becomes the mutator method name. In Example 4-6, the instance variable being changed is `noOfSqYards`; the identifier for the mutator is `SetNoOfSqYards( )`.

Other Instance Methods

You wrote class methods in Chapter 3. Class methods manipulate data by having information passed in as arguments through parameters. That is not necessary with instance methods. Instance method members of a class can directly access private data members of the same class. It is through instance methods that private data is manipulated. Examine the instance method `CalculateAverage( )` shown in Example 4-7. Notice that there are no parameters for the method. `CalculateAverage( )` can use `score1`, `score2`, and `score3` because they belong to the same class.

EXAMPLE 4-7

```
public double CalculateAverage( )
{
     return (score1 + score2 + score3) / 3.0;
}
```

As illustrated in Example 4-7, `CalculateAverage( )` can directly access `score1`, `score2`, and `score3`. It was not necessary to send that data into the method via a parameter.

Also notice that exam average is not one of the data members. The average is not stored. This was done to avoid potential inconsistencies with the data. Normally, any time information can be calculated from other values; it is best to define a method to perform the behavior. By defining a method as opposed to storing the average, it will reduce the chance of inaccurate or inconsistent data. If one of the object's scores is changed, it would be easy to fail to change the average if it were a data member. This is where the potential for inconsistent data pops up. If average is only available through invoking a method, the current values of `score1`, `score2`, and `score3` will always be used.

Property

One of the underlying themes of object-oriented programming is **encapsulation**, which states that the internal representation of an object is generally hidden; thus, member data are defined with `private` access. Typically, the only way to access, inspect, or manipulate the object's data is through the object's `public` methods. As you just read, many languages provide mutators, or setters that enable the data to be changed. They provide accessors or getters that enable the data to be retrieved. Another option is to define and use properties. C# introduced properties. A property looks like a data field, but it does not directly represent a storage location. Properties are more closely aligned to methods. They provide a way to change or retrieve `private` member data. Example 4-8 includes the property for `noOfSqYards` and `pricePerSqYard` data member.

EXAMPLE 4-8

```
public double NoOfSqYards
{
    get
    {
        return noOfSqYards;
    }
    set
    {
        noOfSqYards = value;
    }
}
```

```
public double PricePerSqYard
{
      get
      {
           return pricePerSqYard;
      }
      set
      {
           pricePerSqYard = value;
      }
}
```


Properties are named using Pascal case. A standard naming convention in C# for properties is to use the same name as the instance variable or field but have the property identifier start with an uppercase character. `NoOfSqYards` follows that convention. The property name associated with the `pricePerSqYard` data member would be `PricePerSqYard`.

Using the same name, as shown in Example 4-8, enables the property member to be quickly associated with the data member. The names do not really have to match. `Price`, for example, could have been the name for the property associated with the `pricePerSqYard` data member. No syntax errors would have been created; however, using `Price` as a property name for `pricePerSqYard` does not follow the standard naming convention.

After the properties are defined, they can be used in other classes as if they were fields of the object instantiated. When you define a property, you can define the `set` without the `get` or the `get` without the `set`. It is not necessary to include both. The body of the `get` must return a value of the property type. If you include only the `get`, the property is considered a read-only property because the value of the instance variable cannot be changed through the property. The execution of the `get` is equivalent to reading the value of the field. After the `set` property for a variable is defined, you can change the `private` instance variables data using that property in any `class` that instantiates an `object`. For example, if an instantiated `object` is named `berber`, to change the `pricePerSqYard` you could write:

```
berber.PricePerSqYard = 25.99;
```

The body of the `set` portion in the property is similar to a mutator method. Remember that the mutator method's `return` type is `void`. Mutators normally have one argument representing the value to be assigned to the instance variable. The `set` portion of the property uses an implicit parameter, called `value`. The type of `value` is always the same as the `private` member that is being associated with the property.

get, set, and value are not regular keywords. It is not necessary to declare value, get, or set. They have special meaning when used with properties. They are contextual keywords. Also notice, as shown back in Example 4-8, no parentheses or parameter is placed after the property identifier.

Auto Implemented Properties

There are many shortcuts that can be used by developers; one introduced with C# 3.0 and later is **auto-implemented properties**. With auto-implemented properties, you do not have to include the return and set statements. You simply write get; set; as the body for the property. Auto-implemented properties make property-declaration more concise. They can be used when no additional logic is required in the property accessors other than just returning the value or sending in a new value to change the field. The additional requirement is that you do not define a separate private data member to tie the property to. When you declare a property as shown in the Example 4-10, the compiler creates a private, anonymous backing field that can only be accessed through the property's get and set accessors.

EXAMPLE 4-9

```
//Auto-implemented properties
public string Name { get; set; }

public int EmployeeID { get; set; }
```

As illustrated in Example 4-9, with the auto-implemented property no assignment statement is included with the set portion and no return is written for the get. Another shortcut recently introduced with C# 6.0 is auto property initializers. An **auto property initializer** adds to the auto-implemented concept in that it is used to set the value of read-only properties during the property declaration. This is illustrated in Example 4-10.

EXAMPLE 4-10

```
//Auto property with initializer
public int Salary
{
      get; set;
} = 10000;
public string TypeOfEmployee
{
      get;
} = "Staff";
```

When you define a property member for a class as shown in Example 4-9 and Example 4-10, a backing field is not required, which means no private data members with identifiers like name, employeeID, salary or typeOfEmployee would be defined. You could still initialize the fields in constructors via assignment statements, but you do not have to define separate private data members. With C# 6.0, you now can take it one step further and actually add the assignment to the property definition as is shown with Salary and TypeOfEmployee in Example 4-10. This is referred to as an **Auto-Properties with Initializer**. This shortcut available in C# 6.0 greatly reduces the amount of coding. As previously noted, by including properties for logical member data, the number of mutator and accessor methods needed is reduced. Properties allow access to private data members in a similar way as public members. You will see more examples of their use in the next section.

ToString( ) Method

In Chapter 2, you read that all user-defined classes inherit four methods (ToString( ), Equals( ), GetType( ), and GetHashCode( )) from the object class. Just like you inherit characteristics from your parents, inheritance works similarly in C#. You might have inherited your eye color from your mother or your build from your grandfather. You might even get hair color from your great grandmother. In C#, the very top level class (like your great, great, great, . . . grandparent) is called object. C# supports only single inheritance. As opposed to getting characteristics from two separate parents, in C#, you only get one parent class, but that parent class can also have a parent class. At the very top of this hierarchy is object. When you design your own classes, you can make use of these methods inherited from object by calling them or you can override them and give new definitions for one or more of the methods.

Object's ToString( ) method is a very special method. It is called automatically by several methods, including the Write( ) and WriteLine( ) methods. You can also invoke or call the ToString( ) method directly. ToString( ) returns a human-readable string. However, sometimes, this readable string is not what you intended. For example, if you send an object such as the berber object to the Write( ) method by writing Write(berber);, the ToString( ) method is automatically called and the namespace followed by a dot and the name of the class are displayed (Carpet.CarpetCalculator). This is not very helpful and probably not what you expected.

You could write a new definition for the ToString( ) method to include useful details so that if the berber object is sent to the Write( ) method, useful information is displayed. If you wanted to display the price per square yard, the number of square yards needed, and the total price whenever an object of the Carpet class is referenced, you might write a ToString( ) method similar to what is shown in Example 4-11.

EXAMPLE 4-11

```
public override string ToString( )
{
      return "Price Per Square Yard: " +
             pricePerSqYard.ToString("C") +
             "\nTotal Square Yards needed: " +
             noOfSqYards.ToString("F1") +
             "\nTotal Price: " +
             DetermineTotalCost( ).ToString("C");
}
```

As shown in Example 4-11, the keyword `override` is added to the heading immediately preceding the return type. To override a method, the new method must have the same signature as the one being overridden. After this new `ToString( )` method is defined, it can be called directly using the object with a statement such as `Write(berber.ToString( ));` or because the `Write( )` and `WriteLine( )` methods automatically call the `ToString( )` method, it is automatically invoked with a call such as `Write(berber);`.

You also learned in Chapter 2 that you could add a format specifier as one of the arguments to the `Write( )` and `WriteLine( )` methods. Numeric data types such as `int`, `double`, `float`, and `decimal` have overloaded `ToString( )` methods. One of their `ToString( )` signatures enables you to send as an argument a format specifier. This could be one of the standard numeric format specifiers, as presented in Table 2-16, or you could use one or more of the characters given in Table 2-17 to create a customized user-defined specifier. Example 4-11 illustrated adding the format specifier as an argument to the `ToString( )` method. When the `ToString( )` method is invoked in the `pricePerSqYard.ToString("C")` call, the overloaded `ToString( )` method of the `double class` is called. Now to display the information about the `berber object`, instead of writing a separate `DisplayResults( )`method, a call to the `Write( )` method with the `berber object` as the argument automatically calls the overridden `ToString( )` method of the `CarpetCalculator class`. The `ToString( )` method returns a formatted string that can be displayed.

NOTE In Example 4-11, you do not fully qualify `pricePerSqYard` using a `class` or `object` name. Also notice, the property identifier was not used. The private data member, `pricePerSqYard`, was able to be used because it was included in a member method of the `class`.

Calling Instance Methods

Instance methods are nonstatic methods. When instance methods are defined, you do not use the static keyword. When you invoke an instance method, you do not use the class name. Recall methods in the Math class were identified as class methods. The static keyword was used as part of their heading. In order to invoke the Pow( ) method for example, you had to precede the methods name with the class name (Math.Pow( )). A class method is a static method. The method belongs to the whole class. You must use the class name to call static methods. Instance methods belong to specific objects. You must call or invoke them with an object if you call them outside of the class in which they are defined. To call or invoke an instance method from within the same class where it is defined, simply use the method's name. It is not qualified with an object or class name.

NOTE

Recall with Visual Studio 2015 and C# 6.0, you can add a reference to a class that has static members by adding an additional using statement referencing the namespace and class name. After that, you can invoke the static class method without fully qualifying it with a class name.

After a class template has been defined to include private member data, public methods, and public properties, many different applications can use the class. To do so, objects of the class are instantiated using the class constructor.

Calling the Constructor

Normally, the first method called is the constructor. This is the method that actually creates an object instance of the class. The syntax for this is

```
ClassName objectName = new ClassName(argumentList);
```

Or

```
ClassName objectName;
objectName = new ClassName(argumentList);
```

It is more common to call the constructor in a single statement as shown first.

Example 4-12 creates three objects and calls the three different constructor methods defined in Example 4-4.

EXAMPLE 4-12

```
CarpetCalculator plush = new CarpetCalculator( );
CarpetCalculator pile = new CarpetCalculator(37.90, 17.95);
CarpetCalculator berber = new CarpetCalculator(17.95);
```

Each of the preceding statements does two things:

- Declares an `object` of a specific `class`
- Calls the constructor to create an instance of the class

The keyword `new` is used as an operator to call constructor methods. The first line in Example 4-12 is a call to the default constructor for the `CarpetCalculator` `class`. An `object` named `plush` is created. The `pricePerSqYard` and `noOfSqYards` are both set to 0.0. The system default values for `double` are used to initialize these instance variables. Table 4-2 gives the default values of the value types assigned to variables when no arguments are sent to member data.

TABLE 4-2 Value type defaults

Value type	Default value
`bool`	`false`
`byte`	0
`char`	'\0' (null)
`decimal`	0.0M
`double`	0.0D
`float`	0.0F
`int`	0
`long`	0L
`short`	0
`uint`	0
`ulong`	0
`ushort`	0

NOTE Attempting to add a value to an uninitialized variable in C# is not allowed.

The second call to the constructor sends two arguments. An object named pile is created, and an object named berber is created with the third constructor. The actual argument of 17.95 is used to initialize the private data member pricePerSqYard.

4

Calling Accessor and Mutator Methods

Accessor and mutators are instance methods. All instance methods are called in exactly the same manner as class methods, with one exception. If the method is being called from another class that has instantiated an object of the class, the method name is preceded by the object name. If another member of the same class is invoking the method, all that is needed is the name of the method. You never precede an instance method with the name of the class like you do with static class methods. In order to call the method in another class, a specific object must be associated with it.

One of the methods of the CarpetCalculator class is SetNoOfSqYards( ). Another class, called CarpetCalculatorApp, has instantiated an object of the CarpetCalculator class by using the one argument constructor shown previously in Example 4-4. The call to the constructor to instantiate the berber object is shown again as follows:

```
CarpetCalculator berber = new CarpetCalculator(17.95);
```

A call to the SetNoOfSqYards( ) method requires the name of the object, a dot, and the name of the method, as shown in the following code. This is a nonvalue-returning method. It is a mutator method.

```
berber.SetNoOfSqYards(27.83);
```

If the method is returning a value, as accessors do, there must be a place for the value to be returned. Again the method is called by typing the objectName, a dot, and the methodName. Example 4-13 shows a call to an accessor method, which has a return value.

EXAMPLE 4-13

```
WriteLine("{0:N2}", berber.GetNoOfSqYards( ));
```

The value representing the number of square yards is printed on return from the accessor method.

You read about Property members in the previous section. With C#, properties are often used instead of accessor and mutator methods. Member properties are normally defined with a public access. To reference a set member property, you can use the name of the property field in an assignment statement as in

```
PropertyName = value;
```

You can reference the get portion of the property as if it were an instance variable. Line 2 in Example 4-14 shows how the property PricePerSqYard, which was declared in Example 4-8, is used.

EXAMPLE 4-14

```
Line 1    Write("Total Cost at {0:C} ",
Line 2          berber.PricePerSqYard);
Line 3    WriteLine(" per Square Yard: {0:C}",
Line 4              berber.DetermineTotalCost( ));
```

Notice that the use of the property in Line 2 differs from a method call. No parentheses are used with the property. The complete CarpetCalculatorApp solution is shown near the end of this chapter. Another example, StudentApp, is introduced here.

Calling Other Instance Methods

All behaviors associated with the data are included as method members of the class. These methods are called instance methods as opposed to class methods—because an instance of the class or an object is needed in order to invoke or call the method.

With the Student class, CalculateAverage( ) is an instance method. The body of the CalculateAverage( ) method was shown in Example 4-7. In order to invoke this method, an object must first be instantiated. This is the first statement shown in Example 4-15.

EXAMPLE 4-15

```
Student aStudentObject = new Student("1234", "Maria", "Smith",
                                     97, 75, 87, "CS");
average = aStudentObject.CalculateAverage( );
```

You may want to look back at Example 4-3. The seven argument constructor shown in that example are called here to instantiate the class. The new operator creates the object, aStudentObject. Once a Student object is instantiated, as illustrated in

Example 4-15, `CalculateAverage( )` can now be invoked. A dot separates the object and the instance method name.

Since `CalculateAverage( )` has a return type of `double`, there must be a place for a value to be returned. It is returned through an assignment statement. Another option would be to return it directly to an output statement. However, the only way it can be called or invoked is with an object of the `Student class`. Example 4-16 shows instantiating another `Student object` using the constructor that takes one argument (review Example 4-3). Example 4-16 also illustrates using its properties to assign values to the scores and then invoking the instance method with that object. This time the value from the `CalculateAverage( )` method is returned to a `WriteLine( )` method.

EXAMPLE 4-16

```
Student secondStudentObject = new Student("2345");
secondStudentObject.Score1 = 95;
secondStudentObject.Score2 = 62;
secondStudentObject.Score3 = 87;
WriteLine("Student Number: " +
            secondStudentObject.StudentNumber +
           "\nAverage: {0:F1}",
            secondStudentObject.CalculateAverage( ));
```

Notice that no arguments are needed as parameters to the `CalculateAverage( )` method. This is because `CalculateAverage( )` is a member of the `Student class` and has full access to all of the `Student class` data members. The properties `Score1`, `Score2`, and `Score3` have a `public` access mode. They were used to assign values to the `private` instance data members `score1`, `score2`, and `score3`.

NOTE Recall to clear a console window and reposition the cursor to the top of the display, invoke `Console.Clear( )` or just `Clear( )` if you have the additional `using static System.Console;` reference added at the top of your project and are using Visual Studio 2015 or later versions.

Testing Your New Class

A different class is needed for testing and using your class. If you added your class as a second class to the application, as was recommended earlier, you already have that other class. This other class is the class that has `Main( )` in it. Here, in `Main( )`, you can construct objects of your class, use the properties to assign and retrieve values, and invoke instance methods using the objects you construct. Example 4-17 illustrates testing your class.

EXAMPLE 4-17

```
using System;
using static System.Console;
namespace StudentApp
{
    class StudentApp
    {
        static void Main(string[] args)
        {
            Student firstStudentObject = new Student( );
            firstStudentObject.StudentName =
                             AskForStudentName("First");
            firstStudentObject.StudentFirstName =
                             AskForStudentName("Last");
            firstStudentObject.StudentNumber =
                             AskForStudentNumber( );
            firstStudentObject.Major =
                AskForMajor(firstStudentObject.StudentFirstName);
            firstStudentObject.Score1 = AskForExamScore(1);
            firstStudentObject.Score2 = AskForExamScore(2);
            firstStudentObject.Score3 = AskForExamScore(3);

            Clear( );
            WriteLine("First Student");
            WriteLine(firstStudentObject.ToString( ));


            Student secondStudentObject = new Student("2345");
            secondStudentObject.Score1 = 95;
            secondStudentObject.Score2 = 62;
            secondStudentObject.Score3 = 87;
            WriteLine("\n\nSecond Student");
            WriteLine("Student Number: " +
                       secondStudentObject.StudentNumber +
                     "\nAverage: {0:F1}",
                       secondStudentObject.CalculateAverage( ));

            Student thirdStudentObject = new Student("5432",
                                         "Randolph", "Wonder");
            thirdStudentObject.Major = "Math";
            thirdStudentObject.Score1 = 95;
            thirdStudentObject.Score2 = 87;
            thirdStudentObject.Score3 = 72;
            WriteLine("\n\nThird Student");
            WriteLine(thirdStudentObject);

            Student aStudentObject = new Student("1234","Maria",
                                   "Smith", 97, 75, 87, "CS");
```

```
            WriteLine("\n\nLast Student");
            WriteLine("Student Name: " +
                    aStudentObject.StudentFirstName + " " +
                    aStudentObject.StudentLastName +
                    "\nStudent Number: " +
                    aStudentObject.StudentNumber +
                    "\nMajor: " + aStudentObject.Major +
                    "\nExam Score 1: " + aStudentObject.Score1 +
                    "\nExam Score 2: " + aStudentObject.Score2 +
                    "\nExam Score 3: " + aStudentObject.Score3 +
                    "\nExam Average: " +
                aStudentObject.CalculateAverage( ).ToString("F1"));
            ReadKey( );
        }

        static int AskForExamScore(int whichOne)
        {
            string inValue;
            int aScore;
            Write("Enter a value for Score {0}: ", whichOne);
            inValue = ReadLine( );
            aScore = int.Parse(inValue);
            return aScore;
        }

        static string AskForStudentName(string whichOne)
        {
            string inValue;
            Write("Enter Student {0} Name: ", whichOne);
            inValue = ReadLine( );
            return inValue;
        }

        static string AskForMajor(string name)
        {
            string inValue;
            Write("Enter {0}\' s Major: ", name);
            inValue = ReadLine( );
            return inValue;
        }

        static string AskForStudentNumber( )
        {
            string inValue;
            Write("Enter Student Number: ");
            inValue = ReadLine( );
            return inValue;
        }
    }
}
```

Examine Example 4-17 closely. Each of the constructors are tested and the values are displayed using the `WriteLine( )` method. As you type the program statements, you will be aided with IntelliSense as shown in Figure 4-4.

```
Student firstStudentObject = new Student(
▲ 4 of 4 ▼ Student.Student(int sID, string name, int s1, int s2, int s3, string maj)
```

FIGURE 4-4 IntelliSense displays available constructors

In addition to revealing the available constructor methods as shown in Figure 4-4, IntelliSense also displays all public members of the class once an object is instantiated. As you examine Figure 4-5, notice that none of the data members are present.

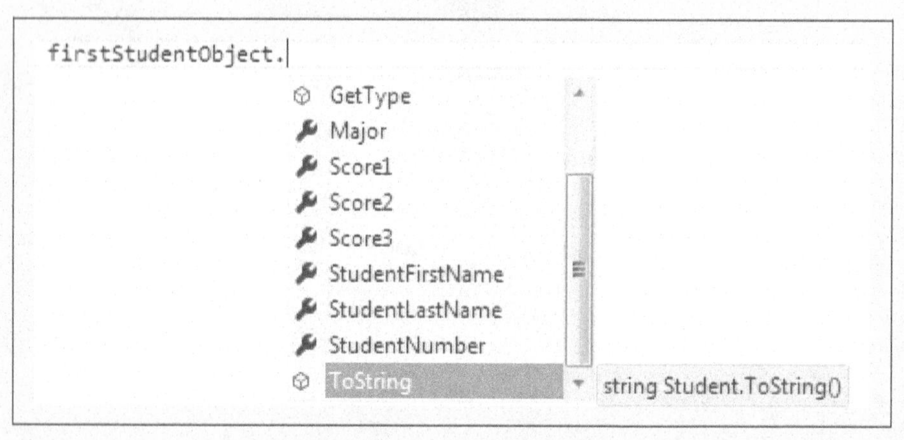

FIGURE 4-5 Public members of the Student class

The data members were defined with an access mode of `private`. They are accessible only inside the `Student class`. You will read more about the two other types of access modifiers, `protected` and `internal`, in Chapter 11. Internal members are accessible only within files in the same assembly. Protected members are accessible to any `class` that is derived from them (child classes), but not to any other classes. With the fourth access specifier, `public`, access is not restrictive.

The `StudentApp class` has a number of class methods that are called from `Main( )`. You will recall that class methods require the keyword `static` and are not associated with a specific object. They are called `static` methods because they are resolved statically, at compile time; thus not associated with any particular instance of an object's data. These `static` or `class` methods, `AskForExamScore( )`, `AskForStudentName( )`, `AskForMajor( )`, and `AskForStudentNumber( )`, are used by `Main( )` to enable the user to input data. The values that are returned are assigned to data members of `firstStudentObject`. However, since the data members of the class are defined as `private`, the `public` properties must be used for the assignments. The output from the application is shown in Figure 4-6.

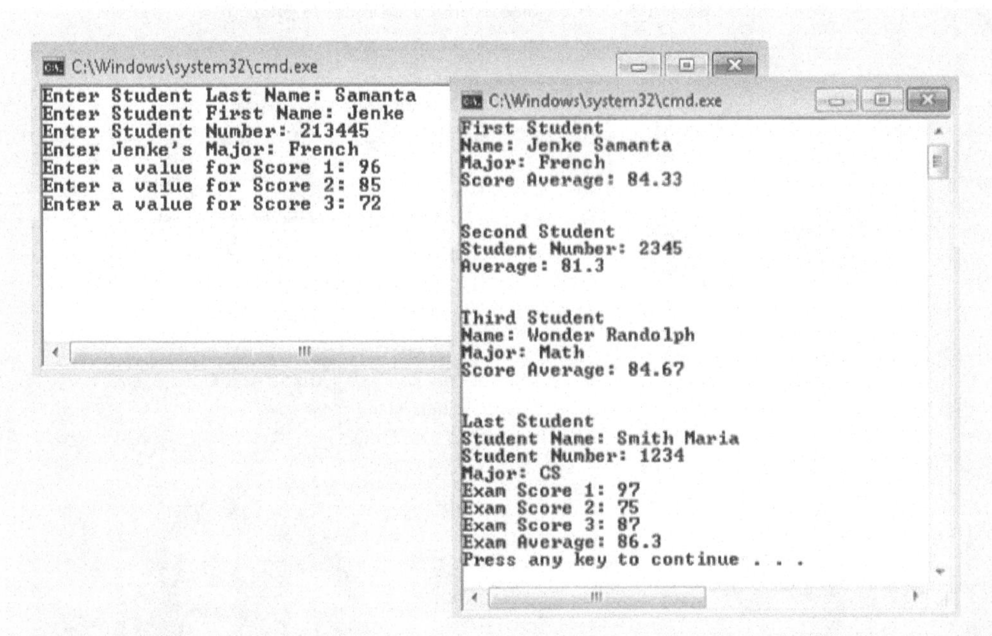

FIGURE 4-6 Output from StudentApp

As you examine the code in Example 4-17, notice that the `firstStudentObject` is displayed by explicitly calling the `ToString( )` method. The same type of information is displayed for both the first and third objects. `ToString( )` is called both times. As you review the code in Example 4-17, notice that the third object is displayed with `WriteLine(thirdStudentObject);`. Here the `ToString( )` method was automatically called. `ToString( )` is also called with the last instantiated student object, `aStudentObject`. This time it is used to format the value returned from the `CalculateAverage( )` method. The format specifer, `"F1,"` is sent as an argument. Here it is the `double.ToString( )` method that is being executed.

When you define a multiclass solution, all input and output of data should be included in the class (file) that has the `Main( )` method. The eventual goal will be to place your class files, such as `Student` and `CarpetCalculator`, in a library so that the classes can be used by different applications. Some of these applications might be Windows applications. Some may be console applications. A Web application could also instantiate objects of your classes. Thus, never include `ReadLine( )` or `WriteLine( )` in your class methods. These methods are only associated with the console application.

NOTE Always override the `ToString( )` method in every class you define. This enables you to decide what should be displayed if the object is printed.

For your review, the code from the `Student class` is displayed in Example 4-18.

EXAMPLE 4-18

```
public class Student
{
      //Data members, data fields, or characteristics
      private string studentNumber;
      private string studentFirstName;
      private string studentLastName;
      private int score1;
      private int score2;
      private int score3;
      private string major;

      //Default constructor
      public Student( )
      {
      }
      //Constructor with one argument
      public Student(string sID)
      {
            studentNumber = sID;
      }

      //Constructor with two arguments
      public Student(string sID, string lastName, string firstName)
      {
            studentNumber = sID;
            studentLastName = lastName;
            studentFirstName = firstName;
      }
```

```
//Constructor with six arguments
public Student(string sID, string lastName, string firstName,
               int s1, int s2, int s3, string maj)
{
     studentNumber = sID;
     studentLastName = lastName;
     studentFirstName = firstName;
     score1 = s1;
     score2 = s2;
     score3 = s3;
     major = maj;
}

//Properties
public string StudentLastName
{
     get
     {
          return studentLastName;
     }
     set
     {
          studentLastName = value;
     }
}

public string StudentFirstName
{
     get
     {
          return studentFirstName;
     }
     set
     {
          studentFirstName = value;
     }
}

public string StudentNumber
{
     get
     {
          return studentNumber;
     }
     set
     {
          studentNumber = value;
     }
}
```

4

```
public string Major
{
     get
     {
          return major;
     }
     set
     {
          major = value;
     }
}

public int Score1
{
     get
     {
          return score1;
     }
     set
     {
          score1 = value;
     }
}

public int Score2
{
     get
     {
          return score2;
     }
     set
     {
          score2 = value;
     }
}

public int Score3
{
     get
     {
          return score3;
     }
     set
     {
          score3 = value;
     }
}

public double CalculateAverage( )
{
     return (score1 + score2 + score3) / 3.0;
}
```

```
        public override string ToString( )
        {
            return "Name: " + studentFirstName + " " +
                   studentLastName + "\nMajor: " + major +
                   "\nScore Average: " +
                   CalculateAverage( ).ToString("F2");
        }
    }
```


In many of the examples, you saw instance methods, instance data fields, and properties defined and called as code snippets for an object-oriented solution to the `CarpetCalculator` problem. The complete listing for the object-oriented solution for the application follows. The solution consists of two files.

When you create an application that has two files, be sure to include only one `Main( )` method. Only one of the files is used as the startup control file. The first file in this solution is the `CarpetCalculator class`, which defines the `class` template for a `carpet object`. It includes `private` data, `public` methods, and `public` property definitions. The second file is a sample application, which instantiates an `object` of the `CarpetCalculator class`.

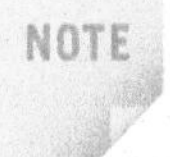

In Visual Studio, add a second file to your application by selecting **Add Class** from the **Project** menu. Only one file in your application can have a `Main( )` method.

The complete program listing follows in Example 4-19.

EXAMPLE 4-19

```
/* CarpetCalculator.cs
 * Author: Doyle
 * Defines the template for the
 * CarpetCalculator class to include constructors,
 * accessors, mutators, and properties
 */
using System;

namespace CarpetCalculatorApp
{
    public class CarpetCalculator
    {
        private double pricePerSqYard;
        private double noOfSqYards;
```

```
// Property for the pricePerSqYard data field
public double PricePerSqYard
{
     get
     {
          return pricePerSqYard;
     }
     set
     {
          pricePerSqYard = value;
     }
}

// Property also associated with
// pricePerSqYard - works, but does
// not follow naming convention
public double Price
{
     get
     {
          return pricePerSqYard;
     }
     set
     {
          pricePerSqYard = value;
     }
}

// Property for noOfSqYards data field
public double NoOfSqYards
{
     get
     {
          return noOfSqYards;
     }
     set
     {
          noOfSqYards = value;
     }
}

// Default constructor
public CarpetCalculator( )
{
          //empty body
}

// One argument constructor
public CarpetCalculator(double price)
{
     pricePerSqYard = price;
}
```

```
        // Two argument constructor
        public CarpetCalculator(double amountNeeded,
                                double price)
        {
            noOfSqYards = amountNeeded;
            pricePerSqYard = price;
        }

        public double DetermineTotalCost( )
        {
            return (pricePerSqYard * noOfSqYards);
        }

        // One of the overloaded mutator methods
        public void SetNoOfSqYards(double length, double width)
        {
            const int SQ_FT_PER_SQ_YARD = 9;
            noOfSqYards = length * width / SQ_FT_PER_SQ_YARD;
        }

        // One of the overloaded mutator methods
        public void SetNoOfSqYards (double squareYards)
        {
            noOfSqYards = squareYards;
        }

        // Accessor method
        public double GetNoOfSqYards( )
        {
             return noOfSqYards;
        }

        public override string ToString( )
        {
             return "Price Per Square Yard: " +
                    pricePerSqYard.ToString("C") +
                    "\nTotal Square Yards: " +
                    noOfSqYards.ToString("F1") +
                    "\nTotal Price: " +
                    DetermineTotalCost( ).ToString("C");
        }
    }
}
```

The following file uses the `CarpetCalculator` `class`:

```
/* CarpetCalculatorApp.cs
 * Author: Doyle
 * This class instantiates an object
 * of the CarpetCalculator class. It
 * demonstrates how to access and use
```

```
* the members of the class.
*/
using System;
using static System.Console;

namespace CarpetCalculatorApp
{
    class CarpetCalculatorApp
    {
        static void Main( )
        {
            CarpetCalculator berber = new
                                    CarpetCalculator(17.95);
            double roomWidth;
            double roomLength;
            DisplayInstructions( );
            // Call GetDimension( ) to get the length
            roomLength = GetDimension("Length");
            // Call GetDimension( ) again to get the width
            roomWidth = GetDimension("Width");
            berber.PricePerSqYard = 25.99;
            berber.SetNoOfSqYards(roomLength, roomWidth);

            Clear( );
            Write(berber);
            ReadKey( );
        }

        static void DisplayInstructions( )
        {
            WriteLine("This program will determine how much " +
                      "carpet to purchase.");
            WriteLine( );
            WriteLine("You will be asked to enter the size " +
                      "of the room and the price of the");
            WriteLine("carpet, in price per " + "square yds.");
            WriteLine( );
        }

        static double GetDimension(string side)
        {
            string inputValue    // local variables
            int feet,            // needed only by this
            inches;              // method

            Write("Enter the {0} in feet: ", side);
            inputValue = ReadLine( );
            feet = int.Parse(inputValue);
```

```
                Write("Enter the {0} in inches: ", side);
                inputValue = ReadLine( );
                inches = int.Parse(inputValue);

                // Note: cast required to avoid int division
                return (feet + (double) inches / 12);
            }
        }
    }
```


As you review Example 4-19, notice that properties were defined in the `CarpetCalculator` `class` called `NoOfSqYards`, `PricePerSqYard`, and `Price`. The `Price` and `PricePerSqYard` properties are both tied to the `pricePerSqYard` data member, which was defined with an access mode of `private`. Rarely will you want to associate two separate properties to a single data member. `Price` was defined to illustrate that you do not have to follow the standard naming convention. Recall that data members are named using Camel case, while property identifiers follow the Pascal case convention; thus, the only difference normally in their names is the first character. `pricePerSqYard` can be referenced in the class where it is defined, but because it is defined with an access mode of `private`, it cannot be referenced outside of the defining class.

In the second class, `CarpetCalculatorApp`, an object of the `CarpetCalculator` `class` is instantiated. The object identifier is `berber`. The object is instantiated with the `new` operator as shown here: `CarpetCalculator berber = new CarpetCalculator(17.95);` Since a double value, 17.95, is sent in as an argument to the constructor, the one argument constructor is used. 17.95 goes into `price` and that value is placed in the `private` data member `pricePerSqYard` as shown here in the constructor:

```
public CarpetCalculator(double price)
{
     pricePerSqYard = price;
}
```

In order to change berber's `pricePerSqYard` in the `CarpetCalculatorApp` `class`, you must use one of the `public` properties, either `Price` or `PricePerSqYard`. The `private` `pricePerSqYard` data member is not accessible in the second class. The `pricePerSqYard` was changed to 25.99 with the statement shown below:

```
berber.PricePerSqYard = 25.99;
```

The `PricePerSqYard` property has `get` and `set` clauses. In order for classes that instantiate objects of the `CarpetCalculator` `class` to change the objects `pricePerSqYard`, they use the `set` clause associated with the public property.

The object's private data members' value (i.e., pricePerSqYard) is retrieved through the public property's get clause.

Next, in the Main( ) method of the CarpetCalculatorApp class, the mutator method SetNoOfSqYards( ) was invoked. Notice that this method, like the property reference above, had to be invoked with an object. The mutator method also offers a public access mode; thus, it is available in classes instantiating objects of the CarpetCalculator class. The object was berber for this example.

NOTE A public property is defined for noOfSqYards in addition to the mutator method. The public property NoOfSqYards is tied to the private noOfSqYards data member. It could have been used as opposed to the mutator method and obtained the same results. Here, in the example, SetNoOfSqYards( ) was used to to illustrate invoking a mutator method with an object.

The last interesting statement in Main( ) for Example 4-19 is the Write(berber) statement. Here the ToString( ) method, defined in the CarpetCalculator class, is automatically invoked with the berber object. The CarpetCalculator class provided a new definition for the object's ToString( ) method. The keyword override was used on the method heading in the CarpetCalculator class.

Figure 4-7 shows the output for the preceding application when the user enters a room measurement of 17 ft. 10 in. for length and 14 ft. 6 in. for the width.

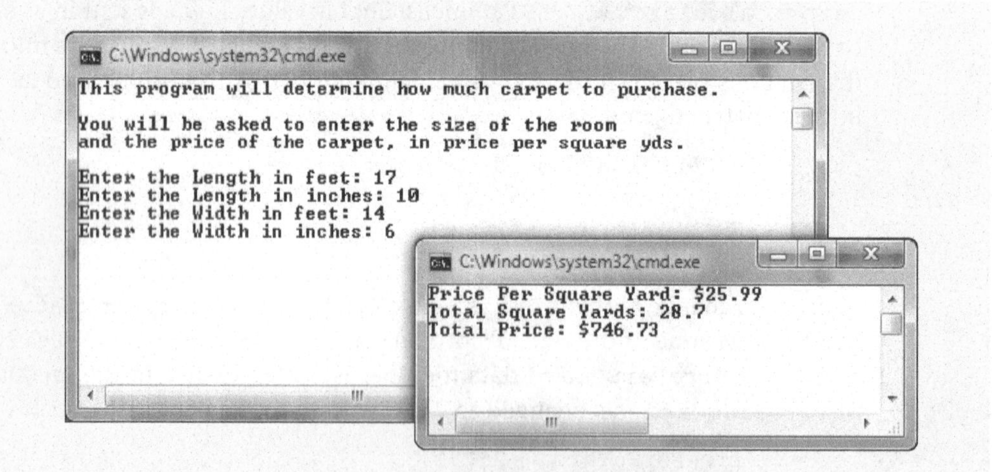

FIGURE 4-7 Output from Carpet example using instance methods

A lot of material is presented in this chapter. The programming example that follows makes use of most of these new concepts.

PROGRAMMING EXAMPLE: RealEstateInvestment

This example demonstrates the use of methods in a program. Both `static` and instance methods are used. Properties are included in the solution. The problem specification is shown in Figure 4-8.

How much cash flow profit is a rental investment generating? Create an application to determine what the cash flow is for a real estate investment used as a rental.

Design an object-oriented solution. Use two classes.

For the real estate property class, characteristics such as the year the home was built, purchase price, and street address will help identify the current state of an object. The real estate object also has a monthly income amount from rent and a monthly expense characteristic. Include a method to determine what the monthly earnings, or cash flow, is based on deducting the total monthly expenses from the monthly rental income.

In the second class, instantiate an object of the real estate property class. Call the constructor that creates an object using year built, purchase price, and street address. Allow the user to input the yearly taxes and insurance expenses. The monthly utilities costs should also be considered. In this application class, calculate a monthly expense based on the inputted values. Set the appropriate data field in the real estate property object.

Write code in the application class to display the property address and the expected cash flow for a given month.

© Cengage Learning

FIGURE 4-8 Problem specification for RealEstateInvestment example

ANALYZE THE PROBLEM

You should review the problem specification in Figure 4-8 and make sure you understand the problem definition. Several values must be entered into the program. These values must be entered as `string` variables and then parsed into numeric fields, so that arithmetic can be performed.

Two separate classes are to be developed. Creating a separate `class` for the real estate `object` enables this `class` to be used by many different applications. One application is to produce a listing showing the cash flow from the investment. Other applications might include determining total investment dollar amounts or locations of investments.

If the characteristics of real estate objects are abstracted out, many applications can reuse the `class`.

VARIABLES

Tables 4-3 and 4-4 list the data items needed for the RealEstateInvestment problem.

TABLE 4-3 Instance variables for the RealEstateInvestment class

Data item description	Type	Identifier
Year the home was built	`int`	`yearBuilt`
Location of the home	`string`	`streetAddress`
Original purchase price	`double`	`purchasePrice`
Total expenses for average month	`double`	`monthlyExpense`
Rental premium per month	`double`	`incomeFromRent`

The `class` that is using the RealEstateInvestment `class` also needs data. As noted in the problem specification, the application `class` allows the user to enter values for expenses. Table 4-4 identifies some of the local variables needed by the application `class`.

TABLE 4-4 Local variables for the property application class

Data item description	Type	Identifier
Cost of insurance per year	`double`	`insurance`
Amount of taxes per year	`double`	`taxes`
Estimated monthly utility costs	`double`	`utilities`
String value for inputting values	`string`	`inValue`

CONSTANTS

To illustrate the use of constants, a default rental rate is set as a constant value. The identifier and preset constant value will be

RENTAL_AMOUNT = 1000.00.

DESIGN A SOLUTION

The desired output is to display the address of a property and the expected cash flow for a given month. Figure 4-9 shows a prototype of the desired final output. The xxx.xx is placed in the prototype to represent the location in which the calculated values should appear.

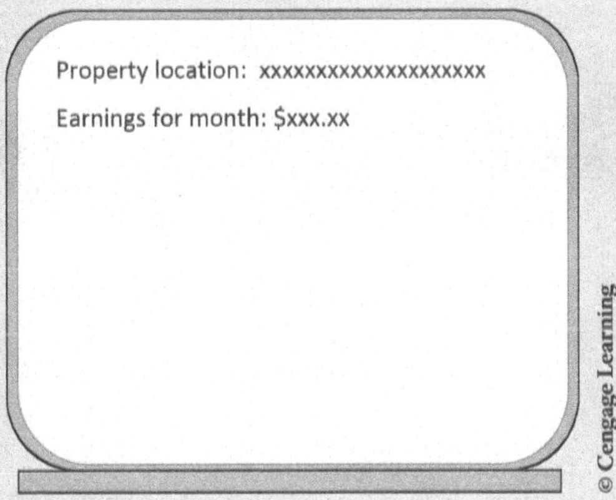

Property location: xxxxxxxxxxxxxxxxxxxx
Earnings for month: $xxx.xx
© Cengage Learning

FIGURE 4-9 Prototype

The object-oriented approach focuses more on the `object`. The real estate property has both data and behavior characteristics that can be identified. Class diagrams are used to help design and document these characteristics. Figure 4-10 shows the `class` diagrams for the RealEstateInvestment example.

FIGURE 4-10 Class diagrams

The class diagrams show neither the properties needed nor the local variables that might be needed by specific class methods. As you learned earlier, properties are new to C# and reduce the need to write mutators and accessors for the private instance variables. Table 4-5 lists the data members that will have properties defined and indicates whether both get and set are needed. The name of the property is also given.

TABLE 4-5 Properties for the RealEstateInvestment class

Data member identifier	Property identifier	Set	Get
yearBuilt	YearBuilt		√
streetAddress	StreetAddress		√
purchasePrice	PurchasePrice		√
monthlyExpense	MonthlyExpense	√	√
incomeFromRent	IncomeFromRent	√	√

The data members of yearBuilt, streetAddress, and purchasePrice are read-only instance variables. After an object of the class is instantiated with these values, they cannot be changed. By making this design choice, no default constructor is provided. It could never be used since no value can later be assigned to yearBuilt, streetAddress, and purchasePrice when the properties are defined with only Gets. No sets were provided for these identifiers. Notice that the identifiers for the properties match the data member with the exception that the first character in the property name is capitalized.

Four constructors were included to provide flexibility in constructing objects. An object can be constructed by sending in either the streetAddress or the yearBuilt as the first argument with the three argument constructors. The two argument constructors accept values for streetAddress or purchasePrice. No constructors were created accepting just year and address. This was part of the design choice made. Signatures of methods must be different; constructors are methods. The identifier yearBuilt is defined to hold an integer; the identifier purchasePrice is defined to hold a floating-point double value. Since C# provides implicit conversion of integers to doubles, a value such as 75000 is automatically converted into 75000.00 if it is stored in a floating-point double memory location. When an object is constructed, a best attempt is made to match the data with the appropriate constructor. Thus, there is the possibility that the wrong constructor might be invoked when a whole number is sent as an argument representing the price. Considering this, no constructors were provided accepting the two arguments of yearBuilt and streetAddress since constructors were provided accepting streetAddress and purchasePrice. One additional caution should be added. It is important to provide additional constructors for flexibility; however, do not attempt to provide a constructor with every possible combination of data fields. Give thought to which ones will really add value and be used.

During design, it is important to develop the algorithm showing the step-by-step process to solve the problem. Structured English, also called pseudocode, is suited for the object-oriented methodology. In addition to the Main( ) method, two additional methods—DetermineMonthlyEarnings( ) and GetExpenses( )—need to be designed. Figure 4-11 shows part of the Structured English design for the RealEstateInvestment example. Additional objects should be instantiated to test the other constructors, properties, and methods of the RealEstateInvestment class.

4

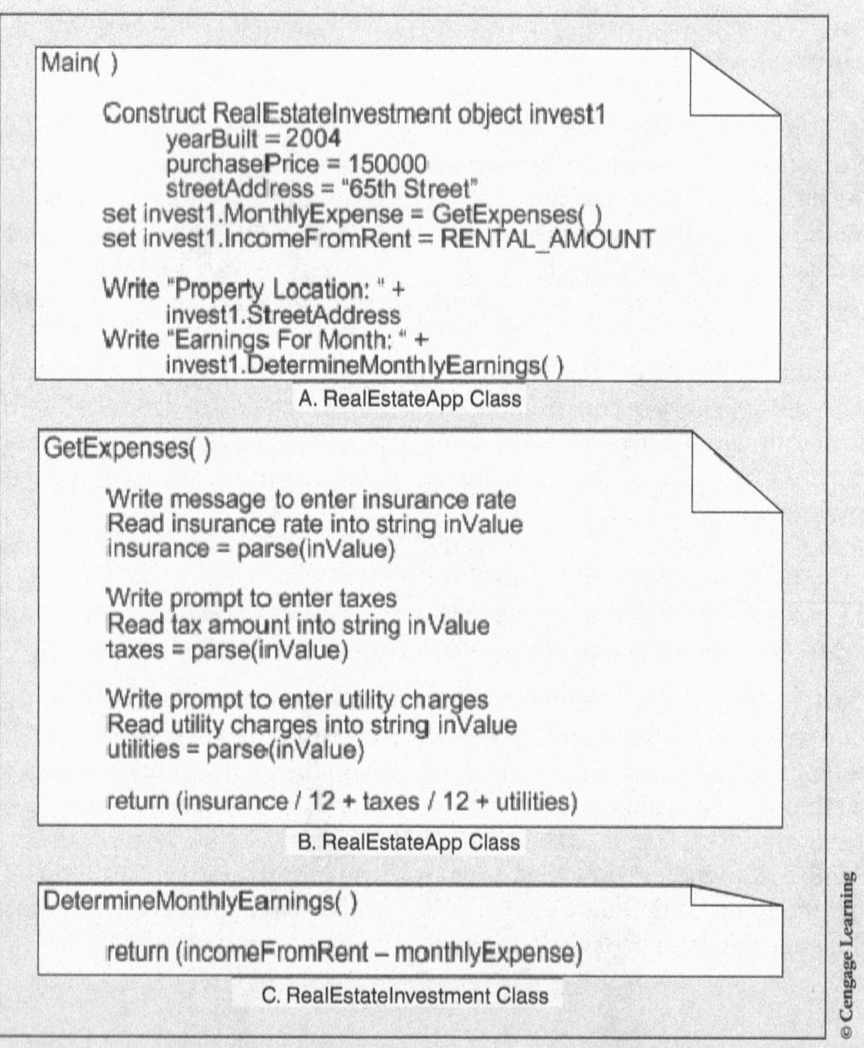

© Cengage Learning

FIGURE 4-11 Structured English for the RealEstateInvestment example

After the algorithm is developed, the design should be checked for correctness. When you desk check your algorithm, begin in `Main( )`. When you encounter method calls, keep your location in that method, go to the called method, and perform the statements. When you finish with the called method, return back to your saved location.

Test your algorithm with the following data:

Insurance: 650.00
Taxes: 1286.92
Utilities: 250.00

Use a calculator and write down the results you obtain. After you implement your design, you can compare these results with those obtained from your program output.

CODE THE SOLUTION

After you complete the design and verify the algorithm's correctness, it is time to translate the design into source code. For this application, you are creating two separate files—one for each `class`. Only one of the classes will have a `Main( )` method. If you create the `RealEstateInvestment class` first, delete the `Main( )` method from that file. To add a second `class`, click **Project, Add Class**. The final application listing for both files appears here:

4

```
/* RealEstateApp.cs                    Author:  Doyle
 * This class constructs an
 * object of the RealEstateInvestment
 * class. It tests several properties and
 * methods of the class.
 * A static method is used in
 * the application class to
 * input expenses.
 * */

using System;
using static System.Console;

namespace RealEstateApp
{
    public class RealEstateApp
    {
        static void Main( )
        {
            const double RENTAL_AMOUNT = 1000.00;
            RealEstateInvestment invest1 = new
              RealEstateInvestment (2004, 150000, "65th Street");
            WriteLine("\tFirst Investment");
            invest1.MonthlyExpense = GetExpenses( );
            invest1.IncomeFromRent = RENTAL_AMOUNT;
            WriteLine( );
            WriteLine("Property Location: {0}",
                      invest1.StreetAddress);
            WriteLine("Earnings For Month: {0:C}",
                      invest1.DetermineMonthlyEarnings( ));

            RealEstateInvestment invest2 = new
                RealEstateInvestment("72 Westchester Dr.",
                                     229000);
            invest2.MonthlyExpense = 900;
            invest2.IncomeFromRent = 1500.00;
            WriteLine("\n\n\tSecond Investment");
            WriteLine(invest2);
            ReadKey( );
        }
```

```
            static double GetExpenses( )
            {
                double insurance;
                double taxes;
                double utilities;
                string inValue;

                Write("Yearly Insurance: ");
                inValue = ReadLine( );
                insurance = double.Parse(inValue);
                Write("Yearly Tax: ");
                inValue = ReadLine( );
                taxes = double.Parse(inValue);
                Write("Monthly Utilities: ");
                inValue = ReadLine( );
                utilities = double.Parse(inValue);
                return (insurance / 12 + taxes / 12 + utilities);
            }
        }
    }

/* RealEstateInvestment.cs
 * Author:       Doyle
 * This class defines a template
 * for a real estate object to
 * include instance data members,
 * public properties,
 * constructors, and a method to
 * determine the monthly earnings.
 */

using System;

namespace RealEstateApp
{
    class RealEstateInvestment
    {
        private string streetAddress;
        private int yearBuilt;
        private double purchasePrice;
        private double monthlyExpense;
        private double incomeFromRent;

        // Read-only property
        public double YearBuilt
        {
            get
            {
                return yearBuilt;
            }
```

```
}
// Read-only property
public string StreetAddress
{
     get
     {
          return streetAddress;
     }
}
// Read-only property
public double PurchasePrice
{
     get
     {
          return purchasePrice;
     }
}
// Property acting as mutator and accessor
public double MonthlyExpense
{
     set
     {
          monthlyExpense = value;
     }
     get
     {
          return monthlyExpense;
     }
}
// Property acting as mutator and accessor
public double IncomeFromRent
{
     set
     {
          incomeFromRent = value;
     }
     get
     {
          return incomeFromRent;
     }
}

// No Default constructor is provided due to the read
// only data fields
// Three parameter constructor with address listed first
public RealEstateInvestment (string address, int year,
                             double price)
{
      streetAddress = address;
```

```
        yearBuilt = year;
        purchasePrice = price;
    }

    // Two parameter constructor with address listed first
    public RealEstateInvestment (string address,
                                 double price)
    {
        streetAddress = address;
        purchasePrice = price;
    }

    // Two parameter constructor with price listed first
    public RealEstateInvestment (double price,
                                 string address)
    {
        streetAddress = address;
        purchasePrice = price;
    }

    // Three parameter constructor with year listed first
    public RealEstateInvestment (int year, double price,
                                 string address)
    {
        yearBuilt = year;
        purchasePrice = price;
        streetAddress = address;
    }

    // Returns the earnings for a given month
    public double DetermineMonthlyEarnings( )
    {
        return incomeFromRent - monthlyExpense;
    }

    public override string ToString( )
    {
        return "Location: " + streetAddress +
               //"\nYear Built: " + yearBuilt +
               //Year omitted - A constructor is
               //provided without year and
               //Year is read only
               "\nPurchase Price: " +
               purchasePrice.ToString("C") +
               "\nMonthly Income: " +
               monthlyExpense.ToString("C") +
               "\nIncome from Rent: " +
```

```
                    incomeFromRent.ToString("C") +
                    "\nMonthly Earnings: " +
                    DetermineMonthlyEarnings( ).ToString("C");
        }
    }
}
```


IMPLEMENT THE CODE

Compile the source code. If you have any rule violations, make corrections until no errors are present. Create a class diagram to go along with the application. You will recall that one option for creating the class diagram is to use the **Solution Explorer** window. When you right click on the source code file, one option is to **View Class Diagram.** Figure 4-12 illustrates the Class Diagram created for the `RealEstateInvestment class`. Run the application entering the values indicated previously (650.00, 1286.92, 250.00).

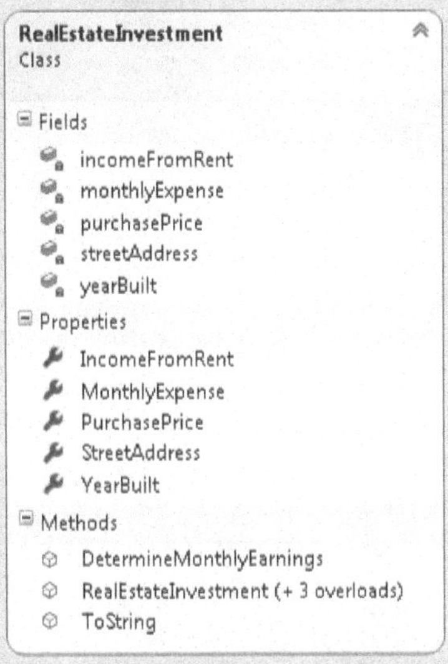

FIGURE 4-12 RealEstateInvestment class diagram

TEST AND DEBUG

During this final step, test the program and ensure you have the correct result. The output for the test values should match your prototype. Figure 4-13 shows the output generated from the preceding source code.

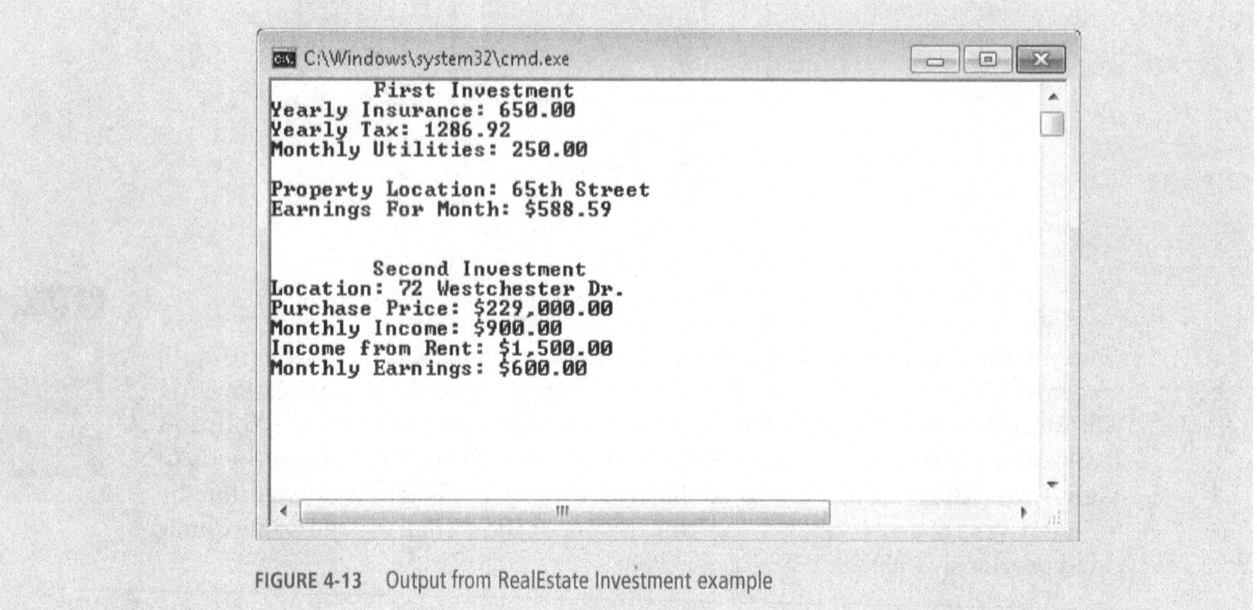

FIGURE 4-13 Output from RealEstate Investment example

Coding Standards

It is important to follow coding standards when you design classes. Developing standards that you consistently adhere to will increase your coding efficiency and make your code more maintainable. The naming conventions, coding standards, and best practices described in this section follow guidelines used in the industry.

Naming Conventions

Classes

- Use a noun or noun phrase to name a class.
- Use Pascal case.
- Use abbreviations sparingly.
- Do not use a type prefix, such as C for class, on a class name. For example, use the class name `Student` rather than `CStudent`.

Properties

- Use a noun or noun phrase to name properties.
- Create a property with the same name as its corresponding data member but use Pascal case.

Methods

- Use Pascal case to name methods.
- Use verbs or verb phrases as part of the name to tell what the method does. Avoid writing long methods. Each method should focus on a single theme. Typically, methods should not have more than 25 lines of code.

Constructor Guidelines

- Constructors use the same identifier as the class.
- Use a consistent ordering for constructors. A common practice is to list constructor methods with the fewest parameters first and the most parameters last. This enables you to provide more details as parameters are added.
- Provide a default constructor if you define even one other constructor.
- Minimize the amount of work done in the constructor. Constructors should not do more than capture the constructor parameter or parameters.

Spacing Conventions

- Use tabs instead of spaces for indentation.
- Use white space (one blank line) to separate and organize logical groups of code within methods. There should be one and only one single blank line between each method inside the class.
- Use white space (one blank line) to separate properties and instance methods.
- Place curly braces ({ }) at the same level as the method name, but on a new line.
- Avoid writing long instance methods.

Resources

Additional sites you might want to explore:

- C# Coding Standards and Best Practices—
http://www.dotnetspider.com/tutorials/BestPractices.aspx
- C# Station Tutorial - Introduction to Classes—
http://www.csharp-station.com/Tutorials/Lesson07.aspx

- Object - Oriented Programming—
  http://msdn.microsoft.com/en-us/library/dd460654.aspx
- Introduction to Objects and Classes in C#—
  http://www.devarticles.com/c/a/C-Sharp/Introduction-to-Objects-and-Classes-in-C-sharp/

QUICK REVIEW

1. A `class` is like a template. It defines the structure for all objects that are going to be of that class type.
2. An object is an instance, example of a class.
3. When you define a class, you describe its attributes in terms of data and its behaviors in terms of methods.
4. Instance methods require that an `object` be instantiated before they can be accessed.
5. Access modifiers specify the level of accessibility for types, or classes, and their members. Public access offers the fewest access limitations.
6. Private members are accessible only within the body of the `class` in which they are declared.
7. Often in object-oriented development, data is defined with a `private` modifier, and methods that access the data are declared to have `public` access.
8. Methods are the members of a `class` that describe the behavior of the data.
9. Many programmers employ the standard convention of using an action verb phrase to name methods.
10. Overloaded methods are methods with the same name but a different number, type, or arrangement of parameters. For example, the `DoSomething( )` method is overloaded with the following headings: `public void DoSomething(int x, string y)` and `public void DoSomething(string y, int x)`.
11. Constructors are special methods that create instances of a `class`. Constructors do not return a value—not even `void`.
12. Constructors use the same identifier as the `class` name. The keyword `new` is used to call the constructors.
13. When you design a class, you normally use `public` access modifiers with constructors and most other methods and `private` access modifiers for data members.
14. The default constructor has an empty body and it is automatically created if you do not write one. If you write even one constructor, you lose the default constructor and have to write it.

15. Accessors are methods that are used to access `private` data members. Accessors are also referred to as getter methods.
16. Mutators are methods that are used to change the current state of `object` member's data. Mutator methods are also referred to as setters.
17. A property looks like a data field and provides a way to set or get `private` member data. You can define the `set` without the `get` or vice versa. It is not necessary to include both.
18. Auto-implemented properties make property-declaration more concise. The body of the property just has two statements, `get; set;`
19. To call nonvalue-returning methods, simply type the method's name. If it is a `static` method, qualify it with the `class` name. If it is an instance method, qualify the identifier with an `object`. If the method has parameters, the call includes actual arguments inside the parentheses, without the types.

EXERCISES

1. Properties are defined with _____ access mode.
   a. `private`
   b. `static`
   c. `public`
   d. `void`
   e. `protected`
2. Objects are instances of:
   a. data members
   b. parameters
   c. properties
   d. methods
   e. classes
3. Which of the following modifiers is the most restrictive?
   a. `private`
   b. `static`
   c. `public`
   d. `internal`
   e. `protected`

4. Which of the following identifiers follows the standard naming convention for naming a class?
   a. `Calculate Final Grade`
   b. `MilesPerGallon`
   c. `Student`
   d. `Reports`
   e. `Employees`

5. Which of the following would be the most appropriate way to invoke the `CalculateAvg( )` method found in the `Student class` if an object named `gradStudent` had been instantiated from the class?

   `public double CalculateAvg( )`

   a. `gradStudent = CalculateAvg( );`
   b. `answer = Student.CalculateAvg( );`
   c. `CalculateAvg( );`
   d. `answer = gradStudent.CalculateAvg( );`
   e. `answer = gradStudent.CalculateAvg(87.2, 90);`

6. Which of the following is one of the user-defined methods inherited from the `object class`?
   a. `ToString( )`
   b. `Main( )`
   c. `CalculateAvg( )`
   d. `EqualsHashCode( )`
   e. `TypeHashCode( )`

7. Properties are associated with the _____ of the class while methods are affiliated with the _____ of the class.
   a. activity, fields
   b. accessors, mutators
   c. objects, instances
   d. data, behavior
   e. behavior, data

8. Which of the following is a valid overloaded method for `CalculateAvg( )`?

   `int CalculateAvg(int val1, int val2)`

   a. `void CalculateAvg(int val1, int val2)`
   b. `int CalculateAvg(int val1, int val2)`
   c. `int CalculateAvg( )`
   d. `double CalculateAvg(int val1, int val2)`
   e. `int CalculateAverage(int val2, int val1)`

9. What operator is used to instantiate the class?
   a. `method`
   b. `plus symbol`
   c. `ToString( )`
   d. `new`
   e. `equal symbol`

10. Instance variables are the same as:
    a. `private` member data
    b. local variables
    c. properties
    d. arguments
    e. parameters

11. Given the `Employee` `class` shown below, which of the following would be the most appropriate heading for its default constructor?

    `public class Employee {`

    a. `public void Employee( )`
    b. `public Employee( )`
    c. `static Employee( )`
    d. `private void Employee( )`
    e. `private Employee( )`

12. The following is probably an example of a(n):

    ```
    public double GetYards( )
    ```

    a. constructor
    b. mutator
    c. property
    d. accessor
    e. `class` definition

13. If you follow the standard C# naming conventions, the property name for the following instance variable would be:

    ```
    private string name;
    ```

    a. `propertyName`
    b. `nameProperty`
    c. `getName`
    d. `name`
    e. `Name`

14. Which of the following would be a valid call to the default constructor for the following `class`?

    ```
    public class Employee {
    ```

    a. `Employee employee1 = new Employee( );`
    b. `Employee employee1 = new undergrad( );`
    c. `Employee employee1;`
    d. `Employee employee1 = new Employee(default);`
    e. Not enough information is given to be able to answer.

15. Given the following `class` definition, what would be a valid heading for a mutator?

    ```
    public class Student
    {
        private string name;
        private double gpa;
    }
    ```

    a. `public double SetGpa(double gpaValue)`
    b. `public void SetGpa(double gpaValue)`
    c. `public double SetGpa( )`
    d. `public void GetGpa(double gpaValue)`
    e. `public double SetGpa( )`

16. With a UML class diagram
    a. the name of the class appears at the bottom section of the diagram
    b. data members show a + to indicate public access
    c. methods are not shown
    d. objects of the class appear in the middle section of the diagram
    e. methods show the return type on the diagram

17. Which of the following modifiers in C# is used with constructors?
    a. `const`
    b. `private`
    c. `public`
    d. `static`
    e. `protected`

18. Normally, member data uses a _____ access modifier, and methods use a _____ access modifier for object-oriented solutions.
    a. `protected`, `public`
    b. `private`, `protected`
    c. `public`, `protected`
    d. `public`, `private`
    e. `private`, `public`

19. For a `class` called `Account` that has data members of `accountNumber`, `balance`, and `transactionAmount`, which would be the most appropriate instance method heading for a method that reduces the transaction amount from the current balance?
    a. `static double ReduceAccount (double accountBalance, double transactionAmount)`
    b. `double ReduceAccount (double accountBalance, double transactionAmount)`
    c. `static ReduceAccount ( )`
    d. `void ReduceAccount ( )`
    e. `static void ReduceAccount ( )`

20. In order to provide a new definition for the `ToString( )` method, what keyword is added to the method heading?

   a. `static`

   b. `override`

   c. `new`

   d. `overload`

   e. `public`

---

21. Given the following code snippet:

```
Line 1   public class Camera
Line 2   {
Line 3       private double zoom;
Line 4       private double lensSpeed;
Line 5       public double Zoom
Line 6       {
Line 7           get
Line 8           {
Line 9               return zoom;
Line 10          }
Line 11      }
Line 12      public Camera ( )
Line 13      {
Line 14      }
Line 15      public Camera (double zCapacity,
Line 16                     double ls)
Line 17      {
Line 18          int xValue = 2;
Line 19          zoom = zCapacity * xValue;
Line 20          lensSpeed = ls;
Line 21      }
Line 22      public double GetLensSpeed( )
Line 23      {
Line 24          return lensSpeed;
Line 25      }
```

   Identify the following items by line number:

   a. method headings

   b. property identifier

   c. default constructors

   d. formal parameters

   e. local variables

22. Explain how instance methods differ from class methods. What differs when you want to invoke each different type? Which one requires an object in order for it to be called?

23. What does it mean to override a method? Why should the `ToString( )` method be overridden for user-defined classes?

24. Explain the role of the constructor. What is the default constructor? When do you automatically get a default constructor?

25. The following program has several syntax errors as well as style inconsistencies. Correct the syntax errors and identify the style violations.

```
public class Chair
{
private string type;
private double weight;
private double cost;
private Chair( )
 {
 }
 private Chair(weight, type, cost)
 {
 }
 public string ChairType
 {
       get
       {
              return type;
       }
       set
       {
              ChairType = value;
          }
      }
      public override ToString( )
         {
            return "Type of Chair: " + ChairType;
         }
   }
}
```

PROGRAMMING EXERCISES

1. Create a `Date class` with integer data members for year, month, and day. Also include a `string` data member for the name of the month. Include a method that returns the month name (as a `string`) as part of the date. Separate the day from the year with a comma in that method.

Include appropriate constructors, properties, and methods. Override the `ToString ( )` method to display the date formatted with slashes (/) separating the month, day, and year. Create a second `class` that instantiates and test the `Date class`.

2. Create a `class` representing a student. Include characteristics such as student number, first and last name, classification, and major. Write at least two constructors. Include properties for each of the data items. Include an instance method that returns a full name (with a space between first and last name). Create a second `class` that instantiates the first `class` with information about yourself. In the second `class`, create a `class` (`static`) method that displays name and major using the instantiated object.

3. Create a Motorway `class` that can be used as extra documentation with directions. Include data members such as name of the highway, type of street (i.e., Road, Street, Avenue, Blvd., Lane, etc.), direction (i.e., E, W, N, or S), surface (i.e., blacktop, gravel, sand, and concrete), number of lanes, toll or no toll, and the party that maintains it. Write instance methods that return the full name of the motorway, full name of the motorway and whether it is toll or not, and full name of the motorway and the number of lanes. Also include a `ToString( )` method that returns all data members with appropriate labels. Include enough constructors to make the class flexible, and experiment with using the class diagram to create the property members. In a second `class` tests the constructors, instance methods, and properties defined in the Motorway `class`.

4. Create an `Employee class`. Items to include as data members are employee number, first name, last name, date of hire, job description, department, and monthly salary. The `class` is often used to display an alphabetical listing of all employees. Include appropriate constructors and properties. Provide two instance methods that return the full name. The first should return first name, space last name. The second method should return the name in a format that it could be used for sorting (last name, followed by a comma, space, and then first name). Override the `ToString ( )` method to return all data members. Create a second `class` to test your `Employee class`.

5. Create a `Receipt class` that could be used by a retail store. Items to include as data members are receipt number, date of purchase, customer number, customer name and address, customer phone number, item number, description, unit price, and quantity purchased. For simplicity,

you may assume each receipt is for a single ticket item and contains a single item number. Include appropriate constructors and properties plus an additional method that calculates the total cost using the quantity and unit price. Override the `ToString ( )` method to return the information about the customer (name and phone number) and the total cost of the item purchased. Create a second `class` to test your `Receipt class`.

6. Create a `Trip class`. Include as data members destination, distance traveled, total cost of gasoline, and number of gallons consumed. Include appropriate constructors and properties. Add additional methods that calculate miles per gallon and the cost per mile. Override the `ToString ( )` method. Create a second `class` to test your `Trip class`.

7. There are a number of national and state parks available to tourists. Create a `Park class`. Include data members such as name of park, location, type of (i.e., national, state, and local) facility, fee, number of employees, number of visitors recorded for the past 12 months, and annual budget. Write separate instance methods that (1) return a string representing name of the park, the location, and type of park; (2) return a string representing the name of the park, the location, and facilities available; (3) compute cost per visitor based on annual budget and the number of visitors during the last 12 months; and (4) compute revenue from fees for the past year based on number of visitors and fee. Also include a `ToString( )` method that returns all data members with appropriate labels. Create a second `class` to test your `Park class`.

8. Write a program that includes an `Employee class` that can be used to calculate and print the take-home pay for a commissioned sales employee. All employees receive 7% of the total sales. Federal tax rate is 18%. Retirement contribution is 10%. Social Security tax rate is 6%. Write instance methods to calculate the commission income, federal and social security tax withholding amounts and the amount withheld for retirement. Use appropriate constants, design an object-oriented solution, and write constructors. Include at least one mutator and one accessor method; provide properties for the other instance variables. Create a second `class` to test your design. Allow the user to enter values for the name of the employee and the sales amount for the week in the second `class`.

9. Write a program that creates a `ProfessorRating class` consisting of professor name, professor ID, and three ratings. The three ratings are used to evaluate easiness, helpfulness, and clarity. Include appropriate

properties. Do not allow the ID to be changed after an object has been constructed. Provide a method in the ProfessorRating class to compute and return the overall rating average. Print all ratings and the average rating formatted with no digits to the right of the decimal from the implementation class. In a separate implementation class, allow the user to enter the values. Use a single class method to enter all data. Test the class by invoking the constructors to create instances of the ProfessorRating class.

10. Create a Money class that has as data members dollars and cents. Include IncrementMoney and DecrementMoney instance methods. Include constructors that enable the Money class to be instantiated with a single value representing the full dollar/cent amount as well as a constructor that enables you to create an instance of the class by sending two separate integer values representing the dollar and cent amounts. Include an instance method that returns as a string the number of dollars, quarters, nickels, dimes, and pennies represented by the object's value. Override the ToString( ) method to return the monetary amount formatted with currency symbols. Create a second class to test your Money class.

© zeljkodan/Shutterstock.com

CHAPTER 5

MAKING DECISIONS

IN THIS CHAPTER, YOU WILL:

- Learn about conditional expressions that return Boolean results and those that use the bool data type
- Examine equality, relational, and logical operators used with conditional expressions
- Write if selection type statements to include one-way, two-way, and nested forms
- Learn about and write switch statements
- Learn how to use the ternary operator to write selection statements
- Revisit operator precedence and explore the order of operations
- Work through a programming example that illustrates the chapter's concepts

General-purpose programming languages provide three categories of programming statements. These categories are referred to as the **basic programming constructs**. They are simple sequence, selection, and iteration or loop statements. **Simple sequence**, which you have already used, is based on the concept that once execution begins in the `Main( )` method, it continues in a linear fashion one statement after the next until the end of your program is encountered. You can alter this sequential flow by invoking or calling other methods. When you do, control transfers to that method. Inside the method, statements are again executed using a linear flow. When you reach the end of the method, control returns back to the place in the calling segment where the call was initiated from. This chapter introduces you to a second construct, which is the selection statement. The **selection statement** is used for decision making and allows your program statements to deviate from the sequential path and perform different statements based on the value of an expression. The third basic construct, iteration, is introduced in Chapter 6. **Iteration**, or looping, enables you to write instructions that can be repeated.

Methods were introduced to you in Chapter 3. In this chapter, you write methods that use two kinds of selection statements: `if...else` and `switch`. You will examine one-way, two-way, nested, multiway, and compound forms of `if` statements. You explore situations where `switch` statements should be used instead of `if...else` statements. You learn about the ternary conditional operator that can be used in your methods to write selection statements. By the time you finish this chapter, your methods include statements that perform simple and complex decisions.

Boolean Expressions

Chapter 3 introduced you to Boolean variables, represented in C# using the `bool` data type. You learned that the `bool` type holds values of either `true` or `false`. Boolean variables are central to both selection and iteration control constructs. Their values can be tested and used to determine alternate paths. However, many times selection statements are written that do not actually use a Boolean variable, but instead produce a Boolean result.

Boolean Results

One of the great powers of the computer is being able to make decisions. You can write program statements that evaluate the contents of a variable. Based on the value of the variable, differing segments of code can be executed. Consider the following statements in Example 5-1. They are written in pseudocode.

You will remember that pseudocode is "near code" but does not satisfy the syntax requirements of any programming language.

EXAMPLE 5-1

1. if (gradePointAverage is greater than 3.80)
   awardType is assigned deansList
2. if (letterGrade is equal to 'F')
   display message "You must repeat course"
3. if (examScore is less than 50)
   display message "Do better on next exam"

The three statements in Example 5-1 have common features. First, they each include a conditional expression, enclosed inside parentheses. **Conditional expressions** produce a Boolean result. The result is either `true` or `false`. The first conditional expression is (`gradePointAverage` is greater than 3.80). Either `gradePointAverage` is greater than 3.8 (`true`) or it is not (`false`); similarly, `letterGrade` is equal to F (`true`) or it is not (`false`). The same holds for `examScore`. It does not matter how close the score is to 50. The result is `true` when `examScore` is less than 50. At other times, it is `false`. That is a requirement of a conditional expression. It must evaluate to `true` or `false`.

The second common feature of the three statements in Example 5-1 is that they each include an additional statement following the conditional expression. This second line is executed when the conditional expression evaluates to `true`. No statement is included for any of the statements in Example 5-1 for the situation when the expression evaluates to `false`. The conditional expression, sometimes called "**the test**," uses English-equivalent words to represent the comparisons to be made. This is because the statements in Example 5-1 are written using pseudocode or Structured English. You will learn how to transpose these words into C# relational and equality operators later in this chapter. First, conditional expressions are examined.

Conditional Expressions

A conditional expression is also referred to as a **test condition**. To determine, for example, who receives an `A` on an exam, a relational test is made between two operands. The first operand is an exam score, and the second is a value such as 90, or some predetermined cutoff value for an `A`. After this conditional expression is written, it can be used with hundreds of different exam scores to determine who gets the `A`.

When you write an expression to be tested, you must first determine the operands. Unless a `bool` data type is used, two operands are required for equality and relational tests. You saw this same requirement of two operands when you used binary arithmetic operators such as multiply `*` and divide `/` to perform multiplication and division.

```
answer = x * y;                  // Here x and y are both operands.
examScore greater than 89        // examScore and 89 are operands.
finalGrade is equal to 'A'       // finalGrade and 'A' are operands.
```

To construct a conditional expression, after you identify the operands, determine what type of comparison to make. In Example 5-1, pseudocode demonstrated how to compare a variable against a value. However, to write those statements in C#, you use special symbols to represent the operations. The next section describes the types of operators that can be used.

Equality, Relational, and Logical Tests

You can use equality, relational, and logical operators in conditional expressions. To determine whether two values are the same, use the equality operator.

EQUALITY OPERATORS

Two equal symbol characters == are used as the **equality operator** in C# for comparing operands. No space is inserted between the symbols. Recall that the single equal symbol (=), called the **assignment operator**, is used to assign the result of an expression to a variable. You cannot use the assignment operator in a selection statement in C#.

Languages such as Java and C++ allow you to use a single equal symbol inside a conditional expression. This often creates an error that takes time to find. Failing to put two equal symbols in a conditional expression leads to an assignment being made. The side effect of this is that the expression always evaluates to `true`, unless the assignment statement assigns zero to a variable. You never have this problem in C# because C# issues a syntax error if you use the assignment operator in a location where the equality operator is expected.

An exclamation point followed by a single equal symbol (!=) represents **NOT equal**. As with the equality operator, no space is embedded between the exclamation point and equal symbol. Table 5-1 gives examples of the use of equality operators.

TABLE 5-1 Equality operators

Symbol	Meaning	Example	Result
==	Equal	(1 == 2)	`false`
!=	NOT equal	(4 != (19 % 5))	`false`

© Cengage Learning

Notice how an arithmetic operator is part of one of the operands in the last row of Table 5-1. The expression 19 % 5 produces 4 as a remainder; thus 4 != (19 % 5) returns `false`. The operand can also include a call to a value-returning method. You can use any valid executable statement that produces or returns a value as an operand.

Consider the next conditional expression. When `operand1` has a value of 25, the expression returns `true` (5^2 is equal to 25). When `operand1` is not 25, the expression returns `false`.

```
(operand1 == Math.Pow(5,2))
```

NOTE Although not a requirement when comparing a variable to a literal value, it is conventional to place the variable in the first operand location with a value in the second location.

5

When you use the equality operator with integral values, such as variables of type `int`, the results produced are what you would expect; however, you need to be cautious of making equality comparisons with floating-point (`float` and `double`) and `decimal` types. In the following code segment, consider the compile-time initialization of `aValue` followed by the conditional expression:

```
double aValue = 10.0 / 3.0;
if (aValue == 3.33333333333333)
```

The expression returns `false`. Floating-point division does not produce a finite value. Because of rounding, you often get unpredictable results when comparing floating-point variables for equality.

The `==` and `!=` are **overloaded operators**. You learned about overloaded methods in Chapter 4. Overloaded operators are defined to perform differently based on their operands. In addition to being defined for numeric data types, `==` and `!=` are defined for strings in C#. The operators perform a completely different function when the operands are of `string` data type in contrast to numeric type. When strings are compared, the first character in the first operand is compared against the first character in the second operand. If they are the same, the comparison moves to the second characters. The characters are compared lexicographically using the Unicode character set.

NOTE Words are placed in a dictionary in lexicographical order. The word "Able" comes before "Ada" in the dictionary. The Unicode uppercase character A comes before the lowercase character a.

EXAMPLE 5-2

```
                 ↓                            ↓
("The class name is CS158" == "The class name is cs158")
```

Example 5-2 returns `false` because the uppercase character `C` at position 19 has a Unicode value of 67, whereas the lowercase `c` at that same position on the right side of the comparison operator has a value of 99.

You might want to review Appendix C, which contains a table showing a subset of the Unicode characters mapped to their numeric equivalent value.

In Example 5-2, up to position 19, the strings are considered equal. When the characters at position 19 are compared, the result of the expression (`false`) is determined, and no additional comparison beyond position 19 is needed.

Many languages require you to use special `string` methods, such as `strcmp( )`, to make equality comparisons on `string` variables. C# makes it much easier for you to write instructions comparing the contents of `string` variables for equality.

RELATIONAL OPERATORS

Relational operators allow you to test variables to see if one is greater or less than another variable or value. Table 5-2 lists the relational symbols used in C#. The symbol's meaning and a sample expression using each operator are included.

TABLE 5-2 Relational symbols

Symbol	Meaning	Example	Result
>	Greater than	(8 > 5)	`true`
		(1 > 2)	`false`
<	Less than	(1 < 2)	`true`
		('z' < 'a')	`false`
>=	Greater than or equal	(100 >= 100)	`true`
		(14 >= 7)	`true`
<=	Less than or equal	(100 <= 100)	`true`
		(27 <= 7)	`false`

© Cengage Learning

For comparing numbers, the relational operators <, >, <=, and >= produce a straightforward result, as given in Table 5-2. When you compare characters declared using `char`, they are compared lexicographically using the Unicode character set. A comparison to determine whether the lowercase character z is less than a produces `false`, because z has a Unicode decimal equivalent of 122 and a has a value of 97.

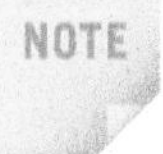

You cannot compare `string` operands using the relational symbols <, >, >=, or <= in C#.

5

Remember from Chapter 2 that strings in C# are reference types. Instead of the `string` character values being stored in binary form at the memory location of the variable's identifier, the memory location of a `string` identifier contains the address in which the string of characters is stored. Normally when you compare reference type variables, you get a comparison of the addresses.

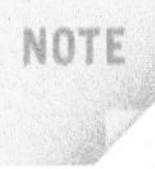

The `string class` in C# has a number of useful methods for dealing with strings. You learn about these methods in Chapter 7. The `Compare( )` method is used for relational comparisons of strings. If you want to look ahead, many methods of the `string class` are listed in Table 7-3.

For debugging, it is often easier to follow and read simple relational comparisons than compound comparisons. You will study this in more detail in a later section in this chapter. With additional thought, most numeric comparisons involving the compound relational operators of <= and >= can be revised. By simply adding or subtracting from the endpoint, the comparison can be written in a simpler form. Consider the following two statements in Example 5-3, which yield exactly the same comparison.

EXAMPLE 5-3

```
(examScore >= 90)     // Avoid compounds if you can.
(examScore > 89)      // Better test – does the same as above.
```

Both of the expressions in Example 5-3 return `true` for integer values larger than 89. The first line contains a compound expression (`examScore greater than 90 or examScore equal to 90`). By simply subtracting 1 from 90, you can write a simpler conditional expression, as shown in Line 2 of Example 5-3.

Develop good style by surrounding operators with a space. This includes arithmetic, logical, and relational symbols. Readability is enhanced if you type a space before and after every operator, for example, `x > 5; y == z; aValue = bValue + 3.`

Table 5-3 in Example 5-4 presents several conditional expressions. Both relational and equality operators are used. A result of the expression with an explanation is included.

EXAMPLE 5-4

For each expression example, use the following declaration of variables:

```
int aValue = 100,
    bValue = 1000;
char cValue = 'A';
string sValue = "CS158";
decimal money = 50.22m;
double dValue = 50.22;
```

TABLE 5-3 Results of sample conditional expressions

Expression	Result	Explanation
(money == 100.00)	Syntax error	Type mismatch. money is decimal, 100.00 is double. Receive an error message that says "Operator '==' cannot be applied to double and decimal"
(money == 50.22m) (money != dValue)	true Syntax error	Must suffix the decimal number with M or m. Type mismatch. money is decimal, dValue is double. Receive an error message that says "Operator '==' cannot be applied to double and decimal"
(aValue > bValue)	false	100 is not greater than 1000
(sValue < "CS")	Syntax error	< cannot be used with string operand
(aValue > (bValue -999))	true	100 is greater than 1

(continues)

TABLE 5-3 Results of sample conditional expressions (*continued*)

Expression	Result	Explanation
`(aValue > dValue)`	`true`	Integer `aValue` is converted into `double` and compared correctly
`(aValue < money)`	`false`	Integer `aValue` is converted into `decimal` and compared correctly
(cValue = 'F')	Syntax error	Cannot use single equal symbol (=) for comparison. Single equal symbol (=) is used for assignment
`(cValue < 'f')`	`true`	Unicode A has a value of 65; Unicode `f` has a value of 102

© Cengage Learning

5

In C#, the `==` and `!=` are defined to work with strings to compare the characters lexicographically. This is not the case for other reference variables. In addition, the relational operators such as <, >, <=, and >= are not defined to work with strings. The relational operators can be used with `char` data types.

LOGICAL OPERATORS

Conditional expressions can be combined with logical conditional operators to form complex expressions. The **logical operators** in C# are `&`, `&&`, `|`, `||`, and `!`. The operands to logical operators must be Boolean expressions. Just as you communicate a compound expression in English, you can combine expressions with AND or OR. C# uses two ampersands && and two pipes || to represent AND and OR, respectively. These two operators are called the **conditional logical operators**. To add two points to `examScore` that range between 70 and 90, you might write the following pseudocode:

```
if (examScore > 69 AND examScore < 91)
    examScore = examScore + 2
```

When expressions are combined with AND, both expressions must evaluate to `true` for the entire compound expression to return `true`. As given in Table 5-4, unless both expression operands are `true`, the compound expression created using the `&&` evaluates to `false`.

TABLE 5-4 Conditional logical AND (&&)

Expression1	Expression2	Expression1 && Expression2
true	true	true
true	false	false
false	true	false
false	false	false

© Cengage Learning

NOTE Table 5-4 is sometimes referred to as a truth table.

When combining logical operators with relational tests, developers often make the mistake of omitting the variable for the second and subsequent conditions being tested. In English, you would probably say, "if examScore is greater than 69 and less than 91." You normally do not repeat the variable being tested. In C#, you must repeat the variable. It is incorrect to write:

```
(examScore > 69 < 91)                          // Invalid
```

It is also incorrect to write:

```
(69 < examScore < 91)                          // Invalid
```

The correct way to write the expression is

```
((examScore > 69) && (examScore < 91))         // Correct way
```

NOTE It is not necessary to use the two innermost parentheses. Later in this chapter, in Table 5-7, you explore the order of operations. The relational operators (< and >) have a higher precedence than the logical && and || operators, meaning that the comparisons would be performed prior to the &&. Including the parentheses adds to the readability.

As presented in Table 5-5, || only returns a `false` result when both of the expressions or operands are `false`. At all other times, when either one of the expressions or operands evaluates to `true`, the entire compound expression evaluates to `true`.

TABLE 5-5 Conditional logical OR (| |)

Expression1	Expression2	Expression1 || Expression2
true	true	true
true	false	true
false	true	true
false	false	false

© Cengage Learning

5

Compound expressions using the || must also have a complete expression on both sides of the logical symbol. The following is invalid:

```
(letterGrade == 'A' || 'B')                                  // Invalid
```

The correct way to write the conditional expression is

```
((letterGrade == 'A') || (letterGrade == 'B'))               // Correct way
```

NOTE Parentheses can be added to conditional expressions to improve readability.

The ! symbol is the **logical negation operator**. It is a unary operator that negates its operand and is called the **NOT operator**. It returns `true` when the expression or operand is `false`. It returns `false` when the expression or operand is `true`. Given the following declaration:

```
char letterGrade = 'A';
```

When the NOT operator (!) is placed in front of the conditional expression, the statement returns `false`, as shown in the following line:

```
( ! (letterGrade == 'A'))
```

The conditional expression first yields a `true` result (`letterGrade is equal to 'A'`). Adding the NOT operator ! negates that result. Thus, the expression evaluates to `false`.

As presented in Table 5-6, the NOT operator ! returns the logical complement, or negation, of its operand.

TABLE 5-6 Logical NOT (!)

Expression	! Expression
true	false
false	true

© Cengage Learning

As with the logical && and ||, the ! operator can also be difficult to follow. It is easier to debug a program that includes only positive expressions. An extra step is required in problem solving if you have to analyze a result that has been reversed or negated.

This section on compound conditions is included to give you an understanding of reading complex expressions. As you learn in the following sections, you can often avoid writing complex expressions that use logical operators with the use of a multiway or nested selection statement. This might take more thought than just combining a number of conditional expressions with a logical operator. However, because compound conditions can be difficult to debug, you should explore other options whenever possible.

Short-Circuit Evaluation

In C#, the && and || operators are also called the **short-circuiting logical operators**. These operators enable doing as little as is needed to produce the final result through short-circuit evaluation. With **short-circuit evaluation**, as soon as the value of the entire expression is known, evaluation stops. A conditional expression is evaluated from left to right. With expressions involving &&, if the first evaluates as false, there is no need to evaluate the second. The result will be false. With expressions involving ||, if the first evaluates as true, there is no need to evaluate the second. The result will be true. Using the initialized variables, consider the expressions that follow in Example 5-5.

EXAMPLE 5-5

```
int examScore = 75;
int homeWkGrade = 100;
double amountOwed = 0;
char status = 'I';
:               // : added to indicate more lines follow
((examScore > 90) && (homeWkGrade > 80))      // Line 1 - false
((amountOwed == 0) || (status == 'A'))        // Line 2 - true
```

When the first part of the expression (examScore > 90) in Line 1 evaluates to false, there is no need to evaluate the second. The result of the entire expression is false. If the first part of the expression in Line 1 evaluates to true, the second expression has to be evaluated. Both must be true for the entire expression to evaluate to true.

Line 2 is a logical OR; thus, if the first part of the expression evaluates to true, there is no need to evaluate the second. The result of the entire expression is true as soon as one of them evaluates to true. With short-circuit evaluation, the computer is able to stop evaluating as soon as the value of the expression is known.

C# also includes the & and | operators. They both compute the logical AND or OR of their operands, just as the && and || do. The difference between them is that && and || do short-circuit evaluation, whereas & and | do not. They are useful for situations that involve compound or complex expressions in which you want the entire expression to be performed, regardless of whether the result of the conditional expression returns true. Consider the following:

```
((aValue > bValue) & (count++ < 100))
```

Using the logical AND (&) always results in 1 being added to count, regardless of whether aValue is greater than bValue. Replacing the & with && produces the same result for the entire expression; however, the side effect of incrementing count might not happen. Using the && and doing short-circuit evaluation would only enable 1 to be added to count when the first part of the expression (aValue > bValue) evaluates to true. With &&, if (aValue > bValue) evaluates to false, the second expression is not executed.

NOTE Because of the visual similarities between the symbols (&, && and |, ||), their use can lead to code that can be difficult to debug. You might want to add comments explaining the conditional expressions.

Consider the code shown in Example 5-6:

EXAMPLE 5-6

```
int x = 0,
    y = 0,
    z = 0;
if (x > 1 && ++y > 0)
    z += 1;
WriteLine("Y is {0}, Z is {1}", y, z);
```

The output for Example 5-6 is

```
Y is 0, Z is 0
```

If you replace the && with a single ampersand (&), as shown in Example 5-7:

EXAMPLE 5-7

```
if (x > 1 & ++y > 0)
```

the variable y gets incremented by one producing the output shown here:

```
Y is 1, Z is 0
```

Boolean Data Type

A variable declared to be of `bool` type holds the value of `true` or `false`. When a `bool` variable is used in a conditional expression, you do not have to add symbols to compare the variable against a value. You simply write the `bool` variable name as the expression. Take, for example, the Boolean variable declared as shown in the following code snippet:

```
bool salariedEmployee;
```

After being declared, a conditional expression could be used to determine whether `salariedEmployee` held the values `true` or `false`. The conditional expression would read:

```
if (salariedEmployee)
```

It is not necessary to write `if (salariedEmployee` is equal to `true)` because `salariedEmployee` is defined as a `bool` type.

NOTE It is OK to test the identifier to see if it is `true`. This is valid and might even be more readable, especially in situations where the variable's identifier is not very descriptive.

BOOLEAN FLAGS

Boolean data types are often used as flags to signal when a condition exists or when a condition changes. To create a flag situation, declare a `bool` data type variable and initialize it to either `true` or `false`. Then use this variable to control processing. As long as the value of the Boolean variable remains the same, processing continues. When some planned condition changes, the Boolean data type is changed and processing stops. For example, `moreData` is declared as a Boolean, is initialized to `true`, but can be changed to `false` when all of the data has been processed.

```
bool moreData = true;
:                           // Other statement(s) that might change
:                           // the value of moreData to false.
if (moreData)               // Execute statement(s) following the
                            // if when moreData is true.
```

The expressions you have seen thus far used English-equivalent words for the conditional expression. In the following sections, you examine operators used for conditional expressions and learn how to implement selection statements in C#.

if. . .else Selection Statements

The **if selection statement**, classified as one-way, two-way, or nested, is used in combination with a conditional expression. The `if` statement facilitates specifying alternate paths based on the result of the conditional expression. The expressions might involve values entered at run time or calculations made using data. The sections that follow illustrate how you can include these types of selection statements in your programs.

One-Way if Statement

A **one-way selection statement** is used when an expression needs to be tested. When the result of the expression is `true`, additional processing is performed. The general format for a one-way `if` statement is

```
if (conditional_expression)
    statement;     // Actions to be performed when the
                   // expression evaluates to true.
```

In C#, the expression must be enclosed in parentheses. Notice that no semicolon is placed at the end of the line containing the expression. The expression must produce a Boolean result when evaluated—a result that can be evaluated as `true` or `false`. Thus, the expression can be a Boolean variable or a conditional expression involving two or more operands. With a one-way `if` statement, when the expression evaluates to `false`, the statement immediately following the conditional expression is skipped or bypassed. No special statement(s) is included for the `false` result. Execution continues with the segment of code following the `if` statement.

If the expression evaluates to `true`, the statement is performed and then execution continues with the same segment of code following the `if` statement as when the expression evaluates to `false`.

With the preceding syntax illustration, `statement` represents the action(s) that takes place when the expression evaluates as `true`. To associate more than one statement with the `true` result, enclose the statements inside curly braces. These statements are referred to as the `true` statements. By enclosing the `true` statements inside curly braces, you are marking the beginning and ending of the statements to be executed when the expression evaluates to `true`.

Consider Example 5-8.

EXAMPLE 5-8

```
if (examScore > 89)
{
     grade = 'A';
     WriteLine("Congratulations — Great job!");
}
WriteLine("I am displayed, whether the expression " +
          "evaluates true or false");
```

When examScore is equal to 89 or any smaller value, the expression evaluates to false, and the true statements inside the curly braces are skipped. The WriteLine( ) method following the closing curly brace is executed. When examScore is equal to 95, the true statements are executed and then the WriteLine( ) following the closing curly brace is executed.

Consider the following revision to Example 5-8:

```
if (examScore > 89)
                        // Missing opening curly brace '{'
    grade = 'A';
    WriteLine("Congratulations — Great job!");
                        // Missing closing curly brace '}'
WriteLine("I am displayed, whether the expression " +
          "evaluates true or false");
```

Here, WriteLine("Congratulations — Great job!"); is always executed. Indentation is for readability only. If the curly braces are omitted, no syntax error or warning is issued. The congratulations message would be displayed for *all* values of examScore (even examScore of zero).

NOTE: Some programmers enclose all statements associated with if statements in curly braces. This includes the single-line true statements. This way, they do not forget to surround the body with { }. You are encouraged as a beginning programmer to follow this guideline.

The flow of execution in a one-way if statement is illustrated in Figure 5-1. When the expression evaluates to true, the true statement(s) is (are) executed. As the figure shows, execution continues at the same location whether the expression evaluates to true or false.

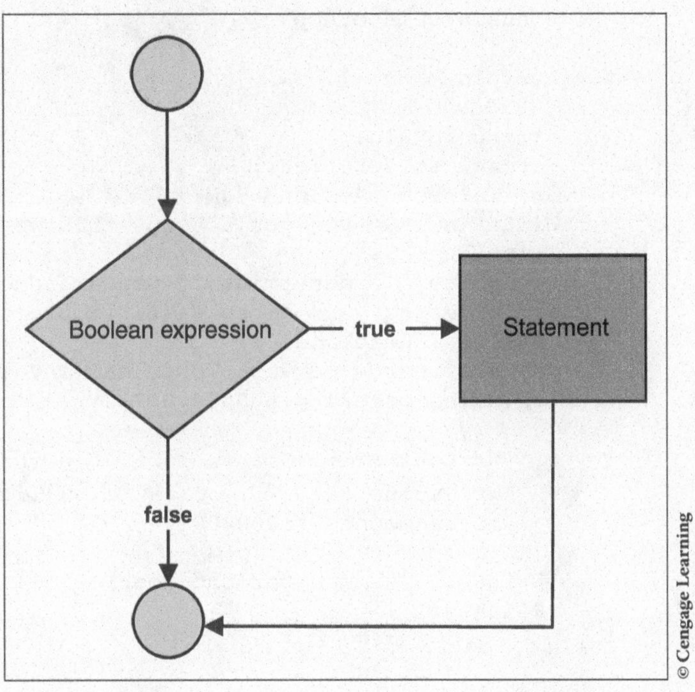

FIGURE 5-1 if One-way statement

5

EXAMPLE 5-9

A company issues $1000.00 bonuses at the end of the year to all employees who have sold over $500,000.00 in products. The following code segment is a program that allows users to enter their sales figure. It determines whether a bonus is due and displays a message indicating whether a bonus is awarded.

```
/* BonusCalculator.cs    Author: Doyle
 * Allows the user to input their
 * gross sales for the year. This value
 * is checked to determine whether
 * a bonus is in order.
 **************************************/

using System;
using static System.Console;

namespace BonusCalculatorApp
```

```
{
        class BonusCalculatorApp
        {
            static void Main( )
            {
                string inValue;
                decimal salesForYear;
                decimal bonusAmount = 0M;
                WriteLine("Do you get a bonus this year?");
                WriteLine( );
                WriteLine("To determine if you are due one,");
                Write("enter your gross sales figure: ");
                inValue = ReadLine( );
                salesForYear = Convert.ToDecimal(inValue);
                if (salesForYear > 500000.00M)
                {
                    WriteLine( );
                    WriteLine("YES. . .you get a bonus!");
                    bonusAmount = 1000.00M;
                }
                 WriteLine("Bonus for the year: {0:C}", bonusAmount);
                 ReadKey( );
            }
        }
}
```

Because this application involves money, the new data type, `decimal`, is used to hold the value entered and the bonus amount. Notice how the special suffix of `M` is placed at the end of the initialization when the variable is declared. The declaration is repeated here:

```
decimal bonusAmount = 0M;
```

It is also necessary to place `M` at the end of the `decimal` numeric literal used as part of the expression being evaluated:

```
if (salesForYear > 500000.00M)
```

It is again necessary to include the `M` when an assignment statement stores the `decimal 1000.00M` in the `bonusAmount` memory location:

```
bonusAmount = 1000.00M;
```

NOTE The special symbols `m` and `M` stand for money. Numeric literals used with `decimal` variables require the `M`; otherwise, a syntax error message is issued.

As you examine Example 5-9, note a call to a method in the `Convert class`. In Chapter 3, you were introduced to the `Parse( )` method to convert values stored in `string` variables into numeric types. You can also use the `Convert class` for this conversion.

`Convert` is in the `System` `namespace` and has methods for converting one `base` type into another `base` type. The `Convert.ToDecimal( )` method was used in Example 5-9 to change the inputted `string` value into a `decimal` value. To convert into an integer, use `Convert.ToInt32( )`, and to convert into a `double`, use `Convert.ToDouble( )`. If you are using Visual Studio, make sure to use the IntelliSense feature. You can explore the many methods and their overloads available in the `Convert` `class`.

For Example 5-9, the output produced when the user enters 600000 is shown in Figure 5-2.

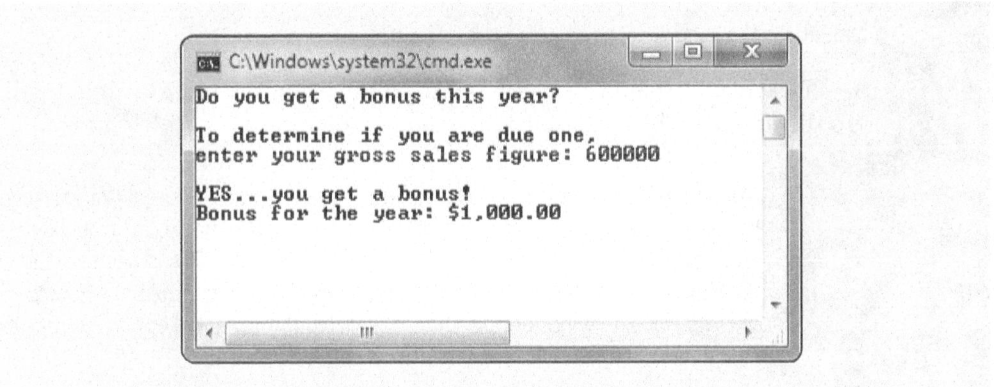

FIGURE 5-2 BonusApp with salesForYear equal to 600000.00

The problem definition indicates that sales must be over $500,000.00 before a bonus is awarded. The output produced when 500000.00 is entered is shown in Figure 5-3.

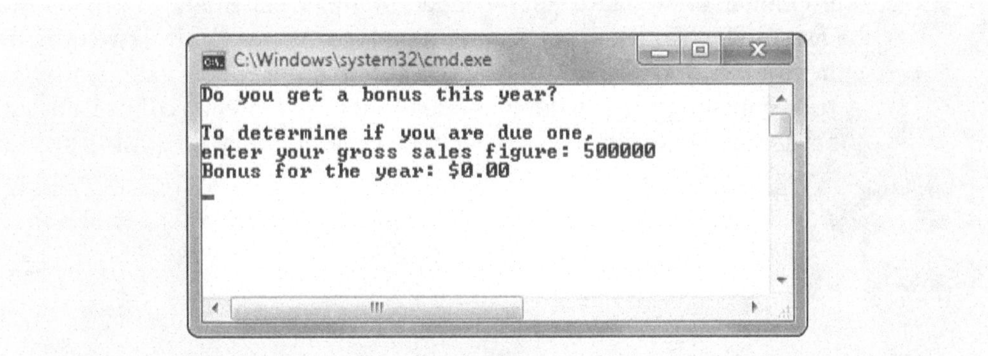

FIGURE 5-3 BonusApp with salesForYear equal to 500000.00

Beginning programmers often mistakenly place a semicolon at the end of the parenthesized expression being evaluated. If you do this, your program runs, and no syntax error message is issued. However, you are creating a **null (empty) statement body** in place of the `true` statement. The logic is basically indicating, "Do nothing when the expression evaluates to `true`." If you are using Visual Studio and place a semicolon in the wrong place, as shown in Figure 5-4, you get a green squiggly indicator, alerting you to the potential problem. Most other language IDEs do not warn you that this problem might exist.

```
if (salesForYear > 500000.00M);
```

Possible mistaken empty statement

FIGURE 5-4 IntelliSense pop-up message

In Visual Studio, when you move your pointer over the red warning, IntelliSense pops up the message, "Possible mistaken empty statement."

Notice that `bonusAmount` was initialized when it was declared. Without this initialization, a syntax error, "Use of unassigned local variable. . ." would be issued when `bonusAmount` is referenced below the `if` statement. This is because there is the possibility that the statements associated with the `if` statements, where `bonusAmount` gets its value, may not be executed. Initializing the variable kept that error from happening.

The one-way `if` statement does not provide an alternate set of steps for a situation in which the expression evaluates to `false`. That option is available with the two-way `if` statement.

Two-Way if Statement

An optional `else` clause can be added to an `if` statement to provide statements to be executed when the expression evaluates to `false`. With a **two-way if statement**, either the `true` statement(s) is (are) executed or the `false` statement(s), but not both. After completing the execution of one of these statements, control always transfers to the statement following the `if` block. The general format for a two-way `if` statement is

```
if (conditional_expression)  // No semicolon is placed on this line
     statement;              // Executed when expression is true
else
     statement;              // Executed when expression is false
```

Notice that there is no need to repeat the expression with the `else`. Many beginning programmers write the following:

```
if (aValue == 100)
    WriteLine("The value is 100");
else (aValue != 100) // INCORRECT! No need to repeat the expression
    WriteLine("The value is not 100");
```

The correct way to include the `else` is to place it on a line by itself without any expression. On the lines that follow the `else`, include the statements that are to be performed when the expression evaluates to `false`. Here is the correct way to write the selection statement:

```
if (aValue == 100)
    WriteLine("The value is 100");
else
    WriteLine("The value is not 100");
```

As with the one-way `if` statement, you can include more than one statement by enclosing statements in curly braces.

Readability is important. Notice the indentation used with one- and two-way `if` statements. The statements are aligned with the conditional expression. Smart indenting can be set in Visual Studio, so that the alignment is automatic.

Figure 5-5 illustrates the flow of execution in a two-way `if` statement.

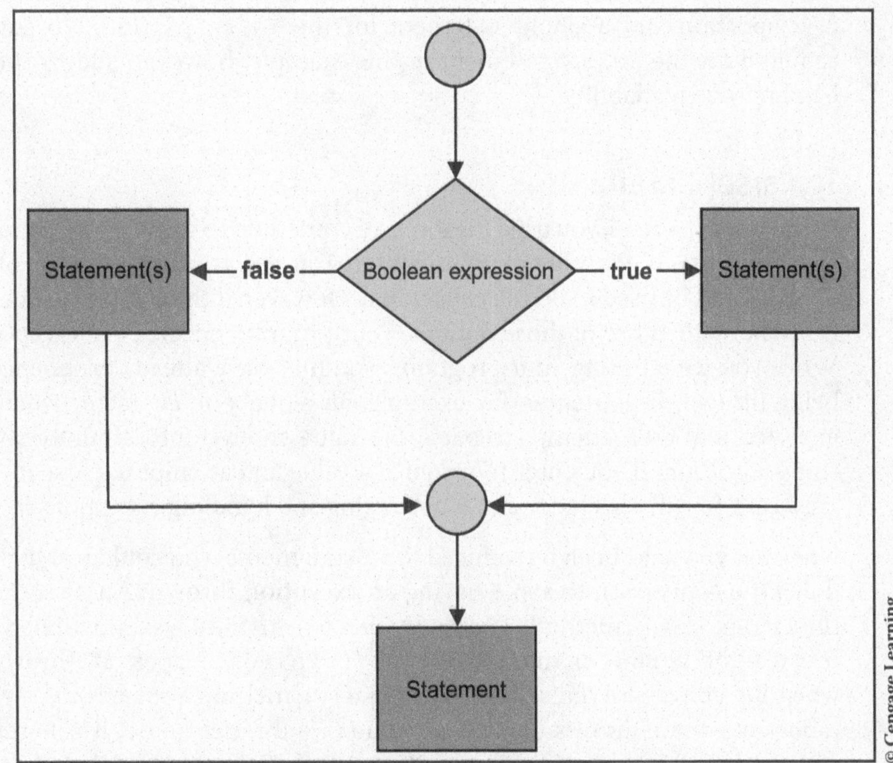

FIGURE 5-5 Two-way if statement

When the expression evaluates to `true`, the `true` statements are executed. As the figure shows, execution continues at the same location for both, whether the `true` statements are executed or the `false` statements are executed. Consider Example 5-10.

EXAMPLE 5-10

```
if (hoursWorked > 40)
{
    payAmount = (hoursWorked - 40) * payRate * 1.5 +
                payRate * 40;
    WriteLine("You worked {0} hours overtime.",
               hoursWorked - 40);
}
else
    payAmount = hoursWorked * payRate;
WriteLine("I am displayed, whether the expression " +
          "evaluates true or false");
```

As shown in Example 5-10, it is permissible to have a block of statements with the `true` portion and a single statement for the `false` portion. No curly braces are required for the `false` statement in this example; however, adding the curly braces can improve readability.

TryParse( ) Method

In previous chapters, you used the `Parse( )` method to convert a string value sent as an argument into its equivalent numeric value. You also saw that members of the `Convert class` could be used to do the conversion. However, if the string value being converted is invalid with either of those options, your program crashes. An exception is thrown. While you were testing your programs, you may have already experienced exceptions being thrown. If you enter, for example, an alphabetic character when a number is expected and then attempt to parse the value entered into a number, your program stops execution. If you enter too large of a value and attempt to parse it, your program crashes. You will read more about debugging and handling exceptions in Chapter 11.

Now that you have been introduced to `if` statements, you could test the value prior to doing the conversion to avoid having an exception thrown. Another option is to use the `TryParse( )` method. The `TryParse( )` method was mentioned in Chapter 3. It is like the `Parse( )` method, except `TryParse( )` does not throw an exception when the conversion fails. The `TryParse( )` method converts the string representation of a value into its equivalent value of a different type. It also returns a Boolean return value indicating whether the conversion succeeded or not. If you examine .NET documentation, you would find that the heading for the `TryParse( )` method for the `bool` data type is as shown in Example 5-11.

EXAMPLE 5-11

```
public static bool TryParse(string someStringValue, out int result)
```

Notice that the `TryParse( )` method returns a boolean indicating whether it was successful or not. After the `TryParse( )` method is executed, `result` either holds the integer value equivalent to the data stored in the string argument, `someStringValue`, or `result` stores a zero. If the string variable's data is in the correct format and range, the conversion succeeds. Zero is only stored in `someStringValue` when the conversion fails. In situations where an alphabetic character is stored in `someStringValue`, the conversion fails, `false` is returned, and zero is stored in `result`. The conversion fails whenever the `someStringValue` parameter is not of the correct format, is null or has no value, or represents a value that can't be stored in the result parameter, such as the number is less than `MinValue` or greater than `MaxValue allowable for the data type`.

5

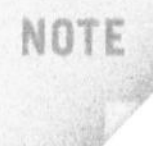

Each of the built-in data types has a `TryParse( )` method. `char.TryParse( )` converts the value of the specified string into its unicode character equivalent; `bool.TryParse( )` converts the specified string representation of a logical value into its Boolean equivalent. There are also `TryParse( )` methods for `decimal`, `double`, and `float`. With each of these, in addition to doing the conversion, a Boolean value is returned indicating whether the conversion was successful or not.

As you review Example 5-11, notice that the parameter `result` has an `out` modifier listed before the data type. `out` parameters are output-only parameters meaning that there is no value in `result` when the method is invoked. The parameter is considered initially unassigned. After the `TryParse( )` method is executed, the `out` parameter `result` will hold either the converted value or zero.

When you input data, instead of just assuming the user will always enter valid characters, you should check and make sure you have valid data before attempting to convert from the string to the appropriate equivalent value. One way to do this is include an `if` statement and test the Boolean value returned from `TryParse( )` as illustrated in Example 5-12. When `TryParse( )` returns `false`, you know there is a problem. The conversion was not successful.

EXAMPLE 5-12

```
if (int.TryParse(inValue, out v1) == false)
    WriteLine("Did not input a valid integer - 0 stored in v1");
```

Recall that when you use the special `out` and `ref` modifiers as part of the parameter, they must appear as part of the heading for the method and also in the call to the method. You saw the heading for one of the `TryParse( )` methods in Example 5-11. It included the `out` modifier. Example 5-12 illustrates a call to `TryParse( )`. It also includes the `out` modifier.

The statement in Example 5-12 attempts to convert the string value stored in `inValue` into an integer, storing the result of the conversion in the variable `v1`. If it is successful, the value is stored in `v1` and `TryParse( )` returns `true`. If there is a problem with the data, `0` is stored in `v1` and `TryParse( )` returns `false`.

Consider Example 5-13, which uses a two-way `if` statement in a `class` method. The user is prompted to enter two values. A two-way `if` statement is used to determine which is the largest. That value and its square root are displayed.

EXAMPLE 5-13

```
/* LargestValue.cs             Author: Doyle
 * Allows the user to input two values.
 * Determine the largest of the two values.
 * Prints the largest and its square root.
 *************************************/

using System;
using static System.Console;

namespace LargestValue
{
    class LargestValue
    {
        static void Main( )
        {
            int value1,
                value2,
                largestOne;
            InputValues(out value1, out value2);
            largestOne = DetermineLargest(value1, value2);
            PrintResults(largestOne);
            ReadKey( );
        }
        public static void InputValues(out int v1, out int v2)
        {
            string inValue;
            Write("Enter the first value: ");
            inValue = ReadLine( );
            if (int.TryParse(inValue, out v1) == false)
                WriteLine("Did not input a " +
                          "valid integer - 0 stored in v1");
```

```
            Write("Enter the second value: ");
            inValue = ReadLine( )
            if (int.TryParse(inValue, out v2) == false)
                    WriteLine("Did not input a " +
                              "valid integer - " +
                              "0 stored in v2");
        }
        public static int DetermineLargest(int value1, int value2)
        {
            int largestOne;      // Local variable declared to
                                 // facilitate single exit from method
            if (value1 > value2)
            {
               largestOne = value1;
            }
            else
            {
               largestOne = value2;
            }
            return largestOne;
        }
        public static void PrintResults(int largestOne)
        {
            WriteLine( );
            WriteLine("The largest value entered was "
                      + largestOne);
            WriteLine("Its square root is {0:f2}",
                      Math.Sqrt(largestOne));
            ReadKey( );
        }
    }
}
```

When you are writing selection statements, try to avoid repeating code. Instead of duplicating statements for both the `true` and `false` statements, pull out common statements and place them before or after the selection statement. You might have been tempted to solve the problem presented for Example 5-13 with the following two-way `if` statement:

```
if (value1 > value2)
{
    WriteLine("The largest value entered was " + value1);
    WriteLine("Its square root is {0:f2}", Math.Sqrt(value1));
}
else
{
    WriteLine("The largest value entered was " + value2);
    WriteLine("Its square root is {0:f2}", Math.Sqrt(value2));
}
```

The calls to the `WriteLine( )` method for displaying the largest value and its square root are included only once in Example 5-13. They appear twice in the last segment.

Another solution that is not modularized, but eliminates the repeating code, is as follows:

```
int largest;
if (value1 > value2)
{
    largest = value1;
}
else
{
    largest = value2;
}
WriteLine("The largest value entered was "+ largest);
WriteLine("Its square root is {0:f2}",
          Math.Sqrt(largest));
```

All three ways of writing the selection statement produce the same output. The modularized version in Example 5-13 is the preferred approach of the three. In this situation, you may not see a clear advantage of one approach over the other. Modularization becomes more important as the complexity of a computer program increases. Figure 5-6 shows the output produced when the program is run with `25` entered for the first value and `15` entered for the second value.

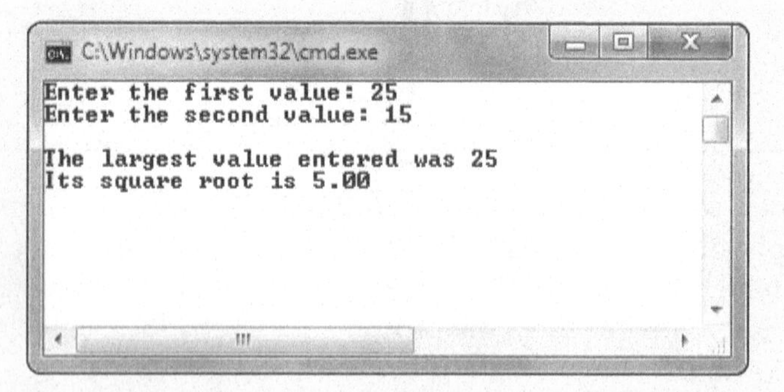

FIGURE 5-6 Output from LargestValue problem

What does the program in Example 5-13 print when the values entered are the same?

Because `value1` is not greater than `value2`, the `else` statement is executed and `value2` is stored in `largestOne`. If you want to display a message indicating their values are the same, you need to add one more conditional expression as part of the `if` statement. This additional test would be to determine whether `value2` is greater than `value1`. The expression would be added as the `else` statement. Adding this second test would enable you to include a second else statement. The last else would not be entered unless both of the conditional expressions evaluated to false—and in this case, the values are the same. If you make this revision, the logic would need to be revised for displaying the largest value. One approach would be to return the negative value of value1 or value2, when they have the same values. It does not matter which one gets returned because their values are the same. The PrintResults( ) method could test the largestOne variable. When it is negative, a message could be printed indicating that the values are the same. The additional test is as follows:

```
if (value1 > value2)
{
    largestOne = value1;
}
else
    if (value1 < value2)
    {
        largestOne = value2;
    }
    else
       largestOne = -(value1);
```


Sometimes, a single variable might need to be tested for multiple values. A nested if...else statement, like that described previously, can be used for this. You might also want to test a different variable inside the true (or false) statements. A nested if...else statement is also used for this. You will learn more about nested if...else statements in the following section.

Nested if. . .else Statement

Any statement can be included with the statements to be executed when the expression evaluates to true. The same holds for the false statements. Therefore, it is acceptable to write an if within an if. Many different expressions can be evaluated in a single if statement. When you place an if within an if, you create a **nested if. . .else statement**, also referred to as a **nested if statement**.

With a nested if statement, multiple expressions can be tested. As long as the expressions evaluate to true, the true statements continue to be evaluated. When another if statement is one of the statements in the block being executed, another evaluation is performed. This continues as long as additional if statements are part of the true statements.

As with the two-way, only one segment of code is executed. You never execute the true and its associated false statements. When the block is completed, all remaining conditional expressions and their statements are skipped or bypassed. After completing the execution of that block, control always transfers to the statement immediately following the if block. The syntax for a nested if. . .else statement, which follows that of the two-way, is repeated here. The difference is that with a nested if. . .else, the statement might be another if statement, as is illustrated next.

```
if (conditional_expression)       // No semicolon placed on this line
    statement;                    // Could be another if statement
else
    statement;                    // Could be another if statement
```

In a nested `if...else`, the inner `if` statement is said to be nested inside the outer `if`. However, the inner `if` may also contain another `if` statement. There are no restrictions on the depth of nesting. The limitation comes in the form of whether you and others can read and follow your code. The mark of a good program is that it is readable.

When you are designing a solution that requires a nested `if...else`, sometimes it is easier to develop your algorithm if you graphically map out the different options. A flowchart could be used. Another option is a **decision tree**, which is a design tool that allows you to represent complex procedures visually. Nodes are used to represent decision points, and lines branch out from the nodes to represent either further conditions or, eventually, the action to be taken based on the conditions expressed to the left. Figure 5-7 shows a decision tree used to calculate bonus for both hourly and salaried employees. Hourly employees working more than 40 hours per week receive $500. Other hourly employees get $100. Salaried employees who have been employed longer than 10 years receive $300, while the others receive $200. Figure 5-7 illustrates this situation in a decision tree.

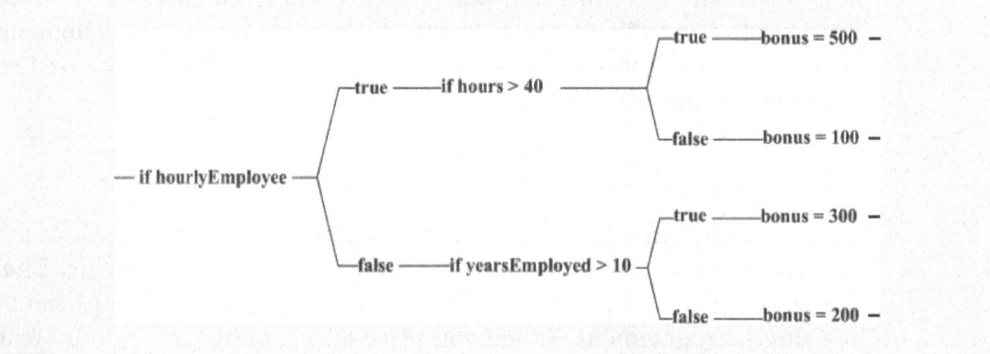

FIGURE 5-7 Bonus decision tree

Example 5-14 shows how a nested `if...else` is used to determine the bonus amount illustrated in Figure 5-7.

EXAMPLE 5-14

```
// For hourlyEmployees working more than 40 hours, a bonus of $500
// is issued. If hourlyEmployee has not worked more than 40 hours,
// issue a bonus of $100. For those non-hourlyEmployees, issue a
// $300 bonus if they have been employed longer than 10 years;
// otherwise, issue a $200 bonus.
```

```
bool hourlyEmployee;
double hours,
       bonus;
int yearsEmployed;
if (hourlyEmployee)
   if (hours > 40)
       bonus = 500;
   else
       bonus = 100;
else
   if (yearsEmployed > 10)
       bonus = 300;
   else
       bonus = 200;
```


No equality operator is needed in the first conditional expression. That is because a Boolean variable, `hourlyEmployee`, is used.

The logic for Example 5-14 could be written using four one-way `if` statements, as shown in Example 5-15. Here, each statement uses the `&&` operator.

EXAMPLE 5-15

```
if (hourlyEmployee && hours > 40)    // Less desirable solution.
    bonus = 500;                     // Example 5-14 preferred.
if (hourlyEmployee && hours <= 40)
    bonus = 100;
if ((!hourlyEmployee) && yearsEmployed > 10)
    bonus = 300;
if ((!hourlyEmployee) && yearsEmployed <= 10)
    bonus = 200;
```

The single nested `if. . .else` solution in Example 5-14 is much more efficient than the four statements in Example 5-15. In Example 5-15, every one of the statements is evaluated, even if the first one evaluates to `true`. In Example 5-14, when the first two lines evaluate to `true`, 500 is assigned to `bonus` and no additional evaluations are performed. Notice how a statement written using a logical `&&` can be rewritten as a nested `if. . .else`.

```
if (hourlyEmployee && hours > 40)
```

produces the same result as

```
if (hourlyEmployee)
    if (hours > 40)
```

When programming a nested `if. . .else` statement, it is important to know which `else` matches which `if` statement. The rule for **lining up**, or matching, elses is that an `else` goes with the closest previous `if` that does not have its own `else`. By properly lining up the `else` clauses with their corresponding `if` clauses, you encounter fewer logic errors that necessitate debugging. Example 5-16 illustrates the importance of properly lining up `if` and `else` clauses. Can you match each `else` with the correct `if`?

EXAMPLE 5-16

```
if (aValue > 10)                    Line 1
if (bValue == 0)                    Line 2
amount = 5;                         Line 3
else                                Line 4
if (cValue > 100)                   Line 5
if (dValue > 100)                   Line 6
amount = 10;                        Line 7
else                                Line 8
amount = 15;                        Line 9
else                                Line 10
amount = 20;                        Line 11
else                                Line 12
if (eValue == 0)                    Line 13
amount = 25;                        Line 14
```

As shown in Example 5-17, the `else` in Line 12 matches the `if` in Line 1; Line 10 matches Line 5. What value would be stored in `amount` if `aValue`, `bValue`, `cValue`, `dValue`, and `eValue` were all equal to `0`? Did you get `25` when you traced the logic? Look at Example 5-17. By properly lining up the `else` clauses with their corresponding `if` clauses, the answer can be determined much more quickly.

EXAMPLE 5-17

```
if (aValue > 10)                    // Line 1
    if (bValue == 0)                // Line 2
        amount = 5;                 // Line 3
    else                            // Line 4
       if (cValue > 100)            // Line 5
           if (dValue > 100)        // Line 6
               amount = 10;         // Line 7
           else                     // Line 8
               amount = 15;         // Line 9
       else                         // Line 10
           amount = 20;             // Line 11
else                                // Line 12
   if (eValue == 0)                 // Line 13
       amount = 25;                 // Line 14
```

The rule indicates that an `else` matches up with the closest previous `if` that does not already have an `else` attached to it. However, you can use braces to attach an `else` to an outer `if`, as shown in Example 5-18.

Be careful about ending a nested `if` statement with an `if` that doesn't have an `else` portion. When the statement involves an identifier that doesn't have a value, a syntax error "Use of unassigned local variable. . ." will be issued.

EXAMPLE 5-18

```
if (average > 59)
{
    if (average < 71)
        grade = 'D';
}
else
   grade = 'F';
```

5

Here `average` is defined as `int`. The braces enclose the `true` statement associated with the expression of (`average > 59`). The inner `if` statement is ended as a statement when the closing curly brace is encountered.

Consider the statements in Example 5-19 that determine a grade based on testing the value in `average`.

EXAMPLE 5-19

```
if (average > 89)
    grade = 'A';
else
    if (average > 79)
        grade = 'B';
    else
        if (average > 69)
            grade = 'C';
        else
            if (average > 59)
                grade = 'D';
            else
                grade = 'F';
```

Pay particular attention to the conditional expressions in Example 5-19. It is not necessary for the second expression to be a compound expression using `&&`. You do not have to write `if (average > 79 && average <= 89)`. Make sure you understand that execution would never have reached the expression of `(average > 79)` unless the first expression was `false`. If the `average` is not greater than `89`, it must be either equal to 89 or less than 89. Similar logic would be developed when average is defined as a floating point data type. Instead of the first conditional expression reading if (average > 89), it might read if (average > 89.4999). The second conditional expression would then read if (average > 79.4999), and so on.

As you reviewed Examples 5-17 and 5-19, you probably wondered what happens when you keep indenting. Your statements soon start to go off to the right, out of sight.

A solution to this problem used by many programmers is to write a series of else...if statements when they have a long, nested, multiway statement.

The lines in Example 5-19 could be written with a series of else...if statements, as shown in Example 5-20. This prevents the indentation problem.

EXAMPLE 5-20

```
if (average > 89)
    grade = 'A';
else if (average > 79)        // More difficult to find matching
    grade = 'B';              // if when 'else if' is placed on
else if (average > 69)        // same line.
    grade = 'C';
else if (average > 59)
    grade = 'D';
else
    grade = 'F';
```

Examples 5-19 and 5-20 are multiway if statements. A single variable is tested using a relational operator.

A nested if...else statement could also be written using the equality operator in the conditional expression. Consider Example 5-21, which displays the weekDay name based on testing an integer variable holding a number representing the day.

EXAMPLE 5-21

```
if (weekDay == 1)
    WriteLine("Monday");
else if (weekDay == 2)          // Less desirable else if (same line)
    WriteLine("Tuesday");       // used here because indentation
else if (weekDay == 3)          // required when else appears on a
    WriteLine("Wednesday");     // line by itself would move
else if (weekDay == 4)          // statements off page.
    WriteLine("Thursday");
else if (weekDay == 5)
    WriteLine("Friday");
else
    WriteLine("Not Monday through Friday");
```

When you have a single variable, such as weekDay, being tested for equality against four or more values, a switch statement can be used. A switch statement is not an option for the nested if...else solution presented in Example 5-20. A switch statement only works for tests of equality. The switch statement could be used to replace the if...else program statements shown in Example 5-21.

Switch Selection Statements

The **switch statement** is considered a multiple selection structure. It also goes by the name **case statement**. The switch or case statement allows you to perform a large number of alternatives based on the value of a single variable. This variable or expression must evaluate to an integral or string value. It cannot be used with a double, decimal, or float. But it is appropriate for short, int, long, char, and string data types. The general format of the switch statement follows:


```
switch (expression)
{
   case value1:
        statement(s);
        break;
   case value2:
        statement(s);
        break;
          . . .              // More case statements could go here
   case valueN:
        statement(s);
        break;
   [default:
        statement(s);
        break;]
}
```

With the switch statement, the expression is sometimes called the **selector**. Its value determines, or selects, which of the cases will be executed. When a switch statement is executed, the expression is evaluated and its result is compared to each case's value.

The case value must be a constant literal of the same type as the expression. You cannot use a variable in the value spot for the case. Nor can you use an expression, such as x < 22, in the value spot for the case. If the expression is a string variable, the value is enclosed in double quotes. If the expression is a char variable, the value is enclosed in single quotes. For integers, the number is typed without any special surrounding symbols.

The comparison to the case values is from top to bottom. The first case value that matches the expression results in that case's statements being executed. If no match is made, the statements associated with default are executed. Default is optional, but usually it is a good idea to include one. The default statements are only executed when there is no match of any of the case values.

The curly braces are required with a `switch` statement. That is different from an `if` statement in which they are only required when more than one statement makes up the `true` statement or the `false` statement body. A syntax error is generated if you fail to use curly braces before the first case and at the end of the last case with the `switch` statement.

The last statement for each `case` and the `default` is a **jump statement**. The `break` keyword is used for this jump. Other types of jump statements are covered in the next chapter. When `break` is encountered, control transfers outside of the `switch` statement.

Unlike other languages that allow you to leave off a `break` and **fall through** executing code from more than one `case`, C# requires the `break` for any `case` that has an executable statement(s). You cannot program a `switch` statement in C# to fall through and execute the code for multiple cases.

C# also differs from some other languages in that it requires that a `break` be included with the `default` statement. If you do not have a `break` with a `default` statement, a syntax error is issued. Many languages do not require the `break` on the last `case` because the `default` is the last statement. A natural fallout occurs.

Switch statements are often used to associate longer text with coded values as is illustrated in Example 5-22. Instead of asking the user to enter the full name for the day of the week, they could enter a number. The `switch` statement would then be used to display the related value.

EXAMPLE 5-22

```
switch(weekDay)
{
    case 1:
        WriteLine("Monday");
        break;
    case 2:
        WriteLine("Tuesday");
        break;
    case 3:
        WriteLine("Wednesday");
        break;
    case 4:
        WriteLine("Thursday");
        break;
    case 5:
        WriteLine("Friday");
        break;
    default:
        WriteLine("Not Monday through Friday");
        break;
}
```

C# allows strings to be used in expressions for `switch` statements. Consider Example 5-23, which displays the full name of a state based on comparing its two-character abbreviation to a series of `string` literals.

EXAMPLE 5-23

```
/* StatePicker.cs        Author: Doyle
 * Allows the user to enter a state
 * abbreviation. A switch statement
 * is used to display the full name
 * of the state.
 * *********************************/

using System;
using static System.Console;

namespace StatePicker
{
    class StatePicker
    {
        static void Main( )
        {
            string stateAbbrev;
            WriteLine("Enter the state abbreviation. ");
            WriteLine("Its full name will" + " be displayed.");
            WriteLine( );
            stateAbbrev = ReadLine( );
            switch(stateAbbrev)
            {
              case "AL":
                  WriteLine("Alabama");
                  break;
              case "FL":
                  WriteLine("Florida");
                  break;
              case "GA":
                  WriteLine("Georgia");
                  break;
              case "IL":
                  WriteLine("Illinois");
                  break;
              case "KY":
                  WriteLine("Kentucky");
                  break;
              case "MI":
                  WriteLine("Michigan");
                  break;
```

5

```
                case "OK":
                    WriteLine("Oklahoma");
                    break;
                case "TX":
                    WriteLine("Texas");
                    break;
                default:
                    WriteLine("No match");
                    break;
            }
            ReadKey( )
        }
    }
}
```

When stateAbbrev has a value of NV, no error message is issued; Nevada is not printed either. Instead, No match is displayed on the console screen. In addition, notice that Alabama is not displayed when stateAbbrev has a value of al. The case value must match the characters exactly; otherwise, the default option executes.

Multiple case values can be associated with the same statement(s), and it is not necessary to repeat the statement(s) for each value. When more than one case is associated with the same statement(s), you group common cases together and follow the last case value with the executable statement(s) to be performed when any of the previous cases match. In Example 5-23, it would be useful to display Alabama for AL, al, Al, and maybe aL. All four of the cases could be associated with the same executable statement that displays Alabama, as shown here:

```
case "AL":
case "aL":
case "Al":
case "al":
     WriteLine("Alabama");
     break;
```

You can place the executable statements for that group with the last case value. When you do this, you have effectively created a logical OR situation.

In Example 5-24, the result of the expression is compared against 1, 2, 3, 4, and 5. If it matches any of those values, Failing Grade is written. Notice that the break statement is required as soon as a case includes an executable statement. No fall through is permitted if the previous case label has code.

EXAMPLE 5-24

```
switch (examScore / 10)
{
    case 1:
    case 2:
    case 3:
    case 4:
    case 5:
         WriteLine("Failing Grade");
         break;
    case 6:
    case 7:
    case 8:
         WriteLine("Passing Grade");
         break;
    case 9:
    case 10:
         WriteLine("Superior Grade");
         break;
    default:
         WriteLine("Problem Grade");
         break;
}
```

The preceding `case` statement could be replaced with the following compound multiway `if` statement:

```
// Not a desirable solution!

if (((examScore / 10) == 1) || ((examScore / 10) == 2) ||
   ((examScore / 10) == 3) || ((examScore / 10) == 4) ||
   ((examScore / 10) == 5))
     WriteLine("Failing Grade");
else if (((examScore / 10) == 6) || ((examScore / 10) == 7) ||
         ((examScore / 10) == 8))
           WriteLine("Passing Grade");
else if (((examScore / 10) == 9) || ((examScore / 10) == 10))
           WriteLine("Superior Grade");
else WriteLine("Problem Grade");
```

NOTE Both the `case` statement and the multiway `if` statements are performing integer division with the previous example. The variable `examScore` is defined as an integer. Neither solution works when `examScore` is defined as a floating point `double` variable.

Which do you find the most readable? A solution for this problem could also be written using 10 separate one-way if statements. When an expression can be designed using the equality operator and involves more than three comparisons, the switch statement is almost always the best choice.

You cannot use the switch statement to test for a range of values. The only way to do this is to list every value using the case keyword. In addition, the case value must be a constant literal; it cannot be a variable. The following code segment creates a syntax error:

```
int score,
    high = 90;
switch (score)
{
     case high:    // Syntax error. Case value must be a constant.
```

You could write case 90:, but not case high.

NOTE You must ensure that the expression type is the same as the case value type. For example, you can use a char variable as the selector. Each character literal value used as the case value must be enclosed in single quotation marks.

Ternary Conditional Operator ? :

Also called the **conditional operator**, the **ternary operator** ? : provides another way to express a simple if...else selection statement. The operator consists of a question mark ? and a colon :. The general format for this conditional expression is

```
expression1 ? expression2 : expression3;
```

The ? : operator is the only ternary operator in C#. The expression that comes before the question mark, expression1, is evaluated first. When expression1 evaluates to true, expression2, following the question mark, is executed; otherwise expression3, following the colon, is executed. An example of a statement using the conditional operator is as follows:

```
grade = examScore > 89 ? 'A' : 'C';
```

This reads if examScore is greater than 89, assign A to grade; otherwise, assign C to grade. When examScore has a value of 75, the first expression, examScore > 89, evaluates to false; thus, expression3, C, following the colon is executed, and C is assigned to the grade memory location.

It performs the same operation as follows:

```
if (examScore > 89)
    grade = 'A';
else
    grade = 'C';
```

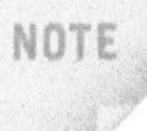

NOTE The ternary conditional operator (? :) is often used in an assignment statement.

Consider Example 5-25.

5

EXAMPLE 5-25

Most service companies have a minimum charge they use for making house calls. Take, for example, a washing machine repairperson. He may charge $50.00 per hour; however, his minimum charge for traveling to your home is $100.00. Thus, when it takes him less than 2 hours, the charge is $100. A conditional expression to calculate the charges follows:

```
double charges,
       timeAtSite = 3.5;
charges = timeAtSite < 2.0 ? 100.00 : timeAtSite * 50.00;
```

The value stored in `charges` would be 175. The first expression (`timeAtSite < 2.0`) evaluates to `false`; thus, the last expression (`timeAtSite * 50.00`) is evaluated and 175 is stored in `charges` since the assignment operator, the equal symbol, has the lowest precedence in the expression and is performed last.

The ternary conditional operator (? :) is not as readable as the `if` statement. The `if` statement is used more often than other forms of the selection statement.

Order of Operations

When an expression contains multiple operators, the **precedence of the operators** controls the order in which the individual operators are evaluated. For example, you saw in Chapter 2 that an expression such as `value1 + value2 * value3` is evaluated as `value1 + (value2 * value3)` because the `*` operator has higher precedence than the `+` operator. Generally speaking, the precedence of operators follows the following order:

1. Unary operators
2. Binary operators

2.1. Arithmetic operators (`* / % before + -`)

2.2. Relational operators (`< <= > >= before == !=`)

2.3. Logical operators (`&& before ||`)

3. Ternary operator (`? :`)
4. Assignment operators (`= *= /= %= += -=`)

In Table 2-14, the operators used primarily for arithmetic were presented. Table 5-7 adds the operators presented in this chapter.

TABLE 5-7 Operator precedence

<table>
<tr><th>Category</th><th>Operator</th><th>Precedence</th></tr>
<tr><td>Unary</td><td>+ - ! ++ --</td><td>Highest</td></tr>
<tr><td>Multiplicative</td><td>* / %</td><td></td></tr>
<tr><td>Additive</td><td>+ -</td><td></td></tr>
<tr><td>Relational</td><td>< > <= >=</td><td></td></tr>
<tr><td>Equality</td><td>== !=</td><td></td></tr>
<tr><td>Logical AND</td><td>&</td><td></td></tr>
<tr><td>Logical OR</td><td>|</td><td></td></tr>
<tr><td>Conditional AND</td><td>&&</td><td></td></tr>
<tr><td>Conditional OR</td><td>||</td><td></td></tr>
<tr><td>Conditional ternary</td><td>? :</td><td></td></tr>
<tr><td>Assignment</td><td>= *= /= %= += -=</td><td>Lowest</td></tr>
</table>

© Cengage Learning

The operators listed in Table 5-7 appear from the highest to the lowest precedence. Except for the assignment operators, all binary operators are **left-associative**, meaning that operations are performed from left to right. For example, `aValue + bValue - cValue` is evaluated as `(aValue + bValue) - cValue`.

The assignment operators and the conditional operator `? :` are **right-associative**, meaning that operations are performed from right to left. For example,

`firstValue = secondValue = thirdValue` is evaluated as `firstValue = (secondValue = (thirdValue)).`

Precedence and associativity can be controlled using parentheses. It is not necessary to include the parentheses in the previous example because the order of operations of the language determines the order. Parentheses can certainly be added to increase readability, but they are not necessary.

Example 5-26 includes an example of a selection statement using many of the operators presented in this chapter. The actual order in which the operations are performed is given following the declaration and conditional expression.

5

EXAMPLE 5-26

```
int value1 = 10, value2 = 20, value3 = 30, value4 = 40, value5 = 50;
if (value1 > value2 || value3 == 10 && value4 + 5 < value5)
    WriteLine("The expression evaluates to true");
```

The preceding expression is evaluated in the following order:

1. (`value4 + 5`) → (40 + 5) → 45
2. (`value1 > value2`) → (10 > 20) → `false`
3. ((`value4 + 5`) < `value5`) → (45 < 50) → `true`
4. (`value3 == 10`) → (30 == 10) → `false`
5. ((`value3 == 10`) && ((`value4 + 5`) < `value5`)) → `false` && `true` → `false`
6. ((`value1 > value2`) || ((`value3 == 10`) && ((`value4 + 5`) < `value5`))) → `false` || `false` → `false`

Because the expression evaluates to `false`, the line following the `if` statement is skipped or bypassed. The executable statement after the `WriteLine( )` would be the next one performed after the expression is evaluated.

PROGRAMMING EXAMPLE: SpeedingTicket

This programming example demonstrates an application that calculates fines for traffic tickets issued on campus. A nested `if...else` selection statement is used in the design. Figure 5-8 shows the problem definition.

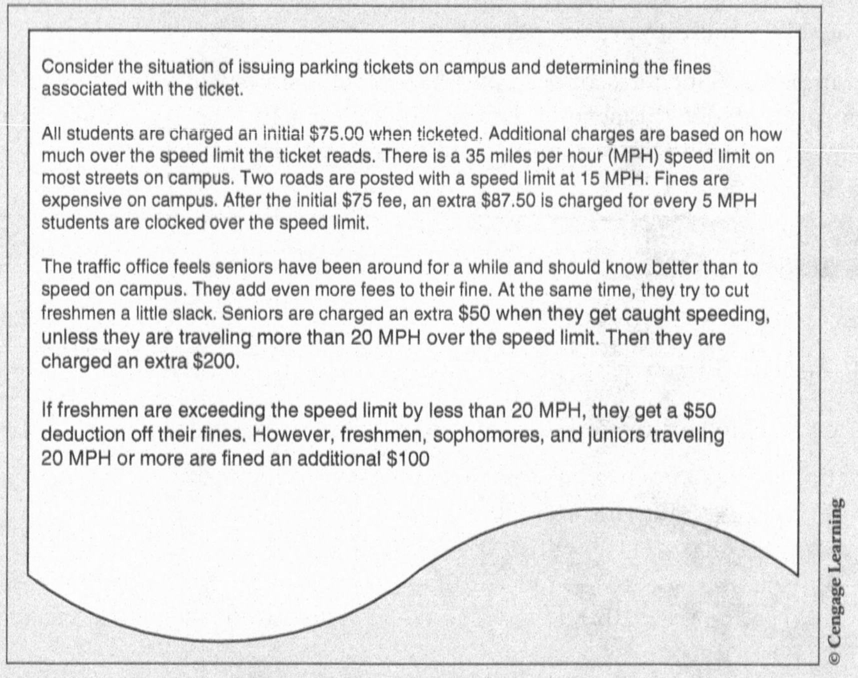

Consider the situation of issuing parking tickets on campus and determining the fines associated with the ticket.

All students are charged an initial $75.00 when ticketed. Additional charges are based on how much over the speed limit the ticket reads. There is a 35 miles per hour (MPH) speed limit on most streets on campus. Two roads are posted with a speed limit at 15 MPH. Fines are expensive on campus. After the initial $75 fee, an extra $87.50 is charged for every 5 MPH students are clocked over the speed limit.

The traffic office feels seniors have been around for a while and should know better than to speed on campus. They add even more fees to their fine. At the same time, they try to cut freshmen a little slack. Seniors are charged an extra $50 when they get caught speeding, unless they are traveling more than 20 MPH over the speed limit. Then they are charged an extra $200.

If freshmen are exceeding the speed limit by less than 20 MPH, they get a $50 deduction off their fines. However, freshmen, sophomores, and juniors traveling 20 MPH or more are fined an additional $100

© Cengage Learning

FIGURE 5-8 Problem specification for SpeedingTicket example

You should review the problem specification in Figure 5-8 and make sure you understand the problem definition. The purpose of the application is to calculate a fine based on the reported speed, speed limit, and classification of a student.

ANALYZE THE PROBLEM

Two separate classes are developed. One `class` is designed to include characteristics of the ticket. The other `class` instantiates objects of the `Ticket` `class` and is used to test the `Ticket` `class` to ensure that all possible situations have been taken into consideration. Several different conditional expressions must be constructed to determine the fine.

The application or client `class` should test for each classification type and for speeds over and under 20 miles over the speed limit. This `class` produces an output listing showing the ticket cost given a number of test cases.

VARIABLES

Tables 5-8 and 5-9 list the data items needed for the `SpeedingTicket` example.

TABLE 5-8 Instance variables for the Ticket class

Data item description	Data type	Identifier
Street speed limit	`int`	`speedLimit`
Speed over the speed limit	`int`	`speed`
Classification of student	`char`	`yrInSchool`

© Cengage Learning

The application `class` that is using the `Ticket` `class` also needs data. The application `class` allows the user to enter values for the speed limit, the speed at which the speeder was traveling, and the speeder's classification. Table 5-9 identifies some of the local variables needed by the application `class`.

TABLE 5-9 Local variables for the SpeedingTicket application class

Data item description	Data type	Identifier
Year in school—classification	`char`	`classif`
Street speed limit	`int`	`speedLimit`
Speed traveling when ticketed	`int`	`speed`
`string` input value	`string`	`inValue`

© Cengage Learning

CONSTANTS

The cost of each 5 miles over the speed limit is a set amount that everyone pays. It is defined as a constant value in the `Ticket` `class`. Setting it as a constant allows quick modification to the memory location when the minimum charges change. The identifier and preset constant value are

```
COST_PER_5_OVER = 87.50
```

DESIGN A SOLUTION

The desired output is to display the fine amount. Figure 5-9 shows a prototype for what the final output should be. The xxx.xx is placed in the prototype to represent the location in which the calculated value should appear. For many applications, it is also useful to display the values used in calculations.

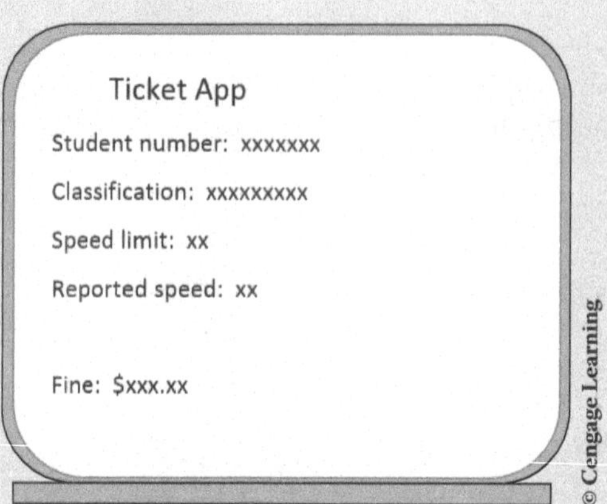

FIGURE 5-9 Prototype for the SpeedingTicket example

As you read in earlier chapters, the object-oriented approach focuses attention on the design of the `object`. A `Ticket` `object` has both data and behavior characteristics that can be identified. Given the characteristics of student classification, speed limit, and ticketed speed, the `Ticket` object's major action or behavior is to set the fine amount. Class diagrams are used to help design and document these characteristics. Figure 5-10 shows the `class` diagrams for the `SpeedingTicket` example.

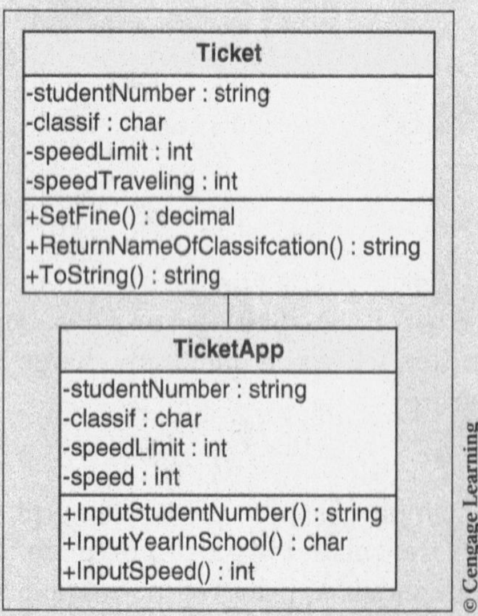

FIGURE 5-10 Class diagrams for the SpeedingTicket example

The `class` diagrams show neither the properties needed nor the local variables that might be needed by specific `class` methods. For example, a `string` value is needed for inputting data in the `TicketApp` `class`. It is not included in the `class` diagram.

As you read earlier, when you are designing a solution that requires a nested `if. . .else`, sometimes it is easier to develop your algorithm if you graphically map out the different options. Figure 5-11 shows a decision tree for part of this application. It pictures the logic involved to determine the additional fee based on classification of student and the number of miles traveling over the speed limit.

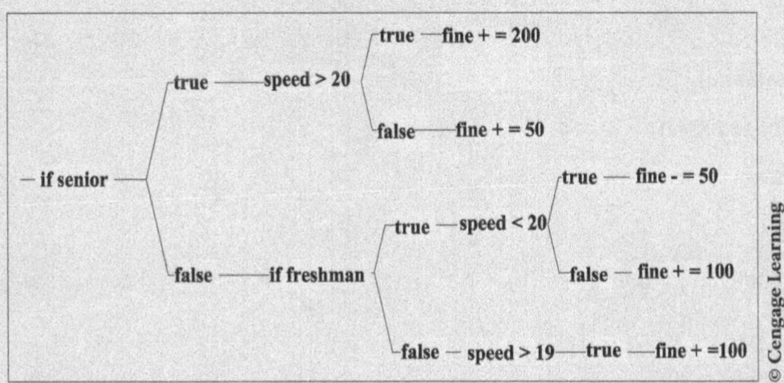

FIGURE 5-11 Decision tree for SpeedingTicket example

During design, it is important to develop an algorithm showing the systematic process to solve the problem. This can be done using any of the design tools presented in previous chapters. Pseudocode for the `SetFine( )` method, which contains a nested `if`, is shown in Figure 5-12.

```
SetFine( )
speed = ticketedSpeed – speedLimit
fine = (speed / 5 * 87.50) + 75.00
if (senior)
   if (speed > 20)
      fine = fine + 200
   else
      fine = fine + 50
else
  if (freshman)
     if (speed < 20)
        fine = fine – 50
     else
        fine = fine + 100
  else
     if (speed > 19)
        fine = fine + 100
```

© Cengage Learning

FIGURE 5-12 Pseudocode for the SetFine( ) method

The problem definition indicates that for every 5 miles over the speed limit the additional fine is $87.50. A whole number value representing the overage is needed. For example, if the `speedLimit` is 35 and the `ticketedSpeed` is 42, only one additional fee of $87.50 is added to the fine. If the `ticketedSpeed` is 45, two additional $87.50 fees are added. This value is determined by doing integer division. An assumption for the pseudocode is that all variables, except `fine`, are of type `int`. This forces the division to be integer division.

42 – 35 = 7 miles over the limit

7 / 5 = 1

Notice that the result is not 1.40, because integer division produces an integer result.

You should always desk check your design. It is especially important when selection statements are included as part of your solution. With the `SpeedingTicket` example, a large number of expressions are combined; thus, it is imperative that you walk through the logic and make sure that the calculations are being performed properly. One way to do this is to develop a table with columns for all inputted and calculated values. Include a row for all possible combinations of unique paths through the nested `if`. If you have developed a decision tree, it is easier to determine which cases need to be tested. Endpoints, such as for speeds over 20 miles per hour above the speed limit, can be especially troublesome. Make sure that you include rows testing those values. After you identify values to be tested, use a calculator to fill in the calculated values. Then, go back and reread the problem definition. Are those the correct calculated values? Table 5-10 includes the values selected to test the `SpeedingTicket` algorithm. This can be considered a test plan. Not only do you want to see how your algorithm handles these specific values, but after you implement your design, be sure to run and test your application using the identified values for speed limit, ticketed speed, and classification. Compare the results with those obtained from your program output.

TABLE 5-10 Desk check of SpeedingTicket algorithm

Speed limit	Ticketed speed	Classification (1=Freshman 2=Sophomore 3=Junior 4=Senior)	Fine
35	42	1	112.50
35	55	2	525.00
35	57	1	525.00
35	47	2	250.00
35	54	1	287.50
35	57	2	525.00
35	44	4	212.50
35	39	4	125.00
35	58	4	625.00
35	55	4	475.00
35	38	1	25.00

© Cengage Learning

CODE THE SOLUTION

After you complete the design and verify the algorithm's correctness, it is time to translate the design into source code. For this application, you are creating two separate files—one for each `class`. As you learned in Chapter 4, only one of the classes has a `Main( )` method.

The final application listing for both files is as follows:

```
/* Ticket.cs     Author:     Doyle
 * Describes the characteristics of a
 * speeding ticket to include the speed
 * limit, ticketed speed and fine amount.
 * The Ticket class is used to set the
 * amount for the fine.
 * **************************************/
using System;

namespace TicketApp
{
    class Ticket
    {
        private const
            decimal COST_PER_5_OVER = 87.50M;
        private string studentNumber;
        private char classif;
        private int speedLimit;
        private int speedTraveling;

        public Ticket( )
        {
        }
        public Ticket(string sNum, char yrInSchool, int speedLmt,
                      int reportedSpeed)
        {
            studentNumber = sNum;
            speedLimit = speedLmt;
            speedTraveling = reportedSpeed;
            classif = yrInSchool;
        }
        public Ticket(string sNum, int speedLmt, int reportedSpeed)
        {
            studentNumber = sNum;
            speedLimit = speedLmt;
            speedTraveling = reportedSpeed - speedLimit;
        }

        public string StudentNumber
        {
            get
            {
```

```
                return studentNumber;
            }
            set
            {
                studentNumber = value ;
            }
        }
        public char Classif
        {
            get
            {
                return classif;
            }
            set
            {
                classif = value ;
            }
        }
        public int SpeedLimt
        {
            get
            {
                return speedLimit;
            }
            set
            {
                speedLimit = value ;
            }
        }
        public int Speed
        {
            get
            {
                return speedTraveling;
            }
            set
            {
                speedTraveling = value ;
            }
        }

        public decimal SetFine( )
        {
            int milesOverSpeedLimit = speedTraveling - speedLimit;
            decimal fine;
            fine = (milesOverSpeedLimit / 5 * COST_PER_5_OVER) +
                    75.00M;
            if (classif == '4')
                if (milesOverSpeedLimit > 20)
                    fine += 200;
```

```
                else
                    fine += 50;
                else
                    if (classif == '1')
                        if (milesOverSpeedLimit < 20)
                            fine -= 50;
                        else
                           fine += 100;
                    else
                        if (milesOverSpeedLimit > 19)
                            fine += 100;
                return fine;
        }

        public string ReturnNameOfClassification( )
        {
             string classificationName;
             switch (classif)
             {
                 case '1':
                      classificationName = "Freshman";
                      break ;
                 case '2':
                      classificationName = "Sophomore";
                      break ;
                 case '3':
                      classificationName = "Junior";
                      break ;
                 case '4':
                      classificationName = "Senior";
                      break ;
                 default :
                      classificationName = "Unspecified";
                      break ;
             }
             return classificationName;
        }

        public override string ToString( )
        {
             return "\tTicket App" +
                "\n\nStudent number: " + studentNumber +
                "\nClassification: " +ReturnNameOfClassification( )+
                "\nSpeed limit: " + speedLimit +
                "\nReported speed: " + speedTraveling +
                "\n\nFine: " + SetFine( ).ToString( "C" );
        }
    }
}
```

```
/* TicketApp.cs              Author:     Doyle
 * Instantiates a Ticket object
 * from the inputted values of
 * speed and speed limit. Uses
 * the year in school classification
 * to set the fine amount.
 * **********************************/

using System;
using static System.Console;

namespace TicketApp
{
     class TicketApp
     {
          static void Main( )
          {
               string studentNumber;
               char classif;
               int speedLimit,
                   speed;
               studentNumber = InputStudentNumber( );
               speedLimit = InputSpeed("Speed Limit");
               speed = InputSpeed("Ticketed Speed");
               classif = InputYearInSchool( );
               Ticket studentTicket = new Ticket(studentNumber,
                                     classif, speedLimit, speed);
               Clear( );
               WriteLine(studentTicket);
               ReadKey( );
          }
          public static string InputStudentNumber( )
          {
              string sNumber;
              Write("Enter Student Number: ");
              sNumber = ReadLine( );
              return sNumber;
          }
          public static int InputSpeed(string whichSpeed)
          {
              string inValue;
              int speed;
              Write("Enter the {0}: ", whichSpeed);
              inValue = ReadLine( );
              if (int.TryParse(inValue, out speed) == false)
                  WriteLine("Invalid entry entered " +
                           "for {0} - 0 was recorded", whichSpeed);
              return speed;
          }
```

5

```
            public static char InputYearInSchool ( )
            {
                string inValue;
                char yrInSchool;
                WriteLine("Enter your classification:" );
                WriteLine("\tFreshmen (enter 1)");
                WriteLine("\tSophomore (enter 2)");
                WriteLine("\tJunior (enter 3)");
                Write("\tSenior (enter 4)");
                WriteLine( );
                inValue = ReadLine( );
                yrInSchool = Convert.ToChar(inValue);
                return yrInSchool;
            }
        }
}
```

Figure 5-13 shows the output produced for a ticket issued to a junior traveling at a speed of 45 MPH in a 35-MPH zone.

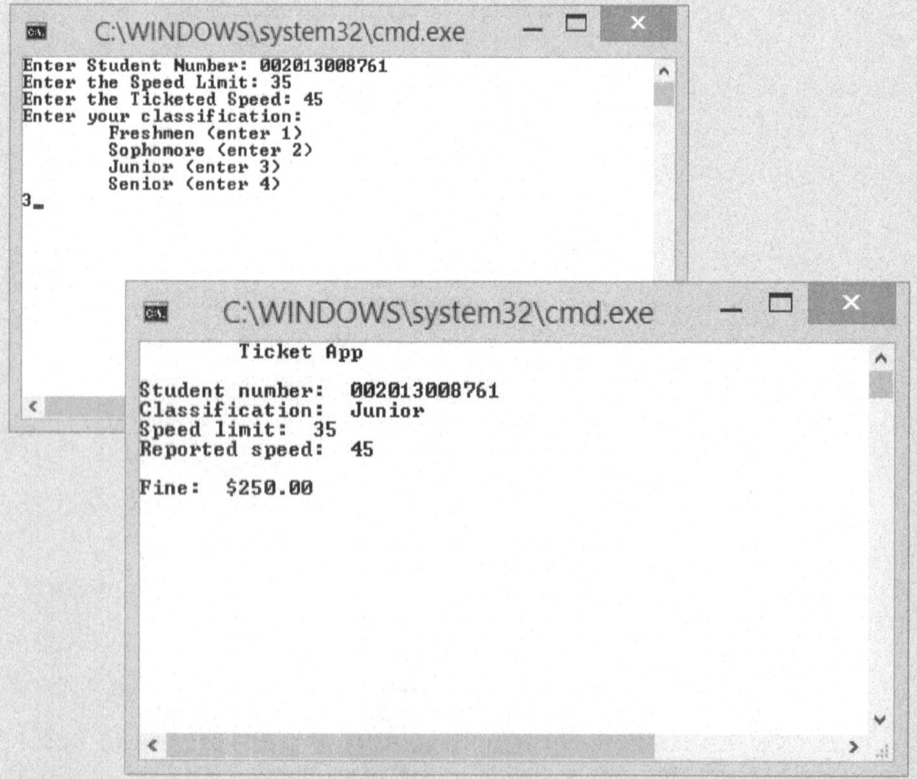

FIGURE 5-13 Output from the SpeedingTicket example

When the user enters an invalid character for speed, the `TryParse( )` method stores zero in `s`. The way it is written the only test is for entering the wrong data type, a null value, or an extreme value that cannot fit in the integer memory location. Additional tests could be performed to make sure a valid range of values were entered. One approach would be to add a compound test as shown below.

```
if ((int.TryParse(inValue, out speed) == false) || speed > 120)
{
    WriteLine("Invalid entry - must be numeric, less than 120");
    Write("Please re-enter speed: ");
    int.TryParse(inValue, out speed);
}
```

5

This approach could also be used to test for the low range. Do this by adding another logical or statement, as in `|| speed < 0`. In the next chapter you will be introduced to loops that will enable you to test the value, and if they enter an invalid data item, ask them for a new value, and continue asking them until a good value is entered. Here once the test is performed, and the `if` statement returns `false`, they get one more chance to input a valid entry.

As indicated in Table 5-10, a number of different test cases should be run to verify the correctness of your solution. Just because you are getting output does not mean that your solution is correct. Compare your results with the desk checked calculated results. Are they the same? Have you considered all possible combinations?

Coding Standards

It is important to follow coding standards when you design solutions involving selection statements. Developing standards that you consistently adhere to will increase your coding efficiency and make your code more maintainable. One of the most important considerations with selection statements relates to readability. The best practices are described next as they relate to the consistent placement of curly braces and the proper use of white space.

Guidelines for Placement of Curly Braces

Curly braces are required when the body following an `if` or `else` statement has more than one statement. Many developers use curly braces with all selection statements—even single `if...else` statements. In this book, curly braces are added when there are two or more executable statements. For single statements, curly braces were omitted. Whether you use curly braces with all cases or just for multi-statement executables, be consistent with your usage.

Open braces should always be at the beginning of the line after the statement that begins the block.

The contents of the brace should be indented by four spaces. For example:

```
if (someExpression)
{
    ExecuteMethod1( );
    ExecuteMethod2( );
}
else
{
    ExecuteMethod3( );
    ExecuteMethod4( );
}
```

Guidelines for Placement of else with Nested if Statements

Many developers place an `else...if` on the same line when a nested `if` is written. In this book, the `else` is placed on a line by itself. The `if` statement appears on the line below as shown in the following example:

```
if (someExpression)
    DoSomething( );
else
    if
    {
        DoSomethingElse( ); // Curly braces are not needed here.
    }
```

Guidelines for Use of White Space with a Switch Statement

Place curly braces on separate lines with a switch statement. Indent the case statements. Do not place curly braces around multiline executables as shown in the following example:

```
switch (someExpression)
{
       case 0:
            DoSomething( );
            break;
       case 1:
            DoSomethingElse( );
            break;
       default:
            break;
}
```

Spacing Conventions

Use a single space before and after comparison operators as shown in the following:

```
if (x == y)
```

Do not place an extra space before or after the expression as shown in the following example:

```
if ( x == y ) // Incorrect – Extraneous spaces before x and after y
```

Use tabs instead of spaces for indentation.

Use white space (one blank line) to separate and organize logical groups of code within the block.

5

Advanced Selection Statement Suggestions

Readability and maintainability are improved when you avoid writing compound selection statements. Instead of writing <= or >=, add or subtract 1 from the endpoint (i.e., `if (a >= 100)` is the same as `if (a > 99)`). Additional thought will normally help you eliminate this type of compound statement.

Write a nested `if` as opposed to combining two expressions with &&. Doing so enables you to provide an `else` clause for each conditional expression. For example, replace `if ((a > b) && (b > c))` with

```
if (a > b)
    if (b > c)
```

When possible use short-circuit evaluation to improve efficiency.

Switch statements should include a `default` label as the last `case` label.

Do not make explicit comparisons to `true` or `false` in a conditional expression.

Do not use the equality operators with floating-point values. Most floating-point values have no exact binary representation and have a limited precision.

Avoid using complex or compound ternary operations. Use the ternary conditional operator only for trivial conditions.

Resources

Additional sites you might want to explore:

- C# Coding Style Guide - TechNotes, HowTo Series—
  http://www.icsharpcode.net/TechNotes/SharpDevelopCodingStyle03.pdf
- Microsoft C# if statement Tutorial—
  http://csharp.net-tutorials.com/basics/if-statement/

- if - else (C# Reference)—
  http://msdn.microsoft.com/en-us/library/5011f09h.aspx
- switch (C# Reference)—
  http://msdn.microsoft.com/en-us/library/06tc147t

QUICK REVIEW

1. The three basic programming constructs include simple sequence, selection, and iteration.
2. The selection statement allows you to deviate from the sequential path and perform different statements based on the value of one or more variables.
3. The two types of selection statements are the `if...else` and `switch` statements. C# also provides the ternary operator ? : for conditional expressions.
4. With selection statements, properly used indentation is for readability only. Curly braces are used when you have more than one expression to be evaluated.
5. The result of expressions used with selection statements is either `true` or `false`.
6. Testing a Boolean variable does not require the use of an equality operator. If `salariedEmployee` is of type `bool`, you can write `if (salariedEmployee)`. It is not necessary to include the == operator.
7. When you compare characters or strings, the Unicode character set is used.
8. You can compare `string` operands using the equality operators == and `!=`.
9. The relational symbols >, <, >=, or <= are not defined for strings.
10. Conditional expressions can be combined with logical conditional operators, && or ||, to form more complex expressions.
11. C# uses the && and || operators to represent AND and OR, respectively.
12. With short-circuit evaluation, as soon as the value of the entire expression is known, the common language runtime (CLR) stops evaluating the expression. For complex expressions using &&, when the first part of the expression evaluates to `false`, there is no need to evaluate the second.
13. In C#, there is no conversion between the `bool` type and other types; thus, when x is defined as `int`, you cannot type `if (x)`.
14. Do not place a semicolon at the end of the `if` statement's parenthesized expression being evaluated. This makes a null (empty) statement but does not create a syntax error.

15. With a two-way `if` statement, either the `true` statement(s) is executed or the `false` statement(s), but not both. After the execution of the statement(s) is (are) finished, control always transfers to the statements following the `if` block.
16. Any statement, including another `if` statement, can be included within the statements to be executed when the expression evaluates to `true`. The same holds for the `false` statements.
17. When determining which `else` matches which `if`, follow this rule: The `else` matches up with the closest previous `if` that does not already have an attached `else`.
18. Use a series of `else...if` for a long, nested, multiway statement.
19. The `switch` statement is considered a multiple selection structure that allows a large number of alternatives to be executed. The `switch` is used for equality comparisons only.
20. The `case` value with a `switch` statement must be a constant literal of the same type as the expression. It cannot be a variable.
21. With a `switch` statement, the occurrence of the first `case` value that matches the expression causes that case's statement(s) to be executed. If no match is made with any of the `case` values, the statements associated with `default` are executed.
22. Having a `default` is not required, but it is a good idea always to include one.
23. There is no way to program a `switch` statement in C# to fall through to the code for the next `case`. After code is associated with a `case`, there must be a `break`. If used, the `default` statements must also end with a `break`.
24. Multiple cases in a `switch` statement can be associated with the same statements. This works like having a logical OR operator between each of the cases.
25. The `switch` statement cannot be used to test for a range of values or to perform a relational test.
26. Also called the conditional operator, the ternary operator `? :` provides a shorthand way to express a simple `if...else` selection statement.
27. When an expression contains multiple operators, the precedence of the operators controls the order in which the individual operators are evaluated.
28. Equality operators have a lower precedence than relational operators; `&&` has a higher precedence than `||`, but both `&&` and `||` have lower precedence than the relational or equality operators. The very lowest precedence is the assignment operators.

EXERCISES

1. The result of the expression `if (aValue == bValue)` is:
   a. `aValue`
   b. `10`
   c. an integer value
   d. `true` or `false`
   e. determined by an input statement

2. Which expression is evaluated first in the following statement?
   `if (a > b && c == d || a == 10 && b > a * b)?`
   a. `a * b`
   b. `b && c`
   c. `d || a`
   d. `a > b`
   e. none of the above

3. What is the output for `total` after the following segment of code executes?

```
int num = 3, total = 0;
switch (num)
{
        case 1:
        case 2:
                total = 5;
                break;
        case 3:
                total = 10;
                break;
        case 4:
                total = total + 3;
                break;
        case 8:
                total = total + 6;
                break;
        default:
                total = total + 4;
                break;
}
WriteLine("The value of total is " + total);
```

   a. 10
   b. 15
   c. 14
   d. 28
   e. none of the above

4. What is displayed when the following code executes?

```
score = 0;
if (score > 95)
    Write("Congratulations! ");
    Write("That's a high score! ");
    Write("This is a test question!");
```

a. `This is a test question!`

b. `Congratulations! That's a high score! This is a test question!`

c. `That's a high score! This is a test question!`

d. `Congratulations! That's a high score!`

e. none of the above

5. Which statement in C# allows you to do the following: Properly check the variable code to determine whether it contains the character C, and if it does, display "This is a check" and then advance to a new line?

a.
```
if code is equal to C
    WriteLine("This is a check");
```

b.
```
if (code = "C")
    WriteLine("This is a check");
```

c.
```
if (code == 'C')
    WriteLine("This is a check");
```

d.
```
if (code == C)
    WriteLine("This is a check");
```

e. none of the above

6. What will be displayed from executing the following segment of code? You may assume `testScore` has a value of 90.

```
int testScore;
if (testScore < 60); // Note the semicolon.
    Write("You failed the test! ");
if (testScore > 60)
    Write("You passed the test! ");
else
    Write("You need to study for the next test!");" +
```

a. `You failed the test!`

b. `You passed the test!`

c. `You failed the test! You passed the test!`

d. `You failed the test! You need to study for the next test!`

e. none of the above

7. The _____ operator represents the logical AND.
   a. `++`
   b. `||`
   c. `&&`
   d. `@`
   e. none of the above
8. The symbol (=) is:
   a. the operator used to test for equality
   b. used for comparing two items
   c. used as part of an assignment statement
   d. considered a logical compound operator
   e. all of the above
9. Incorrect use of spacing with an `if` statement:
   a. detracts from its readability
   b. causes a syntax error message
   c. can change the program logic
   d. causes a logic error message
   e. all of the above
10. What does the following program segment display?

```
int f = 7, s = 15;
f = s % 2;
if (f != 1)
{
    f = 0;
    s = 0;
}
else if (f == 2)
{
    f = 10;
    s = 10;
}
else
{
    f = 1;
    s = 1;
}
WriteLine(" " + f + " " + s);
```

   a. `7 15`
   b. `0 0`
   c. `10 10`
   d. `1 1`
   e. none of the above

11. Which logical operator (op) is defined by the following table? (T and F denote `true` and `false`.)

P	Q	P op Q
T	T	T
T	F	F
F	T	F
F	F	F

a. NOT
b. AND
c. OR
d. not enough information is given
e. none of the above

5

12. Examine the code. When will `C` be assigned `3`? (Be careful.)

```
if (A == B);
    C = 3;
```

a. when `A` is equal to `B`
b. when `A` is not equal to `B`
c. never
d. every time the program is executed
e. not enough information is given

13. Consider the following `if` statement, which is syntactically correct, but uses poor style and indentation:

```
if (x >= y) if (y > 0) x = x * y; else if (y < 4) x = x - y;
```

Assume that x and y are `int` variables containing the values 9 and 3, respectively, before execution of the preceding statement. After execution of the statement, what value does x contain?

a. 9
b. 1
c. 6
d. 27
e. none of the above

14. After execution of the following code, what will be the value of `inputValue`?

```
int inputValue = 0;
if (inputValue > 5)
     inputValue += 5;
else if (inputValue > 2)
         inputValue += 10;
else inputValue += 15;
```

a. 15

b. 10

c. 25

d. 0

e. 5

15. If you intend to place a block of statements within an `if` statement, you must use around the block.

a. parentheses

b. square brackets

c. quotation marks

d. curly braces

e. none of the above

16. Given the following segment of code, what will be the output?

```
int x = 5;
if (x == 2)
   Write("Brown, brown, run aground. ");
else
   Write("Blue, blue, sail on through. ");
Write("Green, green, nice and clean.");
```

a. `Brown, brown, run aground.`

b. `Blue, blue, sail on through.`

c. `Brown, brown, run aground. Blue, blue, sail on through.`

d. `Blue, blue, sail on through. Green, green, nice and clean.`

e. none of the above

17. What is the result of the following conditional expression when aValue = 100 and bValue = 7?

```
result = aValue > bvalue + 100 ? 1000 : 2000;
```

a. 0

b. 1000

c. 2000

d. 7

e. none of the above

18. Given the switch statement, which of the following would be the first if statement to replace the first test in the switch?


```
switch (control)
{
    case 11 :
         WriteLine("eleven");
         break;
    case 12 :
         WriteLine("twelve");
         break;
    case 16 :
         WriteLine("sixteen");
         break;
}
```

a. `if (case = 11)`

b. `if (case == 11)`

c. `if (control == 11)`

d. `if (switch == 11)`

e. none of the above

19. Which of the following statements about logical operators is correct?

a. Logical AND yields true if and only if both of its operands are either true or false.

b. Logical OR yields true if either or both of its operands are true.

c. Logical OR is represented in C# by &&.

d. Logical NOT is represented in C# by |.

e. none of the above

20. The `string` data type can be used:
    a. as an operand for the == or !=
    b. as an expression in the `switch` statement to be evaluated
    c. as an operand for the > or < operator
    d. a and b are correct
    e. all of the above

---

21. Assuming `a` is 5, `b` is 6, and `c` is 8, which of the following is (are) `false`?
    a. `a == 5;`
    b. `7 <= (a + 2);`
    c. `c <= 4;`
    d. `(1 + a) != b;`
    e. `c >= 8;`
    f. `a >= 0;`
    g. `a <= (b * 2);`

22. Could a `switch` statement be designed logically to perform the same tests as the following nested `if` statement? If so, explain how it could be done.

```
if (aValue == 100)
    WriteLine("Value is 100");
else
    if (aValue < 100)
        WriteLine("Value is less than 100");
```

23. Rewrite the following `switch` statement as a nested `if` statement using a series of `else...if` statements:

```
string birdName;
switch (birdName)
{
    case "Pelican":
         WriteLine("Lives near water.");
         break;
    case "Cardinal":
         WriteLine("Beautiful in the snow.");
         break;
    case "Owl":
         WriteLine("Night creature.");
         break;
    case "Eagle":
         WriteLine("Keen vision");
         break;
    case "Flamingo":
         WriteLine("Pretty and pink.");
         break;
    default:
         WriteLine("Can fly.");
         break;
}
```


24. Rewrite the following compound expression as a nested `if` statement:

```
if ((aValue > bValue) && (bValue == 10))
    WriteLine("Test complete");
```

25. Write conditional expressions to perform the following tests:

    a. When `amountOwed` is greater than 1000.00, display an overdue message.

    b. When `amountOfRain` is greater than 5 inches, add 5 to `total`. When it is between 3 and 5 inches, add 3 to `total`. When it is less than 3 inches, add 1 to `total`.

    c. When `middleInitial` is equal to the character `z`, display message "You're one in a thousand"; otherwise, check to see if it is equal to the character 'a'. When it is equal to the character `a`, display the message "You have a common initial".

    d. When `balance` > 100 and `transaction` < 50, subtract `transaction` from `balance`. When `balance` is not greater than 100, add `transaction` to `balance`.

PROGRAMMING EXERCISES

1. Write a program that takes a decimal value between 1 and 10 and displays its equivalent Roman numeral value. Display an error message if the value entered is outside of the acceptable range. Write a two class solution. The second class should allow the user to input a test value.

2. Ever heard of acid rain? This is rainfall with a very low pH. Write an application that will enable you to display the pH level for a swimming pool and whether an additive is needed or not. The pH is a measure of how acidic or basic the water is and is typically given on a 0–14 scale. Below 7.0 is defined as acidic, with 7 being neutral. Levels much above 7 are said to be basic or alkaline. Everything that enters a pool has a pH value. To have pH in balance the water is adjusted with additions of pH increasers (bases) or pH decreasers (acids) to achieve the range of 7.2–7.8. Allow the user to input the pH level number. Display a message indicating the health (i.e., acidic, neutral, or alkaline) and whether an additive is required. If an additive is required, identify the type. The water should be described as acidic, requiring bases, when the pH is lower than 7. Consider the pH level as neutral for pH levels in the range 7–7.8 and alkaline, requiring acid for pH levels greater than 7.8. Display an appropriate message when invalid values are entered.

3. Write a two-class solution to calculate and display a person's body mass index (BMI). BMI is an internationally used measure of obesity. Depending on where you live, the Imperial BMI formula or the Metric Imperial Formula is used. Once the BMI is calculated, display a message of the person's status. Prompt the user for both their weight and height. The BMI status categories, as recognized by the U.S. Department of Health & Human Services, are given in the following table:

BMI	Weight Status
Below 18.5	Underweight
18.5–24.9	Normal
25–29.9	Overweight
30 & above	Obese

   Provide constructors and methods so that both imperial and metric objects can be instantiated. Use the second class to test your design.

4. Write a program that calculates the take-home pay for an employee. The two types of employees are salaried and hourly. Allow the user to

input the employee's first and last name, id, and type. If an employee is salaried, allow the user to input the salary amount. If an employee is hourly, allow the user to input the hourly rate and the number of hours clocked for the week. For hourly employees, overtime is paid for hours over 40 at a rate of 1.5 of the base rate. For all employees' take-home pay, federal tax of 18% is deducted. A retirement contribution of 10% and a Social Security tax rate of 6% should also be deducted. Use appropriate constants. Design an object-oriented solution. Create a second class to test your design.

5. A large Internet merchandise provider determines its shipping charges based on the number of items purchased. As the number increases, the shipping charges proportionally decrease. This is done to encourage more purchases. If a single item is purchased, the shipping charge is $2.99. When customers purchase between 2 and 5 items, they are charged the initial $2.99 for the first item and then $1.99 per item for the remaining items. For customers who purchase more than 5 items but less than 15, they are charged the initial $2.99 for the first item, $1.99 per item for items 2 through 5, and $1.49 per item for the remaining items. If they purchase 15 or more items, they are charged the initial $2.99 for the first item, $1.99 per item for items 2 through 5, and $1.49 per item for items 6 through 14, and then just $0.99 per item for the remaining items. Allow the user to enter the number of items purchased. Define appropriate constants, use the `decimal` data type, and display the shipping formatted charges.

6. Write an application that computes the area of a circle, rectangle, and cylinder. Display a menu showing the three options. Allow users to input which figure they want to see calculated. Based on the value inputted, prompt for appropriate dimensions and perform the calculations using the following formulas:

   Area of a circle = pi * radius^2

   Area of a rectangle = length * width

   Surface area of a cylinder = 2 * pi * radius * height + 2 * pi * radius^2

   Write a modularized solution that includes class methods for inputting data and performing calculations.

7. Create a `Month class` that has a single data member of month number. Include a member method that returns the name of the month and another method that returns the number of days in the month. The `ToString( )` method should return the name and number of

days. Write a second class to test your `Month` `class`. The second class should allow the user to input a month number. Display the name of the month associated with the number entered and the number of days in that month. For this exercise, use 28 for February. If the user inputs an invalid entry, display an appropriate message.

8. Create an application with four classes. Three of the classes should contain data and behavior characteristics for circle, rectangle, and cylinder. You could extend your solution to problem number 6 and provide behaviors based on the type of object instantiated. For example, in addition to calculating the area of a circle, also provide methods to calculate circumference or radius. For the rectangle, consider providing behaviors to calculate perimeter and the polygon diagonals. For cylinder, consider providing behaviors to calculate the volume and surface area for a closed cylinder. The fourth `class` should allow the user to input a figure type from a menu of options. Prompt for appropriate values based on the inputted figure type, instantiate an `object` of the type entered, and display characteristics about the `object`.

9. Design a solution that prints the amount of profit an organization receives based on it sales. The more sales documented, the larger the profit ratio. Allow the user to input the total sales figure for the organization. Compute the profit based on the following table. Display the sales and profit formatted with commas, decimals, and a dollar symbol. Display the profit ratio formatted with a percent symbol.

0	–	$1,000:	3.0%
$1,000.01	–	$5,000:	3.5%
$5,000.01	–	$10,000:	4.0%
over $10,000:			4.5%

Be sure to design your solution so that all possible situations are accounted for and tested. Use the decimal data type for your solution. What values did you enter and test to verify your program's correctness?

10. Two fuel stops, Canadian Fuel and American Fuel, are positioned near the U.S. Canadian border. At the Canadian station, gas is sold by the liter. On the American side, it is sold by the gallon. Write an application that allows the user to input information from both stations and make a decision as to which station offers the most economical fuel price. Test your application with 1.259 per liter against 4.50 per gallon. Once the decision is made, display the equivalent prices.

CHAPTER 6

© zeljkodan/Shutterstock.com

Repeating Instructions

IN THIS CHAPTER, YOU WILL:

- Learn why programs use loops
- Write counter-, state-, and sentinel-controlled while loops
- Examine the conditional expressions that make up a for loop
- Be introduced to the foreach looping structure
- Compare the do . . . while looping structure with the pre-test forms of loops
- Write loops nested inside other loops
- Learn about keywords that can be used for unconditional transfer of control
- Be introduced to recursion and learn how recursive methods work
- Pick appropriate loop structures for different applications
- Work through a programming example that illustrates the chapter's concepts

Chapter 5 introduced you to the second type of programming construct, the selection statement. You learned that the two common forms of selection statements, `if...else` and `switch`, can change the sequential order in which statements are performed. You learned that a conditional expression with a selection statement produces a Boolean result that can be tested and used to determine alternate paths in your program.

Recall that the first programming construct is the simple sequence and that the second construct is the selection statement. The third construct is called repetition, iteration, or looping. In this chapter, you discover why loops are so valuable and how to write loop control structures. You learn about different kinds of loops and determine when one type is more appropriate than another.

Why Use a Loop?

One of the major strengths of programming languages can be attributed to loops. The programming examples you have seen thus far could have been solved more quickly through manual calculations. Take, for example, calculating your course grade average. With a calculator in hand, you could certainly add together your scores and divide by the number of entries. However, if you were assigned this task for everyone in your class or everyone at your school, you could see the value of being able to write one set of instructions that can be repeated with many different sets of data.

C# has a rich set of looping structures. These constructs, sometimes called **repetition** or **iteration structures**, enable you to identify and block together one or more statements to be repeated based on a predetermined condition. For looping, C# includes the C-style traditional `while`, `do...while`, and `for` statements that are found in many other programming languages. New to C-style languages is the `foreach` loop construct used to process collections of data stored under a common name in structures such as arrays, which you will learn about in Chapter 7. The sections that follow introduce you to the different types of loops and show you how they can be used in your programs.

Using the While Statement

Probably the simplest and most frequently used loop structure to write is the `while` statement. The general form of the `while` statement is

```
while (conditional expression)
      statement(s);
```

The conditional expression, sometimes called the **loop condition**, is a logical condition to be tested. It is enclosed in parentheses and is similar to the expressions you use for selection statements. The conditional expression must return a Boolean result of `true` or `false`. An interpretation of the `while` statement is "`while` condition is `true`, perform statement(s)."

The statement(s) following the conditional expression makes up the body of the loop. The body of the loop is performed as long as the conditional expression evaluates to `true`. Like the selection construct, the statement following the conditional expression can be a single statement or a series of statements surrounded by curly braces { }.

Some programmers use curly braces to surround all loop bodies, even loop bodies consisting of a single statement. Consistently using curly braces increases readability. It also reduces the chance of forgetting to include the curly braces when the body contains multiple statements.

Notice that there is no semicolon after the conditional expression. If you place a semicolon there, you do not get a syntax error. Your program will run. If you are using Visual Studio and place a semicolon on the line containing the conditional expression, a squiggly line is placed under the semicolon. This should alert you that there might be a problem. When you move your mouse pointer over the red mark, IntelliSense displays this message: "Possible mistaken empty statement." You saw this same warning when a semicolon was placed at the end of the selection statement expression.

Placing the semicolon at the end of the conditional expression produces a loop that has no body or an **empty bodied loop**. Placing a semicolon at the end of the conditional expression can create an infinite loop situation. Your program will run and run and run, accomplishing nothing. An **infinite loop** is a loop that has no provisions for termination.

You can usually kill an infinite loop by closing the window or pressing the **Esc** key. If that does not work, try the key combinations **Ctrl+C** or **Ctrl+Break**. Press the two keys simultaneously. The easiest way to do this is to hold down the **Ctrl** key and then press the second key. If that does not work, open the **Windows Task Manager** by pressing **Ctrl+Alt+Del**, select **Start Task Manager**, select the Visual Studio application, and press the **End Task** button in the **Windows Task Manager** dialog box. Sometimes, this causes you to lose unsaved work. Thus, it is a good idea to save your work frequently, especially prior to running applications that contain loops.

The `while` statement is a **pretest** loop, which means that the conditional expression is tested before any of the statements in the body of the loop are performed. If the conditional expression evaluates to `false`, the statement(s) in the body of the loop is (are) never performed. If the conditional expression evaluates to `true`, the statements are performed, and then control transfers back to the conditional expression. It is reevaluated and the cycle continues. Figure 6-1 illustrates the flow of execution in a pretest loop.

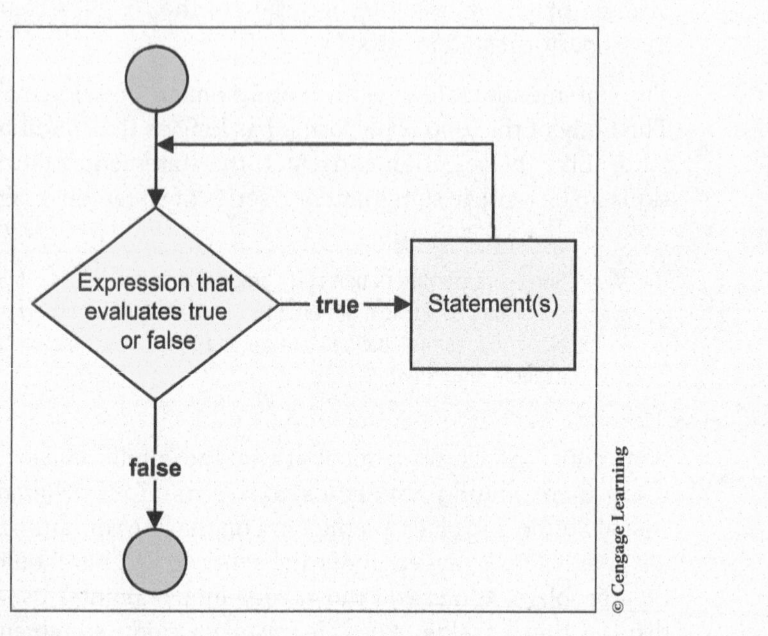

FIGURE 6-1 Pretest loop

Counter-Controlled Loop

Many programs you develop require that you write one or more statements that must be performed more than once. When you know the number of times the statements must be executed, you can create a **counter-controlled loop**. With a counter-controlled loop, a variable simulating a counter is used as the **loop control variable** to keep track of the number of iterations. Example 6-1 adds values to an accumulator. The variable, sum, is initialized to zero and the positive integers 1 through 10 are added to the sum memory location, one value at a time.

EXAMPLE 6-1

```
/* SummedValues.cs        Author: Doyle
 * Demonstrates use of a loop to add 10
 * integers. Displays the total after
 * the loop body is completed.
 */
using System;
using static System.Console;

namespace SummedValues
```

```
{
   class SummedValues
   {
       static void Main( )
       {
          int sum = 0;                                       //Line 1
          int number = 1;                                    //Line 2
          while (number < 11)                                //Line 3
          {                                                  //Line 4
             sum = sum + number;                             //Line 5
             number++;                                       //Line 6
          }                                                  //Line 7
          WriteLine("Sum of values " +                       //Line 8
                    "1 through 10" +                         //Line 9
                    " is " + sum);                           //Line 10
          ReadKey( );                                        //Line 11
       }
   }
}
```

The output of this code is:

```
Sum of values 1 through 10 is 55
```

To include a counter-controlled loop in your program, you must design the conditional expression so that you can exit the loop after a certain number of iterations. Normally on the outside of the loop, before the conditional expression, the loop control variable is initialized. On Line 2 in Example 6-1, `number` is initialized to `1`. The variable `number` is the loop control variable. On Line 3, its value is evaluated and used to determine whether the loop should be executed.

When the `while` statement on Line 3 is reached, the conditional expression of `(number < 11)` produces a `true` result, so the statements in the body of the loop are performed. Notice that the last line in the loop, Line 6, increments the loop control variable, `number`, by one. When the closing curly brace is encountered on Line 7, control transfers back to the conditional expression on Line 3. The conditional expression is reevaluated and again produces a `true` result. This cycle—test, perform body of loop, test—is continued as long as the conditional expression evaluates to `true`. When the loop control variable, `number`, becomes `11`, the conditional expression evaluates to `false` (`11` is not less than `11`). At this point, control transfers to Line 8, the statement following the loop. Here, beginning on Line 8, the `WriteLine( )` method displays the sum of the values.

What would happen if Line 6, the following line, is omitted?

```
number++;
```

If you answered "an infinite loop," you are correct. Without changing the loop control variable used in the conditional expression by increasing its value, the expression would never evaluate to false. Careful thought must focus on how the loop will end with a normal termination. Without incrementing the counter used in the conditional expression, the loop would go on indefinitely.

Why not put the following statement, which began on Line 8, inside the loop body?

```
WriteLine("Sum of values 1 through 10 is " + sum);
```

The final value of sum would be printed if the WriteLine( ) method is placed in the body of the loop. However, you would also have nine additional printed lines. Every time sum changes, a line would be printed showing its new value. Thus, it is better to print the result after all the calculations have been performed.

Visual Studio automatically references and imports a number of namespaces with the using directive. As you review examples, you will notice that the extraneous using statements were deleted and a using static System.Console; directive was added. Being able to reference a static class within a namespace with the using directive is new to Visual Studio 2015. This feature reduces the amount of typing needed when you invoke members of the Console class. If you are using a version prior to Visual Studio 2015, references to members of the Console class, like Write( ), WriteLine( ), ReadKey( ) and Clear( ), require the method name be preceded by the Console class identifier and a dot, as in Console.Write( ).

You could modify Example 6-1 to allow the user to input the first and last values to be summed. Both operands in the conditional expression could be variables. Example 6-2 prompts the user for the boundaries.

EXAMPLE 6-2

```
/* InputEndPointsWithWhile.cs     Author: Doyle
 * Demonstrates use of a loop to add any range
 * of values. User inputs start and stop values.
 * Displays the result after the loop is
 * completed.
 */
using System;
using static System.Console;

namespace InputEndPointsWithWhile
{
    class InputEndPointsWithWhile
    {
        static void Main( )
```

```
        {
            int sum = 0;
            int startValue,
                endValue;
            string inValue;
            Write("Enter the beginning value: ");
            inValue = ReadLine( );
            if (int.TryParse(inValue, out startValue) == false)
                WriteLine("Invalid input - " +
                          "0 recorded for start value");
            Write("Enter the last value: ");
            inValue = ReadLine( );
            if (int.TryParse(inValue, out endValue) == false)
                WriteLine("Invalid input - " +
                          "0 recorded for end value");
            Write("Sum of values {0} through {1} ", startValue,
                  endValue);
            while (startValue < endValue + 1)
            {
                sum = sum + startValue;
                startValue++;
            }
            WriteLine("is {0}", sum);
            ReadKey( );
        }
    }
}
```


There are a couple of interesting issues to consider with Example 6-2. The conditional expression now reads:

```
while (startValue < endValue + 1)
```

The same result could have been achieved using

```
while (startValue <= endValue)
```

Both cases call attention to the fact that the value entered by the user as the last number should be added to the total. If the conditional expression read `while (startValue < endValue)`, the loop would not be executed for the last value. An **off-by-one error** would have occurred. This is a common problem associated with counter-controlled loops. It is important to think through test cases and check endpoints to ensure that they have been taken into consideration. You should always check the initial and final values of the loop control variable and verify that you get the expected results at the boundaries. Without adding one onto the endpoint or using the compound relational operator, the result would be incorrect.

Why did the solution print the range of values (`startValue` and `endValue`) before the loop executed? The following statement appeared before the loop:

```
Write("Sum of values {0} through {1} ", startValue, endValue);
```

The loop control variable, `startValue`, is changed inside the loop. Its original value is lost and no longer available when the loop is finished. Thus, to display the beginning value, you would need either to store it in a different memory location (that does not change) or to print it before the loop body.

If you are going to print the boundaries before the loop, why not go ahead and place the following statement before the loop in Example 6-2?

```
WriteLine("is {0}", sum);
```

Zero would be printed for `sum` if you print it before the loop. The variable `sum` gets the accumulated value from the loop body; thus, it does not make sense to print the value until after the calculations are performed and the loop is completed.

Figure 6-2 shows the results of an execution of Example 6-2 when 14 and 33 are entered as the range of values.

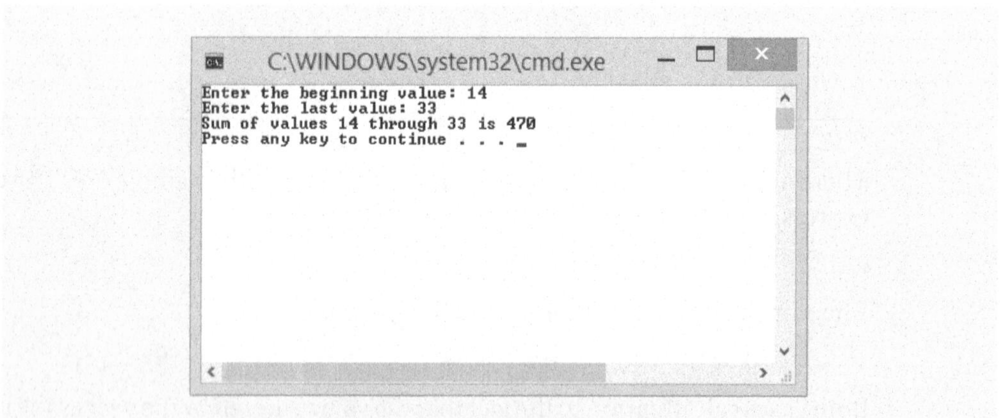

FIGURE 6-2 Example of output from user-entered loop boundaries

With Example 6-2, what happens when the user enters a larger value for the `startValue` than the value entered for `endValue`? If you answered the loop body will not get executed, even one time, you are correct. Because the conditional expression evaluates to `false`, the body is skipped and the lines following the loop are executed.

When you are requesting input from the user, you always run the risk that invalid characters may be entered. You have seen a number of examples that test input using the `TryParse( )` method. You saw statements such as

```
if (int.TryParse(inStringValue, out integerValue) == false)
    WriteLine("Invalid input - 0 recorded for end value");
```

If a character such as "b" is entered by the user and stored in `inStringValue`, `TryParse( )` returns `false`, indicating that it was not able to do the conversion. When `TryParse( )` returns `false`, the conditional expression evaluates to true. Then zero is stored in `integerValue` as a side effect of the `TryParse( )` method not being able to properly do the conversion. There are instances when it is not acceptable to just print an error message. You may want to make sure that valid characters are entered before proceeding with additional statements. Instead of just testing to see whether `TryParse( )` is able to effectively do the conversion, you could use the `TryParse( )` method as your conditional expression for a loop as illustrated in Example 6-3.

6

EXAMPLE 6-3

```
/* ValidInput.cs Author: Doyle
 * Demonstrates testing input to
 * ensure that integers are entered.
 */
using System;
using static System.Console;

namespace ValidInput
{
    class ValidInput
    {
        static void Main(string [] args)
        {
            int integerValue;
            string inStringValue;
            Write("Enter an integer value. ");
            inStringValue = ReadLine( );
            while (int.TryParse(inStringValue,
                                        out integerValue) == false)
            {
                WriteLine("Invalid input");
                Write("Please re-enter an integer value. ");
                inStringValue = ReadLine( );
            }
```

```
            WriteLine("Valid value entered: " + integerValue);
            ReadKey( );
        }
    }
}
```

With Example 6-3, the user is kept inside the loop until an integer is entered. If a character such as "b" is entered by the user, the conditional expression evaluates to `true`. Control goes back inside the loop where the error message is printed and then the user is re-prompted for input. If an integer is entered initially, the `TryParse( )` method returns `true`. Thus, the conditional expression then evaluates to `false` and the loop body is never executed.

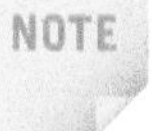

You could add additional tests to the conditional expression to ensure the value fell within a specific range. For example, to ensure that the input value was not only numeric but that it was a positive integer between 1 and 100, the condition expression for the while statement could read:

```
while ((int.TryParse(inStringValue, out integerValue) == false)
                    || integerValue > 100 || integerValue < 1)
```

Three tests are performed. The loop body is executed when a non-integer value is entered and also when the value entered is not within the specified range (greater than 0 and less than 101). This concept was introduced in the discussion following the TicketApp Programming Example at the end of Chapter 5. With the compound tests as part of the conditional expression, to determine exactly what type of invalid input was entered, additional tests might need to be performed inside the loop body.

Sentinel-Controlled Loop

If you are going to use a counter-controlled loop, you must know how many times the loop should be performed. There are situations where you may not know how many iterations are needed. Another looping option is a **sentinel-controlled loop**. Sentinel-controlled loops are often used for inputting data when you do not know the exact number of values to be entered. If your program inputs multiple homework scores, for example, you might display a message telling the users to enter a negative value to indicate they are finished entering scores. You would never have a negative score; thus, this would be an appropriate sentinel value.

Sentinel-controlled loops are also referred to as **indefinite loops** because the number of repetitions is not known before the loop's execution. To design an indefinite loop, select a sentinel value to use in the expression. A **sentinel value** is an extreme value, a dummy value. It is a value that should not be processed—like a negative value when only positive scores are to be processed.

The sentinel value is used as the operand in the conditional expression for an indefinite loop. A sentinel-controlled loop gives you the advantage of not needing to know how many times the loop will be performed. When all the data has been processed, the sentinel value can be entered indicating the loop should terminate normally. Example 6-4 demonstrates how a sentinel-controlled loop can be used to input any number of data values.

EXAMPLE 6-4

```
/* InputValuesLoop.cs        Author: Doyle
 * Demonstrates loop for inputting values.
 */
using System;
using static System.Console;

namespace InputValuesLoop
{
    class InputValuesLoop
    {
        static void Main( )
        {
            string inValue = ""; //Initialized to null
            Write("This program will let you enter");
            Write(" value after value. To Stop, enter");
            WriteLine(" -99");
            while (inValue!= "-99")
            {
                Write("\nEnter value (-99 to exit): ");
                inValue = ReadLine( );
            }
            ReadKey( );
        }
    }
}
```


As with the counter-controlled loop, it is necessary to set up the conditional expression in Example 6-4. This must be done before the loop executes. This time, the variable used to hold the inputted values, `inValue`, is initialized to `null` (`""`); no value is placed between the double quotes. The variable `inValue` could have been initialized to any value, other than `-99`. However, it had to be initialized.

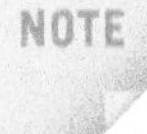

NOTE C# does not allow you to use unassigned values. If you failed to initialize `inValue`, you would have received the error message, "Use of unassigned local variable inValue," when you attempted to use `inValue` in the conditional expression.

In Example 6-4, the conditional expression continues to evaluate as `true` as long as the user does not enter `-99`. Notice how the input statement is placed as the last statement in the loop body. The placement is important. If calculations were part of the loop body, it would have been necessary to **prime the read** on the outside of the loop. This means that you would input a value before going into the body of the loop. Doing this allows the first statements in the loop to be the statements processing that entered value. Then, as the last statement in the body of the loop, another `ReadLine( )` method is included. If you do not place the `ReadLine( )` at the end as the last statement, you end up processing the sentinel value. As soon as the user enters the `-99`, or the sentinel value, you want to stop processing data. Placing the `ReadLine( )` as the last line in the body enables the conditional expression to evaluate to `false` as soon as the `-99` is entered. Example 6-5 illustrates this important point by summing the values entered.

EXAMPLE 6-5

```
/* PrimeRead.cs                          Author:Doyle
 * Sentinel loop to sum values
 */
using System;
using static System.Console;

namespace PrimeRead
{
    class PrimeRead
    {
        static void Main( )
        {
            string inValue = ""; //Initialized to null
            int sum = 0,
                intValue;
            Write("This program will let you enter");
            Write(" value after value. To Stop, enter");
            WriteLine(" -99");
            Write("\nEnter value (-99 to exit): ");
            inValue = ReadLine( ); // Priming read
            while (inValue!= "-99")
            {
                if (int.TryParse(inValue, out intValue) == false)
                    WriteLine("Invalid input - 0 stored in " +
                              "intValue");
                sum += intValue;
                Write("Enter value(-99 to exit): ");
                inValue = ReadLine( );
            }
```

```
            WriteLine("Total values entered {0}", sum);
            ReadKey( );
        }
    }
}
```

Suppose the input is

10

12

40

5

1

-99

The output for this code with the preceding input is

Total values entered 68.

When you implement a sentinel-controlled loop, it is imperative that you tell the user what value to type to end the loop. You should include this information inside the loop body. This is especially true if a large number of values are being entered. You do not want the user to have to guess or try to remember how to terminate the program.

To tell users what value to enter to terminate, you display a message using a `Write( )` or `WriteLine( )` method before the `ReadLine( )`. Otherwise, how will they know what value to enter to stop?

In Chapter 11, you will learn how to process data batched together and stored on a storage medium, such as your hard drive. Sentinel-controlled loops are useful for loops that process data stored in a file. The sentinel value is placed as the last entry in the file. Here, it is unnecessary to display a message indicating how to stop. The loop conditional expression looks exactly like that used for interactive input of data. The conditional expression matches the selected sentinel value.

WINDOWS APPLICATIONS USING LOOPS

Many C# applications developed in industry today create a Windows application designed with a graphical user interface (GUI). So far, the output you have displayed has been in the form of a console window instead of a Windows form or Web page.

Take note that all of the programming concepts you are learning are useful for any type of application; however, as you will learn in later chapters, an event-driven model is used with Windows applications. An **event-driven model** manages the interaction between the user and the GUI by handling the repetition for you. Sending your output to the console made it possible for you to learn the basics of programming before focusing on the interface design.

C# has a predefined `class` called `MessageBox` that can be used to display information to users through its `Show( )` method member. The output generated by the `MessageBox.Show( )` method more closely resembles the windows you are accustomed to seeing and using. In later chapters of this book, all applications are built around windows. The example that follows produces a table showing values 1 through 10 and their squares. The results are displayed in a dialog box window instead of the console to give you the flavor of displaying output to a Windows dialog box.

When you do not want to see the Command window on console applications, you need to indicate that the Output type should be a Windows Application. Do this by selecting the project in the **Solution Explorer** window and then selecting that project's **Properties** option from the **Project** menu. Select **Windows Application** as the **Output type** from the drop-down list. You can also right-click on the project's name in the **Solution Explorer** window. Recall the project name is shown below the solution name in the **Solution Explorer** window. **Properties** is shown as one of the options. The **Alt+Enter** shortcut also displays this dialog box when you have the project selected in the **Solution Explorer** window.

EXAMPLE 6-6

```
/* SquaredValues.cs     Author: Doyle
 * Displays values 1 through 10
 * along with their squares.
 */
using System;
using System.Windows.Forms; //Namespace for Windows Forms class

namespace SquaredValues
{
    class SquaredValues
    {
        static void Main( )
        {
            int counter = 0;
            string result ="\tn       Squared\n";
            while (counter < 10)
```

```
            {
                counter++;
                result += " \t"     // Notice the use of += to build
                        + counter   // the string for the MessageBox.
                        + " \t"
                        + Math.Pow(counter, 2)
                        + "\n";
            }
            MessageBox.Show(result, "1 - 10 and their squares");
        }
    }
}
```

Figure 6-3 shows the output of this program. The figure contains text representing the program's looped output and a title bar. The two buttons, an "X" indicating "close" and an OK button, are added automatically by the predefined `MessageBox.Show( )` method.

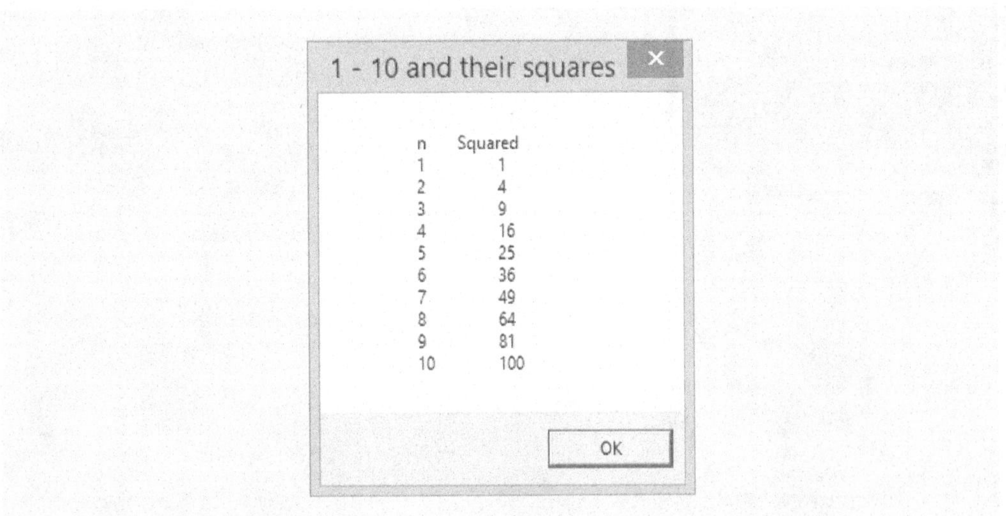

FIGURE 6-3 MessageBox dialog output

To use the `MessageBox` `class` in your console application, you must do two things:

1. Add a reference to the `System.Windows.Forms.dll` assembly in your project. This can be done by opening the **Solution Explorer** tab in Visual Studio and right-clicking on the **References** folder, as shown in Figure 6-4.

Adding a reference to the `System.Windows.Forms.dll` will be done automatically for you when you create Windows applications. You will create Windows Applications in Chapter 9. This is accomplished by selecting a **Windows Forms Application** project type instead of the **Console Application** project type template. Adding the reference is required now because you are adding this `class` to your console application.

If the **Solution Explorer** is not present on your screen, you can open it from the **View** menu.

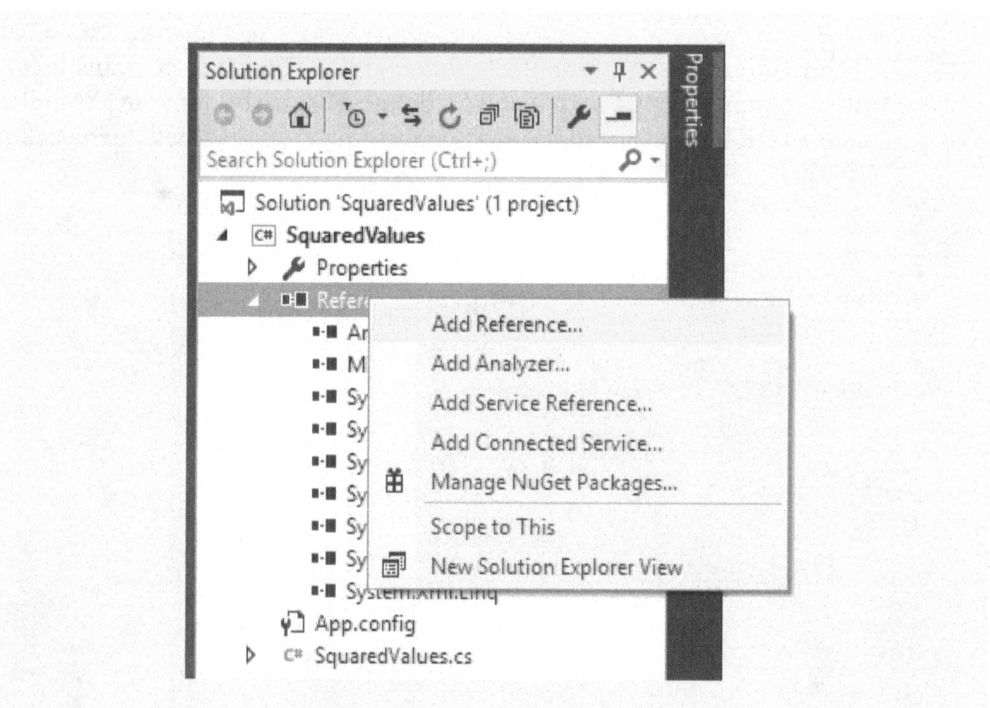

FIGURE 6-4 Add a reference to a project

As shown in Figure 6-5, after you right-click the **References** folder in the **Solution Explorer** window and select **Add Reference**, the **Reference Manager** window opens. If necessary, expand **Assemblies** and select **Framework**. Scroll down the list and select **System.Windows.Forms**. The `MessageBox` `class` is located in this assembly. A check box will appear beside the **System.Windows.Forms**. Click the check box to make that selection and then click **OK** to close the **Reference Manager** dialog box.

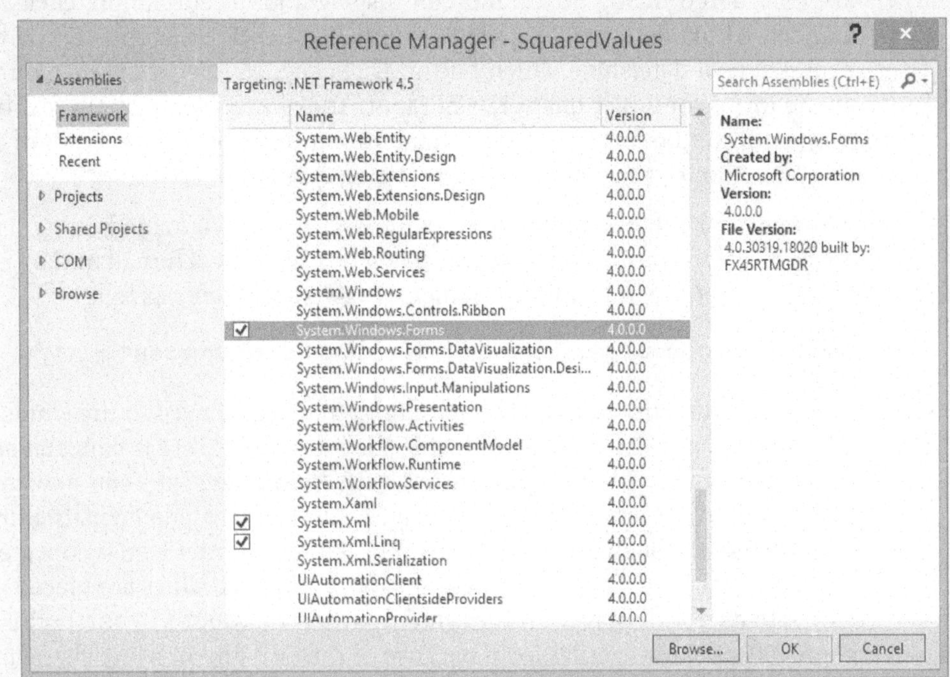

FIGURE 6-5 Class libraries of .NET

After you select the `System.Windows.Forms` component, you can use the `MessageBox` `class`, but you need to specify the full name of the `namespace` in which the `class` is located, starting at the system level. If you do not perform Step 2 that follows, any reference to the `Show( )` message of the `MessageBox` would require the fully qualified name of:

```
System.Windows.Forms.MessageBox.Show( )
```

2. By adding a `using` directive, you can use types defined in the `System.Windows.Forms` `namespace` without qualifying the name. The following `using` directive is added to the Example 6-6 program:

```
using System.Windows.Forms;
```

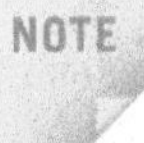

NOTE Notice that it is not enough just to include the `using` directive; you must also add the reference to the assembly.

The `Show( )` method of the `MessageBox` `class` displays a predefined dialog box that can contain text, captions for the title bar, special buttons, and icons. Message boxes are normally used to display small messages but can also be used to accept input in the form of allowing users to make selections from buttons. Message boxes are considered dialog boxes and can display and accept simple clicks on **Yes**, **No**, **Cancel**, **Abort**, and **OK** buttons. Using your selection statement, you can write an expression to determine which button is clicked. In later chapters, you will learn to create forms for larger quantities of input. Your forms will contain text boxes, labels, list boxes, combo boxes, menus, radio buttons, and many other types of controls. For now, the `MessageBox` limits input to dialog types of controls.

The `Show( )` method of the `MessageBox` `class` is overloaded. In its simplest form, a `string` of text is displayed on the dialog box window. The call to the `MessageBox.Show( )` method in Example 6-6 includes two arguments as follows:

```
MessageBox.Show(result, "1 - 10 and their squares");
```

The first argument, `result`, is the `string` that is displayed in the window. The variable `result` gets its value from inside the loop body. Text is concatenated onto the end of the result with each pass through the loop body. Tabs and newline characters (`'\t'` and `'\n'`) are added for spacing. A tab is concatenated as the first character for each pass through the loop. A newline character (Enter key) is concatenated as the last character for each pass through the loop. After all values are placed in the result, its contents are displayed in the window when the `Show( )` method is called. The contents appear in tabular form because of the tabs and newline characters.

The second argument, `"1 - 10 and their squares,"` is placed as a caption in the title bar of the window, as illustrated in Figure 6-3. As noted previously, `Show( )` is overloaded; you can include a button as a third argument. Table 6-1 lists valid options for the buttons that can appear as arguments to the `Show( )` method.

TABLE 6-1 Dialog button arguments

MessageBox buttons	Description of contents
`MessageBoxButtons.AbortRetryIgnore`	Abort, Retry, and Ignore buttons
`MessageBoxButtons.OK`	OK button
`MessageBoxButtons.OKCancel`	OK and Cancel buttons
`MessageBoxButtons.RetryCancel`	Retry and Cancel buttons
`MessageBoxButtons.YesNo`	Yes and No buttons
`MessageBoxButtons.YesNoCancel`	Yes, No, and Cancel buttons

© Cengage Learning

NOTE Using IntelliSense in Visual Studio, you can see the button property values given in Table 6-1, as well as the options for different icons that can be included in the MessageBox.

You can add a button as the third argument, as follows:

```
MessageBox.Show(result, "1 - 10 and their squares", MessageBoxButtons.
                  YesNoCancel);
```

Buttons for Yes, No, and Cancel are included on the MessageBox dialog box.

As you examine Figure 6-3 or Figure 6-6, notice the last line of output is the value 10. However, the conditional expression indicated that the loop is executed as long as the counter is less than 10. The loop terminates when the counter became 10. So why did 10 and its square print? Also, note that the variable counter is initialized to 0, but the first line displayed in Figure 6-3 is for a value of 1. The loop has been included again in Example 6-7 so that you can examine it closely.

EXAMPLE 6-7

```
while (counter < 10)
{
     counter++;
     result += " \t"
             + counter
             + " \t"
             + Math.Pow(counter, 2)
             + "\n";
}
```

Notice where the counter is incremented and where the concatenation occurs. Because the counter is incremented to one as the first statement, the zero is never concatenated. The last time the conditional expression evaluates to true is when counter is equal to 9 because (9 < 10) is true. Because the counter is incremented to 10 inside the loop, before concatenation, the value for 10 is printed. You should pay careful attention to the placement of the update for your loop control variable as well as the conditional expression you write to allow for normal termination.

The MessageBox is a dialog box. As you know, dialog implies conversation between two or more individuals, so a dialog box is designed for user intervention. When the line of code containing the MessageBox.Show( ) method is executed, processing stops until the user responds by clicking the **OK** button on the MessageBox. This method call is placed on the outside of the loop in Example 6-6. Placement inside the loop would have necessitated a click from the user every time the `MessageBox.Show( )` call was executed. The user would have had to click **OK** 10 times if the method call had been included inside the loop body. That is why the values produced inside the loop body were concatenated onto the end of a string variable. Only one call to the `MessageBox.Show( )` method is included and that is on the outside of the loop body.

The overloaded method of `MessageBox.Show( )` can be sent one of the button types from Table 6-1 and a fourth argument of an icon, as shown in Example 6-8.

EXAMPLE 6-8

```
MessageBox.Show(result, "1 - 10 and their squares",
                MessageBoxButtons.YesNoCancel,
                MessageBoxIcon.Information);
```

Figure 6-6 shows the output produced when the `Show( )` method of Example 6-8 replaces that which appears in the full program from Example 6-6.

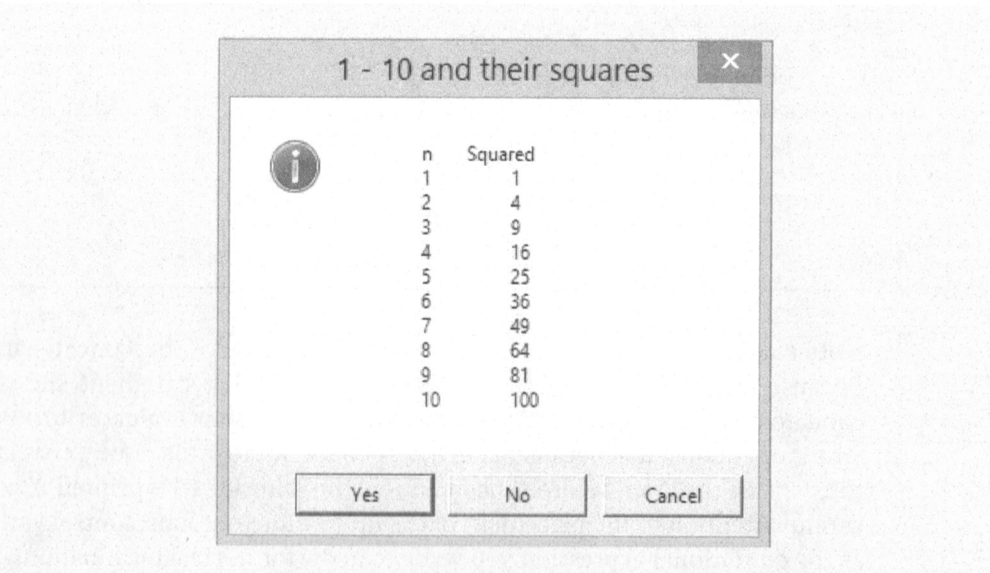

FIGURE 6-6 Button and icon arguments to MessageBox.Show( )

The .NET Framework `class` library includes several predefined icons that can be included as the fourth argument to the `MessageBox.Show( )` method. Table 6-2 lists some you may want to include in your applications.

TABLE 6-2 Dialog icon arguments

MessageBoxIcons	Description of symbol contents
`MessageBoxIcon.Asterisk`	Lowercase letter i in a circle
`MessageBoxIcon.Error`	White X in a circle with a red background
`MessageBoxIcon.Exclamation`	Exclamation point in a triangle with a yellow background
`MessageBoxIcon.Hand`	White X in a circle with a red background
`MessageBoxIcon.Information`	Lowercase letter i in a circle
`MessageBoxIcon.None`	No symbol
`MessageBoxIcon.Question`	Question mark in a circle
`MessageBoxIcon.Stop`	White X in a circle with a red background
`MessageBoxIcon.Warning`	Exclamation point in a circle with a yellow background

© Cengage Learning

6

State-Controlled Loops

Similar to sentinel-controlled loops, **state-controlled loops** stop when a certain state is reached. Instead of requiring that a dummy value be entered after all values are processed, as is often a requirement for a sentinel-controlled loop, another type of special variable is used with a state-controlled loop. This special variable is used in the conditional expression for the loop. It is evaluated to determine when its state changes.

The variable used with a state-controlled loop usually differs from the variable used to store the data that is being processed. It must be initialized and then evaluated to see when it changes state. When it does, the loop is terminated. In Example 6-9, the special Boolean variable `moreData` is used. For this example, a Boolean data type is used; however, that is not a requirement for the variable. It can be of any type.

EXAMPLE 6-9

```
bool moreData = true;
while (moreData)
{
      ...
// moreData is updated inside the loop when a condition
// changes that indicates the loop should stop.
```

```
    if (MessageBox.Show("Do you want another number ?",
                        "State Controlled Loop",
                         MessageBoxButtons.YesNo,
                         MessageBoxIcon.Question)
             == DialogResult.No)// Test to see if No clicked
        {
              moreData = false;
        }
}
```

Sometimes, state-controlled loops are referred to as **flag-controlled loops**. After initializing a variable to a value, flag-controlled loops remain unchanged until it is time for the loops to stop running. In Example 6-9, `moreData` is initialized to `true` when it is declared. Inside the loop, an `if` statement is used to test for a `DialogResult.No` value. The statement `moreData = false;` is executed when the user clicks No on the `MessageBox` dialog box. The next time the conditional expression `while (moreData)` is evaluated, the variable has changed state, so the loop terminates normally.

Example 6-10 illustrates the use of a state-controlled loop to print any number of random positive integers less than 100.

EXAMPLE 6-10

```
/* StateControlled.cs Author: Doyle
 * One or more random integers are
 * printed. User is prompted to
 * determine when to stop printing
 * random values.
 */
using System;
using static System.Console;
using System.Windows.Forms;


namespace StateControlled
{
    class StateControlled
    {
        static void Main( )
        {
            bool moreData = true;
            int s;
            Random numb = new Random( );
            s = numb.Next(100); // Returns positive number < 100.
            while (moreData)
            {
               Write("{0} ", s);
```

```
                if (MessageBox.Show("Do you want another number?",
                                    "State Controlled Loop",
                                    MessageBoxButtons.YesNo,
                                    MessageBoxIcon.Question)
                        == DialogResult.No)
                {
                   moreData = false;
                }
                else
                {
                   s = numb.Next(100);
                }
            }
        }
    }
}
```


One of the overloaded methods of the `Random` `class` is `Next( )`. Used with an `int` argument, it returns a nonnegative random number between zero and the argument included in the call. In Example 6-10, the random number returned is a value less than 100.

Another one of the overloaded `Next( )` methods in the `Random` `class` allows you to send two arguments. These values specify the range of values for the random number.

```
s = numb.Next(300, 1000);      // Returns random number
                               // between 300 and 1000.
```

The random numbers generated during one sample run of the application presented in Example 6-10 are shown in Figure 6-7.

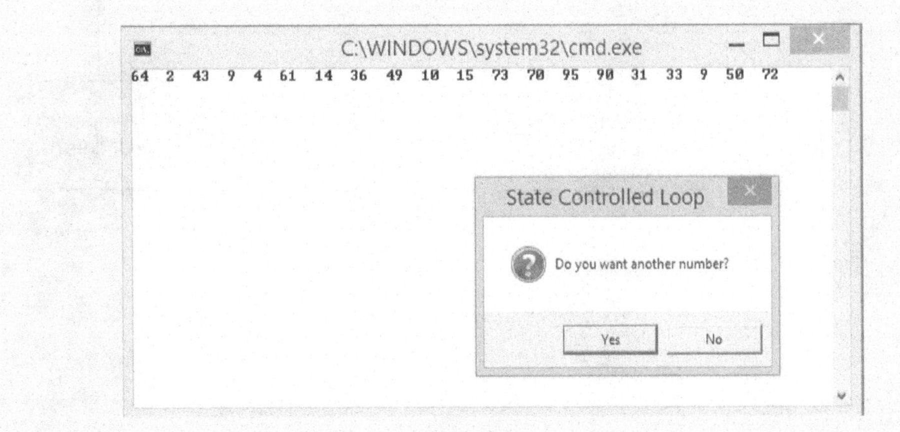

FIGURE 6-7 State-controlled loop of random numbers

Using the for Statement Loop

Another pretest looping structure is the `for` statement. It is considered a specialized form of the `while` statement and is usually associated with counter-controlled types of loops; however, it can be used to create other types of loop structures. The general form of the `for` statement is

```
for (statement; conditional expression; statement)
     statement;
```

The statements and expressions with the `for` loop are interpreted as follows:

```
for (initialize; test; update)
     statement;
```

Figure 6-8 illustrates the flow of execution in a `for` statement.

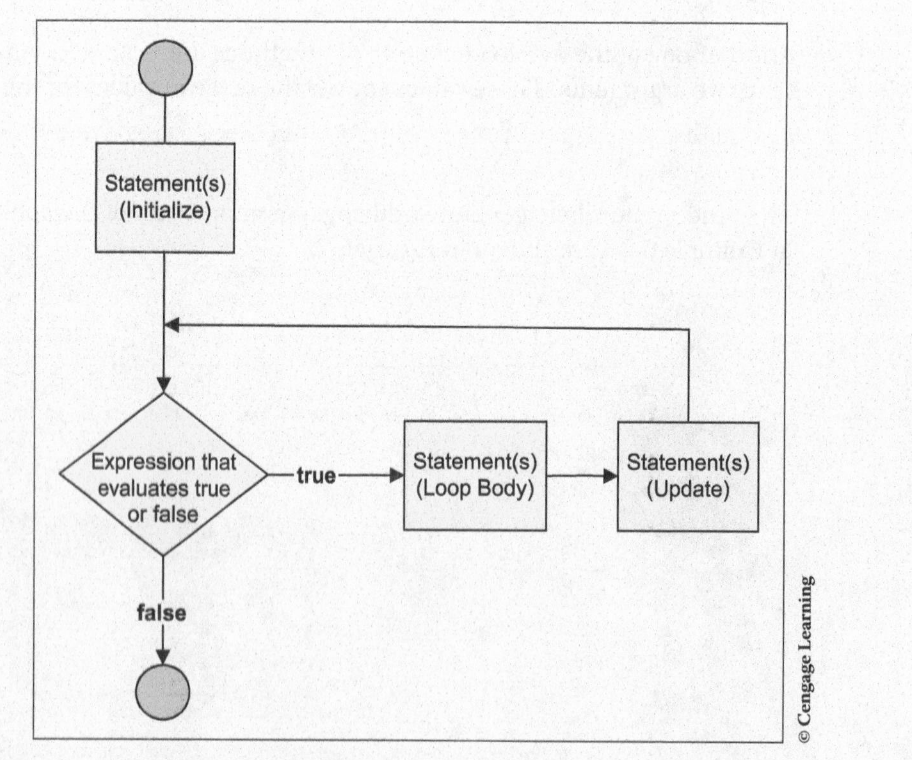

FIGURE 6-8 Flow of control with a for statement

When a variable must be incremented or updated with each pass through the loop, the `for` statement is the preferred loop structure. When a `for` statement is reached in your program, the loop is executed as shown in Figure 6-9.

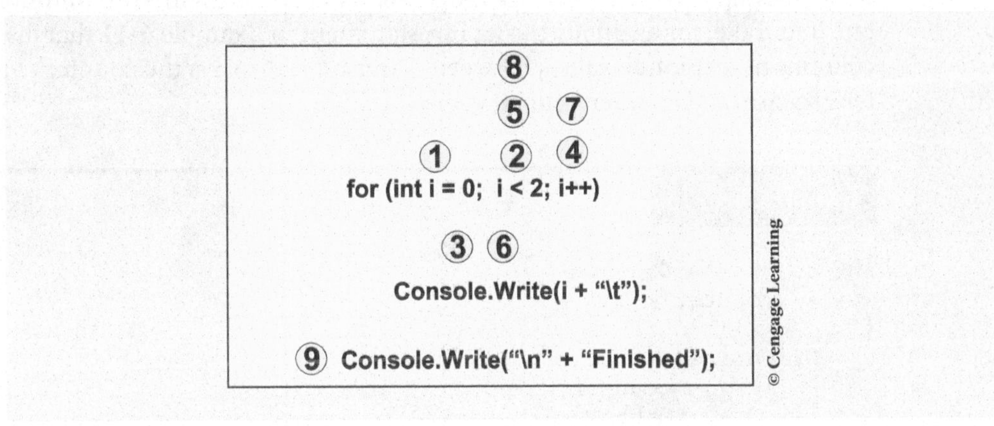

FIGURE 6-9 Steps of the for statement

6

1. The initialize statement is executed first and only once.

NOTE By separating the statements with commas, you can include more than one executable statement in the initialize location. The semicolon ends the initialization portion. Usually, however, the only variable initialized here is the loop control variable.

2. The test is performed. Because the `for` statement is a pretest loop, the test is performed before the loop body is executed. When the conditional expression evaluates to `false`, the rest of the `for` statement (the update and body of the loop) is bypassed and control transfers to the statement following the `for` statement.
3. When the conditional expression evaluates to `true`, the body of the loop is performed.
4. The update statement is executed. Often this involves incrementing a variable.
5. Steps 2–4 are repeated until the conditional expression evaluates to `false`.

As stated, Figure 6-9 numbers the steps that a `for` statement goes through when it executes. The conditional expression is `(i < 2)`. The body of the loop is executed twice for values of `i = 0` and `i = 1`. When `i` is updated to `2`, the conditional expression no longer evaluates to `true`. The body is bypassed and control transfers to the statement following the `for` loop.

The `for` statement is a compact method of writing the same kind of loop that can be written using `while`; it packages together the initialization, test, and update all on one line. Take, for example, the `while` statement in Example 6-11 that displays three columns of text for all values between 0 and 10. It displays the counter's value, counter's square, and counter's cubed value.

EXAMPLE 6-11

```
int counter = 0;
while (counter < 11)
{
    WriteLine("{0,5}\t{1,5}\t{2,5}",
                counter,
                Math.Pow(counter,2),
                Math.Pow(counter,3));
    counter++;
}
```

The output of this code is

```
    0       0       0
    1       1       1
    2       4       8
    3       9      27
    4      16      64
    5      25     125
    6      36     216
    7      49     343
    8      64     512
    9      81     729
   10     100    1000
```

This is a very common type of application. It could be rewritten using a `for` statement, as shown in Example 6-12.

Notice that in addition to a tab being placed between values when they are printed, a 5 is placed inside the curly brace, that is, `"{0,5}\t`. This facilitates number aligning the values.

EXAMPLE 6-12

```
for (int counter = 0; counter < 11; counter++)          //Line 1
{
     WriteLine("{0,5}\t{1,5}\t{2,5}",                   //Loop body
               counter,
               Math.Pow(counter,2),
               Math.Pow(counter,3));
}
```


The output of this code that uses the `for` statement is exactly the same as that shown from the `while` loop in Example 6-11.

In Example 6-12, everything is included on Line 1 except the statements to be looped or the body of the loop. The loop body contains one statement; thus, the curly braces could have been omitted without any change in the output.

In Example 6-12, the loop control variable is declared and initialized at the same time. This is often done with `for` loops when the variable is used only as a loop control variable. Be aware that if you do this, you cannot use the variable that is declared in the `for` statement outside of the `for` statement. The variable `counter` only exists in the `for` block. The scope of the variable declared in the `for` initializer is the initializer, test expression, increment/update portion, and is inside the loop body. Recall that **scope** refers to the region in the program in which you can use the variable. Trying to use it beyond the closing curly brace of the `for` body produces the syntax error shown in Figure 6-10.

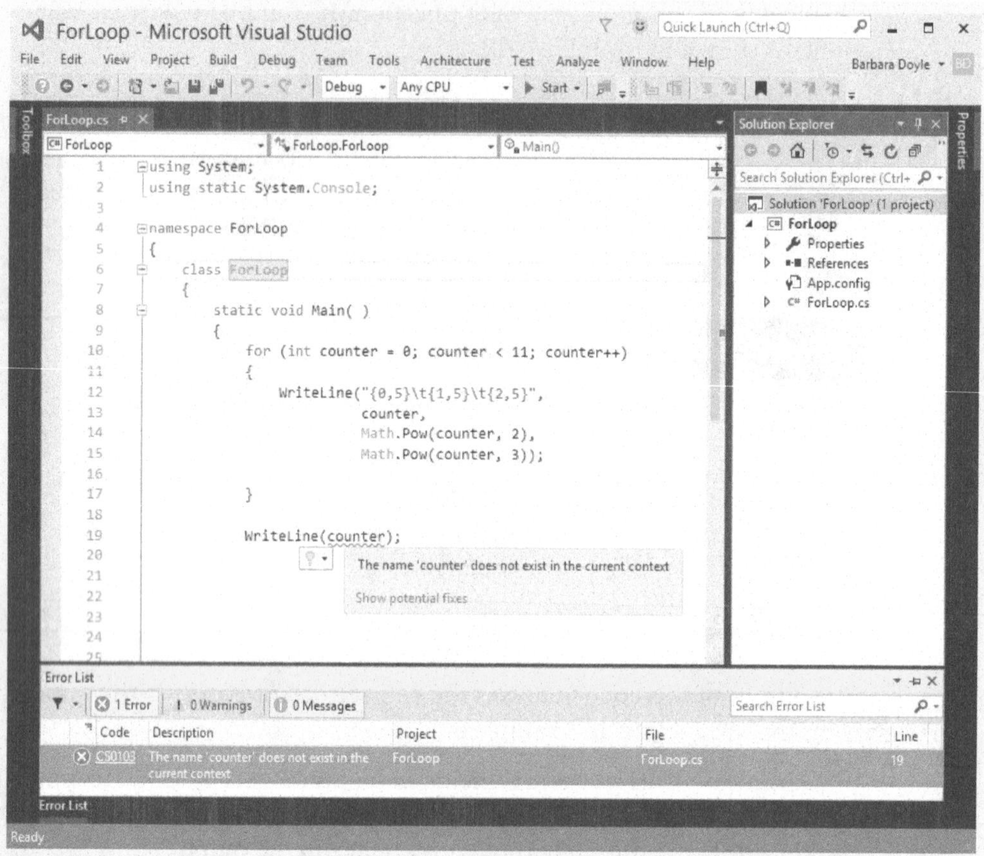

FIGURE 6-10 Syntax error

In addition to declaring variables as part of the initialization of the `for` statement, some programmers declare variables inside the curly braces. You should avoid doing this for two reasons. First, with every iteration through the loop, a new memory location must be set aside for that identifier. Imagine having a loop executed 1000 times. One thousand different memory cells would be declared, but they all hold the same kind of information as that previously declared. It would be best to declare variables on the outside of the loop body.

The second problem involves the visibility of the variable. If it is declared inside a block, it dies or becomes no longer available outside the block. C# performs **automatic garbage collection**. After the loop is finished, the variable is no longer available. Its space is released back to the operating system for reuse. The variable is visible and usable inside the block in which it is defined. If it is needed outside the loop body, it is best to declare the variable outside the loop body.

The conditional expression is located in the center of the `for` statement after the first semicolon. The increment or update of the control variable is placed as the last entry, after the second semicolon. This compact arrangement makes it easier to read and modify because you do not have to go searching through your code to find the lines associated with the loop control variable.

The update does not have to be a simple increment by one. It does not even have to be a single statement. It can be any valid executable statement. This is also true for the initialize statement. You can put multiple entries in the initialize and update portion or you can omit one or both of them. The following six statements illustrate valid ways the initialize, test, and update portions can be written.

```
1.  for (int counter = 0, val1 = 10; counter < val1; counter++)
```

Here, both `counter` and `val1` are declared and initialized as part of the `for` statement. Notice their declaration is separated by a comma and that `int` is not repeated with `val1`. If these identifiers are used in another declaration outside the `for` statement, a syntax error message is issued, such as the one shown in Figure 6-11.

A local variable named 'counter' cannot be declared in this scope because it would give a different meaning to 'counter', which is already used in a 'parent or current' scope to denote something else

FIGURE 6-11 Redeclaration error message

The second statement shows that you do not have to include an expression for the initialize portion. The semicolon is required. When you place a semicolon without anything to the left of it as shown next, it indicates that no statement or a `null` statement is associated with the initialize portion.

```
// Initialization not included as part of for statement

2.  int counter = 0;
    for ( ; counter < 100; counter+=10)
```

The control variable, `counter`, is declared outside of the `for` statement with the second example. The other parts of the `for` statement can also have more than one or no statements for expressions included in the conditional expression, as shown with statement 3.

```
// No conditional expression included

3.  for  (int j = 0; ; j++)
```

The infinite loop created in statement 3 requires an abnormal termination. As you will learn in the sections that follow, either a `break` or `continue` is needed in the body or the user must terminate this running loop; thus, you should rarely omit the conditional expression.

```
// No initialization; but includes compound update
```

4. `for ( ; j < 10; counter++, j += 3)`

The fourth statement indicates that more than one update can be included by separating the statements with commas. Notice that no semicolon is included after the update. No semicolon is placed after the parentheses ending the initialize, test, and update expressions unless you have a `null` body loop or no statements to loop.

NOTE

Syntactically you are permitted to have a null-bodied loop. If you choose to have this, do not hide the semicolon. It is best to place the semicolon on a line by itself (not at the end of the line containing the conditional expression) with a comment indicating that the body is `null`. For example, the following loop adds values 0 through 100 in the update portion of the for statement.

```
for (int aNum = 0; aNum < 101; sum += aNum, aNum++) ;
      // Notice the ; Considered empty loop body
```

Variables declared inside the `for` statement are only accessible within the loop body. They go out of scope when the loop terminates. If the result, `sum`, shown in the Note above is to be displayed outside the loop, it must also be declared outside the loop. It cannot be declared in the initializer portion.

```
// Compound initialization, compound test, and compound update
// Compound test requires logical && or || operator
```

5. `for (int j = 0, k = 10; j < 10 && k > 0; counter++, j += 3)`

To include more than one test as part of the conditional expression, you must use the `&&` operator as a separator between the expressions as shown in statement 5. It is not enough to just separate the conditional expressions by a comma. Of course, the logical OR operator could also be used. However, you should be cautious. With the `||` operator, only one of the expressions must evaluate to `true` for the loop body to be executed. It is easy to create an infinite loop.

```
// Use of floating point variables is permissible
```

6. `for (double d = 15.0; d < 20.0; d += 0.5)`

Floating-point variables can be used for the initialization, conditional expressions, and increments of loops. It is syntactically correct to write:

```
for (double d = 15.0; d < 20.0; d += 0.5)
{
    Write(d + "\t");
}
```

The output produced using the floating-point values is as follows:

15 15.5 16 16.5 17 17.5 18 18.5 19 19.5

You can also change the loop control variable inside the loop and alter the execution. If you add 2.0 to the loop control variable, you change the result produced by the loop as follows:

```
for (double d = 15.0; d < 20.0; d += 0.5)
{
      Write(d + "\t");
      d += 2.0;
}
```

The output produced is

15 17.5

You can even change the value of the variables used in the conditional expression inside the loop body. Each iteration through the loop is an independent activity. If, for example, you modify the variables d and endValue, which are used as the test to terminate the loop, the loop is altered by the new values, as shown in the following code segment:

```
double endValue = 20.0;
for (double d = 15.0; d < endValue; d += 0.5)
{
      Write(d + "\t");
      d += 2;
      endValue = 30;
}
```

The output produced is

15 17.5 20 22.5 25 27.5

NOTE Although it is legal to change endValue, be careful, because it is easy to create an infinite loop. Also notice in the previous example that each iteration through the loop made the same assignment of endValue = 30. This was inefficient.

As noted earlier, the for loop can be used with loop structures that are not counter controlled. For example, applications that retrieve data from an input file could attempt to access the first record in the initialization section. The test section could be used to check to see when the end of file was encountered. The update portion of the for statement could be used to read the next record from the file. The body of the loop could then process the data that was retrieved. You will explore accessing data from an input file in Chapter 13. The for loop is the preferred structure used with arrays. Arrays are the topic of Chapter 7.

Using the Foreach Statement

The `foreach` statement is new to the C++/Java line of programming languages. It is used to iterate or move through a collection, such as an array. You will be working with arrays in Chapter 7. An **array** is a data structure that allows multiple values to be stored under a single identifier. Values are usually accessed in the array using the identifier and an index representing the location of the element relative to the beginning of the first element. The `foreach` loop offers another option for traversing through the array without having to increment indexes or counter-controlled variables like is needed when you use a `for` statement. This chapter introduces the `foreach` loop because it is a looping structure available in C#; however, Chapter 7 explores the concept in greater detail.

To use the `foreach` statement, a collection must be available. You have not used or seen any collections yet; thus, the discussion that follows is brief but is continued in Chapter 7. The general form of the `foreach` statement is

```
foreach (type identifier in expression)
         statement;
```

The expression in the preceding syntax box is the collection, such as the array. The type is the kind of values found in the collection. The identifier is a user-supplied name used as an iteration control variable to reference the individual entries in the collection. The `foreach` statement offers a shortcut to moving through a group of data items. With the `for` statement, you understood that it was necessary to increment a loop control variable and test an expression to determine when all data had been processed. Neither of those statements is required with the `foreach` loop. In Example 6-13, an array called `number` contains five different values. Using the `foreach` statement, all five values are printed.

EXAMPLE 6-13

```
int [ ] number = {2, 4, 6, 8, 10};
foreach(int val in number)
{
     WriteLine(val);
}
```

The output of this code is

2

4

6

8

10

In order to receive the same output using a `for` statement, you would write

```
for (int index = 0; index < 5; index++)
     WriteLine(number[index]);
```

Notice with the `for` statement it is necessary to declare and increment an `index` to reference elements in the collection. You get automatic traversal through the collection with the `foreach` loop.

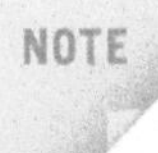

NOTE Note the following restriction on the `foreach` statement: You cannot change values in the collection. The access to the elements is read-only.

Do not be alarmed if you don't totally understand Example 6-13. As mentioned previously, the `foreach` statement will be revisited when you learn about arrays in Chapter 7. For now, recognize that the loop body is executed for every element in the array or collection. Like the other forms of looping structures, after the iteration has been completed for all the elements in the collection, control is transferred to the next statement following the `foreach` block.

Using the Do. . .while Structure

All of the loop structures you have learned up to this point are considered pretests. The `do. . .while` is the only posttest loop structure available in C#. The general form of the `do. . .while` statement is

```
do
{
     statement;
}
while (conditional expression);
```

With a posttest, the statements are executed once before the conditional expression is tested. When the conditional expression evaluates to `true`, the statement(s) are repeated. When the expression evaluates to `false`, control is transferred to the statement following the `do. . .while` loop expression. Notice that the loop body is always executed at least once regardless of the value of the conditional expression.

Figure 6-12 illustrates the flow of execution in a posttest loop.

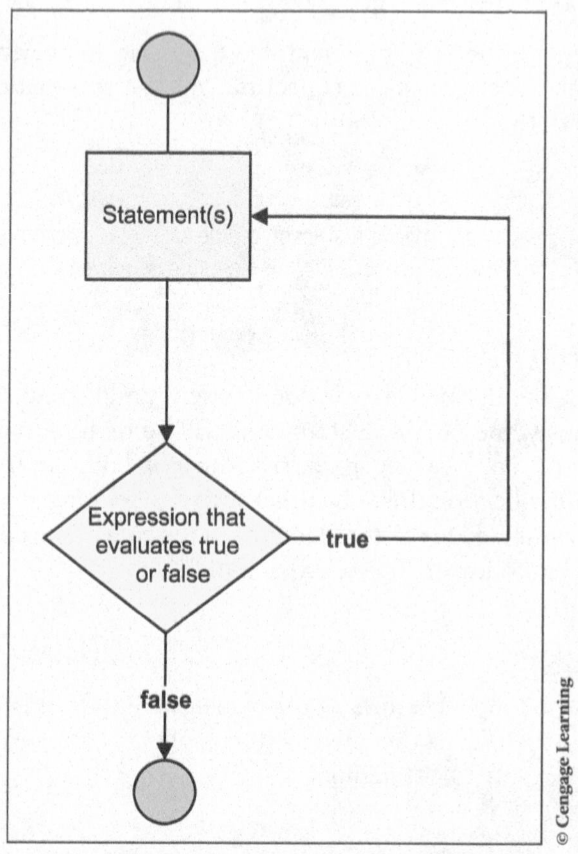

FIGURE 6-12 Do. . .while loop

A do. . .while loop is used in Example 6-14 to display numbers and their squares. The first value printed is 10. Each iteration through the loop decreases the counter by one until the counter reaches zero.

EXAMPLE 6-14

```
int counter = 10;
do                          // No semicolon on this line
{
    WriteLine(counter + "\t" + Math.Pow(counter, 2));
    counter--;
}
while (counter > 0);
```

The output of this code is

```
10    100
 9     81
 8     64
 7     49
 6     36
 5     25
 4     16
 3      9
 2      4
 1      1
```


No semicolon is placed on the line containing the `do` keyword. A semicolon is placed on the last line. It appears on the same line as the `while` keyword. As with the other looping structures, the curly braces are optional; however, with the `do...while` loop you will not forget to block the loop body when you have more than one statement as you might with the other formats. As shown in Figure 6-13, C# issues a syntax error if you have more than one statement between the `do` and `while` without including the curly braces.

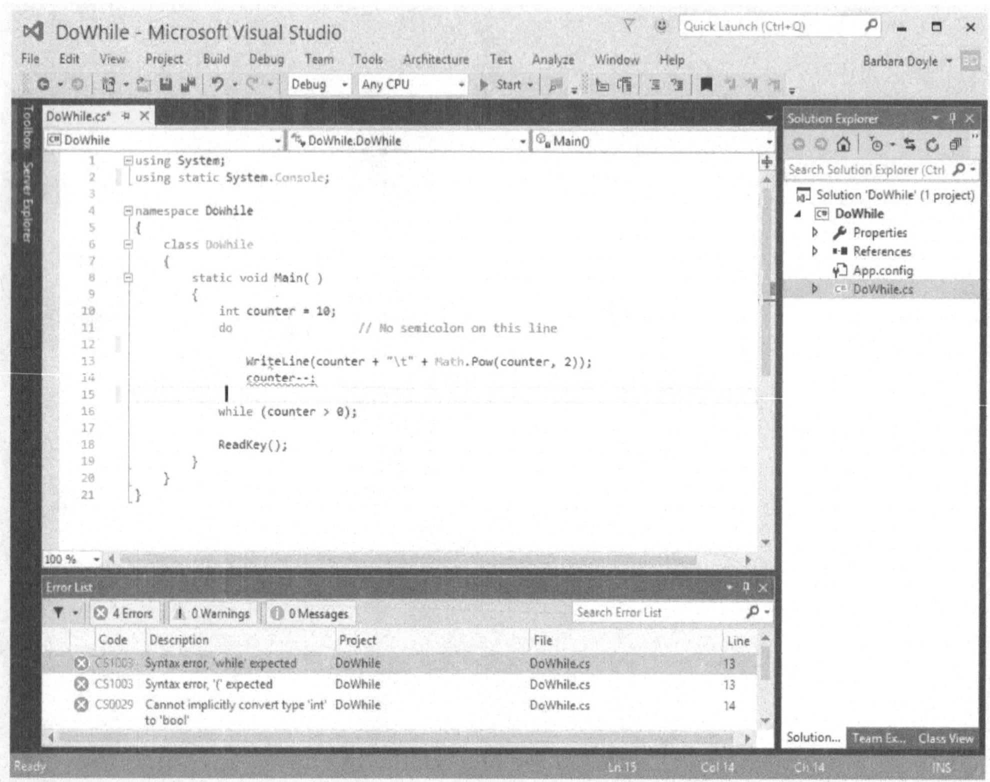

FIGURE 6-13 Curly brace required

The do. . .while loop can be used to implement a counter-controlled loop, as shown in Example 6-14. It can also be used to implement a sentinel- or flag-controlled loop. You will see an example of this in the nested loop section. The only difference between this structure and the while structure is in the placement of the conditional expression. For posttest loops, the conditional expression is placed at the end of the loop body.

Nested Loops

Any statement can be included within the body of a loop, which means another loop can be nested inside an outer loop. When this occurs, the inner nested loop is totally completed before the outside loop is tested a second time. You often need nested loops when working with arrays, especially multidimensional arrays, which are covered in Chapter 8. Example 6-15 illustrates a nested loop using two for statements.

6

EXAMPLE 6-15

```
int inner;
for (int outer = 0; outer < 3; outer++)
{
     for(inner = 10; inner > 5; inner --)
     {
          WriteLine("Outer: {0}\tInner: {1}", outer, inner);
     }
}
```

The output of this code is

Outer: 0	Inner: 10
Outer: 0	Inner: 9
Outer: 0	Inner: 8
Outer: 0	Inner: 7
Outer: 0	Inner: 6
Outer: 1	Inner: 10
Outer: 1	Inner: 9
Outer: 1	Inner: 8
Outer: 1	Inner: 7
Outer: 1	Inner: 6
Outer: 2	Inner: 10
Outer: 2	Inner: 9
Outer: 2	Inner: 8
Outer: 2	Inner: 7
Outer: 2	Inner: 6

In Example 6-15, the `WriteLine( )` method is executed 15 times. As shown from the output, after the variable `outer` is initialized to zero and evaluated to determine whether `outer` is less than 3, the innermost loop is executed five times. The variable `inner` takes on the values of `10`, `9`, `8`, `7`, and `6`. When `inner` is updated to `5`, the second `for` statement, in the innermost loop, evaluates to `false (inner > 5)`. That loop is now completed.

The for statement using the variable inner is the executable statement for the outermost for loop. After the innermost for statement is completed, control transfers back to the update portion of the outside for loop. Here, the variable outer is updated. Another evaluation of outer occurs to determine whether outer is less than 3. Because it is less, control transfers back into the nested innermost for loop. Here, the entire for statement is executed again. Notice the identifier inner is redeclared and reinitialized to 10. The sequence of evaluating the conditional expression using the variable inner, executing the body of the loop and updating inner, which is the control variable, continues until the innermost conditional expression again evaluates to false. At that point, outer, the loop control variable in the outermost loop, is updated and the outermost conditional expression is evaluated again. This cycle continues until the outermost for loop expression evaluates to false.

Example 6-16 shows another nested loop. This program allows any number of n factorial (n!) calculations. First, a loop is used to calculate n!, which represents the product of the first n positive integers. If n, for example, has a value of 3, 3! is 3 * 2 * 1, or 6. When n is 6, n! is 6 * 5 * 4 * 3 * 2 * 1 or 720. One approach to determine the product is to use a loop and multiply n * n–1 * n–2 * . . . 1. Because this is a loop that requires that a variable be updated by decrementing a loop control variable with each pass through the loop, a for loop is used.

A nested loop allows the user to calculate more than one n!. The design choice for Example 6-16 is "at least one calculation should be run." A posttest loop structure is used for the outermost nested loop. At the end of the first pass, the user is asked whether another value is to be calculated. The do...while loop is used as the outer loop control. A for statement is used for the inner loop. The for loop, doing the individual calculations, is placed in a class method. This method is called with each new value entered by the user. Example 6-16 follows:

EXAMPLE 6-16

```
/* NFactorial.cs          Author: Doyle
 * Computes n factorial -
 * the product of the first n
 * positive integers.
 */
using System;
using static System.Console;

namespace NFactorial
{
    class NFactorial
    {
        static void Main( )
        {
```

```
    int result;                                                    //Line 1
    string moreData;                                               //Line 2
    int n;                                                         //Line 3
    DisplayInformation( );                                         //Line 4
    do                                                             //Line 5
    {                                                              //Line 6
        n = InputN( );                                             //Line 7
        CalculateNFactorialIteratively(n, out result);
        DisplayNFactorial(n, result);                              //Line 9
        moreData = PromptForMoreCalculations( );                   //Line 10
    }                                                              //Line 11
    while (moreData == "y" || moreData == "Y");                    //Line 12
    ReadKey( );                                                    //Line 13
}

static void DisplayInformation( )                                  //Line 14
{                                                                  //Line 15
    WriteLine("n! represents the "  +                              //Line 16
              "product of the " +                                  //Line 17
              "first n integers");                                 //Line 18
}

static void CalculateNFactorialIteratively(int n,
                              out int result)                      //Line 19
{                                                                  //Line 20
     result = 1;                                                   //Line 21
     for (int i = n; i > 0; i--)                                   //Line 22
     {                                                             //Line 23
          result *= i;                                             //Line 24
     }                                                             //Line 25
}                                                                  //Line 26

static int InputN( )                                               //Line 27
{                                                                  //Line 28
     string inValue;                                               //Line 29
     int n;                                                        //Line 30
     Write("\nEnter the number to " +                              //Line 31
           "use to compute n! ");                                  //Line 32
     inValue = ReadLine( );                                        //Line 33
     if (int.TryParse(inValue, out n) == false)                    //Line 34
        WriteLine("Invalid input -" +                              //Line 35
                  "0 recorded for n");
     return n;                                                     //Line 36
}

static void DisplayNFactorial(int n, int result)                   //Line 37
{                                                                  //Line 38
     WriteLine("{0}! is {1}.", n, result);                         //Line 39
}                                                                  //Line 40
```

```
//Line 41        static string PromptForMoreCalculations( )
//Line 42        {
//Line 43            string moreData;
//Line 44            WriteLine("\nDo you want to " +
                             "calculate another factorial?");
//Line 45            WriteLine("Enter y for another " +
//Line 46                      "calculation.\nAny other" +
//Line 47                      " character to stop.");
//Line 48            moreData = ReadLine( );
//Line 49            return moreData;
//Line 50        }
//Line 51    }
//Line 52 }
```

Figure 6-14 shows the output of running the program for Example 6-16 with 9, 5, and 3. To exit the outer loop, the character `n` was entered when the user was prompted to "`Enter y for another calculation...`" beginning on Line 45. Any character value, other than the character Y or y, is entered to exit the loop.

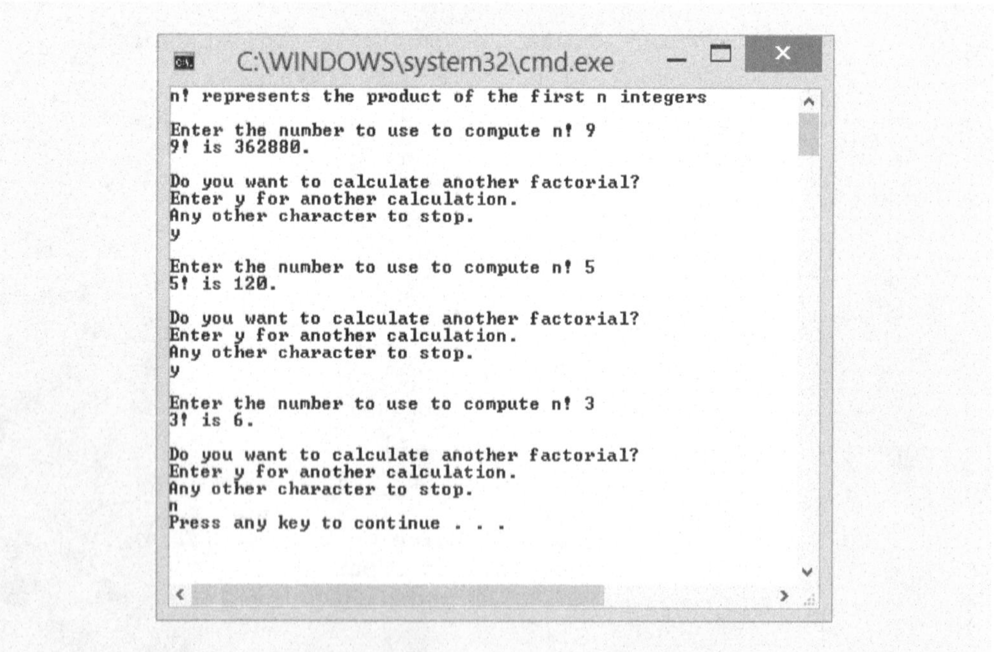

FIGURE 6-14 Nested loop output

Notice that the `CalculateNFactorialIteratively(int n, out int result)` method shown on Lines 19–26 contains the `for` statement used as the inner nested loop. This is where `n!` is calculated. It produces `result` by initializing the loop control variable, `i`, to `n` on Line 22. The variable `n` stores the user-inputted entry that represents the factorial to be calculated. With each iteration of the loop, the loop control variable is multiplied by `result`. The `out` keyword is included in the method call and method heading for the variable `result`, indicating that `result` does not contain a value on entry into the method.

The first statement in the `CalculateNFactorialIteratively( )` method initializes `result` to `1`. During each iteration through the loop, the update portion of the `for` statement decrements the loop counter. The conditional expression is reevaluated to determine whether the calculations are finished. This cycle of execute body, update loop control variable, and evaluate expression continues until the loop control variable reaches `0`. When this occurs, the innermost `for` statement is completed. This also completes the `CalculateNFactorialIteratively( )` method. Control transfers back to the outer loop at Line 9, which calls another method `DisplayNFactorial( )`, to display the original value of `n` and `result`, the product of the calculations. After control returns to the `Main( )` method, the `PromptForMoreCalculations( )` method found on Lines 41–50 is called next. It returns a value indicating whether the loop body should be executed again.

Recursive Calls

Another option for repeating a program statement is recursion. **Recursion** is a technique used where a method calls itself repeatedly until it arrives at the solution. Recursion is somewhat similar to a circular definition, in that the recursive method contains a call to itself. It is a very powerful control mechanism. When you write iteration or looping statements, such as a `while` or `for` statement, you must write statements to deal with the loop variables. With recursion, much of the details of the calls are handled for you behind the scenes. To write a recursive solution, a different problem-solving technique is employed. You must identify a terminating condition so that the method branches to a non-recursive solution at some point.

In C# and most other languages, a method can call itself. Another approach that can be used to solve the `n!` problem, introduced in Example 6-16, is to develop a recursive solution. To write a recursive solution, an algorithm has to be developed so as to avoid an infinite loop. There must be a way for the method to know that it should stop calling itself. This is accomplished by identifying a base case. The base case is a simple, direct answer that is arrived at without another call to the method. The base case is the simplest form of the solution. The other cases are all solved by reducing the value and calling the method again. Example 6-17 illustrates a recursive method that would replace the method `CalculateNFactorialIteratively( )`, which was called iteratively.

EXAMPLE 6-17

```
static int Fact(int n)
{
      if (n == 1 || n == 0)
         return 1;
      else
         return (n * Fact(n-1));
}
```

For this algorithm, the base case is 1. When `Fact( )` is called with an argument of 1, the method returns 1; otherwise, it returns the product of `Fact(n-1)` times `n`. Notice that with each call, 1 is subtracted from `n` so that the new argument is eventually reduced to the simplest or base case. The conditional statement includes the additional compound test of (|| n == 0) because the `int.TryParse( )` method stores 0 in n when invalid data, such as an alphabetic character, is entered.

Both Examples 6-16 and 6-17 solve the `n!` problem. In terms of comparing the code of the iterative to the recursive solution, the `Fact( )` method replaces the `CalculateNFactorialIteratively( )` method and the call in the `Main( )` method would be changed. Because the `Fact( )` method returns a value, a variable was set aside in the `Main( )` method to hold the answer. The call changed from `CalculateNFactorialIteratively(n, out result)` to answer = `Fact(n)`.

When the factorial of `4` is calculated, a test of `n` causes the `Fact( )` method to be called a second time. The value for the `n` argument in the second call is 3 or n−1. Another test of `n`'s value causes a third call to `Fact( )` with `n-1` value, or `2`. The fourth call to `Fact( )` sends in the value of `1`. When this occurs, `1` is returned and that value is used in place of the previous call, which causes `1` to be multiplied by `2` and then that value returned back to the previous call where `n` was equal to `3`. When the `2` is returned, it is multiplied by `n` (or `3`) and `6` is returned. When `6` is returned, it is multiplied by `n`, which is `4` for this call, and the solution for `4!` is `24`. This is illustrated in Figure 6-15.

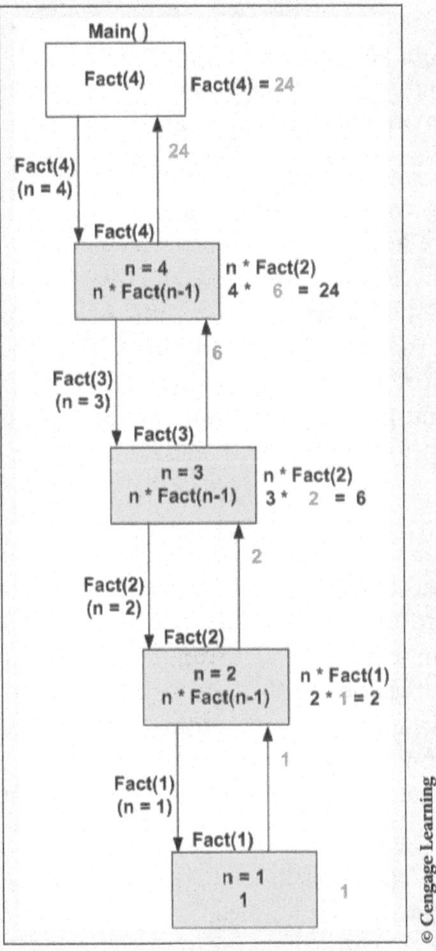

FIGURE 6-15 Recursive evaluation of n!

When a recursive solution is used, the system stack is used to store the values for the local variables. You can think of the memory representation of a stack as analogous to a stack of books. Think of placing the books in a tall, shallow box. The first book is placed in the bottom of the box. The second is placed on top of it. If this were to continue and you placed five books on the stack, to retrieve the first one that went on the stack, you would need to pick up book 5, then book 4, and so on until you finally reached the one on the bottom. As each recursive call is returned, the old variables are removed from the stack and used. They are retrieved, or popped off the stack, using a LIFO (Last In/First Out) approach. When the method is complete, execution always resumes at the point where the call was made and the value returned from the method is used in place of the call.

The n! recursive example shows a simple mathematical use of recursion. Another area where recursion is very useful is with processing lists of items. With this type of application, you can test for an empty list as the base case. Calls to the recursive methods continue with each call sending the list minus its first element. When the call sends in an empty list, the base case is met. Chapter 7 introduces you to collections, such as arrays, where lists of items can be stored.

Recursion is considered an elegant approach for solving problems. It is sometimes less intuitive and more complicated than iterative approaches to solving the same problem. There is also additional overhead required with recursive solutions because multiple method calls are made and with each call, the local variable's data must be saved so that when control returns back, the values of the local variables can be restored. More memory is used with recursive calls. However, it is another tool or approach that programmers can take to solve problems. And, sometimes a shorter, more straightforward solution can be written using recursion.

Unconditional Transfer of Control

C# provides a couple of options to alter the flow of control in a program. You have been introduced to the `break` statement. It is used with the `switch` selection statement to provide an immediate exit from the `switch` structure. You can also place a `break` statement in the body of a loop to provide an immediate exit. If you do, when the `break` statement is reached, control immediately transfers to the statement on the outside of the loop body. The conditional expression is never evaluated again. Example 6-18 illustrates what happens when a `break` statement is placed inside a loop.

NOTE When you use a `break` statement with a nested loop, the `break` takes you out of the innermost loop in which the `break` is placed.

EXAMPLE 6-18

```
int total = 0;
for (int nValue = 0; nValue < 10; nValue++)
{
    if (nValue == 5)
    {
        break;
    }
    total += nValue;
    Write(nValue + "\t");
}
WriteLine("\nTotal is equal to {0}.", total);
```

The output for this code is

0 1 2 3 4

Total is equal to 10.

When the conditional expression associated with the `if` statement inside the loop, `(nValue == 5)`, evaluates to `true`, the `break` statement is executed, which stops the loop body. The loop conditional expression in the `for` statement, `(nValue < 10)`, is never evaluated again. The statement `(WriteLine("\nTotal is equal to {0}.", total);)` is executed.

NOTE For the preceding example, you would get the same result if you modified the conditional expression to `(nValue < 5)`.

6

Another unconditional transfer of control option used with loops is the `continue` statement, discussed in the following section.

Continue Statement

The `continue` statement, like the `break`, is a form of jump statement. When a `continue` is reached, a new iteration of the nearest enclosing `while`, `do...while`, `for`, or `foreach` statement is started. Physically, it does not matter where the execution is. It could be at the top or bottom of the loop body. When `continue` is reached and executed, the rest of that iteration of the loop body is not performed. `continue` immediately transfers control straight to the conditional expression for an evaluation.

NOTE With the `for` statement, transfer is back to the top of the next iteration, which actually causes the update portion to be performed before the reevaluation of the conditional expression.

The general form of the statement is

```
continue;
```

Example 6-19 adds and prints only odd values. When the conditional expression `(nValue % 2 == 0)` evaluates to `true`, the `continue` statement is executed, which causes the loop body to halt at that location. The remaining statements in the loop are skipped and control transfers back to update `nValue`. The variable `total` is not incremented and the `Write(nValue)` is not executed for that iteration through the loop.

EXAMPLE 6-19

```
int total = 0;
for (int nValue = 0; nValue < 10; nValue++)
{
     if (nValue % 2 == 0)
     {
          continue;
     }
     total += nValue;
     Write(nValue + "\t");
}
WriteLine("\nTotal is equal to {0}.", total);
```

The output for this code is

```
1     3     5     7     9
Total is equal to 25.
```

Notice that the difference between the `break` and `continue` statements is that the `continue` statement does not stop the execution of the loop body, but rather, halts that iteration and transfers control to the next iteration of the loop.

The other jump statements in C# are `goto`, `throw`, and `return`. You will learn about the `throw` statement with exception handling in Chapter 12. You have used the `return` statement in your value-returning methods. The `goto` statement transfers control to a statement that is marked by a label. The `goto` statement has a bad reputation. It is associated with poorly designed spaghetti code that is difficult to debug and maintain. You should not use a `goto` jump statement in your programs.

The `break` and `continue` statements should also be used sparingly. It is appropriate and a requirement that you use a `break` statement with a `switch` statement. However, when you use `break` and `continue` statements with a loop, you are violating the **single entry and single exit** guideline for developing a loop. What this means is that there should be only one way to enter a loop and one way to exit. When you exit a loop from multiple locations, it becomes more difficult to debug. The loop might end because the condition evaluates to `false` or it might end prematurely because of the `break`. This adds complications when you are trying to walk through the logic.

Deciding Which Loop to Use

The decision regarding which type of loop to use is sometimes a personal choice; however, there are some considerations you might want to acknowledge and allow to overrule your personal biases. Remember that the body of the `do...while` is always executed at least once. Thus, you should avoid using this form if there is the possibility that the loop body should not be executed when certain types of data are input into your program. Conversely, if you know your loop will always be executed at least once, the `do...while` is a good option.

If a numeric variable is being changed by a consistent amount with each iteration through the loop, the compactness of the `for` statement might work best. The initialization, conditional expression, and update can all be located on the same line. Although the format allows for multiple entries for all three of these entries, a good rule of thumb is that the `for` statement initialization, condition, and update should be able to be placed on one line. Remember, readability is always an important consideration.

The `while` statement can be used to write any type of loop. It can implement counter-controlled loops just as the `for` statement can. The `while` statement is also useful for applications requiring state- and sentinel-controlled loops. So it is always a good option. It offers the advantage of being a pretest type. With all of the loops, you want to ensure that you understand and design the condition that is used to end the loop as well as how the condition is updated or changed.

PROGRAMMING EXAMPLE: LoanApplication

This example demonstrates the use of loops in the analysis, design, and implementation of a program. Both pretest and posttest forms of loops are included in the example. The pretest form is used to calculate individual loan details. It is nested inside the posttest through method calls. Static and instance methods, properties, and selection statements are included. Figure 6-16 outlines the problem specification.

Create an application that will allow a loan amount, interest rate, and number of finance years to be entered for a given loan. Determine the monthly payment amount. Calculate how much interest will be paid over the life of the loan. Display an amortization schedule showing the new balance after each payment is made.

Design an object-oriented solution. Use two classes. For the Loan class, characteristics such as the amount to be financed, rate of interest, period of time for the loan, and total interest paid will identify the current state of a loan object. Include methods to determine the monthly payment amount, return the total interest paid over the life of the loan, and return an amortization schedule.

In the second class, instantiate an object of the loan class. Allow the user to input data about more than one loan. Display in the LoanApp class the payment amount, amortization schedule, and the total amount of interest to be paid.

© Cengage Learning

FIGURE 6-16 Problem specification for the LoanApplication example

ANALYZE THE PROBLEM

You should review the problem specification in Figure 6-16 and make sure that you understand the problem definition. Several values are put into the program to represent the loan amount, rate, and the time period of the loan. These values are entered as `string` variables and then parsed or converted into numeric fields so the calculations can be performed.

Two separate classes are to be developed. Creating a separate `class` for the `Loan` `object` enables the `class` to be used by other applications. The `class` includes an algorithm for producing an amortization schedule. It also includes a stand-alone method to determine the total interest paid over the life of the loan.

DATA

Tables 6-3 and 6-4 list the data field members needed for the `LoanApplication` problem.

TABLE 6-3 Instance field members for the Loan class

Data item description	Type	Identifier
Amount of loan	`double`	`loanAmount`
Interest rate	`double`	`rate`
Total interest paid	`double`	`totalInterestPaid`
Monthly payment amount	`double`	`paymentAmount`
Current balance of the loan	`double`	`balance`
Current amount paid toward principal	`double`	`principal`
Number of payments	`int`	`numPayments`
Interest for the current month	`double`	`monthInterest`

© Cengage Learning

The client `class` that is using the `Loan` `class` will need additional data. As noted in the problem specification, the client or application `class` allows the user to enter values for the loan. Table 6-4 identifies some of the local variables needed by the application `class`.

TABLE 6-4 Local variables for the LoanApp class

Data item description	Type	Identifier
Amount of loan	`double`	`loanAmount`
Interest rate	`double`	`interestRate`
Number of years to finance loan	`int`	`years`
More calculations (loop state-controlled variable)	`char`	`anotherLoan`

© Cengage Learning

6

The top three entries in Table 6-4 will be used to instantiate an `object` of the `Loan` `class`. After the values are entered and converted into numeric values, the loan constructor will be called to create a `Loan` `object`.

CONSTANTS

No constants are used for this application.

FORMULAS

Formulas are needed to calculate the following:

1. numPayments = years * 12
2. term = $(1 + \text{rate} / 12.0)^{\text{numPayments}}$
3. paymentAmount = loanAmount * rate / 12 * term/(term – 1.0)
4. monthInterest = rate / 12 * balance
5. principal = payment – monthInterest
6. balance = balance – principal
7. totalInterestPaid = totalInterestPaid + monthInterest

DESIGN A SOLUTION

The desired output is to display the monthly payment amount, an amortization schedule, and the total interest paid over the life of the loan. Figure 6-17 shows a prototype for the final output. The xxx's are placed in the prototype to represent the location in which the calculated values should appear.

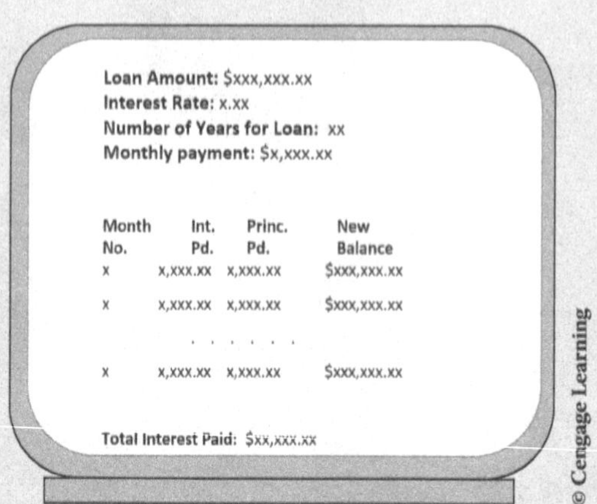

© Cengage Learning

FIGURE 6-17 Prototype for the LoanApplication example

The object-oriented approach focuses on the `object`. The loan application has both data and behavior characteristics that can be identified. Class diagrams are used to help design and document these characteristics. Figure 6-18 shows the `class` diagrams for the Loan Application example.

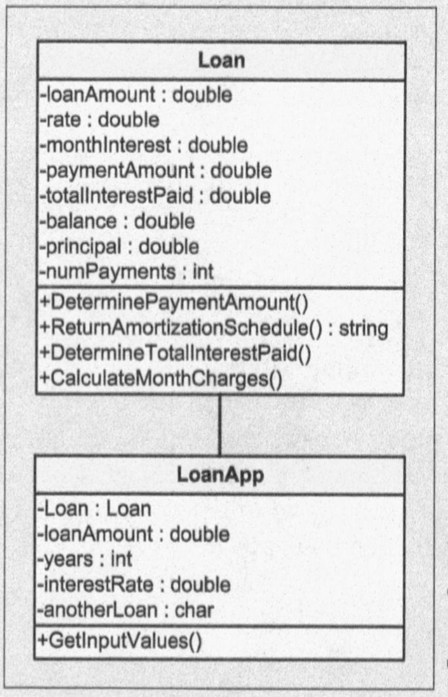

© Cengage Learning

FIGURE 6-18 Class diagrams

The `class` diagrams do not show the properties or the local variables that might be needed by specific methods. Table 6-5 lists the data members that will have properties defined and indicates whether both `get` and/or `set` will be needed. The name of the property is also shown.

TABLE 6-5 Properties for the Loan class

Data member identifier	Property identifier	Set	Get
`paymentAmount`	`PaymentAmount`		√
`loanAmount`	`LoanAmount`	√	√
`rate`	`Rate`	√	√
`numPayments (in months)`	`Years`	√	√
`totalInterestPaid`	`TotalInterestPaid`		√

© Cengage Learning

The property members `PaymentAmount` and `TotalInterestPaid` are set as read-only properties because they are calculated values involving more than just the individual data member.

Figures 6-19 and 6-20 show the Structured English, or pseudocode, used to design the step-by-step processes for the behaviors of the methods for the LoanApplication example.

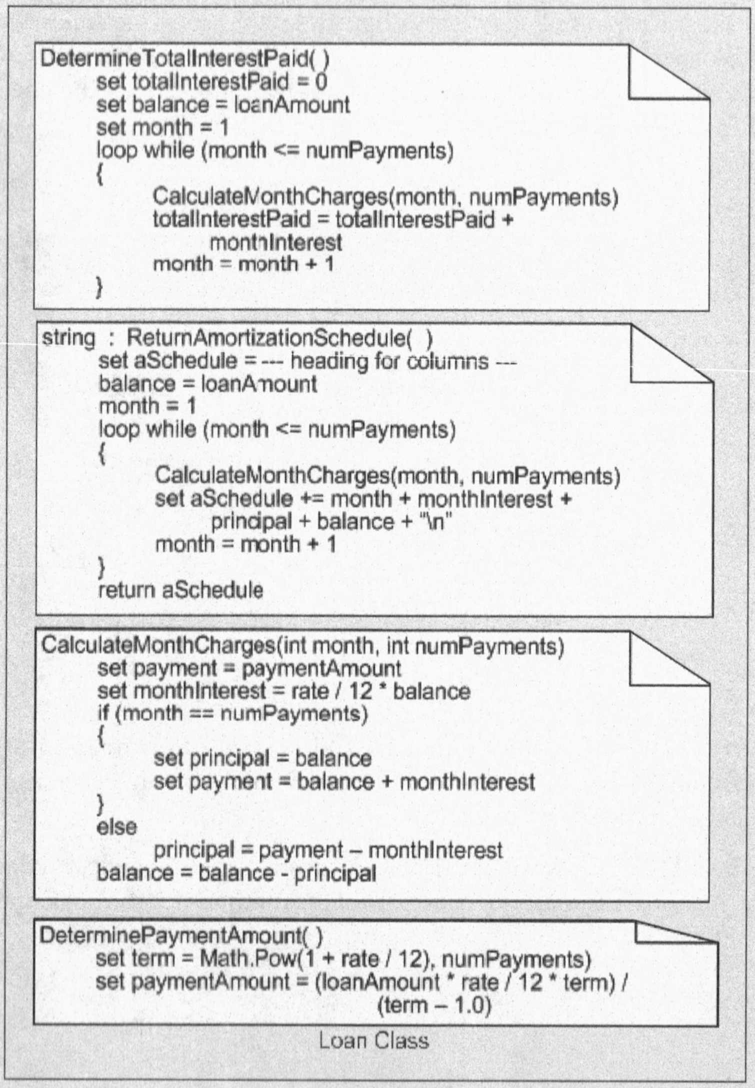

```
DetermineTotalInterestPaid( )
        set totalInterestPaid = 0
        set balance = loanAmount
        set month = 1
        loop while (month <= numPayments)
        {
                CalculateMonthCharges(month, numPayments)
                totalInterestPaid = totalInterestPaid +
                        monthInterest
                month = month + 1
        }
```

```
string : ReturnAmortizationSchedule( )
        set aSchedule = --- heading for columns ---
        balance = loanAmount
        month = 1
        loop while (month <= numPayments)
        {
                CalculateMonthCharges(month, numPayments)
                set aSchedule += month + monthInterest +
                        principal + balance + "\n"
                month = month + 1
        }
        return aSchedule
```

```
CalculateMonthCharges(int month, int numPayments)
        set payment = paymentAmount
        set monthInterest = rate / 12 * balance
        if (month == numPayments)
        {
                set principal = balance
                set payment = balance + monthInterest
        }
        else
                principal = payment – monthInterest
        balance = balance - principal
```

```
DeterminePaymentAmount( )
        set term = Math.Pow(1 + rate / 12), numPayments)
        set paymentAmount = (loanAmount * rate / 12 * term) /
                                        (term – 1.0)
```

Loan Class

© Cengage Learning

FIGURE 6-19 Behavior of Loan class methods

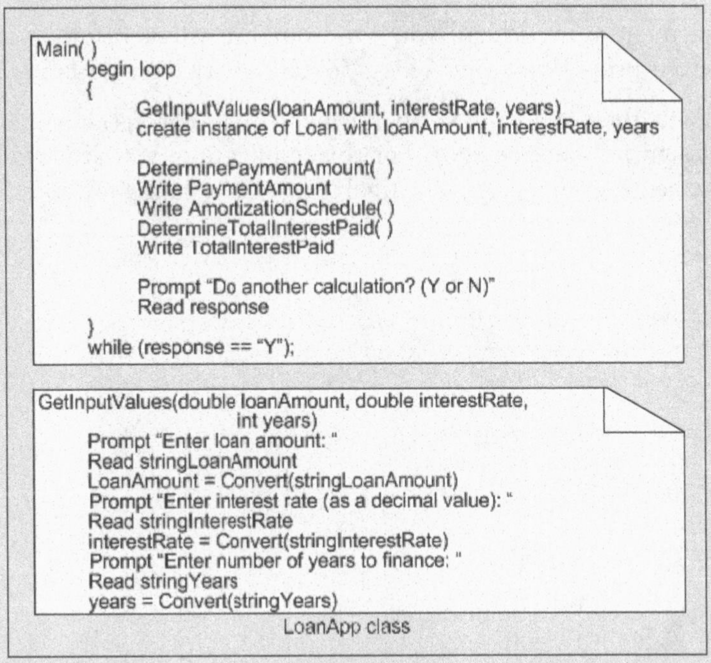

```
Main( )
    begin loop
    {
        GetInputValues(loanAmount, interestRate, years)
        create instance of Loan with loanAmount, interestRate, years

        DeterminePaymentAmount( )
        Write PaymentAmount
        Write AmortizationSchedule( )
        DetermineTotalInterestPaid( )
        Write TotalInterestPaid

        Prompt "Do another calculation? (Y or N)"
        Read response
    }
    while (response == "Y");
```

```
GetInputValues(double loanAmount, double interestRate,
                    int years)
    Prompt "Enter loan amount: "
    Read stringLoanAmount
    LoanAmount = Convert(stringLoanAmount)
    Prompt "Enter interest rate (as a decimal value): "
    Read stringInterestRate
    interestRate = Convert(stringInterestRate)
    Prompt "Enter number of years to finance: "
    Read stringYears
    years = Convert(stringYears)
```

LoanApp class

© Cengage Learning

FIGURE 6-20 Behavior of LoanApp class methods

After the algorithm is developed, the design should be checked for correctness. With previous applications, you have been able to use a standard calculator and compare results you produce with your program against values you produce with a calculator. Sometimes, you need additional resources to verify the correctness of your output. On the Internet, you can find amortization tables and you can also use financial calculators to test your results. Table 6-6 contains values that can be used to verify the correctness of the programming example. For readability here commas are added. They are not entered during testing.

TABLE 6-6 LoanApp test values

Loan amount	Interest rate	Years	Payment amount	Total interest
50,000	0.08	10	606.64	22,796.56
22,000	0.05	5	415.17	2,910.03
150,000	0.055	30	851.68	156,606.06
12,000	0.06	3	365.06	1,142.28
10,000	0.05	2	438.71	529.13

© Cengage Learning

After you implement your design, you can compare these results with those obtained from your program output. This is sometimes called a desk run.

After you complete the design and verify the algorithm's correctness, it is time to translate the design into source code. For this application, you are creating two separate files—one for each class. The final application listing for both files is as follows:

CODE THE SOLUTION

```
/* Loan.cs
 * Creates fields for the amount of loan, interest
 * rate, and number of years. Calculates payment amount
 * and produces an amortization schedule.
 */
using System;

namespace LoanApp
{
   public class Loan
   {
        private double loanAmount;
        private double rate;
        private int numPayments;
        private double balance;
        private double totalInterestPaid;
        private double paymentAmount;
        private double principal;
        private double monthInterest;

        // Default constructor
        public Loan( )
        {

        }

        // Constructor
        public Loan(double loan, double interestRate, int years)
        {
            loanAmount = loan;
            if (interestRate < 1)
               rate = interestRate;
            else     //In case directions aren't followed
                     // convert interest rate to decimal
               rate = interestRate / 100;
            numPayments = 12 * years;
            totalInterestPaid = 0;
            DeterminePaymentAmount( );
        }
```

```
// Property accessing payment amount
public double PaymentAmount
{
    get
    {
         return paymentAmount;
    }
}

// Property setting and returning loan amount
public double LoanAmount
{
    set
    {
         loanAmount = value;
    }
    get
    {
         return loanAmount;
    }
}

// Property setting and returning rate
public double Rate
{
    set
    {
         rate = value;
    }
    get
    {
         return rate;
    }
}

// Property to set the numPayments, given years
// to finance. Returns the number of years using
// number of payments
public int Years
{
    set
    {
         numPayments = value * 12;
    }
    get
    {
         return numPayments / 12;
    }
}
```

```
// Property for accessing total interest
public double TotalInterestPaid
{
     get
     {
          return totalInterestPaid;
     }
}

// Determine payment amount based on number of
// years, loan amount, and rate
public void DeterminePaymentAmount( )
{
     double term;
     term = Math.Pow((1 + rate / 12.0), numPayments);
     paymentAmount = (loanAmount * rate / 12.0 * term) /
                         (term - 1.0);
}

// Returns string containing amortization table
public string ReturnAmortizationSchedule( )
{
     string aSchedule = "Month\t\tInt.\t\tPrin.\t\tNew";
     aSchedule += "\nNo.\t\tPd.\t\tPd.\t\tBalance\n";
     aSchedule += "———\t\t———\t\t————\t" +
                  "—————\n";
     balance = loanAmount;
     for (int month = 1; month <= numPayments;
          month++)
     {
          CalculateMonthCharges(month, numPayments);
          aSchedule += month + "\t" +
                    monthInterest.ToString("N2") + "\t" +
                    principal.ToString("N2") + "\t" +
                    balance.ToString("C") + "\n";
     }
     return aSchedule;
}

// Calculates monthly interest and new balance.
public void CalculateMonthCharges(int month, int
                                   numPayments)
{
     double payment = paymentAmount;
     monthInterest = rate / 12 * balance;
     if (month == numPayments)
     {
          principal = balance;
          payment = balance + monthInterest;
     }
```

```
            else
            {
                principal = payment - monthInterest;
            }
            balance -= principal;
        }

        // Calculates interest paid over life of loan
        public void DetermineTotalInterestPaid( )
        {
            totalInterestPaid = 0;
            balance = loanAmount;
            for (int month = 1; month <= numPayments; month++)
            {
                CalculateMonthCharges(month, numPayments);
                totalInterestPaid += monthInterest;
            }
        }

        //Return information about the loan
        public override string ToString( )
        {
            return "\nLoan Amount: " +
                      loanAmount.ToString("C") +
                      "\nInterest Rate: " + rate +
                      "\nNumber of Years for Loan: " +
                       (numPayments / 12) +
                      "\nMonthly payment: " +
                      paymentAmount.ToString("C");
        }
    }
}

/* LoanApp.cs
 * Used for testing Loan class.
 * Prompts user for loan amount,
 * interest rate, and time period
 * for loan. Calls method to display
 * payment amount and amortization
 * schedule. Allows more than
 * one loan calculation.
 */
using System;
using static System.Console;

namespace LoanApp
{
    class LoanApp
    {
        static void Main( )
```

6

```
{
    int years;
    double loanAmount;
    double interestRate;
    string inValue;
    char anotherLoan = 'N';
    do
    {
       GetInputValues(out loanAmount, out interestRate,
                      out years);
       Loan ln = new Loan(loanAmount, interestRate, years);
       WriteLine( );
       Clear( );
       WriteLine(ln);
       WriteLine( );
       WriteLine(ln.ReturnAmortizationSchedule( ));
       ln.DetermineTotalInterestPaid();
       WriteLine("Payment Amount: {0:C}",ln.PaymentAmount);
       WriteLine("Interest Paid over Life " +
                 "of Loan: {0:C}",
                 ln.TotalInterestPaid);
       Write("Do another Calculation? (Y or N)");
       inValue = ReadLine( );
       anotherLoan = Convert.ToChar(inValue);
    }
    while ((anotherLoan == 'Y')|| (anotherLoan == 'y'));
}

// Prompts user for loan data
static void GetInputValues(out double loanAmount, out
                           double interestRate, out int years)
{
    Clear( );
    loanAmount = GetLoanAmount( );
    interestRate = GetInterestRate( );
    years = GetYears( );
}

static double GetLoanAmount( )
{
    string sValue;
    double loanAmount;
    Write("Please enter the loan amount: ");
    sValue = ReadLine( );
    while ((double.TryParse(sValue,
                out loanAmount) == false)
                || loanAmount < 1 || loanAmount > 500000)
    {
       WriteLine("Invalid data entered " +
                 "for loan amount");
```

```
                Write("\nPlease re-enter the loan amount " +
                      "(less than 500,000): ");
                sValue = ReadLine( );
            }
            return loanAmount;
        }

        static double GetInterestRate( )
        {
            string sValue;
            double interestRate;
            Write("Please enter interest rate (as a " +
                  "decimal value - i.e. .06): ");
            sValue = ReadLine( );
            while ((double.TryParse(sValue,
                         out interestRate)    == false)
                         || interestRate < 0
                         || interestRate > 1)
            {
                Write("\nInvalid data entered for interest rate" +
                      " (decimal value - i.e. 0.06):");
                Write("\nPlease re-enter the interest rate: ");
                sValue = ReadLine( );
            }
            return interestRate;
        }
        static int GetYears( )
        {
            string sValue;
            int years;
            Write("Please enter the number of years " +
                  "for the loan: ");
            sValue = ReadLine( );
            while (int.TryParse(sValue, out years) == false)
                         || years < 1 || years > 30)
            {
                Write("\nInvalid data entered for years");
                Write("\nPlease re-enter the years (1-30): ");
                sValue = ReadLine( );
            }
            return years;
        }
    }
}
```

Using the input values from the last row of Table 6-6, the output is shown in Figure 6-21.

6

```
C:\WINDOWS\system32\cmd.exe

Loan Amount: $10,000.00
Interest Rate: 0.05
Number of Years for Loan: 2
Monthly payment: $438.71

Month       Int.        Prin.       New
No.         Pd.         Pd.         Balance
-------     -------     --------    ----------
1           41.67       397.05      $9,602.95
2           40.01       398.70      $9,204.25
3           38.35       400.36      $8,803.89
4           36.68       402.03      $8,401.86
5           35.01       403.71      $7,998.15
6           33.33       405.39      $7,592.76
7           31.64       407.08      $7,185.69
8           29.94       408.77      $6,776.91
9           28.24       410.48      $6,366.44
10          26.53       412.19      $5,954.25
11          24.81       413.90      $5,540.34
12          23.08       415.63      $5,124.71
13          21.35       417.36      $4,707.35
14          19.61       419.10      $4,288.25
15          17.87       420.85      $3,867.41
16          16.11       422.60      $3,444.81
17          14.35       424.36      $3,020.45
18          12.59       426.13      $2,594.32
19          10.81       427.90      $2,166.41
20          9.03        429.69      $1,736.73
21          7.24        431.48      $1,305.25
22          5.44        433.28      $871.97
23          3.63        435.08      $436.89
24          1.82        436.89      $0.00

Payment Amount: $438.71
Interest Paid over Life of Loan: $529.13
Do another Calculation? (Y or N)_
```

FIGURE 6-21 LoanApplication output

NOTE The output is formatted using the fixed point `N`, which displays a comma with floating-point values and currency `C` format specifiers. They are the arguments to the `ToString( )` method.

Coding Standards

To develop reliable and maintainable applications, you must follow coding standards and the best practices. There are several standards used in the industry today. Some of the standards differ from others: Some are based on personal preferences and some are based on the adage of this is how we have always done it. Differences also exist as they relate to language choices. Some of the standards have recommendations that are in conflict with each other. What is most important is that you select a standard approach and consistently follow it.

One of the most important considerations with looping statements relates to readability. The best practices are described next as they relate to the consistent placement of curly braces and the use of white space.

Guidelines for Placement of Curly Braces

Curly braces should be placed on a separate line and not in the same line as the loop conditional expression as shown in the following:

```
for (int i = 0; i < 10; i++)
{
     //body of the loop
}
```


Line up the opening and closing curly braces as shown above.

Curly braces are optional. They are required when the loop body has more than one statement. As with selection statements (like the `if` statement), many developers use curly braces with all loops—even single statement bodied loops. In this book, curly braces are added when there are two or more executable statements inside the body of the loop. For loops that have a single statement in the body of the loop, curly braces are omitted.

Spacing Conventions

Use a single space before and after comparison operators as shown in the following:

```
while (a < b)
```

Do not place an extra space before or after the parenthesis inside the expression as shown above.

Place each executable statement on a separate line inside the loop body.

Advanced Loop Statement Suggestions

As with selection statements, avoid writing compound loop conditional expressions. Instead of writing `<=` or `>=`, add or subtract 1 from the endpoint (i.e., `while (a >= 100)` is the same as `while (a > 99)`, if a is defined as an integer variable). Additional thought will normally help you to eliminate this type of compound statement.

When displaying error messages, in addition to telling what is wrong, the message should also tell what the user should do to solve the problem.

Use a `for` statement for counter-controlled loops. The counting variable can be declared and incremented as part of the loop structure.

Resources

Additional sites you might want to explore:

- Loops - C# Tutorial—
http://csharp.net-tutorials.com/basics/loops/
- C# Station Tutorial on Control Statements, Loops—
http://www.csharp-station.com/Tutorials/Lesson04.aspx
- C# and Loops—
http://www.homeandlearn.co.uk/csharp/csharp_s3p5.html
- Dot Net Pearls - C# and Loops—
http://www.dotnetperls.com/loop
- You Tube C# Loop Tutorial—
http://www.youtube.com/watch?v=5xlc9qzOQmk
- Net - informations.com How to use C# for loops—
http://csharp.net-informations.com/statements/csharp-for-loop.htm
- msdn for (C# Reference)—
http://msdn.microsoft.com/en-us/library/ch45axte.aspx
- C# Video Tutorial—
http://www.pvtuts.com/csharp/csharp-loops

QUICK REVIEW

1. The three programming constructs found in most programming languages are simple sequence, selection, and iteration.
2. Based on a predetermined condition, iteration enables you to identify and block together one or more statements to be repeated.
3. The looping structures available in C# include `while`, `do...while`, `for`, and `foreach` statements. The `do...while` loop is a posttest. The others are pretest loop structures. With pretest, the conditional expression is tested before any of the statements in the body of the loop are performed.
4. When you know the number of times the statements must be executed, you can use a counter-controlled loop.
5. An infinite loop does not have provisions for normal termination. Infinite loops occur when the loop's conditional expression never evaluates to `false` or there is some inherent characteristic or problem with the loop.

6. With counter-controlled loops, it is important to think through test cases and check endpoints to ensure that they have been used to avoid off-by-one errors.
7. Sentinel-controlled loops are also referred to as indefinite loops. They are useful when the number of repetitions is not known before the loop's execution. For interactive input, a sentinel value is selected and the user is told to input that value to stop. The sentinel value should not be processed.
8. The `MessageBox.Show( )` method is used to display information to users in a format that resembles Windows applications.
9. A state-controlled loop, also referred to a flag-controlled loop, uses a special variable—not the variable used to store the data that is being processed. With a state-controlled loop, the body of the loop is stopped when the special variable's value is changed.
10. The `for` statement is considered a specialized form of the `while` statement. It packages together the initialization, test, and update—all on one line.
11. The `foreach` statement is new and is used to iterate or move through a collection, such as an array. It does not require a loop control variable to be incremented and tested to determine when all data has been processed.
12. With the `do. . .while` posttest loop structure, the statements are executed once before the conditional expression is tested.
13. A loop can be included within the body of another loop. When this occurs, the innermost nested loop is completed totally before the outside loop is tested a second time.
14. C# offers a number of jump statements that can alter the flow of control in a program. They include `break`, `continue`, `goto`, `throw`, and `return` statements.
15. When a `continue` statement is reached, it starts a new iteration of the nearest enclosing `while`, `do...while`, `for`, or `foreach` loop statement.
16. The `break` and `continue` statements should be used sparingly with loops.
17. Regarding decisions about which type of loop to use—if you know your loop will always be executed at least once, then `do. . .while` is a good option. When a numeric variable is being changed by a consistent amount with each iteration through the loop, the `for` statement might be the best option. The `while` statement can be used to write any type of loop.

EXERCISES

1. To write a sentinel-controlled loop to compute the average temperature during the month of July in California, the best option for a sentinel value would be:
   a. 67
   b. 1000
   c. 100
   d. "high temperature"
   e. none of the above
2. Loops are needed in programming languages:
   a. to facilitate sequential processing of data
   b. to enable a variable to be analyzed for additional processing
   c. to allow statements to be repeated
   d. to process files stored on hard drives
   e. all of the above
3. Which loop structure can only be used with a collection such as an array?
   a. `foreach`
   b. `for`
   c. `while`
   d. `do...while`
   e. none of the above
4. If a loop body must be executed at least once, which loop structure would be the best option?
   a. `foreach`
   b. `for`
   c. `while`
   d. `do...while`
   e. none of the above

5. If a loop body uses a numeric value that is incremented by three with each iteration through the loop until it reaches 1000, which loop structure would probably be the best option?
   a. `foreach`
   b. `for`
   c. `while`
   d. `do...while`
   e. none of the above

6. When used with a `while` statement, which jump statement causes execution to halt inside a loop body and immediately transfers control to the conditional expression?
   a. `break`
   b. `goto`
   c. `return`
   d. `continue`
   e. none of the above

7. Which of the following is a valid C# pretest conditional expression that enables a loop to be executed as long as the counter variable is less than 10?
   a. `do while` (counter < 10)
   b. `while` (counter < 10)
   c. `foreach` (counter in 10)
   d. none of the above
   e. all of the above

8. Which of the following `for` statements would be executed the same number of times as the following `while` statement?

```
int num = 10;
while(num > 0)
{
    WriteLine(num);
    num--;
}
```

   a. `for (num = 1; num < 10; num++)`
   b. `for (num = 0; num < 10; num++)`
   c. `for (num = 100; num == 10; num += 10)`
   d. `for (num = 10; num < 0; num--);`
   e. none of the above

9. What would be the output produced from the following statements?

```
int aValue = 1;
do
{
        aValue++;
        Write(aValue++);
}
while (aValue < 3);
```

   a. 23
   b. 234
   c. 1234
   d. 2
   e. none of the above

10. If aValue, i, and n are type int variables, what does the following program fragment do?

```
aValue = 0; n = 10;
for (i = n; i > 0; i--)
     if (i % 2 == 0)
          aValue = aValue + i;
```

   a. computes the sum of the integers from 1 through n
   b. computes the sum of the integers from 1 through n −1
   c. computes the sum of the even integers from 1 through n
   d. computes the sum of the odd integers from 1 through n
   e. none of the above

11. To produce the output

2 4 6 8 10

which should be the loop conditional expression to replace the question marks?

```
int n = 0;
do
{
     n = n + 2;
     Write("{0}\t", n);
}
while (????);
```

   a. n < 11
   b. n < 10
   c. n < 8
   d. n >= 2
   e. n > 8

12. What would be the output produced from the following statements?

```
int i = 0;
while (i < 0)
{
    Write("{0}\t", i);
    i++;
}
Write("{0}\t", i);
```

a. 0
b. an infinite loop
c. an error
d. 0 0
e. none of the above

13. Which of the following represents a pretest loop?

a. `while`
b. `do...while`
c. `for`
d. a and b
e. a and c

14. If you intend to place a block of statements within a loop body, you must use ___________ around the block.

a. parentheses
b. square brackets
c. quotation marks
d. curly braces
e. none of the above

Questions 15–17 refer to the following program segment:

```
int i = 0, g = 0, s = 0, t = 0, z = 0;
string sValue;
while (i < 5)
 {
        inValue = ReadLine( );
        t = Convert.ToInt32(inValue);
        s = s + t;
        if (t > -1)
               g = g + 1;
        else
               z = z + 1;
        i = i + 1;
   }
 }
```

15. How many times is the loop body of the `while` statement executed?
    a. once
    b. never
    c. four times
    d. five times
    e. until a number 5 or larger is entered
16. The value stored in variable z at the end of the execution of the loop could best be described as:
    a. the number of positive items entered
    b. the sum of all positive items entered
    c. the number of negative items entered
    d. the sum of all negative items entered
    e. the sentinel value
17. The loop can best be categorized as a:
    a. counter-controlled loop
    b. sentinel-controlled loop
    c. state-controlled loop
    d. flag-controlled loop
    e. none of the above

18. How many lines of output will be printed by the following program fragment?

```
for (i = 0; i < 5; i++)
    for (j = 0; j < 4; j++)
        WriteLine("{0} {1}", i, j);
```

a. 20

b. 6

c. 9

d. 12

e. none of the above

19. How many lines of output will be printed by the following program fragment?

```
for (i = 0; i < 5; i += 2)
    for (j = 0; j < 4; j = j + 2)
        WriteLine("{0}\n{1}", i, j);
```

a. 20

b. 6

c. 9

d. 12

e. none of the above

20. What would be the result of the following conditional expression?

```
int i = 0;
while (i < 10) ;
i++;
Write(i);
```

a. `123456789`

b. `012345678910`

c. `0123456789`

d. an infinite loop

e. none of the above

21. Convert the following `do. . .while` loop into a `for` loop and a `while` loop. Did the logic change? If so, explain.

```
int counter = 100;
do
{
        WriteLine(counter);
        counter--;
}
while (counter > 0);
```

22. Write a `for` loop to display every third number beginning with 10 and continuing through 100.

23. Write a sentinel-controlled `while` loop that allows any number of temperatures to be entered. The average temperature should be calculated and displayed.

24. Create a loop body that generates random numbers between 25 and 75. Write a state-controlled loop that adds all these randomly generated numbers until a value larger than 60 is generated. When the loop stops, display the number of acceptable generated values and the sum of those values.

25. Desk run or trace the following code segment, showing every value that goes into each variable.

```
for (i = 0; i < 3; i++)
    for (j = 4; j > 0; j--)
        WriteLine ("{0}\t{1}", i, j);
```

PROGRAMMING EXERCISES

1. Create an application that contains a loop to be used for input validation. Valid entries are positive integers less than 100. Test your program with values both less than and greater than the acceptable range as well as non-numeric data. When the user is finished inputting data, display the number of valid and invalid entries entered. For invalid values, identify how many of those values were outside the range and the number of non-numeric invalid values entered.

2. Write an application that will enable a vendor to see what earnings he can expect to make based on what percentage he marks up an item. Allow the user to input the wholesale item price. In a tabular form, show the retail price of the item marked up at 5%, 6%, 7%, 8%, 9%, and 10%.

3. Write a program that generates 1000 random numbers between 0 and 100,000. Display the number of odd values generated as well as the smallest and the largest of values. Output should be displayed in a Windows message box.

4. Write a program to allow multiple sets of scores to be averaged. Valid entries must be numeric and in the range of 0 through 100. Calculate the average of the scores entered. Allow any number of scores to be entered per data set but assume that there will be at least one score entered. Use a sentinel-controlled loop variable to terminate the loop. After values are entered and the average is calculated, test the average to determine whether an A, B, C, D, or F should be recorded. The scoring rubric is as follows:

   A→90–100; B→80–89; C→70–79; D→60–69; F < 60.

5. Create an application that can be used to calculate the total amount due for purchases. Allow any number of items to be entered. Determine the total due including sales tax and shipping. Sales tax of 7.75% is charged against the total purchases. Shipping charges can be determined based on the number of items purchased. Use the following chart to determine the shipping charge.

fewer than 3 items	$3.50
3 to 6 items	$5.00
7 to 10 items	$7.00
11 to 15 items	$9.00
more than 15 items	$10.00

   Display an itemized summary containing the total purchase charge, number of items purchased, sales tax amount, shipping charge, and grand total.

6. Write a program that allows the user to input any number of hexadecimal characters. Sum the values and display the sum as a hexadecimal value. Treat each single inputted character as a separate value. Within the loop, convert each character entered into its decimal equivalent. Display the original hex value and the corresponding decimal value. For example, if the user inputs F, 15 would be displayed as the decimal equivalent. Create a state-controlled loop structure. After all values are entered, display the sum of values entered in both hexadecimal and decimal notation.

7. Write a program that produces a multiplication table with 25 rows of computations. Allow the user to input the first and last base values for the multiplication table. Display a column in the table beginning with the first base inputted value. The last column should be the ending base value entered. The first row should be for 1 times the beginning base, 1 times the (beginning base value + 1), through 1 times the ending base value. The last row should be for 25 times the beginning base, 25 times the (beginning base value + 1), through 25 times the ending base value. Base values can range from 2 to 8. Display an error message if an invalid base is entered. Display an aesthetically formatted multiplication table. An example of output produced when 2 and 8 are entered appears in Figure 6-22.

n	2	3	4	5	6	7	8
1	2	3	4	5	6	7	8
2	4	6	8	10	12	14	16
3	6	9	12	15	18	21	24
4	8	12	16	20	24	28	32
5	10	15	20	25	30	35	40
6	12	18	24	30	36	42	48
7	14	21	28	35	42	49	56
8	16	24	32	40	48	56	64
9	18	27	36	45	54	63	72
10	20	30	40	50	60	70	80
11	22	33	44	55	66	77	88
12	24	36	48	60	72	84	96
13	26	39	52	65	78	91	104
14	28	42	56	70	84	98	112
15	30	45	60	75	90	105	120
16	32	48	64	80	96	112	128
17	34	51	68	85	102	119	136
18	36	54	72	90	108	126	144
19	38	57	76	95	114	133	152
20	40	60	80	100	120	140	160
21	42	63	84	105	126	147	168
22	44	66	88	110	132	154	176
23	46	69	92	115	138	161	184
24	48	72	96	120	144	168	192
25	50	75	100	125	150	175	200

FIGURE 6-22 Output when 2 and 8 are entered

8. Write an application that can be used to determine if three line segments can form a triangle. Prompt the user for the length of three line segments as integers. If non-numeric characters are entered, re-prompt the user for new values. If the three lines could form a triangle, print the integers and a message indicating that they form a triangle. Use a state-controlled loop to allow users to enter as many different combinations as they want.

9. Print isosceles triangles. For each triangle, allow the user to input two values: a character to be used for printing the triangle and the size of the peak for the triangle. Test the input for valid characters. The size of the triangle should not be larger than 10. If an invalid non-numeric character is entered for size or if the value entered for size is larger than 10, use 3 as the default value. If an invalid entry is entered for the character, use an asterisk (*) as the default character. Allow multiple triangles to be printed. For example, if the user inputs # for the character and 6 for the peak, you should produce the following display:

```
#
##
###
####
#####
######
#####
####
###
##
#
```

10. Write an application that enables a user to input the grade and number of credit hours for any number of courses. Calculate the GPA on a 4.0 scale using those values. Grade point average (GPA) is calculated by dividing the total amount of grade points earned, sometimes referred to as quality points, by the total number of credit hours attempted. For each hour, an A receives 4 grade or quality points, a B receives 3 points, a C receives 2 points, and a D receives 1 point. Thus, a three–credit hour course receiving an A would have 12 quality points associated with the course. Allow the user to input any number of courses and associated grades. Display the number of hours earned and the calculated GPA.

CHAPTER 7

© zeljkodan/Shutterstock.com

ARRAYS

IN THIS CHAPTER, YOU WILL:

- Learn array basics.
- Declare arrays and perform compile-time initialization of array elements
- Access elements of an array
- Become familiar with methods of the Array class
- Write methods that use arrays as parameters
- Write classes that include arrays as members and instantiate user-defined array objects
- Work through a programming example that illustrates the chapter's concepts

In previous chapters, you were introduced to the basics of programming. You learned about the three programming constructs of simple sequence, selection, and iteration. You learned to handle data and declare memory locations to store and access values using an identifier. In this chapter, you will discover how to work with collections of data that are referenced by a single identifier name. You will learn about one type of collection, called an array, which is similar to a vector in mathematics or cells in a spreadsheet in that each entry can be referenced by the location of the item in the collection. You will create arrays that can hold multiple data values. Using an index to reference the location of the item, you will learn how to access single values and iterate through collections to process all the values. You will learn about special properties and methods of the .NET `Array class` and learn how to define arrays of user-defined objects. You will learn how to pass arrays to methods and how methods can have arrays as their return type.

Array Basics

It is not always efficient to have unique names for every memory location. Suppose, for example, you have 14 homework scores. A unique identifier could be associated with each one. The declaration would look something like the following:

```
int score1,
    score2,
          . . .
    score14;
```

If you want to allow the user to input the values and compute the average, 14 separate prompts to input a score, 14 calls to the `ReadLine ( )` method, and 14 parse or convert method calls would need to be written. Another option you are probably considering would be to use a loop. You could write a loop body to input a value into a memory location and add that value to an accumulator. The loop body could read all 14 values. If you use the same memory location to store the second value, the second value replaces the first value. The third value replaces the second, and so on. This seems to be the most reasonable approach. Instead of having 14 distinct `ReadLine ( )` statements, you could place one method call inside a counter-controlled loop and have it execute 14 times.

If the only output needed is the average, a loop with a single variable is the most efficient way to write your algorithm. However, what if you want to determine and display how far each score is from the average of all scores? Or, what if you want to drop the lowest score? Or, what if you need all the values for additional processing later in the program? For these situations, using a single value presents a problem. The average cannot be calculated until you accumulate all the values. If all values are read into a single memory location, the first score is no longer available as soon as the second score is read. There is no way to determine how far the first value is from the average, until you calculate the average. For this type of problem, it would be best to retain the values in memory in addition to accumulating them. This brings you back to the need for the 14 different memory locations. What if there were 50 scores, or 1000 scores? You certainly would not want to write declaration statements for `score1`, `score2`, `score3`, `score4`, through `score1000`.

This is where an array is useful. An **array** is a data structure that may contain any number of variables. In the C# language, the variables must be of the same type. A single identifier, or name, is given to the entire structure. The individual variables in the array are called the **elements** of the array and are accessed through an index. The **index**, also called the **subscript** of the array, references the location of the variable relative to the first element in the array. Elements in an array are sometimes referred to as **indexed** or **subscripted variables**.

In C#, all arrays are objects of the base type, `Array class` (`System.Array`). The `Array class` includes a number of built-in methods and properties that add functionality for creating, manipulating, searching, and sorting arrays. You will learn about these members in the sections that follow.

Array Declaration

You create an array in much the same way you instantiate an `object` of a user-defined `class`—by using the `new` keyword at the time of declaration. You can also specify during declaration the number of individual elements for the array. The format for creating an array is as follows:

```
type [ ] identifier = new type[integral value];
```

All data values placed in an array must be of the same **base type**. The type can be one of the predefined types like `int` or `string`, or some other .NET `class`. The type can also be a `class` that you create in C#. The integral value is used to specify the number of elements. This is called the **length** or **size of the array**. This integral value can be a constant literal, a variable, or an expression that produces an integral value. Because the integral value is indicating the actual number of elements for which space will be allocated, the value must be positive. It must represent an integer, a whole number, or an expression that maps to a whole number. To create an array to hold the 14 homework scores discussed previously, you could write:

```
int [ ] score = new int[14];
```

Figure 7-1 shows what happens when you create an array to hold 14 elements of `int` type using `score` as an identifier. When you create the array, you declare the identifier type and also allocate space for a specific number of elements.

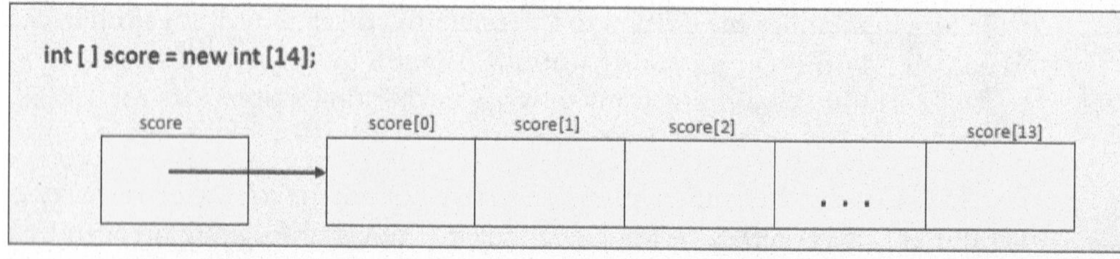

FIGURE 7-1 Creation of an array

The arrow in Figure 7-1 is used to indicate that the identifier, `score`, actually references the first element in the array, `score [0]`, by containing the address in which `score [0]` is located. Array elements are normally stored in contiguous, side-by-side, memory locations. The first index in all arrays is `0`.

Java and all C-style languages use zero-based arrays—meaning the first element is indexed by `0`.

Notice that the last element of all arrays is always referenced by an index with a value of the length of the array minus one. `Length` of `score` is 14; first element is `score [0]`; last element is `score [13]`.

In C#, when creating an array, the location of the square bracket is different from C++, which includes the square brackets after the identifier. Java allows you to place the square bracket before or after the identifier when you declare an array.

C# allows you to declare an array without instantiating it. The general form of the declaration is:

```
type [ ] identifier;
```

No value is placed inside the square bracket `[ ]`. As shown in Figure 7-2, this does not create the array. It simply defines the base type for the array and associates an identifier with it. No values are referenced. When you look at Figure 7-2, remember that arrays are reference types. The identifier `score` declares an array that has no values to reference.

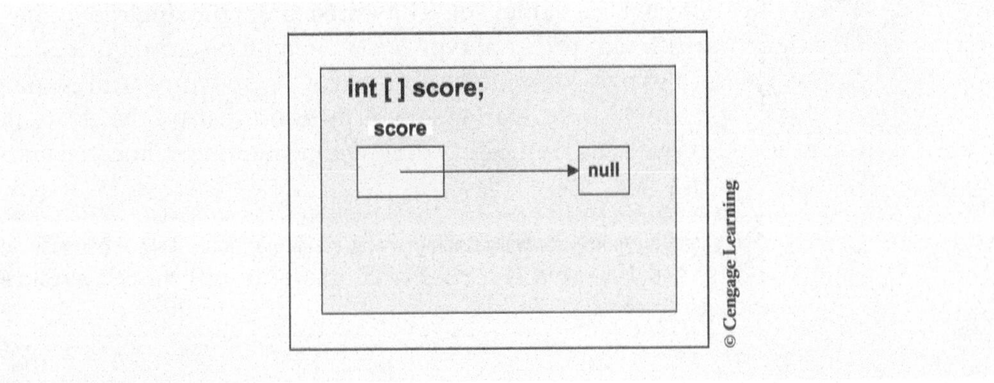

FIGURE 7-2 Declaration of an array

A separate step is required before you can access the array. This step is to instantiate the array by indicating how many elements to allocate. This is sometimes referred to as **dimensioning the array**. The general form of the second step is:

```
identifier = new type[integral value];
```


Adding the additional statement of `score = new int[14];` to the preceding declaration produces the same result you saw in Figure 7-1. The keyword `new` allocated `14` memory locations for `score` to reference.

NOTE You can declare and allocate space for an array in two steps or combine the steps into one statement. When you are declaring an array that will be a field member of a `class`, it is normally declared with the `class`, but instantiated when an `object` of the `class` is created at run time.

With the exception of the first line, which declares an integer used for the length of two of the arrays, the remaining statements in Example 7-1 create different array references.

EXAMPLE 7-1

```
const int SIZE = 15;
string [ ] lastName = new string[25];
double [ ] cost = new double[1000];
double [ ] temperature = new double[SIZE];
int [ ] hmWkScore;
hmWkScore = new int[SIZE + 15];
```

Twenty-five different last names could be stored under the single identifier `lastName`. One thousand different prices of type `double` could be stored using `cost`. Because `SIZE` is declared to be a constant with a value of `15`, 15 temperatures could be stored. As shown with the last declaration, any expression that produces an integral value can be used to create an array. Thirty different locations are allocated for `hmWkScore`.

Array identifiers are normally defined using a singular noun. This is because you normally access individual elements in the array as opposed to using the data structure as a grouped collection.

Some languages, such as C++, do not allow the length of an array to be determined at run time. It is legal in C# to use a variable, such as `arraySize`, as the length indicator. You could prompt the user for the number of values that will be entered and use that entry for the declaration, as shown in Example 7-2.

EXAMPLE 7-2

```
Write("How many scores will you enter? ");
string sSize = ReadLine( );
int arraySize = Convert.ToInt32(sSize);
int [ ] score = new int[arraySize];
```

In C#, the length of an array cannot be changed. After it is instantiated with a length, dynamic resizing is not an option.

Array Initializers

Just as you use **compile-time initialization** with variables, you can initialize the elements of an array during declaration. The general form of the initialization follows:

```
type [ ] identifier = new type[ ] {value1, value2, ...valueN};
```

Values are separated by commas and must be assignment compatible to the element type. Thus, if the type is specified as an `int` and you include values with a decimal point as part of the initialization, you receive an error indicating, "cannot implicitly convert type `double` to `int`." It is legal to have an array defined as a type `double` and include values without decimals. This does not violate the assignment compatibility rule. You get implicit conversion from `int` to `double`.

A more standard way to declare and initialize the elements of an array follows. It is considered a shortcut to specifying the size and at the same time placing values in the array. This option is especially useful when the data will not change.

```
type [ ] identifier = {value1, value2, ...valueN};
```

The length of the array is determined by the number of values placed inside the curly braces. Example 7-3 creates and initializes three arrays of different types. Each statement illustrates a different way to perform the initialization.

EXAMPLE 7-3

```
int [ ] anArray = {100, 200, 400, 600};
char [ ] grade = new char[ ] {'A', 'B', 'C', 'D', 'F'};
double [ ] depth = new double[2] {2.5, 3};
```


The first statement creates an array of four elements. The initial values are `100`, `200`, `400`, and `600`. Notice that the keyword `new` is not included here, and the type is not repeated. The second statement shows that the type of the value used for initialization must be compatible with the declaration type. Because `char` is the specified declaration type, all initialization values are enclosed in single quotes. Five elements are created using the `grade` identifier. No length specifier is required. But notice that this differs from the declaration of `anArray` in that the `new` keyword is used and the type is specified with opening and closing square brackets. The last statement creates an array with a length of two. The value `3` is assignment compatible with the `double` type. Figure 7-3 shows the memory contents after the initialization.

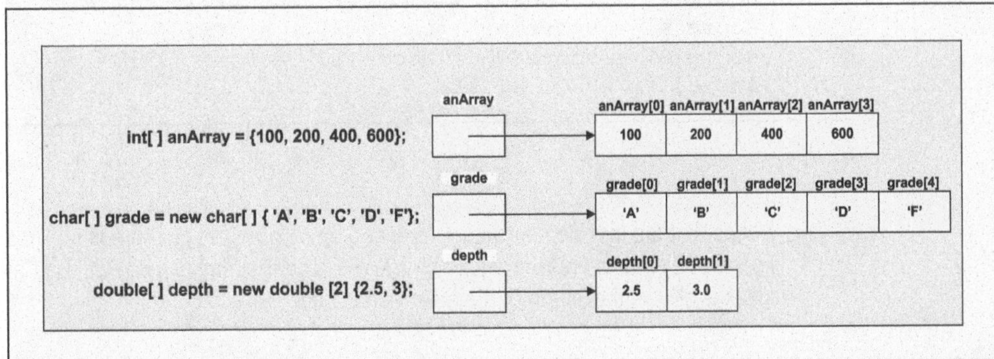

© Cengage Learning

FIGURE 7-3 Methods of creating and initializing arrays at compile time

In Figure 7-3, the depth array is shown with a length indicator of 2, and two initial values are included in the declaration. Remember, the length indicator is not required when you do a compile-time initialization. However, if you include the length indicator, it must match the number of values included. Otherwise, a syntax error is issued. The following example does not compile and generates an error:

```
double [ ] waterDepth = new double[200] {0, 3}; //Invalid
```

Two values were used for initialization; however, the declaration indicated 200 elements were to be allocated.

Array Access

To access an array element, you must specify which element is to be accessed by placing an index inside square brackets following the identifier. This is because the array is now referenced by a single name. To retrieve individual elements, an index or subscript is required. Arrays are zero-based structures; thus, the index of the first element is always 0. The index of the second element is 1 and is referenced using the identifier and a 1 enclosed in square brackets. The index of the last element in the array is always n – 1, where *n* represents the number of elements in the array. The index references the physical location of the element relative to the beginning element. To place a value in the first element of score, the following assignment statement could be made:

```
score [0] = 100;
```

Figure 7-1 shows the index values. The score array can hold 14 elements. Example 7-4 illustrates how the array elements shown in Figure 7-1 could be summed.

EXAMPLE 7-4

```
total = score[0] + score[1] + score[2] + score[3] +
        score[4] + score[5] + score[6] + score[7] +
        score[8] + score[9] + score[10] + score[11] +
        score[12] + score[13];
```

NOTE

Notice that the last element was referenced by score[13]. There is no score[14]. Fourteen elements are referenced by score. The first one is score[0]. The last valid index is always the length of the array minus one.

What if there were 25 scores? Adding all 25 scores to total would take a lot of typing. Example 7-5 shows a better way to sum the values. A counter-controlled loop with a variable for the index is used.

EXAMPLE 7-5

```
for (int i = 0; i < score.Length; i++)
{
      total += score[i];
}
```

This produces exactly the same result as Example 7-4.

NOTE C# always performs bounds checking on array indexes. Some languages let you store or access values outside the originally declared legal bounds of the array. This is not possible in C#.

7

One of the special properties in the `Array` `class` is `Length`. It returns an `int` representing the total number of elements in an array. For Example 7-5, `Length` returned 14. The loop control variable, `i`, is evaluated before each iteration through the loop to determine whether it is less than 14 (`score.Length`).

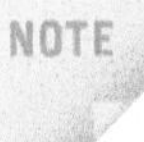

NOTE Notice that the conditional expression that was used with the `for` statement used less than (<) instead of less than or equal to (<=). Because `Length` returns a number representing the size of the array, the last valid index should always be one less than `Length`. Therefore, as soon as the index is equal to `Length`, the loop should terminate.

If you create an array to hold 14 elements and include the following assignment statement:

```
score[14] = 100;          // Run-time error, no location 14
```

a message similar to that shown in Figure 7-4 is generated, which indicates that the index was outside the boundaries of the array.

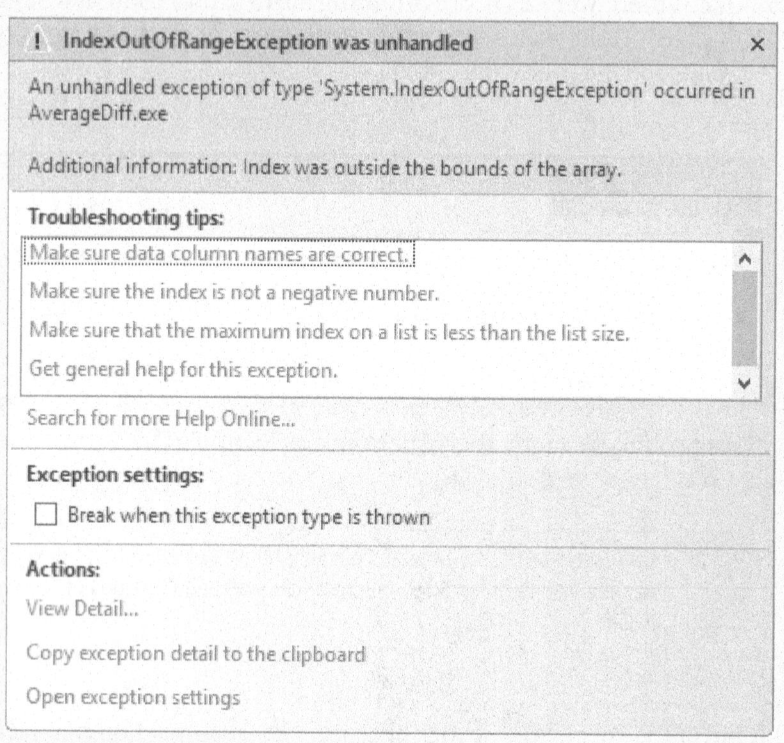

FIGURE 7-4 Index out of range exception

You receive this "unhandled exception" error message if you try to access the array using an index value larger than the array length minus one, a nonintegral index value, or a negative index value. This is a run-time error, not caught during compilation.

Example 7-6 creates an array to hold 10 elements. Values are input, the average is calculated, and then a table is produced showing the original value entered and how far that value is from the overall average.

EXAMPLE 7-6

```
/* AverageDiff.cs                                          Author: Doyle
 * Ten scores are entered. The average is calculated.
 * A table is printed showing how far each value
 * is from the average.
 */
using System;
using static System.Console;

namespace AverageDiff
```

```
{
    class AverageDiff
    {
        static void Main( )
        {
            int total = 0;
            double avg;
            double distance;
            string inValue;
            int [ ] score = new int[10];                    //Line 1
            // Values are entered.
            for (int i = 0; i < score.Length; i++)          //Line 2
            {
                Write("Enter Score{0}: ", i + 1);           //Line 3
                inValue = ReadLine( );
                if (int.TryParse(inValue, out score[i]) == false)
                    WriteLine("Invalid data entered - " +
                            "0 stored in array");           //Line 4
            }
            // Values are summed.
            for (int i = 0; i < score.Length; i++)
            {
                total += score[i];                          //Line 5
            }
            avg = (double) total / score.Length;            //Line 6
            WriteLine( );
            WriteLine("Average: {0}", avg.ToString("F0"));
            // Output is array element and how far value
            // is from the mean (absolute value).
            WriteLine( );
            WriteLine("Score\tDist. from Avg.");
            for (int i = 0; i < score.Length; i++)
            {
                distance = Math.Abs((avg - score[i]));      //Line 7
                WriteLine("{0}\t\t{1}", score[i],
                        distance.ToString("F0"));           //Line 8
            }
            ReadKey( );
        }
    }
}
```


NOTE As you review examples, you'll recall a `using static System.Console;` directive was added. Being able to reference a `static class` within a `namespace` with the `using` directive is new to Visual Studio 2015. This feature reduces the amount of typing needed when you invoke members of the `Console class`. If you are using a version prior to Visual Studio 2015 references to members of the `Console class`, such as `Write( )`, `WriteLine( )`, `ReadKey( )` and `Clear( )`, require the method name be preceded by the `Console class` identifier and a dot, as in `Console.Write( )`.

In Example 7-6 on Line 1, the array is declared and space is allocated for 10 scores. Line 2 uses the `Length` property of the `System.Array class` as the expression for the loop control variable (`i < score.Length`). This loop is used to accumulate scores. `score.Length` returns `10`; thus, 10 iterations of the loop are performed. The property `score.Length` is also used as the divisor representing the number of scores in the calculation of `avg` on Line 6. You should notice that a cast occurs when the `double` is placed in front of `total`. This is done to avoid integer division. When the values are displayed, whole number values, without decimal positions, are shown. The `ToString("F0")` method was invoked with both the `avg` and the `distance` memory locations in Example 7-6.

The loop control variable, `i`, is displayed with `1` added to its value on Line 3. Here, it is used as part of the prompt to the user concerning which score to enter. Instead of first displaying "`Enter Score0`", the display reads "`Enter Score1`". The last prompt displays "`Enter Score10`". Adding 1 to the index produces less confusing output for the user who does not realize that the first score is associated with location zero.

The statement labeled Line 4, also part of the loop body, assigns the converted integer to the array. Notice how the array element is used as an argument to the `TryParse()` method. Line 5 does another assignment statement when the array value is added to `total`. The distance from the average is found in line 7 by first subtracting the individual score from the average, which might yield a positive or negative value. Taking the absolute value `(Math.Abs)` ensures that the distance is positive.

Line 8, inside another loop, displays the contents of each element. The loop control variable serves as the index to the array, indicating which element to access. Figure 7-5 shows the output produced from one test run of Example 7-6.

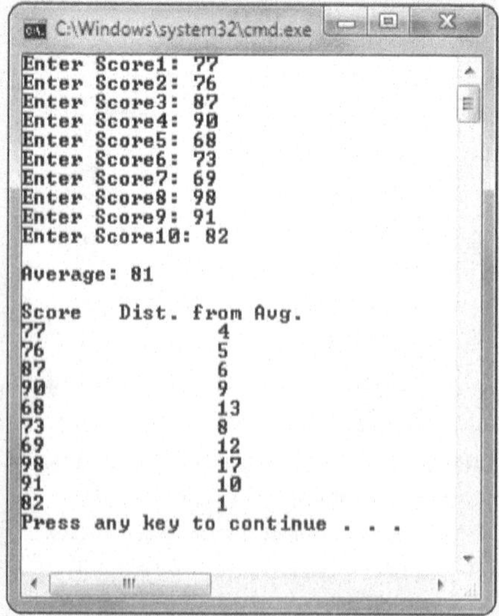

FIGURE 7-5 Output from AverageDiff example

Sentinel-Controlled Access

What if you do not know how many scores will be entered? What size array do you create? The size or length of the array cannot change after it is allocated. If you do not know how many values will be entered, you could ask the user to count the number of entries and use that value for the size when you allocate the array. Another approach is to create the array large enough to hold any number of entries. Then tell users to enter a predetermined sentinel value after they enter the last value. If you use this approach, you need to increment a counter as values are entered so that you know how many elements are stored in your array. The `Length` property would not be helpful for this type of application. It could not be used as a loop control value because `Length` returns whatever the array is dimensioned to hold. Example 7-7 illustrates filling an array when you do not know how many values will be entered. A sentinel value of `-99` is used to terminate the loop.

As you review examples, you'll recall Visual Studio inserts additional `using` statements into your project when you create a new project. Since no classes are needed from these libraries, they were omitted from program listings to conserve space. The parameters to the `Main ( )` method are also removed.

7

EXAMPLE 7-7

```
/* UnknownSize.cs                                    Author: Doyle
 * Any number of scores, up to 100, can be entered.
 */
using System;
using static System.Console;

namespace UnknownSize
{
     class UnknownSize
     {
          static void Main( )
          {
               int [ ] score = new int[100];
               string inValue;
               int scoreCnt = 0;
               Write("Enter Score{0}: ((-99 to exit)) ",
                    scoreCnt + 1);
               inValue = ReadLine( );
               while (inValue != "-99")
               {
                    if (int.TryParse(inValue,
                              out score[scoreCnt]) == false)
                         WriteLine("Invalid data -" +
                              "0 stored in array");
```

```
                    ++scoreCnt;
                    Write("Enter Score{0}: ((-99 to exit)) ",
                           scoreCnt + 1);
                    inValue = ReadLine( );
               }
               WriteLine("The number of scores: " +
                         scoreCnt);
          }
     }
}
```

In Chapter 6, you learned about the importance of priming the read (placing a call to the `ReadLine( )` method on the outside of the loop body) and then placing a second `ReadLine( )` method call as the last statement in the loop body. This keeps you from processing the sentinel value.

Using Foreach with Arrays

The `foreach` loop can be used to iterate through an array. However, it can be used for read-only access to the elements. You were briefly introduced to the `foreach` loop structure in Chapter 6. Remember that the general format is as follows:

```
foreach (type identifier in expression) statement;
```

The `foreach` loop cannot be used to change the contents of any of the elements in an array. You can use it to sum the values. The statements shown in Example 7-8 could be added to the `UnknownSize` `class` introduced in Example 7-7. The new lines use the `foreach` statement to sum the values and calculate a score average.

EXAMPLE 7-8

```
int total = 0;
double avg;
foreach(int val in score)
{
        total += val;
}
WriteLine("Total: " + total);
avg = (double)total / scoreCnt;
WriteLine("Average: " + avg.ToString("F0"));
```

The identifier, `val`, is the iteration variable. It represents a different array element with each loop iteration. Remember that the type used in the `foreach` expression should match the array type. Because the `score` array contains `int` elements, `val` is declared of that type. During the first iteration through the loop, `val` references `score [0]`. A compile-time error occurs if one of the statements in the `foreach` loop body attempts to change the iteration variable or pass the iteration variable as a `ref` or `out` parameter. Example 7-9 displays `red`, `green`, and `blue` on separate lines.

EXAMPLE 7-9

```
string [ ] color = {"red", "green", "blue"};
foreach(string val in color)
        WriteLine(val);
```


Array Class

Through access to the elements using indexed values, C# supports the easy handling of arrays that other languages provide. But you get more than just indexed access. All arrays, of any type, inherit characteristics from the `Array class`, which includes a number of predefined methods and properties. Table 7-1 lists some of these predefined methods from the `System.Array class`. The third column gives examples of the use of each method. You will want to explore methods, especially those that are overloaded, using the online Help features in Visual Studio. Much of the information in Table 7-1 came from that documentation. As you explore the `Array class` methods, you will find a number of other members not listed in Table 7-1. The `Array class` serves as the base array `class` for all languages that target the common language runtime. Having its properties and methods available across languages provides power to each of the .NET languages, and this power is available with minimal programming. For example, an entire collection of data can be sorted with a call to one of the `Array class` member methods.

TABLE 7-1 System.Array methods

Method	Description	Examples

`BinarySearch (System.Array array, object value)`	Class method. Overloaded. Searches a one-dimensional sorted array for a value, using a binary search algorithm. Returns index location or negative value if not found.	`double [ ] waterDepth = {2.4, 3.5, 6.8};`
		`double x = 6.8;`
		`int myIndex = Array.BinarySearch (waterDepth, x);`
		`WriteLine(myIndex);`
		`//Displays index where 6.8 stored`
		2

`Clear (System.Array array, int firstIndex, int length)`	Class method. Sets elements in the array to zero, to false, or to a null reference depending on the element type. Start at `firstIndex`, go length positions.	`double [ ] waterDepth = {2.4, 3.5, 6.8};`
		`Array.Clear(waterDepth, 0, 2);`
		`WriteLine(waterDepth[1]);`
		`//Beginning at index 0, for length of 2.`
		`//Sets waterDepth[0] and`
		`//waterDepth[1] to zero.`
		`//Displays`
		0

`Clone( )`	Creates a copy of the array. Returns an `object`.	`double [ ] waterDepth = {2.4, 3.5, 6.8};`
		`double [ ] w = new double [3];`
		`object o = waterDepth.Clone( );`
		`w = (double [ ]) o;`
		`//object o is cast as a double array.`
		`//Both arrays point to same values.`

`Copy (System.Array sourceArray, int index1Source, System.Array targetArray, int index1Target, int lengthToCopy)`	Class method. Overloaded. Copies a section of one array to another array.	`double [ ] waterDepth = {2.4, 3.5, 6.8};`
		`double [ ] w = new double [3];`
		`Array.Copy(waterDepth, 0, w, 0, 3);`
		`//Copies 3 elements`
		`//from waterDepth to w`
		`//Begins copy at index 0`
		`//in waterDepth;`
		`//Begins placement at index 0 in w.`

`CopyTo(System.Array targetArray, int start)`	Copies elements of a one-dimensional array to another one-dimensional array starting at the specified destination array index. (Destination must be large enough to hold elements.)	`double [ ] waterDepth = {2.4, 3.5, 6.8};`
		`double [ ] w = new double [5];`
		`waterDepth.CopyTo(w, 2);`
		`WriteLine(w[3]);`
		`//Copy started at w[2];`
		`//w[0] = 0, w[1] = 0, w[2] = 2.4,`
		`//w[3] = 3.5, w[4] = 6.8`
		`//Displays`
		3.5

(continues)

TABLE 7-1 System.Array methods (*continued*)

Method	Description	Examples

`GetValue(int index)`	Overloaded. Gets the value of the specified element in the current array.	`double [ ] waterDepth = {2.4, 3.5, 6.8};`
		`WriteLine(waterDepth.GetValue (2));`
		
		`//Displays`
		`6.8`

`IndexOf(System.Array array, object value)`	Class method. Overloaded. Returns the index of the first occurrence of a value in a one-dimensional array or in a portion of the array.	`double [ ] waterDepth = {2.4, 3.5, 6.8};`
		`int i = Array.IndexOf(waterDepth, 3.5);`
		`WriteLine(i);`
		
		`//Returns -1 when`
		`//the value is not`
		`//found in the array`
		
		`//Displays`
		`1`

`LastIndexOf(System.Array array, object value)`	Class method. Overloaded. Returns the index of the last occurrence of a value in a one-dimensional array or in a portion of the array.	`double [ ] waterDepth = {2.4, 3.5, 2.4};`
		`int i = Array.LastIndexOf(waterDepth, 2.4);`
		`WriteLine(i);`
		
		`//Displays`
		`2`

`Reverse(System.Array array)`	Class method. Overloaded. Reverses the order of the elements in a one-dimensional array or in a portion of the array.	`double [ ] waterDepth = {2.4, 3.5, 6.8};`
		`Array.Reverse(waterDepth);`
		`foreach (double wVal in waterDepth)`
		`        Write(wVal + "\t");`
		
		`//Displays`
		`6.8  3.5  2.4`

`SetValue(object value, int indexLocation)`	Overloaded. Sets the specified element in the current array to the specified value.	`double [ ] waterDepth = {2.4, 3.5, 6.8};`
		`waterDepth.SetValue(55, 0);`
		`foreach (double wVal in waterDepth)`
		`        Write(wVal + "\t");`
		
		`//Displays`
		`55  3.5  6.8`

`Sort(System.Array array)`	Class method. Overloaded. Sorts the elements in one-dimensional array objects.	`double [ ] waterDepth = {12.4, 3.5, 6.8};`
		`Array.Sort(waterDepth);`
		`foreach (double wVal in waterDepth)`
		`        Write (wVal + "\t");`
		
		`//Displays`
		`3.5  6.8  12.4`

© Cengage Learning

7

Many of the descriptions listed in the second column of Table 7-1 indicate "Class method." You have used `class` methods from the `Math` `class`. To call a `class` method, you prefix the method name with the `class` name. As you review the examples in the third column, notice that these `class` method calls require `Array` to be listed before the method name.

Example 7-10 demonstrates the use of `Sort ( )`, `Reverse ( )`, and `Copy ( )` methods. Values are concatenated onto a `string` inside a `foreach` loop structure. On the outside of the loop, the `string` is displayed with one call to the `MessageBox.Show ( )` method.

EXAMPLE 7-10

```
/* UsePredefinedMethods.cs                        Author: Doyle
 * Demonstrates use of methods from System.Array class.
 */
using System;
using System.Windows.Forms;


namespace UsePredefinedMethods
{
     class UsePredefinedMethods
     {
          static void Main( )
          {
               double [ ] waterDepth = {45, 19, 2, 16.8, 190,
                                          0.8, 510, 6, 18};
               string outputMsg = "";
               string caption = "System.Array Methods Illustrated";
               double [ ] w = new double [20];

               // Displays contents of Array waterDepth
               outputMsg += "waterDepth Array\n\n";
               foreach(double wVal in waterDepth)
                    outputMsg += wVal + "\n";
               MessageBox.Show(outputMsg, caption);
```

```
                // Copies 5 values from waterDepth,
                // beginning at index location 2.
                // Place values in Array W,
                // starting at index location 0
                Array.Copy(waterDepth, 2, w, 0, 5);

                // Sorts Array w in ascending order
                Array.Sort(w);

                // Displays Array w sorted
                outputMsg = "Array w Sorted\n\n";
                foreach(double wVal in w)
                {
                        if (wVal > 0)
                            outputMsg += wVal + "\n";
                }
                MessageBox.Show(outputMsg, caption);

                // Reverses the elements in Array w
                Array.Reverse(w);

                // Displays Array w in descending order
                outputMsg = "Array w Reversed\n\n";
                foreach(double wVal in w)
                {
                        if (wVal > 0)
                            outputMsg += wVal + "\n";
                }
                MessageBox.Show(outputMsg, caption);
        }
    }
}
```

7

As documented in Example 7-10, five values from `waterDepth`, beginning at indexed location `2`, are placed in array `w`, starting at index location `0`. The last two `foreach` statements both include an `if` statement. The array `w` is dimensioned to hold 20 entries. Only five cells contain data. The `if` statement skips blank entries so they are not concatenated onto the `outputMsg`.

The output produced from Example 7-10 is shown in Figure 7-6.

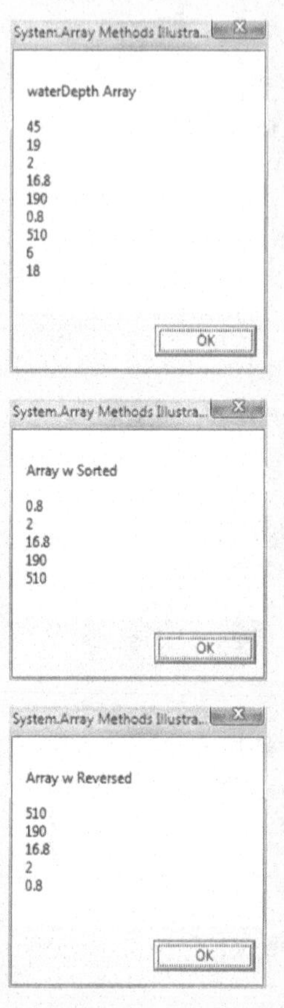

FIGURE 7-6 Output from Examples 7-10 and 7-12

To use the `MessageBox class`, you need to add a reference to the `System.Windows.Forms class` using the Solution Explorer window. Also remember to get rid of the console window in the background; set the **Output type** property for the project to **Windows Application**. Selecting the project in the **Solution Explorer** window and then pressing the **Alt+Enter** shortcut opens the project's properties dialog box.

One of the namespaces automatically imported into your application when you create a new project is `System.Linq`. You will read more about Language-Integrated Query (LINQ, pronounced "link") in Chapter 14. **Linq** defines a set of query operators that can be applied to collection classes like arrays. You often want to determine the average, sum, minimum or maximum value in an array. By including the `using System.Linq;` directive, you have access to `Average( )`, `Sum( )`, `Min( )`, and

Max( ) methods. These methods can be used with an array. They are not members of the Array class; they are members of the Linq class and are called with the array object as in

```
double [ ] waterDepth = {45, 19, 2, 16.8, 190, 0.8, 510, 6, 18};
double averageWaterDepth = waterDepth.Average( );
```

When you are cleaning up your solution and removing extraneous using statements, you may want to consider keeping using System.Linq;

Arrays as Method Parameters

You can write your own methods and send arrays as arguments much as you did with the calls to the predefined methods of the Array class. As you review the code in Example 7-10, notice that three separate segments of code are used for displaying output, and they all look similar. Except for the different headings above the array, the only difference is that the waterDepth array is displayed once. Two other times, the array w is displayed. Why not write one method and call it three times? The general format used for the heading of a method that includes an array as a parameter is: 7

```
modifiers returnType identifier (type [ ] arrayIdentifier...)
```

An illustration of a method heading is shown in Example 7-11.

EXAMPLE 7-11

```
void DisplayArrayContents(double [ ] anArray)
```

The array identifier and type are included in the parameter heading. The length or size of the array is not included. Opening and closing square brackets are required to indicate that the parameter is an array.

NOTE When you work with Visual Studio, the code generator adds an array parameter to the Main( ) method heading (Main(string [ ] args)). This enables arguments to be sent into the program when the application launches. When this occurs, the array identifier args can be used in the program like any other array. Since no values are sent into Main( ), the (string [ ] args) parameter could be deleted.

Pass by Reference

Recall that arrays are reference variables. The array identifier memory location does not actually contain the values, but rather an address indicating the location of the elements in the array. When you pass an array to a method, by default, you pass a reference to the address of the array elements. The importance of this feature is the fact that if the method changes one or more of the elements, the changes are made to the actual data. Thus, any changes made to array elements in a called method change the same array elements created in the calling method.

The actual call to the method expecting an array as an argument simply includes the identifier. It does not include the size or the square brackets. A call to the `DisplayArrayContents( )` method shown in Example 7-11 would be as follows:

```
DisplayArrayContents(waterDepth);
```

Recall that `waterDepth` is a `double [ ]` array.

Example 7-12 illustrates how the output statements can be placed in a method and called three times with different arguments each time. The first call sends the `waterDepth` array. The last two calls send the `w` array.

EXAMPLE 7-12

```
/* StaticMethods.cs                                Author: Doyle
 * Demonstrates use of methods from the
 * System.Array class.
 */
using System;
using System.Windows.Forms;

namespace StaticMethods
{
    class StaticMethods
    {
        private const string CAPTION =
              "System.Array Methods Illustrated";

        static void Main( )
        {
            double [ ] waterDepth = {45, 19, 2, 16.8, 190, 0.8,
                                     510, 6, 18};
            double [ ] w = new double[20];
            DisplayOutput(waterDepth, "waterDepth Array\n\n");

            // Copies values from waterDepth to w
            Array.Copy(waterDepth, 2, w, 0, 5);

            // Sorts Array w in ascending order
            Array.Sort (w);
            DisplayOutput(w, "Array w Sorted\n\n");
```

```
            // Reverses the elements in Array w
            Array.Reverse(w);
            DisplayOutput(w, "Array w Reversed\n\n");
        }

        // Displays an array in a MessageBox
        public static void DisplayOutput(double [ ] anArray,
                                         string msg)
        {
            foreach(double wVal in anArray)
                    if (wVal > 0)
                        msg += wVal + "\n";
            MessageBox.Show(msg, CAPTION);
        }
    }
}
```

Notice how `CAPTION` is defined as a constant data member in the `StaticMethods` `class`. The declaration appears above the `Main( )` method in Example 7-12. Doing this enabled each of the method members to have access to the `string` of characters without having to pass a value for the `CAPTION` to each method.

7

The parameter identifier `anArray` in the `DisplayOutput( )` method is used as a placeholder for an array argument. The arrays are of different lengths, but this does not create a problem. Every element in the array is being processed using the `foreach` statement in the method. When array `w` is sent into the method, it is necessary to use the selection statement (`if (wVal > 0)`); otherwise, 20 lines are displayed. The `foreach` loop traverses through every element in the array. Array `w` is dimensioned to have a length of `20`. Without the `if` statement, a number of `0` values are displayed when no other initialization values are given.

NOTE Zero is used as the default value by the constructor for integer arrays. That includes `sbyte`, `byte`, `short`, `ushort`, `int`, `uint`, `long`, and `ulong`; their default value is `0`. The default constructor values for `decimal`, `float`, and `double` are `0.0M`, `0.0F`, and `0.0D`, respectively. False is the default for `bool`.

Figure 7-6 shows output from Example 7-12. It is exactly the same as the output produced from Example 7-10. The last example, Example 7-12, is more streamlined. Because array parameters are automatically treated as pass by reference, no additional keywords such as `ref` or `out` are required with the argument or parameter list.

NOTE Remember, when you pass by reference, or call by reference, you pass the address of the identifier. A call or pass by value sends the actual data. When you pass a single array element such as an integer, you are passing by value. A copy of the current contents of that array element is made and sent to the method.

Consider the following that allocates memory for five elements:

```
int [ ] temperature = new int[5];
```

The following method could be used to input values into the `temperature` array:

```
public static void InputValues(int [ ] temp)
{
        string inValue;
        for(int i = 0; i < temp.Length; i++)
        {
            Write("Enter Temperature {0}: ", i + 1);
            inValue = ReadLine( );
            temp[i] = int.Parse(inValue);
        }
}
```

A call to the method to input values follows:

```
InputValues(temperature);
```

Figure 7-7 shows the result of inputting 78, 82, 90, 87, and 85.

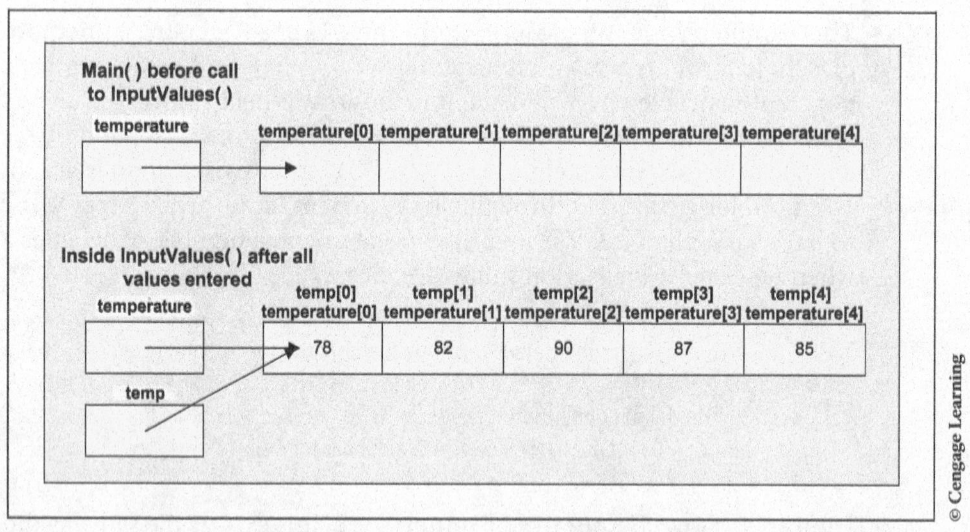

FIGURE 7-7 Array contents after the InputValues( ) method is called

When the `InputValues( )` method is called, a reference to `temperature` is sent.

In Chapter 3, you learned that when an argument is sent using call by value, a copy of the argument's contents is made. The copy of the values is stored in new memory locations accessible only within that method. Changes made to the values do not impact the variables in the calling module. On return from the called method, the original value of the argument is unchanged. It contains the same value it had before the execution of the method.

With call by reference, no copy is made of the contents. A copy is made of the reference (address) to the location in which the array is stored, and the copy is stored in a variable. As shown in Figure 7-7, the formal parameter, `temp`, references the same location in memory as `temperature` does. The values entered into the `temp` array in the `InputValues( )` method are stored in the memory cells referenced by `temperature`.

Array Assignment

The assignment operator = may not work as you would think it should when used with reference types such as arrays. If an additional array is defined and an assignment is made, the assignment operator and the array reference the same elements. Individual elements are not copied to another memory location. Consider the following statements that could be written after the `temperature` array is filled with values:

```
int [ ] t = new int[5];
t = temperature;
t[1] = 44;
```


Figure 7-8 illustrates the result of the assignment statements. Any reference to `temperature[1]` accesses 44.

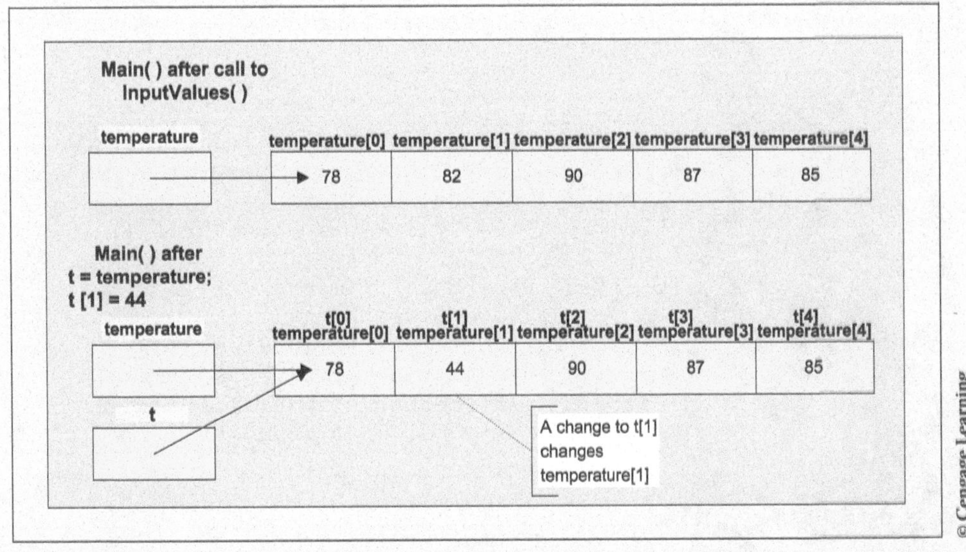

FIGURE 7-8 Assignment of an array to reference another array

Example 7-13 includes the complete code listing from the program statements used in Figures 7-7 and 7-8, which illustrate the assignment and use of arrays as method parameters.

EXAMPLE 7-13

```
/* PassingArray.cs                                   Author: Doyle
 * Demonstrates passing arrays to methods - references
 */
using System;
using static System.Console;

namespace PassingArray
{
     class PassingArray
     {
          static void Main( )
          {
               int [ ] temperature = new int[5];
               int [ ] t = new int[5];
               InputValues(temperature);
               //Array t will reference the same array
               //as the temperature array.
               t = temperature;
               t[1] = 44;
               WriteLine(temperature[1]);
               WriteLine("Value stored in temperature[1]: {0}",
                          temperature[1]);
               ReadKey( );
          }

          public static void InputValues(int [ ] temp)
          {
               string inValue;
               for(int i = 0; i < temp.Length; i++)
               {
                    Write("Enter Temperature {0}: ", i + 1);
                    inValue = ReadLine( );
                    if (int.TryParse(inValue,
                              out temp[i]) == false)
                        WriteLine("Invalid data entered - " +
                                   "0 stored in array element "); +
               }
          }
     }
}
```

Params Parameters

In Chapter 3, you were briefly introduced to the `params` parameter type. When a method uses the `params` modifier, the parameter is considered a **parameter array**. It is used to indicate that the number of arguments to the method may vary.

NOTE

If you include the `params` argument in the method heading, the array identifier it is used with must be the last parameter listed in the method heading. The identifier cannot be defined as a `ref` or `out` parameter.

The keyword `params` appears only in the formal parameter list of the method heading. By including it, the method may be called one time with a single value. Another call to the same method could send 10 or 100 values or an array of values. A variable number of arguments are accepted when `params` is included. It makes the method very flexible. Example 7-14 shows how a method defined with a parameter array can be called with both simple value arguments and with an array.

7

EXAMPLE 7-14

```
/* VaryingArguments.cs                    Author: Doyle
 * This example demonstrates the use
 * of the params keyword. A varying
 * number of arguments can be sent
 * to a method.
 */
using System;
using static System.Console;

namespace VaryingArguments
{
    class VaryingArguments
    {
        public static void Main( )
        {
            DisplayItems(1, 2, 3, 5);
            int[ ] anArray = new int[5] {100, 200, 300, 400,
                                         500};
            DisplayItems(anArray);
            DisplayItems(1500, anArray[1] * anArray[2]);
            ReadKey( );
        }
```

```
        public static void DisplayItems(params int[ ] item)
        {
            for (int i = 0 ; i < item.Length ; i++)
            {
                Write(item[i] + "\t");
            }
            WriteLine( );
        }
    }
}
```

The first call to the `DisplayItems( )` method includes four arguments (`1, 2, 3, 5`). They match the `DisplayItems( )` heading of (`params int [ ] item`). The second call sends an array as an argument during the method call. The last call sends two arguments; the first is `1500`, a constant literal. The second argument for the last call is an expression that involves multiplying 200 times 300 (`anArray[1] * anArray[2]`). This result is an integer; thus, all are acceptable arguments when the `params` keyword is included in the parameter list. The output produced is as follows:

```
1       2       3       5
100     200     300     400     500
1500    60000
```

Arrays in Classes

Arrays can be used as fields or instance variables in classes. Normally, the base type is declared with the other instance variables. But, space is allocated when an `object` of that `class` is instantiated. Consider the following list of data members of the `Player` `class`. In addition to the descriptive characteristics about a player, an array for `pointsScored` is defined. For instance, the player might score 10 points in the first game, 0 in the second, and so on.

```
public class Player
{
    private string lname;
    private string fname;
    private string id;
    private int[ ] pointsScored;
    private int numberOfGames;
```

After the `Player` `class` is defined, any number of games and associated points scored per game could be used to instantiate an `object` of the `class`. As you think about the characteristics of a player, you realize that you cannot say that all team players play 50 games or 5 games; thus, no space is allocated in the `pointsScored` array for a certain number of games. Because this is an instance member, allocate space when you construct an `object` of the `class`. This enables the `class` to be more flexible and usable by a larger number of applications.

Because one player might have played in 50 games and another player only 37, you need to know how many different games to record scores. The `pointsScored[ ]` array is used to hold the player's scores for each game. In addition to the default constructor, a constructor is defined that receives multiple arguments including the number of games a player played. This is sent in as an argument from the application through the `numGames` variable. Thus, if `numGames` has a value of 10, the first 10 elements of the `pointsScored[ ]` array would hold game counts (one per game). The constructor contains parameters for all instance variables.

The heading for the constructor follows:

```
public Player (string ln, string fn, string iden, int [ ] s,
               int numGames)
```

NOTE You might think you could just use the value of `s.Length` to determine the number of games instead of sending in the number of games argument. Remember that `Length` returns the total number of dimensioned elements, even those that are unused. The `Length` value does not represent how many elements are nonzero.

Space is allocated for the `pointsScored` array using the `numGames` argument. The following `Player` member method is used:

```
public void FillPointsScoredArray(int [ ] s)
{
     pointsScored = new int [numberOfGames];
     for (int i = 0; i < pointsScored.Length; i++)
          pointsScored[i] = s[i];
}
```

Before the preceding method can be called, an `object` of the `Player class` has to be constructed. A value would already be associated with the field member `numberOfGames`. The first statement in the body of the `FillPointsScoredArray( )` method instantiates the array `object` by allocating space for the number of elements using that instance field member. The last statement then copies the elements from the array `s`, which was sent into the method, to the instance array member, `pointsScored`.

The length of `s` could not be used as a loop control variable because it does not accurately indicate how many actual values are sent into the method. `Length` is the number of dimensioned elements, which was `1000` in the application using the `Player` class. Remember, one of the goals of creating classes is to be able to reuse the class with different applications. The current Player class determines the average points scored by a player. Additional methods could be written to return the number of games played, the high and low scores, the number of games in which the player scored at least 10 points, and so on. A parallel array could be created to associate pointsScored with the opponent name.

Parallel arrays are two or more arrays that have a relationship. The relationship is established using the same subscript or index to refer to the elements. For example, opponent X's name might be stored in a string array at index location C. Then, the number of points the player made against opponent X would be stored at that same indexed location C in another array. Parallel arrays are especially useful for storing related data when the related data is of different types.

NOTE With parallel arrays, anArrayOne [0] is related to anArrayTwo [0], anArrayOne [1] is related to anArrayTwo [1], anArrayOne [2] is related to anArrayTwo [2], and so on.

Consider the following declarations:

```
string [ ] firstName = new string[3] {"Bill", "Donna", "Peyton"};
string [ ] lastName = new string[3] {"Gates", "Lewis", "Manning"};
```

The two arrays are parallel arrays. firstName [0] goes with lastName [0]. These two memory locations could be concatenated with a separating space to form "Bill Gates". firstName [1] goes with lastName [1], and firstName [2] goes with lastName [2].

Array of User-Defined Objects

Just as you can create arrays of predefined types, such as int, you can create arrays of user-defined classes. What if you had data on 12 different players? Using the Player class, an array of Player objects could be created as follows:

```
Write("How many players? ");
inValue = ReadLine( );
if (int.TryParse(inValue, out playerCnt) == false)
    WriteLine("Invalid data entered - " +
              "0 recorded for number of players.");

Player[ ] teamMember = new Player[playerCnt];
```

First, values are made available for an individual player for the following: last name (ln), first name (fn), identification number (iden), points scored (points), and the number of games played (gameCnt). Then, the constructor for the Player class can be called using the following statement:

```
playerNumber = 1;
teamMember [playerNumber] = new Player(ln, fn, iden, points,
                                         gameCnt);
```

Of course, a loop could be designed to instantiate multiple Player objects. The variable playerCnt could be used as the loop control terminating variable.

Arrays as Return Types

Arrays can be sent to methods as arguments, and methods can have arrays as their return types as well. The following heading to the GetScores( ) method returns an array containing the points scored list for one Player object. Notice the square bracket in the heading preceding the identifier for the method.

```
public static int [ ] GetScores(ref int gameCnt)
```

A call to this method would be as follows:

```
int [ ] points = new int [1000];
points = GetScores(ref gameCnt);
```


GetScores( ) is used by an application that instantiates an object of the Player type. The full code listing appears in Example 7-15. GetScores( ) is defined as a static method (class method) that returns a filled array. An assumption that no player would play more than 1000 games is made. A reference variable, scoreCnt, is included as an argument so that the actual number of games is available when an object of the Player class is constructed.

You will remember that a method can return a single type. A decision had to be made whether to return the array or to return the variable storing gameCnt. The choice was made to use the array as a return type to demonstrate how an array type can be returned. However, a more efficient solution is to send the array into the method as an argument and return gameCnt through the method name. The reason the last option is a better choice is based on the following. To return an array through the return type of the method, another array must be declared and space allocated locally for it in the method. This additional space for the size of the array is unnecessary if the array is sent as an argument because arrays are always passed by reference. Sending the array as an argument passes the address of the one declared in the calling method and eliminates the need to declare a local array.

Example 7-15 contains a listing of the Player application. It consists of two files. The first file describes characteristics of a Player. The second file is an application instantiating an array of Player objects. Recall that you can add a second class to your application in Visual Studio using the **Add Class** option from the **Project** menu. In addition to storing information about multiple Player objects, this file contains code to access the Player members. Player class is listed first.

EXAMPLE 7-15

```
/* Player.cs                              Author:    Doyle
 * Creates class with characteristics about one player.
 * Includes name and ID fields, plus points scored.
 * Any number of games can be used to instantiate an
 * object of this class. Average calculated based on the
 * number of points associated with one player.
 */
using System;

namespace PlayerApp
{
     public class Player
     {
          private string lname;
          private string fname;
          private string id;
          private int[ ] pointsScored;
          private int numberOfGames;

          // Default constructor
          public Player( )
          {
          }
          // Constructor accepts any size
          // pointsScored array.
          public Player (string ln, string fn, string iden,
                         int [ ] s, int numGames)
          {
               numberOfGames = numGames;
               FillPointsScoredArray(s);
               lname = ln;
               fname = fn;
               id = iden;
          }
          public string FName
          {
               get
               {
                    return fname;
               }
               set
               {
                    fname = value;
               }
          }
```

```
public string LName
{
     get
     {
          return lname;
     }
     set
     {
          lname = value;
     }
}
public string ID
{
     get
     {
          return id;
     }
     set
     {
          id = value;
     }
}
public int NumberOfGames
{
     get
     {
          return numberOfGames;
     }
     set
     {
          numberOfGames = value;
     }
}
public int[ ] PointsScored
{
     get
     {
          return pointsScored;
     }
     set
     {
          pointsScored = value;
     }
}

public void FillPointsScoredArray(int [ ] s)
{
     pointsScored = new int [numberOfGames];
     for (int i = 0; i < pointsScored.Length; i++)
         pointsScored[i] = s[i];
}
```

```
        public double ComputeAverage( )
        {
             double total = 0;
             double avg;
             foreach(int s in pointsScored)
                     total += s;
             if (pointsScored.Length > 0)
                 avg = total / pointsScored.Length;
             else
                 avg = 0;
             return avg;
        }

        public override string ToString( )
        {
             return "Player Name: " + fname +
                   " " + lname + "\nPlayer ID: " +
                   id + "\nNumber of Games: " +
                   numberOfGames +
                   "\nAverage PointsScored per Game: " +
                   ComputeAverage( ).ToString("F2");
        }
    }
}

/* PlayerApp.cs Author: Doyle
 * Application that instantiates Player class.
 * Creates an array of player objects that
 * can be used to display individual
 * records or do stats on the entire team.
 */
using System;
using static System.Console;

namespace PlayerApp
{
     class PlayerApp
     {
         static void Main( )
         {
              string ln,
                     fn,
                     iden;
              string inValue;
              int playerCnt,
                  loopCnt = 0,
                  gameCnt;
              int [ ] points = new int [1000];

              Write("How many players? ");
              inValue = ReadLine( );
```

```
        if (int.TryParse(inValue, out playerCnt) == false)
             WriteLine("Invalid data entered - " +
                         "0 recorded for number " +
                         "of players.");
      Player[ ] teamMember = new Player[playerCnt];
      while (loopCnt < playerCnt)
      {
            GetIdInfo(out ln, out fn, out iden);
            gameCnt = 0;
            points = GetScores(ref gameCnt);
            teamMember [loopCnt] = new Player(ln, fn,
                                   iden, points, gameCnt);
            loopCnt++;
      }
      DisplayStats(teamMember);
      ReadKey( );
}

public static int [ ] GetScores(ref int gameCnt)
{
      int [ ] points = new int [1000];
      string inValue;

      Write("Game {0}: ((-99 to exit)) ", gameCnt + 1);
      inValue = ReadLine( );
      while(inValue != "-99")
      {
              if (int.TryParse(inValue,
                      out points[gameCnt]) == false)
                  WriteLine("Invalid data entered" +
                            " - 0 recorded for " +
                            "points array element");
              ++gameCnt;
              Write("Game {0}: ((-99 to exit)) ",
                    gameCnt + 1);
              inValue = ReadLine( );
      }
      return points;
}

public static void GetIdInfo(out string ln,
                 out string fn, out string iden)
{
      WriteLine( );
      Write("Player First Name: ");
      fn = ReadLine( );
      Write("Player Last Name: ");
      ln = ReadLine( );
      Write("Player ID Number: ");
      iden = ReadLine( );
}
```

7

```
        public static void DisplayStats (Player[ ]teamMember)
        {
             WriteLine( );
             WriteLine("{0,12} {1,25}","Player", "Avg Points");
             WriteLine("----------------------------");
             foreach(Player pl in teamMember)
             {
                     WriteLine("{0,-25} {1,7}", (pl.FName + " " +
                               pl.LName),
                               pl.ComputeAverage( ).ToString(
                                                         "F0"));
             }
        }
    }
}
```

NOTE Remember that the properties with the sets and gets are added to enable client applications to access the `private` data members. By including them in your programs, you make your classes more usable.

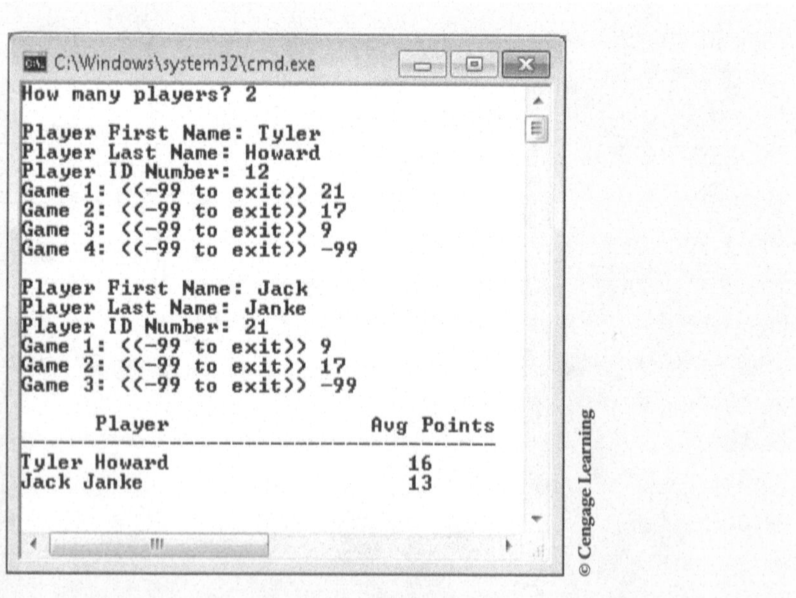

FIGURE 7-9 PlayerApp output

The output from one test run of `PlayerApp` is shown in Figure 7-9.

Notice how Tyler Howard ended up with whole numbers (integers) representing his average points. If you do the arithmetic ((21 + 17 + 9) / 3 = 15.666666667).

As you examine Example 7-15, you should observe that the result is stored in a `double`. To avoid doing integer division in the `ComputeAverage( )` method, `total` was defined as a `double` and then divided by an `int` (`pointsScored.Length`). The result is a `double` and it is then assigned to a `double`. The `ToString( )` method was called in the `DisplayStats( )` method of the `PlayerApp` application sending in "F0" as a format specifier. Another option to produce a floating-point result, both variables could have been defined as integers and then one of them could have been cast to a `double`, that is ((`double`) `total` / `pointsScored.Length`).

Figure 7-10 shows how the data from `PlayerApp` is represented in memory.

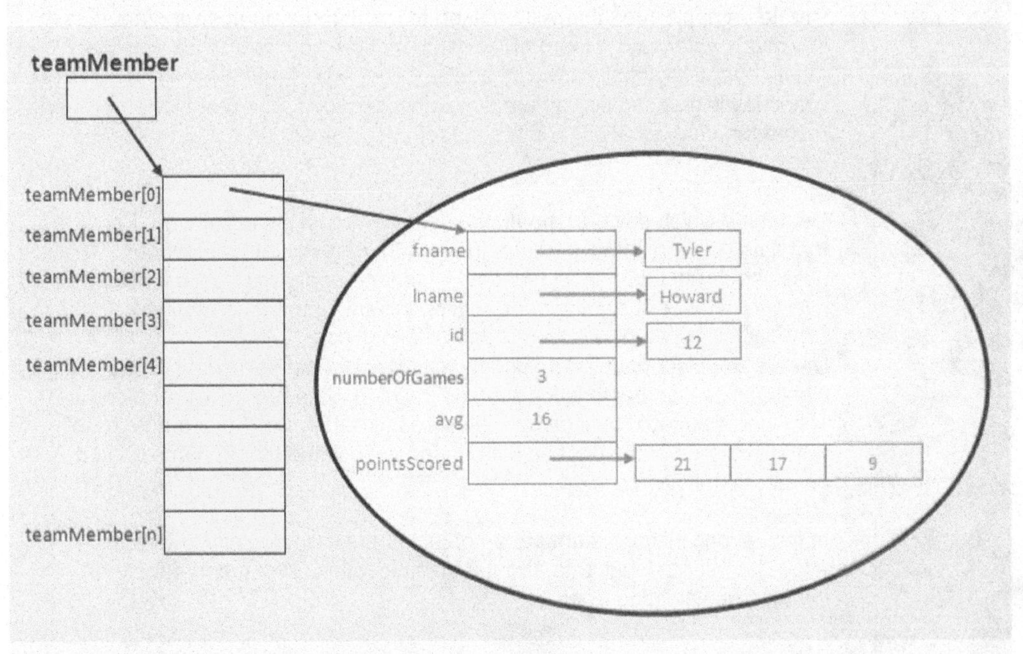

FIGURE 7-10 PlayerApp memory representation

© Cengage Learning

7

As you review the figure, note the difference between value types such as `avg` and `numberOfGames`. Array objects and `string` types contain a reference to the location of the stored values. Many advanced concepts relating to arrays were illustrated in the `PlayerApp` application. Array elements were defined as private data members and local variables. You saw how you could instantiate arrays of user-defined class array objects. Arrays were returned from methods and sent in as arguments to methods. Many of these same features will be revisited with the Programming Example that follows.

PROGRAMMING EXAMPLE: Manatee Application

This example demonstrates the use of collections in the analysis, design, and implementation of a program. `Array` and `string` objects are included. An application is created to monitor manatees, which are still in danger of extinction and are being monitored on a daily basis in some areas. To design this application, a number of instance methods are used. Parallel arrays are created to store the date and number present at each sighting. The application is designed using two classes, and the problem specification is shown in Figure 7-11.

Create an application that will be used to monitor the number of manatees in a given waterway. A team of researchers flies from four to six times per month over a regional waterway and log sightings of manatees. The waterway is mapped into different viewing locations. The researchers record the date, location, and a count of the number present at that location.

Determine which day had the highest sightings at a given location. Print that date with the actual name of the month. Also include the count associated with the highest sighting. Plan your application so that the average number of sightings for a given location can be determined.

Design an object-oriented solution. Use two classes. For the manatee sighting class, characteristics such as location, date of viewing, and count of manatees should be included. Methods to determine the average, date with the highest number of sightings, and associated month name should be part of the class.

In the second class, instantiate an object of the manatee sighting class. Allow the user to input data about a given location. Test the members of the manatee sighting class.

© Cengage Learning

FIGURE 7-11 Problem specification for Manatee example

ANALYZE THE PROBLEM

You should review the problem specification in Figure 7-11 and make sure you understand the problem definition. Several values will be entered into the program to represent location, date, and counts of sighted manatees. These dates and counts will be entered into arrays and used to instantiate an object of the `ManateeSighting` `class`.

DATA

Table 7-2 lists the data field members needed for the manatee sighting problem.

TABLE 7-2 Instance field members for the ManateeSighting class

Data item description	Type	Identifier
Sighting location	string	location
Date of sighting	string [ ]	sightDate
Number of manatees sighted	int [ ]	manateeCount

© Cengage Learning

A second class will be created to test the ManateeSighting class. To do this, additional data is needed by the class using the ManateeSighting class. As noted in the problem specification, the application class allows the user to enter values so that the ManateeSighting class can be instantiated. Local variables for location and arrays for date and count are declared in the application class. The two arrays will be dimensioned to a maximum number of 20 entries. The number of actual records will be used to construct the ManateeSighting object. For testing purposes, a single location is entered and sighting data recorded for that location. The user is able to enter additional location data. The application could be modified to create arrays of data about multiple locations.

DESIGN A SOLUTION

The desired output is to display the location, number of sightings during the most active month, and date (including the month name) in which the most manatees were sighted. Figure 7-12 shows a prototype of what the final output might look like.

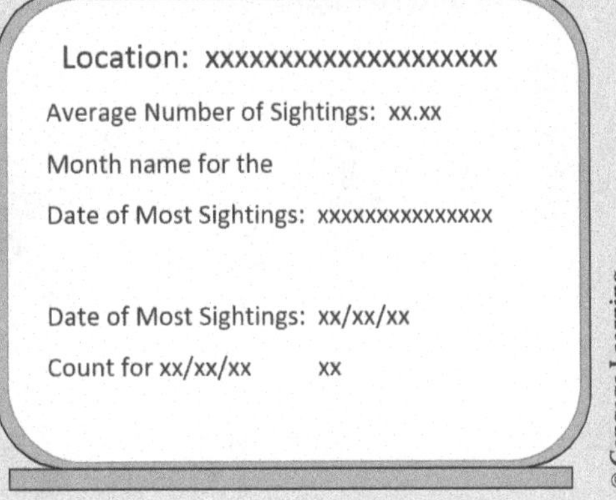

Location: xxxxxxxxxxxxxxxxxxxx
Average Number of Sightings: xx.xx
Month name for the
Date of Most Sightings: xxxxxxxxxxxxxxx
Date of Most Sightings: xx/xx/xx
Count for xx/xx/xx xx
© Cengage Learning

FIGURE 7-12 Prototype for Manatee Application

Class diagrams are used to help design and document both data and behavior characteristics. Figure 7-13 shows the `class` diagrams for the manatee application example.

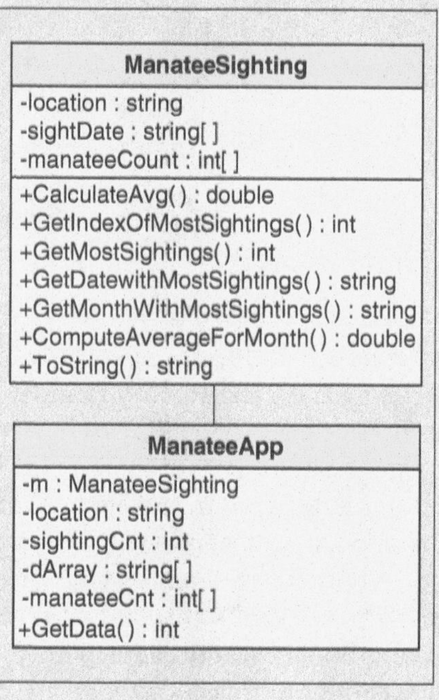

© Cengage Learning

FIGURE 7-13 Class diagrams

The `class` diagrams do not show the properties or the local variables that might be needed by specific methods. Table 7-3 lists the data members that have properties defined indicating whether `get` and/or `set` will be needed. The name of the property is also shown in the table.

TABLE 7-3 Properties for the ManateeSighting class

Data member identifier	Property identifier	Set	Get
location	Location	√	√
sightDate	SightDate	√	√
manateeCount	ManateeCount	√	√

© Cengage Learning

Calculated values such as the average sightings, date with largest sightings, and the name of the month with the largest sightings are instance methods of the `class`. The `ComputeAverageForMonth ( )` method adds additional functionality to the `Manatee class`. It returns the average for a given month.

Figure 7-14 shows the Structured English, or pseudocode, used to design the step-by-step processes for the behaviors of the methods of the `ManateeApp` example.

```
CalculateAvg( )
        set totalCount = 0
        loop while (more manateeCounts)
        {
                totalCount = totalCount + manateeCount
        }
        avg = (double)totalCount / manateeCount.Length
```

```
GetIndexOfMostSightings( )
        maxCntIndex = 0
        index = 1
        loop while(more manateeCounts)
        (
                if (manateeCount[index] > manateeCount[maxCntIndex])
                        maxCntIndex = index
                index++
        }
        return maxCntIndex
```

```
ComputeAverageForMonth(string mon) : monAverage
        total = 0
        days = 0
        index = 0
        loop while(more sightings)
        (
                if (sightDate[index].StartsWith(mon))
                {
                        total += manateeCount[index]
                        days++
                }
        }
        if (days > 0)
                monAverage = (double) total / days
        else
                monAverage = 0
        return monAverage
```

```
ReturnMonth(string someDate) : monthName
        define monthNameArray
        tempArray = someDate.Split('/')
        tempArray = tempArray.Trim(0)
        intMonth = ConvertToInt(tempArray)
        monthName = MonthNameArray[intMonth]
        return monthName
```

© Cengage Learning

FIGURE 7-14 ManateeSighting class methods behavior

7

After the algorithm is developed, the design should be checked for correctness. You might develop a table now with test values using a standard calculator. Desk check the pseudocode to ensure you are getting the results expected. After your program is running, you can validate the correctness by comparing results you produce with your program against values you produced with the calculator during your design walk-through.

CODE THE SOLUTION

After you complete the design and verify the algorithm's correctness, translate the design into source code. For this application, you are creating two separate files—one for each class. The final application listing for both files is as follows:

```
/* ManateeSighting.cs Author: Doyle
 * This class defines manatee characteristics to include
 * location, count, and date of sightings. Methods to
 * determine the month with most sightings and
 * average number of sightings per location included.
 */
using System;

namespace ManateeApp
{
    public class ManateeSighting
    {
        private string location;
        private string [ ] sightDate;
        private int [ ] manateeCount;

        // Constructors
        public ManateeSighting( )
        {
        }
        public ManateeSighting(string loc)
        {
            location = loc;
        }
        public ManateeSighting(string loc, string[ ] date,
                               int[ ] cnt)
        {
            sightDate = new string[date.Length];
            manateeCount = new int[cnt.Length];
            Array.Copy(date, 0, sightDate, 0, date.Length);
            Array.Copy(cnt, 0, manateeCount, 0,
                       manateeCount.LongLength);
            location = loc;
        }
```

```
public ManateeSighting(string loc, string[ ] date,
                       int [ ] cnt, int numOfFlights)
{
     sightDate = new string[numOfFlights];
     manateeCount = new int[numOfFlights];
     Array.Copy(date,0,sightDate, 0, numOfFlights);
     Array.Copy(cnt,0,manateeCount, 0, numOfFlights);
     location = loc;
}

// Properties
public string Location
{
     get
     {
          return location;
     }
     set
     {
          location = value;
     }
}
public string[ ] SightDate
{
     get
     {
          return sightDate;
     }
     set
     {
          sightDate = value;
     }
}
public int [ ] ManateeCount
{
     get
     {
          return manateeCount;
     }
     set
     {
          manateeCount = value;
     }
}

// Determines what the average number of
// sightings is per location
public double CalculateAvg( )
{
     double avg;
```

```
        int cntOfValidEntries;
        int total = 0;
        foreach (int c in manateeCount)
                total += c;
        cntOfValidEntries = TestForZeros( );
        avg = (double)total / cntOfValidEntries;
        return avg;
    }

    // To avoid skewing average, return number
    // of cells with nonzero values
    public int TestForZeros( )
    {
        int numberOfTrueSightings = 0;
        foreach (int cnt in manateeCount)
                if (cnt != 0)
                    numberOfTrueSightings++;
        return numberOfTrueSightings;
    }

    // Returns an index where the largest
    // number of sightings is stored
    public int GetIndexOfMostSightings( )
    {
        int maxCntIndex = 0;
        for (int i = 1; i < manateeCount.Length; i++)
            if (manateeCount[i] >
                        manateeCount[maxCntIndex])
                maxCntIndex = i;
        return maxCntIndex;
    }

    // Returns a count of the most sighted
    public int GetMostSightings( )
    {
        return manateeCount[GetIndexOfMostSightings( )];
    }

    //Returns the date when most sightings occurred
    public string GetDateWithMostSightings( )
    {
        return sightDate[GetIndexOfMostSightings( )];
    }

   // Returns the name of the month when the
   // highest sightings occurred
   public string GetMonthWithMostSightings( )
```

```
{
      return ReturnMonth(
              sightDate[GetIndexOfMostSightings( )]);
}

// Computes the average for a given month
public double ComputeAverageForMonth(string mon)
{
     int total = 0;
     int days = 0;
     double monAverage;
     for (int i = 0; i < sightDate.Length; i++)
     {
          if (sightDate[i].StartsWith(mon))
          {
               total += manateeCount[i];
               days++;
          }
     }
     if (days > 0)
         monAverage = (double)total / days;
     else
         monAverage = 0;
     return monAverage;
}

// Given a date in the format of mm/dd/yyyy
// the name of the month is returned
public string ReturnMonth(string someDate)
{
     string[ ] monthName =
          {"January", "February", "March",
          "April", "May", "June", "July",
          "August", "September", "October",
          "November", "December"};
     string[ ] dateParts = someDate.Split('/');
     dateParts[0] = dateParts[0].TrimStart('0');
     return monthName[Convert.ToInt32(dateParts[0])- 1];
}

public override string ToString( )
{
     return "\tLocation: " + location +
            "\n\nAverage Number " +
            "of Sightings:\t" +
            CalculateAvg( ).ToString("F1") +
            "\n\nMonth name for the" +
```

7

```
                        "\nDate of Most Sightings:\t\t" +
                        GetMonthWithMostSightings( ) +
                        "\n\nDate of Most Sightings:\t\t" +
                        GetDateWithMostSightings( ) +
                        "\nCount for " +
                        GetDateWithMostSightings( ) + ":\t\t" +
                        GetMostSightings( );
        }
    }
}

/* ManateeApp.cs                    Author: Doyle
 * This is the client program that uses the
 * ManateeSighting class. Users are prompted
 * for location, date, and sightings. The
 * ManateeSighting class is tested using
 * this class by calling many of the
 * methods and properties.
 */
using System;
using static System.Console;

namespace ManateeApp
{
     public class ManateeApp
     {
          static void Main(string[] args)
          {
               string location;
               int sightingCnt;
               string [ ] dArray = new String[ 20];
               int [ ] manateeCnt = new int[20];
               char enterMoreData = 'Y';
               ManateeSighting m;
               do
               {
                    sightingCnt = GetData(out location, dArray,
                                             manateeCnt);
                    m = new ManateeSighting(location, dArray,
                                        manateeCnt, sightingCnt);
                    Clear( );
                    WriteLine(m);
                    Write("\n\n\n\nDo you want to enter more " +
                         "data - (Enter y or n)? ");
                    if (char.TryParse(ReadLine( ),
```

```
                        out enterMoreData) == false)
                    WriteLine("Invalid data entered - No " +
                              "recorded for your response ");
        }
        while (enterMoreData == 'Y' || enterMoreData == 'y');
        ReadKey( );
    }

    public static int GetData(out string location, string[ ]
                              dArray, int[ ] manateeCnt)
    {
        int i,
            loopCnt;
        Clear( );
        Write("Location: ");
        location = ReadLine( );
        Write("How many records for {0}? ", location);
        string inValue = ReadLine( );
        if (int.TryParse(inValue, out loopCnt) == false)
            WriteLine("Invalid data entered - " +
                      "0 recorded for number of records");
        for (i = 0; i < loopCnt; i++)
        {
            Write("\nDate (mm/dd/yyyy): ");
            dArray[i] = ReadLine( );
            if (dArray[i] == "")
            {
                WriteLine("No date entered - " +
                          "Unknown recorded " +
                          "for sightings");
                dArray[i] = "Unknown";
            }
            Write("Number of Sightings: ");
            inValue = ReadLine( );
            if (int.TryParse(inValue,
                    out manateeCnt[i]) == false)
                WriteLine("Invalid data entered - 0 " +
                          "recorded for manatee sightings ");
        }
        return i;
      }
    }
}
```

The output displayed during data entry, showing error messages generated when invalid data is entered, is shown in Figure 7-15.

7

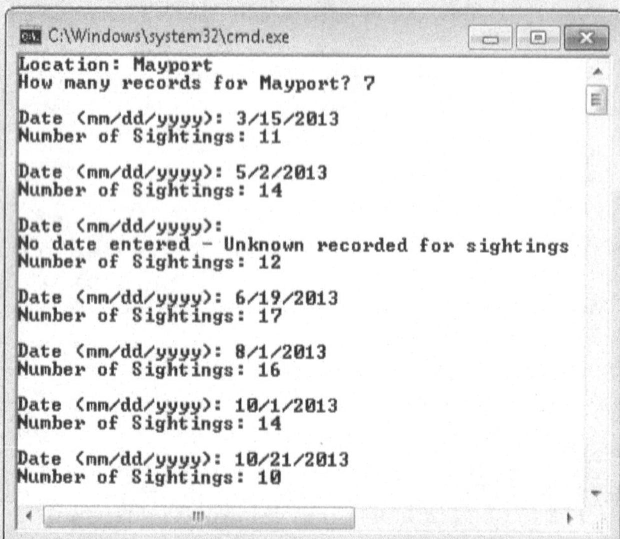

FIGURE 7-15 ManateeApp application during data entry

The output from one iteration during the test run is shown in Figure 7-16.

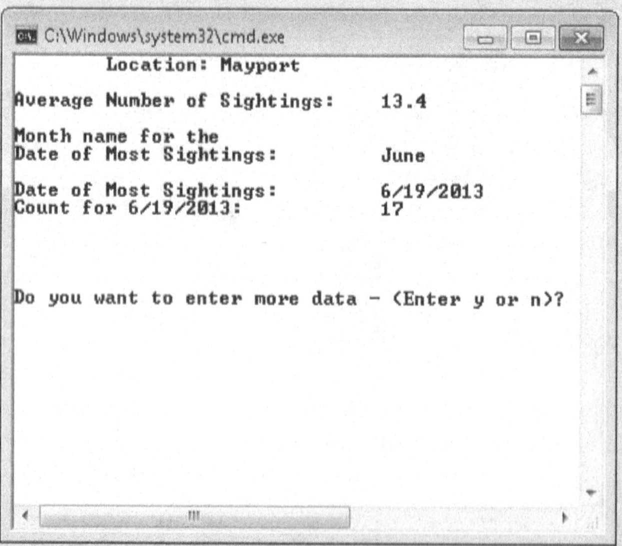

FIGURE 7-16 ManateeApp application output

Coding Standards

Guidelines for Naming Arrays

Use singular nouns as identifiers for arrays. Since arrays are many data items grouped together and you normally reference the data item one data item at a time, it is best to use a singular noun to identify array elements.

Use the Camel case naming convention with arrays.

When you declare an array, place the square brackets ([ ]) after the data type, not after the identifier.

Advanced Array Suggestions

Explicitly initialize arrays either through compile-time initialization or by using a `for` statement or the `Initialize( )` method of the `Array class`.

Use the `foreach` statement when you want read-only access of the data.

Use .NET predefined methods and properties whenever possible as opposed to writing new code.

Resources

Additional sites you might want to explore:

- C# Coding Conventions—
  http://msdn.microsoft.com/en-us/library/ff926074.aspx
- C# Corner - Arrays in C#—
  http://www.c-sharpcorner.com/uploadfile/puranindia/arrays-in-C-Sharp
- Code Project - Doing Arrays - C#—
  http://www.codeproject.com/Articles/161465/Doing-Arrays-C
- C# Dot Net Perls—
  http://www.dotnetperls.com/array
- C# Arrays YouTube Video—
  http://www.youtube.com/watch?v=Shl7TsNMGSE

QUICK REVIEW

1. An array may contain any number of variables of the same type.
2. One common identifier names the entire structure.
3. The individual variables in the array are called the elements of the array.
4. To access an array element, use an index enclosed in square brackets.

5. The index (or subscript) references the location of the variable relative to the beginning location.
6. The first index is always zero.
7. With C#, the size or length of the array cannot change after it is allocated, but you can use a variable to declare the size of an array.
8. During the declaration, specify the number of individual elements for which space must be allocated and use an identifier representative of the contents (normally a singular name).
9. When you use an array as a method parameter, the array identifier and type are specified; however, the length or size of the array is not included. Opening and closing square brackets are required.
10. The call to that method includes the name of the array only.
11. `Array class` has a number of predefined methods that perform sort, binary search, copy, and reverse. All arrays, of any type, inherit them.
12. Include `params` with a parameter to indicate that the number of arguments may vary.
13. Within the `foreach` statement, an identifier represents the array element for the iteration currently being performed.
14. The type used in the `foreach` expression must match the array type.
15. Arrays can be sent as arguments to methods, and in addition, a method can have an array as its return type.
16. Array objects and `string` types are references instead of value types.

EXERCISES

1. An array is a list of data items that:
   a. all have the same type
   b. all have different names
   c. all are integers
   d. all are originally set to `null` (`'\0'`)
   e. none of the above

2. The value contained within the square brackets that is used to indicate the length of the array must be a(n):
   a. `class`
   b. `double`
   c. `string`
   d. integer
   e. none of the above

3. Which of the following array declarations would enable you to store the high temperature for each day of one full week?

   a. `int temp1, temp2, temp3, temp4, temp5, temp6, temp7;`

   b. `int temp [7] = new int[7];`

   c. `temp int [ ] = new temp[7];`

   d. `int [ ] temp = new int[7];`

   e. `int [ ] temp = new temp[8];`

4. Assume an array called num is declared to store four elements. Which of the following statements correctly assigns the value 100 to each of the elements?

   a. `for(x = 0; x < 3; ++x) num[x] = 100;`

   b. `for(x = 0; x < 4; ++x) num[x] = 100;`

   c. `for(x = 1; x < 4; ++x) num[x] = 100;`

   d. `for(x = 1; x < 5; ++x) num[x] = 100;`

   e. none of the above

7

5. Choose the statement that does *not* apply to the following declaration:

```
double [ ] totalCostOfItems = {109.95, 169.95, 1.50,
                                89.95};
```

   a. `declares a one-dimensional array of floating-point values`

   b. specifies the size of the array as five

   c. sets the array element `totalCostOfItems[1]` to `169.95`

   d. declares an area in memory where data of `double` type can be stored

   e. all are correct

6. What value is returned by the method named `result`?

```
int result(int[ ] anArray, int num)
{
    int i,
        r;
    for (r = 0, i = 1; i < num; ++i)
          if (anArray[i] > anArray [r] )
               r = i;
    return (r);
}
```

   a. the index of the largest of the first num elements of array anArray
   b. the value of the largest of the first `num` elements of array `anArray`
   c. the index of the smallest of the first `num` elements of array `anArray`
   d. the value of the smallest of the first `num` elements of array `anArray`
   e. the index of the last element greater than its predecessor within the first `num` elements of array `anArray`

7. What is the effect of the following program segment?

```
int[ ] anArray = new int[50];
int i, j, temp;
string inValue;
for (i = 0; i < 50; ++i)
{
      Write("Enter Value");
      inValue = ReadLine( );
      anArray[i] = int.Parse(inValue);
}
temp = 0;
for (i = 1; i < 50; ++i)
      if (anArray[i] < anArray[0])
           ++temp;
```

   a. arranges the elements of array `anArray` in ascending order
   b. counts the number of elements of array `anArray` less than its initial element
   c. reverses the numbers stored in the array
   d. puts the largest value in the last array position
   e. none of the above

8. Using the following declaration:

```
char [ ] n = {'a', 'b', 'c', 'd', 'e'};
```

What does `n[1]` refer to?

a. `a`

b. `abcde`

c. `b`

d. `'a'`

e. none of the above

9. Using the following declaration:

```
int [ ] x = {12, 13, 14, 15, 16, 17, 18, 19};
```

What does `x[8]` refer to?

a. `19`

b. `18`

c. `'\0'`

d. `0`

e. none of the above

10. Which of the following adds `42` to the element at the fifth physical spot?

```
int [ ] x = {12, 13, 14, 15, 16, 17, 18, 19};
```

a. `x[5] += 42;`

b. `x[4] += 42;`

c. `x[5 + 42];`

d. `x = 42 + 5;`

e. none of the above

11. How many components are allocated by the following statement?

```
double [ ] values = new double[3];
```

a. `32`

b. 3

c. 2

d. 4

e. none of the above

12. What output is produced by the following code?

```
int i;
int [ ] anArray = new int [5];
for (i = 0; i < anArray.Length; i++)
     anArray[i] = 2 * i;
for (i = 0; i < anArray.Length; i++)
     Write(anArray[i] + " ");
```

    a. 22222
    b. 246810
    c. 0246810
    d. 02468
    e. none of the above

13. If you declare an array as `int [ ] anArray = new int[5];` you can double the value stored in `anArray [2]` with the statement:
    a. `anArray[2] = anArray[5] * 2;`
    b. `anArray = anArray * 2;`
    c. `anArray[2] *= anArray[2] * 2;`
    d. `anArray[2] *= 2;`
    e. none of the above

14. With the following declaration:

    `int [ ] points = {550, 700, 900, 800, 100};`

    the statement `points[3] = points[3] + 10;` will
    a. replace the `800` amount with `810`
    b. replace the `550` amount with `560`
    c. replace the `900` amount with `910`
    d. result in an error
    e. none of the above

15. With the following declaration:

    `int [ ] points = {300, 100, 200, 400, 600};`

    the statement `points [4] = points[4 - 2];` will
    a. replace the `400` amount with `2`
    b. replace the `300` and `600` with `2`
    c. replace the `600` with `200`
    d. result in an error
    e. none of the above

16. With the following declaration:

```
int [ ] points = {300, 100, 200, 400, 600};
```

the statement `Write(points[2] + points[3]);` will

a. display 200400

b. display 600

c. display `"points[2] + points[3]"`

d. result in an error

e. none of the above

17. When you pass a single integer array element to a method, the method receives:

a. a copy of the array

b. the address of the array

c. a copy of the value in the element

d. the address of the element

e. none of the above

18. When you pass the entire array to a method, the method receives:

a. a copy of the array

b. the address of the array

c. a copy of the first value in the array

d. the address of each of the elements in the array

e. none of the above

19. A correct method call to a method that has the following heading would be:

```
int result(int [ ] anArray, int num)
```

a. `Write(result(anArray, 3));`

b. `result(anArray, 30);`

c. `Write(result(anArray[ ], 3));`

d. `result(anArray[ ], 30);`

e. none of the above

20. A valid call to the following method using a `params` parameter is:

```
public static void DoSomething(params int[ ] item)
```

   a. `DoSomething(4);`
   b. `DoSomething(anArray);`
   c. `DoSomething(4, 5, 6);`
   d. a and c are correct
   e. all are correct

---

21. Using the following declaration:

```
int [ ] anArray = {34, 55, 67, 89, 99};
```

what would be the result of each of the following output statements?

   a. `WriteLine(anArray.Length);`
   b. `WriteLine(anArray[2]);`
   c. `WriteLine(anArray[anArray.Length - 2]);`
   d. `WriteLine(anArray[2 + 1] * anArray[0]);`
   e. `WriteLine(anArray[1] + 100);`

```
int [ ] bArray = new int [10];
```

22. Using the above declarations write a `foreach` loop to display the contents of `bArray`.

23. Using the above declarations write a `for` loop to increment each element in `bArray` by 5.

24. Using the above declarations, use a member of the Array class to locate the index in the `bArray` array where 14 is stored.

25. Using the above declarations, use a member of the Array class to order the values in the `bArray` array in ascending order.

26. Using the above declarations, use a member of the Array class to change the order of the elements in the `bArray` array. The contents of the first cell should hold what was in the last cell. The second cell should hold what was in the next to last cell.

27. Create array declarations for the following problem specifications.
    a. An array to hold the names of five font strings. Initialize the array with your favorites.
    b. An array to hold 12 state names. Initialize with the 12 states closest to your campus.
    c. An array to hold the 10 most common single character middle initials.
    d. An array to store a key for an exam consisting of 15 true/false questions.
    e. Parallel arrays to hold up to 100 checking account check numbers, dates, and check amounts.
28. Explain the difference between the pass by reference and pass by value. When an array is sent to a method, which one is used?

PROGRAMMING EXERCISES

1. Write an application that allows the user to input monthly rainfall amounts for one year storing the values in an array. Create a second array that holds the names of the month. Produce a report showing the month name along with the rainfall amount and its variance from the mean. Calculate and display the average rainfall for the year.
2. Write a program that allows the user to enter any number of names, last name first. Using one of the predefined methods of the `Array` `class`, order the names in ascending order. Display the results.
3. Create three arrays of type `double`. Do a compile-time initialization and place different values in two of the arrays. Write a program to store the product of the two arrays in the third array. Produce a display using the `MessageBox` `class` that shows the contents of all three arrays using a single line for an element from all three arrays. Design your solution so that the two original arrays have a different number of elements. Use 1 as the multiplier when you produce the third array.
4. Write an application that can be used to test input values to ensure they fall within an established range. Use an array to keep a count of the number of times each acceptable value was entered. Acceptable values are integers between 0 and 10. Your program should display the total number of valid values inputted as well as the number of invalid entries. Show not only the number of values outside the range, but also the number

of non-numeric invalid values entered. For your final display, output a list of distinct valid entries and a count of how many times that entry occurred. Provide your listing in a tabular format, with values number aligned. Do not display the value unless it was entered.
Use the following test data:

7 2 4 2 q 87 4 6 4 4 7

5. The Ion Realty Sales Corporation would like to have an application showing how each monthly sales contributes to their overall total sales. Write a program that accepts as input any number of monthly sales amounts. After all values have been entered, display a report showing each of the monthly sales amounts and the percentage contribution of the individual monthly sales figure to the overall total sales. Your report should show each original value entered and the percentage that value contributes to the total. You may prompt the user for the number of values to be inputted. Be sure your design is aesthetically pleasing with the percentage rounded to one position and all values number aligned.

6. Write an application that provides statistics about temperatures for a given week. Your solution should be a two-class application that has a one-dimensional array as a data member. The array stores temperatures for any given week. Provide constructors for instantiating the class and methods to return the highest temperature, lowest temperature, average temperature, and the average temperature excluding the lowest temperature. Provide a method that accepts as an argument a temperature and returns the number of days the temperatures were below that value. Override the `ToString( )` method to return a listing of all the temperatures in three-column format and the temperature range for the given week. Write a second class to test your class.

7. Write a two-class application that has as a data member an array that can store state area codes. The class should have a member method that enables users to test an area code to determine if the number is one of the area codes in the state exchange. The member method should use one of the predefined methods of the `Array class` and return `true` if the argument to the method is one of the state codes. Override the `ToString( )` method to return the full list of area codes with each surrounded by parentheses. To test the class, store a list of state codes in a one-dimensional array. Send that array as an argument to the class constructor. Test the instance methods. Your application should work with both an ordered list of area codes or an unordered list.

8. Write a program that accepts any number of homework scores ranging in value from 0 through 10. Prompt the user for a new score if they enter a value outside of the specified range. Prompt the user for a new value if they enter an alphabetic character. Store the values in an array. Calculate the average excluding the lowest and highest scores. Display the average as well as the highest and lowest scores that were discarded.

9. Write a program that allows any number of values between 0 and 10 to be entered. When the user stops entering values, display a frequency distribution bar chart. Use asterisks to show the number of times each value was entered. If a given number is not entered, no asterisks should appear on that line. Your application should display error messages if a value outside the acceptable range is entered or if a non-numeric character is entered.

10. Write a program that will produce a report showing the current and maximum enrollments for a number of classes. Your applications should be designed with two classes. The first class should include data members for the name of the course, current enrollment, and maximum enrollment. Include an instance method that returns the number of students that can still enroll in the course. The `ToString( )` method should return the name of the course, current enrollment, and the number of open slots. In the implementation class, declare parallel arrays and do a compile-time initialization for the name of the course, current enrollment, and maximum enrollment. Also declare an array of class objects in your implementation class. Test your application with the following data:

Class name	Current enrollment	Maximum enrollment
CS150	180	200
CS250	21	30
CS270	9	20
CS300	4	20
CS350	20	20

© zeljkodan/Shutterstock.com

ADVANCED COLLECTIONS

IN THIS CHAPTER, YOU WILL:

- Create two-dimensional arrays including rectangular and jagged types
- Use multidimensional arrays
- Use the ArrayList class to create dynamic lists
- Learn about the predefined methods of the string class
- Be introduced to the other collection classes
- Work through a programming example that illustrates the chapter's concepts

In Chapter 7, you were introduced to one-dimensional arrays. These are the basic data structures used for many types of applications. In this chapter, you discover how to work with other types of collections of data. In Chapter 7, you created parallel arrays that can hold multiple data values. In this chapter, you will be introduced to members of the `ArrayList class` for creating collections that can grow and shrink. You learn about special properties and methods of this `class`. You also do additional programming using strings and learn about some of the predefined `string` methods available with the .NET Framework class library for accessing and modifying collections of character data items.

Two-Dimensional Arrays

Two-dimensional and other multidimensional arrays follow the same guidelines you learned about with one-dimensional arrays. One-dimensional arrays are useful for storing lists of data. Because the data is stored in contiguous memory locations, elements are referenced by an index representing the location relative to the beginning element of the array. Two-dimensional arrays, the most common multidimensional arrays, are used to store information that we normally represent in table form. Two kinds of two-dimensional arrays can be created using C#. Rectangular is the first type, and this type is supported by most languages. The second type is called a jagged or ragged array. Two-dimensional arrays are referenced much like you reference a matrix or table.

Rectangular Array

A **rectangular two-dimensional array** is usually visualized as a table divided into rows and columns. Much like a spreadsheet in which the rows and columns intersect, data is stored in individual cells. Figure 8-1 shows a table you might create to store calories consumed for a seven-day period. The table contains three columns and seven rows. Each cell holds one integer value.

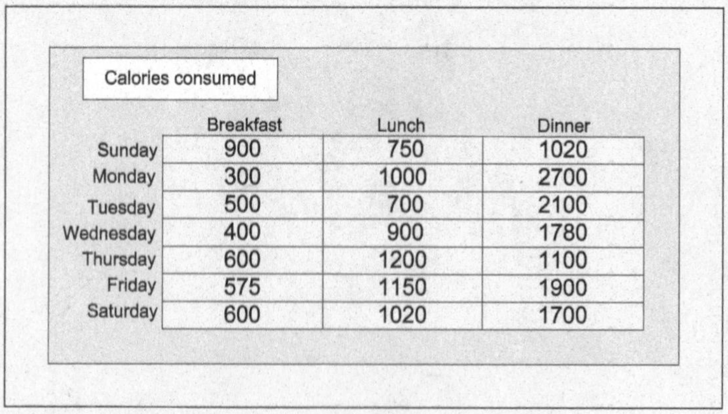

Calories consumed

	Breakfast	Lunch	Dinner
Sunday	900	750	1020
Monday	300	1000	2700
Tuesday	500	700	2100
Wednesday	400	900	1780
Thursday	600	1200	1100
Friday	575	1150	1900
Saturday	600	1020	1700

© Cengage Learning

FIGURE 8-1 Two-dimensional structure

A structure can be created in memory to hold these values using a two-dimensional array. The format for creating such a data structure is

```
type [ , ] identifier = new type[integral value, integral value];
```

As was a requirement for a one-dimensional array, all data values placed in a two-dimensional array must be of the same base type. Two integral values are required for a two-dimensional array. These values specify the number of rows and columns for allocating storage to be referenced by the identifier name. To create an array in C# to hold the data from Figure 8-1, you write

```
int [ , ] calories = new int[7, 3];
```

This allocates storage for 21 elements. The first index represents the number of rows; the second represents the number of columns. Notice how a comma is used as a separator between the row and the column for both the declaration base type and again to separate the number of rows and columns.

You receive a syntax error if you try to use the C-style method for two-dimensional array declaration. The following is not permitted in C#:

```
int anArray [ ] [ ];
```

8

Just as with one-dimensional arrays, you can perform compile-time initialization of the elements. C# is a **row major language**, meaning that data is stored in contiguous memory locations by row. All elements from row 0 are placed in memory first followed by all elements from row 1, and so on. Example 8-1 illustrates how you initialize the calories array with the values shown in Figure 8-1.

EXAMPLE 8-1

```
int [ , ] calories = { {900, 750, 1020},
                       {300, 1000, 2700},
                       {500, 700, 2100},
                       {400, 900, 1780},
                       {600, 1200, 1100},
                       {575, 1150, 1900},
                       {600, 1020, 1700} };
```

Notice how each row is grouped using curly braces. A comma is used to separate rows. Without the curly braces, you receive a syntax error indicating you have an "incorrectly structured array initializer." Figure 8-2 further illustrates the result of the preceding statement.

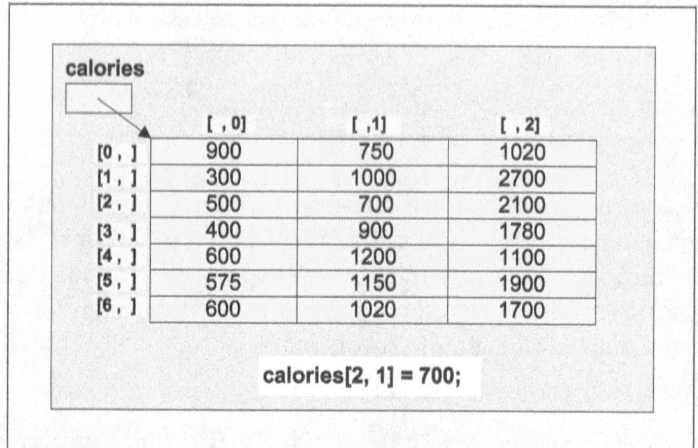

FIGURE 8-2 Two-dimensional calories array

NOTE Data is not really stored in memory in a table such as this. Values are stored side by side in contiguous memory locations using a row major format.

The identifier `calories` contains a reference to `calories[0, 0]`. The `Length` property can be used with multidimensional arrays to get the total number of elements in all dimensions. The following statement displays 21:

```
WriteLine(calories.Length);   // Length returns number of cells
```

Another useful member of the `Array class` is the `GetLength( )` method. It can be called to return the number of rows or columns. Arrays are also zero based for specifying their dimensions. With a two-dimensional array, the first dimension (indexed by 0) represents the number of rows and the second dimension (indexed by 1) represents the number of columns. `GetLength(0)` returns the number of rows and `GetLength(1)` returns the number of columns, as shown in Example 8-2.

EXAMPLE 8-2

```
WriteLine(calories.GetLength(1));   // Displays 3 (columns)
WriteLine(calories.GetLength(0));   // Displays 7 (rows)
WriteLine(calories.Rank);           // Displays 2 (dimensions)
```

NOTE The property `Rank` returns the number of dimensions of the array.

You can also get the upper bounds index using another Array class member. With the array dimensioned as

```
int [ , ] calories = new int[7, 3];
```

the last element (1700) is located at calories[6, 2]. Thus, the upper bound for the row is 6. The upper bound for the column is 2. The lower bound is 0 for both dimensions.

```
WriteLine(calories.GetUpperBound(0));   // Returns 6 (row index)
```

The methods GetUpperBound( ) and GetLowerBound( ) return the upper or lower bounds of the specified dimension. Thus, GetUpperBound(1) returns 2 because the array is dimensioned to have three columns, so the largest index that could be used for the column is 2—the upper bound index for the column.

The foreach loop structure can be used to iterate through a two-dimensional array. Using the same format as noted previously, an identifier of the base type is defined. To display each of the values from the two-dimensional array, a foreach loop could be used as shown in Example 8-3.

8

EXAMPLE 8-3

```
foreach (int cal in calories)
         Write(cal + " ");
```

The output produced from Example 8-3 is in row major format—meaning that every element in row 0 is printed before any element from row 1, as follows:

```
900 750 1020 300 1000 2700 500 700 2100 400 900 1780 600 1200
1100 575 1150 1900 600 1020 1700
```

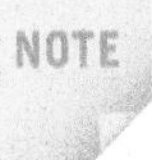

You do not get the whole collection printed if you type Write(calories); instead, the ToString( ) method of the object class is called. ToString( ) is defined in the object class to return an object's type. Thus, you would get System.Int32[ ] printed if you typed Write(calories).

The foreach loop is used for read-only access. To change values, you need a different loop with two indexes. Example 8-4 illustrates how you traverse through the array clearing the contents from each cell.

EXAMPLE 8-4

```
for (int r = 0; r < calories.GetLength(0); r++)
     for (int c = 0; c < calories.GetLength(1); c++)
          calories[r, c] = 0;
```

The nested loop body is executed 21 times. During the last iteration through the loop body, r has a value of six, and c has a value of two.

It is possible to traverse through a two-dimensional array one row at a time or you can process the data by columns. Example 8-5 illustrates adding the values one row at a time. Notice how the nested loop works with this example. The variable r is used to hold the row number; c holds the column number. The outer loop starts r with a value of zero and holds that value constant while performing the innermost loop. The innermost loop starts c with a value of zero and then executes the body for the second loop, which is a single statement (`sum += calories[r, c];`). Still holding r constant at zero, it then increments c to 1 and tests to see if all columns for that row have been processed using the statement `(c < calories.GetLength(1))`. Recall the `GetLength(1)` method returns the number of columns—three for this example.

EXAMPLE 8-5

```
public static double[ ] CalculateAverageByDay(int[ , ] calories)
{
     int sum = 0;
     double[ ] dailyAverage = new double[7];
     for (int r = 0; r < calories.GetLength(0); r++)
     {
          for (int c = 0; c < calories.GetLength(1); c++)
               sum += calories[r, c];
          dailyAverage[r] = (double)sum / calories.GetLength(1);
          sum = 0;
     }
     return dailyAverage;
}
```

The method shown in Example 8-5 returns an array of type double. After all values are added for a given row, the average of those values is stored in the local array named `dailyAverage`. The statement `dailyAverage[r] = (double)sum / calories.GetLength(1);` invokes the `GetLength(1)` method to return the number of columns. This is used as a divisor into sum. An explicit cast is performed on sum so that the result will be a floating-point value. In preparation for the next iteration through the array, sum is reinitialized to zero prior to incrementing r. Notice that the one-dimensional array, dailyAverage is a floating-point data type. This floating-point array is returned at the end of the method.

In order to invoke the above-mentioned method, there must be a one-dimensional array of type double available for the returned array. Example 8-6 illustrates what would be needed in the calling segment.

EXAMPLE 8-6

```
double[ ] dailyAverage = new double[7];
dailyAverage = CalculateAverageByDay(calories);
```

In Example 8-6, CalculateAverageByDay( ) passes the two-dimensional array, calories, in as an argument when it is invoked. Again, notice that there are no square brackets. The call sends the address of the first element of the array. When the method finishes and returns back to Main( ), the address of the first element of the local array, dailyAverage, is sent back through the method call and is then assigned to the local one-dimensional array, dailyAverage, which is defined in the Main( ) method.

C# is a row major language, which means you specify the row index first when you reference elements in the array. In the previous example, the r variable was placed in the outermost loop. It is also possible to process data one column at a time. If you wanted to calculate the average number of calories consumed during all breakfasts, you add all rows for column zero. To calculate the average number of calories during lunch, add all rows for column one. The third physical row, referenced by index 2, holds the calories for dinner. The nested loop shown in Example 8-7 illustrates placing the column variable in the outermost loop.

EXAMPLE 8-7

```
public static double[ ]
     CalculateAverageByMeal(int[ , ] calories)
{
     int sum = 0;
     double[ ] mealAverage = new double[3];
     for (int c = 0; c < calories.GetLength(1); c++)
     {
          for (int r = 0; r < calories.GetLength(0); r++)
               sum += calories[r, c];
          mealAverage[c]=(double)sum / calories.GetLength(0);
          sum = 0;
     }
     return mealAverage;
}
```

Notice in Example 8-7 that when the `calories` array is referenced in the statement `sum += calories[r, c]`, the row is still listed first. As with the previous example, the `CalculateAverageByMeal( )` method returns a one-dimensional array. It is also possible for a method to return a two-dimensional array.

Sometimes, it is more readable to use identifiers for row and column indexes that are more representative of the data. Since the row stores calories for a given day, the identifier `da` is used in Example 8-8, instead of `r` to store the row number. Each column holds the calories for a given meal; thus, the identifier `ml` is used to store the column number. As with the last two examples, Example 8-8 uses a nested loop to add every element in the array. The variable `da` stores the row numbers while `ml` stores the column number.

EXAMPLE 8-8

```
public static void DisplayAverageCaloriesPerMeal(int[ , ] calories)
{
      double sum = 0;
      for (int da = 0; da < calories.GetLength(0); da++)
            for (int ml = 0; ml < calories.GetLength(1); ml++)
                  sum += calories[da, ml];
       WriteLine("\nCaloric Average Per Meal: {0:N0}",
                    (sum / calories.Length));
}
```

In this example, `sum` is divided by the value returned from the `calories.Length` property. The `Length` property was used to return the total number of elements in all dimensions. For Example 8-8, `Length` returns 21.

Example 8-9 displays the entire application. It does a compile-time initialization of the two-dimensional array. The application displays the average number of calories consumed per day, average number consumed per meal type, and the overall average per meal.

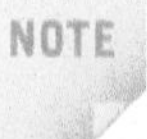

NOTE When you create your solutions in Visual Studio, the code generator adds additional `using` statements. Unnecessary `using` statements were deleted from Example 8-9 and other examples.

EXAMPLE 8-9

```
/* WeeklyCalorieCounter.cs Author: Doyle
 * Demonstrates usage of a two-dimensional array
 * to calculate the average number of calories
 * intake per day, per meal type, and per meal.
 */
using System;
using static System.Console;
```

```
namespace WeeklyCalorieCounter
{
     public class WeeklyCalorieCounter
     {
          public static void Main( )
          {
               int[ , ] calories = { {900, 750, 1020},
                                     {300, 1000, 2700},
                                     {500, 700, 2100},
                                     {400, 900, 1780},
                                     {600, 1200, 1100},
                                     {575, 1150, 1900},
                                     {600, 1020, 1700} };
               double[ ] dailyAverage = new double[7];
               double[ ] mealAverage = new double[3];
               dailyAverage = CalculateAverageByDay(calories);
               mealAverage = CalculateAverageByMeal(calories);
               DisplayDailyAverage(dailyAverage);
               DisplayMealAverage(mealAverage);
               DisplayAverageCaloriesPerMeal(calories);
               ReadKey( );
          }

          public static double[ ] CalculateAverageByDay(int[ , ] calories)
          {
               int sum = 0;
               double[ ] dailyAverage = new double[7];
               for (int r = 0; r < calories.GetLength(0); r++)
               {
                    for (int c = 0; c < calories.GetLength(1); c++)
                         sum += calories[r, c];
                    dailyAverage[r] = (double)sum /
                                             calories.GetLength(1);
                    sum = 0;
               }
               return dailyAverage;
          }

          public static double[ ] CalculateAverageByMeal(int[ , ] calories)
          {
               int sum = 0;
               double[ ] mealAverage = new double[3];
               for (int c = 0; c < calories.GetLength(1); c++)
               {
                    for (int r = 0; r < calories.GetLength(0); r++)
                         sum += calories[r, c];
                    mealAverage[c] = (double)sum /
                                             calories.GetLength(0);
                    sum = 0;
               }
```

8

```
            return mealAverage;
        }

        public static void DisplayDailyAverage(double[ ] dailyAverage)
        {
            int dayNumber = 1;
            WriteLine("Calorie Counter");
            WriteLine("Daily Averages");
            foreach (double avgCalorie in dailyAverage)
            {
                WriteLine("Day {0}: {1,6:N0}", dayNumber,
                        avgCalorie);
                dayNumber++;
            }
        }

        public static void
            DisplayMealAverage(double[ ] mealAverage)
        {
            string[ ] mealTime = {"Breakfast", "Lunch",
                                  "Dinner"};

            WriteLine("\n\nCalorie Counter");
            WriteLine("Meal Averages");
            for (int c = 0; c < mealAverage.Length; c++)
            {
                WriteLine("{0,-10}: {1,6}", mealTime[c],
                        mealAverage[c].ToString("N0"));
            }
        }

        public static void
            DisplayAverageCaloriesPerMeal(int[ , ] calories)
        {
            double sum = 0;
            for (int da = 0; da < calories.GetLength(0); da++)
                for (int ml = 0; ml < calories.GetLength(1);
                                ml++)
                    sum += calories[da, ml];
            WriteLine("\nCaloric Average Per Meal: " +
                    "{0:N0}", sum / calories.Length);
        }
    }
}
```

Example 8-9 includes three separate Display methods. The `DisplayDailyAverage( )` method illustrates using the `foreach` loop. Since no index is included with this loop structure, a separate variable, `dayNumber` was defined and incremented inside the loop body in order to print the day number. The output produced from this example is shown in Figure 8-3.

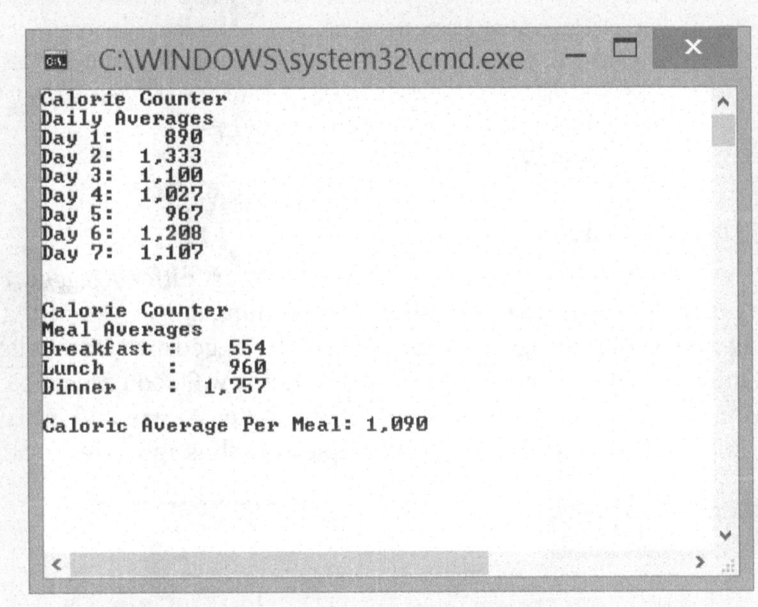

FIGURE 8-3 Output from WeeklyCalorieCounter

As you review Figure 8-3, notice that the numbers are aligned properly. Review the format specifier shown in Example 8-10.

EXAMPLE 8-10

```
WriteLine("{0,-10}: {1,6}", mealTime[c],
          mealAverage[c].ToString("N0"));
```

A comma separates the placeholder index from the width specifier. The `0` references the first argument, `mealTime[c]`. The second argument, the number `10`, specifies the size or the number of positions to use to display the value stored in mealTime[c]. The negative value in front of the 10 indicates that the value stored in `mealTime[c]` should be left justified. Right justification is the default. The one-dimensional array `mealTime` stores the type of meal (i.e., `Breakfast`, `Lunch`, `Dinner`). A colon follows the meal type and then the actual value is displayed in a width of `6` (`{1,6}`) character positions. Since the value `6` is positive, the numbers are right justified and aligned properly.

In Example 8-10, the `ToString()` method is called to convert the double value stored in `mealAverage[c]` into a `string` value. The format specifier `N` is used to convert it into a number with a comma separator. The zero following the `N` indicates that there should be no digits to the right of the decimal.

C# initializes array elements to the `null` value when you create them with the `new` keyword. One way to test to see if a value has been stored is to test for `null`. The following returns `true` when no values have been referenced by the array.

```
string [ ] name = new string[10];
if (name[0] == null)
```

Jagged Array

When the number of columns in the rows must differ, a jagged, or **ragged array**, can be created. **Jagged arrays** differ from rectangular arrays in that rectangular arrays always have a rectangular shape, like a table. Jagged arrays are called "**arrays of arrays**." One row might have five columns; another row 50 columns. To create a jagged array, you can create a one-dimensional array of type `Array` and initialize each of the one-dimensional arrays separately. Example 8-11 illustrates the creation of a jagged array.

EXAMPLE 8-11

```
int[ ] [ ] anArray = new int[4] [ ];
anArray[0] = new int[ ] {100, 200};
anArray[1] = new int[ ] {11, 22, 37};
anArray[2] = new int[ ] {16, 72, 83, 99, 106, 42, 87};
anArray[3] = new int[ ] {1, 2, 3, 4};
```

The `GetLength( )`, `GetUpperBound( )`, and `GetLowerBound( )` methods can be used with jagged arrays. Jagged arrays are used exactly like rectangular arrays, except that rows may have a different number of elements. `anArray.GetLength(0)` returns 4 while `anArray[0].GetLength(0)` returns 2. In order to retrieve the number of columns for a given row, you must specify which row you are referencing with jagged arrays. Similarly `anArray.GetUpperBound(0)` returns 3, the largest valid index that can be used for the row. In order to retrieve the upper bound for a given column, you have to indicate which row you are referencing. `anArray[2].GetUpperBound(0)` returns 6. Notice this is the largest valid column index, since there are seven elements.

Multidimensional Arrays

You are really only limited by your imagination as far as the number of dimensions for which you can allocate arrays in C#. The major requirement is the fact that all data values placed in an array must be of the same base type. A two-dimensional array is actually a multidimensional array; however, it is such a common type of structure that it often is put in its own category.

To declare a three-dimensional array, three integral values are used. They specify the number of planes, rows, and columns to set aside for the array. As with single-dimensional arrays, three-dimensional arrays are referenced by the identifier name.

The format for creating a three-dimensional array is

```
type [ , , ] identifier = new
                        type [integral value, integral value,
                        integral value];
```

What if you wanted to create the calories table to hold four weeks of statistics? A three-dimensional array could be defined to hold the data. The first dimension could represent the number of weeks, the second the number of days, and the third the number of meals. To create the array in C# to hold that extra data, you write

```
int [ , , ] calories = new int [4, 7, 3];
```

Figure 8-4 shows what the array would look like.

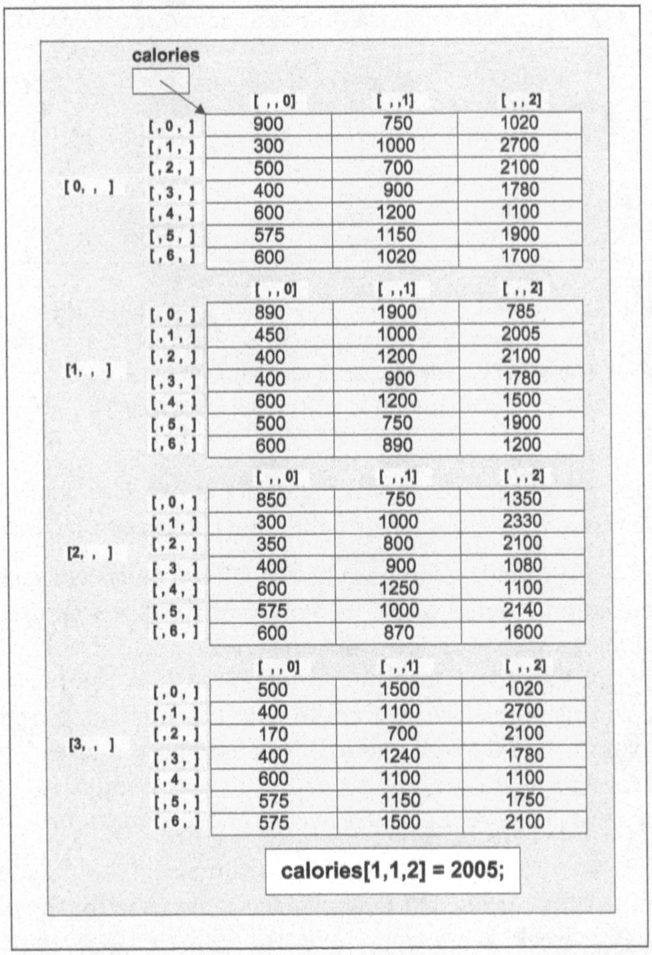

calories

[0, ,]		[, ,0]	[, ,1]	[, ,2]
	[,0,]	900	750	1020
	[,1,]	300	1000	2700
	[,2,]	500	700	2100
	[,3,]	400	900	1780
	[,4,]	600	1200	1100
	[,5,]	575	1150	1900
	[,6,]	600	1020	1700

[1, ,]		[, ,0]	[, ,1]	[, ,2]
	[,0,]	890	1900	785
	[,1,]	450	1000	2005
	[,2,]	400	1200	2100
	[,3,]	400	900	1780
	[,4,]	600	1200	1500
	[,5,]	500	750	1900
	[,6,]	600	890	1200

[2, ,]		[, ,0]	[, ,1]	[, ,2]
	[,0,]	850	750	1350
	[,1,]	300	1000	2330
	[,2,]	350	800	2100
	[,3,]	400	900	1080
	[,4,]	600	1250	1100
	[,5,]	575	1000	2140
	[,6,]	600	870	1600

[3, ,]		[, ,0]	[, ,1]	[, ,2]
	[,0,]	500	1500	1020
	[,1,]	400	1100	2700
	[,2,]	170	700	2100
	[,3,]	400	1240	1780
	[,4,]	600	1100	1100
	[,5,]	575	1150	1750
	[,6,]	575	1500	2100

calories[1,1,2] = 2005;

© Cengage Learning

FIGURE 8-4 Three-dimensional array

This allocates storage for 84 elements (4 * 7 * 3). You will notice that the upper bounds on the indexes are 3, 6, and 2; the lower bound is 0 for all three.

An additional column could be added to the array to hold the total calories for each day by dimensioning the array as shown in Example 8-12. The code in Example 8-12 adds the first three columns and places the sum in the new fourth column.

EXAMPLE 8-12

```
int [ , , ] calories = new int [4, 7, 4];

// Loop to place the row total in the last column, indexed by 3
for (int wk = 0; wk < calories.GetLength(0); wk++)
{
        for (int da = 0; da < calories.GetLength(1); da++)
        {
                for (int ml = 0; ml < calories.GetLength(2) - 1; ml++)
                {
                        calories[wk, da, 3] += calories[wk, da, ml];
                }
        }
}
```

Reexamine the first line in Example 8-12 and note that the dimension representing the number of columns, the last integer, was changed from 3 to 4. This enables the total calories for each row to be stored in the last column.

The last cell for each row holds the total per day. Now each row has the calorie count for breakfast, lunch, dinner, and the total calorie count for the day.

The nested loop adds columns indexed with 0 through 2 of each row and stores the result in the column indexed by 3. The conditional expression used to terminate the innermost loop uses (`calories.GetLength(2) - 1`) for the evaluation. `GetLength(2)` returns the length of the third dimension. This returns 4 because there are now four columns in the row. But notice that 1 is subtracted from that value, because the last column should not be added. It is holding the total. Therefore, the loop is executed for `ml` = 0, `ml` = 1, and `ml` = 2. When `ml` is equal to 3, `ml` is no longer less than 3 (`ml < calories.GetLength(2) - 1`), and the inner loop is complete for that iteration.

`calories.GetLength(0)` returns the dimension for the number of planes or weeks. It returns 4. `GetLength(1)` returns the dimension for the number of rows per plane or days per week. It returns 7. As was noted, `GetLength(2)` returns the dimension for the number of columns per row or meals per day. It returns 4. The program listing for the calorie counter application is included as Example 8-13.

EXAMPLE 8-13

```
/* CalorieCounter.cs Author: Doyle
 * Demonstrates multidimensional array
 * through a calorie counter program.
 * Initializes array with values.
 * Accumulates calories per day and
 * displays report by day.
 */
using System;
using static System.Console;

namespace CalorieCounter
{
      class CalorieCounter
      {
            static void Main( )
            {
                int [ , ,] calories = { {  {900, 750, 1020, 0},
                                           {300, 1000, 2700, 0},
                                           {500, 700, 2100, 0},
                                           {400, 900, 1780, 0},
                                           {600, 1200, 1100, 0},
                                           {575, 1150, 1900, 0},
                                           {600, 1020, 1700, 0} },
                                        {  {890, 1900, 785, 0},
                                           {450, 1000, 2005, 0},
                                           {400, 1200, 2100, 0},
                                           {400, 900, 1780, 0},
                                           {600, 1200, 1500, 0},
                                           {500, 750, 1900, 0},
                                           {600, 890, 1200, 0} },
                                        {  {850, 750, 1350, 0},
                                           {300, 1000, 2330, 0},
                                           {350, 800, 2100, 0},
                                           {400, 900, 1080, 0},
                                           {600, 1250, 1100, 0},
                                           {575, 1000, 2140, 0},
                                           {600, 870, 1600, 0} },
                                        {  {500, 1500, 1020, 0},
                                           {400, 1100, 2700, 0},
                                           {170, 700, 2100, 0},
                                           {400, 1240, 1780, 0},
                                           {600, 1100, 1100, 0},
                                           {575, 1150, 1750, 0},
                                           {575, 1500, 2100, 0} } };
```

8

```
            AccumulateCalories(calories);
            DisplayTotals(calories);
            ReadKey( );
        }

        public static void AccumulateCalories(int [ , , ] calories)
        {
            for (int wk = 0; wk < calories.GetLength(0); wk++)
                for (int da = 0; da < calories.GetLength(1); da++)
                    for (int ml = 0; ml <
                            calories.GetLength(2) - 1; ml++)
                        calories[wk, da, 3] +=
                            calories[wk, da, ml];
        }

        public static void DisplayTotals(int [ , ,] calories)
        {
            string [ ] dayName = {"Sun", "Mon", "Tue",
                                  "Wed", "Thr", "Fri", "Sat"};
            WriteLine("Week#\tDay\tTotal Calories");
            for (int wk = 0; wk < calories.GetLength(0); wk++)
                for (int da = 0; da < calories.GetLength(1);
                        da++)
                    WriteLine(" {0}\t{1}\t {2:N0}",
                            wk + 1, dayName[da],
                            calories[wk, da, 3]);
        }
    }
}
```

The display from this listing includes the name of the day instead of the day number. A selection statement could have been used to test the day number and print the value. A much more efficient solution is to use the index from the calories array for the day number as the index to another one-dimensional `string` array holding the day names. This is illustrated in Example 8-13. Figure 8-5 shows the output.

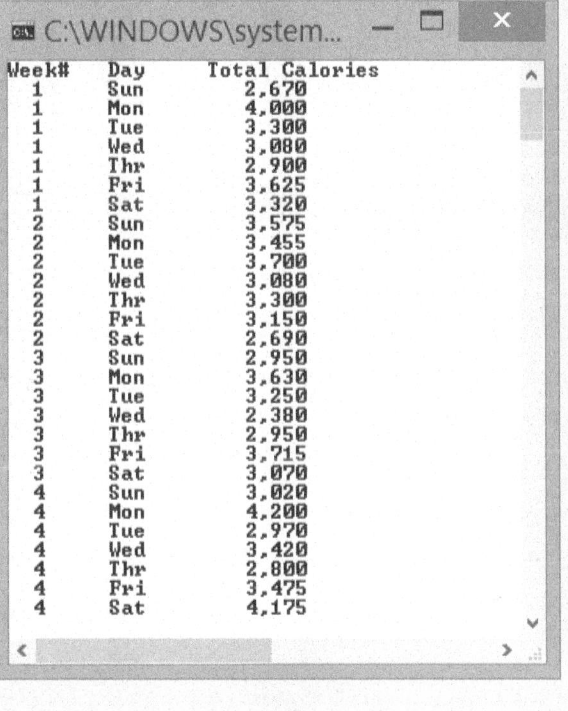

FIGURE 8-5 Sample run from the CalorieCounter application

This section began by stating that you are only limited by your imagination in terms of the number of dimensions you can include in a C# application. Of course, at some point, space becomes an issue. You can now envision creating a `calories` structure for each month, and you might be interested in comparing calorie intake by month. This could be a fourth dimension in your array. The same rules of creation, access, and use with methods that apply to a two-dimensional array apply to fourth- and fifth-dimensional arrays.

ArrayList Class

One of the limitations of the traditional array is the fact that you cannot change the size or length of an array after it is created. To give you more flexibility, .NET includes another `class`, the **ArrayList** `class`, which facilitates creating a listlike structure that can dynamically increase or decrease in length. Like traditional arrays, indexes of `ArrayList` objects are zero based. The `class` includes a large number of predefined methods; Table 8-1 lists some of them. Explore the C# documentation to learn about the parameters of these methods and about the other methods and properties of the `ArrayList` `class`.

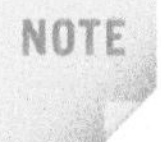

In order to instantiate objects of the `ArrayList class`, add an additional `using` statement.

```
using System.Collections;
```

TABLE 8-1 ArrayList members

Methods or properties	Description
`Add( )`	Adds a value onto the end
`BinarySearch( )`	Overloaded; uses a binary search algorithm to locate a value
`Capacity`	Property; gets or sets the number of elements that the `ArrayList` can contain
`Clear( )`	Removes all elements
`Clone( )`	Creates a copy
`Contains( )`	Determines whether an element is in the `ArrayList`
`Count`	Property; gets or sets the number of elements that the `ArrayList` actually contains
`GetRange( )`	Returns an `ArrayList` that is a subset of another `ArrayList`
`IndexOf( )`	Overloaded; returns the index of the first occurrence of a value
`Insert( )`	Inserts an element at a specified index
`InsertRange( )`	Inserts the elements of an `ArrayList` into another `ArrayList` at the specified index
`Item`	Property; gets or sets the element at the specified index
`LastIndexOf( )`	Overloaded; returns the index of the last occurrence of a value
`Remove( )`	Removes the first occurrence of a specified object
`RemoveAt( )`	Removes the element at the specified index
`RemoveRange( )`	Removes a range of elements
`Repeat( )`	Returns an `ArrayList` whose elements are copies of the specified value
`Reverse( )`	Overloaded; reverses the order of the elements
`Sort( )`	Overloaded; sorts the elements or a portion of them
`ToArray( )`	Overloaded; copies the elements to a new array
`TrimToSize( )`	Sets the capacity to the actual number of elements

© Cengage Learning

NOTE

The ArrayList class is similar to the Vector class found in other languages in that you push and pop elements on and off using the Add( ) and Remove( ) methods.

Example 8-14 includes a program that creates an object of the ArrayList class. String values were added as elements. Any predefined or user-defined type can be used as an ArrayList object.

C# also includes a List<> class. This is a generic class that is very similar to the ArrayList class. The List<> class is also a dynamic structure in that it can grow and shrink in size. The primary difference between the two classes is the List<> class requires that objects are the same type when you place them in the structure. The ArrayList allows you to mix types. The List<> offers the advantage of not having to unbox or cast when you retrieve the values from the structure. For data value types like int, bool, and double, the List<> generic class offers faster access than the ArrayList class. You learn more about generic collection classes in Chapter 11.

NOTE

For this application, three using statements are required. They are the ones shown in Example 8-14.

```
using System;
using static System.Console;
using System.Collections;
```

Recall you need Visual Studio 2015 or later in order to add a reference to a class that exposes static methods like Console. Doing so enables you to then reference its static methods like WriteLine( ) without fully qualifying with the class identifier and a dot.

8

EXAMPLE 8-14

```
/* ArrayListExample.cs Author: Doyle
 * Instantiates the ArrayList class.
 * Adds and removes values. Demonstrates
 * displaying items using an index.
 */
using System;
using static System.Console;
using System.Collections;

namespace ArrayListExample
{
    class ArrayListExample
    {
```

```
        static void Main( )
        {
            ArrayList anArray = new ArrayList( );

            anArray.Add("Today is the first day of the " +
                        "rest of your life!");
            anArray.Add(2);
            anArray.Add("Live it to the fullest!");
            anArray.Add(34.89);
            anArray.Add("ok");
            anArray.Add("You may not get a second chance.");

            WriteLine("Count of elements in array: {0}",
                      anArray.Count);
            anArray.RemoveAt(4);
            WriteLine("New Count (after removing ok): {0}",
                      anArray.Count);
            WriteLine( );
            DisplayContents(anArray);
            ReadKey( );
        }

        public static void DisplayContents(ArrayList ar)
        {
            for(int i = 0; i < ar.Count; i++)
            {
                WriteLine(ar[i]);
                //Arithmetic can be performed with numeric elements
                if (i == 1)
                   WriteLine((int)ar[i] *  100);
            }
            WriteLine( );
        }
}
```

The example demonstrates how items are added and removed from the structure. Notice that data of different types can be stored in an `ArrayList`, one of the advantages of using this type of structure. Also note that arithmetic can be performed on elements that are numeric without boxing/unboxing or casting as is illustrated in the `DisplayContents( )` method with the `if` statement. Since `2` is stored in the `ArrayList` at index position 1, multiplication is performed. This means you must take extra care dealing with elements in an `ArrayList` to make sure you have the correct data type since no type checking occurs when the items are placed in the `ArrayList`. The output from one sample run is shown in Figure 8-6.

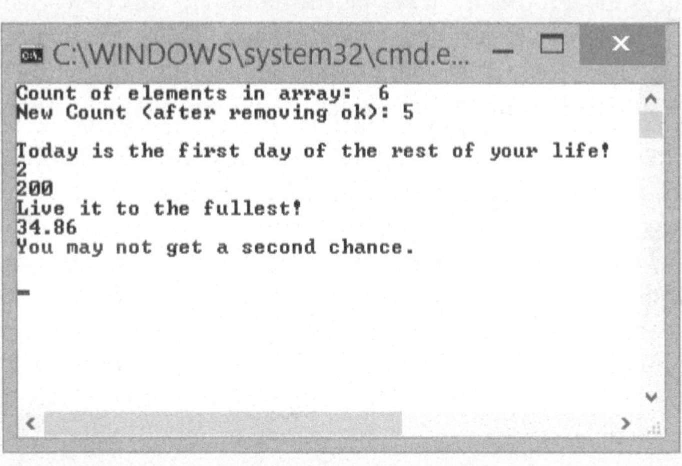

FIGURE 8-6 Sample run from the ArrayList example

By now, you should be fully aware that you must include parentheses ( ) with methods. No parentheses are used with property members in C#.

String Class

You have been using the `string` data type since the beginning of this book. The `string` data type is included in this chapter because strings are used to store a collection of Unicode characters.

Unicode assigns a unique numeric value for characters. It is the universal character encoding scheme used by the .NET languages. Unicode makes it easier to develop applications that can be used around the world because it includes most international characters.

You can instantiate an `object` using `string` or `String`. This works because `string` is an alias for the `System.String` `class` in the .NET Framework. The keyword in C#, which turns blue in Visual Studio, is `string`. It is used throughout the book to represent the type.

You have already learned that the `string` is a reference type. Normally with reference types, equality operators, `==` and `!=`, compare the object's references, instead of their values. However, the equality operators function differently with `string` than with other reference objects. The equality operators are defined to compare the contents or values referenced by the `string` type instead of comparing their addresses. The equality operator is defined to do a lexicographical comparison, which means that it compares each character, one character at a time using its unicode representation.

This is much the same way that the dictionary stores words. The relational operators (>, <, >=, <=) are not defined for strings. There are several methods, including the `Compare( )`, which is illustrated in Table 8-2, which are closely aligned to > and < operations. For the comparison, the Unicode character representation is used.

Unlike some languages that require you to store collections of characters as `char` arrays, the C# `string` type allows individual characters to be accessed using an index with `[ ]`, but you can also process variables of `string` type as a group of characters. As with array objects, when you access an individual element in a `string`, the first character is indexed by zero. However, you have the best of both worlds with strings in C#. You can access the individual characters using an index, but `string` variables are objects of the `string class`. Thus, in addition to `[ ]` and the + used for concatenation, you have many predefined methods and properties that make `string` objects functional and flexible.

Objects of the `string class` store an immutable series of characters. They are considered **immutable** because once you give a `string` a value; it cannot be modified. Methods that seem to be modifying a `string` are actually returning a new `string` containing the modification, so you end up with two different strings. .NET includes another `class`, `StringBuilder`, which represents a mutable string of characters. Objects of this `class` can have data appended onto the same object. The `StringBuilder class` offers many of the same members as the `string class` does. For applications that concatenate or add characters to the string, you will want to consider instantiating objects of the `StringBuilder class`.

String Methods

The `string class` has a lot of built in functionality. Table 8-2 gives some of the members of the `string class`, using the declarations shown in Example 8-15.

EXAMPLE 8-15

```
string sValue = "C# Programming";
object sObj;
string s = "C#";
```

The third column in Table 8-2 illustrates the result produced using some of the methods and properties of the `string class`. The declarations for `sValue`, `sObj`, and `s` from Example 8-15 were used.

TABLE 8-2 Some Members of the string class

Methods and properties	Description	Example

`Clone( )`	Returns a reference to this instance of `string`.	`sObj = sValue.Clone( );`
		`WriteLine(sObj);`
		`//Displays`
		`C# Programming`

`Compare( )`	Overloaded. Class method. Compares two strings.	`if (string.Compare(sValue, s) > 0)`
		`   WriteLine("sValue is lexico" +`
		`         "graphically greater.");`
		`//Displays`
		`sValue is lexicographically greater.`

`Concat( )`	Overloaded. Class method. Concatenates one or more string(s).	`string ns = string.Concat(sValue, s);`
		`WriteLine(ns);`
		`//Displays`
		`C# ProgrammingC#`

`Copy( )`	Class method. Creates a new copy of a `string` with the same values as the source `string`.	`s = string.Copy(sValue);`
		`WriteLine(s);`
		`//Displays`
		`C# Programming`

`EndsWith( )`	Determines whether the end of this instance matches the specified `string`.	`bool result = sValue.EndsWith("#");`
		`WriteLine(result);`
		`//Displays`
		`False`

`Equals( )`	Overloaded. Determines whether two strings have the same value.	`bool result = sValue.Equals(s);`
		`WriteLine(result);`
		`//Displays`
		`False`

`Format( )`	Overloaded. Class method. Replaces each format specification in a `string` with the textual equivalent of the corresponding object's value.	`double nu = 123.45678;`
		`string nn =`
		`      string.Format`
		`      ("{0, 10:F2}", nu);`
		`WriteLine(nn);`
		`//Displays`
		`123.46`

(continues)

8

TABLE 8-2 Some Members of the string class (*continued*)

Methods and properties	Description	Example

`IndexOf( )`	Overloaded. Returns the index of the first occurrence of a `string`, or one or more characters, within this instance.	`WriteLine(sValue.IndexOf("#"));`
		`//Displays`
		`1`

`Insert( )`	Inserts a specified instance of a `string` at a specified index position.	`s = sValue.Insert(3, ".NET ");`
		`WriteLine(s);`
		`//Displays`
		`C# .NET Programming`

`LastIndexOf( )`	Overloaded. Returns the index of the last occurrence of a specified character or `string`.	`WriteLine(sValue.LastIndexOf("P"));`
		`//Displays`
		`3`

`Length - Property`	Gets the number of characters.	`WriteLine(sValue.Length);`
		`//Displays`
		`14`

`PadLeft( )`	Overloaded. Right-aligns the characters in the `string`, padding on the left with spaces or a specified character.	`s = sValue.PadLeft(20, '#');`
		`WriteLine(s);`
		`//Displays`
		`######C# Programming`
		`WriteLine("".PadLeft(10, '-'));`
		`//Displays`
		`----------`

`PadRight( )`	Overloaded. Left-aligns the characters in the `string`, padding on the right with spaces or a specified character.	`s = sValue.PadRight(20, '#');`
		`WriteLine(s);`
		`//Displays`
		`C# Programming######`

(*continues*)

TABLE 8-2 Some Members of the string class (*continued*)

Methods and properties	Description	Example

`Remove( )`	Deletes a specified number of characters beginning at a specified position.	`s = sValue.Remove(3, 8);`
		`WriteLine(s);`
		`//Displays`
		`C# ing`

`Replace( )`	Overloaded. Replaces all occurrences of a character or `string` with another character or `string`.	`s = sValue.Replace("gram", "GRAM");`
		`WriteLine(s);`
		`//Displays`
		`C# ProGRAMming`

`Split( )`	Overloaded. Identifies the substrings in the `string` that are delimited by one or more characters specified in an array, then places the substrings into a `string` array.	`string [ ] sn = sValue.Split(' ');`
		`foreach (string i in sn)`
		`      WriteLine(i);`
		`//Displays`
		`C#`
		`Programming`

`StartsWith( )`	Determines whether the beginning of the `string` matches the specified `string`.	`WriteLine`
		`      (sValue.StartsWith("C#"));`
		`//Displays`
		`True`

`Substring( )`	Overloaded. Retrieves a substring from the `string`.	`WriteLine(sValue.Substring(3, 7));`
		`//Displays`
		`Program`

`ToCharArray( )`	Copies the characters in the `string` to a character array.	`char[ ] cArray =`
		`      sValue.ToCharArray(0, 2);`
		`WriteLine(cArray);`
		`//Displays`
		`C#`

`ToLower( )`	Overloaded. Returns a copy of the `string` in lowercase.	`WriteLine(sValue.ToLower( ));`
		`//Displays`
		`c# programming`

(*continues*)

8

TABLE 8-2 Some Members of the string class (*continued*)

Methods and properties	Description	Example

`ToString( )`	Overloaded. Converts the value of the instance into a `string`.	`int x = 234;`
		`s = x.ToString( );`
		`WriteLine(s);`
		`//Displays`
		`234`

`ToUpper( )`	Overloaded. Returns a copy of the `string` in uppercase.	`WriteLine(sValue.ToUpper( ));`
		`//Displays`
		`C# PROGRAMMING`

`Trim( )`
`TrimEnd( )`
`TrimStart( )`
	Overloaded. Removes all occurrences of a set of specified characters from the beginning and end.	`s = sValue.Trim('g','i','n','m','C');`
		`WriteLine(s);`
		`//Displays`
		`# Progra`

© Cengage Learning

Notice that the methods identified as `class` methods in the second column, such as `Compare( )`, `Concat( )`, and `Copy ( )`, prefix the name of the method in the call with the `string` data type (e.g., s = `string`.Copy(sValue);). Instance methods, like `Clone( )`, `EndsWith( )`, and `Equals( )` are invoked using the `string` identifier, and dot before the name of the method.

Most `string` member arguments that take a `string object` accept a `string` literal. C# has two types of `string` literals. You have used one of them, the quoted literal. Quoted `string` literals appear between double quotation marks (`" "`) and are the most common type found in languages. The other type, @-quoted `string` literals, starts with the at symbol (@) and is also enclosed in double quotation marks. The @-quoted `string` literals are referred to as the **verbatim string literal** because the characters between the double quotes are interpreted verbatim. There are two differences between the quoted and @-quoted string literal. With the @-quoted literal, escape sequence characters, such as `'\t'` and `'\n'`, are not recognized as special characters. The second difference is that the @-quoted literal enables you to use a keyword for an identifier.

String Interpolation

One of the new C# 6.0 features is **string interpolation**. This new feature enables you to put variables directly in a string literal as opposed to using number placeholders to indicate where the string should be inserted. As shown in Example 8-16, precede the string literal with a dollar symbol ($) to indicate string interpolation should occur.

EXAMPLE 8-16

```
string ReturnInterperpolatedString( )
{
        string first = "Joann";
        string first = "Smith";
        double amt = 23.45675;

        return $"{first} {last}\nAmt: {amt : F2}";
}
```

Previously you would have written,

```
return string.Format("{0} {1}\nAmt: {2 :F2}", first, last, amt);
```

As shown above, you would have had to use numeric placeholders to show where the values should be inserted. You also previously needed to invoke the `string.Format()` method to get `amt` formatted. Notice `amt` is formatted as fixed with two positions to the right of the decimal. The value returned from the snippet of code shown in Example 8-16 and the line of code below the example both return 8

Joann Smith

Amt: 23.46

Clearly the new way, shown in Example 8-16, is much more readable. By placing the `$` before the `string` literal, it does string interpolation.

NOTE

Use the verbatim `string` literal, also referred to as the @-quoted literal, when you need to include special characters such as the backslash character. The statement here displays the '\t' as part of the output:

```
WriteLine(@"hello \t world");
//Displays
hello \t world
```

Without the @-quoted literal, a tab is inserted:

```
WriteLine("hello \t world");
//Displays
hello     world
```

Tables 8-1 and 8-2 included a number of extremely useful methods and properties of the `ArrayList` and `String` classes. Other members exist. Do not reinvent the wheel and write code for functions that already exist. These members have been tried and tested. The key to using the members is to experiment and play with them. The C# online documentation with Visual Studio includes many examples that you will want to explore.

Other Collection Classes

Collection classes are classes that enable you to store and retrieve various groups of objects. As you just experienced with arrays, when you have data that is closely related, it is more efficient to group the data together under a common name. This enables you to write code to process all elements in the collection instead of writing code to handle each individual object. There are a number of other collection classes, in addition to ones already introduced, that can be used in C#. You saw that an `ArrayList` offered the advantage of being able to dynamically increase in size as new objects were added. The .NET framework also includes classes for storing bit values. There are predefined classes for creating stacks, queues, and hash tables. As with the `ArrayList class`, in order to instantiate objects of these other collection classes, you need to include a `using System.Collections;` to the list of namespaces. In the section that follows, some of these collection classes are explored.

BitArray

The **BitArray** `class` stores a collection of bit values. These bit values are represented as Booleans, where `true` indicates that the bit is on and `false` indicates that the bit is off. There are several ways to create and initialize BitArrays. Example 8-17 illustrates some of the ways.

EXAMPLE 8-17

```
// Creates and initializes several BitArrays
BitArray firstBitArr = new BitArray(10);
BitArray secondBitArr = new BitArray(10, true);
bool[ ] boolArray = new bool[5] {true, false, true, true, false};
BitArray thirdBitArr = new BitArray(boolArray);
```

There are a number of constructors available with this collection. As shown in the first line in Example 8-17, you can send an integer representing the number of elements. These elements are initially all set to `false`. The second object in Example 8-17 has all values set to `true` when the `secondBitArr` is created. Another constructor option is to use an array of Booleans to set the values. The `thirdBitArr` has a mixture of `true` and `false` values. This is also illustrated in Example 8-17. The `BitArray class` has both `Count` and `Length` properties. Both retrieve the number of elements in the array. `Length` can also be used to set the number of elements thus enabling BitArrays to grow or shrink in size dynamically. An `Item` property is available for setting the actual value. `BitArray` has member methods of `Set( )` and `SetAll( )`, which can be used to change the value of elements. Example 8-18 illustrates accessing elements from the array.

EXAMPLE 8-18

```
// Sets all the elements to true
firstBitArr.SetAll(true);

// Sets the first element to false
firstBitArr[0] = false;

// Sets the last index to false.
secondBitArr.Set(secondBitArr.Count - 1, false);

// Gets the value of the last element
WriteLine(thirdBitArr.Get(thirdBitArray.Count - 1 ));
```


BitArrays are most commonly used to represent a simple group of Boolean flags and are especially useful for working with large data sets. They compactly store individual bits or Boolean values. As shown in Example 8-18, there are several ways to access the elements in the array. There are a number of bitwise operations including OR, AND, XOR, and NOT that can be performed on elements in the array. Surveys or questionnaires that accept responses such as yes/no or true/false are good candidates for using a `BitArray` collection. Data can be stored as Booleans and then a loop could be used to process the results.

Hashtable

Hashing is a technique used for a lot of applications in computer science. One use of hashing is to provide security when data is transmitted across networks. A message is encrypted following some type of algorithm, sent across a network, and then on the other end the same algorithm is used to decrypt or convert the message back into a readable form. This concept is often used in the field of cryptography (i.e., information security) with passwords. Passwords are hashed after the user enters them and then sent to a server and compared against the stored hash values there. This prevents the password from being intercepted in plain text.

Another application of hashing is used with large collections of data. Here instead of encrypting the full record or a password, the key or unique entry associated with the record is hashed or converted into an index and then the record is stored at that index location. Faster retrieval of individual elements or records is afforded using this principle. Instead of having to sequentially compare one record after another to determine if that is the record you want to process, the computer can now use the same algorithm that was used to store the record and go directly to the indexed location. The algorithm used to store the data is called a hash function. The hash function produces a hash code.

.NET includes a specialized collection `class` called a `Hashtable` that represents a collection of key/value pairs that are organized based on the hash code of the key. The hash code is just a number generated using a key with the objective of providing efficient insertion and find operations. There is no requirement that the data be in any specific order. One of the overriding goals is to design an algorithm that provides as few collisions as possible. Collisions occur when the algorithm that's used to create the hash code maps more than one record to the same index position. A good hash function tries to avoid collisions and tends to spread keys evenly in the array. Devising an effective algorithm is said to be an art and sometimes involves some trial and error before an effective algorithm is designed.

The mod operator (`%`) is often used with hashing algorithms. Often, the key is not in numeric form and requires that a conversion occurs so that arithmetic can be performed. The eventual goal is to map the record to an index location in an array. For example, a hash function algorithm might take the Unicode representation for each character in the string and add each of those values. Once a sum is calculated, then the mod operator might be used. That summation could be divided by the first prime number larger than the number of data elements. The result of the mod operation might be the index where the record is stored.

You do not have to create your own algorithm when you use the .NET `Hashtable` `class`. A hash function is used to return a numeric hash code based on a key. The key, of course, is the value of some property of the object being stored. When an object is added to a `Hashtable`, it is stored in the bucket that is associated with the hash code produced by the class. When a value is being searched for in the `Hashtable`, the hash code is generated for that value, and the bucket associated with that hash code is searched.

With the .NET `Hashtable` `class`, a bucket is a virtual subgroup of elements within the `Hashtable`. This bucket concept is what allows or enables multiple keys to hash to the same index. Each bucket is associated with a hash code, generated using a hash function, and based on the key of the element. A hash function must always return the same hash code for the same key. The bucket makes searching and retrieving easier and faster. Example 8-19 illustrates creating a hash table and adding elements. Notice that each element in the hash table is a key and value pair.

EXAMPLE 8-19

```
// Creates a new hash table
Hashtable executableProgram = new Hashtable( );

// Add some elements to the hash table. There are no
// duplicate keys, but some of the values are duplicates.
executableProgram.Add("pdf", "acrord32.exe");
executableProgram.Add("tif", "snagit32.exe");
executableProgram Add("jpg", "snagit32.exe");
executableProgram.Add("sln", "devenv.exe");
executableProgram.Add("rtf", "wordpad.exe");
```

The `Add( )` method takes two arguments. The first is the key and the second is the value. In the example above, file types of `pdf`, `tif`, `sln`, and `rtf` are added as keys. Here, the program `acrord32.exe` is used as the executable program for pdf files.

If you want to write your own hash algorithm, you can use the `Hashtable` `class` and just `override` the `GetHashCode( )` method to provide a new algorithm for the hash function. The method `GetHashCode( )` returns the hash code generated for the key.

If you `override` the `GetHashCode( )` method, you must also `override` the `Equals( )` method to guarantee that two objects considered equal have the same hash code. Both `Equals( )` and `GetHashCode( )` methods are inherited from the `object class`. You have seen them displayed many times from the intellisense popup.

The example of adding together the Unicode representation for each character in the `string` and then mod'ing (%) that result by a large prime number is just one possible algorithm. It might not work well given the data set, but you can get more creative. You could take this accumulated value, square it, subtract an arbitrary number like 73 from it, and then mod that result by a large prime number. The goal is to create an algorithm that maps each data set to a different bucket.

The `Hashtable` `class` has a number of properties and methods including `Count`, `Item`, `Keys`, and `Values`. `Count` gets the number of key/value pairs contained in the `Hashtable`. `Item` gets or sets the value associated with the specified key. `Keys` retrieves all the keys in the collection, and `Values` retrieves all the values from the key/value collection. In addition to the `Add( )` method, there are also `Clear( )`, `Contains( )`, and `Remove( )` methods. You are encouraged to explore and play with this collection class.

Queue

We have all experienced the functionality of a queue. You may have made a phone call and heard a voice on the other end indicating that you had been placed in a queue with an expected wait time of 10 minutes because six people were ahead of you. The calls are answered in the order that they are received. When you go to pay for an item in a department store, you enter a queue. The first one in line gets serviced before the third person that walked up to the counter. Data can be stored and processed in this fashion. One approach to implementing this abstract data type is through using an array and just incrementing a counter as values are added. When you go to process or manipulate the data, simply start at index zero and retrieve the data. Another option is through creating a linked list of elements.

Linked lists are types of data structures that consist of a sequence of data records such that in each record there is an additional field that contains a reference (i.e., a link) to the next record in the sequence. A benefit that a linked list offers over arrays relates to the order of the data. With a linked list, records do not have to be physically stored beside each other to retain their order. For that reason, linked lists allow insertion and removal of records at any point in the list, with a constant number of operations. Insertion of elements into the middle of an ordered list of items in an array requires moving records with key values larger than the one inserted. This is not the case with a linked list. All that is required is an adjustment of the links to point to the newly inserted element. But linked lists by themselves do not allow random access to the data or any form of efficient indexing.

.NET includes a predefined collection `class` called `Queue` with a number of methods and properties. The **Queue** `class` represents a first-in-first-out (FIFO) collection of objects. Queues are useful for storing objects in the order that they were received for sequential processing. That way the first objects added are the first ones to be processed. In C#, a queue is implemented as a circular array. Objects stored in a queue are inserted at one end and removed from the other.

The capacity of a queue is the number of elements that the queue can hold. As elements are added to a queue, the capacity is automatically increased as required through reallocation. The capacity can be decreased by calling its `TrimToSize()` method. Example 8-20 illustrates instantiating an object of the `Queue` `class` and adding elements to the data structure.

EXAMPLE 8-20

```
// Creates and initializes a Queue
Queue firstInFirstOut = new Queue( );
firstInFirstOut.Enqueue("Jill Won");
firstInFirstOut.Enqueue("Donna Abbott");
firstInFirstOut.Enqueue("Jeremy Door");
```

The Enqueue( ) method adds an object to the end of the queue. Dequeue( ) removes and returns the object at the beginning of the queue. So a call to firstInFirstOut.Dequeue( ) would return "Jill Won." The method Peek( ) returns the object at the beginning of the queue without removing it. There are also Clear( ) and Contains( ) methods as well as a Count property that works similarly to the data structures discussed previously. You are encouraged to explore and play with the Queue collection class.

Stack

Do you recall how you place your food tray in the cafeteria on top of your friend's tray if they are in front of you returning a tray? The person behind you places, or stacks, their tray on top of yours. Then the next person stacks theirs on top of the last one. If you now go to get a tray, you do not take one off the bottom. Instead you take the one off the top of the stack. That would be the last one put there. That is the concept behind stacks. The last one placed there becomes the first one processed or used. As with the queue abstract data type, a stack data type can be implemented using an array or a linked list data structure.

Another option is to use the .NET Stack class. The **Stack** class is similar to the Queue class except that it represents a simple last-in-first-out (LIFO) collection of objects. The capacity of a stack is the number of elements the stack can hold. As elements are added to a stack, the capacity is automatically increased. Example 8-21 illustrates instantiating an object of the Stack class and adding elements to that data structure.

8

EXAMPLE 8-21

```
// Creates and initializes a Stack
Stack lastInFirstOut = new Stack( );
lastInFirstOut.Push("Jill Won");
lastInFirstOut.Push("Donna Abbott");
lastInFirstOut.Push("Jeremy Door");
```

The Push( ) method adds an object on to the top of the stack. Pop( ) removes and returns the top or last object placed on of the stack. So a call to lastInFirstOut.Pop( ) would return "Jeremy Door." The method Peek( ) works exactly like it did with the Queue class in that it returns the object at the top of the stack without removing it. There are also Clear( ) and Contains( ) methods as well as a Count property that works similarly to the data structures discussed previously. Example 8-22 shows the complete program invoking the Push( ) and Pop( ) methods.

EXAMPLE 8-22

```
/* StackExample.cs
 * Creates a stack, pushes elements onto it,
 * pops one off, and then displays the contents.
 */
using System;
using static System.Console;
using System.Collections;

namespace StackExample
{
    public class StackExample
    {
        public static void Main( )
        {
            Stack lastInFirstOut = new Stack( );

            lastInFirstOut.Push("Jill Won");
            lastInFirstOut.Push("Donna Abbott");
            lastInFirstOut.Push("Jeremy Door");
            lastInFirstOut.Push("Olivia Rivers");
            lastInFirstOut.Pop( );
            DisplayInfo(lastInFirstOut);
            ReadKey( );
        }

        public static void DisplayInfo(Stack lastInFirstOut)
        {
            WriteLine("Stack - Last In First Out ");
            WriteLine("\nNumber of Elements: {0}",
                      lastInFirstOut.Count);
            Write("Values:");
            foreach (Object obj in lastInFirstOut)
                     Write("     {0}", obj);
            WriteLine( );
        }
    }
}
```

The output from Example 8-22 is shown in Figure 8-7.

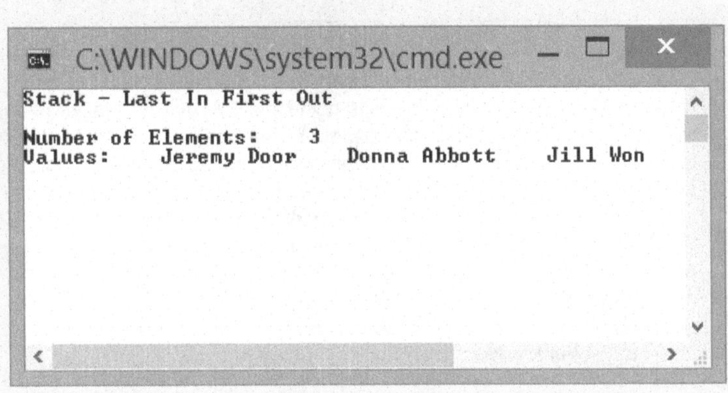

FIGURE 8-7 Output from the StackExample

You might want to explore the `Dictionary` `class`, another example of a `Collection` `class`. `Dictionary` is part of the `System.Collections.Generic` `namespace`, which is imported automatically with later versions of Visual Studio. The `Dictionary` `class` is a generic `class` that provides a mapping from a set of keys to a set of values. When you create a dictionary collection, you place a key and an associated value in the collection using its constructor, its `Add( )` method, or its `Item` property. You can then reference and retrieve these values from the collection using its `Keys` and `Values` properties. The `Dictionary` `class` has much of the same functionality as the `Hashtable` `class`. The `Dictionary` `class` has better performance than a `Hashtable` for value types such as integers. Elements of `Hashtable` are of type `Object` and require boxing and unboxing for storage and retrieval of value types. You are encouraged to explore the MSDN documentation to examine these classes and their members and to see examples of their use. You will also read more about generic classes in Chapter 11.

8

PROGRAMMING EXAMPLE: TempAgency Application

This example demonstrates the use of collections in the analysis, design, and implementation of a program. A two-dimensional array and an array of `string` objects are included. An application is created to produce a sales goal table for a temp agency. To design this application, a two-dimensional array is declared to hold the sales figures and a `string` array for the salesmen names. The problem specification is shown in Figure 8-8.

Create an application that can be used by a temporary job placement office that provides staffing for sales positions. The agency places people in positions for a four month trial period. At the beginning of the placement, an initial sales goal baseline is established for the salesperson. It is expected that each of the temporary salesmen will increase their sales by at least 5% each month over the four month period. After the second month, it is expected the sales will increase 10% from the previous month, the third month sales should increase by 15% from the previous month, and during the fourth month sales should increase by 20% over the previous month. At the end of the trial period, salesmen who met all projected sales are hired.

For testing purposes, allow the user to enter four salesmen. After asking the user for the person's name, use the entered first name as part of the prompt for requesting the initial projected sales goal. Display a table showing the person's name with last name listed first, followed by a comma, and then their first name. Show the projected sales figures for the upcoming four month period so that management may use the report for planning purposes.

Design a modularized solution (with methods) to display the table.

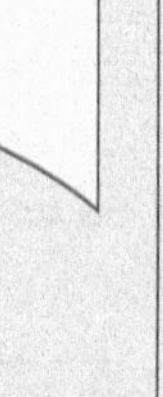

FIGURE 8-8 Problem specification for TempAgency example

ANALYZE THE PROBLEM

You should review the problem specification in Figure 8-8 and make sure you understand the problem definition. Values will be entered into the program to represent each saleman's name and his projected sales goal. The name is stored in a `string` array. The initial sales goal is stored in a two-dimensional array that is also used to hold the target sales for the following four months. Each row stores sales for a different salesperson. The columns store the initial sales and subsequent monthly goals.

DATA

Table 8-3 lists the data field members needed for the temp agency problem.

TABLE 8-3 Instance field members for the TempAgency class

Data item description	Type	Identifier
Names of new salespersons	`string [ ]`	`salesman`
Sales with projected goals	`double [ , ]`	`sales`

© Cengage Learning

DESIGN A SOLUTION

The desired output is to display the salesperson's name formatted last name first along with the initial sales goal and projected sales figures for the following four months. Figure 8-9 shows a prototype of what the final output might look like.

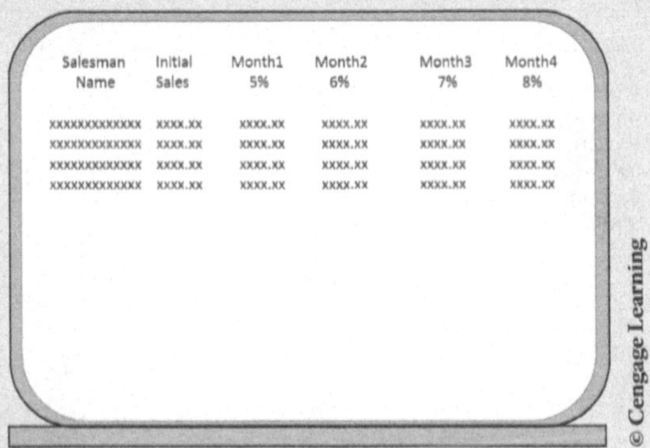

Salesman Name
Initial Sales
Month1 5%
Month2 6%
Month3 7%
Month4 8%
© Cengage Learning

FIGURE 8-9 Prototype for TempAgency Application

Class diagrams are used to help design and document both data and behavior characteristics. Figure 8-10 shows the class diagrams for the `TempAgency` example. Notice that the method `GetSalesData( )` shown in Figure 8-10 adds the **in/out** specifier to both the `salesman` and the `sales` arguments. These are both array arguments. Parameters shown in class diagrams can be **in**, **out**, **in/out**, or not unspecified. Value parameters, by default, use the **in** specifier. With the **in** specifier, an initial value is sent into the method; however, if the method changes the variable, the changed value is not available back in the calling method. When an array is sent as an argument to a method, the address of the first element is passed. If the method changes any of the element's values, the changed value is available when control returns back to the calling method. Thus, arrays are sent by default as **in/out**. The third specifier, **out**, is used with variables to indicate that a value will be sent out when the method ends. No initial value is stored in the variable when it is sent to the method using the **out** specifier.

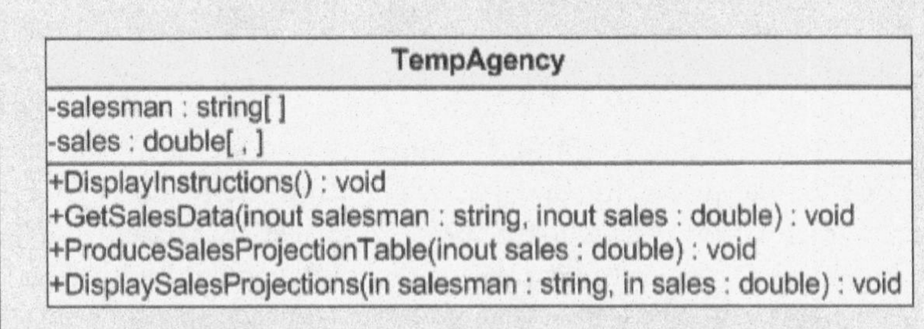

TempAgency
-salesman : string[ ]
-sales : double[,]
+DisplayInstructions() : void
+GetSalesData(inout salesman : string, inout sales : double) : void
+ProduceSalesProjectionTable(inout sales : double) : void
+DisplaySalesProjections(in salesman : string, in sales : double) : void
© Cengage Learning

FIGURE 8-10 Class diagram

Figure 8-11 shows the Structured English, or pseudocode, used to design the step-by-step processes for the behaviors of the methods of the `TempAgency` example.

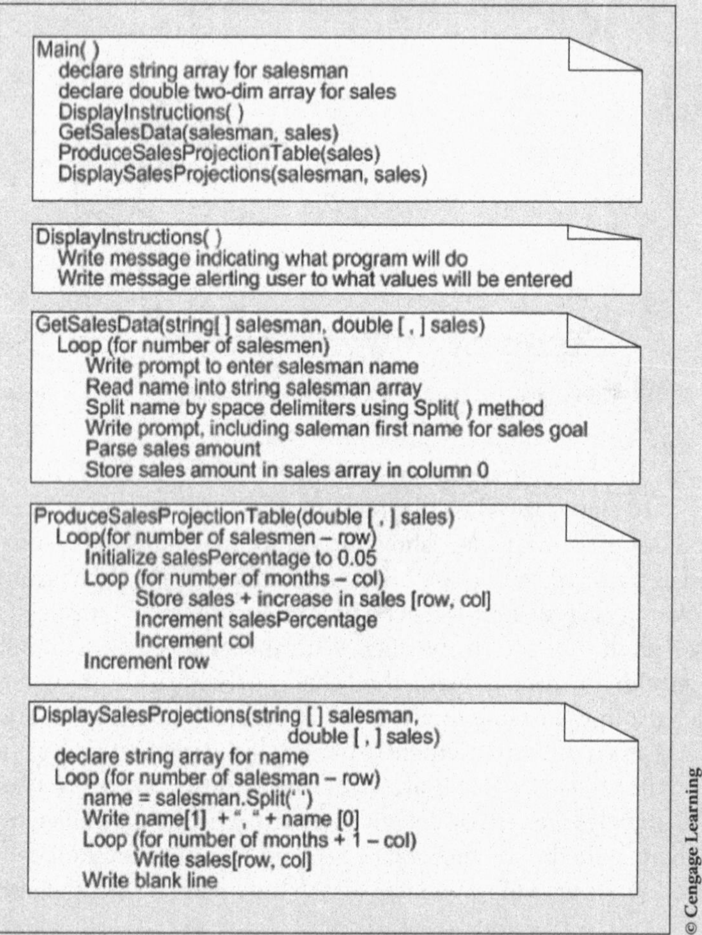

© Cengage Learning

FIGURE 8-11 TempAgency class methods behavior

After the algorithm is developed, the design should be checked for correctness. You might develop a table now with test values using a standard calculator. Desk check the pseudocode to ensure that you are getting the results expected. After your program is run, you can validate the correctness by comparing the results you produce with your program against values you produced with the calculator during your design walk-through.

CODE THE SOLUTION

After you complete the design and verify the algorithm's correctness, translate the design into source code. The final application listing follows:

```
/* TempAgency.cs
 * This application is used by a temporary work agency to
 * set projections for sales for new hires. The program enables the
 * user to input salesmen's names and expected sales goals.
 * The sales figure is placed in a two-dimensional array
 * and expected sales figures for four months are added.
 * These projections are based on increasing sales at
 * least 5% each month over the four-month period.
 * for testing purposes, four salesmen data are entered.
 */
using System;
using System.Console;

namespace TempAgency
{
     public class TempAgency
     {
          public static void Main( )
          {
               double[ , ] sales = new double[4,5];
               string[ ] salesman = new string[4];
               DisplayInstructions( );
               GetSalesData(salesman, sales);
               ProduceSalesProjectionTable(sales);
               DisplaySalesProjections(salesman, sales);
               ReadKey( );
          }

          public static void DisplayInstructions( )
          {
               WriteLine("You will be asked to enter data for " +
                         "four salesmen. \nFor their name, " +
                         "enter their first " +
                         "name followed \nby a space and then " +
                         "their last name." +
                         "\n\nNext you will enter the " +
                         "expected sales for the 1st month." +
                         "\n\n\nFor testing purposes enter " +
                         "data for four (4) salesmen.\n\n");
               WriteLine( );
          }

          public static void GetSalesData(string [ ] salesman,
                                          double[ , ] sales)
          {
```

8

```
        for (int row = 0; row < salesman.Length; row++)
        {
            string fullname;
            string[ ] name = new string[3];
            Write("Name of the New Salesman (first " +
                 " name, space, last name): ");
            salesman[row] = ReadLine( );
            fullname = salesman[row];
            name = fullname.Split(' ');
            Write("Please enter {0}'s Initial Sales " +
                 "Goal: ", name[0]);
            sales[row, 0] = double.Parse (ReadLine( ));
            Clear( );
        }
    }

    public static void ProduceSalesProjectionTable
                          (double[ , ] sales)
    {
        double salesIncrease;
        DisplayHeading(sales);
        for (int row = 0; row < sales.GetLength(0); row++)
        {
            salesIncrease = 0.05;
            for (int col = 1; col < sales.GetLength(1);
                            col++)
            {
                sales[row, col] = sales[row, col-1] *
                     salesIncrease + sales[row, col-1];
                salesIncrease += 0.05;
            }
        }
    }

    public static void DisplayHeading(double[ , ] sales)
    {
        double inc = 0.05;
        Write("{0,-20} {1,-10}", "Salesman", "Initial");
        for (int col = 0; col < sales.GetLength(1) - 1;
                     col++)
        {
            Write("{0,-6}{1,-1} ", "Month", col + 1);
        }
        WriteLine( );
        Write("{0,-20} {1,-7}", " Name", " Sales ");
        for (int col = 0; col < sales.GetLength(1) - 1;
                     col++)
        {
            Write("{0, 8} ", inc.ToString("P0"));
            inc += 0.05;
        }
```

```
            WriteLine( );
        }

        public static void DisplaySalesProjections
                (string[ ] salesman, double[ , ] sales)
        {
            string [ ] name = new string [3];
            WriteLine( );
            for (int row = 0; row < sales.GetLength(0); row++)
            {
                name = salesman[row].Split(' ');
                Write("{0, -20}", (name[1] + "," + name[0]));
                for (int col = 0; col < sales.GetLength(1);
                            col++)
                {
                    Write("{0,11:N2}", sales[row, col] );
                }
                WriteLine( );
            }
        }
    }
}
```

The output from one test run is shown in Figure 8-12.

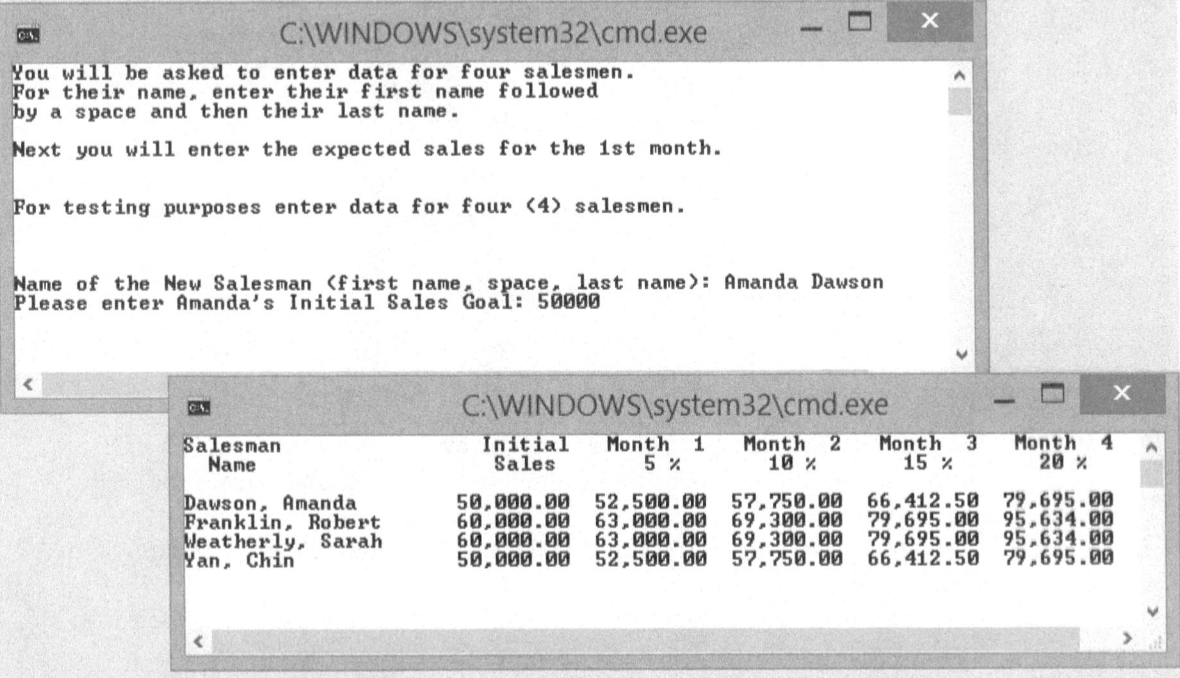

```
You will be asked to enter data for four salesmen.
For their name, enter their first name followed
by a space and then their last name.

Next you will enter the expected sales for the 1st month.

For testing purposes enter data for four (4) salesmen.


Name of the New Salesman (first name, space, last name): Amanda Dawson
Please enter Amanda's Initial Sales Goal: 50000
```

```
Salesman                Initial    Month  1    Month  2    Month  3    Month  4
  Name                   Sales       5 %        10 %        15 %        20 %

Dawson, Amanda        50,000.00  52,500.00  57,750.00  66,412.50  79,695.00
Franklin, Robert      60,000.00  63,000.00  69,300.00  79,695.00  95,634.00
Weatherly, Sarah      60,000.00  63,000.00  69,300.00  79,695.00  95,634.00
Yan, Chin             50,000.00  52,500.00  57,750.00  66,412.50  79,695.00
```

FIGURE 8-12 TempAgency application output

Coding Standards

Each project you develop should follow agreed-upon coding standards. They make your code more readable and help reduce the number of errors.

Guidelines for Naming Collections

Use a singular noun as an identifier for collection objects.

Use the Camel case naming convention when instantiating objects of collections.

Advanced Array Suggestions

If a method returns a collection and there are no values to return, return an empty collection instead of null. As opposed to writing new code, use .NET predefined methods and properties whenever possible when working with collections.

Resources

Additional sites you might want to explore:

- YouTube Video on Coding Multidimensional Arrays in C#—
  http://www.youtube.com/watch?v=XiH1RiGDqdI
- An Extensive Examination of Data Structures—
  http://msdn.microsoft.com/en-us/library/aa289148(VS.71).aspx
- MSDN C# Data Structures series—
  http://www.andrewconnell.com/blog/MSDN-C-Data-Structure-series
- C# String Tutorial—
  http://csharp.net-informations.com/string/csharp_string_tutorial.htm
- Multidimensional Arrays—
  http://www.functionx.com/csharp/Lesson23.htm

QUICK REVIEW

1. Two-dimensional and multidimensional arrays may contain any number of variables of the same type. One common identifier names the entire structure.
2. Two-dimensional and multidimensional arrays should be named using singular nouns.
3. To access a two-dimensional or multidimensional array element, use the number of indexes included in the declaration. Indexes are separated by commas and enclosed in square brackets.

4. When you use a two-dimensional or multidimensional array as a method parameter, the array identifier and type are specified; however, the length or size of the array is not included. Opening, closing square brackets, and commas are required. The call to that method includes the name of the array only.
5. Two-dimensional and multidimensional arrays can be sent as arguments to methods, and in addition, a method can have a two-dimensional or multidimensional array as its return type. The square bracket that is included before the name of the method is empty with the exception of one or more commas. The comma separators identify the number of dimensions.
6. Two-dimensional and other multidimensional arrays follow the same guidelines as one-dimensional arrays.
7. A two-dimensional array is usually visualized as a table divided into rows and columns. The first index represents the number of rows.
8. When the number of columns in rows may need to differ, a jagged, or ragged, array can be used. It is called an "array of arrays."
9. `ArrayList class` creates a listlike structure that can dynamically increase or decrease in length. Like traditional arrays, indexes of `ArrayList` objects are zero based. A number of predefined methods are included.
10. To create a multidimensional array, specify the type and the number of dimensions per rank. These values are separated by commas. A three-dimensional array would be defined with `type [ , , ] identifier = new type [length_of_planes, length_of_rows, length_of_columns]`.
11. The `string class` stores an immutable series of characters. After you give a `string` a value, it cannot be modified.
12. The `string` type is an alias for the `System.String class` in the .NET Framework. You can access the individual characters using an index, with the first index being zero.
13. String variables are objects of the `string class`; thus, a number of predefined methods including the following can be used: `Trim( )`, `ToUpper( )`, `ToLower( )`, `Substring( )`, `Split( )`, `Replace( )`, `Insert( )`, and `Copy( )`.
14. The `Hashtable class` represents a collection of key/value pairs that are organized based on the hash code of the key. Override the `GetHashCode( )` method to provide a new algorithm for the hash function.
15. BitArrays are very useful for working with large data sets. They are most commonly used to represent a simple group of Boolean flags.
16. The `Queue class` represents a first-in-first-out (FIFO) collection of objects. The `Enqueue( )` method adds an object to the end of the queue. `Dequeue( )` removes and returns the object at the beginning of the queue.

17. The `Stack` `class` represents a simple last-in-first-out (LIFO) collection of objects. The `Push( )` method adds an object to the top of the stack. `Pop( )` removes and returns the object at the top of the stack.

EXERCISES

1. When two values are contained within the square brackets, the last number represents the number of:
   a. classes
   b. rows
   c. planes
   d. columns
   e. none of the above

2. Which of the following array declarations would enable you to store the high and low temperatures for each day of one full week?
   a. `int temp1Lo, temp2Lo, temp3Lo, temp4Lo, temp5Lo, temp6Lo, temp7Lo, temp1Hi, temp2Hi, temp3Hi, temp4Hi, temp5Hi, temp6Hi, temp7Hi;`
   b. `int temp [7, 2] = new int [7, 2];`
   c. `temp int [ , ] = new temp [7, 2];`
   d. `int [ , ] temp = new temp [7, 2];`
   e. `int [ , ] temp = new temp [8, 3];`

3. Assume a two-dimensional array called `num` is declared to hold four rows and seven columns. Which of the following statements correctly assigns the value `100` to the third physical column of each row?
   a. `for (x = 0; x < 3; ++x) num [x, 2] = 100`
   b. `for (x = 0; x < 4; ++x) num [x, 2] = 100;`
   c. `for (x = 1; x < 4; ++x) num [x, 2] = 100;`
   d. `for (x = 1; x < 5; ++x) num [x, 2] = 100;`
   e. none of the above

4. Choose the statement that does *not* apply to the following declaration:

```
double [ , ] totalCostOfItems =
                    {{109.95, 169.95, 1.50, 89.95},
                     {27.9, 18.6, 26.8, 98.5}};
```

   a. declares a two-dimensional array of floating-point values
   b. establishes the maximum number of rows as 4
   c. sets the array element `totalCostOfItems[0,1]` to `169.95`
   d. declares an area in memory where data of `double` type can be stored
   e. all are correct

5. What value is returned by the method named `result`?

```
int result(int [ , ] anArray)
{
   int j = 0,
       i = 0;
   for (int r = 0; r < anArray.GetLength(0); r++)
         for (int c = 0; c < anArray.GetLength(1); c++)
              if (anArray[r, c] < anArray[i, j])
              {
                     i = r;
                     j = c;
              }
   return i;
}
```

   a. the row index of the largest element of array `anArray`
   b. the value of the largest element of array `anArray`
   c. the row index of the smallest element of array `anArray`
   d. the column index of the smallest element of array `anArray`
   e. the index of the last element greater than its predecessor

6. What is the largest dimension an array can be declared to store values?
   a. 10
   b. 100
   c. 3
   d. 5
   e. there is no limit

8

7. Using the following declaration:

```
char [ , ] n = {{'a', 'b', 'c', 'd', 'e'},
                {'f', 'g', 'h', 'i', 'j'}};
```

what does `n[1, 1]` refer to?

   a. a
   b. f
   c. b
   d. g
   e. none of the above

8. A two-dimensional array is a list of data items that ______________

   a. all have the same type.
   b. all have different names.
   c. all are integers.
   d. all are originally set to `null` (`'\0'`).
   e. none of the above

9. Using the following declaration:

```
int [ , ] x = {{12, 13, 14, 15 }, {16, 17, 18, 19 }};
```

what does `x[2, 4]` refer to?

   a. 19
   b. 18
   c. '\0'
   d. 0
   e. none of the above

10. Which of the following adds 95 to the array element that is currently storing 14?

```
int [ , , ] x = {{12, 13 }, {14, 15 }, {16, 17 }, {18, 19 }};
```

   a. `x[2] += 95;`
   b. `x[1, 0] += 95;`
   c. `x[1, 0 += 95];`
   d. `x = 14 + 95;`
   e. none of the above

11. How many components are allocated by the following statement?

    `double [ , ] values = new double[3, 2];`

    a. 32
    b. 3
    c. 5
    d. 6
    e. none of the above

12. Given the declaration for values in question #11 above, how would you store 0 in the last physical location?

    a. `values = 0;`
    b. `values[6] = 0;`
    c. `values[3, 2] = 0;`
    d. `values[2, 1] = 0;`
    e. none of the above

13. If you declare an array as `int [ , ] anArray = new int [5, 3];` you can double the value stored in `anArray[2, 1]` with the statement:

    a. `anArray[2, 1] = anArray[5, 1] * 2;`
    b. `anArray = anArray * 2;`
    c. `anArray[2, 1] *= anArray[2, 1] * 2;`
    d. `anArray[2, 1] *= 2;`
    e. none of the above

14. With the following declaration:

    ```
    int [ , ] points = {{300, 100, 200, 400, 600},
                        {550, 700, 900, 800, 100}};
    ```

    the statement `points[1, 3] = points[1, 3] + 10;` will

    a. replace the `300` amount with `310` and `900` with `910`
    b. replace the `500` amount with `510`
    c. replace the `900` amount with `910`
    d. replace the `800` amount with `810`
    e. none of the above

8

15. With the following declaration:

```
int [ , ] points =
            {{300, 100, 200, 400, 600},
             {550, 700, 900, 200, 100}};
```

the statement `points[0, 4] = points[0, 4-2];` will

a. replace the `400` amount with `2`

b. replace the `300` and `600` with `2`

c. replace the `600` with `200`

d. result in an error

e. none of the above

16. With the following declaration:

```
int [ , ] points = {{300, 100, 200, 400, 600},
                    {550, 700, 900, 200, 100}};
```

the statement `Write(points[1, 2] + points[0, 3]);` will

a. display 900400

b. display 1300

c. display `"points[1, 2] + points[0, 3]"`

d. result in an error

e. none of the above

17. When you pass an element from an `ArrayList` to a method, the method receives:

a. a copy of the `ArrayList`

b. the address of the `ArrayList`

c. a copy of the value in the element of the `ArrayList`

d. the address of the element in the `ArrayList`

e. none of the above

18. When you pass the entire `ArrayList` to a method, the method receives:

a. a copy of the `ArrayList`

b. the address of the `ArrayList`

c. a copy of the first value in the `ArrayList`

d. the address of each of the elements in the `ArrayList`

e. none of the above

19. To convert all the uppercase letters in a `string` to their lowercase counterpart, you can use the _______________ method of the `string class`.
    a. `IsLower( )`
    b. `ConvertLower( )`
    c. `Lower( )`
    d. `ToLower( )`
    e. none of the above

20. Which method in the `ArrayList class` can be used to place a value onto the end of the `ArrayList`?
    a. `AddLast( )`
    b. `AddLastIndex( )`
    c. `Add( )`
    d. `Insert( )`
    e. none of the above

21. Which member in the `ArrayList class` can be used to get or set the number of elements that an `ArrayList` can contain?
    a. `Length`
    b. `Size`
    c. `Dimension`
    d. `Rank`
    e. `Capacity`

22. Which `class` includes methods to create a dynamic one-dimensional structure?
    a. `Array`
    b. `string`
    c. `array`
    d. `ArrayList`
    e. all of the above

23. A correct method call to a method that has the following heading would be:

```
int result(int[ , ] anArray, int num)
```

   a. `Write(result(anArray, 3));`
   b. `result(anArray, 30);`
   c. `Write(result(anArray[ ], 3));`
   d. `result(anArray[ ], 30);`
   e. none of the above

24. With two-dimensional arrays a limitation on the `foreach` statement is that it can:
   a. only be used for read-only access
   b. only be used with integral type arrays
   c. not be used with multidimensional arrays
   d. only be used with arrays smaller than 1000 elements
   e. not be used with dynamic arrays

25. In order to retrieve a value stored in an object of the `Queue` `class`, you would use which method?
   a. `Pop( );`
   b. `Push( );`
   c. `Dequeue( );`
   d. `Enqueue( );`
   e. none of the above

---

26. Use the following `string` to answer questions a through e.

```
string sValue =
        "Today is the first day of the rest of your life."
```

   a. Create a new `string` that has all lowercase characters except the word `day`. The word `day` should be set to all uppercase.
   b. Create a new `string` array that contains the eleven elements. Each word from the `sValue` `string` should be in a separate array cell.
   c. Remove the period from the last array element created in Step b. Display the contents of the new array verifying its removal.
   d. Surround the `sValue` `string` with three asterisks on each end.
   e. Replace the word `first` with the word `best` in the `sValue` `string`.

27. Using the following declaration:

```
int [ , ] anArray = {{34, 55, 67, 89, 99}, {22, 68, 11, 19, 45}};
```

what would be the result of each of the following output statements?

a. `WriteLine(anArray.Length);`

b. `WriteLine(anArray[1, 2]);`

c. `WriteLine(anArray[0, anArray.GetLength(0) - 2]);`

d. `WriteLine(anArray[0, 2 + 1] * anArray[0, 0]);`

e. `WriteLine(anArray.Rank);`

28. Using the following declarations, write solutions for Steps a through e.

```
int [ , ] cArray = new int [2, 3];
string [ , , ] dArray = new string [5, 2, 6];
```

a. Write a `foreach` loop to display the contents of `cArray`.

b. Write a `for` loop to increment each element in `cArray` by 5.

c. Write a `foreach` loop to display the contents of `dArray`.

d. Can you use a `foreach` loop to initialize all elements of `dArray` with zero? If so, show your code. If not, explain why.

e. Write a `for` loop to initialize all elements in `dArray` to zero.

8

29. Create array declarations for the following problem specifications.

a. An array to hold the name of the largest 3 cities for 5 states. Initialize with the 5 states closest to your campus.

b. A single array to hold the names of 10 people. You should be able to reference each person's first name without having to use `string` manipulation methods to split the data apart.

c. A single array to store keys for five exams each consisting of 15 true/false questions.

30. Explain the difference between the .NET `Hashtable` and `Dictionary` classes.

PROGRAMMING EXERCISES

1. Write an application that creates and returns a one-dimensional array containing all the elements in the two-dimensional array. Store the values in a row major format. For testing purposes, you may do a compile-time initialization of a 12 x 5 two-dimensional array. Display both the two-dimensional and the one-dimensional array. Be sure that the values in the array are number aligned.

2. Write an application that will let you keep a check on how well six salesmen are performing selling three different products. You should use a two-dimensional array to solve the problem. Allow the user to input any number of sales amounts. Do a compile-time initialization of the salesperson's names and product list. Produce a report by salesman, showing the total sales per product.

3. Revise your solution for problem 2 so that you display the total sales per salesman. As with your solution for exercise #2, include the first and last names for the salesmen in an array. When you display your final output, print the salesman's last name only, sales for each product, and the final sales for the salesman. After you display the tables of sales, display the largest sales figure indicating which salesman sold it and which product was sold. For an added challenge, write your solution so that any number of salesmen and any number of products can be displayed.

4. Write a two-class application that creates a customer code to be placed on a mailing label for a magazine. Allow the user to input their full name with the first name entered first. Prompt them to separate their first and last name with a space. Ask for their birthdate in the format of mm/dd/yyyy. Ask for the month (number) they purchased a subscription and ask for their zip code. Your mailing label should contain the last name, followed by their year of birth, the number of characters in the full name, the first three characters of the month they purchased the subscription, and the last two digits of their zip. The code for Bob Clocksom born 01/22/1993, who purchased his subscription during the 10th month of the year and lists 32226 as his zip code would be Clocksom9312Oct26.

5. Write a program that allows the user to enter any number of names. Your prompt can inform the user to input their first name followed by a space and last name. Order the names in ascending order and display the results with the last name listed first, followed by a comma and then the first name. If a middle initial is entered, it should follow the first name. Your solution should also take into consideration that some users may only enter their last name (one name).

6. Write an application that creates a two-dimensional array. Allow the user to input the size of the array (number of rows and number of columns). Fill the array with random numbers between 0 and 100. Search the array for the largest value. Display the array values, numbers aligned, and the indexes where the largest value is stored.

7. Write a program that creates a two-dimensional array with 10 rows and 2 columns. The first column should be filled with 10 random numbers between 0 and 100. The second column should contain the squared value of the element found in column 1. Using the `Show( )` method of the `MessageBox` `class`, display a table.

8. reAay ouyay aay hizway ithway igPay atin?Lay? (Translated: "Are you a whiz with Pig Latin?") Write a program that converts an English phrase into a pseudo-Pig Latin phrase (that is Pig Latin that doesn't follow all the Pig Latin syntax rules). Use predefined methods of the `Array` and `string` classes to do the work. For simplicity in your conversion, place the first letter as the last character in the word and prefix the characters "ay" onto the end. For example, the word "example" would become "xampleeay," and "method" would become "ethodmay." Allow the user to input the English phrase. After converting it, display the new Pig Latin phrase.

9. Write an application that displays revenue generated for exercise classes at the Tappan Gym. The gym offers two types of exercise classes, zumba and spinning, six days per week, four times per day. Zumba is offered at 1, 3, 5, and 7 p.m.; spinning is offered at 2, 4, 6, and 8 p.m. When attendees sign up, they agree to pay $4.00 per class for zumba and $5.00 for spinning. Produce a table displaying the number of attendees per time slot. Display a row and column of totals showing the total number of attendees by day and also time period. Also include a column showing the revenue generated each day and the overall revenue per type of exercise. Do a compile-time initialization of your data structures using data from the following table.

8

Zumba				
	1:00	3:00	5:00	7:00
Monday	12	10	17	22
Tuesday	11	13	17	22
Wednesday	12	10	22	22
Thursday	9	14	17	22
Friday	12	10	21	12
Saturday	12	10	5	10

Spinning				
	2:00	4:00	6:00	8:00
Monday	7	11	15	8
Tuesday	9	9	9	9
Wednesday	3	12	13	7
Thursday	2	9	9	10
Friday	8	4	9	4
Saturday	4	5	9	3

10. Write an application that enables you to randomly record water depths for five different locations at 0700 (7 a.m.), 1200 (noon), 1700 (5 p.m.), and 2100 (9 p.m.). The locations are Surf City, Solomons, Hilton Head, Miami, and Savannah. For ease of input, you may want to code the locations (i.e., Surf City = 1, Solomons = 2, etc.) and code the time (i.e., 0700 = 1, 1200 = 2, etc.). If the same location and time are entered more than one time, store the last value entered into the array. After the data is entered, display the average depth at each location and the average depth by time period.

© zeljkodan/Shutterstock.com

Introduction to Windows Programming

IN THIS CHAPTER, YOU WILL:

- Differentiate between the functions of Windows applications and console applications
- Learn about graphical user interfaces
- Become aware of some elements of good design
- Use C# and Visual Studio to create Windows-based applications
- Create Windows forms and be able to change form properties
- Add control objects such as buttons, labels, and text boxes to a form
- Work through a programming example that illustrates the chapter's concepts

If you have read and completed the exercises in the previous chapters, you now have a solid programming foundation and can build fairly sophisticated console-based applications. These types of applications are excellent for learning the basic elements of programming and are appropriate for many types of small, utility applications today. However, you probably consider them boring. In your daily life, you have become accustomed to using modern programs that look and act like Windows applications. In this chapter, you learn to create those types of applications.

Building Windows-based applications was a complicated endeavor in the past; this is no longer the case. Included in the .NET Framework class library is an entire subsystem of classes that enables you to create highly interactive, attractive, graphical user interface (GUI) applications. Using Visual Studio, it is easy to perform drag-and-drop constructions. In the following two chapters, you will be introduced to many classes in the `System.Windows.Forms` `namespace`, including control classes such as `Label`, `Button`, and `TextBox` that can be placed on a Windows `Form` container `class`. A different way of programming based on interactively responding to events such as mouse clicks will be introduced. In Chapter 10, you will extend this knowledge by creating applications that are more event-driven and are used for capturing and responding to user input. By the time you complete Chapter 10, you will be building fun, interactive Windows-based applications.

Contrasting Windows and Console Applications

When a Windows application executes, it functions differently from the console-based applications you have been writing. With a console-based application, each line in the `Main( )` method is executed sequentially. Then the program halts. Method calls might branch to different locations in your program; however, control always returns back to the `Main( )` method. When the closing curly brace is encountered in `Main( )`, execution halts with console-based applications. With your console applications, the program initiates interaction with the operating system by calling the operating system to get data using the `ReadLine( )` method. It calls on the operating system to output data through method calls such as `WriteLine( )` or `Write( )`.

For both Windows and console applications, execution begins with the first statement in the `Main( )` method. However, with a Windows application, instead of the program executing sequential statements from top to bottom, the application, once launched, sits in what is called a process loop waiting for an event to execute. An **event** is a notification from the operating system that an action, such as the user clicking the mouse or pressing a key, has occurred. Instead of calling on the operating system with a request, as console applications do, **Windows applications** receive messages from the operating system that an event has occurred. With Windows applications, you write methods called **event handlers** to indicate what should be done when an event such as a mouse click on a button or the press of a key occurs.

You might design a window that includes several locations on your screen where a user could input different values. You might have many different buttons on that same screen, with one labeled Compute. With Windows applications, you register events about which you want your program to receive notification. For example, you might want your program to be notified when the user clicks the Compute button. For this situation, you would write in your program a method called an event handler, indicating what should be done when that Compute button is clicked. If this is the only event-handler method you include, your program, once launched, would be in a process loop—or wait state—until that Compute button was clicked.

The body of the event-handler method for the Compute button might include statements to perform a calculation and then display the formatted results on the Windows form. When the user clicks the Compute button, an event is fired. The operating system sends a message to your program indicating that the event you registered has occurred. The associated method to handle the event is then executed automatically.

Think about your own experience using any Windows-based program. Take, for example, your word-processing program. After being launched, the program appears to be sitting idle allowing you to type forever. However, it is in a process loop after it is launched. When you select an option from one of the menus, an event is fired. Select an option such as Find or Search and a dialog box prompts you to enter the word for the search. Another event is fired when you press the Enter key indicating you have finished typing the search word. This event-handler method performs the search in your document. Until you clicked on the menu bar, the program was just waiting for a notification from the operating system that an event of interest had occurred.

Unlike console-based applications that exit after all statements have been sequentially executed, Windows-based applications, after they are launched, sit idly waiting for notification of a registered event. The program remains in the operating system environment in a process loop. This means your program could be minimized, resized, or closed like other Windows applications. Someone could surf the Web for hours while your program was still running or write an English paper using another application. Your program's code would be ready and still waiting for an event to be fired when the user made the program's window active again.

Another important difference is sequential order. Unlike the sequential nature you expect with console-based applications, in which one statement executes followed by the next, no sequential order exists with methods that handle events for Windows applications. If you have many options on your screen, or many buttons, you do not know which one the user will click first or whether any of them will be clicked. Again, think about your experiences using a Windows-based word processor. Each time you use the program, you select different options or use different menu selections.

With Windows applications, many different types of events can be fired. As a developer, you select actions your program should respond to and write event handlers for those events. If you have five buttons on the screen, button1 might not be the one clicked first every time. These event-handler methods can be executed in a different order every time your application runs.

Windows applications not only function differently but also look different. Windows applications tend to have a consistent user interface—one that is considered more user-friendly than what you find with console-based applications. In many cases, the user interface of a Windows application is considered as important as the application's power behind the scenes.

Graphical User Interfaces

Have you ever tried to use a computer program and said to yourself "Okay, what do I do next?" or been unable to exit a program or perform some function that you knew the program was supposed to be able to do? The culprit was probably the interface. The **interface** is the front end of a program. It is the visual image you see when you run a program. The interface is what allows users to interact with your program. Although a program may be powerful and offer rich functionality, those functions may remain unused unless they present the user with easy methods of interaction. Often users of programs actually identify the interface as the program itself, when in reality, the interface is just one facet of the program.

The interfaces you designed thus far have not been graphical. Your program interaction was primarily limited to accepting input through the `ReadLine( )` method and displaying output in the form of a single font at the DOS console window. In this chapter, the interface changes. Instead of interacting with the black console screen, you will design Windows-based, GUI applications. These types of applications are displayed on a Windows form, as shown in Figure 9-1.

FIGURE 9-1 Windows-based form

A **GUI** can include menus, buttons, pictures, and text in many different colors and sizes. Think of the form in Figure 9-1 as a container waiting to hold additional controls, such as buttons or labels. **Controls** are objects that can display and respond to user interaction. In Figure 9-1, the form has a title bar, complete with an icon on the left, a textual caption in the title bar, and the typical Windows Minimize, Maximize, and Close buttons. The C# code used to create this blank form is shown in Example 9-1.

EXAMPLE 9-1

```
// Windows0.cs                                   Author:   Doyle
// Demonstrates creating a blank container form
using System.Windows.Forms;                                 // Line 1
namespace Windows0
{
     public class Windows0  : Form                          // Line 2
     {
          public Windows0( )                                // Line 3
          {
               Text = "Simple Windows Application";         // Line 4
          }

          public static void Main( )
          {
               Windows0 winForm = new Windows0( );          // Line 5
               Application.Run(winForm);                    // Line 6
          }
     }
}
```


The code in Example 9-1 could be written using an editor such as Notepad and executed from the command line. This is not recommended for developing Windows-based applications. The Visual Studio integrated development environment (IDE) automatically generates all the code needed for a blank Windows form for you. If you do not use the IDE, you lose out on the built-in, drag-and-drop construction capabilities, and the ease of modifying controls during design. The program listing in Example 9-1 is much smaller than what is generated from Visual Studio. Later in the chapter, you have a chance to compare Example 9-1 with the code Visual Studio actually generates. Before doing that and before exploring the rich Visual Studio environment, it is useful to evaluate what is actually required to create a Windows application in C#.

Examine the statements in Example 9-1. Notice that the `using` directive labeled Line 1 imports types or classes from the `System.Windows.Forms` `namespace`.

This is where most of the classes for developing Windows-based applications are organized. By including this directive, you avoid having to fully qualify references to classes organized under the `System.Windows.Forms` `namespace`.

The Windows applications you will be creating will always refer to the `System.Windows.Forms` `namespace`. Visual Studio automatically adds this reference when you select the C# **Windows Forms Application** template, and it makes available for you the data types or classes needed to create a Windows Application Project.

The `class` heading definition labeled Line 2 looks a little different from what you have seen previously. It includes not only the `class` name but also a colon followed by another `class` name. The second `class` is called the **base** `class`; the first is called the **derived** `class`. Look closely at this statement again.

```
public class Form1 : Form                          // Line 2
```

The colon is used in the definition to indicate that the new `class` being defined, `Form1`, is derived from a base `class` named `System.Windows.Forms.Form`. The default name given for a Windows application `class` in Visual Studio is `Form1`. You do not have to change the `class` name, but you might want to so that the name better represents the application.

Because the `namespace` `System.Windows.Forms` was included in the `using` directive, the fully qualified name of `System.Windows.Forms.Form` can be written as `Form`. You will find, however, that Visual Studio often inserts the fully qualified name when you look at the code generated by the IDE.

When a `class` is derived from another `class`, the new `class` inherits the functionality of the base `class`. `Form` is a predefined .NET `class` that includes a number of methods and properties used to create a basic Windows screen. `Form1` inherits the characteristics of the `Form` `class`. You will learn more about inheritance in Chapter 11 when you study advanced object-oriented concepts. For now, think about inheritance as it relates to your family tree. Just as you can inherit traits from your father, such as hair color or height, `Form1` inherits methods and properties from the predefined `System.Windows.Forms.Form` `class`. As you reexamine the form created for Figure 9-1 using Example 9-1, notice that it includes fully functional Close, Minimize, and Maximize buttons in the upper-right corner of the form. No new code had to be written to add these features. `Form1` inherited this functionality from the `Form` `class`. Remember that one of the beauties of object-oriented programming is not having to reinvent the wheel. Inheriting characteristics from base classes adds functionality to your program without the burden of your having to do additional coding.

Unlike your family tree, in which you inherit traits from two distinctively different individuals, your mother and your father, in C# and all .NET languages you are limited to single inheritance. Thus, you cannot just add a second or third colon (e.g., on Line 2 in Example 9-1) and follow that with additional `class` names. You are limited to deriving from one base `class`. You will learn more about this in Chapter 11.

Looking again at Example 9-1, Line 3 begins the section of code defining the constructor for the `Form1` `class`. Remember that a constructor has the same name as the `class` name—`Form1`. Constructors are called automatically when an `object` of the `class` is created. This constructor has one statement in its body, which is

```
Text = "Simple Windows Application";             // Line 4
```

`Text` is a property that can be used to set or get the caption of the title bar for the window. Observe that the `string`

```
"Simple Windows Application"
```

appears on the title bar in Figure 9-1.

You created your own property attributes using `set` and `get` when you defined your own classes. Windows forms and controls offer a wide variety of changeable properties including `Text`, `Color`, `Font`, `Size`, and `Location`. Much of the power of Visual Studio lies in having these properties readily available and easy to change or add through IntelliSense.

9

As with console-based applications, execution for Windows-based programs begins in the `Main( )` method. In Example 9-1, Line 5, the first statement in the `Main( )` method body instantiates or creates an `object` of the `Form1` `class`. The object's identifier is `winForm`. That statement is listed again as follows:

```
Form1 winForm = new Form1( );                    // Line 5
```

The last statement in the body of `Main( )`, on Line 6, calls the `Run( )` method. `Run( )` is a `class` method of the `Application` `class`. The call is as follows:

```
Application.Run(winForm);                        // Line 6
```

The `Application` `class` is also defined as part of the `System.Windows.Forms` `namespace`. The `object` that is instantiated from the `Form1` `class` is sent as the argument to its `Run( )` method. It is this method call that causes the `object`, `winForm`, to be displayed as a window on your screen. This statement displays the form and places the application in a process loop so that it receives messages from the operating system when events of interest to the application are fired.

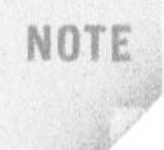

> **NOTE** Unlike instance methods, `class` methods, or `static` methods, are not called with an `object`. Class methods are not owned by any specific `object`. To call `static` methods, the method name is prefixed by the `class` name. `Application` is a `class` that has `static` methods (`class` methods) to start and stop applications. The `Run( )` method starts an application; the `Exit( )` method stops an application and closes all of its windows.

The amount of development time for Windows applications is greatly reduced when you use Visual Studio and C#. Because it is easy to add controls, sometimes beginning programmers get bogged down or carried away designing GUIs. Thus, before jumping into examining the different controls that can be added to the form, the following section presents some design issues that you should think about before dropping any control onto a form using Visual Studio.

Elements of Good Design

As you start developing Windows applications, your goal should be to develop applications that are usable, permit users to spot items in the windows quickly, and enable users to interact with your program. Appearance matters! An attractively laid out screen with good visual organization gives users control. This is of utmost importance.

A large field of research in the field of computing is focused on **human–computer interaction (HCI)**. HCI concentrates on the design and implementation of interactive computing systems for human use. Explaining HCI fully is beyond the scope of this book, but it is a good topic for you to explore further, because it involves issues that you should consider and incorporate into your interfaces from the beginning. A few of the more important HCI considerations are presented in the following sections.

Consistency

This is listed first because it is extremely important. Do you know how to close a Windows-based program? Sure you do. One way is to click the button labeled "X" in the upper-right corner of an active Windows application. The "X" performs the same functionality for all applications and is consistently located in that same place. Do you know which menu option to use to save your work? Again, you probably answered "Yes." Save is almost always located on the File menu for all Windows-based applications. Consistent placement of items is important. Consistent sizing of items is important. Consistent appearance of items that are performing the same functionality is also important. These are good design features to mimic. Buttons that are providing the same functionality should be consistently located in the same general area, be sized consistently, and be designed to look consistent.

Unless you are trying to call attention to an item, keep the item the same as other items. To bring attention to an item, use contrast, make it look different, or place it in a different location; otherwise, you should be consistent with your design of GUIs.

Alignment

Use alignment for grouping items. When you place controls on a form, place similar items together. They can be lined up to call attention to the fact that they belong together. Place similar items together and align them in the same column or same row. Use indentation to show subordination of items.

Use blank spaces to aid in grouping. Adding blank space between controls can make the difference between an attractively laid out GUI and one that is cluttered and difficult to use. Align controls with their identifying labels.

Avoid Clutter

The Windows `Form class` is considered a container on which controls such as buttons, text, labels, text boxes, and pictures can be placed. As you are about to learn, it is easy to fill the window with controls. Pay attention to the amount of information being placed on the form. Do not crowd a form with too many controls. Buttons to be clicked should be large enough for easy use. Make sure that text is readable. Use intuitive labels that are descriptive of the control they are identifying. Fonts should be large enough to be legible.

Color

Think about your color combinations. Background colors and foreground text colors should contrast with each other. Avoid using bright colors (such as reds), especially for backgrounds; this can result in user eye fatigue. You can use color as an attention getter, but do not abuse it. Color can play a significant role in your design. A great deal of research has focused on how colors impact the GUI, and you will probably want to explore this topic further.

Target Audience

You should begin thinking about the design of an interface in terms of who will be using it. Will the user be a child or an adult? Will they be a novice or an expert?

Your target audience should be taken into consideration. Another consideration for the design of an application is where it will be displayed. C# is being used to design mobile applications for handheld devices. A GUI should be different if it is going to be displayed on a WAP (Wireless Access Protocol)-enabled device such as a tablet or a smart phone. You would want to place fewer controls and minimal graphics on such an application. The design of your interface for rich Windows applications that can be run on workstations equipped with large hard drives that hold graphical images should also differ from the design for Web applications that run on thin client systems over a browser. (A thin client is designed to be small because it works with a server designed to perform most of the data processing.) The amount of download overhead should be taken into consideration for a Web application. Thin client systems often do not have much computing power and can be limited in their storage capacity. You will explore Web applications in Chapter 15.

In addition to templates for creating console and Windows applications, Visual Studio includes built-in design templates for creating applications for the Web and Smart devices like Windows Phones. In Chapter 15, you will develop Web applications.

With every application that you design, you should always think about the design considerations discussed in this section. A number of useful websites are focused on HCI. At the time of writing this text, *www.hcibib.org* was one of the more exhaustive sites. It includes a number of software developer resources, such as an online bibliography, published HCI guidelines, plus links to a number of professional affiliations focusing on HCI and personal pages of designers sharing their design suggestions.

Using C# and Visual Studio to Create Windows-Based Applications

Although you could certainly manually create very sophisticated Windows applications in C# using an editor such as Notepad, this is not recommended. Visual Studio automatically generates much of the general service plumbing code that you would have to add to locate your controls on the screen. This makes writing Windows applications using Visual Studio much simpler. To create a Windows application in Visual Studio, click **New**, then **Project** from the **File** menu. Then select **Visual C#, Windows Forms Application** from the **Visual Studio Installed Templates** pane, as shown in Figure 9-2.

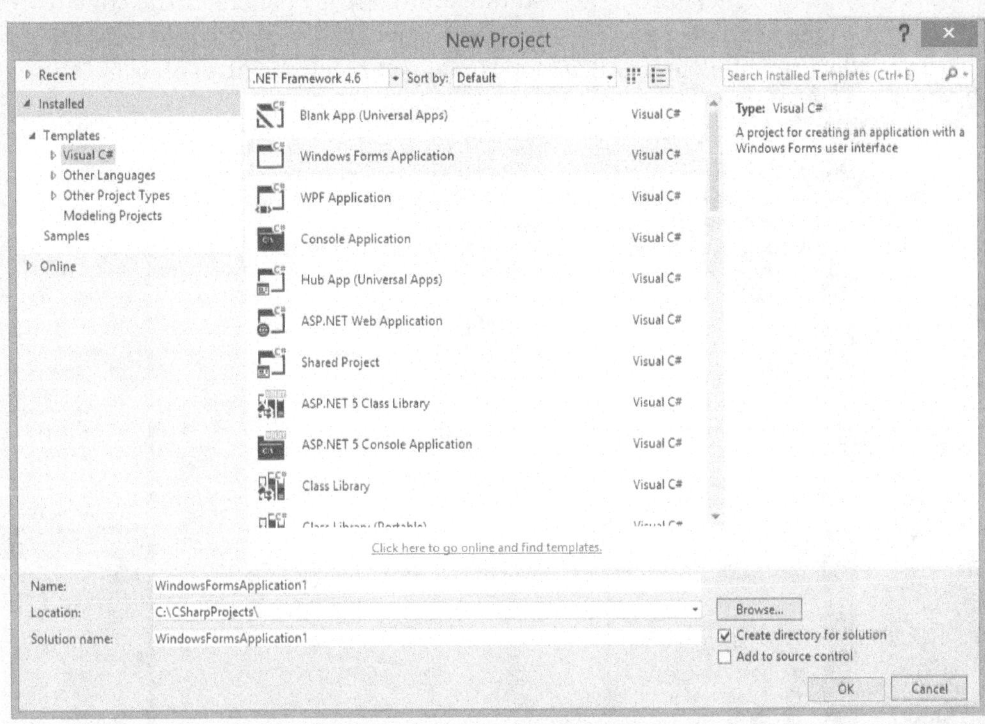

FIGURE 9-2 Visual Studio New Windows application

NOTE

By default a check mark is placed beside **Create directory for solution**, as illustrated in Figure 9-2. This creates a separate folder for the project.

You can browse to the location where you want to store your work and type a name for the project. `FirstWindows` was typed as the name for the project. Whatever value is typed into the **Name** textbox is automatically placed in the textbox for the the **Solution name**.

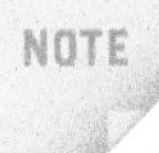

An alternative for creating Windows applications is to use the **Windows Presentation Foundation** (or **WPF**) template. Notice in Figure 9-2, **WPF Application;** is the third option in the middle pane. WPF is an especially great platform to use if your application involves various media types. For example, if you want to incorporate video, 3D content, or animated transitions between a sequence of images, WPF provides a sophisticated layout system that handles the arrangement. You will develop a WPF project in Chapter 10.

After you click **OK**, Visual Studio automatically generates the code to create a blank Windows `Form` `object`. The IDE opens the Form **Designer** showing the form, as illustrated in Figure 9-3, which is ready to receive control objects.

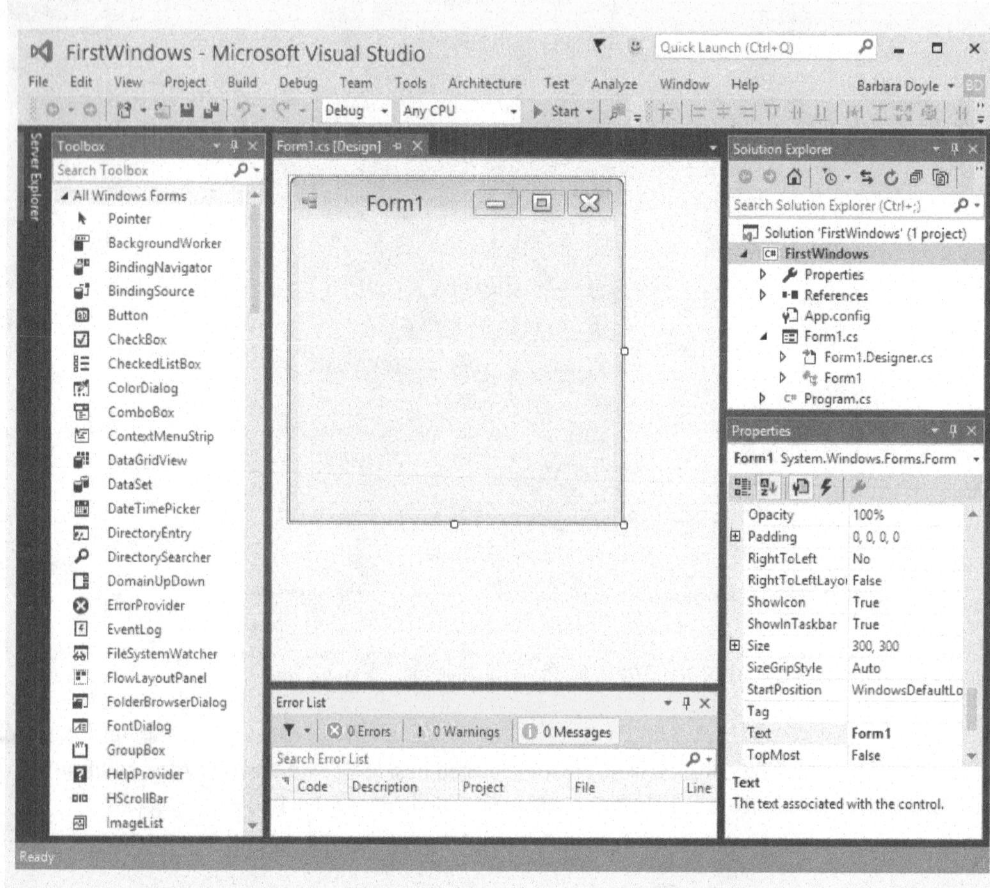

FIGURE 9-3 Initial design screen

If you do not see the constructed form, but instead see the program statements, your system may be set to show the **Code** Editor window first. To see the GUI form, select the **Designer** option from the **View** menu (or press **Shift+F7**). **F7** reveals the **Code** Editor window.

Based on how you have Visual Studio configured, your screen might not look exactly like Figure 9-3. As a minimum, you will probably want to have the **Toolbox** and **Properties** windows accessible when you design your applications. Some developers prefer a larger screen to see their source code or find it distracting to have such a full screen of windows visible. You have many options for docking and hiding the windows shown in Figure 9-3. This figure has the **Toolbox**, **Solution Explorer**, **Properties**, and Form **Designer** windows visible. If you click the pushpin icon on the title bar of a specific window, the Auto Hide feature minimizes that window but leaves a tab for it along the end of the IDE. Figure 9-4 calls attention to the pushpin icon. The **Toolbox** window is displayed in a dockable state snapped in place. The **Solution Explorer** and **Properties** windows are tab docked in Auto Hide state. To put the window in Auto Hide state, click on its pushpin icon, and the pushpin is shown laying on its side. The **Error List** and **Output** windows, which are used when the application runs, are docked near the status bar.

> **NOTE** When a window is in Auto Hide state, if you click the mouse on the tab, the window is redisplayed. At other times, only the tab is visible. To take a window out of Auto Hide, redisplay the window and click the pushpin icon so that it is standing up, as shown in Figure 9-4.

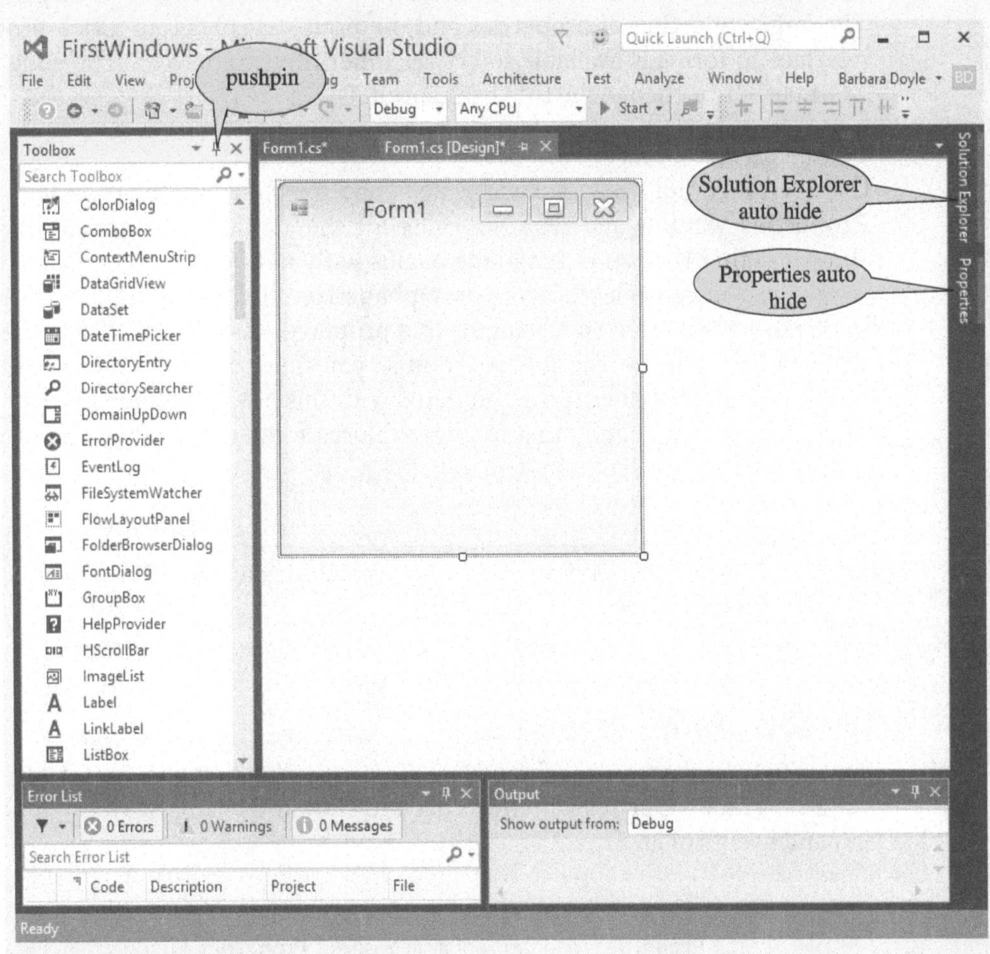

FIGURE 9-4 Dockable windows

NOTE Remember that to display the program statements, you can select **Code** from the **View** menu or press **F7**. If one or more window is accidentally closed during development or is not visible, it can be redisplayed by using the **View** option on the menu and then clicking beside the desired element.

Windows Forms

Windows Forms enable you to use a more modern object-oriented approach to developing Windows applications. The .NET model is based on an extensive collection of `Control` classes available, including a `Form` `class`, which is used as a container to hold other controls. The top-level window for an application is called a "form" in C#. If that top-level window opens another window, it is also considered a "form." The large collection of properties and methods that make up a rich programmable interface to forms is available to classes inheriting from `Form`. The code written for Example 9-1 to change the title bar caption is

```
Text = "Simple Windows Application";              // Line 4
```

Using Visual Studio, all you have to do is find the appropriate property (`Text`) in the **Properties** window and type the value for the caption. You do not have to worry about whether the property's name begins with an uppercase character or is spelled correctly. You can select it from an alphabetized list. In Figure 9-3, notice that the `Text` property is selected. Changing that property is as easy as clicking in the box and typing a new title bar caption. As soon as you finish typing and click outside of the box, the Form **Designer** form is updated with this new caption in place of the default value, `Form1`. The section that follows explores some of the other properties you can change for the `Form` container `class`.

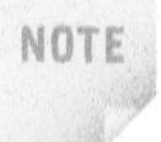

NOTE If the **Designer** window is not visible, select **Designer** from the **View** menu or press **Shift+F7** to show the form.

Windows Forms Properties

Figure 9-5 displays a list of some of the properties that can be set for the `Form1` `object`. The **Properties** window is used to view and change the design time properties and events of an `object`.

NOTE If your **Properties** window is not visible, select **Properties Window** from the **View** menu or press **Alt+Enter**.

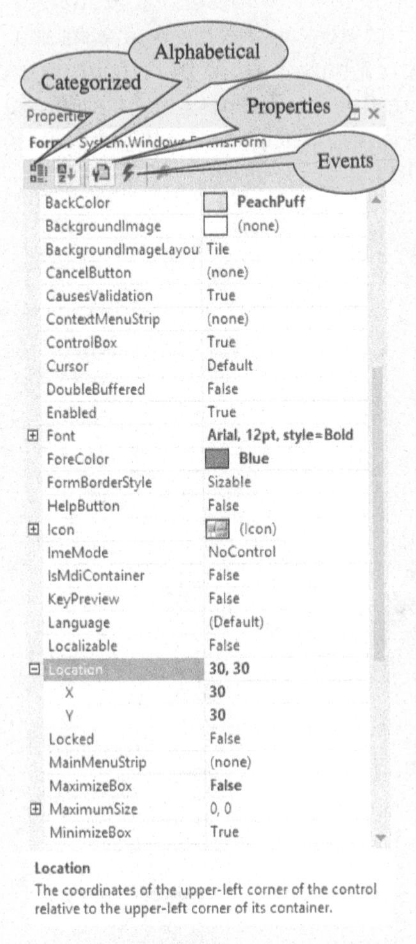

FIGURE 9-5 Properties window

In Figure 9-5, some of the properties have an Expand button to the left of the property name, indicating that the property can be expanded (only one is currently expanded). Groups of properties are collapsed together for easier navigation through the property list. If you click the plus, the group expands. For example, clicking the plus symbol to the left of the `Location` property reveals space where values can be typed for *x* and *y*. These values represent the x-coordinate and y-coordinate, respectively, for the location of the upper-left corner of the form.

In Figure 9-5, there are five buttons or icons immediately above the list of properties. The second button, the Alphabetical button, is selected. Properties appear listed in alphabetical order for this illustration. Many developers prefer to see the properties listed by category. As Figure 9-5 illustrates, the button to the left of the Alphabetical button rearranges the **Properties** window by category. The lightning bolt, labeled **Events**, is used to display the list of events that can be programmed for a selected `object`. The third button from the left in Figure 9-5 is the **Properties** button. This is selected, instead of the Events button, indicating that the list of properties is being displayed. Take a look at Figure 9-6, which contains a partial list of events that can be associated with a `Form1` `object`.

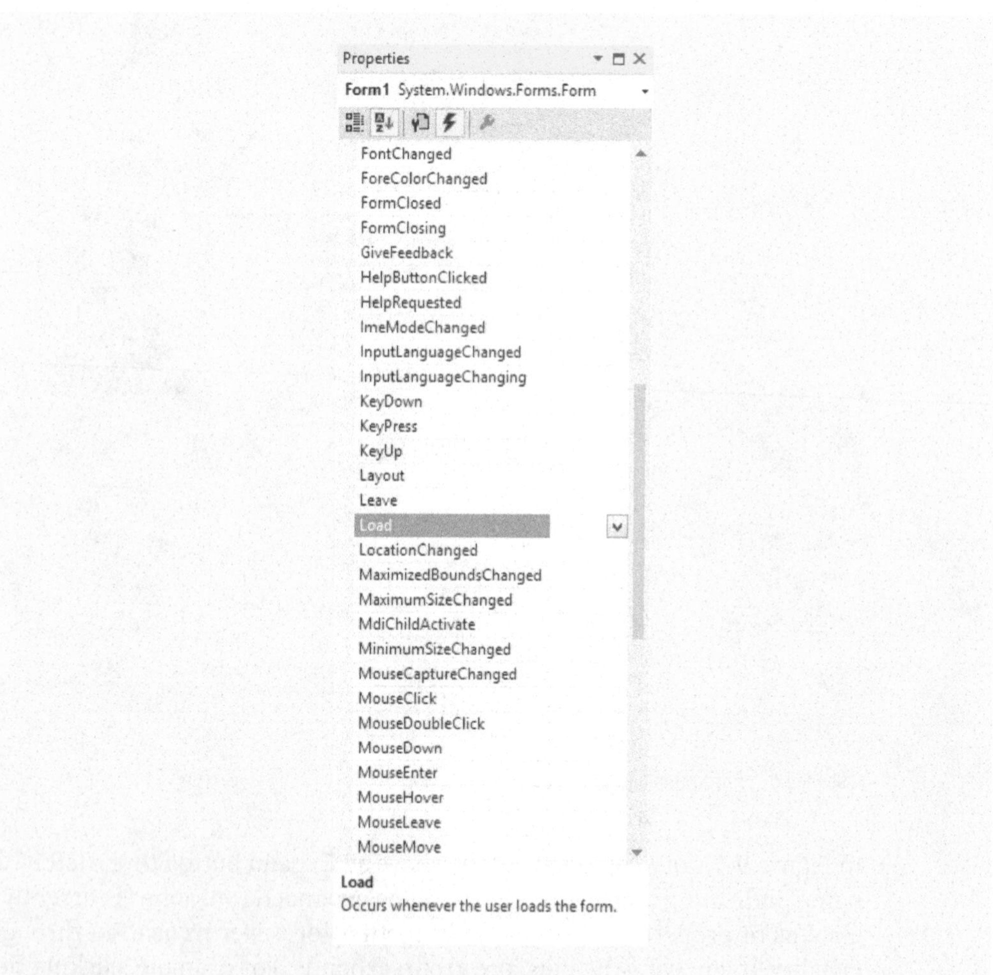

FIGURE 9-6 Form events

To illustrate how Visual Studio automatically generates code when property values are changed, Table 9-1 lists changes made to the respective properties of `Form1`. These changes are applied to the project that was started in Figure 9-2. Changing the property is as simple as moving the cursor to the edit box to the right of the property identifier and typing or selecting a value. Many properties have a drop-down list of values available for selection. All changes to the property values can be made in the **Properties** window at design time. You do not have to enter any source code statements. Properties values set for Form1 are given in Table 9-1.

NOTE You can, however, set the properties using program statements. As you review the code generated by Visual Studio, note how each property that you set by selecting or typing a value in the **Properties** window generates one or more lines of code.

TABLE 9-1 Form1 property changes

Property name	Actions performed on the FirstWindows properties
`AutoScroll`	Selected `true`
`BackColor`	Selected a PeachPuff color from a drop-down color selection window on the Web tab
`Font`	Selected Arial from a list of fonts; changed the size to 12 point; selected bold style
`ForeColor`	Selected a blue color from a drop-down color selection window on the Custom tab
`Location`	Changed the x-coordinate and y-coordinate from 0,0 to 30,30
`MaximizeBox`	Selected `false`
`Size`	Changed the width and height to 400,400
`StartPosition`	Using a drop-down menu option, changed the value from `WindowsDefaultLocation` to `CenterScreen`
`Text`	Typed `"First Windows Application"`

© Cengage Learning

9

As you can see from examining the property names in Table 9-1, the developers of Visual Studio did a good job selecting intuitive names for most of the properties. The names represent what the property would do to the form. Example 9-2 contains the source code listing generated by Visual Studio after the properties are set.

NOTE

Selecting **Code** on the **View** menu reveals the source code associated with the Form1.cs file. Double-clicking the form, while you are in design mode, takes you to the **Code** Editor, but with the undesired side effect that a `Form1_load( )` event-handler method heading and an empty body are added to your code. You will read more about events in Chapter 10. Each control has a default event. Double-clicking on the control adds its default event-handler method to your code. The form's default event is the `Load` event.

Three files are illustrated. The IDE separates the source code into three files when you create a simple Windows application. Initially these files are named `Form1.cs`, `Form1.Designer.cs`, and `Program.cs`. The first two files, `Form1.cs` and `Form1.Designer.cs`, both include `partial class` definitions for the `Form1` `class`. It is recommended that you never edit the `Form1.Designer.cs` file. You will normally only be editing the `Form1.cs` file.

The `Program.cs` file contains the `Main( ) method`, where execution always begins. One of the three lines of code found in the `Main( )` method is a call to `Application.Run( )`, which makes the form visible and ready to receive input from the user. The code shown in Example 9-2 is completely generated by Visual Studio. The full content of the files are included here. The only changes made to Example 9-2 were made to the comments. The XML comments inserted by Visual Studio were deleted and new inline comments added. Much of the auto-generated code and extraneous lines are deleted from the other Windows Forms examples illustrated later in this chapter and in Chapter 10.

NOTE

You will learn more about `partial` classes in Chapter 11. Partial classes allow you to split the definition of a `class` into two or more files.

EXAMPLE 9-2

```
// File#1 - FirstWindows.Form1.cs

using System;
using System.Collections.Generic;
using System.ComponentModel;
using System.Data;
using System.Drawing;
using System.Linq;
using System.Text;
using System.Threading.Tasks;
using System.Windows.Forms;
namespace FirstWindows
```

```
{
     public partial class Form1 : Form
     {
          public Form1( )
          {
               InitializeComponent( );
          }
     }
}    // End of FirstWindows.Form1.cs file


// File#2 - FirstWindows.Form1.Designer.cs
namespace FirstWindows
{
     partial class Form1
     {
          // Required designer variable.
          private System.ComponentModel.IContainer components = null;
          // Clean up any resources being used.
          protected override void Dispose(bool disposing)
          {
               if(disposing && (components != null))
               {
                    components.Dispose( );
               }
               base.Dispose(disposing);
          }
          #region Windows Form Designer generated code
          // Required method for Designer support - do not modify
          // the contents of this method with the code editor.
          private void InitializeComponent( )
          {
              this.SuspendLayout( );
              // Form1
              this.AutoScaleDimensions = new
                   System.Drawing.SizeF(10F,19F);
              this.AutoScaleMode =
                   System.Windows.Forms.AutoScaleMode.Font;
              this.AutoScroll = true;
              this.BackColor = System.Drawing.Color.PeachPuff;
              this.ClientSize = new System.Drawing.Size(384, 356);
              this.Font = new System.Drawing.Font("Arial", 12F,
                    System.Drawing.FontStyle.Bold,
                    System.Drawing.GraphicsUnit.Point,
                    ((System.Byte)(0)));
              this.ForeColor = System.Drawing.Color.Blue;
              this.Location = new System.Drawing.Point(30, 30);
              this.Margin = new
                   System.Windows.Forms.Padding(5,4,5,4);
              this.MaximizeBox = false;
```

9

```
                this.Name = "Form1";
                this.StartPosition =
                  System.Windows.Forms.FormStartPosition.CenterScreen;
                this.Text = "First Windows Application";
                this.ResumeLayout(false);
            }
            #endregion
        }
}           // End of FirstWindows.Form1.Designer.cs file


// File#3 - FirstWindows.Program.cs
using System;
using System.Collections.Generic;
using System.Linq;
using System.Threading.Tasks;
using System.Windows.Forms;
namespace FirstWindows
{
        static class Program
        {
            /// The main entry point for the application.
            static void Main( )
            {
                Application.EnableVisualStyles( );
                Application.SetCompatibleTextRenderingDefault(false);
                Application.Run(new Form1( ));
            }
        }
}                   // End of FirstWindows.Program.cs file
```

You run Windows applications like console applications by selecting **Start Debugging** or **Start Without Debugging** from the **Debug** menu in Visual Studio. You can also use the shortcuts, **F5** and **Ctrl+F5**, or click the **Start** icon on the **Standard** toolbar to run your applications. When you run the program in Example 9-2, a peach-colored window titled `"First Windows Application"` is displayed in the center of your screen. The Maximize button on the title bar is grayed out. The `StartPosition` property overrode the `Location` property values set. As you examine the drop-down menu options for `StartPosition`, notice that `Manual` is one of the values that can be selected. Selecting `Manual` enables the `Location` property to change where the form is displayed.

You can look ahead at Figure 9-8 to see what the form looks like with its title caption added, the Windows Maximize button grayed out, and the color set to peach. Figure 9-8 includes just one additional MessageBox dialog box layered on top of the form. It is added in the examples that follow.

Inspecting the Code Generated by Visual Studio

An examination of the **Solution Explorer** window, which is illustrated in Figure 9-7, reveals three source code files ending with a .cs extension that are part of the application. Console applications just create one source code file.

As you review Figure 9-7, notice that one of the three files is actually shown under the `Form1.cs` structure. This is the `Form1.Designer.cs` file. It is in this file that you will find the Windows Forms Designer generated code associated with the properties that were set for the application.

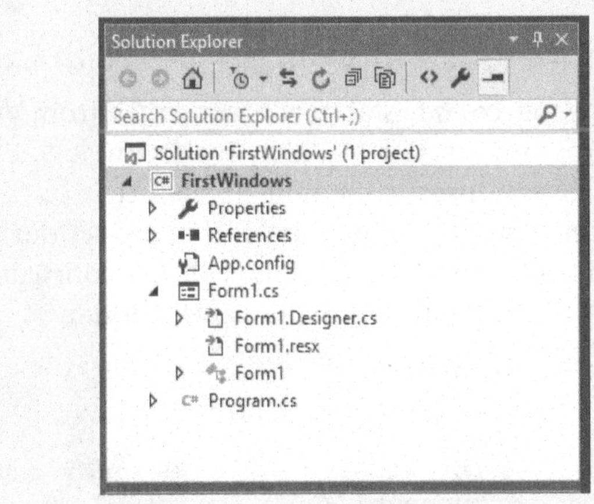

FIGURE 9-7 Solution Explorer window

In Example 9-2, you saw two lines that begin with the pound (#) symbol. These lines were in the `Form1.Designer.cs` file, labeled File#2 in the comment. The first one says `#region Windows Forms Designer generated code`. About 25 lines below that line, you find `#endregion`. This term, `#region`, is one of the preprocessor directives that can be included in C#. A **preprocessor directive** indicates something that should be done before processing. Preprocessor directives are often associated with conditionally skipping sections of source files or reporting certain types of errors.

According to the C# language reference specifications, the term "preprocessor" is used just for consistency. C# does not have the separate preprocessing step you find with C++ and other languages that identify statements that begin with # as preprocessor directives.

The `#region` preprocessor directive in C# is used to explicitly mark sections of source code that you can expand or collapse. If you were viewing the code in the Visual Studio **Code** Editor, observe that to the left of the directive a minus (–) or plus (+)

symbol appears. Clicking the (–) symbol causes the entire block of code between the # symbols to be collapsed and be replaced by a comment labeled "Windows Form Designer generated code". Clicking (+) expands the listing. The **Ctrl+M+M** shortcut can also be used to expand or collapse the region.

You can create your own regions using the #region preprocessor directive. All you have to do is add a label naming your region following #region. To end the block, use #endregion, as is done with the #region Windows Form Designer generated code... #endregion. This can aid the readability and maintainability of the code.

Comparing the Code of Example 9-1 With Example 9-2

Comparing the source code statements generated from Visual Studio for Example 9-2 against the program created manually for Example 9-1 reveals a number of differences. Visual Studio uses a method named InitializeComponent( ) to build the form at run time. All the properties that are set during design are placed in this method. Notice that the only statement in the constructor for Example 9-2 in the Form1.cs file is a call to the InitializeComponent( ) method.

```
// Constructor from Example 9-2
public Form1( )
{
      // Required for Windows Form Designer support.
      InitializeComponent( );
}
```

In Example 9-1, you will remember that the Text property was actually set in the constructor method. No InitializeComponent( ) method was created.

```
// Constructor from Example 9-1
public Form1( )
{
      Text = "Simple Windows Application";
}
```

In the InitializeComponent( ) method of Example 9-2, each of the properties was suffixed with the keyword this, which refers to the current instance of a class. In Example 9-2, this referred to the current instance of Form1. In Example 9-2, the this keyword could have been completely eliminated from the program listing without changing anything.

When you are writing code using the Visual Studio IDE, typing the keyword this followed by a period brings up IntelliSense. A listing of the members of the class is displayed for selection. You will find this extremely useful. It keeps you from having to remember the correct spelling of identifiers associated with your class members.

Notice that Visual Studio imported several other namespaces in the `Form1.cs` file:

```
using System;
using System.Collections.Generic;
using System.ComponentModel;
using System.Data;
using System.Drawing;
using System.Linq;
using System.Text;
using System.Threading.Tasks;
using System.Windows.Forms;
```

No `using` statements were included in the `Form1.Designer.cs` file where the `InitializeComponent( )` method appears. Since the two files (`Form1.Designer.cs` and `Form1.cs`) are designated as `partial` classes, they both have access to namespaces referenced in either file. If the namespaces had been included in the file, it would not be necessary to qualify each `class` name fully. The `InitializeComponent( )` method could read as shown in Example 9-3.

EXAMPLE 9-3

```
private void InitializeComponent( )
{
      SuspendLayout( );
      //
      // Form1
      //
      AutoScaleDimensions = new SizeF(10F, 19F);
      AutoScaleMode = AutoScaleMode.Font;
      AutoScroll = true;
      BackColor = Color.PeachPuff;
      ClientSize = new Size(384, 356);
      Font = new Font("Arial", 12F, FontStyle.Bold,
           GraphicsUnit.Point, ((Byte)(0)));
      ForeColor = Color.Blue;
      Location = new Point(30, 30);
      Margin = new Padding(5,4,5,4);
      MaximizeBox = false;
      Name = "Form1";
      StartPosition = FormStartPosition.CenterScreen;
      Text = "First Windows Application";
      ResumeLayout(false);
      // Additional statements
}
```

This code is much more readable than the code generated from Visual Studio. However, it is not worth your effort to take time to remove the verbage. Do not lose sight of the fact that all of the code was automatically generated from the Visual Studio

Form Designer after properties were set from the **Properties** window. This certainly cuts down on the development time. Nevertheless, it is important that you are able to read the code and make modifications as necessary.

One of the comments in the `Form1.Designer.cs` file (Windows Forms Designer generated code region) reads "do not modify the contents of this method with the code editor." Separating this code into another file helps to discourage modifications.

One additional method, `Dispose( )`, is added in the `Form1.Designer.cs` file by the IDE. This is shown in Example 9-2. The .NET common language runtime (CLR) performs memory management. The CLR's automatic garbage collector releases memory from the application after the program is halted. The purpose of this `Dispose( )` method is to clean up or release unused resources back to the operating system.

Take a look at the call to the `Run( )` method included in the `Program.cs file` generated by Visual Studio. This is one of three statements that appear in the `Main( )` method.

```
Application.EnableVisualStyles( );
Application.SetCompatibleTextRenderingDefault(false);
```

The first two lines of code call methods that enable the text and visual effects to be placed on Windows Forms controls. For the applications you will be creating, they could be removed from the application. However, again it is not worth your effort to take time to remove them. In the call to the `Run( )` method in Example 9-2, no actual identifier was associated with an `object` of the `Form1` type.

```
//From Example 9-2
Application.Run(new Form1( ));
```

The `new` keyword creates an anonymous (unnamed) instance of `Form1`, but notice where this occurs—as an argument to the `Run( )` method. There is really no need to identify an `object` of the `Form1` type by name, and this `Form1 object` identifier is not used anywhere else. Thus, the approach taken in the `Main( )` method in Example 9-2 is more streamlined than in Example 9-1. The two statements that made up the `Main( )` method body from Example 9-1 are displayed again in the following code segment for comparison purposes:

```
// From Example 9-1
Form1 winForm = new Form1( );                          // Line 5
Application.Run(winForm);                              // Line 6
```

One of the first things you may want to do is rename the `Form1.cs` file to something more representative of the application. You can do this using the **Solution Explorer** window. Right-click on the `Form1.cs` file and select the **Rename** option.

Be sure to end the file with the .cs extension. When you rename this file, the `Form1.Designer.cs` file is automatically renamed and all references to `Form1` are automatically changed.

Windows Forms Events

The topic of Chapter 10 is handling events. However, it is useful to have a brief introduction to them here so that you can add some functionality to your Windows form. Figure 9-6 showed a partial list of events to which objects of the `Form1 class` could respond. Visual Studio makes it very simple to add code to respond to events. One way to add a method is to find the event in the list of events (from the **Properties** window with the lightning bolt (**Events**) selected) and double-click on the event name. When you do this, code is automatically added to your program by the Visual Studio Form Designer.

Notice in Figure 9-6 that one of the events listed is `FormClosing`. Double-clicking on the `FormClosing` event adds the following code to the `InitializeComponent( )` method in the `Form1.Designer.cs` file:

```
this.FormClosing += new System.Windows.Forms.FormClosingEventHandler
     (this.Form1_FormClosing);
```

The preceding statement is registering the `FormClosing` event so that your program is notified when a user is closing the application. You will learn more details about events in Chapter 10. For now, just realize that this line is necessary if you want to have your program receive a message from the operating system when a user clicks the "X" to close your application. Visual Studio adds the statement automatically for you when you double-click `FormClosing`, while you are using the Form **Designer** and have the form selected.

9

The other code automatically generated by the Form Designer and added to the program listing for the `Form1.cs` file when you double-click the `FormClosing` event is the actual event-handler method heading and an empty body, as shown in the following code segment:

```
private void Form1_FormClosing(object sender, FormClosingEventArgs e)
{
}
```

Also notice that when you double-click on an event name such as `FormClosing`, the **Code** Editor window for `Form1.cs` becomes the active window.

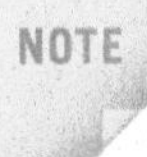

NOTE A tab is created for the **Code** Editor window when the source code file is opened. Clicking the tab allows you to move between the **Code** Editor and the Form **Designer**. The windows can also be opened from the **Solution Explorer** window or from the **View** menu if they are not visible. Both tabs are shown in Figure 9-4. The **Designer** tab is active.

The cursor is placed inside the empty body of the `Form1_FormClosing( )` method. The IDE is waiting for you to program what is to occur when the user is closing your application. Take note! This is the first time you have needed to type any code since you started developing the `FirstWindows` application. The following line is typed as the body for the `Form1_FormClosing( )` method:

```
MessageBox.Show("Hope you are having fun!");
```

Figure 9-8 shows the output produced when the user clicks the Close button.

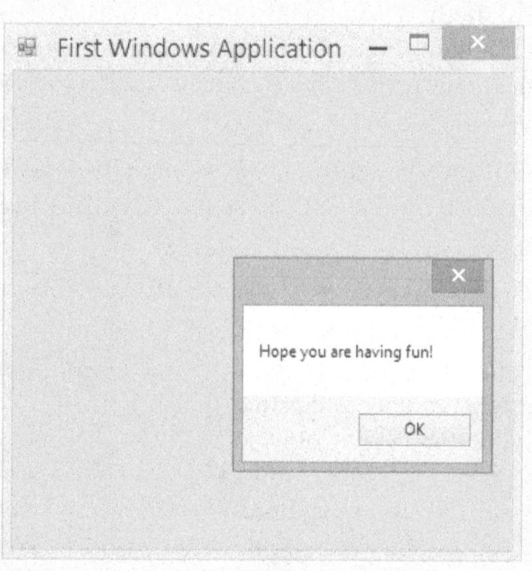

FIGURE 9-8 Output produced when the Close button causes the event-handler

At this point, the form is still blank. The following section introduces you to controls such as buttons and labels that can be placed on the form to add functionality to your Windows application.

Controls

The real strength of using C# for Windows applications lies in the number of controls that you can add to your applications. The `System.Windows.Forms` `namespace` includes many classes that you can add to your form representing controls with names such as `Button`, `Label`, `TextBox`, `ComboBox`, `MainMenu`, `ListBox`, `CheckBox`, `PictureBox`, `MenuStrip`, `RadioButton`, and `MonthCalendar`. It is important to understand the concept that these controls are all classes. Each comes with its own bundle of predefined properties and methods. Each fires events—some of which you should write methods for—indicating what to do when its event is fired. An example is the Button class, which fires click events when an object of the class is clicked. As stated previously, if you use Visual Studio, most of the standard service plumbing code is added automatically for you. All you add is code for the special processing that should occur when a particular Button object is clicked.

NOTE You are going to find it very easy to work with Visual Studio and Windows applications using an object-oriented approach.

All of the control classes that can be added to a form are derived from the System.Windows.Forms.Control class. Figure 9-9 shows the class hierarchy of namespaces for the Control classes. With Object being the base class from which all classes ultimately are derived, Figure 9-9 illustrates that all the Windows control classes derive from a class named Control.

NOTE In C#, object is an alias for System.Object in the .NET Framework. Thus, instead of using Object to refer to this top-level base class, you use object with a lowercase 'o'.

9

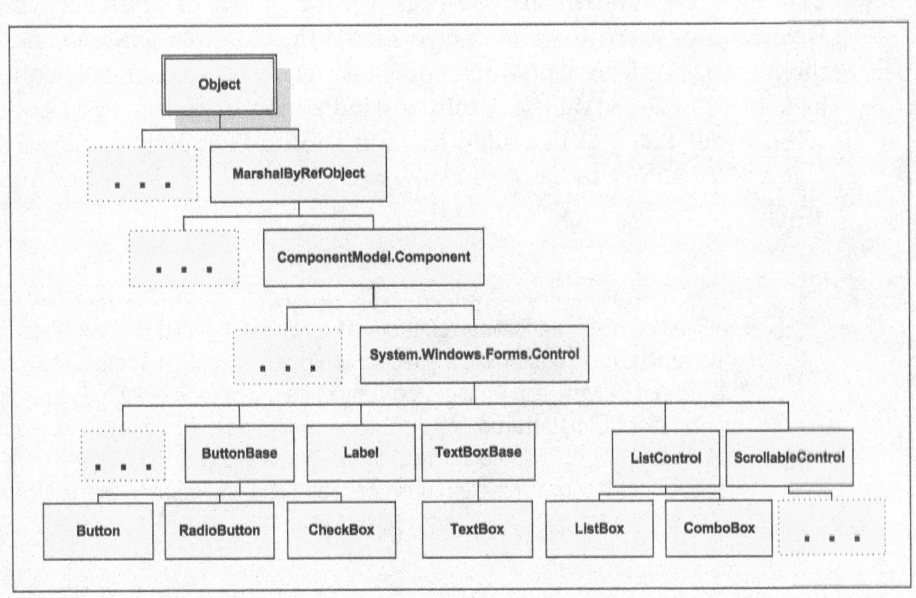

FIGURE 9-9 Control class hierarchy

Remember, when a `class` is derived from another `class`, it inherits the characteristics of all of its ancestor classes—meaning its parent `class`, the parent of the parent, and so on.

The dots on the classes in Figure 9-9 indicate that other classes are derived from the `class`. For example, a number of other classes are derived from the `class Object`; other classes are derived from the `MarshalByRefObject` and `ComponentModel.Component` classes. If you examine the .NET documentation, you find a total of 22 classes that are derived from `System.Windows.Forms.Control`. The classes shown in Figure 9-9 are those that represent some of the more basic GUI controls. They are discussed in the sections that follow and in Chapter 10.

Another important concept to recognize is that the `Form class` is actually a derived `class` of the `ContainerControl class`. The `ContainerControl class` is a derived `class` of the `ScrollableControl class`, which is a derived `class` of `Control`. Figure 9-9 showed the `ScrollableControl class` with dots to indicate that other classes are derived from it. The reason this is important to you will be revealed when you learn about all the properties, methods, and event members that the `Control class` has predefined. Thus, not only `Button`, `Label`, and `TextBox` objects have access to these members but also `Form` objects inherit members of the `Control class`.

The Form **Designer** helps you organize the layout of the form window. While in **Design** view, you can select controls from the **Toolbox** window and drag and drop them onto your form container. You can actually write your own control classes and have them included on the **Toolbox** window. A number of third-party vendors also sell controls that can be added to your **Toolbox** window to increase functionality. Figure 9-10 shows some of the standard controls included when you install Visual Studio.

A large number of additional controls are available, beyond those included when you install Visual Studio. To customize a specific **Toolbox**, select that **Toolbox** tab, such as **All Windows Forms**, and right-click on any of its controls. A menu option is displayed that includes a **Choose Items** option. You can select new .NET predefined controls or deselect those that you do not need access to on your desktop. You can even write your own controls (or buy controls from other vendors) and add them to the **Toolbox**.

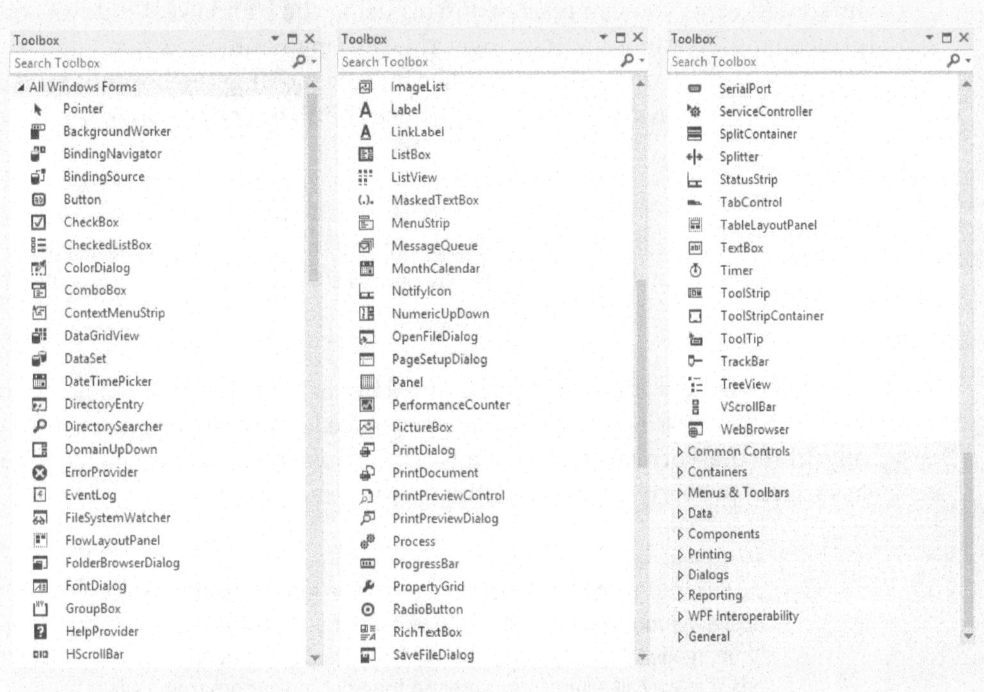

FIGURE 9-10 Windows Forms controls

The illustration shown in Figure 9-10 shows controls available in Visual Studio. You might see a slightly different listing if you are using a different version or if the **Toolbox** has been previously customized.

If your **Toolbox** window is not visible, one way to activate it is to select **Toolbox** from the **View** menu. The **All Windows Forms** controls in the **Toolbox** are only visible when you are using the Designer. If the **Code** Editor window is active, you must select the Designer tab to gain access to the **All Windows Forms** controls.

Placing, Moving, Resizing, and Deleting Control Objects

Two procedures are used to place a control on your form. After the control is selected, you can either double-click the control or drag and drop the control to the correct location. If you use the double-click approach, the control is always placed in the upper-left corner of the form—even if it overlaps other controls. To move the control, position the mouse pointer over the control until you see the standard Windows cross-bars. With the left mouse button pressed, you can drag the control to its new location.

In Design view, you can resize controls using the standard Windows conventions of positioning the mouse pointer over the resizing handles. When you get the double-sided arrow, hold down the left mouse button and drag the border to the desired size. Another option available to you is to use the **Properties** window and set the `Size` property.

Select multiple controls using your mouse by either drawing an outline around the controls that are to be formatted or holding down the **Ctrl** key while you click on the controls.

To delete a control, first select the control by clicking on it. The sizing handles become visible. Now pressing the Delete or Backspace key not only removes the control visually from the Form **Designer** view but also removes all the constructor code and associated property changes relating to the selected `object`.

Just as you spent time designing a prototype for a console-based application, you should design a prototype for your Windows form. Randomly placing controls on your form leads to unorganized source code. It is probably best to place all labels, then all buttons, and so on. That way, like items are grouped together in your program listing.

When you copy and paste controls on the form, you normally must always move the `object` to the new position after it is pasted. Windows Forms **Designer** has a SnapLine feature to help you accomplish precise layout of controls on your form. Horizontal and vertical line segments are dynamically created by the SnapLine feature to assist in the layout of controls. Several menu options from the **Format** menu are also extremely helpful during design, including **Align**, **Make Same Size**, **Horizontal Spacing**, and **Vertical Spacing**. After the control(s) is (are) selected, the **Align** selections include options such as **Lefts**, **Centers**, **Rights**, **Tops**, **Middles**, and **Bottoms**. The **Make Same Size** selection is especially useful for sizing buttons for consistency.

Note that when you select more than one control to format, the last control selected is the one used as the template for the action. For example, if `label1`, `label2`, and `label3` are all large, but `label4` is small, and you click on `label4` last when you are identifying controls to resize, clicking **Make Same Size** changes `label1`, `label2`, and `label3` to the size of `label4`. This also holds true for the **Align** options.

The **Horizontal Spacing** and **Vertical Spacing** options enable you to increase or decrease the amount of blank space displayed between objects. If multiple objects are selected, using these tools helps you have an equal amount of space between your controls.

NOTE Be sure to practice using the tools available from the **Format** menu. Using the **Align**, **Make Same Size**, and **Horizontal Spacing** and **Vertical Spacing** options can greatly reduce your development time for the GUI and lead to more professional looking designs.

Methods and Properties of the Control Class

You recall that classes that derive from the `System.Windows.Forms.Control class` inherit a number of predefined methods and properties from the `Control class`. This includes `Form` objects as well as `Button`, `Label`, `TextBox`, and the other objects from classes shown in Figure 9-9. Table 9-2 describes some of the more interesting properties that the objects have available to them through inheritance from the `Control class`.

NOTE Using the Form Designer, you are able to configure the properties for the form and the controls that are on the form.

TABLE 9-2 System.Windows.Forms.Control class properties

Property	Description
`Anchor`	Gets or sets which edges of the control are anchored to the edges of its container
`BackColor`	Gets or sets the background color for the control
`BackgroundImage`	Gets or sets the background image displayed in the control
`CanFocus`	Gets a value indicating whether the control can receive input focus
`CanSelect`	Gets a value indicating whether the control can be selected
`Enabled`	Gets or sets a value indicating whether the control can respond to user interaction
`Focused`	Gets a value indicating whether the control can have input focus
`Font`	Gets or sets the font of the text displayed by the control
`ForeColor`	Gets or sets the foreground color of the control

(continues)

9

TABLE 9-2 System.Windows.Forms.Control class properties (*continued*)

Property	Description
`Location`	Gets or sets the coordinates of the upper-left corner of the control relative to the upper-left corner of its container
`Name`	Gets or sets the name of the control
`Size`	Gets or sets the height and width of the control
`TabIndex`	Gets or sets the tab order of the control within its container
`Text`	Gets or sets the text associated with the control
`Visible`	Gets or sets a value indicating whether the control is displayed

© Cengage Learning

The `Control class` has over 75 properties and over 100 methods. Not all are useful for every `class` that derives from it. Thus, you will not see all of the `Control` members listed in the **Properties** window for classes that derive from it. For example, the `Label object` has its own `Image`, `ImageIndex`, and `ImageList` properties. It does not use Control's `BackgroundImage` method to get or set its background image.

Table 9-3 includes a short list of methods in the `System.Windows.Forms.Control class` that derived classes inherit. You should explore the online documentation available in Visual Studio to learn about other members. All of the information from Tables 9-2 and 9-3 is developed from the Visual Studio MSDN documentation.

TABLE 9-3 System.Windows.Forms.Control methods

Method	Description
`Focus( )`	Sets the input focus to the control
`Hide( )`	Conceals the control from the user
`Select( )`	Activates a control
`Show( )`	Displays the control to the user

NOTE One of the most powerful features of the Visual Studio IDE is the extensive help available. You can access Visual Studio's online MSDN documentation web page for help or use installed offline help. Manage help settings from the **Help** menu option. You choose **Launch in Browser** or **Launch in Help Viewer** from the **Set Help Preference** menu option. Open the help window using **Ctrl+F1, V**. You can also position your cursor over controls and click on the control or properties and press F1 to cause the documentation to pop up.

The `Show( )` method functions the same way as setting the `Visible` property to `true`; `Hide( )` does the same thing as setting the `Visible` property to `false`. Showing a control is equivalent to setting the `Visible` property to `true`. After the `Show( )` method is called, the `Visible` property returns `true` until the `Hide( )` method is called. When you invoke the `Focus( )` method with an object such as a textbox, the cursor is positioned on that object. This is very useful when you have a control the user will be typing data into. You will be reading about textboxes later in this chapter.

The `System.Windows.Forms.Control class` also has a number of predefined events, many of which you will examine in Chapter 10. The `System.Windows.Forms.Control` click events will be used in this chapter with `Button` objects.

Derived Classes of the System.Windows.Forms.Control Class

All the controls that you add to a form are objects or instances of one of the .NET predefined classes. Figure 9-11 identifies some of the basic user interface controls that can be added to a form. Look at each of the controls. They are named and briefly described. 9

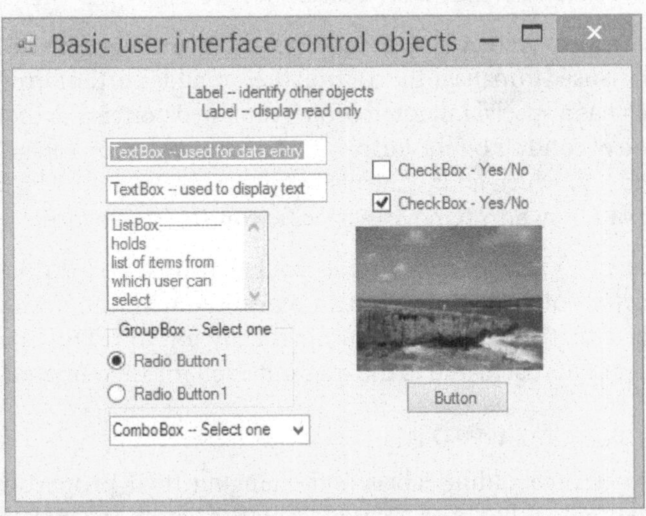

FIGURE 9-11 GUI controls

In the sections that follow, these GUI components are discussed in detail, and you will create a small GUI application that can be used to compute the tax due on a purchase.

LABEL

As the name implies, Label objects are normally used to provide descriptive text or labels for another control. They can also be used to display information at run time. Using Visual Studio, you can drag and drop the Label object onto your form. After it is added, you can set its properties to customize it for your application. The actual text caption that appears on the Label control object is placed there using the Text property. The TextAlign property enables you to position the caption within the label control area. The Label object can be programmed to be visible based on run time dynamics using the Visible property. By default, the Visible property is set to true. Font, Location, and any of the other Control properties given in Table 9-2 can be modified using the Form Designer in Visual Studio.

If you prefer, you can manually add statements to instantiate and place control objects on your Windows forms, instead of using the Form Designer in Visual Studio. As long as the System.Windows.Forms namespace is imported and referenced, you can create a Label object manually (without having to qualify the name fully) by calling the default constructor and instantiating an object as follows:

```
Label labelName = new Label( );
```

If you add a control such as a Label or Button object manually, a second step is required. To make the label viewable on the form, it must be added to the Form object. This is accomplished as follows:

```
this.Controls.Add(labelName);
```

When a form is created, it includes an instance of the ControlCollection class. This class is used to manage the controls that are added to the form. The ControlCollection class has a special inherited property named Controls that can be used to get the collection of controls on the form. The ControlCollection class also has methods such as Add( ), which adds controls to a form; Clear( ), which removes all controls; and Remove( ), which removes a specific control from a form.

If you use Visual Studio to add your controls, you do not have to worry about all the details of getting the control registered with the ControlCollection object, because that code is added automatically for you. This is certainly the easiest, most efficient approach, and is the method used for the remainder of this chapter.

CREATING A TAXAPP FORM

To experience adding labels and changing their properties, a Visual Studio project named TaxApp has been created. Table 9-4 lists the properties set for the Form object.

TABLE 9-4 TaxApp Form1 properties

Property	Changes with explanation
`BackColor`	Selected LightSkyBlue from the Web tab; could have typed an RGB code such as 192, 192, 255 for that selection
`Font`	Selected Microsoft Sans Serif, regular, 12 point; changed the font on the form, so that all controls added to this container would have this value set
`Size`	Changed the size of the window to 320, 300
`Text`	Typed `"Windows Tax App"` for the title bar caption

© Cengage Learning

ADDING LABEL OBJECTS TO YOUR TAXAPP FORM

Four `Label` objects are dragged to the form using the `Label` icon in the **Toolbox**. Figure 9-12 shows the Label objects that are added and formatted.

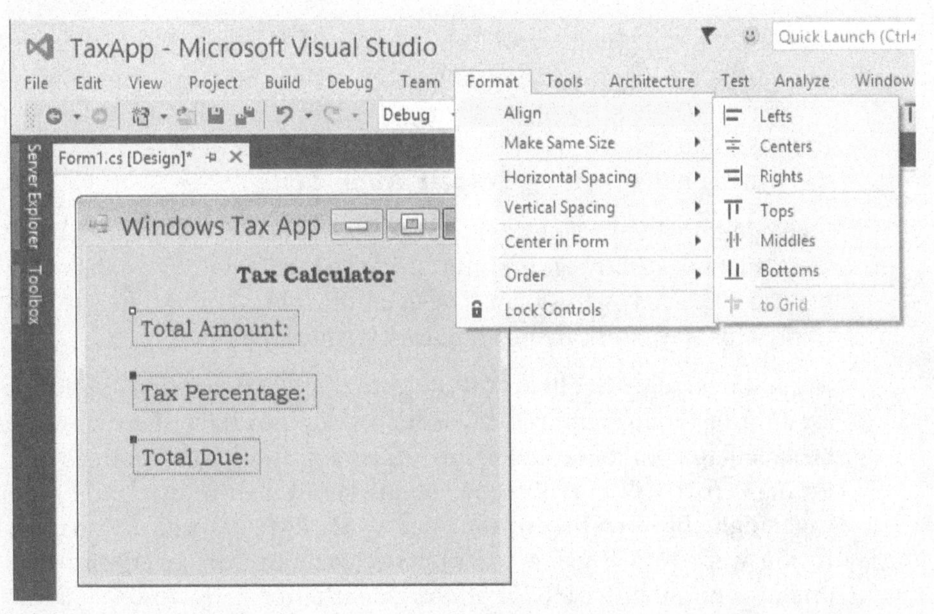

FIGURE 9-12 Formatting Label objects

The `Text` property for each label is selected and values typed. Each of the individual objects needs to be resized so that the text can be displayed. The `label4 object`, which holds the heading "Tax Calculator" for the form, `Font` property is set to a size of 14 points with a bold style. This is done by clicking on the ellipsis beside the `Font` property. A font dialog box is revealed. Bold is selected as the font style and the size was set to 14. The `TextAlign` property for `label1` is set to `TopCenter`.

After `label2`, `label3`, and `label4` object's `Text` properties are changed and they are sized properly, the **Align** option from the **Format** menu can be used to line them up in the same general area. Using the SnapLines, controls can be more easily aligned when they are initially added to the form. If you need to use the **Align** option, you can hold the **Ctrl** key and click on each of the objects you want to format. An alternate approach is to hold down the left mouse button and use the mouse to draw a box around the objects to be impacted. When you release the mouse button, you should ensure that the correct objects are selected.

If you select too many objects, deselect one or more by pressing the **Ctrl** key and clicking on the objects to be deselected. You also have an **Undo** option under the **Edit** menu, which enables you to back out of a step.

While `label2`, `label3`, and `label4` are still selected, the vertical spacing between the labels is formatted using **Format**, **Vertical Spacing**, and **Make Equal**. This is much simpler than trying to align your objects visually and drag them to new locations. As illustrated in Figure 9-12 several controls were selected and then they were all aligned on the left using **Format**, **Align**, **Lefts**.

One additional `Label object`, `label5`, is added to the `TaxApp` form container for the actual tax percentage amount. Because the tax rate is a constant value, the number can be placed on the form at design time. The number can also be used in calculations. This way, users are not required to enter the value.

A good design principle to follow is to keep data entry to a minimum. Limit the amount of typing required by users and do not have them enter values that can be calculated or obtained from other sources. This reduces the chances that typing errors will corrupt your solutions. It also reduces the amount of coding that might have to be done to deal with data entered in inconsistent formats. If you were to ask users to enter the tax rate for seven-and-one-half percent, one user might enter 0.075; others might enter 7.5%, 7.50%, 7.5, or 07.50. Entries stored as constants eliminate the need to program for these potential formatting inconsistencies.

After `label5` is added to the form to the right of Tax Percentage label, its properties are changed, as given in Table 9-5.

TABLE 9-5 TaxApp label5 object properties

Property	Changes with explanation
`BackColor`	Selected medium blue from Custom tab; changed the value to 50, 50, 192 (RGB code for that selection)
`Font`	Selected style of bold italic
`ForeColor`	Selected LightBlue from the Web tab
`Name`	`lblTaxPercent`
`Text`	Typed `"7.5%"`

© Cengage Learning

Because only one label, lblTaxPercent, is programmed for functionality with this application, it is the only label named. The `Name` property of the other `Label` objects are not changed. The default identifier names (`label1`, `label2`, . . .) are left as is.

Labels are sometimes used to display messages to users during run time. They are especially useful for displaying error messages or text that does not appear with each run of an application. However, labels are most often used primarily to describe other controls on the form.

9

TEXTBOX

The `TextBox` control `object`, shown in Figure 9-11, can be used to enter data or display text during run time. This is probably the most commonly used control because it can be used for both input and output. Like most other objects of the `Control class`, the `Text` property is used to get or set the `string` value in the control. Normally, a single line of text is shown in a `TextBox object`; however, by changing the `Multiline` property to `true`, the `TextBox object` can show several lines. There is also a `ScrollBars` property. When this property is used in combination with setting the `Multiline` property to `true`, you can designate whether vertical or horizontal scroll bars are added. You can also restrict the number of characters the `TextBox object` can display by typing a value for the `MaxLength` property.

The `PasswordChar` property is used with `TextBox` objects and is fun to work with. By typing a single character such as an asterisk ( ), you can mask the characters entered by the user. This is perfect for creating or entering data such as passwords. The `PasswordChar` property only works when the `Multiline` property is set to `false`.

Set the value of the `PasswordChar` property to `'0'` if you do not want the control to mask characters as they are typed.

Another property, CharacterCasing, can be set so that all characters retrieved by the TextBox.Text property are converted into uppercase or lowercase. This is useful when you are comparing the results entered from a user against a specific value. By using the CharacterCasing property, you eliminate many of the extra comparisons that might be necessary.

There are many interesting properties that can be used with a TextBox object. Table 9-6 includes some of them. They were adapted from the Visual Studio MSDN documentation.

TABLE 9-6 TextBox properties

Property	Description
AcceptsReturn	Gets or sets a value indicating whether the Enter key creates a new line of text in a multiline TextBox control
AcceptsTab	Gets or sets a value indicating whether the Tab key inserts a tab into text of a multiline TextBox control
CharacterCasing	Gets or sets whether the TextBox control modifies the case of the characters as they are typed
Lines	Gets or sets the lines of text in a TextBox control
MaxLength	Gets or sets the maximum number of characters the user can type or paste into the TextBox control
Modified	Gets or sets a value indicating that the TextBox control has been modified since creation or when its contents were last set
Multiline	Gets or sets a value indicating whether this is a multiline TextBox control
PasswordChar	Gets or sets the character used to mask characters in a single-line TextBox control
ReadOnly	Gets or sets a value indicating whether text in the TextBox is read-only
ScrollBars	Gets or sets which scroll bars should appear in a multiline TextBox control
TextAlign	Gets or sets how text is aligned in a TextBox control
WordWrap	Indicates whether a multiline TextBox control automatically wraps words to the beginning of the next line

© Cengage Learning

NOTE The `Modified` property is not listed in the **Properties** window because it is used to get or set the value indicating whether the contents of the text box control have been modified by the user since the control was created or its contents were last set.

Remember that in addition to the `TextBox` properties listed in Table 9-6, all the `Control` properties and methods given in Tables 9-2 and 9-3 are available for use with `TextBox` objects. Several other methods including `AppendText( )`, which adds text to the end of the current text of the `TextBox`, and `Clear( )` can be used with `TextBox` objects. There are many interesting events that can be responded to with `TextBox` objects, and you will read about many of them in Chapter 10.

ADDING TEXTBOX OBJECTS TO YOUR TAXAPP FORM

Two `TextBox` objects are added to the `TaxApp` form. The first is used as an input control allowing the user to enter the total purchase amount. The second is used to display the results of the calculation. Because the values entered or displayed in the `TextBox` objects must be referenced programmatically, one of the first properties to set is the `Name` property. `textBox1` is renamed `txtPurchase`, and `textBox2` is renamed `txtTotalDue`. If you want blanks in `TextBox` objects, you do not have to clear values. By default, the `Text` property for the `TextBox` object is set to an empty string.

NOTE Remember that to set properties, the **Properties** window must be active. If you do not see it on your screen, it can be displayed from the **View** menu. Then click on the control that you want to change and move down the list of properties in the **Properties** window until you locate the property. Type or select the new setting.

9

Table 9-7 lists the other properties set for the two `TextBox` objects.

TABLE 9-7 TaxApp TextBox objects property changes

Object	Property	Changes with explanation
`textBox1`	`Name`	Typed `txtPurchase`
`textBox2`	`Name`	Typed `txtTotalDue`
`txtPurchase`	`TextAlign`	Selected `Right`
`txtTotalDue`	`Enabled`	Selected `false`
`txtTotalDue`	`TextAlign`	Selected `Right`

© Cengage Learning

The `txtPurchase` `TextBox` object's `TabIndex` property is also set to `1`. You may need to realign it with the `label1` text heading. You can do this by selecting both control objects and clicking **Format, Align, Centers.**

As controls, such as text boxes and labels, are placed on the form, they are aligned and sized using **Format, Align**; **Format, Make Same Size**; **Format, Center in Form**; and the other options available from the **Format** menu. You are encouraged to experiment and learn to use these options.

As you build your Windows applications, in addition to seeing what the output looks like in the Form **Designer**, you can run the application at any stage as soon as you start the project.

The output produced from `TaxApp` (after adding the `Label` and `TextBox` objects and setting their properties) is shown in Figure 9-13.

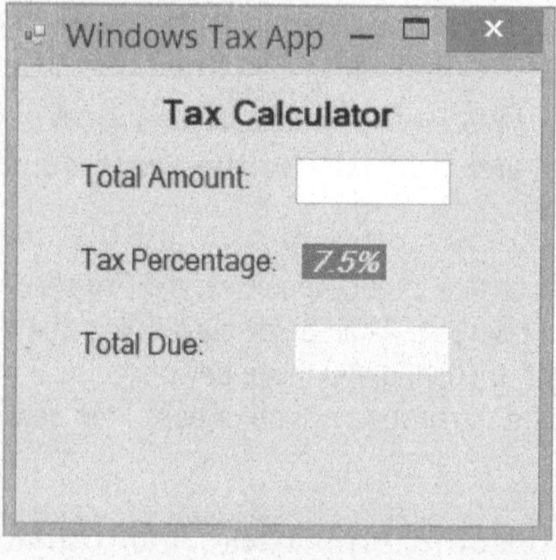

FIGURE 9-13 TaxApp with Label, TextBox, and Button objects

If you accidentally double-click on the form when you are using the Form **Designer**, it brings up the **Code** Editor. Entering the **Code** Editor this way has the undesirable side effect of creating a `Form1_Load( )` method heading for you. The creation of the event does not create an error when you run your application, but it clutters your program listing with an empty method and a statement that registers the event. If you remove the method heading, you should also remove the statement that registered the form load event (`this.Load += new System.EventHandler(this.Form1_Load);`) in the Form1.Designer.cs file. This same side effect occurs if you double-click other controls such as labels or text boxes. The `label_click( )` or `textbox_textChanged( )` methods are added.

At design time, you change the `Text` property by pointing and clicking in the `Text` property box. However, how do you use the Total Amount value entered by the user?

How do you place text in the `TextBox` `object` beside the Total Due `Label` `object`? This cannot be done at design time. It needs to change based on the value the user enters for Total Amount. You are about to experience the programming power of using C# and Visual Studio. Any and all of the properties you changed during design can be accessed as part of a program statement and changed dynamically when your program runs. To experience this powerful characteristic of C#, you will now add a button that performs some calculations and displays the result in the Total Due `TextBox` `object`.

BUTTON

`Button` objects are added to your form to increase functionality. They enable a user to click a button to perform a specific task. When it is clicked by a user, the event-handler method is automatically called up—if the button has an event-handler method—and is registered as an event to which your program is planning to respond. You place code in the event-handler method to perform any action you choose. A click event is normally associated with a mouse click; however, the click event can be fired when the Enter key or Spacebar is pressed if the button has the focus.

NOTE Having **focus** means being selected for the next activity. When an `object` has focus, it often appears different from the other controls. It can appear highlighted or selected with a box surrounding it.

Like other control objects, `Button` objects have a number of properties, methods, and events. They also inherit the properties, methods, and events listed previously in Tables 9-2 and 9-3 from the `Control` `class`. The `Enabled` property, inherited from the `Control` `class`, can be used to get or set a value indicating whether the control can respond to user interaction. The `Focused` property is used to determine whether the control has focus or is the one currently selected. The `Focus( )` method from the `Control` `class` is useful with `Button` objects to set the input focus to that control. `TabIndex`, also inherited from `Control`, is useful for setting or getting the tab order of the controls on a form container. Selecting **Tab Order** from the **View** menu shows the sequential order of how focus moves from control to control if the Tab key is used. By default, the tab order is the same order as the order of how the controls are added to the form. You can change this order when you are in **View, Tab Order** by clicking the controls sequentially to establish the new order. As you do this, a number representing the `TabIndex` property is displayed beside the control.

NOTE You can also set the tab order from the **Properties** window or by writing program statements. A `Label` `object` participates in the tab order in that you can set its `TabIndex`. However, labels never receive focus—meaning that the control is not stopped at when you press the Tab key. Instead, it is skipped and the next control, that can take focus, is selected.

For a complete list and description of the Button members, you should explore the C# documentation provided with Visual Studio.

ADDING BUTTON OBJECTS TO YOUR TAXAPP FORM

A Button object is dragged to the bottom of the form and is center aligned with the center of label1, the heading for the form. This is done using the **Format, Center in Form, Horizontally** option. The Button object's Name property is set to btnCompute. As noted previously, when you plan to name a control object, this should be one of the first things that is done after it is placed on the form container. Under most circumstances, it will not create problems for you if the Name is not set first. However, with buttons, if you add a click event before naming the control, you may have to go into the code generated by Form Designer and manually modify the name of the event-handler methods and registrations to have them match the new button name. Table 9-8 lists the properties that are set at design time for the button1 object.

TABLE 9-8 TaxApp button1 properties

Property	Changes with explanation
Name	Typed btnCompute
BackColor	Selected Navy
Font	Selected style of bold, point size of 14
ForeColor	Selected Yellow
TabIndex	2
Text	Typed "Compute"

© Cengage Learning

After setting the properties, you probably need to resize the Button object so that the text is displayed properly. Remember that it *does* matter what the GUI looks like.

Add a Click event for the btnCompute object. This can be done by double-clicking on the actual Button object in the Form **Designer**. Another option is to display all the events using the lightning bolt on the **Properties** window and then double-click on the `Click` event, as illustrated in Figure 9-14. Double-clicking a control allows the programmer to program the default event. Clicking the lightning bolt allows a choice of all relevant events.

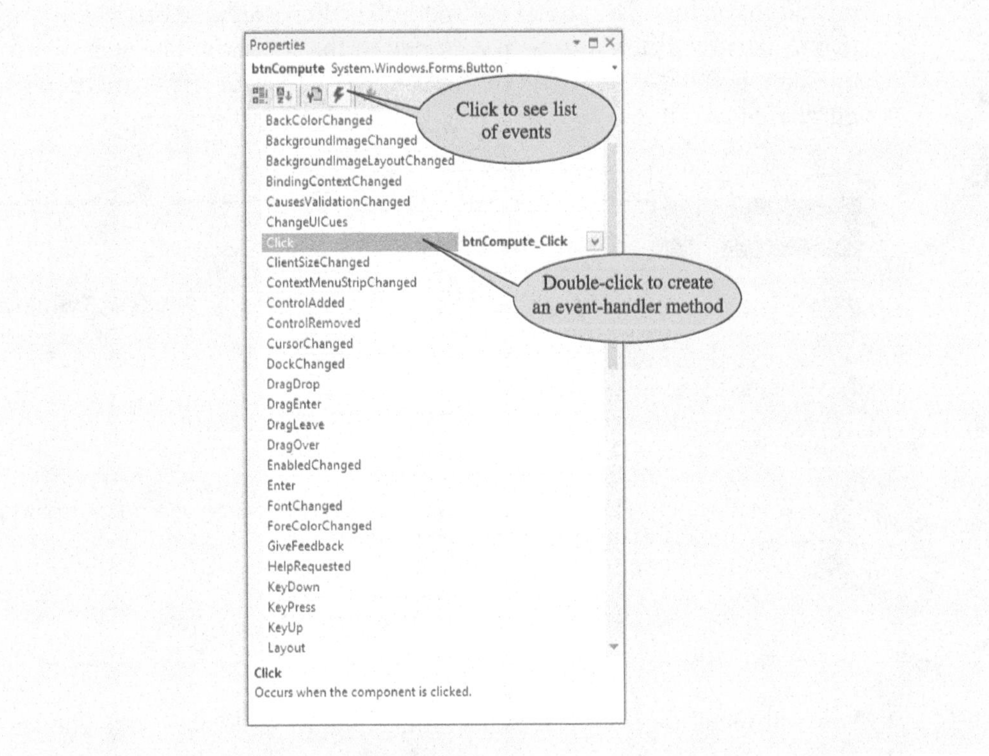

FIGURE 9-14 Events

NOTE If you add the button click event using the list of available events, as shown in Figure 9-14, you need to select the **Properties** icon in that window to reshow the list of properties. The **Properties** icon appears to the left of the lightning bolt.

When you double-click on the `Click` event, you are taken to the `btnCompute_Click( )` method in the **Code** Editor window. This is where you write your program statements describing the actions to be taken when the user clicks the Compute button.

As you think about what program statements need to be written and in what order, you should understand that the first action should be retrieval of the values that are entered into the `txtPurchase TextBox object`. The `Text` property can be used to accomplish this. Values retrieved with the `Text` property are of `string` type and require conversion before arithmetic is performed. A loop can be added to ensure that numeric characters are entered prior to the value being parsed. If a non-numeric character is entered, a message box is displayed reminding the user that numeric characters should be entered. Using the `Text` property, zeros replace the invalid characters. The `Focus( )` method is then executed on the `txtPurchase` control to cause the cursor to be positioned in that textbox. The statements that appear in Example 9-4 can be added to the `btnCompute_Click( )` method to retrieve the purchase price and store it in a `double` variable for processing.

EXAMPLE 9-4

```
private void btnCompute_Click(object sender, System.EventArgs e)
{
    string inValue;
    double purchaseAmt;
    while (double.TryParse(txtPurchase.Text,
                     out purchaseAmt) == false)
    {
        MessageBox.Show("Value entered must be numeric");
        txtPurchase.Text = "0.0";
        txtPurchase.Focus( );
    }
        // More program statements. . .omitted
```

You will recall that the actual percentage value associated with the tax rate is displayed in the `Label` `object` `lblTaxPercent`. The `Text` property for this `object` was used to set the value. The `Text` property can also be used to get the `string` value. However, in addition to the numeric amount representing the tax rate percentage, a special character, the percent symbol (%), was used to set the value. It is displayed and is retrieved with the `Text` property.

You learned about many `string` processing methods in Chapter 8. One of them listed in Table 8-2 is the `Remove( )` method. It can be used to remove characters from a `string` beginning at a specific location. You also learned in Chapter 8 about the `Length` property. `Length` is used to return the number of characters in the `string`. The percent symbol (%) is the last character in the string. Remember that the first character for a `string` is indexed by zero. Thus, the last character of the `string`, where the `'%'` character is located, is indexed by `Length - 1`.

Two arguments are included with the `Remove( )` method. The first argument is the index of where character removal should begin. For this example, removal should start at Length - 1. The second argument, 1, specifies how many characters to remove. Only one character, the '%', needs to be removed before converting the string into a double type for calculations. The statements in Example 9-5 are added to the btnCompute_Click( ) method to retrieve and place the numeric value representing the tax percentage rate into the variable identified by percent.

EXAMPLE 9-5

```
double percent;
inValue = lblTaxPercent.Text;    // inValue previously declared as string
inValue = inValue.Remove(inValue.Length - 1, 1);
percent = double.Parse(inValue) / 100;
```

The last three lines in Example 9-5 could be written in one statement, as shown in Example 9-6. Both produce the same results.

EXAMPLE 9-6

```
percent = (double.Parse(lblTaxPercent.Text.Remove(
              lblTaxPercent.Text.Length - 1, 1))) / 100;
```

9

Now that you have both values stored in the double variable, simple arithmetic can be performed and the result displayed in the txtTotalDue TextBox object. Example 9-7 includes those statements.

EXAMPLE 9-7

```
double ans;
ans = (purchaseAmt * percent) + purchaseAmt;
txtTotalDue.Text = string.Format("{0:C}",ans);
```

Notice that Examples 9-5 and 9-6 invoked the Parse( ) method as opposed to the TryParse( ) method. This is because there is no user input; thus, no concern that a non-numeric character might be entered. Figure 9-15 shows the output produced after the user enters a value and clicks the Compute button.

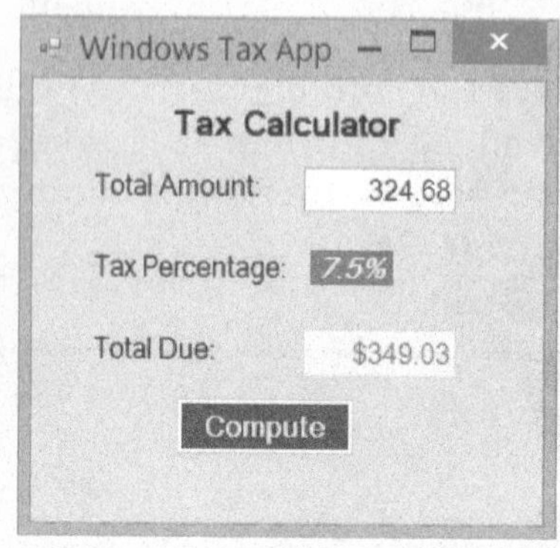

FIGURE 9-15 Tax calculator output

One additional property was set for the form to allow the Enter key to be associated with the `Compute` button. `AcceptButton` was set to `btnCompute`. Now pressing the Enter key is the same as clicking the `Compute Button object`. The complete program listing for `TaxApp` is shown in Example 9-8. Remember that the Form Designer automatically generated the code for the program based on dropping and dragging controls from the **Toolbox** window and setting properties using the **Properties** window during design. The body of the `btnCompute_Click( )` is the only code written manually.

Example 9-8 shows program statements for the source code files. The application is divided into three files. `Program.cs` was renamed `TaxApp.cs` because it contains the `Main( )` method where execution begins. No new code was added to the `TaxApp.cs` file.

NOTE

For the `TaxApp` application and other projects illustrated in Chapters 9 and 10, a number of `using` statements were deleted since the `TaxApp` application did not need to reference their classes. Since no new code was added to the file holding `Main ( )`, it is not shown below.

`Form1.cs` contains the `partial class` definition and includes a call to the `InitializeComponent( )` method. `Form1.cs` also includes methods written to handle any events of interest. `Form1.Designer.cs` is the second `partial class` and contains the rest of the statements defining the `Form object`. `Form1.Designer.cs` holds the Windows generated code responsible for instantiating controls and setting properties for those controls on the form. Tables 9-4, 9-5, 9-7, and 9-8 show the properties set for the Form, Label, Textbox and Button objects for the TaxApp application. The auto-generated code for those property changes are placed in the `InitializeComponent( )` method of the `Form1.Designer.cs` file. That file is shown first in Example 9-8.

EXAMPLE 9-8

```
/* TaxApp              Author:  Doyle
 * A Tax calculator is produced. Labels are used
 * to display descriptive captions. A textbox
 * object is used for input and displaying results.
 * One button click event method is programmed.
 */

// Form1.Designer.cs
namespace TaxApp
{
     public partial class Form1
     {
          // Required designer variable.
          private System.ComponentModel.IContainer components = null;
          // Clean up any resources being used.
          protected override void Dispose(bool disposing)
          {
               if (disposing && (components != null))
               {
                    components.Dispose( );
               }
               base.Dispose(disposing);
          }
          #region Windows Form Designer generated code
          // Required method for Designer support - do not modify
          // the contents of this method with the code editor.
          private void InitializeComponent( )
          {
               this.label1 = new System.Windows.Forms.Label( );
               this.label2 = new System.Windows.Forms.Label( );
               this.label3 = new System.Windows.Forms.Label( );
               this.label4 = new System.Windows.Forms.Label( );
               this.label5 = new System.Windows.Forms.Label( );
               this.txtPurchase = new System.Windows.Forms.TextBox( );
               this.txtTotalDue = new System.Windows.Forms.TextBox( );
               this.btnCompute = new System.Windows.Forms.Button( );
               this.SuspendLayout( );
               //
               // label1
               //
               this.label1.AutoSize = true;
```

9

```
this.label1.Location = new System.Drawing.Point(37, 51);
this.label1.Name = "label1";
this.label1.Size = new System.Drawing.Size(120, 20);
this.label1.TabIndex = 0;
this.label1.Text = "Total Amount:";
//
// label2
//
this.label2.AutoSize = true;
this.label2.Location = new
      System.Drawing.Point(37, 98);
this.label2.Name = "label2";
this.label2.Size = new System.Drawing.Size(133, 20);
this.label2.TabIndex = 1;
this.label2.Text = "Tax Percentage:";
//
// label3
//
this.label3.AutoSize = true;
this.label3.Location = new System.Drawing.Point(37, 145);
this.label3.Name = "label3";
this.label3.Size = new System.Drawing.Size(90, 20);
this.label3.TabIndex = 2;
this.label3.Text = "Total Due:";
//
// label4
//
this.label4.AutoSize = true;
this.label4.Font = new
      System.Drawing.Font("Microsoft Sans Serif",
      14F, System.Drawing.FontStyle.Bold,
      System.Drawing.GraphicsUnit.Point, (byte)(0)));
this.label4.Location = new System.Drawing.Point(109, 13);
this.label4.Name = "label4";
this.label4.Size = new System.Drawing.Size(128, 19);
this.label4.TabIndex = 3;
this.label4.Text = "Tax Calculator";
this.label4.TextAlign =
      System.Drawing.ContentAlignment.TopCenter;
//
// lblTaxPercent
//
this.lblTaxPercent.AutoSize = true;
this.lblTaxPercent.BackColor =
      System.Drawing.Color.RoyalBlue;
this.lblTaxPercent.Font = new
      System.Drawing.Font("Microsoft Sans Serif",
      12F, ((System.Drawing.FontStyle)
      ((System.Drawing.FontStyle.Bold |
      System.Drawing.FontStyle.Italic))),
```

```
        System.Drawing.GraphicsUnit.Point,
        ((byte)(0)));
    this.lblTaxPercent.ForeColor =
        System.Drawing.Color.LightBlue;
    this.lblTaxPercent.Location = new
        System.Drawing.Point(185, 98);
    this.lblTaxPercent.Name = "lblTaxPercent";
    this.lblTaxPercent.Size = new
        System.Drawing.Size(48, 20);
    this.lblTaxPercent.TabIndex = 4;
    this.lblTaxPercent.Text = "7.5%";
    //
    // txtPurchase
    //
    this.txtPurchase.Location = new
        System.Drawing.Point(180, 50);
    this.txtPurchase.Name = "txtPurchase";
    this.txtPurchase.Size = new
        System.Drawing.Size(100, 26);
    this.txtPurchase.TabIndex = 5;
    this.txtPurchase.TextAlign =
        System.Windows.Forms.HorizontalAlignment.Right;
    //
    // txtTotalDue
    //
    this.txtTotalDue.Enabled = false;
    this.txtTotalDue.Location = new
        System.Drawing.Point(180, 144);
    this.txtTotalDue.Name = "txtTotalDue";
    this.txtTotalDue.Size = new
        System.Drawing.Size(100, 26);
    this.txtTotalDue.TabIndex = 6;
    this.txtTotalDue.TextAlign =
        System.Windows.Forms.HorizontalAlignment.Right;
    //
    // btnCompute
    //
    this.btnCompute.BackColor =
        System.Drawing.Color.Navy;
    this.btnCompute.Font = new
        System.Drawing.Font("Microsoft Sans Serif", 14F,
        System.Drawing.FontStyle.Bold,
        System.Drawing.GraphicsUnit.Point, ((byte)(0)));
    this.btnCompute.ForeColor =
        System.Drawing.Color.Yellow;
    this.btnCompute.Location = new
        System.Drawing.Point(114, 196);
    this.btnCompute.Name = "btnCompute";
    this.btnCompute.Size = new
        System.Drawing.Size(119, 34);
```

9

```
                this.btnCompute.TabIndex = 2;
                this.btnCompute.Text = "Compute";
                this.btnCompute.UseVisualStyleBackColor = false;
                this.btnCompute.Click += new
                     System.EventHandler(this.btnCompute_Click);
                //
                // Form1
                //
                this.AcceptButton = this.btnCompute;
                this.AutoScaleDimensions = new
                     System.Drawing.SizeF(10F, 20F);
                this.AutoScaleMode =
                     System.Windows.Forms.AutoScaleMode.Font;
                this.BackColor = System.Drawing.Color.LightSkyBlue;
                this.ClientSize = new System.Drawing.Size(310, 242);
                this.Controls.Add(this.btnCompute);
                this.Controls.Add(this.txtTotalDue);
                this.Controls.Add(this.txtPurchase);
                this.Controls.Add(this.label5);
                this.Controls.Add(this.label4);
                this.Controls.Add(this.label3);
                this.Controls.Add(this.label2);
                this.Controls.Add(this.label1);
                this.Font = new
                     System.Drawing.Font("Microsoft Sans Serif",
                     12F, System.Drawing.FontStyle.Regular,
                     System.Drawing.GraphicsUnit.Point,
                     ((byte)(0)));
                this.Margin = new System.Windows.Forms.Padding(4);
                this.Name = "Form1";
                this.Text = "Windows Tax App";
                this.ResumeLayout(false);
                this.PerformLayout( );
           }
           #endregion

           private System.Windows.Forms.Label label1;
           private System.Windows.Forms.Label label2;
           private System.Windows.Forms.Label label3;
           private System.Windows.Forms.Label label4;
           private System.Windows.Forms.Label lblTaxPercent;
           private System.Windows.Forms.TextBox txtPurchase;
           private System.Windows.Forms.TextBox txtTotalDue;
           private System.Windows.Forms.Button btnCompute;
      }
}  // End of Form1.Designer.cs file

// Form1.cs
using System;                  // Extra using statements omitted.
using System.Windows.Forms;
```

```
namespace TaxApp
{
    public partial class Form1 : Form
    {
        public Form1( )
        {
            InitializeComponent( );
        }

        private void btnCompute_Click(object sender, EventArgs e)
        {
            string inValue;
            double purchaseAmt,
                   percent,
                   ans;
            while (double.TryParse(txtPurchase.Text,
                                   out purchaseAmt) == false)
            {
                MessageBox.Show("Value entered must be numeric");
                txtPurchase.Text = "0.0";
                txtPurchase.Focus( );
            }
            inValue = lblTaxPercent.Text;
            inValue = inValue.Remove(inValue.Length - 1, 1);
            percent = double.Parse(inValue) / 100;
            ans = (purchaseAmt * percent) + purchaseAmt;
            txtTotalDue.Text = string.Format("{0:C}",ans);
        }
    }
}
```

9

PROGRAMMING EXAMPLE: TempAgency Application

This example demonstrates the design and implementation of a GUI for a Windows application. Two classes are constructed to separate the business logic from the presentation details. The first `class` defines a template for a typical payroll employee `object`. It includes the behaviors for determining withholding deductions and calculating the net take-home pay; thus, the business logic is described in this `Employee` `class`. The other `class` instantiates an `object` of the `Employee` `class` and instantiates a Windows `Form` `object` to represent the GUI. Using the .NET predefined `Control` classes, labels, text boxes, and button objects are added to the `Form` `object`. The problem specification for the `TempAgency` application is shown in Figure 9-16.

XYZ JobSource is in the business of matching computer systems analysts and programmers with employers needing temporary help. They pay a flat rate of $150.00 per hour to their contract analysts and programmers. Contractors are paid on a weekly basis or at the completion of a project, whichever comes first. Each contractor logs his or her own hours. They have asked you to develop a Windows application to be used by the contractors to determine how much money they will take home for a given period of time.

XYZ JobSource is located in a city that does not pay local sales tax. The company pays no benefits in terms of insurance or retirement. They are required by law to deduct Social Security taxes and federal income taxes from each check. The amount of Social Security deductions is calculated at 7.85% of the gross pay. The amount of federal withholding is based on the number of dependent allowances. The following formula is used: fed deduction = (grossPay - (grossPay * 5.75% * number of dependents)) * 25%. They also charge a membership fee to each contractor of 13% of their gross pay.

Design a GUI that will accept as input the contractor's name, the number of dependents, and the number of hours worked. Display the gross pay, deductions, and net pay.

© Cengage Learning

FIGURE 9-16 Problem specification for TempAgency

ANALYZE THE PROBLEM

You should review the problem specification in Figure 9-16 and make sure you understand the problem definition. Several values will be entered into the program to represent the name, number of hours worked, and number of dependents for an employee. The business logic is separated from the user interface by using two separate classes. This enables other applications to use the `Employee class`. Actual checks for the XYZ JobSource temp agency may need to be printed, payroll records saved, and other reports generated. By separating the logic from the design of the GUI presentation, the `Employee class` can be reused for many other applications.

DATA

Table 9-9 lists the data field members needed for the `Employee class`. In addition to these entered values, instance variables to store deductions and pay amounts are needed.

TABLE 9-9 Instance field members for the Employee class

Data description	Type	Identifier
Employee last name	`string`	`employeeLastName`
Employee first name	`string`	`employeeFirstName`
Number of dependents	`int`	`noOfDependents`
Number of hours worked	`double`	`noOfHours`

CONSTANTS

For this example, several values such as hourly rate, Social Security, and federal withholding tax rates are the same for all employees. The user does not have to enter these values at run time; instead, constants can be defined for the values in the `Employee` `class` in the methods that use their values. Any objects instantiated of that `class` can then have access to the amounts, as given in Table 9-10.

TABLE 9-10 Constant field members for the Employee class

Data description	Type	Identifier	Value
Hourly rate	`double`	`RATE`	`150.00`
Federal tax deduction percentage	`double`	`FEDERAL_TAX`	`0.25`
Social Security deduction percentage	`double`	`SOCIAL_SECURITY_RATE`	`0.0785`
Dependent allowance percentage	`double`	`DEPENDENT_ALLOWANCE`	`0.0575`
Agency fee for the contract	`double`	`AGENCY_CHARGE`	`0.13`

9

A second `class` is created for the user interface. This `class` allows the user to enter their name, number of dependents, and number of hours worked. Local variables must be declared to hold these values. The employee name can be entered as a single entry. Program statements should be written to separate the first name from last name. You almost always want to have last name separated from first name to facilitate alphabetically ordering records. After values are entered and calculations performed, an area on the form displays the results. Thus, objects that can be used to display gross and net pay along with calculated deductions are needed. During design, a prototype is developed to determine the location of the objects on the form.

DESIGN A SOLUTION

The desired output is to display the gross and net pay along with deductions. Figure 9-17 shows a prototype for the form. It illustrates what types of objects are needed and gives an approximation of where they should be placed.

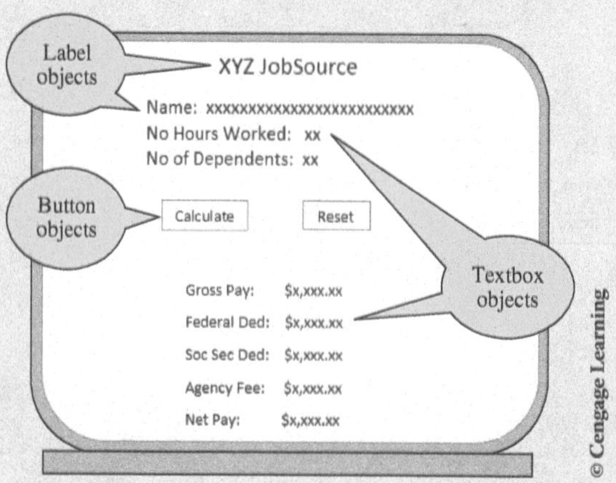

FIGURE 9-17 Prototype for TempAgency example

During design, it is also useful to determine which `object` types are used to create the interface. The GUI is used for both input and output of data. Not all objects show on the screen at the same time. The labels and text boxes below the buttons are initially set to be invisible to the user. Only after the Calculate button is clicked do those objects show on the monitor. When they show, the labels and text boxes associated with the number of hours worked and the number of dependents are hidden.

When the Reset button is pressed, the text box for the name is cleared and the labels and text boxes above the buttons show. All objects below the buttons are hidden.

An abstraction for a typical employee has both data and behavior characteristics that can be identified. For this application, one of the major actions or behaviors of an object of the Employee class is to calculate the net pay using the number of hours and the number of dependents. These values can be retrieved from the TextBox objects. Methods to determine the deductions for the agency, Social Security, and federal tax contributions are needed, as well as a method to calculate the net take-home pay. Class diagrams are used to help design and document these characteristics. Figure 9-18 shows the class diagrams for the TempAgency example.

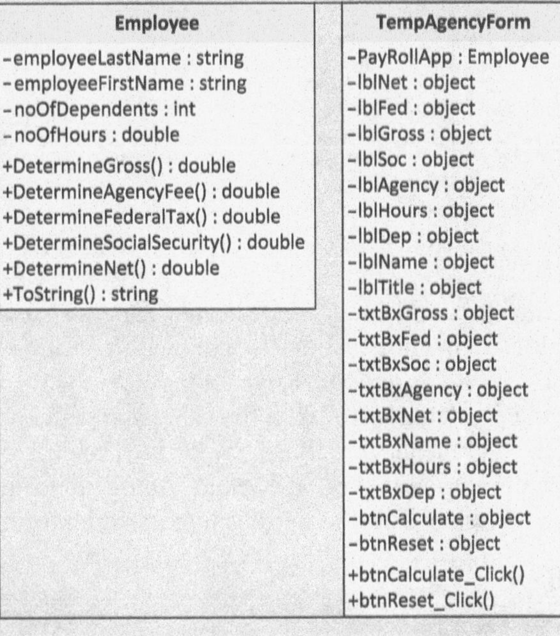

FIGURE 9-18 Class diagrams for TempAgency example

The class diagrams do not show the properties needed or the local variables that might be needed by specific class methods.

During design, it is important to develop an algorithm showing the systematic process for the business logic of the application. Pseudocode for the Employee methods is shown in Figure 9-19.

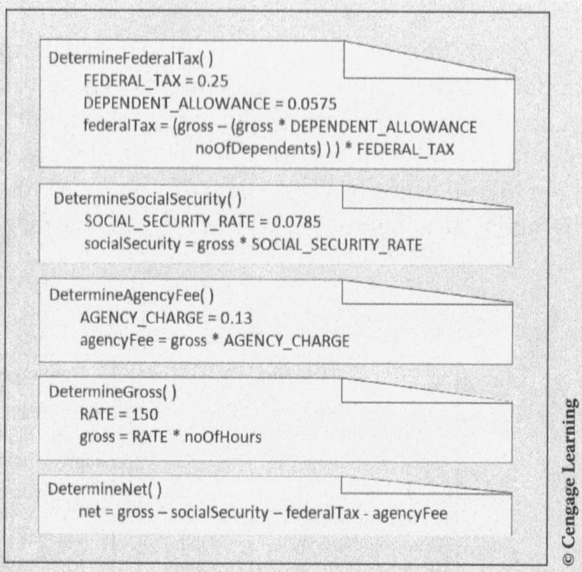

© Cengage Learning

FIGURE 9-19 Pseudocode for the Employee class for the TempAgency example

You should always desk check your design. One way to do this is to develop a test plan of values to use for testing. A table with columns for all entered and calculated values can be developed, as given in Table 9-11. After you identify values to be tested, use a calculator to fill in the calculated values. Then, go back and reread the problem definition. Are those the correct calculated values? Notice that the test plan is developed before any actual coding. This ensures that you design the solution to take all possible situations into consideration.

TABLE 9-11 Desk check test plan of TempAgency example

No Of Dependents	No Of Hours	gross	socialSecurity	federalTax	agencyFee	net
1	10	1500.00	117.75	353.44	195.00	833.81
0	40	6000.00	471.00	1500.00	780.00	3249.00
1	40	6000.00	471.00	1413.75	780.00	3335.25
2	40	6000.00	471.00	1327.50	780.00	3421.50
3	40	6000.00	471.00	1241.25	780.00	3507.75
6	20	3000.00	235.50	491.25	390.00	1883.25
4	40	6000.00	471.00	1155.00	780.00	3594.00
2	30	4500.00	353.25	995.63	585.00	2566.13
0	50	7500.00	588.75	1875.00	975.00	4061.25
2	50	7500.00	588.75	1659.38	975.00	4276.88
3	2	300.00	23.55	62.06	39.00	175.39

© Cengage Learning

After you implement your design, be sure to run and test your application using the values you identified when you developed the test plan. Compare the results you obtain during your desk check using a calculator with the output produced from your program.

CODE THE SOLUTION

After you complete the design and verify the algorithm's correctness, it is time to translate the design into source code.

If you are using Visual Studio, much of the code for the user interface `class` can be generated for you by the Form Designer. It is important to make sure your GUI looks nice. As was noted earlier in the chapter, consistency and alignment of objects on the form are very important. Use of **Align**, **Make Same Size**, **Horizontal Spacing**, **Vertical Spacing**, and **Center in Form** from the **Format** menu will greatly assist you.

Four separate files are created. Visual Studio creates three files for the user interface; one additional file is needed for the `Employee` `class`. If you do not have Visual Studio, you can type assignment statements for the property values. For example, as shown in Table 9-12, to associate the enter key with a specific button you could type

```
AcceptButton = btnCalculate;
```

The statement that the Visual Studio Form Designer generates when you use the **Properties** window to set the `AcceptButton` is

```
this.AcceptButton = this.btnCalculate;
```

Both produce the same result when the application is run. Thus, even though Visual Studio was used to produce the code listing that follows, the program statements could all be written using an editor such as Notepad and executed from the DOS command line. Table 9-12 presents the different `Control` objects' properties and values that are set at design time.

9

TABLE 9-12 Properties set for the TempAgency example

Type of object	Identifier	Property	Value
Form	Form1	Name	TempAgencyForm
Form	TempAgencyForm	AcceptButton	btnCalculate
Form	TempAgencyForm	BackColor	blue (0,0,192)
Form	TempAgencyForm	CancelButton	btnReset

(continues)

TABLE 9-12 Properties set for the TempAgency example (*continued*)

Type of object	Identifier	Property	Value
Form	TempAgencyForm	Font	ComicSansMS, size 12
Form	TempAgencyForm	ForeColor	light yellow(255,255,192)
Form	TempAgencyForm	Text	Typed "PayRoll App"
Label	lblName	Text	Typed "Name: "
Label	lblHours	Text	Typed "No. of Hours Worked: "
Label	lblTitle	Font	Comic Sans MS, size 16, bold
Label	lblTitle	Text	Typed "XYZ JobSource"
Label	lblNet	Text	Typed "Net Pay: "
Label	lblNet	Visible	False
Label	lblFed	Text	Typed "Federal Ded.: "
Label	lblFed	Visible	False
Label	lblGross	Text	Typed "Gross Pay: "
Label	lblGross	Visible	False
Label	lblAgency	Text	Typed "Agency Fee: "
Label	lblAgency	Visible	False
Label	lblSoc	Text	Typed "Soc Sec Ded.: "
Label	lblSoc	Visible	False

(*continues*)

TABLE 9-12 Properties set for the TempAgency example (*continued*)

Type of object	Identifier	Property	Value
TextBox	txtBxHours	Text	0
TextBox	txtBxHours	TabIndex	1
TextBox	txtBxHours	TextAlign	Right
TextBox	txtBxNet	Font	Bold
TextBox	txtBxName	TabIndex	0
TextBox	txtBxDep	AcceptsReturn	True
TextBox	txtBxDep	Text	0
TextBox	txtBxDep	TabIndex	2
TextBox	txtBxDep	TextAlign	Right
TextBox	txtBxGross	TextAlign	Right
TextBox	txtBxGross	Visible	False
TextBox	txtBxGross	BackColor	blue (192,192,255)
TextBox	txtBxFed	TextAlign	Right
TextBox	txtBxFed	Visible	False
TextBox	txtBxFed	BackColor	blue (192,192,255)
TextBox	txtBxSoc	TextAlign	Right
TextBox	txtBxSoc	Visible	False
TextBox	txtBxSoc	BackColor	blue (192,192,255)
TextBox	txtBxAgency	TextAlign	Right

(*continues*)

9

TABLE 9-12 Properties set for the TempAgency example (*continued*)

Type of object	Identifier	Property	Value
TextBox	txtBxAgency	Visible	False
TextBox	txtBxAgency	BackColor	blue (192,192,255)
TextBox	txtBxNet	TextAlign	Right
TextBox	txtBxNet	BackColor	blue (192,192,255)
Textbox	txtBxNet	Visible	False
Button	btnCalculate	Text	Typed "Calculate Take Home Pay"
Button	btnCalculate	ForeColor	Yellow (255, 255, 192)
Button	btnCalculate	BackColor	blue (128,128,255)
Button	btnReset	Text	Typed "Reset"
Button	btnReset	ForeColor	Yellow (255, 255, 192)
Button	btnReset	BackColor	blue (128,128,255)

© Cengage Learning

The final application listing appears in the following code segment. Two of the four source code files are shown. The `Employee class`, which contains the business logic, is shown first. Next the `TempAgencyForm class` is shown. Recall Visual Studio creates three separate .cs files when you create a simple Windows application. Initially, these files are named Form1.cs, Form1.Designer.cs, and Program.cs. Program.cs contains the `Main( )` method and is not shown below. No additional code was added to this file.

The other two files, Form1.cs and Form1.Designer.cs, both include partial class definitions for the Form1 class. The bodies for the methods, `btnCalculate_Click( )`, `btnReset_Click( )`, and `setVisibility( )`, were added to the generated code in the `TempAgencyForm.cs`. The contents of that file are shown after the `Employee` class.

Table 9-12 displayed the properties set for the controls added to the form. Those changes are placed in the `TempAgencyForm.Designer.cs`. This file stores only auto-generated code and since it is recommended that you never edit the .Designer.cs file, it is not shown.

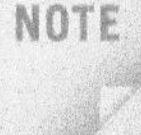

NOTE When you create your application using Visual Studio, your solution might vary from what is shown in the sample code. For example, some of your property value settings might differ because you might drag and drop your controls to different locations, or you might select the controls in a different order. You might see more or different comments than what appears in the code listing. Also, because of space constraints, some lines of code must be formatted to appear on two or more lines.

```
/* Employee.cs                                        Author: Doyle
 * Employee class includes data characteristics of
 * name, employee number, number of dependents and
 * number of hours worked. Methods calculate
 * deductions for social security, federal tax, and
 * agency fee. Both Gross and Net Pay are returned.
 */
using System;
namespace PayRollApp
{
    public class Employee
    {
        private string employeeFirstName;
        private string employeeLastName;
        private int noOfDependents;
        private double noOfHours;

        //Default constructor
        public Employee( )
        {
        }

        public Employee(string first, string last, int dep, double
                     hours)
        {
            employeeFirstName = first;
            employeeLastName = last;
            noOfDependents = dep;
            noOfHours = hours;
        }

        public Employee(string first, string last)
        {
             employeeFirstName = first;
```

9

```
        employeeLastName = last;
    }

    public Employee(string first, string last, int dep)
    {
        employeeFirstName = first;
        employeeLastName = last;
        noOfDependents = dep;
    }

    //Property used to access or change Employee First Name
    public string EmployeeFirstName
    {
        set
        {
            employeeFirstName = value;
        }
        get
        {
            return employeeFirstName;
        }
    }

    //Property used to access or change Employee Last Name
    public string EmployeeLastName
    {
        set
        {
            employeeLastName = value;
        }
        get
        {
            return employeeLastName;
        }
    }

    //Property used to access number of dependents
    public int NoOfDependents
    {
        set
        {
            noOfDependents = value;
        }
        get
        {
            return noOfDependents;
        }
    }
```

```
//Property used to access or change hours worked
public double NoOfHours
{
     set
     {
          noOfHours = value;
     }
     get
     {
          return noOfHours;
     }
}

//Using the same constant value for a flat hourly rate,
//calculate gross pay prior to any deductions
public double DetermineGross( )
{
     const double RATE = 150.00;
     return noOfHours * RATE;
}

//Using the same constant value for the Commission Rate
//for all employees, calculate commission due employee
public double DetermineAgencyFee( )
{
     const double AGENCY_CHARGE = 0.13;
     return DetermineGross( ) * AGENCY_CHARGE;
}

//Calculate federal tax due
public double DetermineFederalTax( )
{
     const double FEDERAL_TAX = 0.25;
     const double DEPENDENT_ALLOWANCE = 0.0575;
     double gross;
     gross = DetermineGross( );
     return (gross - (gross *(DEPENDENT_ALLOWANCE *
            noOfDependents))) * FEDERAL_TAX;
}

//Calculate Social Security taxes
public double DetermineSocialSecurity( )
{
     const double SOCIAL_SECURITY_RATE = 0.0785;
     return DetermineGross( ) * SOCIAL_SECURITY_RATE;
}
```

```
        public double DetermineNet( )
        {
            return DetermineGross( ) - DetermineSocialSecurity( ) -
                   DetermineFederalTax( ) -
                   DetermineAgencyFee( );
        }

        public override string ToString( )
        {
            return employeeFirstName + " " + employeeLastName +
                   "\nTake Home Pay: " +
                   DetermineNet( ).ToString("C");
        }
    }
}  // End of Employee class

/* TempAgencyForm.cs
 * This partial class contains program statements written to handle
 * the two button click events.
 */
using System;
using System.Windows.Forms;

namespace PayRollApp
{
    public partial class TempAgencyForm : Form
    {
        public TempAgencyForm( )
        {
            InitializeComponent( );
        }
        // Button click event handler for the Calculate button
        private void btnCalculate_Click(object sender, EventArgs e)
        {
            int dep;
            double hours;
            string [ ] name = new string[2];
            while (double.TryParse(txtBxHours.Text,
                                   out hours) == false)
            {
                MessageBox.Show("Numeric value should be " +
                                "entered for Hours");
                txtBxHours.Text = "0";
                txtBxHours.Focus( );
            }
            if (int.TryParse(txtBxDep.Text, out dep) == false)
            {
                MessageBox.Show("Dependent default value " +
                         "of 0 used for calculations.");
```

```
            txtBxDep.Text = "0";
            txtBxDep.Focus( );
        }
        name = txtBxName.Text.Split(' ');
        if (name.Length < 2)
        {
            txtBxName.Text = "Please enter full name.";
            txtBxName.Focus( );
        }
        else
            if (hours > 0)
            {
                Employee anEmployee =
                    new Employee(name[0], name[1],
                                    dep, hours);
                txtBxGross.Text =
                    anEmployee.DetermineGross( ).
                        ToString("C"); //continuation line
                txtBxSoc.Text =
                    anEmployee.DetermineSocialSecurity( ).
                        ToString("C");
                txtBxFed.Text =
                    anEmployee.DetermineFederalTax( ).
                        ToString("C");
                txtBxAgency.Text =
                    anEmployee.DetermineAgencyFee( ).
                        ToString("C");
                txtBxNet.Text =
                    anEmployee.DetermineNet( ).
                        ToString("C");
                txtBxName.Enabled = false;
                txtBxHours.Visible = false;
                txtBxDep.Visible = false;
                lblHours.Visible = false;
                lblDep.Visible = false;
                setVisibility(true);
            }
    }

    // Used by both the btnCalculate and btnReset to
    // change the visibility on the objects below the buttons
    private void setVisibility(bool visibilityValue)
    {
        lblGross.Visible = visibilityValue;
        lblSoc.Visible = visibilityValue;
        lblFed.Visible = visibilityValue;
        lblAgency.Visible = visibilityValue;
        lblNet.Visible = visibilityValue;
        txtBxGross.Visible = visibilityValue;
        txtBxSoc.Visible = visibilityValue;
```

9

```
            txtBxFed.Visible = visibilityValue;
            txtBxAgency.Visible = visibilityValue;
            txtBxNet.Visible = visibilityValue;
        }
        private void btnReset_Click(object sender, EventArgs e)
        {
            txtBxName.Clear( );
            txtBxHours.Text = "0";
            txtBxDep.Text = "0";
            txtBxName.Enabled = true;
            txtBxHours.Visible = true;
            txtBxDep.Visible = true;
            lblHours.Visible = true;
            lblDep.Visible = true;
            setVisibility(false);
        }
    }
}
```

Figure 9-20 shows the original user interface as values are entered. Notice that the focus is on the `Calculate` button. The Tab key can be used to move down the form. Also, the Enter key or a mouse click can be used to fire the `btnCalculate_Click( )` event as long as the button has the focus.

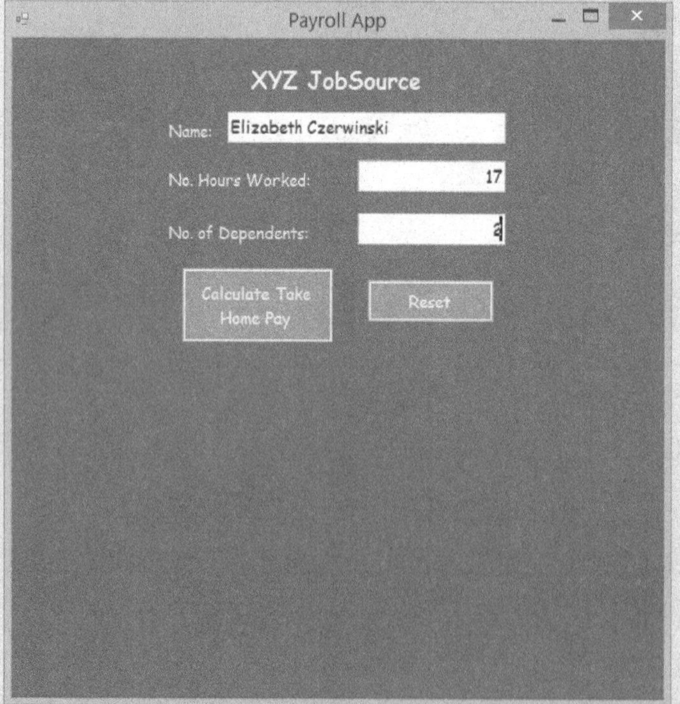

FIGURE 9-20 First user interface for the payroll application

Figure 9-21 shows the result of clicking the `Calculate` button. Comparing Figure 9-20 with Figure 9-21, notice that the number of hours and the number of dependents are hidden, so they are not visible in Figure 9-21. The text box containing the name is also disabled (grayed out) so that no new values can be typed. Values representing the results of the calculations are now displayed in Figure 9-21.

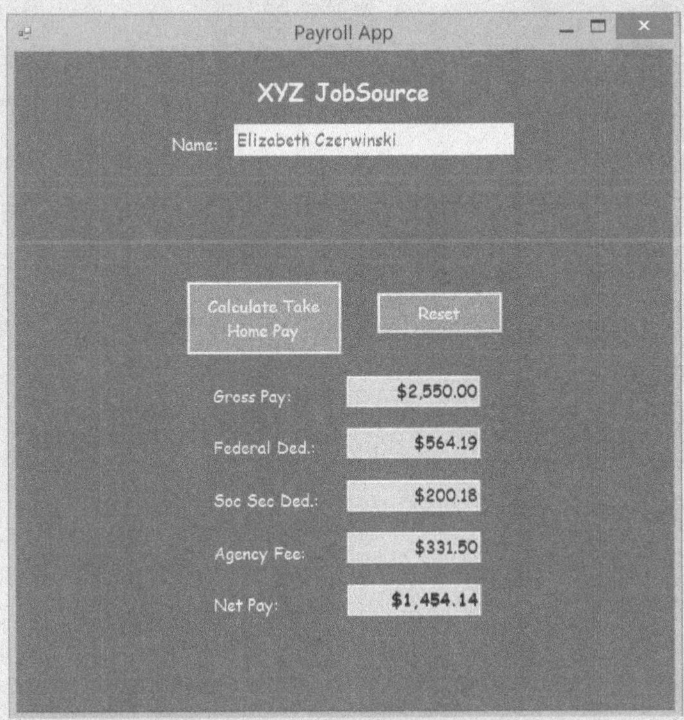

FIGURE 9-21 Output produced when the Calculate button is clicked

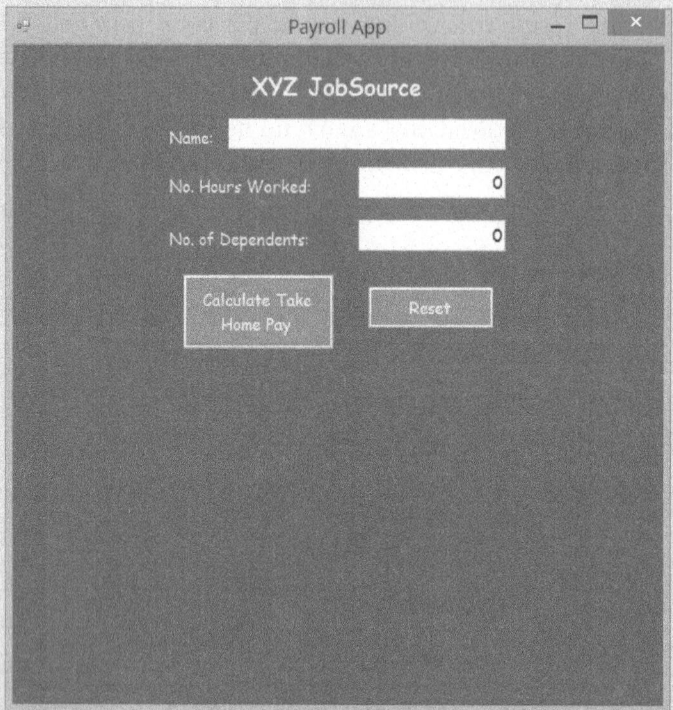

FIGURE 9-22 Output produced when the Reset button is clicked

The `Reset` button clears the text boxes and readies the form for new input. After the values are erased, you will notice that the primary difference between Figure 9-20 (prior to entering the data) and 9-22 is that in Figure 9-22, the focus is on the `Reset` button. As you study the solution, what changes might you make to build the GUI to be more user-friendly? One potential change would be to set the focus to the `Name` text box (where the name is entered) when the `Reset` button is clicked. Another change would be to the size of the form. It could be initially set to be smaller for data entry and then larger for the display of results. A number of other properties could be set to enhance the program. You are encouraged to play, experiment, and experience the effect of modifying properties for the application.

Coding Standards

As you drag and drop controls onto Windows applications, lots of code is automatically generated for you. Following agreed-upon naming standards makes your code more readable and helps to reduce errors.

Guidelines for Naming Controls

Consistently use an appropriate prefix for the user interface elements. For example, a button used to calculate a total could be named btnTotal. This will ensure that you can identify controls from the rest of the variables. Table 9-13 provides examples of some appropriate identifiers. The overriding recommendation is to be consistent.

TABLE 9-13 Example prefix identifiers for controls

Control	Prefix
Button	btn
CheckBox	chkBx
Label	lbl
RadioButton	radBtn
Text Box	txtBx
ListBox	lstBx

Resources

Additional sites you might want to explore:

- C#: Windows Controls—
http://csharpcomputing.com/Tutorials/Lesson9.htm
- Visual C# Tutorials and Lessons - Windows Forms—
http://visualcsharptutorials.com/windows-forms
- Beginners Guide To User Interface Design in C#—
http://www.thetechlabz.com/interfaces/user-interface-design/
- Free C# Tutorials—
http://www.homeandlearn.co.uk/csharp/csharp.html
- YouTube Visual Studio WinForm Windows Calculator Tutorial Example—
http://www.youtube.com/watch?v=Is1EHXFhEe4

QUICK REVIEW

1. Console applications and Windows applications interact differently with the operating system. With console applications, the program calls on the operating system to perform certain functions such as inputting or outputting of data. In contrast, Windows applications are event driven. They register events with the operating system. When the event occurs, they receive notification from the operating system.
2. An event is a notification from the operating system that an action has occurred, such as the user clicking the mouse or pressing a key on the keyboard.
3. With Windows applications, you write methods called event handlers to indicate what should be done when an event such as a click on a button occurs.
4. Another important difference in a Windows application is that unlike the sequential nature you can plan on with console-based applications, in which one statement executes and is followed by the next, no sequential order exists with event-handling methods for Windows applications.
5. As the front end of a program, the interface is the visual image you see when you run a program. Windows applications not only function differently from console applications, they look different, and can, therefore, be used to create a friendlier user interface.
6. Windows-based GUI applications are displayed on a Windows form. `Form` is a container waiting to hold additional controls, such as buttons or labels. Controls are objects that can display and respond to user actions.
7. The Visual Studio integrated development environment (IDE) automatically generates for you all the code needed for a blank Windows form. The amount of development time for Windows applications is greatly reduced when you use Visual Studio and C#, because it is easy to add controls by dropping and dragging them onto the form container.
8. When you have a `class` defined that has the `class` name, followed by a colon and then another `class` name, you have inheritance. The second `class` is called the base `class`; the first is called the derived `class`. The derived `class` inherits the characteristics of the base `class`. In C# and all .NET languages, you are limited to single inheritance.
9. Your design should take into consideration the target audience. Use consistency in the design unless there is a reason to call attention to something. Alignment should be used to group items. Avoid clutter and pay attention to color.
10. Properties of the Form `class` include `AutoScroll`, `BackColor`, `Font`, `ForeColor`, `Location`, `MaximizeBox`, `Size`, `StartPosition`, and `Text`. `Text` is used to set the caption for the title bar of the form.

11. A preprocessor directive indicates that something should be done before processing. C# does not have a separate preprocessing step. The `#region` preprocessor directive in C# is used to explicitly mark sections of source code that you can expand or collapse.
12. The `System.Windows.Forms` `namespace` includes many classes representing controls with names such as `Button`, `Label`, `TextBox`, `ComboBox`, `MainMenu`, `ListBox`, `CheckBox`, `RadioButton`, and `MonthCalendar` that you can add to your form. Each comes with its own bundle of predefined properties and methods, and each fires events.
13. The `Control` `class` has a number of properties, including `Anchor`, `BackColor`, `Enabled`, `Font`, `ForeColor`, `Location`, `Name`, `Size`, `TabIndex`, `Text`, and `Visible`. Names of properties are quite intuitive.
14. The `Control` `class` has a number of methods, including `Focus( )`, `Hide( )`, `Select( )`, and `Show( )`.
15. Controls that you add to a form are objects or instances of one of the predefined classes such as `Label`, `TextBox`, and `Button`. They inherit the properties, methods, and events from the `Control` `class`.
16. `Label` objects are normally used to provide descriptive text for another control. In addition to the inherited members, they have their own unique properties, methods, and events.
17. `TextBox` objects are probably the most commonly used controls, because they can be used for both input and output. In addition to the inherited members, they have their own unique properties, methods, and events.
18. `Button` objects are added to your form to add functionality. Users can click `Button` objects to perform a specific task. In addition to the inherited members, they have their own unique properties, methods, and events.

EXERCISES

1. One of the differences between a console application and a Windows application is:
   a. Classes can only be used with console applications.
   b. One font size is used with console applications.
   c. Variables must be declared with console applications.
   d. Windows applications require that program statements be placed in a `class`.
   e. Execution always begins in the `Main( )` method for console applications.

2. Which `namespace` includes most of the `Control` classes for developing Windows applications?
   a. `System`
   b. `System.Windows.Controls`
   c. `System.Windows.Components.Forms`
   d. `System.Windows.Forms`
   e. `System.Windows.Drawing`
3. Which of the following inherits members from the `Control` `class`?
   a. `Label`
   b. `Form`
   c. `TextBox`
   d. a and c
   e. all of the above
4. The ___________ is the front end of a program that represents the presentation layer or the visual image of the program.
   a. interface
   b. control
   c. Visual Studio
   d. IDE
   e. framework
5. A(n) ___________ is a notification from the operating system that an action has occurred, such as the user clicking the mouse or pressing a key.
   a. method call
   b. statement
   c. event
   d. GUI
   e. handler
6. Which of the `Control` objects is viewed as a container that can hold other objects when you design a Windows application?
   a. `Control`
   b. `Button`
   c. `Window`
   d. `Frame`
   e. `Form`

7. Which property is used to set the caption for the Windows title bar?
   a. `Caption`
   b. `Text`
   c. `Title`
   d. `TitleBar`
   e. `WindowTitle`

8. The `class` heading `public class AForm : Form` indicates that:
   a. `Form` is a derived `class` of the `AForm` `class`.
   b. `AForm` is the base `class` for the `Form` `class`.
   c. The `class` being defined is identified as `Form`.
   d. `AForm` inherits the members of the `Form` `class`.
   e. none of the above

9. If the name of the `class` is `GraphicalForm`, the following: `public GraphicalForm( )` is an example of a(n):
   a. accessor method
   b. property
   c. constructor
   d. mutator method
   e. data member

10. You would use an IDE such as Visual Studio to construct Windows applications because it has the following capability:
   a. drag-and-drop construction
   b. IntelliSense features
   c. access to the Properties window listing properties and events
   d. access to the Toolbox for dropping controls
   e. all of the above

11. `Click` is an example of a(n):
   a. event
   b. property
   c. method
   d. control
   e. handler

12. Visual Studio has a number of windows that can be viewed during design. The window used to hold controls that are dragged and dropped during construction is called the:
    a. Property
    b. Code Editor
    c. Form Designer
    d. Solution Explorer
    e. Class View

13. If the `System.Windows.Forms` `namespace` is imported, the following statement:
    `this.textbox1 = new System.Windows.Forms.TextBox( );`
    `can be written as:`
    a. `this.textbox1 = new TextBox( );`
    b. `textbox1 = new TextBox( );`
    c. `textbox1 = new System.Windows.Forms.TextBox( );`
    d. all of the above
    e. none of the above

14. The statement that actually constructs or instantiates a `Button` `object` is:
    a. `this.button1 = new System.Windows.Forms.Button( );`
    b. `private System.Windows.Forms.Button button1;`
    c. `this.Controls.AddRange(this.button1);`
    d. `button1.Name = "A button";`
    e. `button1.Click += new System.EventHandler (this.button1_Click);`

15. The statement that registers a `Button` `object` click event with the operating system is:
    a. `this.button1ClickEvent = new System.Windows.Forms.Button( );`
    b. `private System.Windows.Forms.Button button1ClickEvent;`
    c. `this.Controls.AddRange(this.button1ClickEvent);`
    d. `button1.Click = "Register Me";`
    e. `button1.Click += new System.EventHandler (this.button1_Click);`

16. The property of the `TextBox` control that is used to set all characters to uppercase as they are typed is:

    a. `CharacterCasing`

    b. `Text`

    c. `ToUpper`

    d. `UpperCase`

    e. `ConvertToUpper`

17. Which of the following might be the heading for an event-handler method?

    a.
    ```
    private void btn1_Click(object sender,
                            System.EventArgs e)
    ```

    b.
    ```
    Application.Run( new TempAgencyForm( ));
    ```

    c.
    ```
    btnCalculate.Click += new
            System.EventHandler(this.btnCalculate_Click);
    ```

    d.
    ```
    this.btnCalculate = new
            System.Windows.Forms.Button( );
    ```

    e. none of the above

18. Which of the following design considerations leads to more user-friendly presentation layers for GUIs?

    a. Avoid clutter.

    b. Be consistent with font, color, and placement.

    c. Design for the target audience.

    d. Use contrast to call attention to something.

    e. all of the above

19. The `#region #endregion` is an example of a C#:

    a. Windows `class` declaration statement

    b. required statement for creating Windows applications

    c. reference to a `namespace` called `region`

    d. preprocessor directive

    e. collapsible segment of code that must be used for Windows applications

20. During design, how can you separate the business logic from the presentation layer?
    a. Create two forms, one for input and the other for output.
    b. Create two objects using an object-oriented approach.
    c. Create at least two methods.
    d. Create separate classes for each.
    e. all of the above

---

21. Describe at least three ways Windows applications differ from console applications.
22. Identify which property could be set so that a `Form` `object` would perform the following function:
    a. Change the background color for the form.
    b. Set the default font to Courier for all controls that are added.
    c. Change the size of the window to 400 by 400.
    d. Associate a name of `designForm` with the `Form` `object`.
    e. Position the window near the center of the screen.
23. Describe what might be done to respond to a button click event.
24. List at least five issues to consider when you plan the design of GUIs.
25. Describe the process that must occur to get a `TextBox` `object` added to a `Form` `object`. In your description, consider not only how the process is performed with Visual Studio, but also what steps would be necessary to do it manually.

PROGRAMMING EXERCISES

1. Create a Windows application that can be used to input a user's name. Include an appropriate label indicator for the name and a textbox for the input entry. A `button` labeled Submit should retrieve and display the value entered on another label positioned near the bottom of the form. The font color for the text for the label object should be yellow. Change the background color of the form to an appropriate one to use with your yellow text. Change the `Font` property to a font of your choice. The size of the font for all objects except the Button should be at least 14 points.

The Button font should be 16 points. Add a title caption of "Name Retrieval App" to the form. Initially clear the text from the label that will display your final answer. When the Submit button is pressed, retrieve the name and concatenate that value with a Congratulatory message. For example, you might display, "Congratulations, Brenda Lewis, you retrieved the data!," if your name was Brenda Lewis. Position the button so it is in the center of the form. Align the other controls so they are aesthetically pleasing. Be sure to change the default names of all controls involved in program statements.

2. Create a Windows application that can be used to change the form color. Your form background color should initially be blue. Provide at least two buttons with two different color choices and a Reset option. Change the font style and size on the buttons. Align the buttons so that they are in the center of the form. The color choice buttons should be the same size. Add event handlers for the buttons so that when the user clicks the button, the form changes color, and a message box is displayed alerting the user as to what color the form is. Be sure to name any controls used in program statements prior to registering your event. Change the default title bar text.

   Hint: This exercise may require you to do some research. You may want to review the code placed in the .Designer.cs file after you set the form's initial color.

3. Create a Windows application that contains two textboxes and three buttons. The textboxes should be used to allow the user to input two positive numeric values. The buttons should be labeled Add and Multiply and Reset. Create event-handler methods that retrieve the values, perform the calculations, and display the result of the calculations on a label. The result label should initially be set to be invisible with a font color of yellow. If invalid data is entered, change the font color to red on the result label and display a message saying "Value must be numeric and > 0." When the final answer is displayed, the font color should be yellow. Additional labels will be needed for the textboxes captions. Do not allow non-numeric characters to be entered. Invoke the `TryParse( )` method to retrieve the values. All controls involved in program statements should be named. Right justify values in the textbox.

4. Create a Windows application that contains two textboxes (with labels) and one button. The textboxes should be used to allow the user to input the x- and y-coordinates to indicate where the form should be positioned. When the user clicks the button, the window should be moved to that new point. Be sure to label the textboxes appropriately. Change the form's background color. Add a title caption to the form.

Include a heading above the textboxes and button. Enlarge the size of the font. Only allow positive integers to be used for the coordinates. If non-numeric or floating point values are entered, place the focus back in the textbox and display a message indicating only positive values are accepted.

Hint: One easy way to do this is to set the location using an instance of the `Point class` when the user clicks the button. To do this, you could allow the user to input values for both x and y into two separate textbox objects. After being retrieved, they would need to be parsed or converted into their integer equivalent. Then use the numeric values for x and y to set the location by typing `Location = new Point(x,y);`.

5. Create a Trip Calculator Windows application that can be used to determine miles per gallon for a given trip. Set the `Form object` properties of `Name, ForeColor, BackColor, Size, Location, Text,` and `AcceptButton`. The form should contain labels and textboxes to allow the user to input trip destination, miles traveled, and gallons of gas consumed. Right justify the number entries. Left justify the destination entry. Two buttons should be placed on the form. Center the text on the button objects. Name all objects used in program statements. When the user clicks the `button` that performs the calculations, display on a label the miles per gallon for that trip. The second button should be used to reset or clear all textbox entries.

6. Create a Windows application that contains two textboxes and three buttons. One of the textboxes and one of the buttons are initially invisible. The first textbox should be used to input a password. The textbox should be masked to some character of your choosing so that the characters entered by the user are not seen on the screen. When the user clicks the first button, the second textbox and button should be displayed with a prompt asking the user to reenter his or her password. Set the focus to the second password textbox. Now, when the user clicks the second button, have the application compare the values entered to make sure that they are the same. Display an appropriate message indicating whether they are the same. Once the check is made, display a third button that resets the form.

7. Create a Windows application that contains a textbox for a person's name. Plan that the user may enter only first and last name, or they may enter first, middle, and last names, or they may enter many parts to their name, as in Jr., Sr., II, or III. Disallow entries of single one word names. If they enter a single first name, prompt them to enter their full name. Include labels to store first, middle, and last names. Disregard names

beyond three words. Two buttons should be included. Both should be positioned in the center of the form. They should overlap. One of the buttons should be used to retrieve the value and the second to reset the form. Initially only the Retrieve button should be displayed. When the Retrieve button is clicked, retrieve the full name, separate it into first, middle (if present), and last names and then display the labeled name values. At this point, the Reset button should be available. When the user clicks the reset button, the form should be readied for new entries.

8. Create a Windows application that can be used to determine distance traveled given speed and time. Provide textboxes for time and speed and a button to calculate the distance. Be sure that only numeric data is able to be entered into the textboxes. Experiment with the controls' properties. Spend time with your design so that your GUI is very user friendly and looks nice.

9. Create a Windows application that functions like a banking account register. The graphical user interface should initially allow the user to input the account name, number, and initial balance. Ensure that the full name is entered for the customer and that only numeric values are entered for number fields when the Create Account button is selected. Separate the business logic from the presentation layer by creating a Customer class. Include a deposit to and withdraw from methods in the Customer class to keep the balance updated. After an object of the Customer class is instantiated, provide textbox objects on your GUI for withdrawals and deposits. A second button should be available to update the account for withdrawal and deposit transactions showing the new balance.

10. Create the higher/lower guessing game using a GUI. Allow users to keep guessing until they guess the number. Keep a count of the number of guesses. Choose two colors for your game: one should be used to indicate that the value the users guessed is higher than the target; the other is used to indicate that the value the users guessed is lower than the target. With each new guess, show the guess count and change the form color based on whether the guess is higher than the target or lower. When they hit the target, display a message on a label indicating the number of guesses it took. Provide a reset button to enable the user to re-start the game without re-running your application. Tie the guess button to the enter key and the reset button to the cancel key. Several approaches can be used to seed the target: One is to generate a random number by constructing an `object` of the `Random` `class`. For example, the following stores a random whole number between 0 and 100 in `target`:

```
Random r = new Random( );
int target = r.Next(0,101);
```

© zeljkodan/Shutterstock.com

Programming Based on Events

IN THIS CHAPTER, YOU WILL:

- Define, create, and use delegates and examine their relationship to events
- Explore event-handling procedures in C# by writing and registering event-handler methods
- Create applications that use the ListBox control object to enable multiple selections from a single control
- Contrast ComboBox to ListBox objects by adding both types of controls to an application
- Add Menu and TabControl options to Windows forms and program their event-handler methods
- Wire multiple RadioButton and CheckBox object events to a single event-handler method
- Design and create a Windows Presentation Foundation (WPF) application
- Work through a programming example that illustrates the chapter's concepts

In Chapter 9, you wrote your first real Windows-based application and learned how easy it is to develop graphical user interfaces using C# and Visual Studio's drag-and-drop construction approach. In addition, you learned that included as part of the .NET Framework `class` library are a number of predefined classes located in the `System.Windows.Forms` `namespace` that enable you to add controls such as `Label`, `Button`, and `TextBox` objects to an `object` of the Windows `Form` container `class`. And, finally, you learned a new way of programming based on interactively responding to events such as button clicks.

In this chapter, you extend this knowledge by writing additional event-handling methods for capturing and responding to user input. You create applications that have menus and other widgets such as list boxes, radio buttons, combo boxes, and check boxes that can be displayed and responded to. You explore other types of events that are triggered or raised for Windows applications.

This chapter begins by introducing you to delegates. An understanding of their use makes you more aware of what goes on behind the scenes with events. The remainder of this chapter focuses on adding controls to Windows applications and programming their events. By the time you complete this chapter, you will be creating very sophisticated, highly interactive, Windows-based applications.

Delegates

Delegates form the foundation for events in C#. **Delegates** are special types of .NET classes whose instances store references (addresses) to methods as opposed to storing actual data. You are used to passing data into methods through the use of parameters. Delegates enable you to pass methods as parameters into other methods. Through the use of a delegate, you are able to encapsulate a reference to a method inside a delegate object. The delegate object can be passed to code which can call the referenced method, without having to know at compile time which method will be invoked. Delegates are used in applications other than Windows applications that respond to GUI events; however, it is their relationship to events that makes them interesting and worth presenting in this section.

Defining Delegates

The `delegate base class` type is defined in the `System` `namespace`. A couple of syntactical differences exist between delegates and the other predefined and user-defined classes that you have already used. First, the declaration for a `delegate` looks more like a method declaration than a `class` definition; however, it has no body. It begins with the keyword `delegate` and it ends with a parenthesized list of parameters followed by a semicolon. Every `delegate` type has a signature, which may include zero or more parameters. Remember that a **signature** for a method includes its name, number of parameters, and parameter types. The signature of a method does not include the `return` type. Like methods, a `delegate` may include a return type or the keyword void as part of its heading. However, unlike a method, the return type of a delegate becomes part of its identifying signature. Example 10-1 defines a delegate type that takes no arguments and returns a string.

EXAMPLE 10-1

```
delegate string ReturnsSimpleString( );
```

When you define a delegate type, you identify what types of methods the delegate represents. This identification is accomplished through the delegate signature, which is very important. It indicates what the method signatures must look like if they are to be referenced by the delegate.

In C#, you can think of the delegate as a way of defining or naming a method signature.

Given the signature for the delegate defined in Example 10-1, any method that has zero parameters and returns a string could be referenced by the ReturnsSimpleString delegate. Example 10-2 shows the heading and body for a prospective method.

EXAMPLE 10-2

```
// Method that returns a string.
static string EndStatement( )
{
    return " in 10 years.";
}
```

Compare the heading for the EndStatement( ) method shown in Example 10-2 with the delegate in Example 10-1. Both return strings. Both have zero parameters. The delegate does not specify what the statements must be in the body of the method, and it does not specify what the name of the method must be, just what the signature must look like.

A delegate is implemented in C# as a class; however, an instance of the delegate class is also referred to as a delegate, rather than as an object. The fact that both the class type and the instance type go by the same name can be confusing.

10

Creating Delegate Instances

To associate the delegate with the method, a delegate instance is defined using the method name as the argument inside the parentheses. One way you have previously identified methods from field and property instances is by recognizing that the method name identifier is followed by a set of parentheses. When you write a method name without parentheses, you are referencing the address of the method. Example 10-3 instantiates the ReturnsSimpleString delegate with the EndStatement( ) method as the argument.

EXAMPLE 10-3

```
ReturnsSimpleString saying3 = new ReturnsSimpleString(EndStatement);
```

NOTE The constructor for a delegate of the delegate class always takes just one parameter. This is because you are sending the name of a method for the constructor to reference.

Notice that the EndStatement argument does not include the parentheses, even though EndStatement is a method. A reference to the address of the method is sent as an argument. The address stored is the entry point in memory where the method begins when it is called.

Using Delegates

After completing the instantiation in Example 10-3, the delegate identifier saying3 references the EndStatement( ) method. Any use of saying3( ) calls the EndStatement( ) method. Example 10-4 illustrates this.

EXAMPLE 10-4

```
MessageBox.Show(saying3( ));
```

A call to the Show( ) method of the MessageBox class calls the delegate instance, saying3( ), which calls the EndStatement( ) method to display "in 10 years." Calling the EndStatement( ) method in the Show( ) method produces the same output. This is a simple example but illustrates how a delegate is used to call a method. Example 10-4 did not directly call the EndStatement( ) method; however, the statements from its body were those executed.

NOTE Recall that you must add a reference to `System.Windows.Forms` in order to use the `MessageBox.Show( )` method. You access the **Reference Manager** from the **Solution Explorer** Window. To avoid fully qualifying the name with your program statements, you should also add another `using` statement, `using System.Windows.Forms;`.

The program in Example 10-5 illustrates defining a single `delegate` type, instantiating three `delegate` instances, and calling up the three delegates. Without looking closely, the arguments to the `Show( )` method appear to be normal method calls. In reality, the methods are called through the delegates. Notice that the `delegate` instance name and a set of parentheses form the argument to the `Show( )` method.

EXAMPLE 10-5

```
// DelegateExample.cs                Author: Doyle
// After defining a delegate class, three delegate
// instances are instantiated. Delegates are
// used as arguments for the Show( ) method.
using System;
using System.Windows.Forms;

namespace DelegateExample
{
      delegate string ReturnsSimpleString( );

      class DelegateExample
      {
            static void Main ( )
            {
                  int age = 18;
                  ReturnsSimpleString saying1 = new
                            ReturnsSimpleString(AHeading);
                  ReturnsSimpleString saying2 = new
                            ReturnsSimpleString((age + 10).ToString);
                  ReturnsSimpleString saying3= new
                            ReturnsSimpleString(EndStatement);
                  MessageBox.Show(saying1( ) + saying2( ) +
                                      saying3( ));
            }

            // Method that returns a string.
            static string AHeading( )
            {
                  return "Your age will be ";
            }
```

10

```
            // Method that returns a string.
            static string EndStatement( )
            {
                return " in 10 years.";
            }
        }
}
```

The signatures for the methods and the delegate class match.

Notice that the second instance of the delegate, saying2, is associated with a .NET predefined method of the object class. Remember that the ToString( ) method takes no arguments and returns a string. Its signature matches the ReturnsSimpleString( ) delegate.

The methods are said to be wrapped by the delegate. When the delegate is used, it passes a method, instead of data, as an argument to the Show( ) method. Figure 10-1 shows the output produced when you execute the program from Example 10-5.

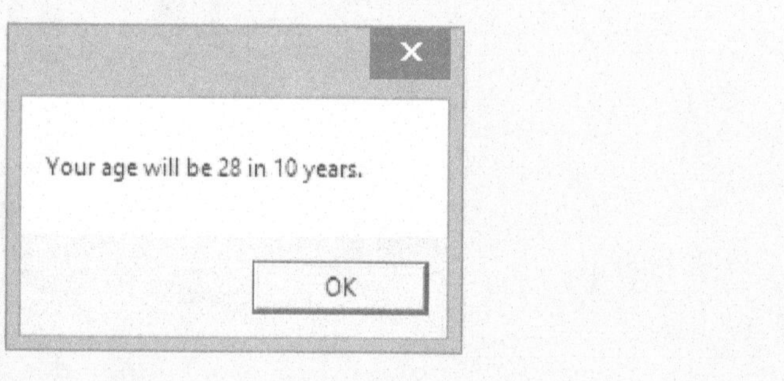

FIGURE 10-1 Output from delegate example

It is possible to have the delegate **wrap** more than one method, so that when a delegate is used, multiple methods are called, one after the other. This type of delegate is called a **multicast delegate**. The += and -= operators are used to add or remove methods to and from the delegate chain or invocation list. One requirement for multicast delegates is that the return type be void.

The real advantage or power of the delegate, however, is that the same delegate can call different methods during run time. When the program is compiled, the method or methods that will be called are not determined. This is why delegates work so well in an event-driven arena, where you do not know, for example, which event occurs first or which control gets attention first.

If the console application template is selected as the type of application, you will see the black command window displayed in the background when you run the program. Remove it by first selecting the project in the **Solution Explorer** window and then select the icon representing Properties in the **Solution Explorer** window. Using the pull-down menu, select **Windows Application** as the **Output type**.

Relationship of Delegates to Events

Think about what the word *delegate* means in the English language; you associate it with something or someone who acts as a bridge between two things. A **delegate** serves as a bridge with event-driven applications. It acts as an intermediary between objects that are raising or triggering an event, and the `object` that captures the event and responds to it. You can think of events as special forms of delegates in C# because they enable you to place a reference to event-handler methods inside a `delegate`. After this reference is made, or the event is registered, the `delegate` is used to call the event-handler method when an event, such as a button click, is fired.

This behind-the-scenes plumbing is dealt with in C# without much programmer intervention. In fact, if you are using Visual Studio, all of the code, with the exception of the statements that appear in the event-handler methods, is automatically generated for you when you identify the events about which your program must receive notification.

Event Handling in C#

In Chapter 9, you wrote program statements for methods that were executed when a button was clicked. The Form Designer in Visual Studio did much of the work for you. Two things were added to your program when you double-clicked on a `Button` control `object` during design (or selected its click event from the **Event** list in the **Properties** window). First, the button click event was registered as being of interest, and second, an event-handler method heading was generated. This process is called **event wiring.** You associate a method in your program to an event, such as the user clicking the button. Then, this method is automatically called when the event occurs.

Now that you know about delegates, if you examine the Windows Forms Designer generated code region, which is generated by Visual Studio, you understand how the `delegate` is used to register the event. The code that appears in Example 10-6 is generated when you double-click a button in the Form Designer. `System.EventHandler` is a `delegate` type. This code associates the two methods, `button1_Click( )` and `button2_Click( )`, with that `delegate`.

EXAMPLE 10-6

```
this.button1.Click += new System.EventHandler(this.button1_Click);
this.button2.Click += new System.EventHandler(this.button2_Click);
```

The keyword `this` is added to code generated by Visual Studio. The `this` keyword is used to indicate the current instance of a `class`. For the Windows applications you are developing in this chapter, think of `this` as the current instance of the form. So, for Example 10-6, when you notice `this.button1.Click`, you should mentally associate that with "the current form's" `button1.Click`.

When Visual Studio adds the event-handler method heading, the body of the method is empty. You add the program statements to the body of the method indicating what actions to perform when the button is clicked. Example 10-7 shows the event-handler method for `button1_Click`.

EXAMPLE 10-7

```
private void button1_Click(object sender, system.EventArgs e)
{
}
```

These methods (`button1_Click( )` and `button2_Click( )`) have a `return` type of `void` with two parameters. The `delegate EventHandler( )` has a `return` type of `void` and two parameters. It's signature is `public delegate void EventHandler(object sender, EventArgs e)`. Their signatures match.

Event-Handler Methods

Example 10-7 includes the heading for the event-handler method. All event-handler methods normally have the same signature. They do not return anything; they have a `return` type of `void`. They take two parameters. The first parameter, `object` sender, represents the source that raises the event, and the second parameter is the data for the event. Accessible data, for example, for a `MouseEventArg` event includes which mouse button (left, right, or both) was clicked, how many clicks, and the x- and y-coordinates for where the mouse pointer was positioned on the screen when the mouse button was clicked. This data can be obtained from the second argument.

The `delegate` maintains a list of the registered event handlers for an event. To identify the events about which you are interested in receiving notification, register the event and specify what actions to perform when the event occurs by typing the body of the event-handler method. The event handlers are called using delegates.

The sections that follow highlight some of the most interesting events that you can include in your application to add functionality. An application will be created using Visual Studio; controls will be added, their properties set, and their events programmed.

ListBox Control Objects

The `ListBox` control is a very powerful widget that can be added to Windows applications. `ListBox` controls can be used to display a list of items from which the user can make single or multiple selections. A scroll bar is automatically added to the control if the total number of items exceeds the number that can be displayed. You can add or remove items to and from the `ListBox` control at design time or dynamically at run time.

Creating a Form to Hold ListBox Controls

To experience working with a `ListBox` `object`, a new project in Visual Studio is created using the Windows application template. Look ahead at Figure 10-5. It shows the completed form. When you select the Windows application template, a blank form is automatically generated. The `Name` property for the form is set to `ClubForm`. The `Font` property for `ClubForm` is set to 12 points. This property is set on the `Form1` `object` so that other objects that are added to `ClubForm` will already be set; this becomes the default font for the application. This procedure ensures consistency in `Font` selection across controls. Of course, the `Font` can be set for individual controls if there is a need for one or more to be different. The `BackColor` Blue `(128, 128, 255)` is set for `ClubForm`. The `Text` property is set to `Computer Club Outing Sign Up`.

NOTE Remember, you need to use the Form **Designer** window to set the properties at design time. If you are in the **Code** Editor instead of the Form **Designer**, select **Designer** from the **View** menu or press **Shift+F7**. Press **F7** to return to the **Code** Editor. If you are using the Express version, you may need to press **Ctrl+Alt+O** to open the **Code** Editor. If you choose not to use the **Properties** window to set properties, program statements could be added to the `FormLoad( )` event-handler method to make the assignments.

A `TextBox` `object` is dragged onto the `ClubForm` `object` and placed at the bottom of the form. The `Name` property is set to `txtBxResult`. This text box stores the result of the list box selection. A `Label` `object` is added to `ClubForm` to the left of the `TextBox` `object` with its `Text` property set to `"Result"`.

ADDING A LISTBOX CONTROL OBJECT

Another `Label` `object` is added to the `ClubForm` in the top-left corner with its `Text` property set to "`Select Event(s)`". A `ListBox` `object` is dragged under the "`Select Event(s)`" label. Its `Name` property is set to `lstBxEvents`. The background color for the control is set using the `BackColor` property. It is set to `Yellow (255,255,192)`. The `ForeColor` property is set to `Blue (0,0,192)` so that the font for characters displays in blue. The `Items` property is used to set the initial values for the list box. Clicking on the button with the ellipsis to the right of the word `Collection` in the `Items` property displays the **String Collection Editor** window. Values for the list box are typed on separate lines using this editor. Figure 10-2 shows the window after values were typed for the list box collection. The following `string` values are typed, each on separate lines; "`Movie`", "`Dance`", "`Boat Tour`", "`Dinner`", "`Hike`", "`Amusement Park`", and "`Sport Event`".

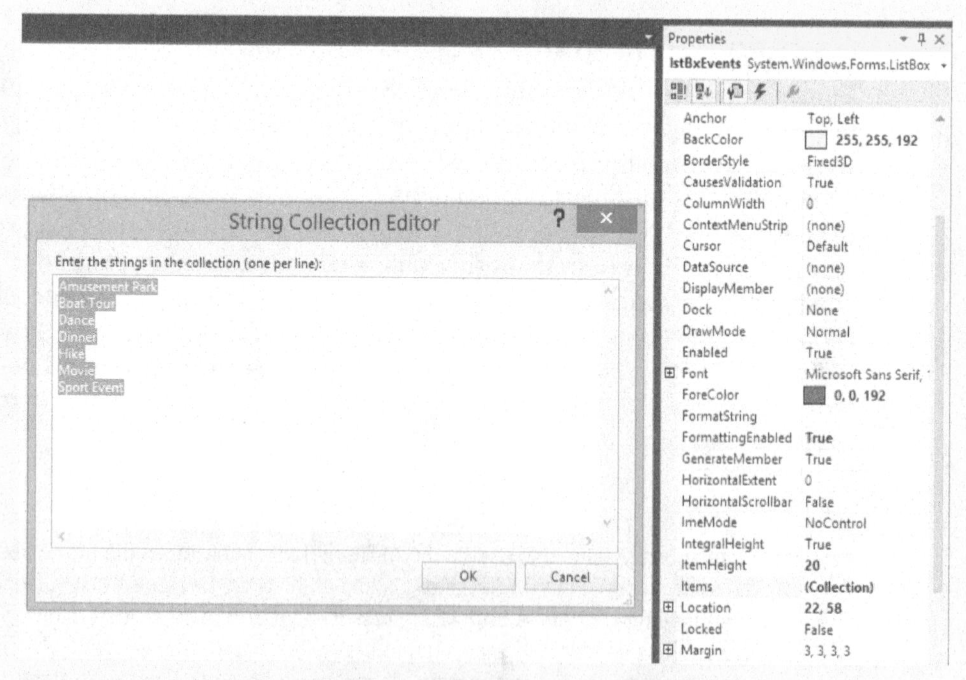

FIGURE 10-2 String Collection Editor

The Sorted property is set to true for the ListBox object. This keeps you from having to type values into the collection as sorted items. By setting the Sorted property to true, they are displayed sorted—as if you had typed them in that order. The control object is sized by clicking on the object and using the standard Windows sizing handles to drag the object so that just four of the strings are shown. If the window is too small to show all choices, a scroll bar is automatically added to ListBox objects when the application is run.

After the controls are placed in their general location, use the **Format**, **Align** menu options to line up associated controls so they are consistently placed on the same row or column. Select multiple controls by drawing a box around the controls using your mouse as the selection tool or hold the **Ctrl** key as you select multiple controls.

REGISTERING A LISTBOX EVENT

To add functionality, you need to register an event for the ListBox control object. To give you an example, you might want to know when the item selection changes. When it does, you might want to display or use the selection. In the Form Designer, when you double-click on a control, you register the default event for that specific control. An event-handler method for that registered event is added to your source code.

You might not want to program a method for the default event for a control. It might be a different event that is of interest. The default event for a Button object is the Button Click event. Thus, when you double-click on a button in the Form Designer, the buttonName_Click event is registered. This is usually the event of interest for Button objects. Clicking on the **Events** icon (lightning bolt) in the **Properties** window shows you a selection of events that can be registered for the object selected.

Double-clicking on the ListBox control adds the line shown in Example 10-8, which registers the SelectedIndexChanged event as being of interest.

EXAMPLE 10-8

```
this.lstBxEvents.SelectedIndexChanged += new
        System.EventHandler(this.lstBxEvents_SelectedIndexChanged);
```

The Form Designer also adds the empty-bodied method shown in Example 10-9 to your program.

EXAMPLE 10-9

```
private void lstBxEvents_SelectedIndexChanged(object sender,
                                              System.EventArgs e)
{
}
```

ListBox Event Handlers

One of the properties of the `ListBox` `class` is `SelectedItem`. It returns an `object` representing the selected `string` item. If you retrieve the selection using this property, the `object` must be converted into a `string` `object` to display it in the Result `TextBox`. The `Text` property of the `txtBxResult` `object` is used to display the selection. The statement in Example 10-10 is added to the body of the `lstBxEvents_SelectedIndexChanged( )` method so that when the event is fired, the selection is displayed.

EXAMPLE 10-10

```
private void lstBxEvents_SelectedIndexChanged(object sender,
                                              System.EventArgs e)
{
     this.txtBxResult.Text =
          this.lstBxEvents.SelectedItem.ToString( );
}
```

The `ToString( )` method was used to convert the item `object` into a `string` for displaying; the `Text` property can also be used to retrieve the data from a `ListBox` control `object`. If you use the `Text` property as opposed to the `SelectedItem` property, there is no requirement of adding the `ToString( )` method. Thus, the body of the `lstBxEvents_SelectedIndexChanged` method could read as shown in Example 10-11.

EXAMPLE 10-11

```
private void lstBxEvents_SelectedIndexChanged(object sender,
                                              System.EventArgs e)
{
     this.txtBxResult.Text = this.lstBxEvents.Text;
}
```

Figure 10-3 shows the output generated from Example 10-11 after the `SelectedIndexChanged` event is fired. Notice that the items appear in alphabetical order. The `Sorted` property rearranged the items.

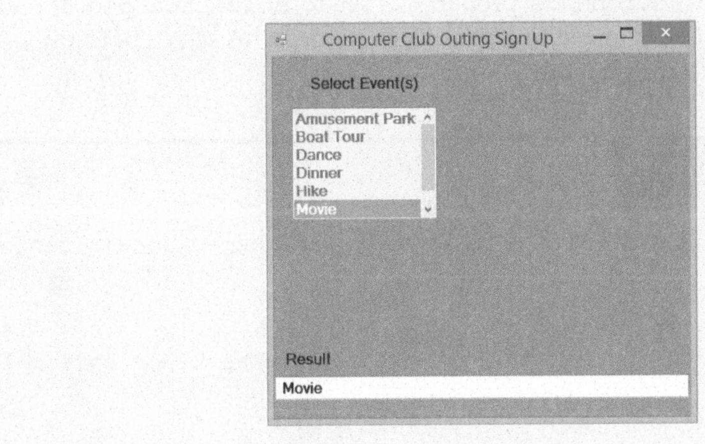

FIGURE 10-3 SelectedIndexChanged event fired

Multiple Selections with a ListBox Object

The `ListBox` control `object` offers the advantage of allowing users to make multiple selections. The `SelectionMode` property has selection values of `MultiSimple` and `MultiExtended`, in addition to `None` and `One`. By default, the property is set to `One`. With a `MultiSimple` selection, the only way to make a selection is by using the Spacebar and clicking the mouse. `MultiExtended` allows users to make selections using the **Ctrl** key, **Shift** key, and arrow keys in addition to using the **Spacebar** and clicking the mouse. Multiple selections are allowed in Figure 10-4. The text box shows that `Boat Tour`, `Dinner`, and `Hike` selections were all highlighted.

10

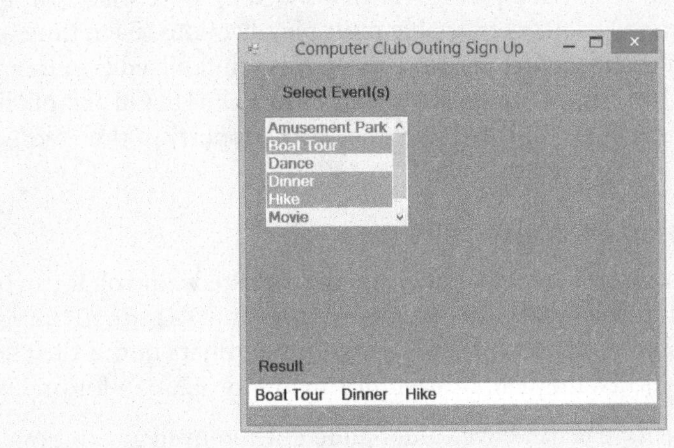

FIGURE 10-4 Multiple selections within a ListBox object

After the SelectionMode property is set to MultiExtended, the event-handler method must be changed to display each of the items selected. Example 10-12 shows the revision to the method.

EXAMPLE 10-12

```
private void lstBxEvents_SelectedIndexChanged(object sender,
                                          System.EventArgs e)
{
     string result = " ";
     foreach(string activity in lstBxEvents.SelectedItems)
     {
          result += activity + " ";
     }
     this.txtBxResult.Text = result;
}
```

Using the foreach loop construct, the selected items are concatenated one item at a time onto a string instance named result.

Remember that when you use + (the plus symbol) with data stored in a string type, the characters are appended onto the end of the result string instead of being used in calculations. The += symbol is used to grow the result string.

Notice that the characters were not appended straight to the Text property of the TextBox object in Example 10-12. Instead, they were placed in an intermediate memory location (result) to enable multiple selections. Each time the event is fired (the selection is changed), the result string is reinitialized (result = " ") and then in the loop, the selected items are added onto result. On the outside of the loop, after values have been concatenated, the Text property of the TextBox object was assigned the string value.

ADDING ITEMS TO A LISTBOX AT RUN TIME

The ListBox control object is a fairly sophisticated control. It can hold data of any type. Values returned using the SelectedItem and SelectedItems properties are returned as objects; thus, you can easily store numbers in the ListBox. After being retrieved as objects, they can be cast into an int or double for processing.

The ListBox control can have values added or removed at run time. To add a value when the program is running, you use the Add( ) method with the Items property, as shown in Example 10-13.

EXAMPLE 10-13

```
lstBxEvents.Items.Add("string value to add");
```

Figure 10-5 shows the form allowing the user to enter another activity to the list of events. A new `Button` and `TextBox` `object` is added to the form. The text from the `TextBox` `object` is added as a selection to the `ListBox`. Two events were fired before the output being displayed in Figure 10-5 was produced. The first event that was fired was the button click. This event-handler method added the user-entered `string` to the `ListBox`. The second event was fired when the user clicked a selection from the list box. The selections are displayed in the Result text box. Notice the new selection that was typed. *Picnic* now appears as an option. It was also selected from the list box.

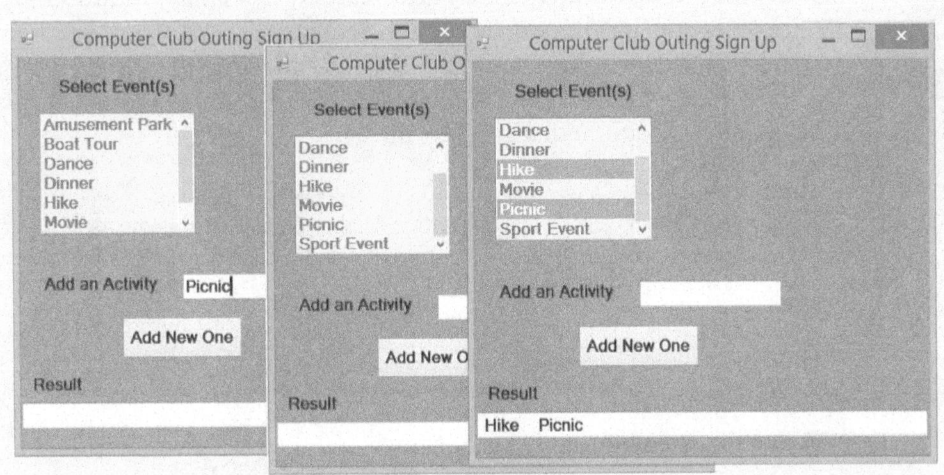

FIGURE 10-5 Picnic inserted from the Add( ) method executed inside the buttonClick event

You may be tempted to double-click the `TextBox` `object` to register its default event handler instead of adding the extra button object. The default event handler for the `TextBox` `object` is the `TextChanged( )` event, which fires with every character that is entered into the textbox. You do not want that to happen with this application. The `btnNew_Click( )` event-handler body retrieves the text that is typed by the user from `txtBxAddNew` and adds it to the `ListBox` `object`. The method is shown in Example 10-14.

EXAMPLE 10-14

```
private void btnNew_Click(object sender, System.EventArgs e)
{
     lstBxEvents.Items.Add(txtBxAddNew.Text);
}
```

Another useful method to use with `ListBox` controls is `AddRange( )`. `AddRange( )` enables you to send an array as an argument. This list of items is used to fill the `ListBox`. You still need to use the `Items` property. A call to `AddRange( )` might look like `listBox1.Items.AddRange(someArray);`.

Example 10-15 shows the program listing for the application with a couple of minor modifications included. The modifications are discussed following the source listing. Example 10-15 shows the program statements typed for the event handlers. Recall that three source code files are created when an application is developed. The Windows Forms Designer contains the generated code added when property values were changed for the form and other controls added to the application. The third file, which includes `Main( )`, is also not shown with Example 10-15. No program statements were typed for either of these files.

Visual Studio automatically inserts a number of `using` statements at the top of a program. Most are not needed for examples illustrated in this chapter. Unnecessary `using` statements have been deleted.

EXAMPLE 10-15

```
/*   ClubForm.cs
     This application illustrates adding
     Button, Label, Textbox and
     ListBox objects. SelectedIndexChanged
     and click events are fired.
*/
using System;
using System.Windows.Forms;

namespace ListBoxExample
{
     public partial class ClubForm : Form
     {
```

```
            public ClubForm( )
            {
                  InitializeComponent( );
            }

            private void lstBxEvents_SelectedIndexChanged (object
                                      sender, EventArgs e)
            {
                  string result = " ";
                  foreach (string activity in
                                 lstBxEvents.SelectedItems)
                              result += activity + " ";
                  this.txtBxResult.Text = result;
            }

            private void btnNew_Click(object sender, EventArgs e)
            {
                  lstBxEvents.Items.Add(txtBxAddNew.Text);
                  txtBxAddNew.Clear( );
            }
      }
}
```

To add functionality, the btnNew Button object was set as the value for the AcceptButton property of the Form object. This enables the user to press the **Enter** key after typing in new entries. Now the **Enter** key functions in the same way as clicking the left mouse button on the btnNew Button object. The btnNew_Click( ) event is fired when the user clicks the mouse or presses the **Enter** key. In the btnNew_Click( ) event-handler method, the TextBox object was also cleared using the Clear( ) method. This was done after the value was typed into the TextBox object, retrieved, and added to the ListBox object. Table 10-1 includes a list of properties set for the ListBoxExample application.

10

TABLE 10-1 ListBoxExample property values

Name	Object type	Property	Value
ClubForm	Form	AcceptButton	btnNew
ClubForm	Form	BackColor	Blue (128,128,255)
ClubForm	Form	Font	Microsoft Sans Serif, 12, Bold

(continues)

TABLE 10-1 ListBoxExample property values (*continued*)

Name	Object type	Property	Value
ClubForm	Form	Text	Typed "Computer Club Outing Sign Up"
lstBxEvents	ListBox	BackColor	Yellow (255, 255, 192)
lstBxEvents	ListBox	ForeColor	Blue (0, 0, 192)
lstBxEvents	ListBox	SelectionMode	MultiExtended
lstBxEvents	ListBox	Sorted	true
lstBxEvents	ListBox	TabIndex	1
lstBxEvents	ListBox	Items (Collection)	Typed "Amusement Park", "Boat Tour", "Dance", "Dinner", "Hike", "Movie", "Sport Event"
label1	Label	Text	Typed "Result"
label2	Label	Text	Typed "Select Event(s)"
Label3	Label	Text	Typed "Add an Activity"
BtnNew	TextBox	Text	Typed "Add New One"

© Cengage Learning

Example 10-15 just touched the surface for what you can do with `ListBox` objects. You will want to explore this `class` further. The `Items`, `SelectedItems`, and `SelectedIndices` properties are useful for getting a collection of selected items from the `ListBox` `object`. The `Count` property can also be used with the `SelectedItems`, and `SelectedIndices` properties to return the number of items selected. To retrieve that value you would type `lstBxEvents.SelectedItems.Count`. To reset the listbox or clear all selections, invoke the `ClearSelected( )` method.

In addition to being useful for entering values at design time, the `ListBox` `object` is a control that can be populated with new values at run time. By including the `Add( )` method with the `Items` property inside a loop, values entered by the user or read from a file or database table can be added to the control while the application is running. The `AddRange( )` method, also used with the `Items` property, allows you to quickly populate the `ListBox` with an array of objects. Table 10-2 describes some of the more interesting properties of the `ListBox` `class`.

NOTE The information included in Tables 10-2 and 10-3 was adapted from the MSDN documentation.

TABLE 10-2 ListBox properties

Property	Description
`Items`	Gets the values (items) in the list box
`MultiColumn`	Gets or sets a value indicating whether the list box supports multiple columns
`SelectedIndex`	Gets or sets the zero-based index of the currently selected item
`SelectedIndices`	Gets a collection that contains the zero-based indexes of all currently selected items
`SelectedItem`	Gets or sets the selected item
`SelectedItems`	Gets a collection containing the currently selected items
`SelectionMode`	Gets or sets the method in which items are selected (`MultiExtended, MultiSimple, One, None`)
`Sorted`	Gets or sets a value indicating whether the items are sorted alphabetically
`Text`	Gets or searches for the text of the currently selected item

© Cengage Learning

Table 10-3 gives a partial list of methods and events of the `ListBox` `object`. Remember that the `ListBox` `object` also inherits members from the `Control` `class`. Tables 9-2 and 9-3, in Chapter 9, listed many of the `Control` `class` members. You should review those tables.

10

TABLE 10-3 ListBox methods

Method (and event)	Description
`ClearSelected( )`	Unselects all items
`Enter( )` Event – [inherited from Control]	Occurs when the control is entered
`FindString( )`	Finds the first item that starts with the specified `string`
`FindStringExact( )`	Finds the first item that exactly matches the specified `string`
`GotFocus( )` Event – [inherited from Control]	Occurs when the control receives focus
`KeyPress( )` Event – [inherited from Control]	Occurs when a key is pressed while the control has focus
`Leave( )` Event – [inherited from Control]	Occurs when the input focus leaves the control
`MouseEnter( )` Event – [inherited from Control]	Occurs when the mouse pointer enters the control
`MouseHover( )` Event – [inherited from Control]	Occurs when the mouse pointer hovers over the control
`MouseLeave( )` Event – [inherited from Control]	Occurs when the mouse pointer leaves the control
`SelectedIndexChanged( )` Event – [default event]	Occurs when the `SelectedIndex` property has changed
`SetSelected( )`	Selects or clears the selection for the specified item

© Cengage Learning

A similar control, but one with additional functionality, is the `ComboBox`. The `ComboBox` `class` is discussed in the following section; the differences between the `ComboBox` `class` and `ListBox` controls are highlighted.

ComboBox Control Objects

In many cases, the `ListBox` controls and `ComboBox` controls can be used interchangeably. They share many of the same properties and methods because they are both derived from the System.Windows.Forms.ListControl class. The ListBox control is usually used when you have all the choices available at design time. You saw in previous code segments that values can be added to the ListBox using the Add( ) method. For the example illustrated in Figure 10-5, an additional control object was required. The TextBox provided a place on the form for the user to enter a new value. After being retrieved, it was then added to the ListBox.

A ComboBox facilitates displaying a list of suggested choices; however, it has an added feature. ComboBox objects contain their own text box field as part of the object. This makes it easy to add a new value at run time. In addition, ComboBox objects save space on a form. Figure 10-6 shows the difference in appearance between the two controls.

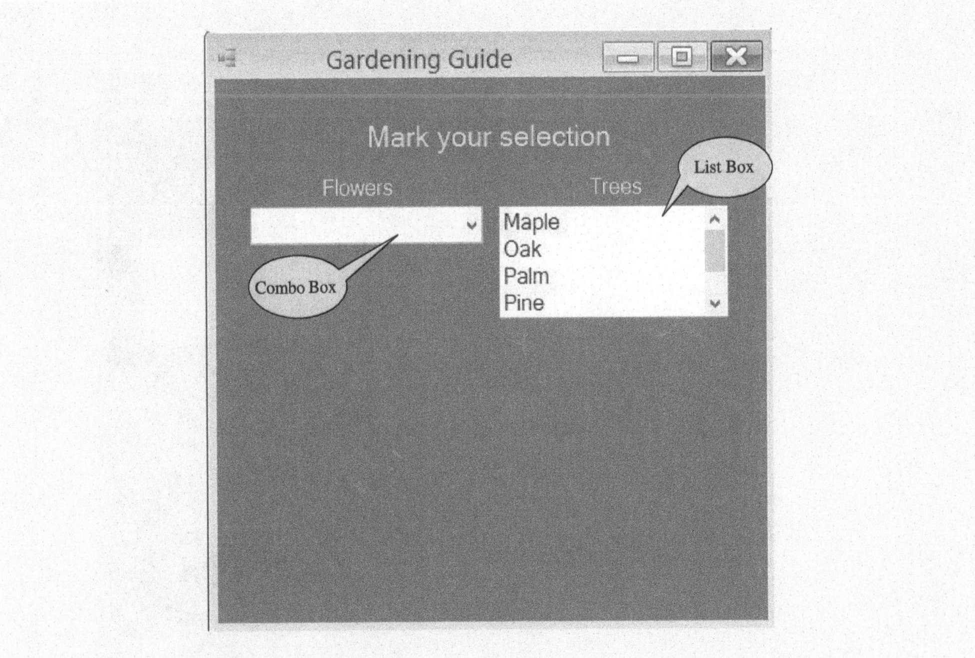

FIGURE 10-6 ComboBox and ListBox objects

NOTE A new Windows application is created to illustrate features of the ComboBox and ListBox. The Text, Name, Font, BackColor, ForeColor, and Size properties were all set for the new Form object.

Adding ComboBox Objects

When you place the ComboBox object on the form, it looks like a TextBox object. The top line of the control is left blank for the entry of typed text. The default setting for the property that determines the combo box's appearance (the DropDownStyle property) is DropDown. If you accept the default setting, the user can either type a new entry into the object or select from the list of items that you assign to the control during design. Another DropDownStyle option, DropDownList, disables new text from being entered into the ComboBox object and offers additional navigational options for viewing the list.

NOTE DropDown, the default value, is set as the DropDownStyle for Figure 10-7. A new entry can be typed and added to the list. The full list of choices is not displayed until the user clicks the down arrow button.

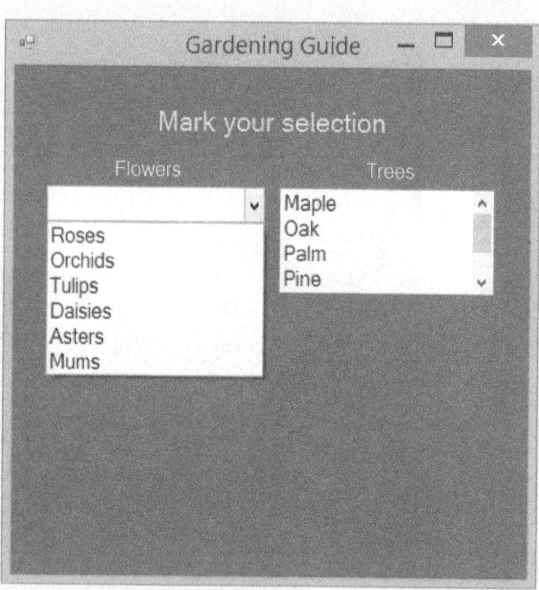

FIGURE 10-7 ComboBox list of choices

Handling ComboBox Events

Another difference between the ComboBox and ListBox is that the ComboBox allows only a single selection to be made. Unlike the ListBox, the ComboBox object does not have a SelectionMode property. Selections from ComboBox objects can be either a new typed value or one of the choices displayed from the drop-down selection. As with the ListBox control object, SelectedIndexChanged( ) is the default event-handler method. When a value such as "Sunflower" is typed into the ComboBox, the SelectedIndexChanged( ) event-handler method is not triggered or raised.

A different event must be registered to respond to values being typed into the text portion. One way to deal with this is to have a `KeyPress( )` or `TextChanged( )` event-handler method executed when new values are entered.

Registering other Events

The `TextChanged( )` event is the default event handler for `Textbox` objects. It is raised if the `Text` property is changed by either a programmatic modification or user interaction. This makes it a great option for `ComboBox` objects. If the `TextChanged( )` event has been registered for the `ComboBox object`, it is fired when the user types a new value into the `ComboBox` open `textbox` area. Values typed into the `text` area can be retrieved and processed when the event fires.

Another option is the `KeyPress( )` event. The `KeyPress( )` event occurs when the user presses a key. Actually, the event is fired with each and every keystroke. The final end result may be the same, but the event handler method will be called many times. It is called each time a key is pressed.

Example 10-16 shows the two events being registered for the `ComboBox` control. Notice that the `Name` property for the `ComboBox object` was set to `cmboFlowers`.

EXAMPLE 10-16

```
this.cmboFlowers.SelectedIndexChanged += new System.EventHandler
                (this.cmboFlowers_SelectedIndexChanged);
this.cmboFlowers.TextChanged += new System.EventHandler
                (this.cmboFlowers_TextChanged);
```

10

NOTE Another option with `ComboBox` objects is the `TextUpdate( )` event. It is fired whenever the text changes.

Programming Event Handlers

To access text from the `ComboBox` and the `ListBox` objects shown in Figure 10-7, three event-handler methods are programmed. New `TextBox` objects are added to store the values retrieved from these controls. Both the `cmboFlowers_SelectedIndexChanged( )` and the `cmboFlowers_TextChanged( )` event handler methods use the `Text` property to get the value from the `ComboBox object`. After retrieving the value, both methods set the text for the associated `TextBox object`. The body for both of those event handlers contains the following statement:

```
this.txtBxResultFlowers.Text = cmboFlowers.Text;
```

USING COLLECTION INDEXES

Because the ListBox object allows multiple selections, the Text property cannot be used. Text retrieves a single selection, the first one selected. To retrieve all of the choices, you have several options. You can use the SelectedItems, SelectedIndices, or Items methods to retrieve a collection of items selected. These collections are zero-based structures such as an array. You can access them as you would access an element from an array by taking advantage of their array-like nature.

NOTE SelectedIndices is a collection of indexes. Thus, if the first, third, and seventh items were selected, the SelectedIndices collection would contain 0, 2, and 6 because the collection is zero-based.

It is possible to use an int to traverse through the collection of SelectedIndices, as shown in Example 10-17.

EXAMPLE 10-17

```
private void lstBxTrees_SelectedIndexChanged(object sender,
                                             System.EventArgs e)
{
      this.txtBxResultTrees.Text = " ";
      foreach(int i in lstBxTrees.SelectedIndices)
      {
            this.txtBxResultTrees.Text +=
                        this.lstBxTrees.Items[i] + " ";
      }
}
```

Compare the event-handler method shown in Example 10-17 to the ListBox SelectedIndexChanged( ) event-handler method shown in Example 10-12. Example 10-12 accessed the items using the SelectedItems property as opposed to the SelectedIndices property. Instead of accessing the selection by retrieving the items, the statements in Example 10-17 retrieved the indexes. The output produced from the application after adding these event-handler methods is shown in Figure 10-8.

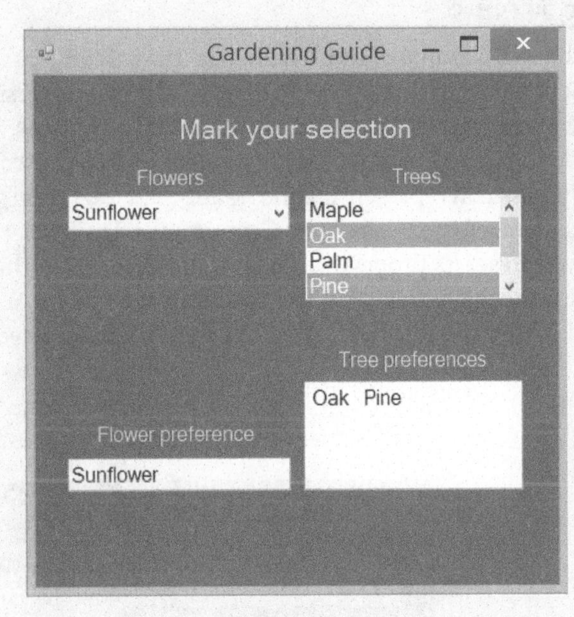

FIGURE 10-8 TextChanged and SelectedIndexChanged events fired

`Sunflower` was not placed in the collection list at design time; it is typed when the program is launched. The `TextChanged( )` event-handler method fired. If the `KeyPress( )` event had been registered, recall it would be fired for each and every character pressed. Thus, it would be fired when the character *S* is typed; it is fired again when the character *u* is typed, and so on. This `TextChanged( )` method uses the `Text` property of the `ComboBox` to get the selection and the `Text` property of the `TextBox object` to set the value for display purposes. Two selections were made from the `ListBox object`. The `SelectionMode` for the `ListBox object` was set to `MultiExtended`. The `SelectedIndexChanged( )` method set the text of the `TextBox object` by concatenating (+=) the selections into the `Text` property. Most Windows applications include a number of menu options. In the following section, you add menus to this application and learn how easy it is to add traditional menus found on most Windows applications.

MenuStrip Control Objects

Menus offer the advantage of taking up minimal space on your window. They enable you to add more functionality to your application through offering additional options to the user. In the `System.Windows.Forms namespace`, a number of classes are available that enable you to add layers of menus to your applications.

Adding Menus

One of the .NET Framework classes is the `MenuStrip` `class`. `MenuStrip` replaces and adds functionality to the `MainMenu` control of previous versions. `MainMenu` is retained for both backward compatibility and future use if you choose. Using the Visual Studio Toolbox window, it is easy to drag and drop a `MenuStrip` control `object` to your form. When you do this, an icon representing the `MenuStrip` `object` is placed below the design window in the grayed area called the **Component Tray**. Selecting the `MenuStrip` `object` enables you to set its properties, such as its `Name`, using the **Properties** window. To add the text for the menu option, select the `MenuStrip` icon and then click on the upper-left corner of the form where the words "Type Here" are displayed as illustrated in Figure 10-9.

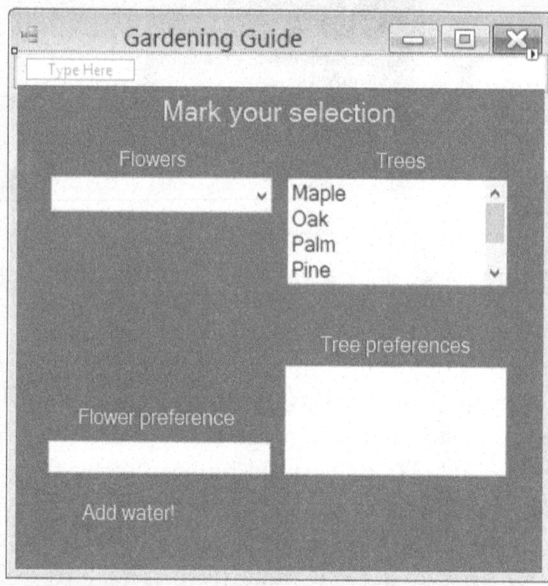

FIGURE 10-9 First step to creating a menu

The menu structure is created by typing the text for each menu option in the prompted text box. This is the blank text box in the upper-left corner immediately below the icon that appears on the title bar, as shown in Figure 10-9. This `class` enables you not only to create the top-level structure but also to type options for drop-down subordinate menus. Notice the phrase "Type Here" in Figure 10-9. Moving to the right or below the current text box selection enables you to type either a subordinate menu option (below it) or another top-level menu option to the right. Additional drop-down options can be typed from the lower layers so that you can create a menu structure exactly like you see in applications such as your word-processing program.

With most Windows application menus, shortcuts are available for selections. Visual Studio enables you to create keyboard shortcuts or access keys. An **access key** is an underlined character in the text of an item or on the label of a control such as a button.

With an access key defined on a button, the user can "click" the button, without using the mouse, by pressing the **Alt** key in combination with the predefined access key character. When you type the text that is to appear in the menu, preceding the character with an ampersand (&) creates an access key. As shown in Figure 10-10, the ampersand is typed between the `F` and `o` for the `Format` option. This makes **Alt+o** the shortcut for **Format**. This enables the option to be selected by pressing the **Alt** key plus the key that you type following the ampersand. For example, instead of typing `File`, type `&File`. This creates a shortcut of **Alt+F** for the **File** menu. You will see **File** displayed when you press the **Alt** key. To the right of `File`, `F&ormat` is typed followed by `&Help`. Under File, `Exit` was typed. As an option under the **Format** menu, `Font` was typed, followed by `Color`. Under `Help`, `About` was typed.

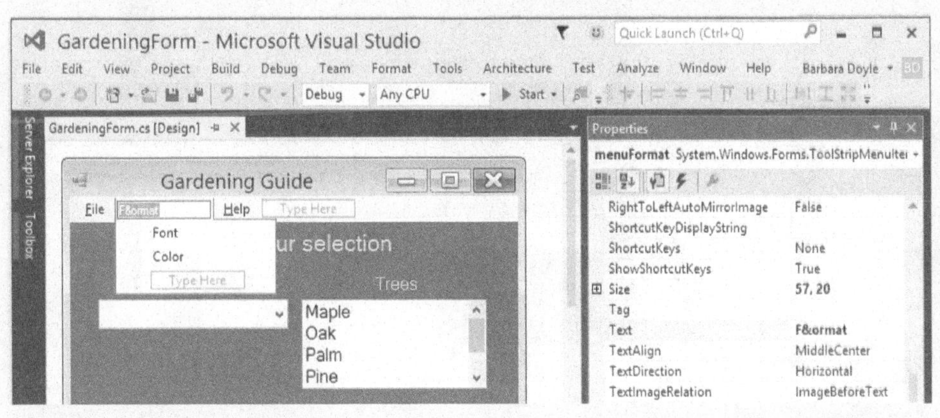

FIGURE 10-10 Creating a shortcut for a menu item

As you review the properties displayed in Figure 10-10, notice three properties, `ShortcutKeyDisplayString`, `SortcutKeys`, and `ShowShortcutKeys`. are shown. They enable you to set a special shortcut for menu items exists. Selecting the box to the right of `ShortcutKeys` in the **Properties** window enables you to select which **Modifier**, **Alt**, **Shift** or **Ctrl** and it reveals a drop-down list of characters to associate with the **Modifer**. You can associate the **Alt**, **Shift**, **Ctrl** or any combination of these three **Modifier** keys, with any of the function keys, alphabetic characters, or many of the other keyboard characters including the keys on the numeric keypad to any menu option. The text to be displayed for the shortcut is set using the `ShortcutKeyDisplayString` property.

If you add shortcuts, you would want to see the shortcut on the menu option. For example, if you associate **Ctrl+S** with save, the text for the menu for save should not just read "**Save**", but should read "**Save Ctrl+S**"; otherwise, how will users know what shortcuts you have programmed for them? The `ShortcutDisplayString` property enables you to identify what additional text should be appended to the right of the menu option's `Text`. The `Text` property would be set to **Save** and the `ShortcutDisplayString` property would be set to **Ctrl+S**.

You are accustomed to seeing separators between menu options. These are easily created in Visual Studio by right-clicking on the text label below the needed separator and selecting **Insert, Separator**, as illustrated in Figure 10-11. When launched, a separator appears between the **Font** and **Color** options.

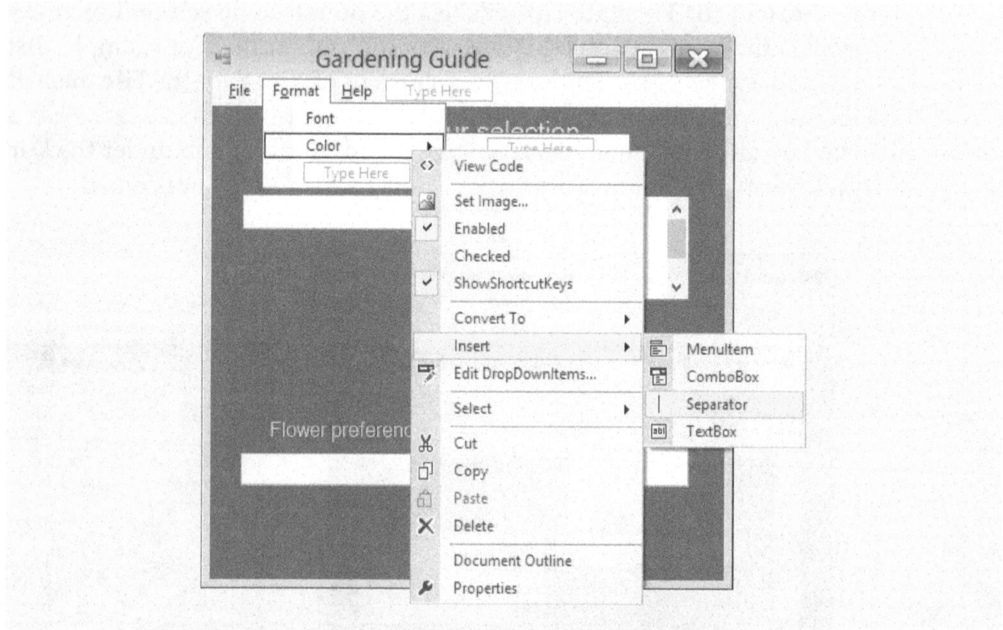

FIGURE 10-11 Adding a separator

If you are using the `MainMenu` control as opposed to the `MenuStrip` control, after you type the text that will appear on the menu, you must set the `Menu` property on the form to the name of the `MainMenu` `object`. Otherwise, the menu does not display when you launch the application. If you use the `MenuStrip` control you do not have to set this property. The association is made automatically for you.

You can assign a tool tip to controls, such as text boxes or menu items, so that text is displayed when the cursor is rested on top of the component. To create a tool tip, drag the `ToolTip` control from the **Toolbox** and drop it anywhere on the form. It will rest in the **Component Tray** below the form. The `ToolTip` is not associated with any specific control object. After it is placed on the form, controls have a new property available in the **Properties** window. To define a tool tip for a specific control, select the control and type what you want to have displayed into the `ToolTip` property in the **Properties** window. For example, to alert the user that multiple selections could be made from the list box holding the tree names, the `ToolTip` property for the `lstBxTrees` control was set to `"Press and Hold the Ctrl Key for Multiple Selections!"`, as shown in Figure 10-12.

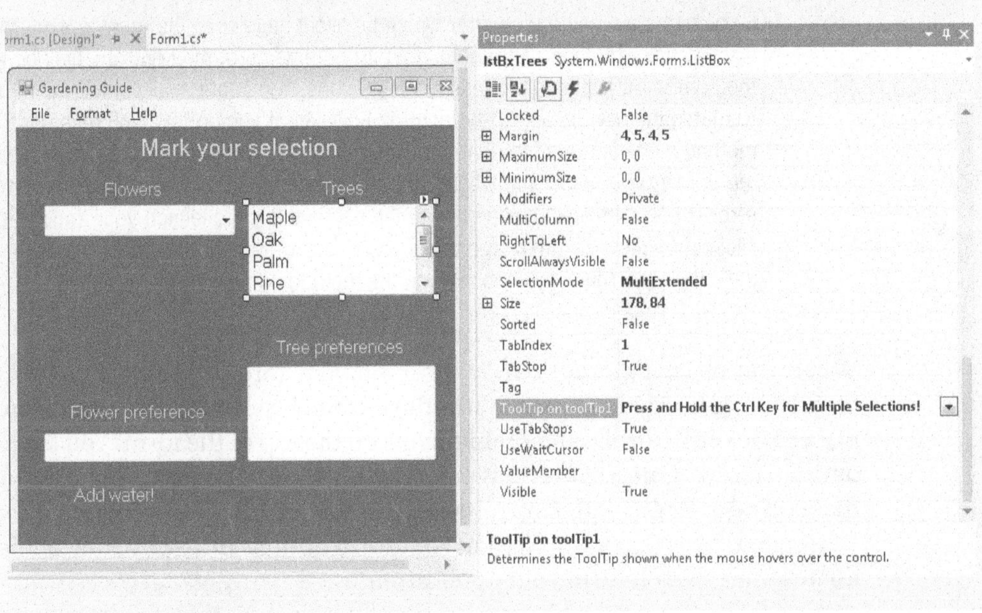

FIGURE 10-12 Setting the ToolTip property

When you create the menu structure using the `MenuStrip` control, separate `ToolStripMenuItem` objects are created for each of the selectable menu options that you type. After you finish laying out the structure, the `Name` property for these `ToolStripMenuItem` objects can be set by selecting the individual menu option prior to selecting the `Name` property in the **Properties** window. This is especially important if the menu item will be wired to an event because the name of the control becomes part of the name of the event-handler method.

To **wire a method to an event** such as a menu option means you are associating the event to a specific method. After the method is wired to the menu option, the method is executed automatically when the menu option is clicked. When the menu option is clicked, it can be said that the event triggers, happens, or is fired. This is one of the underlying concepts behind event-driven applications.

Property names such as `menuExit`, `menuFont`, `menuColor`, and `menuHelp` were set in the **Properties** window after selecting each individual `ToolStripMenuItem` in the Form **Designer**. `Click` events are registered by double-clicking on the option. Form **Designer** generates individual click event-handler methods. The click event method name for the `menuExit` option is `menuExit_Click( );` the event handler for the `menuFont` option is `menuFont_Click( ).`

If you name a menu option after wiring its event handler to the menu option, the event-handler method name does not carry the name of the control. This does not impact the results—it just leads to less readable code. You can actually change the method name to match the new name for the control; however, if you do this, you must also change the method name in the statement that wires the event handler to the `object`. You can use the debugger to show you where that statement appears in the .Designer code. A syntax error is presented when you change the name and try to launch your application. Double clicking on the error message takes you to the statement that wires the event handler to the `object`. There you can replace the method name with the new name.

When you place a `MenuStrip` `object` on your form, the smart tag for the control reveals an option titled "**Insert Standard Items**". Selecting this option automatically places **File**, **Edit**, **Tools**, and **Help** menus on the top of the form. You get the standard options (**New**, **Open**, **Save**, **Save As**, **Print**, **Print Preview**, and **Exit**) on the **File** menu. **Undo**, **Redo**, **Cut**, **Copy**, **Paste**, and **Select All** are automatically added to the **Edit** menu. You can, of course, add additional options or remove any of these that you do not want to include in your application.

The click event-handler methods for the **Exit** and **About** menu options are shown in Example 10-18.

EXAMPLE 10-18

```
private void menuExit_Click(object sender, System.EventArgs e)
{
     Application.Exit( );
}
private void menuAbout_Click(object sender, System.EventArgs e)
{
     MessageBox.Show("Gardening Guide Application\n\n\nVersion" +
                     " 1.0", "About Gardening");
}
```

A message dialog box is displayed when the user clicks the **About** option. All windows are closed and the program is terminated when the user clicks the **Exit** option.

Adding Predefined Standard Windows Dialog Boxes

Included as part of .NET are a number of preconfigured dialog boxes. They include boxes that look like the standard Windows File Open, File Save, File Print, File Print Preview, Format Font, and Format Color dialog boxes. They are added to your application by dragging and dropping the control `object` on your form. Figure 10-13 shows a partial list of controls highlighting the `Dialog` controls.

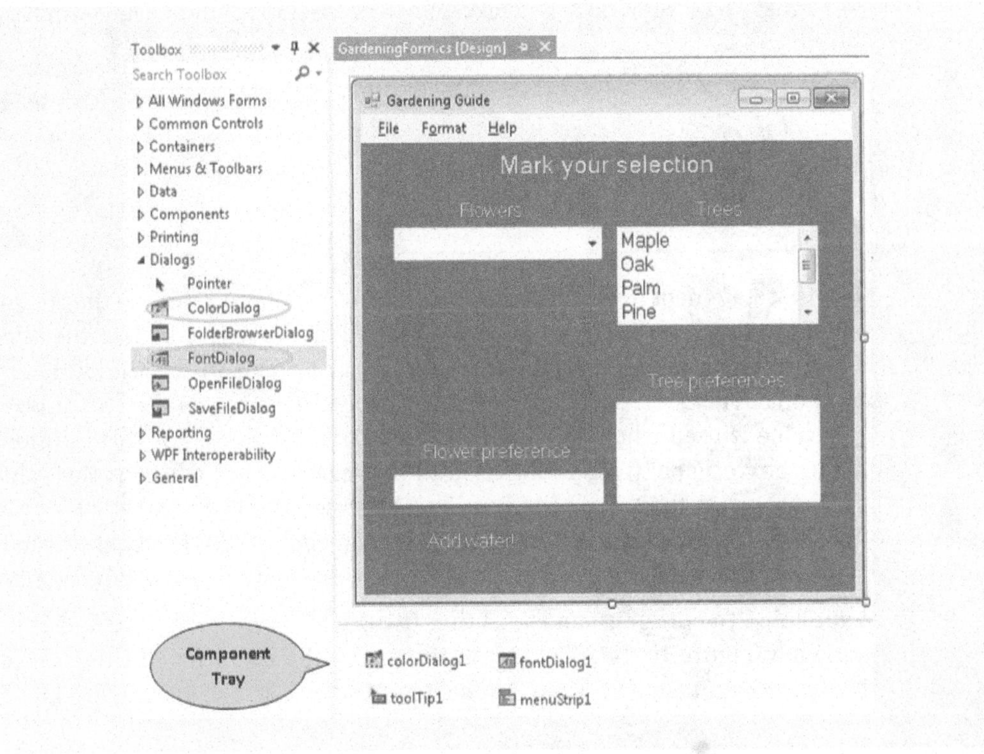

FIGURE 10-13 Adding dialog controls to menu options

As shown in Figure 10-13, objects of the `colorDialog` and `fontDialog` are added to the **ComponentTray** when they are dragged and dropped onto the form. They join the `ToolTip` and `MenuStrip` controls already on the form. To see the effect of the `Font` and `Color` menu options, a new `Label` `object` is placed on the `Form`. Its `Name` property is set to `lblOutput`. The `Text` property for `lblOutput` is set to `"Add Water!"`.

10

Double-clicking on the `Font` and `Color` menu options registers click events and generates event-handler methods. Example 10-19 shows the body of these methods.

EXAMPLE 10-19

```
private void menuFont_Click(object sender, System.EventArgs e)
{
      fontDialog1.Font = lblOutput.Font;
      if (fontDialog1.ShowDialog( ) != DialogResult.Cancel)
      {
          lblOutput.Font = fontDialog1.Font;
      }
}
```

```
private void menuColor_Click(object sender, System.EventArgs e)
{
      colorDialog1.Color = lblOutput.ForeColor;
      if (colorDialog1.ShowDialog( ) != DialogResult.Cancel)
      {
            lblOutput.ForeColor = colorDialog1.Color;
      }
}
```

The first statement in the `menuFont_Click( )` method retrieves the current `Font` setting from the `Label` object's `Font` property. This value is shown as the selected option when the dialog box is displayed. The first statement in the `menuColor_Click( )` method retrieves the current `ForeColor` property setting for the `Label` `object`. Again, this value is used when the Color dialog box is displayed. For this example, the Color dialog box originally has a box around the yellow color, which is the value set as the `ForeColor` on the `Form` property. The `if` statement in Example 10-19 is checking to make sure that the Cancel button has not been clicked. If it has been clicked, no change is made; otherwise, the `Font` and `ForeColor` are set to the selections made by the user.

Launching the program and selecting the `Color` menu option, displays a window, as shown in Figure 10-14. Clicking on the pink color and then clicking OK changes the `ForeColor` for the `Label` to that selection once the dialog box closes.

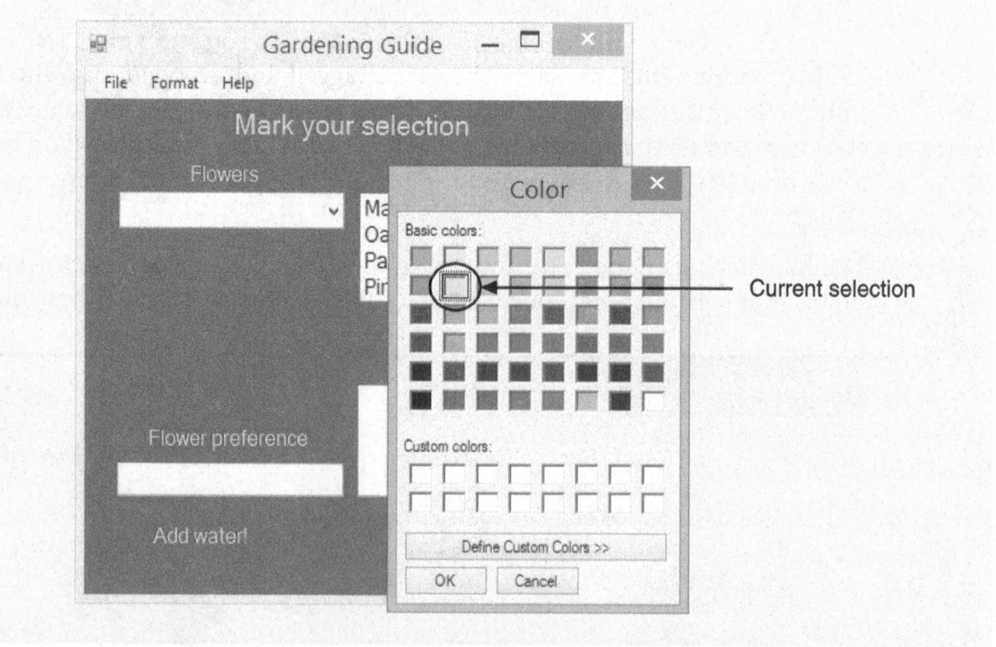

FIGURE 10-14 Color dialog box menu option

The Font dialog box displayed from the Format menu in the Gardening Guide is shown in Figure 10-15. It contains the styles, sizes, effects, and a sample output window for viewing. Notice that Informal Roman, Bold, 28 point, and underline effects were all chosen. The `Label` `object` containing the text "Add water!" is changed to reflect these selections once the dialog box is closed.

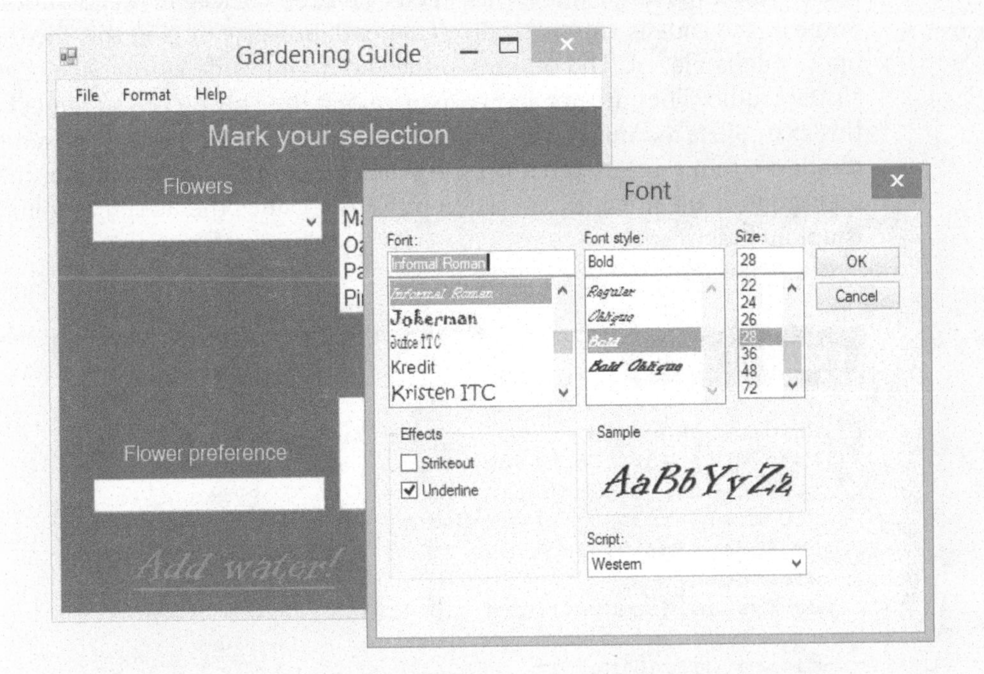

FIGURE 10-15 Font dialog box menu option

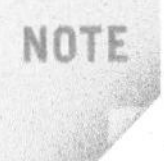

You can add color selections to the `Font` dialog box by setting the `ShowColor` property of the FontDialog `object` to `true`. Your program statement would read: `fontDialog1.ShowColor = true;`. By that same token, you could remove the `Effects` selections by setting the `ShowEffects` property to `false`. Doing this removes the check boxes for Strikeout and Underline.

You could certainly change any or all of the fonts and colors on the form using the name of the control `object` in your program statements. The `lblOutput Label` `object` is the only one modified by the font and color selections at run time. The source code listing for the `GardeningForm.cs` file is given in Example 10-20.

You will recall that three separate source code files are created for each Windows application. One file stores the `Main( )` method. This file has a default name of `Program.cs`. The second and third files, taken together define the `class` for the application. Their heading indicates that each file has a `partial class` definition.

One of these two files is named the GardeningForm.Designer.cs. This file stores all the Visual Studio generated code used to instantiate objects that were dragged and dropped onto the form. No developer code was added to this file. It is now shown here.

The file illustrated in Example 10-20 is named GardeningForm.cs. It stores the code written to handle the events, such as button clicks and menu option selections. Some of the code is automatically generated; however, it is in this file that all developer code is placed. The other two files hold only code automatically generated by Visual Studio. They are not shown. Notice that the only using statement shown with this example is using System.Windows.Forms. EventArgs, for example, is in the System namespace so references to that class in the event handler method headings are fully qualified (System.EventArgs e) since the using System namespace is not included.

EXAMPLE 10-20

```
// GardeningForm.cs                    Author: Doyle
// Menu, ListBox, ComboBox, Label, and TextBox
// objects are included in the design. KeyPress( ),
// Click( ), and SelectedIndexChanged( ) events
// are programmed. Font and Color dialog boxes
// are added.
using System.Windows.Forms;

namespace GardeningForm
{
    public partial class GardeningForm : Form
    {
        public GardeningForm( )
        {
            InitializeComponent( );
        }

        private void cmboFlowers_SelectedIndexChanged
                    (object sender, System.EventArgs e)
        {
            this.txtBxResultFlowers.Text =
            this.cmboFlowers.Text;
        }

        private void cmboFlowers_TextChanged (object sender,
                                 System.EventArgs e)
        {
            this.txtBxResultFlowers.Text =
                              cmboFlowers.Text;
        }
```

```
        private void lstBxTrees_SelectedIndexChanged (object sender,
                                                      System.EventArgs e)
        {
            this.txtBxResultTrees.Text = " ";
            foreach(int i in lstBxTrees.SelectedIndices)
                {
                     this.txtBxResultTrees.Text +=
                 this.lstBxTrees.Items[i] + " ";
                }
        }

        private void menuExit_Click(object sender,
                                    System.EventArgs e)
        {
            Application.Exit( );
        }

        private void menuAbout_Click(object sender,
                                     System.EventArgs e)
        {
             MessageBox.Show("Gardening Guide " +
                             "Application\n\n\nVersion 1.0",
                             "About Gardening");
        }

        private void menuFont_Click(object sender,
                                    System.EventArgs e)
        {
             fontDialog1.Font = lblOutput.Font;
             if (fontDialog1.ShowDialog( ) !=
                            DialogResult.Cancel)
             {
                  lblOutput.Font = fontDialog1.Font;
             }
        }

        private void menuColor_Click(object sender,
                                     System.EventArgs e)
        {
             colorDialog1.Color = lblOutput.ForeColor;
             if (colorDialog1.ShowDialog( ) !=
                             DialogResult.Cancel)
             {
                  lblOutput.ForeColor = colorDialog1.Color;
             }
        }
}
```

As you review the source code for Example 10-20, keep in mind that the Visual Studio Form Designer automatically generated many statements that are stored in the `GardeningForm.Designer.cs` file.

A number of properties were set for the different objects of the `GardeningForm` application. To aid you in reviewing these settings, Table 10-4 includes a list of properties and the values used to set them. The source code for the `GardeningForm.Designer.cs` is not shown; however, the file is available from the publisher like all other examples illustrated in the book.

TABLE 10-4 GardeningForm property values

Name	Object type	Property	Value
GardeningForm	Form	BackColor	Medium Blue (0, 0, 192)
GardeningForm	Form	Font	Microsoft Sans Serif, 12
GardeningForm	Form	Text	Typed "Gardening Guide"
lstBxTrees	ListBox	Items (Collection)	Typed "Maple", "Oak", "Palm", "Pine", "Spruce", "Walnut"
lstBxTrees	ListBox	SelectionMode	MultiExtended
lstBoxTrees	ListBox	ToolTip	Typed "Press and Hold the Ctrl Key for Multiple Selections!"
cmboFlowers	ComboBox	Items (Collection)	Typed "Roses", "Orchids", "Tulips", "Daisies", "Asters", "Mums"

(continues)

TABLE 10-4 GardeningForm property values (*continued*)

Name	Object type	Property	Value
lblFlower	Label	Text	Typed "Flowers"
lblTrees	Label	Text	Typed "Trees"
lblHeading	Label	Text	Typed "Make your Selection"
txtBxResultTrees	TextBox	Multiline	True
txtBxResultTrees	TextBox	ScrollBars	Horizontal
txtBxResultTrees	TextBox	Text	(left blank)
lblFlowerAnswer	Label	Text	Typed "Flower preferences"
lblTreeAnswer	Label	Text	Typed "Tree preferences"
menuFile	ToolStripMenuItem	Text	Typed "&File"
menuExit	ToolStripMenuItem	Text	Typed "Exit"
menuFormat	ToolStripMenuItem	Text	Typed "F&ormat"
menuFont	ToolStripMenuItem	Text	Typed "Font"
menuColor	ToolStripMenuItem	Text	Typed "Color"
menuHelp	ToolStripMenuItem	Text	Typed "&Help"
menuAbout	ToolStripMenuItem	Text	Typed "About"
lblOutput	Label	Text	Typed "Add water!"

© Cengage Learning

10

The program in Example 10-20 wired a number of objects to event-handler methods. Table 10-5 presents the event handlers that are registered for specific objects. Two events are registered for the ComboBox object.

TABLE 10-5 GardeningForm events

Object	Event-handler method
lstBxTrees	SelectedIndexChanged( )
cmboFlowers	SelectedIndexChanged( )
cmboFlowers	TextChanged( )
menuExit	menuExit_Click( )
menuFont	menuFont_Click( )
menuColor	menuColor_Click( )
menuAbout	menuAbout_Click( )

© Cengage Learning

For each entry in the table, a statement was added to the GardeningForm.Designer.cs file that registered the method as being the event handler for the particular object. The actual method is raised when the event is fired.

You have now wired and programmed Click( ), TextChanged( ), and SelectedIndexChanged( ) events. RadioButton and CheckBox objects fire a different type of event. When their values are changed, they raise CheckedChanged( ) events. These types of events are discussed in the following section.

CheckBox and RadioButton Objects

Radio buttons and check boxes are two types of objects commonly used in Windows applications. They are often grouped together for discussion; however, they differ in appearance and functionality. You will first explore CheckBox objects.

CheckBox Objects

CheckBox objects can be added to a Windows form application in the same manner as other objects. If you are using Visual Studio, you drag and drop the control. If you are developing in a simple text editor, such as Notepad, instantiate an object of the CheckBox class using the new operator. Check boxes usually appear as small boxes that allow users to make a yes/no or true/false selection. After the objects are placed on the form, Name and Text properties are normally set for each of the CheckBox objects.

Previous applications used a separate event-handler method for every object added to the form. You can, however, write an event-handler method and wire it to more than one control. This is illustrated in the following example. You might want to look ahead to Figure 10-20 to see an example of what the final solution looks like.

A new project is started. It is also a Windows application. This one allows users to register for swim, snorkel, or dive lessons. The form enables the user to select his or her skill level. The Text property for the Form object is set to "Registration Form". The Name property is set to RegForm and the BackColor property is set to DarkBlue.

Adding CheckBox Objects

A TextBox object is added near the bottom of the form to display the final charge for the lessons. Swim lessons cost $50; snorkel lessons cost $25; scuba diving lessons cost $100. A user can select more than one lesson. Three CheckBox objects are added to the form. Their Name properties are set to ckBxSwim, ckBxSnorkel, and ckBxDive. The Text property on each is set to represent the type of lessons along with a cost (that is, Swim—$50, Snorkel—$25, and Dive—$100). A Label object is used to describe the TextBox where the total charges will be displayed. Another Label object is added near the top of the form describing the TextBox object to its right, which will accept as input the user's name. Additional Label objects are added above and below the check boxes with text of "Select lesson" and "Check all that apply".

After the Text properties are set for the controls, the Checked property of the CheckBox objects is reviewed. The Checked property is set to either true or false depending on whether a check mark appears. This property can be set at design time. At run time, the Checked property can be set or inspected using an if statement to determine which selections are checked by users. All CheckBox objects remain set at their default false value.

10

Registering CheckBox Object Events

The default event-handler method for CheckBox objects is CheckedChanged( ). Double-clicking on one of the CheckBox objects registers a CheckedChanged( ) event for that one CheckBox object. The method that is fired checks all the check boxes to see which are checked. This code could be copied and pasted to different methods or the one method could be wired to all three objects. The last option is a better approach. If you copy and paste the code to three methods, any minor modifications that you make require you to make those changes to all three different methods. A run-time or logic error is easily created by this scenario. It is easy to forget to make those slight changes to all three methods. A better approach is to wire a single method to multiple objects.

In Visual Studio, the Form Designer prefixes the name of the event-handler method with the name of the object to which the method is wired. You can change the name of the method so that the method appears to be used by all three objects and not just associated with one object. If you do this, a second step is required. You cannot just change the name of the method in the method heading. You must also change the name of the method in the statement that registered the method to handle the event.

For this example, the original heading for the event-handler method for the Swim CheckBox object was

```
private void ckBxSwim_CheckedChanged (object sender,
                                      System.EventArgs e)
```

The heading of the ckBxSwim_CheckedChanged( ) method was changed to

```
private void ComputeCost_CheckedChanged (object sender,
                                         System.EventArgs e)
```

NOTE The characters ckBxSwim were replaced by ComputeCost so that the new method name is ComputeCost_CheckedChanged( ). This makes the code more readable. You could have actually wired the other two events to the method without changing any names; however, it would be more difficult to read and modify later because it would appear that the method was associated with the Swim CheckBox object only.

If you change the name of the method, the second step you must take uses the new name to register the event for the Swim CheckBox object. Originally, the statement read:

```
this.ckBxSwim.CheckedChanged += new System.EventHandler
                               (this.ckBxSwim_CheckedChanged);
```

It was changed to

```
this.ckBxSwim.CheckedChanged += new System.EventHandler
                               (this.ComputeCost_CheckedChanged);
```

NOTE A quick way to find the program statement in the .Designer.cs file is to run the application after you made the name change. Double-clicking on the error that's generated will take you directly to the line in the Designer.cs file you need to change. Notice that you are only changing the method name inside the parentheses. You do not change the name of the object on the left side of the += symbols.

After those changes are made, you can write the body for the method that will be fired when any of the CheckBox object states change. This method is shown in the following.

```
// Event handler to be used by all three CheckBoxes.
private void ComputeCost_CheckedChanged (object sender,
                                          System.EventArgs e)
{
    decimal cost = 0;
    if (this.ckBxSwim.Checked)
    {
        cost += 50;
    }
    if (this.ckBxSnorkel.Checked)
    {
        cost += 25;
    }
    if (this.ckBxDive.Checked)
    {
        cost += 100;
    }
    this.txtBxResult.Text = cost.ToString("C");
}
```

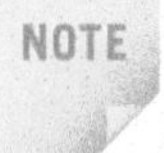

Notice that a nested `if` statement is not used here because the user might click one, two, or all three selections. A nested `if` would exit the selection statement as soon as one condition evaluated to `true`.

Wiring One Event Handler to Multiple Objects

The Swim `CheckBox` `object` is wired to the `ComputeCost_CheckedChanged( )` method. You changed the name associated with the event-handler method. Now with two clicks you can wire the other events. First select the Snorkel `CheckBox` `object`, as shown in Figure 10-16. Using the Visual Studio **Properties** window, click on the **Events** icon (lightning bolt). Move down to the `CheckedChanged` event. Click the down arrow associated with that event and select `ComputeCost_CheckedChanged`. Follow the same steps for the Dive `CheckBox` `object`.

10

Actually, this is the only event-handler method written so far; thus, it is the only one available to choose.

When you launch the application, changes to any of the `CheckBox` objects fire the `ComputeCost_CheckedChanged( )` method.

NOTE A number of Form properties were set. These properties were set when the Form object was initially created. The Name, BackColor, ForeColor, Text, Font, and Size properties should almost always be set.

GroupBox Objects

CheckBox objects can be grouped together using the GroupBox control. This is beneficial for visual appearance. It also helps during design because you can move or set properties that impact the entire group. However, it does not provide any additional functionality for CheckBox objects.

A GroupBox control should be placed on the form before you add the RadioButton objects to it. If you add the RadioButton objects first and then try to add the GroupBox control object on top of the RadioButton objects, it does not work as smoothly. If you add the GroupBox control object last, you need to physically drag the RadioButton objects onto the top of the GroupBox control object.

NOTE Do not forget about the useful tools on the **Format** menu. The **Align**, **Make Same Size**, **Horizontal Spacing**, **Vertical Spacing**, and **Center in Form** tools save you hours of time. Remember, it does matter what your interface looks like!

RadioButton Objects

There are differences between the RadioButton and CheckBox objects, other than their visual representation. RadioButton controls appear as small circles on the Form object. They are used to give users a choice between two or more options. Remember that it is appropriate to select more than one CheckBox object. This is not the case with RadioButton objects. Normally, you group RadioButton objects by placing them on a Panel or GroupBox control. If a radio button is clicked, it is selected and all other radio buttons within the group box are deselected.

Adding RadioButton Objects

To build on the application developed in the previous section containing the CheckBox objects, a GroupBox control is placed on the form. It should be placed there before adding objects to the group. GroupBox control objects provide an identifiable grouping for other controls. After it is dragged onto the form, a GroupBox control object must usually be resized. Using Visual Studio, you can drag three RadioButton objects on top of the GroupBox.

After the `RadioButton` objects are placed on the `GroupBox`, you can set properties of the `GroupBox` and impact all members of the group. Want to make them invisible? Set the `Visible` property of the `GroupBox`. It is not necessary to set all of the members. If you want to change the font color of all radio buttons, just change the `GroupBox Font` property.

Setting the `Text` property for the `GroupBox` adds a labeled heading over the group of radio buttons without you having to add an additional `Label object`. Whatever value you type for the `Text` property for `RadioButton` objects is used to label the control. By default, the text appears to the right of the small circle, as shown in Figure 10-16. If you want the text in the label to display to the left of the small circle, set the `RightToLeft` property to `Yes` for the `RadioButton` control. For this example, the `GroupBox Text` property is set to `"Skill level"`; `RadioButton Text` properties are set to `"Beginner"`, `"Intermediate"`, and `"Advanced"`. An extra `Label object` is added to the bottom right to display messages regarding special discounts or extra charges associated with different skill levels. The new `Label` object's `Text` property is set to `""`. Figure 10-16 shows the form in Design view after the `Text` properties are set for the newly added `GroupBox` and `RadioButton` objects.

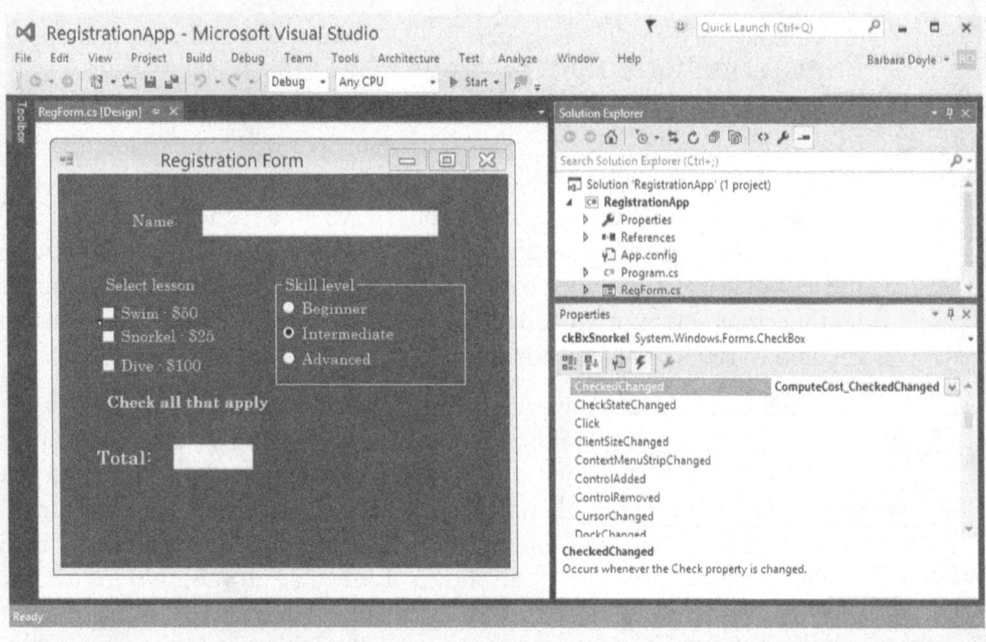

FIGURE 10-16 GroupBox and RadioButton objects added

Notice the box drawn around the RadioButton objects. This is added by the GroupBox control object. The heading that appears over the radio buttons is the Text property for the GroupBox.

The middle RadioButton object is set as the default by selecting true for its Checked property. This is done during design using the Checked property, located in the **Properties** window list of properties. You change the value by selecting true from the drop-down list. Double-clicking on the property name also toggles the setting between false (default) and true. The Visual Studio Form Designer inserts the following line of code in your program: this.radInterm.Checked = true;

If you plan to have more than one set of RadioButton objects on your form, each set must be associated with a different Panel or GroupBox control object. This is necessary to allow mutually exclusive selections from different categories. For example, if you had one set of buttons for skill level and another set for age group (1–5 years; 6–10 years; over 10 years), to allow selection from both categories, the two categories of radio buttons must be connected to two different group boxes or panels.

Registering RadioButton Object Events

Like CheckBox objects, RadioButton objects raise a number of events, including Click( ) and CheckedChanged( ) events. For this application, the skill level helps determine the cost of the lessons. The prices shown on the form are actually for registrants of intermediate skill level. Those with an advanced skill level are discounted $15; beginners are charged an extra $10. Because the skill level is used to determine the cost of lessons, the RadioButton Click event is wired to the same event-handler method that was written for the CheckBox objects. Modifications are made to the method to reflect the additional problem specification.

Wire the Click event for each of the RadioButton objects—just as you wired the Scuba and Dive CheckBox objects. This can be done in Visual Studio by displaying the list of events (click on the Events lightning bolt icon) in the **Properties** window. Select the Click( ) event and then use the down arrow to select the event-handler method ComputeCost_CheckedChanged( ). This is still the only event-handler method available to be displayed, as shown in Figure 10-17. No other event-handler methods have been written for this application. Figure 10-16 shows the ckBxSnorkel CheckBox object being wired to the ComputeCost_CheckedChanged( ) method. That same method, ComputeCost_CheckedChanged( ), is wired to the other CheckBox objects. The Click event for the RadioButton objects is also wired to the ComputeCost_CheckedChanged( ) method shown in Figure 10-17.

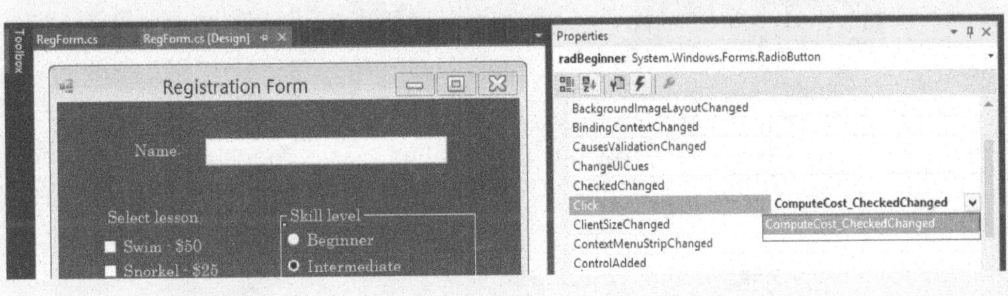

FIGURE 10-17 Wired Click event

Additional statements are added to the end of the `ComputeCost_CheckedChanged( )` method to take the skill level into consideration. The `Checked` property is used again. This time, it is inspected to determine which `RadioButton object` is selected. This is shown in the following.

```
if (this.radBeginner.Checked)
{
      cost +=10;
      this.lblMsg.Text = "Beginner – Extra $10 charge";
}
else
      if (this.radAdvanc.Checked)
      {
            cost -=15;
            this.lblMsg.Text = "Advanced Discount $15";
      }
      else
      {
            this.lblMsg.Text = " ";
      }
```

NOTE Notice that a nested `if` statement is used here with the `RadioButton` objects. Unlike the `CheckBox` objects, only one selection is possible. Thus, as soon as an expression evaluates to `true`, there is no need to test the other expressions.

Example 10-21 includes the `RegForm` program listing. The `RegForm.Designer.cs` file is not shown. The full project is available as a download from the publisher's website. Although the `.Designer.cs` file seems long, the Form Designer in Visual Studio generates the code from selections made in the **Properties** window.

EXAMPLE 10-21

```
/* RegForm.cs
 * This application enables users to register for water
 * activities. GroupBox, RadioButtons, CheckBoxes, TextBoxes,
 * and Labels are added. Several CheckedChanged( ) and Click( )
 * events are wired to a single method.
 */
using System;
using System.Windows.Forms;

namespace RegistrationApp
{
     public partial class RegForm : Form
     {
          public RegForm( )
          {
               InitializeComponent( );
          }

          // Handles CheckChanged( ) events for CheckBox objects
          // and Click( ) events for RadioButton objects
          private void ComputeCost_CheckedChanged(object sender,
                                                  EventArgs e)
          {
               decimal cost = 0;
               this.lblMsg.Text = " ";
               if (this.ckBxSwim.Checked)
               {
                    cost += 50;
               }
               if (this.ckBxSnorkel.Checked)
               {
                    cost += 25;
               }
               if (this.ckBxDive.Checked)
               {
                    cost += 100;
               }
               if (this.radBeginner.Checked)
               {
                    cost += 10;
                    this.lblMsg.Text =
                         "Beginner -- Extra $10 charge";
               }
               else
                    if (this.radAdvanc.Checked)
                    {
                         cost -= 15;
```

```
                this.lblMsg.Text =
                    "Advanced -- Discount $15"
            }
            else
            {
                this.lblMsg.Text = " ";
            }
            this.txtBxResult.Text = cost.ToString("C");
        }
    }
}
```

A sample run of the application appears in Figure 10-18.

As illustrated in Figure 10-18, users can select one or more lessons; however, only one skill level is permissible.

Windows Presentation Foundation (WPF)

In Chapter 9, you read that one of the options for creating Windows applications was to use WPF as opposed to WinForms. The Application Programming Interface (API) is capable of taking full advantage of the multimedia facilities of modern PCs. The power of WPF comes from the fact that it is vector-based and resolution-independent so you get really sharp graphics. Its sophisticated layout system handles arrangement of all visual elements.

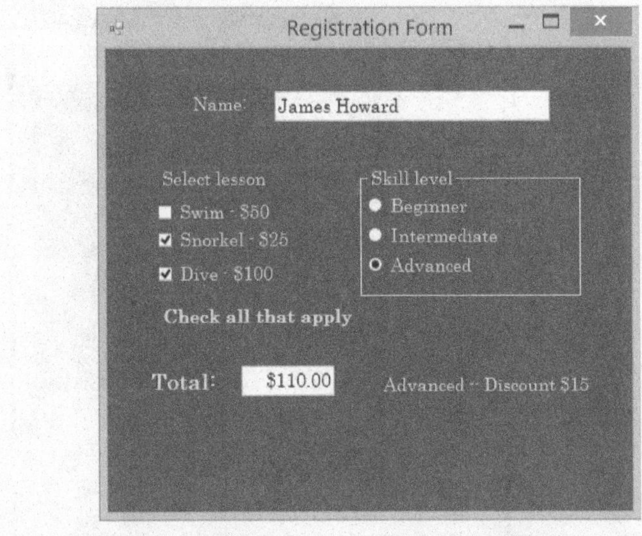

FIGURE 10-18 ComputeCost_CheckedChanged( ) and Click( ) events raised

WPF Application is one of the options available when you create a new Windows project in Visual Studio. Select **File**, **New Project** and the second template listed is **WPF Application**. It is immediately below the **Windows Forms Application** option. You can look back at Figure 9-2 to see that option.

You should try out this platform. You will find many of the controls that you used with Windows Forms Applications, such as buttons, labels, listboxes, textboxes, and comboboxes. As with WinForms applications, you can drag and drop controls from the **Toolbox** onto the window. You can set property values and register events using the **Properties** window. There is not a one-to-one correspondence between properties with WinForms and properties with WPF, but you should explore them. For example, instead of setting the `Text` property for buttons, labels, checkboxes, and radio buttons, you set the `Content` property.

When you are creating a WPF Application, if you do not see `Content` listed as one of the properties, you may want to arrange the properties by name. The **Arrange by:** option is available at the top of the **Properties** window under the **Search Properties** textbox.

A `Header` property is used as identifying text over groupbox objects in WPF. The `Text` property is used for textboxes. The graphics user interface is crisper with WPF. You have greater color control with backgrounds, foregrounds, and images. Figure 10-19 illustrates the design of an application using WPF.

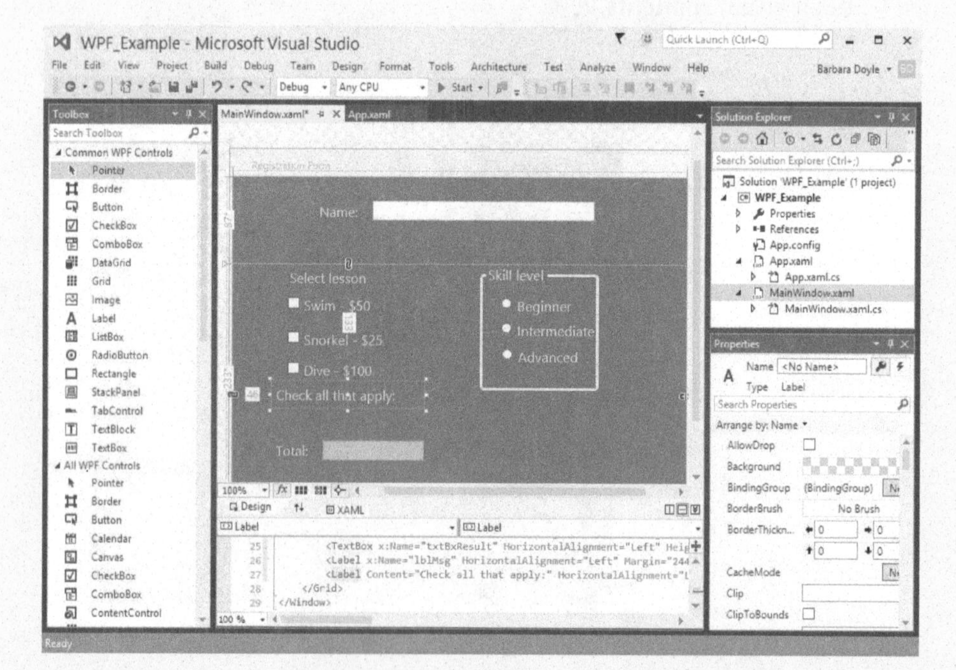

FIGURE 10-19 WPF design

The `RegistrationApp` that you saw earlier in this chapter was recreated using WPF. As shown in Figure 10-19, the **Toolbox** contains many of the same controls you have already experienced. There are two **Toolbox** categories (**Common WPF Controls** and **All WPF Controls**). You have more control placing items on the window with WPF. Notice the slider to the left of the MainWindow. You can zoom in/out for greater precision using this tool. It is not available with WinForms. You can build a more aesthetically appealing window with WPF.

As you review Figure 10-19, you will see different files in the **Solution Explorer** window than you saw with WinForms applications. You will see a new XAML file. WPF files end with the .xaml file extension. WPF's XAML file resembles a Hypertext Markup Language (HTML) file. **XAML** stands for eXtensible Application Markup Language. It is an Extensible Markup Language (XML) file complete with beginning and ending tags. You can think of the XAML file as an HTML file for Windows applications. HTML files are normally associated with Web applications. You will explore these files in Chapter 15. XML is readable and can be easily edited by hand. Below the design window in Figure 10-19, you had a peek at the XAML file. Each of the controls placed on the window appear as separate lines in the XAML file. Content was assigned a value in the **Properties** window for the label. Example 10-22 provides the statements found in that .xaml file.

EXAMPLE 10-22

```
<Window x:Name="RegForm"
     x:Class="WPF_Example.MainWindow"
      xmlns="http://schemas.microsoft.com/" +
            "winfx/2006/xaml/presentation"
      xmlns:x=http://schemas.microsoft.com/" +
            "winfx/2006/xaml"
      Title="Registration Form" Height="350"
             Width="525">
<Grid Background="#FF3B51DC">
     <Grid.BindingGroup>
          <BindingGroup/>
     </Grid.BindingGroup>
     <Grid.RowDefinitions>
          <RowDefinition Height="87*"/>
          <RowDefinition Height="233*"/>
     </Grid.RowDefinitions>
<Label Content="Name:" HorizontalAlignment="Left"
          Margin="97,23,0,0" VerticalAlignment="Top"
          RenderTransformOrigin="-1.877,0.567"
          FontSize="16" Foreground="#FFEBF508"/>
<TextBox HorizontalAlignment="Left"
          Height="23"Margin="165,26,0,0"
          TextWrapping="Wrap" VerticalAlignment="Top"
```

```
            Width="260" FontSize="16"
            Foreground="#FFEBF508" IsTabStop="False"/>
<CheckBox x:Name="ckBxSwim" Content="Swim - $50"
            HorizontalAlignment="Left"
            Margin="64,37,0,0"Grid.Row="1"
            VerticalAlignment="Top"
            FontSize="16" Foreground="#FFEBF508"
            IsTabStop="False" Checked="ComputeCharges"/>
<CheckBox x:Name="ckBxSnorkel"
            Content="Snorkel - $25"
            HorizontalAlignment="Left"
            Margin="64,76,0,0" Grid.Row="1"
            VerticalAlignment="Top" FontSize="16"
            Foreground="#FFEBF508" IsTabStop="False"
            Checked="ComputeCharges"/>
<CheckBox x:Name="ckBxDive"
            Content="Dive - $100"
            HorizontalAlignment="Left"
            Margin="64,111,0,0" Grid.Row="1"
            VerticalAlignment="Top" FontSize="16"
            Foreground="#FFEBF508" IsTabStop="False"
            Checked="ComputeCharges"/>
<GroupBox x:Name="skillGroup" Header="Skill level"
            HorizontalAlignment="Left"
            Margin="292,0,0,0" Grid.Row="1"
            VerticalAlignment="Top" Height="143
            Width="138" FontSize="16"
            Foreground="#FFEBF508">
<RadioButton x:Name="radBeginner"
            Content="Beginner"
            HorizontalAlignment="Left" Height="25"
            VerticalAlignment="Top" Width="104"
            Margin="18,15,0,0" FontSize="16"
            Foreground="#FFEBF508" IsTabStop="False"
            GroupName="skillGroup"
            Checked="ComputeCharges"/>
</GroupBox>
<RadioButton x:Name="radInterm"
            Content="Intermediate"
            HorizontalAlignment="Left"
            Margin="316,65,0,0" Grid.Row="1"
            VerticalAlignment="Top" FontSize="16"
            Foreground="#FFEBF508" IsTabStop="False"
            GroupName="skillGroup"
            Checked="ComputeCharges"/>
<RadioButton x:Name="radAdvanced"
            Content="Advanced"
            HorizontalAlignment="Left"
            Margin="317,95,0,0" Grid.Row="1"
            VerticalAlignment="Top" FontSize="16"
```

```
          Foreground="#FFEBF508" IsTabStop="False
          GroupName="skillGroup" Checked="ComputeCharges"/>
<Label Content="Select lesson"
          HorizontalAlignment="Left" Margin="62,0,0,0"
          Grid.Row="1" VerticalAlignment="Top"
          FontSize="16" Foreground="#FFEBF508"/>
<Label Content="Total: "
          HorizontalAlignment="Left"
          Margin="44,174,0,0" Grid.Row="1"
          VerticalAlignment="Top" FontSize="16
          Foreground="#FFE3F904"/>
<TextBox x:Name="txtBxResult"
          HorizontalAlignment="Left" Height="23"
          Margin="105,178,0,0" Grid.Row="1"
          TextWrapping="Wrap" VerticalAlignment="Top"
          Width="120" FontSize="16"
          Foreground="#FFE3F904" IsEnabled="False"/>
<Label x:Name="lblMsg"
          HorizontalAlignment="Left"
          Margin="244,174,0,0" Grid.Row="1"
          VerticalAlignment="Top" FontSize="16"
          Foreground="#FFE3F904" Width="250"/>
</Grid>
</Window>
```

You do not find the objects, like `RadioButtons`, instantiated. There is no .Designer.cs file. Objects like textboxes and labels are described in the XAML file. As you review the program statements from Example 10-22, you will notice that their appearance is controlled here in the XAML file. There is a beginning and an ending tag for each control placed on the window. Take a look at the label controls shown in the example. It is very easy to read the XML text. The last label is the blank label placed to the right of the result textbox. It does not have any content. Thus, no value was assigned to the `Content` property. The other labels have a value for `Content`. The `Name` property associated with the controls becomes the control's identifier.

10

The **Solution Explorer** window in Figure 10-19 shows a `MainWindow.xaml.cs` file. This is the code behind file. Yes, there is still the code behind file found with WPF applications. This is the main feature that WinForms and WPF applications share in common. With a slight modification of property names, you have the same program statements written for the WPF application as you had with the WinForms application. The primary `namespace` for WPF applications is `System.Windows` as opposed to the `System.Windows.Forms` `namespace` used with Windows Forms applications. Like Windows Forms applications, a number of `using` statements are automatically added. Even more `using` statements are added with WPF applications. Most are not needed. As was done with previous examples, extraneous ones are removed. Example 10-23 shows the program statements found in the code behind file.

EXAMPLE 10-23

```
// WPF_Example.xaml                              Author: Doyle
// CheckBox and RadioButton objects added to the Windows form.
// Illustrates wiring several methods to the same event handler.
using System.Windows;
namespace WPF_Example
{
      public partial class MainWindow : Window
      {
            public MainWindow( )
            {
                  InitializeComponent( );
            }
            private void ComputeCharges(object sender,RoutedEventArgs e)
            {
                  decimal cost = 0M;
                  if (this.ckBxSwim.IsChecked == true)
                  {
                        cost += 50;
                  }
                  if (this.ckBxSnorkel.IsChecked == true)
                  {
                        cost += 25;
                  }
                  if (this.ckBxDive.IsChecked == true)
                  {
                        cost += 100;
                  }
                  if (this.radBeginner.IsChecked == true)
                  {
                        cost += 10;
                        this.lblMsg.Content = "Beginner – – Extra " +
                                              "$10 charge";
                  }
                  else
                        if (this.radAdvanced.IsChecked == true)
                        {
                              cost -= 15;
                              this.lblMsg.Content = "Advanced – – " +
                                                    "Discount $15";
                        }
                        else
                              this.lblMsg.Content = " ";
                  this.txtBxResult.Text = cost.ToString("C");
            }
      }
}
```

When you compile an application that contains XAML files, the markup gets converted into binary XAML (BAML). **BAML** is a tokenized, binary representation of XAML. This binary representation is then stored inside the application's resources and loaded as needed by WPF during the execution of your program. The main advantage of this approach is that you get a faster user interface load time by reading a binary stream than through parsing XML. Figure 10-20 shows the final output when the application runs.

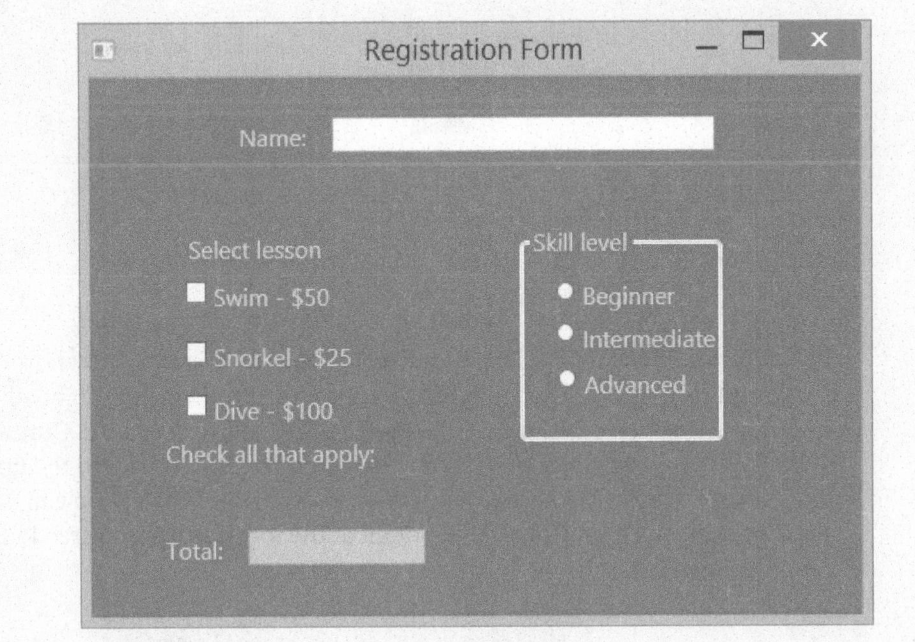

FIGURE 10-20 WPF application

TabControl Objects

There may be times when you build applications that require too many controls for a single screen. You will recall that an important design consideration is to avoid cluttering your graphical user interface (GUI). Readability is very important. An option that you have available is to add tab controls to the page. The `TabControl object` displays multiple tabs, like dividers in a notebook or labels in a set of folders in a filing cabinet. This control makes it possible to create a multiple-page dialog box similar to what you see with many Windows applications. A Windows form using tab controls is illustrated in Figure 10-21.

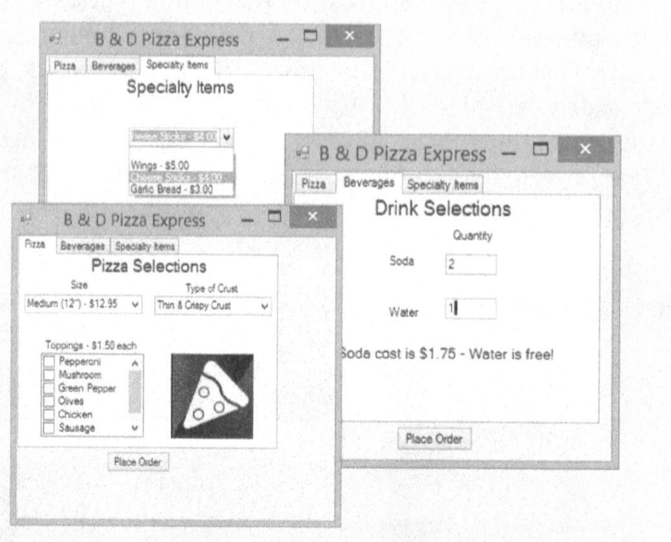

FIGURE 10-21 Tabbed controlled application

Each separate tab can be clicked to display other options, as shown in Figure 10-21. You can place pictures, buttons, labels, or any control on each tabbed page. Add a `TabControl` `object` to the page by dragging the control from the **Container** section of the **Toolbox** onto your blank form. You can move the control to the upper-left corner of the form and use the size handles to stretch the control. You can cover the part of the form as shown in Figure 10-21 or all of the form, as is illustrated in Figure 10-22.

FIGURE 10-22 TabControl object stretched to fill form

When the TabControl object is placed on the form, as shown in Figure 10-22, two tabs are included by default. Additional tabs can be added or removed by right-clicking on a tab and selecting the **Add Tab** option. The most important property the TabControl has is the TabPages property. The TabPages property enables you to format individual tabs. Clicking the ellipsis beside the Collection value displays the **TabPage Collection Editor** shown in Figure 10-23.

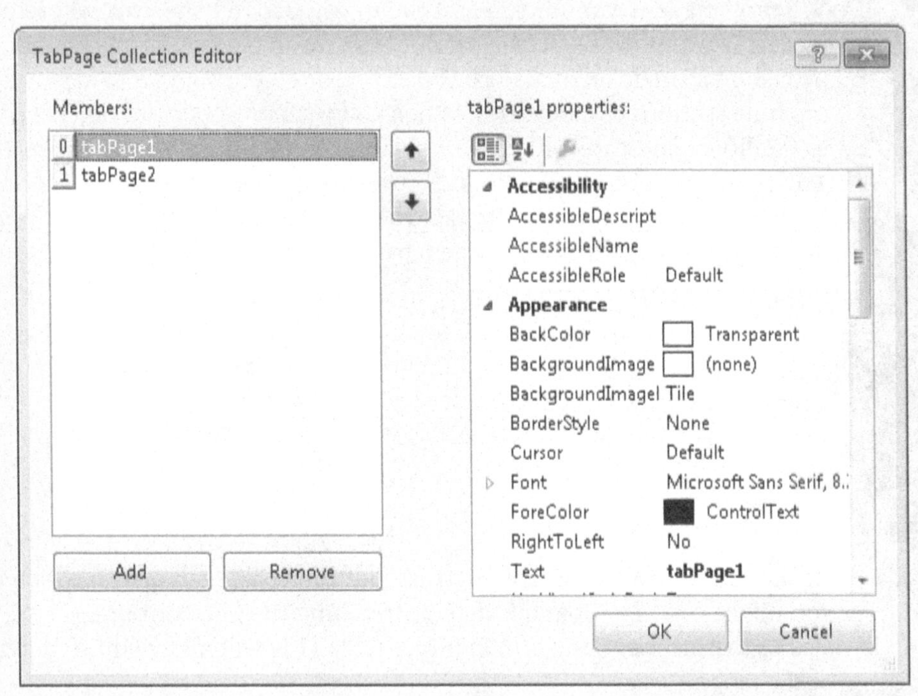

FIGURE 10-23 TabControl's TabPage Collection Editor

You change the appearance of the tabs using the **TabPage Collection Editor**. You can display images on tabs, change the background or foreground colors, or change the text using the Text property. You also change the order of the tabs using the Collection Editor by selecting the tab and using the arrows to the right of the member name to move the tab to its preferred position. Tabs can be displayed vertically instead of horizontally using the Alignment property. Multiple rows of tabs can be displayed by setting the MultiLine property to true. You can also register Click events for each of the tabs so that when an individual tab is selected, its Click event method is executed. If you want to control which tab appears on top, use the SelectedTab property. For example, if you had not changed default names, to indicate tabPage2 should be on top, your program statement would read: tabControl1.SelectedTab = tabPage2;

10

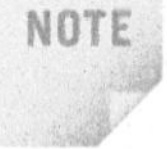

Do not confuse the TabControl objects with the tab order that is used to move from one control to another using the **Tab** key. Each form has its own tab order. By default, the order is the same as the order in which the controls are placed on the form. You can change that order by setting the TabIndex property for each of the controls. Tab-order numbering begins with zero.

When you add a TabControl object, you expand the area where controls can be placed. It is almost like having multiple forms to place controls on, but the tabs are all placed on a single form. TabControl objects enable you to separate the form into separate sections or categories. When you write program statements, you do not have to qualify or indicate which tab holds the controls. All of the controls are available. The pizza application, shown in Figure 10-21, has three categories of items for sale. Each was placed on a separate tab. In order to determine the final amount due, data had to be retrieved from all three tabs.

As you look at the final design for the pizza application, shown in Figure 10-21, you might think it looks pretty plain. It actually is. Very few properties were set for this application. You will get to use your creativity to enhance it since this is one of the programming exercises at the end of this chapter.

If you want to have a control, such as a button, visible, no matter which tab is selected, you might consider not completely stretching the TabControl object over the full size of the form as shown in Figure 10-22. This will allow you to determine the size of the tabbed area.

Figure 10-21 shows the form during design. You are encouraged to be creative when you build the application at the end of this chapter. Example 10-24 provides a listing of the PizzaApp.cs file where the event-handler program statements were added.

EXAMPLE 10-24

```
/* PizzaApp.cs
 * This application illustrates using
 * TabControls, ComboBoxes, Textboxes,
 * CheckListBox. Items can be ordered
 * with a total price displayed.
 */
using System;
using System.Windows.Forms;
```

```
namespace PizzaApp
{
     public partial class PizzaForm : Form
     {
          private string order;
          private double totalCost;

          public PizzaForm( )
          {
               InitializeComponent( );
          }

          private void PizzaForm_Load(object sender, EventArgs e)
          {
               this.cmboSize.SelectedIndex = 1;
               this.cmboCrust.SelectedIndex = 0;
               this.cmboSpeciality.SelectedIndex = 0;
               this.txtBxSodaQty.Text = "0";
               this.txtBxWaterQty.Text = "0";
               order = "";
               totalCost = 0;
          }

          private void btnPlaceOrder_Click(object sender, EventArgs e)
          {
               double drinkCost,
               pizzaCost,
               specialtyCost;
               order = "";
               order += cmboCrust.SelectedItem.ToString( ) +
                         " - ";
               order += cmboSize.SelectedItem.ToString( ) +
                         "\n";
               if (ckBxItems.SelectedItems.Count > 0)
               {
                    order += "Toppings:";
                    foreach (string s in ckBxItems.CheckedItems)
                    {
                         order += "\n" + s;
                    }
               }
               pizzaCost = DeterminePizzaCost( );
               if (pizzaCost != 0)
                    order += "\nPizza Total: " +
                              pizzaCost.ToString("C");
               drinkCost = DetermineDrinkCost( );
               if (drinkCost != 0)
                    order += "\nDrink Total: " +
                              drinkCost;
```

10

```
            specialtyCost = DetermineSpecialtyCost( );
            if (specialtyCost != 0)
            {
                 order += "\n\nSpecialty Items:\ n" +
                   cmboSpeciality.SelectedItem.ToString( );
            }
            order += "\n\nAmount Due: " +
                      (pizzaCost + drinkCost +
                       specialtyCost).ToString("C");
            MessageBox.Show(order,
                           "B & D Pizza Express Order\n");
      }

      private double DetermineDrinkCost( )
      {
            double sodaCnt,
                   waterCnt;
            totalCost = 0;
            if (txtBxSodaQty.Text != "")
            {
                 while (double.TryParse (txtBxSodaQty.Text,
                                      out sodaCnt) == false)
                 {
                       lblErrorMsg.Text =
                                  "Quantity must be numeric";
                       txtBxSodaQty.Text = "0";
                 }
                 order += "\n\nDrink Selections:\ n" + sodaCnt +
                            " soda(s)";
                 totalCost = sodaCnt * 1.75;
            }
            if (txtBxWaterQty.Text != "")
            {
                 while (double.TryParse(txtBxWaterQty.Text,
                                      out waterCnt) == false)
                 {
                       lblErrorMsg.Text =
                                  "Quantity must be numeric";
                       txtBxWaterQty.Text ="0";
                 }
                 order += "\n" + waterCnt + " water(s)";
            }
            return totalCost;
      }

      public double DeterminePizzaCost( )
      {
            double cost;
            if (cmboSize.SelectedIndex == 0)
                cost = 9.95;
            else
```

```
                if (cmboSize.SelectedIndex == 1)
                    cost = 12.95;
                else
                    cost = 15.95;
            return cost +
                (ckBxItems.CheckedItems.Count * 1.50);
        }

        public double DetermineSpecialtyCost( )
        {
            double cost;
            if (cmboSpeciality.SelectedIndex == 1)
            {
                cost = 5.00;
            }
            else
                if (cmboSpeciality.SelectedIndex == 2)
                {
                    cost = 4.00;
                }
                else
                    if (cmboSpeciality.SelectedIndex == 3)
                    {
                        cost = 3.00;
                    }
                    else
                        cost = 0;
            return cost;
        }
    }
}
```

10

As you review Example 10-24, notice that two identifiers, `order` and `totalCost`, are both defined as `private` data members as opposed to being defined as local variables inside an event-handler method. This is to enable all methods in the class to have access to them. The `Form_Load( )` event handler initializes and sets default values for each of the controls on the form. The functionality of the application is controlled from the `btnPlaceOrder_Click ( )` event handler. The total amount due is determined in this method based upon which selections were made on the form.

The auto-generated code in the `PizzaApp.Designer.cs` file is not shown here to conserve space. However, this application, like all the other examples in the book, is available as a fully functioning Visual Studio project. A new control, `CheckedListBox`, is added to this example. The control displays a list of items with a check box on the left. Thus, it places all of the check box items in a group, providing additional functionality of a `GroupBox`, but no `GroupBox` is added. Two new properties are used with the `CheckedListBox` control: `Count` and `CheckedItems`. The `CheckedItems` property returns a collection of the items checked; `Count` returns the number of items checked.

Another control, `PictureBox`, was also dragged onto the top tab on the `PizzaForm`. To associate an image with the `PictureBox` control, the `Image` property is selected. This enables you to browse to the location where the image is stored. You can create a separate folder for your images or as was done with this application place the image in the `bin\debug` directory. Once you select the `Image` property and click the three dot-ellipsis, the **Select Resource** dialog box is revealed. Import the image using the **Local resource** option.

As you review the toolbox, notice that there are over 100 different controls in the **Toolbox**. Details were provided for a small portion of them in this book. You are encouraged to explore, discover, and experiment with the other controls and their properties. Intellisense provides you with a short description. Additional details can be found via the Visual Studio Help system and online resources.

PROGRAMMING EXAMPLE: DinerGUI Application

This example demonstrates event-driven applications that include the design and implementation of a graphical user interface. Two classes are constructed to separate the business logic from the presentation details. The first class defines a template for a food order object. It includes behaviors for processing an order that includes selections for entrée, drink, and special requests. The class assigns prices to each item selected and determines the overall price of the order. The other class instantiates an object of the `Order class` and instantiates a Windows `Form object` to represent the graphical user interface. Using the .NET predefined `Control` classes, `Label`, `ComboBox`, `ListBox`, `RadioButton`, `CheckBox`, and `Menu` objects are added to the `Form object`. The problem specification for the DinerGUI application is shown in Figure 10-24.

The manager of the Diner by the Valley campus deli plans to have a computer available for students to place their orders when they enter the campus center. They have a limited menu selection available that includes sandwiches and drinks. The manager wants the computer screen to allow the students to select from a list of available sandwich and drink options. A large board is located on the wall at the location where the computer will reside. It shows the menu of items available and lists the price of each item.

A user-friendly interface is needed. Water is available for each order at no charge, but it must be ordered. In addition to white bread, they have whole wheat and rye bread. No charge is included for different bread types; however, they do consider that selection a special request. The interface should enable special requests such as bread types to be selected. Students should be able to enter other special requests such as "Hold the onion" or "Hold the mayo."

Design a GUI that accepts as input food and drink selections. The manager would like to have options for showing the total cost of the order, displaying the current order selections, or allowing students to change their minds about each of the selections.

© Cengage Learning

FIGURE 10-24 Problem specification for DinerGUI example

10

ANALYZE THE PROBLEM DATA

You should review the problem specification in Figure 10-24 and make sure you understand the problem definition. Several values will be selected from GUI controls to represent the entree and drink selections, as well as preferences for water and special requests. The business logic is separated from the user interface using two classes. The data members for the `Order class` are given in Table 10-6.

DATA

Table 10-6 lists the data field members needed for the `Order class`.

TABLE 10-6 Order class data fields

Data description	Type	Identifier
Entree selection	`string`	`entree`
Water preference	`bool`	`waterSelection`
Drink preference	`string`	`drinkSelection`
Special requests	`string`	`specialRequest`
Entree price	`decimal`	`entreePrice`
Drink price	`decimal`	`drinkPrice`

© Cengage Learning

A second `class`, `OrderGUI`, is created for the user interface. This `class` allows the user to select an entree and a drink, enter special requests, and request water. During design, a prototype is developed to determine which controls would be most appropriate for each selection.

Drink selections are constant and include `"Milk"`, `"Juice"`, `"Soda"`, `"Lemonade"`, `"Tea"` and `"Coffee"`. Menu options may change occasionally and should not be statically placed on the graphical user interface. Current options are `"Chicken Salad"`, `"Ham and Cheese"`, `"Turkey"`, `"Vegetable Wrap"`, `"Tuna Salad"`, `"Avocado and Cheese"`, `"Club"`, `"Peanut Butter & Jelly"`, `"Grilled Cheese"`, and `"Reuben"`.

DESIGN A SOLUTION

The desired output is to produce a graphical user interface that allows a user to pick from a number of selections while placing an order. According to the problem definition, menu options should be available to clear the entire order or just part of it. After the items are selected, the total price and items selected should be displayed. These options can also appear as selections from the menu bar. Figure 10-25 shows a prototype of the form that illustrates the types of objects to be used and approximates their placement.

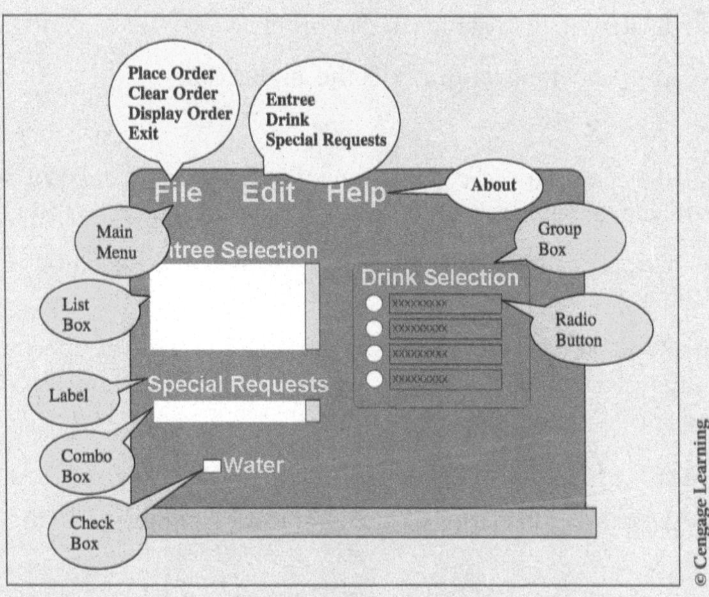

FIGURE 10-25 Prototype for DinerGUI example

During design, determine which `object` types will be used to create the interface. The `MenuStrip` `object` was selected rather than a number of buttons so that the screen does not become cluttered. Menus offer the advantage of requiring less real estate on your screen. The entrees are displayed in a `ListBox` `object`. A scroll bar is automatically added when the number of entries exceeds the available space. The text selections for the `ListBox` `object` are loaded at run time to enable the diner manager to change the menu options in the `class` that deals with the business logic and keep that separate from the actual display.

Special requests are stored in a `ComboBox` `object` because it enables users either to choose from a list of options or to type a new entry. The water selection is a yes/no format; thus, a `CheckBox` `object` is used. `RadioButton` objects are used for drink selection. The buttons are placed in a `GroupBox` so that only one drink is selected.

`Menu` options include the following features:

File

- **Place Order**—Displays the current order and the total price of the order
- **Clear Order**—Deselects all options on the GUI and sets all of the individual selections back to their defaults

10

- **Display Order**—Displays the current order
- **Exit**—Closes all windows and exits the application

Edit

- **Entree**—Displays a message indicating that the entree selection is cleared, clears the entree selection, and deselects the selected entree
- **Drink**—Displays a message indicating that the drink selection is cleared, clears the drink selection, and deselects the selected drink
- **Special Request**—Displays a message indicating that the special request selection is cleared, clears the special request selection, and deselects the selected special request, or clears the text area if a value is typed

Help

- **About**—Displays the name of the application along with the version number.

The `Order` `class` has both data and behavior characteristics that can be identified. The major actions or behaviors of an `Order` `object` are to set instance variables using the selection from the GUI objects, determine the individual prices, and determine the overall charge for the order. Class diagrams are used to help design and document these characteristics. Figure 10-26 shows the `class` diagrams for the `DinerGUI` example.

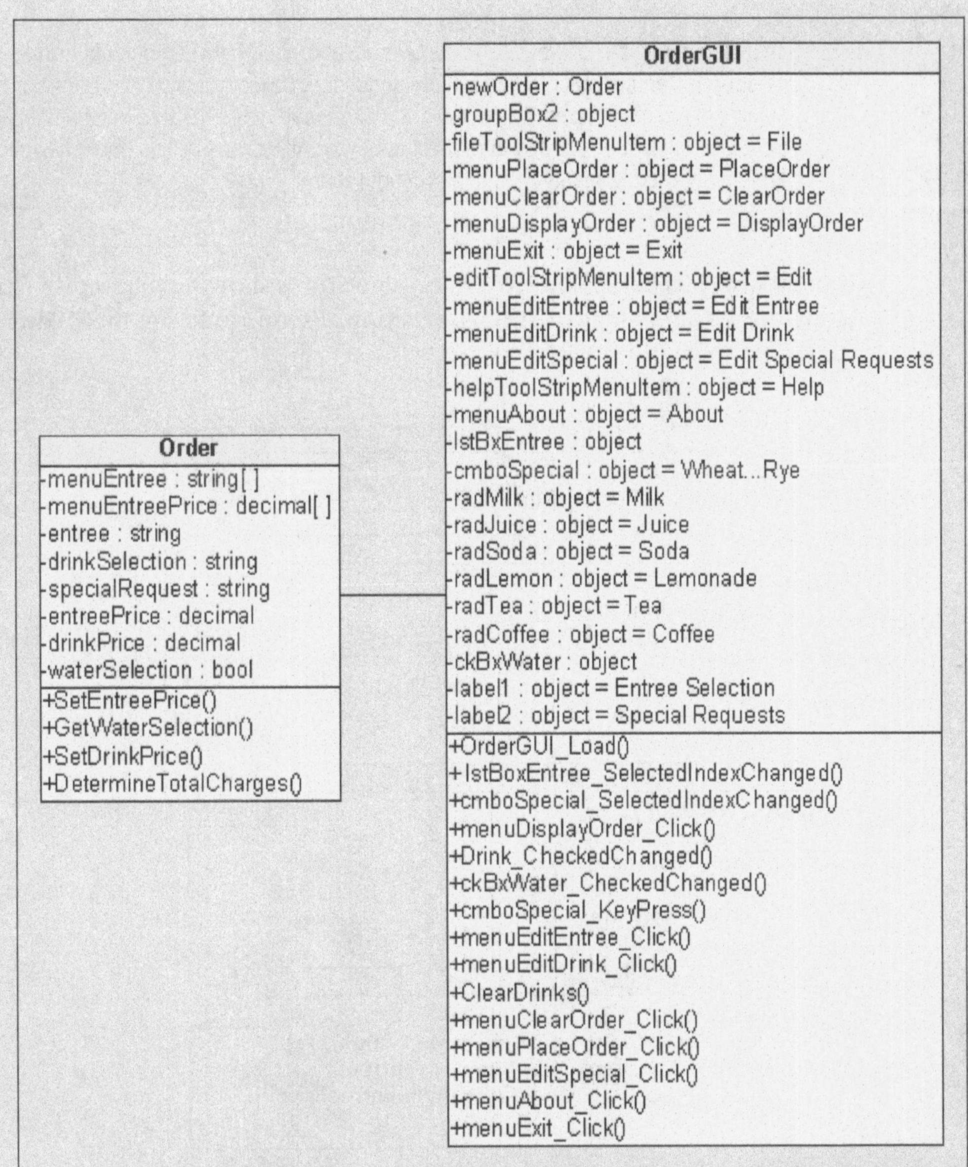

FIGURE 10-26 Class diagrams for DinerGUI example

The `class` diagrams do not show the properties or the local variables that may be required for specific `class` methods. They do not show which event-handler methods are associated with particular objects.

NOTE There are a number of ways to document collaboration between objects using an object-oriented approach. They include sequence, collaboration, state transition, and activity diagrams. Systems analysts often use these diagrams to design an application. Development of these types of models is beyond the scope of this book; however, you are encouraged to research and learn about them.

During design, it is important to develop algorithms showing the step-by-step process for the business logic of the application. Pseudocode for the `Order class` methods is shown in Figure 10-27.

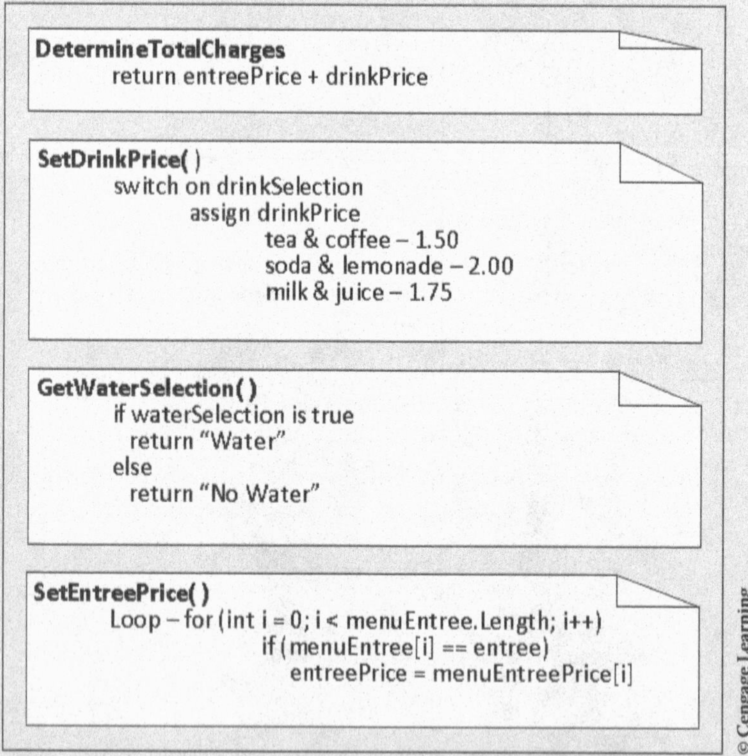

DetermineTotalCharges
return entreePrice + drinkPrice
SetDrinkPrice( )
switch on drinkSelection
assign drinkPrice
tea & coffee – 1.50
soda & lemonade – 2.00
milk & juice – 1.75
GetWaterSelection( )
if waterSelection is true
return "Water"
else
return "No Water"
SetEntreePrice( )
Loop – for (int i = 0; i < menuEntree.Length; i++)
if (menuEntree[i] == entree)
entreePrice = menuEntreePrice[i]
© Cengage Learning

FIGURE 10-27 Pseudocode for the Order class for the DinerGUI example

Many of the objects on the interface must be registered with event-handler methods. It is important that you spend time thinking about what should happen when each event is fired. Figures 10-28–10-30 show pseudocode for the event handlers of the GUI `class`.

Form1_Load( )
{Raised when the form is initially loaded}
  Create an Order object
  Fill the Entree Selections Listbox with entree items from the entree
    array in the order class

lstBoxEntree_SelectedIndexChanged ( )
{Raised when the ListBox object for the Entree selection is changed}
  Get the selection from the entrée list box
  Assign the value to the entrée instance of the order class

cmboBoxSpecial_SelectedIndexChanged ( )
{Raised when ComboBox object for the Special Requests is changed}
  Get the selection from the special requests combo box
  Assign the value to the special requests instance of the order class

cmboBoxSpecial_TextChanged ( )
{Raised when text typed in text area for ComboBox object for Special Requests}
  Retrieve the characters typed into the combo box for the special requests using
    the Text property
  Assign the value to the special requests instance of the order class

Drink_CheckedChanged ( )
{Raised when any RadioButton objects changed. NOTE: one method wired to all radio button objects}
  Using a nested if statement, determine which radio button is checked [use
    Checked property of the RadioButton class]
  Assign the text of the button to the drink selection instance of the order class
    [use Text property of the RadioButton class]

ckBoxWater_CheckedChanged ( )
{Raised when the CheckBox object for the Water is changed}
  Using Checked property of CheckBox class, determine if water checked
    If it is checked, assign true to waterSelection instance of the order class –
      otherwise assign false

© Cengage Learning

FIGURE 10-28 Pseudocode for RadioButton, CheckBox, ListBox, and ComboBox object event handlers

10

```
menuPlaceOrder_Click( )
{Raised when the Place Order option under the File menu is clicked}
        Display a message showing information about the current order
                including what the total charges are.
        Use properties and methods of the order class

menuDisplayOrder_Click( )
{Raised when the Display Order option under the File menu is clicked}
        Display a message showing information about the current order.
        Use properties and methods of the order class

menuEditEntree_Click( )
{Raised when the Edit Entree option under the Edit menu is clicked}
        Display a message indicating user should select a new entrée
        Assign spaces to the entrée instance of the order class
        Clear the selection of the list box [Use ClearSelected( ) method of the listbox class]


menuEditSpecial_Click( )
{Raised when the Edit Special Requests option under the Edit menu is clicked}
        Display a message indicating special request cleared
        Assign spaces to the special requests instance of the order class
        Clear the selection of the combo box [Use the SelectedIndex property of the
                ComboBox class]

menuAbout_Click( )
{Raised when the About option under the Help menu is clicked}
        Display a message with the application name and version number

menuExit_Click( )
{Raised when the Exit option under the File menu is clicked}
        Use the Exit( ) method of the Application class to close all windows
```

© Cengage Learning

FIGURE 10-29 Pseudocode for menu object event handlers

```
menuClearOrder_Click( )
{Raised when the Clear Order option under the File menu is clicked}
        Clear the selection of the list box [use ClearSelected( ) method of the
                listbox class] for the entree.
        Uncheck the check box for Water [set Checked property to false]
        Clear the selection and text from combo box [set the SelectedIndex
                property to -1]
        Clear the selections from the radio buttons by calling ClearDrinks( ) to uncheck all
                button selections
        Set the drinkSelection, entree, and special request instances of the order class to
                blanks
        Set the waterSelection instance of the order class to false

menuEditDrink_Click( )
{Raised when the Edit Drink option under the Edit menu is clicked}
        Display a message indicating user should select a new drink
        Assign spaces to the drink instance of the order class
        Clear the selections from the radio buttons by calling ClearDrinks( ) to uncheck
                all button selections

menuEditEntree_Click( )
{Raised when the Edit Entree option under the Edit menu is clicked}
        Display a message indicating user should select a new entrée
        Assign spaces to the entrée instance of the order class
        Clear the selection of the list box [Use ClearSelected( ) method of the listbox class]

ClearDrinks( )
{ Method created to avoid duplicating code – called from menuEditDrink_Click( ) and
   menuClearOrder_Click( ) }
        Uncheck all radio button selections [set Checked property to false]
```

© Cengage Learning

FIGURE 10-30 Pseudocode for menu object event handlers and the ClearDrinks( ) method

You should always desk check your design. Develop your test plan for testing the application. Walk through your logic and ensure you have accounted for each of the events that need to be programmed. Reread the problem specification and ensure you have taken all issues into consideration.

After you implement your design, be sure to run and test your application using your test plan.

CODE THE SOLUTION

After completing the design and verifying the algorithm's correctness, you translate the design into source code. For this application, two separate files, one for each `class`, are created. Form Designer can generate much of the code for the user interface `class`. Control object's property values are as given in Table 10-7.

TABLE 10-7 DinerGUI property values

Name	Object type	Property	Value
OrderGUI	Form	Text	Typed "Student Union -Diner by the Valley"
OrderGUI	Form	BackColor	Goldenrod
OrderGUI	Form	Menu	menuStrip1
OrderGUI	Form	Font	Arial, 9.75
OrderGUI	Form	Icon	NOTE16.ICO
fileToolStrip MenuItem	ToolStrip MenuItem	Text	Typed "File"
fileToolStrip MenuItem	ToolStrip MenuItem	MenuItems	menuPlaceOrder, menuClearOrder menuDisplayOrder, menuExit
menuPlaceOrder	ToolStrip MenuItem	Text	Typed "Place Order"
menuClearOrder	ToolStrip MenuItem	Text	Typed "Clear Order"
menuDisplayOrder	ToolStrip MenuItem	Text	Typed "Display Order"
menuExit	ToolStrip MenuItem	Text	Typed "Exit"
editTool StripMenuItem	ToolStrip MenuItem	MenuItems	menuEditEntree, menuEditDrink, menuEditSpecial
editTool StripMenuItem	ToolStrip MenuItem	Text	Typed "Edit"

(continues)

TABLE 10-7 DinerGUI property values (*continued*)

Name	Object type	Property	Value
menuEditEntree	ToolStrip MenuItem	Text	Typed "Entree"
menuEditDrink	ToolStrip MenuItem	Text	Typed "Drink"
menuEditSpecial	ToolStrip MenuItem	Text	Typed "Special Requests"
helpToolStrip MenuItem	ToolStrip MenuItem	Text	Typed "Help"
menuAbout	ToolStrip MenuItem	Text	Typed "About"
lstBxEntree	ListBox	BackColor	Khaki
label1	Label	Text	Typed "Entree Selection"
drinkGroup	GroupBox	Controls	radMilk, radJuice, radSoda, radLemon, radTea, radCoffee
radMilk	RadioButton	Text	Typed "Milk"
radJuice	RadioButton	Text	Typed "Juice
radSoda	RadioButton	Text	Typed "Soda"
radLemon	RadioButton	Text	Typed "Lemonade"
radTea	RadioButton	Text	Typed "Tea"
radCoffee	RadioButton	Text	Typed "Coffee"

(*continues*)

TABLE 10-7 DinerGUI property values (*continued*)

Name	Object type	Property	Value
cmboSpecial	ComboBox	Items (Collection)	Typed "Whole Wheat", "Pumpernickel", "Seedless Rye", "Pita", "Sour Dough"
cmboSpecial	ComboBox	BackColor	Khaki
label2	Label	Text	Typed "Special Requests"
ckBxWater	CheckBox	Text	Typed "Water"

If you do not have Visual Studio, you can type assignment statements for the properties, making the assignments indicated in Table 10-7. For example, the first two properties could be set by typing:

```
Text = "Student Union - Diner by the Valley";
BackColor = Color.Goldenrod;
```

If the `System.Drawing` `namespace` is imported and referenced, it is not necessary to fully qualify the name. When the Form Designer generates the code to set these two properties, the statements read:

```
this.Text = "Student Union - Diner by the Valley";
this.BackColor = System.Drawing.Color.Goldenrod;
```

Both produce the same result with this application.

The complete source listing for the application is given in the following. The first `class`, `Order`, was written manually. Much of the code for the second file shown, which is a `partial class` definition for the `OrderGUI` `class`, was created by Visual Studio Form Designer. The third file contains the event-handler methods. Code was written for each of the methods following the pseudocode developed during the design of the application.

```
// Order.cs Author: Doyle
// Creates an order class with entree, drink, and special
// request data members. Methods to calculate total cost
// of order and set each data member included.
using System;
using System.Windows.Forms;

namespace Diner
{
    public class Order
    {
        public string [ ] menuEntree = new string [ ] {"Chicken
              Salad", "Ham and Cheese",
               "Turkey", "Vegetable Wrap", "Tuna Salad",
               "Avocado and Cheese", "Club", "Peanut Butter &
               Jelly", "Grilled Cheese", "Reuben"};
        public decimal [ ] menuEntreePrice = new decimal [ ]
               {4.50m, 5.00m, 4.75m,4.00m, 4.50m, 4.00m, 5.50m,
               3.75m, 3.50m, 5.00m};
        private string entree;
        private bool waterSelection;
        private string drinkSelection;
        private string specialRequest;
        private decimal entreePrice;
        private decimal drinkPrice;

        // Default constructor
        public Order( )
        {
            entree = "";
            waterSelection = false;
            specialRequest = ""; drinkPrice = 0;
            entreePrice = 0;
        }

        // Property for entree
        public string Entree
        {
            get
            {
                return entree;
            }
            set
            {
                entree = value;
                SetEntreePrice( );
            }
        }
```

```
// Property for special requests
public string SpecialRequest
{
     get
     {
          return specialRequest;
     }
     set
     {
          specialRequest = value;
     }
}

// Property for Water selection
public bool WaterSelection
{
     set
     {
          waterSelection = value;
     }
}

// Property for Drink selection
public string DrinkSelection
{
     get
     {
          return drinkSelection;
     }
     set
     {
          drinkSelection = value;
          SetDrinkPrice( );
     }
}

// Read-only property for entree price
public decimal EntreePrice
{
     get
     {
          return entreePrice;
     }
}
```

```
// Read-only property for drink price
public decimal DrinkPrice
{
     get
     {
          return drinkPrice;
     }
}

// After the entree is set, store the entrée price.
public void SetEntreePrice( )
{
     for (int i = 0; i < menuEntree.Length; i++)
     {
          if (menuEntree[i] == entree)
          {
               entreePrice = menuEntreePrice[i];
          }
     }
}

// Return the water selection.
public string GetWaterSelection( )
{
     string waterOrNot;
     if (waterSelection)
     {
          waterOrNot = "Water";
     }
     else
     {
          waterOrNot = "No Water";
     }
     return waterOrNot;
}

// After the drink is set, store the drink price.
public void SetDrinkPrice( )
{
     switch(drinkSelection)
     {
          case "Tea" :
          case "Coffee" :
               drinkPrice = 1.50m;
               break;
          case "Soda" :
          case "Lemonade" :
               drinkPrice = 2.00m;
               break;
```

```
                case "Milk" :
                case "Juice" :
                    drinkPrice = 1.75m;
                    break;
            }
        }

        // return the total cost of the order.
        public decimal DetermineTotalCharges( )
        {
            return entreePrice + drinkPrice;
        }

        public override string ToString( )
        {
            return "Total Due: " +
              DetermineTotalCharges( ).ToString("C");
        }
    }
}
```

The source listing for the two files that comprise the `OrderGUI` `class` is shown in the following.

NOTE Remember that much of the code for the following listing was generated by the Form Designer in Visual Studio. The complete listing is shown so that you can see the program statements added for the set properties. It is also included for those readers developing applications using a simple editor such as Notepad.

```
// OrderGUI Designer.cs Author: Doyle
// Create the graphical user interface
// to take an order and display the total cost.
using System;
using System.Windows.Forms;

namespace Diner
{
    partial class OrderGUI : Form
    {
       // Required designer variable.
         private System.ComponentModel.IContainer
                                        components = null;
       // Clean up any resources being used.
         protected override void Dispose(bool disposing)
```

```
{
    if(disposing && (components != null))
    {
        components.Dispose( );
    }
    base.Dispose(disposing);
}

#region Windows Form Designer generated code
private void InitializeComponent( )
{
  System.ComponentModel.ComponentResourceManager
        resources = new
        System.ComponentModel.ComponentResourceManager
        (typeof(OrderGUI));
  this.lstBxEntree = new System.Windows.Forms.ListBox( );
  this.label1 = new System.Windows.Forms.Label( );
  this.drinkGroup = new System.Windows.Forms.GroupBox( );
  this.radCoffee = new System.Windows.Forms.RadioButton( );
  this.radTea = new System.Windows.Forms.RadioButton( );
  this.radLemon = new System.Windows.Forms.RadioButton( );
  this.radSoda = new System.Windows.Forms.RadioButton( );
  this.radJuice = new System.Windows.Forms.RadioButton( );
  this.radMilk = new System.Windows.Forms.RadioButton( );
  this.cmboSpecial = new
          System.Windows.Forms.ComboBox( );
  this.label2 = new System.Windows.Forms.Label( );
  this.ckBxWater = new System.Windows.Forms.CheckBox( );
  this.menuStrip1 = new System.Windows.Forms.MenuStrip( );
  this.fileToolStripMenuItem = new
          System.Windows.Forms.ToolStripMenuItem( );
  this.menuPlaceOrder = new
          System.Windows.Forms.ToolStripMenuItem( );
  this.menuClearOrder = new
          System.Windows.Forms.ToolStripMenuItem( );
  this.menuDisplayOrder = new
          System.Windows.Forms.ToolStripMenuItem( );
  this.menuExit = new
          System.Windows.Forms.ToolStripMenuItem( );
  this.editToolStripMenuItem = new
          System.Windows.Forms.ToolStripMenuItem( );
  this.menuEditEntree = new
          System.Windows.Forms.ToolStripMenuItem( );
  this.menuEditDrink = new
          System.Windows.Forms.ToolStripMenuItem( );
  this.menuEditSpecial = new
          System.Windows.Forms.ToolStripMenuItem( );
```

10

```
        this.helpToolStripMenuItem = new
                System.Windows.Forms.ToolStripMenuItem( );
        this.menuAbout = new
                System.Windows.Forms.ToolStripMenuItem( );
        this.drinkGroup.SuspendLayout( );
        this.menuStrip1.SuspendLayout( );
        this.SuspendLayout( );
    //
    // lstBoxEntree
    //
        this.lstBxEntree.BackColor =
                System.Drawing.Color.Khaki;
        this.lstBxEntree.ItemHeight = 16;
        this.lstBxEntree.Location = new
                System.Drawing.Point(23, 59);
        this.lstBxEntree.Name = "lstBxEntree";
        this.lstBxEntree.Size = new
                System.Drawing.Size(156, 68);
        this.lstBxEntree.TabIndex = 0;
        this.lstBxEntree.SelectedIndexChanged += new
                System.EventHandler(
                    this.lstBxEntree_SelectedIndexChanged);
    //
    // label1
    //
        this.label1.Location = new System.Drawing.Point(37, 33);
        this.label1.Name = "label1";
        this.label1.Size = new System.Drawing.Size(120, 23);
        this.label1.TabIndex = 1;
        this.label1.Text = "Entree Selection";
    //
    // drinkGroup
    //
        this.drinkGroup.Controls.Add(this.radCoffee);
        this.drinkGroup.Controls.Add(this.radTea);
        this.drinkGroup.Controls.Add(this.radLemon);
        this.drinkGroup.Controls.Add(this.radSoda);
        this.drinkGroup.Controls.Add(this.radJuice);
        this.drinkGroup.Controls.Add(this.radMilk);
        this.drinkGroup.Location = new
                System.Drawing.Point(205, 50);
        this.drinkGroup.Name = "drinkGroup";
        this.drinkGroup.Size = new
                System.Drawing.Size(120, 176);
        this.drinkGroup.TabIndex = 3;
        this.drinkGroup.TabStop = false;
        this.drinkGroup.Text = "Drink Selection";
```

```
//
// radCoffee
//
   this.radCoffee.Location = new
           System.Drawing.Point(8, 144);
   this.radCoffee.Name = "radCoffee";
   this.radCoffee.Size = new
           System.Drawing.Size(104, 24);
   this.radCoffee.TabIndex = 5;
   this.radCoffee.Text = "Coffee";
   this.radCoffee.CheckedChanged += new
           System.EventHandler(this.Drink_CheckedChanged);
//
// radTea
//
   this.radTea.Location = new
           System.Drawing.Point(8, 120);
   this.radTea.Name = "radTea";
   this.radTea.Size = new
           System.Drawing.Size(104, 24);
   this.radTea.TabIndex = 4;
   this.radTea.Text = "Tea";
   this.radTea.CheckedChanged += new
           System.EventHandler(this.Drink_CheckedChanged);
//
// radLemon
//
   this.radLemon.Location = new
           System.Drawing.Point(8, 96);
   this.radLemon.Name = "radLemon";
   this.radLemon.Size = new
           System.Drawing.Size(104, 24);
   this.radLemon.TabIndex = 3;
   this.radLemon.Text = "Lemonade";
   this.radLemon.CheckedChanged += new
           System.EventHandler(this.Drink_CheckedChanged);
//
// radSoda
//
   this.radSoda.Location = new
           System.Drawing.Point(8, 72);
   this.radSoda.Name = "radSoda";
   this.radSoda.Size = new System.Drawing.Size(104, 24);
   this.radSoda.TabIndex = 2;
   this.radSoda.Text = "Soda";
   this.radSoda.CheckedChanged += new
           System.EventHandler(this.Drink_CheckedChanged);
```

```
            //
            // radJuice
            //
               this.radJuice.Location = new System.Drawing.Point(8, 48);
               this.radJuice.Name = "radJuice";
               this.radJuice.Size = new
                      System.Drawing.Size(104, 24);
               this.radJuice.TabIndex = 1;
               this.radJuice.Text = "Juice";
               this.radJuice.CheckedChanged += new System.EventHandler
                                   (this.Drink_CheckedChanged);
            //
            // radMilk
            //
               this.radMilk.Location = new
                      System.Drawing.Point(8, 24);
               this.radMilk.Name = "radMilk";
               this.radMilk.Size = new
                      System.Drawing.Size(104, 24);
               this.radMilk.TabIndex = 0;
               this.radMilk.Text = "Milk";
               this.radMilk.CheckedChanged += new System.EventHandler
                     (this.Drink_CheckedChanged);
            //
            // ckBxWater
            //
               this.ckBxWater.Location = new
                      System.Drawing.Point(69, 210);
               this.ckBxWater.Name = "ckBxWater";
               this.ckBxWater.Size = new
                      System.Drawing.Size(64, 24);
               this.ckBxWater.TabIndex = 6;
               this.ckBxWater.Text = "Water";
               this.ckBxWater.CheckedChanged += new
                  System.EventHandler(this.ckBxWater_CheckedChanged);
            //
            // cmboSpecial
            //
               this.cmboSpecial.BackColor =
                      System.Drawing.Color.Khaki;
               this.cmboSpecial.Items.AddRange(new object[ ] {
                      "Whole Wheat", "Pumpernickel", "Seedless Rye",
                      "Pita", "Sour Dough"} );
               this.cmboSpecial.Location = new
                      System.Drawing.Point(23, 170);
               this.cmboSpecial.Name = "cmboSpecial";
               this.cmboSpecial.Size = new
                      System.Drawing.Size(168, 24);
```

```
        this.cmboSpecial.TabIndex = 4;
        this.cmboSpecial.SelectedIndexChanged += new
                System.EventHandler
                    (this.cmboSpecial_SelectedIndexChanged);
        this.cmboSpecial.TextChanged += new
                System.EventHandler
                    (this.cmboSpecial_TextChanged);
    //
    // label2
    //
        this.label2.Location = new
                System.Drawing.Point(45, 146);
        this.label2.Name = "label2";
        this.label2.Size = new System.Drawing.Size(112, 23);
        this.label2.TabIndex = 5;
        this.label2.Text = "Special Requests";
    //
    // fileToolStripMenuItem
    //
        this.fileToolStripMenuItem.DropDownItems.AddRange (new
                System.Windows.Forms.ToolStripItem[ ]
                {     this.menuPlaceOrder,
                      this.menuClearOrder,
                      this.menuDisplayOrder,
                      this.menuExit
                });
        this.fileToolStripMenuItem.Name =
                "fileToolStripMenuItem";
        this.fileToolStripMenuItem.Size = new
                System.Drawing.Size(35, 20);
        this.fileToolStripMenuItem.Text = "File";
    //
    // menuPlaceOrder
    //
        this.menuPlaceOrder.Name = "menuPlaceOrder";
        this.menuPlaceOrder.Size = new
                System.Drawing.Size(152, 22);
        this.menuPlaceOrder.Text = "Place Order";
        this.menuPlaceOrder.Click += new System.EventHandler
                (this.menuPlaceOrder_Click);
    //
    // menuStrip1
    //
        this.menuStrip1.Items.AddRange(new
                System.Windows.Forms.ToolStripItem[ ]
```

```
            {
                this.fileToolStripMenuItem,
                this.editToolStripMenuItem,
                this.helpToolStripMenuItem
            } );
        this.menuStrip1.Location = new
            System.Drawing.Point(0, 0);
        this.menuStrip1.Name = "menuStrip1";
        this.menuStrip1.Size = new
            System.Drawing.Size(342, 24);
        this.menuStrip1.TabIndex = 7;
        this.menuStrip1.Text = "menuStrip1";
    //
    // menuClearOrder
    //
        this.menuClearOrder.Name = "menuClearOrder";
        this.menuClearOrder.Size = new
            System.Drawing.Size(152, 22);
        this.menuClearOrder.Text = "Clear Order";
        this.menuClearOrder.Click += new System.EventHandler
            (this.menuClearOrder_Click);
    //
    // menuDisplayOrder
    //
        this.menuDisplayOrder.Name = "menuDisplayOrder";
        this.menuDisplayOrder.Size = new
            System.Drawing.Size(152, 22);
        this.menuDisplayOrder.Text = "Display Order";
        this.menuDisplayOrder.Click += new System.EventHandler
            (this.menuDisplayOrder_Click);
    //
    // menuEditEntree
    //
        this.menuEditEntree.Name = "menuEditEntree";
        this.menuEditEntree.Size = new
            System.Drawing.Size(166, 22);
        this.menuEditEntree.Text = "Entree";
        this.menuEditEntree.Click += new System.EventHandler
            (this.menuEditEntree_Click);
    //
    // menuEditDrink
    //
        this.menuEditDrink.Name = "menuEditDrink";
        this.menuEditDrink.Size = new
            System.Drawing.Size(166, 22);
        this.menuEditDrink.Text = "Drink";
        this.menuEditDrink.Click += new System.EventHandler
            (this.menuEditDrink_Click);
```

```
//
// menuExit
//
   this.menuExit.Name = "menuExit";
   this.menuExit.Size = new System.Drawing.Size(152, 22);
   this.menuExit.Text = "Exit";
   this.menuExit.Click += new System.EventHandler
          (this.menuExit_Click);
//
// editToolStripMenuItem
//
   this.editToolStripMenuItem.DropDownItems.AddRange
          (new System.Windows.Forms.ToolStripItem[ ]
          {
               this.menuEditEntree,
               this.menuEditDrink,
               this.menuEditSpecial
          });
   this.editToolStripMenuItem.Name =
          "editToolStripMenuItem";
   this.editToolStripMenuItem.Size = new
          System.Drawing.Size(37, 20);
   this.editToolStripMenuItem.Text = "Edit";
//
// menuEditSpecial
//
   this.menuEditSpecial.Name = "menuEditSpecial";
   this.menuEditSpecial.Size = new
          System.Drawing.Size(166, 22);
   this.menuEditSpecial.Text = "Special Requests";
   this.menuEditSpecial.Click += new System.EventHandler
          (this.menuEditSpecial_Click);
//
// menuAbout
//
   this.menuAbout.Name = "menuAbout";
   this.menuAbout.Size = new
          System.Drawing.Size(152, 22);
   this.menuAbout.Text = "About";
   this.menuAbout.Click += new System.EventHandler
          (this.menuAbout_Click);
//
// helpToolStripMenuItem
//
   this.helpToolStripMenuItem.DropDownItems.AddRange
          (new System.Windows.Forms.ToolStripItem[ ]
          { this.menuAbout });
```

```
            this.helpToolStripMenuItem.Name =
                    "helpToolStripMenuItem";
            this.helpToolStripMenuItem.Size = new
                System.Drawing.Size(40, 20);
            this.helpToolStripMenuItem.Text = "Help";
        //
        // OrderGUI
        //
            this.AutoScaleBaseSize = new
                    System.Drawing.Size(6, 15);
            this.Load += new
                    System.EventHandler(this.OrderGUI_Load);
            this.drinkGroup.ResumeLayout(false);
            this.menuStrip1.ResumeLayout(false);
            this.menuStrip1.PerformLayout( );
                    System.Drawing.Size(6, 15);
            this.BackColor = System.Drawing.Color.Goldenrod;
            this.ClientSize = new System.Drawing.Size(342, 253);
            this.Controls.Add(this.ckBxWater);
            this.Controls.Add(this.label2);
            this.Controls.Add(this.cmboSpecial);
            this.Controls.Add(this.drinkGroup);
            this.Controls.Add(this.label1);
            this.Controls.Add(this.lstBxEntree);
            this.Controls.Add(this.menuStrip1);
            this.Font = new System.Drawing.Font("Arial", 9.75F,
                  System.Drawing.FontStyle.Regular,
                  System.Drawing.GraphicsUnit.Point, ((byte)(0)));
            this.ResumeLayout( false );
            this.PerformLayout( );
            this.ForeColor = System.Drawing.Color.Navy;
            this.Icon = ((System.Drawing.Icon)
                    (resources.GetObject("$this.Icon")));
            this.MainMenuStrip = this.menuStrip1;
            this.Name = "OrderGUI";
            this.Text = "Student Union - Diner by the Valley";
        }
        #endregion // End of Windows Form Designer generated code

        private System.Windows.Forms.Label label1;
        private System.Windows.Forms.GroupBox drinkGroup;
        private System.Windows.Forms.Label label2;
        private System.Windows.Forms.ListBox lstBxEntree;
        private System.Windows.Forms.ComboBox cmboSpecial;
        private System.Windows.Forms.CheckBox ckBxWater;
        private System.Windows.Forms.RadioButton radCoffee;
        private System.Windows.Forms.RadioButton radTea;
        private System.Windows.Forms.RadioButton radLemon;
```

```
            private System.Windows.Forms.RadioButton radSoda;
            private System.Windows.Forms.RadioButton radJuice;
            private System.Windows.Forms.RadioButton radMilk;
            private System.Windows.Forms.MenuStrip menuStrip1;
            private ToolStripMenuItem fileToolStripMenuItem;
            private ToolStripMenuItem menuPlaceOrder;
            private ToolStripMenuItem menuClearOrder;
            private ToolStripMenuItem menuDisplayOrder;
            private ToolStripMenuItem menuExit;
            private ToolStripMenuItem editToolStripMenuItem;
            private ToolStripMenuItem menuEditEntree;
            private ToolStripMenuItem menuEditDrink;
            private ToolStripMenuItem menuEditSpecial;
            private ToolStripMenuItem helpToolStripMenuItem;
            private ToolStripMenuItem menuAbout;
            private System.ComponentModel.IContainer components = null;
      }
} // End of OrderGUI.Designer.cs file

// OrderGUI.cs Author: Doyle
// This file contains the event-handler methods.
using System;
using System.Windows.Forms;

namespace Diner
{
      public partial class OrderGUI : Form
      {
            private Order newOrder;

            public OrderGUI( )
            {
                  InitializeComponent( );
            }

            // Instantiates an object of the Order class when
            // the form is first loaded.
            private void OrderGUI_Load(object sender,
                                             System.EventArgs e)
            {
                  newOrder = new Order( );
                  for (int i = 0; i < newOrder.menuEntree.Length; i++)
                  {
                        this.lstBxEntree.Items.Add
                              (newOrdermenuEntree[i]);
                  }
            }
```

10

```
// Event handler that gets the entree from the
// ListBox and sets the entree price.
private void lstBxEntree_SelectedIndexChanged
                (object sender,System.EventArgs e)
{
     newOrder.Entree = this.lstBxEntree.Text;
}

// Event handler that gets the special request -
// if one is selected from the predefined list.
private void cmboSpecial_SelectedIndexChanged
          (object sender, System.EventArgs e)
{
     newOrder.SpecialRequest = this.cmboSpecial.Text;
}

// Menu item that displays the order.
private void menuDisplayOrder_Click(object sender,
                              System.EventArgs e)
{
    MessageBox.Show (newOrder.Entree + "\n" +
              newOrder.SpecialRequest + " \n" +
              newOrder.DrinkSelection +
              "\n" +
              newOrder.GetWaterSelection( ),
              "Current Order");
}

// Event handler that gets the radio button
// selected and sets the drink selection.
private void Drink_CheckedChanged(object sender,
                                   System.EventArgs e)
{
    if (this.radTea.Checked)
              newOrder.DrinkSelection = radTea.Text;
    else
         if (this.radCoffee.Checked)
              newOrder.DrinkSelection = radCoffee.Text;
         else
              if (this.radSoda.Checked)
                   newOrder.DrinkSelection =
                             radSoda.Text;
              else
                   if (this.radLemon.Checked)
                        newOrder.DrinkSelection =
                                  radLemon.Text;
                   else
```

```
                    if (this.radJuice.Checked)
                        newOrder.DrinkSelection =
                            radJuice.Text;
                    else
                        if (this.radMilk.Checked)
                          newOrder.DrinkSelection =
                               radMilk.Text;
}

// Event handler that gets raised when the check box
// for Water gets clicked.
private void ckBxWater_CheckedChanged
             (object sender, System.EventArgs e)
{
    if (this.ckBxWater.Checked)
       newOrder.WaterSelection = true;
    else
       newOrder.WaterSelection = false;
}

// Event handler that gets raised when the
// user types values into the text area of
// the combo box.
private void cmboSpecial_TextChanged
             (object sender, System.EventArgs e)
{
    newOrder.SpecialRequest = this.cmboSpecial.Text;

}

// Event handler that gets raised when the edit menu
// is clicked to change the entree.
private void menuEditEntree_Click (object sender,
                                   System.EventArgs e)
{
    MessageBox.Show("Please select a new Entree");
    newOrder.Entree = "";
    this.lstBxEntree.ClearSelected( );
}

// Event handler that gets raised when the edit menu
// is clicked to change the drink.
private void menuEditDrink_Click
         (object sender, System.EventArgs e)
{
    MessageBox.Show("Please select a new Drink");
    newOrder.DrinkSelection = "";
    this.ClearDrinks( );
}
```

10

```
// Clears selections for all drink radio buttons.
public void ClearDrinks( )
{
     this.radMilk.Checked = false;
     this.radJuice.Checked = false;
     this.radSoda.Checked = false;
     this.radLemon.Checked = false;
     this.radTea.Checked = false;
     this.radCoffee.Checked = false;
}

// Clears all selections so that a new order
// can be placed. Resets the Order object back
// to its default values.
private void menuClearOrder_Click
          (object sender, System.EventArgs e)
{
     this.lstBxEntree.ClearSelected( );
     this.ckBxWater.Checked = false;
     this.cmboSpecial.SelectedIndex = -1;
     this.cmboSpecial.Text = "";
     this.ClearDrinks( );
     newOrder.DrinkSelection = "";
     newOrder.Entree = "";
     newOrder.SpecialRequest = "";
     newOrder.WaterSelection = false;
}

// Displays the values for the current instance of
// Order object members.
private void menuPlaceOrder_Click
          (object sender, System.EventArgs e)
{
     MessageBox.Show(newOrder.Entree + "\n" +
                    newOrder.SpecialRequest + "\n" +
                    newOrder.DrinkSelection + "\n" +
                    newOrder.GetWaterSelection( ) +
                    "\n\n\n" + newOrder ,
                    "Placed Order" );
}

// Event handler that gets raised when the edit menu
// is clicked to change the special requests.
private void menuEditSpecial_Click
          (object sender, System.EventArgs e)
{
     MessageBox.Show("Special Request cleared.");
     newOrder.SpecialRequest = "";
     this.cmboSpecial.SelectedIndex = -1;
```

```
                this.cmboSpecial.Text ="";
                newOrder.SpecialRequest = "";
            }

            // Event handler that gets raised when the Help
            // menu is clicked to show the About message.
            private void menuAbout_Click
                    (object sender, System.EventArgs e)
            {
                MessageBox.Show("Student Union -" +
                                " Diner by the Valley" +
                                "\n\n\nVersion 1.0");
            }

            // Event handler that gets raised when
            // Exit is clicked.
            private void menuExit_Click
                    (object sender, System.EventArgs e)
            {
                Application.Exit( );
            }
        }
    }
```

Figure 10-31 shows the original user interface with the File menu selections. Notice that a new icon is used in the title bar. The icon was added by setting the `Icon` property for the `OrderGUI` form.

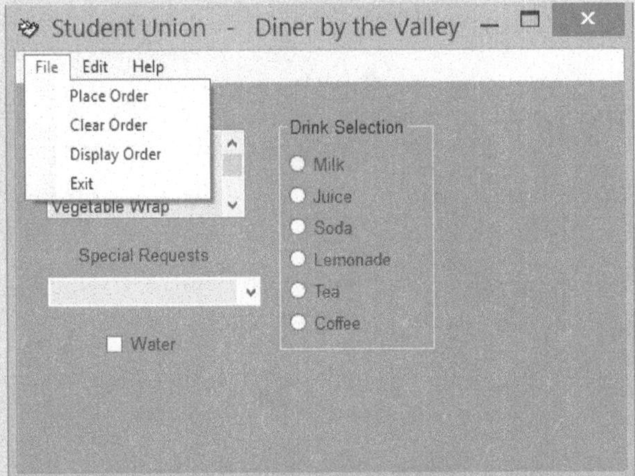

FIGURE 10-31 Interface showing menu selections

10

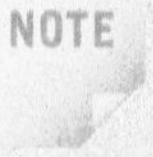

NOTE Any file that ends with an .ico extension can be used as the icon for the application. Many sources on the Internet contain free graphics. They are easily added to your Windows applications.

All that is required to add pictures to a form is to instantiate an `object` of the `PictureBox` `class`. If you are using Visual Studio, drag the `PictureBox` control `object` to your form. Set the `Image` property to the desired picture.

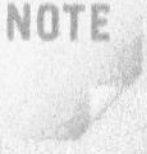

NOTE You can select graphic file types such as *.bmp, *.gif, *.jpeg, *.jpg, *.png, and *.ico or metafile types such as *.emf or *.wmf for the `Image` property. Store the image in the bin\debug subdirectory of the current project.

The `Form` `object` also has a `BackgroundImage` property that can be set to display a picture on the background. To have a picture in the background, using Visual Studio select the form and then use the **Properties** window to select the `BackgroundImage` property. Browse to a location that contains a bitmap or metafile.

When the form is loaded, the `OrderGUI_Load` event is raised. At that time, an `object` of the `Order` `class` is instantiated. Using the entree array of the `Order` `class`, the list box is filled. With each click on the form, a different event is fired. Figure 10-32 shows the message displayed after several options were selected, including the **Place Order** menu option.

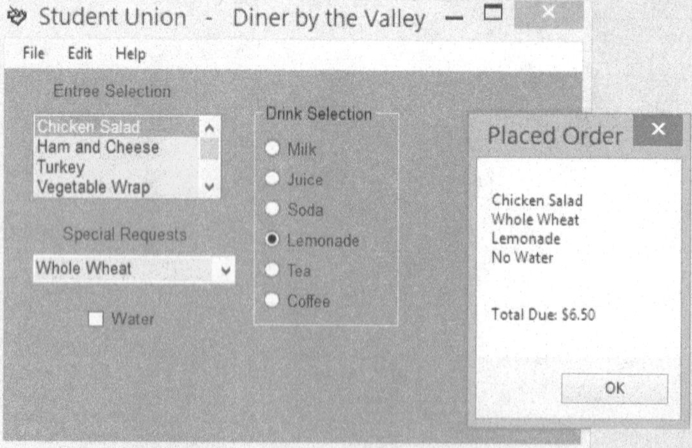

FIGURE 10-32 Message displayed from Place Order menu option

The ComboBox object allows special requests to be typed. Any new selections set new values for the instance of the Order class. When users type values in the text area of the ComboBox object, the TextChanged( ) event is fired. Figure 10-33 illustrates a typed entry for the ComboBox object. The MessageBox.Show( ) method is used to display messages from the menu options. Figure 10-33 is displayed from the **File, Display Order** option.

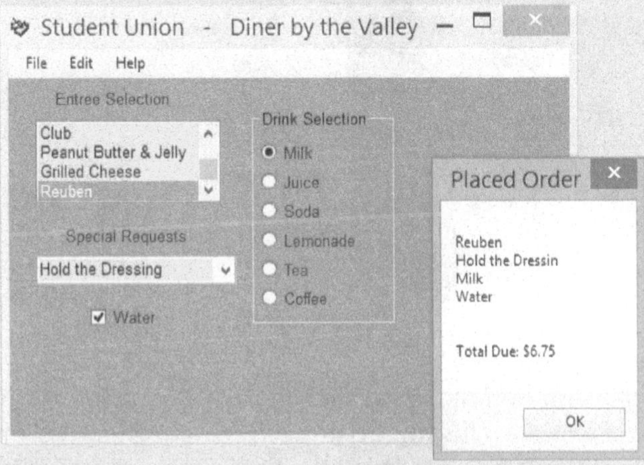

FIGURE 10-33 Message displayed from Display Order menu option

When events are raised from the **Edit** menu, the event-handler methods display a message indicating that the selections are being cleared. Then, the control on the form GUI is cleared and the Order instance data member is set back to its default value. Figure 10-34 shows the result of selecting the **Edit, Special Requests** menu option.

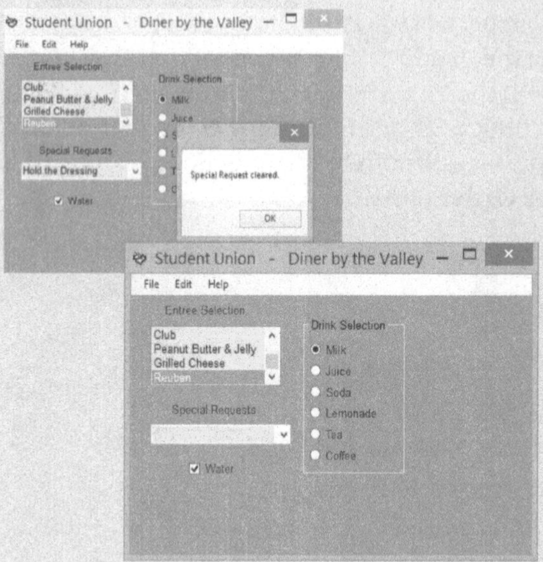

FIGURE 10-34 Special Requests click event fired

Firing the **Clear Order** menu option (shown in Figure 10-35) deselects all entries on the form and resets the `Order` instance data members to their default values. The Windows application is in a `Run` state until the **Exit** menu option is fired or the **Close** button is clicked.

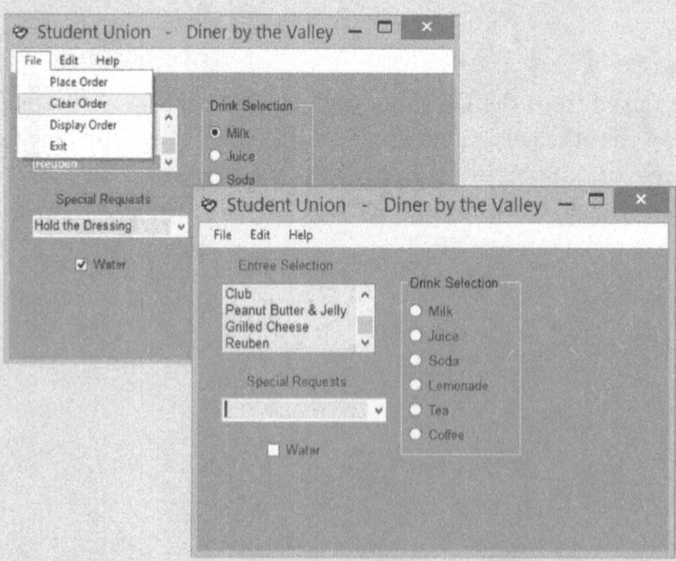

FIGURE 10-35 Clear Order click event fired

A number of event-handler methods are wired to objects for this application. Table 10-8 lists the event-handler methods and their associated objects. These are all instantiated in the OrderGUI class.

TABLE 10-8 DinerGUI events

Event-handler method	Class	Object
ckBxWater_ CheckedChanged	CheckBox	ckBxWater
cmboSpecial_TextChanged	ComboBox	cmboSpecial
cmboSpecial_Selected IndexChanged	ComboBox	cmboSpecial
Drink_CheckedChanged	RadioButton	radTea, radSoda, radLemon, radMilk, radCoffee, radJuice
OrderGUI_Load	OrderGUI	this
lstBxEntree_Selected IndexChanged	ListBox	lstBxEntree
menuAbout_Click	ToolStripMenuItem	menuAbout
menuClearOrder_Click	ToolStripMenuItem	menuClearOrder
menuDisplayOrder_Click	ToolStripMenuItem	menuDisplayOrder
menuEditDrink_Click	ToolStripMenuItem	menuEditDrink
menuEditEntree_Click	ToolStripMenuItem	menuEditEntree
menuEditSpecial_Click	ToolStripMenuItem	menuEditSpecial
menuExit_Click	ToolStripMenuItem	menuExit
menuPlaceOrder_Click	ToolStripMenuItem	menuPlaceOrder

© Cengage Learning

10

Coding Standards

As discussed in Chapter 9, it is important to follow a consistent naming standard for controls added to a Windows form. Before you register events, such as button click events, name the associated control. Then when you register the event handler using Visual Studio, the code that is automatically generated uses the control's identifier as part of the identifier for the method. Naming the control first will make your code more readable and help reduce errors.

Resources

Additional sites you might want to explore:

- Visual Studio - Getting Started Tutorials—
http://msdn.microsoft.com/en-us/library/dd492171.aspx
- Visual C# Windows Forms Tutorials—
http://visualcsharptutorials.com/windows-forms
- Delegates and Events in C#/.NET—
http://www.akadia.com/services/dotnet_delegates_and_events.html
- C# Programmers Reference - Delegates Tutorial—
http://msdn.microsoft.com/en-us/library/aa288459(VS.71).aspx
- Microsoft Virtual Academy - C# Fundamentals for Absolute Beginners—
http://www.microsoftvirtualacademy.com/training-courses/c-fundamentals-for-absolute-beginners

QUICK REVIEW

1. Delegates are special types of .NET classes whose instances store references (addresses) to methods.
2. A declaration for a `delegate` looks more like a method declaration than a `class` definition. Every `delegate` type has a signature, which may include zero or more parameters. The signature indicates what method signatures must look like if they are to be referenced by the `delegate`.
3. Multicast delegates are wired to multiple methods, all of which are executed, one after the other, when an event is raised.
4. Events can be considered special forms of delegates in C# because they enable you to place a reference to event-handler methods inside a `delegate`. After this reference is made, or the event is registered, the `delegate` is used to call the event-handler methods.

5. To respond to events in your program, two things must occur. First, you must register the event as being of interest, and second, an event-handler method must be generated. This process is called event wiring.
6. All event-handler methods normally have the same signature. They do not return anything; they have a `return` type of `void`. They have two parameters.
7. `ListBox` controls can be used to display a list of items from which the user can select. Single or multiple selections can be made. A scroll bar is automatically added to the control if the total number of items exceeds the number that can be displayed.
8. At design time or dynamically at run time, you can add or remove items to and from the `ListBox` control.
9. The default event for the `ListBox` `object` is the `SelectedIndexChanged( )` event. It is raised or triggered when the selection changes for the `ListBox` `object`.
10. The `ListBox` `class` has a number of interesting properties including `Items`, which get the items of the list. `SelectedIndex` and `SelectedItem` properties get or set the selected item.
11. `ListBox` and `ComboBox` objects are zero-based structures. `SelectedIndex` and `SelectedIndices` properties access the `object` by its indexed location.
12. The `Text` property is the most often used property. It receives the text of the currently selected item.
13. `ListBox` controls and `ComboBox` objects share many of the same properties and methods. `ComboBox` objects contain their own text box field as part of the `object`. This makes it easy to add a new value at run time.
14. A `KeyPress( )` event occurs when the user presses a key. Actually, the event is fired with each and every keystroke. This event-handler method is sometimes used with `ComboBox` objects.
15. The `SelectedIndexChanged( )` event-handler method is often wired to `ComboBox` and `ListBox` objects. The `TextChanged( )` event is the default event handler for textboxes. It can also be wired to `ComboBox` objects and fires when the text is entered in the text area.
16. Using the Visual Studio Toolbox window and the `MenuStrip` `class`, it is easy to drag and drop a `MenuStrip` control `object` onto your form.
17. You can create shortcuts to menu options. Shortcuts using the **Alt** key are quickly and easily created. When you type the text that is to appear in the menu (using the `Text` property), preceding the character with an ampersand (&) enables the user to press the Alt key plus the key that follows the ampersand as a shortcut.
18. If you are using the `MainMenu` `object`, to have the menu be displayed on the `Form`, you set the `Menu` property on the `Form` to the name of the `MainMenu` `object`.

19. There are a number of preconfigured dialog boxes that can be added to menus. They include those that resemble the standard Windows File Open, File Save, File Print, File Print Preview, Format Font, and Format Color dialog boxes. These can be added to your application by dragging and dropping the control `object` onto your form.
20. Check boxes appear as small boxes that allow users to make a Yes/No or True/False selection. The default event-handler method for `CheckBox` objects is `CheckedChanged( )`. A `Click( )` event can also be wired to `CheckBox` objects. Double-clicking on one of the `CheckBox` objects registers a `CheckedChanged( )` event for that one `object`.
21. For visual appearances, `CheckBox` objects may be grouped together using the `GroupBox` control. The grouping also aids design because you can move all the objects as a group. However, grouping does not provide any additional functionality for `CheckBox` objects.
22. A `GroupBox` control should be placed on the form for radio buttons. Radio buttons give users a choice between two or more options. Remember that it is appropriate to select more than one `CheckBox` `object`. Not so with `RadioButton` objects.
23. Multiple radio buttons can be wired to the same event-handler method.
24. Windows Presentation Foundation (WPF) applications create a special XAML file with tags to control the appearance of an application. No .Designer.cs is created.
25. The `TabControl` `object` displays multiple tabs on the form, like labels in a set of folders in a filing cabinet. Each tab stores different controls and has a `Click` event.

EXERCISES

1. What `namespace` must be referenced in order to instantiate objects from control classes such as `Label`, `Button`, and `TextBox`?
   a. System
   b. Windows
   c. System.Windows.Forms
   d. System.Windows.Controls
   e. Windows.Forms.Control

2. Given the `delegate` declaration

   `delegate void PerformsSomeTask(int arg1, double arg2);`

   which of the following statements would appear to create a `delegate` instance of `PerformsSomeTask( )` with no syntax errors?

   a.
   ```
   PerformsSomeTask task1 = new
           PerformsSomeTask (CalculateThis);
   ```
   b.
   ```
   PerformsSomeTask task1 = new
           PerformsSomeTask (CalculateThis( ));
   ```
   c.
   ```
   PerformsSomeTask( ) task1 = new
           PerformsSomeTask (CalculateThis( ));
   ```
   d.
   ```
   PerformsSomeTask( ) task1 = new
           PerformsSomeTask (CalculateThis(int, double));
   ```
   e.
   ```
   PerformsSomeTask task1 = new
           PerformsSomeTask (CalculateThis(int arg1, double arg2));
   ```

3. Given the `delegate` declaration

   `delegate void PerformsSomeTask(int arg1, double arg2);`

   which of the following represents a method heading that could be associated with the `delegate`?

   a. `int CalculateThis(int value1, double value2)`
   b. `double CalculateThis(int value1, double value2)`
   c. `void CalculateThis(int value1, double value2)`
   d. `int CalculateThis( )`
   e. all of the above

10

4. The signature for a method includes only the:

   a. `return` type, method name, number of parameters, and the data type of the parameters
   b. method name and `return` type
   c. number of parameters and the data type of the parameters
   d. method name, number of parameters, and the data type of the parameters
   e. `return` type, number of parameters, and the data type of the parameters

5. A multicast `delegate` is one that:
   a. has more than one method wrapped to it
   b. has more than one parameter
   c. has more than one instance of itself created in a program
   d. has more than one `return` type
   e. none of the above
6. What method is used with the `Items` property to populate a `ListBox` control with the contents from an array?
   a. `Populate( )`
   b. `Add( )`
   c. `AddArray( )`
   d. `AddRange( )`
   e. all of the above
7. One distinguishing characteristic between a `ListBox` control `object` and a `ComboBox` control `object` is that:
   a. Multiple selections are possible with `ListBox` objects.
   b. `ComboBox` objects are used for output only.
   c. A scroll bar can be seen with `ComboBox` objects.
   d. It is easier to program the `ComboBox` `object` event-handler method(s).
   e. none of the above
8. A default event-handler method for a `ListBox` `object` is:
   a. `KeyPress( )`
   b. `Click( )`
   c. `SelectedItem( )`
   d. `SelectedIndexChanged( )`
   e. `Selected( )`
9. The property that returns a collection of the indexes selected for a `ListBox` `object` is:
   a. `SelectedIndex`
   b. `SelectedIndices`
   c. `Text`
   d. `Items`
   e. `SelectedItems`

10. `ComboBox` objects offer the added functionality over a `ListBox object` of:
    a. allowing values to be removed at run time
    b. allowing multiple selections to be made
    c. including a scroll bar for moving down the items
    d. containing a text box for values to be entered at run time
    e. none of the above

11. Assuming `comboBoxData` is instantiated as a `ComboBox`, which of the following statements would retrieve its selection and place it in a `string` variable?
    a. `string s = ComboBox.Selection;`
    b. `string s = ComboBox.comboBoxData.Text;`
    c. `string s = comboBoxData.Text;`
    d. `string s.Text = comboBoxData.Text;`
    e. none of the above

12. After you type the text for a menu using the MainMenu control, what else must be done before the menu will be seen on the form?
    a. Set the `Menu` property on the form to the name of the menu.
    b. Set the `Form` property on the menu to the name of the form.
    c. Create `menuItems` subordinate to the menu.
    d. Program the event-handler methods for each `menuItem`.
    e. all of the above

13. When you type the text for the Help menu option, which of the following creates a shortcut of Alt+P for the Help?
    a. Help(Alt p)
    b. &Help
    c. &Hel&p
    d. Hel&p
    e. Help(Alt &p)

10

14. If you want all options to be displayed on the screen, but allow only one of the options to be selected, which type of structure is normally used?
    a. check box
    b. combo box
    c. menu
    d. radio button
    e. text box
15. Which property is used with `CheckBox` and `RadioButton` objects to determine whether their option is selected?
    a. `Selected`
    b. `SelectedIndex`
    c. `SelectedItem`
    d. `Checked`
    e. none of the above
16. Wiring an event handler to multiple objects involves:
    a. using the same method to handle the events fired for more than one `object`
    b. selecting the same objects property for each event-handler method
    c. creating multiple methods that do the same task
    d. naming the object's Event property with an ampersand
    e. none of the above
17. The `GroupBox` provides more functionality for which type of objects?
    a. `ComboBox`
    b. `ListBox`
    c. `CheckBox`
    d. `RadioButton`
    e. `TextBox`
18. `Click( )` events are the default event for which type of `object`?
    a. `Button`
    b. `RadioButton`
    c. `MenuItem`
    d. `CheckBox`
    e. all of the above

19. Which statement could be used in C# to set a `ListBox` object's selection mode to MultiExtended if you did not have Visual Studio's Properties window available? The name for the `ListBox` `object` is `lstBox1`.
    a. `lstBox1.SelectionMode = SelectionMode.MultiExtended;`
    b. `lstBox1 = MultiExtended;`
    c. `SelectionMode = MultiExtended;`
    d. `SelectionMode.MultiExtended;`
    e. all of the above

20. Which property can be set for a form to enable the Enter key to function like a mouse click for a selected `Button` `object`?
    a. `Enter`
    b. `Button_Click`
    c. `EnterKey`
    d. `AcceptButton`
    e. `AcceptKey`

---

21. Describe what is required to make a menu option clickable or a check box functional.

22. When is a `RadioButton` control preferred over a `CheckBox` control? When is a `ComboBox` control preferred over a `ListBox` control?

23. Identify two control options you might add to a Windows form to enable more controls to be available without consuming a lot of additional space.

24. For the following table, identify which properties can be used to set the given values for the controls.

Desired action	Property
Get the selected item from a ComboBox object	
Change the label over a group box	
Arrange the items in a list box in ascending order	
Change the color of the text in a label	
Change the text that appears in the title bar of a form	
Associate a Main menu to a form	

© Cengage Learning

25. From the following partial code listing, identify the name(s) of event-handler method(s) that would need to be written. To what object(s) are they wired?

```
public class Question : System.Windows.Forms.Form
{
      private System.Windows.Forms.Label label1;
      private System.Windows.Forms.TextBox txtBxActivity;
      private System.Windows.Forms.CheckBox ckBxSwim;
      private System.Windows.Forms.CheckBox ckBxSnorkel;
      private System.Windows.Forms.TextBox txtBxResult;

      : // Colon indicates items missing.

      private void InitializeComponent( )
      {
            this.label1 = new System.Windows.Forms.Label( );
            this.ckBxSwim = new
                     System.Windows.Forms.CheckBox( );
            this.ckBxSnorkel = new
                     System.Windows.Forms.CheckBox( );
            this.lstBxEvents.SelectedIndexChanged += new
                     System.EventHandler
                    (this.lstBxEvents_SelectedIndexChanged);
            : // Colon indicates items missing.
            this.label2.Size = new
                     System.Drawing.Size(120, 24);
            this.txtBxResult.Location = new
                     System.Drawing.Point(-2, 240);
```

```
this.btnNew.Text = "Add New One";
this.btnNew.Click += new
        System.EventHandler(this.btnNew_Click);
this.AutoScaleBaseSize = new
        System.Drawing.Size(8, 19);
this.BackColor = System.Drawing.Color.FromArgb
        (((System.Byte)(128)),
        ((System.Byte)(128)),
        ((System.Byte)(255)));
this.ClientSize = new
        System.Drawing.Size(292, 273);
this.Controls.AddRange
        (new System.Windows.Forms.Control[]
        { this.btnNew,
          this.txtBxNewAct,
          this.label3,
          this.label1,
          this.txtBxResult,
          this.label2,
          this.lstBxEvents } );
:    // Colon indicates items missing.
```

PROGRAMMING EXERCISES

1. Create an application that can be used to allow users to enter information such as their names, e-mail addresses, and phone numbers. The application should provide a minimum of four features. The first retrieves and displays the information entered by the user. Output should be displayed in a Windows dialog message box. The second feature clears the entries so that new values can be entered. Provide an "About" feature under a "Help" menu option that displays information about the application such as who developed it and what version it is. Another menu option closes the application. Be creative and be sure to produce an aesthetically pleasing design using options from the Format menu if you are using Visual Studio.

2. The computer club is selling T-shirts. Create an attractive user interface that allows users to select sizes (S, M, L, and XL) and quantity. Which controls would be most appropriate? Remember, the fewer keystrokes required of the user the better. Provide a menu labeled "Process". Display the selections made by the user from a Process menu option under a "Display Order" option. Include an option to exit the application from the Process menu option.

3. Create a Windows application that can be used as a sign-up sheet for ski equipment for the Flyers Sports Club. The club has ski equipment that it makes available to members at a minimal charge. In an attempt to determine what type of equipment members might need for an upcoming trip, they have asked you to design and implement an equipment-needs form. Include `CheckBox` objects that allow users to select the type of gear they will need to purchase for the trip. Include selections of snow gloves, skis, goggles, earmuffs, and other items you feel are appropriate. Include at least one picture image on your application. After all selections are made, display a message indicating what items have been selected. You will probably want to include menu options to display and clear the order for the next user. Also include an option that enables the user to exit the application.

4. Create a graphical user interface that can be used by a community group to enable youths to sign up for different sporting events. Include radio buttons with a minimum of five sports. Wire a single event-handler method to each of the radio buttons. Program the method to display a different message for each different sport. For example, if one of the sports is skiing, the message might say, "Bring warm clothes!" Also include a `PictureBox object` on the form to display a different picture based on which sporting event was selected. One approach would be to layer multiple picture box objects in the same location. When the particular sport is selected, make the associated `PictureBox` visible. You can find free graphics on the Internet to use in your application. Hint: One way to associate a file to the PictureBox control is to Import an image from the Image property.

5. Create an Inspirational Message Displayer that has one `ComboBox object` with a list of at least five of your favorite sayings or inspiration messages. Your design should include the capability of letting users enter their own sayings. When a selection is made or a new entry is typed, display the selection on a `Label object` on your form. Add a menu to the application that includes at least the menu options of "File", "Format", and "Help". Under the "Format" selection, include options of "Font" and "Color". Wire the "Font" and "Color" options to the Windows predefined Font and Color dialog boxes so that when their values are changed, the text in the `Label object` displaying the saying is changed. Provide an "About" selection under the "Help" menu and an "Exit" under the "File" selection.

6. Create an order form that allows bags to be purchased. There are six different types: full decorative, beaded, pirate design, fringed, leather, and plain. Create a `ListBox` `object` for the different styles. Include a ComboBox for quantity. Quantities up to 10 should be provided. After the user makes a selection, display a message indicating which selection was made. Include an option to clear selections. Provide appropriate error messages when selections are not made.

7. Add to the application in Exercise 6 by including a control that allows the user to determine the type of shipping they desire. Include a set of radio buttons that contain shipping options of overnight, three day, and standard. Add the price for each bag to the listbox selection as follows: full decorative—$50.00; beaded—$45.00; pirate design—$40.00; fringed—$25.00; leather—$80.00; and plain—$20.00. Display the items in the listbox in sort order. Using methods of the string class, retrieve the price from the listbox. Display in a Windows dialog message box the total cost for the purchase. Include the selection, quantity, and shipping charge. The shipping charges are based on the total purchase. The following percentages are used: overnight—10%, three day—7%, and standard—5%.

8. Add to your solution in Exercise 2 by including two more sizes, XSmall and XXLarge. Add statements that process the order by calculating the total cost. Each shirt is $16 except the XSmall and XXLarge; their specialty prices are $20.00 each. Include an "Add to Cart" option from the "Process" menu that enables the user to add multiple selections to the order. Allow users to purchase different sizes on the same order. The "Display Order" option should be modified so that it displays the total cost for each selection and the final cost for the order. Include an additional "Help" menu option that displays instructions to the user indicating that they can make multiple size selections on a single order.

9. Create a Windows application for purchasing floor covering. Allow the length and width (feet and inches) of a room to be entered. Be sure to include program statements that will keep your program from crashing if they enter nonnumeric characters for the room dimensions. Using the tab control, provide selections such as Hardwood, Carpet, and Laminate. On each tab allow the user to select a type and price. Have a control that displays different types along with the prices of floor covering. Include, for example, options like Oak, Maple, Walnut, and Cherry Hardwood floors with prices such as $34.95 per square yard for Oak and $41.95 per square yard for Cherry. After the users enter their room dimensions and select the floor covering and price, display the total cost to cover the room. Include an option to clear selections. Place both the type of floor covering and the price in a single control, such as a ComboBox, and use string manipulation techniques to strip the price out of the string.

10. Create an application for a Pizza Delivery Company. You might check out the graphical user interface shown in Figure 10-21. Your solution does not need to resemble this one; however, it might give you some ideas. You must provide a place for the user to enter their contact information (i.e., address, phone number, and e-mail), and some of the contact information should be displayed when an order is placed. Your application should have a picture logo and company name. Provide selections such as Small, Medium, and Large for size. Allow users to select from at least a dozen items to place on their pizza. You might consider offering different types of sauce (i.e., tomato, pesto, or no sauce), different types of crust, different specialty types of pizza (Supreme, Veggie, etc.). BE CREATIVE! You can also sell wings, bread sticks, chicken strips, or something else of your choosing. Consider offering beverages. You must display the price for the order and allow the user to change their mind while they are ordering and reset the order form. Experiment, explore, change properties, and then review the .Designer.cs file.

CHAPTER 11

© zeljkodan/Shutterstock.com

Advanced Object-Oriented Programming Features

IN THIS CHAPTER, YOU WILL:

- Learn the major features of object-oriented languages
- Design and develop multitier applications using component-based development methods
- Use inheritance to extend the functionality of user-defined classes
- Create abstract classes that include abstract methods
- Distinguish the differences between sealed and abstract classes
- Become aware of partial classes
- Design and implement interfaces
- Understand why polymorphic programming is a common goal in .NET
- Explore generics and learn how to create generic classes and generic methods
- Investigate static versus dynamic typing and become aware of when dynamic and var types are used
- Work through a programming example that illustrates the chapter's concepts

In this chapter, you extend your knowledge of programming by exploring advanced features of object-oriented design. You will be introduced to component-based development and learn how to create your own `class` library files. You investigate new ways to write classes and new ways to use the more than 2000 classes that make up the Framework class library (FCL).

In addition, you learn more about inheritance and are introduced to interfaces and `abstract` classes. You explore the differences between extending a `class` through inheritance and implementing an `interface`. You learn how polymorphism relates to object-oriented design and learn how to do polymorphic programming using .NET-supported languages. Advanced features such as overriding, overloading, and the use of `virtual` methods are included in this chapter.

Object-Oriented Language Features

For a language to be considered a true object-oriented programming (OOP) language, it must support the following four major concepts, which C# and the .NET platform embrace:

- **Abstraction**: The language must provide a way to simplify complex problems by generalizing or allowing you to think about something a certain way and then representing only essential features appropriate to the problem, hiding the nonessential complexities.
- **Encapsulation**: The language must provide support for packaging data attributes and behaviors into a single unit, thus hiding implementation details.
- **Inheritance**: The language must provide features that enable reuse of code through extending the functionality of the program units.
- **Polymorphism**: The language must enable multiple implementations of the same behaviors so that the appropriate implementation can be executed based on the situation.

These features form the foundation for object-oriented development. From your first introduction to C#, you have experienced abstraction in your design of applications. Through designing classes, you are able to abstract out common characteristics that all objects of that type possess, including both behavioral and data characteristics. You defined the data in terms of instance fields and the behaviors in terms of methods. You encapsulated or packaged these common characteristics into a single entity labeled a `class`. Through defining the data members as `private`, you protected the data and enabled access only through the object's methods and properties.

Through using read-only properties and methods, you hide the implementation details. You have experienced inheritance, especially when you designed your graphical user interfaces. You extended the `Form` `class` to add to the functionality that was already part of that `class`. In this chapter, you gain a deeper understanding of the power of inheritance and learn how to build your own polymorphic components that can be extended.

Object-oriented development focuses on designing classes that can be reused in many applications. One way to ensure this reuse is through designing and building components that can be stored in a library and called on when needed. The following section describes how to accomplish this through the .NET platform.

Component-Based Development

In the past, applications were developed mainly as single, self-contained, monolithic programs, large programs that combined the user interface and data access code all in the same file. Most new applications are large systems involving development efforts from teams of programmers. These applications often require the packaging together of many different components to respond to business functions. Instead of writing a program that includes all the features in a single file, development today is often geared toward writing multitier applications similar to that shown in Figure 11-1.

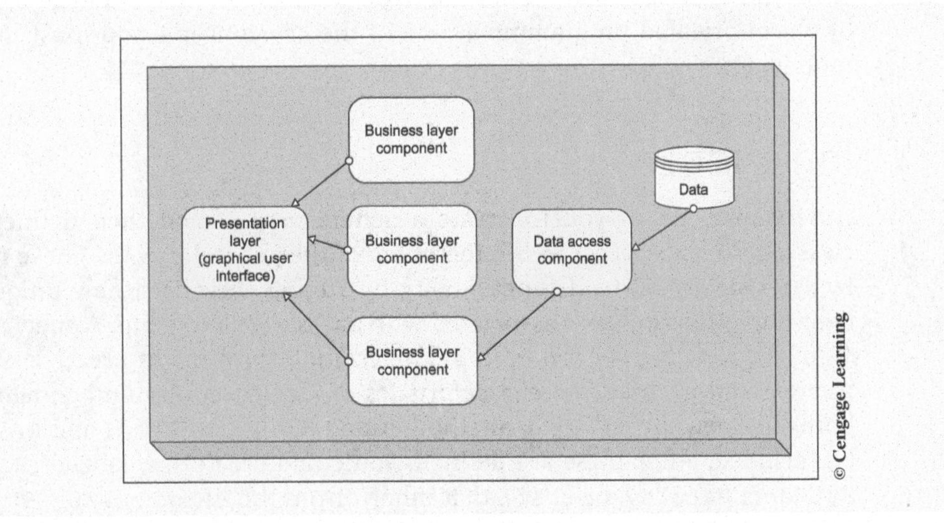

FIGURE 11-1 Component-based development

Component-based development emphasizes a reuse-based approach to defining, implementing, and composing independent components into systems. The business layer components shown in Figure 11-1 might be used in multiple applications. They include the functionality of the system, the processing necessary to prepare the data for presentation. Components are implemented through classes in C#. Software components, thus, often take the form of objects or collections of objects. In Chapters 9 and 10, you learned how to design graphical user interfaces, which enable creating a presentation tier. Chapter 15 introduces you to Web applications that facilitate creating another type of presentation tier, which can be viewed over a browser by different types of platforms. In Chapters 13 and 14, you will learn how to add the data access tier by writing classes that access data from text files and databases such as those created using Microsoft Access or SQL Server. All the work you have accomplished with previous chapters in this book has prepared you to develop the business logic for the center tier of components.

Object-oriented development techniques work well for constructing multitier applications. As you review Figure 11-1, think of each of the components in the diagram as independent classes, separate from each other. Classes can be designed and new subclasses created that extend the functionality of the original `class`. Many different applications can reuse these classes through extending or combining them into new applications. If changes are needed, you can isolate the change and not have to impact other classes.

In C#, in addition to creating .EXE files, you can create `class` library files with a dynamic link library (DLL) extension. These files can become the components that are referenced from any number of applications. To take advantage of the features of object-oriented programming, one of the key concepts you must understand is inheritance.

Inheritance

Inheritance allows you to create a general `class` and then define specialized classes that have access to the members of the general `class`. These new specialized classes can extend functionality by adding their own new unique data and behaviors. Inheritance is associated with an "is a" relationship. A specialized `class` "is a" form of the general `class`. For example, you might create a `class` called `Person` and include data characteristics of identification number, name, age, and home address. Behaviors or methods titled `Eat( )`, `Walk( )`, and `Talk( )` might be included. After these are defined, you could create specialized classes such as `Student`, `Faculty`, or `Staff` that inherit from the `Person` `class`. `Student` "is a" `Person`, just as `Faculty` or `Staff` "is a" `Person`. `Student` might have unique data characteristics of student ID, major, and year in school. `Staff` might have unique data characteristics of employee ID, date of hire, and job title. Through using inheritance, applications instantiating objects of the `Student` `class` would have not only the unique characteristics of the student (student ID, major, and year) but also have access to the characteristics of the Person (identification number, name, age, and address).

Classes can also have a "has a" relationship in which a single `class` is defined to have instances of other `class` types. This is a concept called **containment** or **aggregation**. You experience containment in C# when you define classes that instantiate objects of the `string` or `int` classes. However, "has a" relationships are usually associated with user-defined classes. For example, a Person "has a" medicalRecord and "has a" dentalRecord.

Inheriting from the Object Class

You have been creating your own classes since you wrote your first program in Chapter 1. You learned that every `object` created in C# automatically inherits from a base `class` named `object` that is in the `System` `namespace`. Object has four methods that every `class` written in C# inherits as long as it provides a reference to the `System` `namespace`. One of these, the `ToString( )` method, you have used in many of your programs. Figure 11-2 uses IntelliSense to show the signature for `Object.ToString( )` and the names of the other methods inherited from `object`.

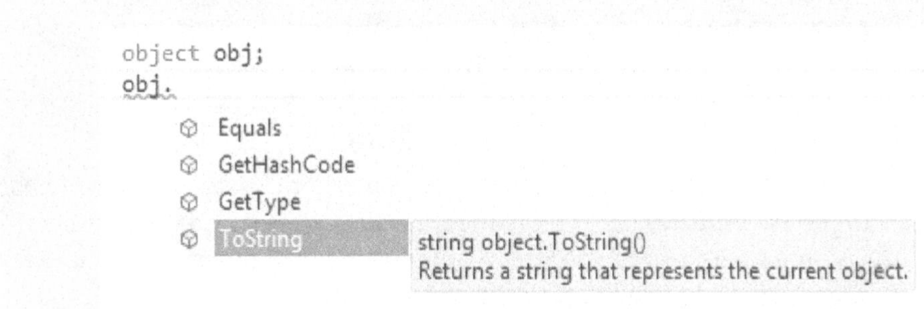

FIGURE 11-2 Methods inherited from an object

11

Inheriting from Other .NET FCL Classes

You also experienced inheritance when you developed Windows-based programs in Chapters 9 and 10. The Windows forms classes that you created inherited from the `System.Windows.Forms.Form` `class`. Extending that `class` enabled you to build on the functionality that was included as part of that .NET Framework `class`. Adding instantiated objects from classes such as `Button`, `Label`, `TextBox`, and `ListBox` enabled you to add functionality to your program with minimal programming. To inherit from the `System.Windows.Forms.Form` `class`, new entries were added to your `class` definition. Figure 11-3 illustrates what Visual Studio adds when you decide to build a Windows application by choosing the **Windows Forms Application** template from the Project Type menu.

```
public partial class PresentationGUI : Form
{
```

FIGURE 11-3 Derived class

In object-oriented terminology, the class listed after the colon in Figure 11-3 is the **base class**. The class to the left of the colon, PresentationGUI, is called the **derived class**. To inherit from a base class, a colon is used as a separator between the derived class and the base class, as shown in Figure 11-3. PresentationGUI is the user-defined name. The Form class belongs to the System.Windows.Forms namespace. For this example, the user-defined class is inheriting from a predefined .NET class; however, the same concepts apply when a user-defined class is inheriting from another user-defined class. By using the colon, you indicate that the PresentationGUI class derives from the Form class. The keyword partial was added by the code generator. The rest of the class is stored in the PresentationGUI.Designer.cs file.

Creating Base Classes for Inheritance

You can define your own classes from which other classes can inherit characteristics. Example 11-1 creates a class named Person with four data members. This class is used as a base class from which other classes can inherit characteristics. The base class is sometimes called the **super** or **parent** class.

EXAMPLE 11-1

```
public class Person
{
    private string idNumber;
    private string lastName;
    private string firstName;
    private int age;

    public Person( ) // Constructor with zero arguments
    {
    }

    // Constructor with four arguments
    public Person(string id, string lname, string fname, int anAge
```

```
    {
        idNumber = id;
        lastName = lname;
        firstName = fname;
        age = anAge;
    }

    // Constructor with three arguments
    public Person(string id, string lname, string fname)
    {
        idNumber = id;
        lastName = lname;
        firstName = fname;
    }

    // Constructor with one argument
    public Person(string id)
    {
        idNumber = id;
    }
}
```

Only data members and constructor methods are shown for the `Person` `class` in Example 11-1. Several examples that follow will build upon Example 11-1 using the Person base `class`. Notice that the data members are defined with a `private` access modifier and constructors are defined with `public` access modifiers. The following section reviews why these choices were made.

ACCESS MODIFIERS

Access to members that have been defined with the `private` access modifier is restricted to members of the current `class`. The `private` members are not accessible to other classes that derive from this `class` or that instantiate objects of this `class`. Using a `private` access modifier enables the `class` to protect its data and only allow access to the data through its methods or properties. This ensures the data-hiding characteristic of encapsulation.

11

CONSTRUCTORS USE PUBLIC ACCESS

Constructors, named the same name as the `class` name, are defined with `public` access. It is important to note that if you do not use a `public` access modifier with constructors, no objects can be instantiated from the `class`. Constructors differ from other methods in that they cannot have a `return` type. Remember that you have an **overloaded method** when you have more than one method using the same identifier. The requirement for an overloaded method is that each of the methods must have a different number and/or type of parameter from the others. Thus, by definition, when you have two or more constructors for a class, you have overloaded methods.

PROPERTIES OFFER PUBLIC ACCESS TO DATA FIELDS

Before creating a specialized `class` to inherit the characteristics of the `Person` `class`, properties are added to the `Person` `class`. By including properties, there is less need to write accessor (getter) and mutator (setter) methods. The `private` member fields can be accessed through these properties.

NOTE Properties look like data fields but are implemented as methods that can be used to get or set a `private` data field instance.

Example 11-2 shows some of the properties added to the `Person` `class`. Due to space constraints, only two of the four properties are shown. The first enables the data field, `firstName`, to be a read-only property; it does not contain a `set` property. Without defining an additional mutator method, `firstName` can never be changed after it is constructed.

NOTE If you were implementing this solution, you might consider some important design issues. First, one or more of the constructors allows an object to be instantiated without assigning values to `lastName` and `firstName`. But, no property is available to change that value for classes that instantiate objects from it. Thus, you would need to write a mutator (`SetFirstName( )`) method; otherwise, the name could never be added.

In Example 11-2, the `FirstName` property is shown as read-only to reinforce the idea that properties do not have to include both a `get` and a `set`. You should probably define read-only properties only for fields that should not be changed, such as identification numbers.

EXAMPLE 11-2

```
// Read-only property. First name cannot be changed.
public string FirstName
{
        get
        {
                return firstName;
        }
}
```

```
// Property for last name
public string LastName
{
    get
    {
        return lastName;
    }
    set
    {
        lastName = value;
    }
}
```

After you add the LastName property to the class, you can retrieve the current contents of lastName using the LastName identifier. Notice you do not declare value. It can be used, almost like magic, to refer to the value that is sent in through an assignment statement.

NOTE Notice how get, set, and value appear in blue code. When you began reading this book, you were told that keywords would be shown in blue. Visual Studio follows this standard with a few exceptions. One exception is that set, value, and get are displayed, by default, in Visual Studio in blue, but they are not regular keywords. They are contextual keywords, not as powerful as regular keywords. They have a special meaning only when used in a specific context. Because you see them in blue in the IDE, they are shown in blue in this book.

Adding properties to your solutions enables access to the private data using the property identifier, as opposed to writing additional methods.

Overriding Methods

Two additional methods are added to the Person class and are shown in Example 11-3. The first overrides the object ToString( ) method. When you override a method, you replace the method defined at a higher level with a new definition or behavior. Notice that the keyword override is added onto the ToString( ) method heading and virtual is added onto the GetSleepAmt( ) method heading. Placing virtual in the method heading allows the method to be overridden.

EXAMPLE 11-3

```
public override string ToString( ) // Defined in Person
{
     return firstName + " " + lastName;
}

public virtual int GetSleepAmt( )
{
     return 8;
}
```

Overriding a method differs from overloading a method. An overridden method must have exactly the same signature as the method it is overriding. New functionality is normally defined with overridden methods. Overloaded methods must have a different signature than others with the same name. Overloaded methods are usually defined to perform a similar behavior but with different data types.

USING THE OVERRIDE KEYWORD

The **override** keyword allows a method to provide a new implementation of a method inherited from a base `class`. When you `override` a method, the signature of the methods must match. To `override` a base method, the base method must be defined as `virtual`, `abstract`, or `override`. Figure 11-4 shows the signature for the `ToString( )` method that belongs to the `object class`. This is taken from the online documentation in Visual Studio.

```
public virtual string ToString()
```

FIGURE 11-4 ToString( ) signature

VIRTUAL METHODS

Because the developers of .NET included the `virtual` modifier as part of the `ToString( )` method signature, the method can be overridden by any C# `class`. Every `class` inherits methods from the `object class`. `ToString( )` does not have to be overridden. It returns a string representing the current object. It is often overridden to offer differing functionality based on which `object` is calling it.

The `ToString( )` method is an example of polymorphism, meaning many forms. You will read more about polymorphism later in this chapter. Think about the meaning of morphing—an object reshapes itself. In that context, the `ToString( )` method can have many different definitions. The definition that is used when you call on the method is determined by which `object` calls it.

In Example 11-3, the `GetSleepAmt( )` method also uses the `virtual` modifier, implying that any `class` that derives from `Person` can `override` that method. To `override` a method, the new method must have exactly the same parameters that are used in the method you plan to `override`.

Creating Derived Classes

Classes that inherit from a base `class` are called derived classes. They are also referred to as subclasses or child classes because they inherit the characteristics of a parent `class`. Any number of classes can inherit from the `Person` `class` that was defined in the previous examples. `Person` is defined using a `public` access modifier.

PROTECTED ACCESS MODIFIERS

Although it is true that derived classes inherit all the characteristics of the base `class`, they do not have direct access to change their `private` members. In addition to `private` and `public` access, C# offers `internal` and `protected` access. Internal members are accessible only within files in the same assembly. Protected members are accessible to any subclass that is derived from them but not to any other classes. So if you want methods in derived classes to have access to change data in the base `class`, define the data members using a `protected` access, instead of a `private` access. This way, the data is still hidden from other classes, but is available for use in subclasses or derived classes.

To demonstrate inheritance, a new file is created in Visual Studio for a `Student` `class`. The `Student` `class` inherits all members of the `Person` `class` and adds two additional data field members. This is an "is a" relationship. `Student` "is a" `Person`. Example 11-4 shows some of the source code from the `Student` `class`.

EXAMPLE 11-4

```
public class Student : Person // Student is derived from Person
{
      private string major;
      private string studentId;

      // Default constructor
      public Student( )
           :base( ) // No arguments sent to base class constructor
      {
      }

      // Constructor sends three arguments to base class constructor
      public Student(string id, string fname, string lname,
                     string maj, string sId)
           :base (id, lname, fname) // Base constructor arguments
      {
           major = maj;
           studentId = sId;
      }

      public override int GetSleepAmt( )
      {
           return 6;
      }
}
```

Example 11-4 includes a number of interesting features. First, the heading for the `class` indicates that `Student` is derived from `Person`. The `class` heading is repeated in Example 11-5.

EXAMPLE 11-5

```
public class Student : Person // Student is derived from Person
```

> **NOTE** Base classes follow the colon. Derived classes appear to the left of the colon.

CALLING THE BASE CONSTRUCTOR

To call the constructor for the base class, an extra entry is added between the constructor heading for the Student subclass and the opening curly brace, as shown in Example 11-6.

EXAMPLE 11-6

```
public Student( )
     :base( ) // No arguments sent to base class constructor
{ ...
```

This calls the default constructor for Person since no arguments appear inside the parentheses. To send data to the base constructor, you must have a matching signature.

To send data to the Person constructor at the same time you instantiate an object of the Student class, the keyword base is followed by arguments that match one of the Person constructors as follows:

```
public Student(string id, string fname, string lname,
               string maj, string sId)
     :base (id, lname, fname) // Base constructor arguments
{ ...
```

The reserved word base, which is shown with a colon and set of parentheses (:base( )) in Example 11-6, is used to indicate which base class constructor should be used when an object of the derived class is created. Notice that it is placed in the class heading before the opening curly brace. The first call to the base constructor uses the default constructor without any arguments for Person.

11

NOTE The call to the constructor, :base( ), could have been omitted on the second line. The default constructor would have been called automatically when an object of the derived class was instantiated. For readability purposes, it is best to include the call to the default base( ) constructor with no arguments.

The second constructor in Example 11-6 indicates that the Person constructor with three string arguments should be used when an object of the Student class is instantiated using that constructor. Notice that to instantiate an object of the

Student class using that constructor, five string arguments are expected. Three of the string arguments are used by the base class. Thus, if an object of the Student class is constructed inside a class that, for example, is taking care of the presentation layer, the code might appear as in Example 11-7.

EXAMPLE 11-7

```
// Student object instantiated in a different class
// such as a PresentationGUI class.
Student aStudent = new
        Student ("123456789", "Maria", "Woo", "CS", "1111");
```

The first three arguments, "123456789", "Maria", and "Woo", are sent to the constructor for the Person class. Remember that this occurred because the Student constructor included as part of its constructor heading the following code:

```
:base (id, lname, fname)// Appears in Student constructor heading
```

The last two arguments ("CS", "1111") are used by the Student class constructor.

The order of the arguments being sent to the base constructor is extremely important. Notice how lname is listed before fname in Example 11-7. The names selected for the identifier do not matter; however, their position does. There must be a constructor accepting three string arguments. The placement of the arguments in the parameter list for the constructor determines the order that must be used by derived classes. Review the constructors for the Person class in Example 11-1. Notice that the three arguments the constructor expects. The constructor expects the first argument to be an identification number, the second argument to be the last name, and the last argument to be the first name.

Objects created using the default constructor do not send any arguments to the Person constructor. Both the Person default constructor and the Student default constructor with no parameters are called when a Student object is instantiated with no arguments, as follows:

```
Student anotherStudent = new Student( );
```

Review Example 11-6. The Person constructor is invoked because :base( ) is included in the heading for the default Student constructor.

USING MEMBERS OF THE BASE CLASS

After objects are instantiated from the Student class, any of the public methods or properties from both the Person class and the Student class can be used with a Student object. You do not have to do anything special to use the public access members of either class. If, in the class that instantiates the anotherStudent object, you want to set a value representing a last name, you can use the property for LastName defined in the Person class as follows:

```
anotherStudent.LastName = "Garcia";
```

CALLING OVERRIDDEN METHODS OF THE BASE CLASS

When you have a method that has the same name in both the base and the derived class, the keyword base can be used in the derived class to refer to methods in the base class that are overridden in the derived class. Example 11-8 shows a method defined in the Student class that calls an overridden method in the Person class. Notice that the method name was qualified with the base keyword. If base had been omitted, the GetSleepAmt( ) method defined in the Student class would have been called.

EXAMPLE 11-8

```
public int CallOverriddenGetSleepAmt( )
{
    return base.GetSleepAmt( ); // Calls method defined in Person
}
```

It is useful to see how the classes are related. Figure 11-5 shows the inheritance relationship between the Person and Student classes. The PresentationGUI class is related through instantiating an object of the Student class. In class diagrams, arrows with empty arrowheads are used to show the inheritance relationship between the Student and Person and PresentationGUI and Form classes.

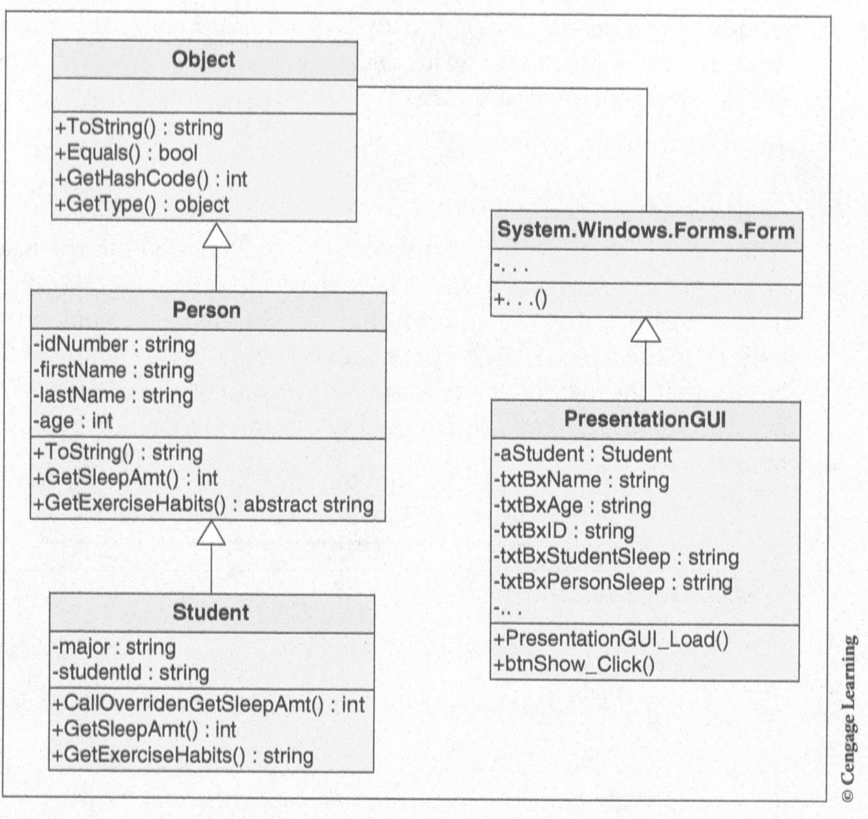

© Cengage Learning

FIGURE 11-5 Inheritance class diagram

NOTE The derived class, Student, has access to the public access members of the base class, Person. But, the base class does not have access to the members of the derived Student class. The base class has no knowledge of any of the derived classes.

As shown in Figure 11-5, Student is derived from Person; PresentationGUI is derived from the Form class in the System.Windows.Forms namespace. Open or unfilled arrows are used in the class diagram to point to the base class. Because Object is the base class of all classes, every class inherits the four methods shown previously in Figure 11-2. A complete solution with `Person`, `Student`, and the `PresentationGUI` classes all stored in a single project is available in the `PresentationGUIWithOneProject_NoDLLs_FirstExample` folder, which is part of the solutions downloaded for this chapter.

Making Stand-Alone Components

The two classes, `Student` and `Person`, can be used with a third `class` that includes a `Main( )` method as was done with the solution appearing in the `PresentationGUIWithOneProject_NoDLLs_FirstExample` folder. The project is compiled just as you have done previously to create a single assembly. By doing this, you associate the `Student` and `Person` with that one assembly.

NOTE **Assemblies** are the units that are configured and deployed in .NET.

The bytecode of an assembly can be reused in other applications, but changes to the `PresentationGUI` require the `Student` and `Person` code be recompiled. Additional applications reusing `Person` and `Student` must include source code for `Person` and `Student` inside the application as part of the project. Figure 11-1, on the other hand, introduced another approach to enabling component-based development. Each of the classes can be compiled and then stored as a dynamic link library (DLL) file, and any number of applications can then reference the classes. That is the beauty of component-based development and object-oriented programming.

DYNAMIC LINK LIBRARY—DLL (OPTIONAL)

Inheritance does not require the use of DLL components. You can create projects similarly to what you have done with all exercises written thus far. This is illustrated later in this chapter. C# and Visual Studio offer the option of creating library components that can be compiled into a dynamic link library (.dll) file instead of into the .exe file type that you have been creating. After you have a .dll, any application that will use that component simply adds a reference to the DLL and that referenced file with the .dll extension becomes part of the application's private assembly. Visual Studio creates the DLL for you. Once the file is stored as a .dll file, it is no longer readable or editable. You can use it in additional applications but you cannot directly modify the .dll file.

When you first start a new solution or a new project, one of the options is to create a `class` library using the **Class Library** template, as shown in Figure 11-6.

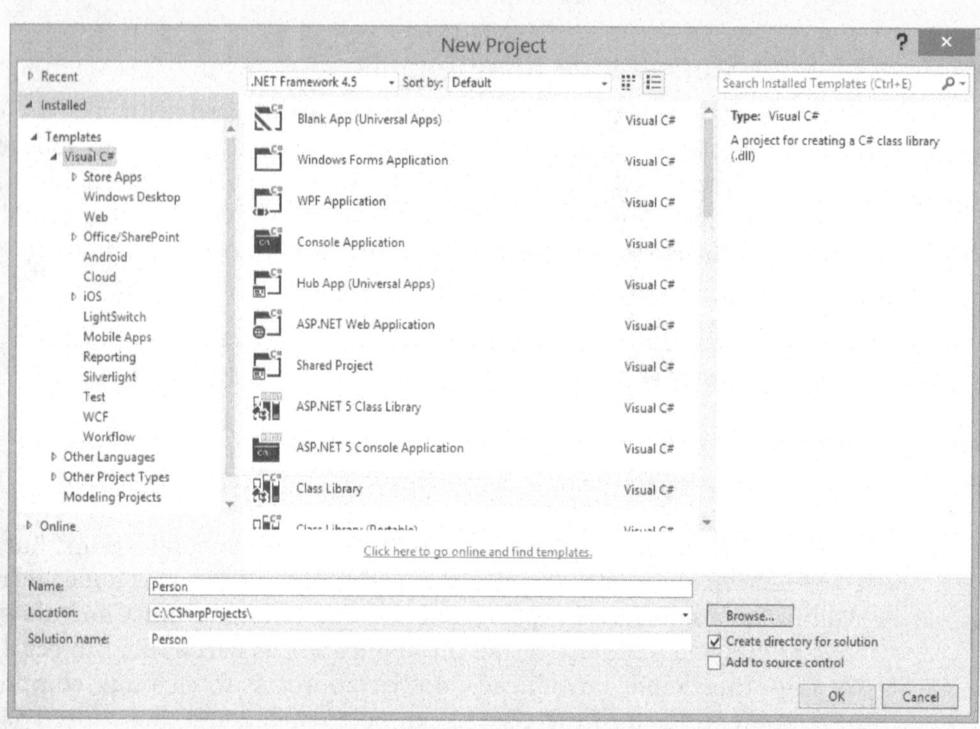

FIGURE 11-6 Creating a DLL component

To illustrate creating and using DLLs, the `Person` `class` is first created. This will enable the `Student` `class` to extend or be derived from it. Creating `Person` first also enables you to use IntelliSense in Visual Studio. After selecting the **Class Library** template option and naming the file, you create the `class` in the same way you have created other files that produce an .exe extension when compiled. Example 11-9 lists the statements in the `Person` `class`.

To illustrate creating stand-alone components, a separate project was created for the `Person` `class` and the `Student` `class` illustrated in Example 11-10. The source code for these projects is stored in `LibraryFiles` folder, which is part of the solutions downloaded for this chapter.

EXAMPLE 11-9

```
// Person.cs
using System;

namespace PersonNamespace
{
     public class Person
     {
          private string idNumber;
          private string lastName;
          private string firstName;
          private int age;

          // Constructor with zero arguments
          public Person( )
          {
          }

          // Constructor with four arguments
          public Person(string id, string lname, string fname, int anAge)
          {
               idNumber = id;
               lastName = lname;
               firstName = fname;
               age = anAge;
          }

          // Constructor with three arguments
          public Person(string id, string lname, string fname)
          {
               idNumber = id;
               lastName = lname;
               firstName = fname;
          }

          // Constructor with one argument
          public Person(string id)
          {
               idNumber = id;
          }

          // Read-only property. ID cannot be changed.
          public string IdNumber
          {
               get
               {
                    return idNumber;
               }
          }
```

```
            // Property for last name
            public string LastName
            {
                get
                {
                    return lastName;
                }
                set
                {
                    lastName = value;
                }
            }

            // Read-only property. First name cannot be changed.
            public string FirstName
            {
                get
                {
                    return firstName;
                }
            }

            public int Age
            {
                get
                {
                    return age;
                }
                set
                {
                    age = value;
                }
            }

            // Overrides ToString( ) method from the Object class
            public override string ToString( )
            {
                return firstName + " " + lastName;
            }

            // Virtual method can be overridden by classes that
            // derive from the Person class.
            public virtual int GetSleepAmt( )
            {
                return 8;
            }
        }
}
```

NOTE By default, Visual Studio assigns the namespace name the same name as the project name (Person). You should change the namespace name; otherwise, when you start adding a reference to a created DLL, it can become quite confusing.

The namespace name selected for this example for the Person class is PersonNamespace. To change the name, just highlight the old namespace name with your mouse and type a new name. No other changes, related to the namespace, need to be made.

BUILD INSTEAD OF RUN THE PROJECT (For Dynamic Link Library files)

When you create a class library file, no executable file is created. You cannot run the project. Instead you build a .dll file. Recall the Person class does not have a Main( ) method. After you finish typing the class, you do not run the application. If you press **F5** or **Ctrl+F5**, an error message is generated similar to that shown in Figure 11-7.

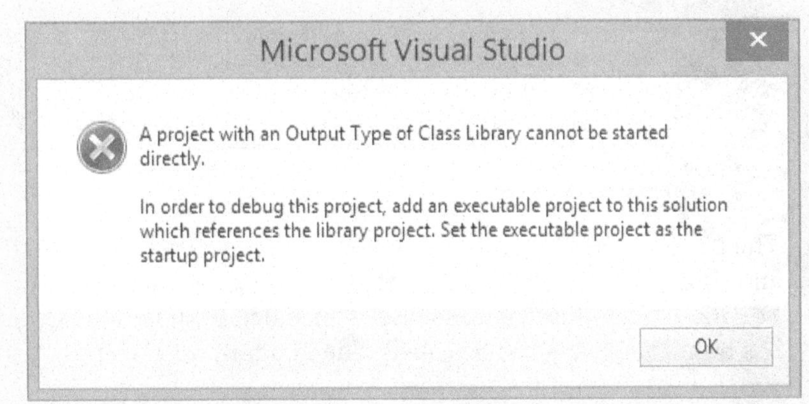

FIGURE 11-7 Attempting to run a class library file

To compile and create the DLL, use one of the Build Solution options under the **Build** menu bar. You can select **Build, Build Solution**, or select **Build** followed by the project name. After you save your work, close the project. A completely new project should be created for the Student class. You will create a class library for the Student class just as you did for the Person class by using the **Class Library** template from the Visual Studio Start page.

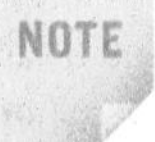

You learned in Chapter 1 that .NET supports having an application include code from multiple .NET languages. This is possible because all .NET-supported and .NET-managed languages use the same common language runtime (CLR) and the same Framework class library (FCL). The `Person class` could be written in C#. The `Student class` could be written in C++. A graphical user interface presentation `class` instantiating the `Student class` that is deriving from the `Person class` could be written in Visual Basic.

The program statements that constitute the `Student class` are shown in Example 11-10. Note that a new `using` statement is added (`using PersonNamespace;`). This is typed manually and matches the name of the `namespace` in the `Person class`. Adding references to other classes is discussed in the following section.

Also, notice that the identifier for the `namespace` in the `Student class` is `StudentNamespace`. This identifier is different from the `namespace` identifier in the `Person class` because two separate projects are developed to demonstrate use of components.

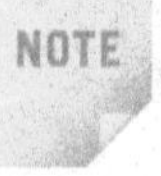

The only requirement for applications with multiple languages is that within the project the source code must use only one language. Thus, if you had a solution file that had three projects, each project could be written in a different language.

The `Student class` includes two additional data fields, properties for those fields, and a `GetSleepAmt()` method that overrides the `GetSleepAmt()` method of the `Person class`. A second method is included to illustrate how a base method that has been overridden can be called. The `Student class` appears in Example 11-10.

EXAMPLE 11-10

```
// Student.cs
using System;
using PersonNamespace; // Added to avoid using fully qualified names

namespace StudentNamespace
{
    public class Student : Person
    {
        private string major;
        private string studentId;
```

```
        // Default constructor
        public Student( )
            : base ( ) // No arguments sent to base constructor
        {
        }

        // Constructor sends arguments to base class constructor
        public Student(string id, string fname, string lname,
                       string maj, string sId)
            : base(id, lname, fname)// Base constructor arguments
        {
            major = maj;
            studentId = sId;
        }

        // Read-only Property for studentID
        public string StudentId
        {
             get
             {
                  return studentId;
             }
        }

       // Property for major data field
        public string Major
        {
             get
             {
                  return major;
             }
             set
             {
                  major = value;
             }
        }

        // Overrides GetSleepAmt( ) method of the Person class
        public override int GetSleepAmt( )
        {
             return 6;
        }

        // Using the base keyword, calls the overridden
        // GetSleepAmt( ) method of the Person class
        public int CallOverriddenGetSleepAmt( )
        {
             return base.GetSleepAmt( );
        }
    }
}
```

11

Since the identification numbers (`IdNumber` in `Person` and `StudentId` in `Student`) have read-only properties, mutator methods need to be defined if you want to enable their values to be changed.

ADDING A REFERENCE TO THE BASE CLASS

Because you are deriving from the `Person` base `class`, one of the first things you should do in the `Student` `class` is add a reference to Person.dll. By doing this first, you gain access to the members of the `Person` `class` inside this newly created `Student` `class`. This can be done several ways in Visual Studio. One option is to use the **Solution Explorer** window. After selecting the project name, right-click it and select **Add Reference**, as shown in Figure 11-8.

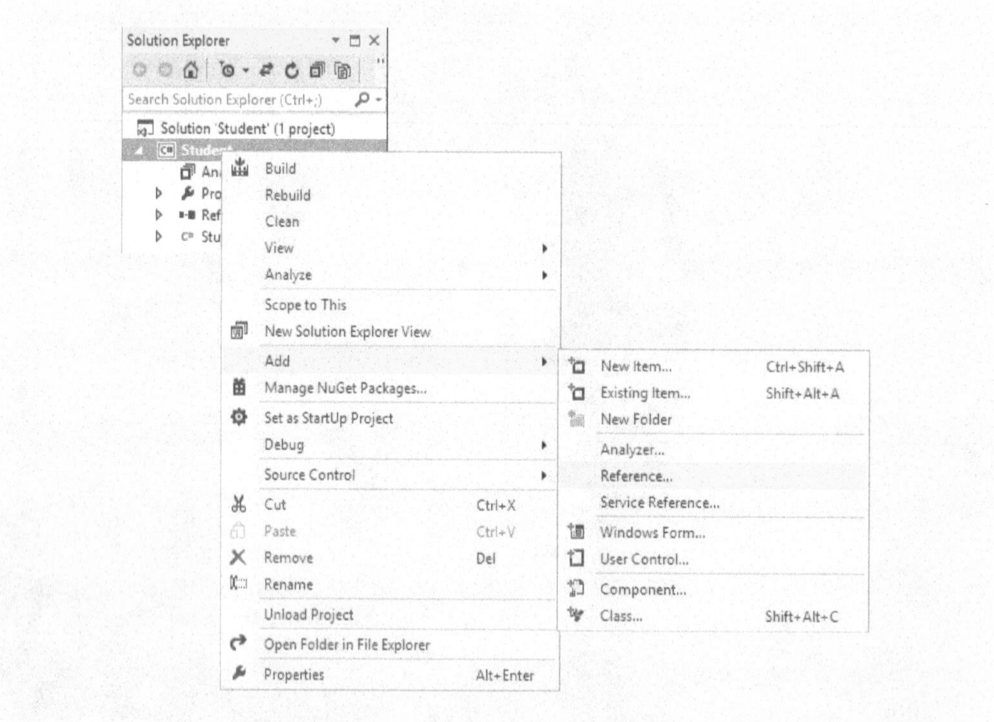

FIGURE 11-8 Adding a reference to a DLL

The **Add Reference** option shown in Figure 11-8 can also be retrieved by right-clicking on the **References** node in the **Solution Explorer** window. A window is displayed similar to that shown in Figure 11-9 that enables you to select one of the .NET predefined components, or you can use the **Browse** tab to locate Person.dll.

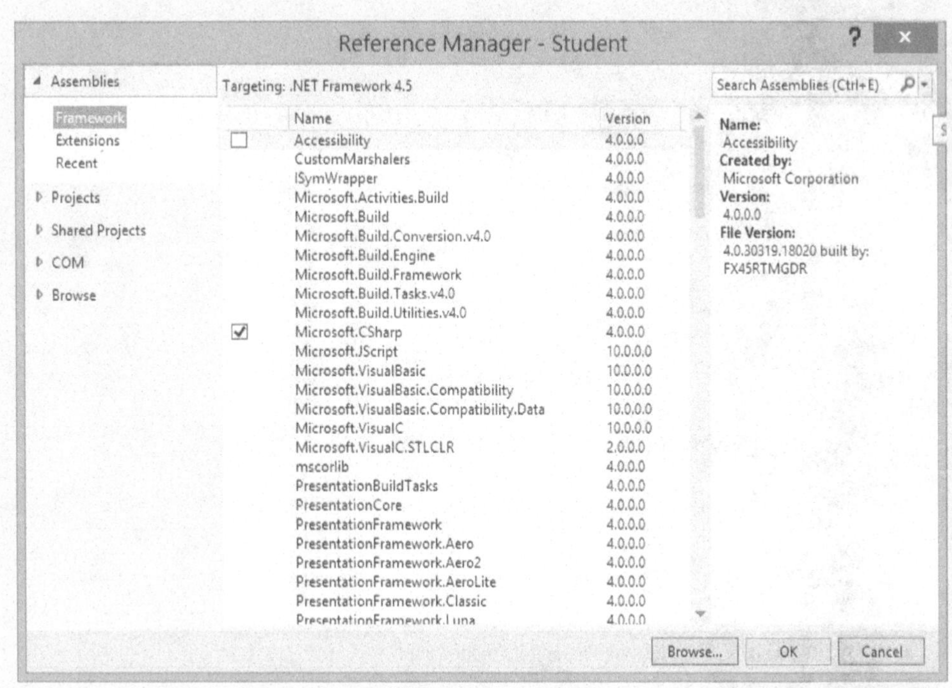

FIGURE 11-9 Add Reference dialog box

After you select the **Browse** button, navigate to the location where the project is located. The DLL is stored in the Debug directory under the bin folder wherever you created your project. For this example, the `Person` project was created in the C:\CSharpProjects\LibraryFiles folder. Thus, it was necessary to navigate into that directory to locate Person.dll, as shown in Figure 11-10.

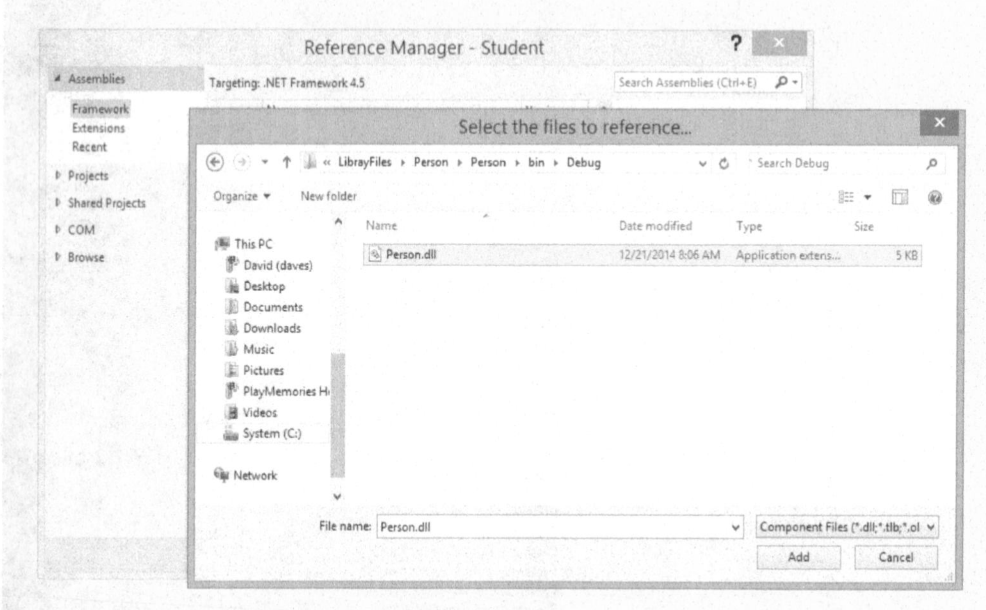

FIGURE 11-10 Locating the Person.dll component

After the reference is made, you can derive new classes from the `class` defined in the component.

ADDING A USING STATEMENT

In the `Student` `class`, if you simply type:

```
public class Student : Person
```

you will receive an error message, as shown in Figure 11-11.

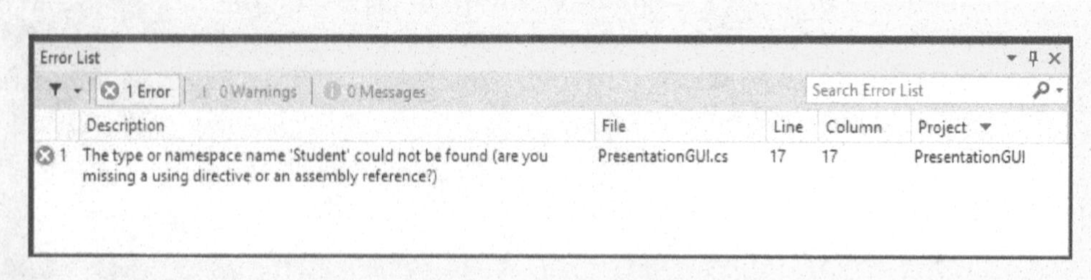

FIGURE 11-11 Namespace reference error

Just adding the reference is not enough—you need to accomplish one more step. You have to qualify `Person` by adding the `namespace` and a dot before the `class` name, as shown in Example 11-11.

EXAMPLE 11-11

```
public class Student : PersonNamespace.Person
```

An even better option is simply to add a `using` directive at the top of the source code file. The `using` statement should indicate the `namespace` identifier for the `Person` `class`. In the `Person` `class`, the name typed for this example was `PersonNamespace`; thus, by adding the `using` statement, you can avoid having to qualify all references to the `Person` `class`. Example 11-12 includes the `using` directive for `PersonNamespace`.

EXAMPLE 11-12

```
using PersonNamespace; // Use whatever name you typed for the
                       // namespace for Person.
```

After adding the `using` statement, your `class` header can now read:

```
public class Student : Person // No need to fully qualify now.
```

After typing your program statements, build the DLL from the **Build** option under the **Build** menu bar. Save your work and close the project.

Creating a Client Application to Use the DLL

You now have two components that can be reused with many different applications. All that is necessary is to add a reference to the components in your program and include a `using` statement with the appropriate `namespace`. To illustrate how a client program could use the `Student` component, a Windows application is developed to instantiate an `object` of the `Student` `class`.

Using Visual Studio, a new solution was created by selecting the **Windows Forms Application** template as the project type. The `solution` is named `PresentationGUI`. To illustrate using these stand-alone components, a new project was created. This project is stored in a separate folder, `PresentationGUIwithDLLs`. Like the solutions presented earlier, this folder is one of the solutions downloaded for this chapter.

ADDING A REFERENCE TO THE DLL

A reference must be added for both the `Person` and `Student` classes. Review Figures 11-8 through 11-10 if you need help adding the references. Both should be referenced in the `PresentationGUI` project, as shown in Figure 11-12.

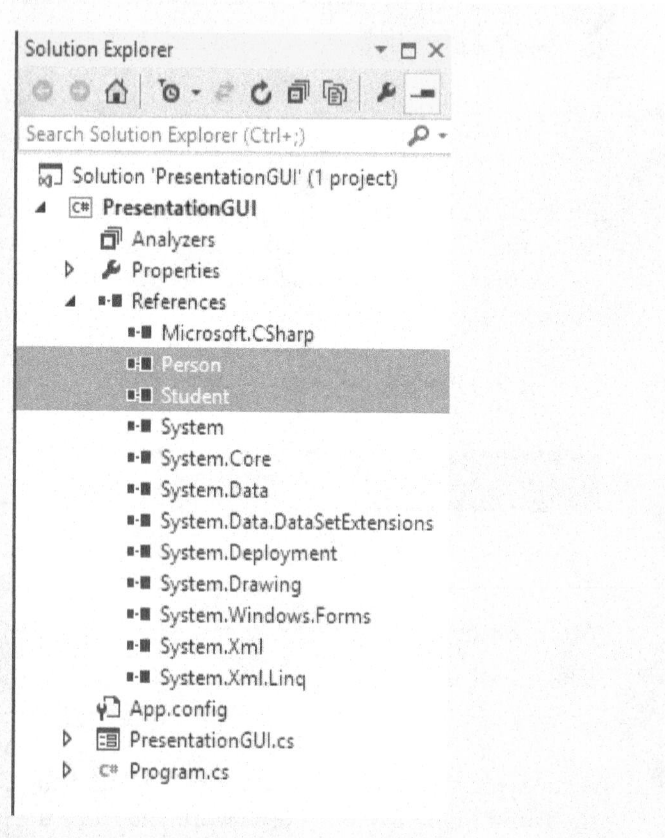

FIGURE 11-12 DLLs referenced in the PresentationGUI class

ADDING A USING STATEMENT FOR THE NAMESPACE

To avoid typing the fully qualified name, add a `using` directive for the `Student` `namespace`. In the previous example, the `namespace` used for the `Student` project was `StudentNamespace`. Thus, Example 11-13 shows how to add a `using` directive for the `StudentNamespace`.

EXAMPLE 11-13

```
using StudentNamespace;
```

Because the `Student` `class` included a `using` statement for `PersonNamespace` and no `Person` `object` is being instantiated, it is not necessary to add a `using` statement for `PersonNamespace` here in the `PresentationGUI` `class`. No syntax error would be generated, however, if `using PersonNamespace;` is also added.

DECLARING AN OBJECT OF THE COMPONENT TYPE

You must declare a `Student` `object`. This is done inside the `PresentationGUI` `class` as a `private` data member, as shown in Example 11-14.

EXAMPLE 11-14

```
public partial class PresentationGUI : System.Windows.Forms.Form
{
     private Student aStudent;
```

The statement in Example 11-14 is declaring one `Student` `object`. Of course, you could define a collection of `Student` `objects` using an array.

INSTANTIATING THE OBJECT

To create or instantiate an actual `object` of the `Student` `class`, one of the `Student` constructors must be used. Remember that there are two constructors defined for the `Student` `class`. Thus, one way to instantiate the `class` is to write:

```
aStudent = new Student("123456789", "Maria", "Woo", "CS", "1111");
```

This instantiation is placed in the method that handles the form load event. It could have also been placed in the `InitializeComponent( )` method where the Windows Forms Designer generated code is placed.

11

USING MEMBERS OF THE DERIVED AND BASE CLASSES

A number of control objects are added to the form. `TextBox` objects are dragged to the form for displaying name, age, student ID, the amount of sleep for the student, and the amount of sleep for others. A `Button` `object` is added for populating the `TextBox` objects. Example 11-15 shows the program statements that were typed for the PresentationGUI. Due to space constraints, the code generated by the Windows Forms Designer and the extraneous `using` statements are not included in the listing.

EXAMPLE 11-15

```
using System;
using System.Windows.Forms;
using StudentNamespace;          // Added for Student class

namespace PresentationGUI
{
    public partial class PresentationGUI: Form
    {
        private Student aStudent;

        public PresentationGUI( )
        {
            InitializeComponent( );
        }

        private void PresentationGUI_Load (object sender,
                                           EventArgs e)
        {
            aStudent = new Student("123456789", "Maria",
                                   "Woo", "CS", "1111");
        }

        private void btnShow_Click(object sender, EventArgs e)
        {
            // Uses Age property defined in the Person class
            aStudent.Age = 25;

            // Calls overridden ToString( ) in Person class
            txtBxName.Text = aStudent.ToString( );

            // Calls ToString( ) defined in object class
            txtBxAge.Text = aStudent.Age.ToString( );

            // Uses StudentID property in Student class
            txtBxID.Text = aStudent.StudentId;

            // Calls GetSleepAmt( ) defined in Student class
            txtBxStudentSleep.Text =
                Convert.ToString(aStudent.GetSleepAmt( ));

            // Calls method defined in Student class that
            // has calls to base.GetSleepAmt( ) in Person class
            txtBxPersonSleep.Text = Convert.ToString
                (aStudent.CallOverriddenGetSleepAmt( ));
        }
    }
}
```

Figure 11-13 shows the output generated from running the `PresentationGUI`. It references the two DLL components.

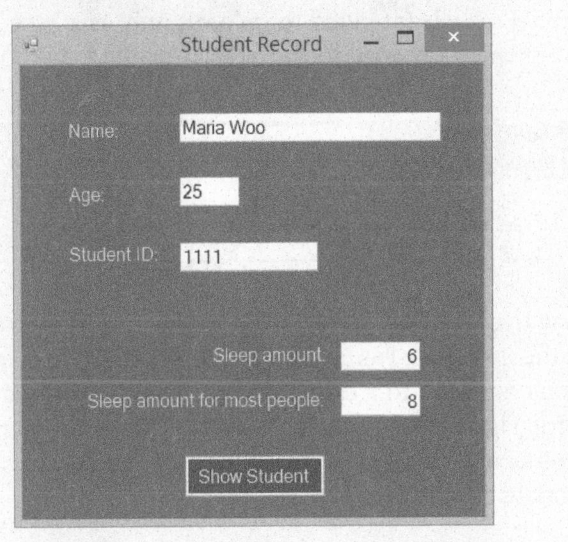

FIGURE 11-13 PresentationGUI output referencing two DLLs

Any number of classes can use the `Student` and `Person` components by instantiating objects of their type. All that is required is that new applications reference the files ending in .dll. A `using` statement can be added for the `namespace` to avoid typing the fully qualified names of the `class` and its members.

Inheritance does not require the use of components. Another option, of course, is to have the actual source code (.cs files) included within the application, as you have been doing with projects you developed in previous chapters. By including the source code files (.cs files), you are able to modify/edit the files. You cannot edit DLLs (.dll files).

11

Abstract Classes

With the preceding examples, you can instantiate objects of the `Person` `class` in the same manner as you construct objects of the `Student` `class`. Most modern languages, including C#, allow you to add an **abstract** modifier to classes that prohibit other classes from instantiating objects of a base `class`. You can still inherit characteristics from this base `class` in subclasses, which enables you to ensure a certain amount of identical functionality from subclasses. This base `class` can have data and method members. To create an `abstract class` in C#, you write

```
[access modifier] abstract class ClassIdentifier // Base class
```

When you use the **abstract modifier** keyword with a class, you mark it so that the class can be used only as the base class from which other classes can be derived. No objects can then be instantiated of the base class type. To indicate that the Person class is intended to be used only as a base class of other classes, you add the abstract keyword to the class heading, as shown in Example 11-16.

EXAMPLE 11-16

```
public abstract class Person
```

Adding the abstract keyword does not keep you from instantiating classes derived from the Person class, such as the Student class. However, after the abstract modifier is added to a class, any attempt to instantiate objects of the class results in an error. Figure 11-14 shows the error "Cannot create an instance of the abstract class or interface PresentationGUI. Person" generated when an attempt was made to instantiate the Person class.

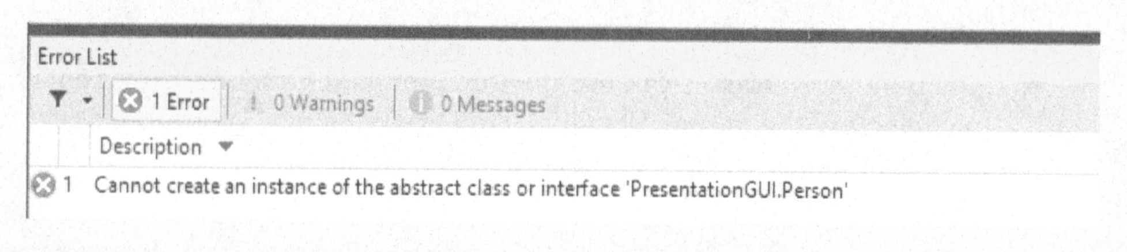

FIGURE 11-14 Error generated for trying to instantiate abstract class

An abstract class may contain one or more abstract methods. Abstract methods are only permitted in abstract classes.

Abstract Methods

An **abstract method** is one that does not include the implementation details for the method. The method has no body. The implementation details of the method are left up to the classes that are derived from the base abstract class. The syntax for creating an abstract method is as follows:

```
[access modifier] abstract returnType
      MethodIdentifier([parameter list]); // No { } included
```

The declaration for an abstract method ends with a semicolon following the signature. No braces ({ }) are used with the method. Example 11-17 illustrates defining Person as an abstract class. An abstract method named GetExerciseHabits( ) was added as the last method in the class. A new solution is created with an abstract class. The solution is stored in the PresentationGUIWithAbstractClassAndInterface folder. This folder is one of the solutions downloaded for this chapter.

EXAMPLE 11-17

```
public abstract class Person
{
    private string idNumber;
    private string lastName;
    private string firstName;
    private int age;

    public Person( )
    {
    }

    public Person(string id, string lname, string fname, int anAge)
    {
        idNumber = id;
        lastName = lname;
        firstName = fname;
        age = anAge;
    }

    public Person(string id, string lname, string fname)
    {
        idNumber = id;
        lastName = lname;
        firstName = fname;
    }

    public Person(string id)
    {
        idNumber = id;
    }

    public string IdNumber
    {
        get
        {
            return idNumber;
        }
    }
```

11

```
        public string LastName
        {
            get
            {
                return lastName;
            }
            set
            {
                lastName = value;
            }
        }

        public string FirstName
        {
            get
            {
                return firstName;
            }
        }

        public int Age
        {
            get
            {
                return age;
            }
            set
            {
                age = value;
            }
        }

        public override string ToString( )
        {
            return firstName + " " + lastName;
        }

        // Virtual method can be overridden
        // by classes that derive from Person
        public virtual int GetSleepAmt( )
        {
            return 8;
        }

        // Classes that derive from Person
        // must provide implementation details
        // (the body for the method)
        public abstract string GetExerciseHabits( );

    }   // End of abstract Person class definition
```

Now any and every `class` that derives from the `Person` `class` must provide the implementation details for the `GetExerciseHabits()` method. That is what adding the `abstract` keyword does. It is like signing a contract. If you derive from an `abstract` base `class`, you sign a contract that details how to implement its `abstract` methods.

You will receive a syntax error if you use the keyword `static` or `virtual` when defining an `abstract` method. There is an implicit assumption that the method will be overridden; thus, the keyword `virtual` is unnecessary in the base `class`.

If the `abstract class` includes more than one `abstract` method, derived classes must provide implementation details for every `abstract` method included in the base `class`. Abstract classes can include regular data field members, regular methods, and `virtual` methods in addition to `abstract` methods. Remember that a `virtual` method tags the method as being capable of being overridden in a derived `class`. This does not mean that all derived classes have to provide new implementation details for those tagged as `virtual`, just that they *can*.

In the derived `class`, all `abstract` methods' headings include the special keyword `override`. Thus, the only change needed for the `Student` `class` is a new method, `GetExerciseHabits()`, which has an `override` keyword added to the method heading. The method body must return a string argument. You can see that new method if you look ahead to Example 11-21, which illustrates the completed `Student` `class`.

All .NET languages only support **single inheritance**, which means that a `class` can extend or derive from at most one `class`. One way languages such as C# and Java work around this is by implementing multiple interfaces, which are the topic for the following section.

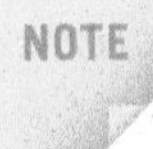

C++ permits multiple inheritances. A `class` can extend from more than one base `class` in C++. This is not possible in C#, Java, or any of the managed .NET languages.

11

Sealed Classes

You learned that the `abstract` keyword enables you to create a class solely for the purpose of inheritance. Abstract classes cannot be instantiated. Objects can only be created using classes derived from the `abstract class`. The purpose of an `abstract class` is to provide a common definition of a base class so that multiple derived classes can share that definition. Sealed classes provide a completely opposite type of restriction. They restrict the inheritance feature of object-oriented programming. When you add the modifier **sealed** to a class, the class cannot be a base class. In order to define a sealed class, add the keyword `sealed` following the access modifier as shown in Example 11-18.

EXAMPLE 11-18

```
public sealed class SealedClassExample
{
    // class members inserted here
}
```

Sealed classes are defined to prevent derivation. The `SealedClassExample` shown in Example 11-18 cannot be inherited. Objects can be instantiated from the class, but subclasses cannot be derived from it. There are a number of .NET classes defined with the `sealed` modifier. The Pen and Brushes classes, for example, are both defined with the `sealed` modifier. The heading for Pen reads

```
public sealed class Pen
```

Objects can be instantiated in the Pen `class`, but no subclasses can be defined.

NOTE If you are working on a large project that has many developers, adding the `sealed` restriction may help keep classes from being used in the wrong way since the functionality cannot be extended.

Sealed Methods

You may also add the keyword `sealed` to class members of nonsealed classes. This is especially helpful when the method has been defined as `virtual` in a base class, indicating that it can be overridden in subclasses. If you do not want subclasses to be able to provide new implementation details, add the keyword `sealed`. Doing so keeps derived classes from being able to override the method.

You should not seal a method unless that method is itself an override of another method in some base class. If it is a new method and you do not want subclasses to override it, do not declare it as virtual in the first place. If however, you have overridden a base class method, the `sealed` keyword provides a way of ensuring that the override supplied to a method is a "final" override. No subclasses can override it again.

Partial Classes

One of the added features of C# is `partial` classes. When you created a Windows application, you may recall that the heading automatically generated by Visual Studio read `partial class Form1`. This was illustrated in Figure 11-3. You also saw the partial keyword listed in Examples 11-14 and 11-15. The definition for the class is split into two files. These two source code files are combined when the application is compiled and run.

When you drag a control onto a Windows form, code is automatically added to initialize the control and set its properties. This code is placed in a somewhat hidden file in a region labeled "Windows Form Designer generated code." A special comment surrounds the code warning the developer to not modify this code. The file is created following a naming convention of "FormName.Designer.cs" or "xxx.Designer.cs." It is stored out of sight and is only visible when you expand the folder or container representing the class file. This is done so that most of the designer-generated code is separated from user code. The intent is to keep the developer from changing the auto-generated code. Although this does somewhat protect the code, the use of partial classes in this instance also shields you from many useful details.

Creating Partial Classes

You can take advantage of this new feature and spread the definition of your classes over multiple files. At compile time, the files are merged together. This might be useful if you were working on a large project and wanted to spread the work among multiple programmers. The requirement for defining a partial class is that all the files must use the `partial` keyword and all of the `partial class` definitions must be defined in the same assembly (.exe or .dll file). Class name and accessibility modifiers, such as `private` or `public`, must also match. Example 11-19 illustrates adding the **partial** keyword to the heading of a `class`, indicating that other parts of the `class` are defined in another file.

EXAMPLE 11-19

```
// class definition split into two or more source files
public partial class ClassIdentifier
```

11

Interfaces

When you use the `abstract` modifier with a `class`, you are indicating that it is intended to be used only as a base `class`. Normally the `class` is incomplete, in that one or more of its methods are declared as `abstract`. No objects can be constructed from an `abstract class`, but it can still perform a number of functions. In addition to having data members, an `abstract class` can have methods that have full implementation details (bodies).

You can think of an **interface** as a `class` that is totally `abstract`. Interfaces contain no implementation details for any of their members; all their members are considered `abstract`. Even more of a contract is required to use an `interface` than was required for the abstract method. By implementing the interface, the class agrees to define details for all of the interface's methods.

One advantage of using interfaces is the fact that a class can implement any number of interfaces. But, you can only inherit from one class, abstract, or nonabstract. An interface may even implement multiple interfaces itself. The syntax for defining an interface is as follows:

```
[modifier] interface InterfaceIdentifier
{
        // Members - no access modifiers are used.
}
```

The members of an interface can be methods, properties, or events. No implementation details are provided by the interface for any of its members. The definition of the interface simply specifies a signature for the members that must be supplied by classes implementing it. Interfaces are usually named using an uppercase I as the first character, such as IComparable, ISearchable, or IPayable.

Interfaces are useful for forcing functionality in classes that implement them. Interfaces are especially good in multiprogrammer environments. They help to guarantee that classes conform to certain set standards and contain required methods. If a class implements the interface, it must provide the details for all of the interface's members. Whereas abstract classes are used with classes that are closely related, interfaces are often best suited for providing some common functionality to unrelated classes. Because the abstract class is used as the base class, the "is a" relationship must exist. Any class derived from that base abstract class "is a" subtype of the abstract class.

Defining an Interface

Interfaces can be defined as members of a namespace or class or by compiling to a DLL. You do this in much the same way that you created the dynamic link library components for Person and Student.

An easy approach is to put the interface in a separate project. In Visual Studio, use the **Class Library** template to start, and after you go into the Code Editor, replace the class definition with your interface definition.

NOTE You could also define the interface inside the file that implements it, like the example first presented with the PresentationGUI project. However, you lose out on the advantages of component-based development. To do this, right-click the project, select **Add**, then **New Item** from the submenu from the **Solution Explorer** window, and then use the **Interface** template.

Figure 11-15 shows an `interface` that is implemented by the `Student class`. It contains three `abstract` methods. Unlike an `abstract class`, it is not necessary to use the `abstract` keyword because all methods are `abstract`. The `ITraveler interface` in Figure 11-15 includes three member methods. Notice that the identifier for the `namespace` is different from the `interface` name.

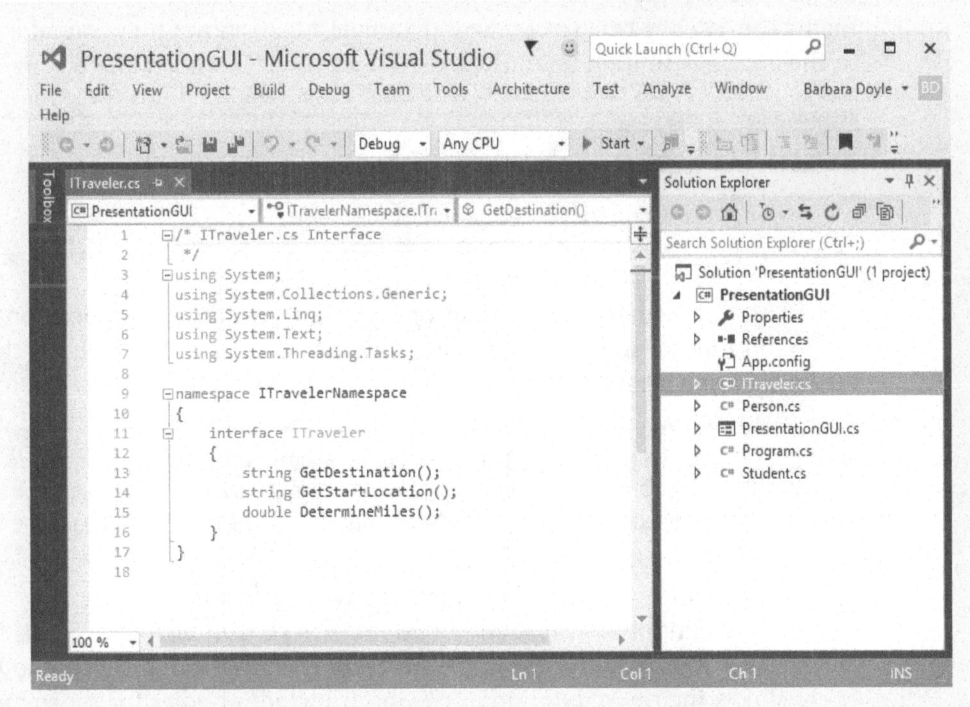

FIGURE 11-15 ITraveler interface

Be sure to change the name of the `namespace` in the `interface` file also. Otherwise, you experience problems when you try to reference the file and add your `using` statement.

After you type the statements, build the interface DLL by using a **Build Solution** option from the **Build** menu bar. You can select **Build, Build Solution**, or **Build** followed by the name of the project. Close the project and get ready to use the `interface`.

Implementing the Interface

If you stored the `interface` as a separate project and created the DLL, to use the `interface`, you follow the same steps as with the `Person` and `Student` DLLs. A separate Interface project was stored in the LibraryFiles folder for this chapter. From the Solution Explorer window, add a reference to the file ending in .dll. Type a `using` statement identifying the `namespace` for the `interface`.

The heading for the class definition can specify not only a base class following the colon but also one or more interfaces as follows:

```
[modifier] class ClassIdentifier : identifier [, identifier]
```

To indicate that the Student class derives from the base class Person and implements the ITraveler interface, Example 11-20 shows that you add ITraveler to the class definition line.

EXAMPLE 11-20

```
public class Student : Person, ITraveler // Base class comes first.
```

If a class implements more than one interface, they all appear on the class definition line separated by commas. The base class is listed first if the class is inheriting from a base class.

NOTE If the interface is part of a project, the namespace for the interface should be the same name as other classes' namespaces in the project. Otherwise, a using statement is needed in classes that implements the interface to reference the interface.

Reviewing Figure 11-15, you see that ITraveler has three abstract methods as part of its definition. Because the Student class is implementing the ITraveler interface, it must define the implementation details for all three methods. Example 11-21 shows the revised Student class. It includes bodies for those methods and the GetExerciseHabits( ) method, which was defined as an abstract method in the Person class. This satisfies the implementation requirements for the methods.

EXAMPLE 11-21

```
public class Student : Person, ITraveler
{
     private string major;
     private string studentId;

     public Student( )
          : base( )
     {
     }

     // Constructor which sends 3 arguments to base class
     public Student(string id, string fname, string lname,
                    string maj, string sId)
          : base(id, lname, fname)
```

```
{
     major = maj;
     studentId = sId;
}

// Read only Property for studentID
public string StudentId
{
     get
     {
          return studentId;
     }
}

// Property for major data field
public string Major
{
     get
     {
          return major;
     }
     set
     {
          major = value;
     }
}

// Overrides GetSleepAmt( )
// method of the Person class
public override int GetSleepAmt( )
{
     return 6;
}

// Using the base keyword, calls the overridden
// GetSleepAmt( ) method of the Person class
public int CallOverriddenGetSleepAmt( )
{
     return base.GetSleepAmt( );
}

// Abstract method in Person
public override string GetExerciseHabits( )
{
     return "Exercises daily";
}

// Abstract method in Itraveler Interface
public string GetDestination( )
{
     return "Home";
}
```

```
        // Abstract method in Itraveler Interface
        public string GetStartLocation( )
        {
             return "School";
        }

        // Abstract method in Itraveler Interface
        public double DetermineMiles( )
        {
             return 75.0;
        }
}
```

No other changes need to be made to the `Student` `class`. Of course, the body of these methods could be as sophisticated as is needed to support the business function. That is all there is to implementing an `interface`. No special changes have to occur to the `Person` or `PresentationGUI` component. They are separate, standalone components. For testing purposes, the `PresentationGUI` `class` in the `PresentationGUIAbtractClassAndInterface` folder is modified to include calls to the three methods defined in the `interface`. Figure 11-16 shows the output generated when the new methods are called. They return the travel details.

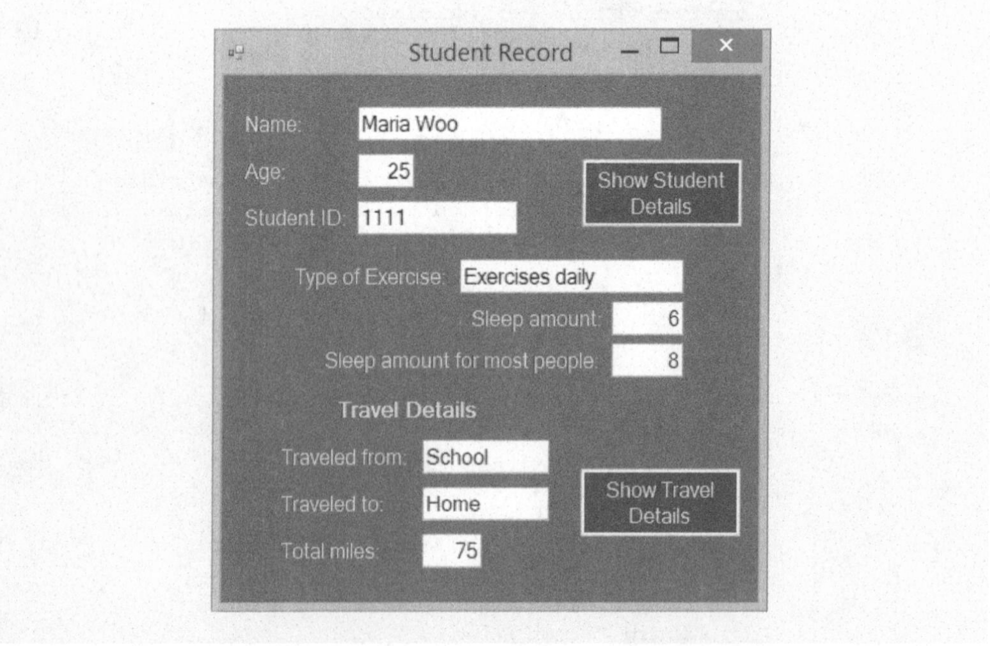

FIGURE 11-16 PresentationGUI output using interface methods

Additional `Label` and `TextBox` objects are added to the `PresentationGUI` `class`. The visibility property for each of these objects is initially set to `false`. When the Show Travel Details button is clicked, the text boxes are populated with data returned from the new `interface` methods that were implemented in the `Student` `class`. Then, the `Visible` property for each of these new controls is set to `true`. The event-handler method for the button click event, where this code is placed, is shown in Example 11-22 along with the other event-handler methods in the `PresentationGUI` `class`. Due to space constraints, the rest of the `partial` `PresentationGUI` `class`, stored in the `PresentationGUI.Designer.cs` file, is not shown.

EXAMPLE 11-22

```
public partial class PresentationGUI : Form
{
     private Student aStudent;

     public PresentationGUI( )
     {
          InitializeComponent( );
     }

     private void btnShow_Click(object sender, EventArgs e)
     {
          aStudent.Age = 25;

          // Calls overridden ToString( ) in Person
          // Returns the first name, a space, and
          // the last name
          txtBxName.Text = aStudent.ToString( );

          // Calls ToString( ) from Object
          // Returns a number representing age
          // in string format
          txtBxAge.Text = aStudent.Age.ToString( );
          txtBxID.Text = aStudent.StudentId;
          txtBxStudentSleep.Text =
          Convert.ToString(aStudent.GetSleepAmt( ));
          txtBxPersonSleep.Text =
                    Convert.ToString
                       (aStudent.CallOverriddenGetSleepAmt( ));

          // GetExerciseHabits( ) method defined as
          // abstract method in Person
          txtBxExercise.Text =
                    aStudent.GetExerciseHabits( );
          btnTravel.Visible = true;
     }
```

11

```
    private void PresentationGUI_Load(object sender, EventArgs e)
    {
        aStudent = new
            Student("123456789", "Maria", "Woo", "CS", "1111");
    }
    private void btnTravel_Click(object sender, EventArgs e)
    {
        // GetStartLocation( ), GetDestination( ) and
        // DetermineMiles( ) methods all defined as
        // abstract methods in ITraveler interface
        txtBxFrom.Text =
            aStudent.GetStartLocation( );
        txtBxTo.Text =
            aStudent.GetDestination( );
        txtBxMiles.Text =
            aStudent.DetermineMiles( ).ToString( );
        txtBxFrom.Visible = true;
        txtBxTo.Visible = true;
        txtBxMiles.Visible = true;
        lblHeading.Visible = true;
        lblMiles.Visible = true;
        lblFrom.Visible = true;
        lblTo.Visible = true;
    }
}
```

`GetStartLocation()`, `GetDestination()`, and `DetermineMiles()` are the members of the `ITraveler` `interface`. When the `Student` `class` implements this `interface`, the body of these methods has to be written. Notice that a call to these methods resembles any other call. The `class` instantiating objects of the `Student` `class` do not make a distinction between those methods, methods inherited from another `class`, or methods that are originally defined in the `Student` `class`.

.NET Framework Interfaces

Interfaces play an important role in the .NET Framework. `Collection` classes such as the `Array` `class`, `ArrayList` `class`, `Hashtable` `class`, `Stack` `class`, and `Queue` `class` implement a number of interfaces. .NET includes these classes to enable you to manage collections of data. Designing the classes to implement interfaces provides common functionality among them. The .NET `Array` `class`, for example, is an `abstract` `class`, used as a base `class` for language implementations that support arrays. If you explore the .NET documentation, you find that the signature for the `Array` `class` shows that it implements several interfaces (`ICloneable`, `IList`, `ICollection`, and `IEnumerable`).

C# and other .NET languages must extend this base `Array` `class` to add constructs for individual arrays in their languages. This includes a requirement for defining the implementation details for the interface methods. For a developer, such as you, all this is happening behind the scenes. But, this base class, Array, provides methods for manipulating arrays, such as iterating through the elements, searching, adding elements to the array, copying, cloning, clearing, removing elements from the array, reversing elements, and sorting. If you examine this functionality closely, you find that much of it is in place because of the contracts the interfaces are enforcing. The cloning functionality is contracted as part of implementing ICloneable. The IList interface requires implementation details for Add( ), Clear( ), Remove( ), Insert( ), plus other methods. The ICollection interface has a method for CopyTo( ). The IEnumerable interface has a method titled GetEnumerator( ) that returns an enumerator that can iterate through a collection.

The signatures for some of the collection classes are shown in Example 11-23.

EXAMPLE 11-23

```
public abstract class Array : ICloneable, IList, ICollection,
         IEnumerable
public class ArrayList : IList, ICollection, IEnumerable,
         ICloneable
public class Queue : ICollection, IEnumerable, ICloneable
public class Stack : ICollection, IEnumerable, ICloneable
public class Hashtable : IDictionary, ICollection, IEnumerable,
         ISerializable, IDeserializationCallback, ICloneable
```

Notice that each of the collection classes implements ICloneable. The Array class is the only one in the collection that is an abstract class. The Hashtable class is the only one that implements the IDeserializationCallback interface. You are encouraged to explore the documentation for these classes and interfaces. By doing so, you can see some of the real power of object-oriented development. As you explore the documentation, you will notice that it includes not only the members that must be implemented but it also gives a description of the class and shows examples in multiple languages.

The documentation provides links to the classes so that you can drill down and uncover additional information.

One of the most powerful features of the .NET Framework class library and Visual Studio is the extensive library of documentation available. In addition to syntax grammar, it includes tutorials and examples of feature use.

The Hashtable class implements Add( ) by adding an element with the specified key and value pair into a collection. The ArrayList class implements Add( ) by adding an object to the end of a collection. Can Add( ) mean something different based on what type of object it is being used with? That is the idea behind polymorphism—the topic of the following section.

Polymorphism

Polymorphism is the ability for classes to provide different implementations of methods that are called by the same name. You already understand and use polymorphism in your everyday life when you determine what situation or object is being used with a verb to determine the verb's true behavior. For example, by itself the meaning of the verb "drive" is vague. Driving a car differs from driving a nail, driving a boat, or driving someone crazy. Only when you put "drive" in context do you know what behavior or activity is associated with it.

You have also experienced the use of polymorphism in your programs a number of times. One quick example is with the ToString( ) method. Remember that this method is defined as one of the four methods of the Object class. This means that for every class in .NET, both user-defined and Framework classes have a ToString( ) method. Based on what kind of object calls the ToString( ) method, it performs a different function. The end result is to convert some object in to its string representation. Converting an integer into a string is a different activity than converting a single character into a string. You can think of it as having a number of different implementations, and the implementation is determined by the type of object that calls it. Example 11-24 shows two calls to the ToString( ) method, which were included in the PresentationGUI class.

EXAMPLE 11-24

```
// Calls overridden ToString( ) defined in Person class
// Returns the first name, a space, and the last name
txtBxName.Text = aStudent.ToString( );

// Calls ToString( ) defined in object class
// Returns a number representing age in string format
txtBxAge.Text = aStudent.Age.ToString( );
```

As is noted in the comment, the first call to the ToString( ) method calls the method defined in the Person class. Remember that the method overrides the object's ToString( ). This implementation of ToString( ) (included in Example 11-9) was to concatenate the first and last name with a space between them. The CLR recognized that it should use this method because it was called with a `Student` `object`. `Student` did not contain an implementation of the `ToString()` method; thus, the CLR looked next to the `class` from which it had been derived, the `Person` `class`.

The second call to the `ToString()` method does not use the `Person` class's implementation. Notice that this call is made with an `int` `object`. The `Age` property returns an `int`. Thus, based on the `object` making the call, the `ToString()` method from the `Object` `class` is called.

Polymorphism allows a method of a `class` to be called without regard to what specific implementation it provides. Thus, in .NET, polymorphism is implemented through interfaces, inheritance, and the use of `abstract` classes.

Polymorphic Programming in .NET

As you saw, multiple classes can implement the same `interface` or implement more than one `interface`. The `interface` describes the methods and the types of parameters each method member needs to receive and return, but it leaves the actual details of the body of the method up to the classes that implement the `interface`. Every `class` that implements the `interface` may have a completely different behavior. The method name is the same in all the classes implementing the `interface`, but the functionality can be much different from one `class` to another.

The black box concept of object-oriented development comes into play here. You do not have to know how the method goes about doing its work. All you need to know is that the method has accomplished its work. This may be to return a value or just an indication that the method is complete.

Through inheritance, polymorphism is made possible by allowing classes to override base `class` members. This makes **dynamic binding** possible. The CLR determines which method to call at run time based on which `object` calls the method. Marking the method with the `virtual` keyword enables derived classes to write their own functionality for the method.

Remember that a `class` does not have to `override` a `virtual` method. The `class` can choose to use the base class's implementation.

Because an `abstract` `class` cannot be instantiated, the features of both interfaces and inheritance come into play with polymorphic programming. Through the use of `abstract` classes, classes that derive from them are forced to include implementation details for any abstract method. Unlike interfaces, which simply provide the heading for the methods that have to be implemented, some or all of the members of an abstract class can be implemented. Abstract classes can also include data members, properties, events, and methods. The methods can be marked as virtual or as abstract or be completely implemented. The determination of which method to use is based on the object that makes the call.

Inheritance is very useful for adding to the functionality of an existing class without having to reinvent the wheel with each new application. With .NET, you have to remember that you only have single inheritance. A class can implement multiple interfaces, but it must provide the implementation details for all of the interface's methods. Component programming is probably the way of the future for development. It is a powerful technique that enables you to implement the multiple interfaces of an object easily. The common goal of all these advanced object-oriented features is to enable polymorphic programming.

Another programming technique, generics, reduces duplication of code by writing common functions or types that differ only in the set of types on which they operate. Generics enables algorithms to be written where a number of details, including the data type can be "specified-later." Generics is the topic of the following section.

Generics

Generics reduces the need to rewrite algorithms for each data type. You can create generic classes, delegates, interfaces, and methods. With each of these, you identify where data will change in the code segment by putting a placeholder in the code for the type parameters. A generic class might use placeholder(s) for the data type of its instance data members or placeholders for return types of one or more of its methods. After the generic class is defined, it could be instantiated using several different types of data.

A generic method might use a generic type for one of its formal parameters and/or use a generic type as the type of its return value. Generic methods can be defined both as part of generic and other classes. First examine what is involved in defining a generic class.

Generic Classes

Prior to the introduction of generics, one way to write reusable code was to use the object data type for instance data members. You will recall that object is the base class from which all other classes are derived. After the data type is defined as an object, then through casting and unboxing the data type can be temporarily made to act like any of the other types. Example 11-25 illustrates defining a Stack class that could be used to store any type of data items. A stack represents a simple last-in-first-out (LIFO) collection. You can think of stacks as analogous to a pile of trays. The Push( ) method places a tray on the top of the others; the Pop( ) method retrieves the one on top. One way stacks are used by applications during execution is to store the address of calling methods so the application will know where to return when it finishes the called method.

> **NOTE** Stack is one of the .NET Framework classes. It includes a number of public methods and properties. You should explore the MSDN documentation to learn more about this class.

Example 11-25 contains a simplified programmer-defined Stack class. The instance data member is an array of object items.

EXAMPLE 11-25

```
public class Stack
{
      private object [ ] items;
      private int stackPointer = 0;

      public Stack(int size)
      {
            items = new object[size];
      }

      public object Pop( )
      {
            return items[--stackPointer];
      }

      public void Push(object anItem)
      {
            items[stackPointer] = anItem; stackPointer++;
      }
}
```

The Push( ) method is used to place items in the stack. You will notice that the class is implemented as an array. The first item added is placed at index location 0. The stackPointer is incremented by one after each item is placed in the stack. The Pop( ) method retrieves the last one placed in the array. Neither of these methods includes any testing to ensure that reference is not made beyond the array boundaries. Example 11-26 illustrates an application that instantiates an object of the Stack class and then pushes data of differing types onto the data structure. Finally, the items are retrieved using the Pop( ) method.

EXAMPLE 11-26

```
using System;
using static System.Console;

namespace Stack
{
    public class TestOfStack
    {
        static void Main(string[] args)
        {
            Stack stack = new Stack(5);
            stack.Push("test");
            stack.Push(100);
            stack.Push(200);
            stack.Push(3.6);
            WriteLine("Values in the Stack are: " +
                      (double)stack.Pop( ) + ", " +
                      (int)stack.Pop( ) + ", " +
                      (int)stack.Pop( ) + ", " +
                      (string)stack.Pop( ));
            ReadKey( );
    }
}
```

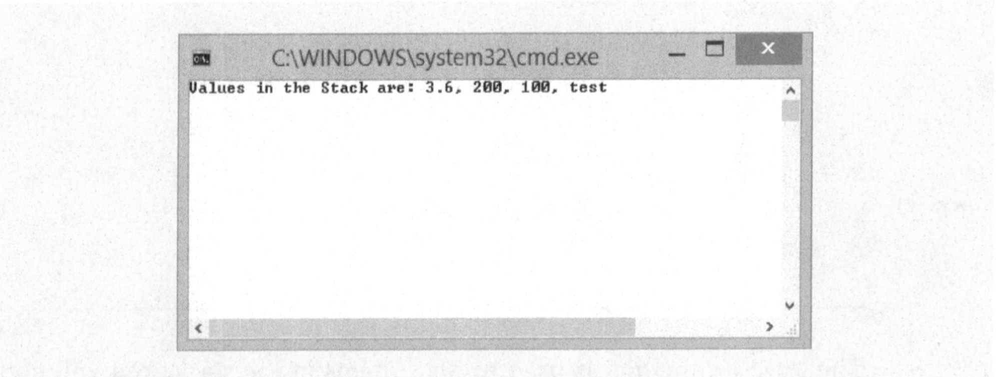

FIGURE 11-17 Output from TestOfStack example

As illustrated in Examples 11-25 and 11-26, without generics, you could define the data type as an object because it can hold any type. To retrieve the items, the last four lines in Example 11-26 show that casts had to be performed to unbox or extract the values from the `object` type. In Example 11-26, because the last item placed on the Stack was a `string`, the first call to `Pop( )` retrieved the string. The program would have terminated abnormally if the order of the casting was changed.

This object-based approach illustrated is not type-safe. Data of `string` type could be pushed onto the same stack that also holds integers. When the data is retrieved, if an attempt is made to do arithmetic with the `string` items, the program will terminate abnormally. To avoid this problem, you could define three separate stack classes: one for integers, another for doubles, and a third one for strings. This could be done by copying and pasting the code. But, if a simple modification is needed, corrections would need to be made to all three classes. This is where generics come into play. They allow you to define type-safe, compiler-generated code that can be defined and consumed with any type. The internal algorithms remain the same, but the `class` can be defined once and reused. Example 11-27 illustrates defining a simple generic `class`.

EXAMPLE 11-27

```
public class GenericClass<T>
{
    public T dataMember;
}
```

Notice that a generic `class` is defined by inserting an identifier between left and right brackets on the `class` definition line. In Example 11-27, `T` is used as the identifier. `T` is the standard identifier used to define a generic type in most of Microsoft's documentation; however, you could use any valid identifier as long as you adhered to the rules for creating an identifier. In the body of the method, the identifier is placed where the data type should be inserted. It can be as a return type in a method, in the parameter list of a method, or as shown in Example 11-27 as the data type for instance data members.

When you create an instance of the `class`, you specify the actual type to substitute for the type parameters. If the `dataMember` was defined as `public` (or if a `public` property was available for the `dataMember`), the `class` could be used as shown in Example 11-28.

EXAMPLE 11-28

```
GenericClass<string> anIdentifer = new GenericClass<string>( );
anIdentifer.dataMember = "A string";
```

You can take advantage of this new feature and redefine the `Stack` `class` as a generic `class`. This is illustrated in Example 11-29.

EXAMPLE 11-29

```
public class Stack<T>
{
      private T[ ] items;
      private int stackPointer = 0;

      public Stack(int size)
      {
            items = new T[size];
      }

      public T Pop( )
      {
            return items[--stackPointer];
      }

      public void Push(T anItem)
      {
            items[stackPointer] = anItem;
            stackPointer++;
      }
}
```

Example 11-30 illustrates the changes needed to implement the `class`. Notice that three separate objects are instantiated. The only values that can be placed in the `int` `Stack` are integers. Thus, a type-safe data structure has been created.

EXAMPLE 11-30

```
public class TestOfGenericStack
{
      static void Main(string[ ] args)
      {
            Stack<int> intStack = new Stack<int>(5);
            Stack<double> doubleStack = new Stack<double>(5);
            Stack<string> stringStack = new Stack<string>(5);

            stringStack.Push("test");
            intStack.Push(100);
            intStack.Push(200);
            doubleStack.Push(3.6);
```

```
            WriteLine("Values in the 3 Stacks are: " +
                      doubleStack.Pop( ) + ", " +
                      intStack.Pop( ) + ", " +
                      intStack.Pop( ) + ", " +
                      stringStack.Pop( ) );
            ReadKey( );
        }
}
```

Notice that no casting was necessary in Example 11-30. The output produced from Examples 11-29 and 11-30 is the same as what was shown in Figure 11-17.

Generic Methods

You can define generic methods that are not part of a generic `class`. This way, the method defers the specification of one or more types until the method is declared and instantiated by client code. Defining a generic method is similar to defining a generic `class`. You insert an identifier between the left and right brackets on the method definition line to indicate that it is a generic method. Then place that identifier either in the parameter list or as a return type or in both places. This is illustrated in Example 11-31.

EXAMPLE 11-31

```
public static void SwapData<T> (ref T first, ref T second)
{
     T temp;

     temp = first;
     first = second;
     second = temp;
}
```

A call to the `SwapData( )` method is shown in Example 11-32.

EXAMPLE 11-32

```
public static void TestSwap( )
{
     string firstValue = "Programming";
     string secondValue = "C#";

     SwapData<string>(ref firstValue, ref secondValue);
     WriteLine(firstValue + " " + secondValue);
}
```

11

As illustrated in Example 11-32, calls to the generic method require that the actual type be specified between the method name and the argument list. For this example, the `string` type was used.

Recall that the `ref` keyword is added to the argument and parameter list to enable the arguments to be passed by reference. The effect is that changes made to the parameter in the `SwapData( )` method will be reflected in that variable when control passes back to the calling method. In C#, the `ref` keyword must be added to the parameter list both in the method heading and in the calling argument list.

Dynamic

C# was originally characterized as being a strongly typed language, requiring all bits of data stored to be associated with a defined type at compile time. This enables the compiler to check to ensure that only compatible values are attempting to be stored. Potential errors can be caught early—before the program actually runs. It also enables the compiler to use the static data type to optimize storage needs and choice of algorithms for operations on the value. Using the static type, explicit casting can occur. Variables can still be defined as objects and then cast as different data types during runtime. But this requires additional boxing/unboxing of the data. With C# 4.0, a new data type of `dynamic` was added to the list of keywords.

Dynamic data type

You first read about the `dynamic` data type in Chapter 2. An object defined using the `dynamic` keyword can store anything. In most cases, it behaves like an `object`. At compile time, an element that is typed as `dynamic` is assumed to support any operation. Example 11-33 declares several variables of type `dynamic`. No unboxing or casting is necessary prior to their use. As shown in Example 11-33, four variables are defined as `dynamic`. Each is initialized with very different data. No special casting is necessary in order to print the contents.

EXAMPLE 11-33

```
dynamic intValue = 1000;
dynamic stringValue = "C#";
dynamic decimalValue = 23.45m;
dynamic aDate = System.DateTime.Today;
WriteLine("{0} {1} {2} {3}" , intValue, stringValue, decimalValue,
          aDate);
```

With `dynamic` data types the type checking occurs at runtime. The output produced from the above-mentioned program statements is:
1000 C# 23.45 6/16/2015 12:00:00 AM

Of even more interest is the fact that once defined as `dynamic`, the memory location can hold any value. Notice in Example 11-34, a single `dynamic` memory location is defined, but then values of four different data types are assigned to the memory location.

EXAMPLE 11-34

```
dynamic aValue;

aValue = 1001;
aValue++;
WriteLine("aValue - int: " + aValue);
aValue = "C#";
WriteLine("aValue - string: " + aValue);
aValue = 23.45m;
WriteLine("aValue - decimal: " + aValue);
aValue = System.DateTime.Today;
WriteLine("aValue - Date/Time: " + aValue);
```

The output produced from the above program statements is

aValue - `int`: 1002
aValue - `string`: C#
aValue - `decimal`: 23.45
aValue - `Date/Time`: 6/16/2015 12:00:00 AM

As you review Example 11-34, notice that arithmetic was able to be performed using the `dynamic` memory location. `aValue` was incremented. The memory location stored both integral values and floating point values and was able to reference both `string` and `object` types. All this was done without any casting or boxing/unboxing. Dynamic types can be used for method parameters or method return types. They offer freedom and speed of coding but should still be used with caution. One of the major advantages of strongly typed languages versus dynamic languages is extensive compile type error checking occurs so that bugs can be found early. With dynamic typing, this is delayed until runtime.

var data type

Another keyword, `var`, may be mistaken as a `dynamic` type. At first glance, it appears to be doing the same thing that dynamic is doing. It enables developers to not associate a specific data type to a group of bits. But `var` is different. It is used to implicitly type variables. Variables that are declared inside a method can be declared using the `var` keyword. The following declarations are functionally equivalent.

```
int someValue = 1000;
var someValue = 1000;
```

The first declaration, `int someValue = 1000;` is explicitly typed by the programmer. The second declaration, `var someValue = 1000;`, is implicitly typed by the compiler. It is said to be an implicitly typed local variable because the compiler determines the type. The keyword instructs the compiler to infer the type of the variable from the expression on the right side of the initialization statement. Instead of writing

```
dynamic aValue = System.DateTime.Today,
```

you would write

```
var aValue = System.DateTime.Today;
```

One of the primary differences between `dynamic` and `var` is that `var` data items must be initialized when they are declared. The compiler determines the memory location's type from the initialized value. If you attempt to declare a `var` type without an initialized value, you will get a compile error: *"Implicitly-typed local variables must be initialized".* This is not the case with `dynamic`. As illustrated in Example 11-34, using `dynamic`, you can declare a `dynamic` memory location and later associate values with it.

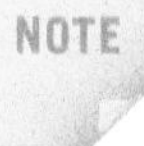

NOTE Dynamic type and the `dynamic` keyword are tied into Microsoft's dynamic language runtime (DLR) environment—a feature of the .NET Framework. The DLR is built on top of the CLR. The DLR adds to the platform a set of services designed explicitly for the needs of dynamic languages, including support to make it easy to generate fast dynamic code.

You will see `var` used again in Chapter 14. It is often used with LINQ query operations.

PROGRAMMING EXAMPLE: StudentGov Application

This example demonstrates developing an application using a number of advanced concepts. An `abstract` base `class` is created to include data members and properties. An `interface` is designed. Three classes are derived from the base `abstract class`; two of those classes implement the `interface`. After these components are stored in a `class` library, they are available for use by any number of applications. To test the design, a Windows application presentation `class` is created. An application is written for the Student Government Association. The problem specification is shown in Figure 11-18.

The Student Government Association (SGA) attempts to get as many students involved in campus activities as possible. They communicate with students about upcoming campus events through clubs and organizations. Each group has a name and a contact person. The contact person is normally a student.

During registration, all students pay a small activity fee, which is transferred into an SGA account. SGA then disperses money from its budget to groups on campus. This enables a number of individual organizations to provide activities for their members. To receive funding, each group registers with the SGA at the end of the academic year for the upcoming year. A preset dollar amount is dispersed to groups based on their classification type. Groups funded include academic clubs at $600 per group and fraternity and sorority organizations at $500 per group. The SGA also keeps records on intramural groups for communication purposes; however, they do not receive any funding.

Design an application that displays on a Windows form the group name and amount of funding, if any, the group receives. Other applications may be designed in the future to display a club's meeting location, date, and time, or the primary sporting event for an intramural group, and the address and status of a fraternity or sorority group.

© Cengage Learning

FIGURE 11-18 Problem specification for StudentGov example

ANALYZE THE PROBLEM

You should review the problem specification in Figure 11-18 to ensure that you understand the problem definition. Objects should be able to be instantiated for the following types of groups:

- Club
- Fraternity and sorority
- Intramural

These groups share some common characteristics. Each has a unique name and a contact person. Two of the groups (clubs, fraternities and sororities) may receive funding from the Student Government Association. Fraternities and sororities that are chartered receive funding; others cannot.

Unique information regarding clubs include the date, time, and place they hold their meetings. The type of sport associated with the intramural group is unique to the Intramural classification. Distinctive characteristics for the fraternity or sorority classification include whether the group is chartered and their house address. After you understand the problem definition, you can begin to abstract out the characteristics for each of the classes. Table 11-1 gives the data fields organized by group. The common data is included with the Organization category.

DATA

TABLE 11-1 Data fields organized by class

Class	Identifier	Data type
`Organization`	`orgName`	`string`
`Organization`	`primaryContact`	`string`
`Organization`	`fundedAmt`	`decimal`
`Club`	`meetingDay`	`string`
`Club`	`meetingTime`	`string`
`Club`	`meetingLocation`	`string`
`FratSorority`	`chartered`	`bool`
`FratSorority`	`houseAddress`	`string`
`Intramural`	`sportType`	`string`

It should not be possible to create a group in this application unless it is associated with a club, fraternity, sorority, or intramural team.

DESIGN A SOLUTION

The desired output is to display data on a Windows form about the different organizations. An application is created using the Windows `Form` `class` to test the design. It should ensure that objects can be instantiated from the `Club`, `FratSorority`, and `Intramural` classes but not from the `Organization` `class`. It should make sure that derived classes have access to base `class` members. Figure 11-19 shows a prototype for the form.

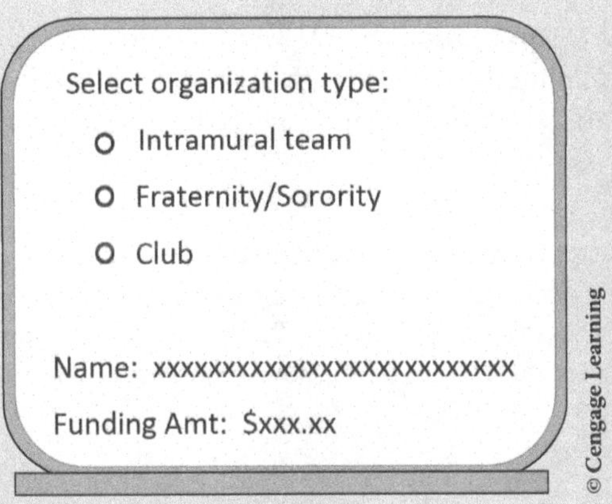

© Cengage Learning

FIGURE 11-19 Prototype for StudentGov example

The business logic is separated into several classes to include an `Organization` `class` that serves as a base `class`. No objects should be instantiated from this `class`, so it is defined as an `abstract class`. Derived classes of `Club`, `Intramural`, and `FratSorority` are defined to inherit from the `Organization` `class`. The `IFunding` `interface` is defined to force functionality of setting the funding amount. `FratSorority` and `Club` both implement this `interface`. Class diagrams are used to help design and document these characteristics. Figure 11-20 shows the `class` diagrams for the `StudentGov` example.

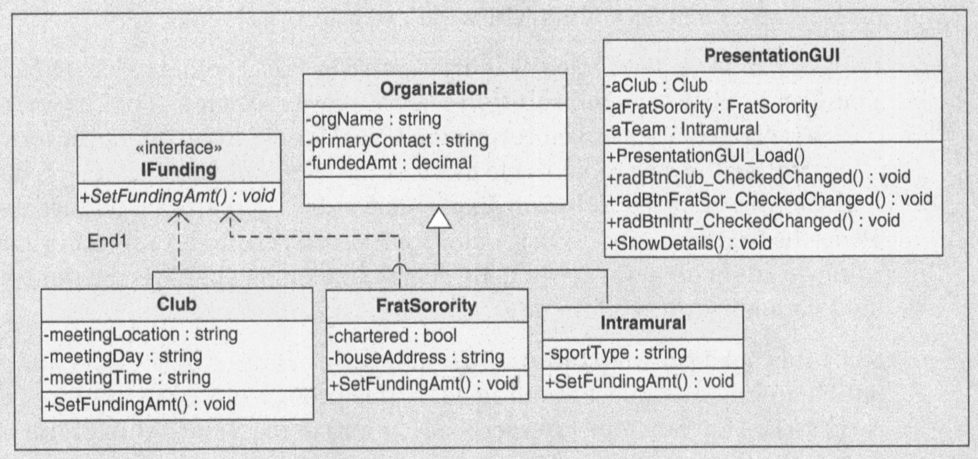

© Cengage Learning

FIGURE 11-20 Class diagrams for StudentGov example

The dotted arrows in Figure 11-20 represent the `interface` link. Notice that the Unified Modeling Language (UML) notation for the interfaces includes the name of the methods in italic, indicating that implementation details must be defined.

NOTE UML is the industry-standard modeling language for specifying and documenting both data and processes. Class diagrams are one of the modeling diagrams used with object-oriented applications. To find out more about UML, visit *www.uml.org*, the Object Management Group's website responsible for the release.

The `interface object` cannot have member data, just methods. The `class` diagrams do not show the properties. No accessor or mutator methods are defined for accessing or changing the `private` data members of the classes. However, during design, it is decided that properties are defined with `get` and `set` behaviors for most data members. Minimal business logic is needed for this application; thus, no pseudo code or additional design tool is constructed.

CODE THE SOLUTION

After you complete the design, it is time to translate the design into source code. For this application, six projects are created inside one solution. It is not necessary to put the files under a single solution umbrella. This was done for ease of demonstration. All of the classes could be defined as stand-alone components. The `interface` and all classes except the `PresentationGUI` could be stored in your library with other DLL files. The PresentationGUI generates an EXE file; all other projects generate files ending with a .dll extension.

For this example, a new Project was first created in Visual Studio called `StudentGov`. The **Create directory for solution** checkbox was selected. The `Organization class` is created first. As you review the Visual Studio **Solution Explorer** window after creating the new project, the name of the solution, `StudentGov`, is displayed at the top level in the **Solution Explorer** window. Projects names are displayed below the solution name. When a new solution was created, a project by that same name, `StudentGov`, was created. By default, the project name is the same name as the solution name (`StudentGov`).

Since this solution will store the C# files for a number of projects and a separate `StudentGov` project is not needed, this project (`StudentGov`) was deleted. A right-click on the project (under the solution) in the **Solution Explorer** window reveals the **Remove** option.

A right-click on the **Solution** `StudentGov` (name at the top of the list) in the **Solution Explorer** window displays a menu that includes an option to **Add > New**

Project. After the program statements are typed, the DLL is built from the **Build** menu. The shortcut for this option is **Shift+F6**. The DLL is built so that other classes can reference it during their design. The source code for the `Organization class` is shown first:

```
// Organization.cs
// Abstract class used as a base class.
using System;

namespace OrganizationNamespace
{
     public abstract class Organization
     {
          private string orgName;
          private string primaryContact;
          private decimal fundedAmt;

          public Organization(string name, string contact)
          {
               orgName = name;
               primaryContact = contact;
          }

          public Organization( )
          {
          }

          // Properties for each private data member follows.
          public decimal FundedAmt
          {
               set
               {
                    fundedAmt = value;
               }
               get
               {
                    return fundedAmt;
               }
          }

          public string OrgName
          {
               set
               {
                    orgName = value;
               }
```

```
                get
                {
                    return orgName;
                }
            }

            private string PrimaryContact
            {
                set
                {
                    primaryContact = value;
                }
                get
                {
                    return primaryContact;
                }
            }
        }
}
```

The namespace was changed to OrganizationNamespace for this class. With the exception of the fact that the Organization class is defined as abstract, nothing else differs in this class from previous exercises. The namespace was changed to OrganizationNamespace. A number of properties are defined.

NOTE A new project for the interface can be added to the solution from the **Solution Explorer** window. Right-click on the solution icon and then select **Add** > **New Project**. Use the **Class Library** template.

The file containing the interface is created next. Like the Organization class, it is a stand-alone component. Using the **Class Library** template in Visual Studio, the following source code is added to the solution:

```
// IFunding.cs      interface
using System;
namespace IFundingNamespace
{
    public interface IFunding
    {
        // No implementation details for SetFundingAmt ( )
        // Method must be defined by classes
        // that implement the interface.
        void SetFundingAmt( );
    }
}
```

The default class name was changed to IFunding.cs. The interface includes one method. Classes that implement it must provide the body for the method. After this DLL is built, the subclasses can reference it.

The Intramural class is defined next. Like the IFunding interface, a new project is created after building and closing the interface. Again by right-clicking on the solution (StudentGov) in the **Solution Explorer** window, selecting **Add** reveals the **New Project** option. The **Class Library** template is selected as the project type. The default class name was changed to Intramural.cs by right-clicking on the class name. This also enables the default class name (Class1) in the source code file to be changed to Intramural.

Intramural inherits from the Organization class but does not implement the interface. To use the Organization component in the Intramural project, a reference had to be made to that DLL before typing the program statements.

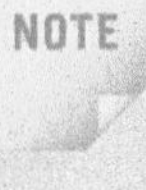

NOTE Recall that one way to add the reference to the Organization.dll is to right-click on the project icon in the **Solution Explorer** window and then choose **Add Reference** from that menu. Because each of the components is stored as a separate project, be sure to browse the project subdirectory to locate the DLL in the bin\Debug directory.

The using OrganizationNamespace; statement is also added to eliminate the need to fully qualify references to the Organization class. The source code for the Intramural class is shown in the following:

```
// Intramural.cs
using System;
// OrganizationNamespace added to avoid fully qualifying
// references
using OrganizationNamespace;

namespace IntramuralNamespace
{
    public class Intramural : Organization
    {
        private string sportType;

        public Intramural(string name, string pContact,
                          string sport)
            // Call to Organization (base) class constructor
            : base (name, pContact)
        {
            sportType = sport;
        }
```

11

```
            // Default constructor
            public Intramural( )
            {
                  sportType = "unknown";
            }

            // Property for sportType
            public string SportType
            {
                  get
                  {
                        return sportType;
                  }
                  set
                  {
                        sportType = value;
                  }
            }
      }
}
```

A number of references were added during design to build the application. With the latest version of Visual Studio, once you browse and locate the .DLL for the first project, the .DLL is available from the list of **Recent .DLLs added**. Each of the classes, with the exception of the `PresentationGUI`, were added using the **Class Library** template. Figure 11-21 shows which references are needed for the six projects in the `StudentGov` solution. In addition to the six projects, `PresentationGUI` is also shown in Figure 11-21. It is discussed in the following. It is best to add the references when you first create the project.

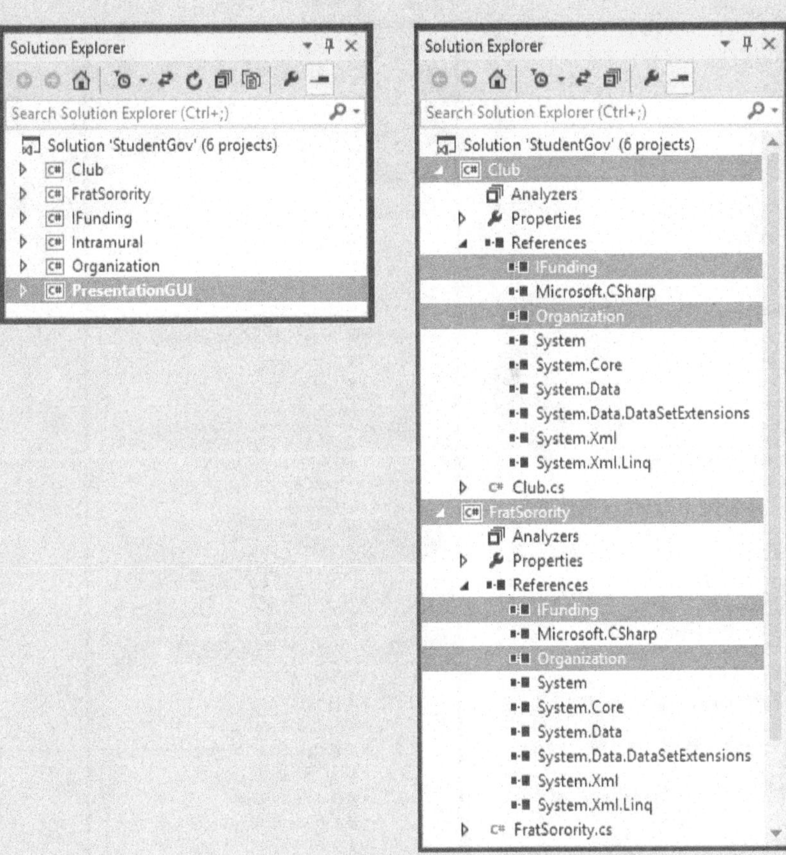

FIGURE 11-21 References added to StudentGov example (*continued*)

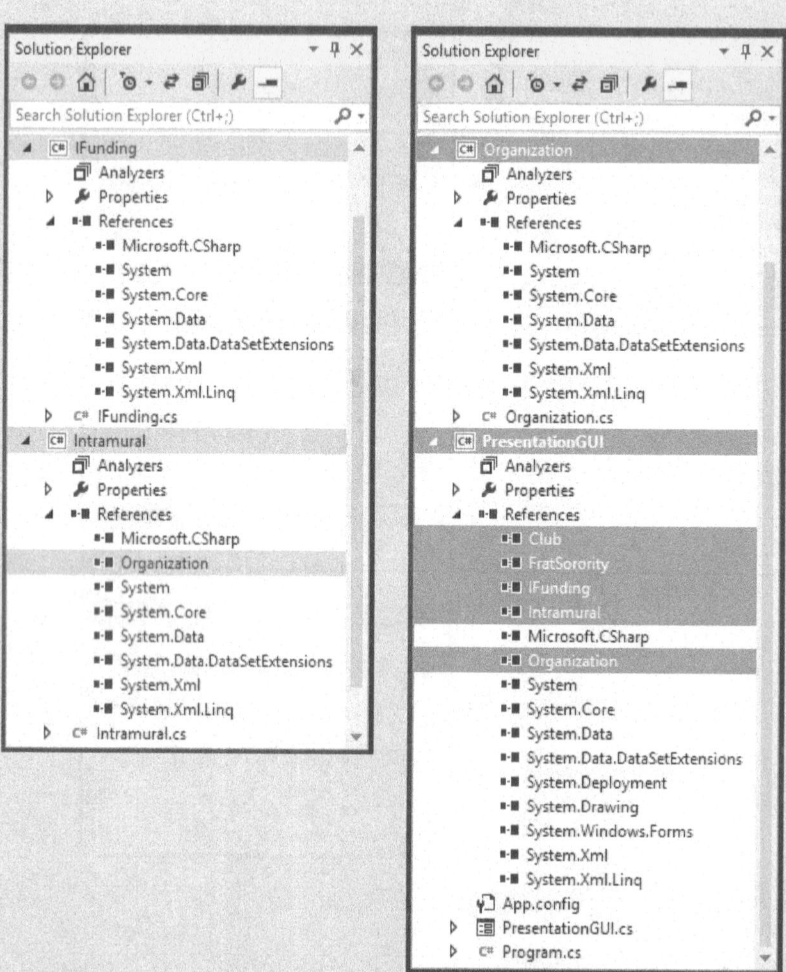

FIGURE 11-21 References added to StudentGov example

Notice that `IFunding` and `Organization` contain no additional references beyond those automatically added by Visual Studio.

Both the `Club` and `FratSorority` classes must add references to `Organization` and `IFunding`. Remember that placing the `using` directive at the beginning of the file allows you to use the unqualified `class` names to reference methods during design. The source code for the `Club` `class` follows:

```
// Club.cs
using System;
// OrganizationNamespace added to avoid fully qualifying references
using OrganizationNamespace;
using IFundingNamespace;

namespace ClubNamespace
{
    public class Club : Organization, IFunding
    {
        // Private member data
        private string meetingLocation;
        private string meetingDay;
        private string meetingTime;

        public Club(string name, string pContact, string mLoc,
                string mDay, string mTime)
            // Call to base constructor
            : base(name, pContact)
        {
            meetingLocation = mLoc;
            meetingDay = mDay;
            meetingTime = mTime;
        }

        // Required method - because of interface
        public void SetFundingAmt( )
        {
            FundedAmt = 600M;
        }
    }
}
```

As you review the code for the `Club`, `FratSorority`, and `Intramural` classes, notice that each one has one constructor that calls the `base` constructor in the `Organization` `class`. They send values for the organization name (`orgName`) and the primary contact person for the group (`primaryContact`).

The `SetFundingAmt( )` method from the `IFunding` `interface` is implemented in the `Club` and `FratSorority` classes. The source code for the `FratSorority` `class` follows:

```
// FratSorority.cs
using System;
using OrganizationNamespace;
using IFundingNamespace;

namespace FratSororityNamespace
{
    public class FratSorority : Organization, IFunding
```

11

```
{
    private bool chartered;
    // Private member data
    private string houseAddress;

    public FratSorority( )
    {
        houseAddress = "unknown";
        chartered = false;
    }

    public FratSorority(string name, string pContact, bool
                isChartered, string address)
        : base(name, pContact)
        // Call to base constructor
    {
        houseAddress = address;
        chartered = isChartered;
    }

    // Required method - because of interface
    public void SetFundingAmt( )
    {
        if(chartered)
        {
            FundedAmt = 500M;
        }
        else
        {
            FundedAmt = 0M;
        }
    }

    // Properties
    private bool Chartered
    {
        get
        {
            return chartered;
        }
        set
        {
            chartered = value; }
        }
    }
```

```
            private string HouseAddress
            {
                get
                {
                    return houseAddress;
                }
                set
                {
                    houseAddress = value;
                }
            }
        }
    }
```

The last class, PresentationGUI, is used to test the components. It is a GUI Windows application. Notice that Figure 11-21 shows that a reference is added to each of the components for the PresentationGUI class. In this class, objects are constructed of the Club, FratSorority, and Intramural classes. The PresentationGUI class includes three RadioButton objects inside a GroupBox object. The radio buttons correspond to the three different types of organization objects being constructed. The PresentationGUI is created similarly to the other classes, except instead of using the **Class Library** template when the **New Project** is added to the solution, the **Windows Forms Application** template is selected. The source listing for this class follows. Due to space constraints, some of the Windows Forms Designer generated code is omitted. Table 11-2 presents what properties are set for the Form and control objects, and extra comments are added to the source code to aid you in following the example.

TABLE 11-2 PresentationGUI property values

Name	Object type	Property	Property value
Form1	Form	Name	PresentationGUI
PresentationGUI	Form	BackColor	Teal
PresentationGUI	Form	Font	12F
PresentationGUI	Form	ForeColor	Yellow
PresentationGUI	Form	Text	Student Government

(continues)

11

TABLE 11-2 PresentationGUI property values (*continued*)

Name	Object type	Property	Property value
groupBox1	GroupBox	Text	Select organization type
radioButton1	RadioButton	Name	radBtnIntr
radBtnIntr	RadioButton	Checked	false
radioButton2	RadioButton	Name	radBtnFratSor
radBtnFratSor	RadioButton	Checked	false
radioButton3	RadioButton	Name	radBtnClub
radBtnClub	RadioButton	Checked	false
radBtnIntr	RadioButton	Text	Intramural team
radBtnFratSor	RadioButton	Text	Fraternity/ Sorority
radBtnClub	RadioButton	Text	Club
label1	Label	Name	lblName
label2	Label	Name	lblFundedAmt
lblName	Label	Text	Name:
lblName	Label	Visible	false
lblFundedAmt	Label	Text	Funding Amt:
lblFundedAmt	Label	Visible	false

(*continues*)

TABLE 11-2 PresentationGUI property values (*continued*)

Name	Object type	Property	Property value
textBox1	TextBox	Name	txtBxName
textBox2	TextBox	Name	txtBxFund
txtBxFund	TextBox	TextAlign	Right
txtBxName	TextBox	Visible	false
txtBxFund	TextBox	Visible	False

The final project source code listing is shown in the following. You will notice that the listing shows the `partial class` representing the `PresentationGUI.cs` file. It does not show the contents of the `PresentationGUI.Designer.cs` file. The `.Designer.cs` file contains the auto-generated code and is available like all the other examples in the book from the publisher.

```
// PresentationGUI.cs
using System;
using System.Windows.Forms;

using ClubNamespace;           // Namespace for Club class
using IntramuralNamespace;     // Namespace for Intramural class
using FratSororityNamespace;   // Namespace for FratSorority class

namespace PresentationGUI
{
     public partial class PresentationGUI : Form
     {
          // Object of Club class declared
          private Club aClub;
          // Object of Intramural class declared
          private Intramural aTeam;
          // Object of FratSorority class declared
          private FratSorority aFratSorority;

          public PresentationGUI( )
          {
               InitializeComponent( );
          }
```

```
// Objects are instantiated when the form is loaded.
// Another GUI could be designed for entering data.
private void PresentationGUI_Load(object sender,
                                  EventArgs e)
{
     aClub = new Club ("ACM", "Jones", "Davis 203",
                       "Tues", "12:30");
     aFratSorority = new FratSorority
          ("Delta PI", "Brenda Wynn", true,
           "86 SmithField");
     aTeam = new Intramural
          ("Winners", "Joe Kitchen", "VolleyBall");
}

// Three CheckedChanged event-handler methods included.
// Double-clicking on the RadioButton adds the method
// heading and registers the event.
private void radBtnClub_CheckedChanged(object sender,
                                       EventArgs e)
{
     txtBxName.Text = aClub.OrgName;
     aClub.SetFundingAmt( );
     txtBxFund.Text = aClub.FundedAmt.ToString("C");
     ShowDetails( );
}

private void radBtnFratSor_CheckedChanged(object sender,
                                          EventArgs e)
{
   txtBxName.Text = aFratSorority.OrgName;
   aFratSorority.SetFundingAmt();
   txtBxFund.Text =
       aFratSorority.FundedAmt.ToString("C");
   ShowDetails();
}

private void radBtnIntr_CheckedChanged(object sender,
                                       EventArgs e)
{
   txtBxName.Text = aTeam.OrgName;
   txtBxFund.Text = aTeam.FundedAmt.ToString("C");
   ShowDetails();
}

// Area at the bottom of the form initally set to
// Visible = false using the Properties window.
// Because each RadioButton objects needed to reset
// the objects to Visible = true, a method is used.
```

```
            public void ShowDetails( )
            {
                txtBxName.Visible = true;
                lblName.Visible = true;
                txtBxFund.Visible = true;
                lblFundedAmount.Visible = true;
            }
        }
}
```

When you complete the `PresentationGUI`, it should be set as the startup project because it is the only project in the solution that contains a `Main( )` method. One way to do this, as illustrated in Figure 11-22, is to right click the `PresentationGUI` project in the **Solution Explorer** window. When you right-click, you see the following option: **Set as StartUp Project**. This is necessary because you have multiple projects in a single solution.

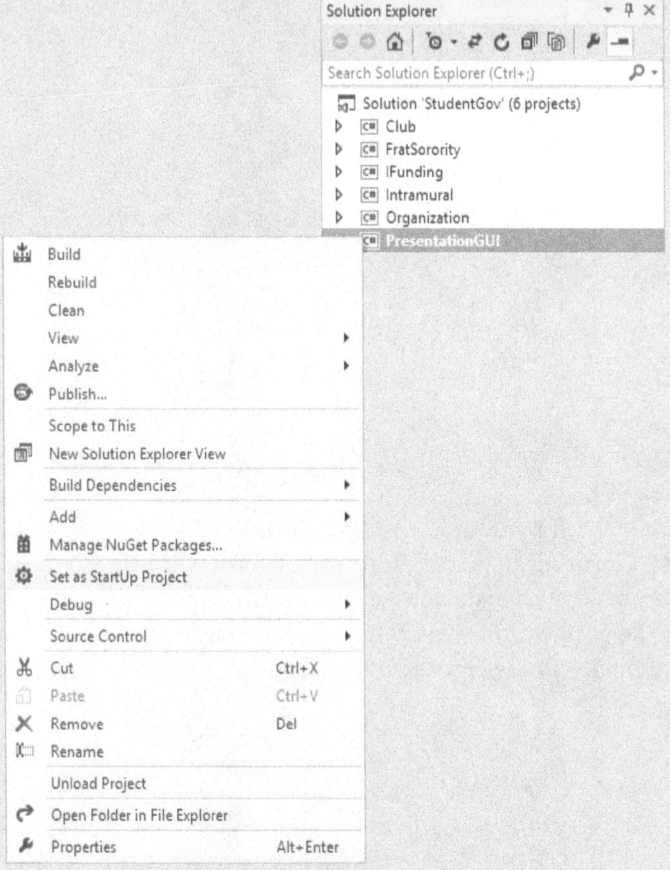

FIGURE 11-22 Setting the StartUp Project

The `PresentationGUI` is considered by many developers an example of a **client application**. It is considered a client because it is using the components that you created. Other client applications can make use of these same components. When you build the solution and run the application, Visual Studio copies the DLL from each of the references that were added into the application's private subdirectory. If you explore the files that are created, you notice you have multiple copies of the DLLs. Actually, each project has its own copy of any referenced DLLs. Figure 11-23 shows the directory listing for the `PresentationGUI` folder. Some files were hidden, but notice that it contains copies of all of the .dlls and the `PresentationGUI.exe`. This makes up the `PresentationGUI` assembly.

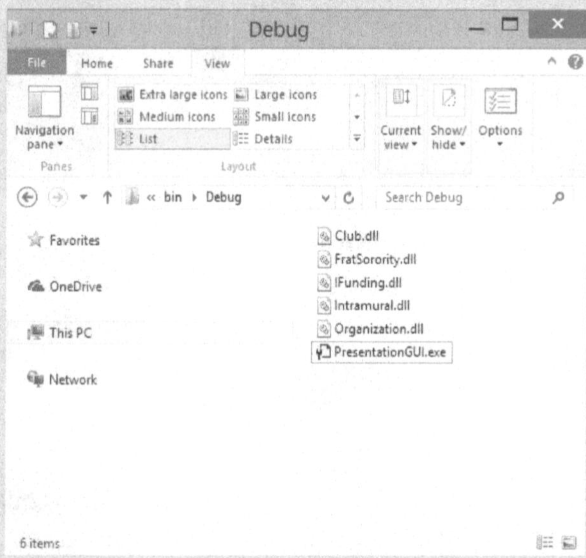

FIGURE 11-23 Part of the PresentationGUI assembly

The application can be run by double-clicking on the .EXE file here in the folder containing the .EXE file, or it can be run from within Visual Studio as you have done with all the applications you have developed previously. The original user interface as it appears when the application is launched is shown in Figure 11-24. The figure contains an overlapping window produced by clicking one of the `RadioButton` objects.

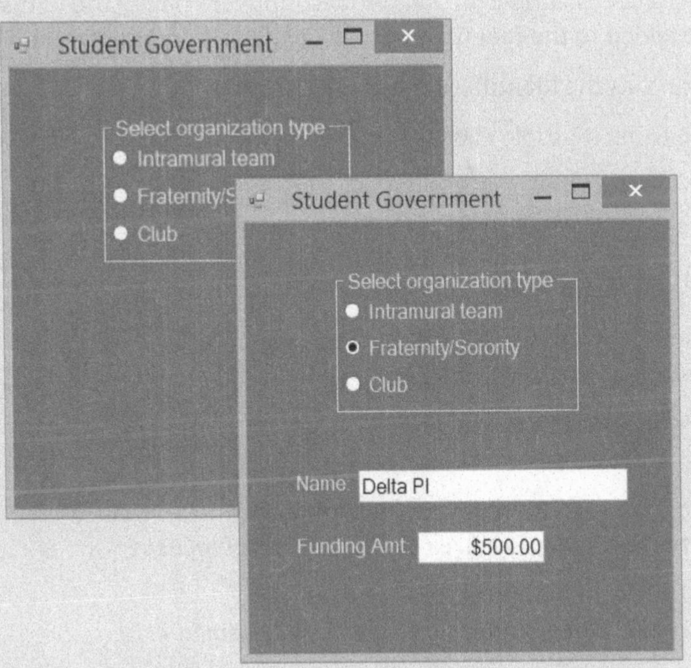

FIGURE 11-24 Output from StudentGov example

Coding Standards

When projects adhere to common standards, others can go into the code and read or modify it. Thus, coding standards make the project go smoother.

11

The following are a list of standards as they relate to creating multiclass solutions:

- Declare members of a class of the same security level together. Place all the `private` members first, followed by `protected` members and then `public` members.
- When declaring methods that have too many arguments to fit on the same line, the leading parenthesis and the first argument should be written on the same line as the method identifier. Additional arguments are written on the following line and indented to the opening parenthesis.
- Data members should never be specified with `public` access.

- Abstract classes should be named descriptively. The suffix "Abstract" may be added to the identifier so as to distinguish it as abstract.
- Use T or K as the identifier for a generic class.
- Avoid putting multiple classes in the same file.

Resources

Additional sites you might want to explore:

- Comparison of Unified Modeling Language Tools—
http://en.wikipedia.org/wiki/List_of_UML_tools
- Code Project for those who code—
http://www.codeproject.com/
- Generic Classes (C# Programming Guide)—
http://msdn.microsoft.com/en-us/library/sz6zd40f.aspx
- C# Station Tutorial: Interfaces—
http://www.csharp-station.com/Tutorials/Lesson13.aspx

QUICK REVIEW

1. For a language to be considered a true object-oriented programming (OOP) language, it must support abstraction, encapsulation, inheritance, and polymorphism.
2. Abstraction enables you to think about something in a certain way and represent only essential features appropriate to the problem. It is used to identify and determine the objects needed for the design.
3. Encapsulation is used to package together common characteristics into a `class` consisting of behaviors and data.
4. Inheritance allows you to create a general `class` and then define specialized classes that have access to the members of the general `class`.
5. Polymorphism is the ability for classes to provide different implementations of methods that are called by the same name.
6. Instead of writing a program that includes all the features in a single file, development today is often geared toward writing multitier applications consisting of a number of components.
7. Components are implemented through classes in C#.
8. A colon is used as a separator between the derived `class` and the base `class`.
9. The base `class` is sometimes called the super or parent `class`.

10. Classes that inherit from a base `class` are called derived classes or subclasses.
11. Constructors, named the same name as the `class` name, are defined with `public` access.
12. Overridden methods must have exactly the same signature as the methods they override. New functionality is normally defined with overridden methods.
13. Overloaded methods must have a different signature. Overloaded methods are often defined to perform a similar behavior but with different data types.
14. The `override` keyword allows a method to provide a new implementation of a method inherited from a base `class`.
15. Base methods are normally defined as `virtual` if they are to be overridden.
16. If you want members of the derived classes to have access to members in the base `class`, define the members using `protected` access.
17. The `private` access modifier restricts access to `class` members only. Public opens access to any `class`. Classes defined with the `internal` access modifier are accessible only within files in the same assembly.
18. To call the base `class` constructor, `base`( ), precede it with a colon and place it in the heading before the opening curly brace. Arguments can be sent inside the parentheses if constructors other than the default are used.
19. Classes can be compiled and stored as a dynamic link library (DLL) file and then referenced by any other applications. To do this in Visual Studio, select the Class Library template option from the Start page.
20. .NET enables multiple languages such as Visual Basic, C++, and C# to be used to create a single application. The only requirement for doing this is that a project must include source code files from only one language.
21. After you create your own DLL file, to use it in an application, one of the first things you should do is add a reference to the DLL. Just adding the reference is not enough. You have to either add a `using` statement at the top of the source code file indicating which `namespace` is used or qualify the `class` and members by using the `namespace` and a dot before each use of the `class` and its members.
22. Add the `abstract` modifier to classes to prohibit other classes from instantiating objects of a base `class`. Add the `sealed` modifier to classes to prohibit subclasses from being derived from the class. Methods having the `sealed` modifier cannot be overridden in subclasses.

23. Abstract classes can include regular data field members, regular methods, and `virtual` methods in addition to `abstract` methods. Derived classes must provide implementation details for every `abstract` method included in the base `class`.
24. Think of an `interface` as a `class` that is totally `abstract`. All of its members are considered `abstract`. No implementation details are provided by the `interface` for any of its members.
25. One advantage of using interfaces is the fact that a `class` can implement any number of interfaces. But, inheritance can only be from one `class`, `abstract`, or nonabstract.
26. Designer-generated code is separated from user code when a Windows application is created through the use of `partial` classes.
27. Spread the definition of your classes over multiple files by using the `partial` keyword as part of the heading for the `class`. All of the `partial class` definitions must be defined in the same assembly.
28. To create an `interface` in C#, you use the Class Library template from the Start page. Interfaces can be compiled to a DLL. Instead of using the keyword `class`, you use `interface` in the heading.
29. If a `class` implements more than one `interface`, they all appear on the `class` definition line separated by commas. The base `class` is listed first.
30. Interfaces play an important role in the .NET Framework. `Collection` classes such as the `Array` `class`, `ArrayList` `class`, `Hashtable` `class`, `Stack` `class`, and `Queue` `class` implement a number of interfaces.
31. One of the most powerful features of the .NET Framework class library and Visual Studio is the extensive library of documentation available. In addition to syntax and grammar, the library includes tutorials and examples of how features are used. You are strongly encouraged to explore this material.
32. Through inheritance and marking the method with the `virtual` keyword, polymorphism is made possible by allowing classes to override base `class` members.
33. Through the use of `abstract` classes, polymorphic programming is possible. Classes that derive from `abstract` classes are forced to include implementation details for any `abstract` method. Polymorphic programming is encouraged with interfaces because interfaces provide the heading for the methods. Classes that implement the `interface` must provide implementation details.
34. Generics enables algorithms to be written where a number of details, including the data type, can be "specified-later."

35. Generics are defined using left and right brackets. An identifier is inserted between them: <T>. The `T` is a user-supplied identifier or name that acts as a placeholder for the type that is going to be used.
36. Once a variable is defined as `dynamic`, the memory location can hold any value. Dynamic types can also be used for method parameters or method return types.
37. `var` is used to implicitly type variables. The compiler determines the type from the expression on the right side of the initialization statement.

EXERCISES

1. Packaging data attributes and behaviors into a single unit so that the implementation details can be hidden describes an object-oriented feature called:
   a. abstraction
   b. inheritance
   c. objects
   d. encapsulation
   e. polymorphism
2. To be considered a true object-oriented language, designers of the language must provide support for:
   a. properties
   b. objects
   c. inheritance
   d. IDEs
   e. command-line tools
3. Components are normally compiled and stored with a file extension of:
   a. .exe
   b. .sno
   c. .proj
   d. .dll
   e. .csc

4. Polymorphism is useful in languages because it facilitates _______________ methods:
   a. overriding
   b. overloading
   c. overstriking
   d. interfacing
   e. inheriting
5. The "is a" relationship is associated with:
   a. inheritance
   b. interfaces
   c. polymorphism
   d. encapsulation
   e. all of the above
6. In C#, the super `class`, or base `class` of all others, is:
   a. super
   b. `base`
   c. value
   d. `class`
   e. `object`
7. Using the following declaration, which of the following statements is true?

   `public class` aClass : bClass, IClass

   a. `IClass` is an `interface`.
   b. `aClass` is the derived `class`.
   c. `bClass` is the base `class`.
   d. all of the above
   e. none of the above

8. If you want to keep classes that instantiate objects of a `class` from changing their data members, but enable derived classes to change base `class` data members, the data members in the base `class` should be defined with a _____________ access modifier.
   a. `private`
   b. `public`
   c. `internal`
   d. `static`
   e. `protected`

9. Constructors are normally defined with a _____________ access modifier; data members with a _____________ access modifier; and properties with a _____________ access modifier.
   a. `public, public, public`
   b. `private, private, private`
   c. `public, public, private`
   d. `public, private, public`
   e. `private, public, public`

10. To enable derived classes to override methods defined in a base `class`, methods of the base class should be defined using a(an) _____________ keyword:
    a. `virtual`
    b. `override`
    c. `static`
    d. `public`
    e. none of the above

11. In .NET, applications are deployed in terms of:
    a. .dll's
    b. .exe's
    c. solutions
    d. assemblies
    e. applications

12. The one constraint for having a solution include code from more than one programming language is the requirement that:
    a. Each project must consist of code in one language only.
    b. Each project must reference all the other projects.
    c. A `using` directive must be placed in the source code files for each project.
    d. The solution can have no more than 10 projects.
    e. Both b and c are correct.

13. To avoid having to use fully qualified referenced classes, you could:
    a. Add a reference to the `class`.
    b. Add an import statement for the `class`.
    c. Add a `using` directive.
    d. Inherit from the `class`.
    e. Package the classes in the same solution.

14. A `class` from which an `object` cannot be instantiated could be a(n):
    a. base `class`
    b. derived `class`
    c. implemented `class`
    d. `virtual class`
    e. `abstract class`

15. Classes can extend or derive from ______________ class(es) and implement ______________ interface(s).
    a. one, one
    b. many, one
    c. many, many
    d. one, many
    e. one, twelve

16. Abstract classes can include:
    a. data members
    b. `abstract` methods
    c. nonabstract methods
    d. properties
    e. all of the above

17. Interfaces can include:
    a. data members
    b. `abstract` methods
    c. nonabstract methods
    d. properties
    e. all of the above

18. _____ allows a method of a `class` to be called without regard to what specific implementation it provides.
    a. Polymorphism
    b. Abstraction
    c. Assemblies
    d. Versioning
    e. Class libraries

19. The feature that enables you to split source code between two or more files is:
    a. generics
    b. base `class`
    c. dynamic link library
    d. `partial classes`
    e. package

20. A multitier application would probably have:
    a. a `class` defined to interact with the user
    b. one or more classes defined to handle the business logic
    c. a `class` defined to deal with the data
    d. a client `class`
    e. all of the above

---

21. Explain the difference between an overloaded and an overridden method. Give an example of each.

22. How does an `abstract` class differ from an `interface`?

```
public class Employee
{
    private int empNumber;
    private decimal pay;
}
```

Given the above program segment, answer Questions 23 through 30.

23. Define a read-only property for the pay data member.

24. Define a default constructor for Employee.

25. Define a more useful constructor that could be used to instantiate objects of the `class`.

26. Define a subclass named `HourlyEmployee` with additional members of `hours` and `payrate`.

27. Define a constructor for `HourlyEmployee` that sends the employee number to the `Employee` `class` when an `object` is instantiated. Are there any changes needed in the `Employee` `class`? If so, what?

28. Create a method in the `Employee` `class` to determine the pay amount. It should be capable of being overridden in subclasses.

29. Provide new implementation details in the `HourlyEmployee` `class` for the method you defined in the preceding question (28).

30. Define the heading for a generic method `ProcessData` that has one generic parameter as part of its signature.

PROGRAMMING EXERCISES

1. Create a ticket reservation `class` for issuing tickets to on-campus events such as plays, musicals, and home basketball games. Design the ticket `class` so that it cannot be instantiated. Create subclasses for at least three different types of events. The subclasses should extend the ticket class. Determine unique characteristics for each of the events. Define a client application to test your `class` designs.

2. Create a base `class` to store characteristics about a loan. Include customer details in the Loan base class such as name, loan number, and amount of loan. Define subclasses of auto loan and home loan. Include unique characteristics in the derived classes. For example, you might

include details about the specific auto in the auto loan class and details about the home in the home loan class. Create a presentation `class` to test your design by displaying information about both types of loans.

3. Create a base `class` to hold information about sporting teams on campus. If you are using Visual Studio to develop your solution, use the class library template. Design the base `class` so that it is not possible to instantiate the `class`. Include characteristics you would find with all sports, such as primary coach's name and the name of the sport. Define properties, a ToString( ) method, and a minimum of one `virtual` method that can be redefined for specific sports. The ToString( ) method should return the name of the sport and coach. Since no class is required to test your base class, be sure to build the solution to ensure that no syntax errors exist.

4. Select two types of sporting teams and define subclasses for them. If you are using Visual Studio to develop your solution, use the class library template. These classes should inherit from a base team `class` such as that created in Exercise 3. Include unique characteristics about the sport. For example, for a sporting team such as a tennis team, the field location and/or the person to contact to restring rackets may be of interest. Be sure to implement any `virtual` methods included in the base `class`. Provide ToString( ) methods in both subclasses that invokes the `ToString( )` method in the base `class` and adds unique characteristics about the individual team to the return value. Since no class is required to test your subclasses, be sure to build the solution to ensure that no syntax errors exist.

5. Provide a test class to demonstrate that your design of a base team `class` and individual sporting team subclasses works. If you completed Exercise 4, provide a reference in your project to the DLLs you designed for Exercise 4; otherwise create the classes for this exercise. Your test `class` can be a console or Windows application. One approach to validate your design would be to instantiate objects of your individual sporting team subclasses when the program launches and then invoke methods and properties to retrieve and display data about the teams. From your test class, be sure to retrieve data from the base class as well as the subclasses.

6. Modify your solution for Exercise 5 so that the source code files for each of the classes you designed are available for edit within the solution project. Enhance the solution by defining an `interface` for the sporting teams relating to budgeting. Any teams that implement the interface

must provide details about how they are budgeted. Modify your test class to verify the interface functions properly.

7. Create a base `class` for a banking account. Decide what characteristics are common for checking and saving accounts and include these characteristics in the base `class`. Define subclasses for checking and savings. In your design, do not allow the banking base account to be instantiated—only the checking and saving subclasses. Include a presentation `class` to test your design.

8. Create a base `class` titled ReadingMaterial. Include subclasses of Online, Book, and Magazine. Design your classes so that common characteristics are placed in the ReadingMaterial `class`. Provide the unique characteristics of the subclasses in the derived classes. Define an `interface` called IPrintable that has a method that returns as a string how it is available in hard copy form (i.e., printable PDF, from a publisher or from a bookstore). Include a presentation `class` to test your design.

9. Define an application to include classes for Student, GraduateStudent, and UndergraduateStudent. Create .DLL files for the three classes. Include characteristics in the Student class that are common to GraduateStudent and UndergraduateStudent students. All three classes should override the ToString( ) method. GraduateStudent should include a data field for the type of undergraduate degree awarded, such as B.A. or B.S., and the location of the institution that awarded the degree. UndergraduateStudent should include classification (for example, freshman, sophomore), and parent or guardian name and address. Create a presentation `class` that instantiates student objects and enables details to be displayed on the form about individual students to test your design.

10. Create a housing application for a property manager. Include a base `class` named Housing. Include data characteristics such as address and year built. Include a `virtual` method that returns the total projected rental amount. Define an `interface` named IUnits that has a method that returns the number of units. The MultiUnit class should implement this interface. Create subclasses of MultiUnit and SingleFamily. SingleFamily should include characteristics such as size in square feet and availability of garage. MultiUnit might include characteristics such as the number of units. Create .DLL components for the housing classes. Define a presentation `class` to test your design.

© zeljkodan/Shutterstock.com

CHAPTER 12

Debugging and Handling Exceptions

IN THIS CHAPTER, YOU WILL:

- Gain an understanding of the different types of errors that are found in programs
- Look at debugging methods available in Visual Studio
- Discover how the Debugger can be used to find run-time errors
- Learn about exceptions, including how they are thrown and caught and filtered
- Become aware of and use exception-handling techniques to include try. . .catch. . .finally clauses
- Explore the many exception classes and learn how to write and order multiple catch clauses

Errors in code will happen. It does not matter how good of a programmer you are or how careful you are when you design your solutions. At some point, your program will not function properly. This chapter introduces you to one of the tools available in Visual Studio, the Debugger, which can be used to observe the run-time environment and locate logic errors. Using the Debugger, you can stop program execution and inspect the values stored in memory. You will explore how the Debugger enables you to take an up-close look at the code.

This chapter also introduces you to a special type of error called an exception. **Exceptions**, as the name implies, are unexpected conditions that happen (hopefully) infrequently. They are usually associated with error conditions or unexpected behaviors that cause abnormal terminations if they are not handled. This chapter introduces you to structured exception-handling techniques. It examines how your program can recover from some of these conditions and which conditions are fatal. You will investigate how the `try...catch...finally` statements, which are available in C# and other languages, are used to separate the program code from the exception-handling code. You will also learn that not all program errors should be treated as exceptions. Exception-handling techniques should be reserved for error conditions from which your program cannot recover.

Errors

The Visual Studio integrated development environment (IDE) reports errors in your program as soon as it is able to detect a problem. You read in Chapter 1 about two major types of errors: compiler or syntax errors and run-time errors. Compiler errors are the easiest to discover and eliminate. A **compiler error** is associated with a language rule violation. C# has about 90 keywords, uses a curly brace notation, and requires that statements end with a semicolon. C# adheres to a fairly sophisticated set of rules known as **C# Language Specifications**, which are the authoritative source for C# grammar and syntax. The specifications detail information on all aspects of the language. As long as you do not violate any rules, no syntax errors are issued. At the time of writing, the specifications are available for download, in Word format, at the MSDN online site: *http://msdn.microsoft.com/en-us/library/ms228593.aspx*. After you install Visual Studio, the specifications are placed on your hard drive. The document is named C# Language Specification. The Language Specifications document is loaded by default under VC#\Specifications under your Visual Studio installation directory.

If you fail to follow the grammar of the language as outlined in the specifications, for example, by misspelling a keyword, failing to place a semicolon at the end of a statement or carelessly placing a semicolon where it shouldn't be placed, Visual Studio places a squiggly line near the location where the error is encountered. This is illustrated in Figure 12-1.

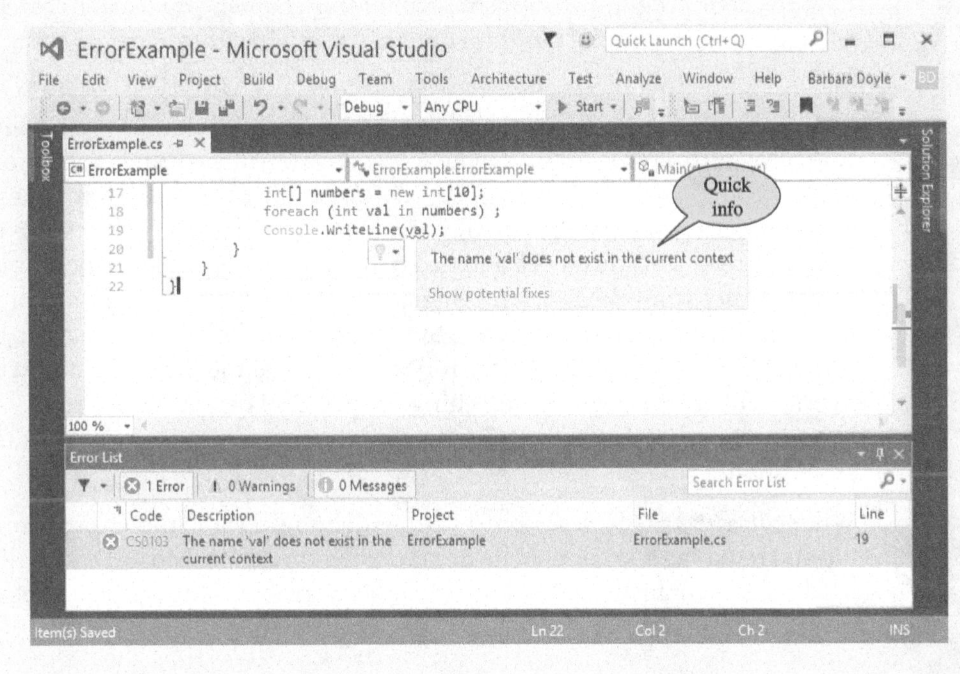

FIGURE 12-1 Syntax error—extraneous semicolon

As shown in the figure, the **Error List** window is displayed when an error is reported. Additional documentation about the error can be retrieved by selecting the error number in the **Error List** window and pressing the **F1** key. If you move the cursor over the problem area, a pop-up box called the **Quick Info** window displays information about the error. Sometimes, as shown in Figure 12-1, the message does not state exactly what the real problem is. Clicking on the light bulb or the link labeled "Show potential fixes" lists a number of possible remedies. None are correct for this example. Sometimes, you have to look beyond what the error message states. In Figure 12-1, for example, an extra semicolon was placed at the end of the `foreach` statement.

Run-Time Errors

Just because your program reports no syntax errors does not necessarily mean that it is running correctly. Sometimes, a program stops during execution. Other times, output is produced, but the output might not be correct. To further complicate matters, a program may sometimes work properly with some data, but crash when a certain value is entered. If a program stops during execution, this is a type of run-time error. For example, if you attempt to divide by zero, your program will crash. If you attempt to access an item outside of your array boundaries, convert an alphabetic character into an `int` using the `Parse( )` method, or try to find the square root of a negative number, your program will crash. Later in this chapter, you learn to catch exceptions such as these, so that the program does not halt when these special types of problems occur.

One form of run-time error is a logic error. **Logic errors** are normally associated with programs that run but produce incorrect results. If the application involves a loop, the loop could be performing one too many or one too few times, producing an incorrect result. It might be that the algorithm you devised to solve the problem is not correct. This produces a logic error. Sometimes variables do not have correct values, either from the user entering acceptable but incorrect values or from incorrectly initialized variables. Finding the types of problems that cause a logic error can sometimes be challenging. As you repeatedly look at the code, you might find yourself saying "This should work! Everything looks OK. There are no errors. . .why doesn't it work properly?" To fix these kinds of problems, you must resort to debugging the application.

Wikipedia (*http://wikipedia.org/*) defines **debugging** as a methodical process of finding and reducing bugs or defects in a computer program. Most IDEs, including Visual Studio, have sophisticated debugging tools available. This chapter explores some of these features.

Debugging in C#

When an application is developed—both during the design and also when the code is implemented—it is extremely important to desk check the solutions to make sure the program is producing consistently accurate results. When problems are discovered, you can use the Visual Studio Debugger to observe the run-time behavior of your program and help locate logic errors. The Debugger lets you break, or halt, the execution of the program to examine the code, evaluate variables in the program, and view the memory space used by your application. You can step through an application, checking the values of variables as each line is executed. Visual Studio lets you also set breakpoints in your program code. A **breakpoint** is a line in your program that you select and when it is reached, the program is suspended or placed in break mode. While in break mode, you have an opportunity to examine, and even change, the value of variables. The Visual Studio Debugger provides a **Debug** menu with access to the Debugger tools.

EXECUTION CONTROL

The Debugger provides commands for controlling the execution of your application. Using the Debugger, you can start or continue execution, break execution, step through an application, or run to a specific point in your program. You can examine the code while it is running to validate that the execution path is what you had intended.

Previously, to run your program, you used the **Debug** menu and selected **Start Without Debugging** or **Start Debugging** or used their shortcuts (**Ctrl+F5** or **F5**). As shown in Figure 12-2, the **Debug** menu offers additional choices.

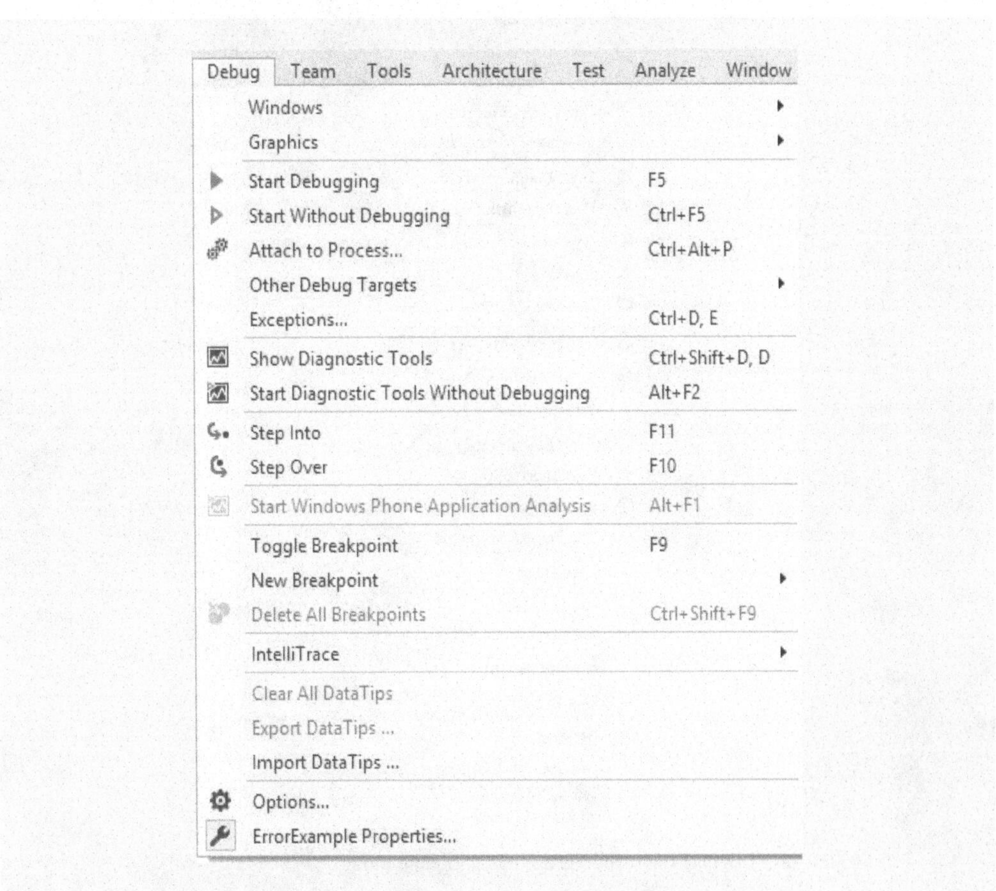

FIGURE 12-2 Debug menu options

12

As soon as you run your program by selecting the **Start Debugging** option, the **Debug** menu changes. The number of options available to you almost doubles. Figure 12-3 shows the options available when a program is running. Several of the options refer to a breakpoint.

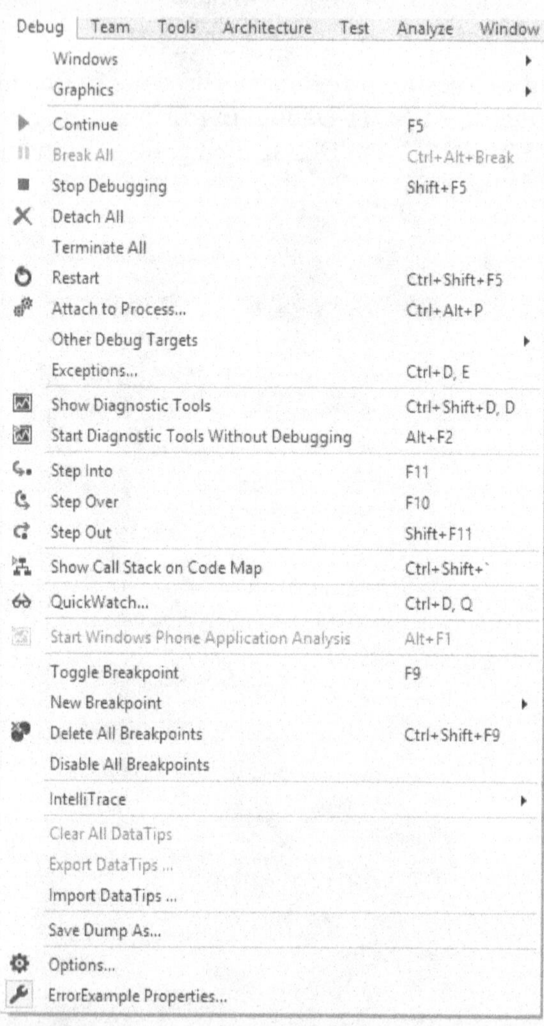

FIGURE 12-3 Debug menu options during debugging mode

BREAKPOINTS

Breakpoints are markers that are placed in an application, indicating that the program should halt execution when it reaches that point. When the break occurs, the program and the Debugger are said to be in break mode. While in break mode, you can examine expressions to see what values are being generated. If your program is not consistently producing correct results, this enables you to check intermediate values.

You can use several methods to add or set a breakpoint. The simplest method is to click anywhere on a line of executable code where you want to set a breakpoint and select **Toggle Breakpoint** from the **Debug** menu or use the **F9** keyboard shortcut. As the menu option name implies, pressing **F9** or selecting **Toggle Breakpoint** a second time turns off the breakpoint. The line of code is also automatically selected, as shown in Figure 12-4. You can place any number of breakpoints in your program following these methods.

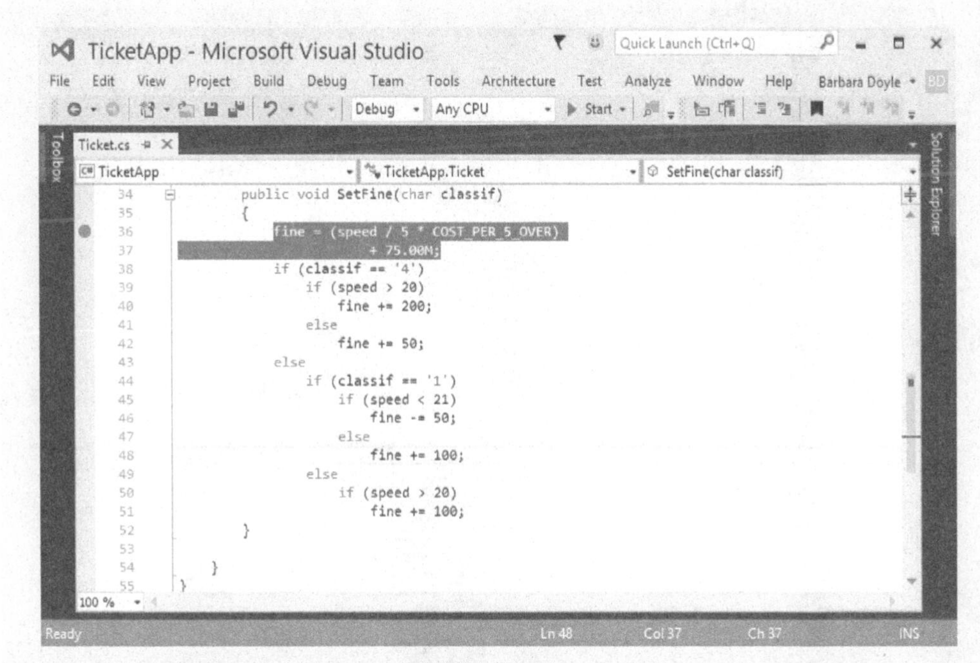

FIGURE 12-4 Breakpoint set

It can be useful to know how many times a breakpoint has been set. When you right-click the selected breakpoint glyph, you can then choose the **Hit Count** option from the shortcut menu.

After a breakpoint is set and you run your program by selecting the **Start Debugging** (**F5**) option, it runs completely as before until it reaches the breakpoint. At that line, the program halts, or pauses, before it executes the line. While the program is paused, you can move the mouse over any variable and see what its current value is. You can also select conditional expressions associated with `if` statements or loop expressions and see whether they have produced a `true` or `false` result at the time the program is halted. In addition to being able to hover over the variable to see its value, the Debugger will also display a **Locals** window near the bottom of the screen. This window automatically shows all variables and their values. This is illustrated in Figure 12-5.

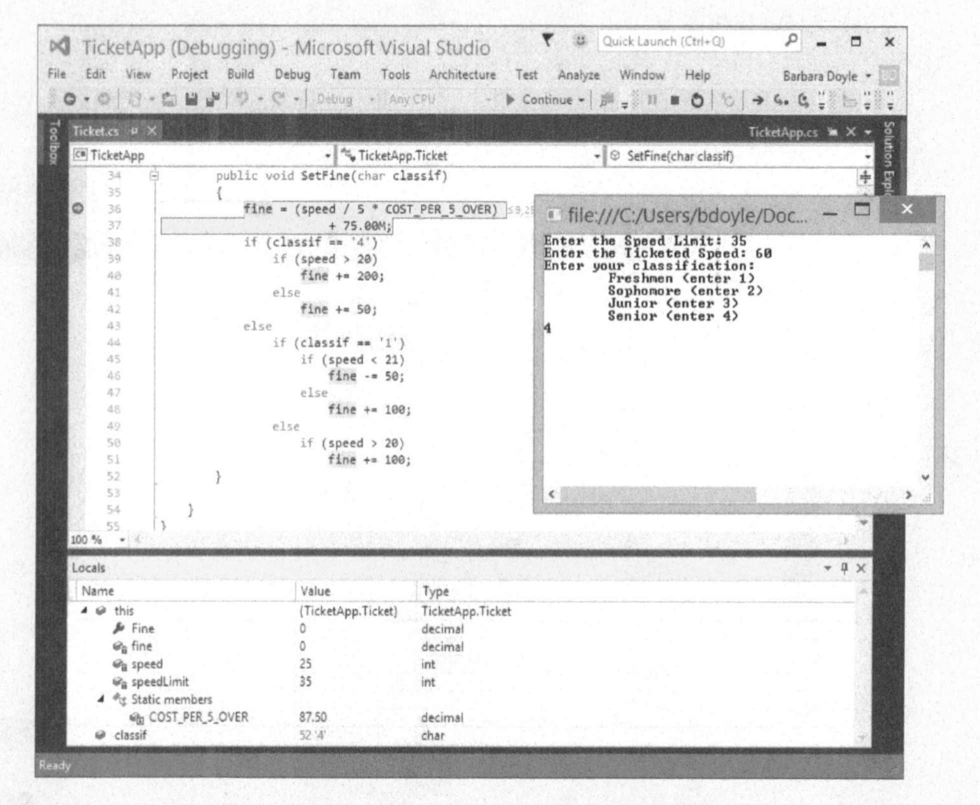

FIGURE 12-5 Locals window at the breakpoint

If you are in debugging mode and do not see the **Locals** window at the bottom of the screen, use the **Windows** option from the **Debug** menu to display the window.

In Chapter 5, an application was developed to calculate a speeding fine. The user was asked to input the speed limit, the speed they were traveling, and the student's classification. A breakpoint was set on the line that calculated the fine. Prior to the breakpoint, in the constructor of the `Ticket class`, the speed for the fine was calculated. As you review the **Locals** window shown in Figure 12-5, you see values for speed, speedLimit, and classif. At that breakpoint, Fine and fine values have not been set. You can see that execution halts prior to the program statements on that line being executed.

CONTINUE

After reviewing the variables and expressions, pressing **F5** or selecting **Continue** from the **Debug** menu takes the program out of break mode and restores it to a runtime mode. If only one breakpoint is set, the **Locals** window closes and the execution continues until the end of the Main( ) method is reached. At that point, the program terminates. However, if more than one breakpoint is set, selecting **Continue** causes the program to execute from the halted line until it reaches the second breakpoint. At that point, the **Locals** window is updated and the program is again paused. To illustrate the changes made to the **Locals** window, a second breakpoint was set on the last line in the SetFine( ) method of the Ticket class. As shown in Figure 12-6, the fine variable and Fine property were changed from 0 to 712.5. The Debugger highlights the line where the program halts. The process of stopping at each breakpoint would continue until the end of the program was encountered.

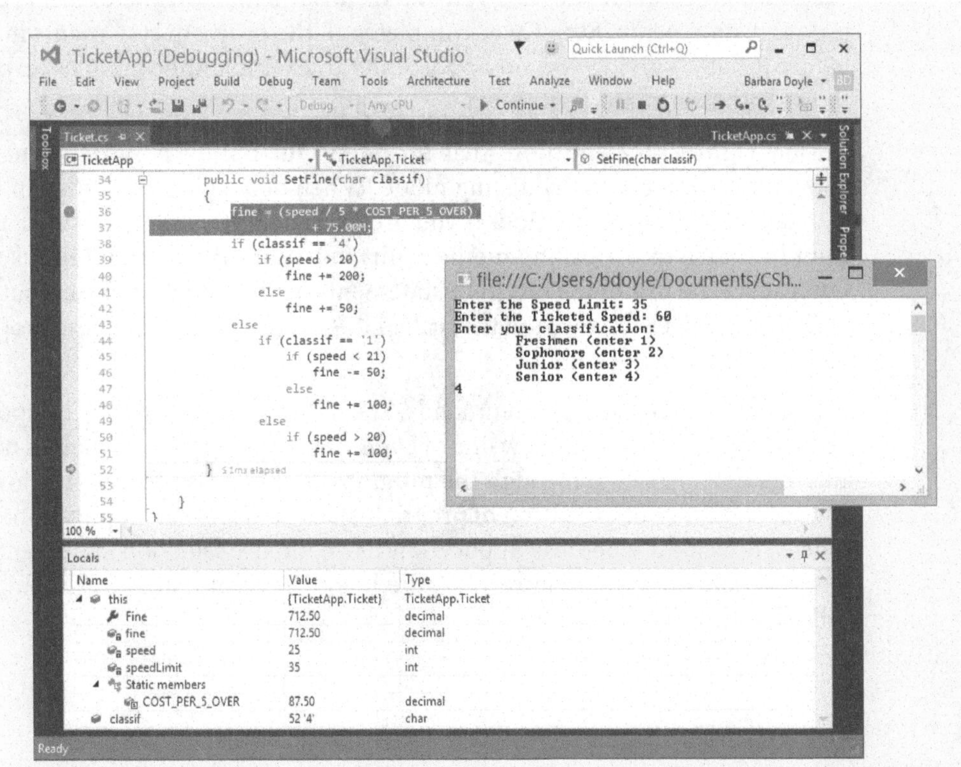

FIGURE 12-6 Next breakpoint

STEPPING THROUGH CODE

Instead of just setting specific breakpoints in your source code, you could step through your code line by line, see the execution path, and examine variable and expression values as they change. The **Debug** menu, which was shown in Figures 12-2 and 12-3, offers three commands for stepping through code while you are in break mode. These commands and their keyboard shortcuts are:

Step Into (F11)
Step Over (F10)
Step Out (Shift+F11)

Both the **Step Into** and **Step Over** commands tell the Debugger to execute the next line of code. The functionality of these two commands differs when a method is invoked. When the **Step Into** command encounters a line that contains a call to a method, the call is executed—then the program halts at the first line of code inside the called method. The **Step Over** command differs in that it executes the entire method called before it halts. It pauses at the first line of code outside the method.

Step Into is useful for allowing you to look inside a method and examine the method's program statements. **Step Over** completes all the program statements in the method before it halts—giving you no opportunity to examine the variables, expressions, or flow of program statements.

Review Figure 12-2 and note that the **Step Out** option is not shown. It does not appear until you are in debugging mode. When debugging, as shown in Figure 12-3, you can see this added option. If you are executing statements inside a method and want to return to the calling method, this third command, **Step Out**, is useful. **Step Out** causes the rest of the program statements in the method to be executed and then returns control to the method that called it. At that point, it halts the program so that you can examine the code.

When you use these step commands, the values are automatically updated in the **Locals** window with each new line of code. You can see the live changes made to variable values as you step through the program. You can also follow the flow of control and see the order of execution of program statements for the application. This can be especially helpful when the application has complex selection statements or nested loops. As illustrated in Figure 12-7, the line of code executed next is highlighted in yellow.

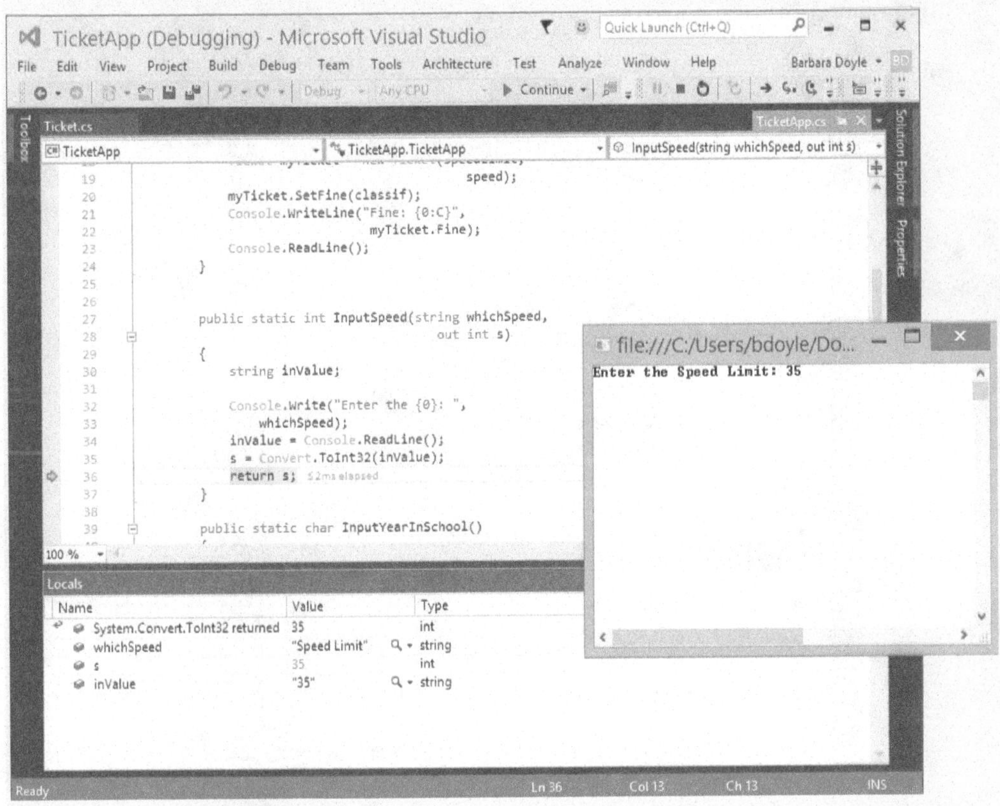

FIGURE 12-7 Breakpoint location

NOTE You can use the keyboard shortcuts **F11**, **F10**, and **Shift+F11**—representing **Step Into**, **Step Over**, and **Step Out**—when you are stepping through an application.

WATCHES

You also have the capability of setting **Watch** windows during debugging sessions. The **Watch** window lets you type in one or more variables or expressions that you want to observe while the program is running. Unlike the **Locals** window, which shows all variables currently in scope, you selectively identify the variables or expressions for the **Watch** window. A **QuickWatch** option on the **Debug** menu lets you type in a single variable or expression and have the Debugger show its value. From the **QuickWatch** dialog box, you can add the identifier to a **Watch** window. This is illustrated in Figure 12-8.

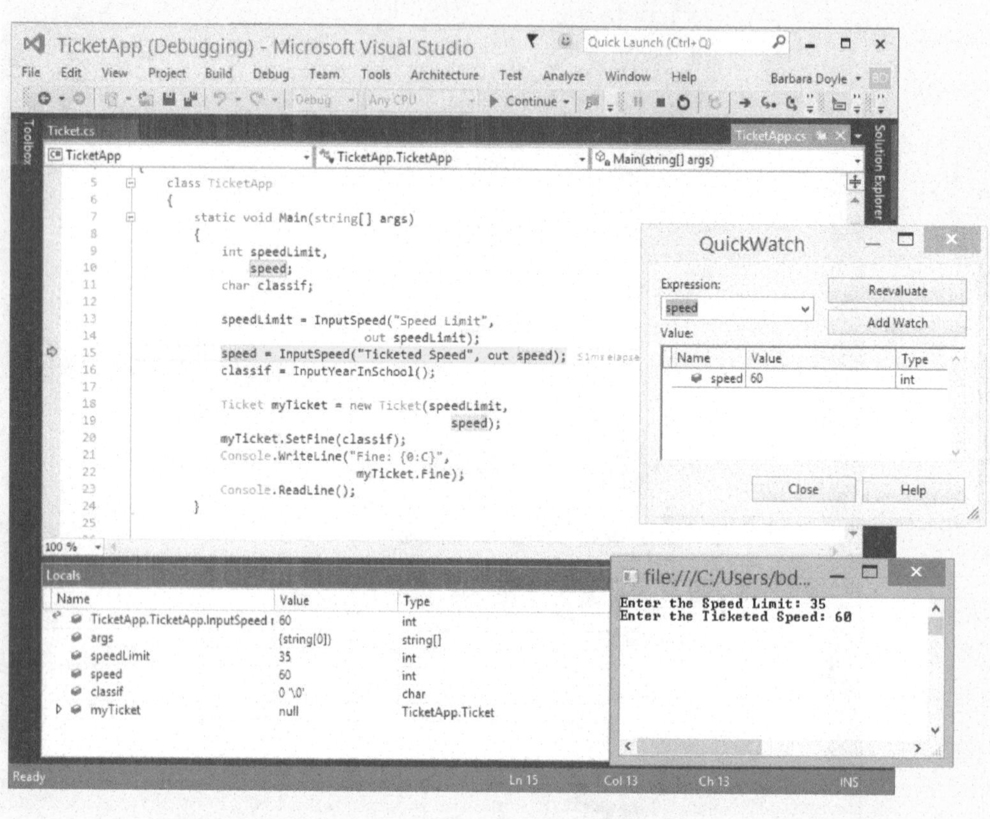

FIGURE 12-8 QuickWatch window

NOTE You can also do an instant watch of variable values. Hover over any variable while in break mode to see its current value.

Exceptions

For most of the programs you have developed to this point, you have assumed nothing unusual would occur. Given perfect situations for running applications, your programs might perform beautifully. However, errors do occur. You can take several actions to keep your program from crashing. You can include `if` statements that check values used as input to ensure that the value is numeric prior to parsing or converting the `string` value into its numeric equivalent. After `string` values are entered for console applications or retrieved from Windows controls, you can use the `IsNumber( )` method of the `char class` to test each character in the `string`, as shown here.

```
string aValue = "1334";
if (char.IsNumber(aValue[0])) // Tests the first character
```

Recall that one of the members of the `string` class is `Length`. Used with a `string` variable, the `Length` property returns the number of characters for that specific instance of the `string`. `Length` would return 4 for the `aValue` variable declared previously. You can use `aValue.Length` to create a loop that traverses through the `string` data, one character at a time, checking to see if each character making up the string is numeric.

You can also use `if` statements to test numeric values for valid ranges prior to using the number in arithmetic. You can use an `if` statement to test numeric values that will be used as divisors in arithmetic expressions to make sure the divisor is not zero prior to doing the division. You can also test subscript or index values used with arrays to make sure they are valid (that is nonnegative and one less than the dimensioned size). With Windows applications, an `if` statement can be included in your event-handling methods to test input controls, such as text boxes, for empty `string` input. You can also disable and make controls invisible by setting the `Enable` and `Visible` properties to `false` until valid entries are entered into other controls. When working with file applications, you can use `if` statements to make sure the file exists prior to attempting to retrieve values from the file. All of these suggestions can be incorporated into your solutions to reduce the likelihood of your program terminating abnormally. Some circumstances are beyond the control of the programmer, and unless provisions are made for handling exceptions, your program might crash or produce erroneous results. It is now time to take your programming skills to the next level and learn how to prevent abnormal terminations.

You have probably experienced unhandled exceptions being thrown while you browsed web pages or during your development of C# programs. Were you ever asked if you wanted to debug some application while you were on the Internet? Have you seen a screen similar to Figure 12-9 while you were developing your C# applications in Visual Studio?

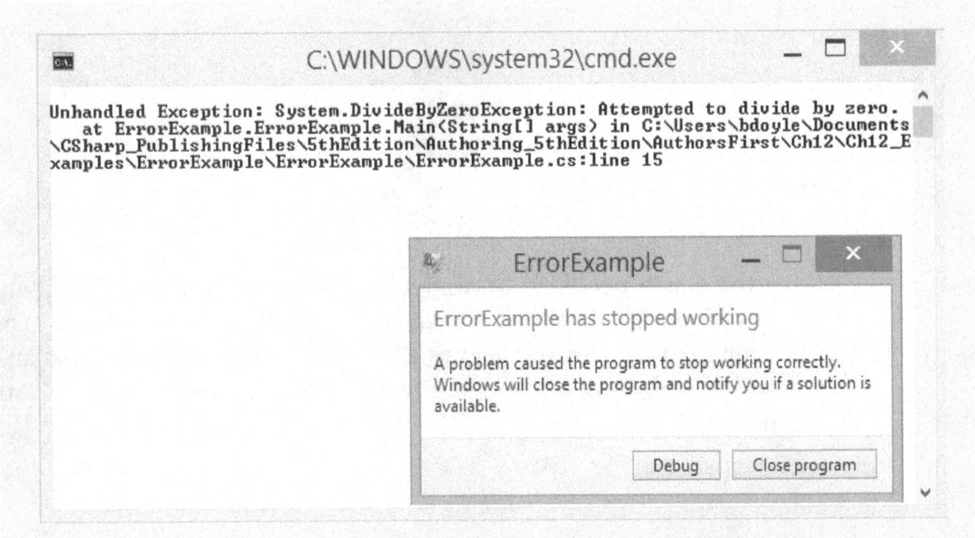

FIGURE 12-9 Microsoft error reporting

The message shown in Figure 12-9 was generated when a console application was run using **Start Without Debugging**. This dialog box asks you whether you want to close the program. You will notice that a button titled Debug is another option on this type of error message. If you select the **Debug** button, a Just-In-Time Debugger dialog box opens. This is illustrated in Figure 12-10. You normally do not want to try to debug the application while it is running.

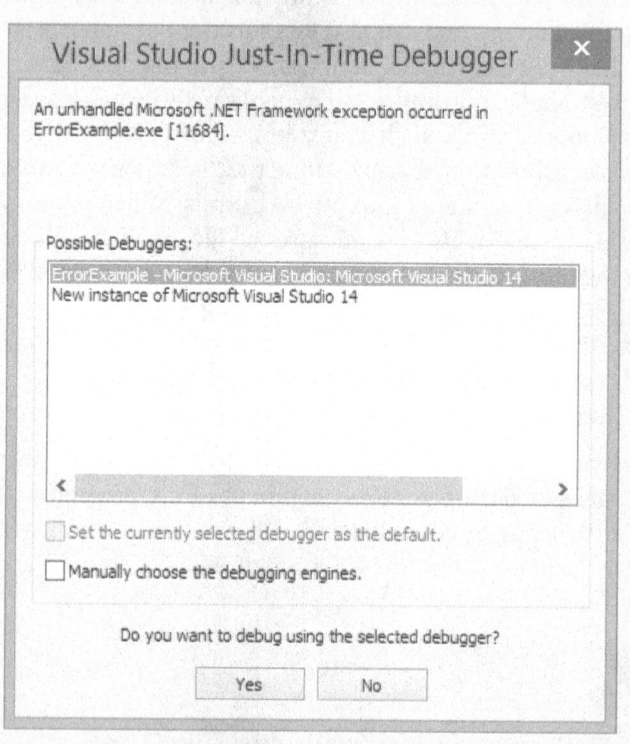

FIGURE 12-10 Just-In-Time Debugger

Clicking the **Close program** button, which is shown in Figure 12-9, when you are creating a console application in Visual Studio, often causes a message to be displayed that is similar to that shown in Figure 12-11. This output indicates that an unhandled exception has occurred. It also identifies what caused the exception ("Attempted to divide by zero.").

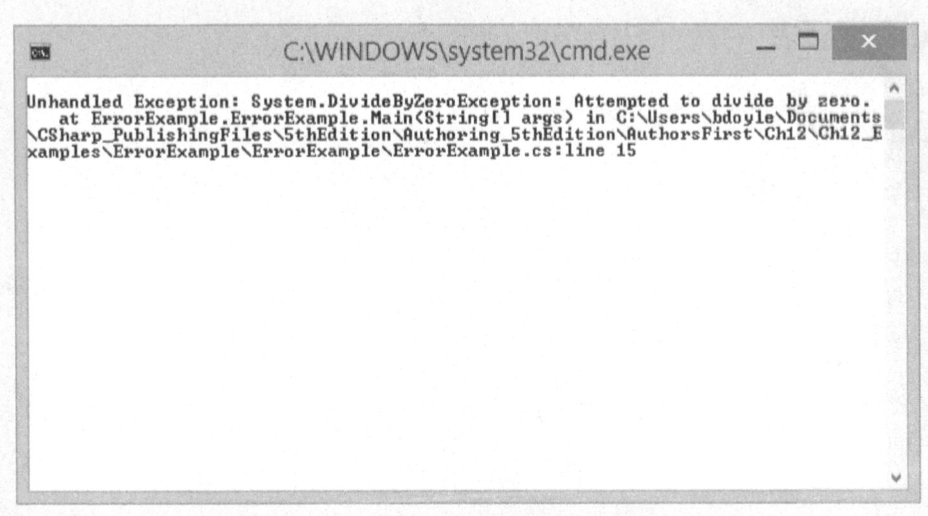

FIGURE 12-11 Unhandled exception in a console application

The messages from Figures 12-9 through 12-11 were generated during run-time, and the entire application halted. No error had been detected when the program was compiled. It was only when the application ran that the program crashed and the message was displayed.

Remember that during the compilation stage, the errors that are detected are those in which specific statements violate the syntax or grammar of the language, such as omission of a semicolon at the end of a statement.

Another type of message you might have seen is shown in Figure 12-12. You learned earlier that you can run applications in Visual Studio by selecting either **Debug, Start Debugging** or **Debug, Start Without Debugging**. If you run this same program and select **Debug, Start Debugging**, it generates a message similar to that shown in Figure 12-12.

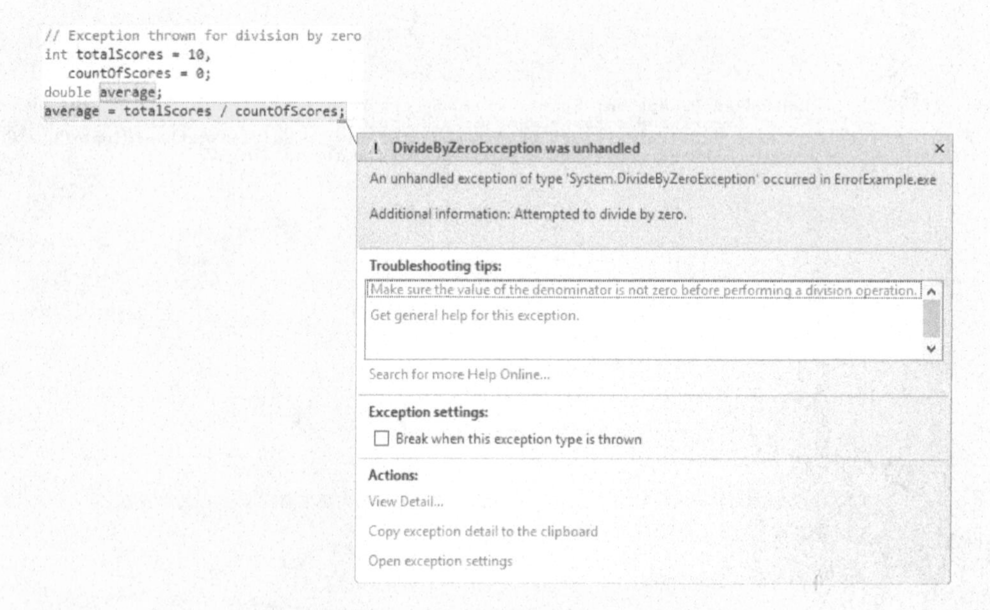

FIGURE 12-12 Unhandled exception thrown—dividing by zero

Notice in Figure 12-12 that the line of the code where the error was found is highlighted in yellow.

The exact message from Figure 12-12 is also generated within a Windows application during run-time when an attempt to divide by zero is reached. The Windows application had a statement in a button event-handler method that tried to divide by zero. Like the console application that generated the messages for Figures 12-9 and 12-11, the divide by zero in the Windows application error was not detected during compilation; the exception was not thrown until the user selected the button wired to the event-handler method that included the division statement. If that button had never been clicked, the application would have run smoothly.

Raising an Exception

If a program encounters an error such as division by zero during run-time, and the program cannot recover from the error, it **raises** or **throws an exception**. When this happens, execution halts in the current method and the common language runtime (CLR) attempts to locate an exception handler to handle the exception. An **exception handler** is a block of code that is executed when an exception occurs. You will learn how to write exception handlers in the following section.

If the CLR finds an exception handler in the current method, control is transferred to that code. If the current method does not contain an exception handler, that method is halted, and the parent method that called the method that threw the exception attempts to handle the exception. The exception is said to be **thrown back** to the calling method. If more than two methods are used, the exception continues to be thrown backward until it reaches the topmost method. If none of the methods includes code to handle the error, the CLR handles the exception—by halting the entire application. This can be very abrupt, as you saw with the messages displayed in Figures 12-9 through 12-12. Because data can be lost, you want to try to avoid such an experience with your programs. If the CLR handles the exception by halting your application, it is called an **unhandled exception**.

Bugs, Errors, and Exceptions

You learned that, in some instances, you can use selection statements, such as `if...else`, to programmatically prevent your programs from crashing. By checking for conditions that are likely to occur and writing statements to manage those situations, you prevent abnormal terminations. You could have avoided the problem presented for Figures 12-9 through 12-12. As you learned in Chapter 5, you can write program statements to test your divisors to make sure they are not zero before using them in division. Example 12-1 shows a statement that would have prevented those unhandled exceptions from being thrown.

EXAMPLE 12-1

```
int countOfScores = 0;
if (countOfScores > 0)
{
     averageTestScore = (examScore1 + examScore2 + examScore3)/
                        countOfScores;
}
else
{
     messageLabel.Text = "Problem with scores—" +
                         "unable to compute average";
}
```

The previous example is easy enough to fix. The problem identified may even be more appropriately labeled a bug instead of an exception. **Bugs** differ from exceptions in that they are normally labeled "programmer mistakes" that should be caught and fixed before an application is released. The problem that created the exception generated for Figures 12-9 through 12-12 was this: `countOfScores` was originally initialized to zero with no provisions made to change it from zero. This oversight caused an unhandled exception to be thrown.

In addition to bugs, programs can experience **errors** because of user actions. These actions can cause exceptions to be thrown. Entering the wrong type of data from the keyboard is an example of a common user mistake. When an application requests numeric data be entered as the program is running, C# initially stores the value entered in a `string` variable. But, as you are aware, to perform calculations with the value, it must be converted from the `string` to a number. If the user types nonnumeric characters when requested to enter numeric values, an exception is thrown. This happens as soon as the statement that has the call to the `Parse( )` method or methods in the `Convert class` is executed with the nonnumeric data. With a Windows application, if no instructions are found in the application for handling the exception, an unhandled exception message similar to that shown in Figure 12-13 is generated.

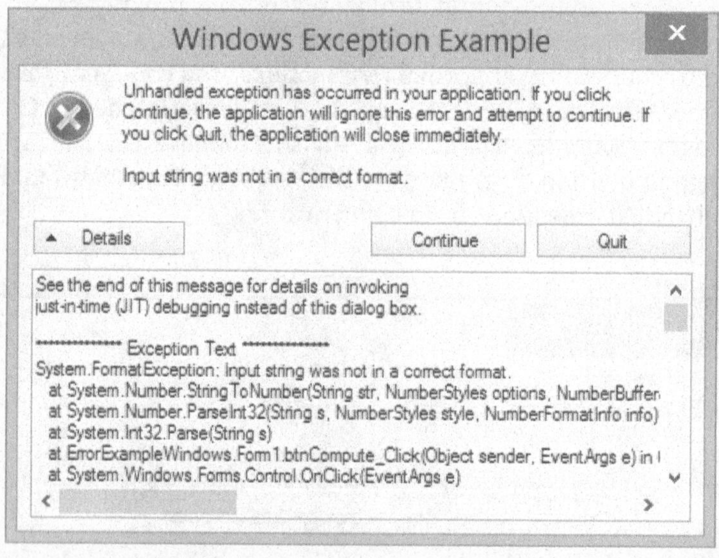

FIGURE 12-13 Unhandled exception raised by incorrect input string

NOTE Figures 12-9 through 12-13 are all examples of messages that are displayed when unhandled exceptions are thrown from a .NET application. They look different because of differences in the programs executed and the type of applications.

When an unhandled exception message is displayed as shown in Figure 12-13, you click on the **Details** button in Visual Studio to view a stack trace of methods with the method that raised the exception listed first. A **stack trace** is a listing of all the methods that are in the execution chain when the exception is thrown.

As you are already aware, when a program first starts, it begins execution in the `Main( )` method. From `Main( )`, it calls on or executes other methods, which can also call on other methods, and so on. When execution reaches the bottom of a given method, control is returned to the method that called it. This continues until control eventually returns to the end of the `Main( )` method, where the program finishes its execution. A stack is used to keep up with the execution chain. Unlike other types of memory, a stack can hold multiple entries. The stack is used as follows: When a method calls on another method, the calling method's identifier is placed on a stack. If another method is called, that calling method's name is placed on the stack. Thus, the first one placed on the stack is always `Main( )`—as the calling method of other methods. This puts `Main( )` on the bottom of the stack execution chain. After a method finishes its execution, the top method name is used (popped off the stack) and control is returned to it. This is the method that previously called the method that just finished. The first one placed on the stack is `Main( )` and the last one that eventually gets popped off the stack is `Main( )`. The stack is used to determine to which method along the execution chain control returns after a method finishes.

The stack used for the execution chain works exactly like the stack of trays at a cafeteria. The top one comes off first. The first one added to the stack is on the bottom. You created a stack in Chapter 11 when you were introduced to generic classes.

The `StringToNumber( )` method threw the exception to the `ParseInt32( )` method. `ParseInt32( )` is the .NET equivalent to the C# `int.Parse( )` method. No exception-handler method was found there, so the exception then bubbled up to the parent method, `Calculate_Click( )`. The CLR again looked for an exception handler in this `Calculate_Click( )` method. Because none was found, it continued bubbling the exception up through the `Windows.Forms.Control.OnClick( )` method, and so on. The stack trace includes all the methods that are still active at the time the exception is raised. Because none of the methods listed in the stack trace included code to handle that type of exception, the unhandled exception message is displayed. So, how do you handle the exception?

Exception-Handling Techniques

First remember that there are bugs, errors, and exceptions. If an event that creates a problem happens frequently, it is best to write program statements, using conditional expressions, to check for the potential error and provide program instructions for what to do when that problem is encountered. This is what you saw listed in Example 12-1. If the CLR has to halt a method and find an appropriate event handler, execution is slowed down. Thus, if a situation that might crash your program occurs frequently, write program statements using conditional expressions to deal with that situation.

Exception-handling techniques are for serious errors that occur infrequently. As stated previously, exceptions are those events from which your program would not be able to recover, such as attempting to read from a data file that does not exist. Included as part of .NET are a number of classes that can be used with your applications to enable them to be less prone to crashing. These exception classes are part of the original design of .NET and, thus, are integrated within the Framework class library (FCL). They facilitate managing exceptions in a consistent, efficient way. They are used with the `try...catch...finally` program constructs to handle unexpected types of conditions.

Realizing the importance of handling exceptions using an object-oriented approach, the developers of C# included provisions for handling exceptions as part of the original design of the FCL. The classes were not just added on as an afterthought as in some languages.

Try. . .Catch. . .Finally Blocks

C#, such as C++, Java, and other languages, handles exceptions through `try...catch...finally` blocks. The code that might create a problem is placed in the `try` block. The code to deal with the problem (the exception handler) is placed in `catch` blocks, which are also called **catch clauses**. The code that you want executed regardless of whether an exception is thrown is placed in the `finally` block. The syntax for a `try...catch...finally` block is as follows:

```
try
{
     // Statements that might create a problem
}
catch [(ExceptionClassName exceptionIdentifier)]
{
     // Exception handler statements
}
:    // [additional catch clauses]
[finally
{
     // Statements to be performed no matter what happens
}]
```

The colon (:) is used in the examples in this book to indicate that additional statements may be added to the program listing. Here, the colon would have to be replaced by additional `catch` clauses.

More than one `catch` clause can be included. A `try` block must include at least one `catch` clause. Notice that a square bracket follows the keyword `catch` to indicate that the parentheses and the argument list are optional. Omitting the argument list makes the catch **generic**—meaning any exception that is thrown is handled by executing the code within that catch block. If you include an exception type as part of the argument list, only exceptions that match the type listed are handled by that catch clause. You will see examples using multiple catch clauses later in this chapter.

The finally clause is also optional. It can be included if there is a segment of code that needs to be executed, no matter what. If, for example, you have an open file or database connection, you can put the close statements in the finally block to make sure the file or connection is closed properly. When code is included in all three blocks for the try...catch...finally construct, the statements inside the try block are attempted first. If no problem exists and the try block code is finished, the catch clause(s) is (are) skipped, and control transfers into the finally block where that code is executed.

If an unexpected error occurs in the try block that throws an exception, the code in the try block is halted at the line that caused the problem. The CLR tries to find a matching exception handler within the current method. If one is found, control transfers to the first listed catch clause that can handle the type of execution thrown. The catch clause statements are executed, and control transfers to the finally block where its code is executed. Notice with both situations (exception thrown and no exception thrown) that if a finally block is included, the statements in it are executed.

Another important point to make sure you understand is the fact that control is never returned to the try block after an exception is thrown. The statement that creates a problem in the try block is the last one tried in the try clause. After control is transferred out of the try block, no other statements inside the try block are ever executed.

Example 12-2 uses a try...catch block to keep the program from terminating abnormally. The example includes a generic catch clause—no specific exception type is listed.

EXAMPLE 12-2

```
// ExceptionExample.cs
// Uses a generic catch block to catch any
// type of exception that is thrown.
using System;
using static System.Console;

namespace ExceptionExample
{
    class ExceptionExample
    {
        static void Main(string[] args)
        {
            int [ ] examScore;
            int totalScores = 0;
```

12

```
            int countOfScores = 0;
            string inValue;
            double averageTestScore;
            try
            {
                Write("How many scores will you enter? ");
                inValue = ReadLine( );
                countOfScores = int.Parse(inValue);
                examScore = new int[countOfScores];
                for (int i = 0; i < countOfScores; i++)
                {
                     Write("Enter score {0}: ",i+1);
                     inValue = ReadLine( );
                     examScore[i] = int.Parse(inValue);
                     totalScores += examScore[i];
                }
                averageTestScore = totalScores / countOfScores;
                WriteLine("Average is {0}", averageTestScore);
            }
            catch
            {
                WriteLine("Problem with scores - " +
                          "Cannot compute average");
            }
            ReadKey( );
        }
    }
}
```

If the application is run and the user types a nonnumeric character, such as the value `9U` (shown entered for score 3 in Figure 12-14), the program does not crash. Instead, the exception-handler code found in the `catch` block is executed and alerts the user of the error.

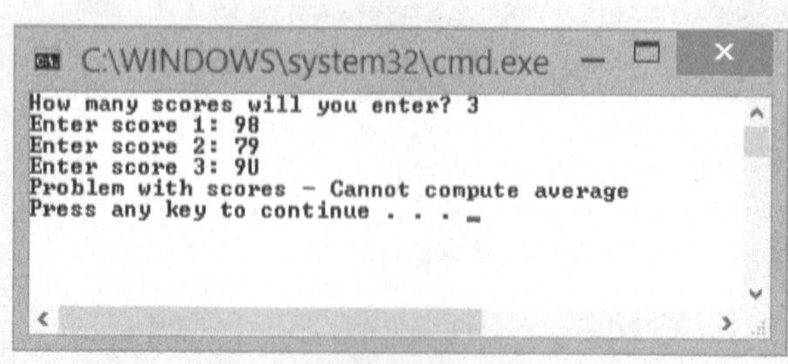

FIGURE 12-14 Generic catch block handles the exception

GENERIC CATCHES

The problem with using a generic `catch` to avoid abnormal termination is that because any type of exception is handled by the `catch` code, you are never quite sure what caused the exception to be thrown. Take, for example, the two output listings shown in Figure 12-15.

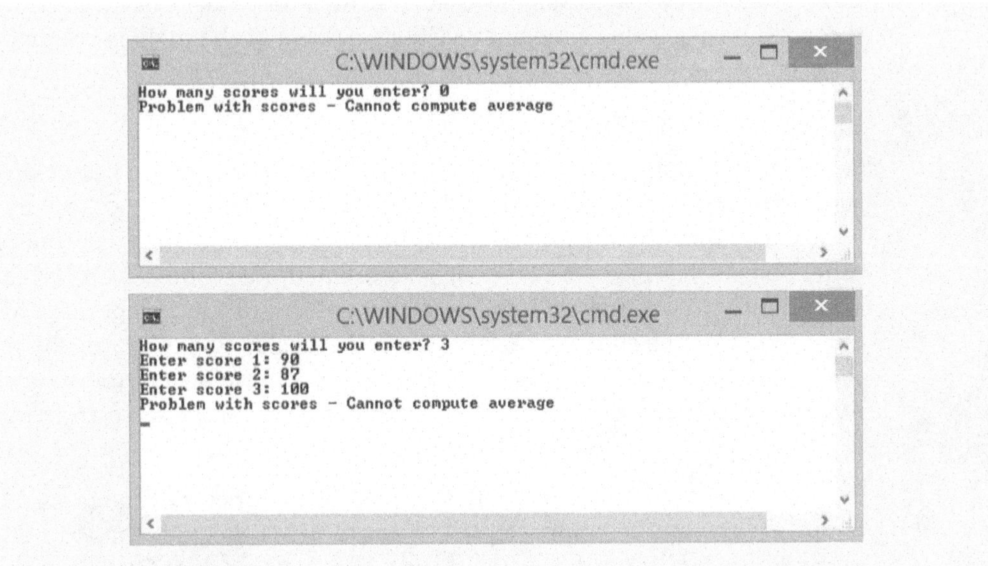

FIGURE 12-15 Exceptions thrown because of division by zero and programmer error

What caused these exceptions to be thrown? The first output in Figure 12-15 is generated because of an attempt to divide by zero. The second one threw an "Index outside the bounds of the array" exception. No message of "Index outside the bounds of the array" is displayed in response to a bug in the program. The exception was thrown when the statement that computes the average from Example 12-2 was changed to the statement shown in Example 12-3.

12

EXAMPLE 12-3

```
averageTestScore = totalScores / examScore [10]; // Invalid
```

There is no `examScore[10]`. Example 12-2 had the correct arithmetic statement; the divisor should be `countOfScores`.

```
averageTestScore = totalScores / countOfScores; // Correct
```

NOTE The computation was modified to illustrate that programmer mistakes (bugs) can lead to exceptions being thrown.

Although you can keep the program from terminating abnormally by using a generic `catch` clause, you can debug more easily if you know what caused the exception to be thrown. Just displaying a message saying there is a problem does not help a lot.

Exception Object

When an exception is raised with .NET languages, an `object` is created to represent the exception. All exception objects inherit from the `base class` for exceptions, named `Exception`. It is part of the `System namespace`. An exception `object`, like other objects, has properties and behaviors (methods). The `catch` clause may list an exception `class` name, and an `object` identifier inside parentheses following the `catch` keyword as shown in Example 12-4. Actually to use any of the properties of the exception `object` that is created, you must have an `object` name. Using the `catch { }` without an exception type does not give you access to an `object`.

One of the properties of the `Exception base class` is `Message`. `Message` returns a `string` describing the exception. Because it is a property of the `base class`, it can be used with any exception `object`. Example 12-4 includes the `Exception class` in the argument list for the `catch` clause. The `object` identifier `e` is used to name an `object` of that `class`. The `object` `e` can now be used with any of the properties or methods of the `Exception class`. The `Message` property, associated with `object` `e`, is used inside the `catch` clause to display a message describing the exception.

NOTE You cannot use the `Message` property or any of the other members of the `class` without an `object`. This is one reason the argument list `(System.Exception e)` needs to be included.

EXAMPLE 12-4

```
catch (System.Exception e)
{
     Error.WriteLine("Problem with scores - " +
                     "Cannot compute average");
     Error.WriteLine(e.Message);
}
```

NOTE Since the `using System; namespace` is automatically added when you create an application, you do not have to fully qualify references to the `Exception class` or other classes in the `System namespace` in order to reference them.

No filtering of exceptions occurs by adding the `(Exception e)` for the argument list. Any exception that is thrown in this method is caught because all exceptions are derived from this `base System.Exception class`. The advantage of typing the argument list following the `catch` is that you have an `object` identifier, such as `e`, to use with properties. In Example 12-4, in addition to displaying the programmer-supplied message indicating that there is a problem, an additional `string`, "Index was outside the bounds of the array," is displayed. That is the current value of the `Message` property for `object e`. Both of these strings are displayed on the `Console.Error` output device. Now if the application is run again and it still contains the programmer error previously entered, the output window lists what caused the exception to be thrown, as shown in Figure 12-16.

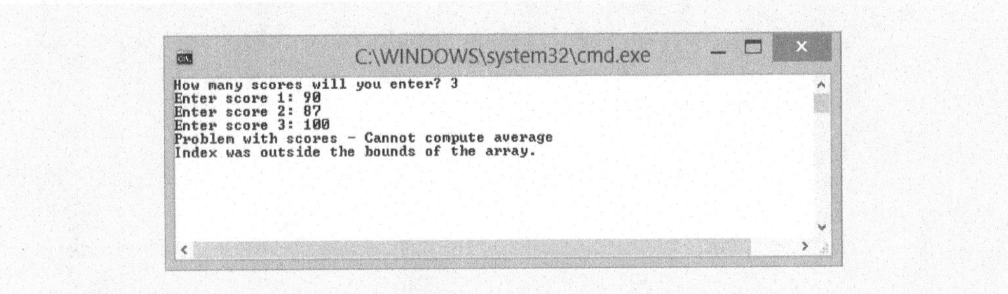

FIGURE 12-16 Use of Message property with the exception object

NOTE Calls were made to the `System.Console.Error.WriteLine( )` method to illustrate that it is probably more appropriate to display error messages to an Error output device. By default, its output goes to the console screen, just as it does with other `Console class` output. However, the `Error` output device can be changed to display to a different device. Like other examples illustrated for this edition, since the `using static System.Console;` directive was added, it is not necessary to precede `Error` with the `Console class` name.

12

The argument list is normally included to filter the exceptions. By specifying more than one exception filter, you can write code in the `catch` clauses that is specific to the particular exception thrown. To do that, you have to know more about the different exception classes that make up the .NET Framework class library, and the following section discusses some of them.

Exception Classes

When an error occurs, it is reported by creating and throwing an `object` that corresponds to the specific type of exception that is thrown. The `object` contains information about the error. There are a number of different types of exceptions that can be thrown.

Derived Classes of the Base Exception Class

Table 12-1 presents some of the derived classes of the `base Exception class`. The `ApplicationException` and `SystemException` classes form the basis for run-time exceptions and are discussed following Table 12-1.

TABLE 12-1 Derived classes of the base System.Exception class

Classes that inherit from Exception
`Microsoft.Build.BuildEngine.InvalidProjectFileException`
`Microsoft.WindowsMobile.DirectX.DirectXException`
`System.ApplicationException`
`System.ComponentModel.Design.ExceptionCollection`
`System.Configuration.SettingsPropertyIsReadOnlyException`
`System.IO.IsolatedStorage.IsolatedStorageException`
`System.Runtime.Remoting.MetadataServices.SUDSGeneratorException`
`System.Runtime.Remoting.MetadataServices.SUDSParserException`
`System.SystemException`
`System.Windows.Forms.AxHost.InvalidActiveXStateException`

© Cengage Learning

NOTE From Table 12-1, the two exception classes of interest are the `ApplicationException` and `SystemException` classes. The other classes listed in the table are not discussed in this chapter; however, you are encouraged to explore the MSDN documentation to learn more about them.

ApplicationException Class

You can write your own exception classes or use one of the many supplied .NET exception classes. The `ApplicationException` `class` was included by the designers of .NET to enable a distinction to be made between user-defined exceptions and exceptions defined by the system. If you write your own exceptions, they should derive from `ApplicationException`. The `ApplicationException` `class` is thrown by a user program, not the CLR.

SystemException Class

The system-supplied exception classes for run-time exceptions derive mainly from the `SystemException` `class`. `SystemException` adds no functionality to classes. Except for its constructor, the `SystemException` `class` has no additional properties or methods other than those derived from the `Exception` and `Object` classes. The `Exception` `class` has several properties. You have already seen the results of two of them—`Message` and `StackTrace`. `StackTrace` returns a `string` that contains the called trace of methods. The `Message` property provides details about the cause of the exception. Another property of the `Exception` `class`, `HelpLink`, can contain a URL to a Help file that can provide additional information about the cause of the exception. The `Source` property gets or sets the name of the application or the `object` that caused the error, and the `TargetSite` property gets the method that threw the exception.

Over 70 classes derive from the `SystemException` `class`. Table 12-2 lists a few of the more common exceptions that are thrown. You might want to consider adding handlers to catch many of these.

TABLE 12-2 Derived classes of SystemException

Exception classes derived from the SystemException class	Description of circumstances causing an exception to be thrown
`System.ArgumentException`	One of the arguments provided to a method is invalid
`System.ArithmeticException`	There are errors in an arithmetic, casting, or conversion operation. Has derived members of `System.DivideByZeroException` and `System.OverflowException`
`System.ArrayTypeMismatchException`	An attempt is made to store an element of the wrong type within an array

(continues)

TABLE 12-2 Derived classes of SystemException (*continued*)

Exception classes derived from the SystemException class	Description of circumstances causing an exception to be thrown
`System.FormatException`	The format of an argument does not meet the parameter specifications
`System.IndexOutOfRangeException`	An attempt is made to access an element of an array with an index that is outside the bounds of the array
`System.InvalidCastException`	There is invalid casting or explicit conversion
`System.IO.IOException`	An I/O error occurs
`System.NullReferenceException`	There is an attempt to dereference a null `object` reference
`System.OutOfMemoryException`	There is not enough memory to continue the execution of a program
`System.RankException`	An array with the wrong number of dimensions is passed to a method

© Cengage Learning

Many of the exception classes included in Table 12-2 have additional classes that are derived from them. You will want to explore the documentation to learn about those derived `class` members. As given in Table 12-2, one derived `class` of the `ArithmeticException` `class` is the `DivideByZeroException` `class`. This is the exception thrown previously in this chapter.

You should be aware that division by zero involving floating-point operands does not throw an exception. Exceptions are only thrown for integral or integer data types. The result of division by zero is reported as positive infinity, negative infinity, or Not-a-Number (NaN). This follows the rules from IEEE 754 arithmetic. .NET languages were designed to implement these rules.

NOTE Because implicit type conversion occurs when you have a floating-point operand with an integer, if either operand is of type `double` or `float`, no exception is thrown when you divide by zero.

Filtering Multiple Exceptions

Following a single try block, you can include multiple catch clauses. This enables you to write code specific to the thrown exception. When you do this, the order of placement of these clauses is important. They should be placed from the most specific to the most generic. Because all exception classes derive from the Exception class, if you are including the Exception class, it should always be placed last. Because the DivideByZeroException class derives from the ArithmeticException class, if both are included, DivideByZeroException should be listed first. Example 12-5 illustrates using several catch clauses to filter the exceptions. A finally clause is also included.

EXAMPLE 12-5

```
// MultipleCatches.cs
// Demonstrates the use of multiple catch
// clauses and a finally clause.
using System;
using static System.Console;

namespace MultipleCatches
{
    class MultipleCatches
    {
        static void Main(string[] args)
        {
            int [ ] examScore;
            int totalScores = 0;
            int countOfScores = 0;
            string inValue;
            double averageTestScore;
            try
            {
                Write("How many scores will you enter? ");
                inValue = ReadLine( );
                countOfScores = int.Parse(inValue);
                examScore = new int[countOfScores];
                for (int i = 0; i < countOfScores; i++)
                {
                    Write("Enter score {0}: ", i+1);
                    inValue = ReadLine( );
                    examScore[i] = int.Parse(inValue);
                    totalScores += examScore[i];
                }
                averageTestScore = totalScores / countOfScores;
                WriteLine("Average is {0}", averageTestScore);
            }
```

12

```
            catch (FormatException e)
            {
                Error.WriteLine("Problem with one of " +
                    "the operands - Cannot compute average!");
                Error.WriteLine("Exception type: {0}", e.Message);
            }
            catch (DivideByZeroException e)
            {
                Error.WriteLine("No scores were " +
                    "entered - Cannot compute average!");
                Error.WriteLine("Exception type: {0}", e.Message);
            }
            catch (ArithmeticException e)
            {
                Error.WriteLine("Error in your " +
                    "arithmetic or casting.");
                Error.WriteLine("Exception type: {0}", e.Message);
            }
            catch (Exception e)
            {
                Error.WriteLine("Any other problem" +
                                 "Cannot compute average!");
                Error.WriteLine("Exception type: {0}", e.Message);
            }
            finally
            {
                WriteLine("...\n...\n...\n" +
                          "Terminated Normally!!!");
            }
            ReadKey( );
        }
    }
}
```

The application in Example 12-5 is poised to avoid terminating abnormally. Because `Exception` is the `base` exception `class`, any exceptions not caught from the previous catch clauses would be caught. It is basically the same as writing the `catch` without the parenthesized arguments.

In Example 12-5, you cannot just remove the `(Exception e)` from the last `catch`. If you do, a syntax error is generated. The error is not generated because of removal of the type; it is because the `catch` block uses the identifier `e` to display the exception type. If you remove `"(Exception e)"`, be sure to modify the code in the `catch` clause so that it does not refer to the `e` `object`.

NOTE You cannot write a `catch` unless you include it within a `try` block.

Now, when the user enters nonnumeric characters, such as the 9U entered during the running of the application shown in Figure 12-14, the output shown in Figure 12-17 is produced.

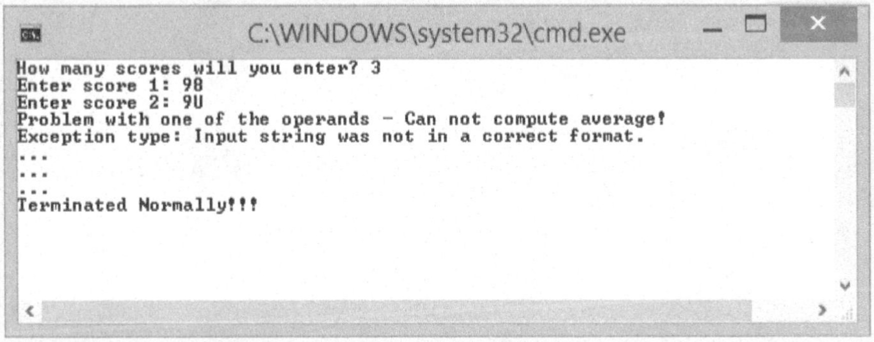

```
C:\WINDOWS\system32\cmd.exe
How many scores will you enter? 3
Enter score 1: 98
Enter score 2: 9U
Problem with one of the operands - Can not compute average!
Exception type: Input string was not in a correct format.
...
...
...
Terminated Normally!!!
```

FIGURE 12-17 Number FormatException thrown

After the statements in the `catch` clause are executed, the `finally` clause is executed as shown in Figure 12-17. Figure 12-18 shows the output produced when no scores are entered.

```
C:\WINDOWS\system32\cmd.exe
How many scores will you enter? 0
No scores were entered - Can not compute average!
Exception type: Attempted to divide by zero.
...
...
...
Terminated Normally!!!
```

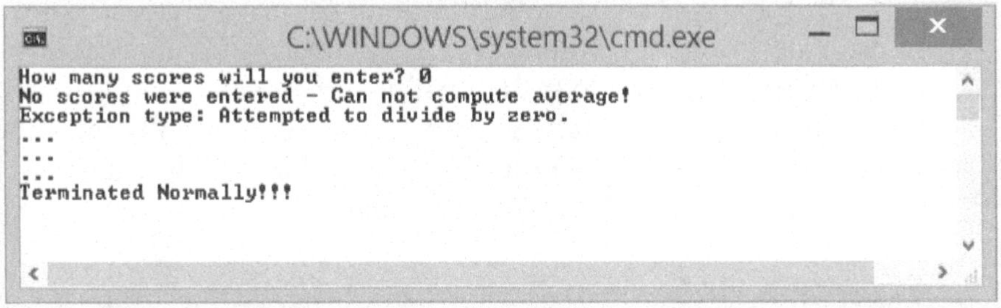

FIGURE 12-18 DivisionByZero exception thrown

When no scores are entered, a different exception is thrown; a different `catch` clause is executed. Normally, division by zero in an application such as this should not be caught by an exception. Instead, it should be dealt with programmatically by checking to ensure that scores are entered before the division occurs. If division by zero errors rarely occur in your programs, you can write an exception-handling technique to deal with those extreme cases.

Integer division was performed for the calculation of the average. No exception would have been thrown when no scores were entered if one of the operands had been cast to a `double` as follows:

```
averageTestScore = totalScores / (double) countOfScores;
```

The application terminates normally. The floating-point division by zero produced the result of NaN, as shown in Figure 12-19.

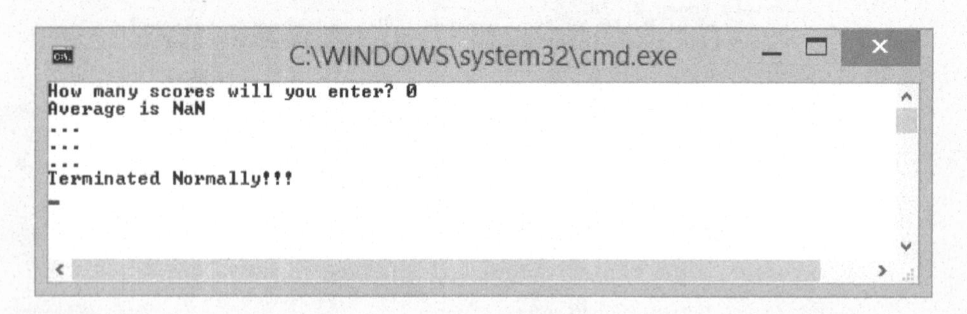

FIGURE 12-19 Floating-point division by zero

No control was transferred into any of the `catch` clauses for this run. The division occurred (division by zero), followed by execution of the last statement in the `try` block, which printed "Average is NaN." The NaN was the result of the floating-point division. From the `finally` clause, "Terminated Normally!!!" is printed.

The `catch` clauses for Example 12-5 simply displayed messages indicating what type of error occurred. You would expect that real-world applications would do much more. Corrective action to ensure that the program not only terminates normally but also produces correct results every time the application is run should be your goal when you are writing programs. If an exception error is caught, you should fix the problem and keep the application running.

Exception Filters

One of the new features available with C# 6.0 are exception filters. **Exception filters** allow you to do another layer of testing before the segment of code included with the catch clause is executed. To add the filter, use an `if` statement to specify the conditional expression you want tested. When the exception is thrown and the associated `catch` clause is identified, additional testing occurs before the block of code is executed. When the conditional expression evaluates to `true`, the body of the corresponding `catch` is executed. When the conditional expression associated with the `if` statement evaluates to `false`, the body of the `catch` clause is not executed, but instead it looks at subsequent listed `catch` clause to handle the exception. To add a filter, place the `if` statement on the heading line before the opening curly braces for the `catch` clause, as is illustrated in Example 12-6.

EXAMPLE 12-6

```
catch (Exception e)  if (countOfScores == 0)
{
     WriteLine("No scores entered - division by zero avoided!");
}
catch (Exception e)
{
     WriteLine("A problem other than division by zero occurred. " +
               "Cannot compute average!");
     WriteLine("Exception type: {0}", e.Message);
}
```

As illustrated in Example 12-6, the `Exception class` can appear in more than one catch clause. Only one of the catch bodies will be executed.

NOTE

As was shown with the multiple catch clause example, Example 12-5, if a `DivideByZeroException` catch clause appeared in the code before the `Exception` class catch clause, the `DivideByZeroException` catch clause would be executed. Only one catch clause is ever executed.

CUSTOM EXCEPTIONS

There are many more exception classes derived from the `System.SystemException class` than you will ever use; however, you also have the opportunity to write your own exception classes. The only requirement is that custom exception classes must derive from the `ApplicationException class`.

NOTE

When defining your own exception classes, it is a good idea to use the word "Exception" as part of the identifier. This adds to the readability and maintainability of the code.

Creating an exception `class` is no different from creating any other `class`. Example 12-7 shows a customized (programmer-defined) exception `class` that can be thrown when floating-point division by zero is attempted. Using the word "Exception" as part of its identifier name, it is named `FloatingPtDivisionException`.

EXAMPLE 12-7

```
public class FloatingPtDivisionException : ApplicationException
{
    public FloatingPtDivisionException(string exceptionType)

        : base (exceptionType)
    {
        // Empty body
    }
}
```

No additional functionality is added by the `FloatingPtDivisionException` `class`—beyond what is available from the parent classes. The constructor for the `FloatingPtDivisionException` `class` has one argument. It is sent to the `base` constructor using the keyword `base`. This argument is a `string` indicating the exception type. The `FloatingPtDivisionException` exception `class` could be saved as a DLL and referenced by numerous applications.

To test the exception, a new `class` is created to include a `try...catch` block. For simplicity, both classes are included in the same file but only `TestOfCustomException` is shown. `TestOfCustomException` is written as shown in Example 12-8.

EXAMPLE 12-8

```
public class TestOfCustomException
{
    static void Main(string[] args)
    {
        double value1 = 0,
               value2 = 0,
               answer;
        try
        {
            // Could include code to enter new values.
            answer = GetResults(value1, value2);
        }
        catch (FloatingPtDivisionException excepObj)
        {
            Error.WriteLine(excepObj.Message);
        }
        catch
        {
            Error.WriteLine("Something else  happened!");
        }
```

```
            ReadKey( );
        }

        static double GetResults(double value1, double value2)
        {
            if (value2 < 0.0000001) // Be careful comparing floating-
                                    // point values for equality.
            {
                FloatingPtDivisionException excepObj = new
                    FloatingPtDivisionException("Exception type: " +
                            "Floating-point division by zero");
                throw excepObj;
            }
            return value1 / value2;
        }
    }
```

The result of one test run of Example 12-8 is shown in Figure 12-20.

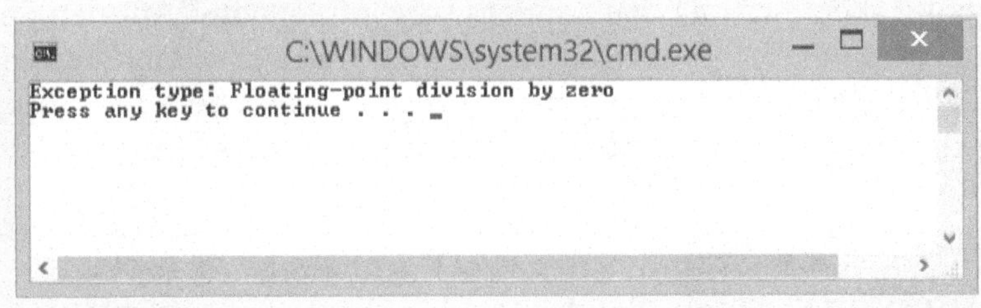

FIGURE 12-20 TestOfCustomException threw FloatingPtDivisionException exception

In the `GetResults( )` method of Example 12-8, the conditional expression of `(value2 < 0.0000001)` was used to determine when `value2` was zero. Notice that a relational test was performed, instead of using an equality expression such as `(value2 == 0)`. Using the equality operator with floating-point variables produces inconsistent results because the value is not stored as a finite value.

To learn more about the IEEE Standard for Binary Floating-Point Arithmetic, explore the website www.ieee.org.

In Example 12-8, two `catch` clauses are included. The first listed is the most specific. Listing the most specific to the most generic is a requirement when you include multiple catches; otherwise, the most specific would never be reached. As soon as one of the filters matches, its block of code is executed and then control either transfers to the bottom of the entire try...catch statement or transfers to a finally statement if one is present.

NOTE Also, had the last catch clause (catch (Exception)) been listed first, C# would issue a syntax error for the second catch clause indicating "A previous catch clause already catches all exceptions of this or a super type."

Remember that writing the catch clause without an argument list is the same as writing catch (Exception), which is the base of all exceptions. The last catch clause catches all other exceptions. If any exceptions other than FloatingPtDivisionException are encountered, Exception is thrown.

Throwing an Exception

In the GetResults( ) method that tested the programmer-defined custom exception, an exception object is instantiated when "an exceptional condition occurs." This exceptional condition is (value2 < 0.0000001). It could be any condition, but it should be one that happens very infrequently. After an object (excepObj) of the FloatingPtDivisionException class is instantiated with a string value of "Exception type: Floating-point division by zero," the excepObj object is thrown. The GetResults( ) method is presented again in Example 12-9 for your review.

EXAMPLE 12-9

```
static double GetResults(double value1, double value2)
{
     if (value2 < 0.0000001)// Be careful comparing floating-
                            // point values for equality.
     {
          FloatingPtDivisionException excepObj = new
               FloatingPtDivisionException
                    ("Exception type: " +
                        "Floating-point division by zero");
          throw excepObj;
     }
     return value1 / value2;
}
```

The CLR is not throwing the exception here. Instead, the exception is thrown by the program using the throw keyword. When the object excepObj is thrown in the GetResults( ) method, the exception object propagates back up the call chain, first stopping at the method that called it to see if a catch is available to handle it.

As you examine Example 12-8, notice that the `GetResults( )` method was called from within the `try` block in the `Main( )` method. When the `object` `excepObj` is thrown in `GetResults( )`, it is thrown back to the `Main( )` method's `catch` clause because that is the position from which it was called.

From inside the `catch` clause, `excepObj.Message` is printed. Observe that the value displayed in Figure 12-20 is exactly the same value as that used to instantiate the `object` in the `GetResults( )` method. The `string` argument, `"Exception type: Floating-point division by zero"`, which is used to construct the `object` in this case, is sent to the `base` constructor. You can also retrieve the error message, exception type, and the line and method name where the exception occurred by calling the `ToString( )` method with the exception object. This invokes the `System.Object` `base` `class` `ToString( )` method. The heading for the `FloatingPtDivisionException` `class` defined in Example 12-7 is shown again as follows:

```
public FloatingPtDivisionException(string exceptionType)
      : base (exceptionType)
```

The argument `exceptionType` sets the `Message` property for the `base` `Exception` `class`. This is why `"Exception type: Floating-point division by zero"` is printed when `excepObj.Message` is displayed in the `catch` clause found in the `Main( )` method.

NOTE The identifier `e` is used by the system as a name for an exception `object` in the `catch` clause. With Windows applications, `e` is also used by the system as the name of the `object` representing the `EventArgs` `class` used for event handling. To avoid confusion and potential syntax errors, you are encouraged to select a different identifier, other than `e`, with your user-defined exception classes.

When no exceptions are thrown in the `GetResults( )` method, the result of dividing `value1` by `value2` is returned back to `Main( )`.

NOTE It is important to write code that can be reused. The `FloatingPtDivisionException` `class` might be stored as a class library and referenced in many different applications. It could be used by Web, console, or Windows applications. Thus, you should always throw the error back to the calling class and enable that class to decide what type of error reporting to perform.

Input Output (IO) Exceptions

Exceptions are extremely useful for applications that process or create stored data. Thus far, your programs have processed only data that was interactively typed while the program was running. All of the output from your programs has been displayed on the console screen. In some situations, it is more appropriate to place the data in a file or use a file for input as opposed to having the user type entries. In other situations, it is best to store the output to a file, as when the input would overflow a single screen or when the output produced by one application is used as input for another application. A lot of support is available in C# for dealing with files. Chapter 13 details how a file is created and processed. First examine the predefined exception classes available for dealing with files.

The primary exception `class` for files is `System.IO.IOException`. It derives from the `SystemException` `class`, which, as you learned, is a direct descendent of `Exception`. An `IO.IOException` exception is thrown for the following types of unexpected errors: a specified file or directory is not found, your program attempts to read beyond the end of a file, or there are problems loading or accessing the contents of a file. Table 12-3 presents the classes derived from the `IO.IOException` `class` and briefly describes the reasons for throwing the exceptions.

TABLE 12-3 Derived classes of IO.IOException

Exception classes derived from the IO.IOException class	Description of circumstances causing an exception to be thrown
`DirectoryNotFoundException`	A directory cannot be found
`EndOfStreamException`	You read past the end of the file
`FileNotFoundException`	A disk fails or you try to access a file that does not exist
`FileLoadException`	The file is found, but it cannot be loaded
`PathTooLongException`	A pathname or filename is longer than the system-defined maximum length

© Cengage Learning

You will experience writing `IO.IOException` exception handlers in Chapter 13 when you work with file streams.

NOTE

In C#, there are none of the checked exceptions that you find in languages such as Java. Java distinguishes between checked and unchecked exceptions. A **checked exception** is one that must be included if you use a specific construct. If you do not include exception-handling techniques for that construct, a syntax error is generated. All file interactions in Java are treated as checked exceptions—meaning you must include your file processing inside `try...catch` blocks in Java. Although you are also encouraged to do this in C#, you do not receive a syntax error if you do not place your file-handling statements in a `try...catch` block. There are no checked exceptions in C#!

PROGRAMMING EXAMPLE: ICW WaterDepth Application

This example demonstrates exception-handling techniques. Three classes are constructed for the application. One of the classes is a programmer-defined custom exception class. It inherits methods and properties from the `ApplicationException` `class` and is included to illustrate throwing an exception using program statements.

Two additional classes are defined. The business logic for the application is separated from the presentation details. The class that defines the graphical user interface makes use of a `try...catch` block with multiple catch clauses. This class is used to input the data. After the data is retrieved, it is used to instantiate an object of the third class, the `ShoalArea` `class`. Output from the application is displayed in a Windows dialog box. The problem specification for the `WaterDepth` application is shown in Figure 12-21.

The United States Coast Guard (USCG) hosts a Navigational Center website that includes a weekly update called the "Local Notice to Mariners." Included in this update is an identification of areas along the waterways where boaters are advised to take warning. This application focuses on the Atlantic Intracoastal Waterway (ICW). The ICW is a 1,095-mile highway of water stretching from Norfolk, Virginia, to Key West, Florida. The route is federally maintained and is connected in many places to inland waterways. The ICW provides shippers, fishermen, and sailors a sheltered route from the storms of the Atlantic Ocean. It is also a scenic byway for yachts and pleasure boating.

The ICW is in trouble in many locations due to silting. Some areas are effectively closed to shipping and even have restricted passage for pleasure boaters. Dredging budgets and the amount spent on waterways have steadily declined. In the "Local Notice to Mariners" update, the USCG identifies problem areas to boaters by using a mile marker (similar to what you see on the highway), name, and state name.

Design an application that can be used to input these potential problem areas. The graphical user interface should enable the user to enter location name, state where it is located, mile number, and four separate days of water depth at low and high tide. When valid data has been entered, display a message showing the location, state, mile number, average depths at low tide, average depths at high tide, and the overall average depth.

© Cengage Learning

FIGURE 12-21 Problem specification for WaterDepth application

12

ANALYZE THE PROBLEM

Review the problem specification in Figure 12-21 to ensure that you understand the problem definition. Values for the location, including location name, state, and mile marker number, are entered. The depths at low and high tide are also input into the application. Four separate days of low and high tidal water values are entered by the user. The `FrmWaterDepth` `class` is created as the user interface. It displays a number of text boxes that are used to enter values into the application. These values are used to instantiate the `ShoalArea` `class`.

Output consists of displaying the location entered and the calculated averages for the water depths at low and high tide. An overall average is calculated using all of the water values entered. The data members for the `ShoalArea` `class` are given in Table 12-4.

DATA

TABLE 12-4 ShoalArea class data fields

Data description	Type	Identifier
Location (town)	`string`	location
State	`string`	state
Mile number	`double`	mileMarker
Low tide depth	`double[ ]`	lowTideDepth
High tide depth	`double[ ]`	hiTideDepth

© Cengage Learning

DESIGN A SOLUTION

The desired output is to produce a message showing the location of the shoal area and data describing the current condition of the reported problem. In Chapter 13, you will be introduced to file-handling techniques. This application will be revisited to illustrate how the records could be stored in a file for later retrieval. Figure 12-22 shows a prototype of the form that will be used for input. As the prototype shows, four different days of water depths are entered by the user along with information relating to the location.

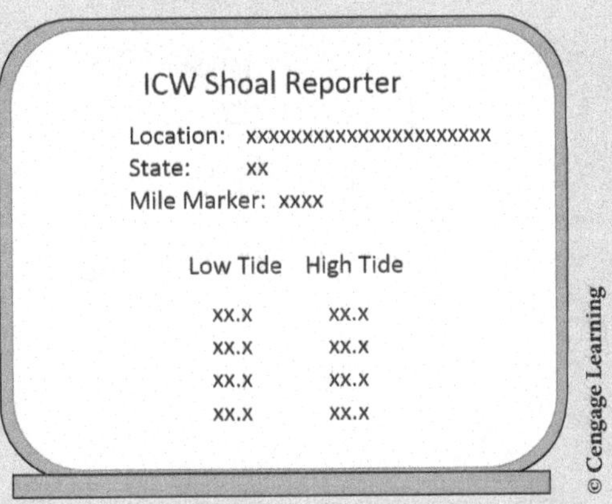

FIGURE 12-22 Prototype for WaterDepth input form

When the Submit button is clicked, the data is retrieved and validated for accurate input and then used to instantiate the `ShoalArea` `object`. Finally, the results are displayed. Figure 12-23 shows a prototype for the projected output.

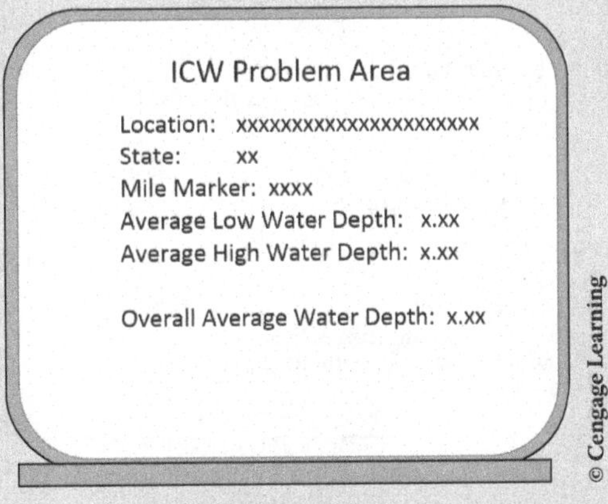

FIGURE 12-23 Prototype for WaterDepth final output

12

The `ShoalArea` `class` has both data and behavior characteristics. The class diagram in Figure 12-24 illustrates its `private` data members and `public` methods. The class diagram does not show its constructors or properties. Figure 12-24 also includes class diagrams for the two other classes, `TestOfStateException` and `FrmWaterDepth` GUI.

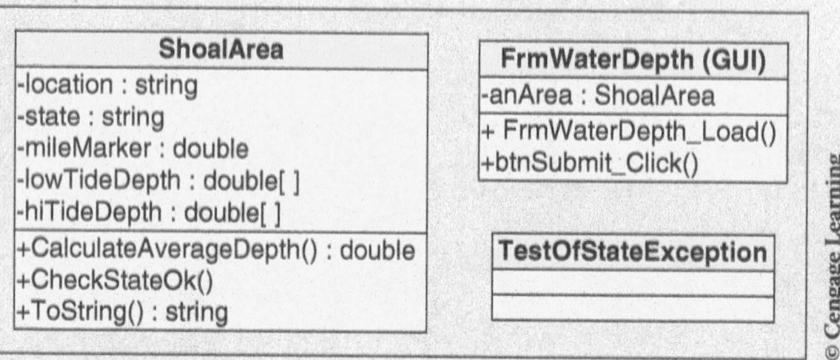

FIGURE 12-24 Class diagrams for WaterDepth application

During design, algorithms for the object's behaviors are developed. Figure 12-25 illustrates the event-handler methods. The form Load( ) and button Click( ) events are included.

```
FrmWaterDepth_Load( )
{Raised when the form is loaded}
        Display the form
        Create an instance of the ShoalArea object

btnSubmit_Click( )
{Raised when the Submit button is clicked}
        Retrieve string values from textbox (using Text property)
        try
        {
                Convert mile marker from string to double
                Convert water depths from string to double
        }
        catch  TestOfStateException,
               FormatException,
               ArithmeticException
               ArrayTypeMismatchException
               IndexOutOfRangeException
               Exception
```

© Cengage Learning

FIGURE 12-25 Behavior for the FrmWaterDepth class

As shown in Figure 12-25, the `btnSubmit_Click( )` method uses exception-handling techniques to make sure valid numeric values are entered. A number of exception classes are included in the `catch` clause since the solution is using arrays to store the values.

Figure 12-26 shows the steps that should be included in several of the instance methods of `ShoalArea` `class`.

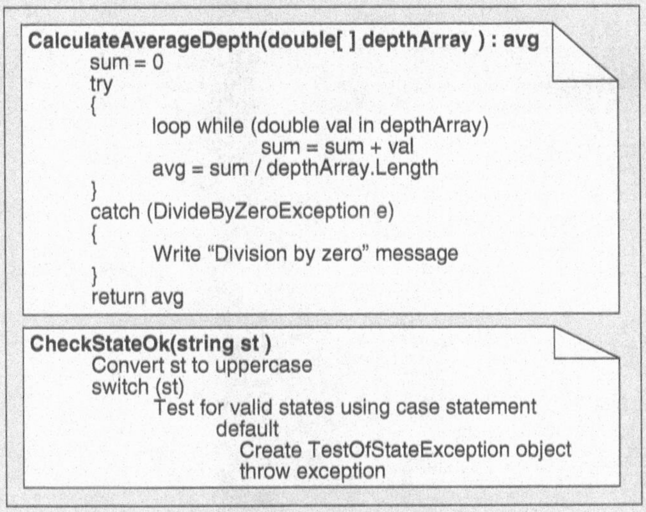

```
CalculateAverageDepth(double[ ] depthArray ) : avg
        sum = 0
        try
        {
                loop while (double val in depthArray)
                        sum = sum + val
                avg = sum / depthArray.Length
        }
        catch (DivideByZeroException e)
        {
                Write "Division by zero" message
        }
        return avg
```

```
CheckStateOk(string st )
        Convert st to uppercase
        switch (st)
                Test for valid states using case statement
                        default
                            Create TestOfStateException object
                            throw exception
```

© Cengage Learning

FIGURE 12-26 Behavior of the ShoalArea class

CODE THE SOLUTION

After completing the design and verifying the algorithm's correctness, you translate the design into source code. Using Visual Studio, you can drag and drop many of the controls from the **Toolbox** to the form when you create the user interface class. When you drag and drop controls, code is auto-generated by Visual Studio and placed in the `FrmWaterDepth.Designer.cs` source code file. This is the semi-hidden file that belongs to the application; it includes the statement ". . . do not modify. . .with the code editor." Because this file is lengthy and auto-generated, it is not shown with the program statements that follow. Instead, Table 12-5 illustrates which property values were set in the design window.

TABLE 12-5 WaterDepth property values

Name	Object type	Property	Value
Form1	Form	Name	Typed "FrmWaterDepth"
FrmWaterDepth	Form	Text	Typed "ICW Shoal Reporter"
FrmWaterDepth	Form	BackgroundImage	Located and selected waterWay.jpg
FrmWaterDepth	Form	AcceptButton	btnSubmit

(*continues*)

12

TABLE 12-5 WaterDepth property values (*continued*)

Name	Object type	Property	Value
FrmWaterDepth	Form	Size	315, 342
txtBxLocation	TextBox	TabIndex	0
txtBxState	TextBox	TabIndex	1
txtBxMile	TextBox	TabIndex	2
txtBxLow1	TextBox	TabIndex	3
txtBxLow2	TextBox	TabIndex	5
txtBxLow3	TextBox	TabIndex	7
txtBxLow4	TextBox	TabIndex	9
txtBxHi1	TextBox	TabIndex	4
txtBxHi2	TextBox	TabIndex	6
txtBxHi3	TextBox	TabIndex	8
txtBxHi4	TextBox	TabIndex	10
btnSubmit	Button	TabIndex	11
btnSubmit	Button	Text	Typed "Submit"
lblError	Label	Text	Typed ""
label1	Label	Text	Typed "Location"
label2	Label	Text	Typed "State"
label3	Label	Text	Typed "Mile Marker"
label4	Label	Text	Typed "Low Tide"
label5	Label	Text	Typed "High Tide"

© Cengage Learning

As you review Table 12-5, you will notice that each of the TextBox objects was named. The Name property was used for this. After the algorithms are designed, they should always be desk checked to ensure that correct output is produced. As with other applications you have developed, you should also devise a plan for testing the application. Walk through your logic, reread the problem specification, and ensure you are fulfilling the problem requirements. Think about the types of exceptions that could be thrown and make sure you have procedures written to handle these types of problems.

The FrmWaterDepth.Designer.cs file includes program statements that instantiate the control objects that are placed on the form. The file includes assignment statements that set the controls' sizes and initial locations. It also includes statements that set the background image for the form as well as program statements that register events of interest such as the Submit button click event.

The program statements for the ShoalArea class follow. A reference to the System.Diagnostics namespace was added so debugging information could be sent to the **Output** window. This namespace includes two classes: Debug and Trace. Both classes have WriteLine( ) methods that work similarly to the Console.WriteLine( ) method. They differ in that the output is sent to the Output window when programs are run in debug mode. The CalculateAverageDepth( ) method in the ShoalArea class calls Trace.WriteLine( ) if an attempt is made to divide by zero.

```
// ShoalArea.cs
// Class representing shoaled area
using System;
using System.Diagnostics;

namespace WaterDepth
{
    public class ShoalArea
    {
        private string location;
        private string state;
        private double mileMarker;
        private double[ ] lowTideDepth;
        private double[ ] hiTideDepth;

        public ShoalArea( )
        {
            lowTideDepth = new double[4];
            hiTideDepth = new double[4];
        }
```

12

```
public ShoalArea(string loc, string st, double mile,
                 double[ ] low, double[ ] hi)
{
     location = loc;
     CheckStateOk(st);
     mileMarker = mile;
     lowTideDepth = low;
     hiTideDepth = hi;
}

public ShoalArea(string loc, string st, double mile)
{
     location = loc;
     state = st;
     mileMarker = mile;
}

//Properties
public string Location
{
     get { return location;}
     set { location = value;}
}
public string State
{
     get { return state; }
     set { CheckStateOk(value ); }
}
public double MileMarker
{
     get { return mileMarker; }
     set { mileMarker = value; }
}
public double[ ] LoTideDepth
{
     get { return lowTideDepth; }
     set { lowTideDepth = value; }
}
public double[ ] HiTideDepth
{
     get { return hiTideDepth; }
     set { hiTideDepth = value; }
}
```

```
public double CalculateAverageDepth(double [ ]
                                          depthArray)
{
     double sum = 0;
     double avg;
     try
     {
          foreach (double val in depthArray)
                    sum += val;
          avg = sum / depthArray.Length;
     }
     catch (DivideByZeroException e)
     {
          avg = 0;
          Trace.WriteLine("Attempted to Divide by Zero" +
                          "\nException Type: " +
                          e.Message);
     }
     return avg;
}

public void CheckStateOk(string st)
{
     switch (st.ToUpper( ))
     {
          case "FL":
          case "GA":
          case "NC":
          case "SC":
          case "VA":
                state = st.ToUpper( );
                break;
          default:
                TestOfStateException ex =
                     new TestOfStateException
                          ("State not Part" +
                           " of Atlantic ICW");
                throw ex;
     }
}

public override string ToString( )
{
     return "Location: " + location +
            "\nState: " + state +
            "\nMile: " + mileMarker +
            "\nAverage Low Water Depth: " +
```

12

```
                                CalculateAverageDepth
                                        (lowTideDepth).ToString("F2") +
                                "\nAverage High Water Depth: " +
                                CalculateAverageDepth
                                        (hiTideDepth).ToString ("F2") +
                                "\n\nOverall Average Water Depth: " +
                                   ((CalculateAverageDepth(lowTideDepth) +
                                CalculateAverageDepth
                                        (hiTideDepth)) / 2.0).ToString("F2");
            }
      }
}
```

The source code listing for the programmer-defined custom exception class is shown in the following. The constructor for this class has one parameter. It accepts a `string` argument representing the type of exception. Notice that value (`exceptionType`) is sent to the `base class` as part of the constructor's heading. The `TestOfStateException class` has access to all of the methods and properties of the `ApplicationException` and Exception classes. No additional functionality was added to the class. An instance of the `TestOfStateException` class is created in the `ShoalArea class` when states other than Florida (FL), Georgia (GA), North Carolina (NC), South Carolina (SC), or Virginia (VA) are entered. The `switch` statement in the `CheckStateOk( )` method throws the exception.

```
// TestOfStateException.cs
// Custom-defined Exception class
using System;

namespace WaterDepth
{
      public class TestOfStateException : ApplicationException
      {
            public TestOfStateException(string exceptionType)
                  : base(exceptionType)
            {
            }
      }
}
```

The source code for the `partial class` that defines the graphical user interface is shown last. Remember that the `FrmWaterDepth.Designer.cs` file contains the code that is auto-generated by Visual Studio. Much of the application's functionality is written into the `btnSubmit_Click ( )` method. The `try` statement includes multiple `catch` clauses. As with the `ShoalArea class`, a reference to the

`System.Diagnostics` `namespace` was added. If an exception is thrown, a message is sent to the **Output** window and also to an invisible label on the form.

```
// FrmWaterDepth.cs
// Graphical User Interface class
using System;
using System.Windows.Forms;
using System.Diagnostics;

namespace WaterDepth
{
    public partial class FrmWaterDepth : Form
    {
        private ShoalArea anArea;

        public FrmWaterDepth( )
        {
            InitializeComponent( );
        }

        private void btnSubmit_Click(object sender, EventArgs e)
        {
            double[ ] lowTides = new double[4];
            double[ ] hiTides = new double[4];
            anArea.Location = txtBxLocation.Text;
            try
            {
                lowTides[0] = double.Parse(txtBxLow1.Text);
                lowTides[1] = double.Parse(txtBxLow2.Text);
                lowTides[2] = double.Parse(txtBxLow3.Text);
                lowTides[3] = double.Parse(txtBxLow4.Text);
                hiTides[0] = double.Parse(txtBxHi1.Text);
                hiTides[1] = double.Parse(txtBxHi2.Text);
                hiTides[2] = double.Parse(txtBxHi3.Text);
                hiTides[3] = double.Parse(txtBxHi4.Text);
                anArea.State = txtBxState.Text;
                anArea.MileMarker=
                    double.Parse(txtBxMile.Text);
                anArea.LoTideDepth = lowTides;
                anArea.HiTideDepth = hiTides;
                MessageBox.Show(anArea.ToString( ),
                                "ICW Problem Area");
            }
            catch (TestOfStateException ex)
            {
                Trace.WriteLine("\nException: " + ex.Message);
                lblError.Text += "\nException: " + ex.Message;
            }
            catch (FormatException ex)
```

```
            {
                Trace.WriteLine("Method\'s actual argument " +
                                "does not match formal " +
                                "parameter.\nException: " +
                                ex.Message);
                lblError.Text += "\nException: " + ex.Message;
            }
            catch (ArithmeticException ex)
            {
                Debug.WriteLine("Errors in an arithmetic, " +
                                "casting, " +
                                "or conversion." +
                                "\nException: " + ex.Message);
                lblError.Text += "\nException: " + ex.Message;
            }
            catch (ArrayTypeMismatchException ex)
            {
                Trace.WriteLine("Trying to store an element " +
                               "of wrong type in an array." +
                               "\nException: " + ex.Message);
                lblError.Text += "\nException: " + ex.Message;
            }
            catch (IndexOutOfRangeException ex)
            {
                Trace.WriteLine("Trying to access element " +
                                "of an array with index " +
                                "outside bounds of the array." +
                                "\nException: " + ex.Message);
                lblError.Text += "\nException: " + ex.Message;
            }
            catch (Exception ex)
            {
                lblError.Text += "\nException: " + ex.Message;
                Trace.WriteLine("Exception: " + ex.Message);
            }
        }

        private void FrmWaterDepth_Load(object sender,
                                        EventArgs e)
        {
            anArea = new ShoalArea( );
        }
    }
}
```

In addition to the `FrmWaterDepth.Designer.cs` partial class (which is not shown), the `Program.cs` file is also part of the application. This is where the `Main( )` method is located. No programmer statements are added to this file. Recall that the `Main( )` method is the entry point into the application. With Windows applications, the method calls the `Application.Run( )` method, which places the program in a process loop.

Figure 12-27 shows the original user interface prior to values being entered. If the user enters correct values, no exception is thrown and the program terminates normally.

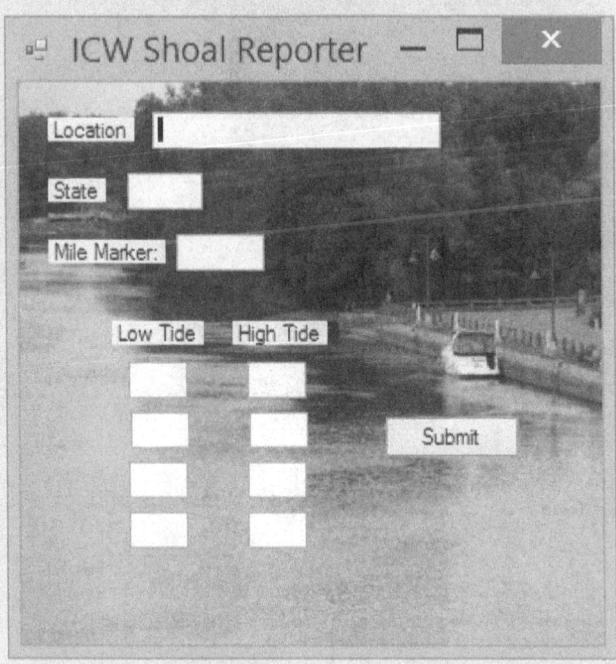

FIGURE 12-27 FrmWaterDepth form

Figure 12-28 illustrates what the output is when the program works correctly. No exceptions are thrown. The output is displayed in a MessageBox.

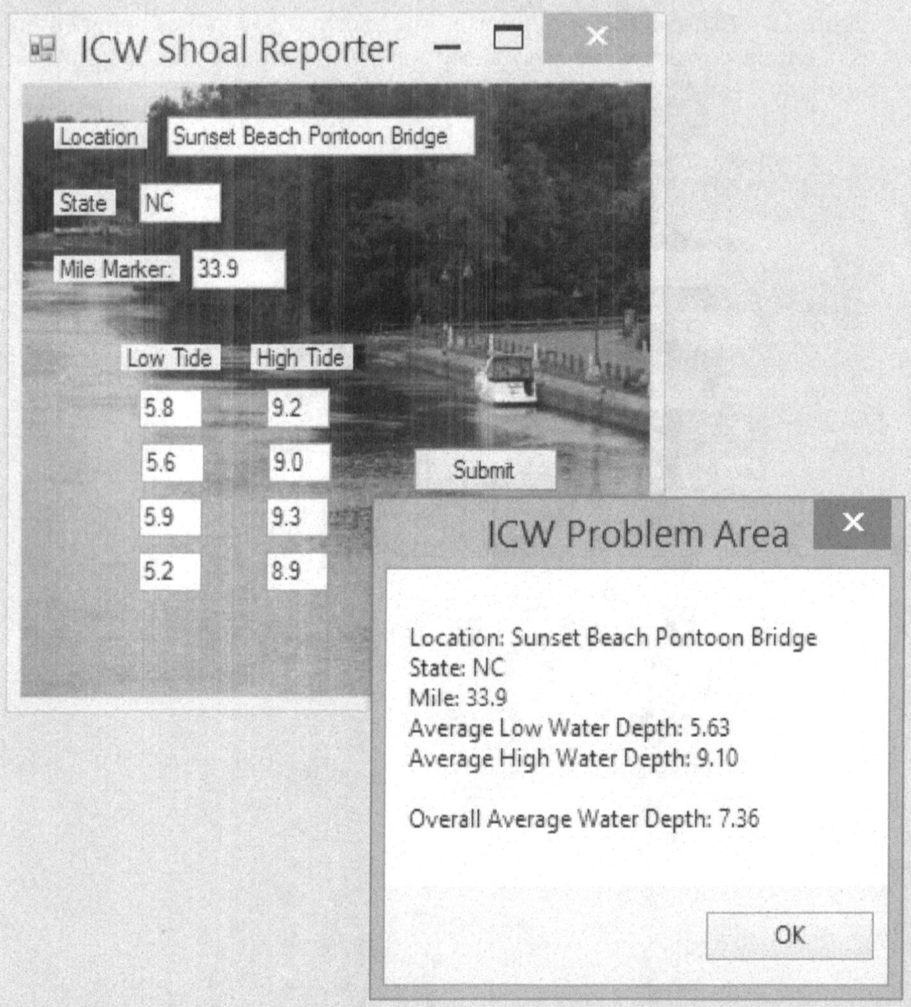

FIGURE 12-28 WaterDepth application output

The problem specification indicates that only valid states along the Atlantic ICW should be entered into the application. An object of the `TestOfStateException` `class` is thrown if the `ShoalArea` objects' state data member is assigned an invalid value for the state. The message property of the `Exception` `class` is displayed in a label named `lblError` on the form object. These points are shown in Figure 12-29.

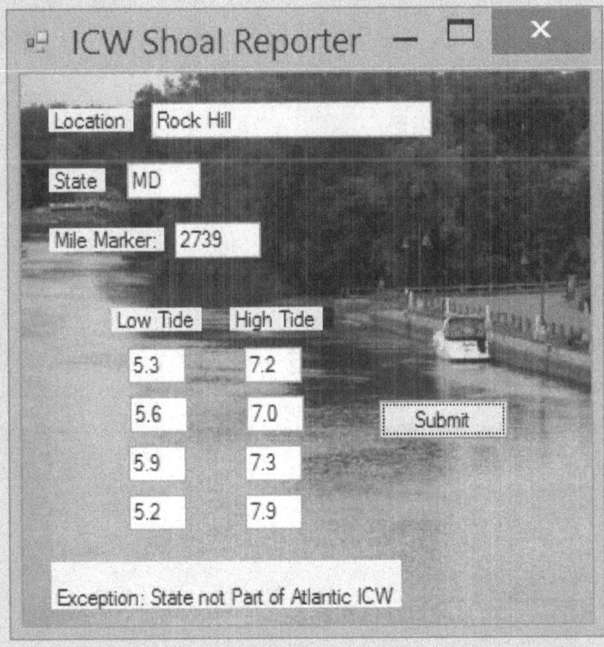

FIGURE 12-29 State exception thrown in WaterDepth application

As you review the program statements, notice that several `catch` clauses were included. Figure 12-30 shows the message displayed in the `lblError` when the user attempts to enter a nonnumeric value for the mile marker.

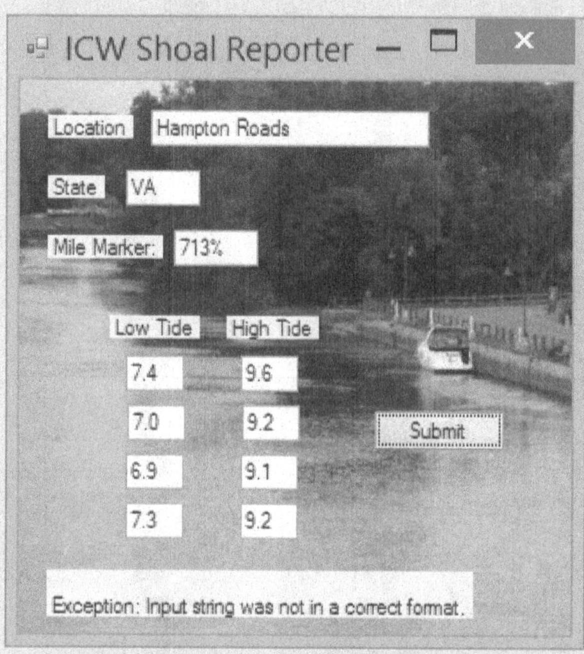

FIGURE 12-30 Invalid input exception thrown in WaterDepth application

Each of the `catch` clauses displays a message on the form in the `lblError` and also sends the same message as an argument to either `Debug.WriteLine( )` or `Trace.WriteLine( )`. The `WriteLine( )` method of the `Debug` or `Trace` class differs from the `Console` class method in that it only works with single-string arguments. No variable values can be inserted inside the parentheses. Both the

`Trace` and `Debug` classes can be used to help you debug your program. `Debug` only works in debug builds. `Trace` can also be used in release builds. They send output to the **Output** window, as shown in Figure 12-31.

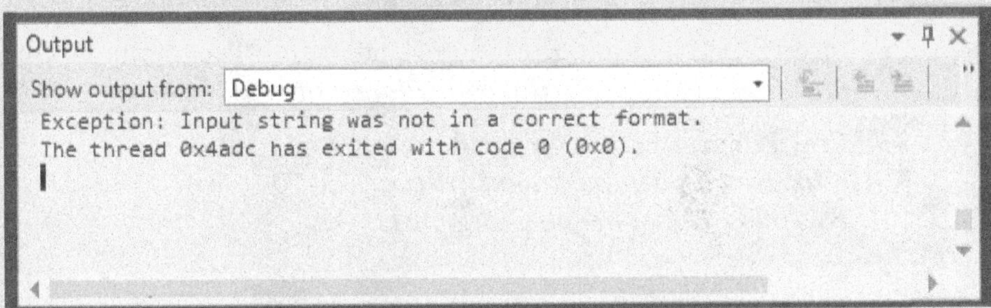

FIGURE 12-31 Debug information sent to Output window

The last two lines in the **Debug Ouput** window, shown in Figure 12-31, were generated by the `FormatException` `catch` clause in the `FrmWaterDepth.cs` `class`. Additional lines, which are not shown, were automatically generated when the form was loaded. As noted previously, a reference to the `System.Diagnostics` `namespace` was added. This enabled debugging information to be sent to the **Output** window.

Coding Standards

Do not use exception-handling techniques to deal with problems that can be handled with reasonable coding effort. Make a clear difference between an error and an exception.

Wrong input data should be an expected situation. Do not handle wrong input data with exception-handling techniques. Use `if...else` statements.

Not all methods throw an exception. Encapsulating all methods in a `try...catch` block will hamper performance.

Always order exceptions from the most specific to the least specific. Putting the general catch clause first will cause all exceptions to be caught by that catch clause.

When creating custom classes, add Exception onto the end of the name for the identifier.

Use meaningful messages with exceptions and avoid grammatical mistakes.

Resources

Additional sites you might want to explore:

- The C# Corner - Exception - Handling articles—
  http://www.c-sharpcorner.com/1/64/exception-handling-C-Sharp.aspx
- msdn Exceptions and Exception Handling (C# Programming Guide)—
  http://msdn.microsoft.com/en-us/library/ms173160.aspx
- CodeProject - Exception Handling in C#—
  http://www.codeproject.com/Articles/125470/Exception-Handling-for-C-Beginners
- C# Exception—
  http://www.dotnetperls.com/exception

QUICK REVIEW

1. Two major types of program errors are compiler or syntax errors and run-time errors.
2. Compiler errors are associated with a violation in one of the rules of the language.
3. C# Language Specifications are the authoritative source for C# grammar and syntax. These specifications detail information on all aspects of the language.
4. Programs with run-time errors may stop during execution or produce output that is not correct.
5. Logic errors are normally associated with programs that run but produce incorrect results.
6. The Debugger lets you break, or halt, the execution of your program to examine your code, and evaluate or change variables in your program.
7. A breakpoint is a line in your program that you select, and when it is reached, the program is suspended or placed in break mode. When the break occurs, the program and the Debugger are said to be in break mode.
8. The **Locals** window shows variables in scope and their values.
9. You could step through your code line by line, see the execution path, and examine variable and expression values as they change using the **Step Into**, **Step Over**, and **Step Out** commands of the Debugger.
10. The **Step Over** command differs from the **Step Into** command in that it executes the entire method called before it halts. **Step Into** halts after each line is executed. **Step Out** returns control back to the calling method.
11. The **Watch** window lets you type one or more variables or expressions that you want to observe while the program is running.

12. Exceptions are unexpected conditions that happen very infrequently. They are usually associated with some type of error condition that causes an abnormal termination if they are not handled.
13. If a program encounters an error during run-time from which it is unable to recover, such as division by zero, it raises or throws an exception.
14. If none of the methods along the call chain include code to handle the error, the CLR handles the exception by halting the entire application.
15. *Bugs* are programmer mistakes that should be caught and fixed before an application is released.
16. In addition to bugs, programs can experience errors because of user actions. These actions can cause exceptions to be thrown.
17. A stack trace is a listing of all the methods that are executing when an exception is thrown.
18. Exception-handling techniques are for serious errors that occur infrequently. Exceptions are those events from which a program is not able to recover, such as attempting to read from a data file that does not exist.
19. For exception handling in C#, `try...catch` blocks are used. Code that might be a problem is placed in a `try` block. The code to deal with the problem, the exception handler, is placed in `catch` blocks, which are also called `catch` clauses. The code found in the `finally` block is executed regardless of whether an exception is thrown.
20. When an exception is raised, an `object` is created to represent the exception. All exception objects inherit from the `base class` named `Exception`, which is part of the `System` `namespace`.
21. If you create your own exception classes, they should derive from the `ApplicationException` `class`. Other system exception classes derive from the `SystemException` `class`. It is a good idea to use the word "Exception" as part of the identifier.
22. When you include filters for multiple exceptions in your `class`, the order of placement of these clauses is very important. They should be placed from most specific to most generic.

EXERCISES

1. _____ are unexpected conditions that happen very infrequently.
   a. Bugs
   b. Conditions
   c. Streams
   d. Exceptions
   e. Objects

2. Raising an exception is the same as:
    a. catching an exception
    b. trying a block of code that might create an exception
    c. throwing an exception
    d. defining a new exception `class`
    e. rolling back an exception
3. A Just-In-Time Debugging window is displayed when a(an):
    a. application is executed
    b. unhandled exception is thrown
    c. handled exception is thrown
    d. unhandled exception is caught
    e. handled exception is caught
4. The segment of code that might create an unexpected problem should be:
    a. placed in a `try` block
    b. placed in a `catch` block
    c. placed in a `finally` block
    d. placed on the outside of the `try...catch...finally` block
    e. included in the `Main( )` method
5. What type of exception would be thrown if the user enters the wrong type of data when requested from the keyboard?
    a. `FormatException`
    b. `Invalid.CastException`
    c. `NullReferenceException`
    d. `IndexOutOfRangeException`
    e. `ArithmeticException`
6. What type of exception would be thrown if a program statement attempted to access location 0 in an array defined to hold 20 elements?
    a. `FormatException`
    b. `Invalid.CastException`
    c. `NullReferenceException`
    d. `IndexOutOfRangeException`
    e. none of the above

7. What type of exception would be thrown if the following arithmetic were performed?

```
double aValue = 0,
       bValue = 0;
int result = (int) aValue / (int) bValue;
```

a. `FormatException`
b. `Invalid.CastException`
c. `ArgumentException`
d. `DivideByZeroException`
e. none of the above

8. If an application is written to filter several exceptions including `Exception`, `DivideByZeroException`, and `ArithmeticException`, in what order should they be listed?

a. `Exception`, `DivideByZeroException`, then `ArithmeticException`
b. `Exception`, `ArithmeticException`, then `DivideByZeroException`
c. `DivideByZeroException`, `Exception`, then `ArithmeticException`
d. `DivideByZeroException`, `ArithmeticException`, then `Exception`
e. It does not matter.

9. To avoid an exception with files, you can use a `try...catch` block and include which exception class in your catch clause?

a. `File.ExistsException`
b. `IOException`
c. `FileException`
d. `ExceptionFile`
e. none of the above

10. Writing a `catch` clause without including the parentheses and an argument list such as `catch` { }:

a. generates a syntax error
b. requires a `finally` clause
c. has the same effect as `catch` (Exception) { }
d. throws an exception
e. none of the above

11. Two major types of errors found in programs are:
    a. compiler and syntax
    b. compiler and exceptions
    c. logic and grammar
    d. compiler and run-time
    e. exceptions and logic
12. _____ errors are the easiest to discover and correct.
    a. Exception
    b. Compiler
    c. Run-time
    d. Logic
    e. Omission
13. C# Language Specifications are:
    a. the authoritative source for C# grammar
    b. the specifications that detail information on all aspects of the language
    c. the authoritative source for C# syntax
    d. available for a free download
    e. all of the above
14. The Debugger can be used to:
    a. observe syntax errors
    b. rewrite the grammar for the program
    c. review what the output should be
    d. step through an application
    e. none of the above
15. A marker that is placed in an application, indicating the program should halt execution when it reaches that point, is called a(n):
    a. exception
    b. debugger
    c. watch
    d. pause
    e. breakpoint

16. If a method throws an exception and the exception is not caught inside the method:
    a. The program automatically crashes.
    b. The rest of the program is executed, but the program statement(s) that caused the problem is skipped.
    c. An exception is thrown.
    d. The method execution returns to the first line in the method.
    e. none of the above
17. Which of the following lines contains information regarding a thrown exception named `e`?
    a. `e.Message`
    b. `e.ExceptionType`
    c. `e.ExceptionInfo`
    d. `e.ExceptionMessage`
    e. `e.Information`
18. The Debugger in Visual Studio offers all of the following options for stepping, except:
    a. Step Into
    b. Step Over
    c. Step Out
    d. Step Through
    e. none of the above
19. The primary difference between using Step Into and Step Over is:
    a. Step Into halts at the last line of code inside a called method.
    b. Step Over halts at the first line of code inside a called method.
    c. Step Over steps into the most deeply nested method.
    d. Step Over executes the called method and halts at the first line of code after the method.
    e. Minimal. They provide the same functionality.

20. The `ApplicationException` `class` is derived from:
    a. `System`
    b. `SystemException`
    c. `System.Exceptions`
    d. `ExceptionApplication`
    e. `Exception`

---

21. The result of division by zero is undefined for both integral and floating-point values. Describe how avoiding floating-point division by zero differs from integral division by zero.

22. Give one example of what would cause an `ArithmeticException` exception to be thrown.

23. Give one example of what would cause a `FormatException` exception to be thrown.

24. Give one example of what would cause an `IndexOutOfRangeException` exception to be thrown.

25. If an application is written to filter Exception, ArgumentException, IndexOutOfRangeException, and ArithmeticException, does it matter which order they should be listed? If so, what is the order?

PROGRAMMING EXERCISES

1. Write an exception tester application that enables you to see the impact of exceptions being thrown. Include multiple `catch` clauses. Include in our investigation the `ArithmeticException`, `FormatException`, `IndexOutOfRangeException`, and `Exception` classes. For each exception, write a `try` block containing errors to throw the exceptions. As you test the application, include an error that throws the exception and then comment it out and program an error that throws the next exception and so on. Your final solution should include at least one statement per exception that throws each exception. The statements should all be commented out by the time you finish testing. Be sure to include documenting comments with each statement.

2. Design an application that enables users to enter two values of type `int`. Write a method that retrieves the values and stores them and their products in separate structures. If you are designing a Windows application, you might allow the user to input the values in a `TextBox` and then retrieve and store the values in a `ListBox`. Their product could be stored in a separate `ListBox`. Your solution should include exception-handling techniques with a minimum of two `catch` clauses and a finally clause. Consider using your finally clause to prepare the GUI for the next set of values.

3. Create a multi-class solution that can be used to calculate body mass index (BMI). The `BodyMassIndexCalculator` `class` should have data members of weight and height. Write an application that lets users enter their weight and height in feet and inches. Calculate their BMI. Include appropriate exception-handling techniques.

4. Include exception-handling techniques with the traditional averaging program. Allow the user to input multiple sets of scores. Ensure that only numeric values are entered and that values fall between 0 and 100. Calculate the average for each set of values. Test the result to determine whether an A, B, C, D, or F should be recorded. The scoring rubric is as follows: A—90–100; B—80–89; C—70–79; D—60–69; F < 60. Your solution should include exception-handling techniques with a minimum of three appropriate `catch` clauses.

5. Create a multi-class solution that includes a `Fraction` class. `Fraction` should have data members of numerator and denominator and be used to represent the ratio of the two integer values. Include appropriate constructors, properties, methods, and a ToString( ) method that returns a fraction using the original integers. Include a method that reduces the fraction to its lowest terms. Include appropriate exception handling techniques. If the denominator is assigned zero, throw and handle an exception. Create an application class to test the `Fraction` `class`. Be sure to test your exception-handling code.

6. Create a multi-class solution that includes a `WeightConverter` `class`. The `WeightConverter` `class` should be used to convert standard weight measurements. In your list of options, include as a minimum grams, kilograms, pounds, and ounces. Create an application class to test the `WeightConverter` `class`. If the user enters a negative number or a nonnumeric value, throw and handle an exception.

7. Create a Windows application that has the functionality of a calculator and works with integral values. Allow the user to select buttons representing numeric values. If the user attempts to divide by zero, throw and handle an exception.

8. Revise the calculator application created in Exercise #7 to enable decimal values to be entered. Recall that an exception is not automatically thrown by the CLR when the divisor operand is a non-integral value. Create a custom exception class that can be thrown if division by zero is attempted. If the divisor becomes zero, instead of doing the division, display a message indicating that division by zero is not possible.

9. Write an application that can be used to count the frequency of characters in a paragraph. Allow the user to input several sentences using a graphical user interface. Display the count for nonzero characters. Use an array as part of your solution. Include appropriate exception-handling techniques so that if the program attempts to access an element outside of the bounds of the array, the exception is handled.

10. Create a `BankAccount` `class` that can be used to maintain a bank account balance. Include appropriate constructors, properties, and methods to enable the account to be originally created and for amounts to be deposited and withdrawn for the account. Write the `NegativeException` `class` to extend the `ApplicationException` `class` to include the additional functionality of a new message detailing the error being sent when the exception is thrown. Throw the `NegativeException` when a negative value is entered to initially create the account or if a negative value is entered for a deposit or withdrawal. Include additional exception-handling techniques. Write an application class and test the exception-handling techniques.

© zeljkodan/Shutterstock.com

Working with Files

IN THIS CHAPTER, YOU WILL:

- Learn about the System.IO namespace
- Explore the File and Directory classes
- Contrast the FileInfo and DirectoryInfo classes to the File and Directory classes
- Discover how stream classes are used
- Read data from text files
- Write data to text files
- Explore appending data to text files
- Use exception-handling techniques to process text files
- Read from and write to binary files

In this chapter, you will discover how to use data from sources other than the keyboard for your applications. You will learn about the major classes used to work with file and directory systems. You will write programs that access stored data and programs that store results in a file. You will also extend your knowledge of handling exceptions as they relate to input and output. In this chapter, you are presented with the basics of creating, opening, closing, reading, and writing files.

System.IO Namespace

A **data file** is a computer file that can be processed, manipulated, or used as input by a computer program. Computer programs also create data files as output. A data file is considered a named collection of bytes having persistent or lasting storage. When working with data files, you think in terms of directory paths, disk storage, and file and directory names. The .NET Framework includes the `System.IO namespace`, which provides basic file and directory support classes. It also contains types that enable you to read and write files and data streams.

When you consider a stream, you think of something flowing in a single direction. A data stream is the flow of data from a source to a single receiver. C#, like many other programming languages, uses streams as a way to write and read bytes to and from a backing medium, such as disk storage. Many types of classes defined as part of the `System.IO namespace` are designed around streams. Table 13-1 lists the types that are explored in this chapter.

TABLE 13-1 System. IO classes

Class	Description
`BinaryReader`	Reads primitive data types as binary values
`BinaryWriter`	Writes primitive types in binary to a stream
`Directory`	Exposes `static` methods for creating and moving through directories and subdirectories
`DirectoryInfo`	Exposes instance methods for creating and moving through directories and subdirectories
`DirectoryNotFoundException`	The exception that is thrown when part of a file or directory cannot be found
`EndOfStreamException`	The exception that is thrown when reading is attempted past the end of a stream

(continues)

TABLE 13-1 System. IO classes (*continued*)

Class	Description
`File`	Provides `static` methods for creating, copying, deleting, moving, and opening files, and aids in the creation of `FileStream` objects
`FileInfo`	Provides instance methods for creating, copying, deleting, moving, and opening files, and aids in the creation of `FileStream` objects
`FileLoadException`	The exception that is thrown when a file is found but cannot be loaded
`FileNotFoundException`	The exception that is thrown when an attempt to access a file that does not exist on disk fails
`FileStream`	Exposes a stream around a file, supporting both synchronous and asynchronous read and write operations
`InvalidDataException`	The exception that is thrown when a data stream is in an invalid format
`IOException`	The exception that is thrown when an I/O error occurs
`Stream`	Provides a generic view of a sequence of bytes
`StreamReader`	Implements a `TextReader` that reads characters from a byte stream
`StreamWriter`	Implements a `TextWriter` for writing characters to a stream
`TextReader`	Represents a reader that can read a sequential series of characters; this `class` is `abstract`
`TextWriter`	Represents a writer that can write a sequential series of characters; this `class` is `abstract`

© Cengage Learning

13

As given in Table 13-1, many of the `System.IO` types are exception classes that can be thrown while accessing information using streams, files, and directories. Others deal with creating and accessing `FileStream` objects. Four of the classes given in Table 13-1 provide methods for copying, deleting, moving, and opening files and directories. These classes are examined first.

File and Directory Classes

The File, FileInfo, Directory, and DirectoryInfo classes are considered utility classes. They normally work with stream objects, allowing you to manipulate files and directory structures. The File and Directory classes expose only static members. Figure 13-1 shows some of the classes in the System.IO namespace.

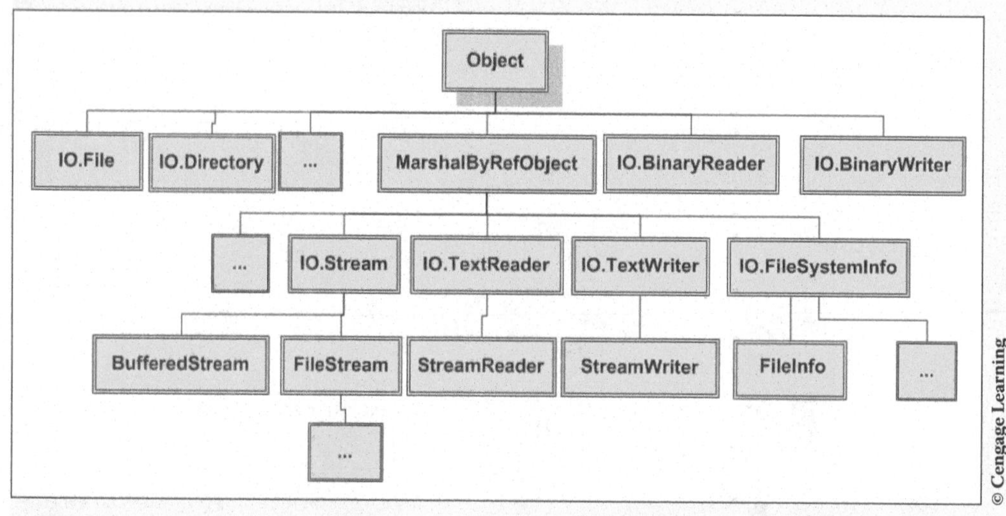

FIGURE 13-1 NET file class hierarchy

As shown in Figure 13-1, the class hierarchy for the System.IO namespace is interesting. Both the File and Directory classes are direct descendants of the Object class, whereas the other classes are descendants of the MarshalByRefObject class. Notice FileInfo and DirectoryInfo extend the FileSystemInfo class. StreamReader and StreamWriter extend the TextReader and TextWriter classes. FileSystemInfo, TextReader, and TextWriter are subclasses of the MarshallByRefObject class. As noted in the MSDN documentation, MarshalByRefObject is the base class for objects that communicate across application domain boundaries by exchanging messages using a proxy. Objects that do not inherit from MarshalByRefObject are implicitly marshal by value. The boxes containing three dots indicate where additional classes are derived.

File Class

The IO.File class shown in Figure 13-1 provides static methods that aid in copying, moving, renaming, creating, opening, deleting, and appending to files. Because they expose only static members, objects cannot be instantiated from the class. Table 13-2 lists the key static members and provides a brief description.

TABLE 13-2 File class static members

Static member	Description
AppendAllText( )	Appends the specified string to the file, creating the file if it does not already exist
AppendText( )	Creates a StreamWriter that appends UTF-8 encoded text to an existing file
Copy( )	Copies an existing file to a new file
Create( )	Creates a file in the specified path
Delete( )	Deletes the specified file
Exists( )	Determines whether the specified file exists
GetCreationTime( )	Returns the date and time when the specified file was created
GetLastAccessTime( )	Gets the date and time when the specified file was last accessed
GetLastWriteTime( )	Gets the date and time when the specified file was last written to
Move( )	Moves a specified file to a new location

© Cengage Learning

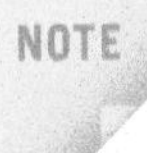

NOTE

Static methods are also available for SetAttributes, SetCreationTime, SetLastAccessTime, and SetLastWriteTime.

Every member of the IO.File class is a method with a public static access modifier. Recall that when a method uses a static modifier, the method belongs to the class itself, not to a specific object of the class. The method does not require that an object of the class be instantiated to invoke it. To invoke the method, the method name is preceded by the class name (as opposed to an object's name). For example, to call the Copy( ) method to make a copy of sourceFile, naming the new file targetFile, you would write:

```
File.Copy("sourceFile", "targetFile");
```

This assumes the using System.IO namespace was included. Otherwise, you would need to fully qualify the name.

13

As was discussed in previous chapters, Visual Studio automatically inserts a number of `using` statements at the top of the source code when you create an application. The `System.IO` is not one of them. You have to manually add `using System.IO;` The extra `using` statements that are not needed are deleted from examples shown in this chapter.

If you use Visual Studio to create the application and include reference to the `System.IO namespace`, the IntelliSense feature provides helpful information while you are developing your application. Figure 13-2 illustrates what is shown as you select methods of the `File class`.

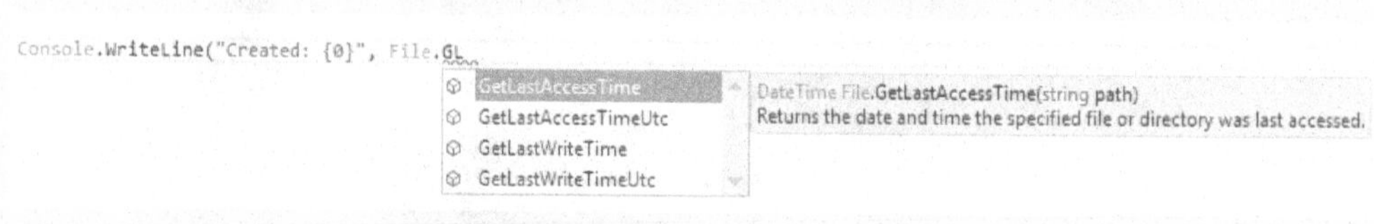

FIGURE 13-2 IntelliSense display

One of the `static` methods of the `File class` is `Exists( )`. Prior to writing program statements that access data in a file, you should always check to make sure the file is available. Example 13-1 illustrates invoking this method and several other methods that return information about the file.

EXAMPLE 13-1

```
/* DirectoryStructure.cs
   Illustrates using File and Directory utilities.
*/
using System;
using System.IO; // Added for File Access

class DirectoryStructure
{
      public static void Main( )
      {
           string fileName = "BirdOfParadise.jpg";
           if (File.Exists(fileName))
           {
                Console.WriteLine("FileName: {0}", fileName);
                Console.WriteLine("Attributes: {0}",
                                       File.GetAttributes(fileName));
                Console.WriteLine("Created: {0}",
                                       File.GetCreationTime(fileName));
```

```
                Console.WriteLine("Last Accessed: {0}",
                                  File.GetLastAccessTime(fileName));
            }
            else
            {
                Console.WriteLine("{0} not found - using current" +
                                  "directory:", fileName);
            }
            Console.ReadKey( );
        }
    }
```

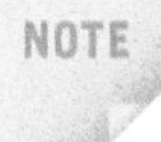

NOTE In previous chapters, `using static` System.Console; was added to eliminated the need to precede calls to Write( ), WriteLine( ), and Read( ), ReadLine( ) with the Console `class` name. This `using` statement was not added for examples in this chapter.

The output produced from the `DirectoryStructure` application is shown in Figure 13-3.

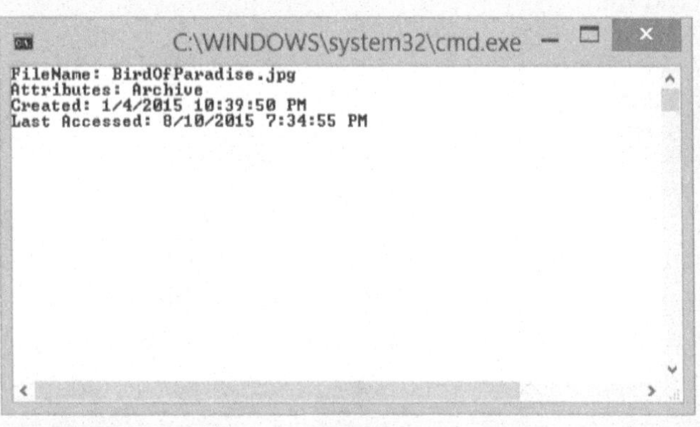

FIGURE 13-3 Output from the DirectoryStructure application

`Archive` is shown as the value for the `Attributes` of the file. Depending on the operating system version you are running, you might see `Normal` instead of `Archive`. `Normal` attribute indicates the file is a standard file that has no special attributes, such as `ReadOnly`. `Archive` indicates the file is a candidate for backup or removal. The method `GetAttributes( )` returns a `FileAttributes` enumeration. Enumerated types are discussed in the next section.

13

ENUMERATED TYPES

An **enumerated type** is a special form of value type that supplies alternate names for the values of an underlying primitive type. An **enumeration type** has a name, an underlying type, and a set of fields. Also called an **enumeration** or an **enum** data type.

It consists of a set of named values called members, **enumerators** or elements of the type. The enumerator names are user-defined identifiers that behave as constants once they are defined. Once a variable is declared of the enumeration type, any of the named values can be assigned to the variable. You've previously seen an enumerated type, the boolean type. Recall `bool` is defined with member elements of `true` and `false`. The Boolean type is a pre-defined enumeration in C#.

C# provides the C-like feature of being able to define specific integer values for enumerations and follows the C style for dealing with enumerators and enables enum value to be explicitly converted to an integer and back again.

One example of a programmer-defined enumeration might be a type called `DayOfWeek`. The possible fields could be `Sunday`, `Monday`, `Tuesday`, `Wednesday`, `Thursday`, `Friday`, and `Saturday`. `Sunday` could be associated with the integer 0, `Monday` with 1 and each consecutive day with 2, 3, 4, 5, and 6, respectively. The enumeration could be defined as follows:

```
public enum DayOfWeek
{
    Sunday,
    Monday,
    Tuesday,
    Wednesday,
    Thursday,
    Friday,
    Saturday
}
```

The enumeration is defined outside of the class, uses the `enum` keyword, and normally offers `public` access. After the enumeration is defined, you may use the values as fields for the data type. For example, to print the string `"Tuesday"`, you could write:

```
WriteLine("Today is {0}!", DayOfWeek.Tuesday);
```

The output produced would be as follows:

```
Today is Tuesday!
```

You can also use explicit type casting to access the associated integer assigned to the value. For example, to display the number associated with Wednesday, you could write:

```
Console.WriteLine("{0} = {1}", DayOfWeek.Wednesday,
                        (int)DayOfWeek.Wednesday);
```

The output produced would be as follows:

```
Wednesday = 3
```

Now look back at Example 13-1. The method `GetAttributes(fileName)` returns the `FileAttributes` for the file. `FileAttributes` is an enumeration. As shown in Figure 13-3, the field it returned was `Archive`. Other enumerated `FileAttributes` values include `Compressed`, `Device`, `Directory`, `Encrypted`, `Hidden`, `Normal`,

ReadOnly, and System. Using enumerations such as this one makes coding simpler and the output more readable.

Directory Class

Like the members of the File class, all members in the Directory class are public static methods. The Directory class provides static methods for creating and moving through directories and subdirectories. Table 13-3 lists some of the more interesting methods of the Directory class.

TABLE 13-3 Directory class members

Public static member	Description
CreateDirectory( )	Creates all the directories in a specified path
Delete( )	Deletes a specified directory
Exists( )	Determines whether the given path refers to an existing directory
GetCreationTime( )	Gets the creation date and time of a directory
GetCurrentDirectory( )	Gets the current working directory of the application
GetDirectories( )	Gets the names of subdirectories in a specified directory
GetFiles( )	Returns the names of files in a specified directory
GetParent( )	Retrieves the parent directory of the specified path, including both absolute and relative paths
GetLastWriteTime( )	Returns the date and time when the specified file or directory was last written to
Move( )	Moves a file or a directory and its contents to a new location
SetCurrentDirectory( )	Sets the application's current working directory to the specified directory

© Cengage Learning

13

.NET also includes DirectoryInfo and FileInfo classes. These classes are very similar to their name counterparts, Directory and File. They differ in that the DirectoryInfo and FileInfo classes both have instance methods instead of static members. They are direct descendents of the FileSystemInfo class.

Objects can be instantiated of the DirectoryInfo and FileInfo classes. No objects can be instantiated of the File and Directory classes.

FileInfo and DirectoryInfo Classes

The FileInfo and DirectoryInfo classes add functionality beyond method members of the File and Directory classes. They both have a number of public properties and, of course, both offer a public constructor. Neither class can be inherited. If you plan to make reference to and use a file or directory several times, you will want to consider instantiating objects of one or both of these classes and use its instance methods. Table 13-4 shows some of the key properties of the FileInfo class.

TABLE 13-4 FileInfo properties

Public member	Description
Attributes	Gets or sets the FileAttributes of the current FileSystemInfo
Directory	Gets an instance of the parent directory
DirectoryName	Gets a string representing the directory's full path
Exists	Gets a value indicating whether a file exists
Extension	Gets the string representing the extension part of the file
FullName	Gets the full path of the directory or file
LastAccessTime	Gets or sets the time when the current file or directory was last accessed
LastWriteTime	Gets or sets the time when the current file or directory was last written to
Length	Gets the size of the current file
Name	Gets the name of the file

© Cengage Learning

The public methods for the FileInfo or DirectoryInfo classes are not shown in the tables. Note, however, that most of the public static methods of the File and Directory classes are available as instance methods in the FileInfo and DirectoryInfo classes.

The DirectoryInfo class adds two other key properties: Parent and Root. Parent gets the parent directory of a specified subdirectory. Root gets the root portion of a path. You should be very careful when you are working with paths in conjunction with files and/or directories. The path must be accurate or an exception is raised.

Example 13-2 adds additional functionality to the `DirectoryStructure` example illustrated in Example 13-1. An object of the `DirectoryInfo` is instantiated, and the `foreach` loop structure uses the `FileInfo` `class`.

EXAMPLE 13-2

```
DirectoryInfo dir = new DirectoryInfo(".");
Console.WriteLine("Current Directory: \n{0}\n",
                  Directory.GetCurrentDirectory( ));
Console.WriteLine("File Name".PadRight(52) + "Size".PadRight(10) +
                  "Creation Time");
foreach (FileInfo fil in dir.GetFiles("*.*"))
{
     string name = fil.Name;
     long size = fil.Length;
     DateTime creationTime = fil.CreationTime;
     Console.WriteLine("{0} {1,12:N0}{2,20:g}", name.PadRight(45),
                       size, creationTime);
}
```

After an `object` of the `DirectoryInfo` is instantiated in Example 13-2, the `GetCurrentDirectory( )` method is invoked to display the current directory. The `GetFiles( )` method of the `FileInfo` `class` is invoked to retrieve a collection of files in the current directory. The `Name`, `Size` or `Length`, and `CreationTime` properties of the `FileInfo` `class` are accessed for the display. The output for the revised example is shown in Figure 13-4.

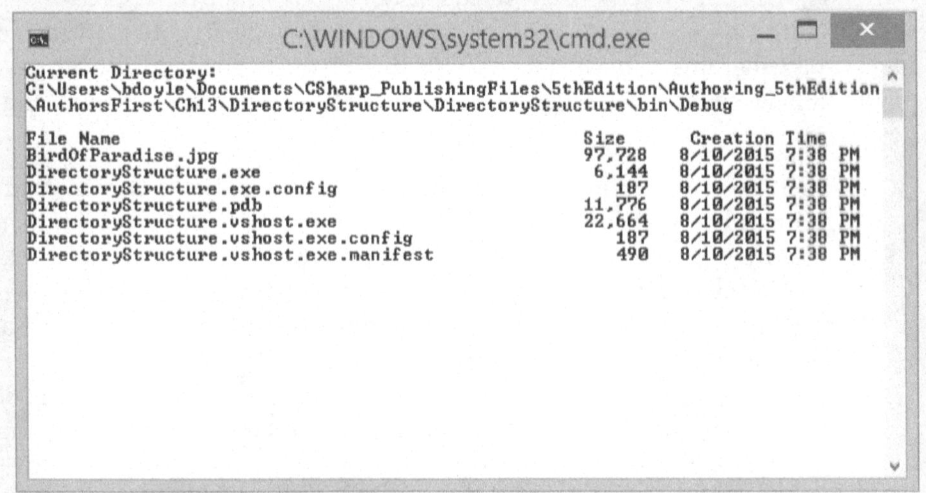

FIGURE 13-4 Output from the revised DirectoryStructure application

As you review the code, you will notice that the `PadRight( )` method of the `string class` was used to format the name of the file returned by the `FileInfo Name` property.

In the last line of the body of the `foreach` loop in Example 13-2, `PadRight( )` left aligned the file names, adding spaces to the right to fill up 45 character positions. The Size or `Length` and `CreationTime` values were right aligned using the format specifiers. The positive integers (12 and 20) in the format specifiers indicate that the values should be right aligned.

You have seen how these classes can be used to obtain information about the files. These classes can also be used to duplicate, move, or delete files or directories. To read data from or write to a file, it is important to understand how streams are used. This is the focus of the next section.

File Streams

C# uses file streams to deal with stored data. Streams represent a chunk of data and provide a way to work with a sequence of bytes. Several `abstract` classes, including `Stream`, `TextWriter`, and `TextReader`, are defined for dealing with files. These classes are defined in the `System.IO namespace`. The stream classes provide generic methods for dealing with input/output, and these methods reduce the need for providing specific details about how the operating system actually accesses data from particular devices. You might want to review Figure 13-1. It shows the hierarchy of many of the classes used for file processing in .NET.

The `IO.Stream class` and its subclasses are used for byte-level data. `IO.TextWriter` and `IO.TextReader` facilitate working with data in a text (readable) format. For the programs you will develop in this chapter, you will use `StreamReader` and `StreamWriter`, which are classes derived from the `TextReader` and `TextWriter` classes.

The `StreamWriter` and `StreamReader` classes make it easy to read or write data from and to text files in C#. The `StreamWriter class` has implementations for `Write( )` and `WriteLine( )` methods similar to the `Console class` methods. `StreamReader` includes implementations of `Read( )` and `ReadLine( )`. The simplest constructor for these classes includes a single argument for the name of the file. The name may include the full path indicating where the file is located or you may use the relative path to the file. Relative paths are relative to the starting location of the project. The starting location is usually located in the `ProjectName\bin\Debug` or `ProjectName\bin\Release` folder. When you specify the relative path, you do not give a drive letter. Instead, you either simply type the filename indicating the file will be stored in the starting location or specify a path relative to the starting location.

If the file is stored in the same Visual Studio folder that holds the project and source code files, you would write `"../../filename"`. This indicates to go up two directory levels from the bin/Debug or bin/Release folders to retrieve the file.

All of the applications you have designed were Debug versions. After an application is debugged and you are ready to deploy or distribute it, you can build a Release version. You switch from Debug to Release versions. The Release version contains no debugging information and is considered an optimized solution. To switch to the Release version, select **Release** from the **Solution Configurations** list box on the Standard Visual Studio toolbar. You can also make that change using the **Properties** dialog box for the project.

If you do not specify the full path for the filename, Visual Studio uses the bin\Debug or bin\Release subdirectory of the current project. To specify the full path, you must use either escape characters for the backslash or the verbatim `string` character `(@)`. To specify that the file is stored at C:\CSharpProjects\Proj1, you would include as an argument either `("c:\\CSharpProjects\\Proj1")` using two backslashes for each backslash, or you would write `(@"C:\CSharpProjects\Proj1")`. When you place an `@` in front of the string, it becomes a verbatim string.

The filename may be sent as a string literal or specified as a variable with a string value. The following statements construct objects of the `StreamWriter` and `StreamReader` classes:

```
StreamWriter outputFile = new StreamWriter ("someOutputFileName");
StreamReader inputFile = new StreamReader ("someInputFileName");
```

The identifiers of `outputFile`, `someOutputFileName`, `inputFile`, and `someInputFileName` are all user-supplied identifiers. `outputFile` and `inputFile` represent the file stream objects. `someOutputFileName` and `someInputFileName` would be replaced by the actual filenames associated with the file—the names you see from **Computer** or **Windows Explorer**. If you are creating a data file, place a file extension such as .dat, .dta, or .txt onto the end of the file so that it can be distinguished from the other files on your system. Files that end in .txt can be easily opened for inspection in Notepad.

To avoid fully qualifying references to objects of these classes, include the `System.IO namespace`.


```
using System.IO;
```

When you use the `Write( )` or `WriteLine( )` methods with the instantiated stream object, the characters are written to the file specified by the filename. The values are stored in the file as text characters—string objects. `ReadLine( )` reads a line of characters and returns the data as a string. The following statements write and read a test message to and from files after an object of the `StreamWriter` `class` has been constructed:

```
outputFile.WriteLine("This is the first line in a text file");
string inValue = inputFile.ReadLine( );
```

Tables 13-5 and 13-6 show members of the `StreamWriter` and `StreamReader` classes.

TABLE 13-5 StreamWriter members

StreamWriter members	Description
AutoFlush	(Property) Gets or sets a value indicating whether the `StreamWriter` flushes its buffer to the underlying stream after calls to the `Write( )` or `WriteLine()` methods
`Close( )`	Closes the current `StreamWriter`
`Dispose( )`	Releases the unmanaged resources used by the `StreamWriter`
`Flush( )`	Clears all buffers for the current writer and causes any buffered data to be written to the underlying stream
`NewLine`	(Property) Gets or sets the line terminator string used by the current `TextWriter`
`Write( )`	Writes the characters to the stream
`WriteLine( )`	Writes the characters to the stream, followed by a line terminator

© Cengage Learning

TABLE 13-6 StreamReader members

StreamReader members	Description
`Close( )`	Closes the current `StreamReader`
`DiscloseBufferedData( )`	Allows the `StreamReader` to discard its current data
`Dispose( )`	Releases the unmanaged resources used by the `StreamReader`
`Peek( )`	Returns the next available character but does not consume it

(*continues*)

TABLE 13-6 StreamReader members (*continued*)

StreamReader members	Description
`Read( )`	Reads the next character or next set of characters from the input stream
`ReadBlock( )`	Reads a specified number of characters from the current stream and writes the data to buffer, beginning at the index
`ReadLine( )`	Reads a line of characters from the current stream and returns the data as a `string`
`ReadToEnd( )`	Reads the stream from the current position to the end of the stream

© Cengage Learning

Recall that in previous chapters, a `using static System.Console;` directive was added at the top of the program in all examples to enable calls to `static` members like `Write( )`, `WriteLine( )`, and `ReadLine( )` to be invoked without fully qualifying the call with the `Console class` name. As given in Tables 13-5 and 13-6, `StreamWriter` and `StreamReader` classes have methods named `Write( )`, `WriteLine( )`, and `ReadLine( )`. Calls made to those methods will be qualified with the `class` name to avoid confusion. In this chapter, that `using` directive, `using static System.Console` is not added.

Writing Text Files

All attempts to access text files should be enclosed inside `try...catch` blocks to check for exceptions. This is not required in C#, but is encouraged to avoid unhandled exceptions being thrown during run time. The constructor for the `StreamWriter class` is overloaded, in that you can include additional arguments such as a Boolean variable indicating whether the file should be appended to or overwritten if it already exists. If you do not include an argument for the `Append` mode, a new file is created by default, overwriting any previously created versions. Using the `Append` mode enables you to add lines onto the end of an existing file.

13

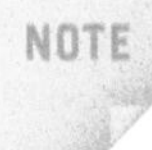

Constructing an object of the `StreamWriter class` using `true` as the second argument enables you to append values onto the end of a file. The following statement opens the file named info.txt, stored in the project subdirectory, so that records will be added onto the end of the file:

```
fileOut = new StreamWriter("../../info.txt", true);
```

Values are placed in the file in a sequential fashion. A pointer moves through the file, keeping up with the current location into which the next values are to be placed in the file. After the file is created, the `Close( )` method is used to finish storing the values. When the `Close( )` method is called, any values waiting in the buffer to be written are flushed to the file and the resources associated with the file are released. Example 13-3 creates a text file containing the user's favorite sayings. This example illustrates using exception-handling techniques with the `StreamWriter class`. For the sake of brevity, the `FrmSayingsGUI.Designer.cs` and `Program.cs` Windows Forms generated code is not included in the listing.

The application includes a `Textbox object` for data entry and a `Label object` for displaying error messages. The label is originally set to `null` (an empty value) at design time. One `Button object` is included. Its event-handler method is used to save the entry to the text file.

EXAMPLE 13-3

```
// FrmSayingGUI.cs
// Windows application that retrieves
// and stores values from a text box
// in a text file.
using System;
using System.Windows.Forms;
using System.IO;      // Added for file access

namespace SayingsApp
{
     public partial class FrmSayingsGUI : Form
     {
          private StreamWriter fil;  // Declares file stream object

          public FrmSayingsGUI( )
          {
               InitializeComponent( );
          }

          // Form load event handler used to construct
          // object of the StreamWriter class, sending the
          // new filename as an argument. Enclosed in
          // try...catch block.
          private void FrmSayingsGUI_Load(object sender,
                                           EventArgs e)
          {
               try
               {
                    fil = new StreamWriter("saying.txt");
               }
```

```
            catch (DirectoryNotFoundException exc)
            {
                lblMessage.Text = "Invalid directory" +
                                     exc.Message;
            }
            catch (System.IO.IOException exc)
            {
                lblMessage.Text = exc.Message;
            }
        }

        // When the button is clicked, write the characters
        // to the text file.
        private void btnStoreSaying_Click(object sender,
                                          EventArgs e)
        {
            try
            {
                fil.WriteLine(txtBxSaying.Text);
                txtBxSaying.Text = "";
                txtBxSaying.Focus( );
            }
            catch (System.IO.IOException exc)
            {
                lblMessage.Text = exc.Message;
            }
        }

        // When the form is closing (default window x
        // box is clicked), close the file associated
        // with the StreamWriter object.
        private void FrmSayingsGUI_FormClosing(object sender,
                                   FormClosingEventArgs e)
        {
            try
            {
                fil.Close( );
            }
            catch
            {
                lblMessage.Text = "File did not close properly: ";
            }
        }
    }
}
```

The application is run and two different sayings are entered by the user, as shown in Figure 13-5.

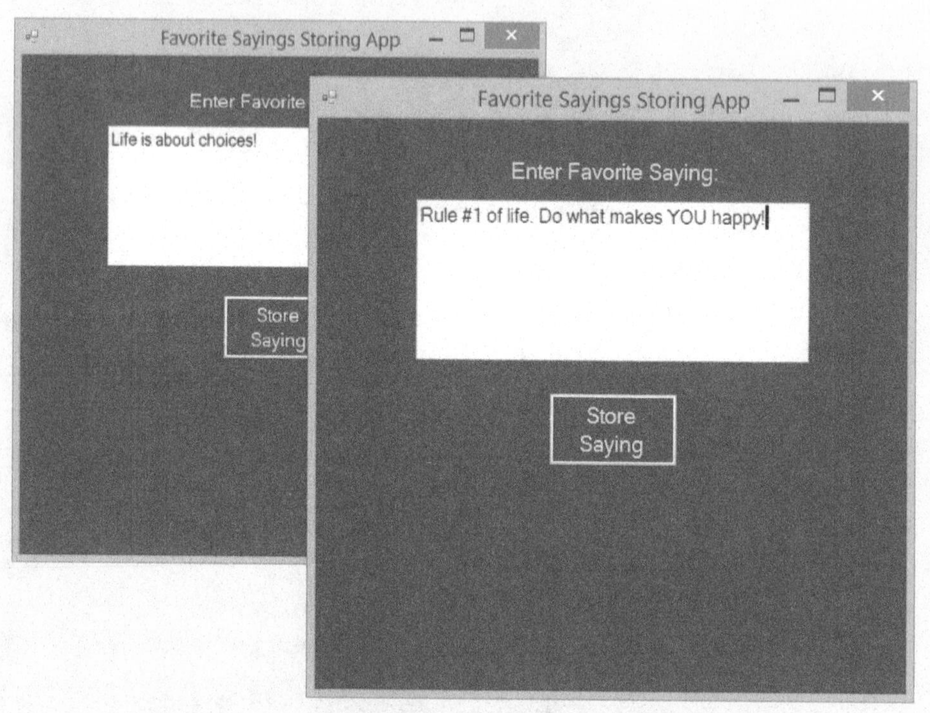

FIGURE 13-5 Data being stored in a text file

As you review the statements in Example 13-3, notice that three event-handler methods are included in the Windows application. In the form-loading event handler, an object of the `StreamWriter` `class` is instantiated. This is included in a `try...catch` clause. The button click event-handler method retrieves the `string` from the text box and writes the text to the file. It is also enclosed in a `try...catch` clause. The third event-handler method is an on form-closing event. In this event-handler method, the file is closed inside another `try...catch` block. Using the data input from Figure 13-5, the contents of the file created from this run of the application are shown in Figure 13-6.

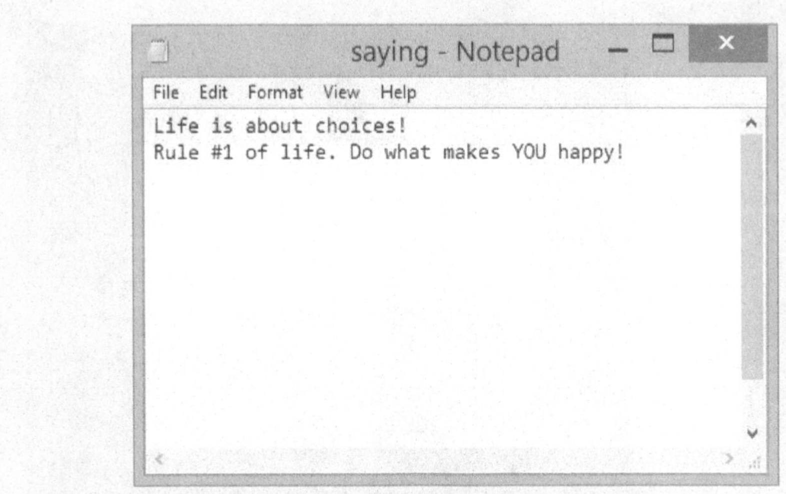

FIGURE 13-6

In Visual Studio, when you create a file (or attempt to access one), if a path is not specified for the filename, the bin\Debug subdirectory for the current project is used. If an invalid path is listed in the constructor for the `StreamWriter` `object`, an `IOException` exception is thrown as soon as the application launches and the form is loaded. To demonstrate this, the call to the constructor was changed in Example 13-3. On the system on which this application is run, there is no C:\Bob subdirectory. Thus, replacing the `object` constructor in the `FrmSayingsGUI_Load( )` method from

```
fil = new StreamWriter("saying.txt");
to:
fil = new StreamWriter(@"C:\Bob\saying.txt");
```

throws an exception as soon as the form is loaded. When the user interface was designed for Example 13-3, a label, initialized with `""` (a null or empty string), was placed on the form to display error messages. Figure 13-7 shows the message displayed when the `DirectoryNotFoundException` exception is thrown.

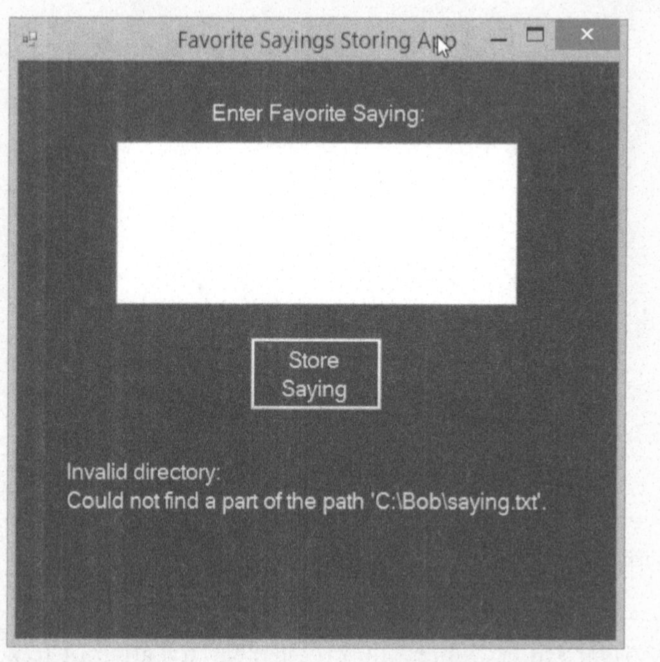

FIGURE 13-7 DirectoryNotFoundException thrown

The `"Invalid directory"` string literal was concatenated onto the string returned from the `Message` property of the `DirectoryNotFoundException` object `exc`. Example 13-4 reprints the `FrmSayingsGUI_Load( )` method that is executed when the form is loaded. This time it includes the invalid path argument used to construct the object when the exception was thrown, as shown in Figure 13-7.

EXAMPLE 13-4

```
private void FrmSayingsGUI_Load(object sender,
                          System.EventArgs e)
{
     try
     {
          fil = new StreamWriter
               (@"C:\Bob\saying.txt");// Invalid path
     }
     catch (DirectoryNotFoundException exc)
     {
          lblMessage.Text = "Invalid directory\n"
                    + exc.Message;
     }
```

```
    catch (System.IO.IOException exc)
    {
        lblMessage.Text = exc.Message;
    }
}
```

Without including the `try...catch` clause in the `FrmSayingsGUI_Load( )` method, the program would have crashed with an unhandled exception, because no file can be created when an invalid path is specified.

You also cannot close a file that does not exist or is not currently open. As you examine the `try...catch` clause in the `FrmSayingsGUI_FormClosing( )` method, notice `inFile.Close( );` in the body of this `catch` is also enclosed in a `try...catch` block. If an exception is thrown and caught when an attempt to close the file is made, `lblMessage.Text = "File did not close properly: ";` is executed in the `catch` clause.

Reading Text Files

The `StreamReader class` was designed to enable lines of text to be read from a file. If you do not specify a different type of encoding (coding representation), the characters read are converted by default to strings of Unicode characters.

NOTE: By default, the Unicode UTF-16 encoding schema is used. This represents characters as sequences of 16-bit integers. You could specify Unicode UTF-8, in which characters are represented as sequences of 8-bit bytes, or use ASCII encoding, which encodes characters as single 7-bit ASCII characters.

Using members of the `StreamReader class`, accessing the contents of a text file is as easy as creating it. As given in Table 13-6, several methods, including the `ReadLine( )` method, are available to read characters from the file. As with the `StreamWriter class`, the constructor for `StreamReader` is overloaded. You may specify a different encoding schema or an initial buffer size for retrieval of data. If you specify a buffer size, it must be given in 16-bit increments.

13

With the `StreamReader` and `StreamWriter` objects, you can use members of parent or ancestor classes or `static` members of the File `class`. As given in Table 13-2, `File.Exists( )` can be used to determine whether the file exists. You can send the filename as an argument to `Exists( )` before attempting to construct an object. This is a way to programmatically avoid having a `FileNotFoundException` or `DirectoryNotFoundException` exception thrown in your applications. This is illustrated in Example 13-5.

Values are read from text files in sequential manner. Just as when you create a text file, a pointer moves through the file keeping track of the current location for the next read.

Example 13-5 reads strings from a text file that contains a list of names. The text file uses those values to populate a list box for a Windows application. This application illustrates using exception-handling techniques with the `StreamReader` `class`. For the sake of brevity, the Windows Forms generated code for the FileAccessApp.Designer.cs and Program.cs files is not included in the listing that follows. The application includes a `Listbox` for data display and a `Label` `object` for displaying error messages. The label is originally set to a `null` empty value.

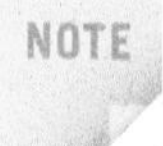

NOTE

Because you often want to read from one or more files and write the output to another file, you can have multiple files open at the same time.

EXAMPLE 13-5

```
// FileAccessApp.cs
// Windows application that retrieves
// and stores values from a text file
// to a list box.
using System;
using System.Windows.Forms;
using System.IO;        // Added for file access

namespace FileAccessApp
{
    public partial class FrmFileGUI : Form
    {
        private StreamReader inFile; //Declares file stream object

        public FrmFileGUI( )
        {
            InitializeComponent( );
        }

        // Form load event handler used to construct
        // object of the StreamReader class, sending the
        // new filename as an argument. Enclosed in
        // try…catch block.
        private void FrmFileGUI_Load(object sender, EventArgs e)
        {
            string inValue;
```

```
                if (File.Exists("name.txt"))
                {
                    try
                    {
                        inFile = new StreamReader("name.txt");
                        while ((inValue =
                                    inFile.ReadLine ( )) != null)
                        {
                            this.lstBxNames.Items.Add(inValue);
                        }
                    }
                    catch (System.IO.IOException exc)
                    {
                        lblMessage.Text = exc.Message;
                    }
                }
                else
                {
                    lblMessage.Text = "File unavailable";
                }
            }

            // When the close X is clicked, as the form is
            // closing, close the file associated with the
            // StreamReader object.
            private void FrmFileGUI_FormClosing(object sender,
                                             FormClosingEventArgs e)
            {
                try
                {
                    inFile.Close( );
                }
                catch
                {
                }
            }
        }
    }
```

NOTE Be sure to close all files before you exit the application. This ensures that the data is usable for the next application. Close the file by calling the `Close( )` method, as shown in Example 13-5. No arguments are sent to the method; however, it must be called with the file object (`inFile.Close( );`).

13

Figure 13-8 shows the contents of the file used for testing the application in Example 13-5. Names were placed in the text file last name first for sorting purposes.

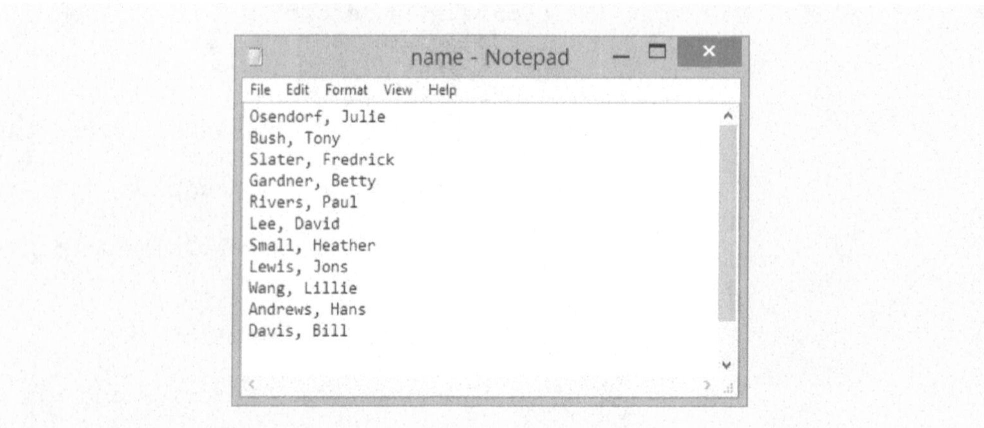

FIGURE 13-8 Content of name.txt file

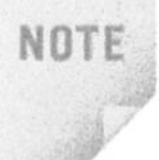

The file is displayed using Notepad. However, it was created in Visual Studio using the **Text File** template found from the **File**, **New File**, **General** Installed template menu option. It is physically located in the project subdirectory under the bin\Debug folder. If you attempt to create it in a word-processing application, such as Microsoft Word, be careful. It must be saved as a plain text file without any special formatting.

A sample run of the application is shown in Figure 13-9.

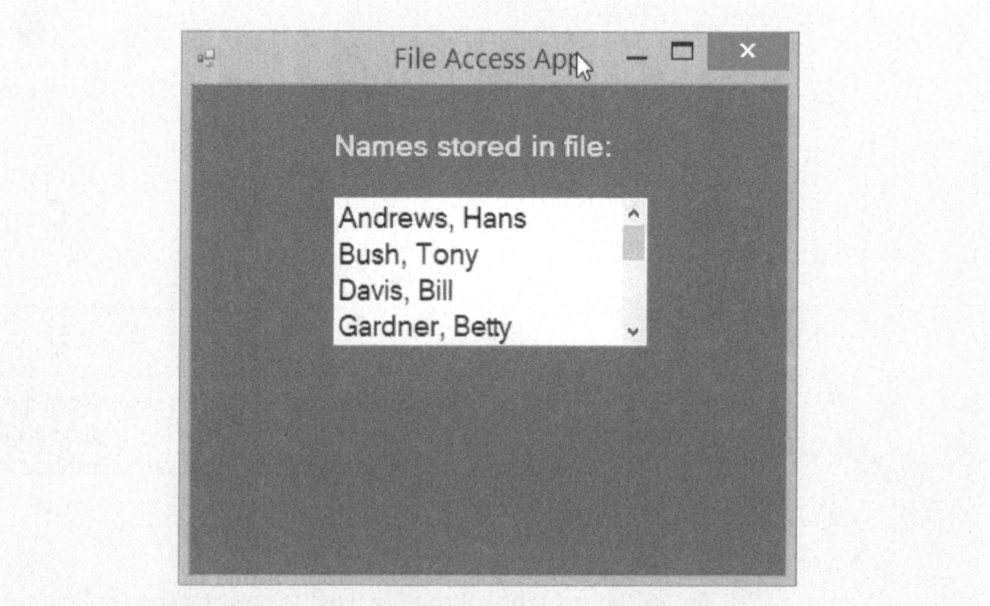

FIGURE 13-9 Output from the FileAccessApp application

One of the properties of the ListBox objects is Sorted. By default, it is set to false; however, you can change that and have the entries in the list box in sort order—even if they are not sorted in the file. For this application, the Sorted property was changed to true.

In Example 13-5, the try...catch block was enclosed inside a selection statement. The if statement was used to check to see if the file existed. When an invalid path was specified, an exception was not thrown and the try...catch block was skipped. Examine the while statement that appears in Example 13-5.

```
while ((inValue = inFile.ReadLine( )) != null)
```

The ReadLine( ) method is used with the infile object to retrieve one line of text from the file. The line is stored in the inValue variable. The while statement tests each access from the file and continues looping until inValue == null, indicating all the lines have been read.

Adding a Using Statement

The using keyword has two major uses. Previously, you added a using clause to your program statements to import types defined in namespaces. By doing this, you were able to avoid fully qualifying references to types. For example, by adding using System, you were able to write Console.WriteLine( ) as opposed to System.Console.WriteLine( ). When working in Visual Studio, you also noticed that once you added reference to a specific namespace with the using statement, IntelliSense was able to list valid members of that type referenced in the namespace.

Recall a new feature introduced as part of Visual Studio 2015 was the option to include a using static statement to add a reference to classes that exposed static members. The Console class is an example of such a class. In previous chapters, using static System.Console; was added. This eliminated the need to precede calls to Write( ), WriteLine( ), and Read( ), ReadLine( ) with the Console class name. The using static System.Console; was not added for examples in this chapter. The file stream classes introduced in this chapter have member methods of Write( ), WriteLine( ), and Read( ), ReadLine( ). To avoid creating confusion, calls to these methods are fully qualified with the class name.

The second major use of the using keyword is to define a scope for an object and have the common language runtime (CLR) automatically dispose of, or release, the resource when the object goes out of scope. This is extremely useful when working with files or databases. For example, if you are writing data to a file, the data is not stored in the file properly until the file is closed. If you fail to close the file, you will find an empty file. The using block, when used with files, ensures the file is closed properly. It is not necessary for you to call the Close( ) method. This is called automatically for you by the CLR when the object goes out of scope. Example 13-6 illustrates adding a using statement to define a StreamReader object.

EXAMPLE 13-6

```
// FileAccessAppWithUsing.cs
using System;
using System.Windows.Forms;
using System.IO;      //Added for file access

namespace FileAccessApp
{
     public partial class FrmFileGUI : Form
     {
          public FrmFileGUI( )
          {
               InitializeComponent( );
          }
          private void FrmFileGUI_Load(object sender, EventArgs e)
          {
               string inValue;
               try
               {
                    using (StreamReader inFile =
                              new StreamReader("name.txt"))
                    {
                         while ((inValue =
                                   inFile.ReadLine( ))!= null)
                         {
                              this.lstBxNames.Items.Add(inValue);
                         }
                    }
               }
               catch (FileNotFoundException exc)
               {
                    lblMessage.Text = "File Not Found !\n" +
                                   exc.Message;
               }
               catch (Exception exc)
               {
                    lblMessage.Text = exc.Message;
               }
          }
     }
}
```

NOTE As with previous examples, the FileAccessApp.Designer.cs and Program.cs files are not shown. These files contain the code automatically generated by Visual Studio. The full application, like all other examples in the textbook, are available from the publisher as fully functioning Visual Studio projects.

Notice in Example 13-6 that the StreamReader object is defined and instantiated inside the using block. This occurs inside a try clause. By instantiating the inFile object here, the object exists only in this block and you are guaranteed that the file is closed when you exit the block. At this point, the inFile object resources are released back to memory. Also note that by placing the declaration and instantiation of the object in the using statement, you no longer need to call the Close( ) method. Thus, you no longer need a Form_Closing( ) event registered.

If you compare Example 13-6 with Example 13-5, you will also notice the if statement, which was used to check whether the file exists or not, was removed. An additional catch clause was added for the FileNotFoundException. It was placed before the catch with the Exception class because the Exception is the base of all exception classes and is more generic than the FileNotFoundException class.

The using statement can be used independent of the try...catch clause. It is extremely useful for dealing with files because it automatically releases the resources and closes the file upon exit. However, when used as shown in Example 13-7, the aFont and c objects only exist inside the block designated by the curly braces, since that is where they are defined. An attempt to reference the objects outside of the block will generate a compiler error.

EXAMPLE 13-7

```
// Adding a using statement
using (Font aFont = new Font("Arial", 12.0f),
                          Customer c = new Customer( ))
{
     // Statements referencing aFont and c
}
```

As shown in Example 13-7, if you want to declare and instantiate more than one object, use a comma between the instantiation.

Random Access

The FileStream class also supports randomly accessing data. Values can be processed in any order. The fifth data record can be retrieved and processed before the first record is processed when random access is used. This is accomplished using a concept called seeking, which modifies the current position. Thus, instead of reading or writing data in a sequential order from the beginning of the file or memory stream, you specify which location or record you want to process.

One of the members of the FileStream class is a Seek( ) method. Seek( ) lets you move the read or write position to any location within the stream using an offset reference parameter. The offset can be specified relative to the beginning, the current position, or the end. The `Seek( )` method takes two arguments. The first specifies the number of bytes from the origin and the second specifies the origin. The enumerated values for the origin are `SeekOrigin.Begin`, `SeekOrigin.End`, and `SeekOrigin.Current`.

Seeking to a location beyond the length of the stream is also supported. When you seek beyond the length of the file, the file size grows. Random access and seeking can be used with the text files and also with the binary files, which is the topic of the next section.

BinaryReader and BinaryWriter Classes

The `BinaryWriter` and `BinaryReader` classes are used for writing and reading binary data, rather than character strings. The files created are readable by the computer but, unlike the files created by the `StreamWriter class`, you cannot simply open and read the contents of a binary file using Notepad. A program is needed to interpret the file contents. It is easy to write to or read from binary files. In addition to constructors, the `BinaryWriter` and `BinaryReader` classes expose a number of instance methods. Tables 13-7 and 13-8 list some of the key instance methods.

TABLE 13-7 BinaryWriter members

Method	Description
`Close( )`	Closes the current BinaryWriter and the underlying stream
`Flush( )`	Clears all buffers for the current writer and causes any buffered data to be written to the underlying device
`Seek( )`	Sets the position within the current stream
`Write( )`	Writes a value to the current stream
`Write7BitEncodedInt( )`	Writes a 32-bit integer in a compressed format

© Cengage Learning

The `BinaryReader` and `BinaryWriter` classes offer streaming functionality that is oriented toward particular data types. As you review the `BinaryReader` methods listed in Table 13-8, you will notice several `Read( )` methods. Each is focused on the type of data that it would be retrieving from a file.

TABLE 13-8 BinaryReader members

Method	Description
`Close( )`	Closes the current `BinaryReader` and the underlying stream
`PeekChar( )`	Returns the next available character and does not advance the byte or character position
`Read( )`	Reads characters from the underlying stream and advances the current position of the stream
`ReadBoolean( )`	Reads a Boolean value from the current stream and advances the current position of the stream by 1 byte
`ReadByte( )`	Reads the next byte from the current stream and advances the current position of the stream by 1 byte
`ReadBytes( )`	Reads count bytes from the current stream into a byte array and advances the current position by count bytes
`ReadChar( )`	Reads the next character from the current stream and advances the current position of the stream
`ReadChars( )`	Reads count characters from the current stream, returns the data in a character array, and advances the current position
`ReadDecimal( )`	Reads a decimal value from the current stream and advances the current position of the stream by 16 bytes
`ReadDouble( )`	Reads an 8-byte floating-point value from the current stream and advances the current position of the stream by 8 bytes
`ReadInt32( )`	Reads a 4-byte signed integer from the current stream and advances the current position of the stream by 4 bytes
`ReadString( )`	Reads a string from the current stream; the string is prefixed with the length

© Cengage Learning

Example 13-8 illustrates using the `BinaryWriter` `class` to create a binary file that stores integers, decimals, and string data types.

EXAMPLE 13-8

```
// BinaryFiles.cs
// Illustrates creating a binary file
using System;
using System.IO;        // Added for file access

namespace BinaryFiles
{
    class BinaryExample
    {
        public static void Main( )
        {
            FileStream filStream;
            BinaryWriter binWriter;

            Console.Write("Enter name of the file: ");
            string fileName = ReadLine( );
            if (File.Exists(fileName))
            {
                Console.WriteLine("File - {0} already exists!",
                                  fileName);
            }
            else
            {
                filStream = new FileStream(fileName,
                            FileMode.CreateNew);
                binWriter = new BinaryWriter (filStream);
                decimal aValue = 2.16M;
                binWriter.Write("Sample Run");
                for (int i = 0; i < 11; i++)
                {
                    binWriter.Write(i);
                }
                binWriter.Write(aValue);
                binWriter.Close( );
                filStream.Close( );
                Console.WriteLine("File Created successfully");
            }
            Console.ReadKey( );
        }
    }
}
```

Example 13-8 first checks to see if the filename entered by the user already exists. This is accomplished using the `static` `Exists( )` method of the `File` `class`. When the name entered is a new file, objects are instantiated of the `FileStream` and `BinaryWriter` classes. Notice that the second argument to the `FileStream` constructor is an enumeration. The `FileMode` enumerated type specifies how the operating system should open the file. As shown in Figure 13-10, the field value member named `CreateNew` indicates that the operating system should create a new file. IntelliSense notes that the `System.IO.IOException` is thrown if the file already exists. Another option for an enumerated value for `FileMode` is `Create`. `Create` differs from `CreateNew` in that it will replace an existing file with a new one, if one already exists, instead of throwing an exception.

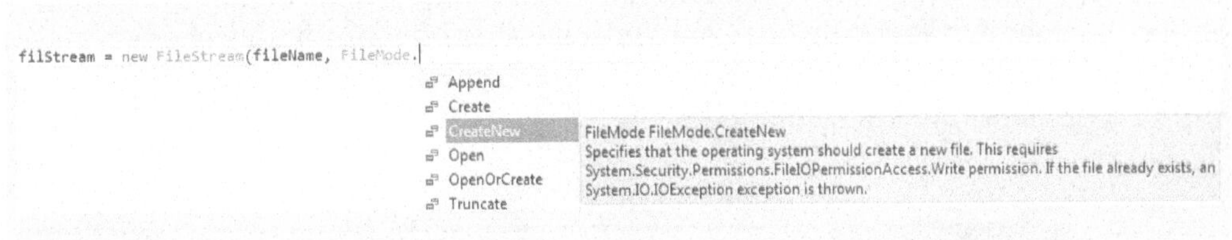

FIGURE 13-10 Enumerated FileMode

The `BinaryWriter` `object` is based on the `FileStream` `object` or wrapped around the `FileStream` `object`. The `FileStream` `object` is sent in as an argument to the `BinaryWriter` constructor.

In Example 13-8, first a string argument is written to the file. This is followed by several integers and a decimal value. Finally, for the file to be created properly, both files must be closed. Figure 13-11 shows the console output produced. In the foreground of the figure, you see the newly created file.

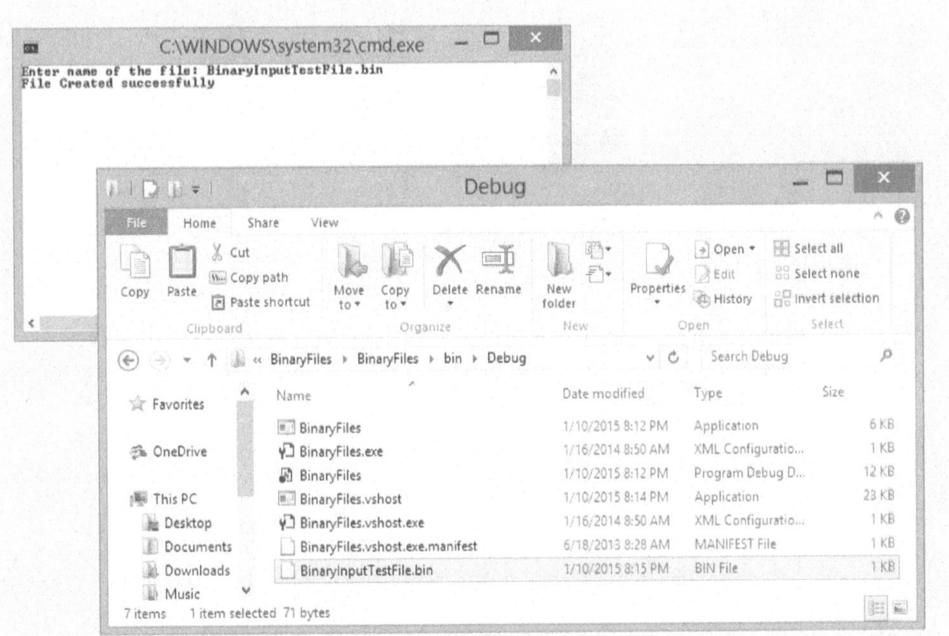

FIGURE 13-11 BinaryInputTestFile.bin file created

When testing the BinaryFiles project shown in Example 13-8, use a name other than BinaryInputTestFile.bin when prompted for a filename. Otherwise you'll have a message "File - BinaryInputTestFile.bin already exists!" displayed.

As you can see from Figure 13-11, because no path was specified, the file is stored in the bin/Debug directory for the project.

After a binary file is created, you cannot simply open the file in Notepad and view its contents. If you do, you will find a number of nonprintable characters. You can write program statements that use the `BinaryReader class` to retrieve the results. This is illustrated in Example 13-9.

EXAMPLE 13-9

```
// BinaryFileAccess.cs
// Illustrates retrieving data from a binary file.
using System;
using System.IO;       // Added for file access

namespace BinaryFileAccess
{
      class BinaryInput
      {
            public static void Main( )
            {
                  FileStream filStream;
                  BinaryReader binReader;

                  Console.Write("Enter name of the file: ");
                  string fileName = Console.ReadLine( );
                  try
                  {
                        filStream = new FileStream(fileName,
                                      FileMode.Open, FileAccess.Read);
                        binReader = new BinaryReader (filStream);
                        RetrieveAndDisplayData(binReader);
                        binReader.Close( );
                        filStream.Close( );
                  }
                  catch (FileNotFoundException exc)
                  {
                        Console.WriteLine(exc.Message);
                  }
                  catch (InvalidDataException exc)
                  {
                        Console.WriteLine(exc.Message);
                  }
```

```
                catch (EndOfStreamException exc)
                {
                    Console.WriteLine(exc.Message);
                }
                catch (IOException exc)
                {
                    Console.WriteLine(exc.Message);
                }
                Console.ReadKey( );
            }

            public static void RetrieveAndDisplayData (BinaryReader
                                                        binReader)
            {
                // Read string data from the file.
                Console.WriteLine(binReader.ReadString( ));
                // Read integer data from the file.
                for (int i = 0; i < 11; i++)
                {
                    Console.WriteLine(binReader.ReadInt32 ( ));
                }
                // Read decimal data from the file.
                Console.WriteLine(binReader.ReadDecimal( ));
            }
        }
    }
```

NOTE The file, BinaryInputTestFile.bin, created from Example 13-8 BinaryInput was moved to the bin/Debug directory for this application. If you do not specify the full path where the file is located, the application looks in the bin/Debug directory.

The code shown in Example 13-9 is used to retrieve the values that were stored in the binary file by the previous application, `BinaryFiles`. The code for `BinaryFiles` was displayed in Example 13-8. With Example 13-9, after the user enters the name of the file, objects of the `FileStream` and `BinaryReader` classes are instantiated. This is done inside a `try...catch` clause.

The constructor for the `FileStream` `object` includes values for two enumerated types (`FileMode.Open` and `FileAccess.Read`). As their names imply, the `FileMode.Open` indicates the operating system should open an existing file. The `FileAccess.Read` indicates the file will be used for input. Recall that the enumerated value of `CreateNew` was used with `FileMode` when the file was created. The three enumerated values for `FileAccess` are `Read`, `Write`, and `ReadWrite`. Figure 13-12 shows the output produced from the run.

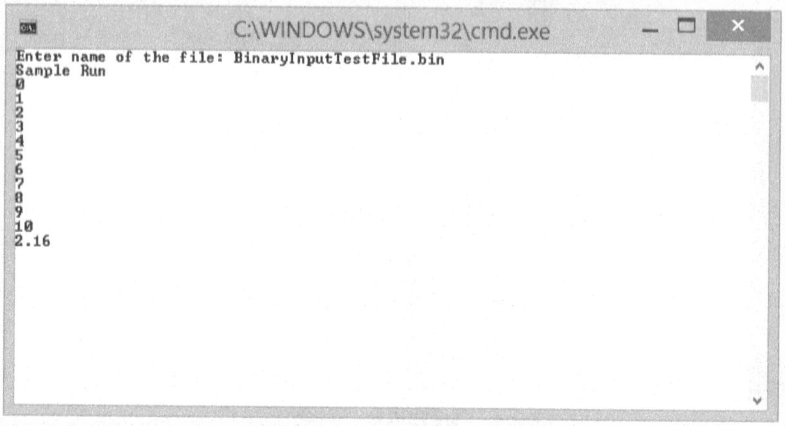

```
C:\WINDOWS\system32\cmd.exe
Enter name of the file: BinaryInputTestFile.bin
Sample Run
0
1
2
3
4
5
6
7
8
9
10
2.16
```

FIGURE 13-12 Reading string, integer, and decimal data from a binary file

Three different methods were invoked to read data from the file. The `ReadInt32( )` method retrieved the 10 integers. The `ReadDecimal( )` reads the decimal value placed in the file, and the `ReadString( )` was invoked to retrieve the string value. You might wonder how it knew to retrieve only the alphabetic characters `"Sample Run"` when the `ReadString( )` method was called. The `ReadString( )` method is the first method invoked. As given in Table 13-8, strings are prefixed with a length when they are stored in the file. The `ReadString( )` method uses that value to determine how many characters to retrieve. Several catch clauses were included. All derived classes of the `IOException` were placed prior to the `IOException catch` because the order of placement is important.

Other Stream Classes

Streams are also used in C# for reading and writing of data on the network and reading and writing to an area in memory. `NetworkStream` works with network connections. `MemoryStream` works directly with data in memory.

The `NetworkStream class` provides methods for sending and receiving data over stream sockets. It is beyond the scope of this book to provide coverage of the `NetworkStream class`. However, this is the class used for both synchronous and asynchronous data transfer. The class has methods similar to the other stream classes, including `Read` and `Write` methods. Also included as part of .NET is a `MemoryStream class`. The `MemoryStream class` is used to create streams that have memory as a backing store instead of a disk or a network connection. The `MemoryStream class` encapsulates data stored as an unsigned byte array and is directly accessible in memory. Memory streams can reduce the need for temporary buffers and files in an application. You are encouraged to explore the MSDN documentation for more details on how to make use of the NetworkStream and MemoryStream classes.

Objects of streams can be wrapped with an object of the BufferedStream class. The unbuffered stream object is passed to the constructor for a buffered stream class, thus enabling buffering of characters. This can improve the speed and performance of file-handling operations. By wrapping a BufferedStream object around a file stream object, you can bring chunks of characters (more than one record) into memory for retrieval. After the data is stored in memory, members of the class read the data from the buffer, reducing the number of actual accesses to secondary storage devices, which slows down applications.

Buffering can also be used for creating files. Here instead of writing every record physically to the secondary storage device, the write stores data in a buffer in memory. After the buffer contains a specified number of characters, the buffer is written to the actual file. All that is required to use buffers is to instantiate an object of the BufferedStream class and send as an argument an object of one of the stream classes. Then use the BufferedStream object to access the data. You are encouraged to explore the MSDN documentation for examples.

Instead of processing values sequentially from top to bottom, values can be processed in any order when random access is used with the FileStream class. Random access is achieved using the Seek( ) method. Seek( ) lets you move the read or write position to any location within the file using offset reference parameters. The offset can be specified relative to the beginning, the current position, or the end of the file.

FileDialog Class

Having worked with Windows applications, you are accustomed to browsing to a specific location to store or retrieve files. It is very easy to include this type of functionality in your applications. Instead of hard coding the actual filename and path as you have seen with most of the examples included in this chapter, you can also add dialog boxes to allow the user to enter the name at run time. If you are accessing a file for input, you can display an **Open** file dialog box and allow the user to traverse to the directory where the file is located and select the file. Or if you are creating a new file, you can display a **Save As** dialog box and allow the user to type or select a filename at run time.

This is accomplished using the OpenFileDialog and SaveFileDialog classes. Both classes are derived from the FileDialog class. FileDialog is an abstract class, which cannot be instantiated but provides much of the functionality for the OpenFileDialog and SaveFileDialog classes. These classes are part of the System.Windows.Forms namespace. The FileDialog class has a property called FileName, which is used by both the OpenFileDialog and SaveFileDialog classes to set or get the name of the file from the dialog box. To add the dialog box behavior to an application, drag the `OpenFileDialog` and/or the `SaveFileDialog` control from the toolbox onto your form. When you release the mouse, the controls are placed in the component tray below the form, as shown in Figure 13-13.

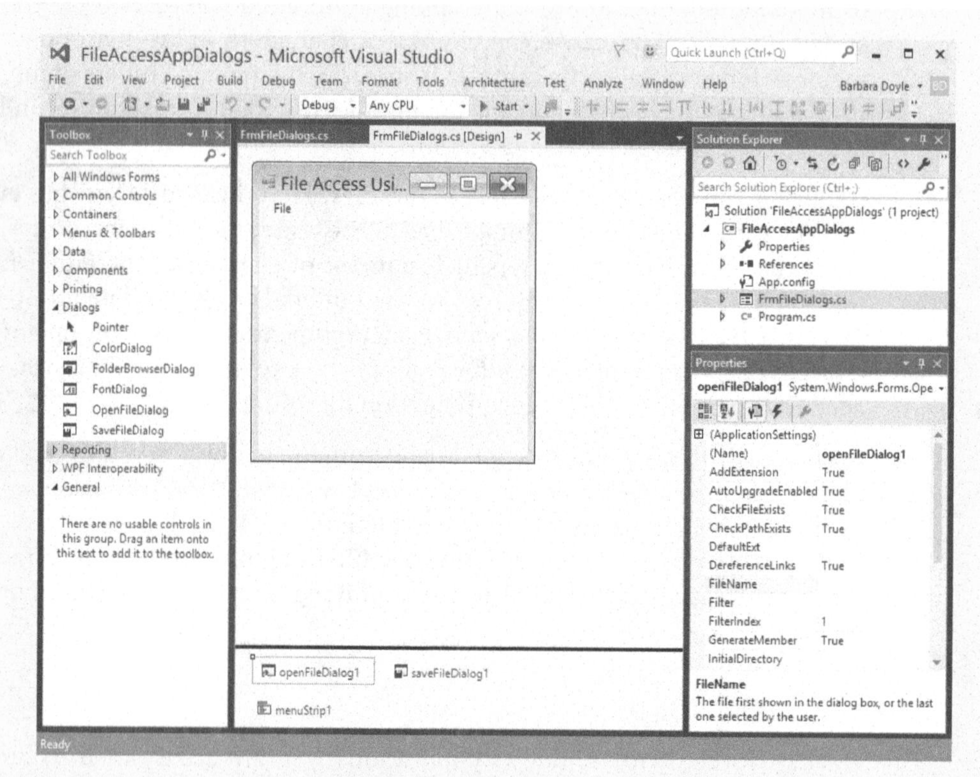

FIGURE 13-13 Placing OpenFileDialog and SaveFileDialog controls

When the `OpenFileDialog` control is placed on your form, the initial default value for the `FileName` property is the name of the object, `openFileDialog1`. You can type a new value for the `FileName` property, or, if you prefer to not have a value for the name, you can erase the value for the `FileName` property. This causes the text box for the filename to be blank. Using the **Properties** window, the text for the filename was removed for this example.

After the dialog controls are placed on the form, the `ShowDialog( )` method is used to cause the dialog boxes to open. The `ShowDialog( )` method is also a member of the abstract FileDialog class. It is available to both of these derived classes. If you do not change the names of the objects, but use the default names, you would include the following statements in your program at the location where you want to display the dialog boxes:

```
openFileDialog1.ShowDialog( );
```

or

```
saveFileDialog1.ShowDialog( );
```

Example 13-10 illustrates using the OpenFileDialog and SaveFileDialog classes.

EXAMPLE 13-10

```
// FileAccessAppDialogs.cs
// Illustrates using file dialogs for
// retrieving and saving files.
using System;
using System.Windows.Forms;
using System.IO;      // Added for file access

namespace FileAccessAppDialogs
{
     public partial class FrmFileDialogs : Form
     {
          StreamReader inFile;
          StreamWriter outFile;

          public FrmFileDialogs( )
          {
               InitializeComponent( );
          }

          private void openToolStripMenuItem_Click (object sender,
                                                    EventArgs e)
          {
              try
              {
                    openFileDialog1.ShowDialog( );
                    inFile = new
                         StreamReader(openFileDialog1.FileName);
                    lblMessage.Text = "File " +
                         openFileDialog1.FileName;
                    inFile.Close( );
              }
```

13

```
                catch (Exception ex)
                {
                    lblMessage.Text = ex.Message;
                }
            }

            private void saveAsToolStripMenuItem_Click (object sender,
                                                        EventArgs e)
            try
            {
                saveFileDialog1.ShowDialog( );
                string testValue =
                    "This is an example using Dialog boxes";
                outFile = new
                          StreamWriter(saveFileDialog1.FileName);
                outFile.WriteLine(testValue);
                outFile.Close( );{
            }
            catch (Exception ex)
            {
                lblMessage.Text = ex.Message;
            }
        }

        private void exitToolStripMenuItem_Click (object sender,
                                                  EventArgs e)
        {
            Application.Exit( );
        }
    }
}
```

Open and **Save** menu options were added to the application. Example 13-10 shows the event-handler methods for these menuStrip objects. If a file is not selected, the `catch` clause is executed. The message property for the exception that is thrown is displayed on the `lblMessage`.

The **Open** file dialog box, shown in Figure 13-14, is displayed when the `ShowDialog( )` method is executed with the `openFileDialog1` `object`.

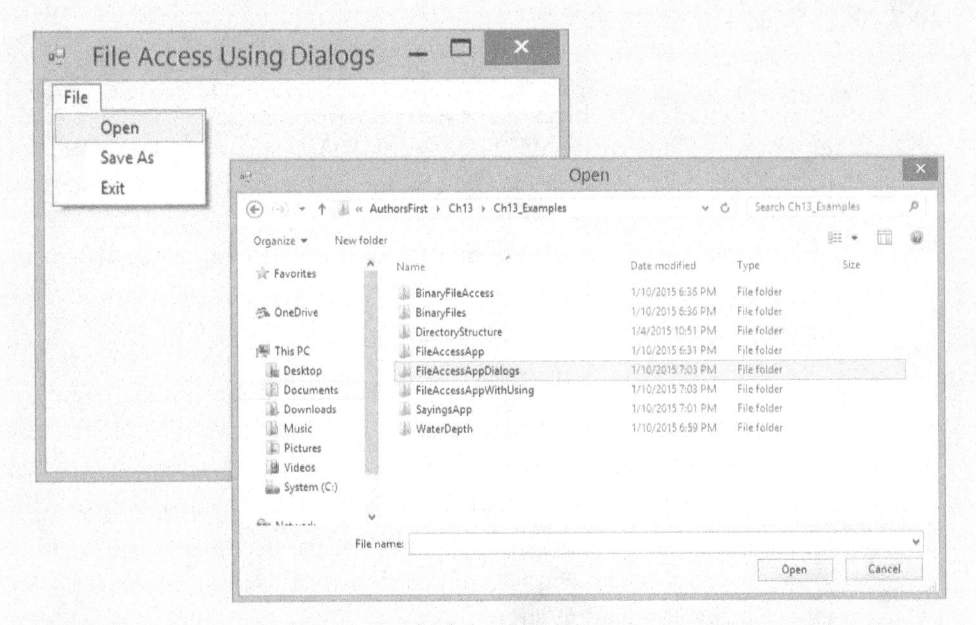

FIGURE 13-14 ShowDialog( ) method executed

A dialog box similar to the one shown in Figure 13-14 would also be displayed when the `ShowDialog( )` method is executed with a `SaveFileDialog` `object`. As shown in Example 13-10, to retrieve the filename from the text box in the dialog box, you use the `FileName` property. This retrieved value can be used as the argument for the stream object instantiation. This is illustrated with the following `inFile` `object`:

```
StreamReader inFile = new StreamReader(openFileDialog1.FileName);
```

Whenever you work with files you should always enclose your access statements in `try...catch` blocks. You read about checked exceptions in Chapter 12. Even though C#, unlike Java, has no checked exceptions, you should still include exception-handling techniques for all file processing applications.

This procedure also works for `StreamWriter` objects. The following two lines cause the **Save As** dialog box to open. The user can browse to the location where the file should be stored and either type a new filename or select a file to replace.

```
saveFileDialog1.ShowDialog( );
StreamWriter outFile = new StreamWriter(saveFileDialog1.FileName);
```

When these lines are executed, instead of the dialog box having the word Open in the title bar, as shown in Figure 13-14, the title bar will contain the words `Save As`.

PROGRAMMING EXAMPLE: ICW WaterDepth File App

In Chapter 12, a graphical user interface solution was designed to enable users to enter areas along the ICW where boaters were advised to take warning because of shoaling or shallow water. The graphical user interface enabled users to enter a location name, state, mile marker number, and four separate days of water depth at low and high tide. When valid data was entered, a message was displayed showing the location and its associated data. However, after the data about a single location was processed and displayed, it was lost when the second and subsequent locations were entered. There was no mechanism available to store the data from one run to another run. For this programming example, the solution presented in Chapter 12 will be modified to allow the results to be captured and stored for future use.

ANALYZE THE PROBLEM

You should review the problem specification in Figure 12-21 and make sure you understand the problem definition. Several values must be entered into the program. Instead of allowing a single set of location and associated depths to be entered, the application should allow multiple locations to be entered. A Windows application was developed as part of the solution for the programming example illustrated in Chapter 12. When a Windows application is run, it is put in a process loop and can handle multiple value sets. Minor modifications will be needed to ready the form for the second and subsequent set of input values.

DATA

Three classes were designed for the solution to the `WaterDepth` application in Chapter 12. You should review Table 12-4. It lists the data field members needed for the `ShoalArea` `class`. No new data members are needed for this class. No changes are needed for the `TestOfStateException` `class`. The `FrmWaterDepth` `class` created the user interface and displayed a message showing the problem area and its water depths. In this class, an `object` of the `StreamWriter` `class` will be created.

DESIGN A SOLUTION

Instead of simply displaying a message showing the location of the shoal area and data describing the current condition of the reported problem, the data will be stored in a text file. Depths will be delimited or separated by a comma and a space. The location will be separated by a comma and a space. The state and the mile marker will be followed by a colon, space, and hyphen, respectively. Averages will be stored inside parentheses and inserted following the raw data they are representing. Usually, you do not store calculated values in a data file or database; there is no need to take up additional storage for calculated values because they can be derived at any time using the raw data. Also, storing calculated values can lead to inconsistent data. If one of the day's depths gets changed and the average does not, the integrity of the data is decreased. Figure 13-15 shows a prototype of what the data file might look like.

```
Location, State: MileMarker- Day1Lo, Day2Lo, Day3Lo, Day4Lo, (LoAvg), Day1Hi, Day2Hi, Day3Hi, Day4Hi, (HiAvg)

Examples:
Jacksonville, FL: 1023- 4.9, 5.6, 5.2, 4.9, (5.15), 7.1, 7.8, 7.7, 7.3, (7.48)
Jeckyl Island, GA: 1232- 4.2, 4.4, 4.4, 4.7, (4.43), 5, 5.1, 5.2, 5.3, (5.15)
Beauford, NC: 2113- 5.2, 5.3, 5.5, 5.5, (5.38), 7.1, 7, 7.4, 7.9, (7.35)
```

FIGURE 13-15 Data file prototype

The first two printed lines would not appear in the file. They are included here to document what the values are. The three lines under Examples are indicative of what the output would look like.

CODE THE SOLUTION

You may want to look ahead at Figure 13-16 to review the form used to collect the data. The revised source code listings for the `ShoalArea` and the `FrmWaterDepth` classes follow.

```
// ShoalArea.cs
// This class defines a ShoalArea location
// where water depths in the ICW are problematic.
// Data stored in a text file includes the
// name of the location, state, mile marker, and
// four days of high and low tide depths, and averages.
using System;
using System.Diagnostics;
namespace WaterDepth
{
    public class ShoalArea
    {
        private string location;
        private string state;
        private double mileMarker;
        private double[ ] lowTideDepth;
        private double[ ] hiTideDepth;

        public ShoalArea( )
        {
            lowTideDepth = new double[4];
            hiTideDepth = new double[4];
        }
        public ShoalArea(string loc, string st, double mile,
                              double[ ] low, double[ ] hi)
        {
           location = loc;
           CheckStateOk(st);
           mileMarker = mile;
```

13

```
        lowTideDepth = low;
        hiTideDepth = hi;
    }
    public ShoalArea(string loc, string st, double mile )
    {
         location = loc;
         state = st;
         mileMarker = mile;
    }

    //Properties
    public string Location
    {
         get { return location; }
         set { location = value; }
    }
    public string State
    {
         get { return state; }
         set { CheckStateOk(value); }
    }
    public double MileMarker
    {
         get { return mileMarker; }
         set { mileMarker = value; }
    }
    public double[ ] LoTideDepth
    {
         get { return lowTideDepth; }
         set { lowTideDepth = value; }
    }
    public double[ ] HiTideDepth
    {
         get { return hiTideDepth; }
         set { hiTideDepth = value; }
    }

    public double CalculateAverageDepth
                          (double [ ] depthArray)
    {
         double sum = 0;
         double avg;
         try
         {
              foreach (double val in depthArray)
                   sum += val;
              avg = sum / depthArray.Length;
         }
```

```
        catch (System.DivideByZeroException e)
        {
            avg = 0;
            Trace.WriteLine("Attempted to Divide by Zero" +
                            "\nException Type: " +
                            e.Message );
        }
        return avg;
    }

    public void CheckStateOk(string st)
    {
        switch(st.ToUpper( ))
        {
            case "FL":
            case "GA":
            case "NC":
            case "SC":
            case "VA":
                state = st.ToUpper( );
                break;
            default:
                TestOfStateException ex =
                    new TestOfStateException
                        ("State not Part of Atlantic ICW");
                throw ex;
        }
    }

    public string ShoalAreaRecord
    {
        get
        {
            string rec = location +"," + state.ToUpper( ) +
                                   ": " + mileMarker + "- ";
            foreach (double val in lowTideDepth)
                rec += val + ", ";
            rec += "(" + CalculateAverageDepth
                         (lowTideDepth).ToString("0.00") +
                         "), " ;
            foreach (double val in hiTideDepth)
                rec += val + ", ";
            rec += "(" + CalculateAverageDepth
                         (hiTideDepth).ToString("0.00") +
                         ") ";
            return rec;
        }
    }
```

13

```
            public override string ToString( )
            {
                return "Location: " + location +
                        "\nState: " + state +
                        "\nMile: " + mileMarker +
                        "\nAverage Low Water Depth: " +
                        CalculateAverageDepth(lowTideDepth).ToString
                        ("F2") + "\nAverage High Water Depth: " +
                        CalculateAverageDepth(hiTideDepth). ToString
                        ("F2") + "\n\nOverall Average Water Depth: " +
                        ((CalculateAverageDepth(lowTideDepth) +
                        CalculateAverageDepth(hiTideDepth))
                        / 2.0).ToString("F2");
            }
        }
}
```

A special property, `ShoalAreaRecord`, was defined to format the raw data with delimiters. Notice how this property resembles the single data member properties you used previously. The keyword `get` is followed by statements that concatenate the data fields onto the string that is returned. The object's `ToString( )` method is overridden to provide a formatted `string` for output.

The `FrmWaterDepth` `class` follows. New event handlers have been added for the form load and form closing events.

```
// FrmWaterDepth.cs
// This class defines the Graphical
// User Interface class. Values retrieved
// from the user are stored in a text file.
using System;
using System.Windows.Forms;
using System.Diagnostics;
using System.IO;

namespace WaterDepth
{
    public partial class FrmWaterDepth : Form
    {
        private ShoalArea anArea;
        private StreamWriter fil;
        public FrmWaterDepth( )
        {
            InitializeComponent( );
        }
```

```
private void FrmWaterDepth_Load(object sender,
                                EventArgs e)
{
    anArea = new ShoalArea( );
    try
    {
        //// To append data onto the end of the file,
        //// as opposed to creating a new file,
        //// add true as the 2nd argument
        //fil = new
        //   StreamWriter("WaterData.txt", true);
        fil = new StreamWriter("WaterData.txt");
    }
    catch (DirectoryNotFoundException exc)
    {
        lblError.Text = "Invalid directory" +
                        exc.Message;
    }
    catch (System.IO.IOException exc)
    {
        lblError.Text = exc.Message;
    }
}

private void btnSubmit_Click(object sender, EventArgs e)
{
    double[ ] lowTides = new double[4];
    double[ ] hiTides = new double[4];

    anArea.Location = txtBxLocation.Text;
    try
    {
        lowTides[0] = double.Parse(txtBxLow1.Text);
        lowTides[1] = double.Parse(txtBxLow2.Text);
        lowTides[2] = double.Parse(txtBxLow3.Text);
        lowTides[3] = double.Parse(txtBxLow4.Text);
        hiTides[0] = double.Parse(txtBxHi1.Text);
        hiTides[1] = double.Parse(txtBxHi2.Text);
        hiTides[2] = double.Parse(txtBxHi3.Text);
        hiTides[3] = double.Parse(txtBxHi4.Text);
        anArea.State = txtBxState.Text;
        anArea.MileMarker =
                double.Parse(txtBxMile.Text);
        anArea.LoTideDepth = lowTides;
        anArea.HiTideDepth = hiTides;
        StoreDataInFile(anArea);
        MessageBox.Show(anArea.ToString( ),
                        "ICW Problem Area");
        ClearForm( );
    }
```

```
            catch (TestOfStateException ex)
            {
                Trace.WriteLine("\nException: " + ex.Message);
                lblError.Text += "\nException: " + ex.Message;
            }
            catch (FormatException ex)
            {
                Trace.WriteLine("Method\'s actual argument " +
                                " does not match formal " +
                                "parameter.\nException: " +
                                ex.Message);
                lblError.Text += "\nException: " + ex.Message;
            }
            catch (ArithmeticException ex)
            {
                Debug.WriteLine("Errors in an arithmetic, " +
                                "casting, or conversion." +
                                "\nException: " + ex.Message);
                lblError.Text += "\nException: " + ex.Message;
            }
            catch (ArrayTypeMismatchException ex)
            {
                Trace.WriteLine("Trying to store an element " +
                                " of wrong type in an array." +
                                "\nException: " + ex.Message);
                lblError.Text += "\nException: " + ex.Message;
            }
            catch (IndexOutOfRangeException ex)
            {
                Trace.WriteLine("Trying to access element " +
                                "of an array with index " +
                                "outside bounds of the " +
                                "array.\nException: " +
                                ex.Message);
                lblError.Text += "\nException: " + ex.Message;
            }
            catch (Exception ex)
            {
                lblError.Text += "\nException: " + ex.Message;
                Trace.WriteLine("Exception: " + ex.Message);
            }
        }
        private void StoreDataInFile(ShoalArea anArea)
        {
            try
            {
                fil.WriteLine(anArea.ShoalAreaRecord);
            }
```

```
            catch (DirectoryNotFoundException exc)
            {
                lblError.Text = "Invalid directory" +
                                    exc.Message;
            }
            catch (InvalidDataException exc)
            {
                lblError.Text = "Invalid format in data stream"
            }
            catch (System.IO.IOException exc)
            {
                lblError.Text = exc.Message;
            }
        }

        private void FrmWaterDepth_FormClosing(object
                      sender,FormClosingEventArgs e)
        {
            try
            {
                fil.Close( );
            }
            catch (IOException exc)
            {
                lblError.Text = exc.Message;
            }
        }

        public void ClearForm( )
        {
            txtBxLocation.Text = string.Empty;
            txtBxState.Text = string.Empty;
            txtBxMile.Text = string.Empty;
            txtBxLow1.Text = string.Empty;
            txtBxLow2.Text = string.Empty;
            txtBxLow3.Text = string.Empty;
            txtBxLow4.Text = string.Empty;
            txtBxHi1.Text = string.Empty;
            txtBxHi2.Text = string.Empty;
            txtBxHi3.Text = string.Empty;
            txtBxHi4.Text = string.Empty;
            lblError.Text = string.Empty;
            txtBxLocation.Focus( );
        }
    }
}
```

13

When the form is loaded, objects of the `ShoalArea` and `StreamWriter` classes are instantiated. When the form is closed, the file is closed. A special method was added to store the data in the file. This method is called from the button-click event handler. Much of the functionality for the application is written in this method. Values are retrieved and parsed. The `StoreDataInFile( )` method is called. In this method, the `ShoalAreaRecord` property is sent as an argument to the `WriteLine( )` method of the `StreamWriter class`. Because the form is used to input multiple records, it was necessary to clear the text box values and refocus the control back into the location text box. Statements were included in the `ClearForm ( )` method to do this. Because no changes were made to the `TestOfStateException class` from the example illustrated in the previous chapter, the source code is not shown. A run of the application is shown in Figure 13-16.

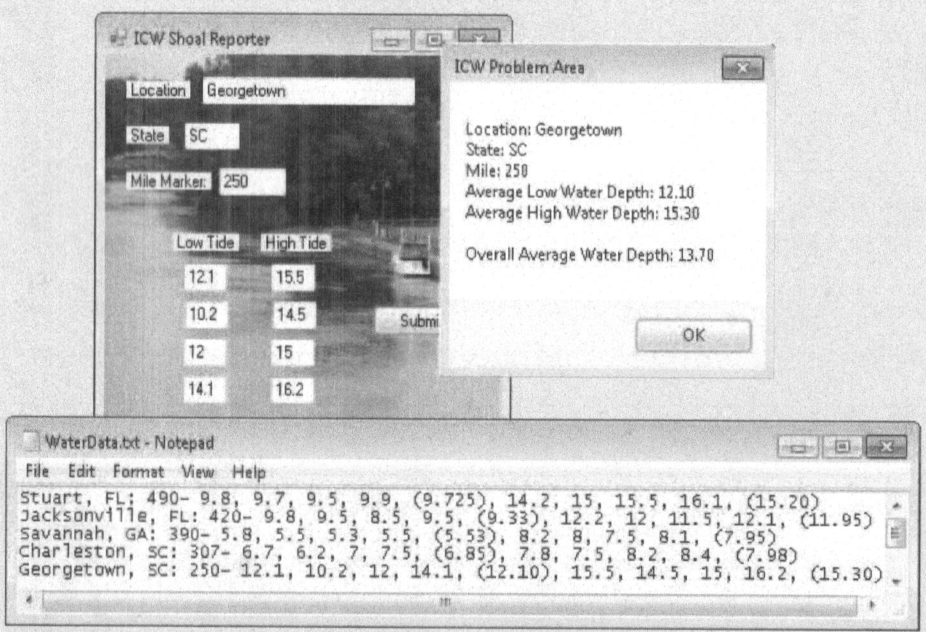

FIGURE 13-16 Values stored in a text file

Figure 13-16 shows the values entered during a single run of the application. If you want to modify the solution so that the next run of the application appends data onto the end of this current data in the text file, only one change is necessary. This change would be made in the `FrmWaterDepth_Load( )` method. Add `true` as the second argument when you instantiate the `StreamWriter( ) object`. It would read:

```
fil = new StreamWriter("WaterData.txt", true);
```

The solution provided in the example did not include a second argument. Thus, by default, a new file is created each time. You get this same effect if you add `false` as the second argument. If the file exists and append is `true`, the data is appended or added onto the end of the file. If the file does not exit, a new file is created.

Coding Standards

Rarely is software maintained for its whole life by the original developer. Using good style improves the maintainability of the software.

Include exception-handling techniques to deal with file or directory not found types of problems. Use specific exception classes, such as `FileIOException`, to handle the exceptions.

`System.IO namespace` should be added when you are reading or writing a file. Always close files that are opened in applications or embed their usage in a `using` statement.

Resources

Additional sites you might want to explore:

- C# Code Style Guide—
  http://www.sourceformat.com/pdf/cs-coding-standard-bellware.pdf
- C# Station - How to: Reading and Writing Text Files—
  http://www.csharp-station.com/HowTo/ReadWriteTextFile.aspx
- Dot Net Perls - C# File Handling—
  http://dotnetperls.com/file-handling

QUICK REVIEW

1. The `System.IO namespace` provides basic file and directory support classes, including `File`, `Directory`, `FileInfo`, `DirectoryInfo`, `StreamReader`, `StreamWriter`, `BinaryReader`, and `BinaryWriter`.
2. The `File` and `Directory` classes expose only `static` members. The `FileInfo` and `DirectoryInfo` classes expose instance methods and properties.
3. An enumeration is a special form of value type that supplies alternate names for the values of an underlying primitive type. An enumeration type has a name, an underlying type, and a set of fields.
4. Streams represent a chunk of data and provide a way to work with a sequence of bytes. Several `abstract` stream classes, including `Stream`, `TextWriter`, and `TextReader`, are defined for dealing with files.
5. `TextWriter` and `TextReader` facilitate working with data in a text (readable) format. `StreamReader` and `StreamWriter` are derived from the `TextReader` and `TextWriter` classes.

6. The `StreamReader` `class` was designed to enable lines of information to be read from a text file.
7. The `StreamWriter` `class` implements methods for `Write( )` and `WriteLine( )` similar to those you learned for the `Console` `class`.
8. `StreamReader` includes implementations of `Read( )` and `ReadLine( )` methods. These methods can be used to retrieve data from the file.
9. To terminate normally, the `Close( )` method is used with the stream classes.
10. `Close( )` is called without arguments, but does require that an `object` be used with the call.
11. Include a using statement for the `System.IO` `namespace`. Otherwise, you will need to fully qualify the name of stream `class` members.
12. If you do not specify the full path for the filename, Visual Studio uses the `bin\Debug` subdirectory of the current project.
13. To specify the full path for a file as a string argument, you must either use escape characters for the backslash or the verbatim string character (@) in front of the string literal.
14. All attempts to access text files should be enclosed inside `try...catch` blocks to check for exceptions. This is not required in C#, but is encouraged to avoid unhandled exceptions being thrown during run time.
15. One of the arguments that can be included with the constructor for the `StreamWriter` `class` is a Boolean variable indicating whether the file should be appended to or overwritten if it already exists. If you do not include an argument for the `Append` mode, a new file is created by default, overwriting any previously created versions.
16. The `StreamReader` `class` was designed to enable lines of text to be read from a file. If you do not specify a different type of encoding (coding representation), the characters read are converted by default to strings of Unicode characters.
17. The `BinaryWriter` and `BinaryReader` classes are used for writing and reading binary data, rather than character strings.
18. The files created by the `BinaryWriter` `class` are readable by the computer but, unlike the files created by the `StreamWriter` `class`, you cannot simply open and read the contents of a binary file using a text editor, such as Notepad.
19. Streams are also used in C# for reading and writing data on the network and reading and writing to an area in memory.

EXERCISES

1. All of the following are exception classes that are thrown in conjunction with files, except:
   a. `DirectoryNotFoundException`
   b. `EndOfStreamException`
   c. `InvalidDataFileException`
   d. `FileNotFoundException`
   e. `IOException`

2. One difference between the `DirectoryInfo class` and the `Directory class` is:
   a. Methods of the `Directory class` allow you to move directories and files; `DirectoryInfo` does not.
   b. The `DirectoryInfo class` also has public properties.
   c. The `DirectoryInfo class` is a `static` class.
   d. The `Directory class` cannot be used with binary files; DirectoryInfo can.
   e. The `DirectoryInfo class` only has methods.

3. To avoid an `IOException` exception with files, you can either use a `try...catch` block or make sure there is a file before attempting to read characters from it. This can be done by:
   a. calling the `File.Exists( )` method
   b. using a loop to cycle through the file structure
   c. throwing an exception
   d. including statements in a finally block
   e. placing a test loop in the `Main( )` method

4. Which class allows you to use the `Read( )` and `ReadLine( )` methods to retrieve data from a text file?
   a. `TextReader`
   b. `FileReader`
   c. `BinaryReader`
   d. `StreamReader`
   e. `File`

5. Which class allows you to use the `Write( )` and `WriteLine( )` methods to write data to a text file?
   a. `TextWriter`
   b. `FileWriter`
   c. `BinaryWriter`
   d. `StreamWriter`
   e. `File`

6. When you are finished processing a text file, you should:
   a. call the `Finished( )` method
   b. call the `Close( )` method
   c. throw an exception
   d. erase the file
   e. reset the file

7. The `File class`:
   a. has only instance members, so to call one of its methods you must have an object
   b. has only instance members, so to call one of its methods you must use the class name
   c. has only static members, so to call one of its methods you must have an object
   d. has only static members, so to call one of its methods you must use the class name
   e. has only static members, so to call one of its methods you must use an instance member

8. To which namespace does the `File class` belong?
   a. `Object`
   b. `System.FileSystem`
   c. `System.Object`
   d. `Object.IO`
   e. `System.IO`

9. The members of the ______________ `class` allow you to create, move, copy, and delete files.
   a. `File`
   b. `FileInfo`
   c. `Directory`
   d. `DirectoryInfo`
   e. `File` and `FileInfo`

10. To append data onto the end of a text file:
    a. use the `AppendStream` `class`
    b. add the `Append` argument to the constructor for the `FileStream` `class`
    c. add the `Append` argument to the constructor for the `StreamWriter` `class`
    d. add `true` as the second argument (Append) to the `StreamWriter` `class`
    e. open the file in an append mode by adding an 'a' onto the end of the identifier

11. Which of the following is an `abstract class`?
    a. `DirectoryInfo`
    b. `Stream`
    c. `StreamReader`
    d. all of the above
    e. none of the above

12. In Visual Studio, if you do not specify the full path of a file, what directory is used?
    a. C:\
    b. the project directory
    c. C:\App_Data
    d. bin\Debug
    e. C:\WorkDirectory

13. Using the verbatim `string`, you could write the full path of C:\CSharpProjects\ Ch13\WorkDirectory as:
    a. `@"C:\CSharpProjects\Ch13\WorkDirectory"@`
    b. `@"C:\\CSharpProjects\\Ch13\\WorkDirectory"`
    c. `@"C:\CSharpProjects\Ch13\WorkDirectory"`
    d. `"@C:\CSharpProjects\Ch13\WorkDirectory"`
    e. none of the above
14. What method in the `StreamReader class` retrieves a full line of text-up until the newline character is encountered?
    a. `Flush( )`
    b. `ReadBlock( )`
    c. `Retrieve( )`
    d. `ReadLine( )`
    e. `Peek( )`
15. To make a duplicate copy of a file, you could use a `static` method in the `class`:
    a. `File`
    b. `StreamWriter`
    c. `Stream`
    d. `TextWriter`
    e. `BinaryWriter`
16. Streams can be used in C# for writing data to:
    a. text files
    b. networks
    c. memory
    d. binary files
    e. all of the above
17. `StreamReader` is a direct descendent of:
    a. `MarshalByRefObject`
    b. `Object`
    c. `File`
    d. `TextReader`
    e. `IO`

18. Which of the following would store an integer in a binary file?
    a. `Write7BitEncodedInt( )`
    b. `WriteInt( )`
    c. `WriteLine( )`
    d. `StoreInt( )`
    e. none of the above

19. Which of the following methods could be used to retrieve a decimal value from a binary file?
    a. `ReadDec( )`
    b. `ReadDecimal( )`
    c. `ReadNumber( )`
    d. `ReadDoubleValue( )`
    e. `ReadDecimalValue( )`

20. All of the following methods of the `BinaryReader` `class` could be used to retrieve data, except:
    a. `ReadChar( )`
    b. `Read( )`
    c. `ReadChars( )`
    d. `ReadInt( )`
    e. `ReadString( )`

---

21. Write a file declaration for a file that holds text characters and can be stored in C:\CSharpProjects\WorkDirectory. The file will be used to store data.

22. For the file declared in Exercise 21, write a method that stores the numbers 10 through 49 in the text file.

23. For the file created in Exercise 22, write a method that retrieves the values from the text file. Display 10 characters per line on the console output screen.

24. Revise the solutions for Exercises 22 and 23 to include a `try` block and at least two appropriate `catch` clauses inside the method.

25. Describe the differences between retrieving data from a text file versus retrieving it from a binary file.

PROGRAMMING EXERCISES

1. Write a C# program that prints the current directory and the name and size of all files that are stored in the directory. Your display should be aesthetically pleasing. Numbers should be number aligned and formatted with a thousand separator. Provide headings over the column listings.

2. Place 10 to 20 integer values in a text file. Write a C# program to retrieve the values from the text file. Display the number of values processed, the average of the values, formatted with two decimal places, and the smallest and largest values. Include appropriate exception-handling techniques with your solution. *Hint:* To simplify the problem, the values can each be placed on separate lines in a Notepad file.

3. Write a program that enables the user to input name, address, and local phone number, including area code. Encourage the user to include dashes between the numbers (i.e. xxx-xxx-xxxx) when they type in the value. Once retrieved, store the values in a text file. For the phone, surround the phone numbers with asterisks in the file and store only the numbers for the phone number. Do not store the hyphens or dashes in the file. Include appropriate exception-handling techniques with your solution. After storing the name, address, and phone number, display a message indicating the data was stored properly. Use Notepad to view the contents.

4. Write a program that stores 50 random numbers in a file. The random numbers should be positive with the largest value being 1000. Store five numbers per line and 10 different lines. Use the `Random` `class` to generate the values. Include appropriate exception-handling techniques in your solution. When the application closes, locate the text file and verify its contents.

5. Write a program that retrieves numbers stored in a text file. Test your solution by retrieving data from a file that contains 10 different rows of data with five values per line. For your test, display the largest and smallest values from each row of data. Include appropriate exception-handling techniques in your solution. *Hint:* If you completed Programming Exercise #4, use the text file created by that exercise.

6. Write a program that displays a graphical user interface (Windows form) that allows multiple names, e-mail addresses, and local phone numbers to be entered. Allow only numbers to be entered for the phone number. Retrieve and store the values entered by the user in a text file and then ready the GUI for the next set of input values. Store each person's data on separate lines. Include appropriate exception-handling techniques in your solution. When the application closes, locate the text file and verify its contents.

7. Write an application that retrieves both string data and numbers from a text file. Test your solution by retrieving names of students and three scores per line from a text file. Process the values by calculating the average of the scores per student. Write the name and average to a different text file. Display on the console screen what is being written to the new file. Test your application with a minimum of eight records in the original file. *Hint:* You might consider adding delimiters between the data values in the original text file to simplify retrieving and processing the data. Include appropriate exception-handling techniques in your solution. When the application closes, locate the text file and verify its contents.

8. Write a program that produces a report showing the number of students who can still enroll in given classes. Test your solution by retrieving the data from a text file that you create using a text editor, such as Notepad. Some sample data follows. Include the name of the class, current enrollment, and maximum enrollment.

Class name	Current enrollment	Maximum enrollment
CS150	18	20
CS250	11	20
CS270	23	25
CS300	4	20
CS350	32	20

Classes should not be oversubscribed. Define a custom exception `class` for this problem so that an exception is thrown if the current enrollment exceeds the maximum enrollment by more than three students. When this unexpected condition occurs, halt the program and display a message indicating which course is overenrolled.

9. Write a graphical user application that accepts employee data to include employee name, number, pay rate, and number of hours worked. Pay is

to be computed as follows: Hours over 40 receive time-and-a-half pay. Store the employee name, number, and the total amount of pay (prior to deductions) in a text file. Close the file and then, in the same application, retrieve the stored values and display the employee name and the formatted total pay. Your application should allow the user to browse to the file location for saving and retrieving the file.

10. Allow the user to enter multiple sets of five numbers. Store the numbers in a binary file. For each set of values, calculate and store the average of the numbers prior to retrieving the next set of values. For example, if the user entered 27 78 120 111 67 as the first set of values, the first values written to the binary file would be 27 78 120 111 67 80.6. For an extra challenge, close the file, reopen it, and display the values from the file in a listbox control.

CHAPTER 14

© zeljkodan/Shutterstock.com

WORKING WITH DATABASES

IN THIS CHAPTER, YOU WILL:

- Be introduced to technologies used for accessing databases
- Become familiar with the ADO.NET classes
- Write program statements that use the DataReader class to retrieve database data
- Access and update databases using the DataSet, DataAdapter, and TableAdapter classes
- Be introduced to Structured Query Language (SQL) query statements
- Retrieve data using Language-Integrated Query (LINQ) expressions
- Use the visual development tools to connect to data sources, populate DataSet objects, build queries, and develop data-bound applications

In the last chapter, you discovered how to use data from sources other than the keyboard for your applications. You wrote programs that created files and that accessed data stored in files. In this chapter, you will learn about databases and the .NET technologies used for accessing and storing data in database tables. You will be introduced to a number of namespaces collectively called ADO.NET, which consist of a managed set of library classes that allow you to interact with databases. **ADO.NET** stands for ActiveX Data Objects for .NET. It refers to the suite of data access technologies used to manipulate databases. You use ADO.NET classes to retrieve and update data in databases, such as those created using Microsoft Access, Oracle, or SQL Server. After being introduced to these classes, you will explore how the visual programming tools and wizards available with Visual Studio can be used to simplify accessing data for your projects. **Language-Integrated Query** (**LINQ**, pronounced "link"), which defines a set of query operators that can be applied to a number of different data sources will also be introduced.

Database Access

For small applications, you can use text files to store data for later processing. However, as the data needs increase, text files become less viable options. It becomes more difficult to manage or relate data that is stored in flat text files. This is where databases come into play. Many applications revolve around reading and updating information in databases.

Databases store information in records, fields, and tables. You can think of a database as an electronic version of a filing cabinet, organized so that you can retrieve and use the data. Wikipedia (*http://en.wikipedia.org/wiki/Database*) defines a **database** as a collection of records stored in a computer in a systematic way, so that a computer program can consult it to answer questions. The computer programs that are used to manage and query a database are known as the **database management system (DBMS)**.

Database Management Systems

Database management systems facilitate storage, retrieval, manipulation, and reporting of large amounts of data. DBMSs include programs such as MySQL, SQL Server, Oracle, DB2, and Microsoft Access. Many of these DBMSs store data in tabular format and are considered relational databases. In a relational database, the rows in the table are referred to as records and the columns are the fields of the table. Look at Figure 14-1 for an example of a database table. A field is a single piece of information, such as StudentID or FirstName. A record is a complete set of fields. When you have the student identification number, student last name, student first name, phone number, and so on about an individual student, this represents a student record.

memberTable

StudentID	LastName	FirstName	PhoneNumber
1234	Smith	Rachel	2677720
1235	Tutle	James	2877790
1237	Winston	Sara	9047089
1257	Bowers	Brenda	5497876
1260	Jones	Gary	8867889
1276	Abbott	Ralph	3207965
1283	Bishop	Linda	8507654
1299	Bennett	Colleen	4568871

FIGURE 14-1 Access database table

A table, as illustrated in Figure 14-1, then is the logical grouping or collection of similar records.

The data in the tables is related through common data field keys. This enables a single database to consist of multiple tables. Because databases are such an important component to many applications, the rest of this chapter is devoted to the topic. Examples of how to retrieve and update data in a database are presented. This should enable you to incorporate stored data from databases into your applications.

C# enables you to view and modify data stored in an Access or SQL Server database. Complete books are written on this subject alone. Thus, it is beyond the scope of this book to provide a discussion on creating databases.

Access creates relational databases. As mentioned previously, data is stored in tabular format for a **relational database**. Each row in the table represents a record, which consists of one or more data fields. Each data field is stored in a single column. For a Student database, one table might contain personal information. In that table, one row might include the student identification number, first name, last name, and local phone number for a single student. A second row in the same table would include exactly the same data fields for a different student. Figure 14-1 displayed a table from an Access database.

All DBMSs provide reporting capabilities; however, these capabilities can be limited, and there is often a need for processing the data beyond what the DBMS package enables. There is also often a need for a single application to process data from multiple vendors. For both of these scenarios, a programming language is required. Typically, when you are programming for database access, you use a query language. One of the most commonly used query languages, **Structured Query Language (SQL)**, includes statements to access, manipulate, and update data in a database. Using SQL queries, you can access single rows, all rows that meet some criteria, or all rows from one or more tables. This retrieval can include one or more of the fields per row.

Most DBMSs include a query language that can be used to interact with the data. The DBMS that you will be using in this chapter includes this feature.

To experience accessing data from an Access database, you do not need the Microsoft Access program, only the table generated using that application. If you are new to databases or do not have Access, your instructor might provide the table for you. One is included with the electronic version of the examples in this chapter.

Programming database access has come a long way and has successfully evolved much as modern DBMSs have. The .NET Framework includes a data access technology called ADO.NET for accessing data in databases. It is discussed in the following section.

ADO.NET

Included as part of ADO.NET namespaces are a number of classes that can be used to retrieve, manipulate, and update data in databases. ADO.NET offers the capability of working with databases in a connected or disconnected mode. ADO.NET was built with the disconnected mode in mind—meaning the entire database table(s) can be retrieved to a temporary file or to a local machine if the database is stored on the network. After the database data is retrieved, you no longer need to stay connected to it. Processing can occur at the local level. If changes are made to the database, the connection can be remade and the changes posted. With multitier applications, the database can be stored on a different computer or across the Internet. With the growth of Web-centric applications, this disconnect feature is extremely important.

To programmatically interact with data from a database, several things are required. First, you must connect to the database. After connecting, you need a mechanism to retrieve the data. The connection can be constant so that as you retrieve one record, you process it, and then retrieve another record. Or, as noted previously, you can work in disconnected mode. For disconnected modes, the data is stored so that your code can work with it. Whether you work in disconnected mode or stay connected to the database, at some point you should release the resources by closing the connection.

Classes that are part of ADO.NET can be used for each of these steps. In the sections that follow, you will see how to incorporate these features into your program.

Data Providers

ADO.NET does not provide a single set of classes that work with all types of database management systems. However, you can use the ADO.NET library of code to access data stored in many different proprietors' database management systems. This is because ADO.NET uses a feature called **data providers** to connect, execute commands, and retrieve results from a database.

The ADO.NET architecture encapsulates the details of differing database structures such as Oracle, as opposed to Access, in the form of data providers. Oracle has its own unique features, just as Access does. But, accessing each of the database management systems involves common sets of functionality—connecting to a database, executing commands, and retrieving results.

A data provider is a set of classes that understands how to communicate with a specific data source or database management system. The data provider database sources currently included with .NET are shown in Table 14-1.

TABLE 14-1 ADO.NET data providers

.NET Framework data providers	Description
SQL Server	Applications using SQL Server 7.0 or later
Oracle	Applications using Oracle data sources
Object Linking and Embedding Database (OLE DB) technology	Applications that use SQL Server 6.5 or earlier and other OLE DB providers, such as the Microsoft Access
Open Database Connectivity (ODBC) technology	Applications supported by earlier versions of Visual Studio, Access Driver (*.mdb), and Microsoft ODBC for Oracle
EntityClient	Applications using Entity Data Model (EDM)
SQL Server Compact	Applications using Microsoft SQL Server Compact 4.0

Each of the data provider classes is encapsulated into a different namespace. Provider classes include classes that allow you to connect to the data source, execute commands against the source, and read the results. The unique namespace for each of the data providers is shown in Table 14-2.

TABLE 14-2 ADO.NET data provider namespaces

Database sources	Data provider namespace
SQL Server	`System.Data.SqlClient`
Oracle	`System.Data.OracleClient`
Object Linking and Embedding Database (OLE DB)	`System.Data.OleDb`
Open Database Connectivity (ODBC)	`System.Data.Odbc`
EntityClient	`System.Data.EntityClient`
SQL Server Compact	`System.Data.SqlServerCe`

A number of third-party vendors also provide ADO.NET data providers for their vendor-specific databases. For example, MySQL Connector/NET is a fully managed ADO.NET driver written in C# that enables developers to easily create .NET applications with MySQL. Sybase includes ASE ADO.NET Data Provider, allowing access to data in ASE using C#. IBM supplies ADO.NET data providers for access to DB2, Informix, and U2 databases. Phoenix offers an open source ADO.NET Data Provider supporting access to SQLite. New providers can also be designed and programmed.

Each data provider includes a collection of classes used to access a data source, such as a database. The four core classes that make up each data provider are listed in Table 14-3.

TABLE 14-3 Core classes that make up ADO.NET data providers

Class	Class description
`Connection`	Establishes a connection to a data source
`Command`	Executes a command against a data source; often in the form of an SQL statement that retrieves data from the data source
`DataReader`	Performs a forward-only (sequential) access of the data in the data source
`DataAdapter`	Populates a dataset and updates the database

Each data provider has its own Connection, Command, DataReader, and DataAdapter classes. Each provider uses different names. For example, the SQL data provider has classes named `SqlConnection`, `SqlCommand`, `SqlDataReader`, and

SqlDataAdapter. The classes are named OleDbConnection, OleDbCommand, OleDbDataReader, and OleDbDataAdapter with the OleDb data provider. The four core classes offer common functionality, primarily due to interfaces implemented by each of the core's base classes.

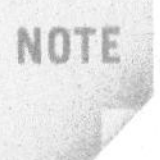

You will recall that when a class implements an interface, it in essence signs a contract indicating it will supply definitions for all of the abstract methods declared in the interface. An interface can also require that any implementing class must also implement one or more other interfaces.

Each provider must provide implementation details for the methods that are exposed in the interface. Table 14-4 lists the core objects, their base classes, and implemented interfaces.

TABLE 14-4 Interfaces implemented by the Core ADO.NET objects

Object	Base class	Implemented interfaces
connection	DbConnection	IDbConnection
command	DbCommand	IDbCommand
dataReader	DbDataReader	IDataReader, IDataRecord
dataAdapter	DbDataAdapter	IDbDataAdapter, IDataAdapter

The base classes listed in Table 14-4 are all abstract. Table 14-5 lists the derived classes from the System.Data.Common.DbConnection class. The other base classes have similarly named derived classes.

TABLE 14-5 Derived classes of DbConnection

Type
System.Data.Odbc.OdbcConnection
System.Data.OleDb.OleDbConnection
System.Data.OracleClient.OracleConnection
System.Data.SqlClient.SqlConnection
System.Data.EntityClient.EntityConnection

As stated in the MSDN documentation, classes that inherit from the `DBConnection class`, such as `OdbcConnection`, must override and provide implementation details for `Close( )`, `BeginDbTransaction( )`, `ChangeDatabase( )`, `CreateDbCommand( )`, and `OpenStateChange( )` methods. Properties must be defined for `ConnectionString`, `Database`, `DataSource`, `ServerVersion`, and `State`. This ensures that all data provider connection objects will have similar functionality, but can also be optimized to interact with their specific DBMS.

In addition to the specific data provider namespaces listed in Table 14-2, namespaces used with ADO.NET classes to access databases include the following:

- `System.Data.Common`—This namespace includes classes shared by all providers.
- `System.Data`—The classes in this namespace represent the ADO.NET architecture, which enables you to build components that use data from multiple data sources.

Each core class is used in subsequent sections of this chapter to retrieve and update data. The first example illustrates using data from an Access database.

CONNECTING TO THE DATABASE

To access a database created with Microsoft Access, use classes from the `System.Data.OleDb namespace`. To avoid fully qualifying references to classes in its `namespace`, the following `using` directive is needed:

```
using System.Data.OleDb;
```

A connection object is instantiated based on the type of database or type of database provider you are using. .NET includes within the `System.Data.OleDb namespace` the `OleDbConnection class` for connection. It represents an open connection to a database. To instantiate an object of this class, you specify a connection string that includes the actual database provider and the data source. The data source is the name of the database. You can include the full path to the database as part of the string argument, or the database can be placed in the bin\Debug subdirectory for the project.

NOTE When specifying the full path as part of the string, the verbatim string is useful. Recall that if you precede the string literal with the `'@'` character, the string is taken as is, verbatim. This eliminates the requirement of using the escape character sequence (`'\\'`) of two backslash characters in the path.

Example 14-1 instantiates an object using a connection string for an `OleDb` data provider. The `"member.accdb"` database is stored in the current project's bin\Debug subdirectory. After an object of the `OleDbConnection class` is instantiated, the connection is opened using the `Open( )` method of the `OleDbConnection class`.

EXAMPLE 14-1

```
string sConnection;
     sConnection = "Provider=Microsoft.ACE.OLEDB.12.0;" +
                   "Data Source=member.accdb";
OleDbConnection dbConn;
dbConn = new OleDbConnection(sConnection);
dbConn.Open( );
```

Connection strings are vendor specific. The syntax for the string begins with a provider or data source name such as `"Provider=someValue"`. The value for later versions of Access at the time the book was published is `"Microsoft.ACE.OLEDB.12.0"`. If you have an older version of Access, the data provider would be different.

NOTE If you are running examples provided with this chapter on a 64-bit processor and get an error indicating "The 'Microsoft.ACE.OLEDB.12.0' provider is not registered on this machine", you may need to install a new driver. At the time the book was written, you could read about the problem and find the download at http://www.connectionstrings.com/the-microsoft-ace-oledb-12-0-provider-is-not-registered-on-the-local-machine/

Example 14-2 illustrates instantiating a `SqlConnection` `object`. The connection string indicates that the `Data Source` is using a local copy of Microsoft SQL Server Express. The database name is RealEstateDb.mdf. The `IntegratedSecurity` property in the connection string is set to `true`, indicating that the current Windows account credentials are used for authentication as opposed to having the User ID and Password specified in the connection string.

EXAMPLE 14-2

```
string sConnection = "Data Source=(localdb)\v11.0;
      IntegratedSecurity=true; AttachDbFileName=RealEstateDb.mdf";
SqlDbConnection dbConn;
dbConn = new SqlDbConnection (sConnection);
dbConn.Open( );
```

Sometimes the more challenging part is determining what should go in the connection string. At the time of writing, *www.connectionstrings.com* listed quite a few strings for different vendors. Another site, *www.carlprothman.net/Default.aspx?tabid=81*, also listed connection strings. If you do not find the specific connection string that you need listed at one of these two sites, you could use your favorite search engine and do a keyword search on .NET, "connection string," and the database vendor name.

Another option is to use one of the ConnectionStringBuilder classes to create the connection string. The OleDbConnectionStringBuilder class can be used to create a connection string for an Access database. There are also classes for SQL Server databases (SqlConnectionStringBuilder) as well as the other providers. These classes enable you to programmatically create a connection string.

NOTE Exceptions can be thrown when you are working with databases. You can enclose statements that establish the connection to the database within a try block and write program statements inside the catch clause for those exceptional times when the connection cannot be made.

Retrieving Data from the Database

After connecting to the database, one way to retrieve records programmatically from the database is to issue an SQL query. Another class, a command class, is available in each of the different data providers' namespaces to hold the SQL statement. The OleDbCommand class is used to hold the SQL statement or stored procedures for OleDb database management systems, such as Microsoft Access. After an object of the OleDbCommand class is constructed, it has several properties that enable you to tie the command (SQL query) to the connection string. Example 14-3 instantiates an object of the OleDbCommand class and sets the CommandText and Connection properties of that class. Example 14-3 assigns the OleDbConnection object, dbConn, instantiated in Example 14-1, to the Connection property of the OleDbCommand object.

EXAMPLE 14-3

```
string sql;
sql = "SELECT * FROM memberTable ORDER BY LastName ASC, " +
      "FirstName ASC;";          // Note the two semicolons.

OleDbCommand dbCmd = new OleDbCommand( );

dbCmd.CommandText = sql;         // Set the command to the SQL string.

dbCmd.Connection = dbConn;       // dbConn is the connection object
                                 // instantiated in Example 14-2.
```

SQL QUERIES

SQL (officially pronounced "S-Q-L," but commonly pronounced "sequel") was developed in the 1970s by a group at IBM as a language that provides an interface to relational database systems. The relational model was invented by Edgar Codd, also at IBM. SQL is a universal language available with many database products, including

SQL Server and Microsoft Access. SQL is a keyword-based language where each statement begins with a unique keyword. SQL syntax is not case sensitive; however, a common practice is to type keywords in uppercase. Each has its own different proprietary extensions or dialects. Queries can be written in SQL that let you SELECT, INSERT, UPDATE, DELETE, and FIND the location of data in tables.

The SELECT statement shown in Example 14-3, `SELECT * FROM memberTable ORDER BY LastName ASC, FirstName ASC;`, is a simple SQL statement that retrieves every row and column in the `memberTable` table. The asterisk (`*`) used in the SQL query specifies the selection of all fields in the database table named `memberTable`. The `ASC` is an abbreviation for ascending—indicating that the result of the query is to be returned with the listing in ascending order by `LastName`. Because `FirstName` also includes `ASC`, any duplicate last names are ordered in ascending order by first name. Notice the SQL query ends with a semicolon and the entire query is placed inside double quotes, which ends with another semicolon. The last semicolon is used to end the assignment statement that assigns the query to a `string` variable named `sql`.

Any valid SQL statement can be used to retrieve data after the connection is open.

If you do not want to retrieve all fields, you replace the asterisk (`*`), shown in Example 14-3, with one or more data field names (separated by commas). The data field names are the column headings in the database table. The SQL statement that retrieves only the first name, last name, and phone number is shown in Example 14-4.

EXAMPLE 14-4

```
SELECT FirstName, LastName, PhoneNumber FROM memberTable;
```

The SQL statement included in Example 14-4 is an example of the most basic format. It retrieves just the identified columns from a single table. All rows are retrieved. To retrieve a single row or just some of the rows from the table, you add a `WHERE` clause to the SQL query. For example, to retrieve the phone number associated with Gary Jones, the SQL statement would read as shown in Example 14-5.

EXAMPLE 14-5

```
SELECT PhoneNumber FROM memberTable
    WHERE FirstName = 'Gary' AND LastName = 'Jones';
```


This returns only the phone number because that is the only field specified following the `SELECT` statement. It does not return the name. Notice that for SQL statements, string literal values ('Gary' and 'Jones') are enclosed in single quotation marks. Also, notice that the database field identifiers do not have spaces as part of the name. If a database table's field has a space, the field name would have to be enclosed in square brackets, as in [Phone Number], for the SQL statement.

The general format for the WHERE clause is as follows:

```
WHERE columnName = value
```

Compound expressions can be combined with AND, OR, or NOT. Relational operators can also be used with WHERE clauses, including >, <, >=, <=, and a single equal symbol used for equality. To test for "not equal to," <> is used. To write conditional expressions that test to determine if a value falls within a specified range, the keyword BETWEEN can be inserted before the first value. The compound expression AND is used between the two values. To use a date as the value, the date value is enclosed in the # symbol for Microsoft Access. As noted previously, DBMSs use slightly different dialects. Microsoft SQL Server uses single apostrophes as date delimiters instead of the # symbol, as follows:

```
WHERE (aDate BETWEEN #10/12/2012# AND #10/12/2013#) – Access
WHERE (aDate BETWEEN '10/12/2012' AND '10/12/2013') – SQL Server
```

In addition to selecting data for viewing using a single table, you can use the SELECT statement to retrieve results from multiple tables by joining them using a common field. One way to combine tables is to use the SQL JOIN clause. The JOIN query combines columns of one table to columns of another to create a single table, matching up a column from one table to a column in the other table. The JOIN query does not alter either table, but temporarily combines data from each table to be viewed as a single table. One type of JOIN statement is an INNER JOIN.

The INNER JOIN used with a SELECT statement returns all rows from both tables where there is a match. If there are rows in one table that do not have matches in the other table, these rows are not returned. To use the JOIN clause, identify the columns from both tables that should be returned. Their names are qualified with a prefixing dot and the table name. Instead of using a WHERE clause to identify the rows to be returned, the keyword INNER JOIN and ON are used with the two tables. Suppose a second table named departmentTable had columns of major_ID, major_Name, and major_Chair; an example illustrating how the two tables could be joined is shown in Example 14-6.

EXAMPLE 14-6

```
SELECT memberTable.FirstName, memberTable.LastName,
       departmentTable.major_Name
    FROM memberTable INNER JOIN departmentTable
         ON memberTable.major_ID = departmentTable.major_ID;
```

Normally, the columns that are used for the join are the primary and/or foreign keys in the two tables. Thus, `major_ID` would need to appear in both tables. It would serve as a foreign key in the `memberTable` table. In Example 14-6, the primary key for the department is `major_ID`. Having common fields in both tables allows the two tables to be linked.

A **primary key** is a column (field) or combination of columns that uniquely identifies a row in a table. A **foreign key** is a column that refers to a column in another table. The foreign key is used to link the two tables.

You selectively choose the columns you want returned from both tables. It is not necessary to return the key that is used to link the tables. However, many applications benefit from retrieving the key columns for later use. For this example, two columns are returned from the `memberTable` (`FirstName` and `LastName`) and one is returned from the `departmentTable` (`major_Name`).

SQL statements can also be written to create tables or to insert, delete, and update data in a table. When you are working with ADO.NET, it is extremely helpful to be able to write SQL statements. To insert values into a table, use the SQL `INSERT INTO` clause followed by the table name and the columns for which you have values. The `VALUES` keyword is used with a parenthesized list of new values, as shown in Example 14-7.

EXAMPLE 14-7

```
INSERT INTO memberTable(StudentID, FirstName, LastName,
                        PhoneNumber)
    VALUES (1123, 'Kathy', 'Weizel', 2345678);
```

The SQL `DELETE` keyword is used to remove rows from a table. To identify which rows to delete, use the `FROM` and `WHERE` clauses. Example 14-8 illustrates removing the last record from the table shown in Figure 14-1.

EXAMPLE 14-8

```
DELETE FROM memberTable
    WHERE (StudentID = 1299);
```

The final example illustrates writing an SQL `UPDATE` statement. The `SET` and `WHERE` clauses are normally used to identify which row and values to change. Referring back to Figure 14-1, to change Rachel Smith's last name to Hakim, you could write an `UPDATE` SQL statement, as shown in Example 14-9.

EXAMPLE 14-9

```
UPDATE memberTable
    SET LastName = 'Hakim'
        WHERE (StudentID = 1234);
```

SQL is a very powerful programming language in itself. To make maximum use of the ADO classes and the tools of Visual Studio, it is helpful to have an understanding of the SQL statements. Many books are available on the topic. You are encouraged to explore and learn the syntax requirements for writing SQL statements. Use your favorite search engine on the Internet. You will find many articles, tutorials, and references relating to SQL.

This chapter does not address database security issues as they relate to accessing database records over the Web using SQL pass-through queries. Applications that allow users to supply values for arguments used to query database tables directly are vulnerable to security hacks and attacks. SQL injection attacks, for example, involve typing or inserting an actual SQL query or command as input (as opposed to a requested value, such as a user login name), gaining access to the tables, and then stealing or destroying data. Use your favorite search engine to locate information about SQL injection attacks. At the time of writing, the following sites offered suggestions for how to keep your code and database more secure from intruders.

- Stop SQL Injection Attacks Before They Stop You—
  http://msdn.microsoft.com/en-us/magazine/cc163917.aspx
- SQL Injection Attacks—
  www.unixwiz.net/techtips/sql-injection.html

Processing the Data

Several classes are available to process the data after it is retrieved through the SQL query. You can retrieve one record at a time in memory and process that record before retrieving another, or store the entire result of the query in a temporary data structure similar to an array and disconnect from the database.

For simple read-only access to the database, ADO.NET includes a data reader class that can be used to read rows of data from a database. Like the connection and command classes, each data provider has a different data reader class defined in its namespace. The data reader class for accessing OleDb providers is the OleDbDataReader class. The SqlDataReader class is used with SQL Server databases.

RETRIEVING DATA USING A DATA READER

The OleDbDataReader and SqlDataReader classes allow read-only forward retrieval of data from the database. Results are returned as the query executes. Using a data reader, you can sequentially loop through the query results. This is an especially good choice for accessing data from the database when you need to retrieve a large amount of data. The data is not cached in memory. By default, only one row is stored in memory at a time when these data reader classes are used. The discussion that follows focuses on the OleDbDataReader class; however, the concepts work equally well when used with the SqlDataReader class.

To process the data using a data reader, you declare an object of the OleDbDataReader class and then call the ExecuteReader( ) method. The ExecuteReader( ) method of the OleDbCommand class is used to build the OleDbDataReader object. You saw in the previous section that the OleDbCommand object contains the SQL command and the connection string representing the data provider.

To position the OleDbDataReader object onto the row of the first retrieved query result, you use the Read( ) method of the OleDbDataReader class. The Read( ) method is also used to advance to the next record after the previous one is processed. To understand the processing of data retrieved using the Read( ) method, you can think about what is retrieved from a single access using a data reader object as a one-dimensional table consisting of the fields from that one row. The fields can be referenced using the actual ordinal index representing the physical location within the record in which the field is located, much as you index through a single-dimensional array. Thus, using the database table shown in Figure 14-1, the first call to the Read( ) method with a data reader object named dbReader references the value "1234" when you write dbReader[0]. dbReader[1] refers to "Smith" or "Hakim" if you had changed the record with the UPDATE command illustrated in Example 14-9. Reference to dbReader[2] refers to "Rachel" and dbReader[3] refers to "2677700".

You can also use the table's field names as indexers to the data reader object. If the table in the database consists of the fields named StudentID, LastName, FirstName and PhoneNumber, as shown in Figure 14-1, dbReader[2] references the first name as does dbReader["FirstName"] when dbReader is instantiated as an object of the OleDbDataReader class. Thus, in addition to pulling out the values using their ordinal location, you can pull out the values using the individual database field names, such as LastName. This is sometimes more convenient and leads to more readable code. However, retrieval using the ordinal index is faster.

The first call to dbReader.Read( ) refers to value 1234 when dbReader["StudentID"] is written. "Rachel" is referenced when dbReader["FirstName"] is referenced. You should note that the field name must be enclosed in double quotes when you use the field name as an indexer.

In addition to accessing the data through indexes, the OleDbDataReader class includes a number of typed accessor method members. The argument sent to each of the methods is the ordinal location of the data field, or the column number with the first column being column 0. Each of these methods returns the value in the type specified by the method. If you do not use these methods, you must perform an additional step, that being to convert the returned object to its correct data type. Table 14-6 lists some of the typed accessor methods and other members of the OleDbDataReader class.

TABLE 14-6 OleDbDataReader class members

OleDbDataReader members	Description
Close( )	Closes an OleDbDataReader object
FieldCount	Property; gets the number of columns in the current row
GetBoolean(int)	Gets the value of the specified column as a Boolean
GetChar(int)	Gets the value of the specified column as a char
GetDecimal(int)	Gets the value of the specified column as a decimal
GetDouble(int)	Gets the value of the specified column as a double
GetInt16(int), GetInt32(int), GetInt64(int)	Gets the value of the specified column as an integer
GetName(int)	Gets the name of the specified column as a Boolean
GetOrdinal(string)	Given the name of the column, gets the ordinal location
GetString(int)	Gets the value of the specified column as a string
GetType(int)	Gets the type of a specified column
Read( )	Advances the OleDbDataReader object to the next record

NOTE Many of the methods listed in Table 14-6 begin with Get followed by a data type, such as GetString( ). These methods are called **typed accessors**.

Example 14-10 illustrates using the data reader to process results retrieved using the SQL command. In this example, the values are first stored in an object, aMember, of the Member class. The Member object is then used to populate a ListBox object for a Windows application.

EXAMPLE 14-10

```
Member aMember;
OleDbDataReader dbReader;
dbReader = dbCmd.ExecuteReader( ); // dbCmd is OleDbCommand object
                                    // instantiated in Example 14-3.
while (dbReader.Read( ))
{
      // Retrieve records 1-by-1. . .
      aMember = new
              Member(dbReader["FirstName"].ToString( ),
                      dbReader["LastName"].ToString( ));
      this.lstBxMembers.Items.Add(aMember);
}
```

Example 14-11 shows the statements that make up the Member class. Notice that one of the constructors of the Member class accepts two string arguments. In Example 14-10, a Member object, aMember, is instantiated using two of the retrieved dbReader objects. The database field names (from Figure 14-1) are used as indexers with the retrieved dbReader object. Notice how the ToString( ) method is called with the dbReader object in Example 14-10. This is because the dbReader returns each data field as an object. You have to do the type conversion before sending it to the Member constructor; otherwise, an exception is thrown. For the sake of brevity, the Member class shown in Example 14-11 contains only the read-only properties, a ToString( ) method, and two constructors.

14

EXAMPLE 14-11

```
// Member.cs
// This class includes private members of
// identification number, first and last
```

```
// names, and local phone number. Read-only
// properties are included. The ToString( )
// method is overridden to return a formatted
// full name.
using System;

namespace DBExample
{
    public class Member
    {
        private string id;
        private string firstName;
        private string lastName;
        private string phoneNumber;

        // Constructors
        public Member( )
        {
        }
        public Member(string fname, string lname)
        {
            firstName = fname;
            lastName = lname;
        }

        // Properties
        public string FirstName
        {
            get
            {
                return firstName;
            }
        }
        public string LastName
        {
            get
            {
                return lastName;
            }
        }
        public string Id
        {
            get
            {
                return id;
            }
        }
        public string PhoneNumber
        {
            get
```

```
            {
                  return phoneNumber;
            }
      }
      public override string ToString( )
      {
                  return firstName + " " + lastName;
      }
   }
}
```

One last thing should be added to your program statements for the class that is accessing the database. You should always close the connections before exiting the application.

CLOSING THE CONNECTION

This is one of the easiest things to do, but is often overlooked. You need to close the reader object and the connection object. By doing this, you unlock the database so that other applications can access it. Example 14-12 includes calls to the `Close( )` method to close the connection and data reader objects instantiated in the previous examples.

EXAMPLE 14-12

```
dbReader.Close( );
dbConn.Close( );
```

An exception can be thrown when you attempt to close connections as well as when you are trying to access data. You can also enclose the close connection statements in a `try...catch` block, alerting the user if problems arise so that corrective action can be taken.

NOTE A special `using` statement can be added to surround the entire block of code accessing a database. When this is added, it is no longer necessary to call the `Close( )` methods. All objects are disposed of when the statements included in the `using` block (surrounded by curly braces) go out of scope.

Example 14-13 pulls together the statements from Examples 14-1, 14-3, 14-11, and 14-12 enclosing them in a `try. . .catch` block. For the sake of brevity, some of the Windows Forms Designer generated code is not included in the listing. The application includes a `ListBox` `object` for data display and a `Label` `object` for displaying error messages. The label is originally set to a `null` value.

EXAMPLE 14-13

```
// DBExample.cs
// A Windows application is used as the
// front end to display records retrieved
// from an Access database.
using System;
using System.Windows.Forms;
using System.Data.OleDb;

namespace DBExample
{
     public partial class DbGUI :Form
     {
          private OleDbConnection dbConn;     // Connection object
          private OleDbCommand dbCmd;         // Command object
          private OleDbDataReader dbReader; // DataReader object
          private Member aMember;
          private string sConnection;
          private string sql;

          public DbGUI( )
          {
               InitializeComponent( );
          }

          private void btnLoad_Click(object sender, EventArgs e)
          {
               try
               {
                    // Construct an object of the OleDbConnection
                    // class to store the connection string
                    // representing the type of data provider
                    // (database) and the source (actual db)
                    sConnection =
                       "Provider=Microsoft.ACE.OLEDB.12.0;" +
                       "Data Source=member.accdb";
                    dbConn = new OleDbConnection(sConnection);
                    dbConn.Open( );
```

```
                    sql = "SELECT * FROM memberTable ORDER " +
                          "BY LastName ASC, FirstName ASC;";

                    // Construct an object of the OleDbCommand
                    // class to hold the SQL query.

                    dbCmd = new OleDbCommand( );
                    dbCmd.CommandText = sql;

                    // Tie the OleDbCommand object
                    // to the OleDbConnection object
                    dbCmd.Connection = dbConn;

                    // Create a dbReader object.
                    dbReader = dbCmd.ExecuteReader( );
                    while (dbReader.Read( ))
                    {
                         aMember = new
                          Member(dbReader["FirstName"].ToString( ),
                                 dbReader["LastName"].ToString( ));
                         this.lstBxMembers.Items.Add(aMember);
                    }
                    dbReader.Close( );
                    dbConn.Close( );
               }
               catch (System.Exception exc)
               {
                    this.lblMessage.Text = exc.Message;
               }
          }
     }
}
```

NOTE Special note: If you do not override the `ToString( )` method in the `Member class`, when you add an object of that class to the list box, you will get a list box full of the member type names.

The output generated from the program listing in Example 14-13, which uses the `Member class` (illustrated in Example 14-11), is shown in Figure 14-2. Remember that the database was previously displayed in Figure 14-1.

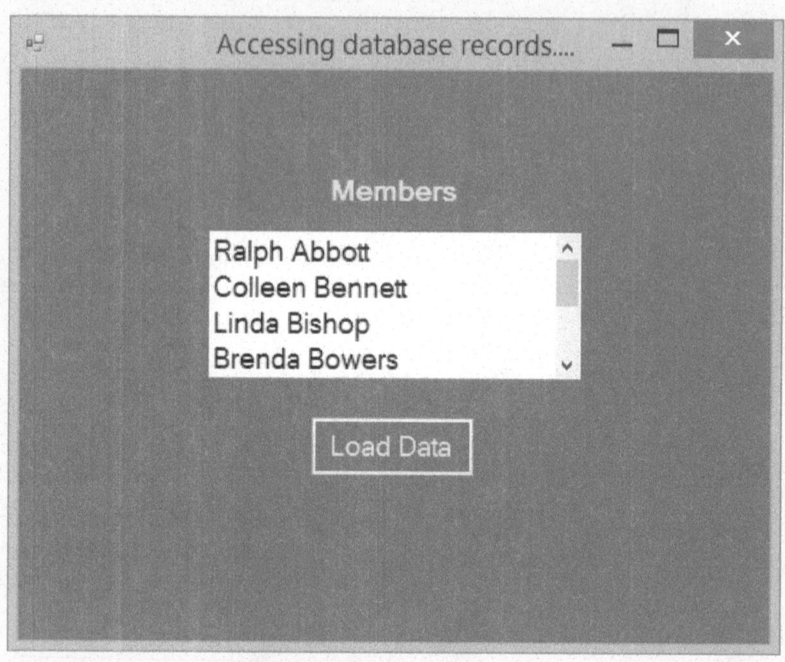

FIGURE 14-2 Accessing the member.accdb database using the database reader object

The data reader class enables read-only access to the database. There are situations that require you to change or update the data in the database. This can be accomplished in several ways. You can write SQL statements that include INSERT, DELETE, and UPDATE statements and then execute those queries by calling the `OleDbCommand.ExecuteNonQuery( )` method. An easier approach is to instantiate objects of the dataset and data adapter classes. You use the data adapter object to populate the dataset object. The data adapter class has methods such as `Fill( )` and `Update( )` that can eliminate the need to write SQL updates. The sections that follow explain how this can be accomplished.

Updating Database Data

ADO.NET does not require that you keep a continuous live connection to the database and process one retrieved record at a time. Additional classes are available that enable you to connect to the database long enough to retrieve records into memory. The data can then be changed and you can reconnect to the database to update the data. This can improve the performance of your applications and allow other applications to access the database while you are working in a disconnected mode. When you do this, you create a temporary copy in memory of the records retrieved from the database and then work with the temporary data as opposed to the live data stored in the database. This is accomplished in .NET using a dataset. A **dataset** is a cache of records retrieved from some data source that may contain one or more tables from the data source. The interaction between the dataset and the actual database is controlled through a data adapter.

Using Datasets to Process Database Records

As with the data reader objects, you use different dataset and data adapter classes in each of the different data provider namespaces depending on the type of database you are accessing. For an Access database provider class, you would still add: `using System.Data.OleDb;`.

Up to the point where you are processing the retrieved data from the SQL query, you need to include the same program statements that you used with the database reader object. You still instantiate a connection object using the connection string for the OleDb data provider and still specify the database name. You will read about this in a later section in this chapter, but it is not necessary to call the `Open( )` method with the connection object when you use a data adapter object. This is handled automatically for you.

You still select the records (and fields) from the database by executing an SQL SELECT statement. As you saw in Example 14-13, the SQL statement is packaged in a data command object. Thus, you still need an object of the `OleDbCommand class` instantiated and the `CommandText` property for the class set to that SQL string. These statements from Example 14-13 are repeated for you here in Example 14-14. The only difference between using the database reader class and the dataset and data adapter classes, thus far, is that `dbConn.Open( )` is omitted. Connection and command objects are needed.

EXAMPLE 14-14

```
private OleDbConnection dbConn;
private OleDbCommand dbCmd;
private string sConnection;
private string sql;

      :     // Colon indicates items missing
```

14

```
// Construct an object of the OleDbConnection
// class to store the connection string
// representing the type of data provider
// (database) and the source (actual db)
sConnection = "Provider=Microsoft.ACE.OLEDB.12.0;" +
              "Data Source=member.accdb";
dbConn = new OleDbConnection(sConnection);

sql = "SELECT * FROM memberTable Order " +
      "BY LastName ASC, FirstName ASC;";

// Construct an object of the OleDbCommand
// class to hold the SQL query.
dbCmd = new OleDbCommand( );
dbCmd.CommandText = sql;

// Tie the OleDbCommand object to the OleDbConnection object
dbCmd.Connection = dbConn;
```

NOTE

Details were provided in an earlier Note in this chapter about how to install a new driver if you are running a 64-bit processor and get an error message indicating "The 'Microsoft.ACE.OLEDB.12.0' provider is not registered on this machine".

DATASET OBJECT

The data reader object held one record of the query result at a time. The dataset object stores an entire relational tablelike structure. More than one table, plus relationships and constraints on the database, can be stored with the dataset object. The dataset is considered a memory-resident representation of the data. An object of the DataSet class can be instantiated, as shown in Example 14-15.

EXAMPLE 14-15

```
DataSet memberDS = new DataSet( );
```

DATAADAPTER OBJECT

An easy way to use a DataSet object is to instantiate an object of the DataAdapter class. Adapters are used to exchange data between a database source and a dataset object. The adapter also makes it easier to update the database if changes are made. An object of the DataAdapter class for an OleDb provider can be instantiated, as shown in Example 14-16.

EXAMPLE 14-16

```
OleDbDataAdapter memberDataAdap = new OleDbDataAdapter( );
```

Several new classes and a **Data Source Configuration Wizard** are available to simplify connecting to a database. A `TableDataAdapter class` is provided for each data provider. You will experience using the wizard and the new classes later in this chapter.

COMMAND BUILDER OBJECT

One additional class can be used to generate SQL statements automatically so that you do not have to do additional SQL programming beyond the initial SELECT statement used to retrieve the records. This is the `OleDbCommandBuilder class`. An `OleDbCommandBuilder object` automatically generates SQL statements for updates after you set the `SelectCommand` property of the `OleDbDataAdapter class`. This property is set to the SQL statement that retrieves the data from the database. Instantiation of the class and setting the property are shown in the following code segment for Example 14-17.

EXAMPLE 14-17

```
private OleDbCommandBuilder cBuilder;

    : // Colon indicates items missing
    cBuilder = new OleDbCommandBuilder(memberDataAdap);
    memberDataAdap.SelectCommand = dbCmd;
```

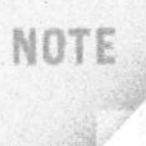

The `CommandBuilder object` can only be used for datasets that map to a single database table. The SQL statement used to set the `SelectCommand` property must also return at least one primary key or unique column. A primary key is a value that uniquely identifies the row. For example, every student has a unique student ID. It makes a good primary key. If none are present, an `InvalidOperation` exception is generated, and the commands are not generated.

FILLING THE DATASET USING THE DATA ADAPTER

After you have objects instantiated of the data adapter, dataset, and command builder classes, you are ready to go. You fill the dataset using the data adapter by specifying the name of the table to use as the data source, as shown in Example 14-18.

EXAMPLE 14-18

```
memberDataAdap.Fill(memberDS, "memberTable");
```

The `Fill( )` method can be used without writing additional SQL statements because you instantiated an object of the command builder class. The command builder automatically generates SQL statements for the `InsertCommand`, `UpdateCommand`, and `DeleteCommand` properties of the `DataAdapter class`. You could set the value for each of these properties in exactly the same manner you set the `SelectCommand` property—using a string containing a SQL statement.

If your application requires that the dataset contain values from two or more tables, you cannot have the command builder class automatically generate the SQL statements for you. In this case, you have to set the `InsertCommand`, `UpdateCommand`, and `DeleteCommand` properties of the `DataAdapter class`. You do this by setting the `DataAdapter` object's `InsertCommand` property with an SQL INSERT statement, `DeleteCommand` property with an SQL DELETE statement, and `UpdateCommand` property with an SQL UPDATE statement.

That is all that is required to retrieve records from a database. To show the contents of the table and enable the user to make changes, a presentation user interface layer is needed. The table values could be displayed on the console screen or on a control in a Windows application. The grid control is especially well suited to dataset objects. The following section explains how to bind a dataset object to a data grid on a Windows application.

Adding a DataGridView Control to Hold the Dataset

To see the data from the database, the records can be placed in a `DataGridView object` on a Windows form. The `DataGridView` control creates a structure that is divided into rows and columns much like the structure you associate with a relational database table. In addition to being able to navigate around in the data grid, you can make changes by editing current records as well as to insert and delete new records. To tie the `DataGridView object` to the dataset, use the `DataSource` and `DataMember` properties of the `dataGridView object`, as shown in Example 14-19.

EXAMPLE 14-19

```
dataGridView1.DataSource = memberDS;
dataGridView1.DataMember = "memberTable";
```

There are over 50 different Windows.Forms controls that can be added to your application. Not all are shown in the drop-down list. Additional ones can be added to the ToolBox using the **Choose ToolBox Items** from the **Tools** menu.

UPDATING THE DATA IN THE DATABASE

Any additional SQL statements needed are generated automatically for you if you instantiated an object of the command builder class. If you load the database into a `DataGridView` `object` and make changes such as adding records or changing the value of one or more fields, you can flush the changes back up to the live database using the `Update( )` method of the `DataAdapter` `class`. There are no additional requirements to write INSERT, DELETE, or UPDATE SQL statements. All you do is write a single statement, as shown in Example 14-20.

EXAMPLE 14-20

```
memberDataAdap.Update(memberDS, "memberTable");
```

This statement is issued after the database table (`"memberTable"`) is tied to the `DataGridView` `object` using the `DataSource` and `DataMember` properties.

Example 14-21 contains the statements that create a Windows application with a `DataGridView` `object` populated from the `Member.accdb` database used previously. The application includes statements that enable the database to be updated with changes made in the `DataGridView` `object`. For the sake of brevity, some of the Windows Forms Designer generated code is not included in the listing for Example 14-21.

EXAMPLE 14-21

```
// DataSetExample.cs
// A Windows application is used as the
// front end to display records retrieved
// from an Access database.
// Values can be changed and the
// database is updated using these changes.
using System;
using System.Data;
using System.Windows.Forms;
using System.Data.OleDb;
```

```
namespace DataSetExample
{
    public partial class FrmUpdate : Form
    {
        private OleDbDataAdapter memberDataAdap;
        private DataSet memberDS;
        private OleDbCommandBuilder cBuilder;
        private OleDbConnection dbConn;
        private OleDbCommand dbCmd;
        private string sConnection;
        private string sql;

        public FrmUpdate( )
        {
            InitializeComponent( );
        }

        private void btnUpdate_Click(object sender, EventArgs e)
        {
            try
            {
                cBuilder =
                    new OleDbCommandBuilder(memberDataAdap);
                memberDataAdap.Update(memberDS, "memberTable");
            }
            catch (System.Exception exc)
            {
                this.lblMessage.Text = exc.Message;
            }
        }

        private void btnLoad_Click (object sender, EventArgs e)
        {
            try
            {
                 // Construct an object of the OleDbConnection
                 // class to store the connection string
                 // representing the type of data provider
                 // (database) and the source (actual db)
                 sConnection =
                    "Provider=Microsoft.ACE.OLEDB.12.0;" +
                    "Data Source=member.accdb";
                 dbConn = new OleDbConnection(sConnection);

                 sql = "SELECT * FROM memberTable ORDER " +
                       "BY LastName ASC, FirstName ASC;";
```

```
                    // Construct an object of the OleDbCommand
                    // class to hold the SQL query.

                    dbCmd = new OleDbCommand( );
                    dbCmd.CommandText = sql;

                    // Tie the OleDbCommand object to the
                    // OleDbConnection object
                    dbCmd.Connection = dbConn;

                    memberDataAdap = new OleDbDataAdapter( );
                    memberDataAdap.SelectCommand = dbCmd;
                    memberDS = new DataSet( );
                    memberDataAdap.Fill(memberDS, "memberTable");
                    dataGridView1.DataSource = memberDS;
                    dataGridView1.DataMember = "memberTable";
                }
                catch (System.Exception exc)
                {
                     lblMessage.Text = exc.Message;
                }
            }
        }
    }
```

Exception-handling techniques were included in Example 14-21. As with previous examples presented in this chapter, a blank `Label` `object` was placed on the form to display error messages.

NOTE Notice how there are no calls to the `Open( )` or `Close( )` methods. When needed, the `Fill( )` and `Update( )` methods implicitly open the connection that the `DataAdapter` is using. These methods also close the connection when they are finished. This simplifies your code.

Figure 14-3 illustrates the application running. The image in the background of Figure 14-3 shows what the form looks like before the **Load Data** button is clicked. Its event-handler method populates the `DataGridView` `object` from the `member.accdb` database by first calling the `Fill( )` method of the `OleDbDataAdapter` `class`. Notice that two arguments to the `Fill( )` method are the `DataSet` `object` and the database table. These two arguments are used to set the `DataGridView` object's `DataSource` and `DataMember` properties.

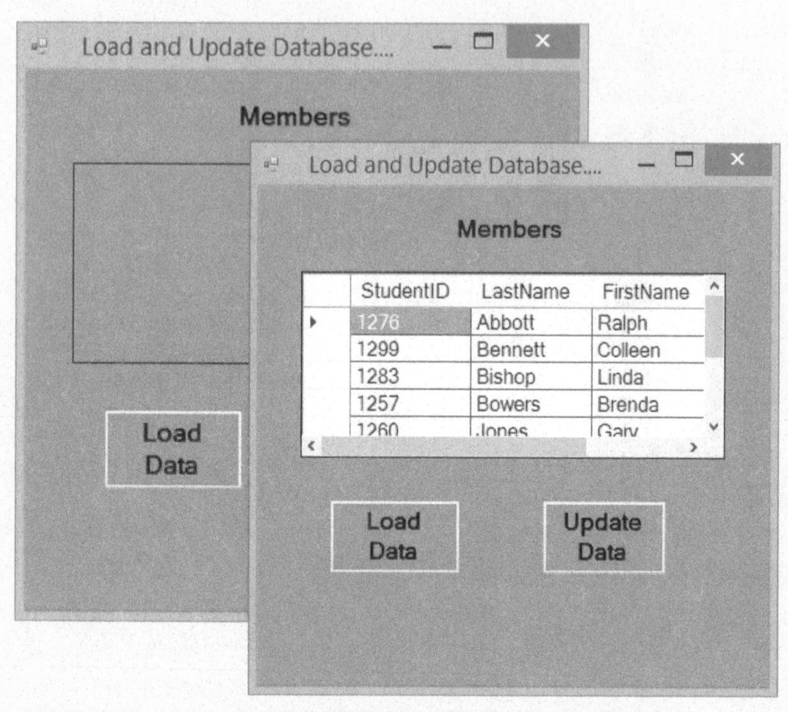

FIGURE 14-3 Output from DataSetExample after the database is loaded

One of the powerful features of the `DataGridView` `object` is that it enables you to delete or insert new records (rows) into the data grid. You can also change the values of individual fields (columns) in the data grid. However, the changes are to the local copy of the database. To update the live database, those changes must be posted back to the `DataMember` database table. This is done in Figure 14-4 when the **Update Data** button is clicked.

This `btnUpdate_Click( )` event-handler method in Example 14-21 included a call to the `Update( )` method of the `OleDbDataAdapter` `class`. The live database connection is reopened, and the current contents of the dataset (bound to the data grid) are written to the database table specified by the `DataMember` property listed as the second argument.

As shown in Figure 14-4, several changes were made to the local database to illustrate that records could be inserted (`Charlene Boswick`), or deleted (`Gary Jones` and `Colleen Bennett`), and values in fields could be changed (`Ralph Abbott` changed to `Ralph Adams`). The back image in Figure 14-4 shows the updated database table. The image in the foreground in Figure 14-4 shows the changed values in the `DataGridView` `object`.

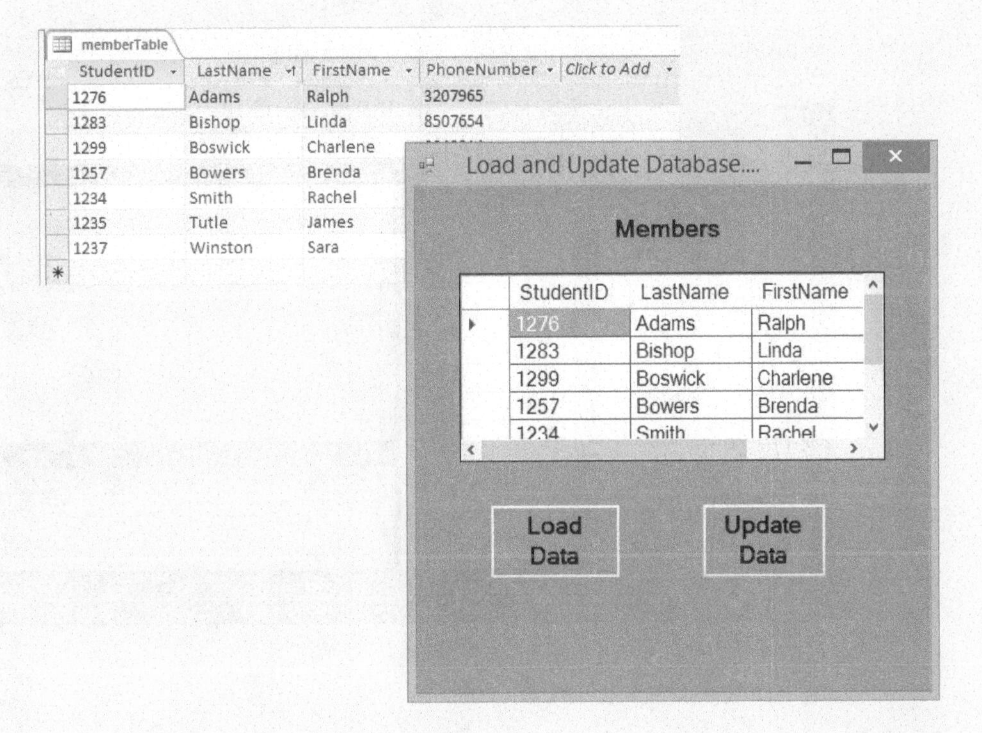

FIGURE 14-4 Updated database records

Visual Studio includes a number of features that make it easier for you to develop applications that access data. Instead of writing code from scratch, the Visual Studio IDE encourages more drag-and-drop development where code is automatically generated for you. The rest of the chapter uses this approach.

Data Source Configuration Tools

The **Data Source Configuration Wizard** simplifies connecting your application to a data source by guiding you through the process, automatically generating the connection string, creating dataset and table adapter objects, and bringing the data into your application. Figure 14-5 shows one way to begin this process.

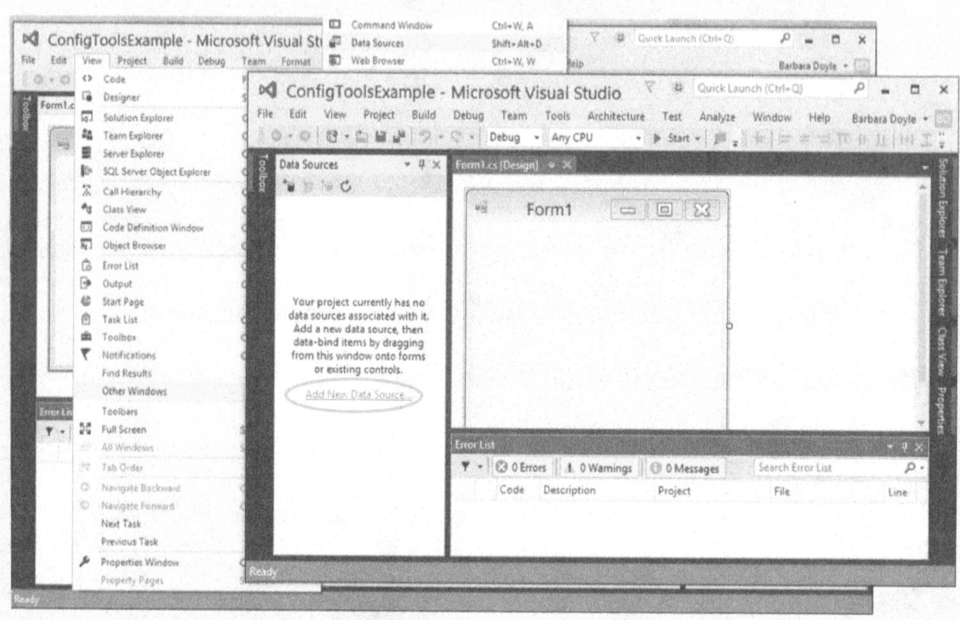

FIGURE 14-5 Data Sources window

Add New Data Source

The **Data Sources** window can be opened from the **View** > **Other Windows** > **Data Sources** menu option as shown in Figure 14-5. To use the configuration tool, select **Add New Data Source** from the **Data Sources** pane. This is shown near the bottom left on the top image for Figure 14-5. **Add New Data Source** is also an option available under the **Project** menu. Whenever you are developing applications that use data, you will find it helpful to have the **Data Sources** window open on your desktop. This window shows you the dataset objects available to your project. You will recall that the data set represents the in-memory cache of data. The data set mimics the database on which it is based.

From the **Data Sources** window, you can drag items (tables and/or columns) onto your form. After the items are placed on the form, you can then customize the way they are displayed. This is illustrated in the sections that follow.

When you select **Add New Data Source** from the **Data Sources** window or the **Project** menu, you are first prompted to choose a data source type. Options of **Database**, **Service**, **Object**, and **SharePoint** are available, as shown in Figure 14-6.

As shown in Figure14-6, selecting **Database** enables you to create a typed dataset object. The typed dataset object corresponds directly to the underlying database table(s). A typed dataset defines a schema that exposes the tables and their columns as object properties. This makes manipulating the dataset much easier because you can reference the tables and columns directly by name.

When a dataset object is available for the application, the **DataSet Designer** tool is available to you. The **DataSet Designer** provides another visual representation of the objects contained in the dataset object. It enables you to set relationships between tables and add additional queries to your application. You will explore the **DataSet Designer** later in this chapter.

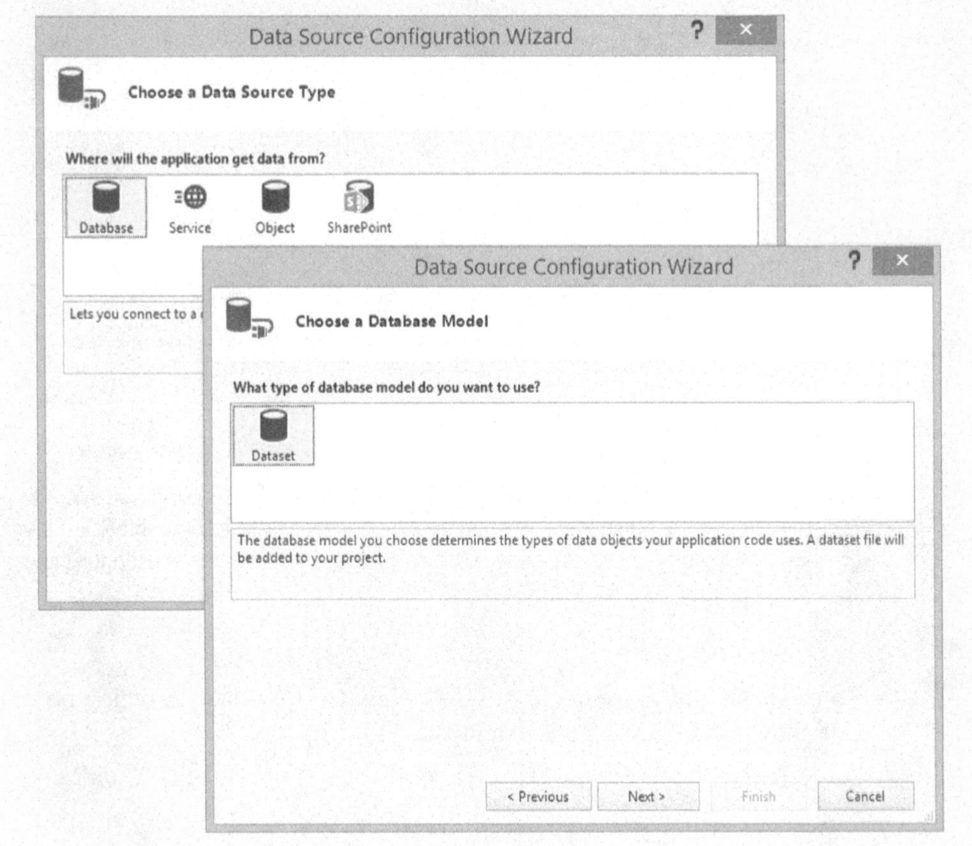

FIGURE 14-6 Data Source Configuration Wizard

NEW CONNECTION

Selecting **Next** reveals the dialog box shown in Figure 14-7. Connections that are already established are available from the drop-down list shown to the left of the **New Connection** button in Figure 14-7. If the database is not already attached, the option to add a **New Connection** is selected, as shown in Figure 14-7.

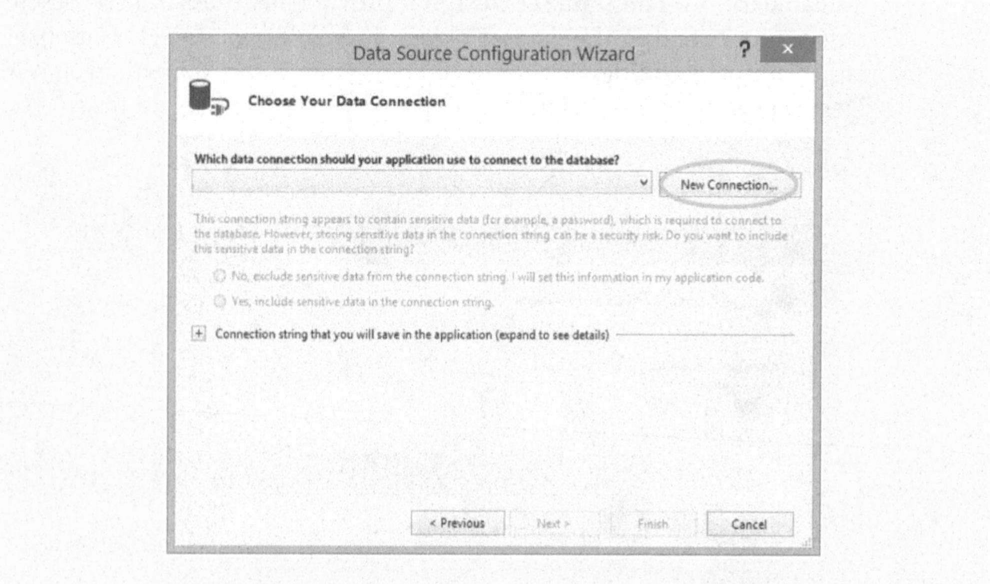

FIGURE 14-7 Choose your Data Connection

You follow these steps whether you are connecting to a Microsoft SQL Server, Oracle, or a Microsoft Access database. Microsoft Access data source is used for the examples in this chapter.

To establish a new connection, select **New Connection**. A dialog box similar to the one shown in Figure 14-8 is displayed.

FIGURE 14-8 Add a New Connection

Selecting the **Change** button beside the **Data Source**, as shown in Figure 14-8, gives you an opportunity to connect to different data sources through the available Data Providers. This opens another dialog box, similar to Figure 14-9, where you would choose **Microsoft Access Database File** as the **Data Source**. This option lets you use the .NET Framework Data Provider for OLE DB. If you select the checkbox in the extreme left corner, **Always use this selection**, Access will become the default data source for future connections.

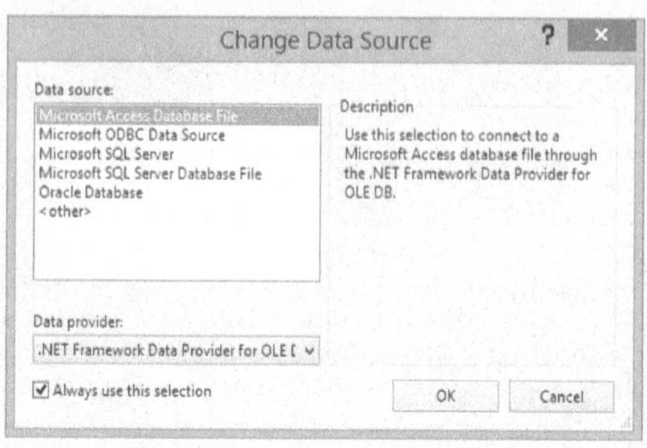

FIGURE 14-9 Change Data Source

A Microsoft Access database file, using the .NET Framework Data Provider for OLE DB is shown selected in Figure 14-9.

Next you are able to enter details regarding the actual database to which you want to connect. Review Figure 14-8. Once the Data Source is determined, you select and enter the name of the database file using the **Browse** button. When connecting to an Access database, you are asked to enter a username and password for the database. The default `(Admin)` is automatically added as the **User name**. You are encouraged to keep this default setting and to leave the **Password** text box blank.

TESTING THE CONNECTION

After you locate the appropriate database, the **Test Connection** button can be used to make sure you are able to connect to the data source. This is illustrated in Figure 14-10. You should perform this test before continuing with the configuration to make sure you are able to connect to the data source.

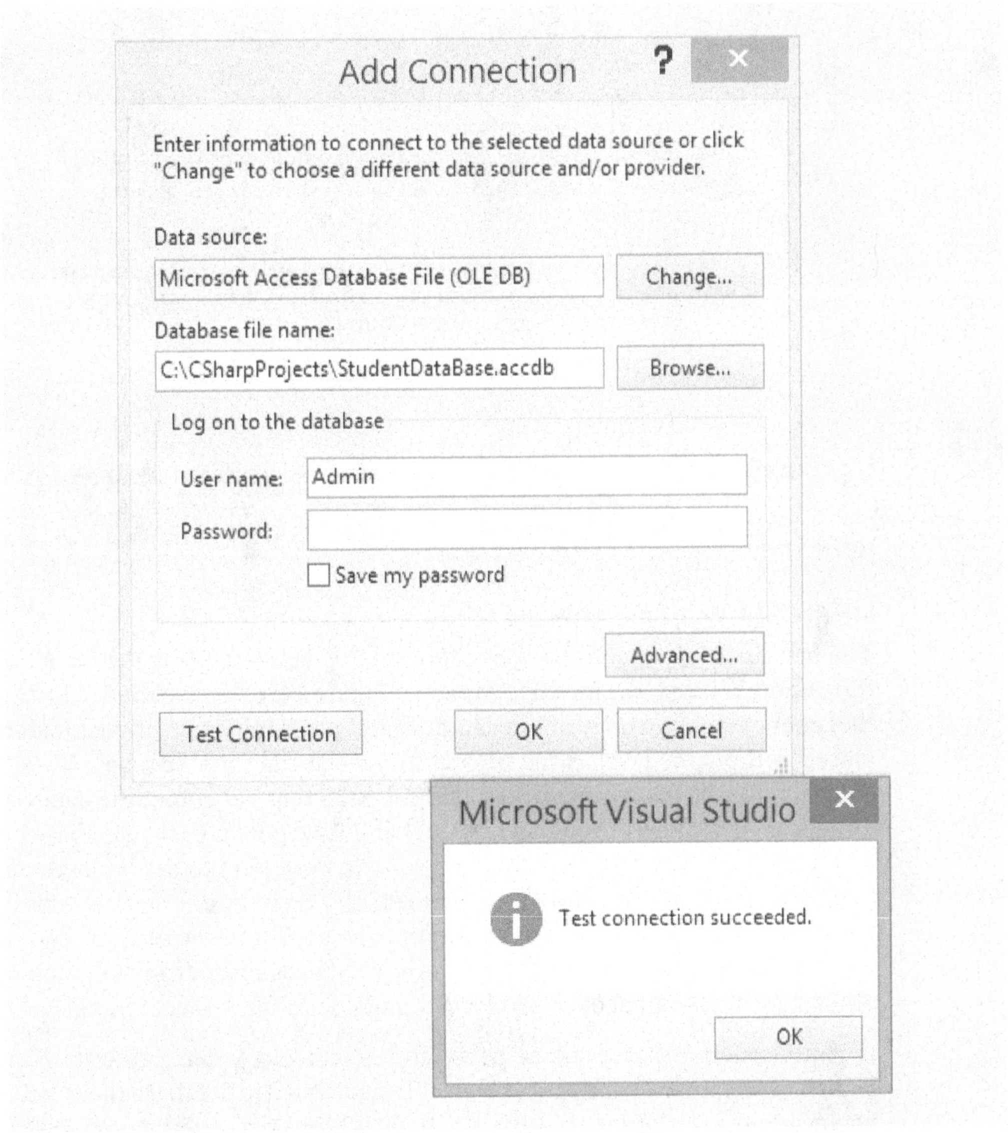

FIGURE 14-10 Locate and test the connection

After testing your connection as shown in Figure 14-10, you are redirected back to the dialog box shown in Figure 14-7. If you are using the **Data Source Configuration Wizard**, you might get a message similar to the one shown in Figure 14-11—especially when you are creating applications that connect to a Microsoft Access database.

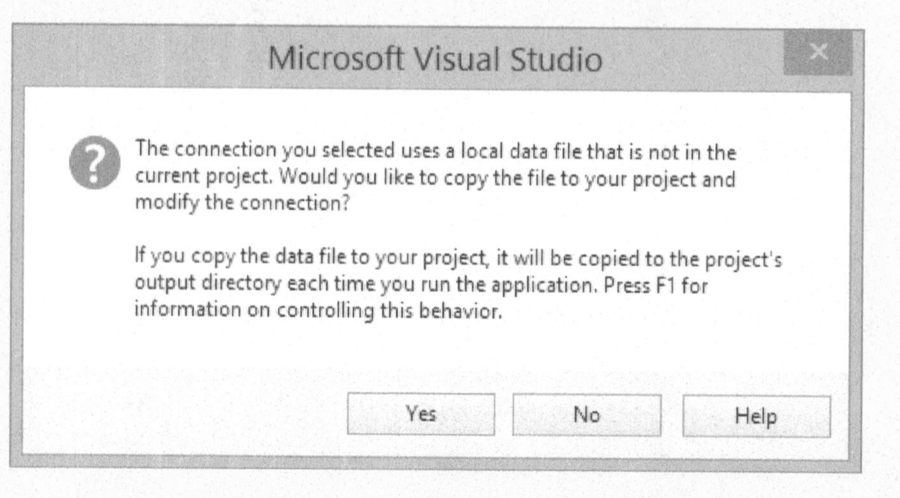

FIGURE 14-11 Copy database file to your project

LOCAL COPY OF YOUR DATABASE

The first time you establish a connection to the database using the **Data Source Configuration Wizard**, the message shown in Figure 14-11 is displayed. The configuration tool offers to make a copy of the database and place it in your project folder. The file is placed at the same level as the project folder—at the same location where the source code files for the Windows form are stored. Selecting **Yes** copies the database into your project and modifies the connection so that it now points to the database in your project. In addition, selecting **Yes** causes the file to be copied to the project's output directory (bin\Debug folder) each time you run the application. So you end up with two copies of the database with your application, when you select **Yes**. The copy of the database in the bin\Debug directory reflects any changes made from your application. The other copy, the original once you located outside of the project remains unchanged.

If you choose not to make a copy, and select **No** when prompted as shown in Figure 14-11, then a connection is established, and the database file is left in its original location. No additional copies are made. Either way, whether you select **Yes** or **No**, the next time you create an application and **Add a Data Source**, the connection to the database that was last accessed is automatically, by default, established. If you want to use a different database, you would **Add New Data Source**. If you wanted to use that same connection, nothing else is required.

NOTE Another option for making a local copy of the database for your project is to use Windows Explorer and drag a copy of the database to the Visual Studio **Solution Explorer** window. The copy should be dropped on top of the project node. When you do this, the **Data Source Configuration Wizard** launches and gives you an opportunity to identify which table(s) to include in the dataset. Access database files end with an .accdb extension.

You can store a local copy of the database with your project. However, if multiple applications are using the same database, you will probably prefer to leave the database in its original location so that changes made by one application are available to all other applications using the database. Thus, you would probably select **No** when asked if you want a copy made for your project as shown in Figure 14-11.

In order to package the database with the project examples for this chapter, a local copy of the each database was included in the project folder. The underlying database does not get changed properly. Having a local copy works fine if you only intend to display the data. If you are using the **Data Source Configuration** and **DataSet Designer** tools and are planning to update or make changes to the database within your application, it is recommended that you do not make a local copy of the database. Select **No** when prompted.

CONNECTION STRING CREATED

Visual Studio offers to store the connection string in a configuration file that contains settings specific to your application. This is illustrated in Figure 14-12. As a final step before you identify the data to be placed in the dataset, you decide whether to store the connection string.

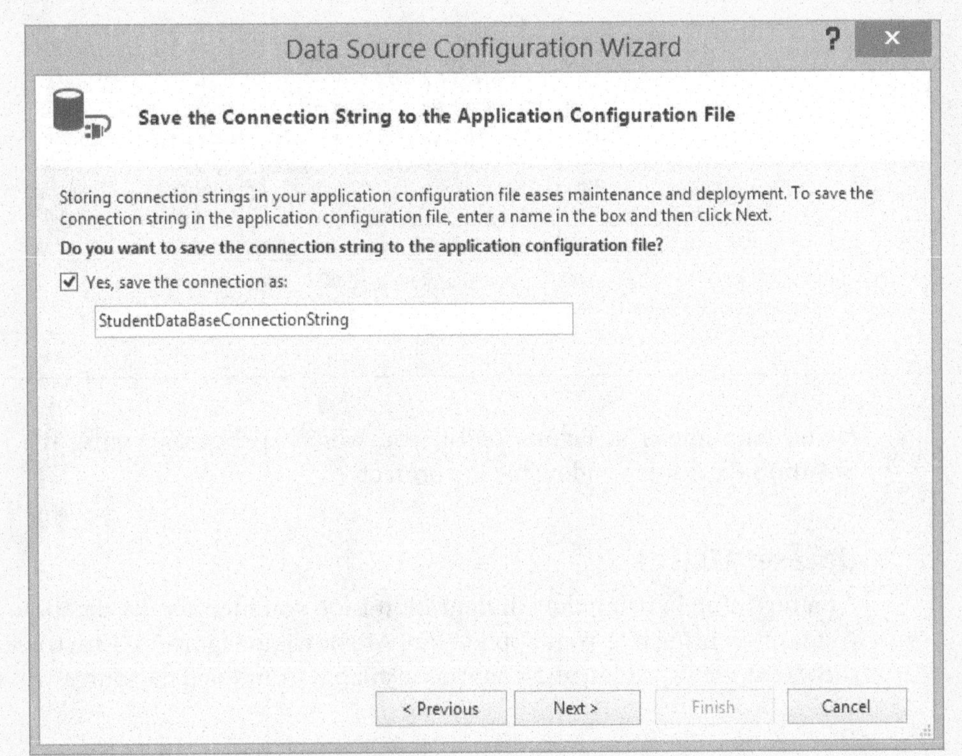

FIGURE 14-12 Save connection string

14

As shown in Figure 14-12, storing the connection string in the application's configuration file makes maintenance and deployment easier. It simplifies the process of maintaining your application if the database connection changes. In the event of a change in the database connection, you can edit the connection string in the application configuration file as opposed to editing the source code and having to recompile your application. The default name for the connection string for the application is the name of the database followed by `ConnectionString`; thus for this example the name is `StudentDataBaseConnectionString`, as shown in Figure 14-12.

If you save the connection string to the application configuration file, as shown in Figure 14-12, an `App.config` file is created. Example 14-22 shows the file contents. It is an XML file that can be viewed and modified in Visual Studio.

EXAMPLE 14-22

```
<?xml version="1.0"encoding="utf-8" ?>
<configuration>
     <configSections>
     </configSections>
     <connectionStrings>
          <add name="ConfigToolsExample.Properties.Settings.
                    StudentDataBaseConnectionString"
          connectionString="Provider=Microsoft.ACE.OLEDB.12.0;
          Data Source=|DataDirectory|\StudentDataBase.accdb"
          providerName="System.Data.OleDb" />
     </connectionStrings>
     <startup>
          <supportedRuntime version="v4.0"
               sku=".NETFramework, Version=v4.5" />
     </startup>
</configuration>
```

If you look ahead at Figure 14-14, you will find the App.config file listed in the **Solution Explorer** window for the project.

Dataset Object

As a final step in using the configuration tool, you identify the database objects that you want to bring into your application. As shown in Figure 14-13, a treelike structure shows the views, tables, and columns available from the data source you selected.

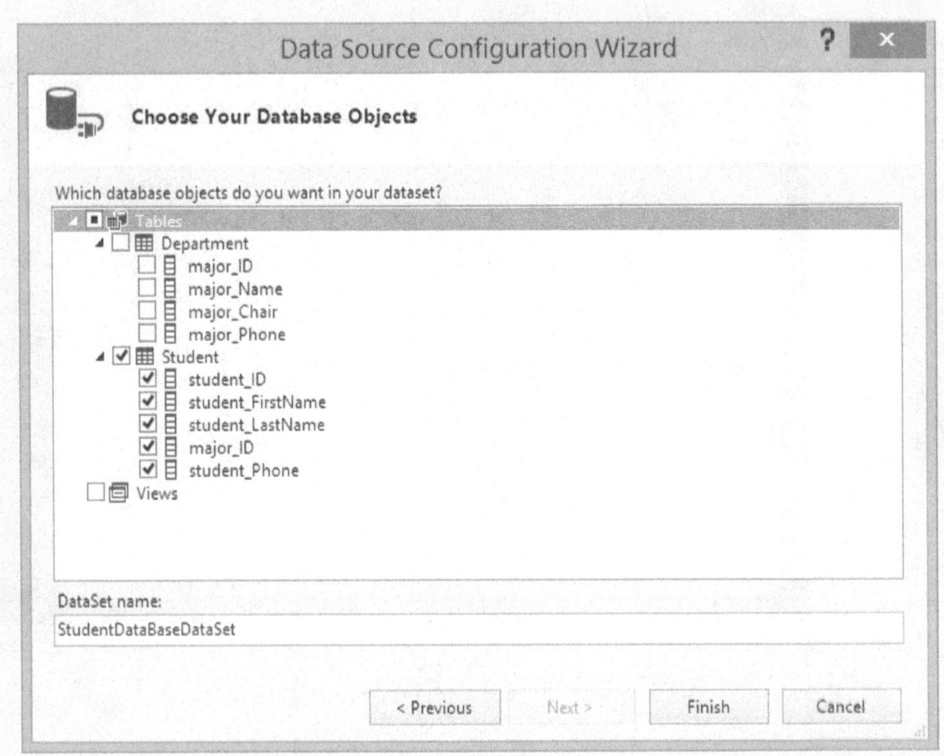

FIGURE 14-13 Choose dataset objects

The chosen objects and their underlying data are brought into your application and become accessible through the dataset object. You can select to include in your dataset all of the tables and/or views of the database. You also have the option of selectively identifying individual tables, as shown in Figure 14-13. Another option is to select certain columns to have available in memory as your dataset object.

The dataset that is created includes not only the collection of one or more data table objects made up of rows and columns of data, but also primary and foreign keys, constraints, and relation information about the data.

You will recall that dataset objects, used with data adapter objects, enable you to update the original data source. As shown in Figure 14-14 in the **Solution Explorer** window, `StudentDataBaseDataSet.xsd` is created.

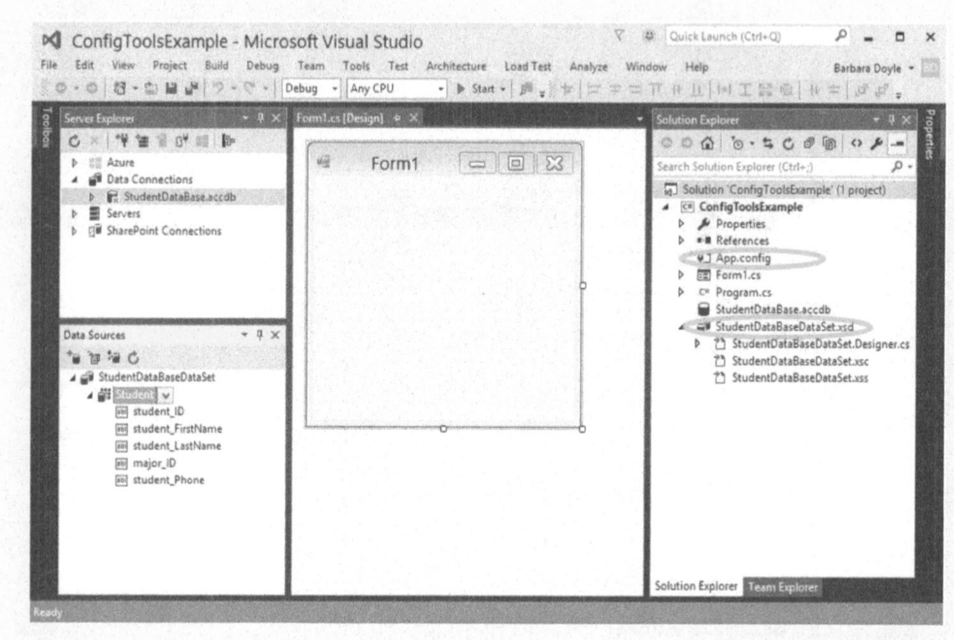

FIGURE 14-14 Data Sources and Solution Explorer windows

As highlighted in Figure 14-14, the `App.config` file, which stores the connection string, is now part of the application. A new set of files defining the dataset object is also included with the application when the configuration wizard terminates normally. These files, independent of the data source, are also named using the database identifier (e.g., `StudentDataBaseDataSet.xsd`) with "DataSet" appended onto the end of the name.

DATA SOURCES WINDOW

Figure 14-14 also shows the new **Data Sources** window to the left of the form. This window enables you to view the data available to your project. It greatly reduces the complexity of binding data from a database to controls on your forms by allowing you to drag complete tables or selectively drag columns from the tables onto forms to create data-bound controls.

Data was placed in rows and columns in an earlier example using the `DataGridView`. The `DataGridView` has additional functionality not used in the previous example. You can specify how data is formatted and displayed using the `DataGridView`. It provides a customizable table that allows you to modify columns, rows, and borders. You can freeze rows and columns to prevent them from scrolling. You can hide rows or columns and provide `ToolTips` and shortcut menus for individual cells, rows, and columns in the grid.

PLACING A DATAGRIDVIEW CONTROL ON THE FORM

The easiest way to add a `DataGridView` control to your application is to drag a table from the **Data Sources** window onto your form. When you do this, an object of the `DataGridView class` is instantiated. You get the added benefit of another control, `BindingNavigator object`, being automatically instantiated. In Figure 14-15, notice the strip of buttons below the title bar. These were all placed when the table from the **Data Sources** window was dragged onto your form; no additional coding was needed. No other objects (other than the table) were dragged onto the form.

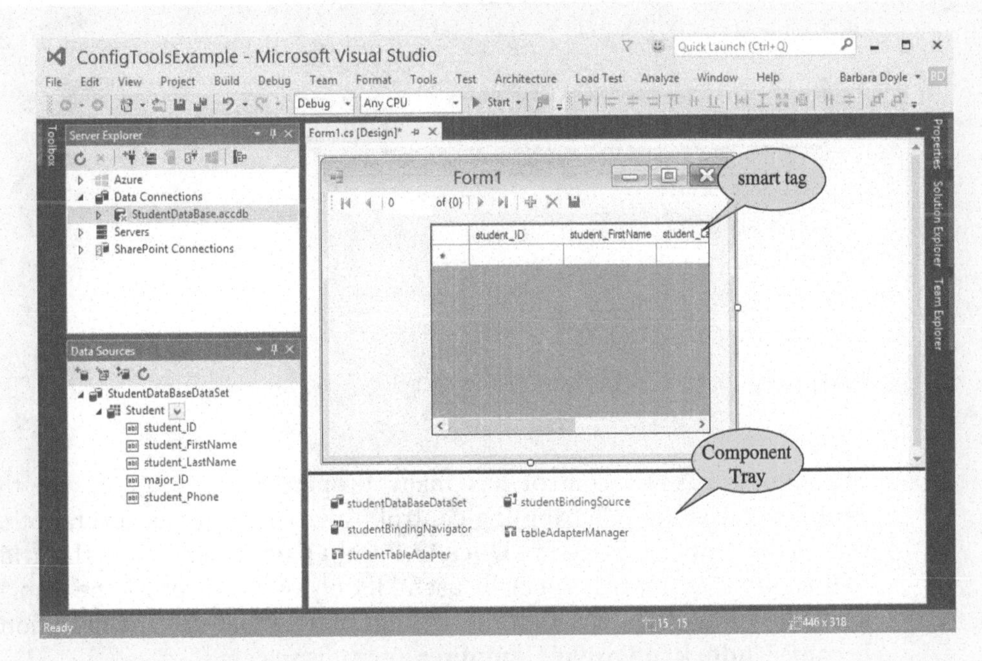

FIGURE 14-15 DataGridView control placed on form

As shown in Figure 14-15, in addition to the grid-like control being placed on the form along with the navigational strip, five objects are placed in the **Component Tray**. These objects will all be explored after you take a closer look at the `DataGridView object`.

CUSTOMIZING THE DATAGRIDVIEW OBJECT

One way to customize the `DataGridView` control is to use its smart tag. You will recall that the smart tag glyphs are displayed when you select the control. They float at the upper-right corner above the control. The `DataGridView` tasks are shown in Figure 14-16.

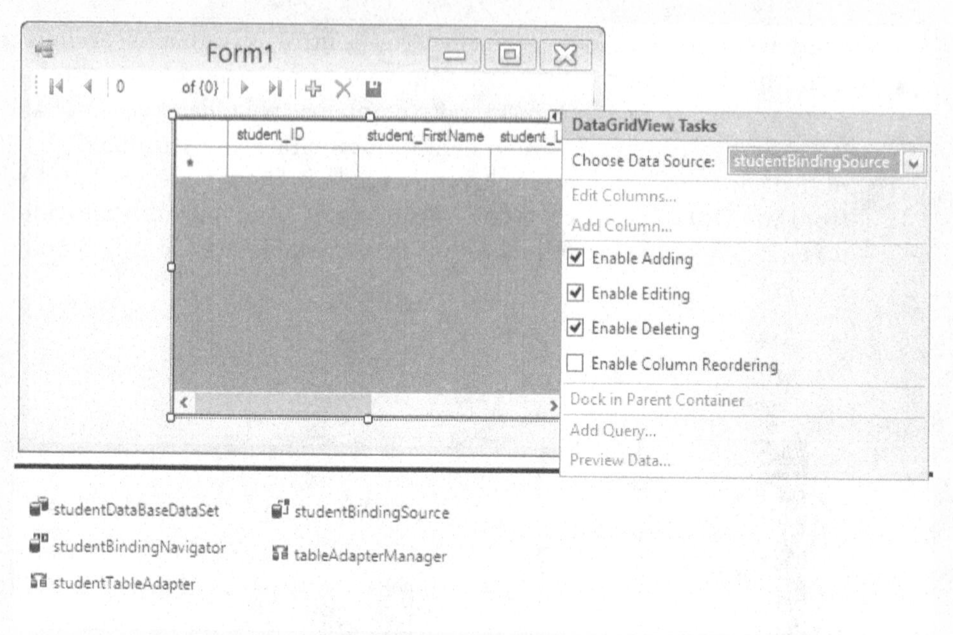

FIGURE 14-16 Customizing the DataGridView control

The `DataGridView` control has many properties that can be set through the **Properties** window. Clicking the control's smart tag reveals several other customization tool options. Selecting **Dock in Parent Container** causes the grid to expand to the form size. This is especially useful if only one control will be displayed on the form. As you experiment with the settings, notice that this menu option toggles to become **Undock in Parent Container** after it is selected.

EDITING COLUMNS

From the `DataGridView`'s smart tag, the **Edit Columns** option displays the columns, allowing you to remove or reorder them. Initially they appear in the same order and by the same name as the columns in the dataset. Recall that the dataset is generated from the table, so the column names are field names in the database. When you click the **Edit Columns** option, you'll see the **Bound Column Properties** for each of the columns. The **Bound Column Properties** option, shown in Figure 14-17, is similar to the **Properties** window but is used to set values specifically for the column objects being displayed on the `DataGridView` control.

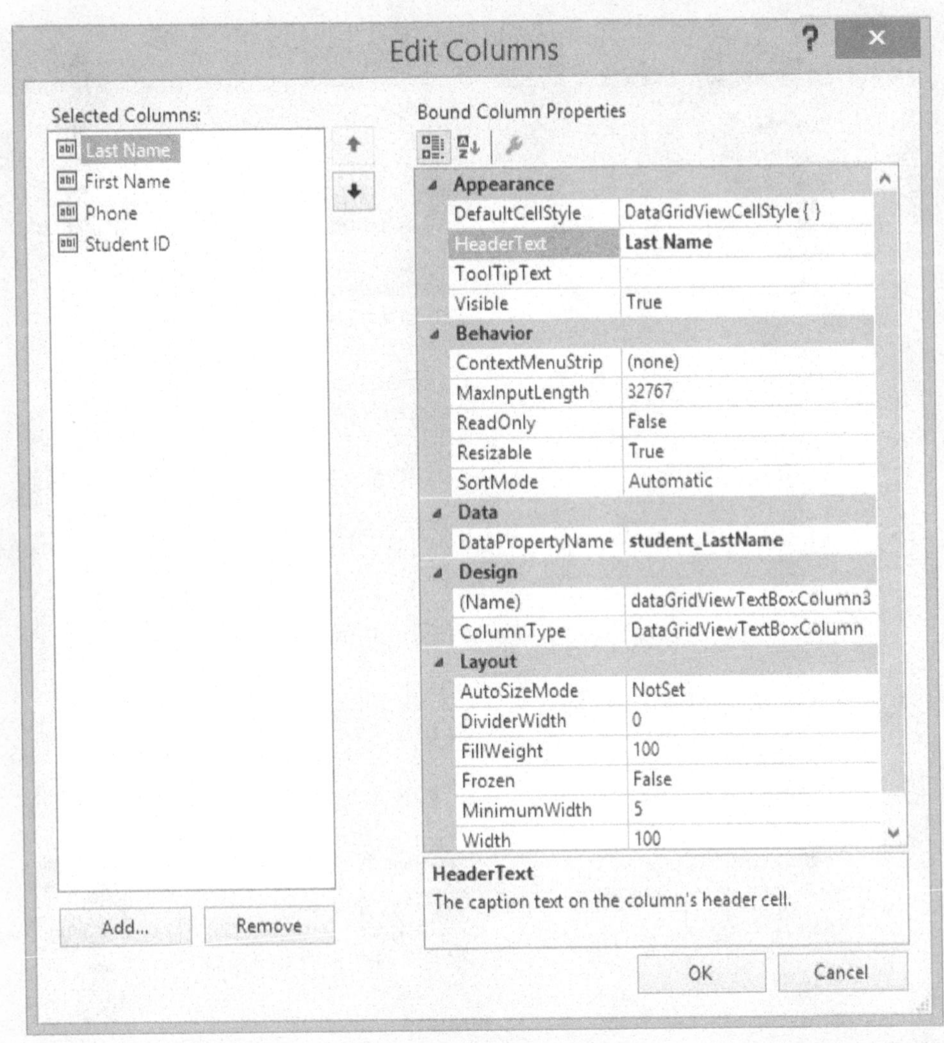

FIGURE 14-17 Edit DataGridView columns

The `major_ID` column was removed from the grid using the smart tag **Edit Columns** option. The `Last Name` was moved up to be displayed in the first column, and the `student_ID` was moved to the end. As shown in Figure 14-17, the `ToolTipText` for the column is set here. You enter column headings for the fields into the `HeaderText` property. Otherwise, the default column names from the database are used as the heading. The `Frozen` property indicates whether the column moves when the `DataGridView` control scrolls horizontally. Table 14-7 lists the properties and changes that were made for this application. 14

TABLE 14-7 ConfigToolsExample property values

Object	Property	Value
Form1	Text	Typed "Example using Configuration Tools"
Form1	BackColor	Ghost White
studentDataGridView	ColumnHeadersDefault CellStyle_BackColor	Blue
studentDataGridView	ColumnHeadersDefault CellStyle_Font	12 pt
studentDataGridView	GridColor	Blue
studentDataGridView	ColumnHeadersHeight SizeMode	Enable Resizing
studentDataGridView	ColumnHeadersHeight	36
studentDataGridView	RowHeadersDefault CellStyle_BackColor	Blue
studentDataGridView	CellBorderStyle	Raised
studentDataGridView	RowHeadersBorderStyle	Raised
student_ID	Bound Column Property_HeaderText	Typed "Student ID"
student_LastName	Bound Column Property_HeaderText	Typed "Last Name"
student_LastName	Bound Column Property_Frozen	True
student_FirstName	Bound Column Property_HeaderText	Typed "First Name"
student_Phone	Bound Column Property_HeaderText	Typed "Phone"
student_Phone	Bound Column Property_ToolTipText	Typed "Campus number"

Figure 14-18 shows the output produced when the application is run. The form and the `DataGridView` control were enlarged using the windows resizing handles. The `DataGridView` was moved to the top-left corner of the form and the `DataGridView` control's **Dock in Parent Container** property was set. The **Dock in Parent Container** property is accessible from the smart tag on the top-right corner of the control.

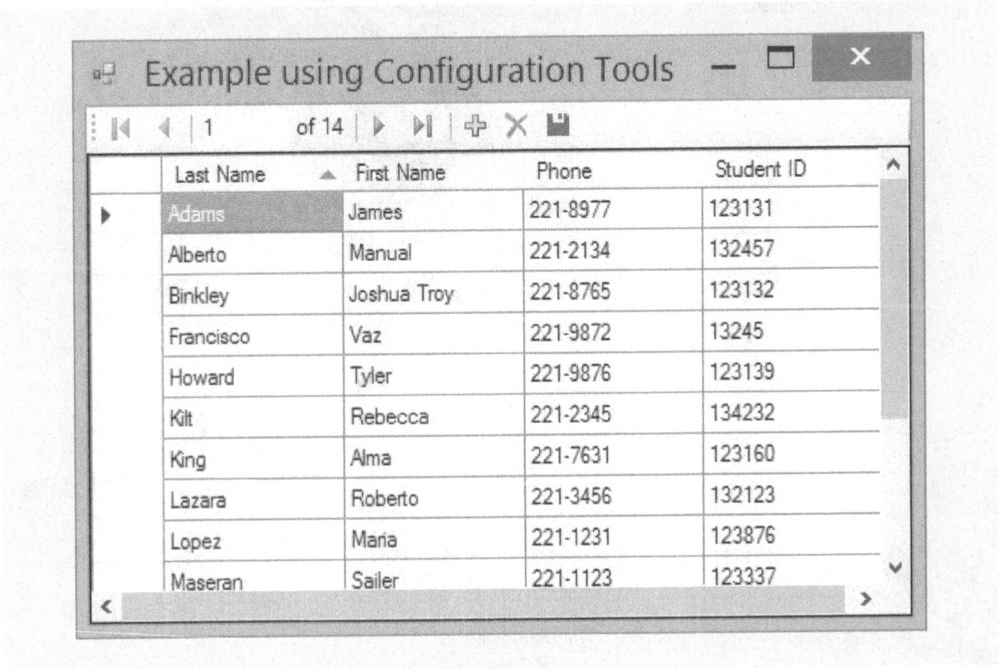

FIGURE 14-18 Example using Configuration Tools output

Values were not stored in alphabetical order by last name in the database. The `DataGridView` control provides the additional functionality of allowing columns to be sorted. The records shown in Figure 14-18 are sorted in ascending order by the last name. Clicking on the column heading for the last name refreshed the display, sorting the records by last name. A second click would rearrange the records in descending order by last name. The sorting capability is available for all of the columns.

FORMATTING DATAGRIDVIEW CELLS

As noted earlier, when you select **Edit Columns** from the smart tag on the `DataViewControl`, the **Bound Columns Properties** window is displayed for individual columns. As shown in Figure 14-19, the appearance of the column can be formatted by selecting the first listed property, `DefaultCellStyle`. A **CellStyle Builder** is opened when you click this property. As shown in the middle window in Figure 14-19, the colors, font, alignment, and format for the cell are set using these properties.

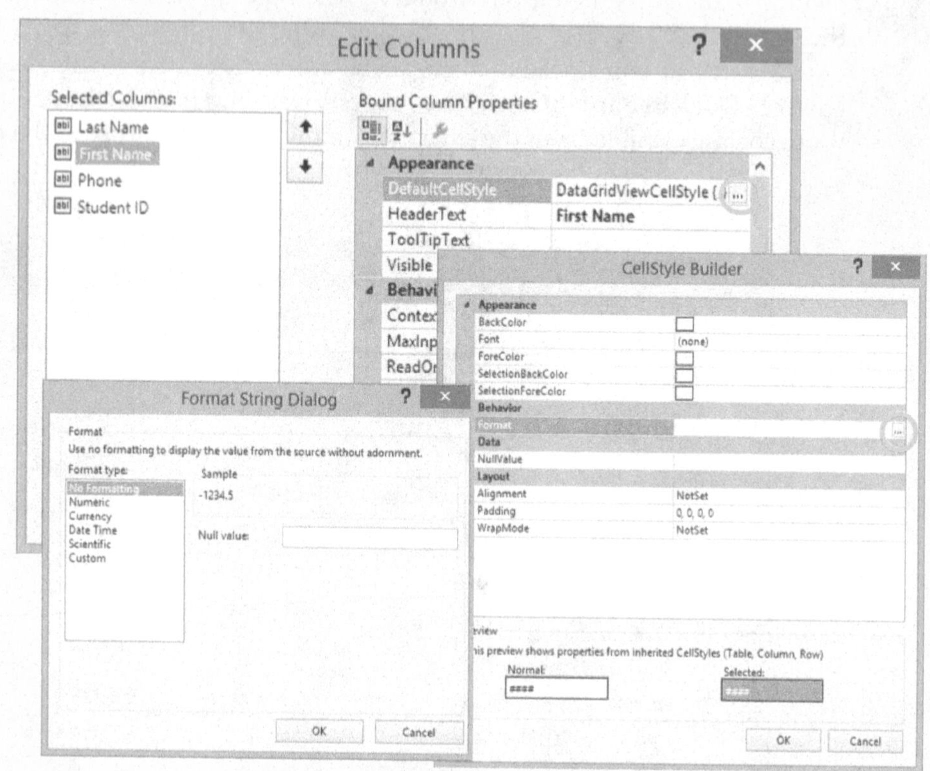

FIGURE 14-19 Formatting DataGridView cells

As shown in Figure 14-19, in addition to having numeric, currency, and scientific notation format options, you can also define custom formats for a cell. Nine options are available from the `Alignment` property, including `TopLeft`, `TopRight`, and `TopCenter`. Similar values (left, right, and center) are found with the middle and bottom options. Four values representing the amount of blank space to insert at the left, right, top, and/or bottom can be set using the `Padding` properties.

Look back at the navigation strip on the form shown in Figure 14-18. This tool strip was automatically added to the form when the table from the **Data Sources** window was dropped onto the form. An object of the `BindingNavigator class` was instantiated; it represents a standardized way to navigate and manipulate data on a form.

BINDINGNAVIGATOR CONTROL

Another class added to the component tray is the `BindingNavigator class`. The `BindingNavigator` control was shown in Figure 14-15. It was one of the five new objects added to the component tray at the bottom of the form when the table from the **Data Sources** pane was placed on the form. The form and component tray are shown again in Figure 14-20.

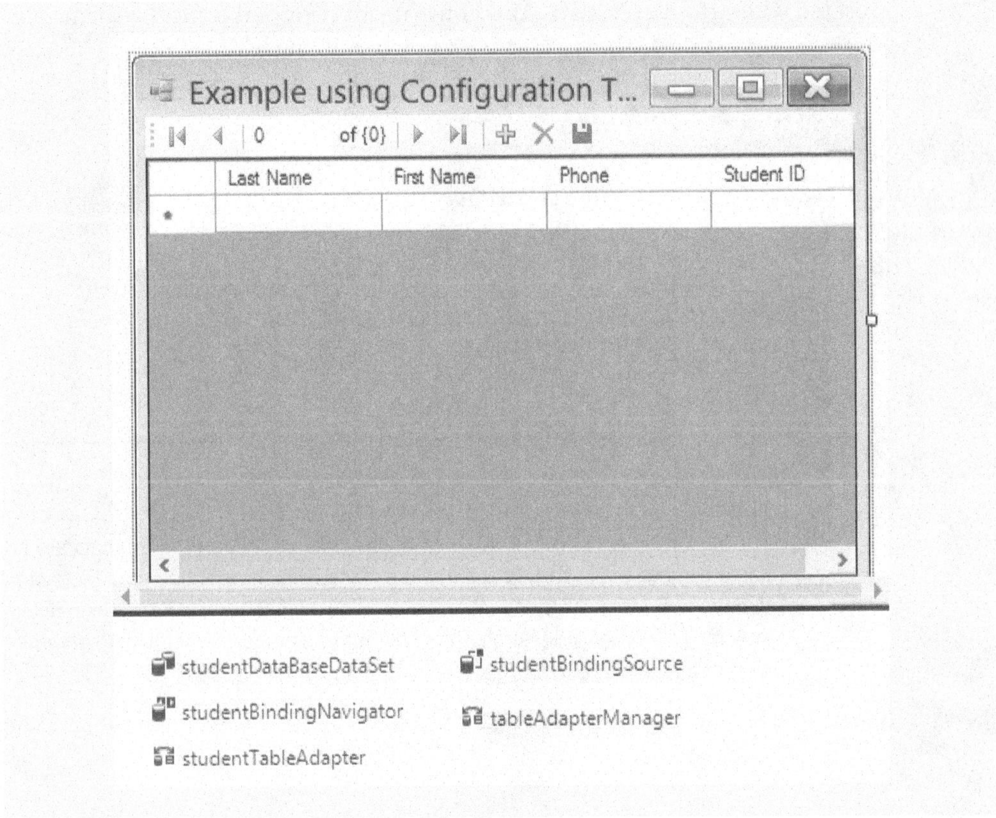

FIGURE 14-20 BindingNavigator and BindingSource objects

The `BindingNavigator` control provides a standardized way to move through and process the data. The user interface for the `BindingNavigator` control includes several buttons and a text box object. The tool strip includes buttons to move to the first, move backward, move forward, and move to the last records. It also allows you to enter a record number and move directly to that record. The plus symbol inserts a new row so that new values can be entered. The **X** symbol deletes the row. The tool strip also includes a **Save** button.

In most cases, a `BindingNavigator` control is paired with a `BindingSource` control to move through data records on a form and interact with them. A `BindingSource object` simplifies binding controls on a form to data. It does this by first attaching the `BindingSource` control to the data source, then each of the individual controls placed on the form can be bound to the `BindingSource object`, as opposed to the actual data source.

Much functionality is automatically programmed into the toolstrip. When the `BindingNavigator` control is first instantiated, the navigational move first, last, forward, and backward arrows work properly. This code was also automatically generated when the `DataGridView` control was dropped onto the form.

EXAMPLE 14-23

```
private void studentBindingNavigatorSaveItem_Click
                    (object sender, EventArgs e)
{
     this.Validate( );
     this.studentBindingSource.EndEdit( );
     this.tableAdapterManager.UpdateAll
          (this.studentDataBaseDataSet);
}
```

NOTE The `DataGridView` is a very rich control that could be programmatically accessed. It has a number of properties and can be treated like a collection of objects stored in a two-dimensional array. `DataGridView` is a column-major structure, which means you would specify the column index first. The following code retrieves the value stored in the first column of the selected row of dataGrid1.

```
dataGrid1[0, dataGrid1.CurrentRow.Index].Value.ToString( );
```

TableAdapterManager

The last statement in the method shown in Example 14-23 calls an `UpdateAll( )` method of a `TableAdapterManager class`. You read earlier in this chapter how a data adapter could be used with a dataset to update a database using a disconnected architecture. The interaction between the dataset and the actual database is controlled through the methods of the data adapter or table adapter objects. Notice that one of the five objects in the component tray, shown in Figure 14-20, is a `TableAdapterManager`. A `TableAdapterManager object` is generated when you create a dataset in a project. The `TableAdapterManager` is extremely useful when an application pulls data from two or more tables. It uses the foreign-key relationships to retrieve and save data in related data tables.

The data or table adapter fills the dataset from the data source (database), and then its update method is used to send the changes back to the database. Data and table adapters read data from a database into a dataset and then write the changed data from the dataset back to the database. They do this using SELECT, INSERT, DELETE, and UPDATE SQL statements.

TABLEADAPTERS

In the previous discussion about writing program statements to use a dataset and data adapter to update a database, we stated that the `CommandBuilder` `class` could be used to generate SQL statements for updates after you set the `SelectCommand` property of the `DataAdapter` `class`. Another approach is to use the `TableAdapter` `SelectCommand`, `InsertCommand`, `UpdateCommand`, and `DeleteCommand` properties. The `CommandText` for each of these properties can be set to an SQL query. For the `TableAdapter` `Update( )` method to work properly, it has to have available SQL INSERT, DELETE, and UPDATE commands. Based on the interaction with the user, one or more of these commands is executed. If data is modified, the UPDATE SQL command is used. When records are deleted, the DELETE SQL command is used. The TableAdapter's `Update( )` method determines which command(s) to use when it is invoked.

When you dropped the `DataGridView` control onto the form, one of the five objects placed in the component tray was `studentTableAdapter`. TableAdapters are designer-generated components that are not technically part of ADO.NET, but like data adapters provide a communication link between an application and a database. They provide all of the functionality of a data adapter. They also have a built-in connection object and enable you to configure the `InsertCommand`, `UpdateCommand`, and `DeleteCommand` SQL queries manually in the **Properties** window.

If you select the `TableAdapter` `object` in the component tray and view its properties, you will not see the `SelectCommand`, `InsertCommand`, `UpdateCommand`, and `DeleteCommand` properties. You need to use the **DataSet Designer** to view and modify the `CommandText` for these properties.

DataSet Designer

The **DataSet Designer** tool is available in Visual Studio to work with `DataSet` objects. The **DataSet Designer** can be used to extend the functionality of datasets. It is also used to create and modify data and table adapters and their queries. To start the designer, double-click a dataset in the **Solution Explorer** window or right-click the dataset in the **Data Sources** window and click **Edit DataSet with Designer**. A visual representation of the dataset and table adapter is presented, as shown in Figure 14-21.

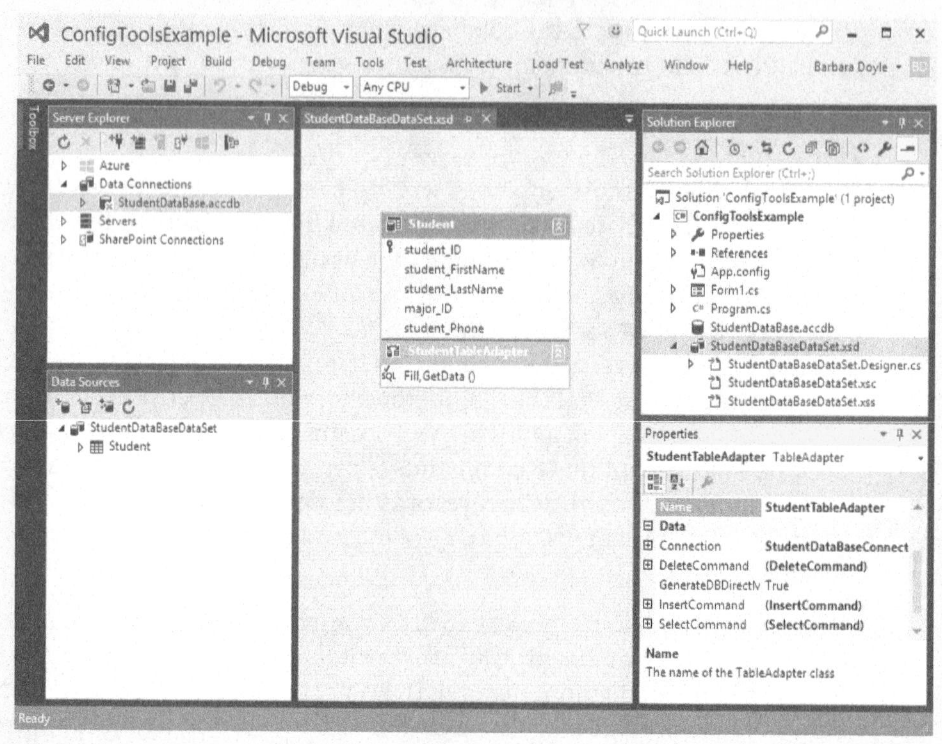

FIGURE 14-21 DataSet Designer opened

The **DataSet Designer** is opened from the **Solution Explorer** window by double-clicking the `StudentDataBaseDataSet.xsd` file. The **Properties** window, shown in Figure 14-21, shows the `StudentTableAdapter` `object`. The `StudentTableAdapter` `object` was selected in the **DataSet Designer**. Notice, there are properties named `InsertCommand`, `DeleteCommand`, `UpdateCommand`, and `SelectCommand`. When the `DataGridView` object was dropped on the form, SQL commands were associated with each of these properties.

REVIEWING THE TABLEADAPTER'S COMMAND PROPERTIES

The `StudentTableAdapter` `object` already has values associated with the SQL commands used to retrieve and update database tables. When you expand each of the properties for the four SQL commands (`DeleteCommand`, `InsertCommand`, `SelectCommand`, and `UpdateCommand`), three additional lines are revealed as shown in Figure 14-22. Options of `CommandText`, `CommandType`, and `Parameters` are displayed. You can use the **Query Builder** to edit or write new SQL statements for each of the CommandTexts.

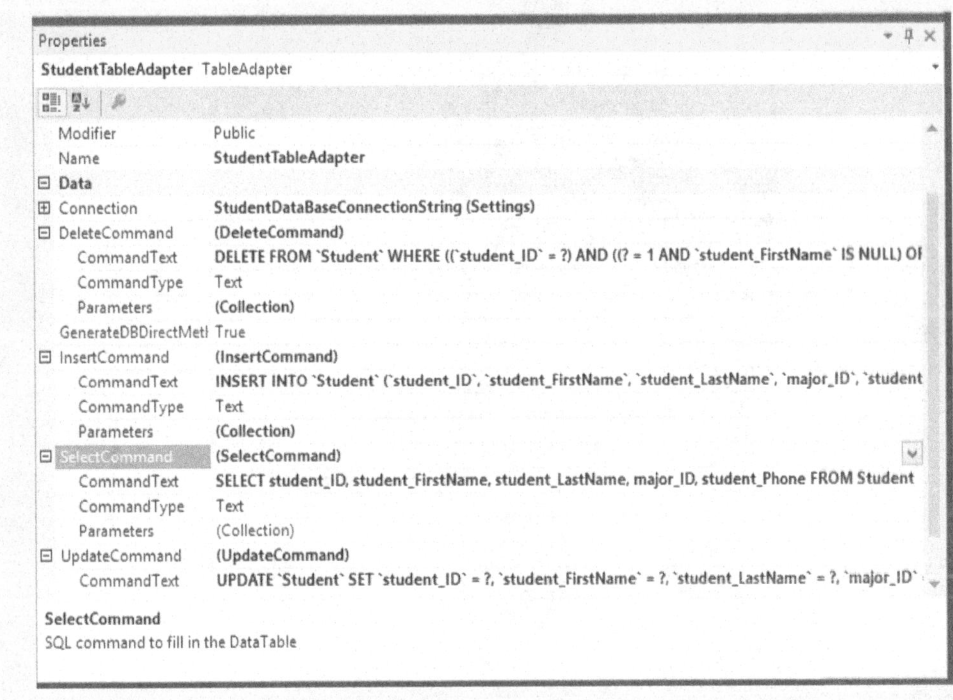

FIGURE 14-22 Updating the SelectCommand

As shown in Figure 14-22, the first property associated with the `SelectCommand`, `CommandText`, holds the SQL statement. The SQL statement can be typed directly into this box, or it can be generated using the **Query Builder**. To open the **Query Builder**, click in the `CommandText` value box. An ellipsis will appear. The Builder is started when you click the ellipsis.

QUERY BUILDER

Clicking the value box beside any of the SQL command properties opens up a drop-down list with options of **Current**, **New**, and **None**. The **Query Builder** can be launched from both **New** or from selecting the ellipsis in the `CommandText` box under the SQL command. If you select **New**, the SQL statement in the `CommandText` box is cleared and then the **Query Builder** is launched. If you select **New** you are first prompted to select the table from which the data is to be retrieved. After you add the table and close the dialog box, you build the query. Instead of selecting **New**, if you select the ellipsis beside the `CommandText` property value, the Query Builder opens with the SQL statement that is automatically generated by Visual Studio. The `SelectCommand` is shown in Figure 14-23.

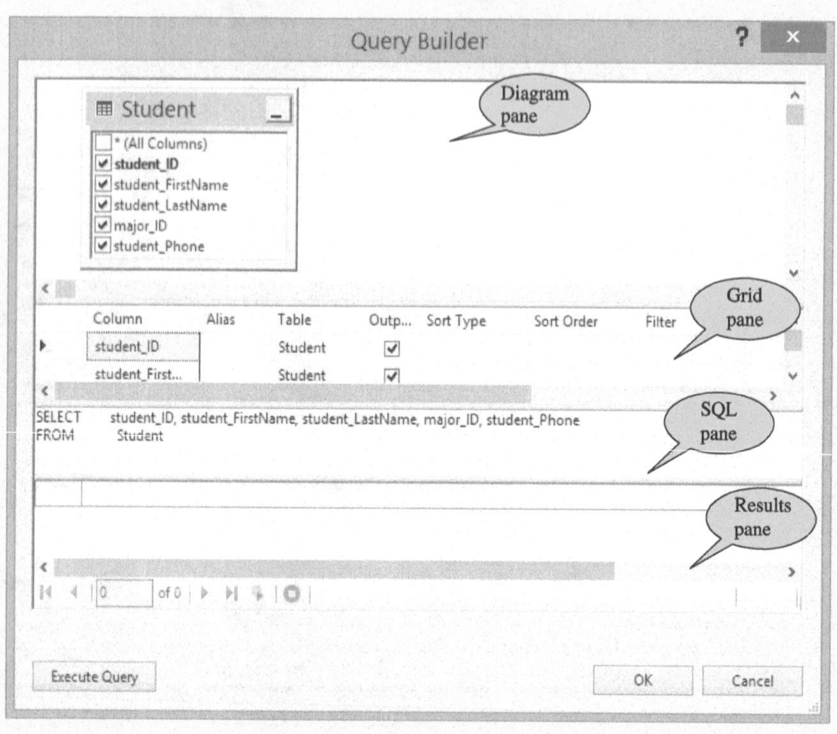

FIGURE 14-23 Identify the table for the update

You can type the SQL statement into the **SQL** pane or use the **Diagram** pane to select the columns you want to update as shown in Figure 14-23. The **Grid** pane in the center is used to filter and enter parameterized expressions. The **Filter** column in the **Grid** pane is used to identify which records should be returned for the query. If you select the **Execute Query** button, the results of the query are displayed in the **Results** pane.

NOTE Normally, all of the columns are selected for an update. Also, if you insert new records, be sure to insert data for any key values.

PARAMETERS

To indicate that the column is to be set by entering a value at run time, a parameterized query can be created. For values that might be provided at run time while the form is being displayed, an "at" symbol (@) is placed in front of an identifier for SQL Server data sources. A question mark (?) is used instead of the @ symbol for Access. No identifier can follow the ? with Access.

Figure 14-24 shows the `SELECT` statement created with the **Query Builder**. Only records that had major_ID = 'CS' or major_ID = 'MS' were retrieved.

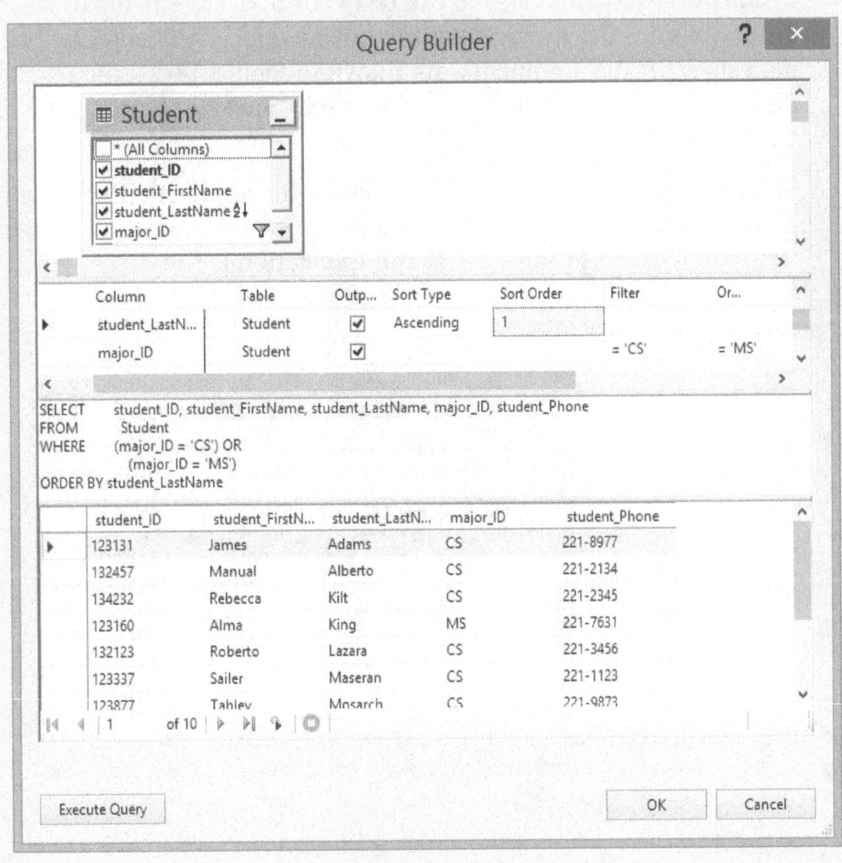

FIGURE 14-24 CommandText property value for the SelectCommand

The `CommandText` for the `SelectCommand` is shown in Example 14-24. When values were entered for the **Filter** and **Or...**, it was not necessary to type the equal symbol or the quotation marks. These symbols were automatically added. Instead of using the **Diagram** or **Grid** pane, this SQL statement was typed directly into the **SQL** pane. The **Sort Order** column was selected for the `student_LastName` data field. **Ascending** was automatically stored in the **SortType** when the **Sort Order** of **1** was selected for last name.

EXAMPLE 14-24

```
SELECT student_ID, student_FirstName, student_LastName,
      major_ID, student_Phone
    FROM Student
       WHERE (major_ID = 'CS') OR (major_ID = 'MS')
             ORDER BY student_LastName
```

Inside the Query Builder, you can test your SQL statements by selecting the **Execute Query** button. If you have parameterized values, a dialog box is displayed requesting values for the arguments. As shown in Figure 14-24, the results of the query are displayed on the **Results** pane in the **Query Builder** window. This enables you to test the SQL statement during development.

With no changes to the SQL statements, the application enables you to insert new rows, modify the existing data, and delete one or more rows. Figure 14-25 shows a snapshot of the user interface as the application is running.

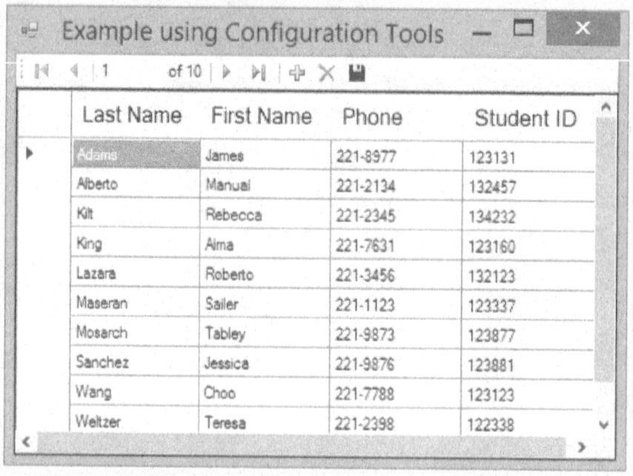

Example using Configuration Tools

1 of 10

Last Name	First Name	Phone	Student ID
Adams	James	221-8977	123131
Alberto	Manual	221-2134	132457
Kilt	Rebecca	221-2345	134232
King	Alma	221-7631	123160
Lazara	Roberto	221-3456	132123
Maseran	Sailer	221-1123	123337
Mosarch	Tabley	221-9873	123877
Sanchez	Jessica	221-9876	123881
Wang	Choo	221-7788	123123
Weltzer	Teresa	221-2398	122338

FIGURE 14-25 Example using Configuration Tools final output

As shown in Figure 14-25, 10 of the records met the `SQL WHERE` clause (`(major_ID = 'CS') OR (major_ID = 'MS')`) and appear in the listing. Records were sorted by last name. Even though the `major_ID` was listed as a field being returned from the `SQL SELECT`, the major did not appear in the listing of Figure 14-25. Recall that the `major_ID` column was removed from the `DataGridControl` using the smart tag **Edit Columns** option. Readable headers were also added during that edit as was illustrated in Figure 14-17.

At this point, the records were changed while the application was running. The record with the name `Manual Alberto` was deleted. `Adam Jones` was inserted. Alma King's name was changed to Alma Norma King. Clicking the **Save** button caused the `tableAdapterManager.UpdateAll( )` method to be called, which used the table adapter's `InsertCommand`, `DeleteCommand`, and `UpdateCommand CommandText` SQL statements to make changes back to the database. The database file was updated. Figure 14-26 shows the changes made while the application was running and the updated Access table.

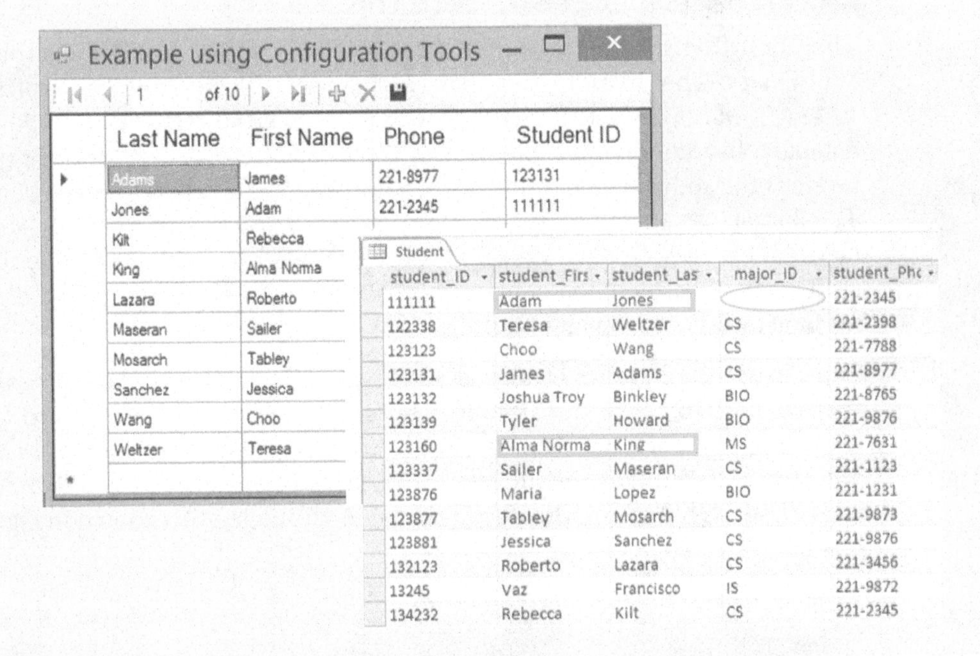

FIGURE 14-26 StudentDataBase Student table updated (from bin\Debug directory)

NOTE As you review Figure 14-26 you will notice that record with the name Adam Jones that was added did not have values associated with the `major_ID`. Recall that the field was deleted from the form during the design so the user could not enter values for it. Be very careful to make sure you include primary key fields on forms when you plan to allow inserts; otherwise, the cell will become `null` and an exception will be thrown.

Figure 14-26 displays the contents of the database stored in the bin\Debug directory. When the database connection was established, **Yes** was selected so that a local copy of the database was copied to the project directory. You may want to again review Figure 14-11. It shows where that selection was made, and any changes made to the database are made to the copy. As the changes are not made to the database stored in the project directory, each time the program launches it loads the original database file.

NOTE If you run the application a second time, you may think your application did not do the updates. This is because the application always reloads the database file stored in the project's directory (not the one stored in the bin\Debug directory). Selecting **No** when prompted about whether you want to make a copy for your project directory would have resulted in the changes being made to the referenced database.

ADDING QUERIES TO TABLEADAPTER OBJECTS

The ConfigToolsExample solution was copied to a new folder, ConfigToolsExampleWithQuery. This section uses that application. `TableAdapters` typically contain `Fill( )` and `Update( )` methods, which are used to retrieve and update data in a database. In addition, multiple queries can be added to `TableAdapter` objects. This is one of the added benefits the `TableAdapter class` offers over the `DataAdapter`. The initial `SELECT` SQL query, used by the `Fill( )` method, is stored in the `SelectCommand CommandText` property. When you add other queries, they are stored as public methods containing SQL statements that are called like any other method or function on an object.

You can use the **DataSet Designer** window to add the additional queries. Right-click the `TableAdapter` in the **DataSet Designer** window and select **Add Query** from the shortcut menu. This displays a **TableAdapter Query Configuration** Wizard. You will first be asked *"How should the TableAdapter query access the database?"* If you select **Use SQL statements** to load the table, the dialog box shown in Figure 14-27 is displayed.

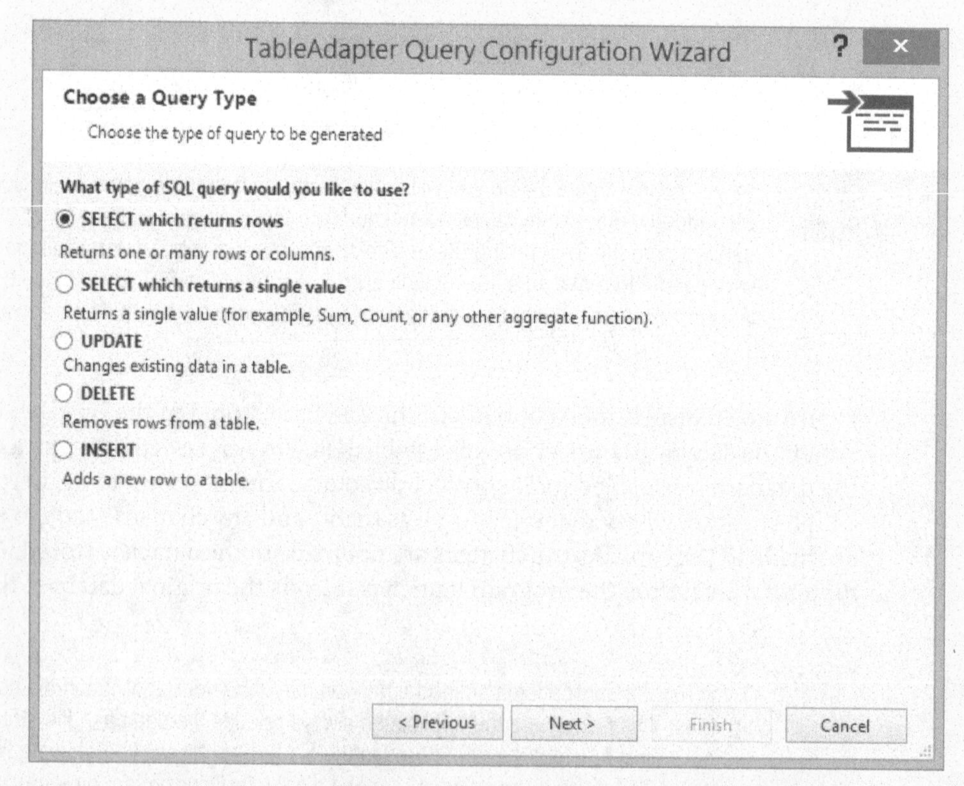

FIGURE 14-27 Multiple queries with the TableAdapter

If you are simply returning values for display, you would select the first option, **SELECT which returns rows**, as shown in Figure 14-27. The next window lets you type the SQL statements and select the **Next** option or click a button that takes you to the **Query Builder**. If you want to retrieve rows based on the user's last name, you could add a parameterized query using the WHERE clause. When you have completed the SQL statement and selected the **Next** option, a dialog box similar to the one shown in Figure 14-28 opens. Notice that two methods are automatically generated.

NOTE For the `ConfigToolsExampleWithQuery`, a WHERE clause was typed onto the end of the auto-generated SQL statement. The SQL statement now reads: `SELECT student_ID, student_FirstName, student_LastName, student_Phone FROM Student WHERE (student_LastName = ?)`

After typing the SQL statement indicating which data should be used to load the table and selecting the **Next** option, the configuration wizard enables you to choose which methods to generate as illustrated in Figure 14-28.

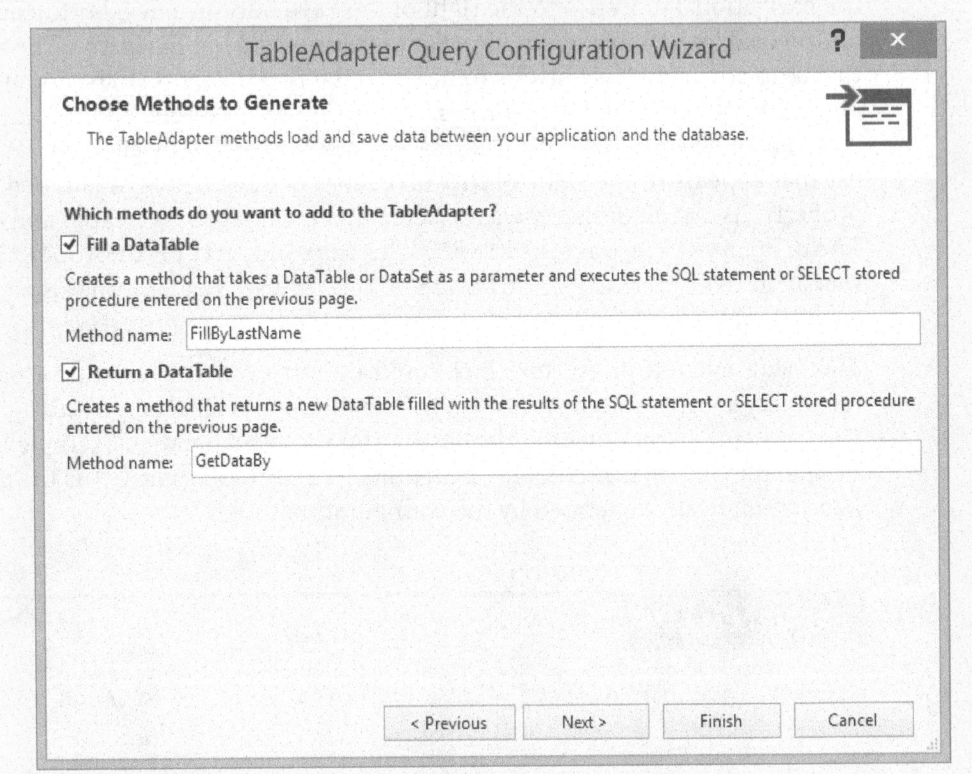

FIGURE 14-28 Naming the new query methods

14

As shown in Figure 14-28, you have the option of naming the methods. The tool automatically populates the method name text boxes with `FillBy` and `GetDataBy`. You can type a completely new name or append onto the end of the default value. A name such as `FillByLastName` would be appropriate if you wanted to show a listing of students with the same user-entered last name. When you click the **Next** button, a message is displayed indicating that the SQL select statement has been generated along with the `Fill` and `Get` methods. Click Finish to complete the process.

A new row, representing the new methods, is added to the class in the **DataSet Designer** for this new query. The row has an SQL icon to the left of the method name. You can look back at the class diagram in Figure 14-21 or ahead at Figure 14-30. Both figures show the **DataSet Designer**. The new row would be added below the `Fill, GetData( )` row.

ADDING A BUTTON AND TEXT BOX FOR THE QUERY

Buttons to execute the new queries that you define using the **DataSet Designer** can be added to the navigational tool strip. In the form design mode, when you click on the navigational tool strip to the right of the **Save** button, a new button appears. This button enables you to add additional controls to the form navigator. The navigational tool strip currently has buttons to move to the first, last, previous, and next records, plus buttons to add and delete rows. You could, for example, add a text box for user input and a new button. A `ToolStripButton` was added by clicking the drop-down list that appears to the right of the **Save** icon; `btnRetrieve` was typed in its `Name` property. Its `Image` property was selected and the image was cleared and set to `none`. The `DisplayStyle` was set to `Text`. The `Text` property for the `ToolStripButton` was set to `"Retrieve By Last Name"`. A `ToolStripTextBox` was also added on the navigational strip; `txtBxLastName` was typed in its `Name` property.

The value entered in the text box could be retrieved and used as a parameter to the query's SQL statement(s) when the button is clicked. Double-clicking the `ToolStripButton` generates the heading for the event handler. Example 14-25 shows a call to the `FillByLastName( )` method. `FillByLastName( )` is the method that was automatically generated by the configuration tool.

EXAMPLE 14-25

```
private void btnRetrieve_Click(object sender, EventArgs e)
{
     studentTableAdapter.FillByLastName
        (studentDataBaseDataSet.Student, txtBxLastName.Text);
}
```

The event-handler method in Example 14-25 invokes the TableAdapter's `FillByLastName( )` method. The last name is retrieved from the `ToolStripTextBox`. It sends as arguments the dataset object and the parameterized value (last name), which was included as part of the SQL query. When the user types a value for last name, records that match that value are displayed. This is illustrated in Figure 14-29.

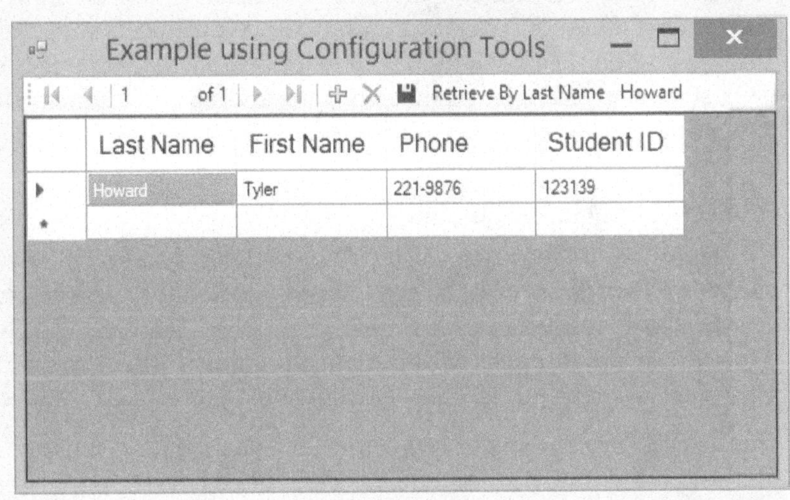

FIGURE 14-29 TableAdapter's Query

Using the smart tag on the `DataViewControl` on the Windows form, the option **Undock in Parent Container** was selected. When the user typed the value `"Howard"` one record was retrieved as illustrated in Figure 14-29.

Two additional controls, a button and a text box, are shown on the navigational tool strip in Figure 14-29. The **Retrieve By Last Name** button uses the value entered in the text box to its right to populate the data grid.

As you review Figure 14-13, you are reminded that the database has two tables. When the solution was originally designed, the dataset was created from a single table, `Student`. It is often necessary to display data from multiple tables on a single form. This can also be accomplished using the visual tools now available with Visual Studio. The `ConfigToolsExample` solution was copied to a new folder, `ConfigToolsExampleWithMultipleTables`. The following section uses that application.

Connecting Multiple Tables

If you plan to retrieve data from multiple tables, it is best to select all of the tables that you will need originally when you create the dataset object. Recall that the dataset created earlier as part of the `ConfigToolsExample` selected a single table for the dataset. Without regenerating the dataset, several options are available to gain access to the database's other table data. One of the simplest approaches is to use the **Query Builder** and add an `INNER JOIN` clause to the `SELECT` statement for the TableAdapter's `SelectCommand`. The **Query Builder** is very sophisticated. You can use the graphical capabilities of the tool on the **Diagram pane**, or you can type the SQL statement straight into the SQL pane and test your statement using the **Execute Query** button.

USING THE DATASET DESIGNER

To follow this approach, use the **Solution Explorer** window to open the **DataSet Designer**. Recall that when you double-click on the dataset file (`StudentDataBaseDataSet.xsd`) from the **Solution Explorer** window, the **DataSet Designer** opens with the `DataSet` and `TableAdapter` objects graphically displayed as a single unit. This was shown in Figure 14-21.

You need to change the `TableAdapter CommandText` for the `SelectCommand` so that when the `Fill( )` method is called, the dataset is populated with results from both tables. Recall that the `TableAdapter object` provides the link between the database and the `DataSet object`. As you have read earlier, the `Fill( )` method uses the SQL command associated with the adapter's `SelectCommand` to populate the dataset object. It is through the `SELECT` command that the `Fill( )` method knows what to put in the dataset. The `TableAdapter's Fill( )` method is called from the page load event handler. This is shown in Example 14-26.

EXAMPLE 14-26

```
private void FrmConfigTools_Load(object sender, EventArgs e)
{
     // This line of code loads data into the
     // 'studentDataBaseDataSet.Student' table.
     this.studentTableAdapter.Fill
          (this.studentDataBaseDataSet.Student);
}
```

Make sure the **Properties** window is visible. Select the `TableAdapter` in **DataSet Designer** and then, using the **Properties** window, expand the Table Adapter's

SelectCommand so that you are able to see the CommandText property, as shown in Figure 14-30.

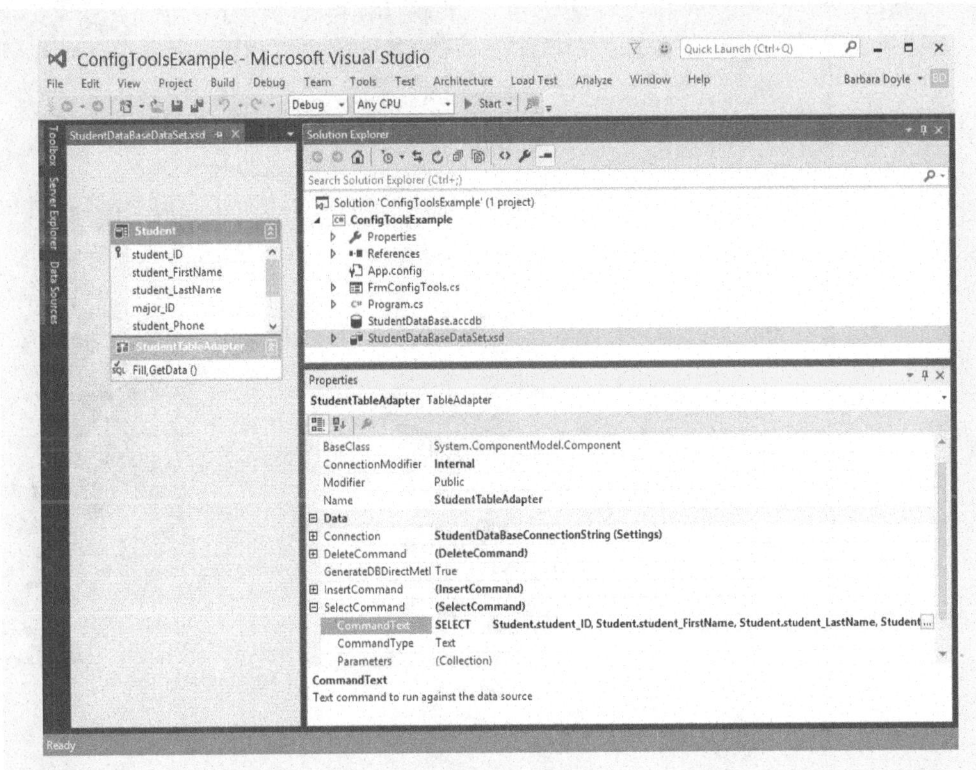

FIGURE 14-30 Revise the CommandText for the SelectCommand

MODIFYING THE SELECTCOMMAND USING THE QUERY BUILDER

To start the **Query Builder** so you can modify the SELECT statement, click the ellipsis in the value box for the CommandText of the SelectCommand, as shown in Figure 14-30.

Because a query already exists, the **Query Builder** takes you immediately to the **Query Builder** designer. When the Builder is first opened, the **Diagram** pane just shows the one table that was used to populate the dataset. If you right-click anywhere in the **Diagram** pane, one of the menu options is **Add Table**. You get a list of tables that belong to the database data source. The Student and Department are both listed. Selecting Department places the Department table in the **Diagram** pane with the Student. It automatically places a relationship line between the two tables as shown in Figure 14-31.

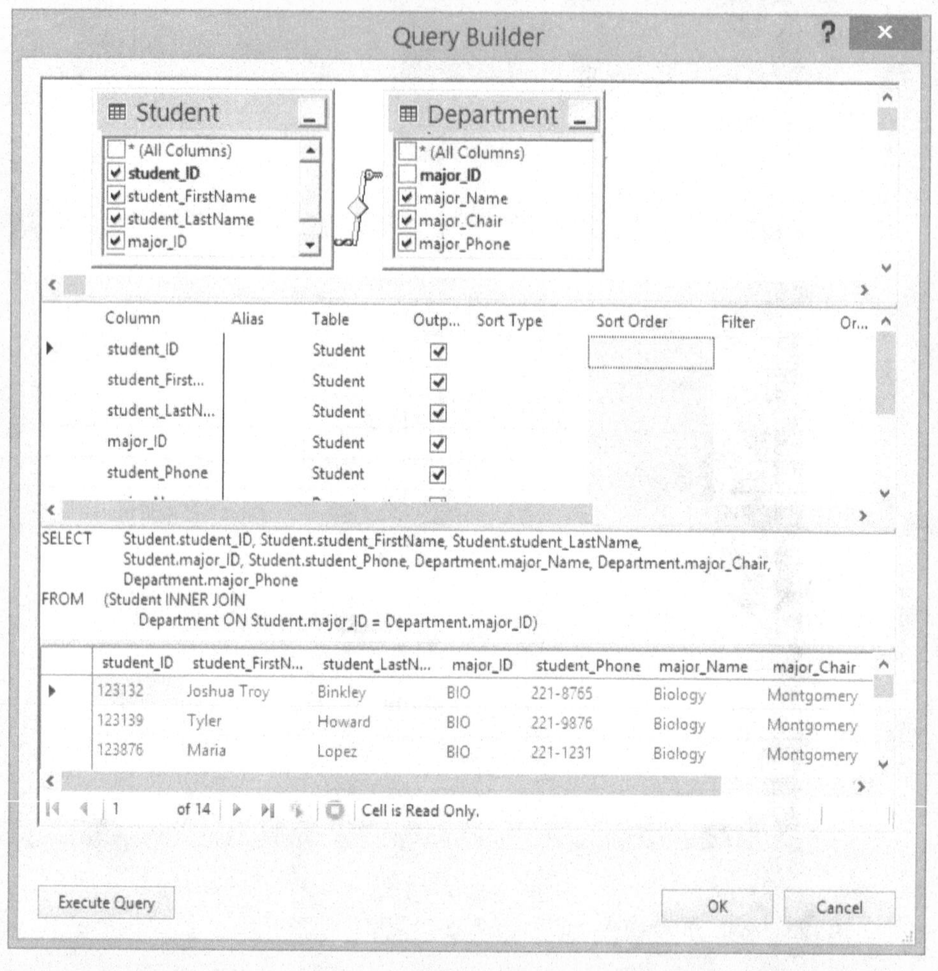

FIGURE 14-31 Use the Query Builder to modify the SelectCommand CommandText

You could type the SQL statement shown in Example 14-27 in the **Query Builder SQL** pane or select the additional fields from the `Department` table to be displayed using the **Diagram** pane. The SQL statement shown in Figure 14-31 looks slightly different from what is shown in Example 14-27. The Query Builder fully qualifies all field name references. Instead of displaying `student_ID` as shown in Example 14-27, the field name is preceded by the table name and a dot (i.e., `Student.student_ID`).

EXAMPLE 14-27

```
SELECT   student_ID, student_FirstName, student_LastName,
         major_ID,student_Phone, major_Name, major_Chair,
         major_Phone
    FROM Student
         INNER JOIN Department
             ON Student.major_ID = Department.major_ID
```

Clicking the **Execute Query** button on the **Query Builder** window displays the records returned as the result of the query in the **Results** pane, near the bottom of the screen as shown in Figure 14-31.

You could actually just type the SQL statement into the **SQL** pane as soon as the **Query Builder** is opened. However, without having the second table displayed, you might not be able to correctly spell the column names.

When you close the **Query Builder**, you will be asked whether you want to have the `UpdateCommand`, `InsertCommand`, and `DeleteCommand` regenerated using the newly added `SelectCommand`. You should select **No** when you see the message. Depending on the application you are building, you might need to go back and revisit one or more of the `INSERT`, `DELETE`, or `UPDATE` SQL commands. It is best not to have them automatically regenerated for you. If you select **Yes**, you may see a message stating that "Dynamic SQL generation is not supported against multiple base tables." The tool is not able to generate dynamic `DELETE`, `UPDATE`, and `INSERT` SQL statements from a `SELECT` statement that involves multiple tables. The update functionality of a `TableAdapter` is dependent on how much information is available to its main SQL `SELECT` query.

Recall that if you have saved a local copy of the database within your project, the database file at the project level is the one that is loaded each time you launch the application. It is not updated. Every time the application runs, a new copy of the database is stored in the bin\Debug directory.

UPDATING THE WINDOWS FORM TO DISPLAY DATA FROM MULTIPLE TABLES

The `DataGridView` `object` was used earlier to display data. You saw how it could be customized to display multiple rows with multiple columns in a grid like structure. Recall that it was originally placed on the form by dragging the `Student` table node from the **Data Sources** window to the form. `DataGridView` is the default control used to display the data when you drag the entire table from the **Data Sources** window. After the relationship is established between the tables, you can add columns from the second table to the data grid. You do this by selecting the data grid's smart tag in the form design mode. The **Edit Columns** option displays the dialog box previously shown in Figure 14-17. The new columns can be added from this dialog box or using the **Add Columns** option from the smart tag. As previously stated, you can also use the **Edit Columns** option dialog box to change any of the property values for the columns. Figure 14-32 illustrates adding columns from the second table.

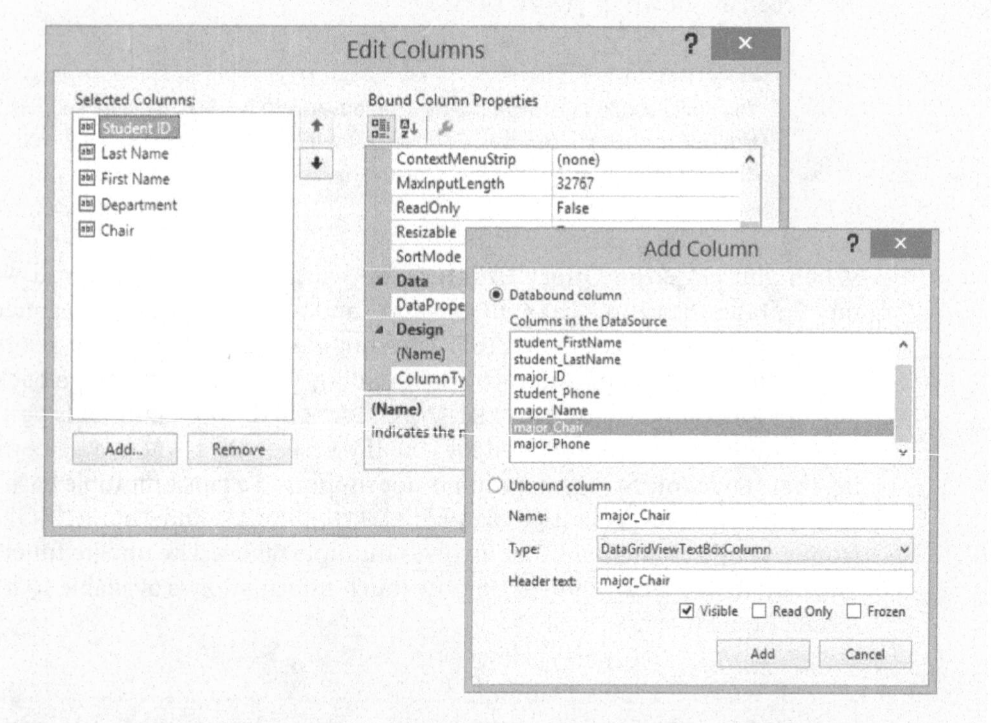

FIGURE 14-32 Adding fields from the second table

The Student ID was moved so that it is displayed in the first column. The name of the major and the major chairman were added to the grid. The `HeaderText` property values for those fields were set to `"Department"` and `"Chair"`. The Phone was removed. Figure 14-33 shows the new design, which retrieves data from multiple tables.

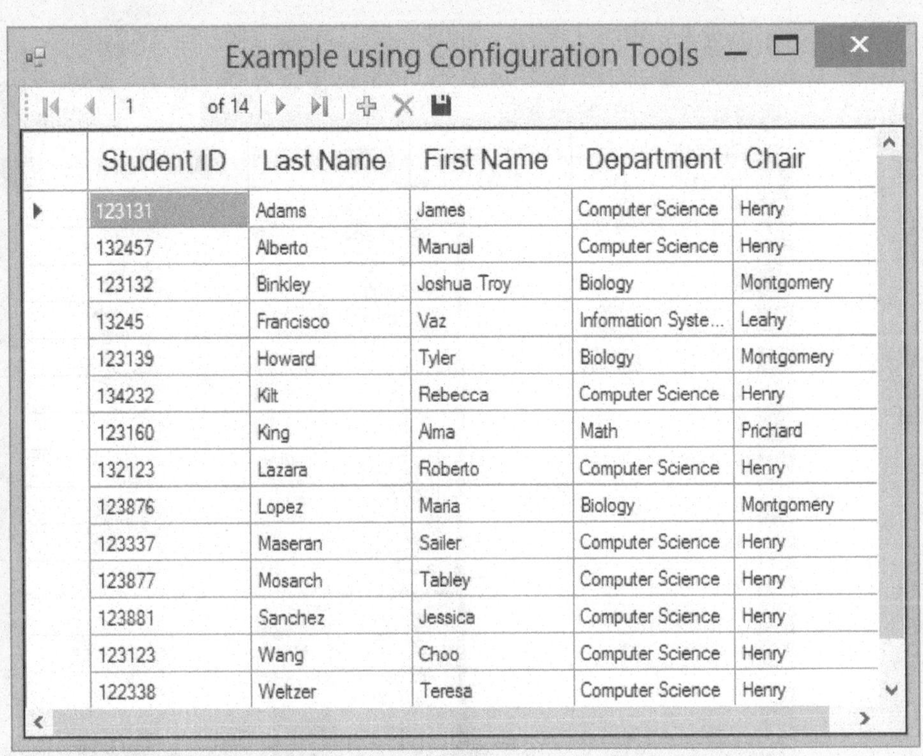

Student ID	Last Name	First Name	Department	Chair
123131	Adams	James	Computer Science	Henry
132457	Alberto	Manual	Computer Science	Henry
123132	Binkley	Joshua Troy	Biology	Montgomery
13245	Francisco	Vaz	Information Syste...	Leahy
123139	Howard	Tyler	Biology	Montgomery
134232	Kilt	Rebecca	Computer Science	Henry
123160	King	Alma	Math	Prichard
132123	Lazara	Roberto	Computer Science	Henry
123876	Lopez	Maria	Biology	Montgomery
123337	Maseran	Sailer	Computer Science	Henry
123877	Mosarch	Tabley	Computer Science	Henry
123881	Sanchez	Jessica	Computer Science	Henry
123123	Wang	Choo	Computer Science	Henry
122338	Weltzer	Teresa	Computer Science	Henry

FIGURE 14-33 Data retrieved from multiple tables

The output generated from the application shown in Figure 14-33 used the original database that was copied into the project directory.

DISPLAYING DATA USING DETAILS VIEW

Instead of displaying data in a grid-like structure, a **Details** view is also available. When you select **Details** and drag the entire table onto the form, you get `Label` and `TextBox` objects for each column in the dataset, as shown in Figure 14-34.

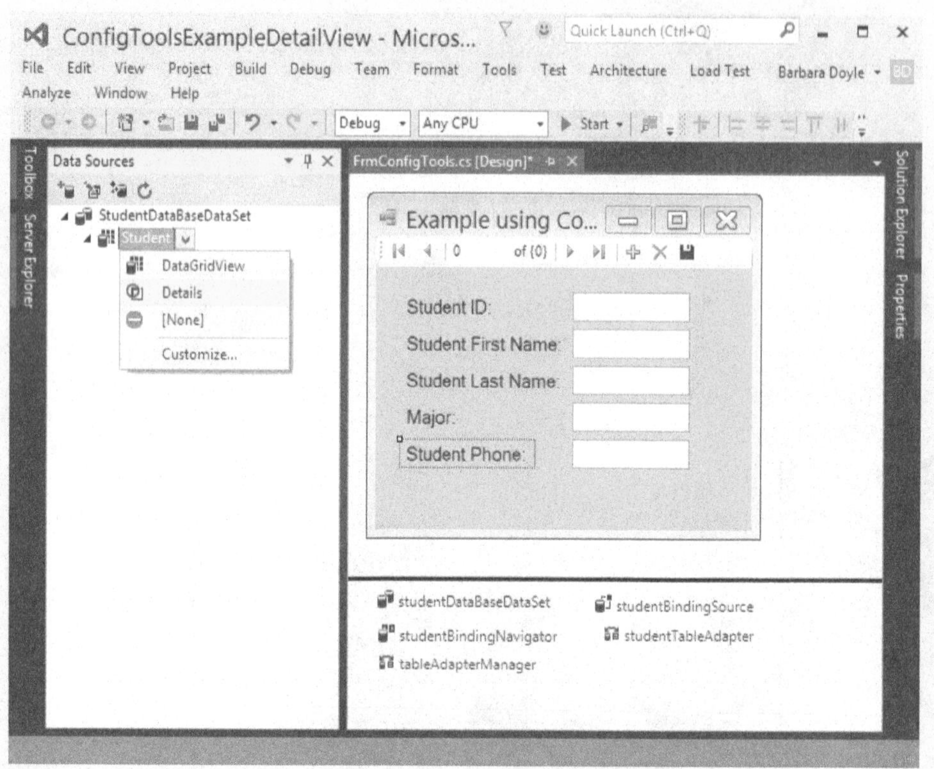

FIGURE 14-34 Details view

If you select the `Label` `object`, you can change its `Text` property from the **Properties** window. You do not have to drag the full set of columns; you can pick and choose from the **Data Sources** window and selectively drag the columns of interest.

ADDING CONTROLS FROM THE TOOLBOX

Using the **Toolbox**, you can also drag any control onto your form. When you select controls from the **Toolbox**, as opposed to using the **Data Sources** window, you will need to set the `DataSource` and `DisplayMember` properties for those controls. These properties can be set in the same way as the `Text` property for a control is set. Select the control on the form with the **Properties** window visible, and type a new value for the property. The value for the `DataSource` is the name of the table within the dataset object. The property value for the `DisplayMember` is the column within the table you want to display. You can also use the smart tag on the control to set the properties.

Figure 14-35 shows the output from the `ConfigToolsExampleDetailView` application.

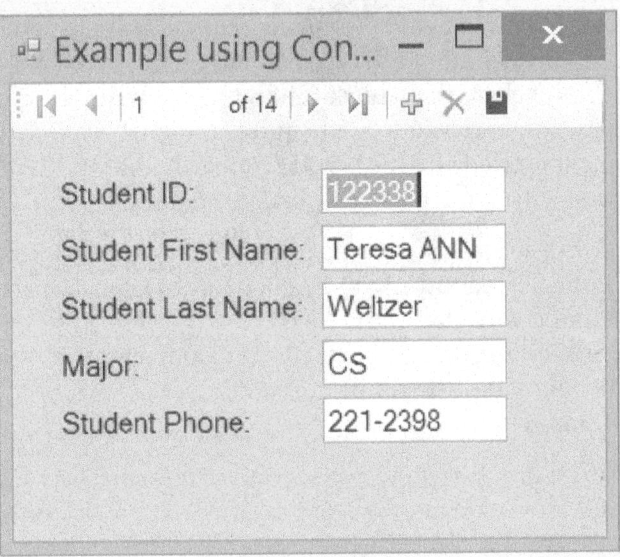

FIGURE 14-35 Output from ConfigToolsExampleDetailView application

No actual program statements were written for these applications. The **Data Source Configuration** tool was used to identify the data source tables. The data-bound controls were placed on the form from the **Data Sources** window. The **DataSet Designer** was used to create the relation between the tables. The `TableAdapter` populated the `DataSet object` with the identified tables' data. `Text` properties for the form and data-bound labels were changed. All of this was completed using the tools of the integrated development environment.

As stated previously, when you attach a database file to your application, you might receive a message asking whether you want a local copy of your database stored with the application. Having a local copy works fine if you only intend to display the data. It also makes testing easier. However, if you are making changes to the database and want the database changes to be available to other applications, you do not want to make a local copy of it.

Language-Integrated Query (LINQ)

As you experienced in this chapter, there is a difference between how programming languages and databases represent and manipulate data. Programs manipulate data as objects, but often information needed by the program is stored in a relational database. As you saw previously, in order for programming languages to access information in databases, they use APIs that require queries to be specified as strings.

When you write the string for the query, there are no checks for errors at compile time or help from IntelliSense. To further complicate the situation, there are slight differences in the query for each type of data source: SQL databases, Access databases, and so on. LINQ changes that by enabling you to write the query using the programming language. It allows you to write queries against strongly typed collections of objects by using language keywords and familiar operators. With LINQ you can query and manipulate data independently of data sources.

LINQ was released as a part of the .NET Framework language specifications for C# 3.0. The goal in adding LINQ to .NET was to provide a general-purpose query facility to the framework that could be used with not only relational data sources, but also XML data, and any class of data that implemented the `IEnumerable<T>` `interface`. IEnumerable supports simple iteration over a collection. For example, arrays implement IEnumerable.

In Chapter 2, you were introduced to a number of new contextual keywords. Fourteen of these contextual keywords are called **Query Contextual Keywords**. These 14 are redisplayed in Table 14-8.

TABLE 14-8 Query contextual keywords

`Ascending`	`by`	`descending`	`equals`	`from`	`group`	`in`
`into`	`join`	`Let`	`on`	`orderby`	`select`	`where`

Recall that contextual keywords have special meaning only when used in a given context. Other times they may be used as simple identifiers. The query contextual keywords shown in Table 14-8 are not considered reserved words in C#.

Query Expressions

When you use one of the contextual keywords in a query expression, they have a special meaning. Most query expressions begin with a `from` clause and end with either a `select` or `group` clause. Each `from` clause identifies the data source and a range variable. The range variable is similar to the iteration variable that you used with a `foreach` statement. A `where` clause is added to filter or exclude items from the result. The other operators shown in Table 14-8 can be added to the expression.

The standard query operators defined in the `System.Linq` `namespace` enable you to select, filter, aggregate, and partition data from any type that implements the `IEnumerable` `interface`. These operators form the backbone for the query functions. Table 14-9 provides a short description of some of the operators. Some are the same as the contextual keywords, but there are additional operators listed.

TABLE 14-9 Some of the LINQ query operators

Query clause keyword	Description
`select`	In a tabular format, picks specific columns and does a projection on the collection retrieving specific data members that make up the object. If no data members are identified, all are returned. Selection creates an object of a different type, which has either some or as many data members as the original class.
`where`	Returns specific objects that meet a set of predicate rules. Objects that do not match the rule are filtered away.
`sum` / `min` / `max` / `average` / `aggregate`	Retrieves a certain numeric value from each element in the collection and uses it to find the sum, minimum, maximum, average, or aggregate values of all the elements in the collection, respectively.
`join` / `groupjoin`	Performs an inner join on two collections by using matching keys for objects in each collection. Like the select operator, the results are instantiations of a different class.
`take` / `takewhile`	The take operator retrieves the first n objects from a collection; takewhile uses a predicate to select those objects that match the predicate.
`skip` / `skipwhile`	Does the opposite of take and takewhile. They both skip the first n objects from a collection, or those objects that match a predicate.
`orderby` / `thenby`	Used to specify the sort order of the elements in a collection according to some key. The default is ascending order. To specify descending order, use the orderbydescending operator. The thenby operator and thenbydescending enables you to do a second sort within the first ordering.
`reverse`	Reverses a collection.
`groupby`	Takes a delegate that extracts a key value and returns a collection of IGrouping<Key, Values> objects, for each distinct key value. The IGrouping objects can then be used to enumerate all the objects for a particular key value.
`distinct`	Removes duplicate instances of a key value from a collection.
`union` / `intersect` / `except`	Used to perform a union, intersection, and difference operation on two sequences, respectively.
`count`	Retrieves the number of elements in the given collection.

Because arrays implement the `IEnumerator interface`, you can use the standard query operators to process the contents of an array. The program shown in Example 14-28 illustrates using a query expression to iterate through an array collection.

EXAMPLE 14-28

```
using System;
using System.Console;
using System.Collections.Generic;
using System.Linq;

namespace LinqArrayExample
{
     class LinqArrayExample
     {
          static void Main(string[] args)
          {
               string[] nameArray = {"Wong", "Abi", "Fredrick",
                     "Davis","Howard","Abbott","Fang","Erlanger",
                     "Halcomb","George","King","Doyle","Mitchell",
                     "Ralph","Barry"};

               IEnumerable<string> queryResult =
                    from aName in nameArray
                         where aName.Length > 5
                         orderby aName descending
                    select aName;
               foreach (string name in queryResult)
                         WriteLine(name);
               ReadKey( );
          }
     }
}
```

In Example 14-28, the identifier `aName` is used with the `from` clause to traverse through the `nameArray` array. It works similarly, to how name works with the `foreach` statement. It is not necessary to increment an index to iterate through the collection. The `where` clause filters out records, so only those names that have more than five characters are added to the `queryResult`. The `select` clause specifies what from the collection will be returned. For this example, it is returning the `aName` element, unchanged in descending order.

The output from Example 14-28 is the list containing `Mitchell`, `Howard`, `Halcomb`, `George`, `Fredrick`, `Erlanger`, and `Abbott`.

Implicitly Typed Local Variables

With Example 14-28, you will receive an error message, if you declare `queryResult` as a `string` data type or even as a `string` array data type. The error message indicates that you cannot implicitly convert from an `OrderedEnumerable <string>` to a `string` argument. With Example 14-28, a generic reference was declared, `IEnumerable <string>`. Another option would be to declare an implicitly typed variable to hold the result. An implicitly typed local variable is strongly typed just as if you had declared the type yourself, but the compiler determines the type. The keyword `var` is used for this type of declaration. As you have read about the var data type in Chapter 11. `var` would replace `IEnumerable<string>`. This is illustrated in Example 14-29.

EXAMPLE 14-29

```
var queryResult =
    from aName in nameArray
         where aName.Length > 5
         orderby aName descending
    select aName;
```

Recall that the keyword `var` indicates the type that will be determined from the expression on the right side of the equal symbol. Nothing else was changed in the program. The output from Example 14-29 is the same as that from Example 14-28.

In addition to using the query operators for collections such as arrays, the query operators can be used to query, project, and filter data in relational databases.

LINQ WITH DATABASES

After a connection is made to a data source, instead of embedding an SQL statement in a `string` argument or using the Query Builder to store SQL statements with the SELECT, INSERT, DELETE, or UPDATE SQL commands, you can include your query expression directly in your C# program. In Example 14-30, a database was attached to the application following the steps described earlier using the **Data Source Configuration Wizard**.

NOTE From the **Project** menu option, **Add New Data Source** was selected. The **DataSet Database Model** was used. When prompted to **Choose Your Data Connection**, the **New Connection** button enables you to select an Access database and browse to its location. For this example, the `member` database was selected. The Access database was copied into the current project. Tables was selected when prompted to **Choose Database Object**. Then the **Data Sources** option was selected from the **View Other Windows** menu.

A DataSet object is displayed from the **Data Sources** window. Expanding the **Table** node shows its data members. When you drag a table from the **Data Sources window**, code is automatically generated. By default, objects are instantiated for a DataGridView object and each record from the table is used to populate the DataGridView object. Objects of the TableAdapter, DataSet, TableAdapterManager, and TableBindingSource are also placed in the component tray, displayed below the form in design view. When you drag the table onto the form, code is automatically generated to load data into the DataSet's table. It is placed in the FormLoad( ) event handler. Example 14-30 shows the auto-generated code.

EXAMPLE 14-30

```
this.memberTableTableAdapter.Fill(this.memberDataSet.memberTable);
```

The code tied to the DataGridView object retrieves all rows from the table. To illustrate use of LINQ with databases, the DataGridView object and the navigation bar were removed and a ListBox object is dragged over to the form. Instead of using an SQL statement to retrieve the data, a query expression traverses through the table producing a list of items to populate the listbox. The query expression is shown in Example 14-31. Basically, it uses the same query expression that was illustrated in Example 14-29. The primary difference was in the identification of the data source.

EXAMPLE 14-31

```
private void FrmLinqExample_Load(object sender, EventArgs e)
{
     // TODO: This line of code loads data into the
     // memberDataSet.MemberTable table.
     // You can move, or remove it, as needed.
     this.memberTableTableAdapter.Fill(
          this.memberDataSet.memberTable);
     var memberResults =
             from member inthis.memberDataSet.memberTable
                  where member.LastName.Length > 4
                  orderby member.LastName
             select member;
     foreach (var aRecord in memberResults)
                  this.lstBxResult.Items.Add(aRecord.FirstName +
                  " " + aRecord.LastName);
}
```

The output from Example 14-31 is illustrated in Figure 14-36. Notice how the keyword `var` is used to create the memberResults collection. Then, `var` is used with the `foreach` loop to traverse through the collection and add the items to the listbox.

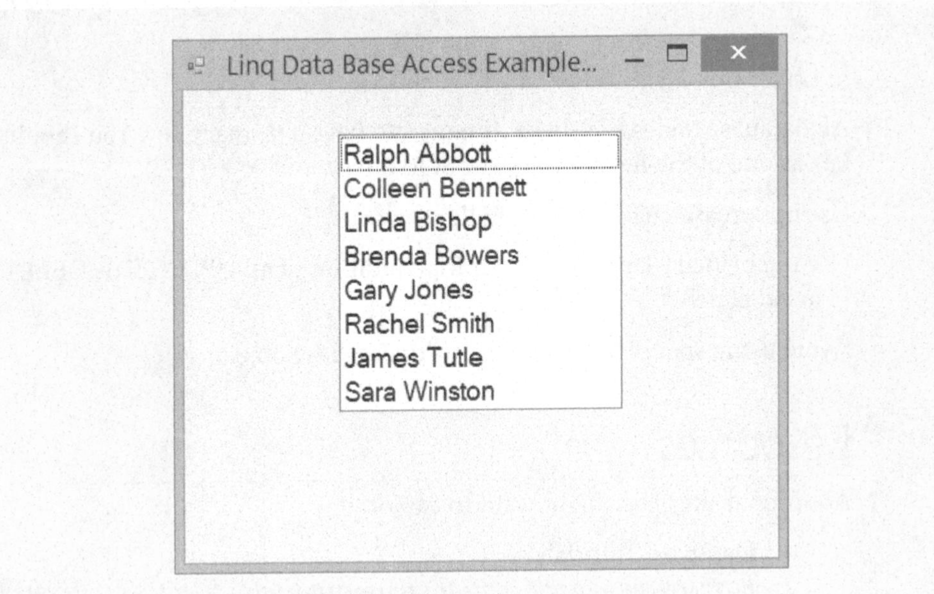

FIGURE 14-36 LINQ database output

LINQ TO SQL

The LINQ to SQL is used to query SQL Server databases. SQL Server data resides on a remote server and includes a querying engine. Since SQL Server database management systems store the data as relational data and LINQ works with data encapsulated in objects, the two representations must be mapped to one another. For this reason, LINQ to SQL defines a mapping framework. The mapping is done by defining classes that correspond to the tables in the database. LINQ-to-SQL defined attributes, like primary keys, are specified. The **DLinq** (also referred to as LINQ to SQL) is specifically the version of LINQ that focuses on querying data from relational data sources. **XLinq** (LINQ to XML) is the aspect of LINQ that is geared toward querying XML data.

Visual Studio includes a mapping designer that can be used to create the mapping between the data schemas in the object and the relational domain. It automatically creates the corresponding classes from a database schema.

14

Many books are written describing how to use C# and the .NET Framework to access databases. This chapter introduced you to the program statements required to make the connections between your program and different data sources. It included program statements that could be used to retrieve and update data from a database. It also focused on how you could use some of the many visual tools available with the IDE to retrieve and display data. With the prevalence of data-driven applications today, you are strongly encouraged to continue your exploration on the topic.

Coding Standards

All database tables should be designed to have a primary key. You should retrieve the key as one of the fields from your SQL query.

Use uppercase characters for SQL keywords.

Use the primary key in the WHERE condition of an UPDATE or DELETE statement to avoid errors.

Avoid using spaces within the name of database objects.

Resources

Additional sites you might want to explore:

- Database Tutorials—
http://www.quackit.com/database/tutorial/
- Accessing Data in Visual Studio—
http://msdn.microsoft.com/en-us/library/wzabh8c4.aspx
- Access Tutorials—
http://databases.about.com/od/tutorials/Tutorials.htm
- Access Connection Strings—
http://www.connectionstrings.com/access/
- 101 LINQ Samples—
http://msdn.microsoft.com/en-us/vcsharp/aa336746.aspx
- LINQ to SQL: .NET Language-Integrated Query for Relational Data—
http://msdn.microsoft.com/en-us/library/bb425822.aspx

QUICK REVIEW

1. .NET includes a number of ActiveX Data Object (ADO.NET) classes that can be used to retrieve, manipulate, and update data in databases.
2. One of the most significant advancements of ADO.NET is the ease with which it is able to work in a disconnected manner—that is, the database table(s) can be retrieved to a client or local machine.

3. To retrieve data from a database programmatically, you must first connect to the database and then use a mechanism to retrieve the data.
4. Four data providers are included with .NET. To connect to an Access database, use the `OleDb` data provider.
5. Connection strings are vendor specific. The syntax for the string begins with a provider or data source name such as
   `"Provider=Microsoft.ACE.OLEDB.12.0;" +`
   `"Data Source=member.accdb";`
6. After connecting, one way to retrieve records programmatically from the database is to issue a SQL query. The `OleDbCommand class` is used to hold the SQL statement.
7. For simple read-only access to the database, .NET includes a data reader class that can be used to read rows of data from a database.
8. The `OleDbDataReader class` allows read-only forward retrieval of data from the database. The data is not cached in memory. By default, only one row is stored in memory at a time when the `OleDbDataReader class` is implemented.
9. To process the data using a data reader, you declare an object of the `OleDbDataReader class` and then call the `ExecuteReader( )` method of the `OleDbCommand class` to build the `OleDbDataReader object`.
10. To position the `OleDbDataReader object` onto the row of the first record retrieved, you use the `Read( )` method of the `OleDbDataReader class`. The `Read( )` method is also used to advance to the next record after the previous one is processed.
11. To understand the processing of the data retrieved using the `Read( )` method, you can think about what is retrieved from a single access attempt using a data reader object as a one-dimensional table consisting of the fields from that one row.
12. You need to close the reader object and the connection object to unlock the database so that others can access it.
13. ADO.NET does not require that you keep a continuous live connection to the database. This is accomplished in .NET using a dataset. A dataset is a cache of records retrieved from some data source that may contain one or more tables from the data source.
14. Using the `DataAdapter object` with the `Fill( )` and/or `Update( )` methods eliminates the need to open and close the connections. Connections are opened and closed automatically when the `Fill( )` or `Update( )` methods are called.
15. Adapters are used to exchange data between a database source and a dataset object.

16. The `OleDbCommandBuilder` object automatically generates SQL statements for updates to the database. It is usable for queries involving one table.
17. The `DataGrid` object is a structure that is divided into rows and columns and can be used to store dataset objects. The `DataGrid` object allows you to change values, or delete or insert new records.
18. To tie the `DataGrid` object to the dataset, the `SetDataBinding( )` method of the `DataGrid` class is used.
19. The `DataGridView` class provides `DataGrid`-like control with added functionality. One way to customize the `DataGridView` control is to click on its smart tag glyph.
20. The **Data Sources** window allows you to drag items (tables and/or columns) onto your form.
21. A typed dataset defines a schema that exposes the tables and their columns as object properties.
22. The **DataSet Designer** enables you to set relationships between tables and add additional queries to your application.
23. To create a new SQL Server database from within Visual Studio, use the **Server Explorer** window. To add tables, right-click on the **Table** and select **Add New Table** from the shortcut menu. Select **Show Table Data** to preview the data.
24. The connection string can be saved to an `App.config` file.
25. The `BindingNavigator` class is normally paired with a `BindingSource` control to enable you to move through data records and interact with them.
26. TableAdapters are designer-generated components that provide a communication link between an application and a database.
27. The **DataSet Designer** is used to create and modify datasets, table adapters, and their queries. To start the designer, double-click a dataset in the **Solution Explorer** window or right-click on the dataset in the **Data Sources** window.
28. Use the **Query Builder** to write the SQL `SELECT`, `INSERT`, `DELETE`, and `UPDATE` statements.
29. The SQL `INNER JOIN` clause used with a `SELECT` statement enables you to retrieve results from two or more tables.
30. With Access, create a parent-child relationship between the tables, using the **DataSet Designer**, to enable data to be retrieved from multiple tables.
31. LINQ enables you to write queries against strongly typed collections of objects by using language keywords and familiar operators.
32. LINQ provides a query facility that can be used with relational data sources, XML data, and any class of data that implemented the `IEnumerable<T>` interface.

33. Most query expressions begin with a `from` clause and end with either a `select` or `group` clause.
34. The keyword `var` indicates that the type will be determined from the expression on the right side of the equal symbol.

EXERCISES

1. An in-memory representation of multiple rows and columns of data from the database is stored in what type of object?
   a. data provider
   b. data reader
   c. datagrid
   d. dataset
   e. data adapter
2. All of the following are examples of ADO.NET data providers except:
   a. OLE DB
   b. Oracle
   c. ODBC
   d. Sql Server
   e. Access
3. Which of the following is the class name of a grid-like structure used to display data from a database?
   a. ComboBox
   b. ListBox
   c. DataGridView
   d. Grid
   e. GridData
4. Databases store information in records, fields, and:
   a. data providers
   b. grids
   c. columns
   d. tables
   e. commands

5. The core classes available with each data provider include all of the following except:
   a. Connection
   b. DataAdapter
   c. Command
   d. DataSet
   e. DataReader

6. Each data provider class is grouped and accessible through its:
   a. namespace
   b. database
   c. data grid
   d. provider
   e. system

7. Which of the following is a valid SQL statement that retrieves all four columns from the customer table?
   a. SELECT ALL FROM customer
   b. SELECT * FROM customer
   c. SELECT customer
   d. SELECT,,,, FROM customer
   e. SELECT @@@@ FROM customer

8. Parameters for SQL Server SQL statements are written slightly different from those written for an Access database. With SQL Server, a parameter is indicated using:
   a. @ followed by an identifier
   b. @ without an identifier
   c. ? followed by an identifier
   d. ? without an identifier
   e. a params keyword

9. The SQL clause that can be added to a SELECT statement to retrieve data from multiple tables is:
   a. BETWEEN
   b. INNER JOIN
   c. CROSS CONNECTION
   d. WHERE
   e. UPDATE

10. The following namespaces (System.Data.OleDB, System.Data.SqlClient, System.Data.Odbc, System.Data.OracleClient) include classes for different:
    a. data providers
    b. file streams
    c. ADO.NET applications
    d. databases
    e. data readers

11. For read-only access to databases, which ADO.NET class is used?
    a. DataSet
    b. DataAdapter
    c. CommandBuilder
    d. Connection
    e. DataReader

12. To provide access to an Access database management system, which data provider is used?
    a. System.Data.OleDb
    b. System.Data.SqlClient
    c. System.Data.Odbc
    d. System.Data.OracleClient
    e. Microsoft ACE.OLEDB.12.0

13. Which class is used with the DataSet class to facilitate using a disconnected database?
    a. DataAdapter
    b. DataReader
    c. Command
    d. OleDbConnection
    e. Fill

14. To avoid writing additional SQL statements to update a live database, you instantiate an object of which class?
    a. DataAdapter
    b. DataReader
    c. Connection
    d. CommandBuilder
    e. DataGrid

15. To release the database so that it can be used by other applications, which method should be invoked?
    a. ReleaseDb( )
    b. Release( )
    c. StopAccess( )
    d. Close( )
    e. none of the above

16. To retrieve specific records from a database, you could create a new query and have it stored as a method using an object of the ______________ class.
    a. DataSet
    b. DataProvider
    c. TableAdapter
    d. Connection
    e. Command

17. Which method is used to originally populate a data-bound control?
    a. `Dataset Fill( )` method
    b. `Dataset Update( )` method
    c. `TableAdapter Fill( )` method
    d. `BindingNavigator Save( )` method
    e. `PageLoad( )` event-handler method
18. Which database wizard in Visual Studio enables you to connect to a database and automatically populate a DataSet object using a TableAdapter object?
    a. Data Source Configuration
    b. Data Source
    c. Query Builder
    d. DataSet Designer
    e. TableAdapter Query Configuration
19. Which window is used in Visual Studio to display dataset tables so they can be dragged and dropped onto the form?
    a. Server Explorer
    b. Properties
    c. DataSet Designer
    d. Data Sources
    e. Solution Explorer
20. A connection string contains:
    a. a using directive
    b. the name of the data source
    c. the version number of database management system
    d. the list of fields in the database
    e. an SQL statement

---

21. Explain how the dataset, table adapter, and data grid objects are used to update a database.

22. Write SQL statements for the following:
    a. Retrieve all partNumber and partDescription columns from a Parts table that has 15 different columns.
    b. Retrieve records from a Parts table for partNumbers 1000 through 2000. Display the partDescription only.
    c. Insert a new record into a Customer table. Store the following values in the columns: LName=Osprey, FName=Teola, CNumber=23456. The columns are ordered as follows: CNumber, LName, FName.
23. What happens when you drag a dataset table from the **Data Sources** window onto a blank form?
24. How can you have controls (other than the default **Data Sources** window controls) display data from a database table?
25. How does a table adapter differ from a data adapter?

PROGRAMMING EXERCISES

1. Create a small BankAccount database with one table storing account details. The Account table should have fields for account number, customer last and first names, and current balance. The type of database (SQL Server or Access) will be determined by your instructor. Populate the table with 8–10 records. Design and create a user interface that will enable you to display all customer records.
2. Create a small Family database with one table to include data about members of your family. Include data fields such as first name, last name, type of relationship, hometown, and age. Include one field that uniquely identifies each record, such as a family member number. You can be creative with the family member number or use the auto-generated number from the database. Populate the database with members of your family. Be sure to include data about yourself in the table. Place at least 10 records in your database table, even if it is necessary to make up information. Write a C# program to display all of the data that appears in the database table on a data grid.
3. Using the database created in Programming Exercise 2, modify your solution to only display the names of the members of your family in a data grid. Dock the grid so that it fills the form. Change the color of the data grid columns, increase the size of the font, choose appropriate headings for your columns, and format the grid control so that it is professionally aesthetically appealing.

4. Using the database created in Programming Exercise 2, write a C# program to only display the names of the members of your family who are over 21 years of age. Display their name, age, and relationship to you. Provide an appropriate heading for the displayed items on the form and format the grid control.

5. Using the database created in Programming Exercise 2, write a C# program to display the names and type of relationship of the members of your family who live in the same hometown as you do. Do not include yourself in the query result. It may be necessary for you to go back into your database and modify some of the records for testing purposes. Display your results in text boxes as opposed to a data grid. Provide appropriate headings and labels.

6. Create a small Sports database with two tables: Team and Athlete. The Team table should include fields for the type of team (e.g., basketball), coach's name (both last and first), and the season the sport is most active (S for spring, F for Fall, or B for both). The Athlete table should include fields for student number, student first and last names, and type of sport. Use the same identifier for type of sport in both tables to enable the tables to be related and linked. Populate the tables with sporting teams from your school. The type of database (SQL Server or Access) will be determined by your instructor. Write a C# program that displays information about each team, including the names of the athletes.

7. Create a Books database to include two tables: BookTable and CourseBookTable. The BookTable table should have fields for ISBN number, title, copyright date, primary author, publisher, and number of pages. The CourseBookTable table should have fields for course number and ISBN. Populate the tables with books in your current collection, including the books you are using for your classes. Books that are not associated with a specific course can be placed in the table with a FUN course number. The type of database (SQL Server or Access) will be determined by your instructor. Write a C# program to display the course number (or FUN) and the ISBN and name of the book on the same screen.

8. Create a small database to include customer data. Include the customer numbers, customer names, and customer directional locations. Place at least eight records in the database. For the customer directional location field, use the designations of N for North, S for South, and so on. The type of database (SQL Server or Access) will be determined by your instructor. Write a C# program to only display the names of all customers. Do not use the database configuration wizard for this application; write program statements.

9. Using the database created in Programming Exercise 8, write a C# program to display the customer number and name in a data grid. Format the grid control so that it is professionally aesthetically appealing. Allow the user to add records to the database. If your designed solution involves the use of a disconnected database, post the changes back to the live database. Check the database records to make sure that the changes have been made. For an added challenge, write program statements, as opposed to using the database configuration tools wizard.

10. Using the database created in Programming Exercise 8, write a C# program that retrieves records from the customer table and displays them in a grid control. Allow the user to select an entry from the data grid and display the values selected in text boxes with appropriate labels. Display the corresponding customer area for the one selected as full text (i.e., display West instead of W, which appears in the database). For an added challenge, write program statements, as opposed to using the database configuration tools wizard.

CHAPTER 15

© zeljkodan/Shutterstock.com

Web-Based Applications

IN THIS CHAPTER, YOU WILL:

- Discover how Web-based applications differ from Windows applications
- Use ASP.NET to create Web applications
- Develop and configure Web Forms pages
- Learn about the different types of controls that can be added to Web applications
- Add HTML and Web Forms server controls to Web applications
- Add validation, custom, and composite controls to verify user input, display calendars, and connect to database tables
- Learn how mobile applications for smart devices are developed using Visual Studio

In previous chapters, you learned how easy it is to develop graphical user interfaces for Windows applications using C# and the drag-and-drop construction approach of Visual Studio. In this chapter, you discover that this same approach can be used to develop applications for the Web. You learn how the design of Web-based applications differs from Windows applications. You discover the differences between HTML and Web server controls. You learn what a Web service is and how to write one. This chapter also includes an introduction to mobile applications.

Web-based applications are often data driven. In Chapter 14, you learned about the rich set of classes that are used to access and update data stored in database tables. You learned about data providers, and the connection, command, data reader, and data adapter core classes included within each data provider. You use these ADO.NET classes with the Web applications you develop. You learn how to use validation controls to check a user's input values. You learn how to add calendar controls to your web pages. By the time you complete this chapter, you are creating very sophisticated, highly interactive, data-driven Web applications.

Web-Based Applications

A Web-based application runs within an Internet browser—which means it is designed to be accessible to multiple users, run over different platforms, and deliver the same content to every user. A **Web application** is simply a collection of one or more related files or components stored on a Web server. Web applications are also called **Web sites**. A **Web server** is software that hosts or delivers the Web application. The hardware on which the Web server software is loaded is often called a Web server, but it is the software that makes the equipment special and thus enables the computer to be called a server.

Web Programming Model

The programming model for web pages is somewhat different from Windows applications, especially in terms of the interaction with users. For example, `MessageBox` dialog boxes, commonly used with Windows applications, are not used with Web applications. Their output is displayed on the server computer instead of at the client computer requesting the page. Messages to users accessing a web page are normally displayed through the `Label object` or other objects on the page.

Each request to view a web page requires a **round-trip to the server** on which the page is stored. This simply means that the user requests the page via Hypertext Transfer Protocol (HTTP) by typing the Web address, the **Uniform Resource Locator (URL)**, into a Web browser. That request is forwarded to the Web server on which the page is stored. The page is then sent back as a Hypertext Markup Language (HTML) document where it is **rendered** (converted from HTML) to a formatted page on the client computer that requested the page.

Second and subsequent requests for the page require a postback to the server. But, not all events are automatically posted back to the server when an event is triggered. Some events such as the `SelectedIndexChanged` or `CheckedChanged` events for `ListBox` and `RadioButton` objects are queued, and their event-handler methods are not executed until an event that causes a postback to the server is fired. `ButtonClick` events are one of the few events that cause an automatic postback.

Every postback trip to the server creates a new object. This causes web pages to be **stateless**—meaning that they do not retain their values from one trip to the Web server to the next. Values that you type into `TextBox` objects, for example, are not automatically saved and redisplayed when a page is sent back to a client computer. Second and subsequent requests for the page may require programmatically retrieving and storing input values and then sending them back to the control when the page is sent back for redisplay on the client computer. Thus, the Web programming model requires some important additional considerations. In the sections that follow, you learn how this model is implemented using C# and ASP.NET.

Static Pages

The files that make up a Web application end with file extensions such as .htm, .html, .jsp, .php, .asp, .aspx, .asmx, or the files may be image, video, music, or data files. Web application pages are commonly categorized as either static or dynamic. **Static web pages** do not require any processing on the client computer or by a Web server. They are previously created, reside on the server's hard drive, and basically are delivered as HTML or XHTML documents. Static web pages are suitable for the contents that rarely need to be updated. An HTML file contains formatting markup tags that are converted (rendered) into their displayed images by browser software such as Microsoft Internet Explorer. Figure 15-1 shows a static HTML document opened within Internet Explorer. As shown in the address bar of the browser software, the file ends with an .htm extension as part of its name.

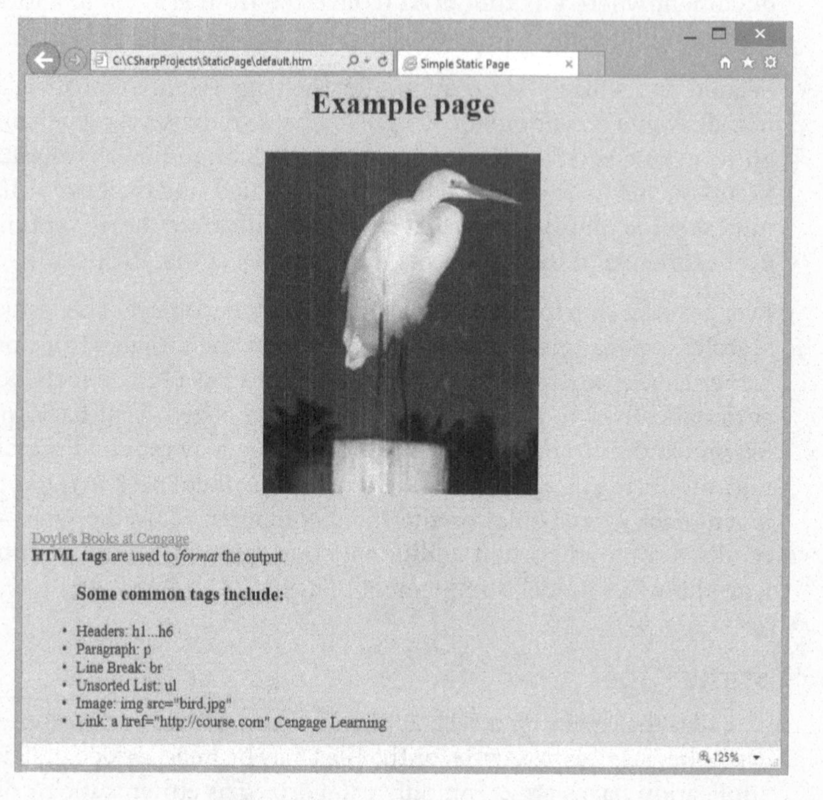

FIGURE 15-1 Output from a static web page

Example 15-1 shows the HTML file used to display the static web page for Figure 15-1.

EXAMPLE 15-1

```
<xhtml>                                   <!-- default.htm -->
  <head>
     <title>
       Simple Static Page
     </title>                             <!-- creates caption -->
  </head>                                 <!-- comments on right -->
<body bgColor="#aabbff">                  <!-- blue background -->
     <center>
     <h1> <p> Example page </p> </h1>
       <br/> <br/>                        <!-- break to next line-->
      <img src="bird.jpg" />
     </center>
       <br/> <br/>
```

15

```
        <a href="http://www.cengage.com/ + ...">
                Doyle's Books at Cengage</a>
        <br/>
        <strong>HTML tags</strong>        <!-- strong - bold-->
        are used to <em>format</em>       <!-- em - italic-->
        the output.
      <ul>                                <!-- unsorted list -->
         <h3>
            Some common tags include:
         </h3>
         <li>                             <!-- element in list -->
            Headers: h1. . .h6            <!-- h1 is the largest -->
         </li>                            <!-- h6 is the smallest -->
         <li>
           Paragraph: p                   <!-- text shown on page -->
         </li>
         <li>
            Line Break: br
         </li>
         <li>
            Unsorted List: ul             <!--ul     and li -->
         </li>
         <li>
            Image: img src="bird.jpg"     <!-- image-->
         </li>                            <!-- end list element -->
         <li>
            Link: a href="http://course.com"
                     Cengage Learning     <!--link      -->
         </li>
       </ui>                              <!-- end unsorted list -->
   </body>
</xhtml>
```

NOTE

XHTML stands for **Extensible Hypertext Markup Language**. XHTML is HTML written as an XML application. It is a stricter, cleaner HTML. With XHTML, all tags or elements are written using lowercase characters. All elements must be closed and properly nested under a single <html> root tag. HTML allows sloppy syntax and assumes that the output will be on a traditional computer running a browser. XHTML cleans up the syntax and makes it easier to display graphical material on not only traditional computers running browsers but also devices such as smart phones and tablets with limited display capability.

The Web server does not have to process any of the statements in Example 15-1. Static pages are client-side applications and, as the name implies, they involve no interaction with the user. The pages are simply displayed as static material on the client's Web browser. Rendering of the pages can occur at the client (local workstation) where the pages are displayed. The Web server simply delivers the requested page as an HTML document.

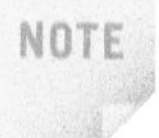

The static page example conforms to XHTML standards. One of the tags used in the example to produce Figure 15-1 is center. The center tag was used to center the heading and image. The center tag is not included in the list of common tags because it is on the deprecated list, which means that on future XHTML versions it may be dropped. Recommendations are included in HTML 4.01 and later versions that Cascading Style Sheets (CSSs) be used to format objects that should be centered. You read more about CSS later in this chapter.

Some Web applications require processing before pages are displayed. Sometimes, information needs to be pulled from a database before the page is rendered. One common way to add functionality to a page is to include code written in a scripting language as part of the HTML file. This creates **dynamic websites**—pages that enable the user to interact and see the result of their interaction. Dynamic websites are discussed in the following.

Dynamic Pages

Dynamic web pages involve processing in addition to rendering the formatting of HTML tags. One programming model for creating dynamic web pages is to extend the HTML file by including script code in the same file. The file may still be able to be executed on the client machine, without additional processing at the server level. In this case, the code that is embedded in the HTML document is called a **client-side script**, and it involves only **client-side processing**. Scripting languages such as JavaScript or ActionScript are often used for these Dynamic HTML (DHTML) and Flash pages.

JavaScript is not a subset of Java. There are some syntax similarities to Java, but it is not a full-featured programming language such as Java. **JScript** is Microsoft's implementation of JavaScript. Using these scripting languages, developers are able to take static pages and add functionality—creating dynamic web pages. JavaScript is one of the components of **AJAX** (Asynchronous JavaScript and XML). Ajax combines several programming and development technologies to create dynamic and interactive Web content. AJAX combines JavaScript with XHTML and CSS standards using XML.

NOTE

Scripting languages are often interpreted, instead of compiled, and the code is embedded directly into the HTML page.

JavaScript, JScript, VBScript, or any one of the other scripting languages could be used to write the embedded code for the HTML document. This code provides functionality beyond the formatting that the HTML tags provide. User input for Web applications is often validated using scripting code. When a request is sent to the server to display a page that contains server-side scripting, the page is interpreted (converted into binary form) and then the scripted code is run to get the output results. The output of the script code is merged with the static HTML output found in the page before sending the output back to the client computer that requested the page. Figure 15-2 illustrates this scenario. The client system requests a page using HTTP—sending the URL as part of the HTTP request. Behind the scenes, the script is executed on the server. The client receives a response back in the form of a displayed HTML document.

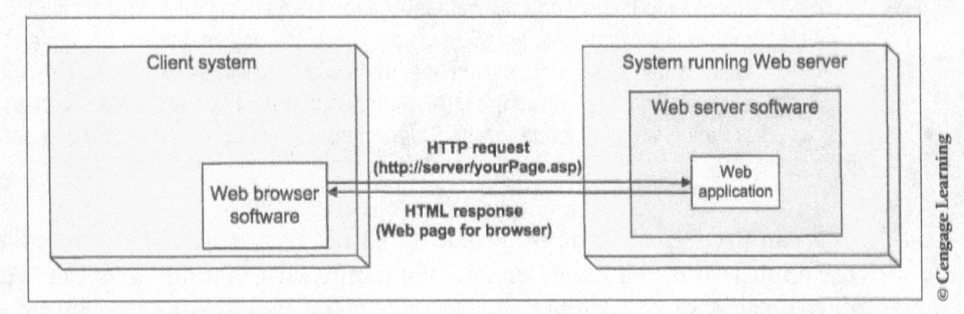

FIGURE 15-2 Server-side processing of a dynamic web page

Figure 15-2 illustrates a **client/server** type of relationship. The client requests a page; the server gets it ready by executing the scripts inside the HTML document; and, lastly, the client sees the result in the form of an HTML document. This is the way traditional ASP is used to enable dynamic web pages to be viewed on client computers. A newer model for Web development is included as part of .NET. That model is called ASP.NET and it is discussed in the following section.

NOTE **Server-side scripts** require the processing to be done at the server level before the page is delivered. PHP, Perl, Ruby on Rails, Python, and ColdFusion languages often use the Common Gateway Interface (CGI) to produce dynamic web pages. PHP is probably the most popular of the other server-side languages. According to Wikipedia in 2014, PHP was used as the server-side programming language on 82% of all websites whose server-side programming language was known. WordPress, Moodle, and the user-facing portion of Facebook were written in PHP.

ASP.NET

ASP.NET is a server-side Web application framework that enables dynamic web pages to be developed. ASP.NET is the successor to the Microsoft's Active Server Pages (ASP). **ASP.NET** is built on the Common Language Runtime (CLR), allowing programmers to write ASP.NET code using any supported languages such as C#. It is a programming model that includes a number of classes as part of the .NET Framework. These classes allow you to take full advantage of the features of the CLR and inheritance. You can use ADO.NET with ASP.NET applications to develop data-driven websites. Using Visual Studio and ASP.NET, you can design the user interface for the Web application using a drag-and-drop approach.

One way to identify an ASP Web application from an ASP.NET Web application is by looking at their file extensions. An ASP web page, which contains the HTML tags and the program logic written in a scripting language, ends with an .asp file extension. The ASP.NET web page file, which contains the HTML tags, ends with an .aspx file extension and includes no scripting language code for the program logic. This logic is stored in a separate file.

You can use Visual Basic or Visual C# to develop ASP.NET Web applications, and the applications you create run on the computer functioning as the Web server. To develop an ASP.NET application, Microsoft Internet Information Services (IIS) needs to be installed or, another option is to use the built-in ASP.NET Development Server. The ASP.NET Development Server works well for applications that are going to be run and tested only for the machine on which they are developed.

Visual Studio for Web Development

Visual Studio provides all the tools you need to build Web applications. The Web development platform is integrated into the Visual Studio IDE. You use a WYSIWYG (what you see is what you get), drag-and-drop approach, which is similar to that used to develop Windows applications. The software enables you to connect to databases and display data in data grid controls using tools and wizards similar to those used for Windows applications. You can run and debug web pages. The product also includes features that enable you to publish your applications on the Web.

NOTE

Students with valid school e-mail addresses can download a number of development software packages, including Visual Studio, for free at http://dreamspark.com/.

Visual Studio has a built-in ASP.NET Development Server for testing and running websites. The ASP.NET Development Server is an excellent tool for building and testing your site; however, the Development Server does not enable the site to be accessed by remote machines or multiple users. To enable this feature, IIS is required. IIS provides the software tools for managing the Web server. You do not have to work directly with IIS; most everything dealing with IIS happens behind the scenes.

With earlier versions of Visual Studio, ASP.NET applications typically were developed using IIS as a Web server, which often requires configuring and setting security permissions. You can continue to create websites that run under your local copy of IIS; however, there is another option. When you create a new Web application, you will see the option to create a File System website. When you select this option, it automatically uses the lightweight test server (ASP.NET Development Server). The File System feature enables you to store and run your Web application in any directory on your local machine. Using the ASP.NET Development Server is simpler and does not leave the system open to security attacks. It is probably the preferred method for classroom use. This File System option is used for the examples illustrated in this chapter.

ASP.NET Programming Models

There are several models used for building ASP.NET websites. You can use the **Model-View-Controller (MVC)**-based pattern or the Web Forms controls model. Both models now enable you to incorporate CSSs into the application. Each features advantages.

MVC enables you to separate the application into three attributes: the Model, the View, and the Controller. Within the Model core, information for the application is described—including the data and validation rules as well as the data access and aggregation logic. The View component encapsulates the presentation of the application and is described through HTML markup. The Controller core contains the control-flow logic, which describes the interaction between the Model and View to control the flow of information and the execution of the application. MVC is really a lower-level programming model. It does not provide higher-level abstractions such as widgets controls. It requires you to know HTML and HTTP more deeply. But, it allows you to use the full power of CSS and JavaScript.

The Web Forms model is the one you are more familiar with. It is closer to the Windows Forms event-based programming model. The **Web Forms model** enables you to use server controls, encapsulating HTML and CSS so dynamic applications can be created. It enables you to incorporate rich user interface controls, such as data grids, into your application. The Web Forms model does not require that you know

HTML and lets you easily use the drag-and-drop approach to development. SharePoint developers use this model to create websites. SharePoint enables you to share content and build websites using a browser-based collaboration. Since both the MVC and Web Forms models are using ASP.NET, you can actually choose to incorporate both models into your Web applications. The Web Forms model is what is used for examples in this chapter.

You have access to all of the Framework class library (FCL) classes and can drag and drop controls in the same manner you did when you created Windows applications. Instead of placing the controls on a Windows Forms page, the controls are dropped onto a Web Forms page.

The `System.Web.UI` `namespace` organizes the classes that are used to create .NET Web applications. This `namespace` includes a `Control` `class`, inherited by the `HTMLControl` and `WebControl` classes. Like the `Control` `class` in the `System.Windows.Forms` `namespace`, `Control` provides some common functionality for all classes that are derived from it. The `System.Web.UI` `namespace` also includes a `Page` `class`, which is instantiated when you create a Web application using Visual Studio.

Web Forms Page

Building ASP.NET Web applications using the Web Forms model involves many of the same concepts you learned when you built Windows applications. They are designed with the event-driven model, but there are fewer events. Websites are created using a Web Forms page. As opposed to dragging and dropping controls onto a Windows form, controls are dropped onto a Web Forms page. There are, however, some significant differences between a Windows and Web application.

When you build an ASP.NET Web application, two separate files are created. Both of these files must be available to the Web server for the page to be displayed. One of the files contains the visual HTML components, and the other contains the logic.

The file storing the logic is referred to as the **code-behind file**. The actual file storing the visual elements is the one referred to as the Web Forms page. This is the container file from which the controls are displayed. The Web Forms page contains static HTML tags and any ASP.NET server controls that have been added to the application. The programming logic resides in a separate file from the file containing the HTML tags. All the event-handler methods are stored in this code-behind file. This file contains the code that enables the user to interact with the page. The following section examines how these two files function when an application is built using Visual Studio.

ASP.NET Web Forms Site

When creating a Web application, instead of selecting **File, New Project** as was used with Windows applications, you select **New Web Site** from the **File** menu. You will notice that there are several installed templates shown in the middle pane in Figure 15-3.

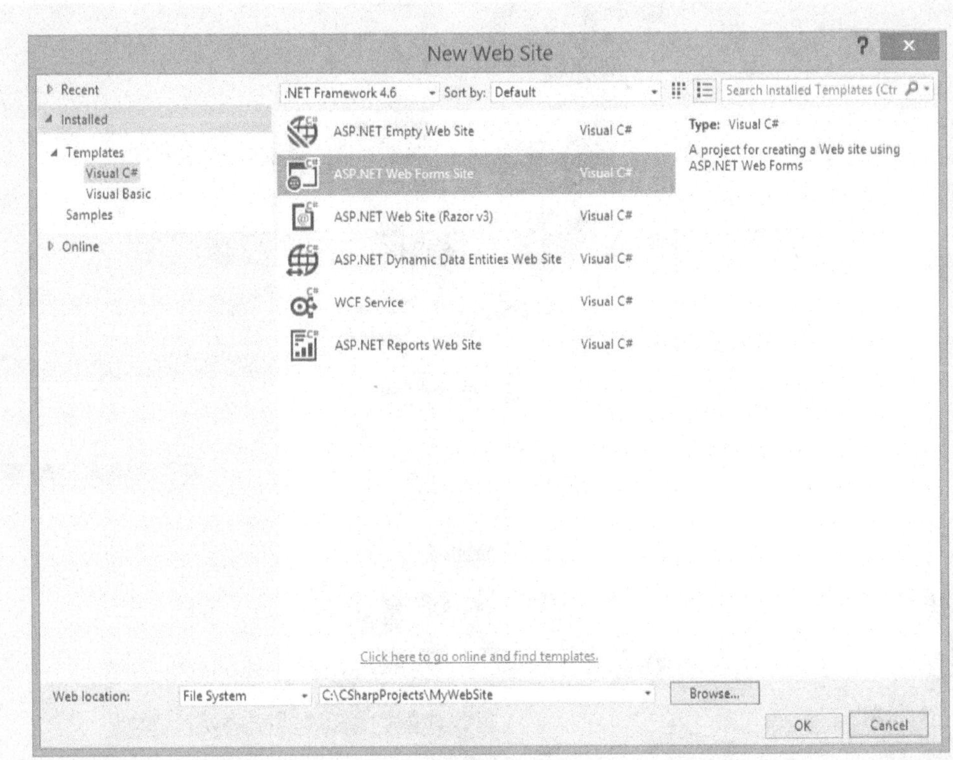

FIGURE 15-3 Web application template for ASP.NET

For this first example, the second option, **ASP.NET Web Forms Site** template is selected. When a new site is created using the **ASP.NET Web Forms Site** template, a number of files and directories are automatically created for you. It creates a website that you can go in and change to fit your needs. This Web Forms template includes features that provide a sleek and responsive look and feel that you can easily customize. Automatically included when you initially create a new project using this template are a Default.aspx web page, a master page, a CSS, login security that uses the ASP.NET membership system, and navigation with a menu control. All of these features are automatically added to the project when a new site is created. In addition, when you use this template to create a Web application, folders are automatically created to contain membership pages and CSS files. A data folder (`App_Data`) with permissions set that allow the file to be read and written to at run time is also added at the time an **ASP.NET Web Forms Site** Web application is created. Figure 15-4 shows what the website looks like before any changes are made. Both the **Register** and **Login** pages are functional and there is consistency among pages.

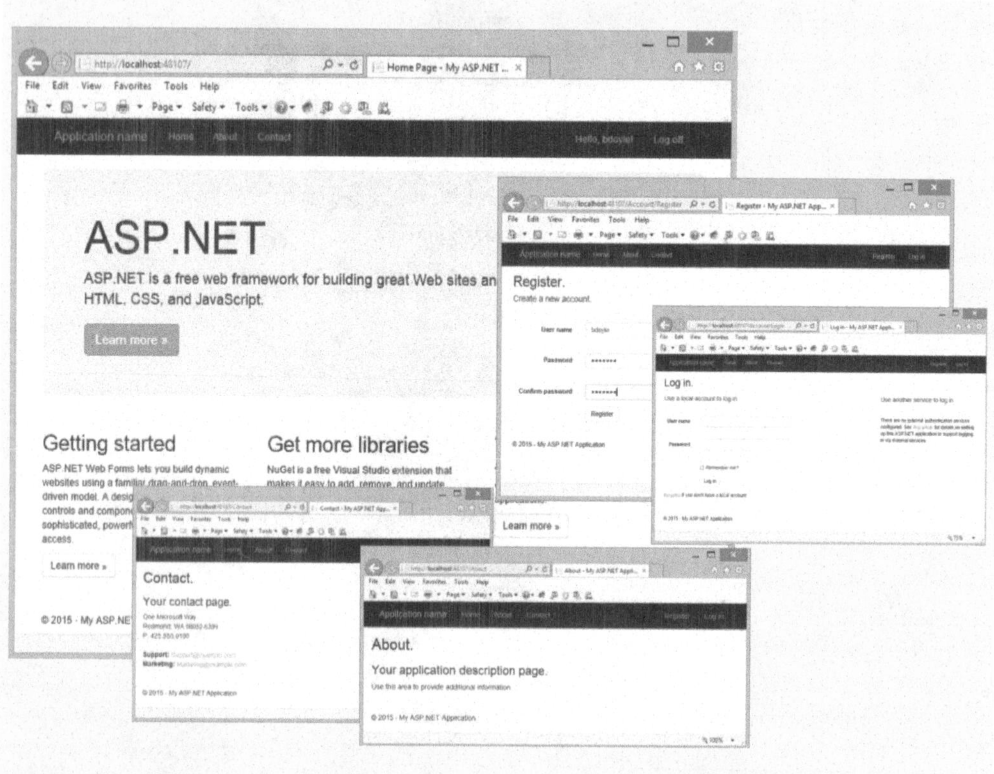

FIGURE 15-4 ASP.NET Web Forms Site

Figure 15-4 was shown to illustrate the robustness of the Web application from the initial selection of the template **ASP.NET Web Forms Site**. Notice that once a user selects the **Register** link, the user name is displayed on the other pages. **Login** changes to **logout**. There is consistent placement of the navigational menus and copyright at the bottom of each page. This is what you start with when a new site is created using the template **ASP.NET Web Forms Site**. The following sections examine some of the features.

Review Figure 15-3. Near the bottom-left corner of the **New Web Site** dialog window shown in Figure 15-3, a drop-down list appears with three options listed for **Web location**. **File System** is used for examples in this chapter. However, note that if you select **FTP**, the last option, you would identify a remote server that you gain access to using File Transfer Protocol. If you select **HTTP** for the File Location, the project is created at *http://localhost.* Whatever name you type for your project name following "http://" becomes the virtual directory name for the website. The files are physically stored at the default home directory for the Web application. Unless you change the **default home directory**, the files are stored at C:\Inetpub\wwwroot. In order to use the **HTTP** option, you need to have IIS components installed and run Visual Studio in the context of an administrative account on the development system.

The first two templates **ASP.NET Empty Web Site** and **ASP.NET Web Forms Site** follow the Web Forms model. The **ASP.NET Web Site (Razor v3)** adheres to the MVC model. The first option has no files or folders associated with it. The second option has a fully functional website that can be edited with your specific details. If you are willing to accept the template's design, you can have a website up quickly.

Selecting **File System**, as shown in Figure 15-3, enables you to **Browse** to the location on your machine where you want to store the files for the website. Visual Studio places the two solution files for the website at a different location from your specified **File Location** designation. A directory is created using the name you typed for the website, and the directory is placed (along with the two solution files) at the location you configured Visual Studio to store all your Visual Studio projects. The two solution files have the same name as the Web application; they end with file extensions of .sln and .suo. Using the **Tools, Options** menu option, you can change the settings for the storage location of your projects.

After a Web application is created, saved, and closed, it is also reopened differently from a Windows application. To reopen a Web application, select **File, Open Web Site** instead of **File, Open Project/Solution**. If you select **Local IIS**, you are shown the list of all Web applications (sites) stored at localhost (`C:\Inetpub\wwwroot`). When you select **File System** option, you are able to browse to the location where the Web application is stored. Unlike Windows applications where you open the .sln file, to reopen a Web application, simply select the folder that contains the Web application. You do not need to locate a specific file in the directory. All of the websites created for the rest of this chapter will be saved using the **File System** option. They were also created using the Visual Studio Development Server as opposed to IIS or IIS Express.

As with Windows applications you still have the option of reopening websites from the **Start Page** with the **Recent Project** selection.

WEB PAGE

Two files are created for each page when you build Web applications. Selecting **File, New Web Site, ASP.NET Web Forms Site** with the **File System** option selection enables you to specify where the website files should be stored on your local machine. The Source code file for the Default.aspx markup file is automatically opened when you first create a website as illustrated in Figure 15-5.

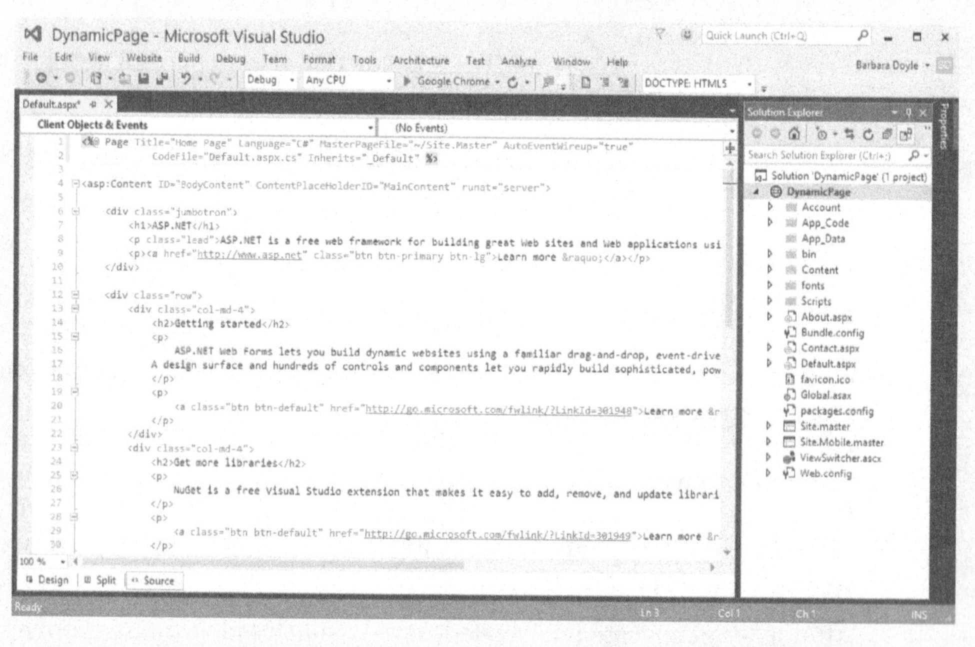

FIGURE 15-5 Source code for HTML file

In Figure 15-5, notice the three buttons, **Design**, **Split**, and **Source**, shown on the bottom-left corner. Initially, the `Default.aspx` file for the `DynamicPage` site is shown in source code; the **Source** button is selected. If you look ahead at Figure 15-6, it illustrates what is shown when the **Design** button is selected for the `Default.aspx` file before any changes are made. Nothing has been added to the file. This is all autogenerated from Visual Studio.

The file (ending in `.aspx`) shown in Figure 15-5 holds the HTML tags. You can view and directly edit the HTML source code here. The tags automatically generated by

Visual Studio are actually XHTML tags. They are referred to as HTML tags for the remainder of this chapter. Tags are automatically inserted when the website is created. The first two lines in the .aspx markup file are called directives. Directives are delimited with <% and %>. They provide information needed by ASP.NET to process the file. Directives are responsible for changing settings that govern the actions of an entire page. The first directive is a page directive. The attribute, @ Page Title="Home Page" identifies the text title that will be associated with the page. This name appears in the title bar or tab for the browser.

When a new website using the **ASP.NET Web Forms Site** template is created, you automatically get a MasterPage added to your site. An ASP.NET MasterPage allows you to set a template for common user interface elements that can be used across the entire website. The attribute, MasterPageFile="~/Site.Master" specifies the path for this file. As you review Figures 15-5 and 15-6, you should see a node labeled Site.master in the **Solution Explorer** window.

Notice that the language used is identified; the name of the CodeFile is provided. The AutoEventWireup indicates how events are to be handled. When this attribute is set to true, the event-handler methods in the class are used. The AutoEventWireup has another special purpose. For any event that has the name Page_ in front of the event, such as the Page_Load( ) event-handler method, ASP.NET automatically binds the event to the page when the AutoEventWireup is set to true. You do not have to do a separate registering of these page events. Therefore, do not double-click the page to register the Page_Load( ) event. This automatic binding is configured by the AutoEventWireUp attribute that is true by default. If you set the AutoEventWireUp to false, the page does not automatically look for methods that use the Page_ event naming convention.

The last attribute, Inherits, identifies the class in the code-behind file from which the ASP.NET class extends. If you change the class name in the code-behind file, it is not automatically changed in the .aspx source file. It is set initially to _Default. When you change the class name in the code-behind file, you must manually change it here for the application to run properly.

In Figure 15-4, Line 4 assigned "server" to the runat attribute, indicating that when a client requests this .aspx file, it should be processed on the server before being rendered and sent back to the client. You will see this again as you build ASP.NET applications.

Although you can change the tags by typing new values, this is not the ideal method. You will probably prefer to drag and drop the controls onto the page much like you did when you created Windows Forms applications, and let Visual Studio generate the tags for you. You can drag and drop controls from the **Toolbox** directly onto the .aspx source file that holds the HTML tags or onto the blank page. Selecting the **Design** tab at the bottom of the screen displays the .aspx page in design mode as illustrated in Figure 15-6.

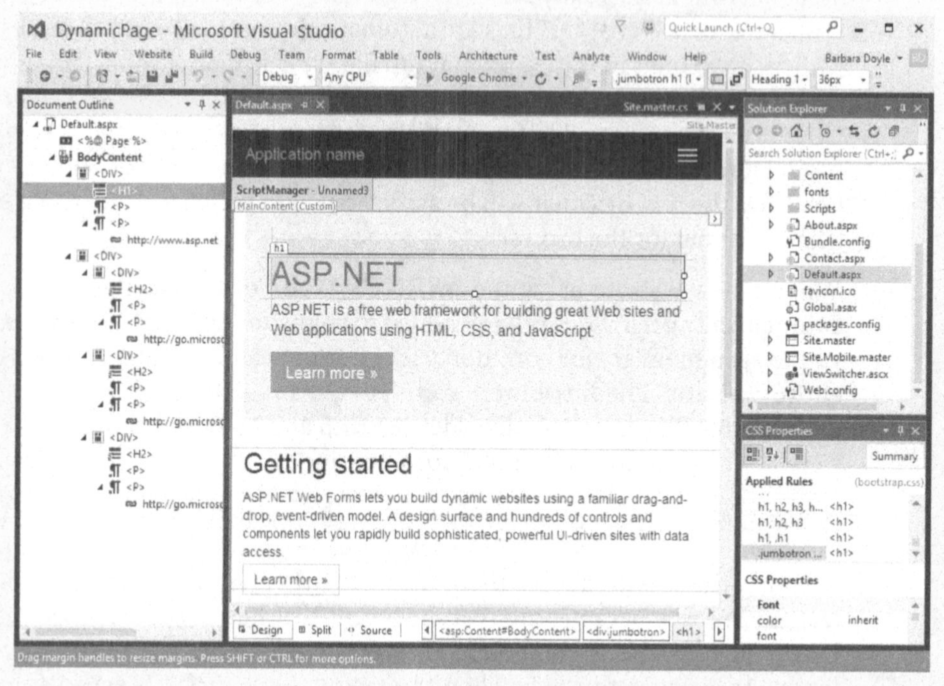

FIGURE 15-6 HTML document in Design mode

New websites that are constructed using Visual Studio's **ASP.NET Web Forms Site** option create all the files shown in Figure 15-6 in the **Solution Explorer** window. The link, text, and HTML tags shown in Figure 15-6 are there when the site is first launched. Also, a master page and CSSs are included.

Additional panes were opened for Figure 15-6. From the **View** menu option, **CSS Properties** were selected. This window is shown in the bottom-right corner of Figure 15-6. **Document Outline**, shown on the left, was made visible from the **View, Other Windows, Document Outline**.

The master page and CSS features are briefly discussed in the following sections.

Master Pages

When you have more than one page associated with a website, a master page can add consistency to your site. You lay out the design, identifying what should appear on each page and indicate on the master page where content will change from one page to the next. For example, on a master page, you might place an HTML table for the layout and include an image element for a logo. You might also include special controls for page navigation for your site. The concept of a master page allows you to create and maintain a constant theme across several pages for a website. As you look back at Figures 15-5 and 15-6, notice that one of the nodes listed in the **Solution Explorer** window is `Site.master`; this is a master page. It is automatically created when you create a new website in Visual Studio and select the **ASP.NET WebForms Site** template. A master page ends with an extension of `.master`.

Figure 15-7 shows most of the `Site.master` file. You will notice that it contains formatting HTML tags. A master page can include static text, HTML elements, and server controls. If you look at the `Site.master` file in Figure 15-7, you will find `html`, `head`, `body`, `form`, and `div` elements on the page. There are a few subtle differences between master pages and other pages, like the `Default.aspx` page. First, the master pages have a special `@ Master` directive instead of the `@ Page` directive you find with files such as `Default.aspx`.

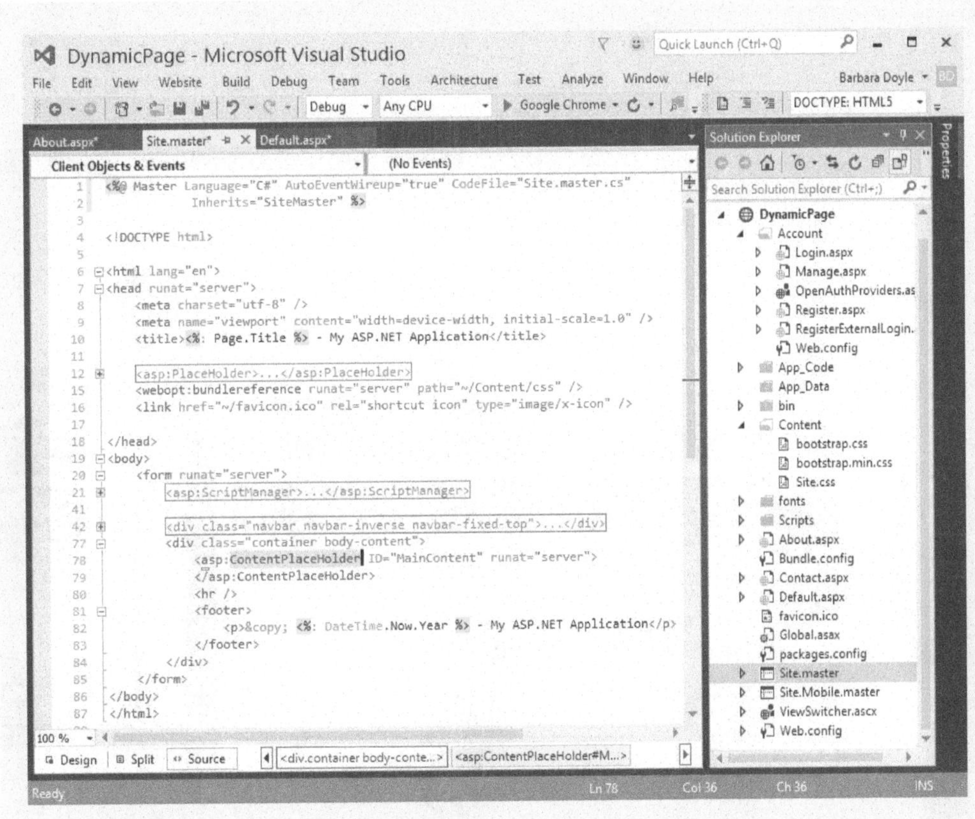

FIGURE 15-7 Site.master master page

Web pages actually consist of two pieces: the master page itself and one or more content pages. Individual content pages contain the content you want to display in the context of the master page template. Each content page contains an `@ Page` directive, which identifies the master page to which the content page is attached. When users request the content pages, the master page is merged with the content page to produce output that combines the layout of the master page with the new material from the content page. There are a number of content pages created and associated with the master page for the `DynamicPage` example. They include `About.aspx`, `Login.aspx`, `Register.aspx`, and `Default.aspx`. Each of these files has a `MasterPageFile="~/Site.Master` attribute as part of its page directive.

The other major difference between a master page and content pages such as `Default.aspx` and `About.aspx` is that the master page has one or more `ContentPlaceHolders` defined with an `ID`. These placeholders define areas where replaceable content will appear. With some areas collapsed, the `MainContent ContentPlaceHolders` is shown on Line 78 in Figure 15-7. Figure 15-8 shows the replaceable content for the `About.aspx` pages. The figure shows both the **Source** and **Design** windows for the `About.aspx` page.

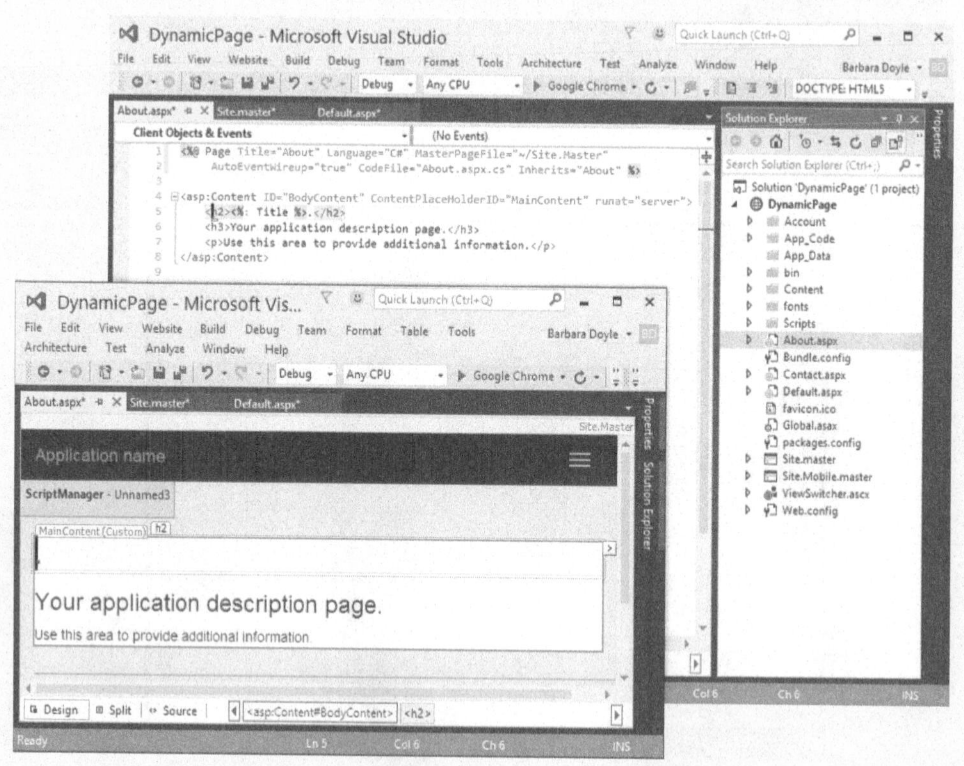

FIGURE 15-8 MainContent in the About.aspx page

Lines 4 through 8 provide the HTML tags for the `BodyContent` shown in Figure 15-8 for the `About.aspx` page. The static text `"Your application description page"` and `"Use this area to provide additional information."` are the text used to fill the white area `(MainContent)` on the page. Figure 15-9 shows the `MainContent` HTML tags that appear in the `Default.aspx` file.

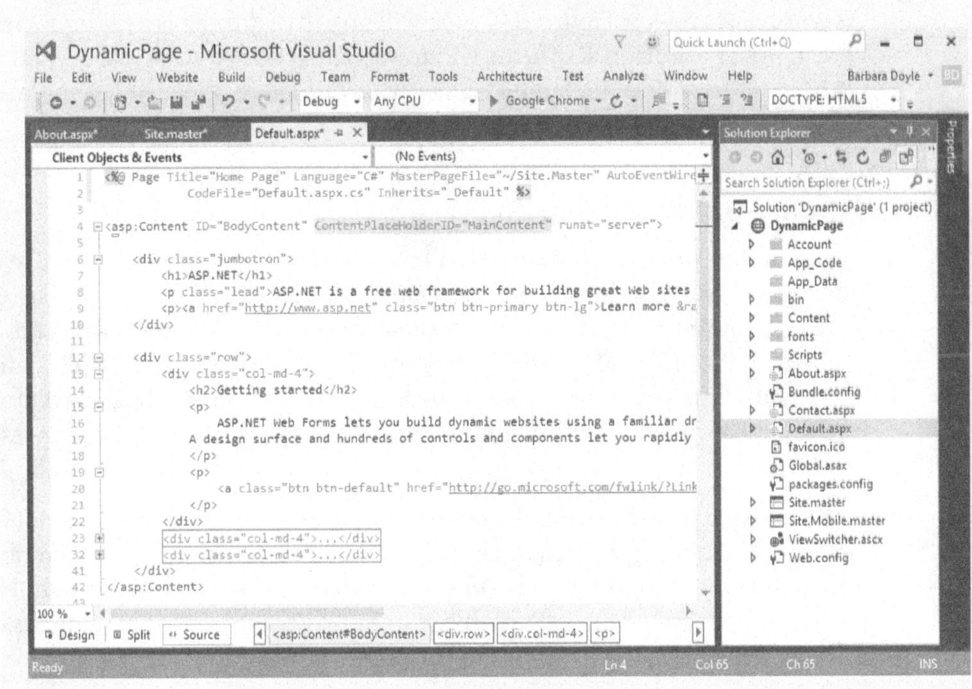

FIGURE 15-9 MainContent in the Default.aspx page

As you review Figure 15-9, notice that the tags for the `BodyContent` are defined beginning on Line 4 and ending on Line 42 for the `Default.aspx` page. The `MainContent` is more lengthy and extensive in the `Default.aspx` page than what is found on the `About.aspx` page because the `Default.aspx` page serves as the opening page and the one that is displayed when **Home** is selected from the navigation bar.

For the content pages shown in Figures 15-8 and 15-9, the line that begins with `<asp:Content ContentPlaceHolders="MainContent"` is what ties the content back to the `Site.master` page.

NOTE As you review the `DynamicPage` Web application, you will discover additional content pages under the `Account` node. `Login.aspx` and `Register.aspx` are both associated with the `Site.master` master page. No changes were made to the `DynamicPage` Web application.

As you closely review Figure 15-7, you will notice that there is a folder named **Content** shown in the **Solution Explorer** window. It is expanded to reveal several files ending with `.css` extension, including `Site.css`. These are style sheets and are automatically added to the project when a Visual Studio website is created.

Cascading Style Sheet (CSS)

Visual Studio provides support for incorporating CSSs into ASP.NET Web applications. CSSs, such as master pages, enable you to provide more consistency across pages on your website. They let you separate the actual content from how it is going to look. Before CSS, all of the presentational attributes, such as sizes and colors of fonts and alignment of text, were included within the HTML markup. You often had to repeat the properties and had to work at providing consistent presentation of elements.

CSS uses style sheets to describe how elements will look in terms of their layout, fonts, and colors. Style sheets enhance your ability to improve the appearance of pages. Most developers feel that style sheets represent a major breakthrough for web page designers because of the added ability to improve the appearance of pages. There is a whole new language for style sheets used to define how an HTML document will look.

The syntax for the language used by CSS is very high level—close to English. CSS uses a number of keywords to describe different style properties. It is beyond the scope of this chapter to describe all of the different properties; however, as you review Figure 15-10, you will find the style sheet very readable and easy to modify.

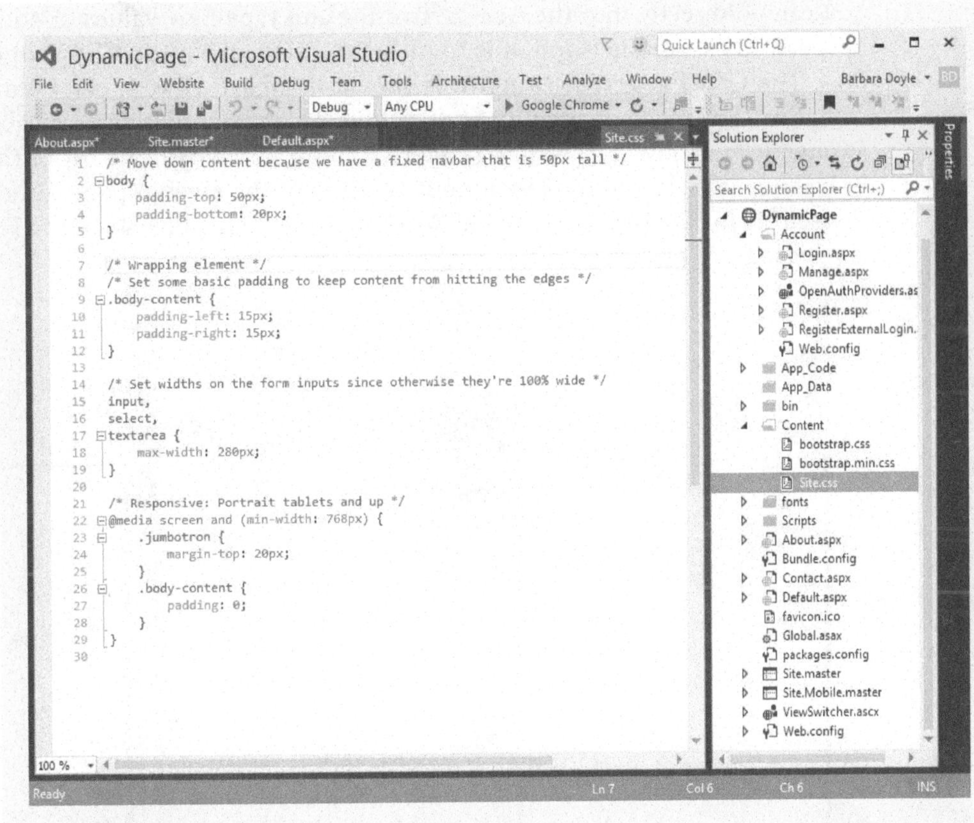

FIGURE 15-10 Site.css

From the **Solution Explorer** window, the Site.css file is opened. By definition, a **style sheet** includes a list of rules. Each rule consists of a selector and one or more declaration blocks. The declaration block is enclosed in curly braces. Inside the block, you will find a property, colon, and a value. Like C#, each property assignment ends with a semicolon. Example 15-2 shows the style rule for body that was included when the `DynamicPage` website was created.

EXAMPLE 15-2

```
body
{
    padding-top: 50px;
    padding-bottom: 20px;
}
```

You can go directly into the `Sites.css` file and type new values or add additional property lines. Another option is to make selections from the **CSS Properties** window. The **CSS Properties** window is shown in Figure 15-6. It can be made visible from the **View** menu. A **Modify Style** configuration wizard is also available from the **Properties** window. The `style` property can be retrieved from any of the elements or classes you select in the **Document Outline** or the **Design** pane. When you click the ellipsis for the `style` value, the **Modify Style** dialog box shown in Figure 15-11 is revealed.

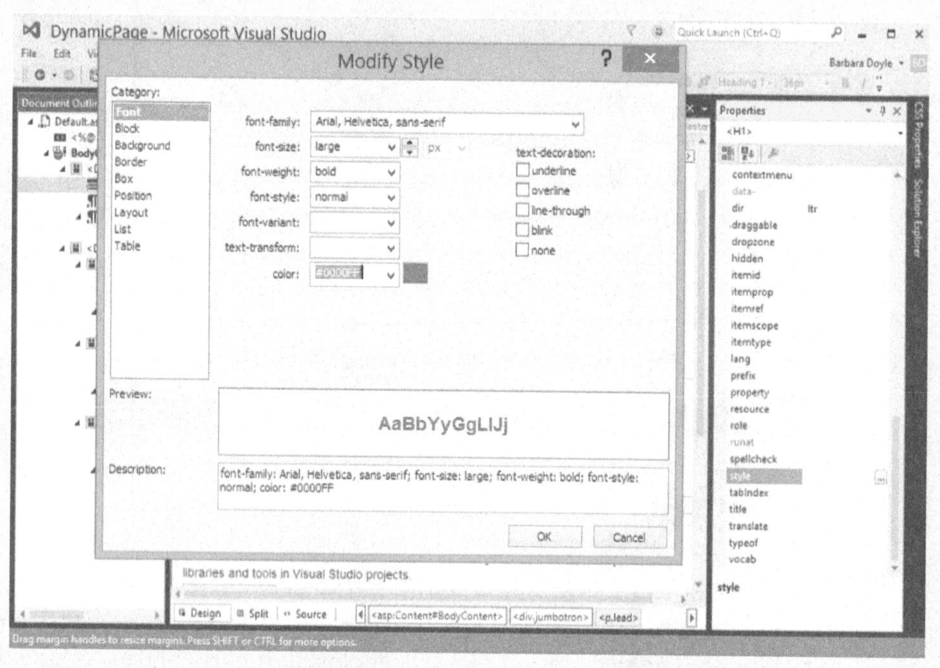

FIGURE 15-11 Modify Style

Each of the **Category** items shown in Figure 15-11, the **Modify Style** dialog box, reveals a number of options you can set for the element. Selections you make are added as new style rules. You are encouraged to explore by making changes and then reviewing the `.css` file and the output you get from your changes when you launch the site.

Figure 15-12 shows modified website example created starting with the **ASP.NET Web Forms Site** template. No C# program statements were added. The default template was kept. Text was changed by typing new values onto the **Design** panes for the `Default.aspx`, `Login.aspx`, `Register.aspx`, `About.aspx`, and

`Contact.aspx` pages. New URLs replaced links in the `.aspx` file using the **Source** pane. An image was dragged from the **Toolbox** to the `site.master` page. Prior to providing a value for the `ImageURL` in the **Properties** windows, a new Images folder was added by right-clicking on the project name in the **Solution Explorer** window. The actual `.jpg` image was copied and pasted into that folder. These changes are shown in Figure 15-12. The Web application is called `RentJaxHomes`.

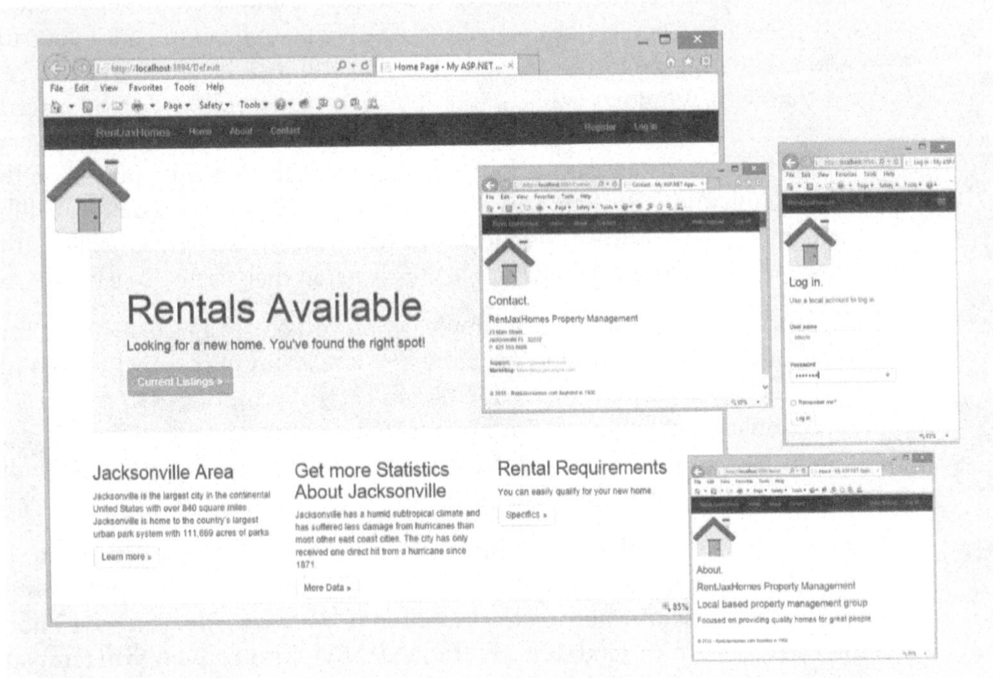

FIGURE 15-12 ASP.NET Web Forms Site modified

Recall that the examples `DynamicPage` and `RentJaxHomes` were created using the **ASP.NET Web Forms Site** template. As you review Figures 15-8–15-10, notice that each of the files ending with `.aspx` is expandable. If you expand any of these `.aspx` files, such as `Default.aspx`, in the **Solution Explorer** window, you will find the code-behind files. They all have `.cs` appended onto the end of their filenames.

CODE-BEHIND FILE

You can open the `.aspx.cs` file from the **Solution Explorer** window. At first glance, the `.aspx.cs` code-behind file looks very similar to a Windows application. However, there are a number of differences. There is no `Main( )` method. Instead there is a `Page_Load( )` event handler. It is added automatically when the project is created.

Recall that a `Form_Load( )` method was added to Windows applications when you double-clicked on the form. You do not need to double-click on the page to get the `Page_Load( )` event handler registered. The `Page_Load( )` event-handler heading is automatically added to the Web application whenever a `default.aspx.cs` file is added to the application.

The code generated by the Web Forms Designer is no longer included. A significant difference exists between an ASP.NET Web Forms and Windows application in that the auto-generated code is not created for ASP.NET applications until you run the application. The heading for the class declaration still includes the `partial` keyword. You saw that with Windows applications. The auto-generated code was placed in another `partial class`. Recall that with Windows applications, the Windows-generated code included object instantiations for the visual controls that were placed on the form and event-handler hookups. These were placed in the `.Designer.cs` file. Unlike Windows applications, one of the differences you will observe when you explore the **Solution Explorer** window for ASP.NET applications is that there is no `.Designer.cs` file listed.

As you saw from the previous example, when you create a website using the **ASP.NET Web Forms Site** template in Visual Studio, a number of files including a master page, style sheet, and content pages for `Default.aspx`, `About.aspx`, and `Login.aspx` are automatically added to the project. If you click the arrow beside each of these content pages in the **Solution Explorer** window, code-behind files (ending in `.cs`) are revealed for each of these `.aspx` files.

The previous examples highlighted what was automatically generated. Using these predesigned templates, you add your own content. If you do not want this design template or these files automatically added to your website, you have another option. You can create from scratch using the **ASP.NET Empty Web Site** template.

ASP.NET Empty Web Site

Look back at Figure 15-3. Listed as the first option in the list of templates available for **Web sites** is the **ASP.NET Empty Web Site** template. Selecting this template does not create any files—not even the `Default.aspx` file. However, it also does not add lots of overhead to the project. This option is used for the remaining examples in this chapter.

When you make the selection **File**, **New Web Site**, **ASP.NET Empty Web Site**, no .aspx files are created. No extra folders are created. For the next project, a website named `HtmlExample` is created. A file is added to the project by right-clicking on the project name in the **Solution Explorer** window and selecting **Add**, **Web Form**. The default name of `Default` is accepted for the **Item Name**. A review of the **Solution Explorer** window reveals that a new file `Default.aspx` has been added. This file is automatically opened in Source view when you first start building a website. Clicking on the arrow beside `Default.aspx` expands to reveal the `Default.aspx.cs` file. This code-behind file was automatically created when you added the new

Web Form item to the project. You will read more about this shortly; however, the `.aspx.cs` file is where your program logic, including your event handlers, is stored.

A CSS was added automatically when you created the ASP.NET Web Forms site in the previous example. A file named Site.css was added. You can add a Site.css CSS to an empty site project by right-clicking the project name in the **Solution Explorer** window and selecting **Add, Style Sheet**.

Another option is to use the **Modify Style** dialog box without adding a style sheet. The **Modify Style** dialog box is shown in Figure 15-11. It is opened by clicking the ellipsis in the `style` value **Properties Window**. You can launch the **Modify Style** dialog box from both the **Source** and the **Design** tabs. To change, for example, the background color for the web page, first the `Default.aspx` window is opened, the **Source** tab is selected, and the mouse is clicked on the line that has the beginning <html tag. When the **Modify Style** dialog box is opened, the **Background Category** is selected. Using the color wheel, a green (`Hex={CC,FF,33}`) is selected for the `background-color`. Under the **Font Category**, the `medium` was set for the `font-size`. Again using the color wheel a darker green (`Hex={00,33,00}`) was selected for the **color** selection under the **Font Category**.

You can also launch the **Modify Style** dialog box from the **Design** tab by selecting the `Form` from the drop-down list of controls in the **Properties Window**. Once the `Form` is selected, clicking the ellipsis in the `Style` value **Properties Window** launches the **Modify Style** dialog box.

As with a Windows application, you can debug and execute a Web application from within the IDE. It is a fully functioning application from the beginning. When you run the application, the default Web browser is launched and the file is opened inside the browser. The first time you run the application, you may receive a message noting **"Debugging Not Enabled."** Selecting **OK** from that dialog box enables debugging.

In addition to running the application from the **Debug, Start Debugging** or **Debug, Start Without Debugging** menu options, you can run the application by right-clicking on the .aspx (HTML) file in the **Solution Explorer** window and selecting **View in Browser**. Another option is to open a browser and then browse to the file using the **Open** menu option. Visual Studio also installs a quick launch icon on the toolbar with a drop-down list of browsers installed on the machine. This enables you to view the page in multiple browsers during testing.

HTML DOCUMENT FILE

The **Page** `object` has a number of properties. In the **Properties** window, you have access to the HTML **Document** properties as well as much of the same functionality that was available for setting a Windows application form; however, differences exist. There are fewer properties available, and they go by different identifiers. Table 15-1 gives some of the page (HTML document) properties that can be set. The table was adapted from the Visual Studio MSDN documentation.

TABLE 15-1 HTML document properties

Property name	Description
`Class`	Defines `class` of the page body
`Culture`	Determines results of culture-dependent functions, such as the date, number, and currency formatting
`Debug`	Indicates whether the `class` should be debugged with debug symbols
`EnableSessionState`	Session state mode
`ID`	Body element ID
`Language`	Specifies the language used when compiling all inline rendering and code declaration blocks within the page
`MasterPageFile`	Master page (read only)
`Style`	Sets style of body element
`StylesheetTheme`	Page style sheet theme
`Theme`	Page theme
`Trace`	Indicates whether tracing is enabled
`TraceMode`	Indicates how traces are to be displayed when tracing is enabled
`UICulture`	Determines which resources are loaded for the page
`Title`	Caption for the title bar

© Cengage Learning

As with Windows applications, you can set some properties during design using the **Properties** window by selecting the individual property and either typing a new value or selecting a value from a drop-down list when available. Doing so adds code to the visual interface file containing the HTML tags (`.aspx` extension). The value typed for the `Text` property becomes text that you see on the tab for the web page when it is launched.

Example 15-3 includes the HTML statements modified as a result of the changes in the property values.

EXAMPLE 15-3

```
<head runat="server">
  <title>HTML Controls Example</title>
</head>
```

As shown in Example 15-3, the property change is made to the .aspx file, which is the file containing the HTML tags. When the pair of attribute names and values were automatically placed in the .aspx markup file, the attribute names were written using lowercase characters.

Controls

Visual Studio groups controls in the **Toolbox** under the following categories:

- Standard
- Data
- Validation
- Navigation
- Login
- WebParts
- AJAX Extensions
- Dynamic Data
- Reporting
- HTML

The **Toolbox** controls are available in both design and source mode. You can drag and drop a control onto the .aspx markup page as easily as you can drop it on the design page. Most of the Web Forms controls you will be using are stored under the **Standard** type on the **Toolbox**. The pure HTML controls appear under the **HTML** type. **HTML** controls are discussed first.

HTML Controls

HTML controls are also called client-side controls. When added to a web page, they map straight to HTML tags. They can be added to your page using a **WYSIWYG** (what you see is what you get) drag-and-drop approach. You can type text directly on the page without placing a control object on the page. To move to the next line, you press the Enter key. For this example, the heading `Computer Club Registration Form` was typed inside the selected div area. Since the labels for text `First name:`, `Last name:`, and `Email:` do not need to be programmatically referenced, they were simply typed directly on the page in design mode. This is shown in Figure 15-13.

You can horizontally center or justify text or controls on the page using the **Justify** option from the **Format** menu. **Format**, **Justify**, **Center** was used to center the heading. The **Format** menu also enables you to change the **Font**, **Background** or **Foreground color** or add a completely **New Style**. You also have the option of inserting tables and merging the cells from the **Table** menu option. Adding a table can give you a little more control over where items are placed on the page. Using the **Format, Set Position** option, you can set the positioning to **Relative** or **Absolute**. Be careful with this setting if you plan to view the page using different browsers. Remember that not all monitors will be set for the same resolution. You have a special **Block Format** tool on the **Formatting** toolbar, as shown in Figure 15-13. This enables you to select a segment of text and apply heading tags or create ordered or unordered lists.

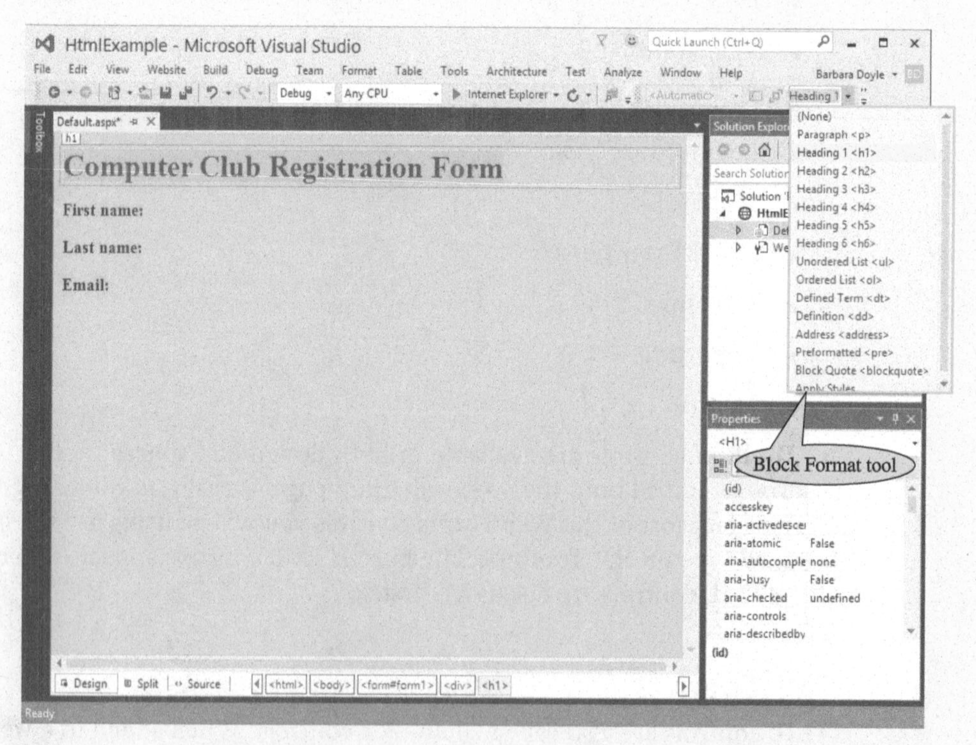

FIGURE 15-13 Block format for design mode

Using the **Block Format** tool shown in Figure 15-13, the heading and labels were formatted using the drop-down list. The heading was set to <h1>. The text or labels for the input boxes were set to <h3> using the **Block Format** tool. You also have support for aligning and placing the items on the page.

The controls and properties, however, associated with the HTML controls are different from those you saw previously with Windows applications. There is not a `Label` or `Text Field` object listed as an HTML control in the **Toolbox**. If you want to place labels over controls and do not need to programmatically reference them, you can simply type the text directly on the page in design mode. When you need to programmatically reference a `Label object`, drag one from the **Standard** group on the **Toolbox**.

To change font type or size with HTML controls, select the control you want to change, choose `Style` in the **Properties** window and select the ellipsis. This brings up a **Modify Style** dialog box where you can define CSS style attributes for these HTML controls. These settings are made by selecting from a group of options. Thus, you can still change these formatting features from within Visual Studio; it is just done a little differently than with Windows applications.

You have the option under **Format, New Style. . .** to create and name a new style. Selecting **Format, New Style. . .** brings up a dialog box containing most of the same options as the **Modify Style. . .** dialog box shown in Figure 15-11. **Format, New Style. . .** adds the capabilities of creating a new named style. You also have an option to apply the new style to the current document selection. Both of these features are not available from the **Modify Style. . .** dialog box.

ADDING HTML CONTROLS

As shown in Figure 15-14, there are a limited number of HTML controls included in the IDE. Most of the HTML controls are based on the `HTML Input` element. These elements are not available to the server, but just treated as markup for the browser.

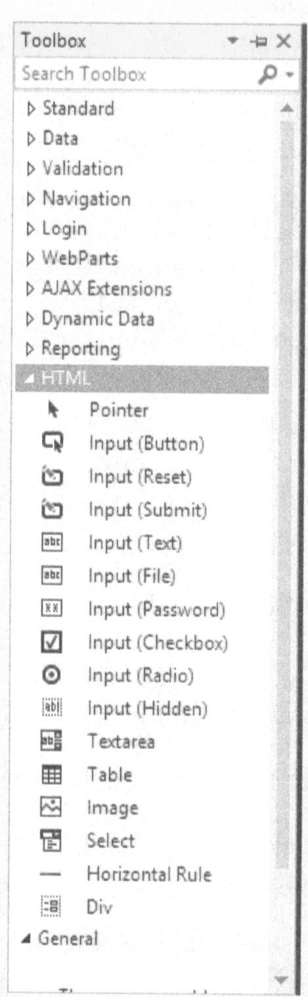

FIGURE 15-14 HTML controls

To illustrate the usage of HTML controls, `Input Text` and `Image` objects were added to the `HTMLExample` Web application. Each `Input Text` control was dragged onto the form and placed to the right of the identifying text. They were moved slightly to the right and resized. All three controls were selected and then the **Set Position** was set to **Relative** from the **Format** menu. Using Visual Studio's Snap lines, the `Input Text` controls were aligned with their identifying text.

Prior to adding the image, a new Images folder was placed in the solution folder for the Web application. The `Happy.jpg` picture was placed inside the folder. In order to center the picture below the input entries, a line was opened up on the **Design** pane and the **Format, Justify, Center** was selected. This was done prior to placing the image on the form. Double-clicking on the **Image** control from the **HTML Toolbox** placed the image in the center of the form. Once the `Image` object was on the form, clicking the ellipsis in the value text box for the **scr** property enabled the control to be tied to the picture. The **Set Position** was set to **Relative** from the **Format** menu.

As you review Figure 15-14, you will notice that there are three HTML button type controls listed in the Toolbox: `Input (Button)`, `Input (Submit)`, and `Input (Reset)`. You cannot double-click and register an event handler with these HTML buttons like you would have done with a Windows application. In order to do that, a Button from the **Standard** section in the **Toolbox** is added. The `Button` was placed on the page in a similar manner that the image was. In the **Design** pane, a line was opened up by pressing the return key, **Justified Center** selected, `Button` from **Standard Toolbox** was double-clicked which placed it on the form in the center of the page. **Relative** was selected for **Set Position** option from the **Format** menu. The `Text` property for the `Button` was set to `Submit` in the **Properties** Window. Like a Windows application, the application can be executed from within Visual Studio. Or, after being built, the page can be opened within a Web browser using the application name—because Visual Studio created a virtual directory for it. Figure 15-15 shows the Web application after values are entered and the `Submit` button is clicked.

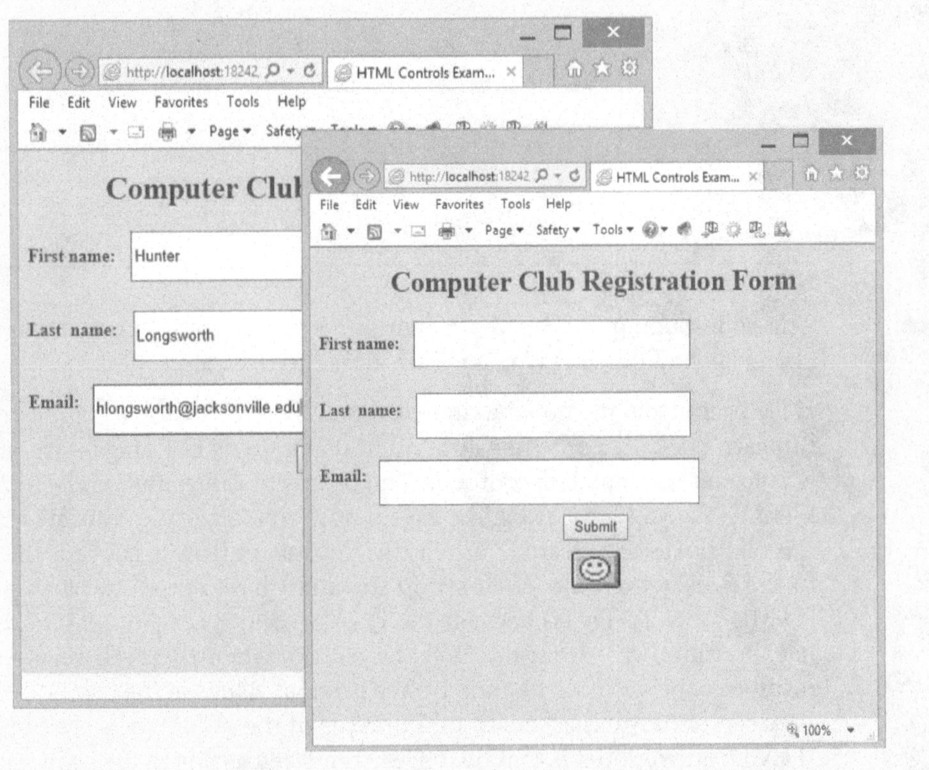

FIGURE 15-15 Submit button clicked

You might think that the illustrations in Figure 15-15 are layered incorrectly, but they are not. As noted previously, web pages are stateless. When the **Submit** button is clicked, a postback to the Web server occurs. When the page is redisplayed upon return from the round-trip to the server, the values in the text box are lost and not available for redisplay.

Adding the text box, button, and image controls to the form alters the code in the file containing the HTML (`.aspx`). It does not add any statements to the file ending in `.aspx.cs` (the code-behind file). The only statements that appear in the `.aspx.cs` file are those originally placed when the page was created. Example 15-4 shows the contents. Notice that a number of namespaces are imported automatically.

EXAMPLE 15-4

```
// HTMLExample Default.aspx.cs
using System;
using System.Collections.Generic;
using System.Linq;
using System.Web;
using System.Web.UI;

public partial class _Default : System.Web.UI.Page
{
   protected void Page_Load(object sender, EventArgs e)
   {
   }
}
```

The code-behind file, `Default.aspx.cs`, for the `HTMLExample` application is not changed. Additional HTML tags are added to the `.aspx` file.

HTML controls do not maintain state. When the page is requested from a Web browser, its static contents—formatted using the HTML tags—are displayed. HTTP is considered a stateless protocol. The property values that are set have a very short lifetime. As you look at Figure 15-15, note that after the **Submit** button is clicked, the text boxes are cleared. When the **Submit** button is clicked, the page is posted to the Web server. The Web server does not have access to what is typed into the HTML controls. This is because the HTML controls do not maintain their state during the round-trip from the Web server. So, when the Web server sends back the results as a new HTML document, the original values in the text boxes disappear. The Web server only has access to the contents of the HTML tags. The biggest advantage HTML controls offer is that the page is rendered as it is to the browser. No processing is necessary by the Web server.

But, if you want to retrieve the values entered by the user, you can programmatically analyze the HTTP request. This has been the traditional method; however, it requires more coding. A better approach is to make the controls available to the Web server, as described in the following section.

HTML Server Controls

To add functionality at run time, you can give the server access to the values entered by the user. One way to do this is to add scripting statements in the HTML file using a scripting language such as JavaScript or VBScript. You could use the HTML `Input(Button)`, `Input(Submit)`, or `Input(Reset)` buttons to do this. This was discussed previously. When using JavaScript or VBScript, however, you miss out on many of the benefits of object-oriented development and the large collection of predefined classes available within .NET. Another approach is to use the ASP.NET Web server controls that appear on the **Standard** tab. Recall that the button added to the form was retrieved from the **Standard Toolbox**. Web Forms server controls are more powerful and closely akin to Windows Forms control objects. These controls are covered in the following section.

.aspx AND .aspx.cs FILES

As you examined the code-behind file in Example 15-4 and Figure 15-12, you should have realized that no code was written for processing the data entered by the user. No event-handler method for the button click was included. When the user clicked the `Submit` button, the page was refreshed from the Web server, which caused the text box objects to be cleared. During design, if you had placed an `Input(Submit)` or an `Input(Button)` from the **HTML Toolbox** tab, and wanted to provide functionality, script code for an `OnClick( )` function would need to be written in the `.aspx` markup file. You probably do not want to do that. That is why the button was retrieved from the **Standard** tab on the **Toolbox**. When it is placed on the form, the `runat="server"` attribute is automatically added to the button tag in the `.aspx` file. The `Button` is a Web Server control.

An additional control, `Label`, was retrieved from the **Standard Toolbox**. To place it on the form, a new line was opened under the `Image` control by pressing the enter key. Once the full paragraph was selected where the `Label` resided, it was left justified using the **Format, Justify** menu. From the **Properties** window, the value for the `Text` property was deleted and its `id` property was set to `lblOutput`.

RUNNING HTML CONTROLS AS SERVER CONTROLS Recall that the `HTMLExample` application had three `Input(Text)` controls placed on the form. These were retrieved from the **HTML** tab on the **Toolbox**. They did not get the `runat="server"` attribute added. The `Label` and `Button` `objects` are pulled over from the **Standard Toolbox**. Because they are a standard ASP.NET control, the `runat="server"` attribute is automatically added to the tags for these controls in the .aspx file. This makes the control visible or accessible to the Web server—meaning that they become programmable. You can double-click on the button and have an event-handler method heading automatically generated for you.

An additional step is needed in order for you to retrieve data from the HTML `Input(Text)` text boxes that you retrieved from the **HTML** tab on the **Toolbox**. These HTML controls are not visible as objects in your aspx.cs file until you add the `runat="server"` attribute to their tag in the .aspx file. Once this is accomplished, the button click event handler can retrieve and store data in those objects. The `id` properties for the three `Input(Text)` text boxes were set to `txtFirst`, `txtLast`, and `txtEmail`. The new tags are shown in Example 15-5.

EXAMPLE 15-5

```
<h3>First name:  <input id="txtFirst" runat="server"
     type="text" /></h3>

<h3>Last  name:  <input id="txtLast" runat="server"
     type="text" /></h3>

<h3>Email:  <input id="txtEmail" runat="server"
     type="text" /></h3>

<p style="text-align: center"> <asp:Button ID=" btnSubmit"
     runat="server" Text="Submit" Height="45px" Width="97px" /p>

<p style="text-align: center"> <img alt="" src="Images/HAPPY.jpg"
     style="height: 34px;  width: 48px; position: relative; top: -2px;
     left: 0px" /></p>

<p style="text-align: center">  </p>
     <asp:Label ID="lblOutput" runat="server"
     style="text-align: left" Font-Size="X-Large"> </asp:Label>
```

The `Label` `object` is used by the Web server to store a message containing the retrieved name and e-mail values from the HTML `Text Field` objects.

The `ID` property is used with ASP.NET applications to set to an appropriate identifier for **Standard** controls. The `ID` property is similar to the Windows application `Name` property. The `Text` property is available for many of the **Standard** controls. The `lblOutput` `Text` property was cleared.

SERVER CONTROL EVENTS

After you select a button from the **Standard** tab on the **Toolbox**, an object is instantiated of the `WebControls.Button class`. You get an object complete with object characteristics. You can register events such as a button click event for the object. Now when you double-click the `Submit` button, you do not get the `function OnClick( )` code added to the .aspx markup file. Instead, double-clicking registers the button click event exactly as it was done when you created button click events for Windows applications. An empty button click event-handler method is added. This code is inserted into the code-behind (`.aspx.cs`) file. Now when the page is requested using HTTP, the Web server has access to all the controls that have `runat="server"` attributes and can retrieve and process the data entered by the user. To demonstrate how the application functions now that the server has access to the controls, the statements shown in Example 15-6 were added to the event-handler method.

EXAMPLE 15-6

```
protected void btnSubmit_Click(object sender, EventArgs e)
{
     lblOutput.Text = "Thanks!! " +
           txtFirst.Value + " " + txtLast.Value +
           " - Information will be forwarded to " +
           txtEmail.Value;
}
```

PROPERTIES OF HTML SERVER CONTROLS As noted previously, the properties of HTML controls are different from those you became accustomed to using Windows applications. This is because they are mapped to HTML elements. Table 15-2 lists the property values set for the HtmlExample application. There is no `Name` property. The `id` property is used to provide an identifier for the HTML controls.

TABLE 15-2 HtmlExample property values

Name	Object type	Property	Value
Document	Page	Title	HTML Controls Example
btnSubmit	Button	ID	btnSubmit
btnSubmit	Button	Height	45px
btnSubmit	Button	Text	Submit

(*continues*)

TABLE 15-2 HtmlExample property values (*continued*)

Name	Object type	Property	Value
btnSubmit	Button	Width	97px
lblOutput	Label	ID	lblOutput
lblOutput	Label	Font - Size	X-Large
txtEmail	HTML - Input (Text)	id	txtEmail
txtFirst	HTML - Input (Text)	id	txtFirst
txtLast	HTML - Input (Text)	id	txtLast
Img	Image	Style	Height: 34px
Img	Image	src	Images/HAPPY.jpg

As you review Table 15-2 and the code illustrated in Example 15-6, notice that the `Text` property is not used to get or set values for the Input text fields. Instead, the `Value` property is used. Figure 15-16 shows the page after it is posted back from the Web server. It is no longer blank after the round-trip to the Web server.

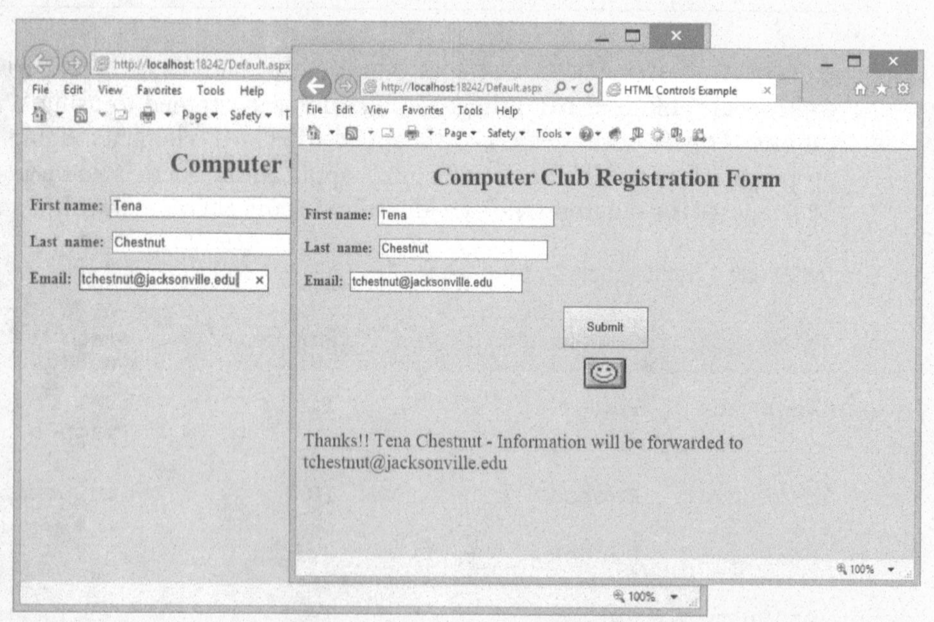

FIGURE 15-16 Web page after postback

Notice in Figure 15-16, that upon return from the server the Input text objects contain the typed values—unlike the illustration shown in Figure 15-15. This is because these HTML controls are now HTML server controls. The only program statements added were those added to retrieve the input values and display their contents in a `Label object`. Those statements were added to the `btnSubmit_Click( )` event and previously shown in Example 15-6. No other changes were made to the .aspx.cs file. The `Font Size` property for the `lblOutput` was set to `X-Large` using the **Properties** window. This caused the following statement to be added as an attribute to the `Label` tag:

```
Font-Size="X-Large"
```

The attribute was placed in the `.aspx` markup file.

The number displayed in the Address bar, shown in Figures 15-15 and 15-16, following local host as the port number is a relatively random number. It is placed in the Address bar when you create a website and specify the location as **File System**. The port number changes.

As you experienced with this example, you can convert traditional HTML controls into server controls. However, there are other options for server-side processing. As part of Visual Studio, you have a whole group of **Standard** Web controls. They are the topic of the following section.

Web Forms Standard Server Controls

Referred to as **Standard** controls, server controls, Web controls, Web Forms server controls, ASP server controls, or simply Web Forms controls, these controls have more built-in features than the HTML controls. They are the controls you want to use in Visual Studio—especially if you need to have the Web server process the data on the page. The Web Forms server controls are designed to look and act like their Windows counterparts. The programming model used for these controls is more closely aligned to the object-oriented model you have used throughout this book. There are fewer of these controls than there are Windows Form controls, but their functionality and many of their properties are similar.

With most **Standard** controls, you have a `Text` property and do not have to learn new identifiers such as `Value`, which was used with the `HTML Input (Text)` control.

Server controls slow applications down because the web page containing them is sent back to the server for processing. Because of this, fewer events can be programmed for server controls.

Available Web Forms Controls

Figure 15-17 shows some of the Web Forms **Standard** controls available in Visual Studio.

If you do not see the **Toolbox**, it can be viewed by selecting **View**, **Toolbox** or by using the **Ctrl+W, X** shortcut. Other controls can be added to the **Toolbox**. Right-click within the Web Forms Toolbar and select **Customize** to add or remove controls.

Notice how the drop-down tabs shown in Figure 15-17 include tabs for **Standard, Data, Validation, Navigation, Login, WebParts, AJAX Extensions, Dynamic Data, Reporting,** and **HTML**. The controls discussed first in this section are the Web Forms **Standard** controls available from the **Toolbox**.

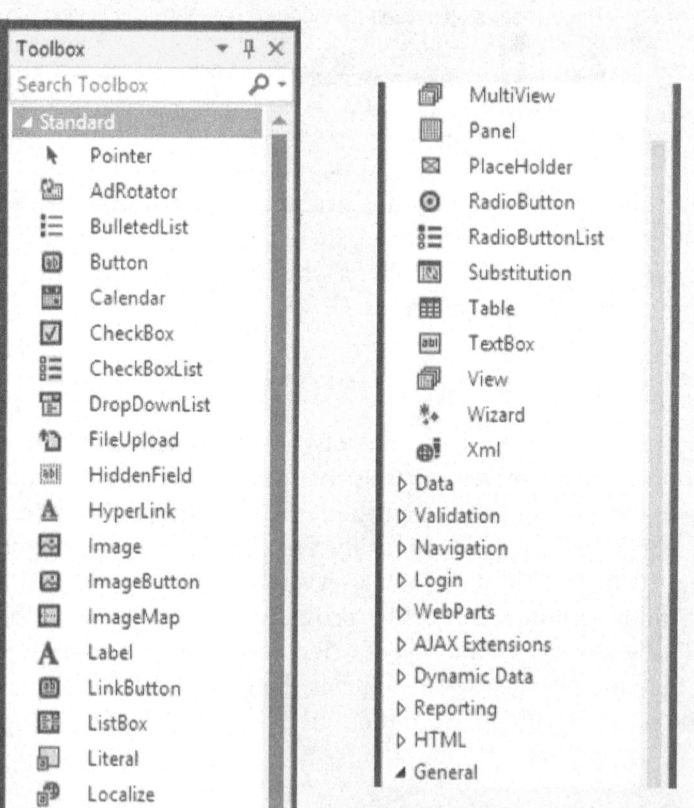

FIGURE 15-17 Web Forms Standard controls

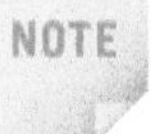

You can mix and match **Navigation** controls, **HTML** controls, and Web Forms **Standard** controls. A single Web application can contain all three.

Web Forms **Standard** controls do not map straight to HTML. Often, it may take several HTML tags to represent one Web Forms Standard control. When you drag and drop a **Standard** control onto the page, an HTML tag is placed in the `.aspx` file representing the control. This tag contains an extra attribute, which is not found on HTML controls, as follows:

```
<asp:controlName>attributes runat="server"
</asp:controlName>
```

To indicate that the control is a Web Forms control, Visual Studio prefixes the control name with `<asp:controlName>` and ends the tag with `</asp:controlName>`. You saw `runat="server"` previously. This attribute is added for Web Forms **Standard** controls.

Other attributes are included with the HTML tags. This is also true for **HTML** controls. When you set the control's property using the **Properties** window in Visual Studio, the settings are stored in the HTML document—the file ending with the `.aspx` extension. Remember that this differs from the operation of Windows applications. With Windows applications, the property settings are placed in the `Windows Forms Designer generated code region`. Web applications do not have a Web Forms Designer generated code section. Property settings are not stored in the code-behind file for Web applications. They are stored in the file containing the HTML tags. All the visual interface settings are stored in this `.aspx` file. You do not need to define and instantiate control variables. You will not find a special auto-generated section, like you found with Windows applications that holds control variable declarations. With Windows applications, when you dropped a button, for example, on the form, you could search through the auto-generated code and find the button being declared and instantiated. When you double-clicked on the button to register a click event, you could again search through the auto-generated code and locate the event wiring code. With Windows applications, all this code was autogenerated and placed in the code-behind file under the `InitializeComponent( )` section. But the ASP.NET run time now automatically performs the code generation that was performed by Visual Studio.

What this means is that the ASP.NET run time automatically inserts the required declaration and event wiring code into the final compiled file. Because the run time takes on this responsibility, you do not need to be concerned with it. The run time creates another `partial class` dynamically from the .aspx page and merges it with the code-behind `partial class`.

Web Forms Controls of the Common Form Type

As you examine Figure 15-17, notice several identifiers that you have seen previously: `Button`, `Label`, `TextBox`, `ListBox`, `CheckBox`, `Image`, and `RadioButton`. These common controls function similarly to their Windows counterpart objects. There are differences, however, between the controls and how their properties are added to an application. First, examine the HTML visual interface file.

HTML (.aspx) FILE

Dragging a Web Forms `Button` `object` onto a form, setting its `ID` (name) to `btnSubmit`, and changing its `Text` value and positioning properties produces the HTML statement shown in Example 15-7.

EXAMPLE 15-7

```
<asp:Button ID="btnSubmit" runat="server"
     style="z-index: 1; left: 400px; top: 321px;
     position: absolute; width: 90px; height: 24px;
     text-align: center" Text="Submit Info"
     OnClick="btnSubmit_Click"
</asp:Button>
```

As you can see from Example 15-7, the settings for the properties are not placed in the code-behind file. These attributes are added to the `.aspx` file—the markup file that contains all the HTML tags. The entries added to the code-behind file (`.aspx.cs` file) include only the declaration of objects and the registration of event handlers along with their methods.

CHANGING PROPERTIES WITHIN VISUAL STUDIO

It is valuable to examine the properties that can be set for the buttons, labels, text boxes, radio buttons, check boxes, and other form type controls. As shown in Figure 15-17, there are fewer controls found with Web Forms types of controls than you find with their Windows Forms counterparts. In addition, there are fewer properties for each control and differences exist between the properties. One obvious difference is in naming the `object`. With Windows Forms controls, the `Name` property is used. With Web Forms controls, the `ID` property is used. The following list shows the number of events and controls that can be registered for different types of control buttons:

- Windows Forms button—60 events
- Web Forms Standard button—8 events
- Windows Forms button—76 properties
- Web Forms Standard button—30 properties

This comparison is representative of all of the other controls.

Take a look at Figure 15-18 to see the properties for the Web Forms `Label` control.

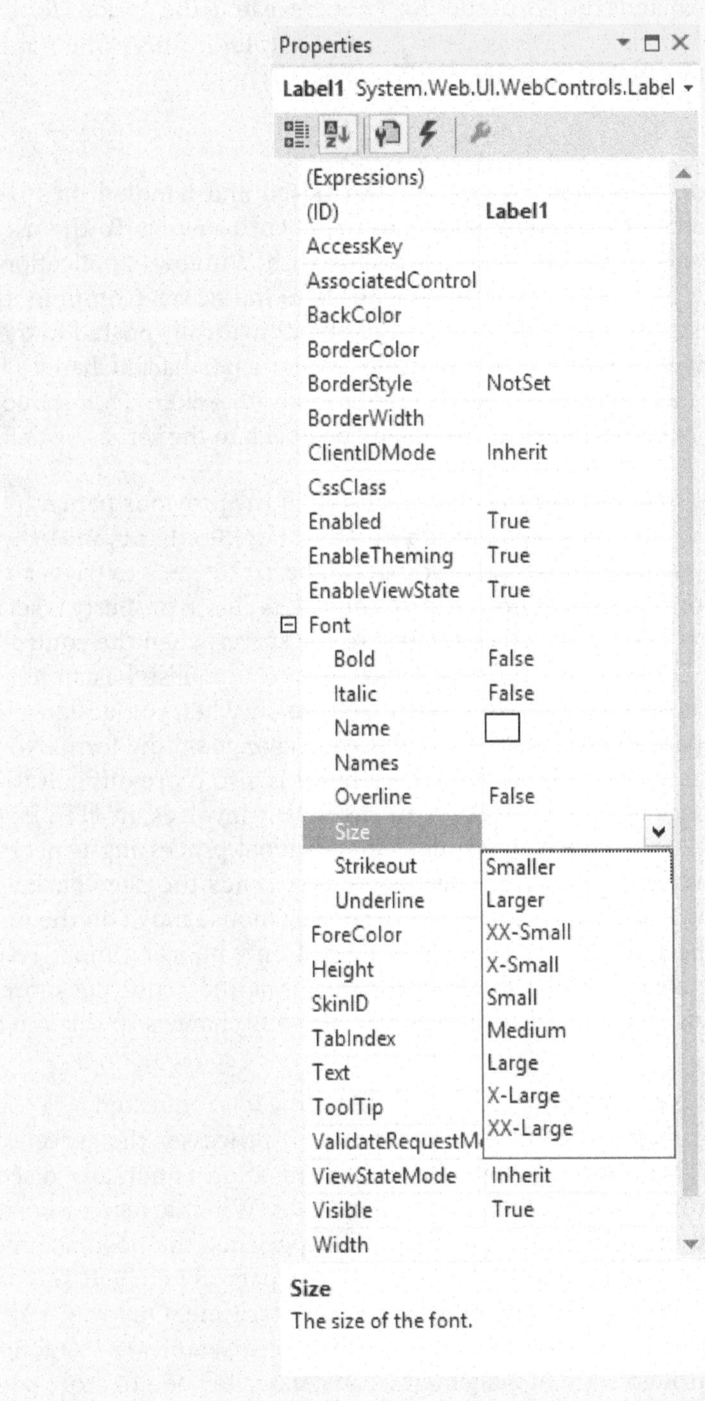

FIGURE 15-18 Properties for the Label control object

Figure 15-18 expands the properties for Font, revealing the options for Size. Instead of typing a point value, Size is set with relative values. This same Font property is found with most Web Forms controls.

EVENTS

The events for Web applications are both raised and handled on the server. The response is sent back through HTML to the client browser. To the user, this event handling appears to be like handling events with Windows applications. However, by default only a few events trigger a postback to the server. Common user interface events such as CheckChanged events are not automatically posted to the server. The click events fired by buttons automatically trigger a postback. Changes in selections to ListBox, RadioButton, RadioButtonList, CheckBox, CheckBoxList, and DropDownList do not cause an automatic postback to the server by default.

AUTOMATIC POSTBACK Each of the controls listed in the previous paragraph (ListBox, RadioButton, RadioButtonList, CheckBox, CheckBoxList, and DropDownList) has a property called AutoPostBack that can be set to true to trigger a postback to the server automatically. When a control's AutoPostBack property is set to true, the control's events trigger an HTTP request to the server when the control's registered event is fired. You will notice that the TextBox object also has an AutoPostBack property. It is also set to false by default. Normally when you design a form, you do not want the page to be posted back after each change on the form. Not only is this an expensive activity involving the server, but it is also more difficult to program. It is expensive because every postback to the server involves an HTTP request with the page's URL. The server determines if additional processing is necessary, and if so, it performs the processing. Then, the server sends the page back as an HTML document. You can imagine that if every click or mouse move on the form required a round-trip back to the server, you would not only be using more resources than necessary but also slowing down your application and requiring more work than necessary. Thus, you should be judicious with your changes to this AutoPostBack property.

The server loads an ASP.NET web page every time it is requested by a client browser and then unloads it back to the browser after it processes the server-side code to render the HTML. Even though this communication is actually disconnected, a feeling of continuity is needed at the client side. When a second postback of the page is sent to the server, the client should experience the postback merely as the next step in the progression of dealing with the page. The client should not know that the page is being reloaded or seen for the first time. One way ASP.NET pages accomplish this transition—so that it seems like a seamless interaction with the website—is through state management. You can write code to store page information between round-trips to the server. State management can occur at the client or server side.

You are encouraged to explore the MSDN documentation to learn more about maintaining state at the client side using the `ViewState` property and cookies. Explore the documentation using the **Help**, **Search** option within Visual Studio. The `HttpApplicationState class` has members for maintaining state for the entire application across many users. For example, you might want to include a counter on a web page to track the number of hits an application (web page) gets. The `HttpSessionState class` provides access to individual user session state values.

Adding Common Form-Type Controls

To illustrate some of the Web Forms controls that can be added to a Web form, a website called WebControls is created to host the Computer Club Inquiry Form. You might want to review Figure 15-3. The website was created using **File, New Web Site, ASP.NET Empty Web Site** with the **Visual C#** template selected. **File System** is selected for the **Web location.** Other than the selection for the **ASP.NET Empty Web Site** and the name for this site, no additional changes were made from what is shown in Figure 15-3.

Figure 15-19 shows the website. It contains some of the controls discussed previously and controls that are added in the sections that follow.

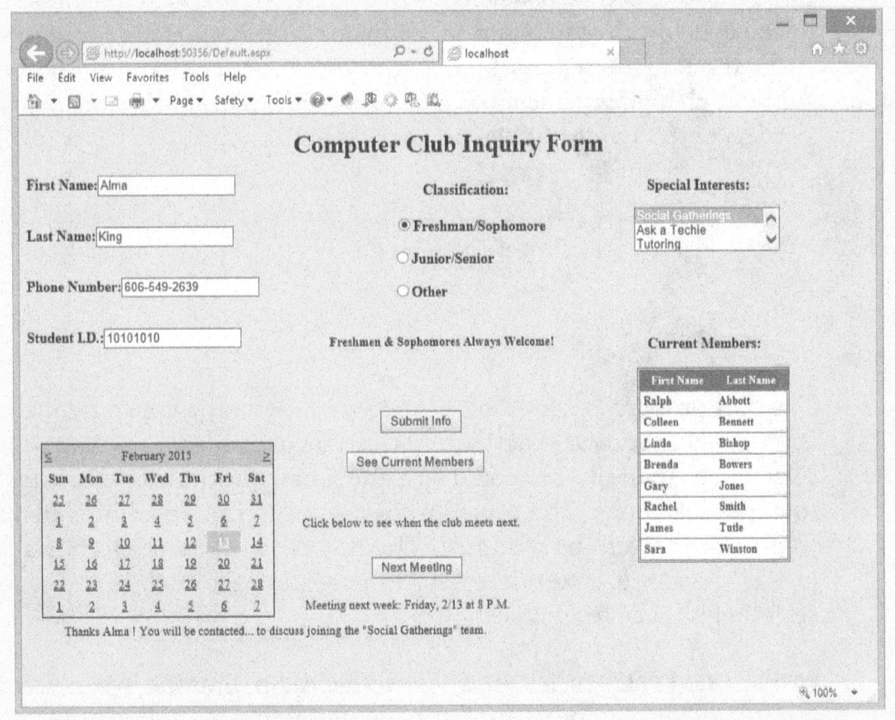

FIGURE 15-19 Website after adding server controls

LABEL, BUTTON, RADIOBUTTON, AND LISTBOX OBJECTS

As shown in Figure 15-19, `Label`, `Button`, `RadioButton`, and `ListBox` objects were added. You should be able to identify those controls on the form from your work with Windows applications. Event-handler methods for button clicks were written for the three buttons in the center of the form. Other than naming the `TextBox` controls using the `ID` property, and sizing them, no other properties were set. Their `AutoPostBack` property was left unchanged (set as `false`).

NOTE The four `TextBox` objects appear in white in Figure 15-19. They are currently storing values for first name, last name, phone number, and student ID.

SETTING THE PROPERTIES OF THE CONTROLS The `ID` properties and the individual `Text` properties were set for the `RadioButton` objects. The `GroupName` property is set for all three `RadioButton` objects. It is set to the same identifier (`Classif`) for all three objects. Adding the three objects to a group creates a **mutually exclusive** set of controls (only one can be selected at a time). If they did not belong to a group, all three could be checked. When one of the buttons is selected, a message is displayed in the label below the radio button. So that the message is displayed as soon as the user clicks the `RadioButton` `object`, and the `AutoPostBack` property is set to `true`. Without changing its default value, the message would not display until one of the `Button` objects triggered the postback event.

NOTE Remember that by default `Button` objects automatically trigger a postback.

The only property set for the `ListBox` `object` in the upper-right corner of the page is the `ID`. `SelectionMode` that was left unchanged (set as `Single`). Thus, only one selection from the list box could be made. Changing the property to `Multiple` enables multiple selections. The program logic for determining which items were selected would also have to be modified. The `AutoPostBack` property was left unchanged (set as `false`). It is not necessary to post the page back to the server as soon as a selection is made from this control.

WIRING EVENT-HANDLER METHODS All three radio buttons were wired to the same event-handler method. This can be done by first selecting all three buttons. Using the **Events** icon on the **Properties** window, the `radButtons_CheckedChanged( )` method was chosen for the `CheckChanged` event handler, as shown in Figure 15-20.

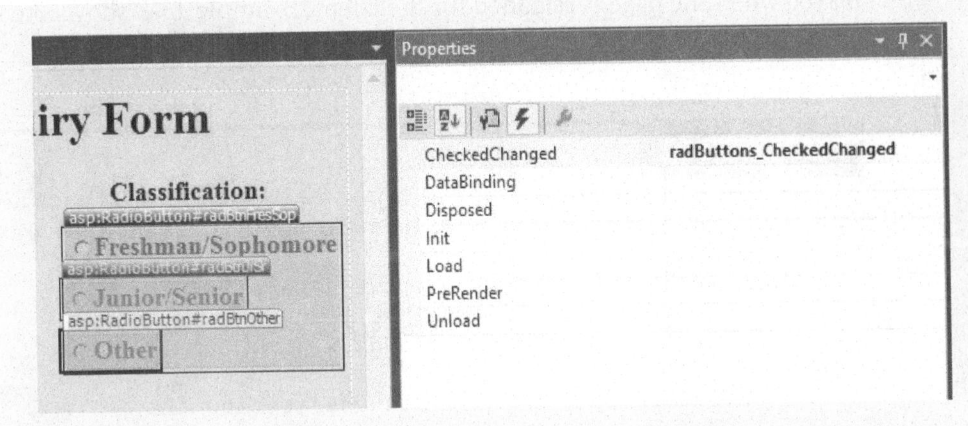

FIGURE 15-20 Wiring the same event to three RadioButton objects

Example 15-8 shows the event-handler method for the `RadioButton CheckedChanged( )` event.

EXAMPLE 15-8

```
protected void radButtons_CheckedChanged(object sender, EventArgs e)
{
   if (radBtnFresSop.Checked)
   {
        lblClassif.Text = "Freshmen & Sophomores ";
   }
   else
        if (radBtnJrSr.Checked)
        {
             lblClassif.Text = "Junior & Seniors ";
        }
        else
             if (radBtnOther.Checked)
             {
                  lblClassif.Text = "Special Students ";
             }
   lblClassif.Text += " Always Welcome!";
}
```

The event-handler method for the **Submit** button is used to retrieve the values entered into the TextBox fields and the selections made from the ListBox object by the user. These values are used to populate the Label controls that are to be displayed when the page is reloaded for the client. Example 15-9 shows the btnSubmit event-handler method.

EXAMPLE 15-9

```
protected void btnSubmit_Click(object sender, EventArgs e)
{
   lblSubmit.Text = "Thanks " + txtBxFname.Text +
                    "! You will be contacted. . . ";
   if (lstBxInterests.SelectedIndex > -1)
   {
       lblSubmit.Text += " to discuss joining the \"" +
                         lstBxInterests.SelectedItem.Text +
                         "\" team.";
   }
}
```

In Figure 15-19, you can see that two other controls were added to the Web application shown: Calendar and GridView. In addition, a validation control was added to the form. These special controls are discussed in the following section.

Validation, Custom, and Composite Controls

As shown in Figure 15-19, a Calendar control is added to the lower-left corner and a GridView control is added to the lower right for data retrieved from a Microsoft Access database. These are special types of controls that are discussed in this section. Also, you did not see it, another type of control, a validation control, is added to the form. Validation controls are discussed first.

NOTE Absolute positioning was used with all of the controls that were placed on the Web form for this example. As soon as the control was dragged to the form, the control was selected and **Set Position, Absolute** was set from the **Format** menu.

Validation Controls

Review Figure 15-17. Notice that there is a special tab labeled **Validation**. Several different types of **validation controls** are listed in the **Toolbox** on this tab. These controls enable input to be validated or checked by the server. Table 15-3 lists these controls in alphabetical order and describes their basic functionality.

TABLE 15-3 Controls of .NET validation

Type of control	Description
`CompareValidator`	Compares an input value against a preset constant value using comparison operators
`CustomValidator`	Checks the input value using program statements that you write
`RequiredFieldValidator`	Compares an input value to see if it is between specified lower and upper boundaries (can check ranges of dates, numbers, or alphabetic characters)
`RegularExpressionValidator`	Matches an input value to a pattern defined as a regular expression (used for entries such as e-mail, telephone numbers, and Social Security numbers to see if the values match a predictable sequence)
`RangeValidator`	Checks that the entry has a value
`ValidationSummary`	Displays a summary of all validation errors found

VALIDATION CONTROL PROPERTIES

To use one of these controls, drag the control to the Web Forms page and place it beside the control you want to validate. You can then treat the validation control object like any other control. It has properties that can be set. Using the `ControlToValidate` property, you tie the validation control to a specific form control object such as a `TextBox object`. The `ErrorMessage` property can be set to the message you want to display when the input control does not pass the validation test and the color for the error message can be changed.

ADDING A RequiredFieldValidator CONTROL

Figure 15-21 illustrates adding a `RequiredFieldValidator` control for the first name.

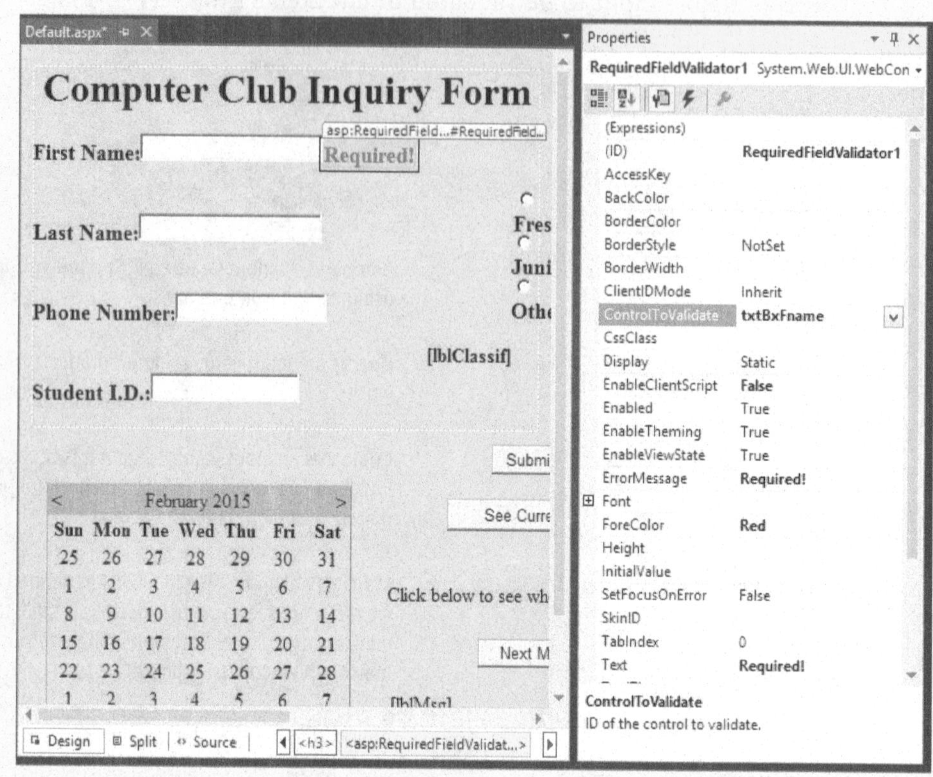

FIGURE 15-21 Adding a RequiredFieldValidator control

Notice that in Figure 15-21, `txtBxFname` is set as the value for the `ControlToValidate` property. "Required!" is set as the `ErrorMessage` value. `Red` is selected for the `Forecolor`. The `EnableClientScript` is set to `false`. The `RequiredField Validator` control is physically placed beside (not on top of) the `TextBox` `object` that it is validating.

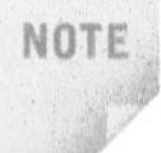

Place the validation control in the location where you want the error message to be displayed; it does not have to be placed beside the control. Sometimes, due to space constraints, the validation control cannot be placed beside the control it is validating. As with other controls, to get it on the form, drag and drop it from the **Toolbox** window.

After you add the `RequiredFieldValidator` control and tie it to the `txtBxFname` `object`, `"Required!"` is displayed in red if the form loads and is submitted to the server with no value entered into the `txtBxFname` control. `"Required!"` is displayed because the `ErrorMessage` property value is set to `"Required!"`. This was just a typed value entered during design.

Using the `Text` property available with validation controls, you can also customize the error information displayed to users. A common practice is to set the `Text` property of the validation control to a red star (asterisk) and place it next to the input box to be validated. If you do this, an asterisk is displayed at run time if the control fails validation.

NOTE Notice that the `Text` property and the `ErrorMessage` property are both used to set the message that prints when validation fails. If you set both, the `Text` property overrides the `ErrorMessage` property.

PAGE VALIDATION

By default, **page validation** occurs when *any* button on the form is clicked. It is called page validation because every control field on the page that has an associated validation control is checked to see if it passes the validation rules. If you do not want one or more of the `Button` objects to cause page validation, you can set a property on the `Button` called `CausesValidation`. By default, every `Button` object's `CausesValidation` property is set to `true`.

NOTE As you design your solutions, give careful thought to which of your buttons should cause page validation of the input controls. Set `CausesValidation` to `false` for all other `Button` objects.

Clicking the **Submit Info** button before typing values into the first name text box causes the validation error message `"Required!"` to be displayed in red, as shown in Figure 15-22.

FIGURE 15-22 Error message from the RequiredFieldValidator control

Review the list of predefined validation controls in Table 15-3. Another one of the validation controls listed is RangeValidator. Using RangeValidator, you can make sure that the value entered by the user falls between a predetermined set of values. This control can be used to test for valid dates to ensure that the dates entered fall within a specific range or to test numeric values to ensure that they fall within the range specified during design. You can do pattern matching with the RegularExpressionValidator control. Checks of e-mail addresses to ensure that the @ symbol is included are performed using the RegularExpressionValidator control. More than one validation control can be associated with an input object. You are encouraged to experiment and review the MSDN documentation.

At run time, you can use the Page.IsValid property to check whether all validation controls on a page are currently valid. The property can be placed in a selection statement with actions performed based on its Boolean result.

PAGE LIFE CYCLE

The nature of Web programming is different from windows application development because of the Page life cycle. There are a number of events that fire up automatically and sequentially on web pages. They includes methods such as Page_Pre_Init( ), LoadViewState( ), LoadPostBackData( ), Page_Load( ), and eventually Page_Unload( ). The sequence of events is somewhat complex. It was noted earlier that a Page_Load( ) method is automatically added when you create a new Web Form page. You do not have to do anything extra or special to register it. As long as you include the word "Page" as part of the name, it, like the other page methods, is triggered when the page is loaded. Bodies for the Page_Load( ) and other methods are included in the code-behind file. You do not have to provide bodies for all these methods, many ASP.NET applications do include a Page_Load( ) event handler. The Page_Load( ) method is the most commonly used method on the server-side application code for an .aspx file.

The last processed method is Page_Unload( ). During this method, data can be released to free up resources on the server for other processes. Once this method is completed, the HTML is sent to the browser for client-side processing.

Recall that the load event with Windows applications, the Form_Load( ) event, is executed once—initially when the application is run. The Page_Load( ) event with Web Forms is not only triggered when the application initially loads, but executed multiple times. It is executed every time a button is clicked and every time the page is loaded. It is sometimes useful to determine if this was the first time the page was loaded or if it is a postback, second, or subsequent loading of the page. ASP.NET provides a special property, IsPostBack property that returns a Boolean value indicating whether it is the first time the page is loaded.

If you want to execute the code in the `Page_Load( )` method only the first time the page is loaded, you can use the `Page.IsPostBack` property. If the `Page.IsPostBack` property returns `false`, the page is loaded for the first time. If it is `true`, the page is posted back to the server, which occurs when a button, for example, is clicked on the form.

15

As was noted earlier, the Web is basically stateless. Each request for a page is treated as a new request. Information from one request is not available by default to the next request, which means that every time you click a button, you lose values from the previous page load. With a web page, for each request, the `Page class` is instantiated every time from "scratch," which means that any values or whatever state it had previously will get lost.

ASP.NET includes a number of features for managing state—that is, for storing information between requests. These include cookies, hidden fields, query strings, application state, and session state. Hidden fields, cookies, and query strings all involve storing data on the client in various ways. However, application state and session state store data in memory on the server. Each option has distinct advantages and disadvantages, depending on the scenario. These topics are beyond the scope of this chapter, but you are encouraged to review the online and MSDN documentation to read more about managing state.

Calendar Control

A `Calendar` control is used to display calendar months on a web page. After being placed on the page, the calendar is live and users can use the calendar to view and select dates. For the application displayed in Figure 15-19, which is being used to demonstrate the server controls, a `Calendar` control is dragged and dropped onto the web page from the **Toolbox**. When the `Calendar object` is dropped on the page, the lines shown in Example 15-10 are added to the HTML (.aspx) file.

EXAMPLE 15-10

```
<asp:Calendar ID="Calendar1" runat="server" style="z-index: 1;
    left: 23px; top: 355px; position: absolute; height: 188px;
    width: 259px">
</asp:Calendar>
```

Remember, after the `.aspx` markup file and the `aspx.cs` code-behind file are opened (using the **Solution Explorer** window), you use the tabs above the page to switch between viewing the files. To switch between HTML (**Source**) and **Design** view, use the tabs at the bottom of the page, as shown in Figure 15-23. The **Split** option enables you to see both Source and Design. Use the **View** menu options, if you have trouble locating any of these tabs.

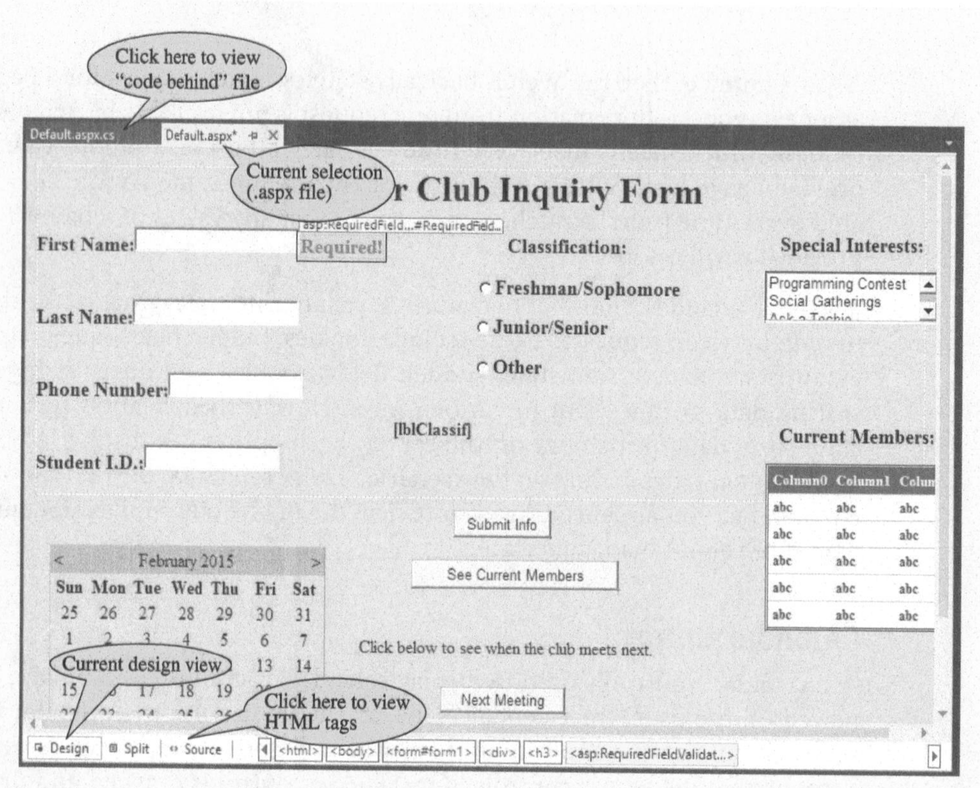

FIGURE 15-23 Switching between .aspx and .aspx.cs files

`Calendar` control has a number of properties including the `SelectedDate` property. `SelectedDate` is used to pick the month, day, and year for display. The `SelectedDate` property is initially set to the current date. This is done when the page is loaded. But, you can also set the date programmatically or during design using the `SelectedDate` property found in the **Properties** window. Setting the date during design enables you to use the built-in `Calendar` control on the **Properties** window, as shown in Figure 15-24.

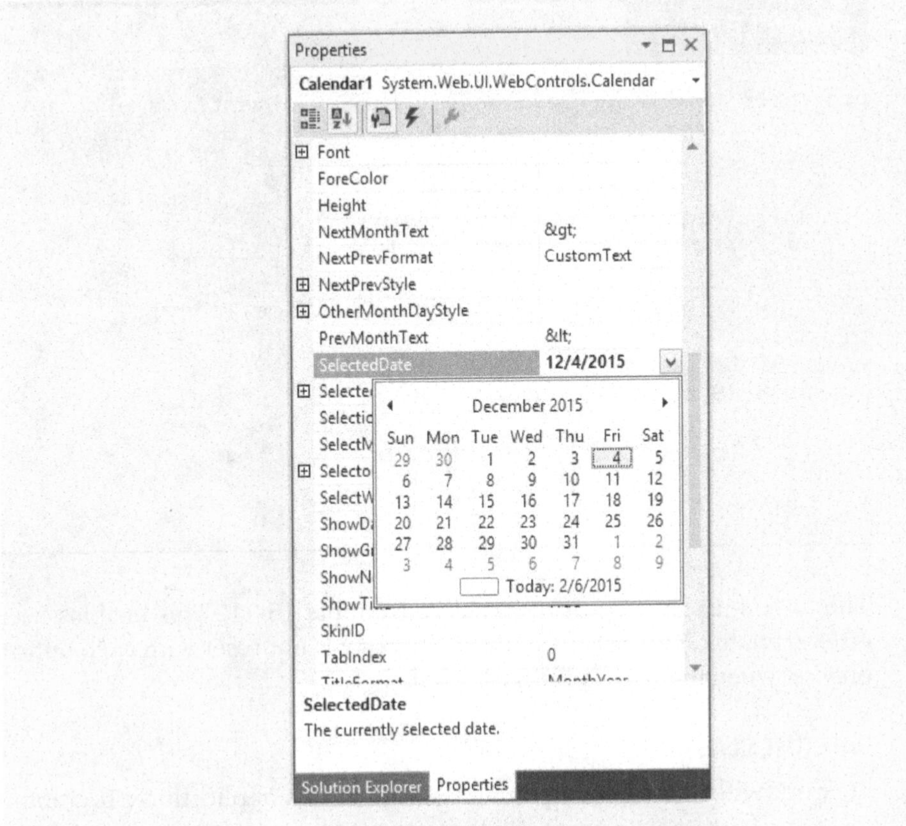

FIGURE 15-24 Using the Properties window to set the SelectedDate property

If you are going to set the date programmatically, use the `Page_Load( )` event-handler method. It is not necessary for you to register the event, since the event name starts with the `Page_` attribute. You can also add a `Page_Unload( )` event if you have activities you need to perform when the application exits, like closing files or database connections. Like the `Page_Load( )` event, it is automatically bound to the page, if the `AutoEventWireup` attribute is set to `true`.

The `Calendar` control is based on the .NET `DateTime` `class`, which enables you to work with dates in different formats. Program statements were added to the `Page_Load( )` event handler to set the date to the current day the application is run. This is shown in Example 15-11. Notice that the statements are placed in a `try...catch` exception block.

EXAMPLE 15-11

```
protected void Page_Load(object sender, EventArgs e)
{
    try
    {
        if (Page.IsPostBack == false)
            // Could also write if(!Page.IsPostBack)
        {
            Calendar1.SelectedDate = DateTime.Today;
        }
    }
    catch (System.Exception exc)
    {
            lblMsg.Text = exc.Message;
    }
}
```

The `IsPostBack` property is used in Example 15-11. This enables users to select different dates. The `SelectedDate` property is not reset with each button click. It is only set when the page is FIRST loaded.

DATETIME CLASS

To work with the calendar for the WebControls application programmatically, an `object` of the `DateTime` `class` is instantiated.

The `DateTime` `class` has a large number of useful members that can be used with `Calendar` control objects. Table 15-4 gives some of the more interesting members of this class.

TABLE 15-4 Members of the `DateTime` class

DateTime members	Description
`AddDays( ), AddHours( ), AddMinutes( ), AddMonths( ), AddYears( )`	Adds a specified number of days, hours, minutes, months, or years
`Compare( ) - (static member)`	Compares two instances of `DateTime`
`Date`	Gets the date

(continues)

TABLE 15-4 Members of the DateTime class (*continued*)

DateTime members	Description
Day	Gets the day of the month
DayOfWeek	Gets the day of the week (0 for Sunday; 6 for Saturday)
DayOfYear	Gets the day of the year
DaysInMonth( )	Returns the number of days in the specified month
Hour	Gets the hour of the date
MaxValue - (static member)	Returns the largest possible value for DateTime
MinValue - (static member)	Returns the smallest possible value for DateTime
Minute	Gets the minute of the date
Month	Gets the month of the date
Now - (static member)	Gets the current date and time
Parse( ) - (static member)	Converts a string into the DateTime format
Subtract( )	Subtracts a specified time from an instance
Today - (static member)	Gets the current date
Year	Gets the current year
+, -, =, ==, <, >, >=, <=	Operators defined to work with DateTime instances

© Cengage Learning

NOTE Property members are given in Table 15-4 without ( ). Members identified as static must be invoked using the DateTime class name (i.e., DateTime.Now).

USING A CALENDAR CONTROL IN APPLICATIONS

To continue creating the `WebControls` application, a button labeled **Next Meeting** was added to the form. Remember that the final result of the application was shown in Figure 15-19. When the button labeled **Next Meeting** is clicked, the calendar changes to show the date of the next computer club meeting. Programmatically, this is set as exactly 7 days from the current date. As you review Example 15-12, notice that the first line of code in the method clears any date selections made by the user. It then uses today's date to set the meeting date. The application could be modified to have the meeting date shown as 7 days from the selected date. However, in order to illustrate properties associated with the current date, the `Today` property is used. A selection statement is then used to test the meeting date to make sure that the date does not fall on Sunday. If it does, the meeting date is set for the following Monday. Example 15-12 shows the event-handler method for this button.

EXAMPLE 15-12

```
protected void btnShowNextMeeting_Click(object sender, EventArgs e)
{
   Calendar1.SelectedDates.Clear( );

   DateTime meetingDate = new DateTime(DateTime.Today.Year,
                  DateTime.Today.Month, DateTime.Today.Day, 8, 0, 0);

   // Meeting is schedule for one week from today!
   meetingDate = meetingDate.AddDays(7);

   // Unless, of course it's Sunday - if so meet on Monday.
   if (meetingDate.DayOfWeek.ToString( ) == "Sunday")
   {
       meetingDate = meetingDate.AddDays(1);
   }

   Calendar1.TodaysDate = meetingDate;
   Calendar1.SelectedDate = Calendar1.TodaysDate;
   lblMsg.Text = ("Meeting next week: " + meetingDate.DayOfWeek +
                ", " + meetingDate.Month + "/" + meetingDate.Day +
                " at " + meetingDate.Hour + " P.M.");
}
```

Figure 15-25 shows the web page before and after the user clicks the **Next Meeting** button.

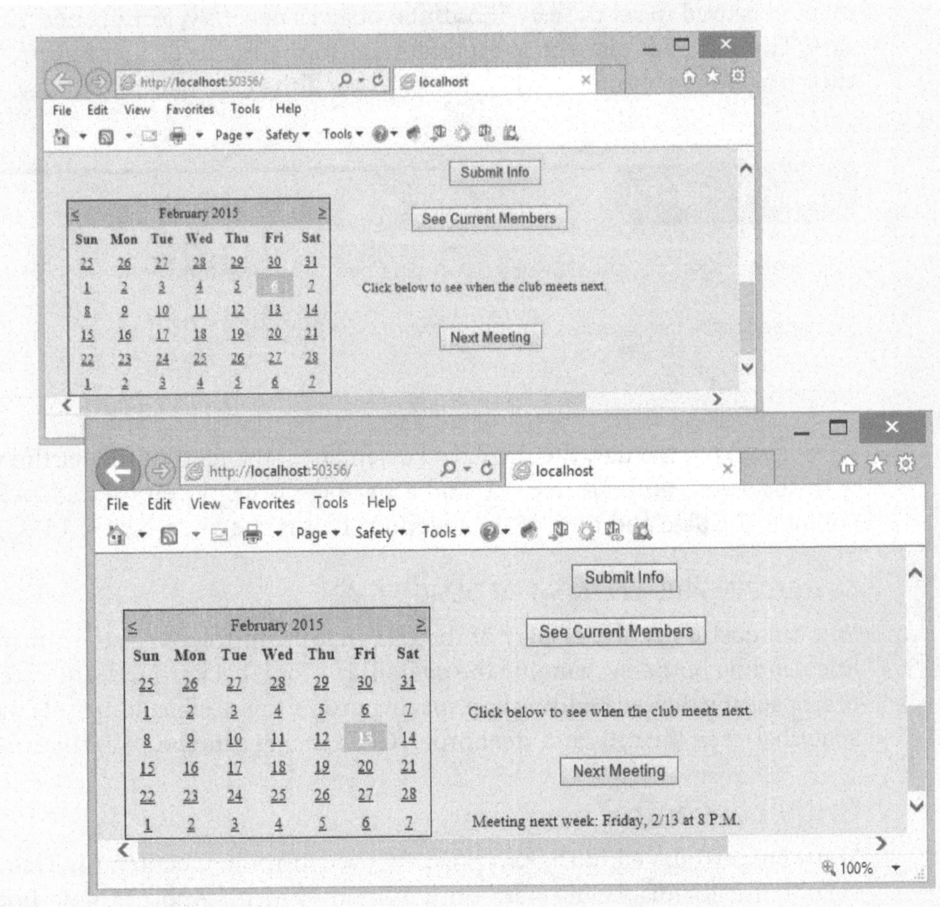

FIGURE 15-25 Calendar showing different dates selected

The `SelectedDate` property of the `Calendar` control is set in the `btnShowNextMeeting_Click( )` method. This method instantiates the `object` of the `DateTime` `class` (`meetingDate`), initializing it using the current year (`Today.Year`), current month (`Today.Month`), and current day (`Today.Day`). As given in Table 15-4, `Today` is a `static` member of the `DateTime` `class`; thus, it must be referenced with the `class` name, as opposed to an `object`. When the `meetingDate` `object` is instantiated, the constructor with six arguments is used. The last three arguments (`8, 0, and 0`) set the `Hour`, `Minute`, and `Second` properties. It displays P.M. because that `string` literal is concatenated onto the end of the value returned from the `Hour` property, as shown in the last line for Example 15-12.

The date of the next Computer Club meeting is 7 days from today's date—unless that date falls on a Sunday. If it does, the meeting date is the following Monday. This is what the code in Example 15-12 accomplishes. In the example, the `AddDays( )`

method is used to set the meetingDate object's new Day, Month, and Year, if necessary. The value of 7 is sent as an argument to the method. The selection statement, shown again in Example 15-13, checks to see if the date falls on Sunday.

EXAMPLE 15-13

```
if (meetingDate.DayOfWeek.ToString( ) == "Sunday")
{
   meetingDate = meetingDate.AddDays(1);
}
```

After checking the day, the displayed calendar is changed to reflect the value stored with the meetingDate object and a message is displayed on a Label object. It contains the date and time of the meeting. This is shown in Figure 15-25.

CUSTOMIZING THE CALENDAR AT DESIGN TIME

You can customize the display of the Calendar control object by turning on gridlines; adding borders; changing the overall size, font, background, and foreground colors; or setting the cell padding and spacing properties. Cell padding sets the amount of space between the cells and the border. Cell spacing sets the space between the cells.

GridView Control

You were introduced to the DataGridView control in Chapter 14. This control was very useful for displaying data on a Windows form. Another data-bound control that you will want to explore is the GridView. The GridView is very similar to the DataGridView you used with Windows applications. It also features automatic data. Both the DataGridView and the GridView are used to display data in a tabular form, with each column representing a field and each row representing a record from a data source. The DataGridView, used with Windows applications, is just a little more sophisticated than the GridView control. You can customize the GridView's appearance. As you learned in Chapter 14, when you used the DataGridView control, you must bind these types of controls to a data source.

DATA BINDING

At design time, you can use the visual configuration tools to bind the data by identifying the data source, selecting the data fields, and setting properties in the **Properties** window, such as the DataSource property. Another option is to write program statements to do this. Two common data source classes used to bind GridView objects to the actual data are the DataReader and DataSet. The actual data used to populate these controls can come from sources such as arrays or database tables. You experienced using both the `DataReader` `object` and the `DataSet` `object` in conjunction with the `DataAdapter` `object` in Chapter 14.

You are encouraged to review the sections in Chapter 14 that relate to accessing data from database tables. You recall, from Chapter 14, that there are a number of visual tools and wizards that can be used to bind data to controls.

USING A GRIDVIEW CONTROL IN APPLICATIONS

The `WebControls` application that is being developed in this chapter includes a `GridView` control, which displays data from an Access database. To add this control to a Web form, you follow the same design guidelines presented previously. You might want to review the `DataSetExample`, Example 14-21, in Chapter 14. It displayed data from an Access database on a standard Windows form. Example 14-21 instantiated objects from the `DataSet` and `DataAdapter` classes. These same classes are used to retrieve data for display on a Web form in this example.

You need to pay particular attention to security issues surrounding data access with websites. Microsoft Access databases include fewer security features than SQL Server databases. Access databases are not recommended for production websites. You would follow the same principles to connect your website to an SQL database. Access was used in this chapter because it was used in Chapter 14. However, you would normally want to connect a website to a database that handles multiple users.

OleDB DATA PROVIDER You learned in Chapter 14 that .NET organizes ADO.NET classes into different provider namespaces. This enables you to work with data from different databases, such as Oracle and Access, using a consistent object-oriented approach. Each of these namespaces has its own classes prefixed with the provider type, one of which is `OleDB` for working with Access databases.

Visual Studio has a **Data** tab as part of the **Toolbox**. Included are controls for displaying data such as the `GridView`, `DataList`, and `DetailsView` controls plus controls that are used to connect to specific databases. These include `AccessDataSource`, `SqlDataSource`, `XmlDataSource`, and `ObjectDataSource`. All of these controls can be dragged to your form in exactly the same manner you drag other control objects, such as buttons.

CONNECTING TO THE DATABASE A button labeled `See Current Members` is added to the `WebControls` application. When the user clicks this button, a table should be displayed with the names of current members. A solution can be developed by writing program statements to populate a control. This approach will be explored first. However, with the visual tools available with Visual Studio, another approach will then be illustrated that minimizes the amount of program statements required.

For the first example, a `Connection` `object` is instantiated. The same connection `string` that you saw in Chapter 14 is used as an argument to the constructor. The connection `string` identifies the provider as an Access database. It also specifies the name of the database—including the full path to the database location. The example that follows, Example 15-14, shows the statements that make up the `btnShowMembers_Click( )` method. As you review the code, notice the comment that appears in the method. Only minor modifications are needed to the code presented in Chapter 14. The `DataBind( )` method call is different for Web applications. To display the data using the `GridView`, objects of the `DataAdapter` and `DataSet` classes are used for both Web and Windows applications.

NOTE Note that the path of the database is listed as

`"C:\\CSharpProjects\\member.accdb"`

You will want to change the path indicating where you have placed a copy of the member.accdb. As noted in Chapter 14, if are running examples provided with this chapter on a 64-bit processor and get an error indicating "The 'Microsoft.ACE.OLEDB.12.0' provider is not registered on this machine", you may need to install a new driver. At the time the book was written, you could read about the problem and find the download at http://www.connectionstrings.com/the-microsoft-ace-oledb-12-0-provider-is-not-registered-on-the-local-machine/

EXAMPLE 15-14

```
protected void btnShowMembers_Click(object sender, EventArgs e)
{
   lblMembers.Visible = true;
   try
   {
     string sConnection =
         "Provider=Microsoft.ACE.OLEDB.12.0;" +
         "Data Source=C:\\CSharpProjects\\member.accdb";
     OleDbConnection dbConn = new OleDbConnection(sConnection);

     string sql =
       "Select FirstName as [First Name], LastName as " +
               "[Last Name] From memberTable " +
               " Order By LastName Asc, FirstName Asc;";
     OleDbCommand dbCmd = new OleDbCommand( );
     dbCmd.CommandText = sql;
     dbCmd.Connection = dbConn;
```

15

```
        OleDbDataAdapter memberDataAdap = new OleDbDataAdapter( );
        memberDataAdap.SelectCommand = dbCmd;
        DataSet memberDS = new DataSet( );
        memberDataAdap.Fill(memberDS, "memberTable");
        grdViewMembers.DataSource = memberDS;

        // Binding is required for web apps
        this.grdViewMembers.DataBind( );

        lblMembers.Visible = true;
        grdViewMembers.Visible = true;
    }
    catch (System.Exception exc)
    {
        this.lblMsg.Text = exc.Message;
    }
}
```

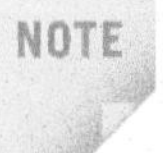

NOTE If you use the Data Source Configuration wizard to connect to the database, an **asp**:AccessDataSource control tag is added to the .aspx file. One of its attributes is DataFile="~/App_Data/member.accdb".

RETRIEVING DATA FROM THE DATABASE

Example 14-21 in Chapter 14 contained statements that created a Windows application with a DataGridView object populated from the Member.accdb database. Example 15-14 is similar but stores the retrieved data on a Web Form. As with Example 14-21, an SQL statement stored in the string identifier, sql, is used to select the records. In this example, the data fields of FirstName and LastName from memberTable are retrieved. The SQL statement arranges the result by LastName. When there are duplicate records with the same last name, the records are arranged in ascending order by FirstName. In order to programmatically change the column heading for the GridView, the as keyword was used. Square brackets were used around the identifier to enable a space to be included as part of the name. Writing Select FirstName as [First Name], retrieves the data field named FirstName and uses "First Name" as the column heading. The sql string object is set as the CommandText property value. The connection string, dbConn, is set as the Connection property as follows:

```
dbCmd.CommandText = sql;
dbCmd.Connection = dbConn;
```

To use the Fill( ) method with the DataSet object, an object of the DataAdapter class is instantiated. Notice that each of these classes is part of the OleDb namespace, thus class names are prefixed with OleDb. Additional using statements were added to include the Data and Data.OleDb namespaces. The SelectCommand property of the DataAdapter class is set to the CommandText object holding the SQL statement. Using the DataAdapter's Fill( ) method, the table from the actual Access database (memberTable) is used to populate the DataSet object (memberDS). The final statements in the try block for Example 15-14 binds the GridView object to the DataSet. Recall that this is the only statement that has changed from the Windows application.

Remember, Figure 15-19 shows this application running after all the controls are added to the page and event-handler methods are wired.

The property values set for the WebControls example are given in Table 15-5.

TABLE 15-5 WebControls properties

Name	Object type	Property	Value
btnShowMembers	Button	ID	btnShowMembers
btnShowMembers	Button	Text	See Current Members
btnShowNextMeeting	Button	ID	btnShowNextMeeting
btnShowNextMeeting	Button	Text	Next Meeting
btnSubmit	Button	ID	btnSubmit
btnSubmit	Button	Text	Submit Info
Calendar1	Calendar	ID	Calendar1
Calendar1	Calendar	SelectedDate	12/4/2015
grdViewMembers	GridView	ID	grdViewMembers
grdViewMembers	GridView	BackColor	White
grdViewMembers	GridView	BorderColor	#336666

(continues)

TABLE 15-5 WebControls properties (*continued*)

Name	Object type	Property	Value
grdViewMembers	GridView	BorderStyle	Double
grdViewMembers	GridView	BroderWidth	3px
grdViewMembers	GridView	CellPadding	4
grdViewMembers	GridView	EmptyDataText	There are no data records to show
grdViewMembers	GridView	Font	Small
grdViewMembers	GridView	GridLines	Horizontal
Label1	Label	ID	Label1
Label1	Label	Text	Classification
Label2	Label	ID	Label2
Label2	Label	Text	Special Interests
Label3	Label	ID	Label3
Label3	Label	Text	Click below to see when the club meets next.
lblClassif	Label	ID	lblClassif
lblMembers	Label	ID	lblMembers
lblMembers	Label	Text	Current Members:
lblMsg	Label	ID	lblMsg
lblSubmit	Label	ID	lblSubmit
lstBxInterests	ListBox	ID	lstBxInterests

(*continues*)

TABLE 15-5 WebControls properties (*continued*)

Name	Object type	Property	Value
lstBxInterests	ListBox	Items	Collection... "Programming Contest", "Ask a Techie", "Tutoring", "Mentoring", "Department Web Site"
radBtnFresSop	RadioButton	ID	radBtnFreSop
radBtnFresSop	RadioButton	Text	Freshman/ Sophomore
radBtnFresSop	RadioButton	AutoPostBack	True
radBtnFresSop	RadioButton	GroupName	Classif
radBtnJrSr	RadioButton	ID	radBtnJrSr
radBtnJrSr	RadioButton	Text	Junior/Senior
radBtnJrSr	RadioButton	AutoPostBack	True
radBtnJrSr	RadioButton	GroupName	Classif
radBtnOther	RadioButton	ID	radBtnJrSr
radBtnJrSr	RadioButton	Text	Other
radBtnJrSr	RadioButton	AutoPostBack	True
radBtnJrSr	RadioButton	GroupName	Classif
RequiredField Validator1	RequiredField Validator	ID	RequiredField Validator1
RequiredField Validator1	RequiredField Validator	ControlTo Validate	txtBxID

(*continues*)

15

TABLE 15-5 WebControls properties (*continued*)

Name	Object type	Property	Value
RequiredField Validator1	RequiredField Validator	ErrorMessage	Required!
RequiredField Validator1	RequiredField Validator	ForeColor	Red
RequiredField Validator1	RequiredField Validator	Text	Required!
txtBxFname	TextBox	ID	txtBxFname
txtBxID	TextBox	ID	txtBxID
txtBxLname	TextBox	ID	txtBxLname
txtBxPhone	TextBox	ID	txtBxPhone

The complete program listing for the code-behind file for the `WebControls` project is shown in Example 15-15.

EXAMPLE 15-15

```
// WebControls
using System;
using System.Collections.Generic;
using System.Linq;
using System.Data;
using System.Web;
using System.Web.UI;
using System.Web.UI.WebControls;
using System.Data.OleDb;

public class _Default : System.Web.UI.Page
{
  protected void Page_Load(object sender, EventArgs e)
  {
     try
     {
        if (Page.IsPostBack == false)
     // Could also write if(!Page.IsPostBack)
```

```
        {
            Calendar1.SelectedDate = DateTime.Today;
        }
    }
    catch (System.Exception exc)
    {
        lblMsg.Text = exc.Message;
    }
}

protected void btnShowNextMeeting_Click (object sender,
                                         EventArgs e)
{
    Calendar1.SelectedDates.Clear( );
    DateTime meetingDate = new
          DateTime(DateTime.Today.Year, DateTime.Today.Month,
                   DateTime.Today.Day, 8,0,0);

    // Meeting is scheduled
    // for one week from today!
    meetingDate = meetingDate.AddDays(7);
    // Unless, of course it's Sunday - if so
    // meet on Monday.
    if (meetingDate.DayOfWeek.ToString( ) == "Sunday")
    {
         meetingDate = meetingDate.AddDays(1);
    }

    Calendar1.TodaysDate = meetingDate;
    Calendar1.SelectedDate = Calendar1.TodaysDate;
    lblMsg.Text = "Meeting next week: " +
                  meetingDate.DayOfWeek + ", " +
                  meetingDate.Month + "/" +
                  meetingDate.Day + " at " +
                  meetingDate.Hour + " P.M.";
}

protected void btnShowMembers_Click (object sender, EventArgs e)
{
      try
      {
            string sConnection =
                 "Provider=Microsoft.ACE.OLEDB.12.0;" +
                 "Data Source=C:\\CSharpProjects\\member.accdb";
            OleDbConnection dbConn = new
                 OleDbConnection (sConnection);
```

```
            string sql = "Select FirstName as [First Name],
                 LastName as [Last name] From " +
                 "memberTable Order " + "By LastName Asc,
                 FirstName Asc;";
            OleDbCommand dbCmd = new OleDbCommand( );
            dbCmd.CommandText = sql;
            dbCmd.Connection = dbConn;
            OleDbDataAdapter memberDataAdap = new
                 OleDbDataAdapter( );
            memberDataAdap.SelectCommand = dbCmd;
            DataSet memberDS = new DataSet( );
            memberDataAdap.Fill(memberDS, "memberTable");
            grdViewMembers.DataSource = memberDS;
            // Binding is required for web apps
            grdViewMembers.DataBind( );
            lblMembers.Visible = true;
            grdViewMembers.Visible = true;
        }
        catch (System.Exception exc)
        {
            lblMsg.Text = exc.Message;
        }
}

protected void btnSubmit_Click(object sender, EventArgs e)
{
   lblSubmit.Text = "Thanks " +
      txtBxFname.Text +
      "! You will be contacted. . . ";
   if (lstBxInterests.SelectedIndex > -1)
   {
        lblSubmit.Text +=
           " to discuss joining" +
           "the \"" +
           lstBxInterests.SelectedItem.Text +
           "\" team.";
   }
}

protected void radButtons_CheckedChanged(object sender,
                                          EventArgs e)
{
   if (radBtnFresSop.Checked)
   {
        lblClassif.Text = "Freshmen & Sophomores ";
   }
```

```
            else if (radBtnJrSr.Checked)
            {
                lblClassif.Text = "Junior & Seniors ";
            }
            else if (radBtnOther.Checked)
            {
                lblClassif.Text = "Special Students ";
            }
            lblClassif.Text += " Always Welcome!"; }
            }
        }
}
```

AccessDataSource

Instead of writing the program statements in the `btnShowMembers_Click( )` method to connect to the database and retrieve the data, you could use the data visual configuration tools and have these statements automatically generated for you. Recall from Chapter 14 that when you drag a data-bound control onto your application using Visual Studio, you get a smart tag on the control that enables you to select the binding data source. .NET includes data source classes that reduce your need for accessing individual Data Provider classes. The `AccessDataSource class` simplifies connecting an ASP.NET web page to an Access database. The `AccessDataSource` is a special class that actually inherits from the `SqlDataSource` and provides additional functionality for working specifically with Access databases.

If the `AccessDataSource` does not show up in your **Toolbox**, it can be added by right-clicking on the **Data Toolbox** and selecting **Choose Items**. Another option is to make the database available to the application from the **Tools**, **Connect to Database** menu option. The **Server Explorer** window will reveal the available database tables once you make the connection. You then drag one of the database tables onto the form. From there, you can use the configuration wizard.

Using Visual Tools to Connect

To illustrate the use of the visual configuration tools, a copy of the `WebControls` website application that was just completed was created. The original `GridView object` was deleted. The `btnShowMembers_Click( )` event-handler method was removed from the code-behind file (`Default.aspx.cs`). One additional change was made to the file before using the configuration tools. On the `btnShowMembers` tag in the `Default.aspx` source code file, the `OnClick="btnShowMembers_Click"` attribute was removed.

Once those items were removed from the application, **Connect to Database** was selected from the **Tools** menu. The members.accdb Access database file was located, selected, and the connection was established. Then using the **Server Explorer** window, the member table is dragged onto the form. This puts a `GridView` `object` on the page. Additional configuring can occur to the grid, but it is that simple. The grid is tied to the database table. As you saw in Chapter 14, the visual tools could be opened a number of different ways. When the control `object` is placed on a page, its smart tag reveals a number of options as shown in Figure 15-26.

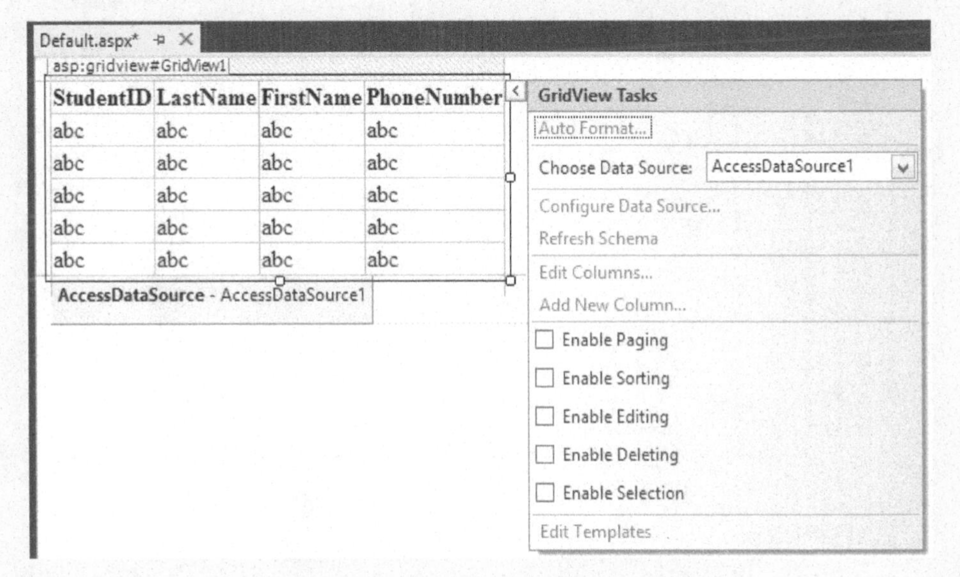

FIGURE 15-26 Binding data source to the GridView

As shown in Figure 15-26, from the smart tag, you can add columns using the **Add New Column** option. Columns can be removed or formatted using the **Edit Columns** option. **Configure Data Source** launches the configuration wizard.

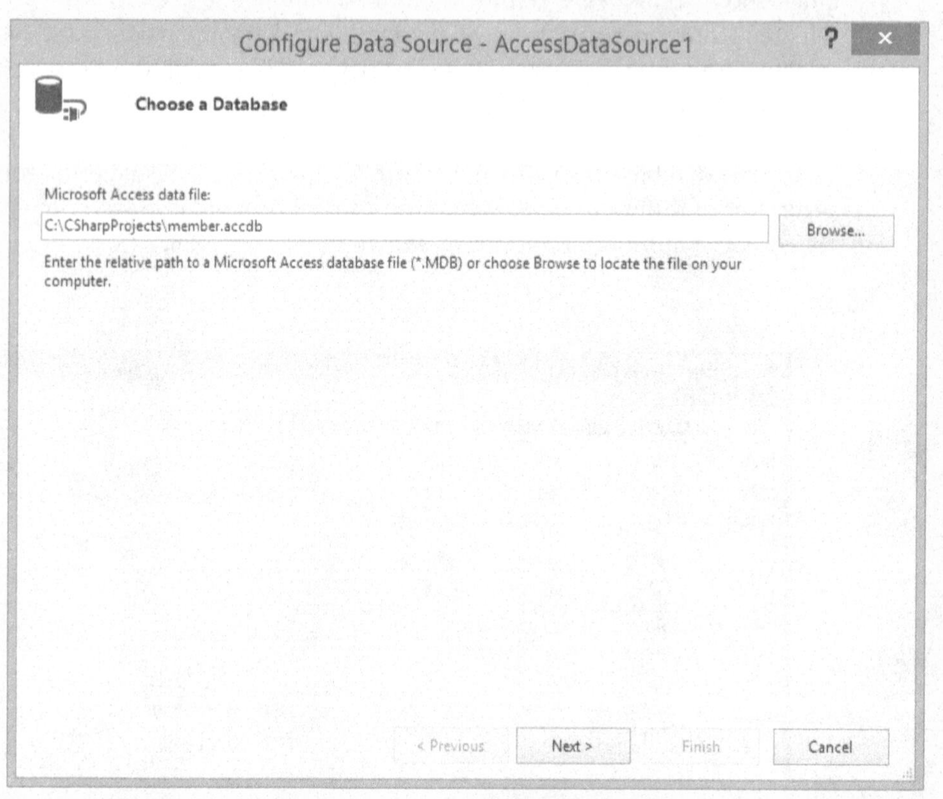

FIGURE 15-27 Connecting to Access Database

The **Browse** button shown in Figure 15-27 enables you to select a different Access Database.

NOTE

Recall that the location or path of the `member.accdb` database was hard-coded in the earlier example. Using the `AccessDataSource` control `object`, you can provide a relative path to the database. This makes deploying or moving the data-driven website easier.

As shown in Figure 15-27, selecting **Configure Data Source** launches the configuration wizard. You could identify a different database where the application should get its data or move to the next step.

Store Databases in App_Data Folder

When the application was first created a Web folder was added, `App_Data`, to hold the database. This is where member.accdb is stored. Recall that this application was started as an **ASP.NET Empty Web Site**. From the **Solution Explorer** window, a **Web Form** was added, `Default.aspx`, and then using the **Solution Explorer** window, `App_Data` was added using the **Add, Add ASP.NET Web Folder** option. The `member.accdb` was then moved into that directory. This makes it easy to locate when you **Select the Microsoft Access Database** to connect to the website, as shown in Figure 15-28. Selecting **Browse** when prompted to **Choose a Database** displays the window shown in Figure 15-28.

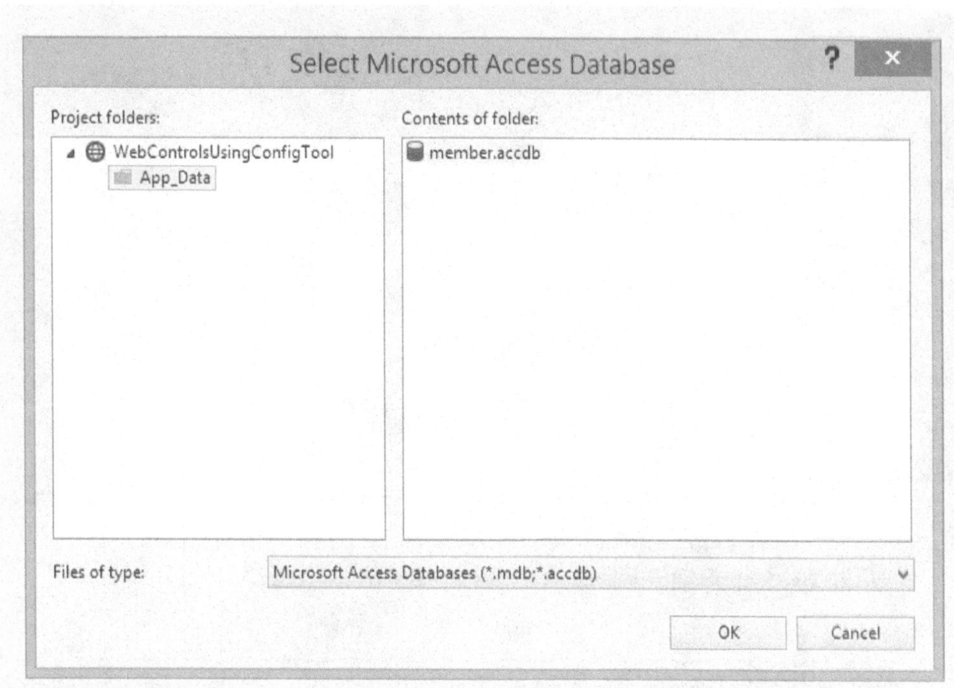

FIGURE 15-28 Database file stored in `App_Data` directory

If the Access database is in the `App_Data` directory, you browse to that location and a relative path is set, as shown in Figure 15-29. You do not have to set the `Connection string` property; you just identify the location of the Access .accdb file.

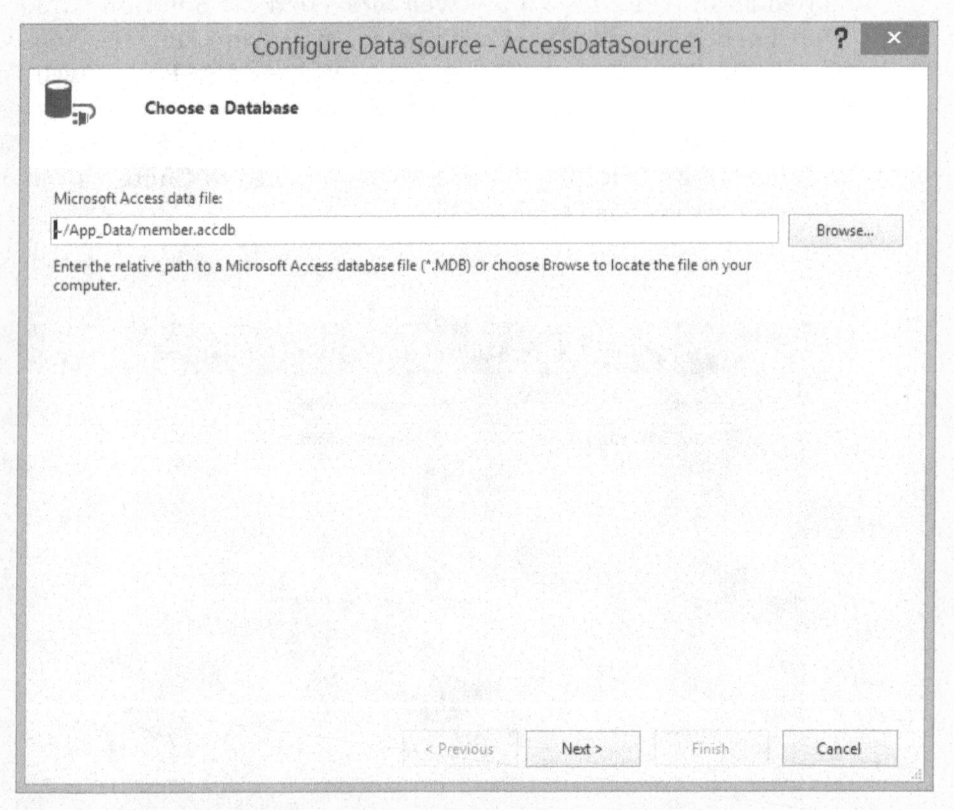

FIGURE 15-29 Relative address for the Access database

NOTE You can place your database in the `App_Data` directory using the **Solution Explorer** window by right-clicking on the `App_Data` folder and selecting **Add, Add Existing Item**. You can then **Browse** to its original location.

The database is now referenced by a relative path (for example, `~/App_Data/member.accdb`). If you move the website, ASP.NET will look for the database in the `App_Data` folder of the application. This is one of the advantages of using the configuration tools. It is no longer necessary for you to locate and change the path for the database in your source code if the website gets moved.

After the file is located, the **Configure Data Source** wizard enables you to identify which table(s) and field(s) to display on the `GridView`. This is shown in Figure 15-30.

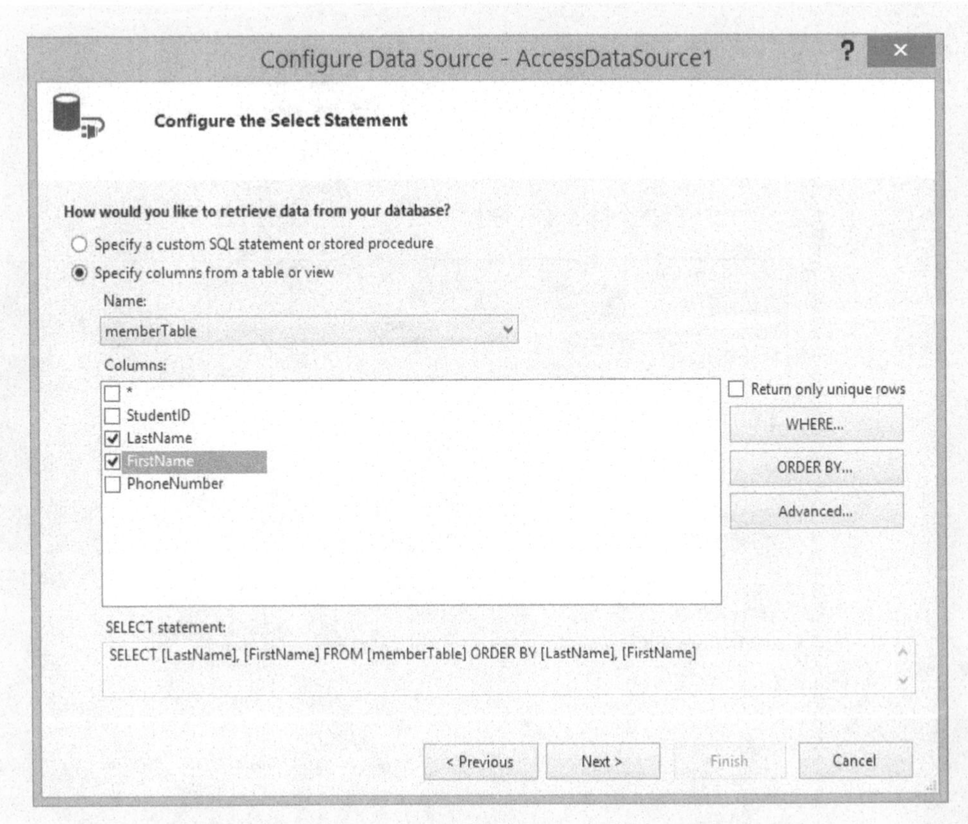

FIGURE 15-30 Identify what data to retrieve

As shown in Figure 15-30, the database table(s) is selected from a drop-down list. The query builder tool is launched if you select the **WHERE** button. To have the items displayed in ascending or descending order by a specific field, the **Order By** option is used. For the `WebControls` application, the records were ordered by `LastName` and then by `FirstName`. As shown at the bottom of the display in Figure 15-30, an SQL select statement is generated based on your selections. The **Test Query** button enables you to see what will be returned from the query. This is illustrated in Figure 15-31.

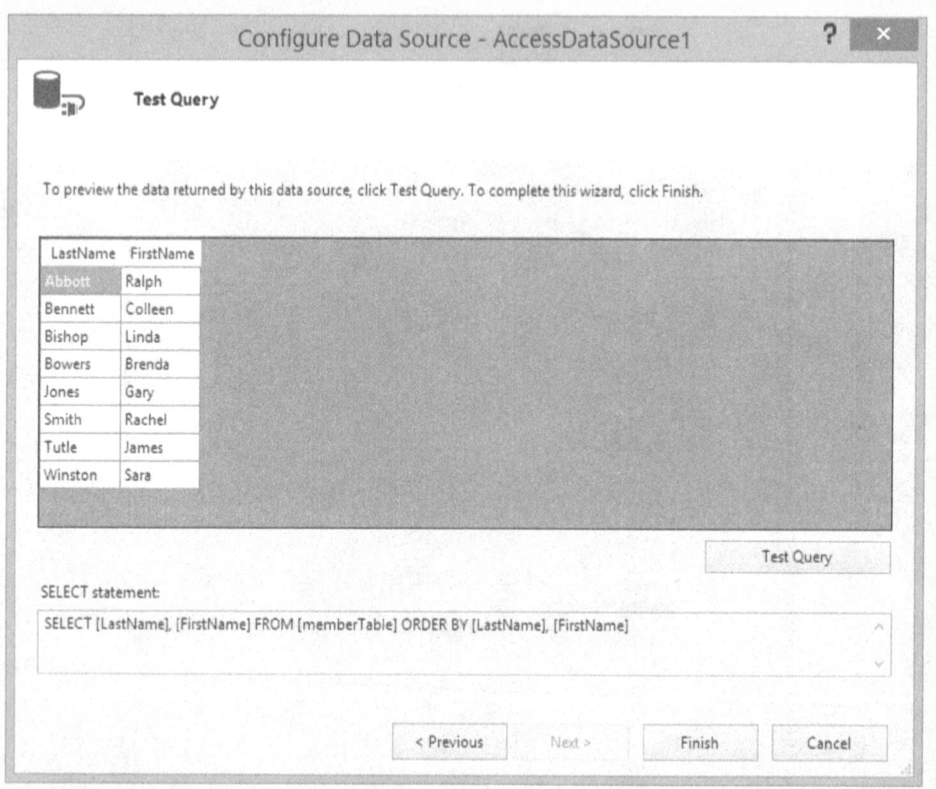

FIGURE 15-31 Test the Query

After you complete the data source configuration, you are returned back to the web page. As shown in Figure 15-26, options are available from the `GridView`'s smart tag to enable paging, sorting, and selection or to change the columns. **Enable Sorting** option makes it possible for you to select a column and have the table reordered by that field. If you want to change the column heading, do this using the **Edit Columns** option. The **Edit Columns** option displays a dialog box where each field's properties can be changed. A number of properties are available for each field grouped by `Accessibility`, `Appearance`, `Behavior`, `Data`, and `Style`. The Header Text was set for both columns and the `BackColor` property for the `HeaderStyle` for both the last and first names was set to yellow (`#FFFFC0`). The FirstName column was moved up so that it appears first.

Setting the Visibility Property

The `btnShowMembers_Click( )` method of the `WebControls` application with the `GridView` no longer needs code to connect to the database and populate the control on the page. Recall that this is done behind the scenes by the **Configure Data Source** wizard. If you review Examples 15-14 and 15-15, you will notice that the first line of code in the `btnShowMembers_Click( )` method for Example 15-14 was a statement that made the label over the table visible when the user clicked the **See Current Members** button. The same line of code (`lblMembers.Visible = true;`) is also part of Example 15-15. If you also want to wait to display the `GridView` `object` after the user clicks this button, the `Visible` property should initially be set to `false` for both the `Label` and the `GridView`. Another line of code needs to be added to this method to make the `GridView` visible. The new `btnShowMembers_Click( )` is shown in Example 15-16. All of the database connection code is deleted.

EXAMPLE 15-16

```
protected void btnShowMembers_Click(object sender, EventArgs e)
{
   lblMembers.Visible = true;
   grdViewMembers.Visible = true;
}
```

MODIFYING THE DATA By default, the `GridView` control displays data on a Web form in a read-only format. To allow users to edit data stored in the `GridView` object, you can use the **Advanced** button to configure the select statement from the **Data Source Configuration** tool. This **Advanced** button is shown in Figure 15-30. Selecting this option generates the additional `Insert`, `Delete`, and `Update` SQL statements needed.

To use this feature, all primary key values must be retrieved as part of the `select` statement during the data source configuration. The key fields do not have to be displayed on the `GridView`. They can be removed using the smart tag after the configuration is complete; however, the query must return their values.

NOTE Be cautious about not including primary key results in your display. If you have specified that a key field cannot be null, you will not be able to add records if no value is entered for the key.

After the SQL statements are available for the `InsertCommand`, `UpdateCommand`, and `DeleteCommand`, the smart tag for the `GridView` reveals additional options of **Enable Editing** and **Enable Deleting**. If you select these options, an additional column is added to the `GridView` table, as shown in Figure 15-32.

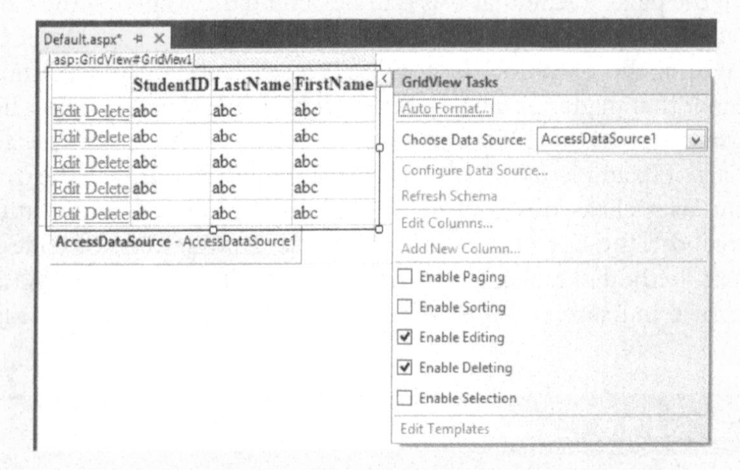

FIGURE 15-32 Modifying the data table

Recall from Chapter 14 that a question mark (`?`) is used as part of the SQL statement to indicate a parameterized value for the insert, delete, and update queries with Access databases. An ampersand (`&`) is used with SQL Server Express.

As shown in Figure 15-32, when the application is run, the column displays buttons labeled **Edit** and **Delete**. Clicking the **Edit** button causes the row of data to be displayed in an editable format. Because the `StudentID` is a primary key, it is not editable. Notice that on the row being modified, the **Edit** button is replaced with **Update** and **Cancel** buttons. After you change the data and click the **Update** button, the `UpdateCommand` event is raised or triggered, and the code written to change the data in the database table is executed.

Other Controls

You are encouraged to review Figure 15-17. It shows the many different Web Forms controls that can be added to a Web Forms page from the **Toolbox** using a drag-and-drop approach. A number of Web Forms server controls are available to you. Explore the `System.Web.UI.WebControls namespace` to find others. Not all of the Web server controls are included in the **Toolbox**.

Because of space constraints, this chapter uses only a small subset of the classes available to you for creating ASP.NET applications. Over 250 classes make up the `System.Web.UI.WebControls namespace`.

NAVIGATION

For navigation purposes, you can add site navigation to your websites by defining a site map. You can do this using one of the navigation controls, such as the `TreeView` and `SiteMapPath` controls. These controls automatically create menu or tree views of pages. There are a number of classes focusing on security and navigation.

DATA

You have a very large selection of controls for working with data. You experienced the `GridView` control in this chapter. You will want to explore the `DetailsView` and `FormView` controls. They are also used to display and edit data from different data sources. You saw in this chapter how the smart tag for the `GridView` enabled you to bind the control to a data source. The connections, queries, and parameters are all now encapsulated with these other data source controls. These data source controls automatically retrieve data when the page runs, cutting down the need to write code to execute commands and manage data sets for common data scenarios.

LOGIN

ASP.NET provides security controls that enable you to authenticate users with a suite of login controls. The `Login` control prompts users for credentials and validates them. The `PasswordRecovery` control helps users change or remember their password. The `LoginStatus` control lets you present a `Login` or `Logout` button.

Entire books are written on ADO.NET and ASP.NET. The intent is to give you a foundation and introduce you to what is available, so that you can continue learning after finishing this chapter. You might want to do that by exploring some of the classes listed in Table 15-6. The table was adapted from the Visual Studio's MSDN documentation—retrievable using the **Help**, **Search** menu option.

TABLE 15-6 Additional Web Forms control classes

Class identifier	Description
`AccessDataSource`	Represents a Microsoft Access database to data-bound controls
`AdRotator`	Displays an advertisement banner on a web page
`ChangePassword`	Provides a user interface that enables users to change their website password
`Content`	Holds text, markup, and server controls to render to a `ContentPlaceHolder` control in a master page
`ContentPlaceHolder`	Defines a region for content in an ASP.NET master page
`DataList`	A data-bound list control that displays items using templates
`DetailsView`	Displays the values of a single record from a data source in a table, where each data row represents a field of the record; the `DetailsView` control allows you to edit, delete, and insert records

(*continues*)

TABLE 15-6 Additional Web Forms control classes (*continued*)

Class identifier	Description
`HiddenField`	Represents a hidden field used to store a non-displayed value
`HyperLink`	Displays a link to another web page
`Image`	Displays an image on a web page
`ImageButton`	Displays an image and responds to mouse clicks on the image
`ImageMap`	Creates a control that displays an image on a page; when a hot spot region defined within the `ImageMap` control is clicked, the control either generates a postback to the server or navigates to a specified URL
`Link-Button`	Displays a hyperlink style button control on a web page
`Login`	Provides user interface (UI) elements for logging in to a website
`LoginStatus`	Detects the user's authentication state and toggles the state of a link to log in to or log out of a website
`SiteMapPath`	Displays a set of text or image hyperlinks that enable users to more easily navigate a website, while taking a minimal amount of page space
`SqlDataSource`	Represents an SQL database to data-bound controls
`Table`	Displays a table on a web page
`TreeView`	Displays hierarchical data, such as a table of contents, in a tree structure
`ValidationSummary`	Displays a summary of all validation errors on a web page, in a message box, or both
`Xml`	Displays an XML document

© Cengage Learning

The examples illustrated in this chapter specified the **File System** for the **Location** argument when the website was created. Moving the files to a different location and reopening the website is not as problematic as attempting to move a website created using **IIS**. You might find that once you move a site, after the website is opened and viewed in a browser, the IDE requests you to create a new solution file. However, it does that for you automatically.

You have dragged and dropped controls on a design surface, typed property values using the properties windows, and directly typed program statements into a file. These same concepts can be applied to creating mobile applications. The following section describes how Visual Studio and C# are used to develop smart device apps.

Mobile Applications

Mobile application development involves writing software for handheld devices such as smartphones or tablets. Today, mobile apps play such an important role in society that when people think about software, they are now often referring to the apps on their phone. There are over a billion smartphones being used around the world today running many different apps. All of these apps are programs providing some type of functionality with a different look and feel from the traditional desktop software you have developed thus far. In addition to a smaller visual interface, there is a different user-interaction model based primarily on touch with a keyboard that pops up only when necessary. The underlying programming concepts are similar but another layer of complexity is added into the picture. There are different platforms that a developer can choose for their applications. Unfortunately, these platforms are pretty much incompatible. Applications developed on one platform will not run on another and most handheld devices only support one particular platform.

MOBILE DEVELOPMENT PLATFORMS

The two dominant current platforms for mobile development are Android and iOS. There is potential for this to change, but currently these are the two giants followed by Microsoft's Windows phone. The Android operating system, developed by Google, is based on the Linux kernel and runs on a variety of phones. For Android development, Eclipse on a variety of platforms is normally used. The Apple family of iPhones and iPads target the iOS operating System. The primary programming language used for developing the iOS has been Objective-C with the XCode IDE on the Mac. Java is the programming language normally used to write for the Android while C# has been used for Windows Phone platforms. In order to have an app available for multiple platforms, the app normally has to be rewritten. There is great potential for this to change. C# combined with Xamarin can be used to write apps that target all three platforms: iOS, Android, and Windows.

XAMARIN

With the Visual Studio 2015 release, Microsoft partnered with a software development company called Xamarin and included their software with the 2015 edition. Xamarin provides add-ins to Visual Studio that not only enable you to build iOS, Android, and Windows apps within the IDE using IntelliSense but also provides support for the building, deploying, and debugging of apps. As part of the Xamarin partnership with Microsoft, Xamarin extensions can be downloaded and added to earlier versions of Visual Studio, back to VS 2010.

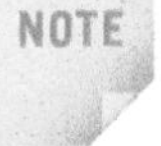

Xamarin was founded in 2011 but has an interesting history that started in the early 2000's when .NET was first announced. Xamarin's creators started an open-source project called Mono as an alternative implementation of C# which could run on Linux. The original company was called Ximian. It was later sold to Novell and when Novell was acquired by Attachmate in 2011, the Mono project came back under the support of its original engineers in a new company named Xamarin. In addition to partnering with Xamarin for the Visual Studio 2015 release, Microsoft also announced that it was embracing open source as a core principal to enable .NET applications to run on multiple operating systems. April 2014 Microsoft published an open-source version of the C# compiler, .NET Compiler Platform.

The Xamarin Starter edition, which includes Xamarin Studio, is bundled with Visual Studio 2015, but has limited functionality. It makes it easy to explore and download the Xamarin product offerings. The first time you attempt to create in Visual Studio an Android app, for example, you receive the message shown in Figure 15-33.

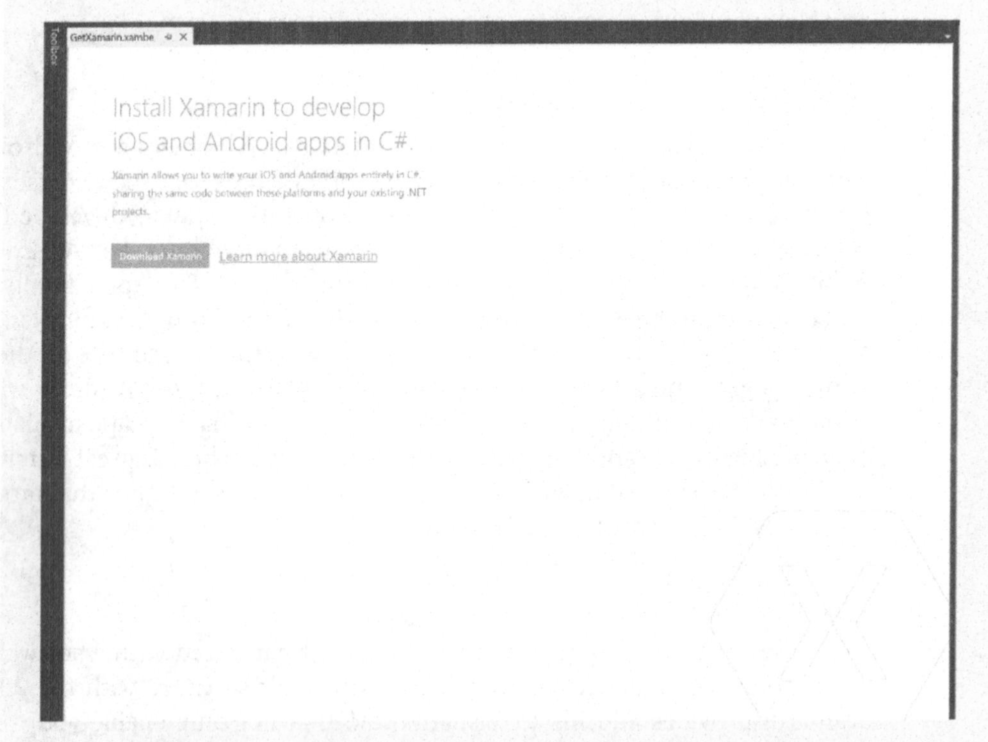

FIGURE 15-33 Download Xamarin

After downloading Xamarin, more functionality including additional templates for building iOS and Android apps with Xamarin directly in Visual Studio 2015 will be available when you create new projects. This is illustrated in Figure 15-34.

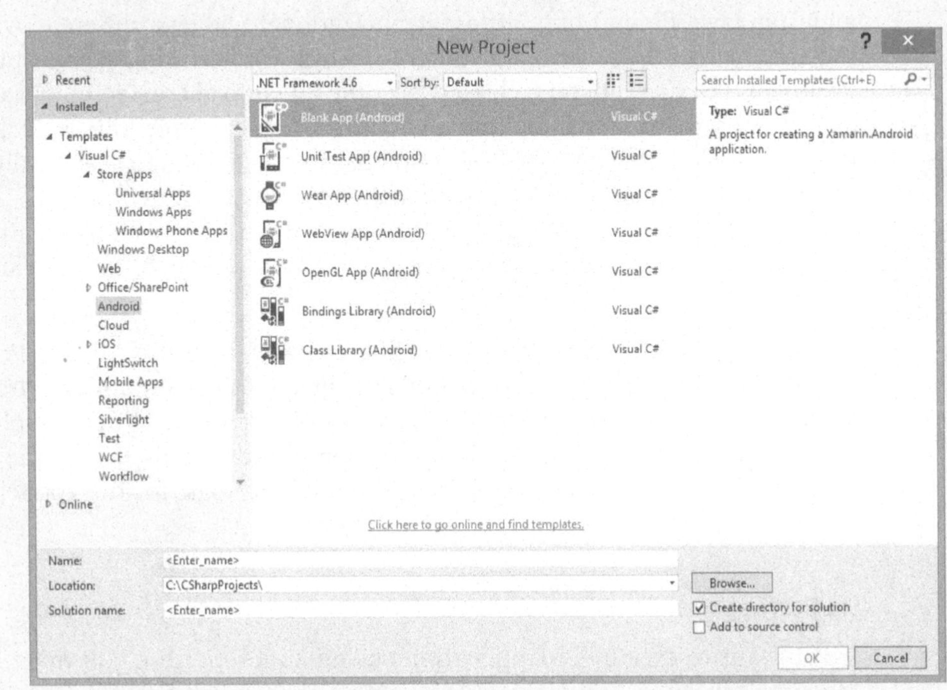

FIGURE 15-34 Mobile app project template

At the time the book was written, Xamarin offered students the free Indie edition, which enables to develop projects of unlimited sized and use `Xamarin.Forms`. Registration at their website (*http://xamarin.com/student*) was a requirement for the download. `Xamarin.Forms` can be used to create stand-alone applications targeted at individual platforms or cross-platform applications targeting two or more of the platforms.

Xamarin.Forms

`Xamarin.Forms` released in May 2014 is a cross-platform natively backed user interface toolkit. Natively backed means the user interface controls are rendered and transformed using the native controls of the target platform, allowing the applications to retain the look and feel you are accustomed to seeing with that platform. `Xamarin.Forms` includes a library of classes that enables developers to build user interfaces for iOS, Android, and Windows Phone and have the different platforms' apps shared C# code. These classes in `Xamarin.Forms` are collections of renderers, classes that change the `Xamarin.Forms` widgets or user interface controls into the platform-specific user interface control. Each of the three platforms has different ways of presenting and interacting with the user. Each platform (Android, iOS, and Windows Phone) uses different navigational widgets, different ways of moving from screen to screen, and different ways of presenting menu options. These `Xamarin.Forms` renderers, classes, take the UI control created in `Xamarin.Forms` and convert them into the platform's control. For example `Xamarin.Forms` has a `Slider` class for displaying a horizontal bar to allow users to select values based on sliding the bar. This `Slider` renders to a `UISlider` for iOS platforms, `SeekBar` on Android platforms, and `Slider` for Windows Phone. They all have different looks, but the functionality is the same. `Xamarin.Forms` is able to take advantage of this shared code.

The sharing of code is done via either a Shared Asset Project (SAP) or a Portable Class Library (PCL) project. If you were building an app to run on both Android and iOS, three separate projects would be built as part of a `Xamarin.Forms` application. The first project would target Android, the second would target iOS, and the third would be a project-containing common code, the business logic for the application. There are differing details that apply to each platform.

iOS Apps

If you want to create iOS applications using Visual Studio, you must have a Mac machine available. Xamarin Studio and Xcode must be installed on the Mac machine. The PC and Mac need to be connected via a network (such as WiFi). You must run the Xamarin.ios **Build Host** on the Mac for this interconnection, and Visual Studio uses that machine to build and deploy the executable on the Mac. When the iOS application is built, Xamarin generates C# Intermediate Language (IL) code and then makes use of the Apple compiler on the Mac to generate the native iOS code, just like an Objective C compiler would. So for developing iOS Apps, you can use Visual Studio on a Windows machine, but you need a Mac available for testing.

Android Apps

You can write apps for Android devices using Xamarin Studio on the Mac, Xamarin Studio on the PC, or Visual Studio on the PC. All that is needed is Visual Studio and Xamarin. There are a number of emulators available for testing or you can perform testing by plugging an Android device directly into a USB port. An **emulator** provides a virtualized environment so that when the application is launched a functioning device is displayed. During development, you interact with the emulator in the same way that you would interact with a phone or tablet device. Several emulators that simulate different Android devices are included in Visual Studio 2015 with Xamarin. The emulators have many of the same features you find on mobile devices. They enable you to see what the output would look like when displayed on the real device. Some are slow to load and one of the issues with Android development is that there are so many different Android devices that it becomes necessary to test on several devices or emulators to ensure that the app will function properly. For the Android apps, Xamarin generates IL, which runs on a version of C# Mono on the device alongside the Java engine, but the API calls from the app are pretty much the same as if the app were written in Java.

Windows Phone Apps

You use Visual Studio 2015 to develop mobile apps to run on Windows 8.1 and later phones. There are a several templates available from which to choose for developing Windows Phone apps. Many target Silverlight.

Silverlight

Silverlight was initially released as a video streaming plugin, but today provides functionality similar to Adobe Flash. It is a Web application framework that enables you to integrate multimedia such as graphics, sounds, and animations into applications. Silverlight user interfaces are declared using Extensible Application Markup Language (XAML) and programmed using a subset of the .NET Framework. You use much of the same programming model you used to develop Web applications. You still have access to the core methods and classes so that the business logic and data access layer can be separated from the GUI. A Silverlight application starts by invoking the Silverlight control from the HTML page, which then loads up an XAML file.

XAML

XAML is a declarative XML-based language developed by Microsoft. It is used for initializing objects and mapping directly to CLR object instances, properties, and events on those objects. XAML files can be created and edited with visual design tools in Visual Studio. The XAML file contains a `Canvas object`, which acts as a placeholder for other elements. XAML is a way of describing the user interface using XML. Like Web applications, you have fewer controls to drag and drop and fewer events to program. You can type tags directly into the XAML file and/or drag and drop controls onto the **Design** pane. Once created, you debug your applications using an actual Windows Phone device or an emulator.

Universal Apps

Another option for creating a Windows Phone App is to select one of the installed **Universal Apps** templates. These templates create a single application that runs on both Windows and Windows phones. The **Store Apps/Universal Apps** template creates a single-page universal app for both Windows and Windows Phone. From the **File, New Project** option you will also find **Hub App (Universal Apps)** available under the **Installed, Templates, Visual C#, Store Apps, Universal Apps** option as shown in Figure 15-35.

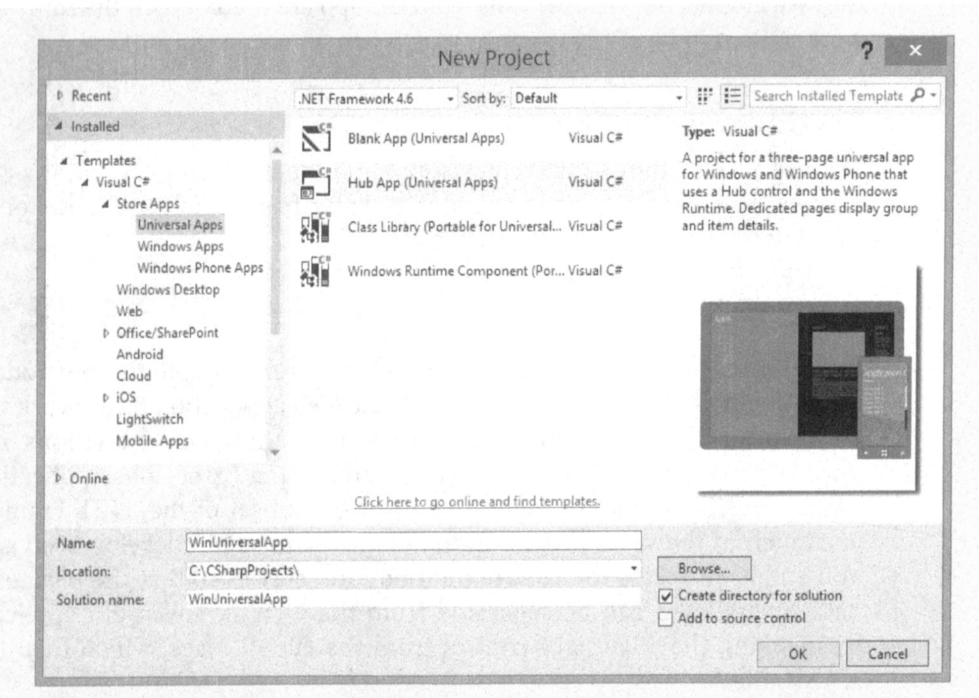

FIGURE 15-35 Windows phone universal app

The **Hub App** creates a three-page universal app that uses a `Hub` control. You could start with a blank Universal App and drag and drop a `Hub` control onto the canvas. It is one of the **XAML Controls** available in the **Toolbox**. A `Hub` control enables a series of sections to be panned side to side. The `Hub` control is part of the native Windows Phone look and feel. Unlike an app designed to fit everything within the confines of a single phone screen, a **Hub App** offers a way to view controls using a wide portrait approach virtual canvas that extends horizontally beyond the confines of a single screen. Selecting this option, as illustrated in Figure 15-35, automatically adds the `Hub` control to the application. Figure 15-36 shows the development environment when a **Hub App** is created.

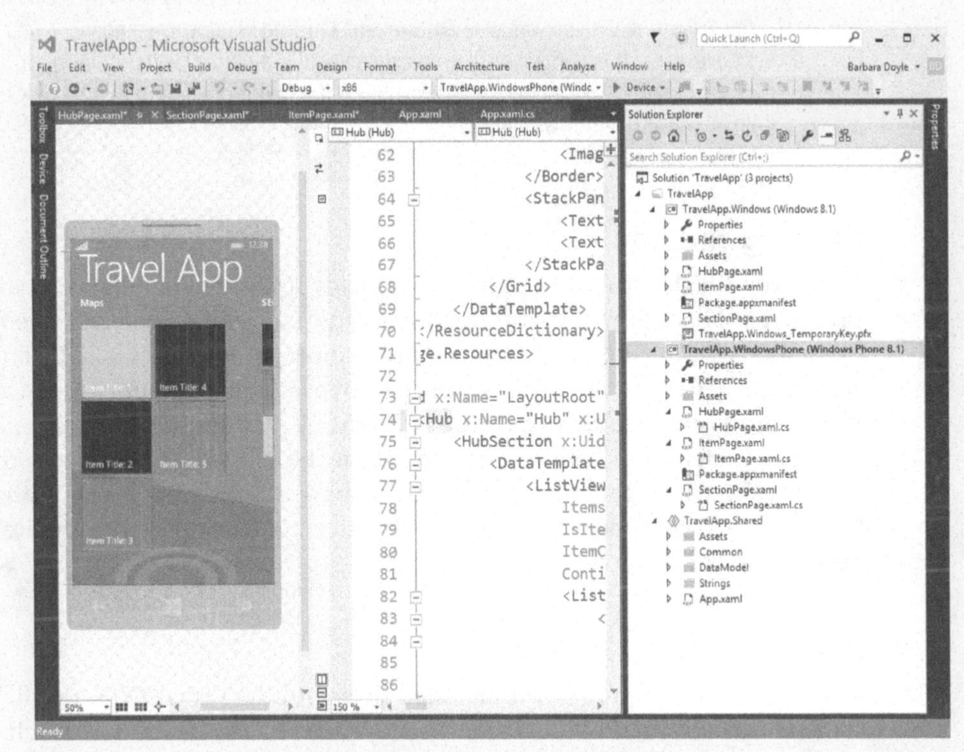

FIGURE 15-36 Windows phone development

As shown in the **Solution Explorer** window in Figure 15-36, three projects are created when you select **Hub App**. The first is a Windows project. The second and the one selected, Windows Phone 8.1, is located in the middle of the **Solution Explorer** pane. A shared project containing items that are used by both the Windows and the Windows Phone projects is stored in the project. Because it is a **Hub App**, three separate XAML files are added to the Windows and Window Phone projects (`HubPage.xaml`, `ItemPage.xaml`, `SectionPage.xaml`). Notice in Figure 15-36 that the Windows Phone `.xaml` files were expanded to reveal the code-behind files (`HubPage.xaml.cs`, `ItemPage.xaml.cs`, `SectionPage.xaml.cs`). Like Windows applications, the code-behind file stores the event-handler methods.

You drag and drop controls on the design surface or directly type XML statements into the `.xaml` files. You can split the screen so that you have access to not only the **Designer** pane but also the `.xaml` file containing the XML Application Markup Language tags. Each of the items on the design screen of an application has a graphical rendering of an object so you will find tags relating to each element that you place on your design surface. These elements contain properties that define how it appears on the screen. Figure 15-36 illustrates that split screen.

You will probably also want the **Document Outline** window opened while you are creating mobile apps. It is very useful for quickly selecting a control without having to use the mouse to click on it. It is unpinned in Figure 15-36. If it is not opened, it can be displayed from the **VIEW**, **Other Windows** menu option.

Running the App

When you finish with the design and are ready to test and debug, you build the solution much the same way you did with other Visual Studio projects. The **Build** menu has options for **Build Solution** and **Build** project, with shortcuts of **F6** and **Shift+F6**. As with other types of projects, you can bypass this step and launch the application using **Start Debugging** or **Start Without Debugging**. Before doing that you will need to determine where your output for the app will be displayed. You have two options. You can deploy it to a device, if you have a Windows Phone. With this option, the Windows phone needs to be connected to your development computer. The other option is to use the emulator.

Deploying to an Emulator

A Windows Phone emulator is included as part of the Visual 2015 install. The emulator runs as a Hyper-V virtual machine on your Windows PC. It has much of the same software as a "real" phone. You can use your PC mouse and/or keyboard to control the emulator. You can perform location and orientation simulation, manage the emulator environment, and even change settings on the emulator.

In order to use the emulator, you must be running a version of Windows 8 Professional Operating System or higher on a 64-bit machine that supports Second Level Address Translation (SLAT). Intel-based processors such as i3, i5, i7, and i9 support SLAT as do CPUs based on Nehalem, Westmere, or Sandybridge microarchitectures. The emulator will not run under Windows 8 Home versions. You can design and create applications running under just the Windows 8 Home version, but in order to launch the emulator you must be on a machine that is running the Windows 8 Pro version. In addition, the emulator requires Hyper-V be enabled, a feature not available in the Home version of Windows 8.

NOTE

Hyper-V is a virtual machine manager, a piece of software that creates and runs a virtual machine. The Hyper-V feature must be enabled. If you get an error message stating "Can't start the Windows Phone Emulator because your PC is missing the Hyper-V pre-requisites," and you are running Windows 8 Pro, you may need to go to the **Control Panel**, **Programs and Features**, **Turn Windows features on or off**, and click the check box beside **Hyper-V** to enable it.

You can easily reuse existing code you have written with mobile apps. A new interface must be designed for these types of applications. You have a much smaller surface for the user interface for mobile applications, so the design is extremely important. There are different controls. Build intuitive interfaces, being careful to not intimidate users, but rather your goal should be to make them feel comfortable with your layout. Focus on the content that your app is delivering. Focus on what you are attempting to achieve as you design and continually strive for creating a clear uncluttered consistent looking app. You should take pride in the craftsmanship and make the application look good.

The business logic, data tiers, and event-driven programming model can all be extended to work with mobile applications. The market for mobile devices is growing by leaps and bounds. You are encouraged to take advantage of the opportunities and continue your exploration of programming these devices using .NET.

It is beyond the scope of this book to illustrate development for the three platforms. However, you are encouraged to take what you have learned here as the first step and keep learning, exploring, and continuing to grow. There are a lot of online resources focusing on mobile application development. Between iOS, Android, and Windows, your C# code can run on billions of devices.

Coding Standards

Use an appropriate classification suffix such as lbl for `Label` or btn for `Button` so that you can differentiate between the control objects and take advantage of IntelliSense during development.

ASPX files should not contain any inline server-side scripting. ASPX files should only contain the visual elements of the page such as the XHTML and static text. The programming logic for the page should be contained in a separate code-behind file. Code-behind files should contain the programming logic for the event handlers.

Resources

Additional sites you might want to explore:

- Official Microsoft ASP.NET site—
  http://www.asp.net/
- Jump Start with ASP.NET Starter Kit—
  http://msdn.microsoft.com/en-us/magazine/cc164097.aspx
- Windows Communication Foundation—
  http://msdn.microsoft.com/en-us/library/dd936243.aspx
- Xamarin—
  http://xamarin.com/

- Windows Phone Silverlight Development—
https://msdn.microsoft.com/library/windows/apps/ff402535(v=vs.105).aspx
- Channel 9 - Xamarin—
http://channel9.msdn.com/Blogs/Videos-DX/Xamarin
- DreamSpark—
https://www.dreamspark.com
- Windows Phone Developer Account—
http://dev.windowsphone.com
- Microsoft Student Developer Program—
https://msdn.microsoft.com/en-us/student-developer-program.aspx

QUICK REVIEW

1. A Web application, also called a website, is simply a collection of one or more related files or components stored on a Web server. Web servers are software that is responsible for hosting or delivering the Web application.
2. When a page is requested using HTTP, the request goes to the Web server, which sends back the document in an HTML format. This is considered a round-trip to the server. Another round-trip is required when changes are made on a dynamic web page.
3. Every trip to the server creates a new object because web pages are considered stateless. They do not retain their values from one trip to the Web server to the next.
4. Static pages do not require any processing by a Web server. They are precreated and reside on the server's hard drive. Dynamic websites involve processing in addition to rendering the formatting HTML.
5. ASP.NET Web application projects are created at *http://localhost* if you select the HTTP option for Location. Physically, the files are stored in the home directory, C:\Inetpub\wwwroot. This is the default for the home directory. A directory is also created with the name you typed for the project, and it is placed (along with the two solution files) at the location you configured Visual Studio to store all of your Visual Studio projects. Choosing the File System option for the Location lets you identify where on your local machine the website application is stored.
6. The Web Forms page `object` has a number of properties, many with the same functionality that was available for setting a Windows application form.

7. Two files are created for Web applications. Code for the visual interface file is placed in the file containing the HTML tags (.aspx extension). The other file, the code-behind file, contains the logic for the application. There is no .Designer.cs file as you find with Windows applications. The ASP.NET code-behind model requires an additional step—compiling the source code when ASP runs the application.
8. HTML controls are also called client-side controls. The biggest advantage HTML controls offer is that the page is rendered "as is" to the browser. Client-side controls require no processing by the Web server.
9. One option for creating a New website, creates a number of files and folders, including a master page. A master page allows you to create and maintain a consistent theme across several pages for a website.
10. Cascading Style Sheets can be used with Web applications. They enable you to separate the actual page content from the visual appearance of the page.
11. Server controls are referred to as Web controls, Web Forms server controls, ASP server controls, or simply Web Forms controls. Visual Studio prefixes the control name with `<asp:control>` and ends the tag with `</asp:control>`.
12. Only a few events trigger a postback to the server. `ListBox`, `RadioButton`, `RadioButtonList`, `CheckBox`, `CheckBoxList`, and `DropDownList` have a property called `AutoPostBack` that can be set to `true` to trigger a postback automatically.
13. Validation controls enable input to be validated or checked by the server. You can check to make sure that values have been entered, that values fall between a range of values, or you can create custom validation checks.
14. You tie the validation control to a specific control such as a `TextBox` `object`, using the `ControlToValidate` property. The `ErrorMessage` property can be set to the message you want to display when the input control does not pass the validation test.
15. A `Calendar` control is used to display a monthly calendar on a web page. After being placed on the page, the calendar is live and users can employ it to view and select dates. To work programmatically with the calendar for the `WebControls` application, you declare an `object` of the `DateTime` `class`.
16. The `GridView` control is very useful for displaying data in a tabular format.
17. To populate the control, the actual data can come from sources such as arrays or database tables.
18. Mobile application development involves writing software for handheld devices such as smartphones or tablets.

19. The two dominant current platforms for mobile development are Android and iOS.
20. Xamarin provides add-ins to Visual Studio that not only enable you to build iOS, Android, and Windows apps within the IDE using IntelliSense but also provides support for building, deploying, and debugging of apps.
21. The hub control is part of the native Windows Phone look and feel and offers a way to view controls using a wide portrait approach extending horizontally beyond the confines of a single screen.
22. You debug Windows Phone applications using an actual Windows Phone device or an emulator. In order to launch the emulator, you must be on a machine that is running the Windows 8 Pro version or late and have Hyper-V enabled.

EXERCISES

1. .NET Web applications differ from Windows applications in that Web applications must take the following into consideration:
    a. Multiple users need to be able to access the application at the same time.
    b. An application must be viewable by multiple types of platforms, including Linux and Windows.
    c. Fewer graphical user interface controls are available for Web applications.
    d. A Web server must be loaded for development of Web applications.
    e. all of the above
2. The term Web application is synonymous with:
    a. Web server
    b. IIS
    c. Web Forms
    d. Web page
    e. Website
3. Interaction with users on Web applications cannot include the use of:
    a. `MessageBox`
    b. `Label`
    c. `TextBox`
    d. `ListBox`
    e. `Button`

4. The term used to reference converting an HTML document into a viewable format for display purposes is:
   a. request
   b. host
   c. illustrate
   d. viewState
   e. render
5. Web pages do not require any processing by the server when they only include which of the following?
   a. HTML controls
   b. HTML server controls
   c. Web Forms controls
   d. HTML controls or HTML server controls
   e. HTML controls, HTML server controls, or Web Forms controls
6. Presentational attributes, such as sizes and colors of fonts and alignment of text, can be placed in a separate file if ___________ are used.
   a. Cascading Style Sheets
   b. Web controls
   c. Master pages
   d. HTML server controls
   e. none of the above
7. ASP.NET applications are characterized by which of the following?
   a. Program statements written in languages such as Java are included inside the HTML file.
   b. A code-behind file is created.
   c. Only formatting HTML tags can be used with the application.
   d. Only static pages can be developed.
   e. Script is embedded in the HTML document.

8. The HTML control property used to set the text on a label is:
   a. `Text`
   b. `Name`
   c. `InnerText`
   d. `ID`
   e. none of the above
9. When you set property values for Web Forms controls, the program statements referencing the settings are:
   a. placed in the code-behind file
   b. placed in the .aspx.cs file
   c. stored in the .aspm file
   d. stored in the file containing the HTML tags
   e. none of the above
10. The default home directory for storing C# Web applications when IIS is used is:
    a. C:\CSharpProjects
    b. C:\localhost
    c. C:\InetPub\wwwroot
    d. C:\WebApps
    e. none of the above
11. Events associated with which of the following automatically trigger a postback to the Web server?
    a. `ListBox`
    b. `TextBox`
    c. `DropDownList`
    d. `Button`
    e. all of the above
12. Which control is often used to display data from a database table?
    a. `DataGrid`
    b. `DataTable`
    c. `Table`
    d. `DataList`
    e. none of the above

13. The validation control used to make sure that values have been entered into a field is:
    a. `RangeValidator`
    b. `FieldRequiredValidator`
    c. `CompareValidator`
    d. `RequiredFieldValidator`
    e. `Required`

14. To work programmatically with the **`Calendar`** control, instantiate an `object` of the __________ `class`.
    a. `Calendar`
    b. `DateTime`
    c. `Date`
    d. `CalendarDate`
    e. none of the above

15. A file ending with the extension of .xaml is associated with which type of application?
    a. `WebService`
    b. `WebClass`
    c. `Web application`
    d. `Mobile application`
    e. all of the above

16. Master pages also require one or more:
    a. content pages
    b. server
    c. Web service
    d. HTML control
    e. none of the above

17. There are a number of events that fire up automatically and sequentially on web pages. They include:
    a. LoadPostBackData( )
    b. Page_Load( )
    c. Page_Pre_Init( )
    d. LoadViewState( )
    e. all of the above

18. Square brackets were used around the identifier with SQL statements to:
    a. enable a space to be included as part of a name
    b. indicate an entry is optional
    c. add multiple arguments
    d. indicate keyword follows
    e. none of the above

19. What software company did Microsoft partner with to provide cross-platform mobile development?
    a. Google
    b. Apple
    c. Xamarin
    d. Mono
    e. Ximirin

20. ___________ includes a library of classes that enables developers to build user interfaces for iOS, Android, and Windows Phone with the different platforms' apps sharing C# code.
    a. content pages
    b. Xamarin.Forms
    c. Web service
    d. HTML control
    e. none of the above

---

21. How do dynamic pages differ from static pages?

22. Compare and contrast HTML controls with Web Forms controls in terms of the code generated and the property values that can be set.

23. Identify and describe three types of validation controls that can be added to a Web application.

24. What are the hardware requirements for developing iOS using Visual Studio?

PROGRAMMING EXERCISES

1. Create a Web application that enables users to select from a `Calendar` control `object` the date of their next exam. Using program statements, retrieve their selection and then display the date along with an appropriate message. If they select a date in the past, display a message and allow them to re-enter a new date. Change background and foreground colors for the web page.

2. The computer club is selling T-shirts. Create a website that allows users to enter their first and last names, phone number, and e-mail address. Allow users to select sizes (S, M, L, XL, and XXL) and quantity. Add statements that process the order by calculating the total cost. All shirts except the XXL are $26; the XXL shirt is $30. Retrieve and display the name of the customer placing the order. Display the total cost of their selection including 7% sales tax.

3. Using Web Forms controls, create a Web application to store a user's To Do List. Include two `TextBox` objects, a `Button` `object` and a `ListBox` `object`. Allow users to input their name in one `TextBox` and To Do tasks into the other `TextBox`. Use those values to populate the `ListBox` `object`. Allow users to make a selection for which item to tackle next from the list. Display their name and the selection on a `Label` `object` and then remove that item from the ListBox.

4. The computer club has decided to take a field trip to the hometown of one of the members during spring vacation. To determine the destination, each member has been charged with creating a web page to highlight the features of his or her hometown. Create a Web application using the ASP.NET Web Forms Site template that contains details about your hometown. If you would prefer that the members visit another location, you may choose a different locale. Set the properties on the form for the controls so the form is aesthetically pleasing. Be sure to change both background and foreground colors, font size, and type.

5. Create a similar application to what you developed in Exercise 4 using the ASP.NET Empty Web Site template. Include an HTML server control that causes a message to be displayed (on a `Label object`) when the user clicks a button. The message should include additional details about the locale.

6. Create a dynamic website that functions like a calculator. Add features for addition, subtraction, multiplication, division, modulation, and so on.

7. Create a Web application that enables the user to enter first name, last name, and e-mail address. Accept those values and store them in a text file. Allow the user to input the path where the file should be stored. After retrieving the values from the user, display on the web page both the full file path (including the name of the file) and all values stored in the file. Confirm that the values are written to the file.

8. Create a website that retrieves and displays the current department chairs from a database. The StudentDataBase.accdb Access database used with examples in this book includes a major table that stores the major id, major name, department chair, and the department phone number. Create a website that references this table, or a database table that you create with similar fields. Display on the website the name of the major and the chair for the department. Enhance the site by changing background and foreground colors of the page and the grid storing the data.

© zeljkodan/Shutterstock.com

APPENDIX A VISUAL STUDIO CONFIGURATION

To increase productivity, you might want to configure the appearance and behavior of the integrated development environment (IDE) for Visual Studio. This appendix presents suggestions for possible settings.

Customizing the Development Environment

When Visual Studio is launched, it opens the current default **Start Page**. As shown in Figure A-1, you have options of **New Project** . . ., **Open Project** . . ., and **Open from Source Control** . . . from the **Start Page**. Shown below that main level of menu options, you see a heading labeled **Recent**. It shows the last 10 projects opened and enables you to quickly reopen the project from that link without having to browse to the location where the project is stored. Also included on this default **Start Page** are sections enabling you to **Connect to Azure, Discover what's new**, view **Product Videos**, and see **Announcements**.

You can choose to have this page opened each time you run Visual Studio or deselect the checkbox in the extreme left corner and not **Show page on startup**. You can begin customizing your environment even at that point. You can also check the **Keep page open after project loads** if you do want to see the **Start Page** listed as one of the available tabs while you are working on your project.

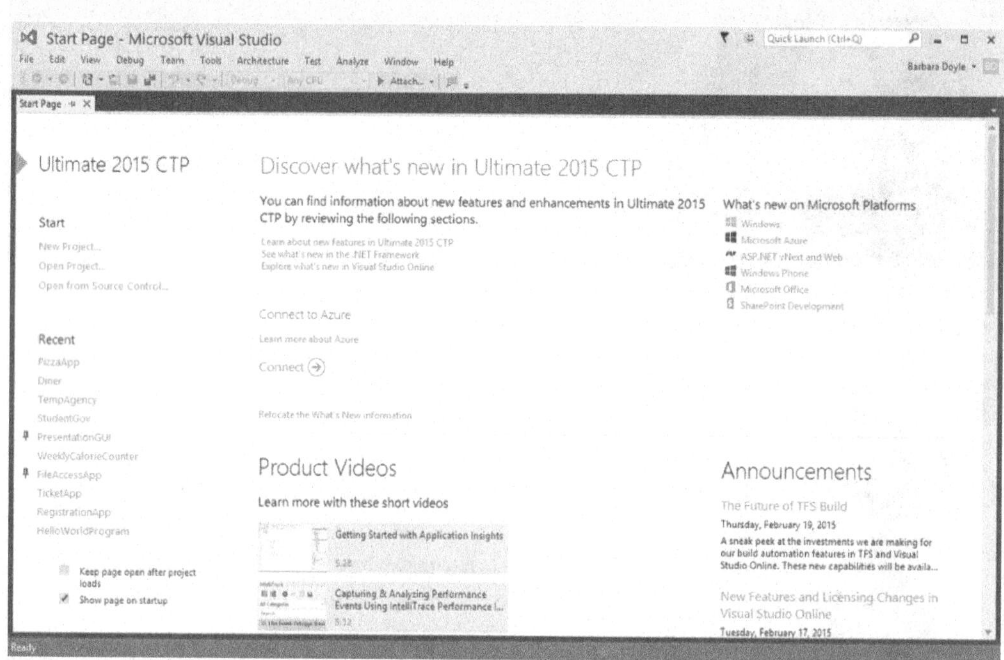

FIGURE A-1 Visual Studio Start Page

You have an option to pin an important project right on the **Start Page** so it will always be there. The pushpin is revealed when you move your mouse over the project in the **Recent** projects area. The `PresentationGUI` and `FileAccessApp` are pinned in Figure A-1. Ten projects are shown under the **Recent** projects area on the left pane in the figure. This number can be changed as described in the following.

You use the **Options** from the **Tools** menu as shown in Figure A-2 to make the most useful changes.

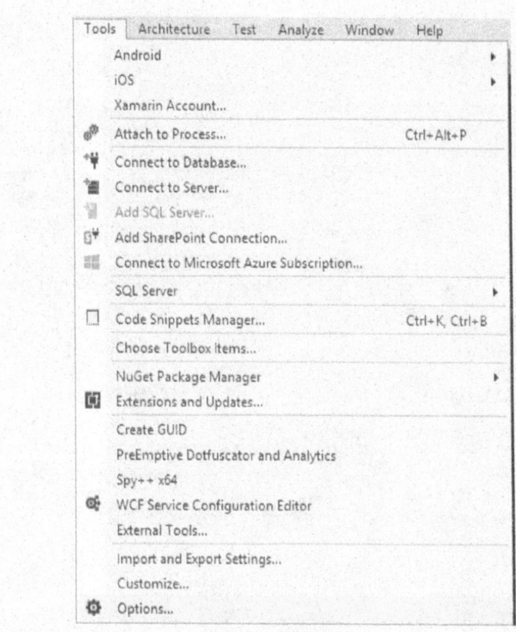

FIGURE A-2 Using Tools, Options to configure Visual Studio

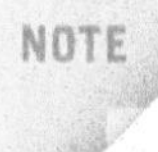

Depending on how the system you are using is configured, the options on your menu may vary slightly from the one displayed in Figure A-2.

Environment

After you select **Options**, the first folder node shown is **Environment**. When you select **Environment**, the right pane of the dialog box changes to reveal options as shown in Figure A-3.

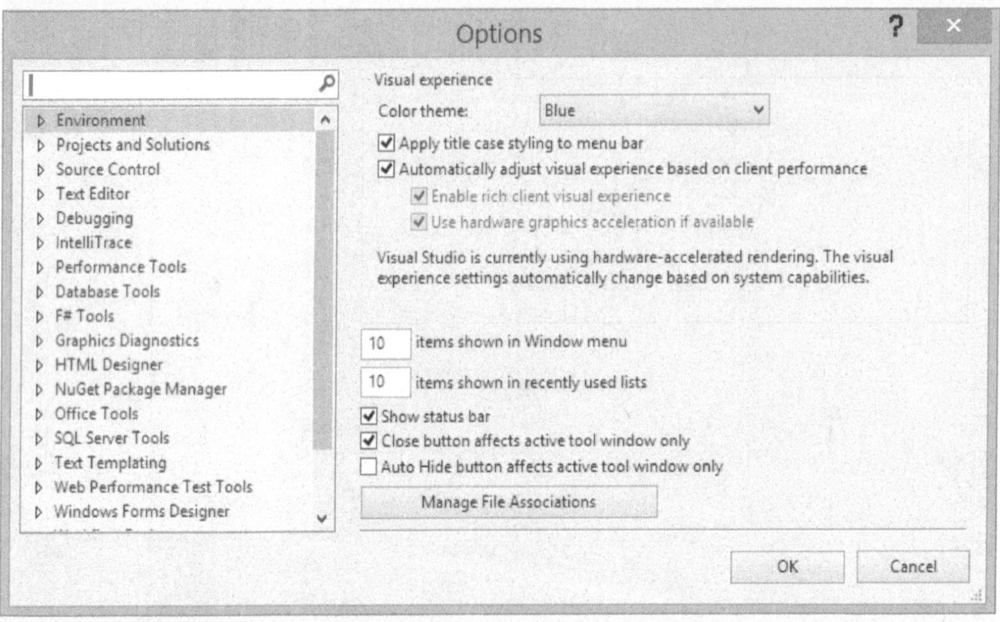

FIGURE A-3 Environment General options

As shown in Figure A-3, the **Environment** node enables you to select either a **Blue, Light** or **Dark Color theme**. You can also indicate how many items should display under the **Window** menu option. You can specify from 1 to 24. The default is **10**. If you have more files open than the number you select, older filenames just fall off the list, which is also the case for the second option under the **Recent** area. The default for **items shown in recently used lists** is also 10. This value impacts the **File** menu option and also the **Start Page** list. Using the **Recent Files** or **Recent Projects and Solutions** option from the **File** menu saves time when you are working with the same project over a long period. It eliminates the need to browse to the same location where the project is stored every time you want to reopen the file. Pinning the project to the list, as was described earlier, is also useful if you have a project that gets worked on often to keep it from falling off the list.

When you select the **Environment** node from the **Options** dialog box, the **General** tab options are displayed. One of the new features with Visual Studio 2015 is the option to **Apply title case styling to menu bar**. If this option is deselected, menu options appear in all upper case characters, which was the default for previous editions. From the **Environment, General** node dialog box, you also specify whether the status bar is displayed and indicate whether the **Close button impacts the active tool window only**. These options are all available when **General** is revealed or by selecting the **Environment** node.

From the **Environment, Fonts and Colors** node, you can change the size and type of the font for almost every item that appears in Visual Studio, including dialog boxes, windows, and text editor's text. It is useful to increase the font size if you are performing paired programming (working as a team of two) at a computer station or if you want to project your source code to a screen for others to view. As shown in Figure A-4, you have the capability of changing the display item's background or foreground.

If you review the list of items available to change in the dropdown list of the **Display Items** control shown on the center pane in Figure A-4, you find that there are over 100 items listed just for the **Text Editor**.

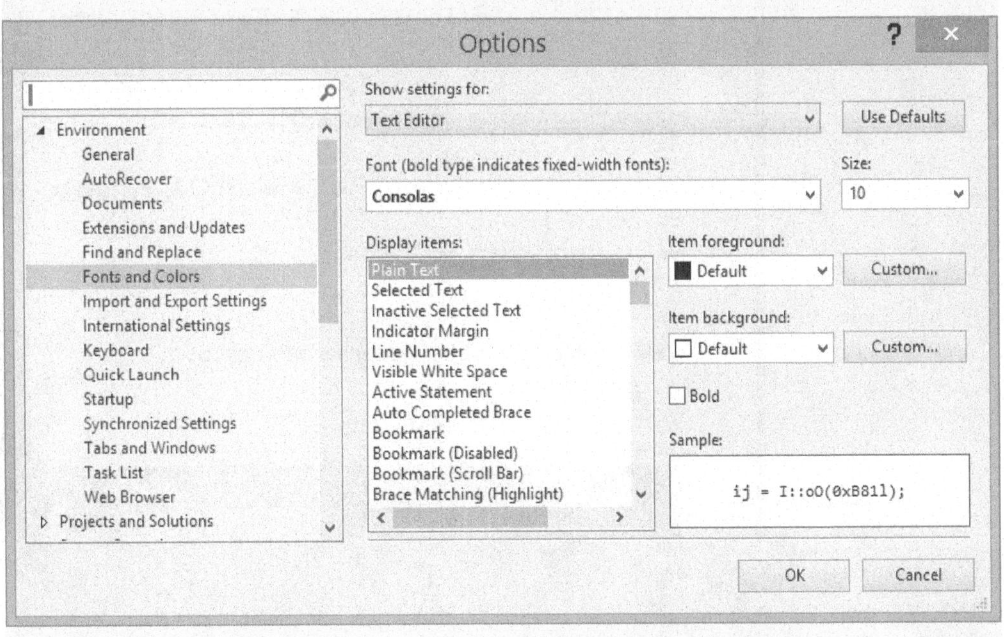

FIGURE A-4 Setting the fonts and colors

The **Environment, Startup** node, shown on the left pane in Figure A-4, lets you determine what is opened when you first start Visual Studio. You can select options such as **Show Start Page, Open Home Page, Load last loaded solution, Show Open Project dialog box, Show New Project dialog box**, or **Show empty environment**. You might also want to make changes at the **Environment, Web Browser** node, where the URLs for your **Home page** and **Search page** are set.

An interesting feature incorporated into the Visual Studio IDE is a zoom control. This feature enables you to increase/decrease the displayed font size of text items.

Figure A-5 illustrates this option. It is extremely useful if you want to quickly enlarge your program statements. Notice the dropdown list in the bottom-left corner. Zoom options from 20% to 400% are available.

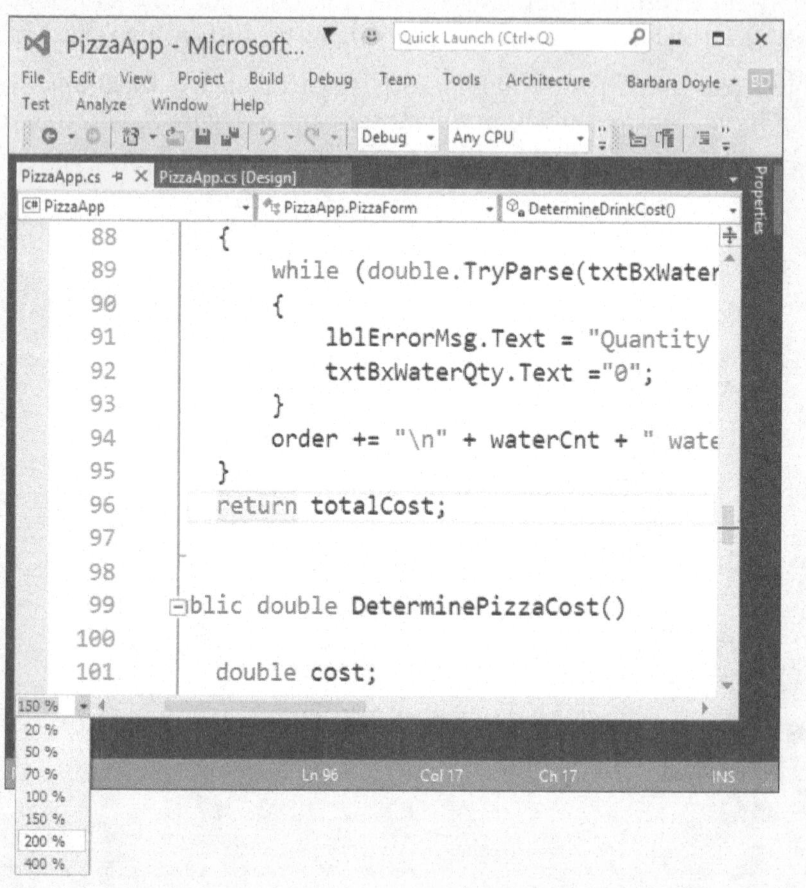

FIGURE A-5 Zoom capability

Projects and Solutions

You identify the default location where your projects should be saved using the **Projects and Solutions** node, as shown in Figure A-6. This selection is found in the top right corner. Clicking the ellipsis associated with this option opens the Project Location dialog box. Like the **Environment** node, when you click **Projects and Solutions**, the options available under the **General** node are displayed. C:\CSharpProjects was the value entered for the **Projects location** for projects created for this book. This is an extremely important setting that you should change. It will enable you to easily locate your saved projects.

You probably do not want to change the default values for the next two options shown in Figure A-6: **User project templates location** and **User item templates location.** It is probably best to store all templates in a common location. From the **Projects and Solutions** dialog box, you also indicate whether you want to **Always show Error List if build finishes with errors** or to **Show Output window when build starts.**

If you are working off a network drive you may want to deselect the option **Warn user when the project location is not trusted.** Otherwise, you may get an annoying dialog message every time you test your applications indicating that the location is not trusted.

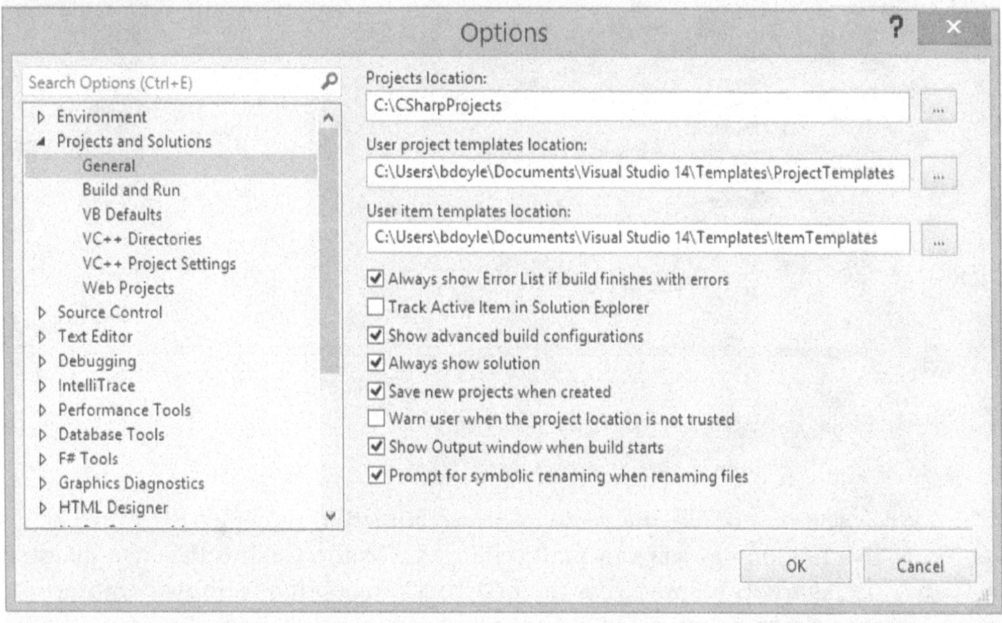

FIGURE A-6 Setting the location for Visual Studio projects

You should definitely configure the Visual Studio **Projects location** setting as shown in Figure A-6. You are encouraged to review and explore the other settings available on the **Environment** and **Projects and Solutions** tabs.

Text Editor

IntelliSense within Visual Studio is a very powerful feature. It can increase your productivity and help you avoid introducing typographical errors in your code. It automatically generates code. You have the option to turn IntelliSense features on/off under the **Text Editor**, **C#**, **IntelliSense** option as shown in Figure A-7. You can adjust the features to fit your preferences.

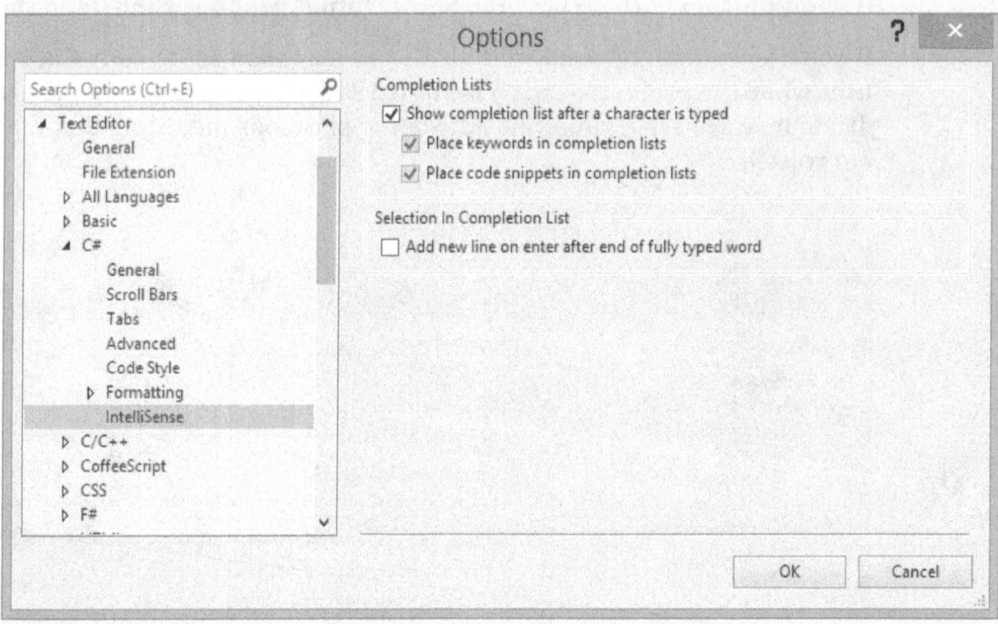

FIGURE A-7 Text Editor IntelliSense settings for C#

If you do not like the way the auto-completion IntelliSense feature of Visual Studio is functioning, you can make changes. On the **C# IntelliSense** dialog box, shown in Figure A-7, notice that the first checkbox option is **Show completion list after a character is typed**. IntelliSense provides code elements that you can select from a drop-down menu when you are coding. Turning on this feature reduces the number of keystrokes required while you are programming.

IntelliSense comes in two modes: Completion and Suggestion. By default, you get Completion mode. Completion mode can be annoying if you try to type the name of something that doesn't exist. IntelliSense tries to help and pops up only available or valid options. Often, you will accidentally get items added you didn't want. You can press **Ctrl** + **Alt** + **Spacebar** to switch to IntelliSense Suggestion mode (as opposed to Completion mode). In suggestion mode, IntelliSense is less aggressive. It does not autocomplete member names after you type open parenthesis or equal symbols. Instead, you are able to choose an existing member from a list.

You can set the editor to display **Line numbers**, **Enable single-click URL navigation**, and display the **Navigation bar** from the **Text Editor**, **C#**, **General** node as shown in Figure A-8.

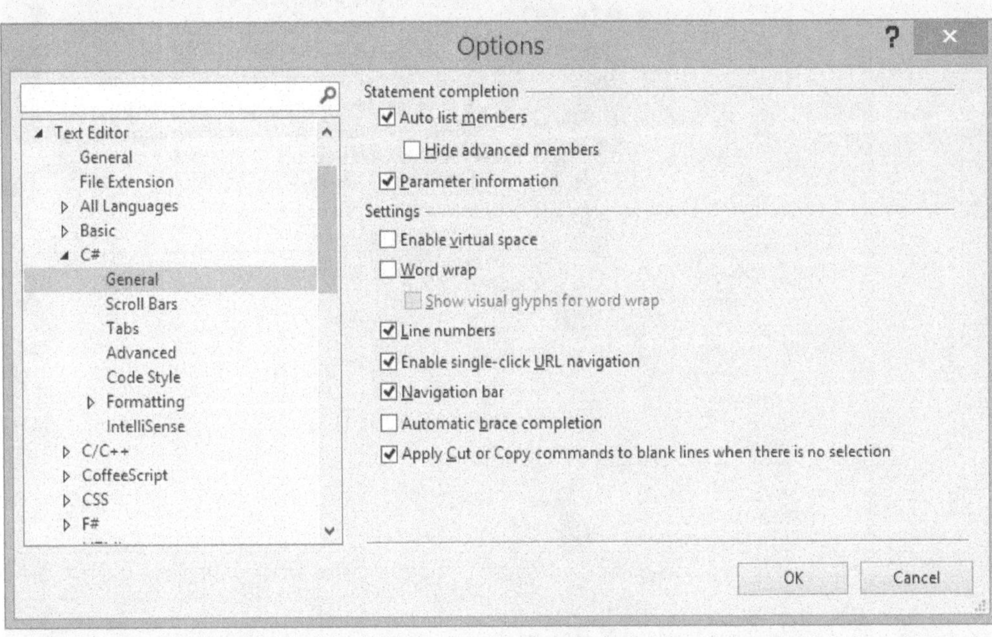

FIGURE A-8 Text Editor display option

You also specify whether you have **Statement completion** to **Auto list members** and/or have **Statement completion** with **Parameter information** displayed from the **Text Editor**, **C#**, **General** option. When you select **Display**, **Line numbers**, the line numbers are displayed to the left of the source code in the IDE.

The **Tabs** node, which appears below the **Scroll Bars** and **General** options, enables you to specify the amount of space inserted when a tab or indent is set and whether tabs or spaces are inserted for tabs. From this option, you can also set **Smart indenting** so that it automatically indents the next line, if a statement doesn't fit on a single line. Smart indenting does not always work the way you think it should. As the name implies, it tries to be smart and sometimes you have to override it.

The **Formatting** option under the **Text Editor** expands to reveal a number of features grouped under **General**, **Indentation**, **New Lines**, **Spacing**, and **Wrapping**. As shown in Figure A-9, from the **Text Editor**, **C#**, **Formatting**, **New Lines** option, you can decide whether you prefer to place your braces on a new line for types, methods, and control blocks. This is how braces have been displayed in this book.

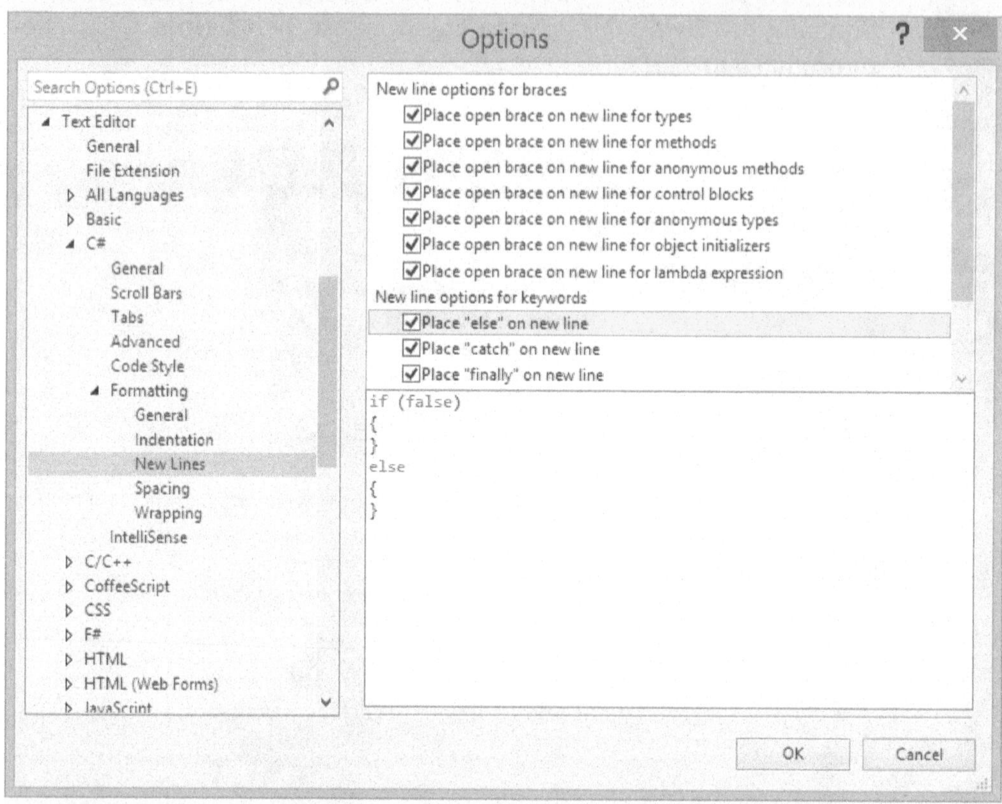

FIGURE A-9 Formatting settings for C# text editing

As illustrated in Figure A-9, this is where you indicate whether keywords such as `else`, `catch`, and `finally` should appear on a separate line. When you make those selections, intellisense places the keywords and braces on separate line and helps with proper indentation.

Selecting **Indent block contents**, **Indent case contents**, and **Indent case labels** causes the indention to occur automatically and can really increase your productivity. You select these settings under the **Indentation** option for **Formatting** within the **Text Editor, C#** node.

Explore the **Spacing** options under the **Text Editor**, **C#**, **Formatting** node. You set spacing for method declarations, method calls, casts, delimiters, and binary operators. You determine whether to have a space inserted between the name and open parenthesis or inside empty square brackets. Some of these settings are shown in Figure A-10.

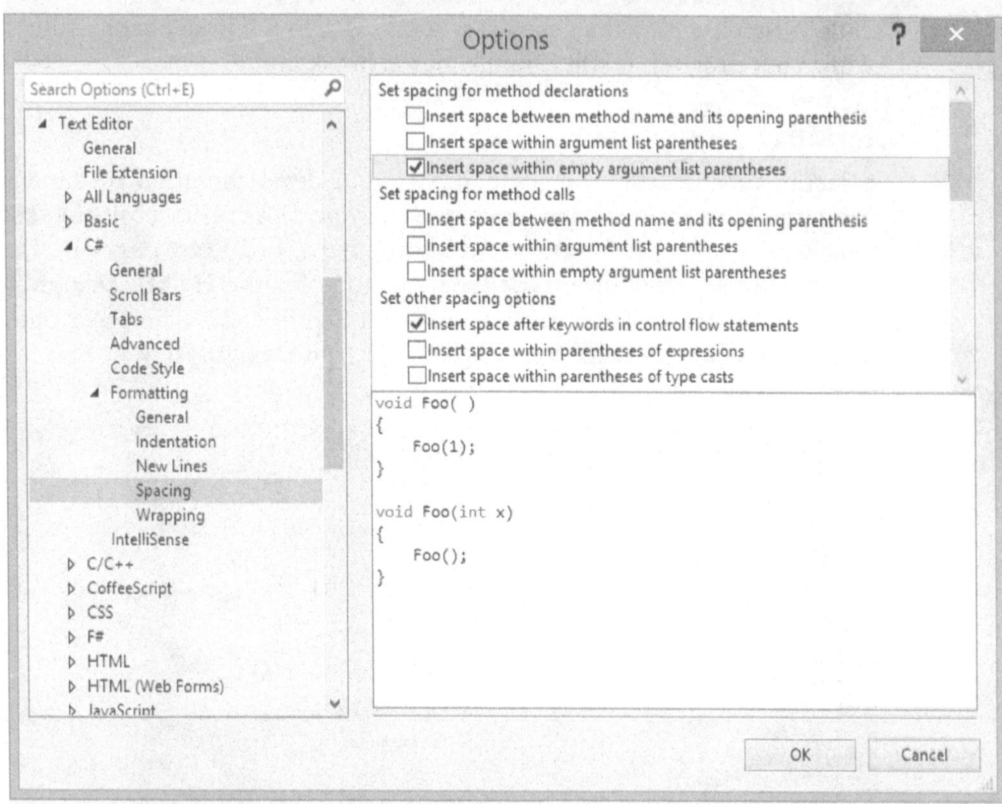

FIGURE A-10 Space settings for C# text editing

You also **Set spacing for operators** under the **TextEditor, C#, Formatting, Spacing node**. The selection **Insert space before and after binary operators** is the last listed option and was used for examples in this book. This enables you to specify whether you want Visual Studio to automatically insert spaces before and after arithmetic operators, such as + and =. As shown in Figure A-10, **Insert space within empty argument list parentheses** was set under **Set spacing for method declarations. Insert space within empty square brackets** was also selected. There are several other options available to configure your environment. You are encouraged to explore **Spacing**.

Debugging

A number of settings can be changed under the **Debugging** folder node. You should review the options that can be set. They include features such as **Ask before deleting all breakpoints**, **Break all processes when one process breaks**, and **Enable breakpoint filters.**

The **Enable Edit and Continue** under the **Edit and Continue** option lets you edit the code without ending the debug session. This allows you to change your source code while your program is still running, but in break mode.

HTML Designer

Selections made using this node impact your development environment when you are designing websites. If you prefer to start your work on a website by first seeing the page where items can be dragged and dropped, select **Start pages in**, **Design View**. You make this selection on the **General** node for the **HTML Designer** or by just selecting **HTML Designer** as illustrated in Figure A-11. The other options for the **Start pages in** are **Source View**, **Split View**, and **Design View**.

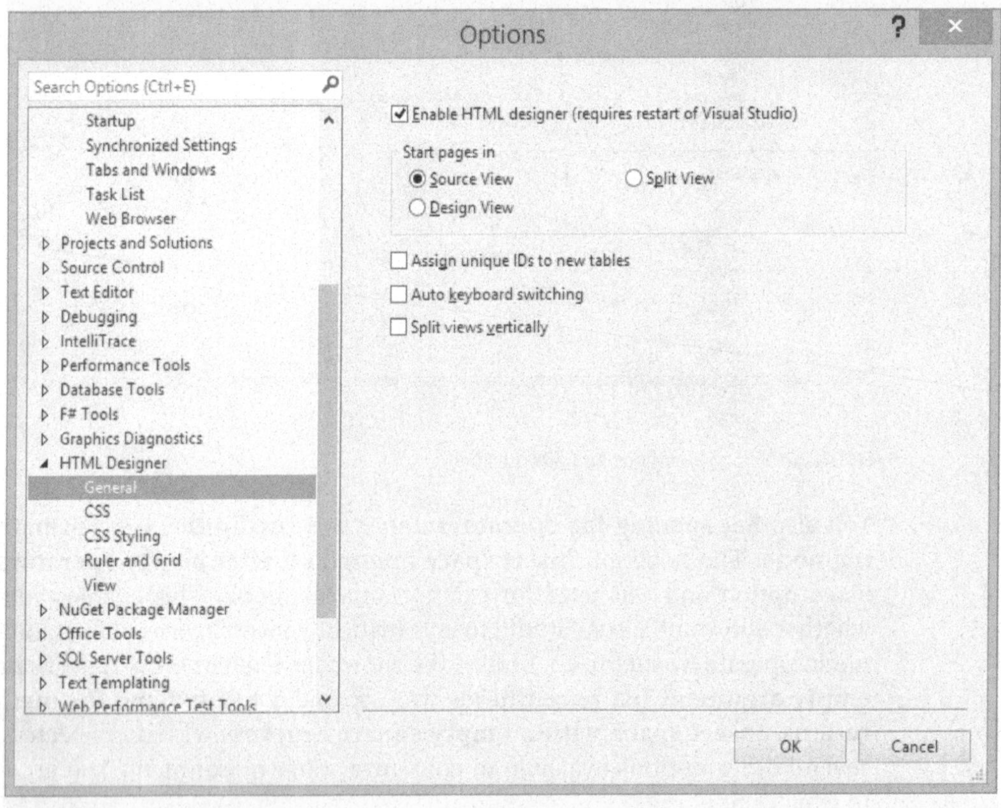

FIGURE A-11 HTML Designer

You determine how much of the screen is used for Design versus Source when you select **Split View**. You can have the majority of your screen show the design of your page with only a few lines revealing HTML if you prefer. As shown in Figure A-11, you can **Split views vertically** or take the default, which places the HTML tags above the design pane.

The **CSS Styling** node for the **HTML Designer**, shown on the left pane in Figure A-11, is used to indicate whether to **Change positioning to absolute for controls added using Toolbox, paste, or drag and drop**. Here, you also indicate whether to **Use <strong> and <em> for bold and italic text.**

The **Ruler and Grid** option under the **HTML Designer** node has options for grid size. You can specify the **Ruler and Grid units** of **pixels**, **inches**, **centimeters**, or **points**. Once that is determined, you can enter measurements for the **Display Grid** and **Snapping Grid** using that unit type. You can also specify the **Line style** and **Line color** from this dialog box.

Windows Forms Designer

Expanding the **Layout Settings** under the **Windows Forms Designer**, **General** node reveals options for **Width** and **Height** for the **Default Grid Cell Size**. The **Layout Mode** has value options of **SnapLines** or **SnapToGrid**. You also specify whether to show the grid and/or to snap objects to the grid when they are placed on the form from the **Show Grid** and **Snap To Grid** options. Positioning elements on the form can be made easier if you select **SnapLines** in the **Layout Mode**. Colored lines appear on the form as you move or resize elements. This allows you to snap the element to vertical or horizontal lines so that you can align them consistently. Some of the **Windows Forms Designer**, **General** options are illustrated in Figure A-12.

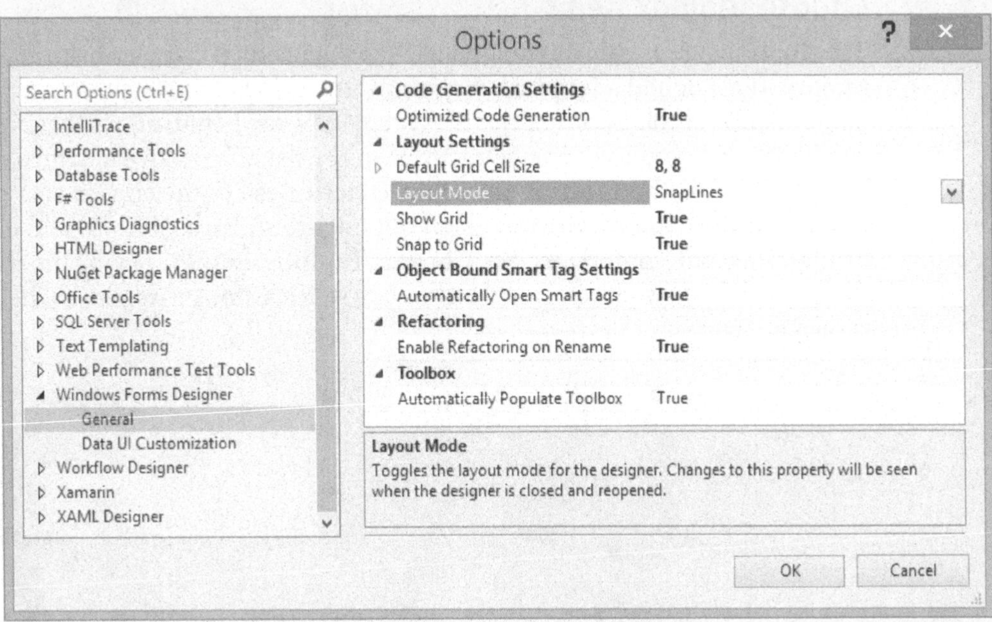

FIGURE A-12 Windows Forms Designer

Another option shown in Figure A-12 under the **Windows Forms Designer** node is the **Data UI Customization**. This dialog box defines which controls appear in the list of available controls for items in the **Data Sources Window**. `TextBox`, `ComboBox`, `Label`, `LinkLabel`, and `ListBox` are originally selected by default for `string` data types. But you can add a number of other ones, such as `CheckBox`, `PictureBox`, `RadioButton`, and `RichTextBox` for the `string` data type. You specify which control for other data type using this dialog box. Then the controls you selected become available for you to drag onto your form from the **Data Sources Window**.

Other Options Settings

Explore the other options on the **Tools, Options** menu. You will want to examine the **Database Tools** settings. From there you can specify the **SQL Server Instance Name** that you will use for your **Data Connections**. You can indicate which **Panes (are) shown by default** (**Diagram**, **Criteria**, **SQL**, or **Results**) from the **Query and View Designers** node. You also specify the **Default Query type** here. It is initially set to the **Select query**. You can change that to an **Insert**, **Delete**, or even a **Make Table query**.

There are lots of options. Spend some time experimenting with them. Change the settings and go into the editor and see what works best for you.

Choose Toolbox Items

The **Toolbox** used with Windows and Web applications can be customized. You can remove items or add additional widgets to the dialog box. When Visual Studio is set up, it installs in the **Toolbox** the most regularly used controls. If there are controls you hardly use, you can remove them from the list. To remove a control, right-click on the control in the **Toolbox** and select **Delete**. Besides the objects currently shown in the **Toolbox**, other controls are left out but are still available. To add one or more of these left out controls, select **Choose Toolbox Items**... from the **Tools** menu or right-click anywhere in the **Toolbox** and click **Choose Items**... The dialog box shown in Figure A-13 is revealed.

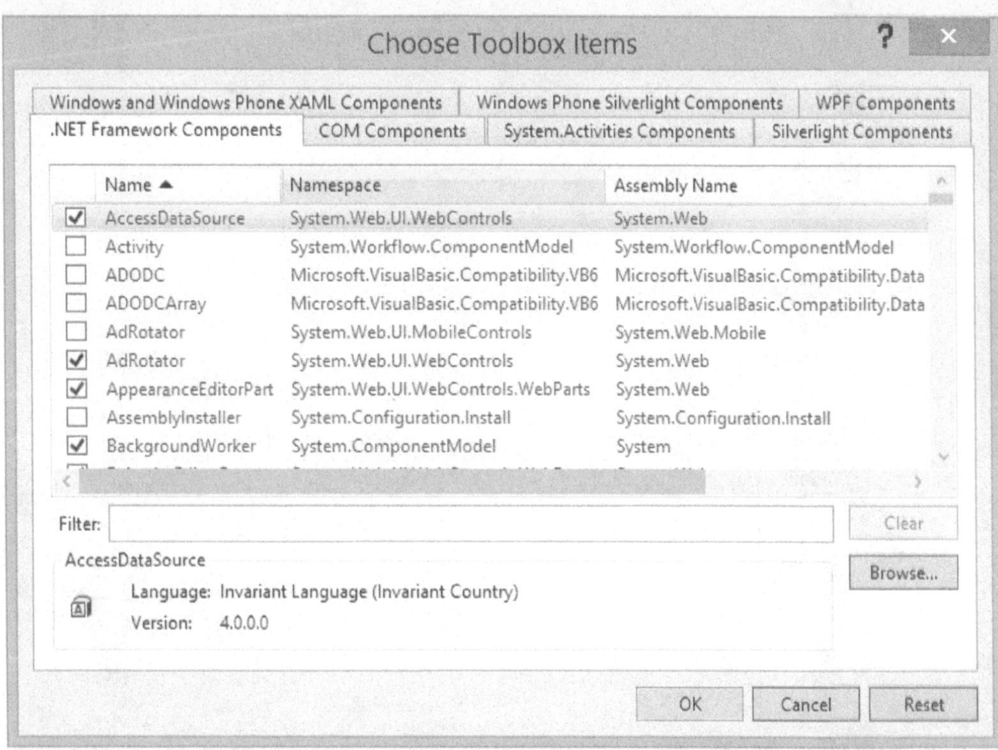

FIGURE A-13 Add Toolbox Items

The **Choose Toolbox Items** dialog box displays tabbed panes listing components that are installed on your local computer. Select the ones you want to appear in the **Toolbox**. When you choose **OK**, any items checked that are not already in the **Toolbox** will be added, and any items whose checkboxes have been cleared will be removed from the **Toolbox**.

Customize the Toolbars

From the **Tools**, **Customize** option you can select which **Toolbars** are displayed in the IDE. Using this option, you not only select the names of the toolbars but you can also specify which **Commands** are to be included within each toolbar. For example, if you choose to display the **Standard** toolbar, you see icons including **Navigate Backward**, **Navigate Forward**, **New Project**, **Open File**, **Save Selected Items**, **Save All**, **MultiLevel Undo**, and **MultiLevel Redo**. To add icons to a toolbar, from the **Commands** tab select **Add Command**. You can move the icon to the position where you want it to appear. The **Standard** toolbar was customized by adding the **Help** category to the toolbar, as shown in Figure A-14.

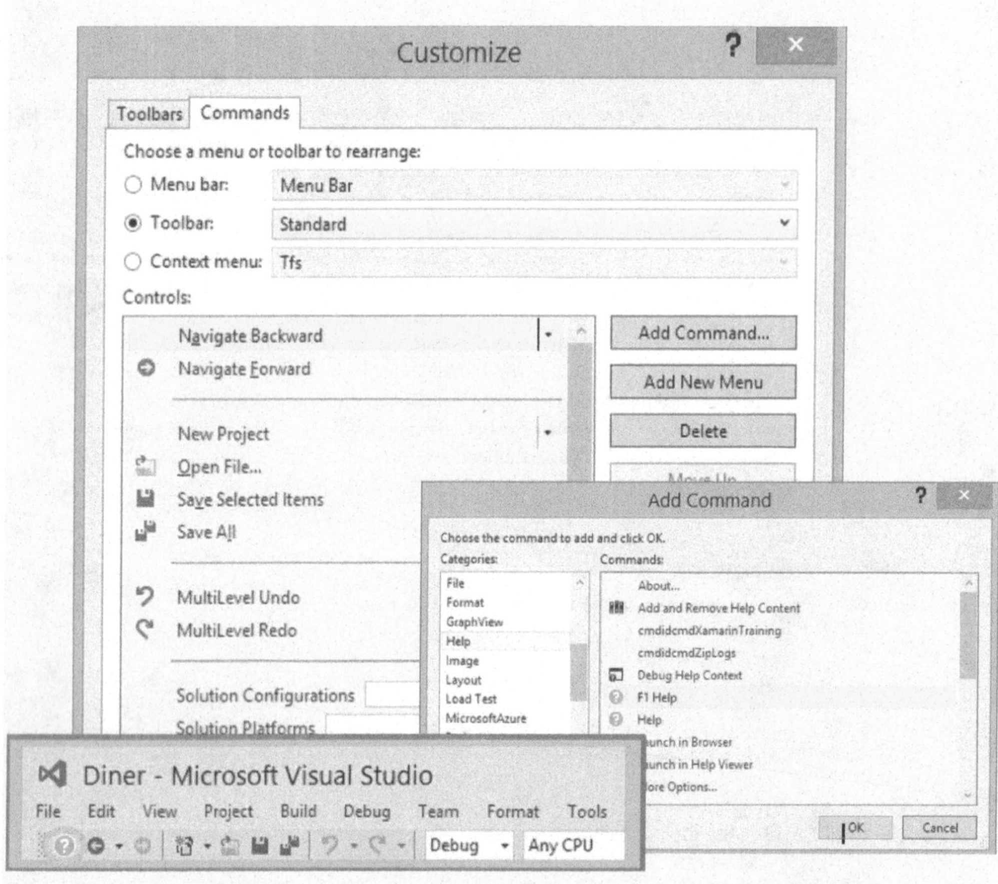

FIGURE A-14 Customizing the IDE

You remove icons in the same manner. As shown in Figure A-14, there is also an option to **Delete** commands from toolbars.

After using the **Tools, Options** and **Tools, Customize** menus, you will want to determine which windows you want open during design. As a minimum, you should have available the **Solution Explorer** and **Properties** windows. During Windows and Web development, the **Toolbox** should be added. For applications involving data connections, the **Data Sources** and **Server Explorer** should be added.

Configure and Save Windows Layouts

One of the new features available from the **Window** menu with Visual Studio 2015 is the option **Save Window Layout**. You can create a number of different types of applications with Visual Studio, from Console Applications, to Windows applications, to mobile applications to Web applications. There are over 40 different templates for different types of applications that can be created. With each of these, you use different windows during design. With this new feature, once the workspace is set up with the windows you want to have visible when you work with a specific type of application, the layout is saved. Then when you want to develop that type of application, simply select **Apply Window Layout** as illustrated in Figure A-15 and all those windows will open for you automatically. Figure A-15 illustrates saving four separate layouts.

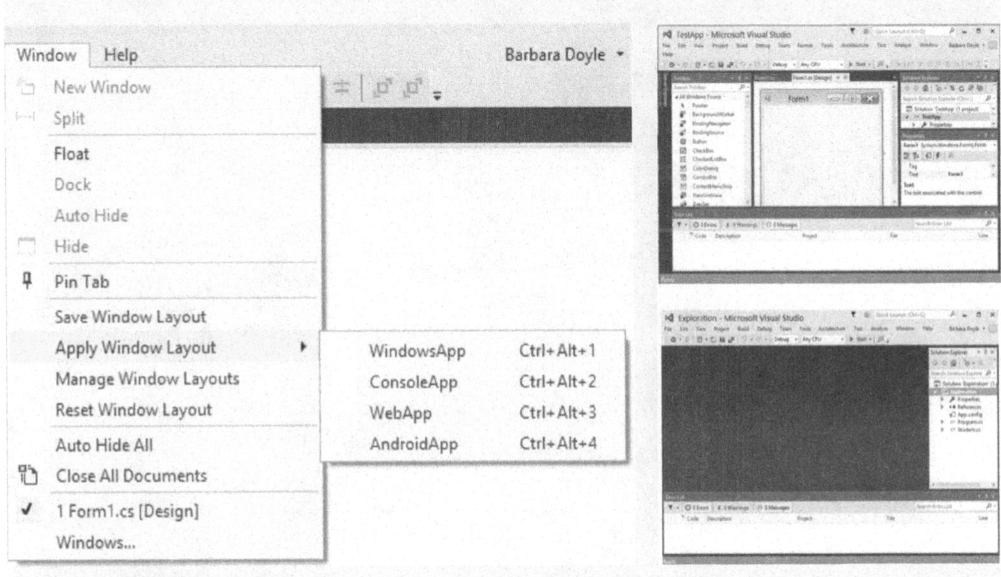

FIGURE A-15 Saving Windows Layout

Two of the layouts, `WindowsApp` and `ConsoleApp`, are shown on the right in Figure A-15. The `WindowsApp` layout, top right, includes not only the **Error List** window but also the **Solutions Explorer** window, **Properties** window, and the **Toolbox**. The `ConsoleApp` layout, bottom right, includes just the **Solution Explorer** and **Error List** windows.

Spend some time customizing the workspace to best meet your needs. You will find that it saves you much time during development and makes you more productive.

© zeljkodan/Shutterstock.com

APPENDIX B
CODE EDITOR TOOLS

There are many features within Visual Studio that make it easier for you to write and manage your code. Using IntelliSense and tooltips and understanding the colored markings offered up from Visual Studio will increase your productivity. This appendix highlights some of these most useful features.

Another time-saving feature is refactoring. If you find that you want to take a segment of code and place it in a method, you can do so using a copy-and-paste approach, or you can use the refactoring tools to restructure your source code. The tools automatically promote local variables to parameters and convert blocks of code into a method. Both of these features are discussed in this appendix.

You write many types of program statements repeatedly. For example, you write `while`, `do`, `for`, `if`, `switch`, `try...catch...finally`, and `foreach` statements. Every time you use these statements, you type curly braces to show the beginning and end of the block, and you spend time formatting to make sure they are syntactically correct and consistently placed in your program. One of the more exciting Visual Studio features in the Code Editor automates their inclusion. This is done through using code snippets. Code snippets are discussed in this appendix.

Class diagrams showing the data members, methods, and relationships between classes can be generated automatically with Visual Studio. You can add blank class diagrams and then add members to the structure or have Visual Studio create diagrams from existing code. This appendix also illustrates the use of class diagrams.

There are many features within Visual Studio that make it easier for you to write and manage your code. IntelliSense guides and enables you to learn more about the code you enter. Some of the features are described later. It begins by discussing IntelliSense.

IntelliSense

IntelliSense, an intelligent code completion context-aware feature is a very powerful aid in Visual Studio. It speeds up and reduces the number of typos you might enter. It guides and enables you to learn about the code you enter. It includes a number of features. One feature is called **List Members**. When you type a trigger character, such as a dot, a list of possible options is displayed. If you keep typing, the list is filtered to include only members that begin with those characters. You can insert the selection into your code by pressing Tab, typing a space, or the character that appears following the word selected. Learning to use this feature can greatly cut down on the amount of typing needed. **Quick Info** is another feature of IntelliSense. This feature is discussed later with the Colorized Tooltip section.

Syntax Coloring

Code elements are colored differently to distinguish them. Keywords are by default shown in blue color in the editor. Types or classes (such as `Console` and `Math`) are a different shade of blue. Other syntax elements are also colorized, such as `string` literals and comments. The default colors are shown in Figure B-1.

```
static void Main(string[] args)
{
    double ans;

    // Returns 5 cubed
    ans = Math.Pow(5, 3);
    Write("Ans: {0}", ans);
```

FIGURE B-1 Syntax colors

As illustrated in Figure B-1, strings are displayed using red text, keywords appear in a royal blue, framework class identifiers appear in a different shade of blue, while comments appear as green. These default colors and all other colors can be changed from the **Fonts and Colors**, **Environment**, **Options** Dialog Box, which you can open from the **Tools** menu.

Colorized Tooltips

You can move your mouse over code segments and get **Quick Info** about any identifier in your program. You get a short description and often times a method heading `or class` declaration. The **Quick Info** feature has been enhanced and color has been brought into the picture with Visual Studio 2015. Hover the mouse over a method call and see its signature as illustrated in Figure B-2.

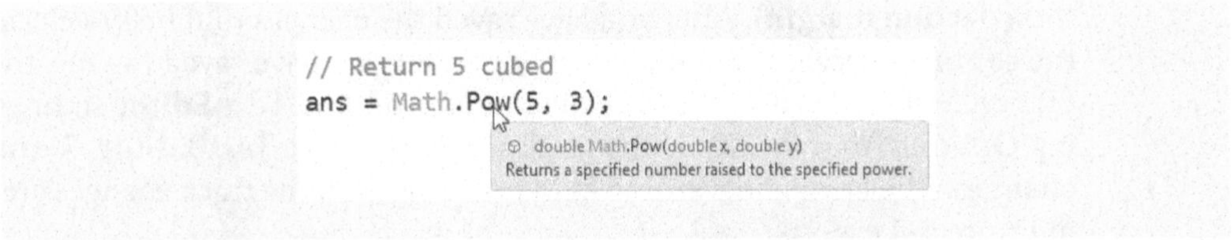

```
// Return 5 cubed
ans = Math.Pow(5, 3);
```

double Math.Pow(double x, double y)
Returns a specified number raised to the specified power.

FIGURE B-2 Colorized tooltip

Positioning the mouse over classes also displays a tooltip in color describing the class. You can create collapsible areas in your code using the `#region/#endregion` directives. Visual Studio also automatically creates collapsible regions for language constructs, such as classes and a methods body. Whenever you see the + or – to the left of code, it can be expanded or collapsed. An ellipsis is placed on the right side of the line, which is shown to also indicate that the segment of code has been collapsed. You can hover over the ellipsis to see the hidden code in a tooltip in colorful code. You don't have to click on the ellipsis and open it; Visual Studio will bring inline a tooltip showing the collapsed region. Figure B-3 shows what is revealed as the mouse is moved over the ellipsis for a collapsed method.

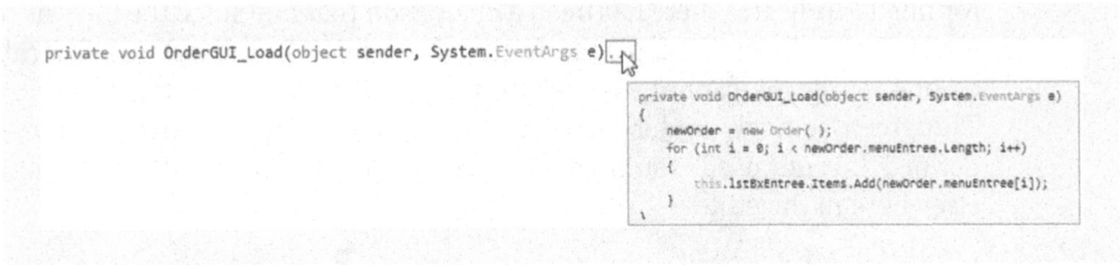

```
private void OrderGUI_Load(object sender, System.EventArgs e)...

private void OrderGUI_Load(object sender, System.EventArgs e)
{
    newOrder = new Order( );
    for (int i = 0; i < newOrder.menuEntree.Length; i++)
    {
        this.lstBxEntree.Items.Add(newOrder.menuEntree[i]);
    }
}
```

FIGURE B-3 Collapsible code revealed in color

Error and Warning Marks

Visual studio uses different-colored wavy underlines (known as **squiggles**) to alert you to problems with your code. Red squiggles or red underlines indicate a syntax error; green squiggles denote warnings such as a variable has been declared but not used. Visual Studio also places yellow or green vertical bars alongside code as alerts or warning. These yellow and green bars are referred to as Change Trackers. They allow you to keep track of the changes you have made in a file. Changes made since the file was opened but not saved are denoted by a yellow bar on the left margin (known as the **selection margin**). After you have saved the changes (but before closing the file), the bar turns green. If you undo a change after you have saved the file, the bar turns orange. You can turn this feature off and on from the **Text Editor** settings by selecting **Options** from the **Tools** menu. From there select **Text Editor**, **Settings**, **Track changes**. The error and warning markers along with the track changes are illustrated in Figure B-4.

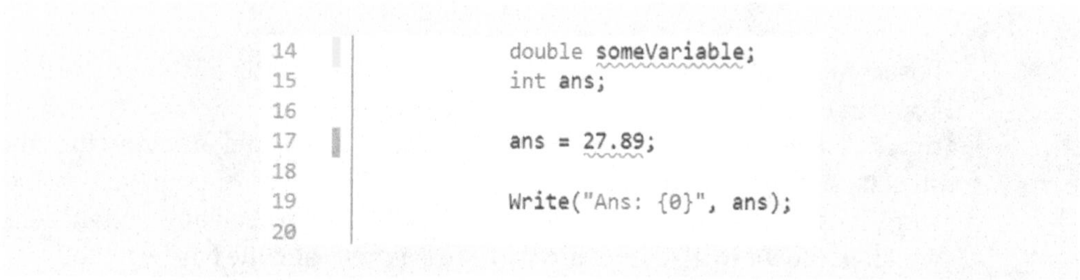

```
14        double someVariable;
15        int ans;
16
17        ans = 27.89;
18
19        Write("Ans: {0}", ans);
20
```

FIGURE B-4 Error and warning marks

The yellow bar in the selection margin of line 14 in Figure B-4 indicates the file has not been saved since making a change on that line. The green bar in the selection margin for line 17 indicates there has been a change on that line since the file was opened, but it has already been saved. The red squiggly on line 17 under `27.89` indicates a syntax error. Clearly you cannot store a floating point value in an integer memory location. The green squiggly under `someVariable` is warning that the memory location is defined, but not used. You might also see a light bulb icon in the selection margin or elsewhere in the editor.

Quick Action Light Bulb Icon

The yellow light bulb is called the Quick Action Light Bulb. This feature is new to Visual Studio 2015. The light bulb provides quick actions, including fixes to syntax errors, removal of unnecessary code, and refactoring help. From clicking the down arrow beside the light bulb icon, multiple options are shown with preview capability.

Recall a number of using statements that are automatically added based on the type of application created. Many times most of these using statements are really not needed. The Quick Action Light Bulb alerts you to these types of unnecessary lines of code in your program. As shown in Figure B-5, a message suggesting you "`Remove unnecessary Usings`" is shown under the light bulb.

```
using System;
using System.Collections.Generic;
using System.Linq;

namespace Exploration
{
    class Program
    {
        static void Main(str
        {
```

Remove Unnecessary Usings

Preview changes

Fix all occurrences in: Document | Project | Solution

FIGURE B-5 Quick Action Light Bulb recommendation

Four of the five using statements are highlighted in pink in Figure B-5, indicating they could be removed. Under that suggestion, a **Preview changes** link is available. The Quick Action Light Bulb also helps with syntax errors. Figure B-6 provides another illustration. This time `itemCnt` was defined, but `cntOfValues` wasn't. As shown in Figure B-6 three possible options are suggested to correct the problem. The preview window shown on the right in Figure B-6 illustrates how the code will be modified if the third option is selected.

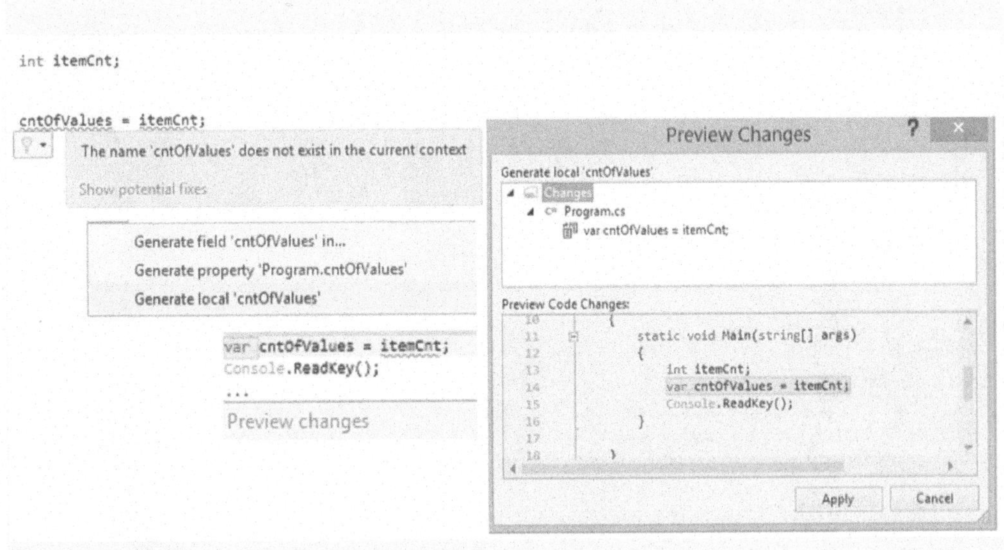

FIGURE B-6 Quick Action Light Bulb changes previewed

The Quick Action Light Bulb is launched automatically when Visual Studio feels it can help. You can also solicit its help by right-clicking the mouse on an area or pressing **Ctrl** + dot (.).

Peek Definition

The **Peek Definition** command enables you to view and edit code without switching away from the code that you are writing. It displays the contents of a method or class right inside the application you are developing. **Peek Definition** and **Go To Definition** show the same information, but **Peek Definition** shows the segment of code in-line in the file you are in, immediately below the existing code. Output from the **Go To Definition** shows the code in a separate code window. Use this feature by selecting the option when you right-click the mouse on an identifier or by using the **Alt** + **F12** shortcut. It is very useful to quickly look at the definition of a class, method, or other structure. Figure B-7 illustrates Peek Definition.

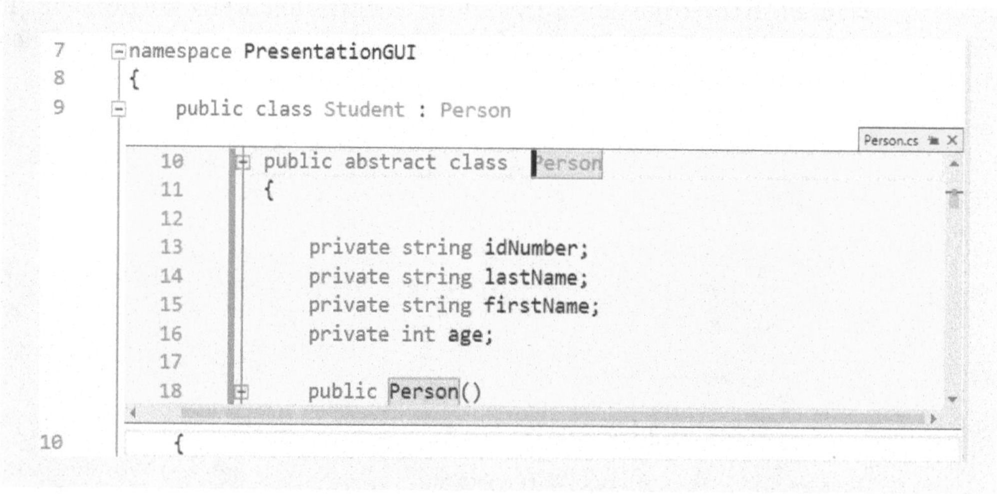

```
namespace PresentationGUI
{
    public class Student : Person
                                                        Person.cs
        public abstract class Person
        {

            private string idNumber;
            private string lastName;
            private string firstName;
            private int age;

            public Person()
    {
```

FIGURE B-7 Peek definition feature

Refactoring

Refactoring lets you improve on your code by modifying the internal structure without changing the logic or the external behavior of your program. Sometimes methods grow to include more than one major theme. Sometimes you can look at your code and see that a method is doing too much. The **Extract Method** option provides an easy way to create a new method from a segment of code.

Extract Method

The `Main( )` method, shown in Figure B-8, does both the calculation and displays the results.

```
12        static void Main(string[] args)
13        {
14            int scoreOne,
15                scoreTwo,
16                scoreThree;
17            double average;
18
19            scoreOne = InputValue("first");
20            scoreTwo = InputValue("second");
21            scoreThree = InputValue("third");
22
23            average = (scoreOne + scoreTwo + scoreThree) / 3.0;
24
25            Clear();
26            WriteLine("Grading App\n");
27            WriteLine("Score #1: {0)\n" +
28                      "Score #2: {1)\n" +
29                      "Score #3: {2)\n",
30                      scoreOne, scoreTwo, scoreThree):
31            WriteLine("\nAverage: {0:F2}", average);
32            ReadKey();
33        }
```

FIGURE B-8 Refactoring a method

Notice that the program statement on Line 23 takes the values entered and performs calculations with them. You can use the **Extract Method** from the **Refactor** menu to create a new method to calculate the average. Line 23 was selected prior to choosing the **Extract Method** from the **Refactor** menu option. **Refactor** is available from the **Edit** menu. As shown in Figure B-9, a new method is added to the program with a call matching the signature for the method. It is initially named "NewMethod." Both the name in the method heading and the method call are highlighted in green and the Rename feature is invoked as illustrated in Figure B-9.

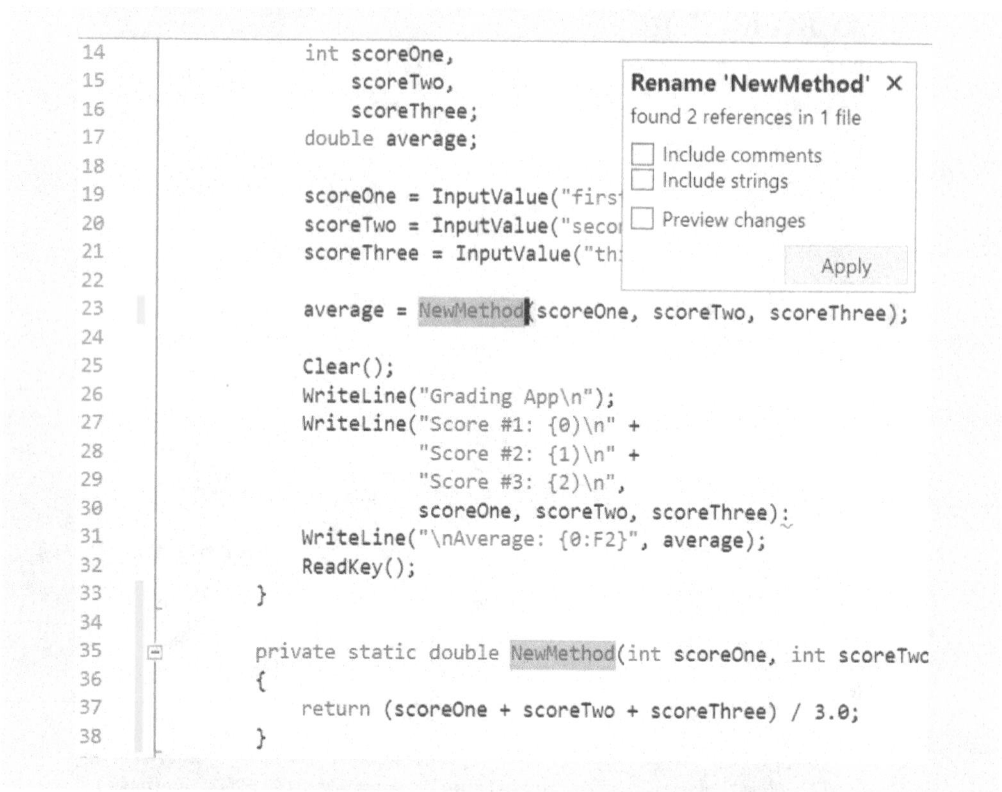

```
            int scoreOne,
                scoreTwo,
                scoreThree;
            double average;

            scoreOne = InputValue("firs
            scoreTwo = InputValue("seco
            scoreThree = InputValue("th

            average = NewMethod(scoreOne, scoreTwo, scoreThree);

            Clear();
            WriteLine("Grading App\n");
            WriteLine("Score #1: {0}\n" +
                      "Score #2: {1}\n" +
                      "Score #3: {2}\n",
                      scoreOne, scoreTwo, scoreThree);
            WriteLine("\nAverage: {0:F2}", average);
            ReadKey();
        }

        private static double NewMethod(int scoreOne, int scoreTwc
        {
            return (scoreOne + scoreTwo + scoreThree) / 3.0;
        }
```

Rename 'NewMethod' ×
found 2 references in 1 file
☐ Include comments
☐ Include strings
☐ Preview changes
Apply

FIGURE B-9 New method name for the extracted code

Rename

Rename is an operation that provides an easy way to change the name of identifiers for data types, local variables, namespaces, methods, and properties. To use this option, position the cursor on the identifier you want to rename and select **Rename** from the **Edit** menu. It changes the identifier throughout the program. The Rename feature has been enhanced in Visual Studio 2015. You can now also rename any text in a string or comment line as is illustrated in Figure B-10. That was not possible in the previous versions of Visual Studio.

```
class Residence
{
    public string PropertyID { get; }
    public string Address { get; }

    public Residence(string id, string add)
    {
        PropertyID = id;
        Address = add;
    }

    public Residence(string id)
    {
        PropertyID = id;
    }

    public override string ToString()
    {
        return "ID: {PropertyID}\nAddress: {Address}";
```

Rename 'PropertyID' ×
found 4 references in 1 file
☐ Include comments
☑ Include strings
☐ Preview changes
Apply

FIGURE B-10 Rename feature

NOTE An additional check box option of **Include overloads** is displayed in the **Rename** dialog box when you select to rename an identifier that is overloaded.

Other Refactoring Options

The **Refactor, Encapsulate Field** option lets you create a property from a local variable and then update your code with references to the new property. There are also options to **Extract Interface** and **Remove** or **Reorder Parameters**. Refactoring lets you quickly reorganize your code for better reuse and readability. You are encouraged to explore the online documentation to learn more about refactoring operations that can increase your productivity.

Code Snippets

Code snippets are templates that you can use to insert code. They can help speed up the entry of common code constructs and make you more productive. When you insert a code snippet, a template is inserted into your program that enables you to fill in unique entries. You can use the built-in snippets or create your own. Snippets are stored as XML files that you can edit and customize. Snippets are grouped into the categories of **NetFX30, Office Development, Other, Test**, and **Visual C#**.

Code snippets are named with a short alias. You activate the snippet by either typing the alias and pressing the **Tab** key twice or by using the IntelliSense menu to insert the code snippet. Pressing **Ctrl** + **K** + **X** activates the code snippet list, as shown in Figure B-11. In order to see the list of available code snippets that you might want to incorporate into your application, select **Visual C#**.

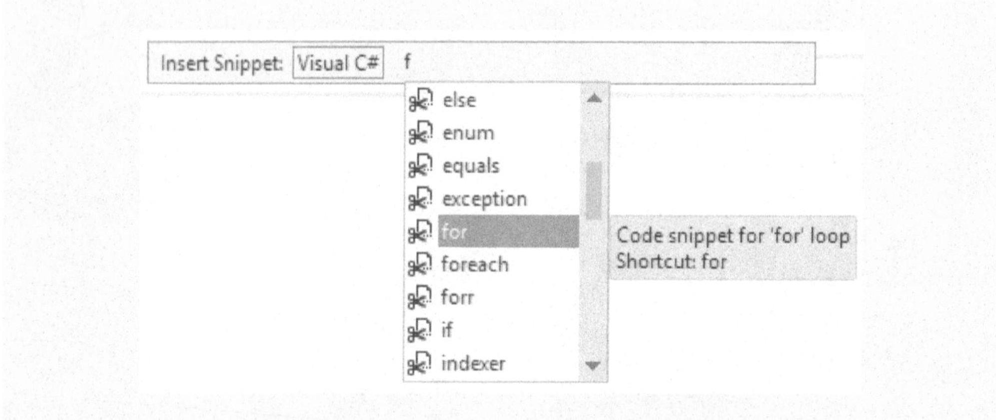

FIGURE B-11 Code snippet list

When the list is displayed, selecting the name inserts a segment of code at the cursor position. The alias for the decrementing `for` is `forr`.

Another shortcut for displaying the list of logical code elements that can be inserted in your program is to press **Ctrl** + **Spacebar**. This pops up a more exhaustive list.

The code snippet aliases are included in the list of available entries. Pressing the **Tab** key twice after selecting the `forr` alias inserts the code snippet text, as shown in Figure B-12.

```
for (int i = length - 1; i >= 0; i--)
{

}
```

FIGURE B-12 Code snippet inserted into text

Notice that the code snippet shown in Figure B-12 inserted the text at the cursor position and created an empty `for` loop. At this point, the editable fields in the code snippet are highlighted and the first editable field is selected automatically. The editable fields for the `for` statement are the initializer variable (`i` by default) and the `Max length` expression (`length` by default). You can type a new value for the field or press the **Tab** key to cycle through the editable fields. Clicking on a field places the cursor in the field, and double-clicking on a field selects it. You can change the fields to reflect the identifiers you use in your program.

Code snippets are simply XML files; you can easily create your own. The file ends with a .snippet filename extension. As you find yourself typing the same segment of code for multiple applications, you are encouraged to explore the online documentation to learn more about creating your own shortcuts.

Working with Class Diagrams

You can view your program in a number of different ways, including graphically. Class diagrams document the structure of an application by showing data members and behaviors of a class. For multiple class applications, they also show the relationship between the classes. Right-clicking on the project in the **Solution Explorer** window reveals **View, View Class Diagram** option. Figure B-13 illustrates the class diagram created for the `PresentationGUI` application created in Chapter 12.

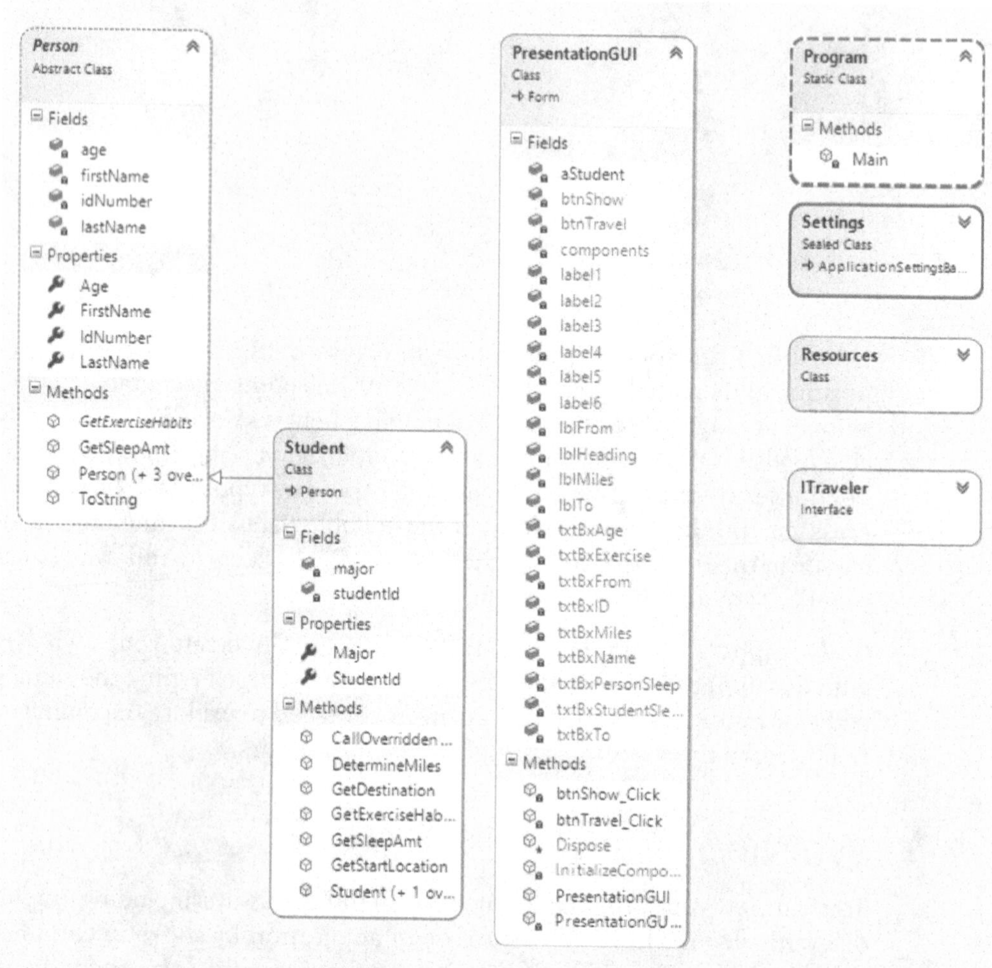

FIGURE B-13 PresentationGUI class diagram

The application shown in Figure B-13 consists of several classes. The `PresentationGUI class` is related to the other classes because it instantiates objects of the `Student class`. No line connects the `PresentationGUI` and `Student` classes. A relationship line connects the `Student` and `Person` classes. These two classes are related through the `Student class` being derived from the `Person class`. Additional classes of `Resources`, `Settings`, and `Program` are shown. The `ITraveler interface` is also shown on the figure.

Class Details View

The methods, or behaviors, of the `Student class` are shown under the class diagram in the **Class Details** pane. This pane can be expanded, as illustrated in Figure B-14.

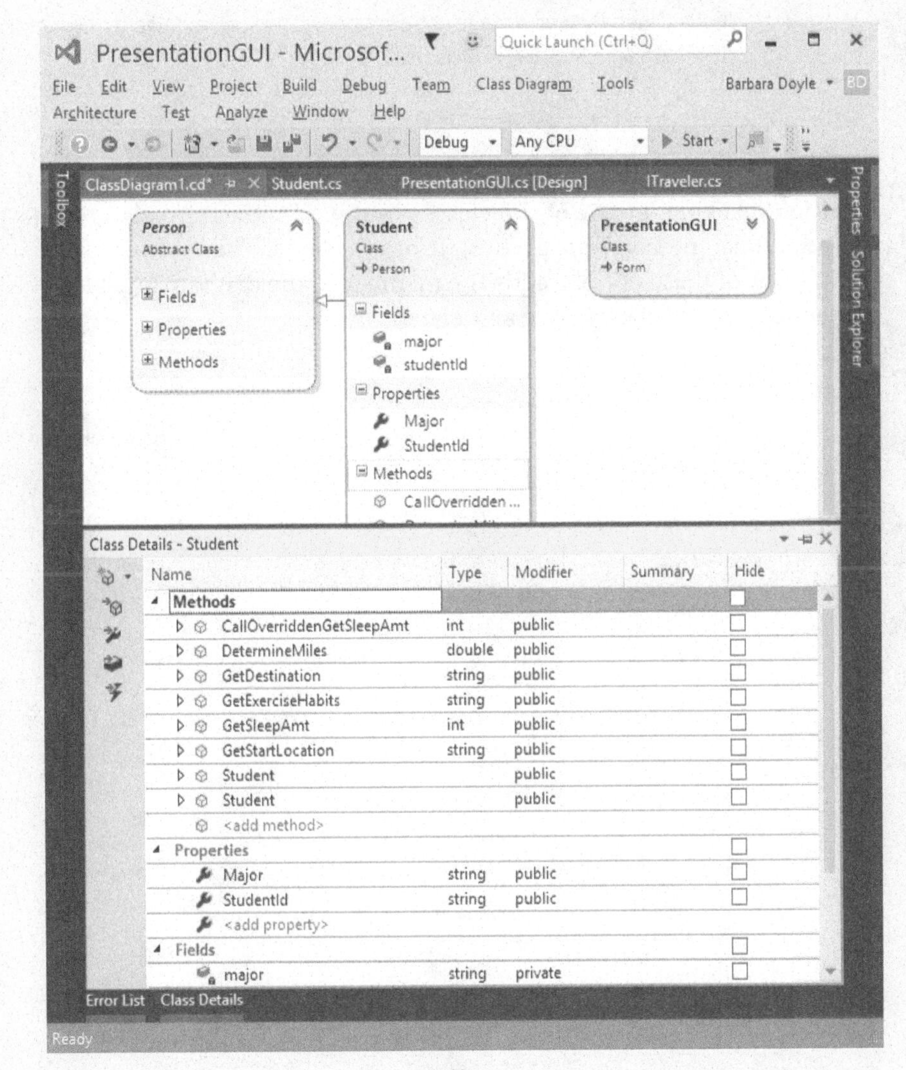

FIGURE B-14 Class Details view

The **Class Details** window provides a considerable amount of information. All of the class methods, properties, fields, and events are included. As shown in Figure B-14, each of these categories can be expanded to provide additional details, including the data type and modifier access level. You can go directly to the code by right-clicking on the diagram and selecting **View Code**.

If the **Class Details** pane is not displayed, it can be revealed by right-clicking the mouse on the class and selecting **Class Details**.

Using the Class Diagram to Add Members

Right-clicking on any of the classes in the class diagram also reveals options to add additional methods, properties, fields, or events. This is shown in Figure B-15. Selecting any of these options adds the member to the diagram and also automatically generates the underlying code associated with it.

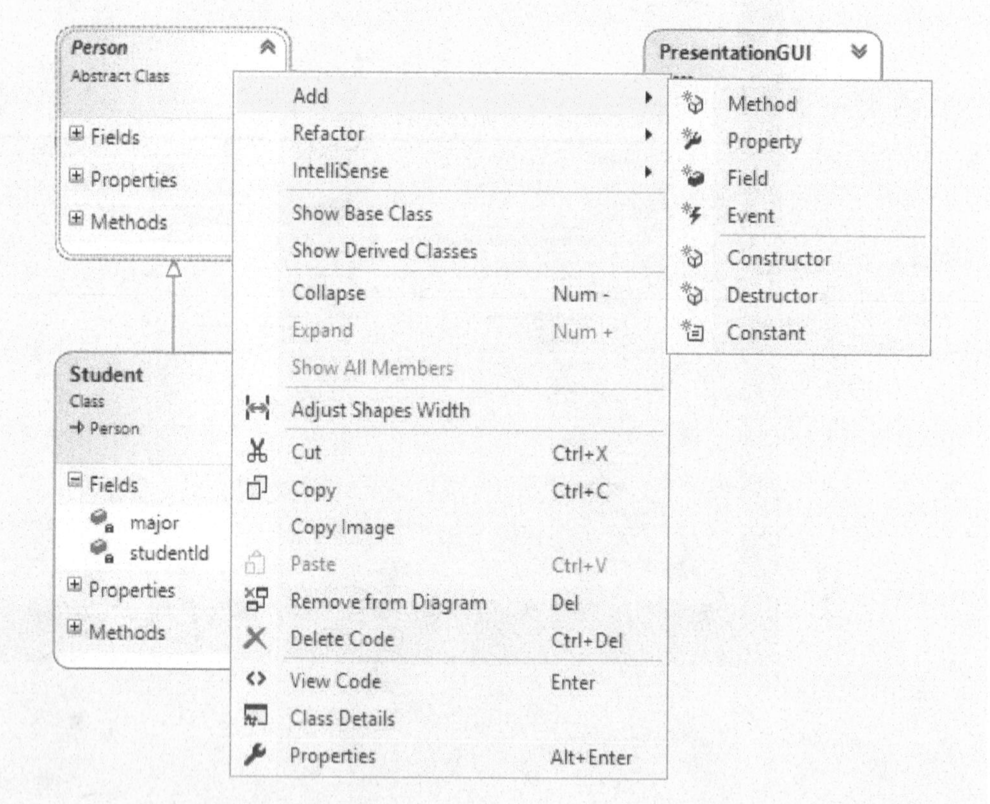

FIGURE B-15 Adding members using the class diagram

As shown in Figure B-15, additional constructors can be added from the class diagram. The **Refactor** option shown in Figure B-15 enables you to extract an interface or rename the class. The **IntelliSense** feature guides you through overriding a method. Figure B-16 illustrates the **Show Base Class** option. The base class for `Person` is `Object`.

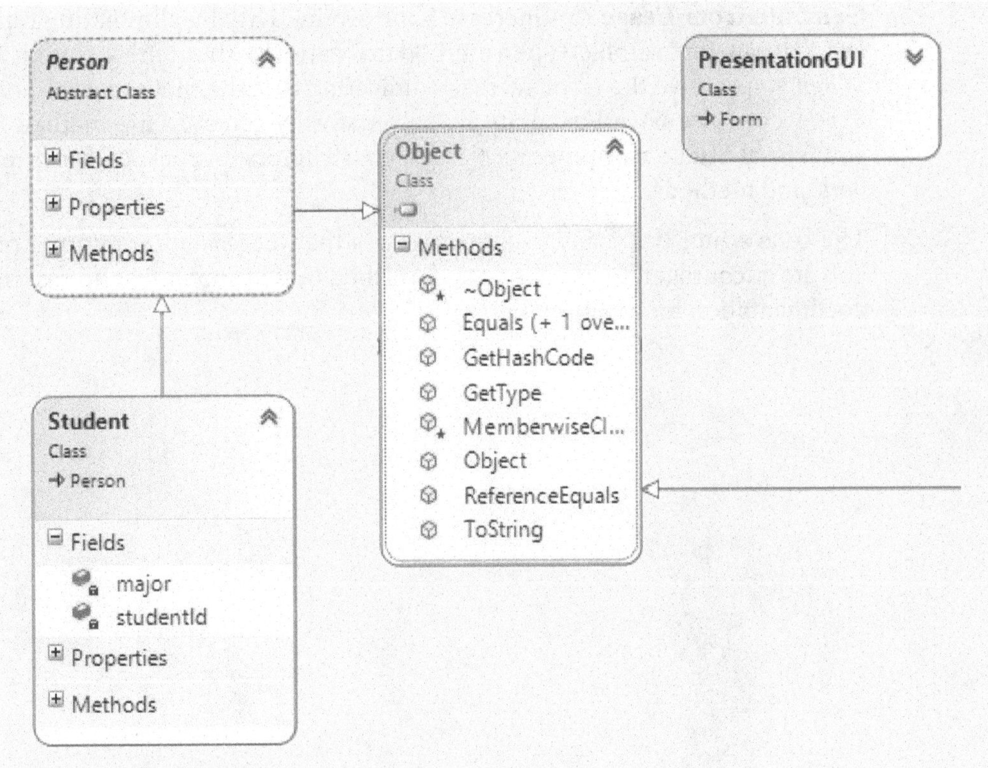

FIGURE B-16 Show base class for Person (Object)

As shown in Figure B-16, `Person` extends the `Object class`. All C# classes inherit from the `Object class`; however, the `Object class` is not automatically shown on the diagram. You must select the **Show Base Class** option to view the `Object class`.

Other Code Editor Tips

Zoom is one of the more interesting features available with Visual Studio. You can press the **Ctrl** + **Mouse** wheel to increase and decrease the font size. There is also zoom capability available in the extreme left corner, near the status line, in code view as was illustrated in Appendix A.

Box Selector is a code editor tool that enables you to select a rectangular region, type a line, and have that line repeated for every line part of the region. To do this, hold the **Alt** key while using the mouse to make a vertical section. Then start typing. Whatever is typed appears on every line that is part of the region. This could be a useful tool for adding comments to blocks of text or to change all data members from `public` to `private` by typing a single `private` keyword once the region has been selected.

Generate from Usage can increase your productivity by eliminating repetitive typing. You can, for example, type a method invocation without first creating the method. When you receive the error message indicating that the method does not exist, type **Ctrl** + dot (.) to have Visual Studio automatically generate the method heading for you. Visual Studio can generate classes, constructors, properties, fields, enum members, and methods.

The code editor has many exciting features that increase programmer productivity. You are encouraged to use the ones described in this appendix and search the online documentation for additional tips.

© zeljkodan/Shutterstock.com

APPENDIX C
CHARACTER SETS

The Unicode standard is a universal character encoding scheme that assigns a unique numeric value, called a code point, to each character used in many of the written languages of the world. Over 65,000 characters can be represented. This appendix shows a subset of the characters commonly used with the English language. The ASCII (American Standard Code for Information Interchange) character set corresponds to the first 128 characters of the Unicode character set. Thus, Table C-1 shows many of the ASCII and Unicode representations. C# and other .NET-supported languages use the Unicode standard.

TABLE C-1 Unicode/ASCII character codes

	0	1	2	3	4	5	6	7	8	9
0	Null							Bell	Back space	Horizontal tab
1	Line feed	Vertical tab	Form feed	Carriage return						
2					Cancel			Escape		
3			(space)	!	"	#	$	%	&	'
4	(	)	*	+	,	-	.	/	0	1
5	2	3	4	5	6	7	8	9	:	;
6	<	=	>	?	@	A	B	C	D	E
7	F	G	H	I	J	K	L	M	N	O
8	P	Q	R	S	T	U	V	W	X	Y
9	Z	[	\	]	^	_	'	a	b	c
10	D	e	f	g	h	i	j	k	l	m
11	N	o	p	q	r	s	t	u	v	w
12	X	y	z	{	|	}	-	De1		

© Cengage Learning

The numbers in the first column represent the first digit(s) for the decimal value. That value is concatenated to the numbers found in the heading row to form the decimal equivalent for that symbol in ASCII and Unicode. For example, the lowercase *s* is located in the row labeled 11 and in the column labeled 5. Its code value is 115. A subset of the characters is shown in the table.

The Unicode standard makes it easier to develop applications that can be implemented worldwide. Developers do not have to keep up with which coding schema is used because it is a worldwide standard. For additional information, see "The Unicode Standard" at *www.unicode.org.*

© zeljkodan/Shutterstock.com

APPENDIX D
OPERATOR PRECEDENCE

When an expression has multiple operations to be evaluated, the order of evaluation of the operators is determined by the precedence and associativity of the operators used in the expression. Most operators are **left-associative**—meaning the operations are performed from left to right. All binary operators are left-associative. The assignment operators and conditional operators are right-associative. Table D-1 shows the C# operators by category of precedence. The operators are shown from highest to lowest precedence.

TABLE D-1 Operator precedence

Category	Example operators
Primary	`[ ]` `( )` `x++` `x--` `new` `typeof` `dot operator(.)`
Unary	`+ - ! ++x --x (cast) size of`
Multiplicative	`* / %`
Additive	`+ -`
Shift	`<< >>`
Relational and type testing	`< > <= >= is as`
Equality	`== !=`
Logical AND	`&`
Logical XOR	`^`

(continues)

TABLE D-1 Operator precedence (*continued*)

<table>
<tr><th>Category</th><th>Example operators</th></tr>
<tr><td>Logical OR</td><td>|</td></tr>
<tr><td>Conditional AND</td><td>&&</td></tr>
<tr><td>Conditional OR</td><td>||</td></tr>
<tr><td>Conditional</td><td>? :</td></tr>
<tr><td>Assignment</td><td>= *= /= %= += -= <<= >>= &= ^= |=</td></tr>
</table>

© Cengage Learning

Operators have equal precedence within the category. Thus, in the expression `answer = aNumber + val1 * val2 / 7`, the order of operations would be *, /, +, and =.

© zeljkodan/Shutterstock.com

APPENDIX E
C# KEYWORDS

This appendix lists the reserved words of C# in Table E-1. Each has a special meaning associated with it. Notice that all keywords begin with a lowercase letter.

TABLE E-1 Keywords

abstract	as	base	bool	break	byte
case	catch	char	checked	class	const
continue	decimal	default	delegate	do	double
else	enum	event	explicit	extern	false
finally	fixed	float	for	foreach	goto
if	implicit	in	int	interface	internal
is	lock	long	namespace	new	null
object	operator	Out	override	params	private
protected	public	readonly	ref	return	sbyte
sealed	short	sizeof	stackalloc	static	string
struct	switch	this	throw	true	try
typeof	uint	ulong	unchecked	unsafe	ushort
using	virtual	void	volatile	while	

© Cengage Learning

There are several other words that have been identified as "contextual keywords." Table E-2 lists these words. Contextual keywords are not as powerful as regular keywords. They have a special meaning only when used in a specific context. Many of these are considered query keywords and are used in query expressions. Some contextual keywords, such as `partial` and `where`, have special meanings in two or more contexts.

TABLE E-2 Contextual keywords

add	alias	ascending	async	await	descending
dynamic	from	Get	global	group	into
join	let	orderby	partial	remove	select
set	value	var	where	yield	

© zeljkodan/Shutterstock.com

GLOSSARY

`abstract class` — Base class that cannot be instantiated. It can only be extended.

`abstraction` — The act of generalizing or thinking about an object in general terms. Through abstraction, data members and behaviors of a class are identified.

`abstract method` — A method that includes no implementation details (no method body) in the declaration. Abstract method declarations are permitted only in abstract classes.

`accessor` — Special type of method used to read or retrieve the current state or value of an object's member's data. Also referred to as getter.

`accumulation` — An operation commonly found in applications that need to add together the values that a single variable holds. A variable initialized to zero is used to hold the running total. For example, to determine the average of a set of values, the values are normally added to an accumulator variable and divided by the number of entries.

`Active Server Pages (ASP)` — A Microsoft programming model for creating dynamic web pages. Using the traditional or classic Active Server Pages (ASP) model, code written in a scripting language, such as JavaScript or VBScript, is added to the HTML file.

`ActiveX Data Objects (ADO.NET)` — Suite of data access technologies used to manipulate databases.

`actual arguments` — The actual data that is sent to a method. Actual argument refers to the variable or literal that is placed inside the parentheses in the method call. Sometimes referred to as actual parameters.

`aggregation` — See containment.

`algorithm` — A clear, unambiguous, step-by-step process for solving a problem. These steps are expressed completely and precisely so that all details are included.

`American Standard Code for Information Interchange (ASCII)` — A subset of Unicode, in which the first 128 characters correspond to the Unicode character set. ASCII consists of the alphabet for the English language, plus numbers and symbols.

`application software` — Programs developed to perform a specific task. A word processor, such as Microsoft Word, is an example of application software.

`argument` — The data included inside the parentheses during a method call. Parameter often refers to items appearing in the heading of the method; argument refers to the data appearing in the call to the method.

`array` — A data structure that allows multiple values of the same data type to be stored under a single identifier.

`ArrayList` — Listlike structure that can dynamically increase or decrease in length.

`array of array` — See ragged array.

`ASCII` — See American Standard Code for Information Interchange.

`ASP` — See Active Server Pages.

`ASP.NET` — The Microsoft programming framework that enables the creation of applications that run on a Web server and delivers functionality through a browser.

`assembler` — Software that converts the assembly programming language, which is a low-level programming language, into machine code.

assemblies — Units that are configured and deployed in .NET.

assignment operator — The equals symbol (=). It is used to perform a compile-time initialization or make an assignment.

attribute — The data member or field of the class. For example, one attribute of a Student class is studentNumber.

auto-implemented property — Property that does not require return or set statements. The body of the property is simply written as get; and set;.

automatic garbage collection — Releasing space back to the operating system for reuse.

automatic postback — An HTTP request to the server that is automatically triggered.

auto-property with initializer — An auto-property with an assignment statement used to initialize the data field.

auxiliary storage — Nonvolatile, permanent memory that can hold data for long periods, even when there is no power to the system. Also called secondary storage.

BAML — Binary XAML or a tokenized, binary representation of XAML. When you compile an application that contains XAML files, the markup gets converted into BAML.

base class — A class from which other classes can inherit characteristics. The base class is sometimes called the super or parent class. The ultimate base class of all classes in C# is object.

base type — The data type of the object. The type can be one of the predefined types such as int or string, a user-defined class that you create, or some other .NET class. All data values placed in an array must be of the same base type.

basic programming constructs — The three categories of programming statements that include simple sequence, iteration, and selection.

behavior — A process data goes through. The class definition uses methods to define the behavior of the data.

beta version — A working version of an application that has not been fully tested and may still contain bugs or errors.

binary numbering system — Base 2 number system that uses two symbols (0 and 1).

binary operator — An operator in C# that requires two operands such as for the operators * or /. There must be divisor and dividend operands with the / operator.

bit — Binary digit that can hold one of two values (0 or 1).

block comment — See multiline comment.

Boolean — A data type that can hold the values of `true` or `false`.

breakpoint — Marker placed in an application, indicating that the program should halt execution when it reaches that point.

bug — An error in a software program that is usually caused by a programmer mistake.

byte code — Form of instruction that the Java virtual machine executes.

call by value — The value of an argument that appears in the method call is copied and stored in a separate, different, memory location in the called method.

camel case — A naming convention used for variable and object identifiers in C#. The first letter of the identifier is lowercase and the first letter of each subsequent concatenated word is capitalized (i.e., amountDue). Also called Hungarian notation.

Cascading Style Sheets(CSS) — Style sheet language used to describe how a document, such as a website, will look in terms of its layout to include elements such as font and colors.

case statement — See switch statement.

cast — The process of making a variable temporarily behave as if it were a different type.

catch block — Code used to deal with a problem (the exception handler); also called a catch clause.

catch clause — See catch block.

central processing unit (CPU) — The brain of the computer. Housed inside the system unit on a silicon chip, it is the most important hardware element.

checked exception — Requirement of including code within a try. . .catch block. All file interactions in Java are treated as checked exceptions.

C# Language Specifications — Authoritative source for C# grammar and syntax. Specification detail information on all aspects of the language.

class — A term denoting the encapsulation of data and behaviors into a single package or unit. Class is the template from which many objects are instantiated.

class diagram — A visual representation of classes and the relationships between them.

client application — A client application that instantiates objects of classes defined elsewhere or uses components that were previously defined and stored as .dlls. Many client applications can make use of these same classes and components.

client-server relationship — Relationship between two computer programs in which one program, the client, makes a service request from another program, the server, which fulfills the request.

client-side controls — See HTML controls.

client-side scripts — Code that is embedded in the HTML document. It is executed on the client computer normally in a Web browser.

CLR — See Common Language Runtime.

COBOL — (Common Business Oriented Language) High-level programming language introduced in the 1950s.

code-behind file — When you build an ASP.NET Web application, two separate files are created for the user interface. The file storing the logic is referred to as the code-behind file.

collection class — Class that enables you to store and retrieve groups of objects, such as an `Array`, `ArrayList`, or `Stack`.

Common Language Runtime (CLR) — The .NET run-time environment that enables the code to be compiled and executed. The CLR is also responsible for loading predefined .NET classes into a program and performing just-in-time (JIT) compilation.

Compact Framework Class Library (FCL) — A new smaller Framework class library that is used with mobile and smart devices such as PDAs, tablets, and cell phones.

compiler — Software that examines an entire program and translates the source code statements written in a programming language such as C# into machine-readable format.

compiler error — Language rule violation.

compile-time initialization — Placing a value in a variable when it is declared or created.

Component-Based Development — Design and develop independent components that can be reused and are packaged together to form the final application.

compound operators — Shortcut way to write an assignment statement that uses the original result as part of the computation.

conditional expression — An expression that produces a Boolean result. Also known as the test condition or simply 'the test'.

conditional logical operators — C# uses two ampersands (&&) and two pipes (||) to represent AND and OR, respectively. Logical && produces a value of `true` if both of its operands are `true`. Logical || produces a value of `true` if either of its operands are `true`.

conditional operator — See ternary operator.

console application — Applications that send requests to the operating system to display text on the command console display or to retrieve data from the keyboard.

constant — A data item defined and initialized to keep the same value throughout the life of the program.

constructor — A method called whenever an object is created. The constructor uses the same identifier as the class name.

containment — Classes can have a "has a" relationship in which a single class is defined to have instances of other class types. This concept is also called aggregation.

controls — Objects that can display and respond to user interactions, such as button clicks.

counter-controlled loop — Used when the loop should be executed a specified number of times. With a counter-controlled loop, a variable simulating a counter is used as the loop control variable to keep track of the number of iterations.

CSS — See Cascading Style Sheets.

data — The raw facts or the basic numbers and characters that are manipulated to produce useful information.

database — An electronic version of a filing cabinet, organized so that you can retrieve and use the data.

Database Management System (DBMS) — A computer program used to manage and query a database.

data file — A computer file that can be processed, manipulated, or used as input or output by a computer program.

data provider — Used for connecting to a database, executing commands, and retrieving results. Each data provider includes a collection of classes. .NET includes data providers for SQL server, OLE DB (Access), ODBC, and Oracle.

dataset — An in-memory cache or representation of data from a database.

debugging — Methodical process of finding and reducing bugs or defects in a computer program.

decimal system — Base-10 numbering system that uses 10 symbols.

decimal value type — A value type appropriate for storing monetary data items because it allows both integral (whole) numbers and a fractional portion.

decision tree — Design tool used when several options are available. It has nodes representing decision points, lines that branch out to represent further conditions, and shows actions based on which route is selected.

declare a variable — The act of allocating memory for a data item in a program. To declare a variable, you select an identifier and determine what type of data will appear in the memory cell.

delegate — Special types of .NET class whose instances store references (addresses) to methods as opposed to storing actual data.

derived — A child class. When a class is derived from another class, the new class inherits all the functionality of the base class.

desk check — The use of sample data to verify programming algorithms by mimicking or walking through each step the computer will take to solve the algorithm.

dimension an array — To instantiate an array by indicating how many elements to allocate.

distributed computing — Computing that takes place when applications are spread over more than one computer system.

divide and conquer design — See top-down design.

DLinq (LINQ to SQL) — Version of LINQ that focuses on querying data from relational data sources.

domain — A range of the values that a data item can store. For example, the domain of letterGrades awarded in most college courses is the characters 'A' through 'F.'

dynamic binding — The determination of which method to call is done at execution time or run time, not during the compile phase. The decision about which method to call is based on what type of data is sent as the argument.

dynamic data type — A type, or class, created at run time that can hold any kind of data.

dynamic web pages — Web pages that involve processing in addition to rendering the formatting of HTML tags.

dynamic website — Web pages that enable users to interact and see the results of their interactions.

element — An individual variable in an array is called an element of the array and is accessed through an index. Elements in an array are sometimes referred to as indexed or subscripted variables.

empty bodied loop — A loop that has no statements to be performed. Placing the semicolon at the end of a conditional expression produces a loop that has no body or an empty bodied loop.

emulator — A device that simulates the operation of some type of hardware, such as a smart phone.

encapsulate — Used in object-oriented programming, the act of combining the attributes and behaviors (characteristics and actions) of data to form a class.

encapsulation — One of the four major concepts that form the basis of an object-oriented programming language. With encapsulation, the language provides support for packaging data attributes and behaviors into a single unit, thus hiding implementation details.

entity — Classes define entities. An entity is usually associated with a person, place, or thing; it is normally a noun. Through defining a class, the entity is described in terms of its current state and behaviors.

enumeration — A type consisting of a set of named constants. Color for example has values such as White, Black, Blue and Green.

equality operator — Two equal symbol characters (==) used as part of a conditional expression for comparing operands. Char and string operands are compared using the dictionary order. No space is inserted between the two equal symbols.

error — Programs may experience an error caused by a user action that may cause an exception to be thrown. Entering the wrong type of data from the keyboard is an example of a common error.

escape character — The backslash('\') character.

escape sequence — Combination of the escape character ('\') followed by another letter to represent an action, such as '\n' for newline.

event — A notification from the operating system that an action, such as the user clicking the mouse or pressing a key has occurred.

event-driven model — The model used by Windows and Web applications wherein, once the program is executed, it sits in a process loop waiting for an event, such as mouse clicks, to occur.

event firing — When a user clicks a button, an event is fired that causes the operating system to send a message to a program indicating that a registered event has occurred.

event handler — Method that defines what should happen when an event such as a mouse click on a button or a click on the keyboard occurs.

event wiring — Associating a method in a program to an event, such as the user clicking a button. The method is automatically called when the event occurs.

exception — An unexpected condition in a computer program that occurs infrequently and is usually associated with error conditions that cause abnormal terminations if they are not handled.

exception handler — A block of code that is executed when an exception occurs.

explicit type coercion — Forcing a variable to be a different type. Explicit type coercion is performed using casting in C#. For example, to store only the integer portion of the following value, an explicit coercion would take the form: int answer = (int) 53.77.

Extensible Markup Language (XML) — A markup language that provides a format for describing data using tags similar to HTML tags.

fall through — A feature associated with switch statements in some languages in which the break statement(s) are optional. Once a match is made, all remaining statements are executed until a break or the end is encountered. C# enforces a "no fall through" rule with switch statements.

flag-controlled loop — A loop that normally uses a Boolean variable in the conditional expression to control the loop. The variable is initialized to a value before entering the loop. When a condition changes, the variable is changed and then the next test of the conditional expression causes the loop to terminate.

floating-point value — One of the types of numbers in C# that may contain a fractional portion. C# supports two types of floating-point values: float and double.

focus — When a control is being selected for the next activity in a Windows or Web application.

foreign key — A common column found in two or more tables used to link data in the tables.

formal parameter — The paired group(s) of identifier and type that appears in the heading of a method.

FORTRAN — (Formula Translator) High-level programming language introduced in the 1950s.

general-purpose computer systems — Electronic devices that process data under the control of a program.

generic catch — No specific exception type is listed. Any exception that is thrown is handled by executing the code within that catch block.

generics — A feature that allows classes and methods to use placeholders, instead of specific types, for the data type.

getters — See accessor.

gigabyte — Approximately 1 billion. 2^{30} (1,073,741,824) bytes abbreviated as GB.

GitHub — Web-based repository hosting service that offers source control management and revision control.

graphical user interface (GUI) — The menus, tabs, buttons, pictures, and text that enable users to interact with applications.

GUI — See graphical user interface.

hashing — Technique used where data is coded or encrypted following some type of algorithm. The same algorithm is used to decrypt or convert the message back to a readable form.

hashTable — A collection of key/value pairs that are organized based on the hash code of the key.

HCI — See human–computer interaction.

heading — The first line of a method. It includes the visibility modifier, return type, and the identifier along with the parameter list enclosed in parentheses.

hexadecimal numbering system — The Base 16 number system with powers of 16. Uses the symbols 0-9 and A-F.

high-level programming language — A modern programming language that is designed to be easy to read and write because it is written in English-like statements. High-level programming languages include C#, Visual Basic, FORTRAN, Pascal, C++, Java, and J#.

HTML — See Hypertext Markup Language.

HTML controls — Controls added to a web page that are rendered by the browser when the page is displayed. When added to a web page, they map straight to HTML formatting tags.

human-computer interaction (HCI) — A field of research that concentrates on the design and implementation of interactive computing systems for human use.

Hungarian notation — See camel case.

Hypertext Markup Language (HTML) — A language, consisting of tags, used to create web pages.

IDE — See Integrated Development Environment.

identifiers — The names of elements that appear in a program, such as the names of data items, variables, objects, classes, or methods. Some identifiers are predefined; others are user defined.

if statement — The selection statement, classified as one-way, two-way, or nested, which is used in combination with a conditional expression to facilitate specifying alternate paths based on the result of the conditional expression.

IL — See Intermediate Language.

immutable — Something that cannot be changed. Objects of the string class store an immutable series of characters.

implicit type coercion — Automatic conversion, without using casting, from one type to another. Normally conversion occurs from less precise to more precise data types. For example, if a binary operation involves a double and an int, implicit type coercion is performed so that both operands are treated as double.

increment/decrement operator — The operator used for the common arithmetic operation of adding or subtracting the number one (1) to or from a memory location. To add or subtract one from an operand, place either two plus (++) or two minus symbols (−−) before or after the identifier. Both are considered binary operators.

indefinite loop — See sentinel-controlled loop.

index — A numeric value, also called the subscript, used to reference the location of the variable relative to the first element in the array. In C#, the index of the first element is always 0.

indexed variable — See element.

infinite loop — A loop that has no provisions for termination. Placing a semicolon at the end of the conditional expression can create an infinite loop situation.

information hiding — Making data private and only accessible to the class.

inheritance — The concept of defining subclasses of data objects that share some or all of the parent's class characteristics.

inline comment — Single-line comment indicated by two forward slashes.

`instance` — An example of something. An object is an instance of a class.

`instance variable` — Data member associated with an object of a class.

`instantiate` — To create an instance of a class. If you define a template (blueprint) for a class (house), you instantiate the class when you create an object (construct the building).

`integer (int)` — One of the types of numbers in C#. A whole number, between a certain range of values, that contains no decimal point and can be positive or negative.

`Integrated Development Environment (IDE)` — A program environment, such as Visual Studio .NET, in which you type your source code statements, debug, compile, and run your application. IDEs include a number of useful development tools: IntelliSense (pop-up windows with completion options), color coding of different program sections, and online help and documentation.

`IntelliSense` — A feature of the Integrated Development Environment (IDE) that attempts to sense what you are going to type before you type it. When the IntelliSense window pops up, you can quickly select from the pull-down menu without having to complete the typing.

`interface` — The front end of a program. It is the visual image you see when you run a program, and it allows users to interact with programs.

`interface keyword` — A type similar to a class that is totally abstract. Interfaces contain no implementation details for any of their members; all their members are considered abstract. Classes that implement the interface must define details for all of the interface's methods.

`Intermediate Language (IL)` — When no syntax errors are found during compilation, .NET source code is converted into the Intermediate Language (IL). All languages targeting the .NET platform compile into an IL. IL code must be compiled a second time before results are seen.

`iteration structure` — A looping structure. Iteration enables you to identify and block together one or more statements to be repeated based on a predetermined condition. Also called repetition.

`iterative approach` — An approach used by programmers, which calls for frequent return to the design and/or analysis phases to make modifications as a program is being developed.

`jagged array` — See ragged array.

`Java` — High-level programming language introduced in 1995, originally called Oak.

`JavaScript` — A scripting language that Web developers use to create interactive websites. The script is embedded in the file that contains the HTML tags.

`JIT` — See just-in-time.

`JITer` — The Common Language Runtime tool used for a just-in-time compilation, which converts the IL code into CPU specific code.

`JScript` — The Microsoft implementation of JavaScript.

`jump statement` — A statement that changes the sequential order of statement execution by transferring control to a different point in the program. The break statement is one jump statement. When encountered inside a switch statement, control is redirected to the statement on the outside of the switch block.

`just-in-time (JIT)` — The second compilation. JIT converts the intermediate language code into the platform's native code.

`keyword` — Predefined reserved identifier that has a specially defined meaning for the compiler.

`kilobyte` — Approximately 1 thousand. 2^{10} (1,024) bytes abbreviated as KB.

`Language Integrated Query` — .NET component that defines a set of query operators that can be applied to a number of different data sources including arrays, databases, and XML data sources.

`language specifications` — See C# Language Specifications.

`left-associative` — Mathematical term used to describe the order of operations in an expression. Expression is performed from left to right. All binary operators, except the equality operators and the conditional operator (?:) are left-associative.

`length of an array` — The number of elements of an array the size of the array.

`LINQ` — See Language Integrated Query.

lining up — Rule related to space alignment with a nested `if...else` statements. The rule for matching `else` is that an `else` goes with the closest previous `if` that does not have its own `else`.

literal — The numbers, characters, and combinations of characters used in a program. They can be assigned to a variable or used in an expression and their values stay constant. For example, 5 is a numeric literal, "A" is a character literal, and "Bob" is a string literal.

logical negation operator — The exclamation symbol (!). It is a unary operator that negates its operand and is called the NOT operator. It returns `true` when operand1 is `false`. It returns `false` when operand1 is `true`.

logical operators — Symbols (&), (&&), (|), (||), and (!) used to connect or negate expressions.

logic error — An error in programs that causes an abnormal termination of a program or produces incorrect results.

loop condition — The conditional expression or the logical condition to be tested. A loop condition is enclosed in parentheses and is similar to the expressions used for selection statements.

loop control variable — Used with a counter-controlled loop. A loop control variable is a variable that simulates a counter.

loop — See iteration.

low-level programming language — Programming language close to machine language, not easy to read or understand.

machine language — Code that can be read by a computer. Also called native code.

main memory — See random-access memory.

Master Page — Web page template that provides a common look for individual content pages.

matching if...else — See lining up.

megabyte — Approximately 1 million. 2^{20} (1,048,576) bytes abbreviated as MB.

methodology — A plan or approach for solving computer-related problems.

method definition — The heading and the body of the method, which includes everything enclosed in curly braces.

method invocation — Method call.

methods — How behaviors are implemented in C#. Similar to functions found in other languages.

Microsoft Intermediate Language (MSIL) — C# code generated by compiler.

mixed mode expression — When an expression has operands of different types.

Model-View-Controller (MVC) — An ASP.NET Web application framework that implements the model-view controller pattern for designing websites where each component can be designed and tested independently.

multicast delegate — Provides functionality to be wired to more than one method. When the multicast delegate is used, multiple methods are called automatically, one after the other. The (+=) and (−=) operators are used to add or remove methods to and from the delegate chain or invocation list.

multiline comment — A remark in code that explains its function. A forward slash followed by an asterisk (/*) marks the beginning of a multiline comment, and the opposite pattern (*/) marks the end. Also called a block comment.

mutator — Special type of method used to change the current state or value of an object's member's data. Also referred to as setter.

mutually exclusive set of controls — A set of controls of which only one can be selected at a time. Radio buttons are often included in this category.

namespace — Container providing context for information created to hold a logical grouping of unique identifiers or symbols.

native code — See machine language.

nested if...else statement — When you place an `if` statement as the statement to be executed within an `if` statement, you create a nested `if...else` statement. If no `else` is included, the construct is referred to as a nested `if` statement.

NET — An environment layer between the operating system and applications for developing and running code.

NET Framework — Large library of coded solutions to common programming problems and a virtual machine that manages the execution of programs written in a variety of programming languages.

`not equal operator` — An exclamation point followed by a single equal symbol (!=). No space is embedded between the exclamation point and equal symbol.

`NOT operator` — See logical negation operator.

`null (empty) statement body` — When you place a semicolon at the end of a parenthesized expression, such as the expression used with a loop or selection statement, you are creating a null (empty) statement body.

`object` — An instance or example of a class. Object is also the base class of all derived classes in C#.

`object-oriented analysis, design, and programming` — A programming methodology that focuses on determining the objects to be manipulated rather than the processes or logic required to manipulate the data.

`object-oriented approach` — An approach to programming that focuses on determining the data characteristics and the methods or behaviors that operate on the data.

`object-oriented programming (OOP) language` — For a language to be considered a true object-oriented programming (OOP) language, it must support the following four major concepts, which C# and the .NET platform embrace: abstraction, encapsulation, inheritance, and polymorphism.

`octal numbering system` — The Base 8 numbering system that uses powers of eight. Uses symbols 0 through 7.

`off-by-one error` — A common programmer error in which a loop body is performed one too many or one too few times.

`one-way selection statement` — A one-way selection statement is used when a single expression needs to be tested. When the result of the expression is `true`, additional processing is performed.

`OOP` — See object-oriented programming.

`operating system` — The system software that is loaded when a computer is powered on and that oversees and coordinates the resources on a computer. Examples of operating systems include Windows 8, Android, and Unix.

`order of operations` — The order in which calculations are performed.

`out` — Used to implement pass by reference. Unlike the ref keyword, out can be used for methods that allow users to enter new values inside the method. The keyword out must be placed both with the parameter and also in the argument list.

`overloaded methods` — Multiple methods with the same name, but each method has a different number or type of parameter.

`overloaded operator` — Operators that behave differently based on the type of operands they receive. The following are overloaded operators: (+), (==), and (!=).

`override keyword` — A keyword that can be added to the method heading to allow a method to provide a new implementation (method body) of a method inherited from a base class.

`page validation` — Every control field on the page that has a validation control is checked when page validation occurs to determine whether it passes the validation rules. By default, page validation occurs when Click events are fired.

`parallel arrays` — Two or more arrays that have a relationship.

`parameter` — The paired data type and identifier that appears in the heading of the method.

`parameter array` — When a method uses the params modifier, the parameter is considered a parameter array. It is used to indicate that the number of arguments to the method may vary.

`parent class` — See base class.

`partial class` — When the definition for a class is split into two or more files. The source code files are combined when the application is compiled and run.

`Pascal case` — A naming convention used for class, method, namespace, and property identifiers. With Pascal case, the first letter in the identifier and the first letters of each subsequent concatenated word are capitalized.

`pass by reference` — Send to a method the address of the variable, so that if changes are made to the variable in the method, the changes will also occur to the calling variable.

`pass by value` — Send to a method a copy of the contents of the variable, so that if changes are made to the variable in the method, the changes will not occur to the calling variable.

polymorphism — The ability of classes to provide different implementations of methods based on what type of argument is used for the call or which object invokes the method behavior. Polymorphism is one of the four major concepts that form the basis of an object-oriented programming language.

precedence of the operators — The order in which the individual operators are evaluated when an expression contains multiple operators.

pre-processor directive — Indicates that an action should be taken before processing. Preprocessor directives are often associated with conditionally skipping sections of source files or reporting certain types of errors. C# does not actually perform a preprocess.

pre-test loop — A conditional expression is tested before any of the statements in the body of the loop are performed. If the conditional expression evaluates to `false`, the statement(s) in the body of the loop is (are) never performed. The `while` and `for` statements are both pretest types of loops.

primary key — A column (field) or combination of columns that uniquely identify a row in a table.

primary storage — The internal or main memory of a computer system.

prime the read — The act of inputting a value before going into the body of the loop.

primitive — The basic set of built-in data types. Data types in C# are implemented as classes.

procedural programming — A programming approach that is process oriented and focuses on the processes that data undergo from input until meaningful output. This approach is effective for small, stand-alone applications.

program — A set of instructions that tells the computer exactly what to do. Also referred to as software.

programming language — A set of syntactical and semantic rules for how to write computer instructions.

property — Considered smart fields, they provide access to private data members.

prototype — A mock-up of screens depicting the look of the final output of a program.

pseudocode — A tool used during the programming design stage to develop an algorithm. As the name implies, with pseudocode, steps are written in "pseudo" or approximate code format, which looks like English statements.

query contextual keyword — Keywords that have special meaning only when used in a query expression.

queue — A simple first-in-first-out (FIFO) collection.

ragged array — A multidimensional array that has a different number of columns in one or more rows. Jagged, or ragged arrays, differ from rectangular arrays in that rectangular arrays always have a rectangular shape, like a table. Jagged arrays are called "arrays of arrays." One row might have 5 columns; another row, 50 columns.

raise an exception — To throw an exception. When a program encounters an error such as division by zero during run time, and the program cannot recover from the error, it raises or throws an exception.

random-access memory (RAM) — The device that holds a computer's instructions and data. Also commonly called main memory.

rectangular two-dimensional array — A two-dimensional array visualized as a table divided into rows and columns. Much like a spreadsheet in which the rows and columns intersect, data is stored in individual cells.

recursion — Technique where a method calls itself repeatedly until it arrives at the solution.

redistributable version — Smaller download that includes CLR and class library.

ref — Used to implement pass by reference. The ref keyword cannot be used unless the original argument is initialized. The keyword ref must be placed both with the parameter and also in the argument list.

relational database — Data structure that stores data in a tabular format with each row representing a record and each column representing a field.

relational operators — Operators used to test variables to see if one is greater or less than another variable or value. The symbols used for relational operators are >, <, >=, and <=.

render — To convert a web page from HTML to a formatted page on the client computer that requested the page.

repetition — See iteration structure.

right-associative — Actions in an expression that are performed from right to left. The assignment operators (such as =, +=, *=) and conditional operator (?:) are right-associative. All other binary operators are left-associative.

round trip to the server — Each request to view a web page requires a round trip to the server on which the page is stored. The user requests the page via Hypertext Transfer Protocol by typing the Web address into a Web browser. That request is forwarded to the Web server on which the page is stored. The page is then sent back as a Hypertext Markup Language document where it is rendered (converted from HTML) to a formatted page on the client computer that requested the page.

row major language — Languages that store data from two-dimensional arrays by row in contiguous memory locations. All elements from row 0 are placed in memory first followed by all elements from row 1 and so on.

run-time error — Errors that surface when the program is executed. Usually the program compiles without any problems, runs, and may even produce some type of result.

scope — The region in the program in which a variable exists. For example, if a variable is declared in a method, it can be used in that method only. It is out of scope in other methods.

sealed class — Class that cannot serve as a base class. It cannot be inherited.

secondary storage — See auxiliary storage.

selection statement — A statement used for decision making that allows you to deviate from the sequential path laid out by a simple sequence and perform instead different statements based on the value of an expression.

selector — With the `switch` statement, this is the expression enclosed inside the parentheses. It follows the word "switch." Its value determines, or selects, which of the cases is executed.

semantic meaning — The meaning of a programming instruction statement rather than the rules for how it should be written.

sentinel-controlled loop — A type of loop that is terminated by entering or encountering a sentinel value. Sentinel-controlled loops are often used for inputting data when you do not know the exact number of values to be entered.

sentinel value — A value used to terminate a loop. It should be an extreme or dummy value that should not be processed, such as a negative value when only positive scores are to be processed.

server controls — Controls that are treated as objects, complete with data, behaviors, and properties. The Web server has access to these controls. Also referred to as Web controls, Web Forms server controls, ASP server controls, or simply Web Forms controls.

server-side scripts — Code that requires processing to be performed at the server level before a web page can be delivered.

setter — See mutator.

short-circuit evaluation — Evaluation of second and subsequent expressions is performed only when necessary. As soon as the value of the entire expression is known, evaluation stops. For example, in a conditional expression combined using &&, when the first expression evaluates to `false`, there is no need to evaluate the second expression.

short-circuiting logical operators — Operators that enable the minimal execution of code to produce the final result. The logical AND (&&) and OR (||) operators are the short-circuiting logical operators in C#.

signature — The name of the method, modifiers, and the types of its formal parameters. Differs from the method heading in that the heading also includes the return type for the method and identifiers for the data type.

simple sequence — One of the three basic programming constructs that causes sequential execution of programming statements. Execution begins with the first statement and continues until the end of the method or until another type of construct (loop or selection) is encountered.

single entry and single exit — Guidelines for providing only one way to enter and exit loops, selection statements, and methods. You violate the single entry and single exit guideline when you use break and continue statements within the loop body or when you write a method that has more than one return statement inside the method body.

single inheritance — Class that can extend or derive from at most one class.

single-line comment — A remark in code that explains its function. Two forward slashes (//) are used to mark the beginning of a single-line comment; the comment is terminated at the end of the current line when the Enter key is pressed.

size of an array — See length of an array.

software — Computer programs or instructions that perform a task or manage the functions of a computer.

software maintenance — Updating or changing an application.

source code — Program statements written using a programming language, such as C#.

specifications — Description of what the program should accomplish.

SQL (Structured Query Language) — A computer language used to create tables, or insert, delete, query, or update data in a table.

stack — A simple last-in-first-out (LIFO) collection.

stack trace — A listing of all the methods that are in an execution chain when an exception is thrown.

state-controlled loop — A variable is initialized to some value before entering the loop. When a condition changes, the variable is changed. The next test of the conditional expression causes the loop to terminate. A state-controlled loop is similar to a sentinel-controlled loop and is sometimes called a flag-controlled loop.

stateless — A stateless web page does not retain its values from one trip to the Web server to the next.

static — Modifier added to methods to indicate the method belongs to the class itself, not to a specific object of the class. To invoke the static methods, the method name is preceded by the class name (as opposed to an object's name).

static web page — A web page that does not require any processing on the client computer or by a Web server. It is precreated, resides on the server's hard drive, and basically is delivered as an HTML document.

Step Into — Debugger command that indicates the program halts at the first line of code inside the called method.

Step Out — Debugger command that causes the rest of the program statements in the called method to be executed. It then returns control to the method that called it and halts so that code can be examined.

Step Over — Debugger command that indicates the entire called method should execute before halting.

stepwise refinement — See top-down design.

string interpolation — A feature that enables you to place variables directly in a string literal as opposed to using number placeholders and arguments.

Structured English — A tool used during the programming design stage to develop an algorithm using a mixture of English and code statements.

style sheet — A file or form that defines the layout of a document to include fonts, text alignment, borders, spacing, and other formatting elements.

subscript — See index.

subscripted variable — See element.

super class — See base class.

switch statement — A multiple selection structure that allows you to perform a large number of alternatives based on the value of a single variable. This variable or expression must evaluate to an integral or `string` value. It cannot be used with `double`, `decimal`, or `float` variables but is appropriate for `short`, `int`, `long`, `char`, and `string` data types. Also called a `case` statement.

syntax — Rules for writing programs.

syntax error — Violation of any of the rules of the language caught by the compiler.

ternary operator — A ternary operator consists of a question mark and a colon (? :) and provides a way to express a simple `if...else` selection statement. Also called the conditional operator.

test condition — See conditional expression.

Test Driven Development (TDD) — Programming methodology that emphasizes fast, incremental development and writing tests before writing code.

test plan — The strategy devised to test code. Usually includes plans for testing extreme values, identifying possible problem cases, and ensuring that these cases are tested.

the test — See conditional expression.

throw an exception — See raise an exception.

throw back — To send an exception backward through the call chain until a method is found that can handle the exception or until it reaches the operating system, which halts the program execution.

top-down design — A design methodology that divides a problem into a number of subproblems. Each subproblem is then further subdivided into smaller units until the method is manageable. Also called the divide-and-conquer approach or step-wise refinement.

truncate — To chop off the fractional part of a number. For example, if the number 3.87 is placed in an integer variable, the integer can only hold the whole number portion; thus, .87 is truncated and 3 is stored in the variable.

two-dimensional array — See rectangular two-dimensional array.

two-way if statement — An if statement with the `else` portion included. With a two-way `if` statement, either the `true` statement(s) following the `if` is (are) executed or the `false` statement(s) following the `else`, but not both.

unary operator — An operator that requires a single operand. Examples in C# are the ++ and -- operators that increment and decrement by one.

unhandled exception — When a computer program runs and encounters an error it cannot handle, it raises an exception. If none of the methods include code to handle the error, the common language run time handles the exception by halting the entire application.

Unicode — The character set used by programmers of C#. The Unicode character set uses 16 bits to represent a character; thus, 2^{16} or 65,536 unique characters can be represented.

uniform resource locator (URL) — An address of a file on the Internet that consists of the protocol, the computer where the file is located, and the file's location on that computer.

uppercase — One of three .NET conventions for naming identifiers. All uppercase characters are used for the names of constant literals and for identifiers that consist of two or fewer letters.

URL — See universal resource locator.

validation controls — Controls that can be added to a web page that enable user input to be validated or checked by the server to ensure that the information entered is valid or is in the right format.

value type — A fundamental data type of the C# language that is copied when passed as an argument to a method. Can include built-in floating and integral types or user-defined types.

variable — The representation of an area in the computer memory in which a value of a particular data type can be stored.

VBScript — A scripting language used to add additional functionality to web pages beyond what HTML formatting tags do. Used with traditional ASP applications. VBScript is a subset of Microsoft Visual Basic 6.0.

verbatim string literal — Take the string exactly as it is. By preceding a string literal with the at symbol (@), the characters are interpreted exactly as they are typed. Using @-quoted string literals eliminates the need to include an extra backslash before the backslash when it is part of the string.

Visual Studio — A suite of products that includes several programming languages, including C# along with a large collection of development and debugging tools.

Web application — A collection of one or more related files or components stored on a Web server. Web applications are also called websites.

Web controls — See server controls.

Web Forms — A tool of ASP.NET technology that enables the building of programmable web pages that serve as a user interface for Web applications.

Web Forms controls — See server controls.

`Web Forms server controls` — See server controls.

`Web server` — Software that hosts or delivers a Web application. The hardware on which the Web server software is loaded is often called a Web server, but it is the software that makes the equipment special and thus enables the computer to be called a server.

`Windows application` — Applications designed for the single platform desktop that receive messages from the operating system when an event occurs.

`Windows Presentation Foundation` — A vector-based, resolution-independent Application Program Interface (API) alternative to using Win Forms for creating Windows interfaces that incorporate documents, media, two- and three-dimensional graphics, and animations into an application. The latest version of the Visual Studio IDE was built using WPF.

`wiring an event` — See event wiring.

`WPF` — See Windows Presentation Foundation.

`wrap` — Associating a delegate to one or more methods, so that when a delegate is used, the method(s) is (are) automatically called.

`WYSIWYG` — Acronym for "What you see is what you get".

`Xamarin` — Software company whose engineers created Mono and later developed cross-platform software to build and design mobile apps.

`XAML` — eXtensible Application Markup Language. Think of the XAML file as an HTML file, with beginning and ending tags, for Windows applications.

`XHTML (Extensible HyperText Markup Language)` — A markup language that extends HTML and is designed to work in conjunction with XML-based documents.

`XLinq (LINQ to XML)` — Version of LINQ that focuses on querying XML data.

`XML` — See Extensible Markup Language.

INDEX

Bold page numbers indicate definitions.